BUSINESS STATISTICS OF THE UNITED STATES

BUSINESS STATISTICS OF THE UNITED STATES

Patterns of Economic Change

Twenty-Sixth Edition
2021

Edited by Susan Ockert

Bernan Press

Lanham • Boulder • New York • London

Published by Bernan Press
An imprint of The Rowman & Littlefield Publishing Group, Inc.
4501 Forbes Boulevard, Suite 200, Lanham, Maryland 20706
www.rowman.com

86-90 Paul Street, London EC2A 4NE

ISBN 978-1-63671-003-7 (hardback)
ISBN 978-1-63671-004-4 (ebook)

CONTENTS

PREFACE

Business Statistics of the United States: Patterns of Economic Change, 26th Edition, 2021 is a basic desk reference for anyone requiring statistics on the U.S. economy. It contains over 3,000 economic time series portraying the period from World War II to December 2020 in industry, product, and demographic detail. In the case of about 200 key series, the period from 1929 through 1948 is depicted as well.

Additionally, for three important statistical series that have been compiled monthly on a continuous basis, monthly and annual data are included going back to 1919 for industrial production and 1913 for consumer and producer prices. Annual data for money and credit have also been taken back before 1929, including money supply figures back to 1892 and some interest rates back to 1919. Annual estimates of the unemployment rate from 1890 to 1929, not official but using a method similar to that used by BLS for its 1929-48 unemployment estimates, are also included.

The National Income and Product Accounts (NIPAs) were comprehensively revised in July 2020, changing some measurement concepts, changing base periods for price indexes and real output, and as a result altering all the data back to 1929. *Business Statistics* incorporates fully revised data for over 700 series from this data set and productivity and costs series that are based on the revised NIPAs, all extended and updated through 2016. The important new concepts introduced in the NIPA revision are explained in the Notes and Definitions to Chapters 1, 4, 5, and 6. In all, this edition provides, in one volume, unparalleled, up-to-date background information on the course of the U.S. economy.

The data are predominantly from federal government sources. Of equal importance are the extensive background notes for each chapter, which help users to understand the data, use them appropriately, and, if desired, seek additional information from the source agencies.

Chapters are organized according to subject matter. For most time series, users will find an initial page displaying the latest two years of monthly data, or three years of quarterly data, for the most recent completed years, along with annual averages for the last completed 40, 50, or even 60 years.

For the most important series for which we have long-term historical data, this initial page will be labeled with "A" after the table number, and identified in the title by the additional words "Recent Data". It will be immediately followed by pages labeled with "B" after the table number and identified by the words "Historical Data", which will show all available historical data annually back as far as possible, and monthly or quarterly back to the earliest available postwar year. In some cases, additional tables of historical data will be included.

The leading article "Cycle and Growth Perspectives" provides other information and techniques to assist in using and interpreting the data.

THE PLAN OF THE BOOK

The history of the U.S. economy is told in major U.S. government sets of statistical data: the national income and product accounts compiled by the Bureau of Economic Analysis (BEA); the data on labor force, employment, hours, earnings, and productivity compiled by the Bureau of Labor Statistics (BLS); the price indexes collected by BLS; and the financial market and industrial production data compiled primarily by the Board of Governors of the Federal Reserve System (FRB). All of these sets exist in annual and either monthly or quarterly form beginning in 1946, 1947, or 1948; many are available, at least annually, as far back as 1929, and a few even farther back; and three are available monthly back to the teens of the 20th century.

In Part A, *Business Statistics* presents the aggregate United States economy in a number of important dimensions. The presentations begin with the national income and product accounts, or NIPAs. The NIPAs comprise a comprehensive, thorough, and internally consistent body of data. They measure the value of the total output of the U.S. economy (the gross domestic product, or GDP) and they allocate that value between its quantity, or "real," and price components. They show how the value of aggregate demand is generated by consumers, business investors, government, and foreign customers; how much of aggregate demand is supplied by imports and how much by domestic production; and how the income generated in domestic production is distributed between labor and capital.

Production estimates covering only the sectors of the economy traditionally labeled "industrial"—manufacturing, mining, and utilities—are shown in Chapter 2, after the presentation of the overall NIPAs in Chapter 1.

Median income—the best measure of the economic well-being of the typical American—income distribution, and poverty statistics from a Census household survey are presented in Chapter 3.

Then, more detail from the NIPAs is presented for the demand components of economic activity. GDP, by its product-side definition, consists of the sum of consumption expenditures, business investment in fixed capital and inventories, government purchases of goods and services, and exports minus imports—as in the elementary economics blackboard identity "GDP = C + I + G + X – M." Chapters on each of these components—consumption, investment, government, and foreign trade--are presented in Part A.

Following these chapters, there are a chapter on prices, two chapters on the compensation of labor and capital inputs and the amount and productivity of labor input, one chapter on energy inputs into production and consumption, and one chapter on money, interest, assets, and debt.

At the end of Part A, comparisons of output, prices, and labor markets among major industrial countries are presented, along with statistics on the value of the dollar against other currencies.

While GDP is initially defined and measured by adding up its demand categories and subtracting imports, this output is produced in industries—some in the old-line heavy industries such as manufacturing, mining, and utilities, but an increasing share in the huge and heterogeneous group known as "service-providing" industries. Part A gives a number of measures of activity classified by industry or industrial sector: industrial production, profits, and employment-related data. Further industry information is provided in Part B, including new quarterly indicators of GDP by industry.

Industry data collection is important because demands for goods and services are channeled into demands for labor and capital through the industries responsible for producing the requested goods and services. These data are reported using the North American Industry Classification System (NAICS). This system, introduced in 1997 to replace the older Standard Industrial Classification System (SIC), delineates industries that are better defined in relation to today's demands and more closely related to each other by technology. Notable examples include more detailed data available on service industries, a more rational grouping of the Computer and electronic product manufacturing subsector, and the creation of the Information sector. See the References at the end of this Preface.

NAICS industries are groupings of producing units—not of products as such—and are grouped according to similarity of production processes. This is done in order to collect consistent data on inputs and outputs, which are then used to measure important concepts, such as productivity and input-output parameters. Emphasis on the production process helps to explain a number of ways in which the NAICS differs from the SIC.

- Manufacturing activities at retail locations, such as bakeries, have been classified separately from retail activity and put into the Food manufacturing industry.

- Central administrative offices of companies have a new sector of their own, Management of companies and enterprises (sector 55). For example, the headquarters office of a food-producing corporation is considered part of the new sector instead of part of the Food manufacturing industry.

- Reproduction of packaged software, which was classified as a business service in the SIC, is now classified in sector 334,

Computer and electronic product manufacturing, as a manufacturing process.

- Electronic markets and agents and brokers, formerly undifferentiated components of wholesale trade industries, have a sector of their own (425).

- Retail trade in NAICS (sectors 44 and 45) now includes establishments such as office supply stores, computer and software stores, building materials dealers, plumbing supply stores, and electrical supply stores, that display merchandise and use mass-media advertising to sell to individuals as well as to businesses, which were formerly classified in wholesale trade.

In Part B, *Business Statistics* shows GDP, income, employment, hours, and earnings by industry, followed by statistics for key sectors such as petroleum, housing, manufacturing, retail trade, and services.

Notes and definitions. Productive use of economic data requires accurate knowledge about the sources and meaning of the data. The notes and definitions for each chapter, shown immediately after that chapter's tables, contain definitions, descriptions of recent data revisions, and references to sources of additional technical information. They also include information about data availability and revision and release schedules, which helps users to readily access the latest current values if they need to keep up with the data month by month or quarter by quarter.

A NOTE ON THE IMPORTANCE OF ECONOMIC STATISTICS

To retrieve money and credit data for earlier years, the editor of *Business Statistics* had to consult old printed volumes, where she encountered some inspiring prefatory words in the Federal Reserve Board volume *Banking and Monetary Statistics* (1943). These words were written by the Fed's longtime statistics chief E. A. Goldenweiser, in the stately cadences of an earlier era, about the financial statistics collected in that volume. But they well express the hope and expectation of statisticians and economists that their work can lead to better economic decisions:

"These serried ranks of organized statistics on banking and finance, even though they may inspire awe, should also inspire confidence. They are an augury that credit policy can be based in the future, as in the past, on fact rather than on fancy."

THE HISTORY OF *BUSINESS STATISTICS*

The history of *Business Statistics* began with the publication, many years ago, of the first edition of a volume with the same name by the U.S. Department of Commerce's Bureau of Economic Analysis (BEA). After 27 periodic editions, the last of which appeared in 1992, BEA found it necessary, for budgetary and other reasons, to discontinue both the publication and the maintenance of the database from which the publication was derived.

The individual statistical series gathered together here are all publicly available. However, the task of gathering them from the numerous different sources within the government and assembling them into one coherent database is impractical for most data users. Even when current data are readily available, obtaining the full historical time series is often time-consuming and difficult. Definitions and other documentation can also be inconvenient to find. Believing that a *Business Statistics* compilation was too valuable to be lost to the public, Bernan Press published the first edition of the present publication, edited by Dr. Courtenay M. Slater, in 1995. The first edition received a warm welcome from users of economic data. Dr. Slater, formerly chief economist of the Department of Commerce, continued to develop *Business Statistics* through four subsequent annual editions. The current editor worked with Dr. Slater on the fourth and fifth editions. In subsequent editions, she has continued in the tradition established by Dr. Slater of ensuring high-quality data, while revising and expanding the book's scope to include significant new aspects of the U.S. economy and longer historical background.

Nearly all of the statistical data in this book are from federal government sources and all are available in the public domain. Sources are given in the applicable notes and definitions.

The data in this volume meet the publication standards of the federal statistical agencies from which they were obtained.

Every effort has been made to select data that are accurate, meaningful, and useful. All statistical data are subject to error arising from sampling variability, reporting errors, incomplete coverage, imputation, and other causes. The responsibility of the editor and publisher of this volume is limited to reasonable care in the reproduction and presentation of data obtained from established sources.

The 2021 edition has been edited by Susan Ockert.

Susan Ockert has worked as an economist in the military, for the federal government, and at regional and state levels. She earned her Masters of Economics at George Mason University in Fairfax, Virginia as well as her Masters of International Management at the Thunderbird University in Glendale, Arizona. She currently teaches economics at the collegiate level.

REFERENCES

The NAICS is explained and laid out in *North American Industry Classification System: United States*, from the Executive Office of the President, Office of Management and Budget. This title is updated every five years. The most recent edition available is 2017. The 2022 edition will be released in January 2022.

These volumes are available from Bernan Press. These volumes fully describe the development and application of the new classification system and are the sources for the material presented in this volume. Information is also available on the NAICS Web site at <https://www.census.gov/naics>.

CYCLE AND GROWTH PERSPECTIVES

This 26th edition of *Business Statistics of the United States* presents comprehensive and detailed data on U.S. economic performance through December 2020, going back to the early 20th century. These numbers show changes in many dimensions—economic growth, employment, inflation, income, to name a few. There are patterns of fluctuation, and, simultaneously, patterns of enduring change. This article will present some ways of looking at these movements and trying to make sense of them. In addition, policy instruments are also described.

The Federal Reserve conducts the nation's <u>monetary policy</u> by managing the level of short-term interest rates and influencing the overall availability and cost of credit in the economy. Monetary policy directly affects short-term interest rates; it indirectly affects longer-term interest rates, currency exchange rates, and prices of equities and other assets and thus wealth. Through these channels, monetary policy influences household spending, business investment, production, employment, and inflation in the United States.

Governments use spending and taxing powers to promote stable and sustainable growth. <u>Fiscal policy</u> is the use of government spending and taxation to influence the economy. Governments typically use fiscal policy to promote strong and sustainable growth and reduce poverty. Fiscal policy aims to stabilize economic growth, avoiding a boom and bust economic cycle. Fiscal policy is often used in conjunction with monetary policy. In fact, governments often prefer monetary policy for stabilizing the economy.

The U.S. economy, even in its infancy, experienced boom or bust periods. The first recorded downturn was the Panic of 1785, which followed the American Revolution when the economy changed from military to industrial. Attempts have been made to date recessions in America beginning in the late 18th century. Economists and historians, because of the lack of economic statistics, didn't always agree on the start and stop of recessions, but they agree that volatility in economic activity and unemployment did exist.

BUSINESS CYCLES IN THE U.S. ECONOMY: RECESSIONS AND EXPANSIONS

The study of economic fluctuations in the United States was pioneered by Wesley C. Mitchell and Arthur F. Burns early in the twentieth century, and was carried on subsequently by other researchers affiliated with the National Bureau of Economic Research (NBER). NBER is an independent, nonpartisan research organization founded in 1920 and is committed to providing unbiased economic research. These analysts observed that indicators of the general state of business activity tended to move up and down over periods that were longer than a year and were therefore not accounted for by seasonal variation. Although these periods of expansion and contraction were not uniform in length, and thus not "cycles" in any strict mathematical sense, their recurrent nature and certain generic similarities caused them to be called "business cycles." NBER has identified 32 complete peak-to-peak business cycles over the period beginning with December 1854.

The first NBER-established business cycle dates, identifying the months in which peaks and troughs in general economic activity occurred, were published in 1929. The dates of current cycles are established, typically within a year or so of their occurrence, by the NBER Business Cycle Dating Committee. This group, first formed in 1978, consists of eight economists who are university professors, associated with research organizations, or both. The peak of the cycle signals the start of a downturn of an economy while the trough signals the beginning of a upturn.

Business cycle dates are based on monthly data, and have been identified for periods long before the availability of quarterly data on real gross national product (GDP). It is important to understand that even in the period since 1947 for which quarterly real GDP exists, the NBER identification of a recession does not always coincide with the frequently cited definition, "two consecutive quarters of decline in real GDP." Because a recession is a broad contraction of the economy, NBER emphasizes economy-wide measures of economic activity such as production, employment, real income, real manufacturing, wholesale-retail sales, and many more indicators. Federal agencies collect the economic data used by NBER. Employment data is provided by the Department of Labor, Bureau of Labor Statistics while the Department of Commerce provides data from the Census Bureau and Bureau of Economic Analysis along with the Federal Reserve Board.

The NBER monthly and quarterly dates of the cycles from 1854 to the latest announced turning point—the June 2009 trough ending the recession that began in December 2007—are shown in Table A-1 below. The quarterly turning points are identified by Roman numerals. NBER considers that the trough month is both the end of the decline and the beginning of the expansion, based on the concept that the actual turning point was some particular day within that month. The longest running contraction, during the Great Depression, lasted from August 1929 to November 1933, for a total of 43 months. The Great Recession ended in June 2009, after 19 months.

Meanwhile, the current expansion began in June 2009 and ended in February 2020, the longest expansion in U.S. history, lasting for 10 years and 8 months. The NBER Business Cycle Dating Committee announced that the U.S. economy had officially ended the Great Recession and the entered another recession. See the Great Recession article for more information on the data used by the NBER.

TABLE A-1 BUSINESS CYCLE REFERENCE DATES 1854–2020

Peak	Trough
	December 1854 (II)
June 1857 (II)	December 1858 (IV)
October 1860 (III)	June 1861 (III)
April 1865 (I)	December 1867 (I)
June 1869 (II)	December 1870 (IV)
October 1873 (III)	March 1879 (I)
March 1882 (I)	May 1885 (II)
March 1887 (II)	April 1888 (I)
July 1890 (III)	May 1891 (II)
January 1893 (I)	June 1894 (II)
December 1895 (IV)	June 1897 (II)
June 1899 (III)	December 1900 (IV)
September 1902 (IV)	August 1904 (III)
May 1907 (II)	June 1908 (II)
January 1910 (I)	January 1912 (IV)
January 1913 (I)	December 1914 (IV)
August 1918 (III)	March 1919 (I)
January 1920 (I)	July 1921 (III)
May 1923 (II)	July 1924 (III)
October 1926 (III)	November 1927 (IV)
August 1929 (III)	March 1933 (I)
May 1937 (II)	June 1938 (II)
February 1945 (I)	October 1945 (IV)
November 1948 (IV)	October 1949 (IV)
July 1953 (II)	May 1954 (II)
August 1957 (III)	April 1958 (II)
April 1960 (II)	February 1961 (I)
December 1969 (IV)	November 1970 (IV)
November 1973 (IV)	March 1975 (I)
January 1980 (I)	July 1980 (III)
July 1981 (III)	November 1982 (IV)
July 1990 (III)	March 1991(I)
March 2001 (I)	November 2001 (IV)
December 2007 (IV)	June 2009 (II)
February 2020 (2019 IV)	April 2020 (II)

Source: National Bureau of Economic Research

Between 1854 to 2020, the American economy experienced over 30 recessions (contractions) and expansions (recoveries). Before the Great Depression, recessions occurred more frequently and in conjunction with financial panics. With such financial instability, the Federal Reserve System was established in 1913 to assert central control of the monetary system. Financial crises during the 1800s occurred due to crop failures, banking failures, drops in cotton prices, rapid speculation in land, sudden plunges in the stock market and currency and credit crises, The United States of America during this period was a very young nation and thus these panics devastated its economy.

THE U.S. ECONOMY 1929–1948

While there has been much discussion in recent years of the "Great Depression," there is surprisingly little familiarity with the basic statistical record of the period between 1929 and the end of World War II. Reproducing material from Chapter 18 of the 15th edition of *Business Statistics,* we present here an explanation of that period from the NBER business cycle perspective, along with a graphic overview and narration of its economic developments as recorded in the statistics now presented in Part A of this volume.

The NBER chronology, presented in Table A-1 in the preceding article "Cycle and Growth Perspectives," may surprise readers who are looking for "The Great Depression" and are not familiar with the NBER approach to business cycles. As NBER perceives it, a downtrend in economic activity began in August 1929 (<u>before</u> the stock market crash) and lasted until March 1933. This 43-month period has been called the "Great Contraction": it was the longest period of economic decline since the 1870s, and more than double the length of the longest recession identified and completed since that time (the one from December 2007 to June 2009, which lasted 18 months). For the rest of the 1930s—excepting a 13-month recession in 1937–1938—the economy is viewed by the NBER as having been in an expansion phase. The NBER chronology does not use the term "depression."

However, the term "Great Depression" is often colloquially used for the entire 1929–1939 period, even though the economy was expanding for most of the period following March 1933. This is because economic activity during that time, though increasing, remained below the likely capacity of the economy, as is indicated in Figures A-1 and A-2 below.

It should also be noted that NBER construes the entire period from June 1938 through February 1945 as a business cycle expansion. The recovery from the 1937–1938 recession merged into a further, continued rise in activity that reflected the outbreak of war in Europe in September 1939, a consequent preparedness effort in the United States, and an increase in demand from abroad for U.S. output. The United States entered the war after being attacked by Japan in December 1941, launching an all-out war production effort at that time.

The February 1945 end of the "wartime expansion" (as NBER terms the period June 1938–February 1945) preceded the end of the war (the European war ended in May 1945 and the Pacific war concluded in August 1945). A brief recession associated with demobilization occurred from February to October 1945, followed by the first postwar expansion, which lasted from October 1945 to November 1948.

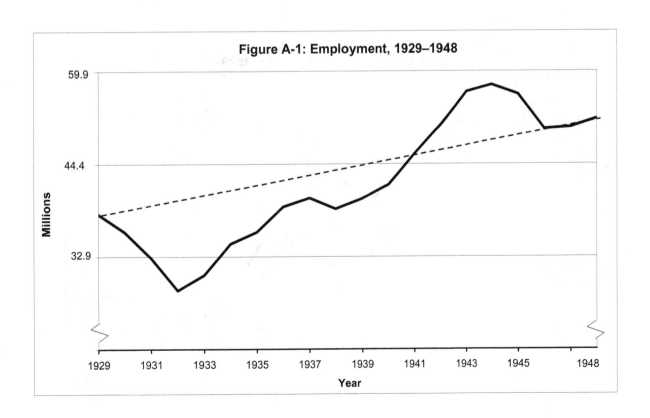

Figure A-1: Employment, 1929–1948

In the graphs that follow, summary annual statistics for the years 1929 through 1948 are presented, depicting the economy during two of its most tumultuous decades. This period encompasses the "great contraction," the economic collapse that began in August 1929 and lasted until March 1933; a subsequent period of recovery, which failed to return many important economic indicators to their expected trend levels and was interrupted by a new, though less severe, recession; apprehension of coming war, then the outbreak of war in Europe in September 1939, leading to increased war-related production; United States participation in all-out war, beginning with the Japanese attack on Pearl Harbor on December 7, 1941, and ending in 1945, with supercharged production and employment rates; then, rapid demobilization, and return to a high peacetime rate of economic activity by 1948.

For a first overall view of the economy during these decades, Figure A-2 shows total U.S. employment as calculated by the Bureau of Economic Analysis, including all private and government jobs, both civilian and military. In this graph a trend line is shown connecting the two peacetime high employment levels of 1929 and 1948.

- More than one-fifth of all the jobs held in the U.S. economy in 1929 were gone by 1932. In the subsequent recovery, total employment was back at the 1929 level by 1936, but only because of government employment, including over 3 ½ million work relief jobs; private industry employment would not recover to its 1929 level until 1941.

- Because the recovery was incomplete and economic activity did not recover to a trend level until after the decade's end, the entire decade of the 1930s is often described as "The Great Depression."

- During the war, men were drafted into the armed forces, practically all of the unemployed were put back to work, and women were drawn into the labor force, resulting in a period of what might be called "super-employment." After the war, employment fell back to a more normal trend level.

- The unemployment rates for the prewar period calculated by the Bureau of Labor Statistics, unlike the employment data used in Figure A-2, count people on government work relief programs as unemployed. By this reckoning, unemployment rose from 3.2 percent of the civilian labor force in 1929 to a peak of 24.9 percent in 1933, and got no lower than 14.3 percent for the rest of the 1930s, as shown in Figure A-2.

- State and local governments started hiring people for work relief in 1930. The federal government's programs began in 1933, and in 1936 and 1938 agencies such as the WPA and the CCC employed over 3 ½ million people. When workers in these programs are counted as employed rather than unemployed, the high point for unemployment was 22.5 percent in 1932, and it was reduced to 9.1 percent in 1937, as shown by the dashed line in Figure A-2; see Notes and Definitions to Chapter 10 for further explanation.

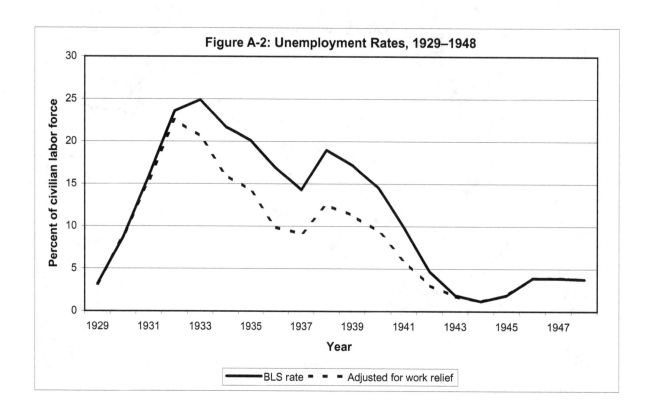

Figure A-2: Unemployment Rates, 1929–1948

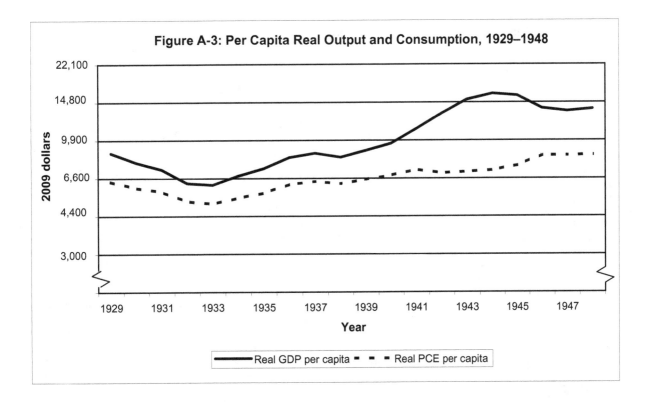

Figure A-3: Per Capita Real Output and Consumption, 1929–1948

- By 1943, the economy reached a state of over-full employ-ment, which would have been associated with runaway infla-tion if not for comprehensive price, wage, and production controls; the years of full wartime production, 1943 through 1945, all saw unemployment rates below 2 percent. After demobilization, the unemployment rate returned to just under 4 percent.

- Real GDP declined 26.7 percent from 1929 to 1933—28.9 percent on a per capita basis. Per capita output recovered almost to the 1929 level in 1937 but fell back 4.1 percent in the 1938 recession. Output then nearly doubled from 1939 to the peak war production year, 1944; the per capita annual growth rate was 12.4 percent. Output fell back during the demobilization, but in 1948 was still at a per capita level representing a 5.0 percent per year growth rate since 1939.

- Per capita personal consumption expenditures fell 20.9 percent from 1929 to 1933. The decline would have been greater if consumers had not dipped into their assets to keep their living standards from declining as steeply as their incomes; the personal saving rate was negative in 1932 and 1933. Real per capita consumption recovered to the 1929 level by 1937. Despite rationing and shortages, real per capita consumption spending declined little during the war years. In 1948, it was 29.3 percent above the 1939 level.

- Why was the 1929-1933 contraction so deep and long-lasting? By some, blame is placed on U.S. government tax increases and imposition of new trade barriers (the Smoot-Hawley Tariff), which undoubtedly made their contribution. A substantial number of well-regarded economists, however, point primarily to deflation and its interaction with debt. The price index for personal consumption expenditures, whose rate of change is shown in Figure A-5, declined 27.2 percent from 1929 to 1933, for an annual average deflation rate of 7.6 percent. Current and prospective price declines make debt more burdensome and debtors more likely to default, as interest payments remain fixed while incomes and asset values decline.

- Current and prospective price declines also make borrowing prohibitively expensive; a low nominal interest rate becomes high in real terms (since the real rate is the nominal rate minus the inflation rate, and subtraction means changing the sign and adding). A dollar in the hands of a prospective lender will be worth more in terms of purchasing power if he simply holds on to it than if he invests it in some real economic asset or activity whose price will be lower at the end of the year. There is no feasible way for a central bank to lower interest rates below zero in order to reduce real rates in the presence of deflation. As Figure A-5 shows, real rates

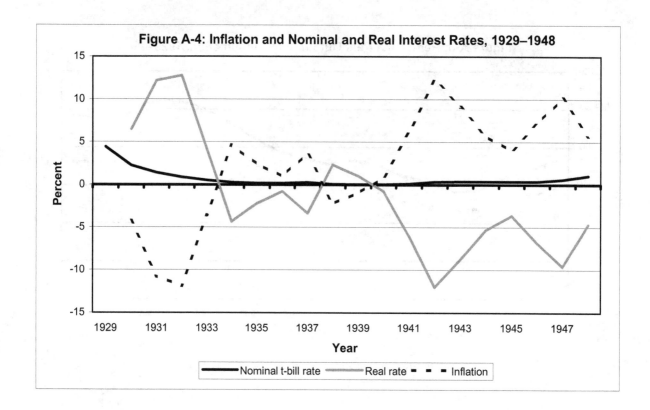

Figure A-4: Inflation and Nominal and Real Interest Rates, 1929–1948

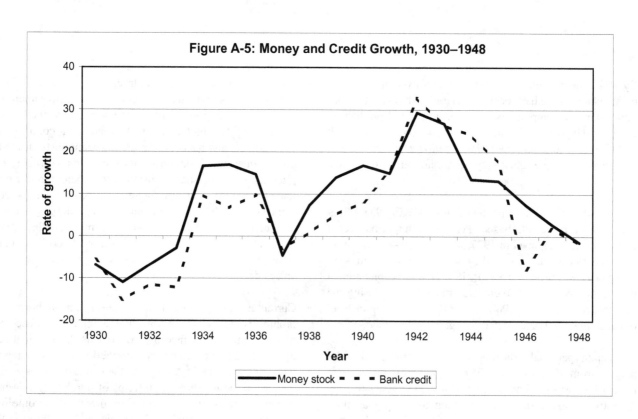

Figure A-5: Money and Credit Growth, 1930–1948

were high from 1930 through 1933 despite near-zero market nominal rates on Treasury bills.

- Deflation was rooted in deep and sustained declines in the dollar volumes of money and credit, as shown in Table 12-1B. The money stock (currency and demand deposits) declined 27 percent from June 30, 1929, to June 30, 1933. Loans and investments at all commercial banks declined 29 percent over the same period. Commercial paper outstanding plunged 76 percent between December 1929 and December 1932, and bankers' acceptances were down 59 percent.

- Positive money and credit growth after 1933 was reflected in moderate rates of price increase and moderately negative—which means stimulative--real interest rates. As can be seen in Figure A-5 and there was a monetary component to the 1937-38 recession. There was also a premature federal budget retrenchment at that time.

- During the war, monetary policy was pre-empted by wartime needs. Interest rates were held low to facilitate the financing of huge federal deficits.

- Worker incomes increased during the wartime boom as employment, average hours, and hourly wages all rose. But inflation and consumer spending were held down by price and production controls and rationing. Personal saving rates soared when there was little to buy and the government emphasized the sale of "war bonds"; the saving rate reached 26 percent in 1943 and 1944, then fell back to 4.2 percent in 1947, almost equal to its 1929 level.

THE GREAT RECESSION, RECOVERY, AND COVID-19

Determining the beginning and ending of economic recessions and expansions depends on data such as GDP growth, unemployment and household income. The National Bureau of Economic Research (NBER) committee also examines other statistics such as industrial production, wholesale-retail sales and real disposal income. The former statistics are provided by the U.S. Department of Commerce, Bureau of Census and Bureau of Economics Analysis (BEA) and Department of Labor, Bureau of Labor Statistics (BLS). Economists at the NBER analyzes this data before announcing any inflection point in the U.S. economy.

The U.S. economy experienced an eight-month decline from March 2001 to November 2001. The dot.com bubble burst was mainly fueled by the excessive speculation in dot.com companies. The NASDAQ sunk significantly between March 2000 and December 2002. One lesson learned was that excessive speculation in internet-related companies with no profits is not sound financial strategy.

The economy recovered after 2001 but the Great Recession began in December 2007 and lasted until June 2009. Numerous consequential actions led to this downturn. Housing prices soared while mortgage lending standards deteriorated. For example, as house prices rose, banks started offering sub-prime mortgages without down payment or income requirements. Housing prices collapsed between 2007 and 2010 as demand for residential construction dropped between 2006 to 2011.

During the Great Depression, demand for construction materials such as wood, carpeting, appliances, etc. led to layoffs which led to increased unemployment. Without jobs, more and more people ended up losing their homes through foreclosures. The domino effect continued as household income, the stock market, and wealth all continued to fall. Millions of people fell below the poverty level in between 2007 to 2009 and household income did not return to its 2007 level until 2016.

Both President Bush and President Obama enacted fiscal and monetary policy to counteract the recession An initial fiscal policy introduced by President Bush in 2008 was the Economic Stimulus Package Act which cost approximately $830 million. As part of the Act, individuals received checks from the government with the amount varying on family size. Next, the Troubled Assets Relief Program (TARP) was a program to purchase assets and equity from financial institutions to strengthen the financial sector. With mortgage foreclosures, high unemployment and declining income created a credit crunch where banks did not have enough reserves to provide loans to businesses and consumers. TARP provided funding to banks to the tune of $431 billion.

The Federal Reserve created the Quantitative Easing (QE) program as an expansionary monetary policy designed to lower interest rates and spur economic growth. QE works by the Federal Reserve buying bank's bonds added to reserves to ease the credit crunch caused by toxic assets.

President Obama continued the QE program and the automobile buyout under TARP, then introduced the American Recovery and Reinvestment Act (ARRA) with a price tag of $787 billion. This program cut taxes, extended unemployment benefits and funded public works projects.

The Financial Crisis Inquiry Commission (FCIC) was a ten-member commission appointed by Congressional leaders with a mission of determining the cause of the financial crisis of 2007 – 2010. Its final report, published in January 2011, concluded that the financial crisis was avoidable. Failures of financial regulation and corporate governance plus risky management actions including excessive borrowing, risky investments and lack of transparency put the financial system on a collision course with the crisis.

Recovery from the Great Recession was slow, sluggish, and at times weak. Between 2010 and 2019, both GDP and median household income grew at a much slower rate than it had historically. Unemployment rose to 9.6 percent in 2010 then receded to 3.7 percent in 2019.

February 2020 became another inflection point. The longest recovery ended after 10 years and 2 months due to the global pandemic. Coronavirus (COVID-19) and its resulting "stay-at-home" orders that were enacted throughout the country caused consumer and business demand to plunge, except for the essential activities, such as health care, groceries, deliveries, truck drivers, etc. Businesses rearranged their work environment such that employees could work at home and many of those companies only retained a small workforce. The unemployment rate reached 14.4 percent in April, 13.0 percent in May and 11.2 percent in June 2020. In the second quarter of 2020, GDP dropped to levels never experienced in U.S. Personal income fared better with the CARES Act through July 2020 but the economic fallout from COVID-19 remains to be seen.

The upcoming sixteen chapters explore topics such as saving and investment, employment, household income, and Gross Domestic Product (GDP). Specifically, Chapters 1, 4, 5, 6, 10 and 12 provide extensive analytics of GDP, Chapter 3 includes detailed information on household income, poverty and health insurance coverage. Meanwhile, Chapter 8 includes information on inflation while Chapter 12 discusses interest rates and housing prices and Chapter 16 addresses key sector statistics. Historical data extending back to 1919 are available for certain series.

GENERAL NOTES

These notes provide general information about the data in Tables 1-1 through 16-14. Specific notes with information about data sources, definitions, methodology, revisions, and sources of additional information follow the tables in each chapter.

MAIN DIVISIONS OF THE BOOK

The tables are presented in two parts:

Part A (Tables 1-1 through 13-2) pertains principally to the U.S. economy as a whole. Generally, each table presents, on its initial page, annual averages as far back as data availability and space permit, and quarterly or monthly values for the most recent year or years. For many important series, this initial page is followed by full annual and quarterly or monthly histories as far back as they are available on a continuous, consistent basis. Some chapters present data for the United States only in aggregate, while others—such as the chapters concerning industrial production and capacity utilization (chapter 2), capital expenditures (chapter 5), profits (chapter 9), and employment, hours, and earnings (chapter 10)—also have detail for industry groups.

Data by industry are classified using the North American Industry Classification System (NAICS), as far back as such data are made available by the source agencies.

Part B focuses on the individual industries that together produce the gross domestic product (GDP).

- Chapter 14 contains data on the value of GDP, quantity production trends, and factor income by NAICS industry group.

- Chapter 15 provides further detail on payroll employment, hours, and earnings classified according to NAICS.

- Chapter 16 presents various data sets for key economic sectors. Some of the tables are based on definitions of products, rather than of producing establishments, and are valid for either classification system. This is the case for Tables 16-1, Petroleum and Petroleum Products; 16-2, New Construction; 16-3, Housing Starts and Building Permits, New House Sales, and Prices; and 16-8, Motor Vehicle Sales and Inventories. Tables 16-4 through 16-7 and 16-9, 16-11, and 16-12, which cover manufacturing and retail and wholesale trade, show data classified according to NAICS. Table 16-15 presents data for services industries classified according to NAICS.

Characteristics of the Tables and the Data

The subtitles or column headings for the data tables normally indicate whether the data are *seasonally adjusted, not seasonally adjusted,* or *at a seasonally adjusted annual rate.* These descriptions refer to the monthly or quarterly data, rather than the annual data; annual data by definition require no seasonal adjustment. Annual values are normally calculated as totals or averages, as appropriate, of unadjusted data. Such annual values are shown in either or both adjusted or unadjusted data columns.

Seasonal adjustment removes from a monthly or quarterly time series the average impact of variations that normally occur at about the same time each year, due to occurrences such as weather, holidays, and tax payment dates.

A simplified example of the process of seasonal adjustment, or deseasonalizing, can indicate its importance in the interpretation of economic time series. Statisticians compare actual monthly data for a number of years with "moving average" trends of the monthly data for the 12 months centered on each month's data. For example, they may find that in November, sales values are usually about 95 percent of the moving average, while in December, usual sales values are 110 percent of the average. Suppose that actual November sales in the current year are $100 and December sales are $105. The seasonally adjusted value for November will be $105 ($100/0.95) while the value for December will be $95 ($105/1.10). Thus, an apparent increase in the unadjusted data turns out to be a decrease when adjusted for the usual seasonal pattern.

The statistical method used to achieve the seasonal adjustment may vary from one data set to another. Many of the data are adjusted by a computer method known as X-12-ARIMA, developed by the Census Bureau. A description of the method is found in "New Capabilities and Methods of the X-12-ARIMA Seasonal Adjustment Program," by David F. Findley, Brian C. Monsell, William R. Bell, Mark C. Otto and Bor-Chung Chen (*Journal of Business and Economic Statistics*, April 1998). This article can be downloaded from the Bureau of the Census Web site at <https://www.census.gov>.

Production and sales data presented at *annual rates*—such as NIPA data in dollars, or motor vehicle data in number of units—show values at their annual equivalents: the values that would be registered if the seasonally adjusted rate of activity measured during a particular month or quarter were maintained for a full year. Specifically, seasonally adjusted monthly values are multiplied by 12 and quarterly values by 4 to yield seasonally adjusted annual rates.

Percent changes at seasonally adjusted annual rates for quarterly time periods are calculated using a compound interest formula, by raising the quarter-to-quarter percent change in a seasonally adjusted series to the fourth power. See the article

"Cycle and Growth Perspectives" for an explanation of compound annual growth rates.

Indexes. In many of the most important data sets presented in this volume, aggregate measures of prices and quantities are expressed in the form of indexes. The most basic and familiar form of index, the original Consumer Price Index, begins with a "market basket" of goods and services purchased in a base period, with each product category valued at its dollar prices—the amount spent on that category by the average consumer. The value weight ascribed to each component of the market basket is moved forward by the observed change in the price of the item selected to represent that component. These weighted component prices—which constitute the quantities in the base period repriced in the prices of subsequent periods—are aggregated, divided by the base period aggregate, and multiplied by 100 to provide an index number. An index calculated in this way is known as a *Laspeyres index.* In general, economists believe that Laspeyres price indexes have an upward bias, showing more price increase than they would if account were taken of consumers' ability to change spending patterns and maintain the same level of satisfaction in response to changing relative prices.

A *Paasche index* is one that uses the weights of the current period. Since the weights in the Paasche index change in each period, Paasche indexes only provide acceptable indications of change relative to the base period. Paasche indexes for two periods neither of which is the base period cannot be correctly compared: for example, a Paasche price index for a recent period might increase from the period just preceding even if no prices changed between those two periods, if there was a change in the composition of output toward prices that had previously increased more from the base period. When the national income and product account (NIPA) measures of real output were Laspeyres measures, using the weights of a single base year, the implicit deflators (current-dollar values divided by constant-dollar values) were Paasche indexes. Just as Laspeyres price indexes are upward-biased, Paasche price indexes are downward-biased because they overestimate consumers' ability to maintain the same level of satisfaction by changing spending patterns.

In recent years, government statisticians--with the aid of complex computer programs--have developed measures of real output and prices that minimize bias by using the weights of both periods and updating the weights for each period-to-period comparison. Such measures are described as chained indexes and are used in the NIPAs, the index of industrial production, and an experimental consumer price index. Chained measures are discussed more fully in the notes and definitions for Chapter 1, Chapter 2, and Chapter 8.

Detail may not sum to totals due to rounding. Since annual data are typically calculated by source agencies as the annual totals or averages of not-seasonally-adjusted data, they therefore will not be precisely equal to the annual totals or averages of monthly seasonally-adjusted data. Also, seasonal adjustment procedures are typically multiplicative rather than additive, which may also prevent seasonally adjusted data from adding or averaging to the annual figure. Percent changes and growth rates may have been calculated using unrounded data and therefore differ from those using the published figures.

The data in this volume are from federal government sources and international organizations and may be reproduced freely. A list of data sources is shown below.

The tables in this volume incorporate data revisions and corrections released by the source agencies through mid-2014, including the July annual revision of the NIPAs and the resulting August revision of productivity and costs.

DATA SOURCES

The source agencies for the data in this volume are listed below. The specific source or sources for each particular data set are identified at the beginning of the notes and definitions for the relevant data pages.

BOARD OF GOVERNORS OF THE FEDERAL RESERVE SYSTEM

20th Street & Constitution Avenue NW
Washington, DC 20551

Data Inquiries and Publication Sales:
Publications Services
Mail Stop 127
Board of Governors of the Federal Reserve System
Washington, DC 20551
Phone: (202) 452-3245

Quarterly Publication:
As of 2006, the *Federal Reserve Bulletin* is available free of charge and only on the Federal Reserve Web site.

URL:
https://www.federalreserve.gov

Census Bureau
U.S. Department of Commerce
4700 Silver Hill Road
Washington, DC 20233

URL:
https://www.census.gov

Ordering Data Products:
Call Center: (301) 763-INFO (4636)

E-mail Questions:
webmaster@census.gov

E-sales:
https://www.census.gov/mp/www/censtore.html

Bureau of Economic Analysis
U.S. Department of Commerce
Washington, DC 20230

Data Inquiries:
Public Information Office
Phone: (202) 606-9900

Monthly Publication:
Survey of Current Business
Available online.

URL:
https://www.bea.gov

Bureau of Labor Statistics
U.S. Department of Labor
2 Massachusetts Avenue NE
Washington, DC 20212-0001
(202) 691-5200

URL:
https://www.bls.gov

Data Inquiries:
Blsdata_staff@bls.gov

Monthly Publications available online:
Monthly Labor Review
Employment and Earnings
Compensation and Working Conditions
Producer Price Indexes
CPI Detailed Report

Employment and Training Administration
U.S. Department of Labor
200 Constitution Avenue NW
Washington, DC 20210
(877) US2-JOBS

URL:
https://www.doleta.gov
https://www.itsc.state.md.us

Energy Information Administration
U.S. Department of Energy
1000 Independence Avenue SW
Washington, DC 20585

Data Inquiries and Publications:
National Energy Information Center
Phone: (202) 586-8800
E-mail: infoctr@eia.doe.gov

Monthly Publication:
Monthly Energy Review, as of 2007 available only on the EIA
Web site, free of charge.

URL:
https://www.eia.doe.gov

Federal Housing Finance Agency
FHFAinfo@FHFA.gov
(202) 414-6921,6922
(202) 414-6376

URL:
https://www.fhfa.gov/hpi

U.S. Department of the Treasury
Office of International Affairs
Treasury International Capital System

URL:
https://www.treas.gov/tic

To order government publications
Superintendent of Documents
Government Printing Office
Washington, DC 20402
(202) 512-1800

URL:
https://bookstore.gpo.gov

PART A: THE U.S. ECONOMY

CHAPTER 1: NATIONAL INCOME AND PRODUCT

SECTION 1A: GROSS DOMESTIC PRODUCT: VALUES, QUANTITIES, AND PRICES

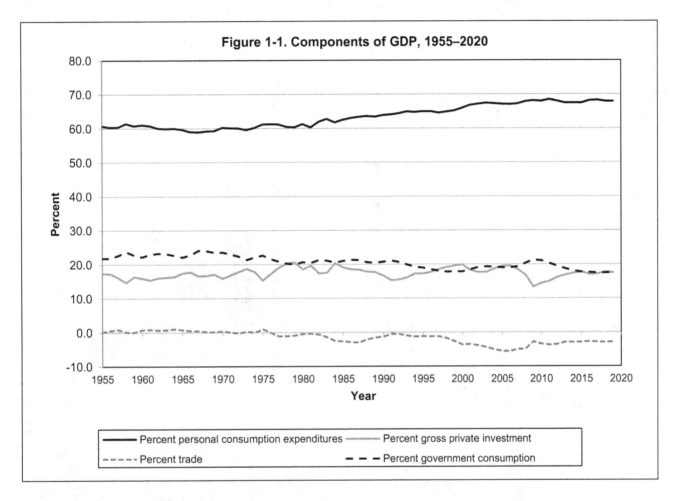

Figure 1-1. Components of GDP, 1955–2020

- As presented in the preface, the output approach to GDP consists of four components: consumption, business investment, government taxes and spending, and the foreign trade balance (exports – imports). GDP is one of the most comprehensive and closely watched economic statistics in not only the United States but also globally. For more details of GDP, see the Notes and Definitions at the end of this chapter.

- As the economy slowed due to COVID-19, the federal government legislated several acts to help consumers, businesses, states, counties, and tribal nations keep afloat. For example, checks were sent directly to Americans. Another program was enhanced unemployment compensation, funding to governmental entities, and more.

- For example, the original CARES Act proposal included $500 billion in direct payments to Americans, $208 billion in loans to major industry, and $300 billion in Small Business Administration loans. As a result of bipartisan negotiations, the bill grew to $2 trillion in the version unanimously passed by the Senate in March 2020.

- Figure 1-1 illustrates the four components of GDP. Consumption's share of GDP rose from 61 percent in 1960 to over 67 percent in 2020. Government's percent share of GDP fell in the same period. (Table 1-1A)

Table 1-1A. Gross Domestic Product: Recent Data

(Billions of dollars, quarterly data are at seasonally adjusted annual rates.)   **NIPA Tables 1.1.5, 1.2.5**

Year and quarter	Gross domestic product	Personal consump-tion expen-ditures	Gross private domestic investment				Exports and imports of goods and services			Government consumption expenditures and gross investment			Addendum: final sales of domestic product
			Total	Fixed investment		Change in private inventories	Net exports	Exports	Imports	Total	Federal	State and local	
				Nonresi-dential	Residential								
1960	542.4	331.2	86.5	56.4	26.9	3.2	4.2	27.0	22.8	120.5	72.9	47.6	539.1
1961	562.2	341.5	86.6	56.6	27.0	3.0	4.9	27.6	22.7	129.2	77.4	51.9	559.2
1962	603.9	362.6	97.0	61.2	29.6	6.1	4.1	29.1	25.0	140.3	85.5	54.8	597.8
1963	637.5	382.0	103.3	64.8	32.9	5.6	4.9	31.1	26.1	147.2	87.9	59.3	631.8
1964	684.5	410.6	112.2	72.2	35.1	4.8	6.9	35.0	28.1	154.8	90.3	64.5	679.6
1965	742.3	443.0	129.6	85.2	35.2	9.2	5.6	37.1	31.5	164.1	93.2	70.9	733.0
1966	813.4	479.9	144.2	97.2	33.4	13.6	3.9	40.9	37.1	185.4	106.6	78.9	799.8
1967	860.0	506.7	142.7	99.2	33.6	9.9	3.6	43.5	39.9	207.0	120.0	87.0	850.1
1968	940.7	556.9	156.9	107.7	40.2	9.1	1.4	47.9	46.6	225.5	128.0	97.6	931.6
1969	1 017.6	603.6	173.6	120.0	44.4	9.2	1.4	51.9	50.5	239.0	131.2	107.8	1 008.4
1970	1 073.3	646.7	170.0	124.6	43.4	2.0	3.9	59.7	55.8	252.6	132.8	119.8	1 071.3
1971	1 164.9	699.9	196.8	130.4	58.2	8.3	0.6	63.0	62.3	267.5	134.5	133.0	1 156.6
1972	1 279.1	768.2	228.1	146.6	72.4	9.1	-3.4	70.8	74.2	286.2	141.6	144.5	1 270.0
1973	1 425.4	849.6	266.9	172.7	78.3	15.9	4.1	95.3	91.2	304.8	146.2	158.6	1 409.5
1974	1 545.2	930.2	274.5	191.1	69.5	14.0	-0.8	126.7	127.5	341.4	158.8	182.5	1 531.3
1975	1 684.9	1 030.5	257.3	196.8	66.7	-6.3	16.0	138.7	122.7	381.1	173.7	207.4	1 691.2
1976	1 873.4	1 147.7	323.2	219.3	86.8	17.1	-1.6	149.5	151.1	404.2	184.8	219.4	1 856.3
1977	2 081.8	1 274.0	396.6	259.1	115.2	22.3	-23.1	159.3	182.4	434.3	200.3	234.0	2 059.5
1978	2 351.6	1 422.3	478.4	314.6	138.0	25.8	-25.4	186.9	212.3	476.3	218.9	257.4	2 325.8
1979	2 627.3	1 585.4	539.7	373.8	147.8	18.0	-22.5	230.1	252.7	524.8	240.6	284.2	2 609.3
1980	2 857.3	1 750.7	530.1	406.9	129.5	-6.3	-13.1	280.8	293.8	589.6	274.9	314.7	2 863.6
1981	3 207.0	1 934.0	631.2	472.9	128.5	29.8	-12.5	305.2	317.8	654.4	314.0	340.4	3 177.2
1982	3 343.8	2 071.3	581.0	485.1	110.8	-14.9	-20.0	283.2	303.2	711.5	348.3	363.1	3 358.7
1983	3 634.0	2 281.6	637.5	482.2	161.1	-5.8	-51.6	277.0	328.6	766.6	382.4	384.2	3 639.8
1984	4 037.6	2 492.3	820.1	564.3	190.4	65.4	-102.7	302.4	405.1	827.9	411.8	416.1	3 972.2
1985	4 339.0	2 712.8	829.7	607.8	200.1	21.8	-114.0	303.2	417.2	910.5	452.9	457.6	4 317.2
1986	4 579.6	2 886.3	849.1	607.8	234.8	6.6	-131.9	321.0	452.9	976.1	481.7	494.4	4 573.1
1987	4 855.2	3 076.3	892.2	615.2	249.8	27.1	-144.8	363.9	508.7	1 031.5	502.8	528.7	4 828.1
1988	5 236.4	3 330.0	937.0	662.3	256.2	18.5	-109.4	444.6	554.0	1 078.9	511.4	567.4	5 218.0
1989	5 641.6	3 576.8	999.7	716.0	256.0	27.7	-86.7	504.3	591.0	1 151.9	534.1	617.8	5 613.9
1990	5 963.1	3 809.0	993.4	739.2	239.7	14.5	-77.9	551.9	629.7	1 238.6	562.4	676.2	5 948.6
1991	6 158.1	3 943.4	944.3	723.6	221.2	-0.4	-28.6	594.9	623.5	1 299.0	582.9	716.0	6 158.5
1992	6 520.3	4 197.6	1 013.0	741.9	254.7	16.3	-34.7	633.1	667.8	1 344.5	588.5	756.0	6 504.0
1993	6 858.6	4 452.0	1 106.8	799.2	286.8	20.8	-65.2	654.8	720.0	1 364.9	580.2	784.8	6 837.7
1994	7 287.2	4 721.0	1 256.5	868.9	323.8	63.8	-92.5	720.9	813.4	1 402.3	574.7	827.6	7 223.5
1995	7 639.7	4 962.6	1 317.5	962.2	324.1	31.2	-89.8	812.8	902.6	1 449.4	576.7	872.7	7 608.6
1996	8 073.1	5 244.6	1 432.1	1 043.2	358.1	30.8	-96.4	867.6	964.0	1 492.8	579.2	913.7	8 042.3
1997	8 577.6	5 536.8	1 595.6	1 149.1	375.6	70.9	-102.0	953.8	1 055.8	1 547.1	583.3	963.8	8 506.6
1998	9 062.8	5 877.2	1 736.7	1 254.1	418.8	63.7	-162.7	953.0	1 115.7	1 611.6	585.5	1 026.1	8 999.1
1999	9 631.2	6 283.8	1 887.1	1 364.5	461.8	60.8	-259.6	992.9	1 252.5	1 719.9	610.7	1 109.2	9 570.4
2000	10 251.0	6 767.2	2 038.4	1 498.4	485.4	54.5	-381.1	1 096.1	1 477.2	1 826.4	633.1	1 193.4	10 196.4
2001	10 581.9	7 073.8	1 934.8	1 460.1	513.1	-38.3	-376.7	1 026.8	1 403.6	1 950.0	670.2	1 279.8	10 620.2
2002	10 929.1	7 348.9	1 930.4	1 352.8	557.6	20.0	-439.7	998.0	1 437.7	2 089.5	743.1	1 346.4	10 909.1
2003	11 456.5	7 740.7	2 027.1	1 375.9	637.1	14.1	-522.0	1 035.2	1 557.1	2 210.6	826.8	1 383.8	11 442.4
2004	12 217.2	8 232.0	2 281.3	1 467.4	749.8	64.1	-634.1	1 176.4	1 810.5	2 338.1	892.1	1 446.0	12 153.1
2005	13 039.2	8 769.1	2 534.7	1 621.0	856.2	57.5	-739.9	1 301.6	2 041.5	2 475.3	947.8	1 527.5	12 981.7
2006	13 815.6	9 277.2	2 701.0	1 793.8	838.2	69.0	-786.5	1 470.2	2 256.6	2 623.8	1 001.2	1 622.7	13 746.6
2007	14 474.2	9 746.6	2 673.0	1 948.6	690.5	34.0	-735.9	1 659.3	2 395.2	2 790.6	1 051.0	1 739.5	14 440.3
2008	14 769.9	10 050.1	2 477.6	1 990.9	516.0	-29.2	-740.9	1 835.3	2 576.2	2 983.0	1 152.0	1 831.1	14 799.1
2009	14 478.1	9 891.2	1 929.7	1 690.4	390.0	-150.8	-419.2	1 582.8	2 001.9	3 076.3	1 220.8	1 855.6	14 628.8
2010	15 049.0	10 260.3	2 165.5	1 735.0	376.6	53.9	-532.3	1 857.2	2 389.6	3 155.6	1 300.2	1 855.4	14 995.1
2011	15 599.7	10 698.9	2 332.6	1 907.5	378.8	46.3	-579.6	2 115.9	2 695.5	3 147.9	1 299.8	1 848.2	15 553.5
2012	16 254.0	11 047.4	2 621.8	2 118.5	432.0	71.2	-551.6	2 217.7	2 769.3	3 136.5	1 287.0	1 849.5	16 182.8
2013	16 843.2	11 363.5	2 826.0	2 211.5	510.0	104.5	-479.4	2 287.0	2 766.4	3 133.0	1 227.2	1 905.9	16 738.7
2014	17 550.7	11 847.7	3 044.2	2 400.1	560.2	84.0	-510.0	2 377.4	2 887.4	3 168.8	1 216.0	1 952.8	17 466.7
2015	18 206.0	12 263.5	3 237.2	2 466.6	633.8	136.8	-526.2	2 268.7	2 794.9	3 231.6	1 221.8	2 009.8	18 069.2
2016	18 695.1	12 693.3	3 205.0	2 469.3	699.4	36.3	-506.3	2 232.1	2 738.4	3 303.1	1 234.5	2 068.5	18 658.8
2017	19 479.6	13 239.1	3 381.4	2 591.6	760.3	29.5	-539.9	2 383.8	2 923.7	3 399.1	1 262.8	2 136.3	19 450.1
2018	20 527.2	13 913.5	3 637.8	2 780.6	798.5	58.7	-596.2	2 533.5	3 129.7	3 572.0	1 339.0	2 233.0	20 468.4
2019	21 372.6	14 428.7	3 826.3	2 938.7	813.9	73.6	-596.3	2 519.7	3 116.0	3 713.9	1 414.9	2 299.0	21 299.0
2020	20 893.7	14 047.6	3 637.8	2 799.6	897.8	-59.6	-651.2	2 123.4	2 774.6	3 859.5	1 501.8	2 357.8	20 953.3
2018													
1st quarter	20 143.7	13 667.4	3 550.8	2 716.0	789.0	45.9	-580.1	2 504.4	3 084.5	3 505.5	1 305.8	2 199.7	20 097.9
2nd quarter	20 492.5	13 864.8	3 603.2	2 770.1	808.9	24.2	-539.8	2 568.3	3 108.1	3 564.3	1 331.7	2 232.6	20 468.3
3rd quarter	20 659.1	14 002.6	3 679.6	2 798.1	804.3	77.1	-624.0	2 534.2	3 158.2	3 600.9	1 350.8	2 250.1	20 582.0
4th quarter	20 813.3	14 119.3	3 717.5	2 838.1	791.8	87.7	-640.9	2 527.1	3 168.1	3 617.4	1 367.7	2 249.7	20 725.7
2019													
1st quarter	21 001.6	14 155.6	3 801.9	2 886.9	796.5	118.5	-606.4	2 524.6	3 131.0	3 650.5	1 387.0	2 263.5	20 883.1
2nd quarter	21 289.3	14 375.7	3 843.0	2 946.1	808.5	88.4	-632.3	2 533.4	3 165.7	3 702.9	1 406.9	2 296.0	21 200.8
3rd quarter	21 505.0	14 529.5	3 858.2	2 969.3	821.9	67.0	-614.0	2 512.1	3 126.1	3 731.3	1 424.1	2 307.2	21 438.0
4th quarter	21 694.5	14 653.9	3 801.9	2 952.6	828.8	20.6	-532.4	2 508.7	3 041.1	3 771.0	1 441.7	2 329.2	21 673.9
2020													
1st quarter	21 481.4	14 439.1	3 752.4	2 900.1	872.9	-20.6	-541.7	2 385.5	2 927.3	3 831.6	1 454.7	2 376.9	21 502.0
2nd quarter	19 477.4	12 989.7	3 167.0	2 659.1	797.8	-289.9	-538.9	1 807.9	2 346.7	3 859.6	1 525.0	2 334.6	19 767.4
3rd quarter	21 138.6	14 293.8	3 708.8	2 776.6	917.2	15.0	-725.7	2 079.6	2 805.3	3 861.7	1 515.1	2 346.5	21 123.6
4th quarter	21 477.6	14 467.6	3 923.2	2 862.7	1 003.2	57.3	-798.4	2 220.7	3 019.1	3 885.3	1 512.3	2 373.0	21 420.3

Table 1-1B. Gross Domestic Product: Historical Data

(Billions of dollars, quarterly data are at seasonally adjusted annual rates.)

NIPA Tables 1.1.5, 1.2.5

| Year and quarter | Gross domestic product | Personal consumption expenditures | Gross private domestic investment | | | | Exports and imports of goods and services | | | Government consumption expenditures and gross investment | | | Addendum: Final sales of domestic product |
| | | | Total | Fixed investment | | Change in private inventories | Net exports | Exports | Imports | Total | Federal | State and local | |
				Nonresidential	Residential								
1929	104.6	77.4	17.2	11.6	4.1	1.5	0.4	5.9	5.6	9.6	1.9	7.7	103.0
1930	92.2	70.1	11.4	9.2	2.5	-0.2	0.3	4.4	4.1	10.3	2.0	8.3	92.4
1931	77.4	60.7	6.5	5.8	1.9	-1.1	0.0	2.9	2.9	10.2	2.1	8.1	78.5
1932	59.5	48.7	1.8	3.3	0.9	-2.4	0.0	2.0	1.9	8.9	2.0	6.9	61.9
1933	57.2	45.9	2.3	3.0	0.7	-1.4	0.1	2.0	1.9	8.9	2.5	6.4	58.6
1934	66.8	51.5	4.3	3.8	1.0	-0.6	0.3	2.6	2.2	10.7	3.5	7.3	67.4
1935	74.2	55.9	7.4	4.8	1.4	1.1	-0.2	2.8	3.0	11.2	3.6	7.6	73.1
1936	84.8	62.2	9.4	6.4	1.8	1.2	-0.1	3.0	3.2	13.4	5.8	7.6	83.7
1937	93.0	66.8	13.0	8.2	2.2	2.6	0.1	4.0	4.0	13.1	5.3	7.8	90.4
1938	87.4	64.3	7.9	6.3	2.2	-0.6	1.0	3.8	2.8	14.2	5.9	8.3	87.9
1939	93.4	67.2	10.2	6.9	3.2	0.2	0.8	4.0	3.1	15.2	6.2	8.9	93.2
1940	102.9	71.3	14.6	8.5	3.6	2.4	1.5	4.9	3.4	15.6	6.8	8.7	100.5
1941	129.3	81.1	19.4	10.8	4.2	4.3	1.0	5.5	4.4	27.8	19.1	8.7	125.0
1942	166.0	89.0	11.8	7.5	2.4	1.9	-0.3	4.4	4.6	65.4	56.7	8.7	164.0
1943	203.1	99.9	7.4	6.6	1.6	-0.7	-2.2	4.0	6.3	98.0	89.5	8.5	203.8
1944	224.4	108.6	9.2	8.6	1.5	-0.9	-2.0	4.9	6.9	108.6	100.1	8.6	225.4
1945	228.0	120.0	12.4	12.1	1.8	-1.5	-0.8	6.8	7.5	96.4	87.2	9.2	229.5
1946	227.5	144.2	33.1	19.2	8.0	6.0	7.2	14.2	7.0	43.0	32.0	11.0	221.5
1947	249.6	161.9	37.1	25.5	12.2	-0.6	10.8	18.7	7.9	39.8	25.7	14.1	250.2
1948	274.5	174.9	50.3	28.9	15.8	5.7	5.5	15.5	10.1	43.8	27.0	16.7	268.8
1949	272.5	178.3	39.1	27.0	14.8	-2.7	5.2	14.5	9.2	49.8	30.4	19.4	275.2
1947													
1st quarter	243.2	156.2	35.9	24.8	10.5	0.5	10.9	18.4	7.5	40.3	27.0	13.3	242.7
2nd quarter	246.0	160.0	34.5	25.2	10.6	-1.2	11.3	19.5	8.2	40.1	26.4	13.7	247.2
3rd quarter	249.6	163.5	34.9	25.4	12.5	-2.9	11.8	19.4	7.7	39.4	25.0	14.3	252.5
4th quarter	259.7	167.7	43.3	26.5	15.3	1.5	9.3	17.6	8.3	39.5	24.5	15.0	258.3
1948													
1st quarter	265.7	170.4	47.2	28.2	15.3	3.6	7.3	16.9	9.6	40.9	25.4	15.5	262.1
2nd quarter	272.6	174.1	50.3	28.1	16.4	5.9	5.2	15.2	10.0	42.9	26.6	16.3	266.7
3rd quarter	279.2	177.1	52.5	29.1	16.3	7.2	4.9	15.4	10.5	44.7	27.5	17.2	272.0
4th quarter	280.4	177.9	51.3	30.2	15.2	6.0	4.5	14.6	10.1	46.6	28.7	17.9	274.4
1949													
1st quarter	275.0	176.8	43.1	28.6	14.2	0.4	6.5	16.1	9.6	48.6	30.2	18.4	274.6
2nd quarter	271.4	178.4	36.2	27.5	13.9	-5.1	6.3	15.6	9.4	50.4	31.2	19.1	276.5
3rd quarter	272.9	177.8	39.5	26.1	14.7	-1.3	5.2	14.1	8.9	50.4	30.5	19.9	274.2
4th quarter	270.6	180.2	37.5	25.6	16.5	-4.7	3.0	12.1	9.1	49.9	29.8	20.1	275.3
1950													
1st quarter	280.8	182.9	46.7	26.4	18.3	2.0	2.2	11.7	9.5	49.0	28.5	20.4	278.8
2nd quarter	290.4	186.8	52.3	28.9	20.6	2.8	1.6	11.9	10.2	49.6	28.9	20.7	287.6
3rd quarter	308.2	200.5	58.6	31.9	22.6	4.2	-0.7	12.3	13.0	49.7	28.4	21.3	304.0
4th quarter	319.9	197.9	68.4	32.9	21.5	14.0	-0.2	13.5	13.7	53.7	31.8	21.9	305.9
1951													
1st quarter	336.0	209.2	64.6	33.1	21.1	10.4	0.2	15.0	14.9	62.0	39.6	22.5	325.6
2nd quarter	344.1	204.9	67.4	34.1	18.5	14.8	1.9	17.1	15.2	69.8	46.6	23.2	329.3
3rd quarter	351.4	207.6	62.0	34.8	17.4	9.7	3.7	18.1	14.3	78.0	54.3	23.7	341.6
4th quarter	356.2	211.6	57.1	34.6	17.7	4.7	4.2	18.2	14.0	83.3	59.3	24.0	351.5
1952													
1st quarter	359.8	213.0	58.1	35.1	18.3	4.7	3.7	18.7	15.0	85.0	60.9	24.1	355.1
2nd quarter	361.0	217.1	53.0	35.8	18.8	-1.5	2.0	16.6	14.6	89.0	64.1	24.9	362.6
3rd quarter	367.7	219.6	57.2	32.9	18.8	5.6	0.0	15.2	15.3	90.9	66.2	24.8	362.1
4th quarter	380.8	227.7	60.7	35.8	19.6	5.3	-1.0	15.3	16.3	93.4	68.1	25.3	375.5
1953													
1st quarter	388.0	231.2	61.7	37.8	20.0	3.9	-0.7	15.1	15.8	95.8	69.7	26.1	384.1
2nd quarter	391.7	233.0	62.1	38.5	20.1	3.6	-1.3	15.2	16.4	97.9	72.0	26.0	388.2
3rd quarter	391.2	233.7	61.4	39.6	19.5	2.3	-0.6	15.8	16.3	96.6	70.0	26.7	388.8
4th quarter	386.0	233.1	56.4	39.2	19.3	-2.0	-0.3	15.2	15.5	96.7	69.5	27.2	388.0
1954													
1st quarter	385.3	235.2	55.7	38.3	19.4	-2.0	-0.4	14.4	14.8	94.8	66.7	28.1	387.3
2nd quarter	386.1	237.9	55.4	38.2	20.7	-3.4	0.3	16.4	16.2	92.5	63.7	28.8	389.5
3rd quarter	391.0	240.3	59.0	38.9	22.2	-2.1	0.6	15.9	15.3	91.1	61.4	29.8	393.1
4th quarter	399.7	245.1	62.1	38.9	23.6	-0.3	1.1	16.6	15.5	91.4	61.2	30.1	400.1
1955													
1st quarter	413.1	251.4	68.7	39.5	25.4	3.8	1.1	17.3	16.2	91.9	60.7	31.1	409.3
2nd quarter	421.5	256.5	72.7	42.1	26.0	4.6	-0.2	16.9	17.1	92.5	60.8	31.7	416.9
3rd quarter	430.2	260.7	74.7	44.8	25.6	4.3	0.7	18.1	17.4	94.1	61.9	32.2	425.9
4th quarter	437.1	264.6	78.9	47.1	24.6	7.2	0.2	18.3	18.1	93.3	60.6	32.8	429.9
1956													
1st quarter	439.7	266.2	78.3	47.8	24.1	6.4	0.4	19.4	18.9	94.8	61.0	33.9	433.3
2nd quarter	446.0	268.8	77.0	49.1	24.4	3.6	1.9	20.9	19.0	98.2	63.5	34.7	442.4
3rd quarter	451.2	272.1	78.3	50.7	24.0	3.6	2.6	21.8	19.3	98.3	62.8	35.5	447.6
4th quarter	460.5	277.4	77.1	51.4	23.5	2.2	4.5	23.1	18.5	101.3	65.2	36.2	458.2
1957													
1st quarter	469.8	281.9	77.7	52.5	23.1	2.2	4.8	24.9	20.1	105.3	67.9	37.5	467.6
2nd quarter	472.0	284.2	77.9	52.6	22.6	2.7	4.1	24.4	20.3	105.8	67.5	38.3	469.4
3rd quarter	479.5	288.8	79.3	54.1	22.5	2.8	4.0	23.8	19.8	107.4	68.4	39.1	476.7
4th quarter	474.9	290.4	71.0	53.2	22.3	-4.5	3.4	23.0	19.6	110.1	70.0	40.0	479.4
1958													
1st quarter	467.5	289.9	66.7	49.4	21.4	-4.0	1.1	20.5	19.5	109.8	68.7	41.1	471.5
2nd quarter	472.0	292.8	65.1	47.8	21.5	-4.2	0.5	20.5	20.1	113.6	71.5	42.1	476.2
3rd quarter	485.8	297.9	72.0	47.4	23.0	1.5	0.9	20.6	19.7	115.1	71.9	43.2	484.3
4th quarter	499.6	301.8	80.0	49.3	25.4	5.2	-0.3	20.6	20.8	118.0	73.9	44.1	494.3

Table 1-1B. Gross Domestic Product: Historical Data—*Continued*

(Billions of dollars, quarterly data are at seasonally adjusted annual rates.)

NIPA Tables 1.1.5, 1.2.5

Year and quarter	Gross domestic product	Personal consumption expenditures	Gross private domestic investment				Exports and imports of goods and services			Government consumption expenditures and gross investment			Addendum: Final sales of domestic product
			Total	Fixed investment		Change in private inventories	Net exports	Exports	Imports	Total	Federal	State and local	
				Nonresidential	Residential								
1959													
1st quarter	510.3	309.4	83.2	50.9	28.3	3.9	0.5	21.9	21.4	117.2	72.4	44.8	506.5
2nd quarter	522.7	315.5	89.4	52.7	29.4	7.3	-0.8	21.8	22.5	118.5	73.6	45.0	515.4
3rd quarter	525.0	320.7	83.6	54.4	28.8	0.4	1.2	24.1	22.9	119.5	74.5	45.0	524.7
4th quarter	528.6	322.8	86.5	54.4	28.0	4.1	0.6	23.1	22.5	118.6	73.8	44.8	524.5
1960													
1st quarter	542.6	326.4	96.5	56.3	29.0	11.2	2.9	26.1	23.3	117.0	71.0	46.0	531.4
2nd quarter	541.1	332.2	87.1	57.2	26.7	3.2	3.4	26.9	23.5	118.4	71.1	47.3	537.9
3rd quarter	545.6	332.1	86.4	56.2	25.9	4.3	4.7	27.6	22.9	122.4	74.2	48.3	541.3
4th quarter	540.2	334.0	76.0	55.9	25.9	-5.8	5.9	27.6	21.7	124.3	75.3	49.0	546.0
1961													
1st quarter	545.0	334.5	78.4	55.0	25.9	-2.5	5.9	27.6	21.7	126.2	75.3	50.9	547.6
2nd quarter	555.5	339.5	84.1	56.2	26.1	1.8	4.7	26.6	21.9	127.3	76.2	51.1	553.8
3rd quarter	567.7	342.3	90.9	56.7	27.6	6.7	4.5	27.8	23.3	130.0	78.1	51.8	561.0
4th quarter	580.6	349.6	92.9	58.5	28.5	6.0	4.6	28.4	23.9	133.5	79.9	53.6	574.6
1962													
1st quarter	594.0	354.8	98.1	59.7	29.0	9.4	4.0	28.3	24.3	137.1	83.3	53.8	584.6
2nd quarter	600.4	360.5	96.7	61.4	29.9	5.4	4.8	29.7	24.9	138.4	84.1	54.3	594.9
3rd quarter	609.0	364.3	98.2	62.1	29.9	6.2	4.5	29.6	25.1	142.1	87.0	55.0	602.8
4th quarter	612.3	370.6	95.0	61.8	29.8	3.4	3.1	28.7	25.6	143.6	87.6	56.0	608.9
1963													
1st quarter	621.7	374.3	99.7	62.0	30.8	6.9	4.0	29.2	25.2	143.7	86.2	57.5	614.8
2nd quarter	629.8	378.4	101.7	63.9	32.9	4.8	5.6	31.4	25.9	144.1	85.8	58.4	624.9
3rd quarter	644.4	385.4	104.6	65.7	33.2	5.7	4.5	31.2	26.7	149.9	89.9	60.1	638.7
4th quarter	653.9	390.0	107.2	67.7	34.5	5.1	5.7	32.5	26.8	151.0	89.7	61.3	648.9
1964													
1st quarter	669.8	399.6	110.5	69.1	36.2	5.1	7.2	34.2	27.0	152.6	90.1	62.5	664.7
2nd quarter	678.7	407.5	110.5	71.1	35.0	4.5	6.3	34.0	27.7	154.3	90.1	64.2	674.2
3rd quarter	692.0	416.4	112.6	73.4	34.5	4.7	6.9	35.4	28.4	156.0	90.8	65.2	687.3
4th quarter	697.3	419.0	115.0	75.3	34.6	5.0	7.2	36.5	29.3	156.2	90.0	66.2	692.3
1965													
1st quarter	717.8	429.7	126.5	80.2	34.8	11.5	4.5	33.0	28.5	157.0	89.5	67.5	706.2
2nd quarter	730.2	436.6	127.1	83.4	35.1	8.6	6.7	38.4	31.7	159.8	90.1	69.7	721.6
3rd quarter	749.3	445.8	131.2	86.7	35.3	9.3	5.5	37.6	32.0	166.8	94.5	72.3	740.0
4th quarter	771.9	459.7	133.8	90.6	35.5	7.6	5.8	39.7	33.9	172.6	98.7	73.9	764.3
1966													
1st quarter	795.7	470.1	144.2	94.4	35.9	13.9	4.4	39.4	35.0	177.0	101.2	75.8	781.9
2nd quarter	805.0	475.2	143.5	96.8	34.4	12.3	4.6	40.9	36.2	181.7	104.0	77.6	792.7
3rd quarter	819.6	484.3	143.2	98.3	33.0	11.9	2.7	40.9	38.2	189.5	109.9	79.5	807.8
4th quarter	833.3	490.1	145.9	99.2	30.2	16.5	3.8	42.6	38.8	193.6	111.2	82.5	816.8
1967													
1st quarter	844.2	494.3	142.8	98.0	29.4	15.4	4.5	43.9	39.4	202.6	117.9	84.7	828.7
2nd quarter	849.0	503.5	137.5	98.3	32.9	6.3	4.2	43.2	39.0	203.8	117.9	85.9	842.6
3rd quarter	865.2	510.7	142.8	98.8	34.8	9.3	3.3	42.8	39.5	208.4	121.0	87.4	856.0
4th quarter	881.4	518.2	147.7	101.7	37.5	8.4	2.2	43.9	41.7	213.3	123.2	90.1	873.0
1968													
1st quarter	909.4	536.3	152.3	105.6	38.3	8.4	1.1	45.5	44.4	219.7	126.4	93.3	900.9
2nd quarter	934.3	550.0	158.9	105.3	39.6	14.1	1.7	47.2	45.4	223.6	127.2	96.5	920.3
3rd quarter	950.8	566.1	155.7	107.6	40.4	7.7	1.7	49.9	48.2	227.4	128.5	98.8	943.1
4th quarter	968.0	575.0	160.8	112.2	42.6	6.0	0.9	49.1	48.2	231.3	129.7	101.6	962.0
1969													
1st quarter	993.3	587.0	172.4	116.0	44.9	11.5	0.2	44.0	43.8	233.7	129.6	104.1	981.8
2nd quarter	1 009.0	598.3	172.7	118.4	45.1	9.2	1.1	53.8	52.7	236.9	129.8	107.1	999.8
3rd quarter	1 030.0	608.6	177.6	122.4	45.0	10.2	1.2	53.6	52.4	242.5	133.4	109.1	1 019.8
4th quarter	1 038.1	620.6	171.6	123.3	42.5	5.8	3.1	56.3	53.1	242.8	132.0	110.8	1 032.4
1970													
1st quarter	1 051.2	631.7	168.1	123.8	42.5	1.8	3.5	57.0	53.5	247.9	133.6	114.3	1 049.4
2nd quarter	1 067.4	641.6	171.5	125.0	41.4	5.1	5.2	60.4	55.2	249.1	131.8	117.4	1 062.3
3rd quarter	1 086.1	653.5	173.9	126.3	42.6	5.1	4.1	60.5	56.4	254.6	132.4	122.2	1 081.0
4th quarter	1 088.6	660.2	166.8	123.5	47.2	-4.0	3.0	60.9	57.9	258.7	133.5	125.2	1 092.6
1971													
1st quarter	1 135.2	679.2	189.5	126.3	51.0	12.3	4.6	63.2	58.7	261.9	133.3	128.6	1 122.9
2nd quarter	1 156.3	693.2	197.3	129.5	57.0	10.9	-0.4	62.9	63.3	266.1	134.3	131.9	1 145.4
3rd quarter	1 177.0	705.6	202.1	131.2	60.7	10.2	0.2	65.7	65.5	269.8	135.6	134.2	1 167.5
4th quarter	1 190.3	721.7	198.4	134.7	64.0	-0.3	-1.9	60.0	61.9	272.1	134.7	137.4	1 190.6
1972													
1st quarter	1 230.6	738.9	213.0	140.6	69.2	3.2	-3.5	68.6	72.2	282.2	141.4	140.8	1 227.4
2nd quarter	1 266.4	757.4	226.8	144.0	70.8	12.0	-4.3	67.2	71.4	286.5	144.2	142.2	1 254.4
3rd quarter	1 290.6	775.8	233.1	147.0	72.4	13.7	-2.6	71.5	74.1	284.3	138.8	145.6	1 276.9
4th quarter	1 328.9	800.5	239.7	155.0	77.3	7.5	-3.1	76.1	79.2	291.7	142.2	149.6	1 321.4
1973													
1st quarter	1 377.5	825.0	254.3	162.8	80.9	10.6	-1.4	84.0	85.4	299.6	146.4	153.2	1 366.9
2nd quarter	1 413.9	840.5	268.2	171.3	78.7	18.2	2.5	91.9	89.5	302.7	146.5	156.2	1 395.7
3rd quarter	1 433.8	858.9	264.3	176.6	77.9	9.8	6.4	97.6	91.1	304.2	144.2	159.9	1 424.1
4th quarter	1 476.3	873.9	280.9	180.1	75.7	25.0	9.0	107.6	98.7	312.6	147.6	165.0	1 451.3
1974													
1st quarter	1 491.2	891.9	268.4	183.4	72.4	12.5	6.4	116.7	110.3	324.6	152.7	171.9	1 478.7
2nd quarter	1 530.1	920.4	277.4	188.8	71.2	17.4	-2.7	126.7	129.4	335.0	154.9	180.1	1 512.6
3rd quarter	1 560.0	949.3	271.0	194.5	70.9	5.6	-7.0	126.6	133.6	346.7	160.4	186.3	1 554.4
4th quarter	1 599.7	959.1	281.3	197.6	63.3	20.4	0.0	136.6	136.6	359.2	167.4	191.9	1 579.2

Table 1-1B. Gross Domestic Product: Historical Data—*Continued*

(Billions of dollars, quarterly data are at seasonally adjusted annual rates.)   NIPA Tables 1.1.5, 1.2.5

Year and quarter	Gross domestic product	Personal consumption expenditures	Gross private domestic investment				Exports and imports of goods and services			Government consumption expenditures and gross investment			Addendum: Final sales of domestic product
			Total	Fixed investment		Change in private inventories	Net exports	Exports	Imports	Total	Federal	State and local	
				Nonresidential	Residential								
1975													
1st quarter	1 616.1	985.2	244.3	193.1	61.2	-10.0	16.5	141.4	124.9	370.1	168.6	201.5	1 626.1
2nd quarter	1 651.9	1 013.6	243.3	193.3	64.0	-14.0	21.6	136.8	115.2	373.4	169.4	204.0	1 665.8
3rd quarter	1 709.8	1 047.2	265.2	197.8	68.8	-1.4	12.0	134.1	122.1	385.4	176.1	209.3	1 711.2
4th quarter	1 761.8	1 076.2	276.2	202.9	73.0	0.3	13.8	142.5	128.7	395.6	180.8	214.8	1 761.5
1976													
1st quarter	1 820.5	1 109.9	304.6	209.5	80.4	14.7	4.7	143.6	138.9	401.3	181.6	219.7	1 805.8
2nd quarter	1 852.3	1 129.5	322.3	215.0	84.8	22.4	-0.5	146.6	147.1	401.0	182.5	218.5	1 829.9
3rd quarter	1 886.6	1 158.8	328.3	222.6	84.9	20.8	-4.1	151.8	155.8	403.5	184.9	218.6	1 865.8
4th quarter	1 934.3	1 192.4	337.7	230.2	96.9	10.5	-6.6	156.1	162.7	410.8	190.2	220.6	1 923.8
1977													
1st quarter	1 988.6	1 228.2	360.3	243.3	102.2	14.8	-21.1	155.4	176.4	421.2	194.2	227.0	1 973.8
2nd quarter	2 055.9	1 256.0	389.7	253.7	116.5	19.5	-21.1	161.9	183.0	431.4	198.9	232.4	2 036.4
3rd quarter	2 118.5	1 286.9	414.1	263.3	120.0	30.9	-20.6	162.3	182.9	438.0	201.9	236.1	2 087.6
4th quarter	2 164.3	1 324.8	422.3	275.9	122.2	24.1	-29.6	157.8	187.4	446.7	206.3	240.5	2 140.1
1978													
1st quarter	2 202.8	1 354.1	434.8	282.4	126.9	25.5	-38.7	164.6	203.3	452.6	208.8	243.8	2 177.3
2nd quarter	2 331.6	1 411.4	470.6	309.4	137.0	24.3	-22.6	186.2	208.8	472.3	217.0	255.3	2 307.4
3rd quarter	2 395.1	1 442.2	492.4	325.1	142.3	25.0	-23.8	191.3	215.1	484.2	222.1	262.2	2 370.1
4th quarter	2 476.9	1 481.4	515.8	341.4	145.8	28.5	-16.4	205.4	221.8	496.2	227.8	268.4	2 448.5
1979													
1st quarter	2 526.6	1 517.1	525.8	356.7	145.3	23.9	-18.2	211.7	229.8	501.8	231.7	270.1	2 502.8
2nd quarter	2 591.2	1 557.6	539.3	364.3	147.6	27.4	-22.2	220.9	243.1	516.5	237.6	278.9	2 563.8
3rd quarter	2 667.6	1 611.9	545.6	383.0	150.5	12.1	-23.0	234.3	257.3	533.1	243.7	289.4	2 655.4
4th quarter	2 723.9	1 655.0	547.9	391.3	148.0	8.6	-26.8	253.7	280.5	547.8	249.3	298.4	2 715.3
1980													
1st quarter	2 789.8	1 702.3	554.6	404.5	140.2	9.9	-35.8	268.5	304.3	568.8	261.1	307.7	2 779.9
2nd quarter	2 797.4	1 704.7	519.3	394.7	116.9	7.8	-15.2	277.4	292.6	588.5	276.5	312.0	2 789.6
3rd quarter	2 856.5	1 763.8	495.1	405.7	123.2	-33.9	5.5	284.7	279.2	592.2	276.1	316.1	2 890.3
4th quarter	2 985.6	1 831.9	551.5	422.8	137.8	-9.1	-6.7	292.5	299.2	608.9	285.8	323.1	2 994.7
1981													
1st quarter	3 124.2	1 885.7	619.4	443.0	137.6	38.8	-14.3	305.5	319.7	633.4	297.2	336.1	3 085.5
2nd quarter	3 162.5	1 917.5	609.8	462.9	135.3	11.7	-13.5	308.5	322.0	648.7	311.9	336.8	3 150.8
3rd quarter	3 260.6	1 958.1	652.3	482.1	126.2	44.0	-7.6	302.3	309.9	657.8	317.4	340.3	3 216.7
4th quarter	3 280.8	1 974.4	643.4	503.8	114.8	24.8	-14.8	304.7	319.4	677.7	329.3	348.4	3 256.0
1982													
1st quarter	3 274.3	2 014.2	588.3	500.1	109.7	-21.5	-16.3	293.2	309.5	688.1	334.9	353.2	3 295.8
2nd quarter	3 332.0	2 039.6	593.6	490.1	107.7	-4.2	-4.4	294.7	299.1	703.1	342.9	360.2	3 336.1
3rd quarter	3 366.3	2 085.7	593.0	478.7	108.4	5.8	-29.6	279.6	309.3	717.3	351.5	365.8	3 360.5
4th quarter	3 402.6	2 145.6	549.2	471.5	117.5	-39.8	-29.6	265.3	294.9	737.4	364.1	373.3	3 442.4
1983													
1st quarter	3 473.4	2 184.6	565.5	462.1	138.5	-35.1	-24.5	270.7	295.3	747.9	370.5	377.4	3 508.5
2nd quarter	3 578.8	2 249.4	613.8	466.5	155.0	-7.7	-45.4	272.5	317.9	761.1	380.3	380.7	3 586.5
3rd quarter	3 689.2	2 319.9	652.3	485.4	171.1	-4.2	-65.2	278.2	343.4	782.2	394.4	387.8	3 693.4
4th quarter	3 794.7	2 372.5	718.5	514.7	179.9	23.9	-71.4	286.6	358.0	775.1	384.2	390.9	3 770.8
1984													
1st quarter	3 908.1	2 418.2	790.9	531.5	186.4	73.0	-95.0	293.0	388.0	794.0	392.4	401.6	3 835.1
2nd quarter	4 009.6	2 475.9	818.9	558.3	191.3	69.3	-104.3	302.2	406.5	819.1	408.3	410.8	3 940.3
3rd quarter	4 084.3	2 513.5	838.9	576.6	190.9	71.3	-103.8	305.7	409.6	835.7	414.0	421.7	4 012.9
4th quarter	4 148.6	2 561.8	831.7	590.9	192.9	48.0	-107.8	308.6	416.4	862.8	432.5	430.2	4 100.6
1985													
1st quarter	4 230.2	2 636.0	809.9	599.4	194.2	16.2	-91.3	306.0	397.3	875.6	434.8	440.8	4 213.9
2nd quarter	4 294.9	2 681.8	827.0	609.1	196.3	21.6	-114.4	304.1	418.6	900.5	447.3	453.2	4 273.2
3rd quarter	4 386.8	2 754.1	822.2	604.4	201.4	16.3	-116.9	297.3	414.2	927.4	463.1	464.3	4 370.5
4th quarter	4 444.1	2 779.4	859.5	618.1	208.4	33.1	-133.4	305.4	438.9	938.6	466.4	472.1	4 411.0
1986													
1st quarter	4 507.9	2 823.6	863.5	613.5	219.5	30.4	-126.0	313.4	439.4	946.8	464.0	482.8	4 477.5
2nd quarter	4 545.3	2 851.5	855.2	605.0	234.6	15.7	-128.9	315.1	444.0	967.5	477.8	489.7	4 529.7
3rd quarter	4 607.7	2 917.2	835.8	602.0	240.9	-7.0	-139.0	320.5	459.4	993.6	495.1	498.5	4 614.7
4th quarter	4 657.6	2 952.8	842.1	610.6	244.3	-12.8	-133.6	335.0	468.6	996.4	489.8	506.6	4 670.4
1987													
1st quarter	4 722.2	2 983.5	871.2	596.6	246.7	28.0	-141.2	336.5	477.7	1 008.7	492.1	516.5	4 694.2
2nd quarter	4 806.2	3 053.3	874.6	608.4	249.7	16.5	-147.0	355.4	502.3	1 025.2	501.2	524.0	4 789.6
3rd quarter	4 884.6	3 117.4	876.5	625.5	250.0	1.0	-145.5	371.9	517.3	1 036.2	504.1	532.1	4 883.5
4th quarter	5 008.0	3 150.9	946.5	630.6	252.8	63.1	-145.4	392.1	537.5	1 056.0	513.7	542.3	4 944.9
1988													
1st quarter	5 073.4	3 231.9	908.6	641.5	250.1	17.0	-124.0	418.7	542.7	1 056.9	505.8	551.1	5 056.4
2nd quarter	5 190.0	3 291.7	934.5	659.4	255.5	19.6	-106.6	439.5	546.1	1 070.4	506.9	563.5	5 170.4
3rd quarter	5 282.8	3 361.9	942.0	666.3	257.5	18.2	-99.3	453.6	552.8	1 078.2	507.4	570.8	5 264.7
4th quarter	5 399.5	3 434.5	962.7	681.9	261.7	19.1	-107.7	466.6	574.3	1 109.9	525.6	584.3	5 380.4
1989													
1st quarter	5 511.3	3 490.2	1 005.5	696.5	260.9	48.1	-101.0	485.2	586.2	1 116.6	519.9	596.7	5 463.1
2nd quarter	5 612.5	3 553.8	1 001.0	709.0	255.8	36.3	-88.2	507.2	595.4	1 145.8	534.3	611.5	5 576.2
3rd quarter	5 695.4	3 609.4	996.5	731.1	255.5	9.8	-75.1	509.4	584.4	1 164.6	541.4	623.2	5 685.5
4th quarter	5 747.2	3 653.7	995.8	727.4	251.9	16.6	-82.8	515.4	598.2	1 180.5	540.8	639.7	5 730.7
1990													
1st quarter	5 872.7	3 737.9	1 010.8	740.9	256.0	14.0	-88.5	538.2	626.8	1 212.5	553.7	658.8	5 858.7
2nd quarter	5 960.0	3 783.4	1 014.7	734.1	246.9	33.7	-68.8	545.9	614.8	1 230.7	563.9	666.8	5 926.3
3rd quarter	6 015.1	3 846.7	1 000.8	744.4	234.5	21.9	-75.0	555.1	630.1	1 242.6	562.2	680.3	5 993.3
4th quarter	6 004.7	3 867.9	947.5	737.5	221.3	-11.3	-79.1	568.2	647.3	1 268.5	569.7	698.8	6 016.1

Table 1-1B. Gross Domestic Product: Historical Data—*Continued*

(Billions of dollars, quarterly data are at seasonally adjusted annual rates.)　　　　　　　　　　　　　　　　NIPA Tables 1.1.5, 1.2.5

Year and quarter	Gross domestic product	Personal consumption expenditures	Gross private domestic investment				Exports and imports of goods and services			Government consumption expenditures and gross investment			Addendum: Final sales of domestic product
			Total	Fixed investment		Change in private inventories	Net exports	Exports	Imports	Total	Federal	State and local	
				Nonresidential	Residential								
1991													
1st quarter	6 035.2	3 873.6	924.6	729.8	210.3	-15.5	-47.1	573.2	620.3	1 284.2	581.4	702.8	6 050.7
2nd quarter	6 126.9	3 926.9	926.5	726.8	217.8	-18.0	-23.2	590.7	613.9	1 296.6	586.6	709.9	6 144.9
3rd quarter	6 205.9	3 973.3	947.5	720.2	226.5	0.8	-21.1	600.6	621.7	1 306.3	586.3	719.9	6 205.1
4th quarter	6 264.5	4 000.0	978.8	717.6	230.1	31.1	-23.1	615.2	638.3	1 308.8	577.4	731.4	6 233.4
1992													
1st quarter	6 363.1	4 100.4	956.8	714.2	242.4	0.2	-20.5	625.3	645.8	1 326.4	580.3	746.1	6 362.9
2nd quarter	6 470.8	4 155.7	1 013.1	736.7	253.2	23.2	-32.8	626.2	659.0	1 334.8	580.9	753.9	6 447.6
3rd quarter	6 566.6	4 227.0	1 024.2	748.5	255.1	20.5	-38.5	639.4	677.9	1 354.0	594.2	759.8	6 546.1
4th quarter	6 680.8	4 307.2	1 058.0	768.3	268.3	21.3	-47.1	641.4	688.5	1 362.8	598.4	764.4	6 659.5
1993													
1st quarter	6 729.5	4 349.5	1 083.8	776.5	271.4	35.9	-55.7	643.6	699.3	1 351.8	580.3	771.5	6 693.5
2nd quarter	6 808.9	4 418.6	1 094.5	792.4	278.0	24.1	-63.2	653.1	716.3	1 359.1	576.7	782.3	6 784.8
3rd quarter	6 882.1	4 487.2	1 095.9	798.3	290.9	6.6	-68.4	650.9	719.3	1 367.4	578.7	788.7	6 875.5
4th quarter	7 013.7	4 552.7	1 153.1	829.6	306.9	16.6	-73.4	671.6	745.0	1 381.4	584.9	796.5	6 997.1
1994													
1st quarter	7 115.7	4 621.2	1 201.7	840.7	315.6	45.4	-80.6	681.2	761.8	1 373.4	567.0	806.3	7 070.3
2nd quarter	7 246.9	4 683.2	1 264.9	855.6	327.9	81.4	-90.6	707.0	797.6	1 389.4	569.4	820.0	7 165.5
3rd quarter	7 331.1	4 752.8	1 251.7	872.1	326.4	53.2	-96.9	736.9	833.8	1 423.4	586.5	836.9	7 277.9
4th quarter	7 455.3	4 826.7	1 307.6	907.0	325.4	75.1	-101.9	758.6	860.6	1 422.9	575.8	847.1	7 380.1
1995													
1st quarter	7 522.3	4 862.4	1 327.6	944.6	321.8	61.2	-105.3	781.6	886.9	1 437.6	579.1	858.5	7 461.1
2nd quarter	7 581.0	4 933.6	1 304.0	956.8	313.5	33.8	-109.5	798.9	908.3	1 452.9	581.0	871.9	7 547.2
3rd quarter	7 683.1	4 998.7	1 303.2	965.5	326.4	11.3	-74.4	831.4	905.8	1 455.7	579.3	876.3	7 671.8
4th quarter	7 772.6	5 055.7	1 335.1	982.1	334.6	18.4	-69.8	839.4	909.2	1 451.6	567.3	884.3	7 754.2
1996													
1st quarter	7 868.5	5 130.6	1 355.4	1 003.7	344.7	6.9	-88.8	847.9	936.7	1 471.3	579.8	891.5	7 861.6
2nd quarter	8 032.8	5 220.5	1 418.4	1 026.5	361.4	30.5	-93.7	859.0	952.8	1 487.7	582.1	905.5	8 002.3
3rd quarter	8 131.4	5 274.5	1 474.4	1 059.0	364.3	51.1	-114.2	859.6	973.8	1 496.7	577.8	919.0	8 080.3
4th quarter	8 259.8	5 352.8	1 480.1	1 083.6	361.8	34.7	-88.8	903.8	992.6	1 515.7	576.9	938.8	8 225.0
1997													
1st quarter	8 362.7	5 433.1	1 522.4	1 107.3	365.4	49.7	-108.8	918.4	1 027.2	1 516.0	570.7	945.3	8 312.9
2nd quarter	8 518.8	5 471.3	1 590.2	1 129.6	372.3	88.4	-85.2	954.5	1 039.7	1 542.5	587.2	955.4	8 430.5
3rd quarter	8 662.8	5 579.2	1 625.3	1 178.4	379.0	67.9	-96.8	974.1	1 070.9	1 555.2	586.0	969.2	8 594.9
4th quarter	8 765.9	5 663.6	1 644.5	1 181.1	385.8	77.7	-117.0	968.3	1 085.3	1 574.8	589.2	985.6	8 688.3
1998													
1st quarter	8 866.5	5 721.3	1 712.3	1 212.4	394.8	105.1	-135.2	963.0	1 098.1	1 568.0	572.2	995.9	8 761.4
2nd quarter	8 969.7	5 832.6	1 695.8	1 247.1	411.3	37.3	-162.3	947.3	1 109.6	1 603.7	587.1	1 016.6	8 932.4
3rd quarter	9 121.1	5 926.8	1 741.6	1 261.7	427.6	52.4	-174.6	935.3	1 109.9	1 627.3	588.6	1 038.6	9 068.7
4th quarter	9 294.0	6 028.2	1 797.0	1 295.4	441.5	60.0	-178.7	966.3	1 145.0	1 647.5	594.2	1 053.2	9 234.0
1999													
1st quarter	9 411.7	6 102.0	1 853.1	1 322.3	447.4	83.4	-212.6	960.8	1 173.3	1 669.1	595.1	1 074.0	9 328.3
2nd quarter	9 526.2	6 230.6	1 848.3	1 354.0	459.3	35.1	-247.5	974.6	1 222.1	1 694.8	599.2	1 095.5	9 491.1
3rd quarter	9 686.6	6 335.3	1 893.7	1 386.6	466.6	40.5	-276.4	1 005.3	1 281.7	1 734.0	614.2	1 119.8	9 646.1
4th quarter	9 900.2	6 467.0	1 953.1	1 395.0	473.8	84.2	-301.7	1 031.0	1 332.7	1 781.7	634.3	1 147.4	9 815.9
2000													
1st quarter	10 002.2	6 618.2	1 950.7	1 450.3	484.2	16.2	-356.6	1 052.9	1 409.5	1 789.9	619.4	1 170.5	9 986.0
2nd quarter	10 247.7	6 711.9	2 075.8	1 498.7	486.6	90.4	-362.5	1 093.4	1 455.9	1 822.5	641.2	1 181.3	10 157.3
3rd quarter	10 318.2	6 820.0	2 060.0	1 519.7	483.1	57.2	-393.9	1 125.0	1 518.9	1 832.1	633.6	1 198.5	10 260.9
4th quarter	10 435.7	6 918.6	2 067.2	1 525.1	487.8	54.3	-411.3	1 113.2	1 524.5	1 861.3	638.2	1 223.1	10 381.4
2001													
1st quarter	10 470.2	6 995.3	1 971.3	1 505.2	496.7	-30.6	-402.7	1 096.8	1 499.5	1 906.3	653.3	1 253.0	10 500.9
2nd quarter	10 599.0	7 042.3	1 973.0	1 473.6	511.0	-11.6	-364.0	1 058.0	1 422.0	1 947.7	666.2	1 281.5	10 610.6
3rd quarter	10 598.0	7 070.3	1 944.9	1 452.6	522.4	-30.1	-370.6	998.9	1 369.5	1 953.4	674.4	1 279.0	10 628.1
4th quarter	10 660.5	7 187.3	1 850.1	1 408.9	522.1	-80.8	-369.7	953.5	1 323.2	1 992.7	686.9	1 305.9	10 741.3
2002													
1st quarter	10 783.5	7 217.7	1 912.7	1 374.0	538.3	0.3	-386.9	969.2	1 356.0	2 040.0	714.0	1 326.0	10 783.2
2nd quarter	10 887.5	7 308.0	1 933.3	1 357.3	554.8	21.2	-428.3	1 004.2	1 432.4	2 074.5	734.8	1 339.7	10 866.3
3rd quarter	10 984.0	7 397.1	1 933.2	1 348.9	558.9	25.4	-447.5	1 015.6	1 463.1	2 101.3	748.4	1 352.9	10 958.6
4th quarter	11 061.4	7 473.0	1 942.5	1 331.2	578.3	33.0	-496.3	1 003.0	1 499.3	2 142.2	775.2	1 367.0	11 028.4
2003													
1st quarter	11 174.1	7 567.2	1 960.2	1 332.7	601.4	26.1	-525.3	1 004.2	1 529.5	2 172.0	792.7	1 379.3	11 148.0
2nd quarter	11 312.8	7 661.5	1 972.4	1 366.8	612.0	-6.5	-519.9	1 007.5	1 527.3	2 198.8	826.0	1 372.8	11 319.3
3rd quarter	11 566.7	7 820.9	2 044.3	1 392.1	651.7	0.4	-519.0	1 037.3	1 556.3	2 220.4	833.3	1 387.2	11 566.2
4th quarter	11 772.2	7 913.5	2 131.3	1 411.9	683.1	36.3	-523.7	1 091.7	1 615.4	2 251.2	855.1	1 396.0	11 735.9
2004													
1st quarter	11 923.4	8 048.8	2 154.1	1 401.8	706.2	46.0	-566.0	1 133.7	1 699.6	2 286.6	871.8	1 414.8	11 877.4
2nd quarter	12 112.8	8 147.1	2 262.6	1 445.5	743.2	74.0	-617.6	1 170.2	1 787.7	2 320.7	884.6	1 436.1	12 038.8
3rd quarter	12 305.3	8 283.3	2 318.3	1 490.5	763.6	64.2	-652.7	1 180.2	1 832.9	2 356.4	902.5	1 453.9	12 241.1
4th quarter	12 527.2	8 448.6	2 390.1	1 531.7	786.3	72.1	-700.3	1 221.4	1 921.8	2 388.8	909.6	1 479.2	12 455.1
2005													
1st quarter	12 767.3	8 551.7	2 486.1	1 568.3	815.3	102.5	-696.7	1 258.4	1 955.1	2 426.1	931.8	1 494.3	12 664.8
2nd quarter	12 922.7	8 701.1	2 476.5	1 603.8	843.8	28.8	-707.2	1 294.9	2 002.1	2 452.2	939.3	1 513.0	12 893.8
3rd quarter	13 142.6	8 868.1	2 531.1	1 643.1	875.6	12.4	-751.0	1 302.3	2 053.3	2 494.6	956.4	1 538.0	13 130.3
4th quarter	13 324.2	8 955.3	2 645.3	1 668.7	890.2	86.4	-804.8	1 350.7	2 155.5	2 528.4	963.7	1 564.8	13 237.8
2006													
1st quarter	13 599.2	9 100.2	2 709.7	1 735.3	896.2	78.2	-790.8	1 414.0	2 204.8	2 580.1	997.1	1 583.0	13 520.9
2nd quarter	13 753.4	9 227.6	2 709.3	1 774.4	859.3	75.5	-794.0	1 459.8	2 253.8	2 610.6	997.2	1 613.4	13 677.9
3rd quarter	13 870.2	9 353.8	2 709.4	1 815.9	814.7	78.8	-823.3	1 475.4	2 298.7	2 630.3	995.4	1 634.8	13 791.4
4th quarter	14 039.6	9 427.4	2 675.4	1 849.5	782.4	43.5	-737.7	1 531.5	2 269.2	2 674.5	1 015.1	1 659.4	13 996.1

Table 1-1B. Gross Domestic Product: Historical Data—*Continued*

(Billions of dollars, quarterly data are at seasonally adjusted annual rates.)   NIPA Tables 1.1.5, 1.2.5

| Year and quarter | Gross domestic product | Personal consumption expenditures | Gross private domestic investment | | | | Exports and imports of goods and services | | | Government consumption expenditures and gross investment | | | Addendum: Final sales of domestic product |
| | | | Total | Fixed investment | | Change in private inventories | Net exports | Exports | Imports | Total | Federal | State and local | |
				Nonresidential	Residential								
2007													
1st quarter	14 215.7	9 572.1	2 664.3	1 892.0	750.9	21.4	-739.3	1 578.0	2 317.3	2 718.5	1 017.5	1 700.9	14 194.3
2nd quarter	14 402.1	9 678.7	2 699.2	1 937.7	719.3	42.2	-745.8	1 622.8	2 368.6	2 770.0	1 042.5	1 727.5	14 359.9
3rd quarter	14 564.1	9 798.4	2 686.0	1 967.4	673.7	44.9	-729.0	1 685.7	2 414.7	2 808.7	1 058.8	1 749.9	14 519.2
4th quarter	14 715.1	9 937.1	2 642.6	1 997.1	618.2	27.3	-729.7	1 750.7	2 480.4	2 865.1	1 085.3	1 779.8	14 687.8
2008													
1st quarter	14 706.5	10 004.4	2 563.7	2 013.7	566.7	-16.7	-771.2	1 813.3	2 584.6	2 909.6	1 111.2	1 798.5	14 723.2
2nd quarter	14 865.7	10 129.9	2 540.6	2 024.0	538.8	-22.3	-776.4	1 905.3	2 681.7	2 971.6	1 146.6	1 825.0	14 888.0
3rd quarter	14 899.0	10 159.1	2 498.2	2 007.0	507.1	-15.8	-787.4	1 922.2	2 709.6	3 029.0	1 170.2	1 858.8	14 914.8
4th quarter	14 608.2	9 906.9	2 307.9	1 918.7	451.4	-62.2	-628.5	1 700.3	2 328.8	3 021.8	1 179.8	1 842.0	14 670.4
2009													
1st quarter	14 430.9	9 815.0	2 014.9	1 761.4	404.5	-151.0	-421.0	1 511.8	1 932.8	3 022.0	1 185.2	1 836.8	14 581.9
2nd quarter	14 381.2	9 805.5	1 863.7	1 685.0	374.7	-196.0	-358.4	1 521.1	1 879.5	3 070.5	1 213.5	1 857.0	14 577.2
3rd quarter	14 448.9	9 939.4	1 841.4	1 656.0	389.4	-204.0	-424.0	1 594.7	2 018.7	3 092.1	1 228.3	1 863.8	14 652.9
4th quarter	14 651.2	10 005.0	1 998.7	1 659.3	391.5	-52.1	-473.3	1 703.5	2 176.8	3 120.8	1 256.2	1 864.6	14 703.3
2010													
1st quarter	14 764.6	10 101.8	2 038.2	1 660.0	379.4	-1.2	-509.2	1 759.9	2 269.1	3 133.8	1 278.4	1 855.5	14 765.8
2nd quarter	14 980.2	10 208.1	2 148.8	1 715.7	396.3	36.7	-542.5	1 819.7	2 362.3	3 165.8	1 305.1	1 860.7	14 943.5
3rd quarter	15 141.6	10 300.8	2 236.5	1 762.4	361.2	112.9	-553.9	1 877.3	2 431.2	3 158.3	1 304.3	1 854.0	15 028.7
4th quarter	15 309.5	10 430.3	2 238.4	1 801.9	369.3	67.3	-523.6	1 972.1	2 495.7	3 164.3	1 312.9	1 851.4	15 242.2
2011													
1st quarter	15 351.4	10 558.2	2 206.0	1 805.1	368.8	32.1	-568.5	2 040.4	2 608.9	3 155.8	1 306.0	1 849.8	15 319.4
2nd quarter	15 557.5	10 673.0	2 297.4	1 862.0	374.3	61.0	-581.1	2 116.1	2 697.2	3 168.3	1 312.7	1 855.5	15 496.5
3rd quarter	15 647.7	10 755.0	2 322.8	1 953.8	381.1	-12.0	-567.1	2 156.8	2 723.9	3 136.9	1 288.7	1 848.3	15 659.7
4th quarter	15 842.3	10 809.2	2 504.1	2 009.0	391.2	104.0	-601.8	2 150.1	2 751.9	3 130.8	1 291.7	1 839.1	15 738.3
2012													
1st quarter	16 068.8	10 959.3	2 567.8	2 073.4	414.1	80.3	-602.3	2 190.0	2 792.3	3 144.0	1 296.1	1 847.9	15 988.5
2nd quarter	16 207.1	11 005.1	2 636.9	2 126.2	419.3	91.4	-565.2	2 215.6	2 780.8	3 130.5	1 288.6	1 841.8	16 115.7
3rd quarter	16 319.5	11 059.4	2 644.1	2 126.0	433.7	84.4	-523.1	2 227.7	2 750.8	3 139.1	1 293.8	1 845.3	16 235.1
4th quarter	16 420.4	11 165.7	2 638.3	2 148.6	460.9	28.7	-515.9	2 237.5	2 753.4	3 132.3	1 269.5	1 862.7	16 391.7
2013													
1st quarter	16 629.1	11 265.6	2 738.2	2 170.9	485.1	82.3	-500.2	2 255.1	2 755.3	3 125.4	1 240.5	1 884.9	16 546.8
2nd quarter	16 699.6	11 291.0	2 775.3	2 180.3	507.2	87.8	-499.3	2 260.4	2 759.8	3 132.6	1 232.9	1 899.8	16 611.8
3rd quarter	16 911.1	11 379.2	2 880.0	2 220.7	523.1	136.2	-483.0	2 284.2	2 767.2	3 134.8	1 219.0	1 915.8	16 774.9
4th quarter	17 133.1	11 518.4	2 910.5	2 274.0	524.6	111.9	-435.1	2 348.2	2 783.3	3 139.3	1 216.3	1 923.0	17 021.2
2014													
1st quarter	17 144.3	11 618.1	2 899.2	2 314.9	532.1	52.3	-511.3	2 342.4	2 853.7	3 138.2	1 211.8	1 926.4	17 092.0
2nd quarter	17 462.7	11 784.7	3 030.4	2 383.6	550.4	96.4	-506.5	2 394.1	2 900.6	3 154.1	1 210.0	1 944.1	17 366.3
3rd quarter	17 743.2	11 934.3	3 107.6	2 439.8	568.4	99.4	-490.5	2 398.1	2 888.5	3 191.8	1 229.3	1 962.5	17 643.8
4th quarter	17 852.5	12 053.8	3 139.5	2 462.0	589.7	87.8	-531.9	2 375.1	2 907.0	3 191.2	1 212.9	1 978.3	17 764.8
2015													
1st quarter	17 991.3	12 083.9	3 245.1	2 464.3	605.1	175.6	-526.9	2 297.4	2 824.4	3 189.3	1 216.0	1 973.3	17 815.7
2nd quarter	18 193.7	12 224.7	3 245.8	2 472.5	623.3	150.0	-508.8	2 298.7	2 807.5	3 232.0	1 220.6	2 011.4	18 043.7
3rd quarter	18 307.0	12 347.8	3 251.7	2 479.2	645.7	126.8	-543.0	2 258.4	2 801.4	3 250.6	1 221.2	2 029.4	18 180.2
4th quarter	18 332.1	12 397.5	3 206.1	2 450.3	661.1	94.7	-526.1	2 220.1	2 746.1	3 254.5	1 229.3	2 025.2	18 237.4
2016													
1st quarter	18 425.3	12 495.1	3 174.4	2 435.5	684.4	54.5	-514.4	2 179.2	2 693.6	3 270.2	1 229.3	2 040.9	18 370.8
2nd quarter	18 611.6	12 637.4	3 178.5	2 454.1	694.1	30.3	-491.7	2 218.9	2 710.6	3 287.4	1 225.8	2 061.6	18 581.3
3rd quarter	18 775.5	12 759.1	3 185.7	2 481.6	700.7	3.4	-485.1	2 265.4	2 750.5	3 315.8	1 238.1	2 077.7	18 772.0
4th quarter	18 968.0	12 881.6	3 281.5	2 506.2	718.6	56.8	-533.8	2 264.9	2 798.7	3 338.8	1 244.8	2 094.0	18 911.3
2017													
1st quarter	19 153.9	13 046.4	3 283.5	2 545.4	742.7	-4.6	-533.3	2 334.4	2 867.7	3 357.3	1 242.5	2 114.8	19 158.5
2nd quarter	19 322.9	13 144.4	3 357.4	2 579.7	756.7	21.0	-557.1	2 346.2	2 903.3	3 378.2	1 257.6	2 120.6	19 301.9
3rd quarter	19 558.7	13 268.1	3 413.2	2 592.7	761.5	59.1	-523.5	2 383.1	2 906.6	3 400.8	1 263.3	2 137.5	19 499.6
4th quarter	19 883.0	13 497.5	3 471.4	2 648.6	780.4	42.4	-545.8	2 471.3	3 017.1	3 459.9	1 287.7	2 172.2	19 840.5
2018													
1st quarter	20 143.7	13 667.4	3 550.8	2 716.0	789.0	45.9	-580.1	2 504.4	3 084.5	3 505.5	1 305.8	2 199.7	20 097.9
2nd quarter	20 492.5	13 864.8	3 603.2	2 770.1	808.9	24.2	-539.8	2 568.3	3 108.1	3 564.3	1 331.7	2 232.6	20 468.3
3rd quarter	20 659.1	14 002.6	3 679.6	2 798.1	804.3	77.1	-624.0	2 534.2	3 158.2	3 600.9	1 350.8	2 250.1	20 582.0
4th quarter	20 813.3	14 119.3	3 717.5	2 838.1	791.8	87.7	-640.9	2 527.1	3 168.1	3 617.4	1 367.7	2 249.7	20 725.7
2019													
1st quarter	21 001.6	14 155.6	3 801.9	2 886.9	796.5	118.5	-606.4	2 524.6	3 131.0	3 650.5	1 387.0	2 263.5	20 883.1
2nd quarter	21 289.3	14 375.7	3 843.0	2 946.1	808.5	88.4	-632.3	2 533.4	3 165.7	3 702.9	1 406.9	2 296.0	21 200.8
3rd quarter	21 505.0	14 529.5	3 858.2	2 969.3	821.9	67.0	-614.0	2 512.1	3 126.1	3 731.3	1 424.1	2 307.2	21 438.0
4th quarter	21 694.5	14 653.9	3 801.9	2 952.6	828.8	20.6	-532.4	2 508.7	3 041.1	3 771.0	1 441.7	2 329.2	21 673.9
2020													
1st quarter	21 481.4	14 439.1	3 752.4	2 900.1	872.9	-20.6	-541.7	2 385.5	2 927.3	3 831.6	1 454.7	2 376.9	21 502.0
2nd quarter	19 477.4	12 989.7	3 167.0	2 659.1	797.8	-289.9	-538.9	1 807.9	2 346.7	3 859.6	1 525.0	2 334.6	19 767.4
3rd quarter	21 138.6	14 293.8	3 708.8	2 776.6	917.2	15.0	-725.7	2 079.6	2 805.3	3 861.7	1 515.1	2 346.5	21 123.6
4th quarter	21 477.6	14 467.6	3 923.2	2 862.7	1 003.2	57.3	-798.4	2 220.7	3 019.1	3 885.3	1 512.3	2 373.0	21 420.3

Table 1-2A. Real Gross Domestic Product: Recent Data

(Billions of chained [2012] dollars, quarterly data are at seasonally adjusted annual rates.)   NIPA Tables 1.1.6, 1.2.6

Year and quarter	Gross domestic product	Personal consumption expenditures	Gross private domestic investment				Exports and imports of goods and services			Government consumption expenditures and gross investment			Residual	Adden-dum: final sales of domestic product
			Total	Fixed investment		Change in private inventories	Net exports	Exports	Imports	Total	Federal	State and local		
				Nonresidential	Residential									
1960	3 262.1	2 014.3	352.7	...	...	...	...	112.7	135.7	1 086.3	...	...	-183.6	3 268.6
1961	3 345.7	2 055.6	353.8	...	...	...	...	113.3	134.8	1 145.1	...	...	-201.1	3 354.6
1962	3 550.7	2 157.3	395.9	...	...	...	...	119.0	150.1	1 220.0	...	...	-219.8	3 542.5
1963	3 705.3	2 246.3	422.8	...	...	...	...	127.5	154.2	1 249.6	...	...	-212.9	3 701.0
1964	3 918.8	2 380.0	456.1	...	...	...	...	142.6	162.4	1 280.2	...	...	-200.0	3 920.6
1965	4 173.4	2 531.0	519.2	...	...	...	...	146.6	179.6	1 321.1	...	...	-207.4	4 151.9
1966	4 448.7	2 674.5	565.9	...	...	...	...	156.7	206.3	1 436.3	...	...	-239.2	4 405.7
1967	4 570.7	2 754.4	546.1	...	...	...	...	160.3	221.4	1 550.2	...	...	-262.8	4 549.6
1968	4 795.4	2 913.1	578.7	...	...	...	...	172.9	254.3	1 603.0	...	...	-257.9	4 780.2
1969	4 945.2	3 021.8	610.9	...	...	...	...	181.4	268.8	1 604.7	...	...	-243.9	4 931.0
1970	4 954.4	3 092.9	573.8	...	...	...	...	200.7	280.3	1 570.8	...	...	-210.7	4 975.2
1971	5 117.6	3 211.0	632.9	...	...	...	...	204.2	295.3	1 541.4	...	...	-208.9	5 111.6
1972	5 386.7	3 407.7	704.2	...	...	...	...	220.1	328.5	1 533.5	...	...	-183.4	5 379.4
1973	5 690.9	3 576.3	781.3	...	...	...	...	261.5	343.7	1 528.5	...	...	-163.5	5 659.1
1974	5 660.1	3 546.4	729.5	...	...	...	...	282.3	335.9	1 562.1	...	...	-161.9	5 643.0
1975	5 648.5	3 626.8	611.4	...	...	...	...	280.5	298.6	1 596.5	...	...	-151.6	5 701.7
1976	5 952.8	3 828.9	728.0	...	...	...	...	292.7	357.0	1 604.9	...	...	-189.0	5 929.6
1977	6 228.1	3 990.7	831.9	...	...	...	...	299.8	396.0	1 624.2	...	...	-178.2	6 191.7
1978	6 572.8	4 165.4	928.1	...	...	...	...	331.4	430.4	1 670.8	...	...	-151.4	6 530.7
1979	6 780.9	4 264.4	960.7	...	...	...	...	364.2	437.5	1 700.8	...	...	-107.9	6 766.0
1980	6 763.5	4 251.1	864.0	...	...	...	...	403.4	408.4	1 731.6	...	...	-66.1	6 809.1
1981	6 935.2	4 310.0	940.1	...	...	...	...	408.4	419.1	1 748.4	...	...	-103.0	6 904.6
1982	6 810.1	4 373.1	822.0	...	...	...	...	377.1	413.7	1 779.8	...	...	-102.7	6 869.9
1983	7 122.3	4 620.7	898.7	...	...	...	...	367.3	465.9	1 846.2	...	...	-134.6	7 164.6
1984	7 637.7	4 863.8	1 144.0	...	...	...	...	397.3	579.3	1 911.1	...	...	-199.6	7 546.4
1985	7 956.2	5 115.6	1 143.2	...	...	...	...	410.6	616.9	2 038.6	...	...	-167.3	7 945.4
1986	8 231.7	5 326.8	1 145.0	...	...	...	...	442.0	669.6	2 149.3	...	...	-172.5	8 246.4
1987	8 516.4	5 507.6	1 177.6	...	...	...	...	490.3	709.4	2 211.7	...	...	-204.1	8 498.0
1988	8 872.2	5 737.7	1 206.6	...	...	...	...	569.8	737.2	2 239.2	...	...	-171.9	8 866.3
1989	9 198.0	5 905.0	1 255.4	...	...	...	...	635.8	769.7	2 302.8	...	...	-170.3	9 178.2
1990	9 371.5	6 023.9	1 223.0	...	...	...	...	691.9	797.2	2 376.5	...	...	-167.7	9 371.2
1991	9 361.3	6 034.8	1 142.1	...	...	...	...	737.7	796.0	2 405.0	...	...	-159.9	9 385.0
1992	9 691.1	6 256.9	1 225.3	...	...	...	...	788.8	851.8	2 416.1	...	...	-167.0	9 689.4
1993	9 957.7	6 474.8	1 323.3	...	...	...	...	814.5	925.5	2 396.3	...	...	-154.0	9 949.9
1994	10 358.9	6 725.7	1 479.8	...	...	...	...	886.5	1 035.9	2 398.3	...	...	-184.0	10 290.7
1995	10 637.0	6 924.1	1 527.3	...	...	...	...	977.6	1 118.7	2 410.6	...	...	-124.4	10 615.2
1996	11 038.3	7 164.4	1 660.8	...	...	...	...	1 057.5	1 216.0	2 432.9	...	...	-101.0	11 015.6
1997	11 529.2	7 434.2	1 850.2	...	...	...	...	1 183.5	1 379.8	2 472.8	...	...	-127.1	11 449.5
1998	12 045.8	7 829.0	2 026.3	...	...	...	...	1 211.1	1 541.1	2 532.8	...	...	-104.1	11 974.5
1999	12 623.4	8 250.3	2 198.7	...	...	...	...	1 271.5	1 719.8	2 615.7	...	...	-80.4	12 556.0
2000	13 138.0	8 665.8	2 346.7	...	...	...	...	1 377.2	1 943.3	2 663.3	...	...	-50.3	13 075.1
2001	13 263.4	8 880.4	2 214.6	...	...	...	...	1 300.3	1 895.5	2 763.7	...	...	53.1	13 311.0
2002	13 488.4	9 106.2	2 195.5	1 472.7	692.6	24.3	-690.3	1 274.8	1 965.1	2 886.6	969.5	1 929.1	-86.6	13 471.8
2003	13 865.5	9 394.4	2 290.4	1 509.4	755.5	19.9	-764.2	1 301.6	2 065.8	2 945.7	1 033.1	1 920.3	-46.9	13 851.3
2004	14 399.7	9 748.6	2 502.6	1 594.0	830.9	82.6	-865.6	1 427.0	2 292.6	2 991.1	1 077.7	1 918.2	-5.2	14 329.2
2005	14 901.3	10 093.8	2 670.6	1 716.4	885.4	63.7	-915.4	1 526.1	2 441.4	3 013.8	1 099.2	1 918.3	36.0	14 841.2
2006	15 315.9	10 386.2	2 752.4	1 854.2	818.9	87.1	-927.6	1 670.5	2 598.2	3 061.8	1 125.3	1 939.6	33.3	15 240.9
2007	15 623.9	10 638.7	2 684.1	1 982.1	665.8	40.6	-847.9	1 816.9	2 664.8	3 116.9	1 147.3	1 972.7	26.8	15 586.7
2008	15 643.0	10 654.7	2 462.9	1 994.2	504.6	-32.7	-685.7	1 921.9	2 607.6	3 195.8	1 220.0	1 977.6	-1.7	15 678.0
2009	15 236.3	10 515.6	1 942.0	1 704.3	395.3	-177.3	-516.3	1 762.5	2 278.8	3 310.7	1 296.0	2 015.9	-15.3	15 400.3
2010	15 649.0	10 716.0	2 216.5	1 781.0	383.0	57.3	-589.4	1 989.5	2 578.9	3 308.0	1 348.4	1 959.8	-11.3	15 596.8
2011	15 891.5	10 898.3	2 362.1	1 935.4	382.5	46.7	-571.0	2 132.1	2 703.1	3 202.7	1 312.0	1 890.8	-3.7	15 847.4
2012	16 254.0	11 047.4	2 621.8	2 118.5	432.0	71.2	-551.6	2 217.7	2 769.3	3 136.5	1 287.0	1 849.5	0.0	16 182.8
2013	16 553.3	11 211.7	2 801.5	2 206.0	485.5	108.7	-519.3	2 283.6	2 802.9	3 060.7	1 215.8	1 844.5	-0.3	16 444.1
2014	16 932.1	11 515.3	2 959.2	2 365.3	504.1	86.3	-575.3	2 372.3	2 947.6	3 033.2	1 184.7	1 847.6	0.6	16 842.3
2015	17 390.3	11 892.9	3 121.8	2 420.3	555.4	137.6	-721.7	2 378.7	3 100.4	3 088.4	1 184.5	1 902.2	10.7	17 248.3
2016	17 680.3	12 187.7	3 089.9	2 442.0	592.1	35.7	-757.1	2 388.4	3 145.4	3 148.8	1 190.5	1 956.3	15.3	17 630.6
2017	18 079.1	12 483.7	3 212.5	2 541.4	615.9	33.6	-799.5	2 485.8	3 285.2	3 165.2	1 194.7	1 968.5	11.8	18 030.4
2018	18 606.8	12 845.0	3 394.8	2 704.4	612.3	65.7	-864.2	2 555.6	3 419.9	3 208.8	1 231.0	1 976.4	-7.2	18 528.8
2019	19 032.7	13 126.3	3 510.6	2 822.0	606.7	75.1	-905.3	2 554.0	3 459.2	3 279.5	1 277.2	2 001.5	-32.3	18 944.4
2020	18 384.7	12 629.9	3 316.2	2 671.1	648.0	-42.3	-942.7	2 207.6	3 150.3	3 360.2	1 340.7	2 019.9	-83.7	18 395.9
2018														
1st quarter	18 436.3	12 707.6	3 346.3	2 654.0	616.5	63.5	-826.4	2 551.6	3 378.0	3 189.7	1 213.0	1 974.9	-2.2	18 363.5
2nd quarter	18 590.0	12 816.4	3 352.5	2 698.0	621.5	11.1	-807.2	2 582.9	3 390.1	3 212.2	1 228.1	1 982.5	-4.5	18 558.0
3rd quarter	18 679.6	12 900.6	3 430.9	2 716.7	612.2	101.0	-896.9	2 542.5	3 439.4	3 220.0	1 238.5	1 980.2	-15.9	18 577.9
4th quarter	18 721.3	12 955.5	3 449.6	2 749.0	599.0	87.3	-926.5	2 545.6	3 472.1	3 213.4	1 244.2	1 968.1	-6.3	18 615.8
2019														
1st quarter	18 833.2	12 975.1	3 503.4	2 780.7	599.1	131.7	-906.7	2 565.3	3 472.0	3 235.2	1 248.7	1 985.4	-33.8	18 704.8
2nd quarter	18 982.5	13 088.8	3 526.0	2 826.0	605.2	84.3	-935.3	2 551.3	3 486.6	3 274.9	1 275.5	1 998.7	-20.7	18 881.4
3rd quarter	19 112.7	13 192.3	3 535.9	2 846.5	610.6	68.3	-931.5	2 545.9	3 477.4	3 291.7	1 286.8	2 004.3	-29.3	19 027.1
4th quarter	19 202.3	13 249.0	3 477.1	2 834.7	612.2	16.3	-847.6	2 553.3	3 400.9	3 316.3	1 298.0	2 017.6	-45.4	19 164.4
2020														
1st quarter	18 952.0	13 014.5	3 430.1	2 775.5	641.2	-30.4	-841.9	2 442.1	3 283.9	3 346.3	1 305.8	2 039.7	-25.5	18 940.1
2nd quarter	17 258.2	11 756.4	2 901.9	2 535.7	584.9	-252.8	-774.8	1 943.0	2 717.7	3 378.1	1 368.4	2 011.0	-95.1	17 471.0
3rd quarter	18 560.8	12 820.8	3 371.0	2 646.9	657.8	25.3	-1 021.3	2 166.3	3 187.5	3 360.2	1 349.6	2 011.4	-117.5	18 508.0
4th quarter	18 767.8	12 927.9	3 561.9	2 726.2	708.2	88.8	-1 132.8	2 279.0	3 411.8	3 356.0	1 338.8	2 017.6	-96.7	18 664.8

Note: Chained (2012) dollar series are calculated as the product of the chain-type quantity index and the 2012 current-dollar value of the corresponding series, divided by 100. Because the formula for the chain-type quantity indexes uses weights from more than one period, the corresponding chained-dollar estimates are usually not additive. The residual column is the difference between the total and the sum of the most detailed components shown in the Bureau of Economic Analysis (BEA) published data.

. . . = Not available.

Table 1-2B. Real Gross Domestic Product: Historical Data

(Billions of chained [2012] dollars, quarterly data are at seasonally adjusted annual rates.)

NIPA Tables 1.1.6, 1.2.6

Year and quarter	Gross domestic product	Personal consump- tion expen- ditures	Gross private domestic investment				Exports and imports of goods and services			Government consumption expenditures and gross investment			Residual	Adden- dum: Final sales of domestic product
			Total	Fixed investment		Change in private inventories	Net exports	Exports	Imports	Total	Federal	State and local		
				Nonresi- dential	Residential									
1929	1 110.2	832.4	120.4	...	...	...	...	43.4	58.1	180.4	...	...	-21.6	1 122.0
1930	1 015.8	787.8	82.0	...	...	...	...	35.9	50.6	198.7	...	...	-32.2	1 046.3
1931	950.7	763.2	53.3	...	...	...	...	29.8	44.1	206.8	...	...	-44.7	985.5
1932	828.1	694.9	19.7	...	...	...	...	23.4	36.6	200.2	...	...	-42.7	874.6
1933	817.8	679.6	26.6	...	...	...	...	23.5	38.1	193.8	...	...	-51.7	848.7
1934	906.2	728.1	44.0	...	...	...	...	26.2	39.0	217.8	...	...	-63.3	929.1
1935	986.9	772.3	76.5	...	...	...	...	27.6	51.1	224.5	...	...	-72.8	987.2
1936	1 114.1	850.9	96.8	...	...	...	...	29.0	50.5	259.9	...	...	-82.0	1 116.0
1937	1 171.1	882.4	119.2	...	...	...	...	36.5	56.8	249.7	...	...	-76.5	1 162.8
1938	1 132.3	868.3	82.0	...	...	...	...	36.1	44.1	268.7	...	...	-74.6	1 147.4
1939	1 223.2	916.8	103.1	...	...	...	...	38.1	46.4	292.3	...	...	-82.8	1 231.7
1940	1 331.1	964.3	140.4	...	...	...	...	43.3	47.5	302.9	...	...	-93.3	1 316.2
1941	1 566.8	1 032.5	171.9	...	...	...	...	44.4	58.4	509.7	...	...	-167.4	1 536.3
1942	1 862.8	1 008.0	95.7	...	...	...	...	29.3	53.0	1 183.8	...	...	-414.4	1 862.6
1943	2 179.9	1 036.1	59.7	...	...	...	...	24.7	66.8	1 774.8	...	...	-643.9	2 208.7
1944	2 353.2	1 065.5	71.3	...	...	...	...	26.6	69.9	1 992.1	...	...	-726.8	2 384.9
1945	2 330.2	1 131.4	91.7	...	...	...	...	37.2	74.4	1 749.4	...	...	-594.8	2 368.7
1946	2 059.8	1 271.3	220.3	...	...	...	...	80.4	61.6	615.9	...	...	-99.4	2 030.6
1947	2 036.2	1 295.6	212.1	...	...	...	...	91.7	58.5	522.6	...	...	-22.6	2 066.5
1948	2 120.0	1 324.9	267.3	...	...	...	...	72.2	68.3	551.7	...	...	-52.8	2 100.8
1949	2 108.0	1 361.7	206.7	...	...	...	...	71.5	65.9	611.0	...	...	-63.9	2 148.4
1947														
1st quarter	2 034.5	1 277.4	218.1	...	...	...	...	97.6	60.4	524.0	...	...	-28.8	2 051.2
2nd quarter ...	2 029.0	1 298.7	201.4	...	...	...	...	96.4	61.6	523.6	...	...	-25.0	2 061.7
3rd quarter	2 024.8	1 302.9	195.5	...	...	...	...	91.5	54.6	523.5	...	...	-16.5	2 075.4
4th quarter	2 056.5	1 303.3	233.3	...	...	...	...	81.1	57.5	519.2	...	...	-20.0	2 077.7
1948														
1st quarter	2 087.4	1 309.8	257.2	...	...	...	...	77.4	64.9	527.0	...	...	-33.7	2 085.5
2nd quarter ...	2 121.9	1 325.1	273.1	...	...	...	...	70.2	67.5	545.6	...	...	-52.4	2 097.2
3rd quarter	2 134.1	1 327.0	275.9	...	...	...	...	71.8	71.0	556.9	...	...	-59.2	2 101.7
4th quarter	2 136.4	1 337.6	262.7	...	...	...	...	69.3	69.8	577.5	...	...	-66.0	2 118.6
1949														
1st quarter	2 107.0	1 339.8	223.5	...	...	...	...	77.6	67.7	592.8	...	...	-56.4	2 126.7
2nd quarter ...	2 099.8	1 360.3	193.8	...	...	...	...	76.9	66.7	618.5	...	...	-60.4	2 154.1
3rd quarter	2 121.5	1 363.4	209.9	...	...	...	...	70.5	64.0	621.8	...	...	-75.1	2 151.7
4th quarter	2 103.7	1 383.4	199.5	...	...	...	...	61.0	65.0	610.9	...	...	-63.6	2 161.2
1950														
1st quarter	2 186.4	1 406.4	246.9	...	...	...	...	60.0	66.8	599.6	...	...	-69.3	2 194.5
2nd quarter ...	2 253.0	1 429.6	273.3	...	...	...	...	60.8	70.5	610.5	...	...	-64.5	2 253.8
3rd quarter	2 340.1	1 503.0	296.8	...	...	...	...	62.3	87.0	600.7	...	...	-53.9	2 334.0
4th quarter	2 384.9	1 457.7	334.5	...	...	...	...	67.4	87.1	643.1	...	...	-88.9	2 313.5
1951														
1st quarter	2 417.3	1 492.9	300.4	...	...	...	...	70.8	87.2	711.5	...	...	-107.3	2 383.3
2nd quarter ...	2 459.2	1 450.8	307.3	...	...	...	...	77.7	84.3	806.4	...	...	-151.3	2 397.0
3rd quarter	2 509.9	1 467.7	284.7	...	...	...	...	79.6	77.1	895.0	...	...	-174.7	2 477.3
4th quarter	2 515.4	1 476.2	262.0	...	...	...	...	78.9	75.1	942.4	...	...	-183.8	2 514.6
1952														
1st quarter	2 542.3	1 479.6	268.9	...	...	...	...	83.1	83.8	970.4	...	...	-194.5	2 536.9
2nd quarter ...	2 547.8	1 508.6	248.6	...	...	...	...	74.0	83.4	1 003.5	...	...	-198.9	2 579.8
3rd quarter	2 566.2	1 515.8	261.9	...	...	...	...	68.1	88.5	1 013.6	...	...	-225.5	2 557.0
4th quarter	2 650.4	1 569.3	280.8	...	...	...	...	68.6	96.4	1 030.5	...	...	-223.1	2 641.3
1953														
1st quarter	2 699.7	1 587.7	286.8	...	...	...	...	67.4	94.1	1 063.2	...	...	-228.2	2 697.9
2nd quarter ...	2 720.6	1 597.3	288.4	...	...	...	...	67.8	98.9	1 085.0	...	...	-235.5	2 719.6
3rd quarter	2 705.3	1 593.5	282.4	...	...	...	...	70.6	98.6	1 073.4	...	...	-226.1	2 714.0
4th quarter	2 664.3	1 582.8	262.0	...	...	...	...	68.2	93.7	1 070.8	...	...	-217.3	2 699.8
1954														
1st quarter	2 651.6	1 588.7	260.1	...	...	...	...	65.2	88.3	1 042.9	...	...	-209.4	2 684.0
2nd quarter ...	2 654.5	1 609.3	259.5	...	...	...	...	74.5	96.2	1 007.6	...	...	-188.0	2 694.3
3rd quarter	2 684.4	1 631.1	272.0	...	...	...	...	72.1	90.4	985.8	...	...	-176.4	2 721.2
4th quarter	2 737.0	1 665.3	284.0	...	...	...	...	75.5	91.3	979.9	...	...	-172.8	2 765.5
1955														
1st quarter	2 815.1	1 702.7	312.3	...	...	...	...	78.3	96.7	980.5	...	...	-176.4	2 818.3
2nd quarter ...	2 860.9	1 735.3	331.3	...	...	...	...	76.4	102.2	970.9	...	...	-172.2	2 854.8
3rd quarter	2 899.6	1 756.7	336.4	...	...	...	...	81.5	103.9	977.1	...	...	-167.8	2 896.7
4th quarter	2 917.0	1 778.8	344.2	...	...	...	...	81.8	107.7	957.7	...	...	-164.8	2 904.4
1956														
1st quarter	2 905.7	1 781.7	334.4	...	...	...	...	85.7	112.2	957.4	...	...	-164.1	2 899.8
2nd quarter ...	2 929.7	1 787.6	331.8	...	...	...	...	91.5	111.6	976.8	...	...	-162.1	2 932.9
3rd quarter	2 927.0	1 791.6	328.8	...	...	...	...	94.5	112.6	968.2	...	...	-155.8	2 935.0
4th quarter	2 975.2	1 816.3	325.7	...	...	...	...	98.8	107.4	992.8	...	...	-161.9	2 986.0
1957														
1st quarter	2 994.3	1 829.0	320.7	...	...	...	...	105.2	115.9	1 014.1	...	...	-164.6	3 012.7
2nd quarter ...	2 987.7	1 832.1	320.4	...	...	...	...	102.1	116.8	1 008.9	...	...	-167.3	3 002.4
3rd quarter	3 017.0	1 846.6	327.7	...	...	...	...	99.2	114.6	1 017.4	...	...	-171.8	3 025.6
4th quarter	2 985.8	1 847.4	302.5	...	...	...	...	96.3	115.0	1 034.2	...	...	-168.1	3 024.6

Note: Chained (2012) dollar series are calculated as the product of the chain-type quantity index and the 2012 current-dollar value of the corresponding series, divided by 100. Because the formula for the chain-type quantity indexes uses weights from more than one period, the corresponding chained-dollar estimates are usually not additive. The residual column is the difference between the total and the sum of the most detailed components shown in the Bureau of Economic Analysis (BEA) published data.

. . . = Not available.

Table 1-2B. Real Gross Domestic Product: Historical Data—*Continued*

(Billions of chained [2012] dollars, quarterly data are at seasonally adjusted annual rates.)   **NIPA Tables 1.1.6, 1.2.6**

| Year and quarter | Gross domestic product | Personal consumption expenditures | Gross private domestic investment | | | | Exports and imports of goods and services | | | Government consumption expenditures and gross investment | | | Residual | Addendum: Final sales of domestic product |
| | | | Total | Fixed investment | | Change in private inventories | Net exports | Exports | Imports | Total | Federal | State and local | | |
				Nonresidential	Residential									
1958														
1st quarter	2 908.3	1 821.8	282.1	...	...	...	...	86.7	116.7	1 025.2	...	...	-176.6	2 950.4
2nd quarter	2 927.4	1 836.9	276.4	...	...	...	...	87.1	121.7	1 050.8	...	...	-189.7	2 967.1
3rd quarter	2 995.1	1 867.4	297.6	...	...	...	...	87.4	119.8	1 056.9	...	...	-200.7	3 010.2
4th quarter	3 065.1	1 892.7	323.0	...	...	...	...	87.1	126.1	1 078.2	...	...	-206.4	3 068.9
1959														
1st quarter	3 124.0	1 927.4	340.6	...	...	...	...	93.4	129.4	1 067.2	...	...	-188.8	3 129.0
2nd quarter	3 194.4	1 957.2	367.1	...	...	...	...	92.6	135.7	1 080.4	...	...	-201.5	3 175.2
3rd quarter	3 196.7	1 977.6	343.4	...	...	...	...	101.6	137.0	1 089.7	...	...	-182.6	3 218.7
4th quarter	3 205.8	1 979.9	354.6	...	...	...	...	96.6	133.6	1 080.7	...	...	-192.5	3 205.2
1960														
1st quarter	3 277.8	1 998.8	390.2	...	...	...	...	109.0	138.6	1 062.3	...	...	-194.1	3 241.5
2nd quarter	3 260.2	2 024.0	353.8	...	...	...	...	112.1	139.6	1 074.2	...	...	-178.8	3 268.6
3rd quarter	3 276.1	2 015.9	352.9	...	...	...	...	114.6	135.5	1 100.5	...	...	-192.6	3 275.0
4th quarter	3 234.1	2 018.5	313.8	...	...	...	...	115.2	129.1	1 108.1	...	...	-168.9	3 289.2
1961														
1st quarter	3 255.9	2 017.8	322.0	...	...	...	...	114.4	128.5	1 124.6	...	...	-183.6	3 295.0
2nd quarter	3 311.2	2 047.8	344.5	...	...	...	...	109.1	130.1	1 127.4	...	...	-196.9	3 325.5
3rd quarter	3 374.7	2 057.8	371.3	...	...	...	...	114.0	138.7	1 151.5	...	...	-212.0	3 362.1
4th quarter	3 440.9	2 099.2	377.5	...	...	...	...	115.9	142.0	1 176.7	...	...	-211.9	3 435.7
1962														
1st quarter	3 502.3	2 121.4	397.8	...	...	...	...	115.2	146.3	1 199.4	...	...	-225.7	3 477.9
2nd quarter	3 533.9	2 147.5	394.7	...	...	...	...	121.8	149.5	1 205.5	...	...	-211.4	3 529.4
3rd quarter	3 577.4	2 164.8	401.4	...	...	...	...	121.6	151.4	1 233.3	...	...	-222.1	3 567.8
4th quarter	3 589.1	2 195.4	389.7	...	...	...	...	117.6	153.2	1 241.9	...	...	-219.9	3 595.0
1963														
1st quarter	3 628.3	2 210.8	410.2	...	...	...	...	119.4	149.7	1 225.0	...	...	-222.1	3 611.9
2nd quarter	3 669.0	2 231.7	416.7	...	...	...	...	129.0	153.2	1 225.9	...	...	-203.9	3 667.9
3rd quarter	3 749.7	2 261.9	429.5	...	...	...	...	128.3	157.1	1 280.3	...	...	-220.5	3 744.7
4th quarter	3 774.3	2 280.8	434.7	...	...	...	...	133.3	156.6	1 267.0	...	...	-204.9	3 779.4
1964														
1st quarter	3 853.8	2 325.6	451.0	...	...	...	...	140.1	156.5	1 271.0	...	...	-198.6	3 856.9
2nd quarter	3 895.8	2 366.7	449.4	...	...	...	...	139.5	160.0	1 282.4	...	...	-202.6	3 900.4
3rd quarter	3 956.7	2 410.4	459.9	...	...	...	...	143.9	164.3	1 283.9	...	...	-201.5	3 956.8
4th quarter	3 968.9	2 417.3	464.2	...	...	...	...	146.8	168.7	1 283.4	...	...	-197.4	3 968.4
1965														
1st quarter	4 064.9	2 471.2	508.5	...	...	...	...	129.7	162.6	1 281.9	...	...	-217.2	4 030.7
2nd quarter	4 116.3	2 498.5	509.8	...	...	...	...	151.4	181.8	1 297.1	...	...	-197.2	4 099.2
3rd quarter	4 207.8	2 541.4	527.6	...	...	...	...	148.0	182.6	1 340.1	...	...	-210.1	4 184.5
4th quarter	4 304.7	2 612.8	531.1	...	...	...	...	157.1	191.5	1 365.5	...	...	-205.1	4 293.2
1966														
1st quarter	4 409.5	2 651.4	573.5	...	...	...	...	153.2	196.4	1 390.9	...	...	-224.2	4 365.2
2nd quarter	4 424.6	2 658.2	565.0	...	...	...	...	157.8	201.3	1 417.2	...	...	-231.1	4 385.2
3rd quarter	4 462.1	2 688.5	560.8	...	...	...	...	155.9	212.6	1 455.9	...	...	-238.7	4 429.6
4th quarter	4 498.7	2 699.7	564.1	...	...	...	...	159.8	215.0	1 481.0	...	...	-262.9	4 442.7
1967														
1st quarter	4 538.5	2 715.3	550.3	...	...	...	...	161.8	218.3	1 543.6	...	...	-281.3	4 488.9
2nd quarter	4 541.3	2 752.4	530.4	...	...	...	...	159.6	216.6	1 537.2	...	...	-251.2	4 536.6
3rd quarter	4 584.2	2 766.5	545.9	...	...	...	...	158.4	219.5	1 554.2	...	...	-261.1	4 566.6
4th quarter	4 618.8	2 783.4	557.7	...	...	...	...	161.3	231.0	1 566.0	...	...	-257.4	4 606.4
1968														
1st quarter	4 713.0	2 850.2	568.9	...	...	...	...	165.9	244.6	1 594.0	...	...	-256.7	4 702.0
2nd quarter	4 791.8	2 893.6	590.6	...	...	...	...	168.6	248.4	1 602.3	...	...	-277.0	4 749.2
3rd quarter	4 828.9	2 947.8	574.5	...	...	...	...	180.6	263.3	1 607.1	...	...	-251.7	4 820.5
4th quarter	4 847.9	2 961.1	580.8	...	...	...	...	176.6	261.1	1 608.6	...	...	-246.2	4 848.9
1969														
1st quarter	4 923.8	2 993.9	615.0	...	...	...	...	156.1	236.5	1 612.2	...	...	-264.1	4 899.3
2nd quarter	4 938.7	3 013.2	611.4	...	...	...	...	190.3	283.1	1 607.2	...	...	-239.6	4 923.7
3rd quarter	4 971.3	3 027.9	623.8	...	...	...	...	187.1	279.4	1 610.5	...	...	-244.0	4 950.8
4th quarter	4 947.1	3 052.1	593.7	...	...	...	...	192.0	276.4	1 588.8	...	...	-227.7	4 950.1
1970														
1st quarter	4 939.8	3 071.1	576.0	...	...	...	...	194.5	275.5	1 581.1	...	...	-212.0	4 963.2
2nd quarter	4 946.8	3 085.0	577.2	...	...	...	...	202.1	280.9	1 562.8	...	...	-220.2	4 952.3
3rd quarter	4 992.4	3 112.0	586.6	...	...	...	...	202.9	280.3	1 569.4	...	...	-219.2	4 998.2
4th quarter	4 938.9	3 103.6	555.5	...	...	...	...	203.3	284.6	1 570.1	...	...	-191.5	4 987.0
1971														
1st quarter	5 073.0	3 163.1	620.2	...	...	...	...	205.2	281.2	1 547.1	...	...	-230.8	5 049.1
2nd quarter	5 100.4	3 192.2	637.8	...	...	...	...	203.6	302.5	1 543.6	...	...	-216.4	5 082.5
3rd quarter	5 142.4	3 217.7	645.5	...	...	...	...	213.8	309.2	1 542.8	...	...	-208.2	5 128.3
4th quarter	5 154.5	3 271.1	628.2	...	...	...	...	194.1	288.2	1 531.9	...	...	-180.2	5 186.4
1972														
1st quarter	5 249.3	3 314.2	669.6	...	...	...	...	216.1	330.3	1 540.4	...	...	-175.1	5 261.8
2nd quarter	5 368.5	3 377.3	707.6	...	...	...	...	209.8	318.6	1 546.6	...	...	-201.6	5 344.9
3rd quarter	5 419.2	3 429.4	717.6	...	...	...	...	222.5	325.2	1 517.1	...	...	-192.8	5 392.5
4th quarter	5 509.9	3 509.8	722.1	...	...	...	...	231.9	339.9	1 529.7	...	...	-164.1	5 518.3

Note: Chained (2012) dollar series are calculated as the product of the chain-type quantity index and the 2012 current-dollar value of the corresponding series, divided by 100. Because the formula for the chain-type quantity indexes uses weights from more than one period, the corresponding chained-dollar estimates are usually not additive. The residual column is the difference between the total and the sum of the most detailed components shown in the Bureau of Economic Analysis (BEA) published data.

. . . = Not available.

Table 1-2B. Real Gross Domestic Product: Historical Data—*Continued*

(Billions of chained [2012] dollars, quarterly data are at seasonally adjusted annual rates.)   **NIPA Tables 1.1.6, 1.2.6**

Year and quarter	Gross domestic product	Personal consumption expenditures	Gross private domestic investment Total	Fixed investment Nonresidential	Fixed investment Residential	Change in private inventories	Net exports	Exports	Imports	Government consumption expenditures and gross investment Total	Federal	State and local	Residual	Addendum: Final sales of domestic product
1973														
1st quarter	5 646.3	3 573.9	764.5	...	...	...	...	248.9	355.6	1 542.9	...	...	-161.6	5 635.3
2nd quarter ...	5 707.8	3 572.3	797.0	...	...	...	...	260.9	345.3	1 532.0	...	...	-174.3	5 660.1
3rd quarter	5 677.7	3 584.9	768.1	...	...	...	...	261.7	335.8	1 514.0	...	...	-146.3	5 666.5
4th quarter	5 731.6	3 574.2	795.5	...	...	...	...	274.6	338.3	1 525.3	...	...	-171.8	5 674.2
1974														
1st quarter	5 682.4	3 542.2	750.1	...	...	...	...	278.2	326.8	1 552.9	...	...	-149.3	5 667.0
2nd quarter ...	5 695.9	3 555.0	747.1	...	...	...	...	291.7	344.1	1 560.7	...	...	-160.5	5 672.4
3rd quarter	5 642.0	3 570.2	708.4	...	...	...	...	276.0	338.1	1 563.8	...	...	-153.0	5 656.3
4th quarter	5 620.1	3 518.1	712.7	...	...	...	...	283.2	334.8	1 571.3	...	...	-184.7	5 576.3
1975														
1st quarter	5 551.7	3 547.6	597.9	...	...	...	...	285.2	301.2	1 588.4	...	...	-144.2	5 616.4
2nd quarter ...	5 591.4	3 605.9	580.1	...	...	...	...	276.9	277.1	1 574.9	...	...	-130.9	5 670.8
3rd quarter	5 687.1	3 657.2	625.0	...	...	...	...	272.2	300.1	1 604.4	...	...	-165.5	5 724.6
4th quarter	5 763.7	3 696.5	642.5	...	...	...	...	287.6	316.1	1 618.4	...	...	-165.6	5 794.8
1976														
1st quarter	5 893.3	3 770.4	704.5	...	...	...	...	285.6	335.9	1 621.0	...	...	-192.9	5 874.8
2nd quarter ...	5 936.5	3 805.1	732.4	...	...	...	...	288.5	350.5	1 602.9	...	...	-203.0	5 894.2
3rd quarter	5 969.1	3 845.1	734.9	...	...	...	...	296.9	364.8	1 598.2	...	...	-196.5	5 933.9
4th quarter	6 012.4	3 895.0	740.4	...	...	...	...	299.9	376.8	1 597.3	...	...	-163.6	6 015.7
1977														
1st quarter	6 083.4	3 940.9	774.7	...	...	...	...	295.1	394.7	1 610.8	...	...	-177.8	6 073.8
2nd quarter ...	6 201.7	3 962.3	830.3	...	...	...	...	303.0	398.3	1 625.6	...	...	-172.4	6 169.3
3rd quarter	6 313.6	3 999.8	872.3	...	...	...	...	305.4	392.8	1 632.1	...	...	-193.1	6 236.4
4th quarter	6 313.7	4 059.9	850.4	...	...	...	...	295.6	398.3	1 628.2	...	...	-169.4	6 287.5
1978														
1st quarter	6 333.8	4 082.7	867.0	...	...	...	...	302.6	425.1	1 628.6	...	...	-178.3	6 294.3
2nd quarter ...	6 578.6	4 170.0	923.3	...	...	...	...	334.1	426.4	1 669.5	...	...	-147.3	6 539.6
3rd quarter	6 644.8	4 187.5	950.2	...	...	...	...	337.8	432.0	1 684.9	...	...	-140.1	6 601.3
4th quarter	6 734.1	4 221.3	972.1	...	...	...	...	351.2	437.9	1 700.1	...	...	-139.9	6 687.7
1979														
1st quarter	6 746.2	4 243.2	973.8	...	...	...	...	351.5	436.7	1 683.3	...	...	-119.5	6 709.4
2nd quarter ...	6 753.4	4 240.4	972.9	...	...	...	...	352.4	439.1	1 699.7	...	...	-130.3	6 710.1
3rd quarter	6 803.6	4 281.7	956.5	...	...	...	...	365.1	432.4	1 704.6	...	...	-93.1	6 807.7
4th quarter	6 820.6	4 292.3	939.5	...	...	...	...	388.0	441.8	1 715.9	...	...	-88.6	6 836.8
1980														
1st quarter	6 842.0	4 286.2	933.1	...	...	...	...	398.8	442.1	1 741.0	...	...	-91.9	6 849.8
2nd quarter ...	6 701.0	4 189.7	853.8	...	...	...	...	406.4	410.0	1 744.5	...	...	-97.6	6 714.6
3rd quarter	6 693.1	4 235.6	797.4	...	...	...	...	405.5	380.5	1 720.7	...	...	-23.6	6 804.3
4th quarter	6 817.9	4 292.9	871.7	...	...	...	...	403.0	400.9	1 720.3	...	...	-51.5	6 867.7
1981														
1st quarter	6 951.5	4 307.2	952.4	...	...	...	...	410.6	418.0	1 743.3	...	...	-115.8	6 895.9
2nd quarter ...	6 900.0	4 307.6	912.9	...	...	...	...	412.8	418.6	1 746.7	...	...	-79.4	6 912.0
3rd quarter	6 982.6	4 327.5	964.4	...	...	...	...	404.1	413.8	1 740.7	...	...	-114.2	6 920.7
4th quarter	6 906.5	4 297.9	930.4	...	...	...	...	405.9	425.7	1 762.8	...	...	-102.4	6 889.8
1982														
1st quarter	6 799.2	4 329.5	842.4	...	...	...	...	388.3	413.5	1 760.8	...	...	-73.0	6 873.9
2nd quarter ...	6 830.3	4 342.7	841.8	...	...	...	...	390.6	406.8	1 767.5	...	...	-98.7	6 866.2
3rd quarter	6 804.1	4 371.8	834.1	...	...	...	...	373.3	425.6	1 781.7	...	...	-138.8	6 821.9
4th quarter	6 806.9	4 448.4	769.6	...	...	...	...	356.2	408.9	1 809.2	...	...	-100.1	6 917.8
1983														
1st quarter	6 896.6	4 492.4	796.3	...	...	...	...	361.9	418.3	1 826.6	...	...	-99.4	6 996.3
2nd quarter ...	7 053.5	4 583.9	866.8	...	...	...	...	363.0	450.5	1 841.6	...	...	-141.4	7 098.8
3rd quarter	7 194.5	4 666.1	921.1	...	...	...	...	368.5	485.6	1 873.4	...	...	-145.5	7 232.7
4th quarter	7 344.6	4 740.1	1 010.7	...	...	...	...	375.9	509.4	1 843.4	...	...	-152.1	7 330.5
1984														
1st quarter	7 488.2	4 779.8	1 108.3	...	...	...	...	383.7	550.3	1 863.0	...	...	-210.0	7 383.1
2nd quarter ...	7 617.5	4 846.7	1 144.4	...	...	...	...	393.3	573.4	1 903.4	...	...	-203.8	7 518.4
3rd quarter	7 691.0	4 882.7	1 169.1	...	...	...	...	401.9	588.2	1 918.8	...	...	-205.0	7 587.2
4th quarter	7 754.1	4 945.9	1 154.0	...	...	...	...	410.1	605.5	1 959.1	...	...	-179.8	7 697.0
1985														
1st quarter	7 829.3	5 030.0	1 122.3	...	...	...	...	411.2	592.1	1 980.5	...	...	-144.3	7 827.9
2nd quarter ...	7 898.2	5 076.1	1 141.4	...	...	...	...	410.3	621.2	2 024.4	...	...	-164.8	7 890.3
3rd quarter	8 018.8	5 172.6	1 133.7	...	...	...	...	404.3	615.2	2 070.6	...	...	-173.9	8 015.5
4th quarter	8 078.4	5 183.7	1 175.5	...	...	...	...	416.4	639.3	2 079.1	...	...	-186.2	8 047.8
1986														
1st quarter	8 153.8	5 229.0	1 175.1	...	...	...	...	429.5	638.6	2 095.5	...	...	-180.3	8 128.2
2nd quarter ...	8 190.6	5 286.0	1 154.6	...	...	...	...	434.1	665.8	2 139.2	...	...	-178.8	8 192.8
3rd quarter	8 268.9	5 379.5	1 123.5	...	...	...	...	444.0	684.3	2 185.8	...	...	-167.5	8 306.3
4th quarter	8 313.3	5 412.5	1 126.9	...	...	...	...	460.6	689.6	2 176.8	...	...	-163.5	8 358.2
1987														
1st quarter	8 375.3	5 417.9	1 157.3	...	...	...	...	461.0	685.5	2 189.5	...	...	-212.0	8 353.2
2nd quarter ...	8 465.6	5 491.8	1 157.9	...	...	...	...	480.0	702.7	2 206.5	...	...	-194.3	8 466.0
3rd quarter	8 539.1	5 554.5	1 158.1	...	...	...	...	500.8	716.4	2 208.8	...	...	-164.5	8 565.6
4th quarter	8 685.7	5 566.3	1 237.0	...	...	...	...	519.5	732.8	2 241.9	...	...	-245.3	8 607.2

Note: Chained (2012) dollar series are calculated as the product of the chain-type quantity index and the 2012 current-dollar value of the corresponding series, divided by 100. Because the formula for the chain-type quantity indexes uses weights from more than one period, the corresponding chained-dollar estimates are usually not additive. The residual column is the difference between the total and the sum of the most detailed components shown in the Bureau of Economic Analysis (BEA) published data.

. . . = Not available.

Table 1-2B. Real Gross Domestic Product: Historical Data—*Continued*

(Billions of chained [2012] dollars, quarterly data are at seasonally adjusted annual rates.)   **NIPA Tables 1.1.6, 1.2.6**

| Year and quarter | Gross domestic product | Personal consumption expenditures | Gross private domestic investment | | | | Exports and imports of goods and services | | | Government consumption expenditures and gross investment | | | Residual | Addendum: Final sales of domestic product |
| | | | Total | Fixed investment | | Change in private inventories | Net exports | Exports | Imports | Total | Federal | State and local | | |
				Nonresidential	Residential									
1988														
1st quarter	8 730.6	5 664.6	1 177.6	...	...	...	...	548.4	729.4	2 223.2	...	...	-175.6	8 732.0
2nd quarter	8 845.3	5 706.4	1 205.7	...	...	...	...	563.7	721.0	2 229.9	...	...	-169.7	8 839.8
3rd quarter	8 897.1	5 757.1	1 212.4	...	...	...	...	574.9	738.0	2 230.1	...	...	-164.5	8 890.2
4th quarter	9 015.7	5 822.6	1 230.9	...	...	...	...	592.4	760.5	2 273.4	...	...	-177.7	9 003.3
1989														
1st quarter	9 107.3	5 849.6	1 272.6	...	...	...	...	610.1	764.0	2 263.4	...	...	-192.7	9 054.6
2nd quarter	9 176.8	5 876.9	1 260.3	...	...	...	...	636.8	767.6	2 298.2	...	...	-180.1	9 142.5
3rd quarter	9 244.8	5 933.8	1 249.0	...	...	...	...	643.3	766.6	2 318.9	...	...	-148.1	9 253.1
4th quarter	9 263.0	5 959.6	1 239.7	...	...	...	...	653.0	780.5	2 330.5	...	...	-160.4	9 262.6
1990														
1st quarter	9 364.3	6 009.7	1 252.1	...	...	...	...	681.4	805.2	2 367.8	...	...	-160.8	9 366.9
2nd quarter	9 398.2	6 028.0	1 252.4	...	...	...	...	689.9	803.9	2 371.5	...	...	-188.0	9 369.0
3rd quarter	9 404.5	6 051.9	1 228.2	...	...	...	...	695.1	800.6	2 375.3	...	...	-177.0	9 393.4
4th quarter	9 318.9	6 005.9	1 159.5	...	...	...	...	701.2	779.2	2 391.2	...	...	-144.9	9 355.6
1991														
1st quarter	9 275.3	5 983.3	1 120.9	...	...	...	...	705.5	770.3	2 405.4	...	...	-146.1	9 319.8
2nd quarter	9 347.6	6 032.9	1 120.9	...	...	...	...	731.2	784.0	2 415.2	...	...	-140.8	9 396.6
3rd quarter	9 394.8	6 063.0	1 143.1	...	...	...	...	748.5	806.0	2 408.5	...	...	-163.4	9 417.7
4th quarter	9 427.6	6 059.9	1 183.6	...	...	...	...	765.4	823.8	2 390.8	...	...	-189.2	9 406.0
1992														
1st quarter ...	9 540.4	6 173.4	1 161.7	...	...	...	...	779.2	829.8	2 412.0	...	...	-159.2	9 562.1
2nd quarter ...	9 643.9	6 215.3	1 227.4	...	...	...	...	779.6	843.5	2 407.4	...	...	-172.1	9 631.8
3rd quarter ...	9 739.2	6 281.9	1 237.2	...	...	...	...	796.1	856.8	2 422.7	...	...	-169.3	9 732.3
4th quarter ...	9 840.8	6 356.8	1 274.9	...	...	...	...	800.1	877.3	2 422.4	...	...	-167.5	9 831.4
1993														
1st quarter	9 857.2	6 381.2	1 305.0	...	...	...	...	801.9	896.3	2 392.4	...	...	-181.0	9 822.5
2nd quarter	9 914.6	6 439.2	1 312.5	...	...	...	...	811.5	914.8	2 392.6	...	...	-162.9	9 898.5
3rd quarter	9 961.9	6 510.9	1 303.6	...	...	...	...	809.3	926.8	2 396.0	...	...	-133.5	9 981.3
4th quarter	10 097.4	6 568.0	1 372.1	...	...	...	...	835.4	964.1	2 404.4	...	...	-138.8	10 097.4
1994														
1st quarter	10 195.3	6 643.2	1 424.4	...	...	...	...	843.6	986.5	2 374.7	...	...	-168.1	10 151.6
2nd quarter	10 333.5	6 694.8	1 494.4	...	...	...	...	872.1	1 023.3	2 386.5	...	...	-206.8	10 238.5
3rd quarter	10 393.9	6 745.9	1 470.0	...	...	...	...	904.7	1 052.0	2 426.7	...	...	-173.7	10 342.6
4th quarter	10 513.0	6 818.8	1 530.5	...	...	...	...	925.6	1 081.6	2 405.6	...	...	-187.5	10 430.0
1995														
1st quarter	10 550.3	6 835.8	1 546.5	...	...	...	...	943.4	1 105.4	2 414.0	...	...	-169.1	10 484.9
2nd quarter	10 581.7	6 895.7	1 514.4	...	...	...	...	956.6	1 115.9	2 422.1	...	...	-139.8	10 554.0
3rd quarter	10 671.7	6 958.2	1 505.4	...	...	...	...	998.0	1 119.7	2 415.7	...	...	-97.0	10 679.8
4th quarter	10 744.2	7 006.7	1 542.8	...	...	...	...	1 012.3	1 134.0	2 390.5	...	...	-91.8	10 742.3
1996														
1st quarter	10 824.7	7 071.4	1 567.6	...	...	...	...	1 024.5	1 170.9	2 406.2	...	...	-76.5	10 839.7
2nd quarter	11 005.2	7 147.4	1 642.9	...	...	...	...	1 041.1	1 197.1	2 436.2	...	...	-100.1	10 988.6
3rd quarter	11 103.9	7 190.7	1 717.5	...	...	...	...	1 049.5	1 235.9	2 436.2	...	...	-131.0	11 042.5
4th quarter	11 219.2	7 248.0	1 715.2	...	...	...	...	1 115.0	1 260.3	2 453.0	...	...	-96.5	11 191.5
1997														
1st quarter	11 291.7	7 324.4	1 749.9	...	...	...	...	1 136.2	1 314.1	2 440.2	...	...	-82.1	11 260.1
2nd quarter	11 479.3	7 357.4	1 857.0	...	...	...	...	1 181.6	1 358.2	2 471.9	...	...	-174.8	11 361.4
3rd quarter	11 622.9	7 482.7	1 883.0	...	...	...	...	1 208.9	1 408.3	2 483.3	...	...	-122.8	11 546.7
4th quarter	11 722.7	7 572.1	1 911.0	...	...	...	...	1 207.3	1 438.7	2 495.8	...	...	-128.6	11 629.8
1998														
1st quarter	11 839.9	7 648.7	1 994.4	...	...	...	...	1 212.9	1 492.6	2 486.8	...	...	-166.6	11 713.2
2nd quarter	11 949.5	7 783.4	1 982.1	...	...	...	...	1 199.5	1 526.8	2 530.4	...	...	-75.5	11 910.0
3rd quarter	12 099.2	7 884.9	2 033.0	...	...	...	...	1 193.9	1 547.4	2 549.4	...	...	-85.9	12 044.1
4th quarter	12 294.7	7 998.8	2 095.8	...	...	...	...	1 238.1	1 597.5	2 564.5	...	...	-88.4	12 230.7
1999														
1st quarter	12 410.8	8 081.0	2 153.3	...	...	...	...	1 234.5	1 642.6	2 582.9	...	...	-116.3	12 321.9
2nd quarter	12 514.4	8 204.8	2 154.7	...	...	...	...	1 249.6	1 689.8	2 592.2	...	...	-47.0	12 479.5
3rd quarter	12 680.0	8 297.0	2 213.8	...	...	...	...	1 287.2	1 750.9	2 623.4	...	...	-52.9	12 634.1
4th quarter	12 888.3	8 418.3	2 273.1	...	...	...	...	1 314.6	1 795.7	2 664.2	...	...	-105.6	12 788.7
2000														
1st quarter	12 935.3	8 545.6	2 257.1	...	...	...	...	1 333.7	1 863.5	2 645.3	...	...	-4.4	12 923.2
2nd quarter	13 170.7	8 625.4	2 390.7	...	...	...	...	1 374.3	1 922.9	2 671.4	...	...	-91.8	13 065.1
3rd quarter	13 183.9	8 708.1	2 367.3	...	...	...	...	1 407.3	1 992.0	2 660.1	...	...	-54.2	13 115.5
4th quarter	13 262.3	8 784.2	2 371.8	...	...	...	...	1 393.3	1 995.0	2 676.4	...	...	-50.9	13 196.7
2001														
1st quarter	13 219.3	8 816.0	2 264.2	...	...	...	...	1 375.8	1 969.2	2 718.3	...	...	59.7	13 257.7
2nd quarter	13 301.4	8 833.7	2 267.4	...	...	...	...	1 335.4	1 906.2	2 765.4	...	...	8.3	13 306.8
3rd quarter	13 248.1	8 864.5	2 218.4	...	...	...	...	1 267.0	1 863.0	2 762.7	...	...	45.3	13 289.4
4th quarter	13 284.9	9 007.5	2 108.5	...	...	...	...	1 222.9	1 843.7	2 808.5	...	...	99.0	13 390.2
2002														
1st quarter	13 394.9	9 027.5	2 170.7	1 492.6	675.9	-7.8	-646.4	1 249.6	1 896.0	2 857.3	946.8	1 923.7	-103.6	13 411.4
2nd quarter	13 477.4	9 073.2	2 206.4	1 475.8	692.6	33.1	-672.8	1 286.8	1 959.6	2 879.3	965.2	1 926.3	-92.4	13 452.5
3rd quarter	13 531.7	9 136.7	2 203.1	1 471.0	694.7	28.7	-693.6	1 290.9	1 984.5	2 894.2	974.7	1 931.5	-68.2	13 506.9
4th quarter	13 549.4	9 187.5	2 201.7	1 451.2	707.2	43.4	-748.3	1 271.8	2 020.1	2 915.6	991.3	1 935.3	-82.1	13 516.2

Note: Chained (2012) dollar series are calculated as the product of the chain-type quantity index and the 2012 current-dollar value of the corresponding series, divided by 100. Because the formula for the chain-type quantity indexes uses weights from more than one period, the corresponding chained-dollar estimates are usually not additive. The residual column is the difference between the total and the sum of the most detailed components shown in the Bureau of Economic Analysis (BEA) published data.

. . . = Not available.

Table 1-2B. Real Gross Domestic Product: Historical Data—*Continued*

(Billions of chained [2012] dollars, quarterly data are at seasonally adjusted annual rates.) **NIPA Tables 1.1.6, 1.2.6**

| Year and quarter | Gross domestic product | Personal consumption expenditures | Gross private domestic investment | | | | Exports and imports of goods and services | | | Government consumption expenditures and gross investment | | | Residual | Addendum: Final sales of domestic product |
| | | | Total | Fixed investment | | Change in private inventories | Net exports | Exports | Imports | Total | Federal | State and local | | |
				Nonresidential	Residential									
2003														
1st quarter	13 619.4	9 232.8	2 218.7	1 458.4	720.2	39.9	-743.4	1 267.9	2 011.3	2 917.9	1 002.5	1 925.3	-79.6	13 589.3
2nd quarter	13 741.1	9 338.5	2 234.0	1 498.7	731.7	-9.2	-770.5	1 270.1	2 040.7	2 944.7	1 037.1	1 914.9	-48.5	13 751.1
3rd quarter	13 970.2	9 470.5	2 315.4	1 530.5	773.6	2.8	-767.8	1 304.8	2 072.6	2 951.2	1 036.8	1 921.9	-32.5	13 970.9
4th quarter	14 131.4	9 535.7	2 393.4	1 549.8	796.6	46.2	-774.9	1 363.5	2 138.4	2 969.1	1 056.1	1 919.2	-26.9	14 093.7
2004														
1st quarter	14 212.3	9 624.6	2 398.2	1 534.4	805.9	58.7	-804.0	1 394.3	2 198.3	2 982.7	1 067.6	1 920.6	-20.7	14 162.7
2nd quarter	14 323.0	9 677.2	2 493.9	1 572.8	831.4	97.7	-861.4	1 423.5	2 284.9	2 990.8	1 073.9	1 922.1	-13.3	14 239.4
3rd quarter	14 457.8	9 790.8	2 532.6	1 617.8	837.4	83.1	-888.4	1 428.2	2 316.6	2 996.3	1 085.7	1 914.9	0.6	14 387.8
4th quarter	14 605.6	9 901.6	2 585.5	1 651.0	848.9	91.1	-908.5	1 462.1	2 370.6	2 994.6	1 083.7	1 915.3	12.5	14 527.0
2005														
1st quarter	14 767.8	9 964.5	2 658.2	1 675.0	868.9	124.9	-901.5	1 489.5	2 391.0	3 009.6	1 095.8	1 917.6	11.7	14 658.3
2nd quarter	14 839.7	10 074.9	2 622.8	1 702.0	885.0	24.7	-900.2	1 522.7	2 423.0	3 007.8	1 094.6	1 917.0	38.9	14 815.3
3rd quarter	14 956.3	10 158.5	2 657.5	1 737.5	894.7	7.9	-914.2	1 522.4	2 436.6	3 017.8	1 103.1	1 918.2	55.0	14 943.6
4th quarter	15 041.2	10 177.2	2 743.8	1 750.9	892.9	97.4	-945.5	1 569.6	2 515.1	3 020.1	1 103.5	1 920.2	38.4	14 947.7
2006														
1st quarter	15 244.1	10 288.2	2 784.6	1 809.7	884.6	102.7	-933.7	1 633.2	2 566.9	3 058.5	1 132.2	1 928.9	33.5	15 160.5
2nd quarter	15 281.5	10 341.6	2 766.6	1 841.3	840.3	92.7	-929.0	1 663.4	2 592.5	3 057.6	1 124.4	1 936.2	33.4	15 201.6
3rd quarter	15 304.5	10 408.0	2 756.0	1 872.9	793.8	97.3	-957.1	1 661.2	2 618.4	3 053.1	1 114.3	1 942.4	34.1	15 217.5
4th quarter	15 433.6	10 507.2	2 702.5	1 892.7	756.9	55.7	-890.7	1 724.3	2 615.0	3 078.2	1 130.4	1 951.0	32.1	15 384.1
2007														
1st quarter	15 479.0	10 572.1	2 683.9	1 926.8	722.7	27.5	-894.6	1 758.4	2 653.1	3 082.5	1 123.7	1 962.4	41.3	15 447.1
2nd quarter	15 577.8	10 599.8	2 713.5	1 969.6	694.3	56.4	-882.1	1 785.1	2 667.2	3 110.7	1 142.1	1 971.8	28.8	15 527.4
3rd quarter	15 671.6	10 670.5	2 686.1	2 000.5	650.1	43.4	-841.3	1 840.8	2 682.1	3 124.9	1 152.1	1 975.8	22.2	15 634.2
4th quarter	15 767.1	10 712.6	2 653.1	2 031.3	596.1	35.0	-773.7	1 883.1	2 656.8	3 149.5	1 171.3	1 980.8	15.1	15 738.0
2008														
1st quarter	15 702.9	10 697.9	2 583.3	2 039.4	548.7	1.6	-753.7	1 913.0	2 666.7	3 156.9	1 189.1	1 970.0	4.8	15 705.2
2nd quarter	15 792.8	10 727.3	2 536.4	2 043.5	523.8	-25.4	-672.3	1 969.2	2 641.5	3 184.3	1 214.5	1 971.6	1.5	15 822.7
3rd quarter	15 709.6	10 644.7	2 485.5	2 005.4	497.2	-19.3	-647.8	1 960.4	2 608.2	3 210.0	1 230.3	1 981.5	5.6	15 724.6
4th quarter	15 366.6	10 548.9	2 246.4	1 888.6	448.8	-87.6	-668.9	1 845.0	2 513.8	3 231.9	1 246.3	1 987.3	-18.5	15 459.7
2009														
1st quarter	15 187.5	10 522.1	1 986.8	1 746.3	405.3	-179.0	-577.3	1 697.6	2 274.9	3 268.8	1 262.8	2 007.7	-23.5	15 359.8
2nd quarter	15 161.8	10 470.4	1 872.3	1 693.2	380.4	-228.3	-473.7	1 708.8	2 182.5	3 316.6	1 292.8	2 025.2	-21.0	15 371.4
3rd quarter	15 216.6	10 540.8	1 868.0	1 683.3	398.1	-245.1	-500.5	1 772.0	2 272.5	3 325.7	1 304.6	2 022.3	-1.0	15 437.6
4th quarter	15 379.2	10 529.2	2 040.7	1 694.5	397.2	-56.8	-513.6	1 871.5	2 385.1	3 331.6	1 324.0	2 008.4	-15.9	15 432.4
2010														
1st quarter	15 456.1	10 590.2	2 087.2	1 706.4	384.4	-5.0	-531.8	1 916.2	2 448.0	3 317.3	1 338.8	1 978.9	-13.7	15 460.9
2nd quarter	15 605.6	10 685.1	2 196.7	1 762.3	404.4	33.3	-601.3	1 958.4	2 559.7	3 327.6	1 356.4	1 971.3	-10.9	15 576.4
3rd quarter	15 726.3	10 761.4	2 294.7	1 810.1	368.6	128.8	-634.9	2 014.2	2 649.1	3 304.1	1 350.2	1 953.9	-14.3	15 609.5
4th quarter	15 808.0	10 827.3	2 287.4	1 845.2	374.7	72.1	-589.5	2 069.3	2 658.9	3 283.0	1 348.0	1 934.9	-6.4	15 740.4
2011														
1st quarter	15 769.9	10 868.7	2 244.2	1 842.7	373.4	32.8	-584.8	2 087.1	2 671.9	3 242.8	1 329.0	1 913.8	-5.3	15 742.1
2nd quarter	15 876.8	10 879.9	2 336.1	1 890.4	377.6	71.3	-559.5	2 122.3	2 681.9	3 220.8	1 323.9	1 896.9	-4.6	15 808.8
3rd quarter	15 870.7	10 913.0	2 343.8	1 978.9	384.4	-17.7	-560.1	2 151.5	2 711.6	3 174.8	1 295.1	1 879.8	-4.0	15 890.5
4th quarter	16 048.7	10 931.8	2 524.4	2 029.4	394.4	100.4	-579.6	2 167.7	2 747.2	3 172.5	1 299.9	1 872.6	-0.8	15 948.0
2012														
1st quarter	16 180.0	11 010.7	2 577.2	2 081.3	418.3	72.8	-566.7	2 194.1	2 760.7	3 158.9	1 299.9	1 859.0	4.6	16 102.3
2nd quarter	16 253.7	11 030.0	2 636.5	2 128.0	421.9	87.1	-555.3	2 215.8	2 771.0	3 142.4	1 289.5	1 852.9	-0.3	16 167.1
3rd quarter	16 282.2	11 052.4	2 648.5	2 120.9	432.7	98.0	-556.5	2 229.4	2 785.9	3 137.7	1 292.2	1 845.5	-2.8	16 187.3
4th quarter	16 300.0	11 096.4	2 624.9	2 144.0	455.2	27.0	-528.0	2 231.6	2 759.6	3 106.9	1 266.4	1 840.5	-1.5	16 274.3
2013														
1st quarter	16 441.5	11 155.5	2 722.8	2 171.6	471.8	81.2	-515.0	2 242.3	2 757.3	3 078.9	1 237.4	1 841.3	-3.1	16 362.5
2nd quarter	16 464.4	11 172.6	2 753.2	2 177.5	486.8	85.8	-534.8	2 262.5	2 797.3	3 073.7	1 227.4	1 846.0	2.3	16 376.4
3rd quarter	16 594.7	11 214.4	2 859.8	2 214.7	495.5	147.6	-535.4	2 282.0	2 817.4	3 057.2	1 209.6	1 847.0	0.8	16 446.7
4th quarter	16 712.8	11 304.3	2 870.1	2 260.0	487.7	120.0	-492.1	2 347.6	2 839.7	3 033.1	1 188.9	1 843.4	-1.0	16 591.0
2014														
1st quarter	16 654.2	11 347.6	2 838.3	2 291.7	484.5	58.3	-551.5	2 324.8	2 876.3	3 020.6	1 187.7	1 832.2	2.9	16 591.3
2nd quarter	16 868.1	11 453.0	2 958.1	2 353.3	499.8	98.6	-566.7	2 375.1	2 941.8	3 024.4	1 180.7	1 842.7	3.8	16 763.1
3rd quarter	17 064.6	11 565.7	3 018.6	2 400.8	507.1	106.3	-562.6	2 384.8	2 947.4	3 044.7	1 193.9	1 849.9	-1.4	16 953.8
4th quarter	17 141.2	11 694.9	3 021.9	2 415.5	525.2	82.0	-620.3	2 404.4	3 024.7	3 043.2	1 176.5	1 865.4	-2.9	17 061.0
2015														
1st quarter	17 280.6	11 772.9	3 127.3	2 412.6	535.5	177.3	-683.6	2 384.8	3 068.5	3 059.0	1 181.3	1 876.3	4.5	17 104.4
2nd quarter	17 380.9	11 852.7	3 136.7	2 423.6	548.9	156.5	-699.9	2 391.1	3 091.1	3 085.1	1 183.5	1 900.0	9.0	17 220.5
3rd quarter	17 437.1	11 943.0	3 130.4	2 432.4	563.7	125.2	-746.6	2 371.2	3 117.8	3 099.1	1 182.3	1 915.1	11.8	17 307.2
4th quarter	17 462.6	12 003.1	3 092.7	2 412.8	573.6	91.4	-756.7	2 367.7	3 124.4	3 110.3	1 191.1	1 917.5	17.4	17 361.0
2016														
1st quarter	17 565.5	12 091.6	3 079.4	2 410.4	591.2	59.1	-759.3	2 360.7	3 120.0	3 142.8	1 194.0	1 946.9	14.9	17 494.9
2nd quarter	17 618.6	12 152.6	3 063.3	2 426.1	592.0	23.0	-744.6	2 378.6	3 123.2	3 137.9	1 184.3	1 951.6	17.8	17 579.7
3rd quarter	17 724.5	12 223.8	3 069.3	2 457.8	588.9	-6.2	-730.4	2 415.6	3 146.0	3 153.9	1 191.5	1 960.4	19.4	17 706.5
4th quarter	17 812.6	12 283.1	3 147.6	2 473.6	596.3	66.9	-794.0	2 398.6	3 192.5	3 160.5	1 192.3	1 966.2	9.0	17 741.3
2017														
1st quarter	17 896.6	12 372.2	3 137.7	2 505.1	611.8	-13.0	-783.2	2 455.6	3 238.8	3 153.8	1 183.8	1 967.8	32.4	17 882.3
2nd quarter	17 996.8	12 430.1	3 192.8	2 531.0	615.7	18.5	-808.0	2 465.4	3 273.4	3 163.2	1 193.7	1 967.5	24.0	17 957.5
3rd quarter	18 126.2	12 500.4	3 241.0	2 538.7	612.7	83.4	-790.3	2 481.9	3 272.2	3 160.7	1 193.4	1 965.3	-9.6	18 043.5
4th quarter	18 296.7	12 632.0	3 278.4	2 590.5	623.2	45.6	-816.3	2 540.1	3 356.5	3 183.0	1 207.7	1 973.4	0.4	18 238.3

Note: Chained (2012) dollar series are calculated as the product of the chain-type quantity index and the 2012 current-dollar value of the corresponding series, divided by 100. Because the formula for the chain-type quantity indexes uses weights from more than one period, the corresponding chained-dollar estimates are usually not additive. The residual column is the difference between the total and the sum of the most detailed components shown in the Bureau of Economic Analysis (BEA) published data.

Table 1-3A. U.S. Population and Per Capita Product and Income: Recent Data

(Dollars, except as noted; quarterly data are at seasonally adjusted annual rates.)

Year and quarter	Population (mid-period, thousands)	Current dollars							Chained (2012) dollars					
		Gross domestic product	Personal income	Disposable personal income	Personal consumption expenditures				Gross domestic product	Disposable personal income	Personal consumption expenditures			
					Total	Durable goods	Nondurable goods	Services			Total	Durable goods	Nondurable goods	Services
1960	180 760	3 001	2 335	2 080	1 832	252	727	853	18 046	12 654	11 144	444	4 024	7 232
1961	183 742	3 060	2 398	2 141	1 858	241	733	885	18 209	12 886	11 188	422	4 039	7 376
1962	186 590	3 237	2 513	2 236	1 943	265	748	930	19 029	13 307	11 562	463	4 099	7 607
1963	189 300	3 367	2 603	2 315	2 018	286	760	971	19 574	13 612	11 866	498	4 128	7 818
1964	191 927	3 566	2 752	2 481	2 140	310	796	1 034	20 418	14 378	12 400	537	4 262	8 169
1965	194 347	3 819	2 936	2 640	2 279	342	840	1 098	21 474	15 081	13 023	596	4 421	8 515
1966	196 599	4 137	3 155	2 818	2 441	365	905	1 171	22 628	15 702	13 604	638	4 614	8 834
1967	198 752	4 327	3 350	2 982	2 549	372	931	1 246	22 997	16 213	13 859	641	4 662	9 097
1968	200 745	4 686	3 641	3 208	2 774	423	995	1 356	23 888	16 781	14 512	705	4 811	9 485
1969	202 736	5 019	3 948	3 432	2 977	446	1 057	1 475	24 392	17 181	14 905	724	4 895	9 808
1970	205 089	5 233	4 218	3 715	3 153	439	1 116	1 599	24 157	17 768	15 081	697	4 947	10 077
1971	207 692	5 609	4 491	4 002	3 370	493	1 154	1 723	24 640	18 357	15 460	757	4 976	10 296
1972	209 924	6 093	4 880	4 291	3 659	555	1 226	1 878	25 660	19 036	16 233	842	5 123	10 770
1973	211 939	6 725	5 383	4 758	4 009	616	1 350	2 043	26 851	20 028	16 874	921	5 220	11 172
1974	213 898	7 224	5 852	5 146	4 349	609	1 502	2 238	26 462	19 621	16 580	854	5 046	11 282
1975	215 981	7 801	6 340	5 657	4 771	658	1 617	2 497	26 153	19 908	16 792	848	5 040	11 594
1976	218 086	8 590	6 890	6 098	5 262	773	1 732	2 757	27 296	20 346	17 557	945	5 229	11 975
1977	220 289	9 450	7 532	6 634	5 783	871	1 854	3 058	28 272	20 780	18 116	1 019	5 295	12 345
1978	222 629	10 563	8 371	7 340	6 388	958	2 022	3 408	29 524	21 497	18 710	1 061	5 428	12 776
1979	225 106	11 672	9 252	8 057	7 043	1 005	2 273	3 765	30 123	21 672	18 944	1 044	5 507	13 022
1980	227 726	12 547	10 204	8 888	7 688	994	2 518	4 176	29 700	21 584	18 668	950	5 434	13 082
1981	230 008	13 943	11 326	9 823	8 408	1 061	2 719	4 628	30 152	21 891	18 739	950	5 448	13 154
1982	232 218	14 399	12 021	10 494	8 919	1 090	2 783	5 047	29 326	22 156	18 832	939	5 452	13 299
1983	234 333	15 508	12 721	11 216	9 737	1 259	2 897	5 581	30 394	22 714	19 718	1 064	5 579	13 855
1984	236 394	17 080	13 929	12 330	10 543	1 447	3 052	6 043	32 309	24 062	20 575	1 205	5 759	14 261
1985	238 506	18 192	14 779	13 027	11 374	1 595	3 175	6 605	33 358	24 565	21 449	1 314	5 880	14 858
1986	240 683	19 028	15 510	13 691	11 992	1 751	3 217	7 024	34 201	25 268	22 132	1 427	6 035	15 179
1987	242 843	19 993	16 313	14 297	12 668	1 820	3 353	7 494	35 070	25 597	22 680	1 442	6 084	15 725
1988	245 061	21 368	17 479	15 414	13 589	1 939	3 519	8 131	36 204	26 559	23 413	1 511	6 187	16 283
1989	247 387	22 805	18 698	16 403	14 458	1 998	3 757	8 703	37 181	27 080	23 869	1 530	6 294	16 642
1990	250 181	23 835	19 641	17 264	15 225	1 987	3 974	9 264	37 459	27 303	24 078	1 506	6 297	16 939
1991	253 530	24 290	20 056	17 734	15 554	1 882	4 024	9 648	36 924	27 138	23 803	1 406	6 195	16 977
1992	256 922	25 379	21 099	18 714	16 338	1 978	4 107	10 253	37 720	27 895	24 353	1 467	6 232	17 423
1993	260 282	26 350	21 738	19 245	17 104	2 119	4 191	10 795	38 258	27 990	24 876	1 557	6 308	17 729
1994	263 455	27 660	22 574	19 943	17 919	2 305	4 325	11 290	39 320	28 411	25 529	1 661	6 475	18 052
1995	266 588	28 658	23 600	20 792	18 615	2 385	4 426	11 805	39 900	29 011	25 973	1 706	6 558	18 363
1996	269 714	29 932	24 762	21 658	19 445	2 507	4 603	12 335	40 926	29 586	26 563	1 812	6 669	18 675
1997	272 958	31 424	25 984	22 570	20 284	2 621	4 730	12 933	42 238	30 304	27 236	1 937	6 782	19 044
1998	276 154	32 818	27 545	23 806	21 283	2 822	4 813	13 647	43 620	31 712	28 350	2 145	6 953	19 679
1999	279 328	34 480	28 665	24 684	22 496	3 063	5 125	14 308	45 192	32 409	29 536	2 393	7 224	20 229
2000	282 398	36 300	30 651	26 274	23 963	3 232	5 455	15 276	46 523	33 645	30 687	2 570	7 373	21 001
2001	285 225	37 100	31 599	27 255	24 801	3 301	5 554	15 946	46 502	34 216	31 135	2 678	7 427	21 243
2002	287 955	37 954	31 814	28 160	25 521	3 422	5 603	16 496	46 842	34 894	31 624	2 848	7 493	21 422
2003	290 626	39 420	32 683	29 230	26 635	3 502	5 866	17 267	47 709	35 474	32 325	3 026	7 685	21 699
2004	293 262	41 660	34 250	30 674	28 070	3 685	6 211	18 175	49 102	36 325	33 242	3 247	7 865	22 159
2005	295 993	44 052	35 828	31 732	29 626	3 813	6 603	19 210	50 343	36 526	34 101	3 395	8 052	22 661
2006	298 818	46 234	38 099	33 558	31 046	3 876	6 965	20 205	51 255	37 570	34 758	3 512	8 238	23 001
2007	301 696	47 976	39 846	34 899	32 306	3 938	7 222	21 146	51 787	38 093	35 263	3 645	8 298	23 292
2008	304 543	48 498	40 971	36 021	33 001	3 608	7 436	21 957	51 365	38 188	34 986	3 403	8 091	23 494
2009	307 240	47 123	39 319	35 568	32 194	3 294	7 056	21 843	49 591	37 814	34 226	3 167	7 887	23 193
2010	309 774	48 580	40 657	36 662	33 122	3 386	7 324	22 411	50 517	38 290	34 593	3 316	7 945	23 341
2011	312 010	49 998	42 753	38 094	34 290	3 505	7 771	23 014	50 933	38 804	34 929	3 460	7 958	23 514
2012	314 212	51 729	44 602	39 797	35 159	3 642	7 936	23 582	51 729	39 797	35 159	3 642	7 936	23 582
2013	316 357	53 241	44 866	39 567	35 920	3 760	8 031	24 130	52 325	39 038	35 440	3 838	8 024	23 582
2014	318 631	55 082	47 003	41 402	37 183	3 898	8 225	25 060	53 140	40 240	36 140	4 085	8 176	23 894
2015	320 918	56 731	48 876	42 831	38 214	4 075	8 150	25 989	54 189	41 537	37 059	4 364	8 394	24 336
2016	323 186	57 846	49 807	43 748	39 275	4 162	8 189	26 924	54 706	42 005	37 711	4 567	8 542	24 656
2017	325 220	59 897	51 812	45 511	40 708	4 294	8 492	27 921	55 590	42 914	38 385	4 822	8 715	24 937
2018	326 949	62 784	54 155	47 805	42 556	4 494	8 823	29 239	56 910	44 133	39 288	5 133	8 881	25 403
2019	328 527	65 056	56 082	49 370	43 919	4 606	9 027	30 286	57 933	44 913	39 955	5 326	9 095	25 702
2020	330 152	63 285	59 450	52 800	42 549	4 896	9 200	28 453	55 685	47 471	38 255	5 707	9 330	23 651
2018														
1st quarter	326 325	61 729	53 340	46 977	41 883	4 441	8 731	28 711	56 497	43 678	38 942	5 050	8 811	25 201
2nd quarter	326 703	62 725	53 867	47 593	42 438	4 503	8 825	29 110	56 902	43 994	39 230	5 131	8 862	25 367
3rd quarter	327 167	63 145	54 471	48 079	42 800	4 518	8 849	29 433	57 095	44 295	39 431	5 172	8 902	25 491
4th quarter	327 602	63 532	54 940	48 567	43 099	4 511	8 886	29 702	57 146	44 564	39 546	5 179	8 948	25 555
2019														
1st quarter	327 923	64 044	55 619	49 004	43 167	4 493	8 873	29 802	57 432	44 918	39 568	5 164	8 992	25 548
2nd quarter	328 270	64 853	55 885	49 114	43 792	4 598	9 048	30 147	57 826	44 717	39 872	5 293	9 094	25 650
3rd quarter	328 730	65 419	56 170	49 462	44 199	4 659	9 069	30 471	58 141	44 910	40 131	5 394	9 151	25 769
4th quarter	329 186	65 903	56 650	49 897	44 516	4 676	9 118	30 722	58 333	45 113	40 248	5 452	9 144	25 839
2020														
1st quarter	329 529	65 188	57 179	50 377	43 817	4 506	9 244	30 068	57 512	45 406	39 494	5 275	9 291	25 140
2nd quarter	329 898	59 041	61 682	55 319	39 375	4 451	8 735	26 189	52 314	50 067	35 637	5 249	8 940	21 878
3rd quarter	330 368	63 985	59 865	53 261	43 266	5 307	9 426	28 534	56 182	47 772	38 808	6 146	9 565	23 656
4th quarter	330 815	64 923	59 072	52 241	43 733	5 318	9 395	29 020	56 732	46 682	39 079	6 156	9 525	23 932

Table 1-3B. U.S. Population and Per Capita Product and Income: Historical Data

(Dollars, except as noted; quarterly data are at seasonally adjusted annual rates.) NIPA Table 7.1

Year and quarter	Population (mid-period, thousands)	Current dollars							Chained (2012) dollars					
		Gross domestic product	Personal income	Disposable personal income	Personal consumption expenditures				Gross domestic product	Disposable personal income	Personal consumption expenditures			
					Total	Durable goods	Nondurable goods	Services			Total	Durable goods	Nondurable goods	Services
1929	121 878	858	700	686	635	81	278	276	9 109	7 375	6 830	251	2 769	4 074
1930	123 188	748	621	609	569	62	248	260	8 246	6 836	6 395	206	2 597	3 947
1931	124 149	623	529	521	489	48	208	233	7 658	6 552	6 148	177	2 549	3 817
1932	124 949	476	403	397	390	32	161	197	6 627	5 659	5 562	133	2 310	3 563
1933	125 690	455	376	369	366	30	159	177	6 507	5 463	5 407	129	2 288	3 411
1934	126 485	528	428	421	407	36	189	182	7 165	5 950	5 757	147	2 459	3 556
1935	127 362	583	478	469	439	43	205	191	7 749	6 481	6 064	177	2 582	3 655
1936	128 181	662	540	530	485	53	228	205	8 691	7 251	6 638	214	2 858	3 855
1937	128 961	721	579	564	518	57	240	221	9 081	7 451	6 842	224	2 911	4 011
1938	129 969	672	532	517	495	47	230	217	8 712	6 988	6 681	184	2 930	3 948
1939	131 028	713	562	551	513	55	235	224	9 335	7 511	6 997	217	3 039	4 069
1940	132 122	779	601	588	540	63	245	232	10 074	7 957	7 299	246	3 143	4 190
1941	133 402	969	734	716	608	77	279	252	11 745	9 123	7 740	281	3 299	4 397
1942	134 860	1 231	940	903	660	57	322	282	13 813	10 232	7 474	176	3 272	4 589
1943	136 739	1 485	1 142	1 020	731	55	357	319	15 942	10 576	7 577	156	3 248	4 887
1944	138 397	1 622	1 226	1 099	785	56	381	348	17 004	10 775	7 699	142	3 276	5 098
1945	139 928	1 629	1 256	1 117	857	65	418	374	16 653	10 537	8 086	156	3 441	5 312
1946	141 389	1 609	1 291	1 169	1 020	121	489	410	14 568	10 309	8 992	279	3 713	5 487
1947	144 126	1 732	1 349	1 212	1 123	151	538	433	14 128	9 702	8 989	322	3 621	5 404
1948	146 631	1 872	1 456	1 325	1 193	167	566	460	14 458	10 039	9 036	337	3 586	5 453
1949	149 188	1 826	1 415	1 303	1 195	178	546	471	14 130	9 947	9 128	358	3 577	5 488
1947														
1st quarter	143 143	1 699	1 325	1 191	1 091	145	523	423	14 213	9 746	8 924	311	3 603	5 395
2nd quarter	143 790	1 711	1 319	1 184	1 113	148	535	430	14 111	9 608	9 032	317	3 648	5 449
3rd quarter	144 449	1 728	1 369	1 233	1 132	151	544	437	14 018	9 820	9 020	319	3 648	5 413
4th quarter	145 122	1 790	1 383	1 240	1 155	162	551	443	14 171	9 637	8 981	339	3 584	5 360
1948														
1st quarter	145 709	1 824	1 417	1 272	1 169	162	560	448	14 326	9 777	8 989	336	3 581	5 395
2nd quarter	146 289	1 863	1 449	1 319	1 190	164	569	458	14 505	10 040	9 058	337	3 602	5 458
3rd quarter	146 921	1 900	1 480	1 356	1 205	172	568	465	14 525	10 160	9 032	341	3 565	5 464
4th quarter	147 607	1 899	1 478	1 353	1 205	169	567	469	14 474	10 170	9 062	334	3 595	5 493
1949														
1st quarter	148 254	1 855	1 430	1 310	1 193	165	558	470	14 212	9 926	9 037	327	3 593	5 503
2nd quarter	148 847	1 823	1 417	1 303	1 199	177	550	471	14 107	9 935	9 139	354	3 588	5 509
3rd quarter	149 485	1 826	1 408	1 299	1 189	183	537	470	14 192	9 957	9 121	369	3 542	5 474
4th quarter	150 167	1 802	1 404	1 299	1 200	189	539	472	14 009	9 968	9 212	382	3 583	5 465
1950														
1st quarter	150 786	1 862	1 501	1 391	1 213	195	540	478	14 500	10 693	9 327	395	3 614	5 511
2nd quarter	151 319	1 919	1 505	1 388	1 235	197	547	490	14 889	10 624	9 448	397	3 644	5 630
3rd quarter	151 973	2 028	1 553	1 429	1 319	246	570	503	15 398	10 711	9 890	489	3 691	5 693
4th quarter	152 658	2 096	1 604	1 457	1 297	218	568	511	15 623	10 728	9 549	426	3 592	5 704
1951														
1st quarter	153 291	2 192	1 658	1 499	1 365	232	600	532	15 769	10 694	9 739	438	3 643	5 836
2nd quarter	153 902	2 236	1 710	1 538	1 332	200	594	538	15 979	10 889	9 426	374	3 576	5 852
3rd quarter	154 610	2 273	1 730	1 551	1 343	195	603	545	16 234	10 962	9 493	365	3 634	5 898
4th quarter	155 344	2 293	1 752	1 561	1 362	196	614	552	16 192	10 891	9 503	362	3 659	5 885
1952														
1st quarter	155 976	2 307	1 758	1 561	1 365	197	608	561	16 299	10 842	9 486	363	3 614	5 935
2nd quarter	156 587	2 306	1 777	1 574	1 386	198	617	571	16 271	10 937	9 634	369	3 684	6 003
3rd quarter	157 267	2 338	1 814	1 609	1 396	187	626	583	16 317	11 109	9 639	345	3 733	6 056
4th quarter	157 986	2 410	1 848	1 639	1 441	213	635	593	16 776	11 296	9 933	403	3 770	6 113
1953														
1st quarter	158 574	2 447	1 869	1 658	1 458	222	634	602	17 025	11 387	10 013	415	3 779	6 150
2nd quarter	159 160	2 461	1 886	1 676	1 464	220	632	612	17 093	11 494	10 036	411	3 783	6 201
3rd quarter	159 889	2 447	1 877	1 670	1 461	216	624	621	16 920	11 386	9 966	407	3 731	6 209
4th quarter	160 639	2 403	1 868	1 663	1 451	210	622	619	16 586	11 295	9 853	393	3 719	6 133
1954														
1st quarter	161 328	2 389	1 860	1 673	1 458	204	628	626	16 436	11 304	9 847	379	3 739	6 165
2nd quarter	161 983	2 384	1 851	1 666	1 469	208	626	635	16 387	11 269	9 935	396	3 714	6 245
3rd quarter	162 731	2 403	1 854	1 670	1 477	204	628	644	16 496	11 336	10 023	396	3 744	6 324
4th quarter	163 524	2 445	1 878	1 692	1 499	214	633	652	16 737	11 498	10 184	418	3 788	6 369
1955														
1st quarter	164 204	2 516	1 909	1 718	1 531	234	636	661	17 144	11 636	10 369	454	3 812	6 417
2nd quarter	164 864	2 557	1 947	1 751	1 556	247	644	665	17 353	11 846	10 525	477	3 866	6 438
3rd quarter	165 612	2 598	1 983	1 782	1 574	256	646	672	17 508	12 010	10 607	490	3 875	6 474
4th quarter	166 419	2 626	2 004	1 799	1 590	249	655	686	17 528	12 091	10 688	475	3 934	6 571
1956														
1st quarter	167 109	2 632	2 029	1 817	1 593	237	661	694	17 388	12 162	10 662	451	3 962	6 607
2nd quarter	167 788	2 658	2 055	1 839	1 602	237	663	702	17 461	12 228	10 654	450	3 936	6 644
3rd quarter	168 573	2 677	2 077	1 858	1 614	235	667	712	17 364	12 234	10 628	440	3 921	6 682
4th quarter	169 416	2 718	2 112	1 888	1 638	245	671	722	17 562	12 361	10 721	452	3 932	6 736
1957														
1st quarter	170 172	2 761	2 129	1 903	1 656	250	678	728	17 595	12 345	10 748	458	3 939	6 733
2nd quarter	170 869	2 762	2 148	1 920	1 663	247	682	735	17 485	12 382	10 723	446	3 937	6 763
3rd quarter	171 638	2 794	2 165	1 937	1 682	244	695	743	17 578	12 388	10 759	441	3 974	6 781
4th quarter	172 417	2 754	2 150	1 925	1 684	241	690	753	17 317	12 250	10 715	433	3 930	6 824

Table 1-3B. U.S. Population and Per Capita Product and Income: Historical Data—*Continued*

(Dollars, except as noted; quarterly data are at seasonally adjusted annual rates.)   NIPA Table 7.1

Year and quarter	Population (mid-period, thousands)	Current dollars							Chained (2012) dollars					
		Gross domestic product	Personal income	Disposable personal income	Personal consumption expenditures				Gross domestic product	Disposable personal income	Personal consumption expenditures			
					Total	Durable goods	Nondurable goods	Services			Total	Durable goods	Nondurable goods	Services
1958														
1st quarter	173 064	2 702	2 145	1 925	1 675	228	693	755	16 805	12 096	10 527	403	3 880	6 789
2nd quarter	173 729	2 717	2 151	1 934	1 685	222	698	766	16 850	12 134	10 573	395	3 901	6 862
3rd quarter	174 483	2 784	2 193	1 970	1 707	226	705	776	17 166	12 347	10 702	402	3 955	6 927
4th quarter	175 288	2 850	2 215	1 990	1 722	232	708	782	17 486	12 479	10 798	415	3 991	6 942
1959														
1st quarter	176 045	2 899	2 238	2 006	1 758	248	716	794	17 745	12 497	10 949	435	4 025	6 998
2nd quarter	176 727	2 957	2 277	2 039	1 785	257	719	809	18 075	12 650	11 075	450	4 043	7 075
3rd quarter	177 481	2 958	2 280	2 040	1 807	261	722	824	18 011	12 579	11 143	457	4 041	7 140
4th quarter	178 268	2 965	2 302	2 057	1 811	247	726	837	17 983	12 613	11 106	433	4 048	7 195
1960														
1st quarter	179 319	3 026	2 324	2 071	1 820	253	723	844	18 279	12 683	11 147	444	4 035	7 217
2nd quarter	180 401	2 999	2 338	2 083	1 842	257	731	853	18 072	12 689	11 220	452	4 054	7 253
3rd quarter	181 301	3 009	2 341	2 084	1 832	253	726	853	18 070	12 650	11 119	446	4 010	7 209
4th quarter	182 019	2 968	2 339	2 084	1 835	246	727	862	17 768	12 595	11 090	433	3 997	7 250
1961														
1st quarter	182 634	2 984	2 355	2 101	1 832	231	730	870	17 828	12 671	11 048	408	4 008	7 296
2nd quarter	183 337	3 030	2 380	2 124	1 852	236	732	883	18 061	12 814	11 170	415	4 046	7 374
3rd quarter	184 103	3 083	2 409	2 151	1 859	242	731	886	18 331	12 931	11 177	423	4 032	7 366
4th quarter	184 894	3 140	2 446	2 186	1 891	252	736	902	18 610	13 126	11 353	442	4 069	7 465
1962														
1st quarter	185 553	3 201	2 475	2 209	1 912	257	743	912	18 875	13 209	11 433	449	4 088	7 508
2nd quarter	186 203	3 224	2 507	2 233	1 936	263	745	927	18 979	13 305	11 533	460	4 090	7 594
3rd quarter	186 926	3 258	2 522	2 242	1 949	265	749	935	19 138	13 324	11 581	461	4 106	7 629
4th quarter	187 680	3 262	2 546	2 260	1 975	275	754	946	19 124	13 389	11 698	480	4 113	7 694
1963														
1st quarter	188 299	3 302	2 566	2 279	1 988	279	757	952	19 269	13 461	11 741	488	4 122	7 703
2nd quarter	188 906	3 334	2 584	2 296	2 003	285	756	962	19 422	13 541	11 814	497	4 122	7 760
3rd quarter	189 631	3 398	2 611	2 323	2 032	288	766	978	19 774	13 637	11 928	501	4 144	7 865
4th quarter	190 362	3 435	2 651	2 361	2 049	293	763	993	19 827	13 806	11 981	507	4 123	7 942
1964														
1st quarter	190 954	3 508	2 693	2 411	2 093	304	778	1 010	20 182	14 032	12 179	525	4 181	8 043
2nd quarter	191 560	3 543	2 733	2 474	2 127	310	791	1 026	20 337	14 365	12 355	537	4 247	8 130
3rd quarter	192 256	3 600	2 773	2 505	2 166	319	806	1 041	20 580	14 499	12 537	553	4 314	8 208
4th quarter	192 938	3 614	2 809	2 533	2 172	308	808	1 056	20 571	14 613	12 529	534	4 307	8 293
1965														
1st quarter	193 467	3 710	2 858	2 564	2 221	336	815	1 070	21 011	14 744	12 773	582	4 336	8 365
2nd quarter	193 994	3 764	2 900	2 599	2 251	334	829	1 088	21 219	14 870	12 879	581	4 366	8 468
3rd quarter	194 647	3 850	2 964	2 671	2 290	343	843	1 105	21 618	15 225	13 056	599	4 417	8 555
4th quarter	195 279	3 953	3 022	2 724	2 354	354	873	1 127	22 044	15 482	13 380	622	4 566	8 672
1966														
1st quarter	195 763	4 065	3 080	2 765	2 402	369	889	1 143	22 525	15 596	13 544	650	4 587	8 740
2nd quarter	196 277	4 101	3 122	2 788	2 421	355	903	1 163	22 543	15 597	13 543	623	4 619	8 812
3rd quarter	196 877	4 163	3 180	2 835	2 460	367	913	1 179	22 664	15 739	13 656	641	4 638	8 857
4th quarter	197 481	4 220	3 239	2 882	2 482	368	913	1 200	22 780	15 875	13 671	639	4 611	8 927
1967														
1st quarter	197 967	4 264	3 286	2 926	2 497	359	921	1 217	22 926	16 075	13 716	625	4 651	8 986
2nd quarter	198 455	4 278	3 314	2 956	2 537	375	927	1 234	22 883	16 162	13 869	651	4 674	9 051
3rd quarter	199 012	4 348	3 375	3 004	2 566	375	933	1 257	23 035	16 270	13 901	644	4 657	9 149
4th quarter	199 572	4 417	3 423	3 043	2 597	379	941	1 276	23 144	16 343	13 947	643	4 665	9 200
1968														
1st quarter	199 995	4 547	3 513	3 120	2 682	404	968	1 310	23 566	16 580	14 251	682	4 746	9 326
2nd quarter	200 452	4 661	3 604	3 196	2 744	414	987	1 343	23 905	16 815	14 435	695	4 794	9 449
3rd quarter	200 997	4 731	3 688	3 231	2 817	436	1 009	1 372	24 025	16 823	14 666	724	4 857	9 543
4th quarter	201 538	4 803	3 759	3 283	2 853	436	1 017	1 400	24 054	16 908	14 692	718	4 845	9 622
1969														
1st quarter	201 955	4 919	3 824	3 316	2 907	446	1 034	1 427	24 380	16 915	14 825	730	4 889	9 686
2nd quarter	202 419	4 985	3 906	3 384	2 956	447	1 048	1 461	24 399	17 041	14 886	726	4 888	9 784
3rd quarter	202 986	5 074	3 998	3 485	2 998	446	1 064	1 488	24 491	17 340	14 917	722	4 893	9 835
4th quarter	203 584	5 099	4 061	3 542	3 048	446	1 079	1 523	24 300	17 421	14 992	717	4 911	9 928
1970														
1st quarter	204 086	5 151	4 124	3 612	3 095	439	1 100	1 556	24 204	17 561	15 048	705	4 941	10 010
2nd quarter	204 721	5 214	4 201	3 686	3 134	445	1 107	1 583	24 163	17 722	15 069	711	4 923	10 041
3rd quarter	205 419	5 287	4 258	3 768	3 181	448	1 118	1 615	24 303	17 944	15 150	711	4 941	10 120
4th quarter	206 130	5 281	4 287	3 795	3 203	424	1 138	1 641	23 960	17 839	15 056	661	4 982	10 137
1971														
1st quarter	206 763	5 490	4 371	3 895	3 285	474	1 141	1 670	24 535	18 140	15 298	730	4 987	10 176
2nd quarter	207 362	5 576	4 471	3 985	3 343	487	1 152	1 704	24 597	18 351	15 394	744	4 984	10 249
3rd quarter	208 000	5 662	4 525	4 033	3 392	497	1 156	1 739	24 723	18 390	15 470	762	4 958	10 314
4th quarter	208 642	5 705	4 598	4 092	3 459	514	1 168	1 777	24 705	18 547	15 678	792	4 977	10 443
1972														
1st quarter	209 142	5 884	4 717	4 144	3 533	529	1 181	1 823	25 099	18 588	15 847	808	4 981	10 594
2nd quarter	209 637	6 041	4 790	4 202	3 613	544	1 213	1 856	25 608	18 736	16 110	827	5 104	10 696
3rd quarter	210 181	6 140	4 901	4 310	3 691	559	1 237	1 894	25 783	19 051	16 316	846	5 161	10 813
4th quarter	210 737	6 306	5 111	4 507	3 799	586	1 272	1 941	26 146	19 763	16 655	888	5 244	10 977

Table 1-3B. U.S. Population and Per Capita Product and Income: Historical Data—*Continued*

(Dollars, except as noted; quarterly data are at seasonally adjusted annual rates.)   **NIPA Table 7.1**

Year and quarter	Population (mid-period, thou-sands)	Current dollars							Chained (2012) dollars					
		Gross domestic product	Personal income	Dispos-able personal income	Personal consumption expenditures				Gross domestic product	Dispos-able personal income	Personal consumption expenditures			
					Total	Durable goods	Nondur-able goods	Services			Total	Durable goods	Nondur-able goods	Services
1973														
1st quarter	211 192	6 522	5 185	4 587	3 906	624	1 304	1 978	26 735	19 870	16 923	943	5 264	11 094
2nd quarter	211 663	6 680	5 314	4 704	3 971	620	1 329	2 021	26 966	19 993	16 877	929	5 208	11 163
3rd quarter	212 191	6 757	5 432	4 800	4 048	616	1 366	2 065	26 758	20 033	16 895	919	5 220	11 209
4th quarter	212 708	6 940	5 598	4 940	4 108	603	1 399	2 106	26 946	20 203	16 803	895	5 186	11 223
1974														
1st quarter	213 144	6 996	5 662	4 992	4 184	594	1 449	2 141	26 660	19 827	16 619	872	5 106	11 179
2nd quarter	213 602	7 163	5 772	5 075	4 309	611	1 489	2 209	26 666	19 600	16 643	875	5 062	11 267
3rd quarter	214 147	7 285	5 926	5 203	4 433	637	1 530	2 266	26 347	19 568	16 672	878	5 060	11 298
4th quarter	214 700	7 451	6 048	5 314	4 467	592	1 541	2 334	26 177	19 492	16 386	792	4 957	11 384
1975														
1st quarter	215 135	7 512	6 128	5 394	4 579	613	1 563	2 404	25 806	19 423	16 490	808	4 956	11 467
2nd quarter	215 652	7 660	6 260	5 698	4 700	634	1 599	2 467	25 928	20 273	16 721	821	5 054	11 577
3rd quarter	216 289	7 905	6 410	5 704	4 842	679	1 646	2 517	26 294	19 919	16 909	870	5 088	11 597
4th quarter	216 848	8 125	6 561	5 830	4 963	707	1 659	2 597	26 579	20 023	17 046	893	5 063	11 734
1976														
1st quarter	217 314	8 377	6 701	5 953	5 107	751	1 691	2 665	27 119	20 222	17 350	936	5 154	11 845
2nd quarter	217 776	8 506	6 802	6 024	5 187	762	1 713	2 712	27 260	20 293	17 472	938	5 222	11 898
3rd quarter	218 338	8 641	6 954	6 148	5 307	778	1 743	2 786	27 339	20 399	17 611	946	5 249	12 011
4th quarter	218 917	8 836	7 102	6 268	5 447	801	1 780	2 866	27 464	20 474	17 792	959	5 290	12 144
1977														
1st quarter	219 427	9 063	7 241	6 380	5 597	838	1 807	2 952	27 724	20 472	17 960	993	5 274	12 264
2nd quarter	219 956	9 347	7 424	6 535	5 710	860	1 835	3 014	28 195	20 615	18 014	1 014	5 261	12 280
3rd quarter	220 573	9 604	7 606	6 706	5 834	879	1 858	3 096	28 623	20 843	18 134	1 026	5 272	12 376
4th quarter	221 201	9 784	7 854	6 912	5 989	907	1 915	3 167	28 543	21 181	18 354	1 044	5 370	12 458
1978														
1st quarter	221 719	9 935	8 020	7 063	6 107	894	1 944	3 269	28 567	21 297	18 414	1 014	5 381	12 623
2nd quarter	222 281	10 490	8 270	7 266	6 350	973	2 001	3 376	29 596	21 468	18 760	1 087	5 408	12 780
3rd quarter	222 933	10 743	8 490	7 430	6 469	972	2 044	3 453	29 806	21 572	18 784	1 069	5 434	12 835
4th quarter	223 583	11 078	8 704	7 598	6 626	994	2 099	3 532	30 119	21 651	18 880	1 075	5 488	12 865
1979														
1st quarter	224 152	11 272	8 947	7 815	6 768	996	2 162	3 610	30 096	21 857	18 930	1 059	5 499	12 966
2nd quarter	224 737	11 530	9 101	7 936	6 931	988	2 225	3 718	30 050	21 603	18 868	1 033	5 474	13 012
3rd quarter	225 418	11 834	9 364	8 145	7 151	1 024	2 317	3 809	30 182	21 636	18 994	1 058	5 521	13 021
4th quarter	226 117	12 046	9 593	8 331	7 319	1 013	2 385	3 921	30 164	21 607	18 983	1 028	5 533	13 089
1980														
1st quarter	226 754	12 303	9 843	8 587	7 507	1 023	2 469	4 014	30 174	21 621	18 902	1 009	5 515	13 075
2nd quarter	227 389	12 302	9 980	8 696	7 497	932	2 489	4 076	29 470	21 371	18 425	897	5 425	12 956
3rd quarter	228 070	12 525	10 297	8 972	7 733	988	2 528	4 218	29 347	21 546	18 572	934	5 396	13 066
4th quarter	228 689	13 055	10 690	9 296	8 010	1 033	2 585	4 392	29 813	21 784	18 772	960	5 402	13 230
1981														
1st quarter	229 155	13 634	10 948	9 504	8 229	1 074	2 680	4 476	30 335	21 709	18 796	986	5 439	13 128
2nd quarter	229 674	13 770	11 145	9 653	8 349	1 049	2 712	4 588	30 042	21 685	18 755	945	5 450	13 187
3rd quarter	230 301	14 158	11 546	9 997	8 502	1 094	2 732	4 677	30 319	22 093	18 791	971	5 448	13 153
4th quarter	230 903	14 209	11 661	10 134	8 551	1 026	2 753	4 772	29 911	22 059	18 613	899	5 454	13 147
1982														
1st quarter	231 395	14 150	11 789	10 265	8 704	1 065	2 765	4 874	29 384	22 066	18 711	926	5 453	13 188
2nd quarter	231 906	14 368	11 954	10 403	8 795	1 075	2 754	4 966	29 453	22 150	18 726	927	5 431	13 232
3rd quarter	232 498	14 479	12 097	10 591	8 971	1 084	2 795	5 092	29 265	22 199	18 804	932	5 441	13 301
4th quarter	233 074	14 599	12 244	10 714	9 205	1 134	2 818	5 254	29 205	22 214	19 086	972	5 483	13 473
1983														
1st quarter	233 546	14 872	12 385	10 882	9 354	1 151	2 813	5 389	29 530	22 378	19 236	980	5 490	13 625
2nd quarter	234 028	15 292	12 571	11 035	9 612	1 237	2 876	5 499	30 140	22 487	19 587	1 050	5 543	13 782
3rd quarter	234 603	15 725	12 793	11 320	9 889	1 289	2 934	5 665	30 667	22 769	19 889	1 087	5 613	13 951
4th quarter	235 153	16 137	13 134	11 622	10 089	1 358	2 962	5 769	31 233	23 221	20 159	1 138	5 668	14 062
1984														
1st quarter	235 605	16 587	13 493	11 960	10 264	1 407	2 998	5 858	31 783	23 640	20 287	1 179	5 672	14 097
2nd quarter	236 082	16 984	13 821	12 252	10 487	1 446	3 060	5 982	32 267	23 984	20 530	1 204	5 784	14 180
3rd quarter	236 657	17 258	14 102	12 479	10 621	1 445	3 062	6 114	32 498	24 241	20 632	1 201	5 774	14 323
4th quarter	237 232	17 487	14 297	12 628	10 799	1 492	3 089	6 218	32 686	24 380	20 848	1 237	5 805	14 445
1985														
1st quarter	237 673	17 798	14 538	12 720	11 091	1 548	3 124	6 419	32 941	24 271	21 163	1 278	5 829	14 680
2nd quarter	238 176	18 032	14 676	13 045	11 260	1 567	3 161	6 532	33 161	24 692	21 313	1 290	5 862	14 783
3rd quarter	238 789	18 371	14 838	13 072	11 534	1 660	3 185	6 689	33 581	24 551	21 662	1 369	5 895	14 944
4th quarter	239 387	18 564	15 062	13 270	11 610	1 603	3 231	6 777	33 746	24 749	21 654	1 319	5 933	15 026
1986														
1st quarter	239 861	18 794	15 291	13 513	11 772	1 633	3 249	6 891	33 994	25 025	21 800	1 343	5 997	15 058
2nd quarter	240 368	18 910	15 430	13 643	11 863	1 694	3 193	6 976	34 075	25 291	21 991	1 388	6 037	15 117
3rd quarter	240 962	19 122	15 592	13 768	12 106	1 850	3 200	7 057	34 316	25 390	22 325	1 502	6 035	15 206
4th quarter	241 539	19 283	15 728	13 839	12 225	1 826	3 225	7 173	34 418	25 368	22 408	1 475	6 069	15 336
1987														
1st quarter	242 009	19 512	15 933	14 071	12 328	1 729	3 295	7 304	34 607	25 552	22 387	1 385	6 065	15 555
2nd quarter	242 520	19 818	16 153	14 044	12 590	1 811	3 349	7 430	34 907	25 259	22 645	1 439	6 099	15 676
3rd quarter	243 120	20 091	16 406	14 394	12 822	1 894	3 376	7 552	35 123	25 648	22 847	1 494	6 089	15 776
4th quarter	243 721	20 548	16 758	14 678	12 928	1 846	3 392	7 690	35 638	25 930	22 839	1 450	6 081	15 892

Table 1-3B. U.S. Population and Per Capita Product and Income: Historical Data—*Continued*

(Dollars, except as noted; quarterly data are at seasonally adjusted annual rates.)   NIPA Table 7.1

| Year and quarter | Population (mid-period, thousands) | Current dollars | | | | | | | Chained (2012) dollars | | | | | |
| | | Gross domestic product | Personal income | Disposable personal income | Personal consumption expenditures | | | | Gross domestic product | Disposable personal income | Personal consumption expenditures | | | |
					Total	Durable goods	Nondurable goods	Services			Total	Durable goods	Nondurable goods	Services
1988														
1st quarter	244 208	20 775	17 037	14 981	13 234	1 926	3 433	7 875	35 751	26 258	23 196	1 516	6 135	16 077
2nd quarter	244 716	21 208	17 305	15 271	13 451	1 934	3 488	8 030	36 145	26 473	23 319	1 513	6 170	16 185
3rd quarter	245 354	21 531	17 633	15 568	13 702	1 917	3 549	8 236	36 262	26 659	23 465	1 490	6 197	16 386
4th quarter	245 966	21 952	17 937	15 834	13 963	1 977	3 603	8 384	36 654	26 844	23 672	1 525	6 246	16 482
1989														
1st quarter	246 460	22 362	18 410	16 166	14 161	1 974	3 662	8 526	36 953	27 095	23 734	1 515	6 262	16 561
2nd quarter	247 017	22 721	18 593	16 299	14 387	1 997	3 756	8 634	37 151	26 954	23 791	1 531	6 257	16 590
3rd quarter	247 698	22 993	18 767	16 459	14 572	2 041	3 780	8 750	37 323	27 059	23 956	1 562	6 302	16 653
4th quarter	248 374	23 139	19 018	16 684	14 710	1 980	3 830	8 900	37 295	27 213	23 994	1 510	6 356	16 764
1990														
1st quarter	248 936	23 591	19 358	17 018	15 016	2 070	3 913	9 032	37 617	27 361	24 142	1 570	6 334	16 813
2nd quarter	249 711	23 868	19 620	17 238	15 151	1 996	3 928	9 227	37 636	27 465	24 140	1 514	6 321	16 964
3rd quarter	250 595	24 003	19 787	17 390	15 350	1 970	4 003	9 378	37 529	27 359	24 150	1 493	6 309	17 040
4th quarter	251 482	23 877	19 797	17 408	15 380	1 912	4 051	9 417	37 056	27 030	23 882	1 447	6 224	16 939
1991														
1st quarter	252 258	23 925	19 791	17 489	15 356	1 870	4 020	9 465	36 769	27 014	23 719	1 403	6 207	16 874
2nd quarter	253 063	24 211	19 972	17 656	15 518	1 878	4 038	9 602	36 938	27 125	23 839	1 405	6 224	16 988
3rd quarter	253 965	24 436	20 109	17 785	15 645	1 907	4 034	9 704	36 993	27 139	23 873	1 422	6 212	17 001
4th quarter	254 835	24 583	20 351	18 001	15 697	1 874	4 005	9 818	36 995	27 271	23 780	1 394	6 138	17 044
1992														
1st quarter	255 585	24 896	20 728	18 424	16 043	1 941	4 060	10 042	37 328	27 739	24 154	1 444	6 211	17 272
2nd quarter	256 439	25 233	21 036	18 668	16 205	1 954	4 084	10 168	37 607	27 920	24 237	1 450	6 216	17 349
3rd quarter	257 386	25 513	21 199	18 805	16 423	1 990	4 122	10 311	37 839	27 947	24 407	1 475	6 230	17 468
4th quarter	258 277	25 867	21 430	18 957	16 677	2 025	4 161	10 490	38 102	27 977	24 612	1 499	6 271	17 601
1993														
1st quarter	259 039	25 979	21 467	19 085	16 791	2 038	4 166	10 587	38 053	27 999	24 634	1 509	6 259	17 616
2nd quarter	259 826	26 206	21 691	19 214	17 006	2 108	4 181	10 716	38 158	28 001	24 783	1 554	6 290	17 651
3rd quarter	260 714	26 397	21 777	19 249	17 211	2 135	4 191	10 886	38 210	27 930	24 973	1 566	6 330	17 795
4th quarter	261 547	26 816	22 014	19 432	17 407	2 194	4 226	10 987	38 606	28 034	25 112	1 598	6 354	17 853
1994														
1st quarter	262 250	27 133	22 147	19 578	17 621	2 245	4 259	11 117	38 876	28 144	25 331	1 632	6 422	17 952
2nd quarter	263 020	27 553	22 480	19 827	17 805	2 276	4 289	11 240	39 288	28 344	25 454	1 644	6 454	18 027
3rd quarter	263 870	27 783	22 657	20 021	18 012	2 309	4 357	11 346	39 390	28 417	25 565	1 656	6 488	18 089
4th quarter	264 678	28 167	23 007	20 342	18 236	2 387	4 394	11 455	39 720	28 737	25 763	1 709	6 537	18 141
1995														
1st quarter	265 388	28 344	23 291	20 561	18 322	2 341	4 397	11 584	39 754	28 905	25 758	1 670	6 543	18 217
2nd quarter	266 142	28 485	23 486	20 680	18 538	2 356	4 422	11 760	39 760	28 905	25 910	1 682	6 557	18 346
3rd quarter	267 000	28 776	23 705	20 888	18 722	2 407	4 433	11 882	39 969	29 076	26 061	1 724	6 559	18 421
4th quarter	267 820	29 022	23 913	21 038	18 877	2 435	4 449	11 992	40 117	29 157	26 162	1 748	6 572	18 466
1996														
1st quarter	268 487	29 307	24 288	21 302	19 109	2 458	4 511	12 141	40 317	29 359	26 338	1 763	6 599	18 603
2nd quarter	269 251	29 834	24 698	21 579	19 389	2 512	4 604	12 273	40 873	29 545	26 546	1 814	6 664	18 657
3rd quarter	270 128	30 102	24 899	21 776	19 526	2 515	4 614	12 396	41 106	29 687	26 620	1 821	6 690	18 697
4th quarter	270 991	30 480	25 158	21 971	19 753	2 545	4 680	12 527	41 401	29 750	26 746	1 850	6 723	18 742
1997														
1st quarter	271 709	30 778	25 540	22 220	19 996	2 597	4 715	12 685	41 558	29 954	26 957	1 895	6 745	18 858
2nd quarter	272 487	31 263	25 771	22 409	20 079	2 556	4 689	12 833	42 128	30 133	27 001	1 884	6 729	18 947
3rd quarter	273 391	31 687	26 099	22 657	20 407	2 644	4 745	13 018	42 514	30 387	27 370	1 961	6 814	19 110
4th quarter	274 246	31 964	26 520	22 991	20 652	2 688	4 769	13 195	42 745	30 739	27 611	2 005	6 840	19 259
1998														
1st quarter	274 950	32 248	27 040	23 417	20 809	2 683	4 752	13 373	43 062	31 305	27 819	2 016	6 872	19 431
2nd quarter	275 703	32 534	27 425	23 716	21 155	2 790	4 787	13 578	43 342	31 649	28 231	2 112	6 936	19 629
3rd quarter	276 564	32 980	27 726	23 954	21 430	2 839	4 826	13 765	43 748	31 868	28 510	2 165	6 965	19 801
4th quarter	277 400	33 504	27 984	24 134	21 731	2 975	4 885	13 871	44 321	32 024	28 835	2 286	7 039	19 852
1999														
1st quarter	278 103	33 842	28 260	24 384	21 942	2 948	4 980	14 013	44 627	32 292	29 058	2 286	7 151	19 982
2nd quarter	278 864	34 161	28 411	24 484	22 343	3 065	5 086	14 192	44 876	32 242	29 422	2 388	7 199	20 139
3rd quarter	279 751	34 626	28 734	24 728	22 646	3 114	5 148	14 384	45 326	32 385	29 658	2 438	7 209	20 294
4th quarter	280 592	35 283	29 248	25 136	23 048	3 123	5 284	14 641	45 932	32 720	30 002	2 460	7 334	20 500
2000														
1st quarter	281 304	35 556	30 015	25 718	23 527	3 274	5 305	14 949	45 983	33 208	30 379	2 590	7 252	20 759
2nd quarter	282 002	36 339	30 447	26 084	23 801	3 198	5 444	15 159	46 704	33 521	30 586	2 536	7 377	20 950
3rd quarter	282 769	36 490	30 933	26 521	24 119	3 224	5 508	15 387	46 624	33 863	30 796	2 572	7 406	21 083
4th quarter	283 518	36 808	31 206	26 766	24 403	3 230	5 564	15 608	46 777	33 983	30 983	2 583	7 457	21 211
2001														
1st quarter	284 169	36 845	31 704	27 122	24 617	3 261	5 533	15 822	46 519	34 182	31 024	2 620	7 396	21 253
2nd quarter	284 838	37 211	31 711	27 116	24 724	3 228	5 584	15 911	46 698	34 014	31 013	2 611	7 413	21 237
3rd quarter	285 584	37 110	31 548	27 649	24 758	3 235	5 572	15 950	46 390	34 665	31 040	2 634	7 428	21 213
4th quarter	286 311	37 234	31 434	27 132	25 103	3 478	5 525	16 100	46 400	34 003	31 461	2 847	7 472	21 271
2002														
1st quarter	286 935	37 582	31 511	27 764	25 155	3 402	5 526	16 226	46 683	34 725	31 462	2 809	7 487	21 319
2nd quarter	287 574	37 860	31 788	28 133	25 412	3 399	5 597	16 417	46 866	34 929	31 551	2 821	7 475	21 407
3rd quarter	288 303	38 099	31 870	28 249	25 658	3 475	5 608	16 575	46 936	34 892	31 691	2 898	7 469	21 439
4th quarter	289 007	38 274	32 084	28 491	25 857	3 412	5 681	16 764	46 883	35 028	31 790	2 865	7 540	21 524

Table 1-3B. U.S. Population and Per Capita Product and Income: Historical Data—*Continued*

(Dollars, except as noted; quarterly data are at seasonally adjusted annual rates.)   NIPA Table 7.1

Year and quarter	Population (mid-period, thousands)	Current dollars							Chained (2012) dollars					
		Gross domestic product	Personal income	Disposable personal income	Personal consumption expenditures				Gross domestic product	Disposable personal income	Personal consumption expenditures			
					Total	Durable goods	Nondurable goods	Services			Total	Durable goods	Nondurable goods	Services
2003														
1st quarter	289 609	38 584	32 159	28 633	26 129	3 365	5 811	16 953	47 027	34 935	31 880	2 861	7 585	21 577
2nd quarter	290 253	38 976	32 474	28 957	26 396	3 472	5 754	17 170	47 342	35 295	32 174	2 985	7 629	21 656
3rd quarter	290 974	39 752	32 852	29 584	26 878	3 580	5 927	17 372	48 012	35 825	32 548	3 109	7 750	21 745
4th quarter	291 669	40 362	33 242	29 741	27 132	3 590	5 972	17 570	48 450	35 838	32 694	3 146	7 776	21 818
2004														
1st quarter	292 237	40 801	33 508	30 045	27 542	3 642	6 088	17 813	48 633	35 927	32 934	3 195	7 821	21 956
2nd quarter	292 875	41 358	34 000	30 494	27 818	3 640	6 156	18 022	48 905	36 221	33 042	3 196	7 835	22 052
3rd quarter	293 603	41 911	34 412	30 787	28 213	3 696	6 220	18 297	49 243	36 390	33 347	3 271	7 872	22 229
4th quarter	294 334	42 561	35 073	31 365	28 704	3 761	6 379	18 564	49 623	36 759	33 641	3 324	7 932	22 399
2005														
1st quarter	294 957	43 285	35 073	31 099	28 993	3 763	6 414	18 816	50 068	36 237	33 783	3 333	7 990	22 478
2nd quarter	295 588	43 718	35 579	31 532	29 437	3 850	6 494	19 093	50 204	36 510	34 084	3 414	8 036	22 634
3rd quarter	296 340	44 350	36 060	31 925	29 925	3 887	6 702	19 337	50 470	36 570	34 280	3 472	8 045	22 748
4th quarter	297 086	44 850	36 595	32 368	30 144	3 752	6 799	19 593	50 629	36 784	34 257	3 360	8 137	22 782
2006														
1st quarter	297 736	45 675	37 554	33 119	30 564	3 876	6 861	19 827	51 200	37 442	34 555	3 486	8 203	22 860
2nd quarter	298 408	46 089	37 989	33 461	30 923	3 851	6 960	20 112	51 210	37 500	34 656	3 479	8 201	22 973
3rd quarter	299 180	46 361	38 223	33 682	31 265	3 879	7 062	20 323	51 155	37 478	34 788	3 520	8 227	23 032
4th quarter	299 946	46 807	38 626	33 967	31 430	3 899	6 977	20 554	51 455	37 858	35 030	3 561	8 320	23 137
2007														
1st quarter	300 609	47 289	39 334	34 455	31 842	3 922	7 083	20 838	51 492	38 054	35 169	3 601	8 330	23 218
2nd quarter	301 284	47 802	39 792	34 827	32 125	3 935	7 190	21 000	51 705	38 141	35 182	3 630	8 293	23 231
3rd quarter	302 062	48 216	39 956	34 994	32 438	3 946	7 244	21 248	51 882	38 109	35 325	3 665	8 298	23 330
4th quarter	302 829	48 592	40 298	35 316	32 814	3 948	7 372	21 494	52 066	38 072	35 375	3 683	8 270	23 387
2008														
1st quarter	303 494	48 457	40 644	35 586	32 964	3 801	7 423	21 740	51 740	38 053	35 249	3 556	8 188	23 489
2nd quarter	304 160	48 875	41 654	36 550	33 304	3 741	7 581	21 983	51 923	38 706	35 269	3 523	8 183	23 554
3rd quarter	304 902	48 865	41 025	36 114	33 319	3 594	7 649	22 076	51 523	37 840	34 912	3 396	8 044	23 475
4th quarter	305 616	47 799	40 563	35 836	32 416	3 298	7 091	22 027	50 281	38 158	34 517	3 139	7 948	23 459
2009														
1st quarter	306 237	47 123	39 372	35 445	32 050	3 280	6 908	21 862	49 594	37 999	34 359	3 138	7 929	23 319
2nd quarter	306 866	46 865	39 390	35 704	31 954	3 241	6 973	21 739	49 408	38 124	34 120	3 109	7 866	23 172
3rd quarter	307 573	46 977	39 123	35 432	32 316	3 365	7 131	21 819	49 473	37 576	34 271	3 252	7 873	23 156
4th quarter	308 285	47 525	39 392	35 692	32 454	3 290	7 211	21 953	49 886	37 562	34 154	3 168	7 880	23 125
2010														
1st quarter	308 901	47 797	39 887	36 029	32 702	3 306	7 268	22 129	50 036	37 771	34 283	3 201	7 906	23 194
2nd quarter	309 460	48 408	40 537	36 617	32 987	3 373	7 262	22 352	50 429	38 328	34 528	3 296	7 935	23 309
3rd quarter	310 062	48 834	40 902	36 850	33 222	3 394	7 298	22 530	50 720	38 498	34 707	3 341	7 949	23 425
4th quarter	310 675	49 278	41 298	37 148	33 573	3 471	7 469	22 633	50 883	38 562	34 851	3 428	7 992	23 435
2011														
1st quarter	311 176	49 334	42 342	37 758	33 930	3 496	7 652	22 782	50 678	38 868	34 928	3 452	8 006	23 473
2nd quarter	311 684	49 914	42 609	37 970	34 243	3 474	7 801	22 967	50 939	38 706	34 907	3 422	7 976	23 513
3rd quarter	312 293	50 106	42 953	38 241	34 439	3 493	7 804	23 143	50 820	38 803	34 945	3 446	7 933	23 569
4th quarter	312 887	50 633	43 105	38 404	34 547	3 555	7 826	23 165	51 292	38 839	34 939	3 522	7 916	23 502
2012														
1st quarter	313 385	51 275	43 991	39 306	34 971	3 632	7 947	23 392	51 630	39 490	35 135	3 602	7 962	23 571
2nd quarter	313 888	51 633	44 429	39 690	35 060	3 611	7 910	23 539	51 782	39 780	35 140	3 603	7 940	23 597
3rd quarter	314 488	51 892	44 271	39 469	35 166	3 630	7 918	23 618	51 774	39 444	35 144	3 643	7 928	23 573
4th quarter	315 085	52 114	45 710	40 721	35 437	3 693	7 968	23 777	51 732	40 468	35 217	3 718	7 914	23 586
2013														
1st quarter	315 539	52 700	44 430	39 201	35 703	3 767	8 059	23 877	52 106	38 818	35 354	3 808	8 007	23 541
2nd quarter	316 020	52 843	44 785	39 461	35 729	3 751	7 955	24 023	52 099	39 048	35 354	3 820	7 987	23 551
3rd quarter	316 626	53 410	44 987	39 697	35 939	3 755	8 027	24 157	52 411	39 123	35 419	3 845	8 024	23 555
4th quarter	317 244	54 006	45 259	39 906	36 308	3 765	8 082	24 460	52 681	39 164	35 633	3 878	8 078	23 681
2014														
1st quarter	317 760	53 954	46 026	40 535	36 563	3 788	8 138	24 637	52 411	39 591	35 711	3 933	8 084	23 701
2nd quarter	318 287	54 865	46 733	41 209	37 025	3 894	8 243	24 889	52 997	40 049	35 983	4 068	8 148	23 782
3rd quarter	318 921	55 635	47 346	41 706	37 421	3 937	8 285	25 199	53 507	40 418	36 265	4 134	8 200	23 949
4th quarter	319 557	55 867	47 901	42 154	37 720	3 973	8 236	25 511	53 641	40 899	36 597	4 204	8 273	24 142
2015														
1st quarter	320 058	56 213	48 422	42 471	37 755	4 011	8 074	25 670	53 992	41 378	36 784	4 273	8 334	24 205
2nd quarter	320 578	56 753	48 787	42 726	38 133	4 085	8 166	25 882	54 217	41 425	36 973	4 356	8 365	24 286
3rd quarter	321 205	56 995	49 056	42 993	38 442	4 105	8 225	26 112	54 286	41 584	37 182	4 406	8 433	24 382
4th quarter	321 831	56 962	49 238	43 133	38 522	4 097	8 134	26 291	54 260	41 760	37 296	4 422	8 442	24 470
2016														
1st quarter	322 354	57 159	49 382	43 412	38 762	4 122	8 083	26 557	54 491	42 009	37 509	4 473	8 500	24 579
2nd quarter	322 871	57 644	49 562	43 543	39 141	4 138	8 204	26 799	54 568	41 873	37 639	4 510	8 555	24 623
3rd quarter	323 473	58 043	49 932	43 836	39 444	4 188	8 204	27 052	54 794	41 997	37 789	4 614	8 559	24 676
4th quarter	324 048	58 535	50 348	44 198	39 752	4 201	8 266	27 285	54 969	42 145	37 905	4 670	8 552	24 746
2017														
1st quarter	324 496	59 027	51 008	44 829	40 205	4 224	8 397	27 584	55 152	42 513	38 128	4 696	8 621	24 876
2nd quarter	324 948	59 465	51 515	45 338	40 451	4 238	8 428	27 785	55 384	42 874	38 253	4 740	8 699	24 890
3rd quarter	325 475	60 093	52 024	45 706	40 765	4 294	8 486	27 985	55 692	43 061	38 407	4 843	8 724	24 932
4th quarter	325 963	60 998	52 695	46 168	41 408	4 421	8 657	28 329	56 131	43 208	38 753	5 011	8 814	25 051

Table 1-4. Contributions to Percent Change in Real Gross Domestic Product: Recent Data

(Percent, percentage points.)   NIPA Table 1.1.2

| Year and quarter | Percent change at seasonally adjusted annual rate, real GDP | Personal consump-tion expen-ditures | Gross private domestic investment | | | | Exports and imports of goods and services | | | Government consumption expenditures and gross investment | | |
| | | | Total | Fixed investment | | Change in private inventories | Net exports | Exports | Imports | Total | Federal | State and local |
				Nonresi-dential	Residential							
1960	2.6	1.67	0.06	0.56	-0.37	-0.13	0.70	0.76	-0.06	0.14	-0.23	0.37
1961	2.6	1.25	0.05	0.08	0.02	-0.05	0.05	0.03	0.03	1.21	0.66	0.54
1962	6.1	3.00	1.82	0.81	0.46	0.55	-0.21	0.25	-0.45	1.51	1.24	0.27
1963	4.4	2.48	1.08	0.59	0.57	-0.07	0.23	0.34	-0.11	0.57	0.03	0.53
1964	5.8	3.57	1.27	1.09	0.31	-0.12	0.35	0.57	-0.22	0.57	-0.05	0.62
1965	6.5	3.80	2.26	1.76	-0.13	0.64	-0.29	0.14	-0.44	0.73	0.10	0.63
1966	6.6	3.38	1.56	1.40	-0.40	0.56	-0.28	0.35	-0.63	1.94	1.34	0.60
1967	2.7	1.76	-0.62	-0.04	-0.11	-0.47	-0.21	0.12	-0.33	1.81	1.32	0.49
1968	4.9	3.39	0.99	0.55	0.53	-0.09	-0.29	0.40	-0.68	0.82	0.21	0.61
1969	3.1	2.20	0.93	0.79	0.14	0.00	-0.03	0.25	-0.28	0.02	-0.34	0.36
1970	0.2	1.39	-1.03	-0.10	-0.23	-0.70	0.33	0.54	-0.21	-0.50	-0.80	0.30
1971	3.3	2.29	1.63	-0.01	1.08	0.56	-0.18	0.10	-0.28	-0.45	-0.80	0.35
1972	5.3	3.66	1.90	0.97	0.87	0.06	-0.19	0.42	-0.61	-0.12	-0.37	0.25
1973	5.6	2.97	1.95	1.51	-0.04	0.48	0.80	1.08	-0.28	-0.07	-0.39	0.32
1974	-0.5	-0.50	-1.24	0.10	-1.08	-0.26	0.73	0.56	0.17	0.47	0.06	0.41
1975	-0.2	1.36	-2.91	-1.13	-0.54	-1.24	0.86	-0.05	0.91	0.49	0.05	0.43
1976	5.4	3.41	2.91	0.66	0.88	1.37	-1.05	0.36	-1.41	0.12	0.01	0.10
1977	4.6	2.59	2.47	1.26	0.97	0.24	-0.70	0.19	-0.89	0.26	0.21	0.05
1978	5.5	2.68	2.22	1.72	0.38	0.12	0.05	0.80	-0.76	0.60	0.23	0.37
1979	3.2	1.44	0.72	1.34	-0.22	-0.40	0.64	0.80	-0.16	0.36	0.20	0.16
1980	-0.3	-0.19	-2.07	0.00	-1.19	-0.89	1.64	0.95	0.69	0.36	0.38	-0.02
1981	2.5	0.85	1.64	0.87	-0.37	1.13	-0.15	0.12	-0.26	0.20	0.43	-0.23
1982	-1.8	0.88	-2.46	-0.43	-0.72	-1.31	-0.59	-0.71	0.12	0.37	0.35	0.01
1983	4.6	3.51	1.60	-0.06	1.38	0.28	-1.32	-0.22	-1.10	0.79	0.65	0.14
1984	7.2	3.30	4.73	2.18	0.65	1.90	-1.54	0.61	-2.16	0.74	0.33	0.41
1985	4.2	3.20	-0.01	0.91	0.11	-1.03	-0.39	0.24	-0.63	1.37	0.78	0.59
1986	3.5	2.58	0.03	-0.24	0.58	-0.31	-0.29	0.53	-0.82	1.14	0.61	0.53
1987	3.5	2.15	0.53	0.01	0.10	0.41	0.17	0.77	-0.60	0.62	0.38	0.24
1988	4.2	2.65	0.45	0.63	-0.05	-0.13	0.81	1.23	-0.41	0.26	-0.15	0.42
1989	3.7	1.86	0.72	0.71	-0.16	0.17	0.51	0.97	-0.46	0.58	0.15	0.43
1990	1.9	1.28	-0.45	0.14	-0.38	-0.21	0.40	0.78	-0.37	0.65	0.20	0.45
1991	-0.1	0.12	-1.09	-0.48	-0.35	-0.26	0.62	0.61	0.01	0.25	0.01	0.24
1992	3.5	2.36	1.11	0.33	0.49	0.28	-0.04	0.66	-0.70	0.10	-0.15	0.25
1993	2.8	2.24	1.24	0.84	0.32	0.07	-0.56	0.31	-0.87	-0.17	-0.32	0.15
1994	4.0	2.51	1.90	0.91	0.38	0.61	-0.41	0.84	-1.25	0.02	-0.31	0.32
1995	2.7	1.91	0.55	1.15	-0.15	-0.44	0.12	1.02	-0.90	0.10	-0.21	0.31
1996	3.8	2.26	1.49	1.13	0.35	0.02	-0.15	0.86	-1.01	0.18	-0.09	0.27
1997	4.4	2.45	2.01	1.38	0.11	0.52	-0.31	1.26	-1.57	0.30	-0.06	0.36
1998	4.5	3.42	1.76	1.44	0.38	-0.07	-1.14	0.26	-1.39	0.44	-0.06	0.50
1999	4.8	3.49	1.62	1.36	0.29	-0.03	-0.90	0.52	-1.42	0.59	0.12	0.47
2000	4.1	3.29	1.31	1.31	0.03	-0.03	-0.85	0.86	-1.71	0.33	0.02	0.31
2001	1.0	1.63	-1.11	-0.31	0.04	-0.84	-0.24	-0.59	0.35	0.67	0.24	0.43
2002	1.7	1.70	-0.16	-0.94	0.29	0.48	-0.67	-0.19	-0.48	0.82	0.47	0.35
2003	2.8	2.13	0.76	0.30	0.47	-0.02	-0.49	0.19	-0.68	0.39	0.45	-0.06
2004	3.9	2.54	1.64	0.67	0.57	0.41	-0.63	0.88	-1.51	0.30	0.31	-0.01
2005	3.5	2.38	1.26	0.92	0.41	-0.07	-0.31	0.67	-0.98	0.15	0.15	0.00
2006	2.8	1.95	0.60	1.00	-0.50	0.10	-0.06	0.95	-1.01	0.30	0.17	0.13
2007	2.0	1.63	-0.48	0.89	-1.13	-0.25	0.52	0.94	-0.42	0.34	0.14	0.20
2008	0.1	0.10	-1.52	0.08	-1.14	-0.46	1.04	0.67	0.37	0.49	0.46	0.03
2009	-2.6	-0.88	-3.51	-1.95	-0.74	-0.82	1.07	-1.00	2.07	0.72	0.48	0.24
2010	2.7	1.31	1.85	0.52	-0.08	1.42	-0.43	1.43	-1.86	-0.02	0.34	-0.36
2011	1.5	1.16	0.94	0.99	0.00	-0.05	0.12	0.90	-0.79	-0.67	-0.23	-0.44
2012	2.3	0.94	1.64	1.16	0.31	0.17	0.12	0.54	-0.42	-0.42	-0.16	-0.26
2013	1.8	1.01	1.10	0.53	0.33	0.23	0.20	0.40	-0.20	-0.47	-0.44	-0.03
2014	2.3	1.82	0.95	0.95	0.12	-0.12	-0.31	0.52	-0.84	-0.17	-0.19	0.02
2015	2.7	2.20	0.95	0.32	0.33	0.31	-0.78	0.04	-0.81	0.33	0.00	0.33
2016	1.7	1.67	-0.18	0.12	0.23	-0.53	-0.17	0.05	-0.22	0.35	0.03	0.31
2017	2.3	1.65	0.68	0.53	0.15	-0.01	-0.16	0.49	-0.65	0.09	0.02	0.07
2018	2.9	1.96	0.98	0.85	-0.02	0.16	-0.27	0.35	-0.62	0.24	0.20	0.04
2019	2.3	1.48	0.60	0.59	-0.04	0.05	-0.18	-0.01	-0.17	0.38	0.25	0.14
2020	-3.4	-2.55	-0.99	-0.73	0.26	-0.52	-0.29	-1.57	1.28	0.43	0.33	0.10
2018												
1st quarter	3.1	1.64	1.45	1.31	-0.17	0.31	-0.16	0.24	-0.40	0.15	0.12	0.03
2nd quarter	3.4	2.34	0.14	0.90	0.13	-0.89	0.40	0.62	-0.22	0.49	0.32	0.17
3rd quarter	1.9	1.79	1.64	0.38	-0.24	1.50	-1.66	-0.78	-0.88	0.17	0.22	-0.05
4th quarter	0.9	1.16	0.39	0.65	-0.34	0.08	-0.51	0.05	-0.57	-0.14	0.12	-0.26
2019												
1st quarter	2.4	0.43	1.13	0.63	0.00	0.49	0.39	0.36	0.02	0.47	0.09	0.38
2nd quarter	3.2	2.37	0.48	0.90	0.15	-0.57	-0.50	-0.26	-0.24	0.86	0.57	0.29
3rd quarter	2.8	2.12	0.22	0.40	0.14	-0.32	0.07	-0.08	0.15	0.36	0.23	0.12
4th quarter	1.9	1.13	-1.18	-0.23	0.04	-0.99	1.43	0.17	1.26	0.52	0.23	0.28
2020												
1st quarter	-5.1	-4.79	-0.92	-1.14	0.73	-0.51	-0.05	-1.95	1.90	0.63	0.16	0.47
2nd quarter	-31.2	-24.10	-9.64	-4.28	-1.36	-4.01	1.53	-8.34	9.87	0.97	1.42	-0.45
3rd quarter	33.8	25.51	11.71	2.72	2.16	6.84	-3.25	4.64	-7.89	-0.19	-0.32	0.13
4th quarter	4.5	2.26	4.01	1.57	1.34	1.10	-1.65	2.07	-3.73	-0.09	-0.22	0.14

Table 1-5A. Chain-Type Quantity Indexes for Gross Domestic Product and Domestic Purchases: Recent Data

(Index numbers, 2012 = 100.)

NIPA Tables 1.1.3, 1.4.3, 2.3.3

Year and quarter	Gross domestic product											Gross domestic purchases
	Gross domestic product, total	Personal consumption expenditures		Private fixed investment			Exports and imports of goods and services		Government consumption expenditures and gross investment			
		Total	Excluding food and energy	Total	Nonresidential	Residential	Exports	Imports	Total	Federal	State and local	
1960	20.1	18.2	14.9	13.9	8.8	49.9	5.1	4.9	34.6	41.5	27.7	19.8
1961	20.6	18.6	15.2	13.9	8.8	50.1	5.1	4.9	36.5	43.5	29.4	20.3
1962	21.8	19.5	16.2	15.1	9.5	54.9	5.4	5.4	38.9	47.4	30.3	21.6
1963	22.8	20.3	16.9	16.3	10.1	61.3	5.8	5.6	39.8	47.5	32.1	22.5
1964	24.1	21.5	18.1	17.8	11.2	65.0	6.4	5.9	40.8	47.3	34.2	23.7
1965	25.7	22.9	19.3	19.7	13.0	63.4	6.6	6.5	42.1	47.7	36.5	25.3
1966	27.4	24.2	20.5	20.9	14.6	58.0	7.1	7.5	45.8	52.8	38.7	27.1
1967	28.1	24.9	21.1	20.7	14.6	56.5	7.2	8.0	49.4	58.1	40.7	27.9
1968	29.5	26.4	22.4	22.1	15.3	64.2	7.8	9.2	51.1	59.0	43.1	29.3
1969	30.4	27.4	23.3	23.4	16.4	66.2	8.2	9.7	51.2	57.5	44.6	30.3
1970	30.5	28.0	23.7	23.0	16.2	62.7	9.1	10.1	50.1	54.0	45.9	30.2
1971	31.5	29.1	24.8	24.5	16.2	79.4	9.2	10.7	49.1	50.5	47.3	31.3
1972	33.1	30.8	26.5	27.3	17.6	93.2	9.9	11.9	48.9	48.9	48.4	33.0
1973	35.0	32.4	28.2	29.7	19.9	92.6	11.8	12.4	48.7	47.2	49.7	34.6
1974	34.8	32.1	28.1	28.0	20.1	74.5	12.7	12.1	49.8	47.5	51.5	34.1
1975	34.8	32.8	28.8	25.3	18.3	65.5	12.6	10.8	50.9	47.8	53.4	33.8
1976	36.6	34.7	30.4	27.8	19.3	80.0	13.2	12.9	51.2	47.8	53.9	36.0
1977	38.3	36.1	31.9	31.5	21.4	96.4	13.5	14.3	51.8	48.9	54.1	37.9
1978	40.4	37.7	33.6	35.2	24.4	102.8	14.9	15.5	53.3	50.0	55.9	39.9
1979	41.7	38.6	34.6	37.2	26.8	98.9	16.4	15.8	54.2	51.1	56.7	40.9
1980	41.6	38.5	34.6	35.0	26.8	78.2	18.2	14.7	55.2	53.3	56.6	40.1
1981	42.7	39.0	35.3	35.9	28.5	71.8	18.4	15.1	55.7	55.6	55.4	41.2
1982	41.9	39.6	35.8	33.7	27.6	58.8	17.0	14.9	56.7	57.6	55.5	40.7
1983	43.8	41.8	38.2	36.3	27.5	83.5	16.6	16.8	58.9	61.2	56.2	43.1
1984	47.0	44.0	40.5	42.1	32.1	95.8	17.9	20.9	60.9	63.2	58.4	46.8
1985	48.9	46.3	42.8	44.4	34.2	98.0	18.5	22.3	65.0	68.0	61.7	48.9
1986	50.6	48.2	44.8	45.2	33.6	110.1	19.9	24.2	68.5	72.0	64.8	50.7
1987	52.4	49.9	46.6	45.5	33.6	112.3	22.1	25.6	70.5	74.7	66.2	52.3
1988	54.6	51.9	48.6	47.0	35.3	111.3	25.7	26.6	71.4	73.5	68.7	54.0
1989	56.6	53.5	50.2	48.5	37.3	107.7	28.7	27.8	73.4	74.7	71.4	55.7
1990	57.7	54.5	51.3	47.8	37.7	98.6	31.2	28.8	75.8	76.3	74.4	56.5
1991	57.6	54.6	51.4	45.3	36.2	89.8	33.3	28.7	76.7	76.4	76.0	56.1
1992	59.6	56.6	53.6	47.8	37.3	102.2	35.6	30.8	77.0	75.2	77.6	58.1
1993	61.3	58.6	55.7	51.5	40.1	110.5	36.7	33.4	76.4	72.5	78.6	60.0
1994	63.7	60.9	58.0	55.7	43.2	120.4	40.0	37.4	76.5	69.9	80.8	62.7
1995	65.4	62.7	59.9	59.1	47.4	116.3	44.1	40.4	76.9	68.0	83.0	64.3
1996	67.9	64.9	62.2	64.3	51.7	125.9	47.7	43.9	77.6	67.2	84.9	66.8
1997	70.9	67.3	64.8	69.8	57.3	128.9	53.4	49.8	78.8	66.7	87.6	69.9
1998	74.1	70.9	68.6	77.0	63.5	140.0	54.6	55.6	80.8	66.1	91.5	73.8
1999	77.7	74.7	72.5	84.0	69.8	148.8	57.3	62.1	83.4	67.3	95.3	77.9
2000	80.8	78.4	76.5	89.9	76.3	149.8	62.1	70.2	84.9	67.5	97.8	81.6
2001	81.6	80.4	78.6	88.7	74.6	151.2	58.6	68.4	88.1	70.1	101.4	82.6
2002	83.0	82.4	80.8	85.6	69.5	160.3	57.5	71.0	92.0	75.3	104.3	84.5
2003	85.3	85.0	83.5	89.4	71.2	174.9	58.7	74.6	93.9	80.3	103.8	87.1
2004	88.6	88.2	86.9	95.7	75.2	192.3	64.3	82.8	95.4	83.7	103.7	90.9
2005	91.7	91.4	90.1	102.7	81.0	204.9	68.8	88.2	96.1	85.4	103.7	94.1
2006	94.2	94.0	92.9	105.3	87.5	189.5	75.3	93.8	97.6	87.4	104.9	96.7
2007	96.1	96.3	95.4	104.0	93.6	154.1	81.9	96.2	99.4	89.1	106.7	98.0
2008	96.2	96.4	95.9	98.0	94.1	116.8	86.7	94.2	101.9	94.8	106.9	97.2
2009	93.7	95.2	94.5	82.3	80.5	91.5	79.5	82.3	105.6	100.7	109.0	93.8
2010	96.3	97.0	96.4	84.9	84.1	88.7	89.7	93.1	105.5	104.8	106.0	96.6
2011	97.8	98.7	98.4	90.9	91.4	88.5	96.1	97.6	102.1	101.9	102.2	98.0
2012	100.0	100.0	100.0	100.0	100.0	100.0	100.0	100.0	100.0	100.0	100.0	100.0
2013	101.8	101.5	101.5	105.6	104.1	112.4	103.0	101.2	97.6	94.5	99.7	101.6
2014	104.2	104.2	104.4	112.5	111.6	116.7	107.0	106.4	96.7	92.1	99.9	104.2
2015	107.0	107.7	108.1	116.8	114.2	128.6	107.3	112.0	98.5	92.0	102.9	107.7
2016	108.8	110.3	110.8	119.2	115.3	137.1	107.7	113.6	100.4	92.5	105.8	109.6
2017	111.2	113.0	113.6	124.1	120.0	142.6	112.1	118.6	100.9	92.8	106.4	112.2
2018	114.5	116.3	116.9	130.0	127.7	141.7	115.2	123.5	102.3	95.6	106.9	115.7
2019	117.1	118.8	119.6	134.1	133.2	140.4	115.2	124.9	104.6	99.2	108.2	118.5
2020	113.1	114.3	114.2	130.5	126.1	150.0	99.5	113.8	107.1	104.2	109.2	114.9
2018												
1st quarter	113.4	115.0	115.6	128.3	125.3	142.7	115.1	122.0	101.7	94.3	106.8	114.5
2nd quarter	114.4	116.0	116.6	130.2	127.4	143.9	116.5	122.4	102.4	95.4	107.2	115.3
3rd quarter	114.9	116.8	117.5	130.5	128.2	141.7	114.6	124.2	102.7	96.2	107.1	116.3
4th quarter	115.2	117.3	117.9	131.1	129.8	138.6	114.8	125.4	102.5	96.7	106.4	116.7
2019												
1st quarter	115.9	117.5	118.2	132.2	131.3	138.7	115.7	125.4	103.1	97.0	107.3	117.3
2nd quarter	116.8	118.5	119.3	134.2	133.4	140.1	115.0	125.9	104.4	99.1	108.1	118.3
3rd quarter	117.6	119.4	120.2	135.2	134.4	141.3	114.8	125.6	105.0	100.0	108.4	119.1
4th quarter	118.1	119.9	120.8	134.9	133.8	141.7	115.1	122.8	105.7	100.9	109.1	119.2
2020												
1st quarter	116.6	117.8	118.1	134.1	131.0	148.4	110.1	118.6	106.7	101.5	110.3	117.7
2nd quarter	106.2	106.4	105.5	122.4	119.7	135.4	87.6	98.1	107.7	106.3	108.7	107.4
3rd quarter	114.2	116.1	116.0	130.1	124.9	152.3	97.7	115.1	107.1	104.9	108.8	116.3
4th quarter	115.5	117.0	117.3	135.5	128.7	163.9	102.8	123.2	107.0	104.0	109.1	118.1

Table 1-5B. Chain-Type Quantity Indexes for Gross Domestic Product and Domestic Purchases: Historical Data

(Index numbers, 2012 = 100.)   **NIPA Tables 1.1.3, 1.4.3, 2.3.3**

Year and quarter	Gross domestic product, total	Personal consumption expenditures		Private fixed investment			Exports and imports of goods and services		Government consumption expenditures and gross investment			Gross domestic purchases
		Total	Excluding food and energy	Total	Nonresi-dential	Residential	Exports	Imports	Total	Federal	State and local	
1929	6.8	7.5	6.2	5.9	4.1	18.6	2.0	2.1	5.8	2.3	11.3	6.8
1930	6.2	7.1	5.8	4.6	3.4	11.5	1.6	1.8	6.3	2.5	12.4	6.2
1931	5.8	6.9	5.5	3.3	2.3	9.8	1.3	1.6	6.6	2.6	13.0	5.8
1932	5.1	6.3	5.0	2.0	1.4	5.5	1.1	1.3	6.4	2.6	12.4	5.1
1933	5.0	6.2	4.8	1.8	1.3	4.6	1.1	1.4	6.2	3.2	11.1	5.0
1934	5.6	6.6	5.1	2.3	1.7	6.0	1.2	1.4	6.9	4.2	11.6	5.6
1935	6.1	7.0	5.4	2.9	2.1	8.2	1.2	1.8	7.2	4.3	12.0	6.1
1936	6.9	7.7	5.9	3.8	2.7	10.2	1.3	1.8	8.3	6.4	12.0	6.9
1937	7.2	8.0	6.2	4.4	3.2	11.0	1.6	2.1	8.0	5.8	12.0	7.2
1938	7.0	7.9	6.0	3.6	2.5	11.0	1.6	1.6	8.6	6.4	12.7	6.9
1939	7.5	8.3	6.4	4.2	2.7	15.4	1.7	1.7	9.3	6.9	14.0	7.4
1940	8.2	8.7	6.7	5.0	3.3	17.3	2.0	1.7	9.7	7.8	13.6	8.1
1941	9.6	9.3	7.3	5.8	4.0	18.4	2.0	2.1	16.3	20.6	12.7	9.6
1942	11.5	9.1	7.1	3.4	2.5	9.5	1.3	1.9	37.7	61.6	11.6	11.5
1943	13.4	9.4	7.5	2.7	2.1	5.9	1.1	2.4	56.6	98.1	10.6	13.6
1944	14.5	9.6	7.7	3.2	2.6	5.1	1.2	2.5	63.5	111.6	10.2	14.6
1945	14.3	10.2	8.2	4.3	3.6	5.8	1.7	2.7	55.8	96.5	10.6	14.4
1946	12.7	11.5	9.1	7.6	5.2	23.5	3.6	2.2	19.6	27.0	11.6	12.2
1947	12.5	11.7	9.3	9.1	6.0	30.1	4.1	2.1	16.7	20.2	13.2	11.9
1948	13.0	12.0	9.6	9.9	6.3	35.9	3.3	2.5	17.6	21.3	14.0	12.7
1949	13.0	12.3	9.9	9.1	5.7	33.3	3.2	2.4	19.5	23.0	16.1	12.6
1947												
1st quarter	12.5	11.6	. . .	8.9	6.1	27.6	4.4	2.2	16.7	20.6	12.8	11.9
2nd quarter	12.5	11.8	. . .	8.7	6.0	26.2	4.3	2.2	16.7	20.4	13.0	11.9
3rd quarter	12.5	11.8	. . .	9.0	5.9	30.3	4.1	2.0	16.7	20.1	13.3	11.8
4th quarter	12.7	11.8	. . .	9.7	6.0	36.1	3.7	2.1	16.6	19.7	13.5	12.2
1948												
1st quarter	12.8	11.9	. . .	10.0	6.4	35.6	3.5	2.3	16.8	20.2	13.5	12.4
2nd quarter	13.1	12.0	. . .	10.0	6.2	37.7	3.2	2.4	17.4	21.0	13.9	12.7
3rd quarter	13.1	12.0	. . .	9.9	6.2	36.5	3.2	2.6	17.8	21.5	14.1	12.8
4th quarter	13.1	12.1	. . .	9.8	6.3	33.8	3.1	2.5	18.4	22.4	14.4	12.9
1949												
1st quarter	13.0	12.1	. . .	9.3	6.0	31.3	3.5	2.4	18.9	22.8	15.0	12.6
2nd quarter	12.9	12.3	. . .	9.0	5.8	30.8	3.5	2.4	19.7	23.7	15.9	12.5
3rd quarter	13.1	12.3	. . .	9.0	5.5	33.4	3.2	2.3	19.8	23.3	16.5	12.7
4th quarter	12.9	12.5	. . .	9.3	5.5	37.5	2.8	2.3	19.5	22.3	16.8	12.7
1950												
1st quarter	13.5	12.7	. . .	9.9	5.6	41.7	2.7	2.4	19.1	21.2	17.2	13.2
2nd quarter	13.9	12.9	. . .	10.7	6.1	45.7	2.7	2.5	19.5	21.8	17.4	13.6
3rd quarter	14.4	13.6	. . .	11.5	6.6	48.2	2.8	3.1	19.2	21.2	17.4	14.3
4th quarter	14.7	13.2	. . .	11.3	6.6	45.9	3.0	3.1	20.5	23.8	17.4	14.5
1951												
1st quarter	14.9	13.5	. . .	10.8	6.4	43.6	3.2	3.1	22.7	28.2	17.2	14.7
2nd quarter	15.1	13.1	. . .	10.4	6.5	37.7	3.5	3.0	25.7	33.8	17.5	14.8
3rd quarter	15.4	13.3	. . .	10.2	6.6	35.4	3.6	2.8	28.5	39.3	17.6	15.1
4th quarter	15.5	13.4	. . .	10.1	6.5	35.7	3.6	2.7	30.0	42.3	17.6	15.1
1952												
1st quarter	15.6	13.4	. . .	10.3	6.5	36.6	3.7	3.0	30.9	44.0	17.6	15.3
2nd quarter	15.7	13.7	. . .	10.5	6.6	37.3	3.3	3.0	32.0	45.8	18.0	15.4
3rd quarter	15.8	13.7	. . .	9.9	6.1	37.0	3.1	3.2	32.3	46.9	17.5	15.6
4th quarter	16.3	14.2	. . .	10.6	6.7	38.9	3.1	3.5	32.9	47.6	17.9	16.2
1953												
1st quarter	16.6	14.4	. . .	11.1	7.0	39.6	3.0	3.4	33.9	49.3	18.3	16.5
2nd quarter	16.7	14.5	. . .	11.2	7.1	39.7	3.1	3.6	34.6	50.7	18.3	16.6
3rd quarter	16.6	14.4	. . .	11.2	7.2	38.2	3.2	3.6	34.2	49.5	18.8	16.5
4th quarter	16.4	14.3	. . .	11.1	7.2	37.9	3.1	3.4	34.1	48.8	19.2	16.3
1954												
1st quarter	16.3	14.4	. . .	10.9	7.0	38.3	2.9	3.2	33.3	46.4	19.9	16.2
2nd quarter	16.3	14.6	. . .	11.1	6.9	40.8	3.4	3.5	32.1	44.1	20.0	16.2
3rd quarter	16.5	14.8	. . .	11.5	7.1	43.3	3.3	3.3	31.4	42.1	20.5	16.3
4th quarter	16.8	15.1	. . .	11.8	7.1	46.0	3.4	3.3	31.2	41.7	20.6	16.6
1955												
1st quarter	17.3	15.4	. . .	12.2	7.2	49.4	3.5	3.5	31.3	40.9	21.5	17.1
2nd quarter	17.6	15.7	. . .	12.7	7.7	50.1	3.4	3.7	31.0	40.0	21.8	17.4
3rd quarter	17.8	15.9	. . .	13.0	8.0	49.0	3.7	3.8	31.2	40.4	21.7	17.6
4th quarter	17.9	16.1	. . .	13.1	8.3	47.0	3.7	3.9	30.5	39.1	21.9	17.8

. . . = Not available.

Table 1-5B. Chain-Type Quantity Indexes for Gross Domestic Product and Domestic Purchases: Historical Data—*Continued*

(Index numbers, 2012 = 100.) **NIPA Tables 1.1.3, 1.4.3, 2.3.3**

Year and quarter	Gross domestic product, total	Personal consumption expenditures Total	Excluding food and energy	Private fixed investment Total	Nonresidential	Residential	Exports	Imports	Government Total	Federal	State and local	Gross domestic purchases
1956												
1st quarter	17.9	16.1	...	12.9	8.2	45.8	3.9	4.1	30.5	38.8	22.1	17.7
2nd quarter	18.0	16.2	...	13.0	8.3	45.6	4.1	4.0	31.1	39.8	22.4	17.8
3rd quarter	18.0	16.2	...	13.0	8.4	44.7	4.3	4.1	30.9	39.1	22.5	17.7
4th quarter	18.3	16.4	...	12.9	8.4	44.0	4.5	3.9	31.7	40.5	22.7	18.0
1957												
1st quarter	18.4	16.6	...	12.9	8.4	43.4	4.7	4.2	32.3	41.3	23.3	18.1
2nd quarter	18.4	16.6	...	12.8	8.4	42.4	4.6	4.2	32.2	40.7	23.4	18.1
3rd quarter	18.6	16.7	...	13.0	8.6	41.8	4.5	4.1	32.4	41.0	23.8	18.3
4th quarter	18.4	16.7	...	12.7	8.4	41.8	4.3	4.2	33.0	41.4	24.4	18.1
1958												
1st quarter	17.9	16.5	...	12.0	7.9	40.1	3.9	4.2	32.7	40.2	25.1	17.7
2nd quarter	18.0	16.6	...	11.7	7.6	40.3	3.9	4.4	33.5	41.5	25.4	17.9
3rd quarter	18.4	16.9	...	11.9	7.5	43.2	3.9	4.3	33.7	41.3	26.0	18.3
4th quarter	18.9	17.1	...	12.6	7.8	47.7	3.9	4.6	34.4	42.2	26.4	18.7
1959												
1st quarter	19.2	17.4	14.1	13.4	8.0	53.1	4.2	4.7	34.0	41.4	26.6	19.1
2nd quarter	19.7	17.7	14.4	13.8	8.2	54.9	4.2	4.9	34.4	42.2	26.6	19.5
3rd quarter	19.7	17.9	14.6	13.9	8.5	53.9	4.6	4.9	34.7	42.7	26.6	19.5
4th quarter	19.7	17.9	14.6	13.7	8.4	52.4	4.4	4.8	34.5	42.3	26.5	19.6
1960												
1st quarter	20.2	18.1	14.8	14.2	8.7	54.0	4.9	5.0	33.9	40.7	27.0	19.9
2nd quarter	20.1	18.3	15.0	13.9	8.9	49.5	5.1	5.0	34.3	40.8	27.6	19.8
3rd quarter	20.2	18.2	14.9	13.6	8.7	48.1	5.2	4.9	35.1	42.1	28.0	19.8
4th quarter	19.9	18.3	14.9	13.6	8.7	48.0	5.2	4.7	35.3	42.2	28.4	19.5
1961												
1st quarter	20.0	18.3	14.9	13.5	8.6	48.2	5.2	4.6	35.9	42.4	29.3	19.7
2nd quarter	20.4	18.5	15.1	13.7	8.8	48.4	4.9	4.7	35.9	42.8	29.1	20.1
3rd quarter	20.8	18.6	15.3	14.1	8.8	51.0	5.1	5.0	36.7	44.0	29.3	20.5
4th quarter	21.2	19.0	15.6	14.5	9.1	52.8	5.2	5.1	37.5	44.9	30.1	20.9
1962												
1st quarter	21.5	19.2	15.8	14.8	9.3	53.7	5.2	5.3	38.2	46.5	29.9	21.3
2nd quarter	21.7	19.4	16.1	15.2	9.6	55.4	5.5	5.4	38.4	46.7	30.1	21.4
3rd quarter	22.0	19.6	16.2	15.3	9.7	55.3	5.5	5.5	39.3	48.1	30.5	21.7
4th quarter	22.1	19.9	16.5	15.3	9.6	55.2	5.3	5.5	39.6	48.3	30.8	21.8
1963												
1st quarter	22.3	20.0	16.6	15.5	9.7	57.2	5.4	5.4	39.1	46.7	31.3	22.0
2nd quarter	22.6	20.2	16.8	16.2	10.0	61.3	5.8	5.5	39.1	46.5	31.6	22.2
3rd quarter	23.1	20.5	17.1	16.6	10.2	62.5	5.8	5.7	40.8	49.1	32.5	22.7
4th quarter	23.2	20.6	17.3	17.1	10.5	64.4	6.0	5.7	40.4	47.8	32.9	22.8
1964												
1st quarter	23.7	21.1	17.6	17.6	10.7	68.4	6.3	5.6	40.5	47.6	33.4	23.3
2nd quarter	24.0	21.4	18.0	17.6	11.0	65.0	6.3	5.8	40.9	47.6	34.1	23.6
3rd quarter	24.3	21.8	18.3	17.9	11.4	63.9	6.5	5.9	40.9	47.3	34.5	23.9
4th quarter	24.4	21.9	18.4	18.1	11.6	62.8	6.6	6.1	40.9	46.9	34.9	24.0
1965												
1st quarter	25.0	22.4	18.8	18.9	12.3	63.1	5.8	5.9	40.9	46.5	35.2	24.7
2nd quarter	25.3	22.6	19.0	19.4	12.8	63.7	6.8	6.6	41.4	46.6	36.1	24.9
3rd quarter	25.9	23.0	19.4	19.9	13.3	64.0	6.7	6.6	42.7	48.3	37.1	25.5
4th quarter	26.5	23.7	19.9	20.4	13.8	62.7	7.1	6.9	43.5	49.4	37.6	26.1
1966												
1st quarter	27.1	24.0	20.3	21.2	14.4	64.3	6.9	7.1	44.3	50.6	38.1	26.8
2nd quarter	27.2	24.1	20.3	20.9	14.6	59.3	7.1	7.3	45.2	52.0	38.3	26.9
3rd quarter	27.5	24.3	20.6	21.0	14.8	57.3	7.0	7.7	46.4	54.0	38.8	27.2
4th quarter	27.7	24.4	20.7	20.4	14.8	51.3	7.2	7.8	47.2	54.6	39.8	27.4
1967												
1st quarter	27.9	24.6	20.8	20.0	14.6	49.9	7.3	7.9	49.2	58.1	40.3	27.6
2nd quarter	27.9	24.9	21.1	20.5	14.5	55.6	7.2	7.8	49.0	57.5	40.5	27.7
3rd quarter	28.2	25.0	21.2	20.8	14.5	58.6	7.1	7.9	49.6	58.4	40.6	28.0
4th quarter	28.4	25.2	21.3	21.4	14.8	62.0	7.3	8.3	49.9	58.5	41.3	28.2
1968												
1st quarter	29.0	25.8	21.9	21.9	15.2	62.2	7.5	8.8	50.8	59.5	42.1	28.8
2nd quarter	29.5	26.2	22.2	21.8	15.0	63.7	7.6	9.0	51.1	59.2	42.9	29.3
3rd quarter	29.7	26.7	22.7	22.2	15.2	65.0	8.1	9.5	51.2	58.8	43.5	29.5
4th quarter	29.8	26.8	22.8	22.7	15.7	65.9	8.0	9.4	51.3	58.5	43.9	29.7

. . . = Not available.

Table 1-5B. Chain-Type Quantity Indexes for Gross Domestic Product and Domestic Purchases: Historical Data—*Continued*

(Index numbers, 2012 = 100.)   NIPA Tables 1.1.3, 1.4.3, 2.3.3

Year and quarter	Gross domestic product, total	Personal consumption expenditures		Private fixed investment			Exports and imports of goods and services		Government consumption expenditures and gross investment			Gross domestic purchases
		Total	Excluding food and energy	Total	Nonresi-dential	Residential	Exports	Imports	Total	Federal	State and local	
1969												
1st quarter	30.3	27.1	23.0	23.3	16.1	68.1	7.0	8.5	51.4	58.4	44.3	30.2
2nd quarter	30.4	27.3	23.2	23.4	16.2	67.5	8.6	10.2	51.2	57.6	44.7	30.2
3rd quarter	30.6	27.4	23.3	23.8	16.6	66.9	8.4	10.1	51.3	57.7	44.8	30.4
4th quarter	30.4	27.6	23.5	23.2	16.5	62.3	8.7	10.0	50.7	56.4	44.7	30.2
1970												
1st quarter	30.4	27.8	23.6	23.1	16.4	62.4	8.8	9.9	50.4	55.5	45.1	30.1
2nd quarter	30.4	27.9	23.7	22.6	16.3	58.5	9.1	10.1	49.8	54.0	45.4	30.2
3rd quarter	30.7	28.2	23.9	23.0	16.4	61.9	9.1	10.1	50.0	53.3	46.4	30.4
4th quarter	30.4	28.1	23.8	23.0	15.8	68.2	9.2	10.3	50.1	53.1	46.6	30.1
1971												
1st quarter	31.2	28.6	24.3	23.5	15.9	71.7	9.3	10.2	49.3	51.4	46.8	30.9
2nd quarter	31.4	28.9	24.6	24.4	16.1	78.6	9.2	10.9	49.2	50.8	47.2	31.2
3rd quarter	31.6	29.1	24.9	24.8	16.2	82.2	9.6	11.2	49.2	50.6	47.3	31.4
4th quarter	31.7	29.6	25.4	25.5	16.5	85.3	8.8	10.4	48.8	49.3	47.9	31.5
1972												
1st quarter	32.3	30.0	25.8	26.5	17.1	90.9	9.7	11.9	49.1	49.7	48.1	32.2
2nd quarter	33.0	30.6	26.2	27.0	17.3	92.6	9.5	11.5	49.3	50.2	48.0	32.9
3rd quarter	33.3	31.0	26.7	27.3	17.6	93.0	10.0	11.7	48.4	47.9	48.4	33.1
4th quarter	33.9	31.8	27.4	28.5	18.4	96.3	10.5	12.3	48.8	48.0	49.0	33.7
1973												
1st quarter	34.7	32.4	28.1	29.6	19.2	99.6	11.2	12.8	49.2	48.6	49.2	34.5
2nd quarter	35.1	32.3	28.2	29.8	19.9	94.4	11.8	12.5	48.8	47.8	49.3	34.7
3rd quarter	34.9	32.5	28.3	29.8	20.2	90.3	11.8	12.1	48.3	46.2	49.8	34.4
4th quarter	35.3	32.4	28.3	29.5	20.4	86.2	12.4	12.2	48.6	46.3	50.5	34.7
1974												
1st quarter	35.0	32.1	28.2	28.9	20.4	80.6	12.5	11.8	49.5	47.4	51.1	34.2
2nd quarter	35.0	32.2	28.3	28.5	20.3	77.4	13.2	12.4	49.8	47.2	51.7	34.3
3rd quarter	34.7	32.3	28.3	28.1	20.1	74.8	12.4	12.2	49.9	47.5	51.6	34.1
4th quarter	34.6	31.8	27.8	26.6	19.6	65.1	12.8	12.1	50.1	48.0	51.6	33.9
1975												
1st quarter	34.2	32.1	28.1	25.1	18.5	61.4	12.9	10.9	50.6	47.5	53.2	33.1
2nd quarter	34.4	32.6	28.5	24.8	18.0	63.1	12.5	10.0	50.2	47.0	52.8	33.3
3rd quarter	35.0	33.1	29.0	25.4	18.2	67.3	12.3	10.8	51.2	48.2	53.5	34.1
4th quarter	35.5	33.5	29.5	25.9	18.4	70.2	13.0	11.4	51.6	48.4	54.2	34.5
1976												
1st quarter	36.3	34.1	30.0	26.9	18.8	76.8	12.9	12.1	51.7	47.9	54.8	35.5
2nd quarter	36.5	34.4	30.2	27.4	19.1	78.7	13.0	12.7	51.1	47.7	53.8	35.8
3rd quarter	36.7	34.8	30.6	27.7	19.5	77.5	13.4	13.2	51.0	47.8	53.5	36.1
4th quarter	37.0	35.3	30.9	29.0	19.9	86.8	13.5	13.6	50.9	47.9	53.3	36.4
1977												
1st quarter	37.4	35.7	31.4	30.0	20.6	89.4	13.3	14.3	51.4	48.2	53.8	37.0
2nd quarter	38.2	35.9	31.7	31.6	21.2	99.2	13.7	14.4	51.8	48.9	54.2	37.7
3rd quarter	38.8	36.2	32.0	32.0	21.6	98.9	13.8	14.2	52.0	49.3	54.1	38.3
4th quarter	38.8	36.8	32.5	32.5	22.3	97.8	13.3	14.4	51.9	49.0	54.2	38.4
1978												
1st quarter	39.0	37.0	32.7	32.8	22.5	98.7	13.6	15.3	51.9	49.0	54.2	38.7
2nd quarter	40.5	37.7	33.7	35.1	24.2	103.4	15.1	15.4	53.2	50.0	55.8	39.9
3rd quarter	40.9	37.9	33.9	36.0	25.0	104.6	15.2	15.6	53.7	50.3	56.5	40.3
4th quarter	41.4	38.2	34.2	36.8	25.8	104.4	15.8	15.8	54.2	50.7	57.0	40.8
1979												
1st quarter	41.5	38.4	34.3	37.1	26.4	101.9	15.8	15.8	53.7	50.7	56.0	40.8
2nd quarter	41.5	38.4	34.4	36.9	26.4	100.1	15.9	15.9	54.2	51.2	56.6	40.9
3rd quarter	41.9	38.8	34.9	37.6	27.2	98.9	16.5	15.6	54.3	51.3	56.7	41.0
4th quarter	42.0	38.9	34.9	37.2	27.2	94.9	17.5	16.0	54.7	51.3	57.4	41.0
1980												
1st quarter	42.1	38.8	34.8	36.7	27.5	87.6	18.0	16.0	55.5	52.7	57.7	41.0
2nd quarter	41.2	37.9	33.9	33.7	26.3	71.4	18.3	14.8	55.6	53.8	56.9	39.8
3rd quarter	41.2	38.3	34.5	34.1	26.4	73.5	18.3	13.7	54.9	53.1	56.0	39.4
4th quarter	41.9	38.9	35.2	35.4	27.0	80.4	18.2	14.5	54.8	53.4	55.7	40.4
1981												
1st quarter	42.8	39.0	35.4	35.7	27.5	78.4	18.5	15.1	55.6	54.5	56.2	41.3
2nd quarter	42.5	39.0	35.3	36.0	28.1	75.9	18.6	15.1	55.7	55.9	55.1	41.0
3rd quarter	43.0	39.2	35.5	36.0	28.8	70.0	18.2	14.9	55.5	55.6	54.9	41.5
4th quarter	42.5	38.9	35.1	35.9	29.4	62.7	18.3	15.4	56.2	56.6	55.4	41.1

Table 1-5B. Chain-Type Quantity Indexes for Gross Domestic Product and Domestic Purchases: Historical Data—*Continued*

(Index numbers, 2012 = 100.)   NIPA Tables 1.1.3, 1.4.3, 2.3.3

Year and quarter	Gross domestic product, total	Gross domestic product											Gross domestic purchases
		Personal consumption expenditures		Private fixed investment			Exports and imports of goods and services		Government consumption expenditures and gross investment			
		Total	Excluding food and energy	Total	Nonresi-dential	Residential	Exports	Imports	Total	Federal	State and local	
1982												
1st quarter	41.8	39.2	35.4	34.9	28.8	59.1	17.5	14.9	56.1	56.7	55.2	40.5
2nd quarter	42.0	39.3	35.5	33.8	27.9	57.2	17.6	14.7	56.4	56.9	55.4	40.7
3rd quarter	41.9	39.6	35.9	33.0	27.1	57.2	16.8	15.4	56.8	57.8	55.4	40.8
4th quarter	41.9	40.3	36.6	33.1	26.6	61.7	16.1	14.8	57.7	59.2	55.8	40.9
1983												
1st quarter	42.4	40.7	37.0	33.8	26.2	72.3	16.3	15.1	58.2	60.1	56.0	41.4
2nd quarter	43.4	41.5	37.9	35.1	26.6	80.7	16.4	16.3	58.7	61.2	55.9	42.6
3rd quarter	44.3	42.2	38.5	37.0	27.7	88.6	16.6	17.5	59.7	62.8	56.4	43.7
4th quarter	45.2	42.9	39.3	39.1	29.4	92.3	16.9	18.4	58.8	60.8	56.4	44.7
1984												
1st quarter	46.1	43.3	39.8	40.3	30.3	95.1	17.3	19.9	59.4	61.3	57.2	45.8
2nd quarter	46.9	43.9	40.3	41.9	31.8	96.7	17.7	20.7	60.7	63.2	57.9	46.7
3rd quarter	47.3	44.2	40.7	42.7	32.7	95.6	18.1	21.2	61.2	63.1	58.9	47.2
4th quarter	47.7	44.8	41.3	43.5	33.5	95.7	18.5	21.9	62.5	65.1	59.5	47.6
1985												
1st quarter	48.2	45.5	42.0	43.9	33.9	95.9	18.5	21.4	63.1	65.7	60.3	48.0
2nd quarter	48.6	45.9	42.5	44.5	34.4	96.7	18.5	22.4	64.5	67.5	61.3	48.6
3rd quarter	49.3	46.8	43.4	44.3	34.0	98.5	18.2	22.2	66.0	69.5	62.3	49.3
4th quarter	49.7	46.9	43.4	45.1	34.6	100.7	18.8	23.1	66.3	69.5	62.8	49.8
1986												
1st quarter	50.2	47.3	43.9	45.2	34.2	104.8	19.4	23.1	66.8	69.3	64.0	50.1
2nd quarter	50.4	47.8	44.4	45.3	33.5	110.8	19.6	24.0	68.2	71.6	64.6	50.5
3rd quarter	50.9	48.7	45.4	45.1	33.2	112.3	20.0	24.7	69.7	74.0	65.2	51.0
4th quarter	51.1	49.0	45.6	45.4	33.5	112.6	20.8	24.9	69.4	73.2	65.4	51.2
1987												
1st quarter	51.5	49.0	45.7	44.6	32.7	112.4	20.8	24.8	69.8	73.6	65.7	51.5
2nd quarter	52.1	49.7	46.4	45.3	33.3	112.8	21.6	25.4	70.4	74.6	65.9	52.1
3rd quarter	52.5	50.3	47.1	46.1	34.3	111.9	22.6	25.9	70.4	74.5	66.1	52.4
4th quarter	53.4	50.4	47.2	46.1	34.2	112.1	23.4	26.5	71.5	75.8	67.0	53.3
1988												
1st quarter	53.7	51.3	48.0	46.1	34.5	110.1	24.7	26.3	70.9	73.6	67.7	53.3
2nd quarter	54.4	51.7	48.3	47.0	35.3	111.4	25.4	26.0	71.1	73.1	68.6	53.8
3rd quarter	54.7	52.1	48.8	47.2	35.5	111.5	25.9	26.6	71.1	72.7	68.9	54.2
4th quarter	55.5	52.7	49.4	47.8	36.0	112.2	26.7	27.5	72.5	74.7	69.7	54.9
1989												
1st quarter	56.0	53.0	49.7	48.2	36.6	111.1	27.5	27.6	72.2	73.4	70.3	55.3
2nd quarter	56.5	53.2	50.0	48.3	37.1	107.7	28.7	27.7	73.3	74.9	71.1	55.6
3rd quarter	56.9	53.7	50.5	49.1	38.0	107.2	29.0	27.7	73.9	75.5	71.7	55.9
4th quarter	57.0	53.9	50.6	48.5	37.6	104.9	29.4	28.2	74.3	75.1	72.7	56.1
1990												
1st quarter	57.6	54.4	51.3	49.0	38.1	105.8	30.7	29.1	75.5	76.4	73.8	56.6
2nd quarter	57.8	54.6	51.3	48.1	37.6	101.6	31.1	29.0	75.6	76.5	74.0	56.8
3rd quarter	57.9	54.8	51.5	47.7	37.9	96.2	31.3	28.9	75.7	76.1	74.4	56.7
4th quarter	57.3	54.4	51.2	46.4	37.3	90.6	31.6	28.1	76.2	76.2	75.3	56.0
1991												
1st quarter	57.1	54.2	51.0	45.2	36.5	85.8	31.8	27.8	76.7	77.1	75.4	55.7
2nd quarter	57.5	54.6	51.3	45.3	36.3	88.5	33.0	28.3	77.0	77.4	75.7	56.0
3rd quarter	57.8	54.9	51.6	45.4	36.0	91.5	33.8	29.1	76.8	76.4	76.1	56.3
4th quarter	58.0	54.9	51.7	45.6	36.0	93.3	34.5	29.7	76.2	74.5	76.7	56.5
1992												
1st quarter	58.7	55.9	52.9	46.1	35.9	98.6	35.1	30.0	76.9	74.8	77.7	57.1
2nd quarter	59.3	56.3	53.2	47.6	37.0	102.0	35.2	30.5	76.8	74.6	77.6	57.8
3rd quarter	59.9	56.9	53.9	48.1	37.6	102.0	35.9	30.9	77.2	75.6	77.6	58.4
4th quarter	60.5	57.5	54.5	49.5	38.6	105.9	36.1	31.7	77.2	75.7	77.5	59.1
1993												
1st quarter	60.6	57.8	54.8	49.9	39.0	106.0	36.2	32.4	76.3	73.2	77.8	59.3
2nd quarter	61.0	58.3	55.4	50.8	39.7	107.4	36.6	33.0	76.3	72.4	78.4	59.7
3rd quarter	61.3	58.9	56.0	51.6	40.1	111.4	36.5	33.5	76.4	72.2	78.8	60.1
4th quarter	62.1	59.5	56.5	53.7	41.5	117.2	37.7	34.8	76.7	72.3	79.2	61.0
1994												
1st quarter	62.7	60.1	57.2	54.3	41.9	118.9	38.0	35.6	75.7	69.8	79.5	61.7
2nd quarter	63.6	60.6	57.6	55.4	42.6	122.8	39.3	37.0	76.1	69.5	80.5	62.5
3rd quarter	63.9	61.1	58.2	55.8	43.3	121.0	40.8	38.0	77.4	71.1	81.4	62.9
4th quarter	64.7	61.7	58.9	57.2	45.0	119.1	41.7	39.1	76.7	69.3	81.7	63.6
1995												
1st quarter	64.9	61.9	59.1	58.4	46.7	116.4	42.5	39.9	77.0	69.1	82.3	63.9
2nd quarter	65.1	62.4	59.6	58.4	47.1	112.8	43.1	40.3	77.2	68.8	83.0	64.1
3rd quarter	65.7	63.0	60.2	59.2	47.4	117.0	45.0	40.4	77.0	68.3	83.1	64.3
4th quarter	66.1	63.4	60.7	60.3	48.3	119.2	45.6	41.0	76.2	66.0	83.5	64.8

Table 1-5B. Chain-Type Quantity Indexes for Gross Domestic Product and Domestic Purchases: Historical Data—*Continued*

(Index numbers, 2012 = 100.)   **NIPA Tables 1.1.3, 1.4.3, 2.3.3**

Year and quarter	Gross domestic product, total	Personal consumption expenditures		Private fixed investment			Exports and imports of goods and services		Government consumption expenditures and gross investment			Gross domestic purchases
		Total	Excluding food and energy	Total	Nonresidential	Residential	Exports	Imports	Total	Federal	State and local	
1996												
1st quarter	66.6	64.0	61.2	61.9	49.6	122.3	46.2	42.3	76.7	67.3	83.4	65.4
2nd quarter	67.7	64.7	61.9	63.8	50.9	127.7	46.9	43.2	77.7	67.9	84.6	66.5
3rd quarter	68.3	65.1	62.5	65.2	52.5	127.4	47.3	44.6	77.7	67.0	85.3	67.3
4th quarter	69.0	65.6	63.0	66.3	53.8	126.0	50.3	45.5	78.2	66.7	86.5	67.7
1997												
1st quarter	69.5	66.3	63.7	67.5	55.1	126.6	51.2	47.5	77.8	65.7	86.5	68.4
2nd quarter	70.6	66.6	64.1	68.8	56.2	128.4	53.3	49.0	78.8	67.2	87.2	69.5
3rd quarter	71.5	67.7	65.3	71.2	58.7	129.6	54.5	50.9	79.2	66.9	88.0	70.5
4th quarter	72.1	68.5	66.1	71.8	59.1	131.0	54.4	52.0	79.6	66.8	88.8	71.3
1998												
1st quarter	72.8	69.2	66.9	73.9	61.0	133.7	54.7	53.9	79.3	65.1	89.6	72.2
2nd quarter	73.5	70.5	68.1	76.4	63.0	138.3	54.1	55.1	80.7	66.4	91.1	73.2
3rd quarter	74.4	71.4	69.1	77.9	64.0	142.4	53.8	55.9	81.3	66.2	92.4	74.2
4th quarter	75.6	72.4	70.3	80.0	65.9	145.7	55.8	57.7	81.8	66.6	92.9	75.4
1999												
1st quarter	76.4	73.1	70.9	81.4	67.4	146.3	55.7	59.3	82.4	66.5	94.0	76.4
2nd quarter	77.0	74.3	72.0	83.4	69.1	148.6	56.3	61.0	82.6	66.4	94.6	77.2
3rd quarter	78.0	75.1	72.9	85.3	71.1	149.7	58.0	63.2	83.6	67.4	95.6	78.3
4th quarter	79.3	76.2	74.1	85.8	71.4	150.8	59.3	64.8	84.9	68.8	96.8	79.7
2000												
1st quarter	79.6	77.4	75.5	88.2	74.1	151.5	60.1	67.3	84.3	66.5	97.5	80.2
2nd quarter	81.0	78.1	76.1	90.2	76.4	150.8	62.0	69.4	85.2	68.6	97.4	81.7
3rd quarter	81.1	78.8	76.9	90.6	77.2	148.4	63.5	71.9	84.8	67.3	97.7	82.0
4th quarter	81.6	79.5	77.5	90.8	77.5	148.6	62.8	72.0	85.3	67.5	98.5	82.6
2001												
1st quarter	81.3	79.8	77.9	90.3	76.8	149.2	62.0	71.1	86.7	69.0	99.7	82.3
2nd quarter	81.8	80.0	78.2	89.2	75.2	151.5	60.2	68.8	88.2	70.0	101.6	82.7
3rd quarter	81.5	80.2	78.5	88.6	74.3	152.5	57.1	67.3	88.1	70.4	101.1	82.5
4th quarter	81.7	81.5	79.9	86.6	72.2	151.5	55.1	66.6	89.5	71.2	103.1	82.9
2002												
1st quarter	82.4	81.7	80.2	85.8	70.5	156.4	56.3	68.5	91.1	73.6	104.0	83.7
2nd quarter	82.9	82.1	80.5	85.7	69.7	160.3	58.0	70.8	91.8	75.0	104.2	84.3
3rd quarter	83.3	82.7	81.1	85.6	69.4	160.8	58.2	71.7	92.3	75.7	104.4	84.7
4th quarter	83.4	83.2	81.5	85.2	68.5	163.7	57.3	72.9	93.0	77.0	104.6	85.2
2003												
1st quarter	83.8	83.6	81.9	86.0	68.8	166.7	57.2	72.6	93.0	77.9	104.1	85.6
2nd quarter	84.5	84.5	83.0	88.1	70.7	169.4	57.3	73.7	93.9	80.6	103.5	86.4
3rd quarter	85.9	85.7	84.3	91.0	72.2	179.1	58.8	74.8	94.1	80.6	103.9	87.8
4th quarter	86.9	86.3	84.9	92.6	73.2	184.4	61.5	77.2	94.7	82.1	103.8	88.8
2004												
1st quarter	87.4	87.1	85.7	92.4	72.4	186.5	62.9	79.4	95.1	83.0	103.8	89.4
2nd quarter	88.1	87.6	86.2	94.9	74.2	192.5	64.2	82.5	95.4	83.4	103.9	90.4
3rd quarter	89.0	88.6	87.4	96.9	76.4	193.8	64.4	83.7	95.5	84.4	103.5	91.3
4th quarter	89.9	89.6	88.4	98.7	77.9	196.5	65.9	85.6	95.5	84.2	103.6	92.3
2005												
1st quarter	90.9	90.2	88.9	100.4	79.1	201.1	67.2	86.3	96.0	85.1	103.7	93.3
2nd quarter	91.3	91.2	89.9	102.1	80.3	204.9	68.7	87.5	95.9	85.1	103.7	93.7
3rd quarter	92.0	92.0	90.7	103.9	82.0	207.1	68.6	88.0	96.2	85.7	103.7	94.5
4th quarter	92.5	92.1	90.9	104.3	82.6	206.7	70.8	90.8	96.3	85.7	103.8	95.1
2006												
1st quarter	93.8	93.1	92.2	106.3	85.4	204.8	73.6	92.7	97.5	88.0	104.3	96.3
2nd quarter	94.0	93.6	92.5	105.7	86.9	194.5	75.0	93.6	97.5	87.4	104.7	96.5
3rd quarter	94.2	94.2	93.1	105.0	88.4	183.7	74.9	94.5	97.3	86.6	105.0	96.8
4th quarter	95.0	95.1	94.1	104.3	89.3	175.2	77.8	94.4	98.1	87.8	105.5	97.2
2007												
1st quarter	95.2	95.7	94.6	104.2	91.0	167.3	79.3	95.8	98.3	87.3	106.1	97.4
2nd quarter	95.8	95.9	95.0	104.7	93.0	160.7	80.5	96.3	99.2	88.7	106.6	98.0
3rd quarter	96.4	96.6	95.7	104.1	94.4	150.5	83.0	96.9	99.6	89.5	106.8	98.3
4th quarter	97.0	97.0	96.2	103.1	95.9	138.0	84.9	95.9	100.4	91.0	107.1	98.5
2008												
1st quarter	96.6	96.8	96.1	101.5	96.3	127.0	86.3	96.3	100.7	92.4	106.5	98.0
2nd quarter	97.2	97.1	96.6	100.7	96.5	121.2	88.8	95.4	101.5	94.4	106.6	98.0
3rd quarter	96.7	96.4	96.1	98.1	94.7	115.1	88.4	94.2	102.3	95.6	107.1	97.4
4th quarter	94.5	95.5	94.9	91.7	89.1	103.9	83.2	90.8	103.0	96.8	107.5	95.4
2009												
1st quarter	93.4	95.2	94.6	84.4	82.4	93.8	76.5	82.1	104.2	98.1	108.6	93.8
2nd quarter	93.3	94.8	94.1	81.3	79.9	88.1	77.1	78.8	105.7	100.4	109.5	93.1
3rd quarter	93.6	95.4	94.8	81.6	79.5	92.1	79.9	82.1	106.0	101.4	109.3	93.6
4th quarter	94.6	95.3	94.5	82.0	80.0	92.0	84.4	86.1	106.2	102.9	108.6	94.6

Table 1-5B. Chain-Type Quantity Indexes for Gross Domestic Product and Domestic Purchases:
Historical Data—*Continued*

(Index numbers, 2012 = 100.)   NIPA Tables 1.1.3, 1.4.3, 2.3.3

| Year and quarter | Gross domestic product, total | Gross domestic product | | | | | | | | | | Gross domestic purchases |
| | | Personal consumption expenditures | | Private fixed investment | | | Exports and imports of goods and services | | Government consumption expenditures and gross investment | | | |
		Total	Excluding food and energy	Total	Nonresidential	Residential	Exports	Imports	Total	Federal	State and local	
2010												
1st quarter	95.1	95.9	95.1	82.0	80.5	89.0	86.4	88.4	105.8	104.0	107.0	95.1
2nd quarter	96.0	96.7	96.1	85.0	83.2	93.6	88.3	92.4	106.1	105.4	106.6	96.4
3rd quarter	96.8	97.4	96.8	85.4	85.4	85.3	90.8	95.7	105.3	104.9	105.6	97.3
4th quarter	97.3	98.0	97.4	87.0	87.1	86.7	93.3	96.0	104.7	104.7	104.6	97.6
2011												
1st quarter	97.0	98.4	98.0	86.9	87.0	86.4	94.1	96.5	103.4	103.3	103.5	97.3
2nd quarter	97.7	98.5	98.2	88.9	89.2	87.4	95.7	96.8	102.7	102.9	102.6	97.8
3rd quarter	97.6	98.8	98.5	92.7	93.4	89.0	97.0	97.9	101.2	100.6	101.6	97.8
4th quarter	98.7	99.0	98.8	95.0	95.8	91.3	97.7	99.2	101.2	101.0	101.3	98.9
2012												
1st quarter	99.5	99.7	99.8	98.0	98.2	96.8	98.9	99.7	100.7	101.0	100.5	99.7
2nd quarter	100.0	99.8	99.7	100.0	100.4	97.6	99.9	100.1	100.2	100.2	100.2	100.0
3rd quarter	100.2	100.0	99.9	100.1	100.1	100.2	100.5	100.6	100.0	100.4	99.8	100.2
4th quarter	100.3	100.4	100.5	101.9	101.2	105.4	100.6	99.7	99.1	98.4	99.5	100.1
2013												
1st quarter	101.2	101.0	100.9	103.7	102.5	109.2	101.1	99.6	98.2	96.1	99.6	100.9
2nd quarter	101.3	101.1	101.1	104.5	102.8	112.7	102.0	101.0	98.0	95.4	99.8	101.2
3rd quarter	102.1	101.5	101.6	106.3	104.5	114.7	102.9	101.7	97.5	94.0	99.9	101.9
4th quarter	102.8	102.3	102.3	107.7	106.7	112.9	105.9	102.5	96.7	92.4	99.7	102.4
2014												
1st quarter	102.5	102.7	102.6	108.8	108.2	112.1	104.8	103.9	96.3	92.3	99.1	102.4
2nd quarter	103.8	103.7	103.9	111.8	111.1	115.7	107.1	106.2	96.4	91.7	99.6	103.7
3rd quarter	105.0	104.7	105.1	114.0	113.3	117.4	107.5	106.4	97.1	92.8	100.0	104.9
4th quarter	105.5	105.9	106.2	115.3	114.0	121.6	108.4	109.2	97.0	91.4	100.9	105.7
2015												
1st quarter	106.3	106.6	106.8	115.6	113.9	124.0	107.5	110.8	97.5	91.8	101.5	106.8
2nd quarter	106.9	107.3	107.7	116.6	114.4	127.1	107.8	111.6	98.4	92.0	102.7	107.5
3rd quarter	107.3	108.1	108.6	117.6	114.8	130.5	106.9	112.6	98.8	91.9	103.5	108.1
4th quarter	107.4	108.7	109.3	117.3	113.9	132.8	106.8	112.8	99.2	92.5	103.7	108.3
2016												
1st quarter	108.1	109.4	110.0	118.0	113.8	136.9	106.4	112.7	100.2	92.8	105.3	109.0
2nd quarter	108.4	110.0	110.4	118.6	114.5	137.0	107.3	112.8	100.0	92.0	105.5	109.2
3rd quarter	109.0	110.6	111.1	119.7	116.0	136.3	108.9	113.6	100.6	92.6	106.0	109.8
4th quarter	109.6	111.2	111.7	120.6	116.8	138.0	108.2	115.3	100.8	92.6	106.3	110.6
2017												
1st quarter	110.1	112.0	112.7	122.5	118.2	141.6	110.7	117.0	100.6	92.0	106.4	111.0
2nd quarter	110.7	112.5	113.0	123.7	119.5	142.5	111.2	118.2	100.9	92.8	106.4	111.8
3rd quarter	111.5	113.2	113.7	123.8	119.8	141.8	111.9	118.2	100.8	92.7	106.3	112.5
4th quarter	112.6	114.3	114.8	126.3	122.3	144.3	114.5	121.2	101.5	93.8	106.7	113.6
2018												
1st quarter	113.4	115.0	115.6	128.3	125.3	142.7	115.1	122.0	101.7	94.3	106.8	114.5
2nd quarter	114.4	116.0	116.6	130.2	127.4	143.9	116.5	122.4	102.4	95.4	107.2	115.3
3rd quarter	114.9	116.8	117.5	130.5	128.2	141.7	114.6	124.2	102.7	96.2	107.1	116.3
4th quarter	115.2	117.3	117.9	131.1	129.8	138.6	114.8	125.4	102.5	96.7	106.4	116.7
2019												
1st quarter	115.9	117.5	118.2	132.2	131.3	138.7	115.7	125.4	103.1	97.0	107.3	117.3
2nd quarter	116.8	118.5	119.3	134.2	133.4	140.1	115.0	125.9	104.4	99.1	108.1	118.3
3rd quarter	117.6	119.4	120.2	135.2	134.4	141.3	114.8	125.6	105.0	100.0	108.4	119.1
4th quarter	118.1	119.9	120.8	134.9	133.8	141.7	115.1	122.8	105.7	100.9	109.1	119.2
2020												
1st quarter	116.6	117.8	118.1	134.1	131.0	148.4	110.1	118.6	106.7	101.5	110.3	117.7
2nd quarter	106.2	106.4	105.5	122.4	119.7	135.4	87.6	98.1	107.7	106.3	108.7	107.4
3rd quarter	114.2	116.1	116.0	130.1	124.9	152.3	97.7	115.1	107.1	104.9	108.8	116.3
4th quarter	115.5	117.0	117.3	135.5	128.7	163.9	102.8	123.2	107.0	104.0	109.1	118.1

Table 1-6A. Chain-Type Price Indexes for Gross Domestic Product and Domestic Purchases: Recent Data

(Index numbers, 2012 = 100.)   NIPA Tables 1.1.4, 1.6.4, 2.3.4

Year and quarter	Gross domestic product, total	Personal consumption expenditures		Private fixed investment			Exports and imports of goods and services		Government consumption expenditures and gross investment			Gross domestic purchases
		Total	Excluding food and energy	Total	Nonresidential	Residential	Exports	Imports	Total	Federal	State and local	
1960	16.6	16.4	17.2	24.5	30.4	12.5	24.0	16.8	11.1	13.7	9.3	16.2
1961	16.8	16.6	17.4	24.5	30.3	12.5	24.4	16.8	11.3	13.8	9.5	16.4
1962	17.0	16.8	17.6	24.5	30.3	12.5	24.4	16.6	11.5	14.0	9.8	16.5
1963	17.2	17.0	17.8	24.4	30.3	12.4	24.4	17.0	11.8	14.4	10.0	16.8
1964	17.5	17.3	18.1	24.6	30.5	12.5	24.6	17.3	12.1	14.8	10.2	17.0
1965	17.8	17.5	18.3	25.0	30.9	12.8	25.3	17.6	12.4	15.2	10.5	17.3
1966	18.3	17.9	18.7	25.5	31.3	13.3	26.1	18.0	12.9	15.7	11.0	17.8
1967	18.8	18.4	19.3	26.1	32.1	13.8	27.1	18.0	13.4	16.0	11.6	18.3
1968	19.6	19.1	20.1	27.1	33.2	14.5	27.7	18.3	14.1	16.9	12.2	19.1
1969	20.6	20.0	21.1	28.4	34.6	15.5	28.6	18.8	14.9	17.7	13.1	20.0
1970	21.7	20.9	22.1	29.6	36.3	16.0	29.8	19.9	16.1	19.1	14.1	21.1
1971	22.8	21.8	23.1	31.1	38.0	16.9	30.8	21.1	17.4	20.7	15.2	22.2
1972	23.7	22.5	23.9	32.4	39.3	18.0	32.2	22.6	18.7	22.5	16.2	23.1
1973	25.0	23.8	24.8	34.2	40.9	19.6	36.4	26.5	19.9	24.1	17.2	24.5
1974	27.3	26.2	26.7	37.6	44.9	21.6	44.9	37.9	21.9	26.0	19.2	27.0
1975	29.8	28.4	29.0	42.1	50.8	23.6	49.5	41.1	23.9	28.3	21.0	29.4
1976	31.5	30.0	30.7	44.4	53.6	25.1	51.1	42.3	25.2	30.0	22.0	31.0
1977	33.4	31.9	32.7	47.7	57.1	27.7	53.2	46.1	26.7	31.9	23.4	33.1
1978	35.8	34.1	34.9	51.5	60.9	31.1	56.4	49.3	28.5	34.0	24.9	35.4
1979	38.7	37.2	37.4	56.1	65.8	34.6	63.2	57.8	30.9	36.6	27.1	38.5
1980	42.3	41.2	40.8	61.4	71.6	38.3	69.6	71.9	34.0	40.1	30.1	42.6
1981	46.2	44.9	44.4	67.1	78.5	41.4	74.7	75.8	37.4	43.8	33.2	46.5
1982	49.1	47.4	47.3	70.7	82.9	43.6	75.1	73.3	40.0	47.0	35.4	49.2
1983	51.0	49.4	49.7	70.9	82.8	44.7	75.4	70.5	41.5	48.5	37.0	50.9
1984	52.9	51.2	51.8	71.7	83.0	46.0	76.1	69.9	43.3	50.6	38.5	52.6
1985	54.5	53.0	53.9	72.5	83.9	47.3	73.9	67.6	44.7	51.7	40.1	54.1
1986	55.6	54.2	55.8	74.2	85.4	49.4	72.6	67.6	45.4	52.0	41.3	55.3
1987	57.0	55.9	57.5	75.7	86.3	51.5	74.2	71.7	46.6	52.3	43.2	56.8
1988	59.0	58.0	60.0	77.6	88.5	53.3	78.0	75.1	48.2	54.0	44.6	58.9
1989	61.3	60.6	62.5	79.6	90.6	55.0	79.3	76.8	50.0	55.5	46.8	61.2
1990	63.6	63.2	65.0	81.3	92.5	56.3	79.8	79.0	52.1	57.3	49.2	63.6
1991	65.8	65.3	67.3	82.6	94.3	57.0	80.7	78.3	54.0	59.3	51.0	65.6
1992	67.3	67.1	69.4	82.6	94.0	57.7	80.3	78.4	55.6	60.8	52.7	67.1
1993	68.9	68.8	71.3	83.6	94.2	60.1	80.4	77.8	57.0	62.2	54.0	68.6
1994	70.3	70.2	72.9	84.9	94.9	62.2	81.3	78.5	58.5	63.9	55.4	70.1
1995	71.8	71.7	74.5	86.2	95.8	64.5	83.1	80.7	60.1	65.8	56.9	71.6
1996	73.1	73.2	75.9	86.2	95.3	65.9	82.0	79.3	61.4	66.9	58.2	72.8
1997	74.4	74.5	77.2	86.2	94.7	67.4	80.6	76.5	62.6	68.0	59.5	73.9
1998	75.2	75.1	78.2	85.6	93.2	69.2	78.7	72.4	63.6	68.9	60.6	74.4
1999	76.3	76.2	79.2	85.7	92.3	71.8	78.1	72.8	65.8	70.5	63.0	75.5
2000	78.0	78.1	80.6	86.8	92.7	75.0	79.6	76.0	68.6	72.9	66.0	77.5
2001	79.8	79.7	82.2	87.6	92.3	78.6	79.0	74.0	70.6	74.2	68.3	79.0
2002	81.0	80.7	83.5	87.8	91.9	80.5	78.3	73.2	72.4	76.6	69.8	80.1
2003	82.6	82.4	84.9	88.6	91.2	84.3	79.5	75.4	75.0	80.0	72.1	81.8
2004	84.8	84.4	86.5	91.1	92.1	90.2	82.4	79.0	78.2	82.8	75.4	84.2
2005	87.5	86.9	88.4	94.8	94.4	96.7	85.3	83.6	82.1	86.2	79.6	87.1
2006	90.2	89.3	90.6	98.2	96.7	102.4	88.0	86.9	85.7	89.0	83.7	89.9
2007	92.7	91.6	92.6	99.7	98.3	103.7	91.3	89.9	89.5	91.6	88.2	92.3
2008	94.4	94.3	94.4	100.5	99.8	102.2	95.5	98.8	93.3	94.4	92.6	94.9
2009	95.0	94.1	95.3	99.3	99.2	98.7	89.8	87.9	92.9	94.2	92.0	94.5
2010	96.2	95.7	96.7	97.7	97.4	98.3	93.4	92.7	95.4	96.4	94.7	96.0
2011	98.2	98.2	98.2	98.7	98.6	99.0	99.2	99.7	98.3	99.1	97.7	98.3
2012	100.0	100.0	100.0	100.0	100.0	100.0	100.0	100.0	100.0	100.0	100.0	100.0
2013	101.8	101.4	101.5	101.0	100.3	105.1	100.1	98.7	102.4	100.9	103.3	101.5
2014	103.7	102.9	103.2	102.9	101.5	111.1	100.2	98.0	104.5	102.6	105.7	103.2
2015	104.7	103.1	104.5	103.5	101.9	114.1	95.4	90.1	104.6	103.1	105.7	103.5
2016	105.7	104.1	106.1	103.5	101.1	118.1	93.5	87.1	104.9	103.7	105.7	104.2
2017	107.7	106.1	107.9	105.2	102.0	123.5	95.9	89.0	107.4	105.7	108.5	106.2
2018	110.3	108.3	110.1	107.2	102.8	130.4	99.1	91.5	111.3	108.8	113.0	108.6
2019	112.3	109.9	112.0	108.9	104.1	134.1	98.7	90.1	113.2	110.8	114.9	110.3
2020	113.7	111.2	113.6	110.2	104.8	138.5	96.2	88.1	114.9	112.0	116.7	111.7
2018												
1st quarter	109.3	107.6	109.3	106.4	102.3	128.0	98.2	91.3	109.9	107.7	111.4	107.8
2nd quarter	110.2	108.2	109.9	107.0	102.7	130.2	99.4	91.7	111.0	108.4	112.6	108.5
3rd quarter	110.6	108.5	110.3	107.5	103.0	131.4	99.7	91.8	111.8	109.1	113.6	108.9
4th quarter	111.2	109.0	110.8	107.8	103.2	132.2	99.3	91.2	112.6	109.9	114.3	109.4
2019												
1st quarter	111.5	109.1	111.1	108.4	103.8	132.9	98.4	90.2	112.8	111.1	114.0	109.6
2nd quarter	112.1	109.8	111.8	108.9	104.3	133.6	99.3	90.8	113.1	110.3	114.9	110.2
3rd quarter	112.5	110.1	112.3	109.1	104.3	134.6	98.7	89.9	113.4	110.7	115.1	110.5
4th quarter	112.9	110.6	112.6	109.1	104.2	135.4	98.3	89.4	113.7	111.1	115.4	110.9
2020												
1st quarter	113.4	111.0	113.1	109.6	104.5	136.2	97.8	89.2	114.5	111.4	116.5	111.3
2nd quarter	113.0	110.5	112.9	109.7	104.9	136.5	93.2	86.4	114.3	111.4	116.1	111.0
3rd quarter	114.0	111.5	113.9	110.5	104.9	139.6	96.2	88.1	114.9	112.3	116.7	111.9
4th quarter	114.6	111.9	114.3	111.0	105.0	141.8	97.6	88.6	115.8	113.0	117.6	112.4

Table 1-6B. Chain-Type Price Indexes for Gross Domestic Product and Domestic Purchases: Historical Data

(Index numbers, 2012 = 100.)

Year and quarter	Gross domestic product, total	Personal consumption expenditures		Private fixed investment			Exports and imports of goods and services		Government consumption expenditures and gross investment			Gross domestic purchases
		Total	Excluding food and energy	Total	Nonresidential	Residential	Exports	Imports	Total	Federal	State and local	
1929	9.4	9.3	9.6	14.0	13.5	5.1	13.7	9.6	5.3	6.6	3.7	9.1
1930	9.0	8.9	9.2	13.4	12.8	5.0	12.4	8.1	5.2	6.3	3.6	8.8
1931	8.1	7.9	8.5	12.3	11.9	4.5	9.7	6.6	4.9	6.2	3.4	7.9
1932	7.2	7.0	7.5	10.4	10.8	3.7	8.4	5.3	4.5	5.9	3.0	7.0
1933	7.0	6.8	7.2	9.5	10.6	3.6	8.4	5.1	4.6	6.0	3.1	6.8
1934	7.4	7.1	7.3	9.5	10.9	4.0	9.8	5.7	4.9	6.4	3.4	7.1
1935	7.5	7.2	7.4	9.4	11.0	4.0	10.0	5.8	5.0	6.4	3.4	7.3
1936	7.6	7.3	7.5	9.5	11.0	4.1	10.4	6.3	5.2	7.0	3.4	7.4
1937	7.9	7.6	7.8	10.2	11.9	4.5	11.1	7.0	5.3	7.1	3.5	7.6
1938	7.7	7.4	7.8	9.9	12.0	4.7	10.6	6.4	5.3	7.1	3.5	7.5
1939	7.6	7.3	7.7	9.9	11.9	4.7	10.4	6.8	5.2	7.0	3.5	7.4
1940	7.7	7.4	7.8	10.1	12.1	4.9	11.3	7.2	5.1	6.8	3.5	7.5
1941	8.2	7.9	8.2	10.8	12.9	5.3	12.3	7.6	5.5	7.2	3.7	7.9
1942	8.9	8.8	9.1	12.0	14.3	5.7	14.9	8.7	5.5	7.2	4.1	8.6
1943	9.3	9.3	9.6	12.6	14.9	6.2	16.3	9.4	5.5	7.1	4.4	9.0
1944	9.5	10.2	10.5	13.1	15.4	6.8	18.4	9.9	5.5	7.0	4.5	9.2
1945	9.8	10.6	11.0	13.4	15.8	7.2	18.2	10.1	5.5	7.0	4.7	9.4
1946	11.0	11.3	11.7	14.7	17.4	7.8	17.6	11.3	7.0	9.2	5.1	10.7
1947	12.2	12.5	12.7	17.4	20.1	9.4	20.4	13.6	7.6	9.9	5.8	11.9
1948	12.9	13.2	13.4	18.8	21.8	10.2	21.5	14.7	7.9	9.9	6.5	12.6
1949	12.9	13.1	13.4	19.0	22.3	10.3	20.2	14.0	8.2	10.3	6.5	12.6
1947												
1st quarter	12.0	12.2	. . .	16.5	19.3	8.9	18.8	12.4	7.7	10.2	5.6	11.6
2nd quarter	12.1	12.3	. . .	17.2	19.9	9.4	20.1	13.3	7.7	10.1	5.7	11.8
3rd quarter	12.3	12.6	. . .	17.7	20.4	9.6	21.2	14.0	7.5	9.7	5.8	11.9
4th quarter	12.6	12.9	. . .	18.0	20.8	9.8	21.7	14.5	7.6	9.7	6.0	12.2
1948												
1st quarter	12.7	13.0	. . .	18.2	20.9	10.0	21.8	14.8	7.8	9.8	6.2	12.3
2nd quarter	12.9	13.1	. . .	18.6	21.5	10.1	21.7	14.9	7.9	9.8	6.4	12.5
3rd quarter	13.1	13.3	. . .	19.1	22.2	10.3	21.5	14.7	8.0	9.9	6.6	12.7
4th quarter	13.1	13.3	. . .	19.2	22.5	10.4	21.1	14.5	8.1	10.0	6.7	12.7
1949												
1st quarter	13.0	13.2	. . .	19.1	22.4	10.5	20.8	14.2	8.2	10.3	6.6	12.7
2nd quarter	13.0	13.1	. . .	19.1	22.3	10.4	20.4	14.0	8.1	10.3	6.5	12.6
3rd quarter	12.9	13.0	. . .	18.9	22.3	10.2	20.0	14.0	8.1	10.2	6.5	12.5
4th quarter	12.9	13.0	. . .	18.8	22.1	10.2	19.8	14.0	8.2	10.4	6.5	12.5
1950												
1st quarter	12.8	13.0	. . .	18.8	22.2	10.2	19.5	14.3	8.2	10.4	6.4	12.5
2nd quarter	12.9	13.1	. . .	19.1	22.4	10.5	19.5	14.6	8.1	10.3	6.4	12.6
3rd quarter	13.2	13.3	. . .	19.6	22.8	10.9	19.7	15.1	8.3	10.4	6.6	12.9
4th quarter	13.4	13.6	. . .	20.0	23.6	10.8	20.1	15.8	8.4	10.4	6.8	13.1
1951												
1st quarter	13.8	14.0	. . .	20.8	24.4	11.2	21.3	17.1	8.7	10.9	7.0	13.5
2nd quarter	13.9	14.1	. . .	21.1	24.8	11.3	22.1	18.0	8.7	10.7	7.2	13.6
3rd quarter	13.9	14.1	. . .	21.2	25.0	11.4	22.7	18.5	8.7	10.7	7.3	13.7
4th quarter	14.1	14.3	. . .	21.4	25.3	11.5	23.1	18.6	8.8	10.9	7.4	13.8
1952												
1st quarter	14.1	14.4	. . .	21.5	25.4	11.5	22.5	17.8	8.8	10.7	7.4	13.8
2nd quarter	14.2	14.4	. . .	21.5	25.4	11.6	22.4	17.5	8.9	10.9	7.5	13.9
3rd quarter	14.3	14.5	. . .	21.5	25.4	11.8	22.4	17.2	9.0	11.0	7.6	14.0
4th quarter	14.3	14.5	. . .	21.4	25.4	11.7	22.4	16.9	9.1	11.1	7.6	14.0
1953												
1st quarter	14.4	14.6	. . .	21.4	25.4	11.7	22.4	16.8	9.0	11.0	7.7	14.0
2nd quarter	14.4	14.6	. . .	21.5	25.6	11.7	22.4	16.6	9.0	11.0	7.7	14.1
3rd quarter	14.5	14.7	. . .	21.7	25.8	11.8	22.3	16.5	9.0	11.0	7.7	14.1
4th quarter	14.5	14.7	. . .	21.6	25.8	11.8	22.2	16.6	9.0	11.1	7.7	14.2
1954												
1st quarter	14.6	14.8	. . .	21.7	25.9	11.7	22.1	16.7	9.1	11.2	7.6	14.2
2nd quarter	14.6	14.8	. . .	21.7	26.0	11.7	22.1	16.8	9.2	11.2	7.8	14.3
3rd quarter	14.6	14.7	. . .	21.7	25.8	11.9	22.0	16.9	9.2	11.3	7.9	14.2
4th quarter	14.6	14.7	. . .	21.7	25.9	11.9	22.0	16.9	9.3	11.4	7.9	14.3
1955												
1st quarter	14.6	14.8	. . .	21.7	25.8	11.9	22.1	16.7	9.4	11.5	7.8	14.3
2nd quarter	14.7	14.8	. . .	21.9	26.0	12.0	22.2	16.7	9.5	11.8	7.9	14.4
3rd quarter	14.8	14.8	. . .	22.1	26.4	12.1	22.3	16.8	9.6	11.9	8.0	14.5
4th quarter	14.9	14.9	. . .	22.4	26.9	12.1	22.4	16.8	9.7	12.0	8.1	14.6
1956												
1st quarter	15.1	14.9	. . .	22.9	27.6	12.2	22.6	16.9	9.9	12.2	8.3	14.7
2nd quarter	15.2	15.0	. . .	23.1	27.9	12.4	22.8	17.0	10.1	12.4	8.4	14.9
3rd quarter	15.4	15.2	. . .	23.5	28.5	12.4	23.1	17.1	10.2	12.5	8.5	15.0
4th quarter	15.5	15.3	. . .	23.7	28.9	12.4	23.4	17.3	10.2	12.5	8.6	15.1
1957												
1st quarter	15.7	15.4	. . .	23.9	29.3	12.3	23.7	17.3	10.4	12.8	8.7	15.3
2nd quarter	15.8	15.5	. . .	24.0	29.5	12.3	23.9	17.4	10.5	12.9	8.8	15.4
3rd quarter	15.9	15.6	. . .	24.1	29.7	12.4	23.9	17.2	10.6	13.0	8.9	15.5
4th quarter	16.0	15.7	. . .	24.2	29.9	12.4	23.9	17.1	10.6	13.1	8.9	15.6

. . . = Not available.

Table 1-6B. Chain-Type Price Indexes for Gross Domestic Product and Domestic Purchases: Historical Data—*Continued*

(Index numbers, 2012 = 100.)   NIPA Tables 1.1.4, 1.6.4, 2.3.4

Year and quarter	Gross domestic product, total	Personal consumption expenditures		Private fixed investment			Exports and imports of goods and services		Government consumption expenditures and gross investment			Gross domestic purchases
		Total	Excluding food and energy	Total	Nonresidential	Residential	Exports	Imports	Total	Federal	State and local	
1958												
1st quarter	16.1	15.9	. . .	24.0	29.6	12.3	23.7	16.7	10.7	13.3	8.9	15.7
2nd quarter	16.2	15.9	. . .	24.1	29.8	12.3	23.6	16.5	10.8	13.4	9.0	15.8
3rd quarter	16.2	16.0	. . .	24.2	29.9	12.3	23.6	16.5	10.9	13.5	9.0	15.8
4th quarter	16.2	15.9	. . .	24.2	30.0	12.3	23.6	16.5	10.9	13.6	9.0	15.8
1959												
1st quarter	16.3	16.1	16.7	24.2	30.0	12.4	23.5	16.5	11.0	13.6	9.1	15.9
2nd quarter	16.4	16.1	16.8	24.3	30.2	12.4	23.5	16.6	11.0	13.6	9.1	15.9
3rd quarter	16.4	16.2	16.9	24.4	30.3	12.4	23.7	16.7	11.0	13.6	9.1	16.0
4th quarter	16.5	16.3	17.0	24.5	30.4	12.4	24.0	16.8	11.0	13.6	9.1	16.1
1960												
1st quarter	16.5	16.3	17.1	24.5	30.4	12.4	24.0	16.8	11.0	13.5	9.2	16.1
2nd quarter	16.6	16.4	17.1	24.5	30.4	12.5	23.9	16.8	11.0	13.5	9.3	16.2
3rd quarter	16.7	16.5	17.2	24.5	30.4	12.5	24.1	16.9	11.1	13.7	9.3	16.2
4th quarter	16.7	16.5	17.2	24.5	30.3	12.5	24.0	16.8	11.2	13.9	9.4	16.3
1961												
1st quarter	16.8	16.6	17.3	24.5	30.3	12.4	24.1	16.9	11.2	13.8	9.4	16.3
2nd quarter	16.8	16.6	17.3	24.5	30.3	12.5	24.4	16.8	11.3	13.8	9.5	16.3
3rd quarter	16.8	16.6	17.4	24.5	30.3	12.5	24.4	16.8	11.3	13.8	9.6	16.4
4th quarter	16.9	16.7	17.4	24.5	30.3	12.5	24.5	16.8	11.3	13.8	9.6	16.4
1962												
1st quarter	16.9	16.7	17.5	24.5	30.3	12.5	24.6	16.6	11.4	13.9	9.7	16.5
2nd quarter	17.0	16.8	17.6	24.5	30.3	12.5	24.4	16.6	11.5	14.0	9.8	16.5
3rd quarter	17.0	16.8	17.6	24.5	30.3	12.5	24.3	16.6	11.5	14.1	9.8	16.6
4th quarter	17.1	16.9	17.7	24.5	30.3	12.5	24.4	16.7	11.6	14.1	9.8	16.6
1963												
1st quarter	17.2	16.9	17.7	24.5	30.3	12.5	24.4	16.8	11.7	14.3	9.9	16.7
2nd quarter	17.2	17.0	17.8	24.4	30.3	12.4	24.4	16.9	11.8	14.3	10.0	16.7
3rd quarter	17.2	17.0	17.9	24.4	30.3	12.3	24.3	17.0	11.7	14.2	10.0	16.7
4th quarter	17.3	17.1	18.0	24.4	30.3	12.4	24.4	17.1	11.9	14.6	10.1	16.9
1964												
1st quarter	17.4	17.2	18.0	24.4	30.4	12.3	24.4	17.2	12.0	14.7	10.1	16.9
2nd quarter	17.4	17.2	18.1	24.6	30.5	12.5	24.4	17.3	12.0	14.7	10.2	17.0
3rd quarter	17.5	17.3	18.1	24.6	30.5	12.5	24.6	17.3	12.2	14.9	10.2	17.1
4th quarter	17.6	17.3	18.2	24.8	30.7	12.8	24.9	17.4	12.2	14.9	10.3	17.1
1965												
1st quarter	17.7	17.4	18.2	24.8	30.7	12.8	25.4	17.5	12.3	15.0	10.4	17.2
2nd quarter	17.7	17.5	18.3	24.9	30.8	12.8	25.3	17.4	12.3	15.0	10.5	17.3
3rd quarter	17.8	17.5	18.4	24.9	30.9	12.8	25.4	17.5	12.4	15.2	10.5	17.3
4th quarter	17.9	17.6	18.4	25.2	31.0	13.1	25.3	17.7	12.6	15.5	10.6	17.5
1966												
1st quarter	18.0	17.7	18.5	25.1	31.0	12.9	25.7	17.8	12.7	15.6	10.8	17.6
2nd quarter	18.2	17.9	18.7	25.5	31.3	13.4	25.9	18.0	12.8	15.6	11.0	17.7
3rd quarter	18.4	18.0	18.8	25.5	31.4	13.3	26.2	18.0	13.0	15.8	11.1	17.9
4th quarter	18.5	18.2	19.0	25.8	31.6	13.6	26.7	18.1	13.1	15.8	11.2	18.0
1967												
1st quarter	18.6	18.2	19.1	25.9	31.8	13.6	27.1	18.1	13.1	15.8	11.4	18.1
2nd quarter	18.7	18.3	19.2	26.0	32.0	13.7	27.1	18.0	13.3	15.9	11.5	18.2
3rd quarter	18.9	18.5	19.4	26.1	32.2	13.8	27.1	18.0	13.4	16.1	11.6	18.3
4th quarter	19.1	18.6	19.6	26.4	32.5	14.0	27.2	18.0	13.6	16.4	11.8	18.5
1968												
1st quarter	19.3	18.8	19.8	26.7	32.7	14.3	27.4	18.2	13.8	16.5	12.0	18.7
2nd quarter	19.5	19.0	20.0	26.9	33.1	14.4	28.0	18.3	14.0	16.7	12.2	18.9
3rd quarter	19.7	19.2	20.3	27.1	33.3	14.4	27.6	18.3	14.1	17.0	12.3	19.1
4th quarter	20.0	19.4	20.5	27.7	33.8	15.0	27.8	18.5	14.4	17.2	12.5	19.4
1969												
1st quarter	20.2	19.6	20.7	28.0	34.1	15.3	28.2	18.5	14.5	17.3	12.7	19.6
2nd quarter	20.4	19.9	21.0	28.3	34.4	15.5	28.3	18.6	14.7	17.5	13.0	19.8
3rd quarter	20.7	20.1	21.2	28.5	34.8	15.5	28.7	18.7	15.1	17.9	13.2	20.1
4th quarter	21.0	20.3	21.5	28.9	35.2	15.8	29.3	19.2	15.3	18.2	13.4	20.4
1970												
1st quarter	21.3	20.6	21.7	29.1	35.6	15.8	29.3	19.4	15.7	18.7	13.7	20.7
2nd quarter	21.6	20.8	21.9	29.7	36.2	16.3	29.9	19.7	15.9	19.0	14.0	21.0
3rd quarter	21.8	21.0	22.2	29.7	36.4	15.9	29.8	20.1	16.2	19.3	14.3	21.2
4th quarter	22.0	21.3	22.5	30.0	36.9	16.0	29.9	20.3	16.5	19.5	14.5	21.4
1971												
1st quarter	22.4	21.5	22.8	30.5	37.4	16.5	30.8	20.9	16.9	20.1	14.8	21.8
2nd quarter	22.7	21.7	23.0	31.0	37.9	16.8	30.9	20.9	17.2	20.5	15.1	22.1
3rd quarter	22.9	21.9	23.3	31.3	38.2	17.1	30.7	21.2	17.5	20.8	15.3	22.3
4th quarter	23.1	22.1	23.4	31.6	38.5	17.4	30.9	21.5	17.8	21.2	15.5	22.5
1972												
1st quarter	23.5	22.3	23.6	31.9	38.9	17.6	31.8	21.9	18.3	22.1	15.8	22.8
2nd quarter	23.6	22.4	23.8	32.2	39.2	17.7	32.0	22.4	18.5	22.3	16.0	23.0
3rd quarter	23.8	22.6	23.9	32.5	39.4	18.0	32.1	22.8	18.7	22.5	16.3	23.2
4th quarter	24.1	22.8	24.1	33.0	39.7	18.6	32.9	23.3	19.1	23.0	16.5	23.5

. . . = Not available.

Table 1-6B. Chain-Type Price Indexes for Gross Domestic Product and Domestic Purchases: Historical Data—*Continued*

(Index numbers, 2012 = 100.)   NIPA Tables 1.1.4, 1.6.4, 2.3.4

Year and quarter	Gross domestic product, total	Personal consumption expenditures		Private fixed investment			Exports and imports of goods and services		Government consumption expenditures and gross investment			Gross domestic purchases
		Total	Excluding food and energy	Total	Nonresidential	Residential	Exports	Imports	Total	Federal	State and local	
1973												
1st quarter	24.4	23.1	24.3	33.3	40.0	18.8	33.8	24.0	19.4	23.4	16.8	23.8
2nd quarter	24.8	23.5	24.6	33.8	40.6	19.3	35.3	25.9	19.8	23.8	17.1	24.2
3rd quarter	25.3	24.0	24.9	34.6	41.2	19.9	37.4	27.1	20.1	24.3	17.4	24.7
4th quarter	25.7	24.4	25.3	35.0	41.7	20.3	39.3	29.1	20.5	24.8	17.7	25.2
1974												
1st quarter	26.2	25.2	25.7	35.7	42.5	20.7	42.0	33.8	20.9	25.0	18.2	25.8
2nd quarter	26.8	25.9	26.3	36.8	43.8	21.2	43.4	37.6	21.5	25.5	18.8	26.5
3rd quarter	27.6	26.6	27.1	38.2	45.6	21.9	45.9	39.6	22.2	26.2	19.5	27.3
4th quarter	28.5	27.3	27.8	39.6	47.6	22.5	48.2	40.8	22.9	27.1	20.1	28.1
1975												
1st quarter	29.1	27.8	28.3	41.0	49.3	23.1	49.6	41.5	23.3	27.6	20.5	28.7
2nd quarter	29.5	28.1	28.7	41.9	50.6	23.5	49.4	41.6	23.7	28.0	20.9	29.2
3rd quarter	30.1	28.6	29.2	42.4	51.2	23.7	49.3	40.6	24.0	28.4	21.2	29.6
4th quarter	30.6	29.1	29.6	43.0	51.9	24.1	49.6	40.7	24.4	29.0	21.4	30.1
1976												
1st quarter	30.9	29.4	30.1	43.4	52.5	24.3	50.3	41.4	24.8	29.5	21.7	30.5
2nd quarter	31.2	29.7	30.4	44.1	53.2	25.0	50.8	42.0	25.0	29.7	21.9	30.8
3rd quarter	31.6	30.1	30.9	44.7	53.9	25.4	51.1	42.8	25.2	30.0	22.1	31.2
4th quarter	32.1	30.6	31.4	45.4	54.7	25.8	52.0	43.2	25.7	30.9	22.4	31.7
1977												
1st quarter	32.7	31.2	31.9	46.3	55.7	26.5	52.6	44.7	26.1	31.3	22.8	32.3
2nd quarter	33.2	31.7	32.4	47.2	56.6	27.2	53.4	46.0	26.5	31.6	23.2	32.8
3rd quarter	33.6	32.2	33.0	48.1	57.6	28.1	53.2	46.6	26.8	31.8	23.6	33.3
4th quarter	34.2	32.6	33.4	49.1	58.6	29.0	53.4	47.0	27.4	32.7	24.0	33.9
1978												
1st quarter	34.8	33.2	34.0	50.0	59.4	29.8	54.5	47.8	27.8	33.1	24.3	34.4
2nd quarter	35.5	33.9	34.6	51.0	60.4	30.7	55.8	49.0	28.3	33.7	24.7	35.1
3rd quarter	36.1	34.4	35.1	52.0	61.4	31.5	56.7	49.8	28.7	34.3	25.1	35.7
4th quarter	36.8	35.1	35.8	53.1	62.5	32.3	58.6	50.7	29.2	34.9	25.5	36.4
1979												
1st quarter	37.5	35.8	36.3	54.2	63.8	33.0	60.3	52.6	29.8	35.5	26.1	37.1
2nd quarter	38.4	36.7	37.1	55.5	65.2	34.1	62.8	55.4	30.4	36.1	26.7	38.1
3rd quarter	39.2	37.7	37.7	56.9	66.6	35.2	64.2	59.5	31.3	36.9	27.6	39.0
4th quarter	39.9	38.6	38.5	58.0	67.8	36.1	65.4	63.5	31.9	37.7	28.1	39.9
1980												
1st quarter	40.8	39.7	39.5	59.4	69.3	37.0	67.3	68.8	32.7	38.5	28.9	41.0
2nd quarter	41.7	40.7	40.4	60.8	70.9	37.9	68.3	71.2	33.7	40.0	29.6	42.1
3rd quarter	42.7	41.6	41.3	62.0	72.4	38.8	70.2	73.3	34.4	40.4	30.5	43.0
4th quarter	43.8	42.7	42.3	63.4	73.9	39.6	72.6	74.5	35.4	41.6	31.3	44.1
1981												
1st quarter	45.0	43.8	43.2	65.2	76.0	40.6	74.4	76.4	36.3	42.4	32.3	45.3
2nd quarter	45.8	44.5	44.0	66.6	77.8	41.2	74.7	76.9	37.1	43.4	33.0	46.1
3rd quarter	46.7	45.2	44.8	67.7	79.2	41.7	74.8	74.9	37.8	44.4	33.5	46.9
4th quarter	47.5	45.9	45.6	69.0	80.9	42.3	75.1	75.1	38.5	45.2	34.0	47.6
1982												
1st quarter	48.2	46.5	46.3	69.8	81.9	42.9	75.5	74.8	39.1	45.9	34.6	48.3
2nd quarter	48.8	47.0	46.9	70.6	82.9	43.6	75.5	73.5	39.8	46.8	35.2	48.9
3rd quarter	49.5	47.7	47.7	71.1	83.3	43.9	74.9	72.7	40.3	47.2	35.7	49.5
4th quarter	50.0	48.2	48.3	71.2	83.5	44.1	74.5	72.1	40.8	47.8	36.2	50.0
1983												
1st quarter	50.4	48.6	49.0	71.0	83.1	44.4	74.8	70.6	40.9	47.9	36.4	50.3
2nd quarter	50.7	49.1	49.3	70.8	82.7	44.5	75.1	70.6	41.3	48.3	36.8	50.6
3rd quarter	51.3	49.7	50.1	70.8	82.6	44.7	75.5	70.7	41.8	48.8	37.2	51.1
4th quarter	51.7	50.1	50.5	71.0	82.6	45.1	76.2	70.3	42.1	49.1	37.5	51.4
1984												
1st quarter	52.2	50.6	51.0	71.2	82.7	45.4	76.3	70.5	42.6	49.7	38.0	52.0
2nd quarter	52.6	51.1	51.6	71.6	83.0	45.8	76.8	70.9	43.0	50.2	38.4	52.4
3rd quarter	53.1	51.5	52.1	71.9	83.2	46.2	76.1	69.6	43.6	51.0	38.7	52.8
4th quarter	53.5	51.8	52.5	72.0	83.3	46.6	75.2	68.8	44.0	51.6	39.1	53.2
1985												
1st quarter	54.0	52.4	53.2	72.2	83.5	46.9	74.4	67.1	44.2	51.4	39.6	53.6
2nd quarter	54.4	52.8	53.6	72.3	83.7	47.0	74.1	67.4	44.5	51.5	40.0	54.0
3rd quarter	54.7	53.3	54.2	72.6	84.0	47.3	73.5	67.3	44.8	51.8	40.3	54.3
4th quarter	55.0	53.6	54.6	73.1	84.4	47.9	73.3	68.7	45.1	52.1	40.7	54.7
1986												
1st quarter	55.3	54.0	55.2	73.4	84.6	48.5	73.0	68.8	45.2	52.0	40.8	55.0
2nd quarter	55.5	53.9	55.5	73.9	85.1	49.0	72.6	66.7	45.2	51.9	41.0	55.0
3rd quarter	55.7	54.2	55.9	74.5	85.7	49.7	72.2	67.1	45.5	52.0	41.4	55.4
4th quarter	56.1	54.6	56.4	75.0	86.1	50.2	72.7	67.9	45.8	52.0	41.9	55.7
1987												
1st quarter	56.4	55.1	56.7	75.3	86.1	50.8	73.0	69.7	46.1	51.9	42.5	56.2
2nd quarter	56.8	55.6	57.3	75.5	86.1	51.2	74.1	71.5	46.5	52.2	43.0	56.6
3rd quarter	57.2	56.1	57.8	75.7	86.1	51.7	74.3	72.3	46.9	52.5	43.5	57.1
4th quarter	57.6	56.6	58.4	76.4	87.0	52.2	75.5	73.4	47.1	52.7	43.8	57.5

Table 1-6B. Chain-Type Price Indexes for Gross Domestic Product and Domestic Purchases: Historical Data—*Continued*

(Index numbers, 2012 = 100.)　　　　　　　　　　　　　　　　　　　　　　　　　　NIPA Tables 1.1.4, 1.6.4, 2.3.4

Year and quarter	Gross domestic product, total	Personal consumption expenditures Total	Excluding food and energy	Private fixed investment Total	Nonresidential	Residential	Exports and imports of goods and services Exports	Imports	Government consumption expenditures and gross investment Total	Federal	State and local	Gross domestic purchases
1988												
1st quarter	58.1	57.1	58.9	76.9	87.8	52.6	76.4	74.4	47.5	53.4	44.0	58.0
2nd quarter	58.7	57.7	59.7	77.4	88.2	53.1	78.0	75.7	48.0	53.9	44.4	58.6
3rd quarter	59.4	58.4	60.3	77.7	88.6	53.5	78.9	74.9	48.4	54.2	44.8	59.1
4th quarter	59.9	59.0	61.0	78.5	89.4	54.0	78.8	75.5	48.8	54.6	45.3	59.7
1989												
1st quarter	60.5	59.7	61.7	78.9	89.9	54.3	79.5	76.7	49.3	55.1	45.9	60.3
2nd quarter	61.2	60.5	62.2	79.4	90.3	55.0	79.6	77.6	49.9	55.5	46.5	61.0
3rd quarter	61.6	60.8	62.7	79.8	90.8	55.2	79.2	76.2	50.2	55.7	47.0	61.4
4th quarter	62.0	61.3	63.3	80.2	91.3	55.6	78.9	76.6	50.7	55.9	47.6	61.9
1990												
1st quarter	62.7	62.2	64.0	80.7	91.8	56.0	79.0	77.8	51.2	56.3	48.3	62.6
2nd quarter	63.4	62.8	64.7	81.0	92.1	56.2	79.1	76.4	51.9	57.3	48.8	63.2
3rd quarter	64.0	63.6	65.4	81.5	92.8	56.4	79.9	78.7	52.3	57.4	49.4	63.9
4th quarter	64.5	64.4	65.9	81.8	93.4	56.5	81.0	83.0	53.0	58.1	50.2	64.6
1991												
1st quarter	65.1	64.7	66.5	82.6	94.3	56.7	81.2	80.5	53.4	58.6	50.4	65.0
2nd quarter	65.5	65.1	67.0	82.7	94.4	57.0	80.8	78.3	53.7	58.9	50.7	65.3
3rd quarter	66.1	65.5	67.6	82.8	94.3	57.3	80.2	77.1	54.2	59.6	51.1	65.8
4th quarter	66.4	66.0	68.2	82.5	94.1	57.1	80.4	77.5	54.7	60.2	51.6	66.2
1992												
1st quarter	66.7	66.4	68.7	82.4	94.0	56.9	80.2	77.8	55.0	60.3	51.9	66.5
2nd quarter	67.1	66.9	69.2	82.5	93.9	57.5	80.3	78.1	55.4	60.5	52.6	66.9
3rd quarter	67.4	67.3	69.6	82.7	94.0	57.9	80.3	79.1	55.9	61.1	53.0	67.3
4th quarter	67.9	67.8	70.1	83.0	94.0	58.6	80.2	78.5	56.3	61.4	53.3	67.7
1993												
1st quarter	68.3	68.2	70.6	83.2	94.1	59.3	80.3	78.0	56.5	61.6	53.6	68.1
2nd quarter	68.7	68.6	71.1	83.6	94.1	59.9	80.5	78.3	56.8	61.9	53.9	68.5
3rd quarter	69.0	68.9	71.5	83.8	94.1	60.4	80.4	77.6	57.1	62.3	54.1	68.8
4th quarter	69.5	69.3	71.9	84.0	94.4	60.6	80.4	77.3	57.5	62.9	54.4	69.1
1994												
1st quarter	69.8	69.6	72.2	84.5	94.6	61.4	80.8	77.2	57.8	63.2	54.8	69.5
2nd quarter	70.1	70.0	72.7	84.7	94.8	61.8	81.1	78.0	58.2	63.7	55.1	69.8
3rd quarter	70.5	70.5	73.1	85.0	95.0	62.5	81.5	79.3	58.7	64.1	55.6	70.3
4th quarter	70.9	70.8	73.5	85.4	95.1	63.3	82.0	79.6	59.2	64.6	56.1	70.7
1995												
1st quarter	71.3	71.1	73.9	85.9	95.5	64.0	82.9	80.2	59.6	65.1	56.4	71.1
2nd quarter	71.7	71.5	74.3	86.2	95.8	64.3	83.5	81.4	60.0	65.6	56.8	71.5
3rd quarter	72.0	71.8	74.6	86.5	96.1	64.6	83.3	80.9	60.3	65.9	57.0	71.7
4th quarter	72.3	72.2	75.0	86.4	95.9	65.0	82.9	80.2	60.7	66.8	57.3	72.0
1996												
1st quarter	72.7	72.6	75.3	86.2	95.6	65.2	82.7	80.0	61.1	67.0	57.8	72.4
2nd quarter	73.0	73.0	75.7	86.0	95.2	65.5	82.5	79.6	61.1	66.6	57.9	72.6
3rd quarter	73.3	73.4	76.0	86.3	95.2	66.2	81.9	78.8	61.4	67.0	58.3	73.0
4th quarter	73.6	73.9	76.5	86.2	95.0	66.5	81.0	78.7	61.8	67.2	58.7	73.3
1997												
1st quarter	73.9	74.2	76.8	86.2	94.9	66.8	80.8	78.1	62.1	67.5	59.1	73.6
2nd quarter	74.3	74.4	77.2	86.3	94.9	67.1	80.8	76.5	62.4	67.9	59.3	73.8
3rd quarter	74.5	74.6	77.3	86.3	94.8	67.7	80.6	76.0	62.6	68.1	59.5	74.0
4th quarter	74.8	74.8	77.6	86.2	94.4	68.2	80.2	75.4	63.1	68.5	60.0	74.2
1998												
1st quarter	74.9	74.8	77.8	85.8	93.8	68.4	79.4	73.5	63.1	68.2	60.1	74.1
2nd quarter	75.1	74.9	78.0	85.6	93.4	68.8	79.0	72.7	63.4	68.7	60.3	74.2
3rd quarter	75.4	75.2	78.3	85.5	93.0	69.5	78.3	71.7	63.8	69.1	60.8	74.5
4th quarter	75.6	75.4	78.6	85.6	92.8	70.1	78.0	71.7	64.2	69.4	61.3	74.7
1999												
1st quarter	75.8	75.5	78.8	85.6	92.7	70.8	77.8	71.5	64.6	69.6	61.8	74.9
2nd quarter	76.1	75.9	79.0	85.7	92.4	71.6	78.0	72.4	65.4	70.1	62.6	75.3
3rd quarter	76.4	76.4	79.3	85.6	92.0	72.2	78.1	73.2	66.1	70.8	63.4	75.7
4th quarter	76.8	76.8	79.7	85.8	92.2	72.7	78.4	74.2	66.9	71.6	64.1	76.2
2000												
1st quarter	77.3	77.5	80.1	86.4	92.4	74.0	79.0	75.7	67.7	72.3	64.9	76.8
2nd quarter	77.8	77.8	80.4	86.7	92.6	74.7	79.6	75.7	68.2	72.6	65.6	77.2
3rd quarter	78.3	78.3	80.8	87.0	92.9	75.3	79.9	76.3	68.9	73.1	66.3	77.7
4th quarter	78.7	78.8	81.2	87.2	92.9	76.0	79.9	76.4	69.5	73.5	67.1	78.2
2001												
1st quarter	79.2	79.3	81.7	87.2	92.5	77.1	79.7	76.2	70.1	73.6	67.9	78.7
2nd quarter	79.8	79.7	82.0	87.5	92.5	78.1	79.3	74.6	70.4	74.0	68.2	79.0
3rd quarter	80.0	79.8	82.2	87.7	92.3	79.3	78.9	73.6	70.7	74.5	68.4	79.1
4th quarter	80.3	79.8	82.6	87.8	92.1	79.8	78.0	71.8	71.0	74.9	68.5	79.2
2002												
1st quarter	80.5	80.0	82.9	87.9	92.1	79.7	77.6	71.6	71.4	75.4	68.9	79.4
2nd quarter	80.8	80.5	83.3	87.7	92.0	80.1	78.0	73.1	72.1	76.1	69.6	79.9
3rd quarter	81.2	81.0	83.8	87.6	91.7	80.5	78.7	73.7	72.6	76.8	70.1	80.3
4th quarter	81.6	81.3	84.1	88.1	91.7	81.8	78.9	74.2	73.5	78.2	70.6	80.7

Table 1-6B. Chain-Type Price Indexes for Gross Domestic Product and Domestic Purchases: Historical Data—*Continued*

(Index numbers, 2012 = 100.)   NIPA Tables 1.1.4, 1.6.4, 2.3.4

Year and quarter	Gross domestic product, total	Personal consumption expenditures		Private fixed investment			Exports and imports of goods and services		Government consumption expenditures and gross investment			Gross domestic purchases
		Total	Excluding food and energy	Total	Nonresidential	Residential	Exports	Imports	Total	Federal	State and local	
2003												
1st quarter	82.1	82.0	84.3	88.5	91.4	83.5	79.2	76.0	74.4	79.1	71.6	81.4
2nd quarter	82.3	82.0	84.7	88.4	91.2	83.7	79.3	74.8	74.7	79.7	71.7	81.5
3rd quarter	82.8	82.6	85.1	88.4	91.0	84.3	79.5	75.1	75.2	80.4	72.2	81.9
4th quarter	83.3	83.0	85.4	89.0	91.1	85.8	80.1	75.5	75.8	81.0	72.7	82.4
2004												
1st quarter	83.9	83.6	85.9	89.8	91.4	87.7	81.3	77.3	76.7	81.7	73.7	83.1
2nd quarter	84.6	84.2	86.4	90.8	91.9	89.4	82.2	78.3	77.6	82.4	74.7	83.8
3rd quarter	85.1	84.6	86.7	91.6	92.1	91.2	82.6	79.2	78.6	83.1	75.9	84.4
4th quarter	85.8	85.3	87.2	92.4	92.8	92.7	83.6	81.1	79.8	83.9	77.2	85.2
2005												
1st quarter	86.4	85.8	87.8	93.4	93.6	93.9	84.5	81.8	80.6	85.0	77.9	85.9
2nd quarter	87.1	86.4	88.2	94.3	94.2	95.4	85.0	82.7	81.5	85.8	78.9	86.6
3rd quarter	87.9	87.3	88.6	95.3	94.6	97.9	85.6	84.3	82.7	86.7	80.2	87.5
4th quarter	88.6	88.0	89.2	96.4	95.3	99.7	86.1	85.7	83.7	87.3	81.5	88.4
2006												
1st quarter	89.2	88.5	89.7	97.3	95.9	101.3	86.6	85.9	84.4	88.1	82.1	88.9
2nd quarter	90.0	89.2	90.4	97.9	96.4	102.2	87.8	86.9	85.4	88.7	83.3	89.7
3rd quarter	90.7	89.9	90.9	98.4	97.0	102.6	88.8	87.8	86.2	89.3	84.2	90.4
4th quarter	91.0	89.7	91.3	99.2	97.7	103.3	88.8	86.8	86.9	89.8	85.1	90.5
2007												
1st quarter	91.9	90.5	91.9	99.7	98.2	103.9	89.8	87.3	88.2	90.6	86.7	91.4
2nd quarter	92.5	91.3	92.3	99.7	98.4	103.6	90.9	88.8	89.1	91.3	87.6	92.0
3rd quarter	92.9	91.8	92.7	99.7	98.3	103.6	91.6	90.0	89.9	91.9	88.6	92.5
4th quarter	93.3	92.8	93.4	99.6	98.3	103.7	93.0	93.4	91.0	92.7	89.9	93.3
2008												
1st quarter	93.7	93.5	93.9	99.7	98.7	103.4	94.8	97.0	92.2	93.4	91.3	94.1
2nd quarter	94.1	94.4	94.3	99.8	99.0	102.9	96.8	101.6	93.3	94.4	92.6	94.9
3rd quarter	94.8	95.4	94.8	100.3	100.0	102.1	98.1	104.0	94.4	95.1	93.8	95.8
4th quarter	95.0	93.9	94.7	102.1	101.6	100.6	92.2	92.7	93.5	94.7	92.7	94.9
2009												
1st quarter	95.0	93.3	94.7	101.3	100.9	99.8	89.1	85.0	92.5	93.9	91.5	94.2
2nd quarter	94.9	93.7	95.0	99.7	99.5	98.5	89.0	86.2	92.6	93.9	91.7	94.2
3rd quarter	94.9	94.3	95.4	98.3	98.4	97.8	90.0	88.9	93.0	94.2	92.2	94.6
4th quarter	95.3	95.0	96.0	98.0	97.9	98.5	91.1	91.3	93.7	94.9	92.8	95.2
2010												
1st quarter	95.5	95.4	96.3	97.6	97.3	98.7	91.9	92.7	94.5	95.5	93.8	95.5
2nd quarter	96.0	95.5	96.6	97.6	97.4	98.0	93.0	92.3	95.1	96.2	94.4	95.7
3rd quarter	96.3	95.7	96.7	97.6	97.4	98.0	93.2	91.8	95.6	96.6	94.9	96.0
4th quarter	96.9	96.3	97.0	98.0	97.7	98.6	95.3	93.9	96.4	97.4	95.7	96.6
2011												
1st quarter	97.3	97.1	97.4	98.2	98.0	98.8	97.8	97.6	97.3	98.3	96.7	97.3
2nd quarter	98.0	98.1	98.0	98.7	98.5	99.1	99.7	100.6	98.4	99.2	97.8	98.2
3rd quarter	98.6	98.6	98.5	98.9	98.7	99.1	100.3	100.5	98.8	99.5	98.3	98.7
4th quarter	98.7	98.9	98.8	99.0	99.0	99.2	99.2	100.2	98.7	99.4	98.2	98.9
2012												
1st quarter	99.3	99.5	99.4	99.4	99.6	99.0	99.8	101.1	99.5	99.7	99.4	99.5
2nd quarter	99.7	99.8	99.8	99.9	99.9	99.4	100.0	100.4	99.6	99.9	99.4	99.8
3rd quarter	100.3	100.1	100.1	100.3	100.2	100.3	99.9	98.7	100.0	100.1	100.0	100.1
4th quarter	100.7	100.6	100.6	100.4	100.2	101.3	100.3	99.8	100.8	100.2	101.2	100.6
2013												
1st quarter	101.1	101.0	101.0	100.5	100.0	102.8	100.6	99.9	101.5	100.2	102.4	101.0
2nd quarter	101.4	101.1	101.3	100.8	100.1	104.2	99.9	98.7	101.9	100.4	102.9	101.2
3rd quarter	102.0	101.5	101.7	101.1	100.3	105.6	100.1	98.2	102.5	100.8	103.7	101.6
4th quarter	102.6	101.9	102.2	101.6	100.6	107.6	100.0	98.0	103.5	102.3	104.3	102.1
2014												
1st quarter	103.0	102.4	102.5	102.3	101.0	109.9	100.7	99.2	103.9	102.0	105.1	102.6
2nd quarter	103.6	102.9	103.0	102.6	101.3	110.2	100.8	98.6	104.3	102.5	105.5	103.1
3rd quarter	104.0	103.2	103.4	103.2	101.6	112.1	100.6	98.0	104.8	103.0	106.1	103.5
4th quarter	104.1	103.1	103.7	103.6	101.9	112.3	98.8	96.1	104.9	103.1	106.1	103.5
2015												
1st quarter	104.1	102.6	103.9	103.6	102.1	113.0	96.3	92.0	104.3	102.9	105.2	103.1
2nd quarter	104.7	103.1	104.4	103.5	102.0	113.6	96.1	90.8	104.8	103.1	105.9	103.5
3rd quarter	104.9	103.4	104.7	103.6	101.9	114.6	95.2	89.8	104.9	103.3	106.0	103.7
4th quarter	104.9	103.3	104.9	103.4	101.6	115.3	93.8	87.9	104.6	103.2	105.6	103.5
2016												
1st quarter	104.9	103.3	105.4	102.9	101.0	115.8	92.3	86.3	104.1	103.0	104.8	103.4
2nd quarter	105.6	104.0	105.9	103.4	101.2	117.3	93.3	86.8	104.8	103.5	105.6	104.0
3rd quarter	105.9	104.4	106.4	103.6	101.0	119.0	93.8	87.4	105.1	103.9	106.0	104.4
4th quarter	106.5	104.9	106.8	104.1	101.3	120.5	94.4	87.7	105.6	104.4	106.5	104.9
2017												
1st quarter	107.0	105.5	107.3	104.5	101.6	121.4	95.1	88.6	106.5	105.0	107.5	105.5
2nd quarter	107.4	105.8	107.7	105.1	101.9	122.9	95.2	88.7	106.8	105.4	107.8	105.8
3rd quarter	107.9	106.1	108.1	105.5	102.1	124.3	96.0	88.8	107.6	105.9	108.8	106.3
4th quarter	108.7	106.9	108.6	105.8	102.2	125.2	97.3	89.9	108.7	106.6	110.1	107.0

Table 1-7. Final Sales

(Quarterly dollar data are at seasonally adjusted annual rates.)   **NIPA Tables 1.4.4, 1.4.5, 1.4.6**

Year and quarter	Final sales of domestic product			Final sales to domestic purchasers		
	Billions of dollars	Billions of chained (2012) dollars	Chain-type price index, 2012 = 100	Billions of dollars	Billions of chained (2012) dollars	Chain-type price index, 2012 = 100
1960	539.1	3 268.6	16.5	534.9	3 329.7	16.1
1961	559.2	3 354.6	16.7	554.3	3 416.2	16.2
1962	597.8	3 542.5	16.9	593.7	3 616.5	16.4
1963	631.8	3 701.0	17.1	626.9	3 770.8	16.6
1964	679.6	3 920.6	17.3	672.7	3 982.8	16.9
1965	733.0	4 151.9	17.7	727.4	4 232.1	17.2
1966	799.8	4 405.7	18.2	795.9	4 505.0	17.7
1967	850.1	4 549.6	18.7	846.5	4 662.8	18.2
1968	931.6	4 780.2	19.5	930.2	4 913.7	18.9
1969	1 008.4	4 931.0	20.5	1 007.0	5 070.6	19.9
1970	1 071.3	4 975.2	21.5	1 067.4	5 099.3	20.9
1971	1 156.6	5 111.6	22.6	1 156.0	5 248.9	22.0
1972	1 270.0	5 379.4	23.6	1 273.4	5 533.7	23.0
1973	1 409.5	5 659.1	24.9	1 405.4	5 776.2	24.3
1974	1 531.3	5 643.0	27.1	1 532.1	5 717.1	26.8
1975	1 691.2	5 701.7	29.7	1 675.2	5 726.9	29.3
1976	1 856.3	5 929.6	31.3	1 857.9	6 018.6	30.9
1977	2 059.5	6 191.7	33.3	2 082.6	6 326.5	32.9
1978	2 325.8	6 530.7	35.6	2 351.2	6 666.1	35.3
1979	2 609.3	6 766.0	38.6	2 631.9	6 860.2	38.4
1980	2 863.6	6 809.1	42.1	2 876.7	6 791.5	42.4
1981	3 177.2	6 904.6	46.0	3 189.8	6 896.3	46.3
1982	3 358.7	6 869.9	48.9	3 378.7	6 902.7	48.9
1983	3 639.8	7 164.6	50.8	3 691.4	7 287.8	50.7
1984	3 972.2	7 546.4	52.6	4 074.9	7 781.8	52.4
1985	4 317.2	7 945.4	54.3	4 431.2	8 213.1	54.0
1986	4 573.1	8 246.4	55.5	4 704.9	8 539.3	55.1
1987	4 828.1	8 498.0	56.8	4 972.8	8 778.2	56.7
1988	5 218.0	8 866.3	58.9	5 327.3	9 078.1	58.7
1989	5 613.9	9 178.2	61.2	5 700.6	9 345.3	61.0
1990	5 948.6	9 371.2	63.5	6 026.5	9 501.3	63.4
1991	6 158.5	9 385.0	65.6	6 187.1	9 456.7	65.4
1992	6 504.0	9 689.4	67.1	6 538.7	9 765.8	67.0
1993	6 837.7	9 949.9	68.7	6 902.9	10 081.6	68.5
1994	7 223.5	10 290.7	70.2	7 315.9	10 464.2	69.9
1995	7 608.6	10 615.2	71.7	7 698.3	10 777.2	71.4
1996	8 042.3	11 015.6	73.0	8 138.7	11 195.6	72.7
1997	8 506.6	11 449.5	74.3	8 608.6	11 666.5	73.8
1998	8 999.1	11 974.5	75.2	9 161.8	12 328.5	74.3
1999	9 570.4	12 556.0	76.2	9 829.9	13 026.4	75.5
2000	10 196.4	13 075.1	78.0	10 577.5	13 658.6	77.4
2001	10 620.2	13 311.0	79.8	10 997.0	13 928.6	79.0
2002	10 909.1	13 471.8	81.0	11 348.9	14 180.8	80.0
2003	11 442.4	13 851.3	82.6	11 964.3	14 630.8	81.8
2004	12 153.1	14 329.2	84.8	12 787.3	15 201.7	84.1
2005	12 981.7	14 841.2	87.5	13 721.6	15 761.3	87.1
2006	13 746.6	15 240.9	90.2	14 533.0	16 172.3	89.9
2007	14 440.3	15 586.7	92.6	15 176.2	16 439.9	92.3
2008	14 799.1	15 678.0	94.4	15 540.0	16 368.5	94.9
2009	14 628.8	15 400.3	95.0	15 048.0	15 922.7	94.5
2010	14 995.1	15 596.8	96.1	15 527.4	16 186.2	95.9
2011	15 553.5	15 847.4	98.1	16 133.1	16 418.5	98.3
2012	16 182.8	16 182.8	100.0	16 734.4	16 734.4	100.0
2013	16 738.7	16 444.1	101.8	17 218.1	16 963.8	101.5
2014	17 466.7	16 842.3	103.7	17 976.8	17 415.7	103.2
2015	18 069.2	17 248.3	104.8	18 595.4	17 957.7	103.6
2016	18 658.8	17 630.6	105.8	19 165.1	18 374.6	104.3
2017	19 450.1	18 030.4	107.9	19 990.1	18 809.7	106.3
2018	20 468.4	18 528.8	110.5	21 064.6	19 365.4	108.8
2019	21 299.0	18 944.4	112.4	21 895.2	19 822.0	110.5
2020	20 953.3	18 395.9	113.9	21 604.5	19 319.8	111.8
2018						
1st quarter	20 097.9	18 363.5	109.4	20 677.9	19 166.3	107.9
2nd quarter	20 468.3	18 558.0	110.3	21 008.1	19 345.3	108.6
3rd quarter	20 582.0	18 577.9	110.8	21 206.0	19 443.7	109.1
4th quarter	20 725.7	18 615.8	111.3	21 366.6	19 506.1	109.5
2019						
1st quarter	20 883.1	18 704.8	111.6	21 489.5	19 578.0	109.8
2nd quarter	21 200.8	18 881.4	112.3	21 833.1	19 781.9	110.4
3rd quarter	21 438.0	19 027.1	112.7	22 052.0	19 928.0	110.7
4th quarter	21 673.9	19 164.4	113.1	22 206.3	20 000.2	111.0
2020						
1st quarter	21 502.0	18 940.1	113.5	22 043.7	19 777.4	111.5
2nd quarter	19 767.4	17 471.0	113.2	20 306.3	18 264.4	111.2
3rd quarter	21 123.6	18 508.0	114.1	21 849.3	19 498.9	112.1
4th quarter	21 420.3	18 664.8	114.8	22 218.8	19 738.3	112.6

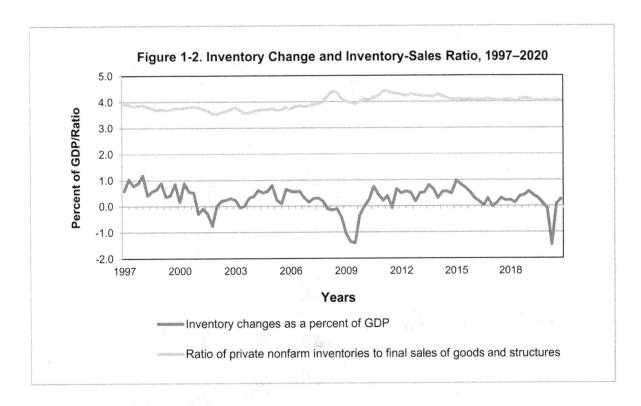

Figure 1-2. Inventory Change and Inventory-Sales Ratio, 1997–2020

- The change in inventories is part of business investment component that, although small, can be volatile and even negative, reflecting the fact that production is frequently more variable than sales. When inventory change is positive, the economy is producing more than is sold. This is the normal condition, as inventories grow to accommodate a growing level of sales. When inventory change is negative, production is below the rate of sales—which could be because sales rose faster than anticipated, causing involuntary inventory reduction, or on the other hand because production was deliberately cut back in order to get rid of unwanted stocks. Furthermore, it is the <u>change</u> in inventory —the change in an already volatile number—that drives the GDP's <u>growth rate</u>.

- In 2009, following a rapid and unwanted rise in inventories, stocks were reduced at a record rate of $144 billion (2012 dollars), contributing to the 2.6 percent decline in GDP. In 2010, the resumption of inventory-building contributed significantly to the 2.7 percent GDP increase. (Tables 1-2A, 1-8A and 1-4).

- The impact that COVID-19 had on industrial production is illustrated in the 2nd and 3rd quarters of 2020. This disruption to production hampered supply chains in 2021.

Table 1-8A. Inventory Change and Inventory-Sales Ratios: Recent Data

(Quarterly dollar data are at seasonally adjusted annual rates.)   NIPA Tables 5.7.5B, 5.7.6B, 5.8.5B, 5.8.6B

Year and quarter	Change in private inventories				Ratio, inventories at end of quarter to monthly rate of sales during the quarter					
	Billions of current dollars		Billions of chained dollars[1]		Total private inventories to final sales of domestic business		Nonfarm inventories to final sales of domestic business		Nonfarm inventories to final sales of goods and structures	
	Farm	Nonfarm	Farm	Nonfarm	Current dollars	Chained dollars[1]	Current dollars	Chained dollars[1]	Current dollars	Chained dollars[1]
OLD BASIS										
1960	0.6	2.7	1.7	9.9	4.22	3.37	2.89	2.34	3.93	4.10
1961	0.9	2.1	2.5	7.8	4.12	3.30	2.81	2.29	3.84	4.03
1962	0.6	5.5	1.7	20.4	4.14	3.32	2.82	2.34	3.87	4.11
1963	0.5	5.1	1.4	19.0	3.95	3.25	2.78	2.32	3.81	4.07
1964	-1.2	6.0	-3.8	21.8	3.79	3.17	2.75	2.31	3.79	4.07
1965	0.8	8.4	2.5	30.5	3.77	3.09	2.72	2.29	3.71	3.99
1966	-0.5	14.1	-1.4	50.2	3.92	3.26	2.92	2.50	4.01	4.38
1967	0.9	9.0	2.5	31.5	3.90	3.35	2.99	2.59	4.14	4.57
1968	1.4	7.7	4.1	26.5	3.79	3.33	2.90	2.58	4.03	4.56
1969	0.0	9.2	0.0	30.9	3.88	3.40	2.98	2.68	4.18	4.76
1970	-0.8	2.8	-2.4	8.6	3.81	3.39	2.96	2.68	4.23	4.83
1971	1.7	6.6	4.1	20.6	3.76	3.33	2.88	2.64	4.12	4.75
1972	0.3	8.8	0.4	26.7	3.74	3.18	2.77	2.55	3.94	4.53
1973	1.5	14.4	1.8	40.5	4.20	3.22	2.98	2.62	4.22	4.67
1974	-2.8	16.8	-4.4	39.0	4.52	3.46	3.54	2.88	5.11	5.26
1975	3.4	-9.6	5.8	-21.4	4.04	3.26	3.16	2.66	4.59	4.88
1976	-0.8	18.0	-1.6	37.6	3.95	3.23	3.19	2.68	4.68	4.92
1977	4.5	17.8	7.2	35.7	3.89	3.22	3.16	2.67	4.63	4.87
1978	1.4	24.4	2.1	44.9	3.98	3.14	3.15	2.63	4.54	4.73
1979	3.6	14.4	4.2	23.8	4.19	3.16	3.34	2.64	4.85	4.75
1980	-6.1	-0.2	-7.2	-0.4	4.24	3.13	3.44	2.65	5.08	4.82
1981	8.8	21.0	10.1	28.2	4.17	3.28	3.49	2.75	5.20	5.03
1982	5.8	-20.7	7.5	-27.4	3.97	3.23	3.30	2.68	5.10	4.99
1983	-15.4	9.6	-17.4	10.7	3.69	2.98	3.08	2.52	4.77	4.64
1984	5.7	59.7	6.3	72.3	3.72	3.05	3.16	2.60	4.89	4.72
1985	5.8	16.1	7.0	18.4	3.51	2.98	3.01	2.53	4.74	4.65
1986	-1.5	8.0	-2.3	10.4	3.25	2.90	2.82	2.47	4.49	4.53
1987	-6.4	33.6	-9.1	41.1	3.33	2.90	2.90	2.50	4.65	4.62
1988	-11.9	30.4	-13.1	35.4	3.29	2.81	2.86	2.47	4.63	4.55
1989	0.0	27.7	0.0	30.8	3.23	2.80	2.83	2.47	4.63	4.56
1990	2.4	12.2	2.5	14.0	3.22	2.83	2.82	2.49	4.71	4.66
1991	-1.3	0.9	-1.8	0.4	3.06	2.83	2.70	2.50	4.62	4.74
1992	6.3	10.1	7.1	11.0	2.92	2.73	2.56	2.39	4.41	4.53
1993	-6.2	27.0	-7.5	29.8	2.85	2.68	2.51	2.38	4.33	4.47
1994	12.0	51.8	13.7	55.9	2.89	2.72	2.56	2.40	4.39	4.47
1995	-11.1	42.2	-13.0	44.3	2.88	2.69	2.58	2.40	4.45	4.46
1996	8.6	22.1	8.3	23.2	2.76	2.62	2.47	2.33	4.24	4.28
1997	3.3	67.7	3.7	73.6	2.70	2.65	2.42	2.37	4.17	4.32
NEW BASIS										
1998	1.3	62.5	2.8	86.5	2.47	2.92	2.25	2.54	3.69	4.56
1999	-2.7	63.5	-6.3	87.7	2.49	2.90	2.27	2.54	3.75	4.56
2000	-1.4	55.9	-3.0	77.6	2.51	2.90	2.29	2.56	3.82	4.61
2001	0.0	-38.3	0.2	-51.4	2.33	2.81	2.13	2.47	3.55	4.44
2002	-2.5	22.5	-5.2	27.1	2.38	2.84	2.17	2.50	3.71	4.56
2003	0.1	14.0	0.2	19.2	2.33	2.71	2.10	2.39	3.57	4.29
2004	8.8	55.3	13.5	70.3	2.39	2.73	2.17	2.40	3.71	4.31
2005	0.2	57.3	0.4	61.5	2.42	2.71	2.20	2.39	3.80	4.29
2006	-3.6	72.6	-6.3	89.1	2.42	2.72	2.21	2.41	3.83	4.32
2007	0.6	33.3	-1.4	40.6	2.51	2.70	2.28	2.40	4.01	4.32
2008	-0.5	-28.7	-0.6	-31.5	2.50	2.76	2.28	2.46	4.14	4.56
2009	-6.7	-144.1	-10.0	-165.2	2.38	2.59	2.17	2.29	4.00	4.28
2010	-12.2	66.1	-17.8	70.2	2.49	2.58	2.26	2.31	4.20	4.31
2011	-2.1	48.3	-2.2	48.4	2.58	2.57	2.32	2.30	4.29	4.25
2012	-18.7	89.9	-18.7	89.9	2.55	2.56	2.32	2.33	4.26	4.27
2013	11.7	92.8	10.4	98.2	2.52	2.60	2.29	2.36	4.19	4.27
2014	-3.2	87.2	-3.5	90.1	2.47	2.59	2.24	2.36	4.10	4.26
2015	1.5	135.3	1.1	136.5	2.40	2.68	2.21	2.46	4.09	4.45
2016	-5.9	42.2	-6.7	41.2	2.38	2.65	2.22	2.44	4.13	4.39
2017	-5.2	34.6	-6.4	38.6	2.36	2.58	2.20	2.38	4.07	4.25
2018	-7.9	66.7	-9.1	72.7	2.36	2.58	2.22	2.39	4.14	4.27
2019	-15.3	88.9	-17.2	89.0	2.31	2.56	2.18	2.39	4.02	4.21
2020	-6.0	-53.6	-7.7	-35.3	2.38	2.62	2.26	2.45	3.95	4.06
2018										
1st quarter	-4.9	50.8	-4.9	67.5	2.37	2.58	2.21	2.38	4.11	4.24
2nd quarter	-6.1	30.3	-6.7	17.0	2.35	2.55	2.20	2.35	4.07	4.17
3rd quarter	-9.0	86.2	-10.9	108.5	2.36	2.57	2.22	2.38	4.14	4.24
4th quarter	-11.7	99.4	-14.1	97.8	2.36	2.58	2.22	2.39	4.14	4.27
2019										
1st quarter	-18.7	137.2	-17.1	145.7	2.39	2.60	2.24	2.41	4.15	4.28
2nd quarter	-16.5	104.9	-17.3	98.7	2.35	2.59	2.22	2.41	4.10	4.26
3rd quarter	-15.1	82.1	-20.1	83.7	2.32	2.58	2.20	2.41	4.06	4.24
4th quarter	-10.8	31.4	-14.3	27.8	2.31	2.56	2.18	2.39	4.02	4.21
2020										
1st quarter	-10.9	-9.7	-16.8	-15.4	2.30	2.60	2.18	2.43	3.95	4.19
2nd quarter	-7.2	-282.7	-8.1	-242.3	2.53	2.84	2.41	2.66	4.12	4.33
3rd quarter	-3.6	18.6	-2.1	26.4	2.35	2.63	2.24	2.46	3.89	4.07
4th quarter	-2.2	59.4	-3.9	90.2	2.38	2.62	2.26	2.45	3.95	4.06

[1]Before 1997, 2005 dollars; 1997 forward, 2012 dollars.

Table 1-8B. Inventory Change and Inventory-Sales Ratios: Historical Data

(Quarterly dollar data are at seasonally adjusted annual rates.)   **NIPA Tables 5.7.5B, 5.7.6B, 5.8.5B, 5.8.6B**

Year and quarter	Change in private inventories				Ratio, inventories at end of quarter to monthly rate of sales during the quarter					
	Billions of current dollars		Billions of chained dollars [1]		Total private inventories to final sales of domestic business		Nonfarm inventories to final sales of domestic business		Nonfarm inventories to final sales of goods and structures	
	Farm	Nonfarm	Farm	Nonfarm	Current dollars	Chained dollars[1]	Current dollars	Chained dollars[1]	Current dollars	Chained dollars[1]
OLD BASIS										
1929	-0.1	1.7	-0.6	10.6	...	...	...	...	...	...
1930	-0.3	0.0	-1.7	-2.4	...	...	...	...	...	...
1931	0.5	-1.6	3.1	-13.4	...	...	...	...	...	...
1932	0.1	-2.5	0.8	-21.2	...	...	...	...	...	...
1933	-0.1	-1.3	-1.1	-9.4	...	...	...	...	...	...
1934	-0.8	0.2	-5.7	1.0	...	...	...	...	...	...
1935	0.7	0.4	4.0	2.5	...	...	...	...	...	...
1936	-0.9	2.0	-5.4	15.5	...	...	...	...	...	...
1937	0.9	1.7	4.1	7.9	...	...	...	...	...	...
1938	0.4	-1.0	2.8	-6.0	...	...	...	...	...	...
1939	-0.1	0.3	-1.1	2.7	...	...	...	...	...	...
1940	0.5	1.9	2.8	12.4	...	...	...	...	...	...
1941	0.4	3.9	1.9	24.3	...	...	...	...	...	...
1942	1.3	0.6	5.6	3.0	...	...	...	...	...	...
1943	-0.2	-0.5	-1.1	-2.3	...	...	...	...	...	...
1944	-0.3	-0.6	-1.5	-2.5	...	...	...	...	...	...
1945	-0.9	-0.6	-3.3	-3.8	...	...	...	...	...	...
1946	-0.2	6.2	-1.0	31.8	...	...	...	...	...	...
1947	-1.8	1.2	-4.5	4.4	...	...	...	...	...	...
1948	2.7	3.0	6.1	12.4	...	...	...	...	...	...
1949	-0.6	-2.1	-1.9	-8.6	...	...	...	...	...	...
1950	-0.1	5.9	-0.3	22.8	...	...	...	...	...	...
1951	1.0	8.9	2.1	28.4	5.81	3.67	3.04	2.30	3.94	3.97
1952	1.4	2.1	3.1	7.4	5.85	3.76	3.15	2.46	4.07	4.24
1953	0.7	1.2	2.0	4.5	5.24	3.74	3.06	2.45	3.98	4.23
1954	0.2	-2.1	0.5	-7.5	4.74	3.52	2.88	2.28	3.81	3.94
1948										
1st quarter	1.3	2.4	1.6	11.7	6.00	3.76	2.87	2.27	3.71	3.96
2nd quarter	2.8	3.0	7.7	11.9	6.02	3.81	2.89	2.30	3.76	4.03
3rd quarter	3.4	3.7	8.3	15.0	5.88	3.88	2.97	2.34	3.85	4.10
4th quarter	3.1	2.9	6.6	11.1	5.74	3.91	3.00	2.36	3.90	4.13
1949										
1st quarter	-0.2	0.6	-1.2	-0.4	5.66	3.90	2.97	2.36	3.88	4.14
2nd quarter	-1.2	-4.0	-3.0	-15.1	5.38	3.82	2.83	2.30	3.70	4.02
3rd quarter	-0.9	-0.4	-2.3	-0.6	5.39	3.81	2.82	2.29	3.69	4.00
4th quarter	-0.2	-4.5	-0.9	-18.4	5.23	3.73	2.77	2.23	3.61	3.87
1950										
1st quarter	-0.1	2.2	-1.0	9.7	5.26	3.69	2.76	2.22	3.61	3.84
2nd quarter	-1.3	4.2	-2.5	16.2	5.27	3.62	2.75	2.20	3.57	3.79
3rd quarter	0.5	3.7	0.6	15.2	5.21	3.47	2.72	2.12	3.50	3.63
4th quarter	0.7	13.4	1.5	50.2	5.81	3.67	3.04	2.30	3.94	3.97
1951										
1st quarter	1.2	9.2	2.6	29.0	5.94	3.68	3.12	2.33	4.01	4.01
2nd quarter	0.9	13.8	2.5	44.3	5.99	3.81	3.25	2.45	4.23	4.28
3rd quarter	0.8	9.0	1.6	29.3	5.89	3.79	3.20	2.47	4.16	4.29
4th quarter	1.1	3.6	1.7	11.0	5.85	3.76	3.15	2.46	4.07	4.24
1952										
1st quarter	1.0	3.8	2.7	12.8	5.77	3.79	3.16	2.49	4.11	4.31
2nd quarter	1.9	-3.4	3.6	-10.5	5.63	3.75	3.08	2.44	4.01	4.24
3rd quarter	2.2	3.4	4.5	11.2	5.63	3.85	3.15	2.51	4.13	4.38
4th quarter	0.5	4.8	1.5	16.2	5.24	3.74	3.06	2.45	3.98	4.23
1953										
1st quarter	0.8	3.1	2.5	10.6	5.06	3.69	3.02	2.42	3.93	4.17
2nd quarter	-0.7	4.3	-0.2	14.1	5.00	3.69	3.06	2.43	3.99	4.20
3rd quarter	0.7	1.6	1.8	5.8	4.99	3.72	3.09	2.45	4.05	4.23
4th quarter	2.1	-4.1	3.8	-12.3	5.04	3.74	3.08	2.45	4.04	4.22
1954										
1st quarter	0.8	-2.8	2.1	-9.2	5.02	3.72	3.04	2.42	4.01	4.20
2nd quarter	-0.2	-3.2	0.5	-10.8	4.91	3.66	2.98	2.38	3.93	4.11
3rd quarter	0.7	-2.8	0.8	-9.1	4.85	3.59	2.93	2.32	3.89	4.04
4th quarter	-0.5	0.2	-1.5	-0.9	4.74	3.52	2.88	2.28	3.81	3.94
1955										
1st quarter	-0.1	3.9	-1.7	14.0	4.68	3.46	2.86	2.25	3.77	3.88
2nd quarter	-1.1	5.7	-2.1	20.0	4.57	3.44	2.87	2.26	3.73	3.83
3rd quarter	-1.3	5.6	-2.0	17.9	4.47	3.42	2.89	2.26	3.77	3.85
4th quarter	0.3	6.9	-1.6	22.7	4.43	3.44	2.95	2.29	3.87	3.94
1956										
1st quarter	0.0	6.4	-2.9	20.8	4.50	3.48	3.00	2.33	3.96	4.02
2nd quarter	-1.5	5.0	-3.4	16.2	4.57	3.48	3.03	2.35	3.99	4.04
3rd quarter	-0.8	4.3	-3.2	13.2	4.50	3.48	3.02	2.36	3.98	4.07
4th quarter	-1.6	3.9	-3.3	12.1	4.47	3.45	3.03	2.35	4.00	4.07
1957										
1st quarter	0.3	1.9	-0.9	5.7	4.44	3.44	3.02	2.35	3.97	4.05
2nd quarter	0.7	2.0	-0.2	6.8	4.48	3.48	3.04	2.38	4.00	4.11
3rd quarter	0.5	2.3	1.8	7.5	4.46	3.47	3.03	2.38	3.99	4.10
4th quarter	-1.0	-3.5	1.1	-10.2	4.46	3.48	3.01	2.37	4.01	4.14

[1]Before 1997, 2005 dollars; 1997 forward, 2009 dollars.
. . . = Not available.

Table 1-8B. Inventory Change and Inventory-Sales Ratios: Historical Data—*Continued*

(Quarterly dollar data are at seasonally adjusted annual rates.)   **NIPA Tables 5.7.5B, 5.7.6B, 5.8.5B, 5.8.6B**

Year and quarter	Change in private inventories				Ratio, inventories at end of quarter to monthly rate of sales during the quarter					
	Billions of current dollars		Billions of chained dollars [1]		Total private inventories to final sales of domestic business		Nonfarm inventories to final sales of domestic business		Nonfarm inventories to final sales of goods and structures	
	Farm	Nonfarm	Farm	Nonfarm	Current dollars	Chained dollars[1]	Current dollars	Chained dollars[1]	Current dollars	Chained dollars[1]
1958										
1st quarter	2.2	-6.3	7.6	-20.4	4.67	3.56	3.04	2.41	4.06	4.20
2nd quarter	1.6	-5.8	6.9	-18.6	4.65	3.56	3.00	2.38	4.00	4.17
3rd quarter	2.2	-0.7	6.2	-2.5	4.58	3.48	2.92	2.32	3.92	4.07
4th quarter	1.8	3.4	2.5	10.6	4.50	3.44	2.90	2.30	3.88	4.00
1959										
1st quarter	-0.3	4.2	-3.5	14.9	4.37	3.35	2.83	2.25	3.79	3.93
2nd quarter	-1.9	9.2	-5.3	33.8	4.33	3.34	2.86	2.27	3.85	3.98
3rd quarter	-2.3	2.6	-5.4	9.6	4.25	3.31	2.84	2.27	3.82	3.96
4th quarter	-1.8	5.9	-4.6	21.1	4.26	3.37	2.90	2.32	3.94	4.08
1960										
1st quarter	0.6	10.6	0.4	39.0	4.29	3.37	2.93	2.35	3.96	4.10
2nd quarter	0.9	2.4	1.9	9.0	4.21	3.36	2.91	2.34	3.95	4.11
3rd quarter	1.0	3.3	3.1	12.1	4.27	3.41	2.95	2.38	3.99	4.15
4th quarter	-0.2	-5.6	1.5	-20.2	4.22	3.37	2.89	2.34	3.93	4.10
1961										
1st quarter	0.6	-3.1	2.5	-11.3	4.19	3.35	2.86	2.32	3.90	4.07
2nd quarter	0.6	1.2	2.2	4.7	4.12	3.33	2.83	2.30	3.89	4.07
3rd quarter	0.9	5.7	2.6	21.0	4.17	3.35	2.85	2.32	3.89	4.08
4th quarter	1.4	4.6	2.8	16.8	4.12	3.30	2.81	2.29	3.84	4.03
1962										
1st quarter	1.5	7.9	2.5	29.0	4.15	3.32	2.82	2.32	3.85	4.07
2nd quarter	0.2	5.2	0.8	19.2	4.09	3.29	2.80	2.31	3.84	4.06
3rd quarter	0.2	5.9	1.4	22.0	4.17	3.32	2.83	2.33	3.87	4.09
4th quarter	0.4	3.0	2.2	11.3	4.14	3.32	2.82	2.34	3.87	4.11
1963										
1st quarter	1.9	4.9	7.5	18.2	4.12	3.34	2.83	2.35	3.87	4.12
2nd quarter	0.1	4.8	0.7	17.4	4.04	3.29	2.79	2.32	3.83	4.08
3rd quarter	-0.6	6.4	-1.7	23.6	4.00	3.27	2.79	2.33	3.81	4.07
4th quarter	0.6	4.5	-0.8	16.7	3.95	3.25	2.78	2.32	3.81	4.07
1964										
1st quarter	-0.6	5.8	-3.9	21.1	3.85	3.19	2.74	2.29	3.75	4.01
2nd quarter	-1.2	5.7	-4.3	20.7	3.79	3.17	2.73	2.29	3.75	4.02
3rd quarter	-1.8	6.5	-4.2	23.8	3.78	3.15	2.73	2.29	3.74	4.00
4th quarter	-1.1	6.1	-3.1	21.7	3.79	3.17	2.75	2.31	3.79	4.07
1965										
1st quarter	0.3	11.2	0.9	40.8	3.81	3.17	2.76	2.33	3.79	4.08
2nd quarter	1.1	7.4	2.9	26.9	3.82	3.15	2.75	2.32	3.79	4.08
3rd quarter	0.8	8.5	3.1	30.5	3.78	3.14	2.76	2.32	3.78	4.06
4th quarter	1.0	6.6	3.2	23.7	3.77	3.09	2.72	2.29	3.71	3.99
1966										
1st quarter	0.6	13.2	1.1	46.8	3.80	3.09	2.73	2.31	3.71	4.00
2nd quarter	-1.7	14.0	-2.7	50.2	3.86	3.16	2.80	2.38	3.83	4.16
3rd quarter	-0.6	12.4	-1.7	43.7	3.91	3.19	2.84	2.42	3.88	4.22
4th quarter	-0.4	16.9	-2.3	59.9	3.92	3.26	2.92	2.50	4.01	4.38
1967										
1st quarter	1.7	13.7	3.4	48.6	3.94	3.32	2.98	2.55	4.11	4.50
2nd quarter	2.1	4.2	7.6	14.7	3.92	3.31	2.95	2.54	4.07	4.46
3rd quarter	0.5	8.7	1.4	29.7	3.92	3.34	2.97	2.57	4.10	4.52
4th quarter	-0.9	9.3	-2.2	33.1	3.90	3.35	2.99	2.59	4.14	4.57
1968										
1st quarter	3.0	5.4	7.3	19.1	3.87	3.32	2.94	2.57	4.08	4.51
2nd quarter	4.3	9.8	13.4	33.9	3.87	3.34	2.93	2.58	4.07	4.55
3rd quarter	0.2	7.5	1.2	25.1	3.81	3.32	2.90	2.56	4.03	4.51
4th quarter	-2.0	8.0	-5.5	27.8	3.79	3.33	2.90	2.58	4.03	4.56
1969										
1st quarter	1.8	9.7	3.9	33.0	3.79	3.32	2.90	2.59	4.02	4.54
2nd quarter	1.4	7.8	4.4	26.6	3.83	3.35	2.91	2.61	4.06	4.61
3rd quarter	-1.2	11.4	-2.5	38.6	3.83	3.38	2.94	2.64	4.10	4.67
4th quarter	-1.9	7.7	-5.8	25.5	3.88	3.40	2.98	2.68	4.18	4.76
1970										
1st quarter	1.6	0.2	3.4	0.0	3.86	3.38	2.96	2.66	4.18	4.74
2nd quarter	0.4	4.7	1.9	14.9	3.85	3.40	2.96	2.68	4.20	4.80
3rd quarter	-1.8	6.9	-4.4	21.9	3.84	3.39	2.97	2.67	4.22	4.79
4th quarter	-3.5	-0.5	-10.3	-2.2	3.81	3.39	2.96	2.68	4.23	4.83
1971										
1st quarter	2.5	9.7	6.6	31.3	3.83	3.38	2.95	2.68	4.21	4.81
2nd quarter	4.2	6.7	10.7	20.6	3.81	3.39	2.94	2.68	4.20	4.81
3rd quarter	2.3	7.9	5.8	25.2	3.80	3.38	2.93	2.68	4.18	4.80
4th quarter	-2.3	2.0	-6.8	5.4	3.76	3.33	2.88	2.64	4.12	4.75
1972										
1st quarter	-0.5	3.7	0.1	11.1	3.72	3.30	2.84	2.62	4.06	4.69
2nd quarter	2.0	10.0	6.8	30.6	3.75	3.27	2.83	2.60	4.03	4.64
3rd quarter	1.0	12.7	1.9	38.5	3.77	3.26	2.83	2.60	4.05	4.66
4th quarter	-1.4	8.9	-7.1	26.5	3.74	3.18	2.77	2.55	3.94	4.53

[1] Before 1997, 2005 dollars; 1997 forward, 2009 dollars.

Table 1-8B. Inventory Change and Inventory-Sales Ratios: Historical Data—*Continued*

(Quarterly dollar data are at seasonally adjusted annual rates.)

NIPA Tables 5.7.5B, 5.7.6B, 5.8.5B, 5.8.6B

Year and quarter	Change in private inventories				Ratio, inventories at end of quarter to monthly rate of sales during the quarter					
	Billions of current dollars		Billions of chained dollars [1]		Total private inventories to final sales of domestic business		Nonfarm inventories to final sales of domestic business		Nonfarm inventories to final sales of goods and structures	
	Farm	Nonfarm	Farm	Nonfarm	Current dollars	Chained dollars[1]	Current dollars	Chained dollars[1]	Current dollars	Chained dollars[1]
1973										
1st quarter	-4.2	14.8	-10.7	42.9	3.86	3.11	2.79	2.52	3.92	4.45
2nd quarter	5.0	13.2	12.0	38.3	4.03	3.15	2.86	2.54	4.02	4.51
3rd quarter	2.6	7.2	3.5	20.0	4.11	3.16	2.87	2.56	4.05	4.55
4th quarter	2.8	22.2	2.3	60.9	4.20	3.22	2.98	2.62	4.22	4.67
1974										
1st quarter	-3.3	15.9	-5.2	39.7	4.26	3.27	3.13	2.68	4.42	4.76
2nd quarter	1.0	16.4	0.9	39.6	4.29	3.31	3.28	2.72	4.67	4.86
3rd quarter	-0.1	5.7	1.7	11.7	4.45	3.34	3.40	2.75	4.84	4.93
4th quarter	-8.7	29.2	-15.0	64.9	4.52	3.46	3.54	2.88	5.11	5.26
1975										
1st quarter	7.1	-17.1	16.4	-38.3	4.32	3.42	3.41	2.82	4.94	5.16
2nd quarter	3.1	-17.1	5.4	-38.6	4.26	3.35	3.30	2.75	4.81	5.06
3rd quarter	0.8	-2.2	-1.0	-5.0	4.18	3.31	3.24	2.71	4.69	4.95
4th quarter	2.5	-2.1	2.3	-3.7	4.04	3.26	3.16	2.66	4.59	4.88
1976										
1st quarter	-0.5	15.2	0.1	33.2	4.00	3.22	3.14	2.64	4.56	4.83
2nd quarter	-1.8	24.3	-1.9	51.8	4.07	3.26	3.21	2.69	4.67	4.91
3rd quarter	2.0	18.8	5.4	38.9	4.04	3.28	3.23	2.70	4.74	4.96
4th quarter	-3.0	13.6	-9.8	26.5	3.95	3.23	3.19	2.68	4.68	4.92
1977										
1st quarter	-1.3	16.1	-7.0	33.0	3.96	3.22	3.21	2.68	4.72	4.92
2nd quarter	5.3	14.2	11.3	27.8	3.88	3.19	3.16	2.65	4.62	4.84
3rd quarter	4.4	26.5	16.3	53.8	3.86	3.22	3.16	2.67	4.63	4.88
4th quarter	9.8	14.4	8.4	28.1	3.89	3.22	3.16	2.67	4.63	4.87
1978										
1st quarter	-0.6	26.1	-3.6	48.9	4.02	3.26	3.21	2.72	4.78	5.00
2nd quarter	0.4	23.9	0.2	44.2	3.92	3.14	3.12	2.62	4.55	4.75
3rd quarter	7.2	17.8	11.1	32.3	3.95	3.15	3.13	2.62	4.54	4.74
4th quarter	-1.5	30.0	0.5	54.1	3.98	3.14	3.15	2.63	4.54	4.73
1979										
1st quarter	4.2	19.6	6.6	33.0	4.15	3.17	3.22	2.65	4.66	4.78
2nd quarter	3.1	24.3	5.3	40.4	4.19	3.21	3.29	2.69	4.78	4.87
3rd quarter	6.6	5.5	7.0	8.2	4.16	3.16	3.28	2.64	4.74	4.73
4th quarter	0.3	8.3	-1.9	13.4	4.19	3.16	3.34	2.64	4.85	4.75
1980										
1st quarter	-0.6	10.5	-2.6	17.4	4.25	3.17	3.45	2.66	5.02	4.78
2nd quarter	-5.2	13.0	-5.9	19.3	4.40	3.28	3.57	2.76	5.26	5.02
3rd quarter	-12.5	-21.4	-14.2	-32.6	4.34	3.18	3.50	2.68	5.15	4.88
4th quarter	-6.1	-3.0	-6.0	-5.8	4.24	3.13	3.44	2.65	5.08	4.82
1981										
1st quarter	6.8	31.9	10.3	44.6	4.26	3.17	3.48	2.67	5.13	4.84
2nd quarter	9.9	1.8	10.9	1.7	4.24	3.18	3.47	2.67	5.15	4.87
3rd quarter	11.8	32.1	14.5	42.6	4.20	3.22	3.48	2.71	5.16	4.93
4th quarter	6.5	18.3	4.5	23.8	4.17	3.28	3.49	2.75	5.20	5.03
1982										
1st quarter	5.1	-26.5	6.7	-34.3	4.19	3.28	3.46	2.74	5.20	5.03
2nd quarter	4.3	-8.5	6.4	-12.2	4.15	3.28	3.42	2.74	5.17	5.04
3rd quarter	9.0	-3.2	12.0	-5.5	4.12	3.33	3.43	2.77	5.26	5.15
4th quarter	4.6	-44.4	4.9	-57.5	3.97	3.23	3.30	2.68	5.10	4.99
1983										
1st quarter	-7.3	-27.8	-10.4	-37.3	3.89	3.15	3.19	2.62	4.98	4.89
2nd quarter	-13.0	5.3	-12.6	6.5	3.81	3.09	3.14	2.58	4.89	4.80
3rd quarter	-32.4	28.2	-37.7	34.3	3.73	3.03	3.12	2.55	4.86	4.73
4th quarter	-8.8	32.7	-9.0	39.4	3.69	2.98	3.08	2.52	4.77	4.64
1984										
1st quarter	5.5	67.5	7.4	81.9	3.78	3.02	3.15	2.56	4.87	4.71
2nd quarter	5.6	63.7	6.4	77.2	3.76	3.03	3.16	2.57	4.88	4.69
3rd quarter	6.8	64.5	8.1	78.9	3.75	3.06	3.18	2.60	4.93	4.75
4th quarter	5.0	43.0	3.3	51.0	3.72	3.05	3.16	2.60	4.89	4.72
1985										
1st quarter	7.9	8.3	8.4	8.8	3.60	3.00	3.06	2.55	4.77	4.65
2nd quarter	4.2	17.4	4.8	20.3	3.55	2.99	3.04	2.55	4.76	4.66
3rd quarter	6.6	9.7	9.1	12.0	3.47	2.96	2.98	2.51	4.67	4.60
4th quarter	4.3	28.8	5.9	32.7	3.51	2.98	3.01	2.53	4.74	4.65
1986										
1st quarter	2.5	27.8	1.7	33.3	3.42	2.97	2.94	2.52	4.65	4.63
2nd quarter	-3.5	19.1	-5.9	22.3	3.37	2.97	2.92	2.53	4.63	4.65
3rd quarter	-3.1	-3.9	-4.3	-5.5	3.29	2.92	2.85	2.49	4.52	4.55
4th quarter	-1.8	-11.0	-0.6	-8.5	3.25	2.90	2.82	2.47	4.49	4.53
1987										
1st quarter	-7.7	35.6	-9.7	44.5	3.31	2.94	2.86	2.51	4.62	4.66
2nd quarter	-10.7	27.2	-14.5	33.1	3.30	2.90	2.86	2.49	4.60	4.60
3rd quarter	-4.0	5.0	-5.2	4.1	3.25	2.85	2.82	2.45	4.52	4.51
4th quarter	-3.3	66.4	-7.0	82.5	3.33	2.90	2.90	2.50	4.65	4.62

[1] Before 1997, 2005 dollars; 1997 forward, 2009 dollars.

Table 1-8B. Inventory Change and Inventory-Sales Ratios: Historical Data—*Continued*

(Quarterly dollar data are at seasonally adjusted annual rates.)   **NIPA Tables 5.7.5B, 5.7.6B, 5.8.5B, 5.8.6B**

Year and quarter	Change in private inventories				Ratio, inventories at end of quarter to monthly rate of sales during the quarter					
	Billions of current dollars		Billions of chained dollars [1]		Total private inventories to final sales of domestic business		Nonfarm inventories to final sales of domestic business		Nonfarm inventories to final sales of goods and structures	
	Farm	Nonfarm	Farm	Nonfarm	Current dollars	Chained dollars[1]	Current dollars	Chained dollars[1]	Current dollars	Chained dollars[1]
1988										
1st quarter	-4.4	21.4	-7.6	25.1	3.30	2.86	2.86	2.47	4.61	4.56
2nd quarter	-12.2	31.9	-15.2	38.0	3.29	2.83	2.85	2.46	4.60	4.52
3rd quarter	-11.2	29.4	-11.4	32.6	3.30	2.83	2.85	2.47	4.63	4.57
4th quarter	-19.7	38.8	-18.3	45.9	3.29	2.81	2.86	2.47	4.63	4.55
1989										
1st quarter	7.2	41.0	7.8	46.6	3.32	2.83	2.89	2.48	4.70	4.58
2nd quarter	2.9	33.2	3.6	37.6	3.28	2.83	2.87	2.48	4.65	4.56
3rd quarter	-5.5	15.5	-5.8	16.9	3.21	2.79	2.82	2.45	4.55	4.49
4th quarter	-4.6	21.2	-5.6	22.3	3.23	2.80	2.83	2.47	4.63	4.56
1990										
1st quarter	1.8	12.1	1.7	13.3	3.18	2.78	2.78	2.45	4.53	4.50
2nd quarter	-1.5	35.3	-2.6	39.9	3.17	2.81	2.78	2.47	4.58	4.60
3rd quarter	4.0	17.9	4.4	20.3	3.20	2.82	2.82	2.48	4.67	4.63
4th quarter	5.2	-16.6	6.7	-17.7	3.22	2.83	2.82	2.49	4.71	4.66
1991										
1st quarter	0.0	-15.6	0.7	-18.1	3.18	2.85	2.78	2.51	4.65	4.71
2nd quarter	-0.7	-17.3	-0.5	-20.6	3.08	2.81	2.70	2.47	4.55	4.66
3rd quarter	-10.9	11.7	-13.8	13.1	3.04	2.81	2.69	2.48	4.54	4.67
4th quarter	6.4	24.7	6.1	27.1	3.06	2.83	2.70	2.50	4.62	4.74
1992										
1st quarter	8.0	-7.8	10.5	-7.5	3.00	2.78	2.63	2.44	4.52	4.64
2nd quarter	9.4	13.8	10.9	13.2	2.99	2.77	2.62	2.43	4.50	4.61
3rd quarter	5.1	15.4	4.7	16.6	2.96	2.75	2.60	2.41	4.47	4.57
4th quarter	2.5	18.9	2.4	21.6	2.92	2.73	2.56	2.39	4.41	4.53
1993										
1st quarter	-5.6	41.6	-6.2	46.5	2.95	2.75	2.58	2.42	4.47	4.60
2nd quarter	-4.9	29.0	-5.3	32.3	2.92	2.74	2.57	2.41	4.44	4.56
3rd quarter	-12.5	19.1	-14.2	20.6	2.89	2.72	2.54	2.40	4.42	4.55
4th quarter	-1.7	18.3	-4.1	19.9	2.85	2.68	2.51	2.38	4.33	4.47
1994										
1st quarter	16.5	28.8	19.4	31.1	2.87	2.69	2.51	2.38	4.33	4.48
2nd quarter	17.1	64.3	21.0	70.0	2.86	2.71	2.53	2.39	4.37	4.49
3rd quarter	10.7	42.5	10.6	46.1	2.86	2.71	2.53	2.39	4.36	4.48
4th quarter	3.7	71.5	3.7	76.3	2.89	2.72	2.56	2.40	4.39	4.47
1995										
1st quarter	-5.8	67.0	-5.9	71.2	2.93	2.75	2.62	2.43	4.49	4.52
2nd quarter	-13.7	47.4	-13.6	50.1	2.94	2.75	2.64	2.44	4.55	4.55
3rd quarter	-20.4	31.7	-26.4	32.8	2.90	2.71	2.60	2.41	4.49	4.50
4th quarter	-4.4	22.8	-6.2	22.9	2.88	2.69	2.58	2.40	4.45	4.46
1996										
1st quarter	1.1	5.8	-2.9	6.2	2.84	2.66	2.55	2.38	4.39	4.42
2nd quarter	11.8	18.6	7.4	19.8	2.81	2.63	2.51	2.35	4.30	4.35
3rd quarter	17.1	34.0	27.4	35.0	2.81	2.65	2.50	2.35	4.29	4.34
4th quarter	4.5	30.2	1.3	31.7	2.76	2.62	2.47	2.33	4.24	4.28
1997										
1st quarter	-0.5	50.3	-10.8	53.3	2.74	2.62	2.45	2.33	4.21	4.28
2nd quarter	0.8	87.6	8.2	95.7	2.73	2.65	2.44	2.36	4.21	4.33
3rd quarter	8.3	59.6	10.1	65.5	2.69	2.63	2.41	2.34	4.14	4.27
4th quarter	4.7	73.1	7.2	79.8	2.70	2.65	2.42	2.37	4.17	4.32
1998										
1st quarter	-0.6	50.3	-13.5	45.4	2.66	2.93	2.37	2.54	3.91	4.62
2nd quarter	0.8	87.6	13.1	130.9	2.64	2.97	2.36	2.57	3.90	4.67
3rd quarter	8.3	59.6	15.1	82.4	2.60	2.94	2.33	2.55	3.83	4.61
4th quarter	4.6	73.0	10.0	93.4	2.60	2.97	2.34	2.57	3.86	4.65
NEW BASIS										
1998										
1st quarter	5.6	99.5	9.4	144.4	2.60	2.99	2.34	2.60	3.87	4.71
2nd quarter	-4.9	42.2	-4.0	57.0	2.55	2.96	2.30	2.57	3.81	4.66
3rd quarter	0.5	51.9	4.5	65.5	2.51	2.95	2.28	2.56	3.75	4.63
4th quarter	3.8	56.2	1.3	79.1	2.47	2.92	2.25	2.54	3.69	4.56
1999										
1st quarter	4.1	79.3	-2.9	114.9	2.48	2.94	2.25	2.56	3.71	4.61
2nd quarter	-0.2	35.3	1.6	46.9	2.46	2.91	2.24	2.54	3.68	4.56
3rd quarter	-9.1	49.6	-18.1	71.1	2.46	2.89	2.25	2.53	3.70	4.55
4th quarter	-5.7	90.0	-5.9	118.0	2.49	2.90	2.27	2.54	3.75	4.56
2000										
1st quarter	-17.7	33.9	-30.9	40.7	2.48	2.86	2.26	2.52	3.75	4.52
2nd quarter	5.9	84.5	10.4	112.1	2.48	2.87	2.27	2.53	3.76	4.55
3rd quarter	-1.1	58.4	-3.5	86.1	2.48	2.89	2.28	2.55	3.79	4.59
4th quarter	7.3	47.0	11.8	71.5	2.51	2.90	2.29	2.56	3.82	4.61
2001										
1st quarter	5.6	-36.2	10.0	-50.7	2.48	2.88	2.26	2.54	3.80	4.57
2nd quarter	-3.0	-8.6	-5.0	0.8	2.44	2.88	2.23	2.53	3.72	4.56
3rd quarter	1.8	-31.9	2.6	-46.8	2.41	2.88	2.20	2.53	3.69	4.56
4th quarter	-4.3	-76.6	-6.9	-108.8	2.33	2.81	2.13	2.47	3.55	4.44

[1] Before 1997, 2005 dollars; 1997 forward, 2009 dollars.

Table 1-8B. Inventory Change and Inventory-Sales Ratios: Historical Data—*Continued*

(Quarterly dollar data are at seasonally adjusted annual rates.) NIPA Tables 5.7.5B, 5.7.6B, 5.8.5B, 5.8.6B

| Year and quarter | Change in private inventories | | | | Ratio, inventories at end of quarter to monthly rate of sales during the quarter | | | | | |
| | Billions of current dollars | | Billions of chained dollars [1] | | Total private inventories to final sales of domestic business | | Nonfarm inventories to final sales of domestic business | | Nonfarm inventories to final sales of goods and structures | |
	Farm	Nonfarm	Farm	Nonfarm	Current dollars	Chained dollars[1]	Current dollars	Chained dollars[1]	Current dollars	Chained dollars[1]
2002										
1st quarter	4.1	-3.8	4.1	-10.2	2.31	2.81	2.11	2.47	3.54	4.46
2nd quarter	-10.3	31.5	-16.4	43.0	2.32	2.82	2.12	2.48	3.60	4.51
3rd quarter	-2.9	28.3	-5.6	31.5	2.35	2.82	2.14	2.48	3.65	4.51
4th quarter	-0.8	33.8	-3.0	44.1	2.38	2.84	2.17	2.50	3.71	4.56
2003										
1st quarter	2.8	23.2	4.9	35.1	2.42	2.83	2.21	2.49	3.78	4.54
2nd quarter	-1.4	-5.1	-1.5	-7.9	2.37	2.79	2.15	2.46	3.70	4.46
3rd quarter	0.9	-0.4	0.3	2.5	2.33	2.73	2.10	2.40	3.58	4.31
4th quarter	-2.1	38.4	-2.9	47.3	2.33	2.71	2.10	2.39	3.57	4.29
2004										
1st quarter	4.4	41.6	8.6	50.7	2.36	2.73	2.13	2.40	3.65	4.32
2nd quarter	18.4	55.5	23.7	77.1	2.39	2.74	2.15	2.41	3.69	4.34
3rd quarter	7.7	56.5	12.6	71.5	2.39	2.73	2.17	2.40	3.71	4.31
4th quarter	4.7	67.4	9.0	82.0	2.39	2.73	2.17	2.40	3.71	4.31
2005										
1st quarter	-6.7	109.2	-7.6	126.7	2.41	2.74	2.19	2.42	3.76	4.33
2nd quarter	0.9	27.9	1.2	23.0	2.37	2.71	2.16	2.39	3.70	4.27
3rd quarter	4.3	8.0	5.0	4.1	2.38	2.68	2.17	2.37	3.70	4.22
4th quarter	2.3	84.1	2.9	92.4	2.42	2.71	2.20	2.39	3.80	4.29
2006										
1st quarter	3.7	74.5	2.6	98.0	2.38	2.70	2.18	2.38	3.73	4.23
2nd quarter	-8.1	83.6	-11.0	97.5	2.42	2.71	2.22	2.40	3.81	4.28
3rd quarter	-6.3	85.1	-9.4	101.2	2.44	2.74	2.23	2.43	3.85	4.35
4th quarter	-3.6	47.1	-7.1	59.7	2.42	2.72	2.21	2.41	3.83	4.32
2007										
1st quarter	7.9	13.4	5.3	22.6	2.44	2.71	2.22	2.41	3.85	4.33
2nd quarter	-4.1	46.4	5.9	50.4	2.46	2.71	2.24	2.41	3.89	4.32
3rd quarter	-1.7	46.6	-15.5	54.3	2.46	2.71	2.24	2.41	3.91	4.33
4th quarter	0.4	26.9	-1.4	35.2	2.51	2.70	2.28	2.40	4.01	4.32
2008										
1st quarter	-8.6	-8.1	-6.1	6.5	2.61	2.72	2.37	2.42	4.21	4.38
2nd quarter	3.8	-26.1	2.1	-26.6	2.71	2.69	2.46	2.39	4.39	4.33
3rd quarter	4.1	-20.0	2.3	-20.7	2.68	2.72	2.44	2.42	4.37	4.39
4th quarter	-1.5	-60.8	-0.8	-85.0	2.50	2.76	2.28	2.46	4.14	4.56
2009										
1st quarter	-4.8	-146.2	-8.6	-168.1	2.43	2.75	2.21	2.44	4.02	4.56
2nd quarter	-6.3	-189.7	-9.5	-215.3	2.40	2.69	2.19	2.38	3.98	4.45
3rd quarter	-10.9	-193.1	-13.5	-228.3	2.35	2.60	2.14	2.30	3.91	4.29
4th quarter	-4.6	-47.4	-8.4	-49.0	2.38	2.59	2.17	2.29	4.00	4.28
2010										
1st quarter	-6.6	5.3	-14.0	6.1	2.42	2.59	2.21	2.29	4.10	4.29
2nd quarter	-11.7	48.4	-16.5	45.2	2.40	2.57	2.19	2.28	4.07	4.26
3rd quarter	-16.5	129.4	-20.6	141.9	2.45	2.60	2.24	2.31	4.18	4.35
4th quarter	-13.9	81.2	-20.0	87.7	2.49	2.58	2.26	2.31	4.20	4.31
2011										
1st quarter	-2.1	34.2	-2.1	34.3	2.60	2.59	2.34	2.31	4.37	4.33
2nd quarter	-5.7	66.8	-4.1	74.4	2.62	2.59	2.37	2.32	4.41	4.33
3rd quarter	-1.2	-10.8	-2.2	-15.4	2.58	2.56	2.33	2.29	4.32	4.26
4th quarter	0.7	103.2	-0.4	100.2	2.58	2.57	2.32	2.30	4.29	4.25
2012										
1st quarter	-6.4	86.7	-10.8	83.7	2.57	2.55	2.32	2.29	4.27	4.22
2nd quarter	-15.4	106.8	-16.4	103.3	2.54	2.56	2.30	2.31	4.22	4.23
3rd quarter	-29.9	114.3	-25.1	122.8	2.57	2.58	2.34	2.34	4.28	4.29
4th quarter	-23.1	51.8	-22.5	49.8	2.55	2.56	2.32	2.33	4.26	4.27
2013										
1st quarter	2.4	79.9	0.1	80.7	2.51	2.56	2.30	2.33	4.21	4.24
2nd quarter	15.0	72.7	12.4	73.7	2.51	2.58	2.30	2.35	4.21	4.27
3rd quarter	17.4	118.8	15.0	132.5	2.52	2.60	2.30	2.36	4.20	4.29
4th quarter	11.9	100.0	14.1	105.9	2.52	2.60	2.29	2.36	4.19	4.27
2014										
1st quarter	-3.5	55.7	-5.1	63.3	2.57	2.62	2.33	2.38	4.28	4.31
2nd quarter	0.0	96.3	-3.1	102.0	2.54	2.60	2.30	2.37	4.21	4.27
3rd quarter	-2.0	101.5	-1.5	108.1	2.51	2.59	2.28	2.36	4.15	4.25
4th quarter	-7.4	95.2	-4.4	87.0	2.47	2.59	2.24	2.36	4.10	4.26
2015										
1st quarter	5.9	169.7	4.8	173.1	2.45	2.63	2.22	2.40	4.10	4.36
2nd quarter	2.2	147.8	2.2	154.7	2.44	2.65	2.23	2.42	4.09	4.38
3rd quarter	-1.9	128.7	-1.5	126.4	2.41	2.67	2.22	2.44	4.07	4.41
4th quarter	-0.1	94.8	-1.2	91.8	2.40	2.68	2.21	2.46	4.09	4.45
2016										
1st quarter	-12.5	67.0	-11.8	69.7	2.39	2.67	2.20	2.45	4.07	4.43
2nd quarter	-3.2	33.6	-4.3	26.7	2.39	2.66	2.22	2.45	4.11	4.41
3rd quarter	-0.6	4.0	-1.7	-4.7	2.36	2.64	2.20	2.42	4.08	4.36
4th quarter	-7.4	64.2	-8.9	73.1	2.38	2.65	2.22	2.44	4.13	4.39
2017										
1st quarter	-5.4	0.8	-6.4	-7.5	2.38	2.61	2.21	2.41	4.11	4.32
2nd quarter	-5.1	26.2	-5.7	23.3	2.38	2.61	2.20	2.40	4.10	4.30
3rd quarter	-5.4	64.5	-6.9	88.2	2.36	2.61	2.21	2.41	4.09	4.30
4th quarter	-4.7	47.1	-6.8	50.5	2.36	2.58	2.20	2.38	4.07	4.25

[1]Before 1997, 2005 dollars; 1997 forward, 2009 dollars.

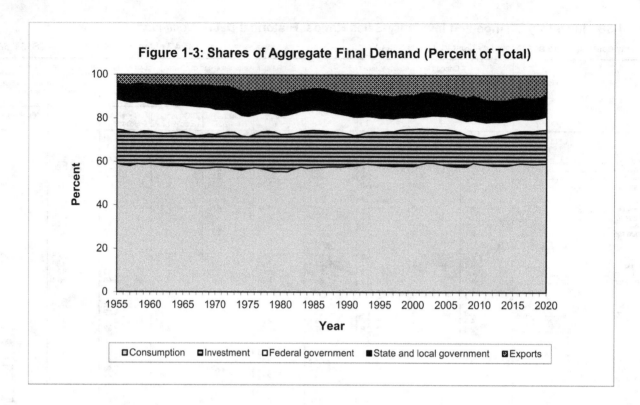

Figure 1-3: Shares of Aggregate Final Demand (Percent of Total)

- People often want to know how various sources of demand, especially consumption spending, affect GDP. Often, it is said that consumption "accounts for" about 70 percent, or sometimes two-thirds, of GDP. That is based on a NIPA table showing the components of GDP as a percent of total GDP. In such a calculation, personal consumption expenditures (PCE) amounted to slightly more than 67 percent of total GDP in 2020, up from a range of 60 to 65 percent earlier in the postwar period but a slight decline from 2019. (Table 1-1A)

- Is "amounted to" the same as "accounted for"? No, because the value of PCE includes imported goods and services—coffee, cocoa, and bananas; crude oil from the Middle East, transformed into gasoline; clothing, cars, and toys manufactured overseas— even the money that U.S. consumers spend when they travel. These imports included in PCE don't account for demand for U.S. GDP, which excludes imports; instead, they account for demand for GDP in China and other countries that export to us.

- It is not possible with NIPA data to precisely estimate and subtract out the import content of PCE, and so there is no way to precisely estimate PCE's contribution to GDP. What we can do is calculate PCE and the other sources of aggregate final demand for U.S. output as shares of <u>total final demand</u>; this is shown in Table 1-10 and Figure 1-3. These shares also approximate their contributions to GDP (excluding inventory change) if each final demand source has, in aggregate, about the same percentage import content as total GDP.

- The share of imports in the total supply of goods and services in the U.S. market rose from around 4 percent in the 1950s to a high of 14.9 percent in 2008. By 2020, the import share decreased to 11.7 percent. Only in 2009, the year of maximum inventory liquidation, did the import share temporarily dip back to 12.1 percent. (Table 1-9)

Table 1-9. Shares of Aggregate Supply

(Billions of dollars, quarterly dollar data are at seasonally adjusted rates, percents.)   NIPA Table 1.1.5

Year and quarter	Aggregate supply (billions of dollars)			Shares of aggregate supply (percent)	
	Total	GDP	Imports	Domestic production (GDP)	Imports
1955	442.7	425.5	17.2	96.1	3.9
1956	468.3	449.4	18.9	96.0	4.0
1957	493.9	474.0	19.9	96.0	4.0
1958	501.2	481.2	20.0	96.0	4.0
1959	544.0	521.7	22.3	95.9	4.1
1960	565.2	542.4	22.8	96.0	4.0
1961	584.9	562.2	22.7	96.1	3.9
1962	628.9	603.9	25.0	96.0	4.0
1963	663.6	637.5	26.1	96.1	3.9
1964	712.6	684.5	28.1	96.1	3.9
1965	773.8	742.3	31.5	95.9	4.1
1966	850.5	813.4	37.1	95.6	4.4
1967	899.9	860.0	39.9	95.6	4.4
1968	987.3	940.7	46.6	95.3	4.7
1969	1 068.1	1 017.6	50.5	95.3	4.7
1970	1 129.1	1 073.3	55.8	95.1	4.9
1971	1 227.2	1 164.9	62.3	94.9	5.1
1972	1 353.3	1 279.1	74.2	94.5	5.5
1973	1 516.6	1 425.4	91.2	94.0	6.0
1974	1 672.7	1 545.2	127.5	92.4	7.6
1975	1 807.6	1 684.9	122.7	93.2	6.8
1976	2 024.5	1 873.4	151.1	92.5	7.5
1977	2 264.2	2 081.8	182.4	91.9	8.1
1978	2 563.9	2 351.6	212.3	91.7	8.3
1979	2 880.0	2 627.3	252.7	91.2	8.8
1980	3 151.1	2 857.3	293.8	90.7	9.3
1981	3 524.8	3 207.0	317.8	91.0	9.0
1982	3 647.0	3 343.8	303.2	91.7	8.3
1983	3 962.6	3 634.0	328.6	91.7	8.3
1984	4 442.7	4 037.6	405.1	90.9	9.1
1985	4 756.2	4 339.0	417.2	91.2	8.8
1986	5 032.5	4 579.6	452.9	91.0	9.0
1987	5 363.9	4 855.2	508.7	90.5	9.5
1988	5 790.4	5 236.4	554.0	90.4	9.6
1989	6 232.6	5 641.6	591.0	90.5	9.5
1990	6 592.8	5 963.1	629.7	90.4	9.6
1991	6 781.6	6 158.1	623.5	90.8	9.2
1992	7 188.1	6 520.3	667.8	90.7	9.3
1993	7 578.6	6 858.6	720.0	90.5	9.5
1994	8 100.6	7 287.2	813.4	90.0	10.0
1995	8 542.3	7 639.7	902.6	89.4	10.6
1996	9 037.1	8 073.1	964.0	89.3	10.7
1997	9 633.4	8 577.6	1 055.8	89.0	11.0
1998	10 178.5	9 062.8	1 115.7	89.0	11.0
1999	10 883.7	9 631.2	1 252.5	88.5	11.5
2000	11 728.2	10 251.0	1 477.2	87.4	12.6
2001	11 985.5	10 581.9	1 403.6	88.3	11.7
2002	12 366.8	10 929.1	1 437.7	88.4	11.6
2003	13 013.6	11 456.5	1 557.1	88.0	12.0
2004	14 027.7	12 217.2	1 810.5	87.1	12.9
2005	15 080.7	13 039.2	2 041.5	86.5	13.5
2006	16 072.2	13 815.6	2 256.6	86.0	14.0
2007	16 869.4	14 474.2	2 395.2	85.8	14.2
2008	17 346.1	14 769.9	2 576.2	85.1	14.9
2009	16 480.0	14 478.1	2 001.9	87.9	12.1
2010	17 438.6	15 049.0	2 389.6	86.3	13.7
2011	18 295.2	15 599.7	2 695.5	85.3	14.7
2012	19 023.3	16 254.0	2 769.3	85.4	14.6
2013	19 609.6	16 843.2	2 766.4	85.9	14.1
2014	20 438.1	17 550.7	2 887.4	85.9	14.1
2015	21 000.9	18 206.0	2 794.9	86.7	13.3
2016	21 433.5	18 695.1	2 738.4	87.2	12.8
2017	22 403.3	19 479.6	2 923.7	86.9	13.1
2018	23 656.9	20 527.2	3 129.7	86.8	13.2
2019	24 488.6	21 372.6	3 116.0	87.3	12.7
2020	23 668.3	20 893.7	2 774.6	88.3	11.7
2018					
1st quarter	23 228.2	20 143.7	3 084.5	86.7	13.3
2nd quarter	23 600.6	20 492.5	3 108.1	86.8	13.2
3rd quarter	23 817.3	20 659.1	3 158.2	86.7	13.3
4th quarter	23 981.4	20 813.3	3 168.1	86.8	13.2
2019					
1st quarter	24 132.6	21 001.6	3 131.0	87.0	13.0
2nd quarter	24 455.0	21 289.3	3 165.7	87.1	12.9
3rd quarter	24 631.1	21 505.0	3 126.1	87.3	12.7
4th quarter	24 735.6	21 694.5	3 041.1	87.7	12.3
2020					
1st quarter	24 408.7	21 481.4	2 927.3	88.0	12.0
2nd quarter	21 824.1	19 477.4	2 346.7	89.2	10.8
3rd quarter	23 943.9	21 138.6	2 805.3	88.3	11.7
4th quarter	24 496.7	21 477.6	3 019.1	87.7	12.3

Table 1-10. Shares of Aggregate Final Demand

(Billions of dollars, quarterly dollar data are at seasonally adjusted rates, percents.)

NIPA Table 1.1.5

Year and quarter	Aggregate final demand (billions of dollars)							Shares of aggregate final demand (percent)					
	Total	Consumption (PCE)	Nonresidential fixed investment	Residential investment	Exports	Government consumption and gross investment Federal	State and local	PCE	Nonresidential investment	Residential investment	Exports	Federal government	State and local government
1955	437.7	258.3	43.4	25.4	17.7	61.0	31.9	59.0	9.9	5.8	4.0	13.9	7.3
1956	464.3	271.1	49.7	24.0	21.3	63.1	35.1	58.4	10.7	5.2	4.6	13.6	7.6
1957	493.2	286.3	53.1	22.6	24.0	68.5	38.7	58.0	10.8	4.6	4.9	13.9	7.8
1958	501.6	295.6	48.5	22.8	20.6	71.5	42.6	58.9	9.7	4.5	4.1	14.3	8.5
1959	540.0	317.1	53.1	28.6	22.7	73.6	44.9	58.7	9.8	5.3	4.2	13.6	8.3
1960	562.0	331.2	56.4	26.9	27.0	72.9	47.6	58.9	10.0	4.8	4.8	13.0	8.5
1961	582.0	341.5	56.6	27.0	27.6	77.4	51.9	58.7	9.7	4.6	4.7	13.3	8.9
1962	622.8	362.6	61.2	29.6	29.1	85.5	54.8	58.2	9.8	4.8	4.7	13.7	8.8
1963	658.0	382.0	64.8	32.9	31.1	87.9	59.3	58.1	9.8	5.0	4.7	13.4	9.0
1964	707.7	410.6	72.2	35.1	35.0	90.3	64.5	58.0	10.2	5.0	4.9	12.8	9.1
1965	764.6	443.0	85.2	35.2	37.1	93.2	70.9	57.9	11.1	4.6	4.9	12.2	9.3
1966	836.9	479.9	97.2	33.4	40.9	106.6	78.9	57.3	11.6	4.0	4.9	12.7	9.4
1967	890.0	506.7	99.2	33.6	43.5	120.0	87.0	56.9	11.1	3.8	4.9	13.5	9.8
1968	978.3	556.9	107.7	40.2	47.9	128.0	97.6	56.9	11.0	4.1	4.9	13.1	10.0
1969	1 058.9	603.6	120.0	44.4	51.9	131.2	107.8	57.0	11.3	4.2	4.9	12.4	10.2
1970	1 127.0	646.7	124.6	43.4	59.7	132.8	119.8	57.4	11.1	3.9	5.3	11.8	10.6
1971	1 219.0	699.9	130.4	58.2	63.0	134.5	133.0	57.4	10.7	4.8	5.2	11.0	10.9
1972	1 344.1	768.2	146.6	72.4	70.8	141.6	144.5	57.2	10.9	5.4	5.3	10.5	10.8
1973	1 500.7	849.6	172.7	78.3	95.3	146.2	158.6	56.6	11.5	5.2	6.4	9.7	10.6
1974	1 658.8	930.2	191.1	69.5	126.7	158.8	182.5	56.1	11.5	4.2	7.6	9.6	11.0
1975	1 813.8	1 030.5	196.8	66.7	138.7	173.7	207.4	56.8	10.9	3.7	7.6	9.6	11.4
1976	2 007.5	1 147.7	219.3	86.8	149.5	184.8	219.4	57.2	10.9	4.3	7.4	9.2	10.9
1977	2 241.9	1 274.0	259.1	115.2	159.3	200.3	234.0	56.8	11.6	5.1	7.1	8.9	10.4
1978	2 538.1	1 422.3	314.6	138.0	186.9	218.9	257.4	56.0	12.4	5.4	7.4	8.6	10.1
1979	2 861.9	1 585.4	373.8	147.8	230.1	240.6	284.2	55.4	13.1	5.2	8.0	8.4	9.9
1980	3 157.5	1 750.7	406.9	129.5	280.8	274.9	314.7	55.4	12.9	4.1	8.9	8.7	10.0
1981	3 495.0	1 934.0	472.9	128.5	305.2	314.0	340.4	55.3	13.5	3.7	8.7	9.0	9.7
1982	3 661.8	2 071.3	485.1	110.8	283.2	348.3	363.1	56.6	13.2	3.0	7.7	9.5	9.9
1983	3 968.5	2 281.6	482.2	161.1	277.0	382.4	384.2	57.5	12.2	4.1	7.0	9.6	9.7
1984	4 377.3	2 492.3	564.3	190.4	302.4	411.8	416.1	56.9	12.9	4.3	6.9	9.4	9.5
1985	4 734.4	2 712.8	607.8	200.1	303.2	452.9	457.6	57.3	12.8	4.2	6.4	9.6	9.7
1986	5 026.0	2 886.3	607.8	234.8	321.0	481.7	494.4	57.4	12.1	4.7	6.4	9.6	9.8
1987	5 336.7	3 076.3	615.2	249.8	363.9	502.8	528.7	57.6	11.5	4.7	6.8	9.4	9.9
1988	5 771.9	3 330.0	662.3	256.2	444.6	511.4	567.4	57.7	11.5	4.4	7.7	8.9	9.8
1989	6 205.0	3 576.8	716.0	256.0	504.3	534.1	617.8	57.6	11.5	4.1	8.1	8.6	10.0
1990	6 578.4	3 809.0	739.2	239.7	551.9	562.4	676.2	57.9	11.2	3.6	8.4	8.5	10.3
1991	6 782.0	3 943.4	723.6	221.2	594.9	582.9	716.0	58.1	10.7	3.3	8.8	8.6	10.6
1992	7 171.8	4 197.6	741.9	254.7	633.1	588.5	756.0	58.5	10.3	3.6	8.8	8.2	10.5
1993	7 557.8	4 452.0	799.2	286.8	654.8	580.2	784.8	58.9	10.6	3.8	8.7	7.7	10.4
1994	8 036.9	4 721.0	868.9	323.8	720.9	574.7	827.6	58.7	10.8	4.0	9.0	7.2	10.3
1995	8 511.1	4 962.6	962.2	324.1	812.8	576.7	872.7	58.3	11.3	3.8	9.5	6.8	10.3
1996	9 006.4	5 244.6	1 043.2	358.1	867.6	579.2	913.7	58.2	11.6	4.0	9.6	6.4	10.1
1997	9 562.4	5 536.8	1 149.1	375.6	953.8	583.3	963.8	57.9	12.0	3.9	10.0	6.1	10.1
1998	10 114.7	5 877.2	1 254.1	418.8	953.0	585.5	1 026.1	58.1	12.4	4.1	9.4	5.8	10.1
1999	10 822.9	6 283.8	1 364.5	461.8	992.9	610.7	1 109.2	58.1	12.6	4.3	9.2	5.6	10.2
2000	11 673.6	6 767.2	1 498.4	485.4	1 096.1	633.1	1 193.4	58.0	12.8	4.2	9.4	5.4	10.2
2001	12 023.8	7 073.8	1 460.1	513.1	1 026.8	670.2	1 279.8	58.8	12.1	4.3	8.5	5.6	10.6
2002	12 346.8	7 348.9	1 352.8	557.6	998.0	743.1	1 346.4	59.5	11.0	4.5	8.1	6.0	10.9
2003	12 999.5	7 740.7	1 375.9	637.1	1 035.2	826.8	1 383.8	59.5	10.6	4.9	8.0	6.4	10.6
2004	13 963.7	8 232.0	1 467.4	749.8	1 176.4	892.1	1 446.0	59.0	10.5	5.4	8.4	6.4	10.4
2005	15 023.2	8 769.1	1 621.0	856.2	1 301.6	947.8	1 527.5	58.4	10.8	5.7	8.7	6.3	10.2
2006	16 003.3	9 277.2	1 793.8	838.2	1 470.2	1 001.2	1 622.7	58.0	11.2	5.2	9.2	6.3	10.1
2007	16 835.5	9 746.6	1 948.6	690.5	1 659.3	1 051.0	1 739.5	57.9	11.6	4.1	9.9	6.2	10.3
2008	17 375.4	10 050.1	1 990.9	516.0	1 835.3	1 152.0	1 831.1	57.8	11.5	3.0	10.6	6.6	10.5
2009	16 630.8	9 891.2	1 690.4	390.0	1 582.8	1 220.8	1 855.6	59.5	10.2	2.3	9.5	7.3	11.2
2010	17 384.7	10 260.3	1 735.0	376.6	1 857.2	1 300.2	1 855.4	59.0	10.0	2.2	10.7	7.5	10.7
2011	18 249.1	10 698.9	1 907.5	378.8	2 115.9	1 299.8	1 848.2	58.6	10.5	2.1	11.6	7.1	10.1
2012	18 952.1	11 047.4	2 118.5	432.0	2 217.7	1 287.0	1 849.5	58.3	11.2	2.3	11.7	6.8	9.8
2013	19 505.1	11 363.5	2 211.5	510.0	2 287.0	1 227.2	1 905.9	58.3	11.3	2.6	11.7	6.3	9.8
2014	20 354.2	11 847.7	2 400.1	560.2	2 377.4	1 216.0	1 952.8	58.2	11.8	2.8	11.7	6.0	9.6
2015	20 864.2	12 263.5	2 466.6	633.8	2 268.7	1 221.8	2 009.8	58.8	11.8	3.0	10.9	5.9	9.6
2016	21 397.1	12 693.3	2 469.3	699.4	2 232.1	1 234.5	2 068.5	59.3	11.5	3.3	10.4	5.8	9.7
2017	22 373.9	13 239.1	2 591.6	760.3	2 383.8	1 262.8	2 136.3	59.2	11.6	3.4	10.7	5.6	9.5
2018	23 598.1	13 913.5	2 780.6	798.5	2 533.5	1 339.0	2 233.0	59.0	11.8	3.4	10.7	5.7	9.5
2019	24 414.9	14 428.7	2 938.7	813.9	2 519.7	1 414.9	2 299.0	59.1	12.0	3.3	10.3	5.8	9.4
2020	23 728.0	14 047.6	2 799.6	897.8	2 123.4	1 501.8	2 357.8	59.2	11.8	3.8	8.9	6.3	9.9
2018													
1st quarter	23 182.3	13 667.4	2 716.0	789.0	2 504.4	1 305.8	2 199.7	59.0	11.7	3.4	10.8	5.6	9.5
2nd quarter	23 576.4	13 864.8	2 770.1	808.9	2 568.3	1 331.7	2 232.6	58.8	11.7	3.4	10.9	5.6	9.5
3rd quarter	23 740.1	14 002.6	2 798.1	804.3	2 534.2	1 350.8	2 250.1	59.0	11.8	3.4	10.7	5.7	9.5
4th quarter	23 893.7	14 119.3	2 838.1	791.8	2 527.1	1 367.7	2 249.7	59.1	11.9	3.3	10.6	5.7	9.4
2019													
1st quarter	24 014.1	14 155.6	2 886.9	796.5	2 524.6	1 387.0	2 263.5	58.9	12.0	3.3	10.5	5.8	9.4
2nd quarter	24 366.6	14 375.7	2 946.1	808.5	2 533.4	1 406.9	2 296.0	59.0	12.1	3.3	10.4	5.8	9.4
3rd quarter	24 564.1	14 529.5	2 969.3	821.9	2 512.1	1 424.1	2 307.2	59.1	12.1	3.3	10.2	5.8	9.4
4th quarter	24 714.9	14 653.9	2 952.6	828.8	2 508.7	1 441.7	2 329.2	59.3	11.9	3.4	10.2	5.8	9.4
2020													
1st quarter	24 429.2	14 439.1	2 900.1	872.9	2 385.5	1 454.7	2 376.9	59.1	11.9	3.6	9.8	6.0	9.7
2nd quarter	22 114.1	12 989.7	2 659.1	797.8	1 807.9	1 525.0	2 334.6	58.7	12.0	3.6	8.2	6.9	10.6
3rd quarter	23 928.8	14 293.8	2 776.6	917.2	2 079.6	1 515.1	2 346.5	59.7	11.6	3.8	8.7	6.3	9.8
4th quarter	24 439.5	14 467.6	2 862.7	1 003.2	2 220.7	1 512.3	2 373.0	59.2	11.7	4.1	9.1	6.2	9.7

SECTION 1B: INCOME AND VALUE ADDED

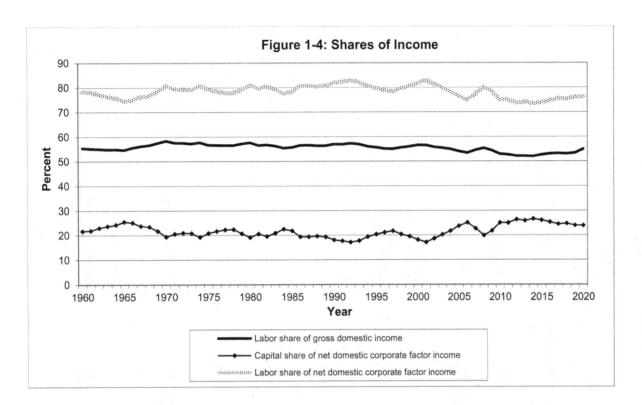

Figure 1-4: Shares of Income

- Recent years have seen a decline in the share of national income paid to workers—not just the share paid out as worker wages, but in total compensation, including all health and other benefits. One indicator of this can be seen in a later chapter, in Tables 9-3A and B, where Bureau of Labor Statistics calculations (based on BEA data) document a declining labor share in the value of output of private nonfarm business. In the tables in Section 1B immediately following this page, BEA compilations show the composition of domestic income, national income, and corporate value added. Table 1-16 shows income share percentages calculated by the editors based on these data. Labor shares rise temporarily in recession years (when the "pie" is smaller) but aside from that effect they have declined over much of the period, and the decline has accelerated in recent years.

- Employee compensation has fallen since the early 1970s to a record low of 52.0 percent in 2014, as shown in the middle line in Figure 1-4. In 2020, the share grew to 55.0 percent. One factor in this decline has been a rising share of output required to replace used-up capital ("consumption of fixed capital"), reflecting increased use of capital per unit of production. In addition, the "net operating surplus" which is largely profits, interest, and proprietor's income, reached a peak in 2014 but has declined or remained the same each year since then. (Tables 1-12 and 1-16)

- Narrowing the focus to the corporate business sector, net income shares become clearer. (Proprietor's, i.e. unincorporated business; income includes a labor compensation component of uncertain size.) Total net factor income (that is, net of capital consumption) can be completely attributed to either labor or capital. These shares are also charted in Figure 1-4. Between 1959 and 2004, the shares vary cyclically but seem stable over time, averaging around 78 percent for labor and 22 percent for capital. Since then, they have broken out of that range. (Tables 1-14 and 1-16)

Table 1-11. Relation of Gross Domestic Product, Gross and Net National Product, National Income, and Personal Income

(Billions of dollars, quarterly data are at seasonally adjusted annual rates.)

NIPA Table 1.7.5

Year and quarter	Gross domestic product	Plus: Income receipts from the rest of the world	Less: Income payments to the rest of the world	Equals: Gross national product	Less: Consumption of fixed capital									Equals: Net national product
					Total	Private					Government			
						Total	Domestic business			House-holds and institutions	Total	General government	Govern-ment enter-prises	
							Total	Capital consump-tion allow-ances	Less: Capital consump-tion ad-justment					
1960	542.4	4.9	1.8	545.5	67.9	48.2	40.0	39.7	-0.3	8.2	19.7	18.6	1.1	477.6
1961	562.2	5.3	1.8	565.7	70.6	49.8	41.3	41.7	0.4	8.5	20.8	19.7	1.1	495.1
1962	603.9	5.9	1.8	608.0	74.1	51.8	42.9	46.6	3.6	8.8	22.3	21.1	1.2	533.9
1963	637.5	6.5	2.1	641.9	78.0	54.2	44.9	49.9	5.0	9.3	23.9	22.6	1.3	563.9
1964	684.5	7.2	2.3	689.4	82.4	57.3	47.4	53.2	5.8	9.9	25.1	23.7	1.4	607.0
1965	742.3	7.9	2.6	747.6	88.0	61.6	50.9	57.0	6.1	10.7	26.4	25.0	1.5	659.6
1966	813.4	8.1	3.0	818.5	95.3	67.2	55.6	61.9	6.2	11.5	28.1	26.5	1.6	723.2
1967	860.0	8.7	3.3	865.4	103.6	73.3	60.9	66.9	6.0	12.4	30.2	28.5	1.8	761.8
1968	940.7	10.1	4.0	946.7	113.4	80.6	67.0	72.5	5.6	13.6	32.8	30.8	2.0	833.4
1969	1 017.6	11.8	5.7	1 023.7	124.9	89.4	74.2	79.7	5.5	15.2	35.5	33.3	2.2	898.8
1970	1 073.3	12.8	6.4	1 079.7	136.8	98.3	81.8	85.9	4.1	16.5	38.6	36.1	2.5	942.9
1971	1 164.9	14.0	6.4	1 172.4	148.9	107.6	89.4	92.3	2.9	18.2	41.3	38.5	2.8	1 023.5
1972	1 279.1	16.3	7.7	1 287.7	161.0	117.5	97.2	102.3	5.2	20.3	43.5	40.4	3.1	1 126.7
1973	1 425.4	23.5	10.9	1 438.0	178.7	131.5	108.2	111.9	3.7	23.3	47.2	43.7	3.5	1 259.3
1974	1 545.2	29.8	14.3	1 560.8	206.9	153.2	126.1	123.9	-2.2	27.0	53.7	49.4	4.3	1 353.9
1975	1 684.9	28.0	15.0	1 697.9	238.5	178.8	147.9	135.9	-12.0	30.9	59.7	54.6	5.1	1 459.4
1976	1 873.4	32.4	15.5	1 890.3	260.2	196.5	162.2	147.4	-14.8	34.3	63.7	58.2	5.5	1 630.0
1977	2 081.8	37.2	16.9	2 102.1	289.8	221.1	181.5	167.0	-14.5	39.6	68.7	62.7	6.0	1 812.3
1978	2 351.6	46.3	24.7	2 373.2	327.2	252.1	205.5	189.4	-16.2	46.6	75.1	68.5	6.6	2 046.0
1979	2 627.3	68.3	36.4	2 659.3	373.9	290.7	236.4	216.1	-20.2	54.4	83.1	75.6	7.5	2 285.4
1980	2 857.3	79.1	44.9	2 891.5	428.4	335.0	272.8	245.8	-26.9	62.2	93.5	84.7	8.7	2 463.1
1981	3 207.0	92.0	59.1	3 240.0	487.2	381.9	313.5	301.2	-12.3	68.5	105.3	95.4	9.9	2 752.7
1982	3 343.8	101.0	64.5	3 380.3	537.0	420.4	347.5	343.1	-4.4	72.9	116.6	105.7	10.8	2 843.3
1983	3 634.0	101.9	64.8	3 671.1	562.6	438.8	362.8	385.6	22.8	76.0	123.8	112.4	11.4	3 108.5
1984	4 037.6	121.9	85.6	4 073.9	598.4	463.5	382.7	435.6	52.9	80.9	134.9	122.8	12.1	3 475.5
1985	4 339.0	112.7	87.3	4 364.3	640.1	496.4	410.3	493.5	83.2	86.2	143.7	130.9	12.8	3 724.2
1986	4 579.6	111.3	94.4	4 596.6	685.3	531.6	438.1	512.0	73.9	93.4	153.7	140.1	13.6	3 911.3
1987	4 855.2	123.3	105.8	4 872.7	730.4	566.3	464.5	533.1	68.6	101.8	164.1	149.6	14.5	4 142.3
1988	5 236.4	152.1	129.5	5 259.1	784.5	607.9	499.2	563.7	64.5	108.8	176.6	161.1	15.5	4 474.6
1989	5 641.6	177.7	152.9	5 666.4	838.3	649.6	532.6	589.5	56.9	117.0	188.6	172.0	16.6	4 828.1
1990	5 963.1	188.8	154.2	5 997.8	888.5	688.4	564.6	596.0	31.4	123.8	200.1	182.3	17.8	5 109.3
1991	6 158.1	168.4	136.8	6 189.7	932.4	721.5	592.3	611.6	19.3	129.2	210.9	192.1	18.8	5 257.3
1992	6 520.3	152.1	121.0	6 551.4	960.2	742.9	608.2	628.4	20.2	134.7	217.4	197.6	19.8	5 591.2
1993	6 858.6	155.6	124.4	6 889.7	1 003.5	778.2	634.2	658.9	24.7	144.0	225.3	204.2	21.1	5 886.2
1994	7 287.2	184.5	161.2	7 310.2	1 055.6	822.5	669.0	701.6	32.6	153.5	233.1	210.9	22.2	6 254.6
1995	7 639.7	229.8	201.9	7 667.7	1 122.4	880.7	717.8	753.9	36.1	162.9	241.7	218.2	23.5	6 545.3
1996	8 073.1	246.4	215.5	8 104.0	1 175.3	929.1	758.5	808.3	49.8	170.6	246.2	221.6	24.6	6 928.7
1997	8 577.6	280.1	256.8	8 600.9	1 239.3	987.8	807.9	877.0	69.2	179.9	251.6	225.9	25.7	7 361.5
1998	9 062.8	286.8	269.4	9 080.2	1 309.7	1 052.4	860.1	941.4	81.3	192.1	257.6	230.8	26.8	7 770.5
1999	9 631.2	324.6	293.7	9 662.1	1 398.9	1 132.2	924.0	1 023.8	99.8	208.2	266.7	238.3	28.4	8 263.1
2000	10 251.0	390.6	352.2	10 289.4	1 511.2	1 231.5	1 004.6	1 096.1	91.5	227.0	279.7	249.4	30.3	8 778.2
2001	10 581.9	339.6	289.3	10 632.3	1 599.5	1 311.7	1 064.9	1 180.1	115.2	246.8	287.8	256.0	31.8	9 032.8
2002	10 929.1	335.8	290.0	10 974.9	1 658.0	1 361.8	1 098.8	1 283.9	185.1	263.0	296.2	262.9	33.2	9 316.9
2003	11 456.5	377.4	318.9	11 514.9	1 719.1	1 411.9	1 125.4	1 303.5	178.1	286.6	307.1	272.2	34.9	9 795.9
2004	12 217.2	464.7	388.0	12 293.9	1 821.8	1 497.1	1 178.8	1 332.0	153.2	318.3	324.7	286.9	37.9	10 472.1
2005	13 039.2	569.3	494.5	13 114.0	1 971.0	1 622.6	1 266.4	1 169.5	-97.0	356.2	348.4	307.0	41.4	11 143.0
2006	13 815.6	702.6	656.2	13 862.0	2 124.1	1 751.8	1 362.6	1 245.1	-117.4	389.2	372.3	327.6	44.7	11 737.9
2007	14 474.2	850.2	754.5	14 569.9	2 252.8	1 852.5	1 446.7	1 326.8	-119.8	405.8	400.3	352.1	48.2	12 317.1
2008	14 769.9	855.2	710.0	14 915.1	2 358.8	1 931.8	1 524.9	1 584.1	59.3	427.0	427.0	375.7	51.3	12 556.2
2009	14 478.1	689.3	539.0	14 628.3	2 371.5	1 928.7	1 531.2	1 562.1	30.9	442.8	442.8	389.8	53.0	12 256.8
2010	15 049.0	760.0	554.3	15 254.6	2 390.9	1 933.8	1 537.1	1 605.9	68.8	396.7	457.2	402.2	55.0	12 863.7
2011	15 599.7	827.9	589.9	15 837.7	2 474.5	1 997.3	1 595.1	1 831.3	236.2	402.2	477.2	419.3	57.8	13 363.2
2012	16 254.0	827.4	594.7	16 486.7	2 576.0	2 082.4	1 670.4	1 665.9	-4.5	412.0	493.6	433.0	60.7	13 910.7
2013	16 843.2	847.2	616.9	17 073.5	2 681.2	2 176.6	1 738.8	1 753.6	14.8	437.8	504.6	441.8	62.9	14 392.3
2014	17 550.7	881.6	646.4	17 785.9	2 815.0	2 298.5	1 831.2	1 866.4	35.2	467.3	516.6	451.4	65.2	14 970.9
2015	18 206.0	860.8	640.4	18 426.4	2 911.4	2 388.5	1 903.1	1 981.9	78.8	485.4	522.9	455.8	67.1	15 515.0
2016	18 695.1	893.5	661.5	18 927.1	2 987.1	2 459.9	1 950.9	2 075.3	124.3	509.0	527.1	458.1	69.0	15 940.0
2017	19 479.6	1 032.7	738.2	19 774.2	3 118.2	2 576.1	2 037.6	2 303.3	265.6	538.4	542.1	470.0	72.1	16 656.0
2018	20 527.2	1 142.1	847.9	20 821.3	3 273.4	2 708.1	2 133.3	2 566.2	433.0	574.8	565.4	489.3	76.1	17 547.9
2019	21 372.6	1 160.3	893.9	21 639.0	3 435.6	2 848.6	2 248.3	2 712.2	463.9	600.3	586.9	506.7	80.3	18 203.4
2020	20 893.7	992.9	770.6	21 116.1	3 575.9	2 969.6	2 338.6	2 754.7	416.1	631.0	606.4	523.5	82.8	17 540.2
2018														
1st quarter	20 143.7	1 113.5	796.9	20 460.3	3 209.7	2 654.6	2 092.2	2 522.5	430.3	562.4	555.1	480.8	74.3	17 250.6
2nd quarter	20 492.5	1 151.1	850.4	20 793.2	3 256.3	2 693.0	2 120.7	2 537.3	416.6	572.3	563.3	487.7	75.6	17 536.9
3rd quarter	20 659.1	1 134.5	863.0	20 930.7	3 295.7	2 726.9	2 147.4	2 573.4	426.0	579.5	568.8	492.1	76.7	17 635.0
4th quarter	20 813.3	1 169.3	881.5	21 101.1	3 332.0	2 757.7	2 172.6	2 631.7	459.1	585.1	574.3	496.4	77.9	17 769.1
2019														
1st quarter	21 001.6	1 140.8	888.1	21 254.3	3 378.0	2 798.1	2 207.4	2 629.4	421.9	590.6	580.0	501.1	78.9	17 876.3
2nd quarter	21 289.3	1 184.4	908.8	21 564.9	3 421.0	2 836.1	2 239.5	2 695.6	456.1	596.5	584.9	504.9	80.0	18 143.9
3rd quarter	21 505.0	1 168.8	893.0	21 780.8	3 457.9	2 867.9	2 264.0	2 745.7	481.7	604.0	589.9	509.1	80.8	18 322.9
4th quarter	21 694.5	1 147.3	885.8	21 956.0	3 485.5	2 892.5	2 282.0	2 778.1	495.8	610.1	593.0	511.6	81.4	18 470.5
2020														
1st quarter	21 481.4	1 048.9	809.0	21 721.3	3 522.3	2 924.5	2 308.7	2 735.2	426.6	615.9	597.8	515.8	82.0	18 198.9
2nd quarter	19 477.4	883.5	711.5	19 649.4	3 550.9	2 949.0	2 327.5	2 744.7	417.2	621.5	601.9	519.8	82.1	16 098.6
3rd quarter	21 138.6	996.1	769.2	21 365.4	3 591.0	2 981.5	2 345.3	2 757.6	412.3	636.2	609.6	526.4	83.2	17 774.4
4th quarter	21 477.6	1 043.2	792.5	21 728.2	3 639.4	3 023.3	2 372.9	2 781.3	408.5	650.4	616.1	532.1	84.0	18 088.8

Table 1-12. Gross Domestic Income by Type of Income

(Billions of dollars, quarterly data are at seasonally adjusted annual rates.)   NIPA Tables 1.10

Year and quarter	Gross domestic income	Compensation of employees			Taxes on production and imports	Less: Subsidies	Net operating surplus					
							Total	Private enterprises				
		Total	Wages and salaries	Supplements to wages and salaries				Total	Net interest and miscellaneous payments, domestic industries	Business current transfer payments, net	Proprietors' income with IVA and CCAdj	Rental income of persons with CCAdj
1960	543.7	301.4	273.0	28.4	44.5	1.1	130.9	130.5	10.1	1.7	50.6	16.5
1961	563.1	310.6	280.7	29.9	47.0	2.0	137.0	136.7	11.7	1.9	53.2	17.2
1962	603.9	332.3	299.5	32.8	50.4	2.3	149.4	149.0	13.4	2.1	55.2	18.0
1963	638.9	350.5	314.9	35.6	53.4	2.2	159.3	158.5	14.4	2.5	56.4	18.7
1964	684.5	376.0	337.8	38.2	57.3	2.7	171.6	170.7	16.5	3.0	59.1	18.8
1965	741.5	405.4	363.8	41.7	60.7	3.0	190.4	189.6	18.6	3.5	63.7	19.3
1966	808.3	449.2	400.3	48.9	63.2	3.9	204.5	204.2	21.3	3.4	67.9	19.9
1967	856.6	481.8	429.0	52.8	67.9	3.8	207.2	206.9	24.3	3.6	69.5	20.3
1968	937.5	530.7	472.0	58.8	76.4	4.2	221.2	220.7	26.5	4.2	73.8	20.1
1969	1 016.0	584.4	518.3	66.1	83.9	4.5	227.4	227.2	33.2	4.8	77.0	20.3
1970	1 068.0	623.3	551.5	71.8	91.4	4.8	221.2	222.2	40.2	4.4	77.8	20.7
1971	1 155.3	665.0	584.5	80.4	100.5	4.7	245.6	247.1	44.4	4.2	83.9	21.8
1972	1 271.9	731.3	638.8	92.5	107.9	6.6	278.3	279.2	49.0	4.8	95.1	22.7
1973	1 419.2	812.7	708.8	103.9	117.2	5.2	315.9	317.8	58.0	5.7	112.5	23.1
1974	1 537.8	887.7	772.3	115.4	124.9	3.3	321.6	324.0	73.6	6.8	112.2	23.2
1975	1 671.6	947.3	814.9	132.4	135.3	4.5	355.0	359.0	85.3	9.0	118.2	22.3
1976	1 852.8	1 048.4	899.8	148.6	146.4	5.1	402.9	405.3	87.1	9.1	131.0	20.3
1977	2 062.4	1 165.9	994.2	171.7	159.7	7.1	454.1	457.1	101.9	8.1	144.5	15.9
1978	2 328.3	1 316.9	1 120.7	196.2	170.9	8.9	522.3	524.6	116.0	10.4	166.0	16.5
1979	2 582.3	1 477.3	1 253.4	223.9	180.1	8.5	559.5	562.2	139.6	12.8	179.4	16.1
1980	2 812.9	1 622.3	1 373.5	248.8	200.3	9.8	571.6	576.0	183.4	14.0	171.6	19.0
1981	3 169.0	1 792.7	1 511.5	281.2	235.6	11.5	664.9	669.6	231.4	16.9	179.7	23.8
1982	3 335.0	1 893.2	1 587.7	305.5	240.9	15.0	678.9	682.2	270.7	19.3	171.2	23.8
1983	3 577.1	2 012.7	1 677.7	335.0	263.3	21.3	759.8	761.7	284.6	21.7	186.3	24.4
1984	3 996.0	2 216.1	1 845.1	371.0	289.8	21.1	912.8	913.7	330.3	29.2	228.2	24.7
1985	4 284.7	2 387.5	1 982.8	404.8	308.1	21.4	970.3	968.4	350.7	34.1	241.1	26.2
1986	4 499.6	2 543.8	2 104.1	439.7	323.4	24.9	972.0	969.4	373.8	36.0	256.5	18.3
1987	4 811.4	2 723.8	2 257.6	466.1	347.5	30.3	1 040.0	1 037.2	382.9	33.3	286.5	16.6
1988	5 233.4	2 948.9	2 440.6	508.2	374.5	29.5	1 155.1	1 149.6	411.3	32.8	325.5	22.5
1989	5 573.6	3 140.9	2 584.3	556.6	398.9	27.4	1 223.0	1 215.8	467.7	38.3	341.1	21.5
1990	5 867.6	3 342.7	2 743.5	599.2	425.0	27.0	1 238.4	1 234.7	472.5	39.2	353.2	28.2
1991	6 065.2	3 453.3	2 817.2	636.0	457.1	27.5	1 249.9	1 241.7	433.9	38.9	354.2	38.6
1992	6 404.4	3 671.2	2 968.5	702.7	483.4	30.1	1 319.6	1 309.2	404.7	39.7	400.2	60.6
1993	6 702.6	3 820.6	3 082.7	737.9	503.1	36.7	1 412.1	1 400.6	395.5	39.4	428.0	90.1
1994	7 147.3	4 010.2	3 240.6	769.6	545.2	32.5	1 568.7	1 556.1	398.3	40.7	456.6	113.7
1995	7 546.7	4 202.2	3 422.1	780.1	557.9	34.8	1 699.1	1 682.6	418.3	45.0	481.2	124.9
1996	8 015.0	4 421.1	3 620.6	800.5	580.8	35.2	1 873.1	1 855.4	428.9	52.6	543.8	142.5
1997	8 566.0	4 713.2	3 881.2	832.0	611.6	33.8	2 035.6	2 017.5	474.3	50.1	584.0	147.1
1998	9 118.1	5 075.7	4 186.2	889.5	639.5	36.4	2 129.5	2 112.6	537.5	64.1	640.2	165.2
1999	9 659.5	5 409.9	4 465.2	944.8	673.6	45.2	2 222.2	2 205.4	549.6	67.7	696.4	178.5
2000	10 345.2	5 854.6	4 832.4	1 022.2	708.6	45.8	2 316.6	2 305.2	641.8	85.2	753.9	183.5
2001	10 695.7	6 046.3	4 961.6	1 084.7	727.7	58.7	2 380.9	2 375.2	652.7	99.2	831.0	202.4
2002	11 006.4	6 143.4	5 004.1	1 139.3	760.0	41.4	2 486.5	2 478.9	564.7	80.8	870.0	208.4
2003	11 476.3	6 362.3	5 147.0	1 215.3	805.6	49.1	2 638.4	2 633.3	535.3	76.0	897.5	227.1
2004	12 240.9	6 729.3	5 430.8	1 298.5	868.1	46.4	2 868.1	2 868.0	485.9	82.2	962.9	242.8
2005	13 091.7	7 077.7	5 703.0	1 374.7	942.4	60.9	3 161.4	3 166.0	611.1	91.7	979.1	221.1
2006	14 019.9	7 491.3	6 068.3	1 422.9	997.0	51.5	3 459.0	3 466.0	746.5	80.9	1 050.9	181.1
2007	14 454.4	7 889.4	6 407.3	1 482.1	1 036.8	54.6	3 330.0	3 344.2	868.5	98.5	995.5	186.3
2008	14 572.9	8 068.7	6 545.9	1 522.7	1 049.7	52.6	3 148.2	3 166.4	906.6	114.3	959.7	290.3
2009	14 276.0	7 767.2	6 257.3	1 509.9	1 026.8	58.3	3 168.9	3 185.0	735.1	126.6	937.6	347.6
2010	14 966.4	7 933.0	6 380.1	1 552.9	1 063.1	55.8	3 635.3	3 655.4	643.6	127.9	1 107.3	433.7
2011	15 612.0	8 234.0	6 634.0	1 600.0	1 103.7	60.0	3 859.3	3 879.3	616.4	131.7	1 227.4	506.5
2012	16 442.8	8 575.4	6 936.1	1 639.2	1 136.1	58.0	4 213.4	4 228.8	658.6	97.3	1 346.4	534.5
2013	16 958.0	8 843.6	7 122.6	1 721.0	1 188.7	59.7	4 304.2	4 320.2	619.2	109.5	1 402.2	577.4
2014	17 807.9	9 259.7	7 485.8	1 773.9	1 240.8	58.1	4 550.4	4 561.4	665.0	132.7	1 445.6	602.7
2015	18 440.5	9 709.5	7 869.6	1 839.9	1 275.2	57.2	4 601.6	4 606.9	755.8	155.6	1 420.8	609.5
2016	18 788.5	9 977.1	8 102.2	1 874.9	1 311.6	61.7	4 574.5	4 578.4	744.3	166.9	1 423.3	626.6
2017	19 598.5	10 436.7	8 485.3	1 951.5	1 366.3	59.9	4 737.2	4 743.9	806.2	149.1	1 505.8	652.7
2018	20 652.6	10 969.8	8 910.8	2 059.0	1 461.7	63.3	5 011.0	5 019.5	815.9	158.0	1 580.4	681.9
2019	21 442.2	11 459.4	9 335.3	2 124.2	1 532.3	73.0	5 087.8	5 101.1	793.5	162.3	1 598.9	692.1
2020	21 064.3	11 580.1	9 452.0	2 128.0	1 534.7	761.4	5 135.0	5 152.5	843.3	158.6	1 650.0	711.6
2018												
1st quarter	20 276.4	10 794.3	8 772.5	2 021.8	1 427.2	58.7	4 903.8	4 910.7	819.2	150.9	1 567.0	671.8
2nd quarter	20 497.4	10 902.0	8 853.1	2 048.9	1 448.6	58.2	4 948.7	4 956.4	816.0	148.7	1 572.1	677.3
3rd quarter	20 823.8	11 054.9	8 980.4	2 074.5	1 468.9	57.8	5 062.2	5 071.1	809.5	173.6	1 581.3	689.8
4th quarter	21 012.9	11 128.1	9 037.2	2 090.9	1 502.2	78.5	5 129.1	5 139.8	819.0	158.9	1 601.4	688.6
2019												
1st quarter	21 195.6	11 347.4	9 237.7	2 109.7	1 504.8	69.0	5 034.4	5 046.6	804.2	170.8	1 585.5	687.0
2nd quarter	21 361.6	11 405.9	9 287.2	2 118.7	1 520.9	58.8	5 072.7	5 086.3	801.9	162.5	1 572.8	691.0
3rd quarter	21 481.9	11 465.8	9 338.7	2 127.1	1 547.4	81.2	5 092.0	5 105.9	776.4	168.2	1 610.6	691.5
4th quarter	21 729.8	11 618.8	9 477.6	2 141.2	1 556.3	82.8	5 152.2	5 165.6	791.3	147.5	1 626.8	699.0
2020												
1st quarter	21 755.9	11 764.8	9 613.3	2 151.4	1 577.1	80.9	4 972.6	4 987.1	796.8	149.4	1 638.3	712.2
2nd quarter	19 620.2	11 036.1	8 985.9	2 050.2	1 460.5	1 124.3	4 696.9	4 716.4	848.7	152.8	1 471.1	709.5
3rd quarter	20 908.5	11 547.2	9 417.8	2 129.4	1 544.0	1 221.2	5 447.5	5 465.1	843.1	165.8	1 760.7	714.5
4th quarter	21 972.6	11 972.3	9 791.1	2 181.1	1 557.0	619.2	5 423.2	5 441.3	884.4	166.3	1 730.0	710.0

Table 1-13A. National Income by Type of Income: Recent Data

(Billions of dollars, quarterly data are at seasonally adjusted annual rates.) NIPA Tables 1.7.5, 1.12

Year and quarter	National income, total	Compensation of employees								Proprietors' income with IVA and CCAdj			Rental income of persons with CCAdj
		Total	Wages and salaries			Supplements to wages and salaries				Total	Farm	Nonfarm	
			Total	Government	Other	Total	Employer contributions for:						
							Total	Employee pension and insurance funds	Government social insurance				
1960	478.9	301.3	272.9	49.2	223.7	28.4	19.2	9.3	50.6	10.6	39.9	16.5
1961	496.0	310.4	280.5	52.5	228.0	29.9	20.3	9.6	53.2	11.2	42.0	17.2
1962	533.9	332.2	299.4	56.3	243.0	32.8	21.7	11.2	55.2	11.2	44.0	18.0
1963	565.4	350.4	314.9	60.0	254.8	35.6	23.2	12.4	56.4	11.0	45.4	18.7
1964	607.0	376.0	337.8	64.9	272.9	38.2	25.6	12.6	59.1	9.8	49.4	18.8
1965	658.8	405.4	363.8	69.9	293.8	41.7	28.6	13.1	63.7	12.0	51.6	19.3
1966	718.1	449.2	400.3	78.4	321.9	48.9	32.1	16.8	67.9	13.0	54.9	19.9
1967	758.4	481.8	429.0	86.5	342.5	52.8	34.8	18.0	69.5	11.6	57.8	20.3
1968	830.2	530.8	472.0	96.7	375.3	58.8	38.8	20.0	73.8	11.7	62.2	20.1
1969	897.2	584.5	518.3	105.6	412.7	66.1	43.4	22.8	77.0	12.8	64.2	20.3
1970	937.5	623.3	551.6	117.2	434.3	71.8	47.9	23.8	77.8	12.9	64.9	20.7
1971	1 014.0	665.0	584.5	126.8	457.8	80.4	54.0	26.4	83.9	13.4	70.5	21.8
1972	1 119.5	731.3	638.8	137.9	500.9	92.5	61.4	31.2	95.1	17.0	78.1	22.7
1973	1 253.2	812.7	708.8	148.8	560.0	103.9	64.1	39.8	112.5	29.1	83.4	23.1
1974	1 346.4	887.7	772.3	160.5	611.8	115.4	70.7	44.7	112.2	23.5	88.7	23.2
1975	1 446.0	947.2	814.8	176.2	638.6	132.4	85.7	46.7	118.2	22.0	96.2	22.3
1976	1 609.4	1 048.3	899.7	188.9	710.8	148.6	94.2	54.4	131.0	17.2	113.8	20.3
1977	1 792.8	1 165.8	994.2	202.6	791.6	171.7	110.6	61.1	144.5	16.0	128.5	15.9
1978	2 022.7	1 316.8	1 120.6	220.0	900.6	196.2	124.7	71.5	166.0	19.9	146.1	16.5
1979	2 240.3	1 477.2	1 253.3	237.1	1 016.2	223.9	141.3	82.6	179.4	22.2	157.3	16.1
1980	2 418.6	1 622.2	1 373.4	261.5	1 112.0	248.8	159.9	88.9	171.6	11.7	159.9	19.0
1981	2 714.7	1 792.5	1 511.4	285.8	1 225.5	281.2	177.5	103.6	179.7	19.0	160.7	23.8
1982	2 834.5	1 893.0	1 587.5	307.5	1 280.0	305.5	195.7	109.8	171.2	13.3	157.9	23.8
1983	3 051.5	2 012.5	1 677.5	324.8	1 352.7	335.0	215.1	119.9	186.3	6.2	180.1	24.4
1984	3 433.9	2 215.9	1 844.9	348.1	1 496.8	371.0	231.9	139.0	228.2	20.9	207.3	24.7
1985	3 669.9	2 387.3	1 982.6	373.9	1 608.7	404.8	257.0	147.7	241.1	21.0	220.1	26.2
1986	3 831.2	2 542.1	2 102.3	397.2	1 705.1	439.7	281.9	157.9	256.5	22.8	233.7	18.3
1987	4 098.5	2 722.4	2 256.3	423.1	1 833.2	466.1	299.9	166.3	286.5	28.9	257.6	16.6
1988	4 471.6	2 948.0	2 439.8	452.0	1 987.7	508.2	323.6	184.6	325.5	26.8	298.7	22.5
1989	4 760.1	3 139.6	2 583.1	481.1	2 101.9	556.6	362.9	193.7	341.1	33.0	308.1	21.5
1990	5 013.8	3 340.4	2 741.2	519.0	2 222.2	599.2	392.7	206.5	353.2	32.2	321.0	28.2
1991	5 164.4	3 450.5	2 814.5	548.8	2 265.7	636.0	420.9	215.1	354.2	26.8	327.4	38.6
1992	5 475.2	3 668.2	2 965.5	572.0	2 393.5	702.7	474.3	228.4	400.2	34.8	365.4	60.6
1993	5 730.3	3 817.3	3 079.3	589.0	2 490.3	737.9	498.3	239.7	428.0	31.4	396.6	90.1
1994	6 114.6	4 006.2	3 396.6	609.5	2 627.1	769.6	515.5	254.1	456.6	34.7	422.0	113.7
1995	6 452.3	4 198.1	3 418.0	629.0	2 789.0	780.1	515.9	264.1	481.2	22.0	459.2	124.9
1996	6 870.6	4 416.9	3 616.5	648.1	2 968.4	800.5	525.7	274.8	543.8	37.3	506.4	142.5
1997	7 349.9	4 708.8	3 876.8	671.9	3 205.0	832.0	542.4	289.6	584.0	32.4	551.6	147.1
1998	7 825.7	5 071.1	4 181.6	701.3	3 480.3	889.5	582.3	307.2	640.2	28.5	611.7	165.2
1999	8 291.5	5 402.7	4 457.9	733.8	3 724.2	944.8	621.4	323.3	696.4	28.1	668.3	178.5
2000	8 872.4	5 847.1	4 824.9	779.8	4 045.2	1 022.2	677.0	345.2	753.9	31.5	722.4	183.5
2001	9 146.6	6 038.3	4 953.6	822.0	4 131.6	1 084.7	726.7	358.0	831.0	32.1	798.9	202.4
2002	9 394.2	6 135.1	4 995.8	872.9	4 123.0	1 139.3	773.2	366.0	870.0	20.2	849.8	208.4
2003	9 815.8	6 353.6	5 138.3	914.0	4 224.3	1 215.3	832.8	382.5	897.5	37.1	860.4	227.1
2004	10 495.8	6 719.5	5 421.0	952.3	4 468.7	1 298.5	889.7	408.8	962.9	52.4	910.5	242.8
2005	11 195.5	7 066.1	5 691.4	991.3	4 700.1	1 374.7	946.7	428.1	979.1	47.9	931.2	221.1
2006	11 942.3	7 479.7	6 056.7	1 034.5	5 022.2	1 422.9	975.6	447.3	1 050.9	34.3	1 016.6	181.1
2007	12 297.3	7 878.5	6 396.4	1 088.5	5 307.8	1 482.1	1 020.4	461.7	995.5	41.7	953.8	186.3
2008	12 359.3	8 056.8	6 534.1	1 143.9	5 390.2	1 522.7	1 051.3	471.4	959.7	38.9	920.7	290.3
2009	12 054.8	7 759.0	6 249.1	1 175.2	5 073.9	1 509.9	1 051.8	458.1	937.6	27.2	910.5	347.6
2010	12 781.1	7 925.4	6 372.5	1 191.2	5 181.3	1 552.9	1 083.9	469.0	1 107.3	37.6	1 069.7	433.7
2011	13 375.5	8 226.2	6 626.2	1 194.9	5 431.3	1 600.0	1 107.3	492.7	1 227.4	63.0	1 164.4	506.5
2012	14 099.6	8 567.4	6 928.1	1 198.3	5 729.8	1 639.2	1 125.9	513.3	1 346.4	59.9	1 286.4	534.5
2013	14 507.1	8 835.0	7 114.0	1 208.0	5 906.0	1 721.0	1 194.7	526.3	1 402.2	87.0	1 315.3	577.4
2014	15 228.1	9 250.2	7 476.3	1 236.9	6 239.4	1 773.9	1 227.5	546.4	1 445.6	67.7	1 377.9	602.7
2015	15 749.5	9 699.4	7 859.5	1 275.8	6 583.7	1 839.9	1 270.6	569.4	1 420.8	54.1	1 366.7	609.5
2016	16 033.4	9 966.1	8 091.2	1 308.0	6 783.2	1 874.9	1 293.9	580.9	1 423.3	34.1	1 389.2	626.6
2017	16 774.9	10 426.0	8 474.7	1 348.0	7 126.7	1 951.5	1 346.5	604.9	1 505.8	39.5	1 466.4	652.7
2018	17 673.3	10 959.0	8 900.5	1 401.4	7 499.1	2 059.0	1 434.3	624.7	1 580.4	38.9	1 541.5	681.9
2019	18 273.1	11 447.0	9 323.5	1 450.2	7 873.3	2 124.2	1 474.6	649.6	1 598.9	38.4	1 560.5	692.1
2020	17 710.7	11 572.0	9 444.1	1 494.5	7 949.6	2 128.0	1 464.4	663.7	1 650.0	70.2	1 579.9	711.6
2018												
1st quarter	17 383.2	10 784.0	8 762.3	1 381.3	7 381.0	2 021.8	1 404.6	617.2	1 567.0	37.4	1 529.5	671.8
2nd quarter	17 541.8	10 891.0	8 842.9	1 394.2	7 448.7	2 048.9	1 427.7	621.1	1 572.1	39.5	1 532.6	677.3
3rd quarter	17 799.7	11 044.0	8 969.8	1 411.1	7 558.7	2 074.5	1 445.8	628.7	1 581.3	30.1	1 551.1	689.8
4th quarter	17 968.6	11 118.0	9 027.1	1 419.0	7 608.1	2 090.9	1 459.0	631.9	1 601.4	48.6	1 552.8	688.6
2019												
1st quarter	18 070.4	11 336.0	9 226.3	1 423.6	7 802.7	2 109.7	1 466.6	643.2	1 585.5	33.1	1 552.4	687.0
2nd quarter	18 216.3	11 394.0	9 275.4	1 435.0	7 840.4	2 118.7	1 472.5	646.2	1 572.8	23.6	1 549.2	691.0
3rd quarter	18 299.7	11 453.0	9 326.8	1 459.1	7 867.8	2 127.1	1 477.4	649.6	1 610.6	46.4	1 564.1	691.5
4th quarter	18 505.9	11 606.0	9 465.6	1 483.3	7 982.4	2 141.2	1 481.8	659.4	1 626.8	50.6	1 576.1	699.0
2020												
1st quarter	18 473.4	11 755.0	9 604.1	1 515.2	8 088.9	2 151.4	1 483.7	667.7	1 638.3	58.1	1 580.2	712.2
2nd quarter	16 241.3	11 029.0	8 979.0	1 467.7	7 511.3	2 050.2	1 410.5	639.7	1 471.1	44.9	1 426.2	709.5
3rd quarter	17 544.3	11 539.0	9 410.3	1 498.8	7 911.5	2 129.4	1 464.9	664.5	1 760.7	69.2	1 691.5	714.5
4th quarter	18 583.8	11 964.2	9 783.0	1 496.4	8 286.6	2 181.1	1 498.3	682.8	1 730.0	108.5	1 621.5	710.0

Table 1-13A. National Income by Type of Income: Recent Data—*Continued*

(Billions of dollars, quarterly data are at seasonally adjusted annual rates.)

NIPA Tables 1.7.5, 1.12

| Year and quarter | Corporate profits with IVA and CCAdj | | | | | Net interest and miscellaneous payments | Taxes on production and imports | Less: Subsidies | Business current transfer payments, net | | | Current surplus of government enterprises | Addendum: Net national factor income |
| | Total | Taxes on corporate income | Profits after tax | | | | | | Total¹ | To persons | To government | | |
			Total	Net dividends	Undistributed corporate profits								
1960	54.7	21.9	32.8	14.3	18.5	10.3	44.5	1.1	1.7	1.3	0.4	. . .	433.3
1961	55.9	22.2	33.7	14.6	19.2	12.1	47.0	2.0	1.9	1.4	0.5	. . .	448.8
1962	64.0	23.3	40.7	15.8	24.9	13.8	50.4	2.3	2.1	1.5	0.6	. . .	483.3
1963	70.5	25.5	45.0	17.1	27.9	14.8	53.4	2.2	2.5	1.9	0.7	. . .	510.9
1964	77.7	26.6	51.1	19.8	31.4	17.0	57.3	2.7	3.0	2.2	0.8	. . .	548.6
1965	89.3	29.8	59.5	21.5	38.0	19.1	60.7	3.0	3.5	2.3	1.2	. . .	596.8
1966	96.1	32.2	63.9	22.3	41.6	21.8	63.2	3.9	3.4	2.1	1.3	. . .	655.1
1967	93.9	31.0	62.9	23.4	39.5	24.9	67.9	3.8	3.6	2.3	1.4	. . .	690.4
1968	101.7	37.2	64.6	26.0	38.6	27.0	76.4	4.2	4.2	2.8	1.4	. . .	753.4
1969	98.4	37.0	61.5	27.3	34.2	32.7	83.9	4.5	4.8	3.3	1.5	. . .	813.0
1970	86.2	31.3	55.0	27.8	27.2	39.5	91.4	4.8	4.4	2.9	1.4	. . .	847.6
1971	100.6	34.8	65.8	28.4	37.5	44.2	100.5	4.7	4.2	2.7	1.5	. . .	915.5
1972	117.2	39.1	78.1	30.1	48.0	48.0	107.9	6.6	4.8	3.1	1.7	. . .	1 014.4
1973	133.4	45.6	87.8	34.2	53.5	55.7	117.2	5.2	5.7	3.9	1.8	. . .	1 137.4
1974	125.7	47.2	78.5	38.8	39.7	71.7	124.9	3.3	6.8	4.7	2.1	. . .	1 220.5
1975	138.9	46.3	92.6	38.3	54.3	83.7	135.3	4.5	9.0	6.8	2.2	. . .	1 310.3
1976	174.3	59.4	114.9	44.9	70.0	87.4	146.4	5.1	9.1	6.7	2.4	. . .	1 461.4
1977	205.8	68.5	137.3	50.7	86.6	103.2	159.7	7.1	8.1	5.1	3.0	. . .	1 635.2
1978	238.6	77.9	160.7	57.8	102.9	114.8	170.9	8.9	10.4	6.5	3.9	. . .	1 852.7
1979	249.0	80.7	168.2	66.8	101.4	137.0	180.1	8.5	12.8	8.2	4.5	. . .	2 058.7
1980	223.6	75.5	148.1	75.8	72.3	182.2	200.3	9.8	14.0	8.6	5.4	. . .	2 218.6
1981	247.5	70.3	177.2	87.8	89.4	234.8	235.6	11.5	16.9	11.2	5.7	. . .	2 478.3
1982	229.9	51.3	178.6	92.9	85.6	274.8	240.9	15.0	19.3	12.4	6.9	. . .	2 592.7
1983	279.8	66.4	213.3	97.7	115.7	286.8	263.3	21.3	21.7	13.8	7.9	. . .	2 789.8
1984	337.9	81.5	256.4	106.9	149.5	330.2	289.8	21.1	29.2	19.7	9.4	. . .	3 136.9
1985	354.5	81.6	272.9	115.3	157.5	338.2	308.1	21.4	34.1	22.3	11.8	. . .	3 347.2
1986	324.4	91.9	232.5	124.0	108.5	353.1	323.4	24.9	36.0	22.9	13.0	. . .	3 494.3
1987	366.0	112.7	253.3	130.1	123.2	353.7	347.5	30.3	33.3	20.2	13.1	. . .	3 745.2
1988	414.5	124.3	290.2	147.3	142.9	377.9	374.5	29.5	32.8	20.6	12.2	. . .	4 088.3
1989	414.3	124.4	289.9	179.6	110.3	426.6	398.9	27.4	38.3	23.2	15.1	. . .	4 343.2
1990	417.7	121.8	295.9	192.7	103.2	433.4	425.0	27.0	39.2	22.2	17.0	. . .	4 572.9
1991	452.6	117.8	334.8	201.3	133.5	391.8	457.1	27.5	38.9	17.6	21.3	. . .	4 687.6
1992	477.2	131.9	345.3	206.3	139.0	365.6	483.4	30.1	39.7	16.3	23.6	-0.1	4 971.8
1993	524.6	155.0	369.5	221.3	148.2	353.1	503.1	36.7	39.4	14.1	25.6	-0.3	5 213.0
1994	624.8	172.7	452.1	256.4	195.7	347.3	545.2	32.5	40.7	13.3	27.9	-0.4	5 548.6
1995	706.2	194.4	511.8	282.3	229.4	357.4	557.9	34.8	45.0	18.7	24.9	1.4	5 867.7
1996	789.5	211.4	578.1	323.6	254.5	361.9	580.8	35.2	52.6	22.9	30.7	-1.0	6 254.7
1997	869.7	224.8	645.0	360.1	284.9	394.4	611.6	33.8	50.1	19.4	29.8	0.8	6 704.0
1998	808.5	221.8	586.6	383.6	203.0	456.7	639.5	36.4	64.1	26.0	34.3	3.8	7 141.7
1999	834.9	227.4	607.5	373.5	234.0	466.0	673.6	45.2	67.7	34.0	36.5	-2.7	7 578.6
2000	786.6	233.4	553.1	410.2	142.9	542.1	708.6	45.8	85.2	42.4	41.9	0.8	8 113.1
2001	758.7	170.1	588.6	397.9	190.7	542.2	727.7	58.7	99.2	46.8	43.9	8.6	8 372.7
2002	911.7	160.7	751.0	424.9	326.2	462.0	760.0	41.4	80.8	34.2	46.2	0.3	8 587.3
2003	1 056.3	213.8	842.5	456.0	386.5	443.6	805.6	49.1	76.0	26.3	48.3	1.5	8 978.0
2004	1 289.3	278.5	1 010.8	582.2	428.6	377.3	868.1	46.4	82.2	16.8	52.4	13.1	9 591.8
2005	1 488.6	379.7	1 108.9	602.0	506.9	471.8	942.4	60.9	91.7	25.8	53.4	12.5	10 226.0
2006	1 646.3	430.1	1 216.1	755.1	461.1	564.8	997.0	51.5	80.9	20.8	57.5	2.6	10 922.0
2007	1 533.2	391.8	1 141.4	853.5	287.9	637.3	1 036.8	54.6	98.5	30.8	60.9	6.9	11 230.0
2008	1 285.8	255.9	1 029.9	840.3	189.6	673.4	1 049.7	52.6	114.3	35.8	69.5	9.0	11 266.0
2009	1 386.8	203.9	1 182.9	622.1	560.8	544.7	1 026.8	58.3	126.6	39.0	86.1	1.5	10 975.0
2010	1 728.7	272.3	1 456.5	643.2	813.3	471.0	1 063.1	55.8	127.9	43.7	84.1	0.0	11 666.1
2011	1 809.8	280.8	1 529.0	779.1	749.9	449.6	1 103.7	60.0	131.7	48.5	86.8	-3.7	12 219.5
2012	1 997.4	334.6	1 662.8	948.7	714.1	494.0	1 136.1	58.0	97.3	40.4	69.0	-12.1	12 939.6
2013	2 010.7	362.6	1 648.1	1 009.0	639.1	459.2	1 188.7	59.7	109.5	38.4	84.7	-13.6	13 284.6
2014	2 120.2	407.1	1 713.1	1 096.1	617.1	504.8	1 240.8	58.1	132.7	42.9	98.1	-8.3	13 923.6
2015	2 060.5	396.3	1 664.2	1 164.9	499.3	591.1	1 275.2	57.2	155.6	50.3	110.5	-5.2	14 381.2
2016	2 037.7	376.2	1 661.5	1 189.4	472.1	567.3	1 311.6	61.7	166.9	59.7	105.3	1.9	14 621.1
2017	2 128.9	312.3	1 816.6	1 264.1	552.5	612.5	1 366.3	59.9	149.1	48.7	99.7	0.7	15 326.0
2018	2 305.0	281.5	2 023.4	1 338.4	685.0	598.7	1 461.7	63.3	158.0	50.2	103.8	4.1	16 125.4
2019	2 367.8	302.2	2 065.6	1 386.4	679.2	558.2	1 532.3	73.0	162.3	56.0	95.7	10.6	16 664.7
2020	2 243.8	275.6	1 968.1	1 394.9	573.3	618.8	1 534.7	761.4	158.6	59.9	97.8	0.9	16 796.3
2018													
1st quarter	2 240.1	256.8	1 983.3	1 288.6	694.7	607.7	1 427.2	58.7	150.9	48.0	105.8	-2.9	15 870.7
2nd quarter	2 264.4	282.9	1 981.4	1 314.5	666.9	604.9	1 448.6	58.2	148.7	49.4	98.8	0.5	16 010.4
3rd quarter	2 320.3	287.2	2 033.1	1 355.7	677.3	588.3	1 468.9	57.8	173.6	50.9	117.5	5.2	16 223.9
4th quarter	2 395.0	299.2	2 095.9	1 394.8	701.1	593.8	1 502.2	78.5	158.9	52.5	92.9	13.4	16 396.8
2019													
1st quarter	2 297.2	297.4	1 999.8	1 367.5	632.3	570.2	1 504.8	69.0	170.8	54.2	90.3	26.4	16 475.9
2nd quarter	2 387.2	303.8	2 083.2	1 393.7	689.5	560.4	1 520.9	58.8	162.5	55.6	92.9	14.1	16 605.3
3rd quarter	2 381.8	291.5	2 090.3	1 387.0	703.2	541.6	1 547.4	81.2	168.2	56.7	109.2	2.4	16 679.3
4th quarter	2 405.1	316.0	2 089.2	1 397.4	691.8	560.7	1 556.3	82.8	147.5	57.5	90.7	-0.7	16 898.4
2020													
1st quarter	2 169.5	245.4	1 924.0	1 417.7	506.3	566.9	1 577.1	80.9	149.4	58.0	93.3	-1.9	16 842.4
2nd quarter	1 942.6	241.2	1 701.5	1 395.7	305.8	619.3	1 460.5	1 124.3	152.8	63.3	95.1	-5.6	15 771.8
3rd quarter	2 435.4	300.3	2 135.1	1 368.6	766.5	623.0	1 544.0	1 221.2	165.8	58.9	99.7	7.2	17 073.4
4th quarter	2 427.5	315.6	2 111.9	1 397.5	714.4	666.1	1 557.0	619.2	166.3	59.2	103.2	3.9	17 497.8

¹Includes net transfer payments to the rest of the world, not shown separately.
. . . = Not available.

Table 1-13B. National Income by Type of Income: Historical Data

(Billions of dollars, quarterly data are at seasonally adjusted annual rates.)   **NIPA Tables 1.7.5, 1.12**

Year and quarter	National income, total	Compensation of employees							Proprietors' income with IVA and CCAdj			Rental income of persons with CCAdj
		Total	Wages and salaries			Supplements to wages and salaries			Total	Farm	Nonfarm	
			Total	Government	Other	Total	Employer contributions for:					
							Employee pension and insurance funds	Government social insurance				
1929	94.2	51.4	50.5	5.0	45.5	0.9	0.9	0.0	14.0	5.7	8.4	6.1
1930	83.1	47.2	46.2	5.2	41.0	1.0	0.9	0.0	10.9	3.9	7.0	5.4
1931	67.7	40.1	39.2	5.3	33.9	0.9	0.9	0.0	8.3	3.0	5.3	4.4
1932	51.3	31.3	30.5	5.0	25.5	0.8	0.8	0.0	5.0	1.8	3.3	3.6
1933	48.9	29.8	29.0	5.2	23.9	0.8	0.8	0.0	5.3	2.2	3.0	2.9
1934	58.3	34.6	33.7	6.1	27.6	0.8	0.8	0.0	7.0	2.6	4.4	2.5
1935	66.3	37.7	36.7	6.5	30.2	0.9	0.9	0.0	10.1	4.9	5.2	2.6
1936	75.1	43.3	42.0	7.9	34.1	1.3	1.1	0.2	10.4	3.9	6.4	2.7
1937	83.7	48.3	46.1	7.5	38.6	2.2	1.1	1.0	12.5	5.6	6.9	3.0
1938	77.0	45.4	43.0	8.3	34.8	2.4	1.2	1.2	10.6	4.0	6.6	3.5
1939	82.4	48.6	46.0	8.2	37.7	2.6	1.3	1.3	11.1	4.0	7.1	3.7
1940	91.5	52.7	49.9	8.5	41.4	2.9	1.5	1.4	12.2	4.1	8.2	3.8
1941	117.3	66.2	62.1	10.2	51.9	4.1	2.4	1.7	16.7	6.0	10.6	4.4
1942	152.4	88.0	82.1	16.0	66.1	5.9	3.9	2.0	23.3	9.7	13.7	5.5
1943	187.2	112.7	105.8	26.6	79.2	6.9	4.6	2.3	28.2	11.5	16.7	6.0
1944	200.9	124.3	116.7	33.0	83.8	7.6	5.0	2.5	29.3	11.4	17.9	6.3
1945	201.3	126.3	117.5	34.9	82.6	8.8	5.3	3.5	30.8	11.8	19.0	6.6
1946	201.3	122.5	112.0	20.7	91.3	10.5	5.4	5.1	35.7	14.2	21.5	6.9
1947	218.7	132.4	123.1	17.5	105.6	9.3	5.3	3.9	34.6	14.3	20.2	6.9
1948	244.8	144.3	135.6	19.0	116.5	8.8	5.8	3.0	39.3	16.7	22.6	7.5
1949	239.7	144.3	134.7	20.8	113.9	9.6	6.3	3.3	34.7	12.0	22.7	7.8
1947												
1st quarter	213.0	129.0	118.9	17.1	101.7	10.1	5.5	4.7	36.2	16.0	20.2	6.7
2nd quarter	215.6	130.8	121.3	17.3	103.9	9.5	5.2	4.3	33.3	12.4	20.9	6.8
3rd quarter	219.2	132.8	124.0	17.6	106.4	8.8	5.2	3.5	33.9	14.1	19.8	7.0
4th quarter	227.2	136.9	128.3	18.0	110.3	8.6	5.4	3.2	35.0	14.9	20.0	7.2
1948												
1st quarter	235.8	140.4	131.7	18.3	113.4	8.7	5.5	3.2	36.4	14.5	21.9	7.3
2nd quarter	244.0	142.1	133.4	18.6	114.7	8.7	5.7	3.0	40.2	18.0	22.3	7.5
3rd quarter	248.8	146.8	138.1	19.3	118.8	8.8	5.8	2.9	40.6	17.9	22.7	7.5
4th quarter	250.7	147.9	139.1	19.9	119.2	8.8	6.0	2.9	39.9	16.4	23.5	7.6
1949												
1st quarter	243.3	146.3	136.7	20.4	116.4	9.5	6.0	3.5	35.4	12.7	22.7	7.5
2nd quarter	239.7	144.7	135.0	20.7	114.3	9.7	6.1	3.5	34.9	12.1	22.8	7.7
3rd quarter	239.9	143.6	134.0	21.1	112.9	9.6	6.3	3.3	34.2	11.6	22.6	7.9
4th quarter	236.0	142.8	133.2	21.2	112.0	9.6	6.5	3.0	34.2	11.5	22.7	8.1
1950												
1st quarter	246.3	147.0	136.9	21.2	115.6	10.1	6.9	3.3	36.2	12.2	24.0	8.5
2nd quarter	258.5	153.6	143.0	21.8	121.2	10.6	7.3	3.3	36.8	12.2	24.6	8.7
3rd quarter	275.6	162.3	151.0	23.0	128.1	11.3	7.9	3.4	38.5	13.1	25.4	8.8
4th quarter	286.1	170.2	158.1	24.5	133.5	12.1	8.5	3.6	38.5	13.9	24.6	9.1
1951												
1st quarter	297.8	178.6	165.3	26.7	138.6	13.2	9.2	4.0	40.9	15.0	25.9	9.3
2nd quarter	305.2	184.9	171.0	28.5	142.5	13.9	9.8	4.1	42.5	15.4	27.1	9.6
3rd quarter	310.6	187.9	173.5	30.2	143.3	14.4	10.3	4.1	43.2	15.1	28.1	9.9
4th quarter	317.0	191.5	176.6	31.5	145.1	14.9	10.7	4.1	43.7	15.7	28.0	10.1
1952												
1st quarter	318.5	196.1	181.0	32.4	148.6	15.1	11.0	4.1	41.7	13.7	28.0	10.4
2nd quarter	320.4	197.4	182.1	33.1	149.0	15.3	11.2	4.1	43.0	14.5	28.4	10.7
3rd quarter	327.0	201.5	186.0	33.8	152.2	15.6	11.4	4.1	44.7	16.0	28.8	10.9
4th quarter	338.5	209.3	193.5	34.2	159.3	15.9	11.6	4.2	42.8	13.0	29.7	11.3
1953												
1st quarter	344.5	213.1	197.1	34.3	162.7	16.1	11.9	4.2	42.9	13.0	29.9	11.6
2nd quarter	347.3	216.2	200.0	34.4	165.7	16.2	12.0	4.2	42.3	12.4	29.9	11.9
3rd quarter	345.6	216.5	200.1	34.3	165.9	16.4	12.1	4.3	41.2	11.7	29.5	12.2
4th quarter	338.0	215.1	198.7	34.4	164.3	16.4	12.2	4.2	41.6	11.5	30.0	12.5
1954												
1st quarter	339.6	213.1	196.4	34.4	162.0	16.7	12.1	4.6	42.7	12.9	29.8	12.8
2nd quarter	339.9	212.7	196.0	34.7	161.2	16.7	12.1	4.6	42.1	11.7	30.4	13.0
3rd quarter	343.3	213.2	196.3	35.1	161.2	16.9	12.3	4.6	42.2	11.8	30.5	13.1
4th quarter	352.2	217.5	200.4	35.4	165.0	17.2	12.5	4.6	42.0	10.7	31.3	13.3
1955												
1st quarter	364.6	221.9	204.1	35.5	168.6	17.8	12.8	5.0	43.7	10.9	32.7	13.3
2nd quarter	374.0	228.1	209.9	36.2	173.6	18.2	13.1	5.1	44.3	11.3	33.0	13.4
3rd quarter	381.4	233.9	215.2	37.4	177.8	18.7	13.4	5.2	44.6	10.7	33.9	13.4
4th quarter	387.7	238.4	219.5	37.3	182.2	18.9	13.7	5.3	44.5	10.0	34.5	13.5
1956												
1st quarter	391.2	242.8	223.3	37.8	185.4	19.5	14.0	5.6	44.9	10.2	34.7	13.6
2nd quarter	397.0	247.5	227.5	38.5	189.0	20.0	14.3	5.7	45.3	10.4	34.9	13.6
3rd quarter	401.9	250.4	230.0	39.2	190.8	20.5	14.8	5.7	46.4	10.9	35.5	13.7
4th quarter	410.1	256.4	235.4	39.7	195.7	21.0	15.2	5.8	46.8	10.9	35.8	13.8
1957												
1st quarter	416.8	260.2	238.3	40.2	198.0	22.0	15.6	6.4	46.9	9.9	37.0	13.9
2nd quarter	418.9	262.1	239.6	40.7	198.9	22.4	16.0	6.4	47.7	10.5	37.2	14.0
3rd quarter	422.6	264.7	241.8	41.5	200.3	22.9	16.5	6.4	48.8	11.0	37.8	14.1
4th quarter	415.8	263.3	240.1	41.6	198.5	23.2	16.9	6.3	47.7	10.7	37.0	14.3

Table 1-13B. National Income by Type of Income: Historical Data—*Continued*

(Billions of dollars, quarterly data are at seasonally adjusted annual rates.)   **NIPA Tables 1.7.5, 1.12**

| Year and quarter | Corporate profits with IVA and CCAdj | | | | | Net interest and miscellaneous payments | Taxes on production and imports | Less: Subsidies | Business current transfer payments, net | | | Current surplus of government enterprises | Addendum: Net national factor income |
| | Total | Taxes on corporate income | Profits after tax | | | | | | Total 1 | To persons | To government | | |
			Total	Net dividends	Undistributed corporate profits								
1929	10.8	1.4	9.5	5.8	3.7	4.6	6.8	0.0	0.5	0.4	0.1	...	86.9
1930	7.5	0.8	6.7	5.5	1.2	4.8	7.0	0.1	0.5	0.4	0.1	...	75.7
1931	3.0	0.5	2.5	4.1	-1.6	4.8	6.7	0.1	0.5	0.4	0.1	...	60.6
1932	-0.2	0.4	-0.6	2.5	-3.1	4.5	6.6	0.1	0.6	0.5	0.1	...	44.2
1933	-0.2	0.5	-0.7	2.0	-2.7	4.0	6.9	0.2	0.5	0.4	0.1	...	41.7
1934	2.5	0.7	1.8	2.6	-0.8	4.0	7.6	0.5	0.5	0.4	0.1	...	50.6
1935	4.0	1.0	3.1	2.8	0.2	4.1	8.0	0.6	0.5	0.4	0.1	...	58.4
1936	6.2	1.4	4.8	4.5	0.3	3.8	8.5	0.3	0.5	0.4	0.1	...	66.4
1937	7.1	1.5	5.6	4.7	0.9	3.7	8.9	0.3	0.5	0.4	0.1	...	74.5
1938	5.0	1.0	4.0	3.2	0.8	3.6	8.9	0.5	0.4	0.3	0.2	...	68.1
1939	6.6	1.4	5.2	3.8	1.4	3.6	9.1	0.8	0.4	0.3	0.2	...	73.6
1940	9.9	2.8	7.0	4.0	3.0	3.3	9.8	0.7	0.5	0.3	0.2	...	82.0
1941	15.7	7.6	8.1	4.4	3.7	3.3	11.1	0.5	0.5	0.4	0.2	...	106.2
1942	20.8	11.4	9.4	4.3	5.1	3.2	11.5	0.5	0.5	0.3	0.2	...	140.8
1943	24.9	14.1	10.8	4.4	6.4	2.9	12.4	0.6	0.6	0.4	0.3	...	174.7
1944	25.0	12.9	12.0	4.6	7.4	2.4	13.7	1.0	0.8	0.4	0.4	...	187.4
1945	20.5	10.7	9.8	4.6	5.2	2.3	15.1	1.1	0.9	0.5	0.4	...	186.5
1946	18.2	9.1	9.1	5.6	3.6	1.8	16.8	1.4	0.7	0.4	0.3	...	185.1
1947	24.2	11.2	13.0	6.4	6.6	2.3	18.1	0.4	0.7	0.4	0.3	...	200.3
1948	31.4	12.3	19.1	7.2	11.9	2.5	19.7	0.5	0.7	0.4	0.3	...	225.0
1949	29.1	10.0	19.0	7.4	11.6	2.8	20.9	0.5	0.7	0.4	0.3	...	218.6
1947													
1st quarter	21.5	11.5	10.0	6.1	3.9	2.0	17.7	0.5	0.5	0.2	0.3	...	195.3
2nd quarter	24.5	10.9	13.6	6.4	7.2	2.3	17.7	0.4	0.7	0.4	0.3	...	197.6
3rd quarter	24.6	10.7	13.9	6.6	7.3	2.5	18.0	0.4	0.8	0.5	0.3	...	200.7
4th quarter	26.1	11.7	14.5	6.6	7.9	2.5	19.0	0.3	0.9	0.5	0.3	...	207.6
1948													
1st quarter	30.0	12.0	18.0	7.2	10.8	2.4	19.0	0.4	0.7	0.4	0.4	...	216.5
2nd quarter	31.8	12.6	19.1	6.8	12.3	2.4	19.7	0.3	0.7	0.4	0.3	...	224.0
3rd quarter	31.2	12.4	18.8	7.3	11.5	2.5	20.0	0.6	0.7	0.4	0.3	...	228.7
4th quarter	32.7	12.0	20.7	7.6	13.1	2.5	20.3	0.9	0.7	0.4	0.3	...	230.6
1949													
1st quarter	31.0	10.8	20.2	7.4	12.7	2.7	20.4	0.6	0.7	0.3	0.3	...	222.9
2nd quarter	28.7	9.5	19.1	7.4	11.7	2.7	20.8	0.4	0.7	0.3	0.3	...	218.7
3rd quarter	29.9	9.9	20.0	7.3	12.7	2.8	21.3	0.5	0.7	0.4	0.3	...	218.5
4th quarter	26.6	9.7	16.9	7.6	9.3	2.8	21.2	0.5	0.7	0.4	0.3	...	214.5
1950													
1st quarter	30.1	13.4	16.6	8.5	8.1	3.0	21.6	0.7	0.7	0.4	0.3	...	224.8
2nd quarter	33.9	16.1	17.8	8.6	9.2	3.1	22.5	0.8	0.8	0.5	0.3	...	236.0
3rd quarter	38.4	19.7	18.7	9.4	9.4	3.1	24.4	0.8	0.9	0.6	0.3	...	251.1
4th quarter	41.8	21.6	20.2	9.7	10.5	3.1	23.4	1.1	0.9	0.7	0.3	...	262.8
1951													
1st quarter	40.7	26.0	14.7	8.6	6.1	3.3	25.1	1.2	1.1	0.8	0.3	...	272.8
2nd quarter	40.6	22.0	18.6	8.9	9.7	3.5	24.1	1.1	1.2	0.9	0.3	...	281.1
3rd quarter	41.1	19.9	21.2	8.8	12.4	3.7	24.5	0.9	1.2	0.9	0.3	...	285.8
4th quarter	42.4	21.3	21.1	9.0	12.2	3.8	25.3	1.0	1.2	0.9	0.3	...	291.5
1952													
1st quarter	40.0	19.5	20.5	8.4	12.1	3.8	26.1	0.8	1.2	0.9	0.3	...	292.0
2nd quarter	38.1	18.4	19.8	9.0	10.8	3.9	26.9	0.8	1.2	0.9	0.3	...	293.1
3rd quarter	38.1	18.3	19.8	8.9	10.9	4.0	27.3	0.8	1.2	0.9	0.3	...	299.3
4th quarter	42.4	20.2	22.2	9.1	13.1	4.1	28.1	0.7	1.2	0.9	0.3	...	309.9
1953													
1st quarter	43.3	21.3	22.1	8.8	13.3	4.3	28.7	0.7	1.2	0.9	0.3	...	315.3
2nd quarter	42.5	21.4	21.1	9.5	11.6	4.4	29.2	0.5	1.2	0.9	0.3	...	317.4
3rd quarter	41.3	20.9	20.4	9.4	11.0	4.6	29.3	0.7	1.2	0.8	0.3	...	315.8
4th quarter	34.0	16.2	17.8	9.2	8.5	4.8	29.2	0.2	1.1	0.8	0.3	...	307.9
1954													
1st quarter	36.5	16.1	20.4	9.7	10.7	5.0	28.7	0.1	1.0	0.6	0.3	...	310.1
2nd quarter	37.8	16.6	21.2	9.2	12.1	5.3	28.8	0.7	0.9	0.5	0.3	...	310.9
3rd quarter	39.9	17.7	22.2	9.6	12.7	5.5	28.7	0.3	0.9	0.5	0.4	...	314.0
4th quarter	43.6	19.0	24.6	9.7	14.8	5.7	29.3	0.2	0.9	0.6	0.4	...	322.1
1955													
1st quarter	48.8	21.1	27.7	10.3	17.4	5.8	30.2	0.3	1.1	0.7	0.4	...	333.5
2nd quarter	50.1	21.4	28.7	10.4	18.3	6.0	31.2	0.3	1.2	0.9	0.4	...	341.8
3rd quarter	50.2	21.9	28.3	11.0	17.2	5.9	31.9	0.0	1.4	1.0	0.4	...	348.1
4th quarter	51.6	22.8	28.8	11.2	17.6	5.9	32.5	0.2	1.5	1.1	0.4	...	354.0
1956													
1st quarter	49.4	21.7	27.7	11.5	16.2	6.2	33.0	0.3	1.6	1.2	0.4	...	356.9
2nd quarter	49.6	22.1	27.5	11.6	16.0	6.4	33.6	0.6	1.6	1.2	0.4	...	362.3
3rd quarter	49.3	20.7	28.6	11.6	17.0	6.7	34.6	0.9	1.7	1.3	0.4	...	366.5
4th quarter	50.2	21.9	28.4	12.0	16.3	6.7	35.7	1.2	1.7	1.3	0.4	...	373.8
1957													
1st quarter	51.7	22.3	29.3	12.1	17.2	7.5	36.1	1.3	1.8	1.4	0.4	...	380.2
2nd quarter	50.3	21.4	28.9	12.3	16.6	7.7	36.6	1.2	1.8	1.4	0.4	...	381.7
3rd quarter	49.3	20.9	28.5	12.5	16.0	7.8	37.0	1.1	1.8	1.4	0.4	...	384.8
4th quarter	45.3	19.0	26.3	12.3	14.0	7.6	36.7	1.0	1.8	1.4	0.4	...	378.2

1Includes net transfer payments to the rest of the world, not shown separately.
. . . = Not available.

Table 1-13B. National Income by Type of Income: Historical Data—Continued

(Billions of dollars, quarterly data are at seasonally adjusted annual rates.)   NIPA Tables 1.7.5, 1.12

Year and quarter	National income, total	Compensation of employees							Proprietors' income with IVA and CCAdj			Rental income of persons with CCAdj
		Total	Wages and salaries			Supplements to wages and salaries			Total	Farm	Nonfarm	
			Total	Government	Other	Total	Employer contributions for:					
							Employee pension and insurance funds	Government social insurance				
1958												
1st quarter	409.7	259.8	236.7	42.0	194.7	23.0	16.7	6.3	50.3	13.3	36.9	14.6
2nd quarter	411.6	259.4	236.3	43.1	193.2	23.2	16.9	6.3	50.3	13.0	37.3	14.8
3rd quarter	424.5	267.2	243.8	46.1	197.7	23.4	17.0	6.4	50.1	12.1	38.0	14.9
4th quarter	437.2	272.3	248.4	45.3	203.2	23.8	17.4	6.4	49.9	11.2	38.7	15.0
1959												
1st quarter	448.3	279.7	254.0	45.5	208.6	25.7	18.0	7.8	50.1	10.9	39.2	15.0
2nd quarter	462.4	286.5	260.6	45.8	214.7	25.9	18.0	7.9	50.3	9.9	40.5	15.4
3rd quarter	459.6	286.9	260.9	46.2	214.7	26.0	18.2	7.9	50.4	9.4	41.0	15.8
4th quarter	464.8	290.2	263.9	46.7	217.2	26.3	18.4	7.9	50.6	10.1	40.5	16.0
1960												
1st quarter	478.1	298.7	270.7	47.7	223.0	28.0	18.7	9.3	49.7	9.6	40.1	16.2
2nd quarter	478.8	301.7	273.4	48.6	224.8	28.3	19.1	9.3	50.7	10.6	40.1	16.4
3rd quarter	480.2	302.6	274.0	49.9	224.1	28.6	19.3	9.3	50.9	11.0	39.9	16.5
4th quarter	478.5	302.1	273.3	50.5	222.8	28.8	19.6	9.2	51.0	11.3	39.7	16.7
1961												
1st quarter	480.3	303.1	273.8	51.1	222.7	29.3	19.9	9.5	52.3	11.5	40.8	16.9
2nd quarter	489.9	307.3	277.6	51.8	225.8	29.7	20.1	9.6	52.6	10.9	41.8	17.1
3rd quarter	499.7	312.3	282.3	52.8	229.5	30.1	20.4	9.6	53.3	11.0	42.3	17.3
4th quarter	514.2	318.9	288.4	54.2	234.2	30.5	20.7	9.8	54.5	11.5	43.0	17.5
1962												
1st quarter	523.4	325.5	293.3	55.3	238.0	32.2	21.2	11.0	55.3	11.9	43.5	17.7
2nd quarter	530.5	331.4	298.7	56.0	242.8	32.7	21.5	11.2	55.0	11.1	43.9	18.0
3rd quarter	536.9	334.2	301.2	56.5	244.7	33.1	21.8	11.2	54.9	10.7	44.2	18.2
4th quarter	544.9	337.7	304.2	57.6	246.6	33.4	22.1	11.3	55.8	11.3	44.5	18.3
1963												
1st quarter	551.8	342.7	308.0	58.6	249.3	34.7	22.5	12.2	56.0	11.4	44.6	18.5
2nd quarter	560.9	347.6	312.4	59.4	253.0	35.2	22.9	12.3	55.8	10.8	45.0	18.7
3rd quarter	569.4	352.6	316.8	60.2	256.7	35.8	23.3	12.5	56.2	10.7	45.6	18.8
4th quarter	579.4	358.8	322.2	61.9	260.3	36.5	23.9	12.6	57.6	11.1	46.5	18.8
1964												
1st quarter	591.7	365.2	328.2	63.1	265.1	37.0	24.5	12.4	57.9	9.9	48.0	18.8
2nd quarter	601.8	372.6	334.8	64.2	270.7	37.8	25.2	12.6	58.8	9.5	49.3	18.8
3rd quarter	613.2	380.0	341.4	65.7	275.7	38.6	25.9	12.7	59.3	9.3	50.0	18.9
4th quarter	621.4	386.1	346.7	66.8	279.9	39.4	26.6	12.8	60.5	10.4	50.1	18.8
1965												
1st quarter	640.0	392.9	352.8	67.5	285.4	40.1	27.3	12.8	61.9	11.4	50.5	19.1
2nd quarter	651.2	399.9	358.9	68.5	290.3	41.0	28.1	13.0	63.2	12.0	51.2	19.3
3rd quarter	662.4	408.3	366.2	70.5	295.7	42.1	29.0	13.2	64.0	12.2	51.8	19.5
4th quarter	681.8	420.5	377.1	73.2	304.0	43.3	29.9	13.4	65.6	12.5	53.0	19.5
1966												
1st quarter	702.0	433.1	385.8	74.9	310.8	47.3	30.9	16.5	69.2	14.9	54.4	19.8
2nd quarter	711.8	444.4	395.9	76.9	319.0	48.5	31.8	16.7	67.2	12.7	54.5	19.8
3rd quarter	723.1	455.7	406.1	79.8	326.3	49.5	32.5	17.0	67.2	12.3	54.9	20.0
4th quarter	735.5	463.8	413.5	82.0	331.5	50.3	33.1	17.2	68.1	12.2	55.9	20.0
1967												
1st quarter	741.8	470.0	418.8	83.5	335.4	51.2	33.6	17.6	68.9	11.9	57.0	20.3
2nd quarter	748.4	475.6	423.6	85.0	338.6	52.0	34.3	17.8	68.5	11.1	57.4	20.4
3rd quarter	763.8	485.3	432.0	87.1	344.9	53.3	35.1	18.2	70.5	12.0	58.6	20.4
4th quarter	779.7	496.2	441.6	90.4	351.2	54.7	36.1	18.6	70.0	11.5	58.4	20.3
1968												
1st quarter	800.5	510.9	454.2	92.8	361.5	56.7	37.2	19.4	71.7	11.6	60.1	20.1
2nd quarter	821.5	524.0	465.9	95.2	370.7	58.1	38.3	19.8	73.2	11.2	61.9	20.1
3rd quarter	841.0	537.8	478.3	98.7	379.6	59.5	39.4	20.1	75.0	11.8	63.2	20.2
4th quarter	858.0	550.3	489.4	100.1	389.4	60.9	40.4	20.5	75.5	12.0	63.5	20.0
1969												
1st quarter	874.6	562.8	499.1	101.3	397.8	63.7	41.6	22.1	75.6	11.6	64.1	20.2
2nd quarter	890.1	576.7	511.4	103.1	408.3	65.3	42.8	22.5	77.1	12.5	64.6	20.3
3rd quarter	908.1	593.4	526.4	108.2	418.3	67.0	44.0	23.0	78.0	13.1	64.8	20.4
4th quarter	916.3	604.9	536.5	109.8	426.6	68.5	45.1	23.4	77.3	14.1	63.2	20.4
1970												
1st quarter	921.1	615.0	545.1	114.4	430.7	69.9	46.2	23.7	77.1	13.5	63.5	20.4
2nd quarter	933.2	620.2	549.1	116.5	432.6	71.2	47.3	23.9	76.7	12.4	64.3	20.2
3rd quarter	947.7	628.2	555.7	118.3	437.4	72.5	48.5	23.9	78.5	13.2	65.3	20.9
4th quarter	948.0	630.0	556.4	119.7	436.6	73.7	49.8	23.9	78.9	12.5	66.4	21.2
1971												
1st quarter	984.6	647.9	570.5	123.9	446.6	77.4	51.3	26.1	80.3	13.1	67.2	21.1
2nd quarter	1 004.4	659.8	580.4	125.6	454.8	79.3	52.9	26.4	82.8	13.3	69.6	21.7
3rd quarter	1 022.4	670.1	588.8	128.0	460.8	81.3	54.8	26.5	84.6	13.0	71.6	22.0
4th quarter	1 044.7	682.2	598.4	129.6	468.8	83.7	56.9	26.8	87.9	14.2	73.6	22.5
1972												
1st quarter	1 077.9	708.4	618.5	134.2	484.3	89.9	59.3	30.6	87.9	13.1	74.8	23.1
2nd quarter	1 098.2	722.5	630.4	135.7	494.7	92.1	61.1	31.0	91.3	15.4	75.9	20.2
3rd quarter	1 127.9	735.7	642.3	138.4	503.9	93.4	62.3	31.2	95.5	17.2	78.4	23.9
4th quarter	1 174.0	758.8	664.0	143.3	520.7	94.8	63.0	31.8	105.6	22.4	83.3	23.8

Table 1-13B. National Income by Type of Income: Historical Data—*Continued*

(Billions of dollars, quarterly data are at seasonally adjusted annual rates.)   **NIPA Tables 1.7.5, 1.12**

Year and quarter	Corporate profits with IVA and CCAdj					Net interest and miscellaneous payments	Taxes on production and imports	Less: Subsidies	Business current transfer payments, net			Current surplus of government enterprises	Addendum: Net national factor income
	Total	Taxes on corporate income	Profits after tax						Total 1	To persons	To government		
			Total	Net dividends	Undistributed corporate profits								
1958													
1st quarter	39.5	16.3	23.1	12.1	11.0	8.1	36.8	1.1	1.8	1.3	0.5	...	372.2
2nd quarter	40.6	16.7	23.9	12.2	11.7	8.7	37.3	1.3	1.7	1.3	0.5	...	373.8
3rd quarter	44.8	18.9	25.9	12.1	13.7	9.5	37.8	1.5	1.7	1.2	0.5	...	386.5
4th quarter	50.6	21.8	28.7	11.8	16.9	10.6	38.9	1.6	1.6	1.2	0.4	...	398.3
1959													
1st quarter	54.3	22.8	31.5	12.8	18.7	8.5	39.8	1.1	1.6	1.3	0.3	...	407.5
2nd quarter	59.1	25.0	34.1	13.2	20.9	9.5	40.3	0.9	1.7	1.3	0.3	...	420.8
3rd quarter	54.2	22.1	32.1	13.8	18.3	9.5	41.7	1.1	1.7	1.3	0.3	...	416.8
4th quarter	54.5	21.4	33.1	14.1	19.0	9.8	42.4	1.1	1.7	1.4	0.3	...	421.2
1960													
1st quarter	58.6	24.2	34.4	14.1	20.3	9.8	43.7	1.0	1.7	1.3	0.4	...	433.1
2nd quarter	54.8	22.1	32.7	14.2	18.5	9.9	44.3	1.3	1.7	1.3	0.4	...	433.5
3rd quarter	53.8	21.1	32.7	14.4	18.2	10.5	44.9	1.0	1.7	1.3	0.4	...	434.3
4th quarter	51.5	20.1	31.4	14.3	17.1	10.9	45.3	1.2	1.8	1.3	0.5	...	432.3
1961													
1st quarter	50.2	20.0	30.3	14.3	16.0	11.3	45.8	1.6	1.9	1.3	0.5	...	433.9
2nd quarter	54.5	21.4	33.1	14.3	18.7	11.9	46.5	2.0	1.9	1.3	0.5	...	443.4
3rd quarter	57.2	22.7	34.5	14.6	19.9	12.2	47.3	2.2	1.9	1.4	0.5	...	452.4
4th quarter	61.8	24.7	37.1	15.2	21.9	12.9	48.4	2.3	2.0	1.4	0.6	...	465.7
1962													
1st quarter	62.6	23.1	39.4	15.3	24.1	12.7	49.4	2.3	2.0	1.5	0.6	...	473.8
2nd quarter	62.5	22.9	39.7	15.8	23.9	13.7	49.9	2.4	2.1	1.5	0.6	...	480.6
3rd quarter	64.2	23.6	40.7	16.0	24.7	14.2	50.9	2.2	2.1	1.6	0.6	...	485.7
4th quarter	66.9	23.6	43.2	16.2	27.0	14.6	51.3	2.2	2.2	1.6	0.6	...	493.2
1963													
1st quarter	67.2	23.7	43.5	16.6	26.9	14.3	52.0	2.0	2.4	1.8	0.6	...	498.7
2nd quarter	70.2	25.4	44.8	16.9	27.9	14.5	52.9	2.2	2.5	1.8	0.7	...	506.8
3rd quarter	71.7	26.1	45.5	17.2	28.3	15.0	53.9	2.3	2.5	1.9	0.7	...	514.4
4th quarter	73.0	26.7	46.2	17.7	28.5	15.5	54.7	2.4	2.6	2.0	0.7	...	523.6
1964													
1st quarter	77.1	26.4	50.7	19.0	31.7	16.2	55.7	2.7	2.7	2.1	0.6	...	535.1
2nd quarter	77.3	26.4	50.9	19.6	31.3	16.7	56.7	2.9	2.8	2.2	0.6	...	544.3
3rd quarter	78.4	27.0	51.5	20.0	31.4	17.5	57.9	2.6	3.2	2.2	1.0	...	554.1
4th quarter	78.0	26.5	51.5	20.5	31.0	17.6	58.8	2.7	3.3	2.3	1.0	...	561.1
1965													
1st quarter	85.8	28.3	57.5	20.4	37.1	18.6	60.2	2.9	3.5	2.3	1.2	...	578.4
2nd quarter	88.0	29.2	58.8	21.2	37.7	19.0	60.3	3.0	3.5	2.3	1.2	...	589.4
3rd quarter	89.3	29.8	59.5	21.9	37.6	19.5	60.5	3.0	3.5	2.2	1.2	...	600.6
4th quarter	94.0	31.7	62.3	22.6	39.7	19.5	61.8	3.1	3.4	2.2	1.3	...	619.0
1966													
1st quarter	97.4	32.7	64.7	22.7	41.9	20.7	61.4	3.6	3.4	2.2	1.3	...	640.2
2nd quarter	96.4	32.6	63.7	22.5	41.3	21.3	62.8	3.9	3.4	2.1	1.3	...	649.1
3rd quarter	94.8	32.2	62.7	22.2	40.4	22.1	63.7	4.1	3.4	2.1	1.3	...	659.8
4th quarter	95.9	31.4	64.5	21.8	42.6	23.2	64.9	4.2	3.4	2.1	1.3	...	671.1
1967													
1st quarter	93.3	30.6	62.7	22.9	39.8	24.0	65.6	4.0	3.5	2.2	1.3	...	676.4
2nd quarter	92.2	30.3	61.8	23.5	38.3	24.8	66.8	3.9	3.6	2.2	1.4	...	681.5
3rd quarter	93.2	30.6	62.6	23.9	38.7	25.2	68.7	3.7	3.7	2.3	1.4	...	694.7
4th quarter	96.8	32.4	64.4	23.2	41.1	25.7	70.6	3.7	3.8	2.4	1.4	...	709.0
1968													
1st quarter	98.1	36.5	61.7	24.9	36.8	26.0	73.4	4.0	3.9	2.5	1.4	...	726.7
2nd quarter	102.1	37.1	65.1	25.8	39.2	26.3	75.4	4.2	4.1	2.7	1.4	...	745.7
3rd quarter	102.6	37.1	65.5	26.5	39.0	27.1	77.7	4.2	4.3	2.9	1.4	...	762.8
4th quarter	104.1	38.0	66.1	26.8	39.3	28.4	79.1	4.2	4.4	3.0	1.4	...	778.3
1969													
1st quarter	103.5	38.7	64.8	26.7	38.1	31.4	80.6	4.3	4.7	3.3	1.5	...	793.5
2nd quarter	100.3	37.5	62.9	27.1	35.8	32.2	82.9	4.5	4.8	3.4	1.5	...	806.6
3rd quarter	97.4	36.1	61.4	27.3	34.0	33.3	85.2	4.7	4.8	3.4	1.5	...	822.6
4th quarter	92.4	35.6	56.8	27.9	29.0	34.1	86.7	4.7	4.8	3.3	1.5	...	829.2
1970													
1st quarter	84.7	31.1	53.6	27.9	25.7	36.2	88.5	4.7	4.6	3.1	1.5	...	833.3
2nd quarter	88.5	31.2	57.3	27.8	29.6	38.5	90.5	4.8	4.5	3.0	1.5	...	844.2
3rd quarter	88.4	32.1	56.2	27.8	28.4	40.9	92.5	4.7	4.2	2.8	1.4	...	856.8
4th quarter	83.5	30.7	52.8	27.7	25.1	42.4	94.1	4.8	4.1	2.8	1.4	...	855.9
1971													
1st quarter	96.6	34.4	62.2	28.5	33.8	43.4	97.7	4.8	4.1	2.7	1.5	...	889.4
2nd quarter	98.7	35.3	63.4	28.2	35.2	44.3	98.9	4.8	4.1	2.7	1.4	...	907.4
3rd quarter	101.4	34.6	66.9	28.5	38.4	44.4	101.7	4.5	4.2	2.7	1.5	...	922.6
4th quarter	105.8	35.0	70.8	28.3	42.5	44.5	103.7	4.6	4.2	2.8	1.5	...	942.8
1972													
1st quarter	111.5	37.1	74.4	29.3	45.0	45.4	104.6	6.1	4.5	2.9	1.6	...	976.3
2nd quarter	113.4	37.5	76.0	29.6	46.3	46.6	106.8	6.2	4.7	3.0	1.7	...	994.0
3rd quarter	118.2	38.8	79.4	30.3	49.1	48.9	108.9	7.2	4.9	3.2	1.7	...	1 022.2
4th quarter	125.7	43.1	82.7	31.0	51.7	51.1	111.5	7.1	5.0	3.3	1.7	...	1 065.0

1Includes net transfer payments to the rest of the world, not shown separately.
. . . = Not available.

Table 1-13B. National Income by Type of Income: Historical Data—*Continued*

(Billions of dollars, quarterly data are at seasonally adjusted annual rates.)   **NIPA Tables 1.7.5, 1.12**

Year and quarter	National income, total	Compensation of employees							Proprietors' income with IVA and CCAdj			Rental income of persons with CCAdj
		Total	Wages and salaries			Supplements to wages and salaries			Total	Farm	Nonfarm	
			Total	Government	Other	Total	Employer contributions for:					
							Employee pension and insurance funds	Government social insurance				
1973												
1st quarter	1 211.0	785.4	683.4	145.0	538.3	102.1	63.3	38.7	104.1	21.8	82.4	23.5
2nd quarter	1 235.7	803.2	700.2	147.2	553.0	103.0	63.7	39.3	109.9	27.6	82.4	23.3
3rd quarter	1 264.0	820.4	716.2	149.6	566.6	104.2	64.3	39.9	113.8	29.5	84.3	22.3
4th quarter	1 301.9	841.7	735.3	153.4	582.0	106.4	65.3	41.1	122.2	37.5	84.7	23.3
1974												
1st quarter	1 313.9	858.3	748.2	155.6	592.5	110.2	66.6	43.6	115.7	28.6	87.1	23.5
2nd quarter	1 334.6	878.5	765.3	158.2	607.1	113.2	68.7	44.5	108.6	20.1	88.5	22.9
3rd quarter	1 360.6	900.2	783.1	161.3	621.8	117.1	71.8	45.3	111.0	21.5	89.5	23.3
4th quarter	1 376.5	913.8	792.5	166.9	625.6	121.3	75.9	45.4	113.5	23.7	89.8	23.0
1975												
1st quarter	1 383.4	918.4	791.9	170.5	621.4	126.5	80.7	45.7	112.7	19.7	93.0	22.7
2nd quarter	1 413.8	931.2	800.4	174.5	625.9	130.8	84.8	46.0	114.3	20.1	94.2	22.4
3rd quarter	1 471.7	956.0	821.3	177.8	643.5	134.7	87.7	47.0	120.7	23.8	96.9	22.2
4th quarter	1 515.3	983.4	845.8	182.2	663.6	137.6	89.4	48.2	125.2	24.3	100.8	21.9
1976												
1st quarter	1 565.6	1 014.7	871.2	184.8	686.4	143.5	90.4	53.1	126.4	19.4	107.0	21.6
2nd quarter	1 591.3	1 035.5	889.4	187.3	702.1	146.1	92.2	53.9	128.6	17.0	111.6	20.5
3rd quarter	1 623.6	1 058.4	908.5	189.5	719.0	149.9	95.1	54.9	132.7	16.1	116.6	20.0
4th quarter	1 656.9	1 084.8	929.9	194.1	735.8	154.9	99.2	55.7	136.2	16.3	119.9	19.1
1977												
1st quarter	1 704.1	1 113.3	950.0	196.7	753.3	163.2	104.2	59.1	138.6	16.0	122.6	16.4
2nd quarter	1 770.3	1 150.3	980.9	199.7	781.2	169.4	108.8	60.6	140.5	14.1	126.4	16.3
3rd quarter	1 825.0	1 182.1	1 007.5	203.7	803.8	174.6	112.9	61.7	142.4	11.8	130.6	15.6
4th quarter	1 871.9	1 217.6	1 038.2	210.3	827.9	179.4	116.4	63.0	156.5	22.0	134.5	15.1
1978												
1st quarter	1 910.5	1 250.9	1 063.8	213.6	850.3	187.1	119.4	67.6	158.5	18.5	140.0	15.9
2nd quarter	2 006.3	1 299.1	1 106.0	217.3	888.8	193.1	122.6	70.4	166.1	20.9	145.2	15.6
3rd quarter	2 054.8	1 336.9	1 138.0	222.4	915.6	198.9	126.3	72.6	168.3	20.8	147.6	17.1
4th quarter	2 119.1	1 380.2	1 174.4	226.8	947.6	205.8	130.3	75.4	170.9	19.5	151.4	17.5
1979												
1st quarter	2 172.6	1 422.5	1 208.6	231.3	977.2	214.0	134.7	79.2	180.1	23.8	156.3	17.3
2nd quarter	2 212.5	1 454.7	1 234.4	233.5	1 000.9	220.4	139.0	81.4	179.2	21.8	157.3	15.6
3rd quarter	2 264.9	1 496.7	1 269.4	239.4	1 030.0	227.3	143.5	83.9	180.7	22.3	158.5	15.4
4th quarter	2 311.3	1 534.9	1 300.9	244.3	1 056.6	234.0	148.1	85.9	177.8	20.8	157.0	16.1
1980												
1st quarter	2 353.0	1 573.6	1 333.8	250.2	1 083.6	239.8	152.9	86.9	167.6	13.3	154.3	15.8
2nd quarter	2 356.2	1 599.2	1 353.9	260.6	1 093.3	245.3	157.7	87.6	160.3	3.1	157.2	17.1
3rd quarter	2 422.8	1 628.6	1 377.3	264.2	1 113.1	251.3	162.2	89.1	173.4	11.7	161.7	19.9
4th quarter	2 542.6	1 687.6	1 428.7	270.8	1 157.9	258.9	166.7	92.2	185.0	18.7	166.3	23.2
1981												
1st quarter	2 630.5	1 739.6	1 467.7	277.3	1 190.3	271.9	171.0	100.9	188.2	17.6	170.6	24.0
2nd quarter	2 676.3	1 774.8	1 496.7	282.6	1 214.1	278.1	175.3	102.7	176.4	18.2	158.2	23.3
3rd quarter	2 769.4	1 815.1	1 530.6	288.6	1 241.9	284.5	179.7	104.8	182.3	23.3	158.9	23.1
4th quarter	2 782.5	1 840.7	1 550.6	294.8	1 255.8	290.1	184.1	106.0	171.8	17.0	154.9	24.7
1982												
1st quarter	2 786.1	1 864.7	1 567.5	300.8	1 266.8	297.1	188.5	108.6	165.2	14.4	150.8	23.5
2nd quarter	2 833.6	1 884.4	1 581.7	305.4	1 276.3	302.6	193.2	109.5	169.4	12.8	156.6	21.1
3rd quarter	2 852.9	1 904.8	1 596.4	309.5	1 286.9	308.3	198.0	110.3	170.7	11.9	158.8	24.4
4th quarter	2 865.4	1 918.1	1 604.4	314.5	1 289.9	313.8	203.1	110.7	179.5	14.2	165.3	26.3
1983												
1st quarter	2 924.4	1 947.2	1 622.4	318.7	1 303.7	324.8	208.4	116.4	183.3	12.9	170.4	25.8
2nd quarter	3 004.2	1 986.3	1 654.7	322.6	1 332.1	331.6	213.2	118.4	182.6	7.9	174.8	24.7
3rd quarter	3 085.1	2 029.6	1 691.4	326.7	1 364.7	338.2	217.5	120.7	183.8	0.2	183.6	23.7
4th quarter	3 192.4	2 086.8	1 741.5	331.2	1 410.4	345.3	221.3	124.0	195.3	3.8	191.5	23.5
1984												
1st quarter	3 320.8	2 143.8	1 784.0	337.8	1 446.2	359.8	224.7	135.1	221.9	19.5	202.4	23.2
2nd quarter	3 408.8	2 195.2	1 828.1	344.8	1 483.4	367.0	228.9	138.1	231.8	21.3	210.5	21.7
3rd quarter	3 474.3	2 241.6	1 867.1	351.9	1 515.2	374.6	234.0	140.5	232.4	20.4	211.9	24.4
4th quarter	3 531.6	2 282.9	1 900.5	358.1	1 542.4	382.4	240.0	142.4	226.9	22.5	204.4	29.3
1985												
1st quarter	3 593.1	2 323.5	1 932.1	363.9	1 568.2	391.4	247.0	144.4	240.7	22.8	217.8	26.9
2nd quarter	3 641.2	2 363.6	1 963.6	370.4	1 593.2	400.0	253.8	146.2	238.5	20.4	218.0	25.3
3rd quarter	3 702.9	2 406.4	1 997.4	378.1	1 619.3	409.0	260.4	148.6	240.7	19.3	221.5	27.1
4th quarter	3 742.5	2 455.7	2 037.0	383.0	1 654.0	418.7	266.9	151.8	244.3	21.4	223.0	25.6
1986												
1st quarter	3 793.2	2 491.1	2 063.5	387.9	1 675.6	427.6	273.1	154.5	245.6	18.3	227.4	22.0
2nd quarter	3 804.1	2 517.2	2 081.8	393.6	1 688.3	435.4	279.1	156.3	251.6	19.6	232.0	21.1
3rd quarter	3 842.3	2 555.2	2 111.5	399.4	1 712.0	443.8	284.9	158.9	264.4	26.6	237.8	16.6
4th quarter	3 885.3	2 604.7	2 152.5	407.9	1 744.6	452.2	290.4	161.8	264.2	26.6	237.6	13.4
1987												
1st quarter	3 953.9	2 647.8	2 192.7	413.5	1 779.1	455.1	292.4	162.7	275.4	27.3	248.2	14.5
2nd quarter	4 053.1	2 692.0	2 229.9	419.9	1 810.0	462.1	297.5	164.6	282.3	29.0	253.3	14.1
3rd quarter	4 146.6	2 740.3	2 270.8	425.1	1 845.7	469.5	302.4	167.1	289.5	28.8	260.7	17.5
4th quarter	4 239.9	2 809.6	2 331.7	433.9	1 897.8	477.8	307.2	170.6	298.6	30.4	268.2	20.3

Table 1-13B. National Income by Type of Income: Historical Data—*Continued*

(Billions of dollars, quarterly data are at seasonally adjusted annual rates.)   **NIPA Tables 1.7.5, 1.12**

Year and quarter	Corporate profits with IVA and CCAdj					Net interest and miscellaneous payments	Taxes on production and imports	Less: Subsidies	Business current transfer payments, net			Current surplus of government enterprises	Addendum: Net national factor income
	Total	Taxes on corporate income	Profits after tax						Total 1	To persons	To government		
			Total	Net dividends	Undistributed corporate profits								
1973													
1st quarter	133.5	46.0	87.5	32.1	55.4	51.6	114.6	5.9	5.6	3.6	1.9	. . .	1 098.1
2nd quarter	131.2	46.0	85.2	33.5	51.7	53.4	116.2	5.7	5.9	3.9	2.0	. . .	1 121.1
3rd quarter	133.0	44.0	89.0	35.0	54.0	57.3	118.4	4.7	5.6	4.1	1.6	. . .	1 146.8
4th quarter	135.8	46.5	89.3	36.4	52.9	60.5	119.7	4.6	5.8	4.2	1.6	. . .	1 183.5
1974													
1st quarter	130.3	44.6	85.7	37.7	48.0	64.9	120.8	3.6	6.3	4.3	2.0	. . .	1 192.8
2nd quarter	128.9	46.7	82.3	38.8	43.5	69.8	124.1	2.9	6.6	4.5	2.1	. . .	1 208.8
3rd quarter	124.3	51.5	72.8	39.4	33.4	73.4	127.1	3.2	7.0	4.9	2.1	. . .	1 232.2
4th quarter	119.3	46.2	73.2	39.2	33.9	78.5	127.7	3.6	7.3	5.2	2.1	. . .	1 248.1
1975													
1st quarter	117.8	38.3	79.4	38.4	41.0	82.6	128.8	4.2	8.4	6.1	2.2	. . .	1 254.1
2nd quarter	128.9	41.4	87.5	38.0	49.5	83.1	133.0	4.3	9.1	6.9	2.2	. . .	1 279.9
3rd quarter	149.8	52.0	97.7	38.0	59.7	84.3	138.2	4.6	9.3	7.1	2.2	. . .	1 333.0
4th quarter	159.0	53.3	105.7	38.9	66.8	84.7	141.1	4.9	9.4	7.2	2.2	. . .	1 374.1
1976													
1st quarter	175.1	60.8	114.3	41.9	72.3	84.1	141.7	5.1	9.5	7.0	2.5	. . .	1 422.0
2nd quarter	173.2	59.4	113.8	43.9	69.9	86.6	144.9	4.8	9.4	7.0	2.4	. . .	1 444.4
3rd quarter	174.7	59.0	115.8	45.8	69.9	88.4	147.7	5.1	9.1	6.7	2.4	. . .	1 474.3
4th quarter	174.3	58.5	115.9	47.9	68.0	90.4	151.3	5.5	8.6	6.1	2.5	. . .	1 504.9
1977													
1st quarter	184.1	62.9	121.2	48.6	72.6	97.1	154.8	5.8	8.2	5.5	2.7	. . .	1 549.6
2nd quarter	204.9	68.4	136.5	49.9	86.6	101.0	158.0	5.9	7.8	5.0	2.8	. . .	1 613.0
3rd quarter	219.6	70.8	148.8	51.5	97.3	105.3	161.5	6.4	8.0	4.9	3.2	. . .	1 665.1
4th quarter	214.5	71.8	142.6	52.8	89.8	109.3	164.3	10.3	8.3	5.0	3.3	. . .	1 713.0
1978													
1st quarter	209.9	66.2	143.7	54.6	89.2	110.8	166.9	8.7	9.4	5.6	3.7	. . .	1 746.1
2nd quarter	239.7	80.0	159.7	56.1	103.7	113.7	173.1	8.4	10.0	6.2	3.9	. . .	1 834.3
3rd quarter	246.2	80.2	166.0	59.0	107.0	115.4	169.7	8.3	10.7	6.7	4.0	. . .	1 884.0
4th quarter	258.4	85.0	173.4	61.6	111.8	119.4	173.9	10.4	11.4	7.3	4.1	. . .	1 946.4
1979													
1st quarter	249.7	81.9	167.8	63.6	104.2	125.0	176.4	8.4	12.3	7.9	4.4	. . .	1 994.5
2nd quarter	252.1	82.1	170.0	65.8	104.3	130.8	178.5	8.8	12.7	8.2	4.5	. . .	2 032.5
3rd quarter	250.1	81.0	169.0	67.6	101.4	138.9	180.9	8.1	13.0	8.4	4.6	. . .	2 081.8
4th quarter	244.0	77.9	166.1	70.2	95.9	153.1	184.6	8.9	13.1	8.5	4.6	. . .	2 126.0
1980													
1st quarter	237.5	85.4	152.1	73.4	78.7	168.6	189.5	9.2	13.2	8.2	5.0	. . .	2 163.1
2nd quarter	207.0	64.9	142.1	76.6	65.5	176.1	196.9	9.6	13.4	8.3	5.1	. . .	2 159.8
3rd quarter	214.6	72.1	142.5	75.7	66.8	182.9	204.3	10.1	13.7	8.7	5.0	. . .	2 219.4
4th quarter	235.1	79.5	155.6	77.4	78.2	201.3	210.6	10.3	15.7	9.3	6.4	. . .	2 332.2
1981													
1st quarter	244.4	78.1	166.2	81.7	84.5	203.8	230.8	10.6	16.4	10.4	6.1	. . .	2 399.9
2nd quarter	240.8	69.1	171.8	86.3	85.5	223.7	235.5	10.7	16.6	11.0	5.6	. . .	2 439.0
3rd quarter	257.8	71.6	186.2	90.4	95.8	252.3	237.5	11.1	17.1	11.5	5.6	. . .	2 530.6
4th quarter	246.9	62.4	184.5	92.8	91.8	259.5	238.8	13.5	17.5	11.9	5.7	. . .	2 543.7
1982													
1st quarter	221.8	50.6	171.2	92.8	78.4	272.2	237.4	14.0	18.6	12.0	6.6	. . .	2 547.5
2nd quarter	236.2	52.7	183.5	92.2	91.2	282.1	238.3	13.6	19.2	12.3	6.9	. . .	2 593.1
3rd quarter	233.7	53.2	180.5	92.5	87.9	274.6	241.8	13.0	19.5	12.5	7.0	. . .	2 608.1
4th quarter	227.7	48.6	179.1	94.1	85.0	270.3	246.3	19.4	20.0	12.7	7.2	. . .	2 621.9
1983													
1st quarter	244.6	50.2	194.3	95.0	99.4	275.1	250.7	19.9	20.3	12.8	7.5	. . .	2 676.0
2nd quarter	274.7	65.3	209.4	96.0	113.4	277.4	261.2	21.6	20.9	13.2	7.7	. . .	2 745.7
3rd quarter	291.2	74.0	217.3	98.6	118.6	291.2	267.5	22.2	21.9	14.0	7.9	. . .	2 819.7
4th quarter	308.6	76.1	232.4	101.2	131.3	303.6	273.7	21.5	23.6	15.3	8.4	. . .	2 917.8
1984													
1st quarter	336.6	88.4	248.2	104.0	144.1	309.8	281.6	21.2	26.7	17.6	9.1	. . .	3 035.4
2nd quarter	338.2	87.1	251.1	106.6	144.5	327.6	287.7	21.0	28.6	19.2	9.4	. . .	3 114.5
3rd quarter	333.6	74.7	258.8	107.4	151.5	341.7	292.2	20.9	30.1	20.6	9.6	. . .	3 173.7
4th quarter	343.1	75.6	267.5	109.4	158.1	341.9	297.5	21.2	31.2	21.5	9.7	. . .	3 224.1
1985													
1st quarter	347.9	80.5	267.4	113.6	153.8	341.3	301.0	21.1	32.2	21.9	10.3	. . .	3 280.2
2nd quarter	351.5	78.8	272.7	115.2	157.6	337.3	305.7	21.0	38.1	22.1	16.0	. . .	3 316.3
3rd quarter	368.9	84.7	284.1	115.8	168.3	334.1	311.9	21.3	32.8	22.3	10.5	. . .	3 377.2
4th quarter	349.7	82.4	267.3	116.8	150.5	340.0	313.9	22.0	33.1	22.6	10.5	. . .	3 415.3
1986													
1st quarter	340.7	87.8	252.9	122.0	130.9	354.9	317.5	23.1	42.1	23.3	18.7	. . .	3 454.3
2nd quarter	326.6	88.4	238.2	124.3	113.9	355.3	319.5	24.2	34.5	23.5	11.1	. . .	3 471.8
3rd quarter	315.6	90.0	225.6	124.8	100.8	354.0	326.2	25.5	33.2	23.0	10.2	. . .	3 505.8
4th quarter	314.7	101.2	213.4	124.9	88.6	348.1	330.4	26.8	34.0	22.0	12.0	. . .	3 545.1
1987													
1st quarter	325.9	101.5	224.3	126.0	98.3	345.6	336.0	28.3	34.0	21.3	12.7	. . .	3 609.1
2nd quarter	362.9	115.1	247.8	127.5	120.2	351.0	344.4	30.4	34.4	20.6	13.8	. . .	3 702.4
3rd quarter	386.4	119.9	266.5	131.3	135.2	356.9	352.4	31.3	32.5	19.7	12.8	. . .	3 790.5
4th quarter	388.8	114.3	274.5	135.3	139.2	361.4	357.4	31.1	32.3	19.3	13.0	. . .	3 878.7

1Includes net transfer payments to the rest of the world, not shown separately.
. . . = Not available.

Table 1-13B. National Income by Type of Income: Historical Data—*Continued*

(Billions of dollars, quarterly data are at seasonally adjusted annual rates.)   NIPA Tables 1.7.5, 1.12

Year and quarter	National income, total	Compensation of employees							Proprietors' income with IVA and CCAdj			Rental income of persons with CCAdj
		Total	Wages and salaries			Supplements to wages and salaries			Total	Farm	Nonfarm	
			Total	Government	Other	Total	Employer contributions for:					
							Employee pension and insurance funds	Government social insurance				
1988												
1st quarter	4 329.2	2 857.6	2 366.2	441.7	1 924.4	491.4	312.1	179.2	319.2	33.3	285.9	21.1
2nd quarter	4 421.4	2 923.1	2 421.5	448.5	1 973.0	501.6	318.6	183.0	322.5	27.4	295.1	20.3
3rd quarter	4 514.3	2 975.8	2 462.9	454.5	2 008.3	513.0	326.8	186.2	333.6	28.8	304.8	21.2
4th quarter	4 621.4	3 035.4	2 508.6	463.4	2 045.2	526.9	336.8	190.0	326.8	17.7	309.2	27.4
1989												
1st quarter	4 697.6	3 079.1	2 540.8	469.5	2 071.3	538.3	348.1	190.1	348.1	36.7	311.4	23.1
2nd quarter	4 732.4	3 114.6	2 563.5	476.9	2 086.6	551.1	358.8	192.3	339.5	32.6	306.9	21.2
3rd quarter	4 785.4	3 155.0	2 592.3	485.1	2 107.1	562.8	368.2	194.6	337.2	30.3	306.9	20.0
4th quarter	4 825.0	3 209.7	2 635.7	493.0	2 142.7	574.1	376.4	197.7	339.7	32.5	307.2	21.8
1990												
1st quarter	4 927.3	3 272.8	2 684.4	503.5	2 180.9	588.3	386.3	202.0	345.6	34.5	311.1	23.1
2nd quarter	5 014.2	3 334.7	2 738.8	518.7	2 220.1	595.9	390.3	205.6	351.1	32.7	318.4	26.7
3rd quarter	5 042.9	3 372.5	2 769.3	523.9	2 245.5	603.2	394.7	208.5	358.9	31.8	327.2	31.6
4th quarter	5 070.6	3 381.5	2 772.2	530.1	2 242.1	609.3	399.6	209.6	357.0	29.7	327.3	31.3
1991												
1st quarter	5 093.1	3 387.5	2 771.7	539.6	2 232.1	615.8	405.2	210.6	347.5	26.2	321.3	33.0
2nd quarter	5 133.7	3 427.6	2 800.1	546.0	2 254.1	627.5	413.6	213.9	353.0	27.9	325.2	35.5
3rd quarter	5 185.5	3 469.9	2 828.1	551.6	2 276.5	641.8	425.1	216.8	353.6	24.5	329.1	39.4
4th quarter	5 245.1	3 517.0	2 858.0	557.8	2 300.2	659.0	439.7	219.3	362.6	28.6	333.9	46.4
1992												
1st quarter	5 369.1	3 595.7	2 912.9	564.2	2 348.7	682.8	456.8	226.0	378.7	32.9	345.8	50.0
2nd quarter	5 451.9	3 651.9	2 952.0	569.8	2 382.2	699.9	471.0	229.0	395.2	35.4	359.8	57.3
3rd quarter	5 492.3	3 688.5	2 976.6	575.2	2 401.4	712.0	481.4	230.6	407.9	36.7	371.1	64.3
4th quarter	5 587.6	3 736.9	3 020.8	578.8	2 442.0	716.1	488.1	228.0	418.8	34.1	384.8	70.7
1993												
1st quarter	5 596.5	3 745.6	3 015.9	582.8	2 433.1	729.6	491.7	238.0	418.9	28.6	390.3	80.7
2nd quarter	5 696.8	3 800.2	3 066.5	586.6	2 479.8	733.8	495.6	238.2	429.6	34.9	394.6	86.9
3rd quarter	5 744.2	3 834.1	3 093.6	591.8	2 501.9	740.5	500.2	240.3	423.4	26.1	397.4	92.5
4th quarter	5 883.6	3 889.3	3 141.4	594.8	2 546.5	747.9	505.7	242.2	440.0	35.8	404.2	100.2
1994												
1st quarter	5 949.8	3 913.4	3 152.7	601.1	2 551.6	760.7	511.4	249.3	450.2	41.8	408.4	109.0
2nd quarter	6 073.8	3 991.5	3 223.3	607.2	2 616.2	768.2	515.4	252.8	454.1	36.7	417.5	113.5
3rd quarter	6 163.9	4 031.8	3 258.7	612.5	2 646.2	773.0	517.6	255.5	456.8	32.1	424.6	116.3
4th quarter	6 271.1	4 088.1	3 311.6	617.2	2 694.4	776.5	517.4	259.0	465.5	28.1	437.4	115.9
1995												
1st quarter	6 331.9	4 134.4	3 358.1	622.4	2 735.7	776.3	515.6	260.8	467.4	20.3	447.1	118.3
2nd quarter	6 397.0	4 172.9	3 395.2	627.5	2 767.7	777.7	514.9	262.8	472.0	18.4	453.6	121.6
3rd quarter	6 497.6	4 219.7	3 438.9	630.9	2 808.0	780.8	515.6	265.3	484.5	21.4	463.1	125.7
4th quarter	6 582.7	4 265.3	3 479.9	635.3	2 844.6	785.4	517.8	267.7	501.0	28.1	472.9	134.0
1996												
1st quarter	6 701.0	4 314.5	3 524.4	640.0	2 884.4	790.1	521.0	269.1	523.3	36.9	486.4	139.5
2nd quarter	6 827.4	4 387.5	3 590.0	645.6	2 944.3	797.6	524.4	273.2	547.5	44.2	503.3	141.6
3rd quarter	6 909.7	4 451.2	3 647.2	650.7	2 996.5	804.0	527.3	276.7	547.5	33.5	514.0	143.7
4th quarter	7 044.3	4 514.5	3 704.3	656.0	3 048.2	810.2	530.0	280.3	556.8	34.7	522.1	145.3
1997												
1st quarter	7 159.1	4 592.4	3 776.4	662.3	3 114.1	816.0	532.7	283.3	575.6	37.8	537.8	144.2
2nd quarter	7 273.8	4 660.0	3 835.6	668.0	3 167.7	824.3	537.4	286.9	575.1	28.1	547.0	144.6
3rd quarter	7 422.5	4 738.9	3 903.0	674.1	3 228.9	835.9	544.7	291.2	588.5	32.4	556.1	147.4
4th quarter	7 544.4	4 844.0	3 992.4	683.2	3 309.2	851.6	554.7	297.0	596.6	31.2	565.4	152.1
1998												
1st quarter	7 641.9	4 942.0	4 074.9	689.8	3 385.1	867.1	566.7	300.4	617.4	27.9	589.5	156.8
2nd quarter	7 767.1	5 028.3	4 145.5	697.4	3 448.1	882.8	578.0	304.9	629.6	26.4	603.2	162.6
3rd quarter	7 898.7	5 114.9	4 217.4	705.6	3 511.8	897.4	587.9	309.5	645.0	26.6	618.4	168.0
4th quarter	7 995.3	5 199.4	4 288.7	712.4	3 576.2	910.7	596.6	314.1	668.7	33.0	635.7	173.4
1999												
1st quarter	8 149.3	5 287.0	4 364.6	718.1	3 646.5	922.3	604.1	318.2	681.9	33.6	648.3	176.1
2nd quarter	8 213.5	5 343.9	4 409.3	727.0	3 682.3	934.6	613.9	320.7	690.1	28.1	661.9	179.6
3rd quarter	8 314.1	5 424.0	4 473.7	738.6	3 735.1	950.3	626.3	324.0	699.8	26.2	673.6	179.4
4th quarter	8 488.9	5 555.9	4 584.1	751.4	3 832.7	971.8	641.4	330.5	713.9	24.5	689.4	178.9
2000												
1st quarter	8 710.9	5 749.2	4 751.5	765.2	3 986.3	997.7	657.1	340.6	720.9	27.1	693.9	179.8
2nd quarter	8 817.3	5 791.7	4 779.1	778.6	4 000.5	1 012.7	671.3	341.4	751.3	33.4	717.9	180.2
3rd quarter	8 946.1	5 903.9	4 871.3	783.8	4 087.5	1 032.7	684.6	348.1	760.8	31.9	728.9	182.9
4th quarter	9 015.4	5 943.7	4 898.0	791.5	4 106.4	1 045.8	694.9	350.8	782.4	33.7	748.7	191.0
2001												
1st quarter	9 157.9	6 050.1	4 979.5	801.8	4 177.7	1 070.7	712.9	357.8	809.8	34.0	775.7	197.1
2nd quarter	9 183.2	6 040.9	4 961.4	814.0	4 147.4	1 079.5	721.6	358.0	827.7	32.5	795.2	202.6
3rd quarter	9 124.8	6 024.6	4 935.9	828.9	4 107.0	1 088.6	731.2	357.4	845.6	32.6	813.0	204.8
4th quarter	9 120.3	6 037.8	4 937.8	843.3	4 094.4	1 100.0	741.3	358.7	840.9	29.2	811.7	205.1
2002												
1st quarter	9 237.4	6 060.7	4 945.9	855.1	4 090.7	1 114.9	753.2	361.6	859.5	17.7	841.8	207.3
2nd quarter	9 345.3	6 129.1	4 998.3	868.2	4 130.2	1 130.8	764.8	366.0	864.5	13.6	850.9	208.9
3rd quarter	9 425.1	6 156.9	5 012.1	879.8	4 132.3	1 144.8	777.3	367.5	872.9	21.8	851.2	207.7
4th quarter	9 569.2	6 193.7	5 027.1	888.4	4 138.7	1 166.6	797.6	369.0	883.3	27.8	855.5	209.9

Table 1-13B. National Income by Type of Income: Historical Data—*Continued*

(Billions of dollars, quarterly data are at seasonally adjusted annual rates.) NIPA Tables 1.7.5, 1.12

Year and quarter	Corporate profits with IVA and CCAdj					Net interest and miscellaneous payments	Taxes on production and imports	Less: Subsidies	Business current transfer payments, net			Current surplus of government enterprises	Addendum: Net national factor income
	Total	Taxes on corporate income	Profits after tax						Total¹	To persons	To government		
			Total	Net dividends	Undistributed corporate profits								
1988													
1st quarter	394.2	112.6	281.6	138.5	143.1	369.1	365.2	30.4	31.1	19.6	11.5	. . .	3 961.1
2nd quarter	408.6	120.0	288.6	143.1	145.5	366.4	372.5	29.8	31.7	20.1	11.6	. . .	4 040.9
3rd quarter	415.2	129.1	286.1	150.3	135.8	380.4	377.5	29.2	33.2	20.8	12.4	. . .	4 126.3
4th quarter	439.8	135.4	304.5	157.3	147.2	395.5	382.6	28.6	35.1	21.9	13.2	. . .	4 225.0
1989													
1st quarter	423.7	137.2	286.5	169.2	117.3	416.3	391.0	28.0	37.2	23.3	14.0	. . .	4 290.2
2nd quarter	415.8	123.0	292.9	177.8	115.1	426.5	397.5	27.4	37.7	23.1	14.5	. . .	4 317.6
3rd quarter	416.6	118.9	297.7	182.5	115.2	433.4	403.9	27.1	39.1	23.2	15.9	. . .	4 362.2
4th quarter	401.0	118.6	282.4	189.0	93.4	430.3	403.0	27.3	39.0	23.1	16.0	. . .	4 402.6
1990													
1st quarter	413.9	116.8	297.1	192.7	104.4	435.0	419.5	27.1	39.4	23.3	16.1	. . .	4 490.3
2nd quarter	433.9	121.7	312.2	193.1	119.1	432.8	419.5	27.0	39.0	22.9	16.0	. . .	4 579.2
3rd quarter	407.7	125.1	282.6	194.7	87.9	430.0	426.8	26.9	38.9	21.9	17.0	. . .	4 600.8
4th quarter	415.4	123.7	291.7	190.1	101.6	435.9	434.2	27.0	39.5	20.7	18.8	. . .	4 621.1
1991													
1st quarter	455.0	120.2	334.8	196.7	138.1	407.7	444.0	27.1	39.8	19.2	20.6	. . .	4 630.6
2nd quarter	452.7	116.0	336.7	200.9	135.7	393.8	451.6	27.2	38.7	17.9	20.7	. . .	4 662.6
3rd quarter	450.7	116.9	333.8	203.6	130.2	390.9	461.3	27.5	38.5	17.0	21.5	. . .	4 704.6
4th quarter	452.0	118.2	333.8	203.9	129.9	374.8	471.5	28.1	38.7	16.4	22.2	. . .	4 752.7
1992													
1st quarter	478.2	130.4	347.8	202.9	144.8	370.3	476.4	28.6	38.6	16.5	22.4	-0.2	4 872.9
2nd quarter	479.6	132.4	347.3	205.5	141.7	367.0	481.2	29.2	38.4	16.5	22.0	-0.1	4 951.0
3rd quarter	465.2	127.8	337.4	207.3	130.1	360.6	486.0	30.4	38.9	16.3	22.7	-0.1	4 986.5
4th quarter	485.7	137.1	348.6	209.4	139.2	364.6	489.9	32.2	43.0	15.9	27.1	0.0	5 076.7
1993													
1st quarter	483.6	141.7	341.9	213.0	128.9	363.5	489.7	35.5	40.2	15.1	25.1	-0.1	5 092.4
2nd quarter	511.9	154.1	357.8	217.1	140.7	357.3	497.6	37.6	39.3	14.4	25.1	-0.2	5 185.8
3rd quarter	526.3	146.4	379.9	223.3	156.5	350.1	504.9	37.7	38.7	13.7	25.4	-0.4	5 226.5
4th quarter	576.5	178.0	398.5	231.8	166.7	341.5	520.3	36.0	39.3	13.1	26.9	-0.6	5 347.4
1994													
1st quarter	584.3	155.9	428.4	244.2	184.2	341.5	531.5	33.6	40.7	12.8	28.7	-0.8	5 398.4
2nd quarter	607.3	164.1	443.2	253.3	189.9	342.9	544.4	32.4	39.7	12.8	27.7	-0.8	5 509.3
3rd quarter	641.4	180.2	461.2	260.9	200.3	345.1	550.5	31.9	41.3	13.2	28.4	-0.4	5 591.3
4th quarter	666.0	190.4	475.6	267.4	208.3	359.6	554.6	32.2	41.2	14.2	26.8	0.2	5 695.2
1995													
1st quarter	667.8	194.7	473.0	270.6	202.4	362.6	555.3	34.0	43.6	16.0	25.9	1.7	5 750.5
2nd quarter	692.4	191.0	501.4	277.0	224.4	358.1	553.6	34.6	44.9	17.8	25.1	1.9	5 816.9
3rd quarter	726.4	198.0	528.4	285.4	243.0	355.1	558.9	35.1	45.8	19.6	24.6	1.6	5 911.4
4th quarter	738.3	194.0	544.3	296.4	247.9	353.7	563.8	35.5	45.5	21.4	23.9	0.2	5 992.2
1996													
1st quarter	772.3	201.7	570.6	306.2	264.4	352.5	570.4	35.5	46.8	22.8	24.7	-0.7	6 102.1
2nd quarter	784.8	213.4	571.4	318.7	252.6	358.2	577.7	35.4	48.2	23.5	25.8	-1.1	6 219.6
3rd quarter	790.0	213.7	576.3	329.9	246.4	363.6	581.8	35.2	48.9	23.2	26.8	-1.2	6 296.0
4th quarter	810.9	216.8	594.1	339.6	254.5	373.4	593.2	34.8	66.7	21.9	45.5	-0.8	6 401.0
1997													
1st quarter	839.0	218.2	620.8	347.7	273.2	381.8	595.7	34.4	46.9	19.7	27.8	-0.6	6 532.9
2nd quarter	861.6	222.5	639.2	356.2	282.9	389.8	610.4	33.6	47.4	18.7	28.5	0.1	6 631.1
3rd quarter	896.6	234.2	662.4	364.4	298.0	396.4	616.6	33.4	53.5	19.0	33.4	1.2	6 767.8
4th quarter	881.6	224.2	657.4	372.2	285.3	409.8	623.8	33.8	52.5	20.4	29.6	2.5	6 884.2
1998													
1st quarter	812.7	222.1	590.5	383.5	207.0	442.0	629.1	33.8	58.9	22.8	31.1	5.0	6 970.9
2nd quarter	809.4	218.9	590.5	386.4	204.1	459.0	635.5	35.0	60.4	25.1	30.4	4.9	7 088.9
3rd quarter	817.6	225.5	592.2	385.2	207.0	467.0	643.0	36.8	62.6	27.1	31.8	3.7	7 212.6
4th quarter	794.1	220.7	573.4	379.4	194.0	458.8	650.3	39.9	74.3	28.9	43.9	1.6	7 294.3
1999													
1st quarter	847.1	226.5	620.6	368.7	251.8	459.0	657.5	42.4	65.4	31.2	35.6	-1.4	7 451.0
2nd quarter	840.2	223.6	616.7	366.6	250.1	453.3	667.1	45.0	67.1	32.8	36.2	-1.9	7 507.0
3rd quarter	823.7	227.6	596.1	372.1	224.1	469.9	679.0	46.4	67.9	34.8	36.2	-3.1	7 596.8
4th quarter	828.7	231.9	596.7	386.6	210.2	482.0	690.7	46.9	70.3	37.1	37.8	-4.5	7 759.4
2000													
1st quarter	808.5	243.3	565.2	400.6	164.6	503.1	698.6	45.1	81.0	39.8	41.0	0.2	7 961.5
2nd quarter	798.1	241.7	556.4	412.0	144.4	536.2	707.3	45.5	84.3	41.5	41.8	1.0	8 057.6
3rd quarter	781.2	222.8	558.4	416.0	142.4	555.5	711.3	45.8	86.3	43.3	42.0	1.0	8 184.2
4th quarter	758.4	226.0	532.4	412.3	120.2	573.6	717.1	47.0	89.0	45.2	42.8	1.1	8 249.0
2001													
1st quarter	748.0	188.6	559.4	404.2	155.2	579.1	724.2	55.2	98.6	47.9	42.8	7.9	8 384.1
2nd quarter	778.0	182.7	595.3	396.5	198.8	567.1	724.1	62.0	100.2	48.3	43.2	8.6	8 416.3
3rd quarter	746.7	162.8	583.9	393.7	190.2	539.3	725.3	71.2	100.5	47.0	44.2	9.3	8 361.0
4th quarter	762.2	146.5	615.7	397.1	218.6	483.4	737.1	46.4	97.7	43.9	45.2	8.5	8 329.3
2002													
1st quarter	852.5	147.4	705.1	412.3	292.8	463.5	744.0	42.6	87.8	39.1	46.5	2.2	8 443.5
2nd quarter	883.2	153.7	729.6	424.3	305.3	461.1	751.3	39.8	81.6	35.2	45.9	0.5	8 546.8
3rd quarter	914.6	161.8	752.8	428.2	324.6	458.0	768.5	41.3	77.5	32.3	45.8	-0.6	8 610.1
4th quarter	996.5	179.9	816.7	434.7	382.0	465.3	776.3	41.9	76.2	30.2	46.8	-0.8	8 748.8

¹Includes net transfer payments to the rest of the world, not shown separately.
. . . = Not available.

Table 1-13B. National Income by Type of Income: Historical Data—*Continued*

(Billions of dollars, quarterly data are at seasonally adjusted annual rates.)

NIPA Tables 1.7.5, 1.12

Year and quarter	National income, total	Compensation of employees								Proprietors' income with IVA and CCAdj			Rental income of persons with CCAdj
		Total	Wages and salaries			Supplements to wages and salaries				Total	Farm	Nonfarm	
			Total	Government	Other	Total	Employer contributions for:						
							Total	Employee pension and insurance funds	Government social insurance				

Year and quarter	National income, total	Comp. Total	W&S Total	W&S Government	W&S Other	Suppl. Total	Empl. pension and insurance funds	Government social insurance	Prop. Total	Prop. Farm	Prop. Nonfarm	Rental income
2003												
1st quarter	9 589.5	6 213.2	5 027.0	901.2	4 125.8	1 186.2	812.2	374.0	876.3	29.9	846.4	218.7
2nd quarter	9 721.0	6 307.3	5 101.4	911.9	4 189.4	1 205.9	826.2	379.8	892.4	37.3	855.1	223.2
3rd quarter	9 889.3	6 393.7	5 168.7	917.8	4 251.0	1 225.0	839.9	385.0	905.3	39.8	865.5	227.5
4th quarter	10 063.2	6 500.2	5 256.0	924.9	4 331.0	1 244.3	852.8	391.4	916.1	41.5	874.5	239.0
2004												
1st quarter	10 237.0	6 541.3	5 274.5	936.6	4 337.9	1 266.8	868.0	398.8	946.5	56.3	890.3	243.0
2nd quarter	10 414.2	6 668.5	5 380.7	948.3	4 432.5	1 287.7	881.6	406.1	963.0	55.3	907.8	243.4
3rd quarter	10 617.0	6 803.7	5 492.8	956.6	4 536.1	1 310.9	897.1	413.9	964.2	47.1	917.1	241.8
4th quarter	10 715.1	6 864.5	5 536.1	967.9	4 568.2	1 328.4	912.2	416.2	977.8	50.9	926.8	242.9
2005												
1st quarter	10 920.0	6 926.3	5 574.6	977.8	4 596.8	1 351.6	930.6	421.1	957.1	47.6	909.5	233.7
2nd quarter	11 085.7	7 005.6	5 637.8	986.1	4 651.7	1 367.7	943.1	424.6	964.1	51.2	913.0	231.2
3rd quarter	11 270.1	7 122.6	5 738.3	995.5	4 742.8	1 384.4	953.4	430.9	988.1	49.6	938.5	213.6
4th quarter	11 506.3	7 209.9	5 814.8	1 005.8	4 809.0	1 395.2	959.5	435.6	1 007.2	43.3	963.9	206.0
2006												
1st quarter	11 776.8	7 379.7	5 971.4	1 014.6	4 956.8	1 408.3	964.7	443.6	1 049.1	34.8	1 014.2	194.5
2nd quarter	11 909.7	7 428.0	6 012.6	1 025.8	4 986.8	1 415.4	970.1	445.3	1 052.1	33.9	1 018.2	183.4
3rd quarter	12 014.7	7 487.3	6 061.9	1 041.9	5 019.9	1 425.4	978.5	447.0	1 049.0	33.7	1 015.3	177.8
4th quarter	12 067.8	7 623.6	6 181.1	1 055.8	5 125.3	1 442.6	989.2	453.3	1 053.3	34.8	1 018.5	168.7
2007												
1st quarter	12 163.7	7 806.0	6 343.8	1 071.6	5 272.1	1 462.2	1 002.5	459.7	1 017.5	43.1	974.4	162.5
2nd quarter	12 322.2	7 845.2	6 370.3	1 080.5	5 289.8	1 474.8	1 015.0	459.8	997.9	38.5	959.3	180.3
3rd quarter	12 309.3	7 885.2	6 397.6	1 093.6	5 304.0	1 487.6	1 026.8	460.9	986.8	38.8	947.9	193.6
4th quarter	12 394.0	7 977.5	6 473.9	1 108.5	5 365.5	1 503.6	1 037.3	466.3	979.8	46.3	933.5	208.7
2008												
1st quarter	12 399.1	8 054.9	6 539.4	1 124.8	5 414.6	1 515.5	1 045.8	469.7	964.1	48.0	916.1	249.2
2nd quarter	12 423.7	8 054.9	6 532.7	1 136.0	5 396.7	1 522.2	1 051.9	470.4	967.2	44.2	923.1	280.9
3rd quarter	12 506.0	8 074.4	6 547.2	1 151.2	5 396.0	1 527.2	1 054.4	472.8	956.6	33.8	922.8	305.3
4th quarter	12 108.2	8 043.2	6 517.2	1 163.4	5 353.8	1 526.0	1 053.3	472.7	950.7	29.7	921.0	325.7
2009												
1st quarter	11 889.4	7 730.4	6 225.6	1 162.8	5 062.8	1 504.8	1 048.8	456.0	913.2	22.9	890.3	326.6
2nd quarter	11 933.3	7 762.0	6 254.5	1 176.0	5 078.4	1 507.5	1 048.1	459.4	901.5	23.6	878.0	335.9
3rd quarter	12 076.5	7 746.5	6 237.2	1 179.0	5 058.2	1 509.3	1 051.5	457.8	934.5	26.7	907.9	355.8
4th quarter	12 320.0	7 797.2	6 279.2	1 183.1	5 096.1	1 518.1	1 058.9	459.2	1 001.3	35.5	965.7	372.0
2010												
1st quarter	12 467.7	7 767.6	6 233.2	1 185.8	5 047.5	1 534.4	1 070.3	464.1	1 055.8	30.4	1 025.4	404.9
2nd quarter	12 676.4	7 910.6	6 360.7	1 196.6	5 164.1	1 549.9	1 080.4	469.5	1 102.7	34.0	1 068.7	428.9
3rd quarter	12 929.6	7 982.0	6 422.5	1 191.3	5 231.3	1 559.7	1 088.9	470.8	1 128.0	39.8	1 088.2	442.6
4th quarter	13 050.9	8 041.0	6 473.6	1 191.1	5 282.5	1 567.4	1 095.9	471.5	1 142.7	46.0	1 096.7	458.3
2011												
1st quarter	13 130.8	8 170.1	6 577.3	1 193.1	5 384.2	1 592.8	1 102.0	490.8	1 179.0	64.8	1 114.2	489.1
2nd quarter	13 319.3	8 206.4	6 608.2	1 199.2	5 409.0	1 598.2	1 106.4	491.8	1 210.2	59.2	1 151.0	501.4
3rd quarter	13 447.6	8 287.3	6 681.6	1 197.6	5 484.0	1 605.7	1 109.5	496.2	1 251.6	64.6	1 187.1	510.1
4th quarter	13 604.3	8 240.9	6 637.6	1 189.5	5 448.1	1 603.3	1 111.1	492.2	1 268.9	63.6	1 205.3	525.6
2012												
1st quarter	13 999.2	8 456.4	6 836.3	1 198.7	5 637.6	1 620.1	1 112.1	508.0	1 321.8	59.9	1 261.9	526.7
2nd quarter	14 081.0	8 503.8	6 876.0	1 195.8	5 680.2	1 627.8	1 117.8	510.0	1 355.6	58.1	1 297.5	532.4
3rd quarter	14 016.5	8 546.1	6 906.1	1 196.8	5 709.2	1 640.0	1 128.8	511.2	1 344.9	59.4	1 285.5	536.1
4th quarter	14 301.7	8 763.2	7 094.2	1 202.0	5 892.2	1 669.0	1 145.1	523.9	1 363.2	62.4	1 300.8	542.8
2013												
1st quarter	14 324.1	8 732.6	7 043.9	1 206.4	5 837.5	1 688.7	1 168.4	520.4	1 387.2	93.0	1 294.2	560.8
2nd quarter	14 464.7	8 819.6	7 103.0	1 206.8	5 896.2	1 716.6	1 190.7	525.9	1 410.6	94.1	1 316.5	573.1
3rd quarter	14 536.1	8 845.6	7 112.9	1 204.8	5 908.0	1 732.7	1 205.9	526.8	1 411.0	92.8	1 318.2	585.1
4th quarter	14 703.6	8 942.5	7 196.3	1 214.0	5 982.3	1 746.2	1 214.0	532.1	1 400.0	67.9	1 332.0	590.7
2014												
1st quarter	14 825.9	9 114.2	7 358.6	1 221.9	6 136.8	1 755.6	1 216.1	539.5	1 411.4	66.3	1 345.1	598.1
2nd quarter	15 140.7	9 172.4	7 409.4	1 230.6	6 178.8	1 763.1	1 221.3	541.8	1 450.6	77.0	1 373.6	602.6
3rd quarter	15 412.4	9 280.6	7 503.0	1 241.5	6 261.6	1 777.6	1 229.9	547.7	1 466.2	63.9	1 402.2	604.6
4th quarter	15 533.3	9 433.5	7 634.3	1 253.7	6 380.6	1 799.2	1 242.5	556.7	1 454.4	63.7	1 390.7	605.5
2015												
1st quarter	15 604.6	9 563.8	7 746.2	1 263.2	6 483.0	1 817.7	1 256.2	561.5	1 434.9	54.5	1 380.4	596.2
2nd quarter	15 746.9	9 666.2	7 830.8	1 273.0	6 557.8	1 835.4	1 267.9	567.5	1 411.3	54.5	1 356.8	611.3
3rd quarter	15 807.8	9 751.7	7 903.0	1 280.2	6 622.8	1 848.7	1 276.3	572.4	1 423.2	55.8	1 367.4	614.9
4th quarter	15 838.8	9 816.0	7 958.0	1 286.7	6 671.3	1 858.0	1 281.9	576.1	1 413.8	51.6	1 362.3	615.6
2016												
1st quarter	15 905.1	9 851.7	7 992.7	1 294.4	6 698.3	1 858.9	1 284.4	574.5	1 410.1	38.0	1 372.1	619.8
2nd quarter	15 911.1	9 905.2	8 039.2	1 302.6	6 736.7	1 866.0	1 288.7	577.3	1 409.6	37.6	1 372.0	626.7
3rd quarter	16 056.2	9 998.5	8 119.3	1 314.1	6 805.2	1 879.2	1 296.5	582.7	1 431.0	33.7	1 397.4	627.6
4th quarter	16 261.2	10 109.1	8 213.7	1 321.0	6 892.7	1 895.3	1 306.1	589.2	1 442.5	27.1	1 415.4	632.5
2017												
1st quarter	16 479.9	10 225.4	8 311.4	1 331.5	6 979.9	1 914.0	1 319.2	594.9	1 484.4	44.0	1 440.3	643.9
2nd quarter	16 639.7	10 337.9	8 402.5	1 340.1	7 062.4	1 935.4	1 334.7	600.7	1 498.5	42.2	1 456.3	645.1
3rd quarter	16 841.6	10 480.5	8 518.5	1 352.9	7 165.5	1 962.0	1 354.3	607.7	1 502.9	35.5	1 467.4	654.9
4th quarter	17 138.5	10 660.7	8 666.4	1 367.4	7 298.9	1 994.3	1 377.8	616.5	1 537.5	36.1	1 501.4	667.0

Table 1-13B. National Income by Type of Income: Historical Data—*Continued*

(Billions of dollars, quarterly data are at seasonally adjusted annual rates.)   **NIPA Tables 1.7.5, 1.12**

| Year and quarter | Corporate profits with IVA and CCAdj | | Profits after tax | | | Net interest and miscellaneous payments | Taxes on production and imports | Less: Subsidies | Business current transfer payments, net | | | Current surplus of government enterprises | Addendum: Net national factor income |
	Total	Taxes on corporate income	Total	Net dividends	Undistributed corporate profits				Total ¹	To persons	To government		
2003													
1st quarter	988.6	199.9	788.7	435.3	353.4	466.3	788.6	47.1	77.8	29.6	47.1	1.1	8 763.1
2nd quarter	1 024.8	196.5	828.3	435.6	392.8	449.2	800.0	57.1	75.6	28.0	47.7	-0.1	8 896.9
3rd quarter	1 075.7	217.7	858.0	457.8	400.3	440.2	813.0	45.9	75.7	25.5	48.6	1.7	9 042.3
4th quarter	1 135.9	241.0	894.9	495.4	399.5	418.6	820.9	46.0	75.0	22.0	49.8	3.2	9 209.8
2004													
1st quarter	1 242.4	251.4	991.0	532.7	458.3	378.4	847.3	44.2	80.3	17.5	51.3	11.5	9 351.7
2nd quarter	1 271.7	271.6	1 000.1	560.3	439.7	370.5	859.9	43.7	79.8	15.4	52.5	11.9	9 517.1
3rd quarter	1 330.4	292.7	1 037.7	567.2	470.5	373.0	871.3	45.4	78.8	15.7	53.0	10.1	9 713.1
4th quarter	1 312.9	298.3	1 014.5	668.5	346.0	387.3	893.8	52.3	90.0	18.4	52.6	19.0	9 785.3
2005													
1st quarter	1 442.1	375.7	1 066.3	575.2	491.2	420.4	915.1	56.7	85.0	23.7	52.0	9.3	9 979.6
2nd quarter	1 457.0	364.0	1 093.0	592.1	501.0	457.7	937.3	60.7	97.6	26.7	53.2	17.7	10 115.6
3rd quarter	1 483.0	370.2	1 112.8	598.4	514.3	485.0	952.1	62.0	93.2	27.3	53.5	12.5	10 292.3
4th quarter	1 572.5	409.0	1 163.4	642.3	521.1	524.0	965.3	64.2	91.1	25.6	55.0	10.6	10 519.7
2006													
1st quarter	1 629.6	421.4	1 208.2	714.1	494.2	523.4	981.8	55.7	77.9	21.6	56.0	0.3	10 776.3
2nd quarter	1 643.1	432.6	1 210.5	747.2	463.3	591.3	991.7	51.5	77.4	19.7	57.1	0.6	10 898.0
3rd quarter	1 688.7	451.3	1 237.4	765.6	471.8	582.2	1 004.1	49.9	83.8	19.9	58.0	5.9	10 985.0
4th quarter	1 623.6	415.3	1 208.4	793.4	415.0	562.5	1 010.5	48.7	84.6	22.1	58.9	3.6	11 031.8
2007													
1st quarter	1 528.8	418.6	1 110.2	820.3	289.9	586.6	1 025.9	49.5	99.0	26.5	59.2	13.2	11 101.4
2nd quarter	1 593.0	413.3	1 179.7	858.8	320.9	648.2	1 033.1	58.2	96.3	30.0	59.9	6.5	11 264.5
3rd quarter	1 525.9	376.5	1 149.4	868.1	281.3	651.7	1 035.8	55.9	99.8	32.5	60.8	6.5	11 243.2
4th quarter	1 485.0	358.7	1 126.3	866.8	259.5	662.6	1 052.6	54.7	99.0	34.1	63.7	1.3	11 313.6
2008													
1st quarter	1 388.4	298.0	1 090.4	903.0	187.4	652.9	1 045.7	51.9	113.4	34.7	65.2	13.5	11 309.5
2nd quarter	1 364.6	285.2	1 079.4	866.5	212.9	664.6	1 054.7	51.7	107.0	35.4	66.1	5.5	11 332.3
3rd quarter	1 372.6	270.7	1 101.9	820.8	281.2	702.1	1 058.5	52.0	107.1	36.1	65.3	5.7	11 410.9
4th quarter	1 017.8	169.8	848.0	770.9	77.0	674.1	1 040.0	54.6	129.5	36.9	81.2	11.4	11 011.4
2009													
1st quarter	1 255.1	172.0	1 083.1	702.8	380.3	598.3	1 015.9	55.4	122.5	37.8	82.3	2.4	10 823.5
2nd quarter	1 283.8	195.3	1 088.4	620.7	467.7	561.8	1 017.3	55.5	142.3	38.6	99.1	4.6	10 844.9
3rd quarter	1 456.5	206.4	1 250.1	584.1	666.0	516.8	1 028.8	67.1	119.7	39.4	81.2	-1.0	11 010.2
4th quarter	1 551.9	242.0	1 309.9	580.5	729.3	502.0	1 045.3	55.5	122.1	40.2	81.8	0.0	11 224.4
2010													
1st quarter	1 642.6	256.3	1 386.2	593.9	792.4	497.2	1 044.6	54.8	127.5	41.0	82.4	4.0	11 368.1
2nd quarter	1 640.8	262.2	1 378.5	613.0	765.5	482.5	1 062.1	55.5	124.2	42.4	81.4	0.4	11 565.5
3rd quarter	1 802.8	279.2	1 523.6	661.7	861.9	451.1	1 069.1	56.0	130.9	44.1	86.1	0.7	11 806.7
4th quarter	1 828.8	291.3	1 537.5	704.3	833.2	453.3	1 076.4	56.9	128.8	47.4	86.5	-5.1	11 924.1
2011													
1st quarter	1 670.4	285.1	1 385.2	748.0	637.2	463.6	1 091.5	58.9	147.1	48.8	88.9	9.5	11 972.1
2nd quarter	1 791.8	285.1	1 506.6	761.0	745.6	451.7	1 105.5	59.9	132.0	49.5	87.2	-4.7	12 161.6
3rd quarter	1 818.5	256.4	1 562.1	787.5	774.6	425.9	1 103.9	60.2	129.6	48.9	87.9	-7.2	12 293.4
4th quarter	1 958.5	296.4	1 662.1	819.8	842.2	457.2	1 114.0	61.1	118.0	47.0	83.3	-12.3	12 451.0
2012													
1st quarter	2 025.6	319.9	1 705.7	879.7	826.0	502.7	1 130.9	58.4	109.8	43.5	77.0	-10.7	12 833.0
2nd quarter	2 006.9	334.2	1 672.7	902.1	770.6	523.4	1 133.9	58.1	98.6	41.0	69.9	-12.3	12 922.1
3rd quarter	1 985.4	341.7	1 643.7	906.9	736.9	455.6	1 131.3	56.3	88.3	39.1	63.0	-13.8	12 868.1
4th quarter	1 971.7	342.5	1 629.2	1 106.1	523.2	494.4	1 148.4	59.4	92.5	38.1	66.0	-11.5	13 135.3
2013													
1st quarter	1 983.5	360.7	1 622.8	870.8	751.9	459.5	1 174.6	59.4	100.5	37.8	78.8	-16.1	13 123.6
2nd quarter	2 000.2	357.2	1 643.1	1 127.8	515.3	452.0	1 180.8	60.1	104.8	37.9	80.6	-13.7	13 255.5
3rd quarter	2 011.1	364.8	1 646.4	958.4	688.0	460.2	1 195.0	60.0	104.3	38.5	77.3	-11.6	13 313.1
4th quarter	2 047.9	367.9	1 680.0	1 079.0	601.0	465.1	1 204.1	59.4	128.5	39.5	102.0	-13.1	13 446.1
2014													
1st quarter	1 967.4	403.7	1 563.7	1 052.4	511.3	473.7	1 220.5	58.7	111.8	40.9	81.8	-10.9	13 564.9
2nd quarter	2 138.3	425.8	1 712.5	1 093.2	619.3	494.0	1 237.5	58.5	115.3	42.2	82.3	-9.3	13 857.8
3rd quarter	2 191.0	397.9	1 793.1	1 105.6	687.6	516.3	1 248.4	58.2	174.0	43.6	137.9	-7.5	14 058.7
4th quarter	2 184.2	400.9	1 783.3	1 133.1	650.2	535.3	1 257.0	57.0	130.0	45.0	90.2	-5.3	14 212.8
2015													
1st quarter	2 121.3	414.4	1 706.9	1 149.4	557.5	565.2	1 262.2	56.0	123.8	46.4	85.9	-8.4	14 281.6
2nd quarter	2 108.8	419.6	1 689.2	1 129.5	559.7	603.8	1 273.1	56.4	134.9	48.5	93.4	-7.0	14 401.3
3rd quarter	2 066.3	390.7	1 675.6	1 157.0	518.6	600.9	1 275.5	57.7	137.5	51.3	88.9	-2.7	14 456.9
4th quarter	1 945.5	360.3	1 585.2	1 223.7	361.5	594.3	1 289.9	58.7	226.0	54.8	173.9	-2.8	14 385.2
2016													
1st quarter	2 040.0	375.1	1 664.9	1 176.7	488.2	586.1	1 295.9	60.7	165.1	59.2	105.2	0.7	14 507.6
2nd quarter	2 003.2	378.9	1 624.2	1 178.2	446.0	562.4	1 301.0	62.4	170.2	61.2	110.0	-0.9	14 507.0
3rd quarter	2 035.7	385.7	1 649.9	1 198.7	451.3	558.2	1 320.8	63.0	152.3	60.7	92.2	-0.6	14 651.0
4th quarter	2 072.0	364.9	1 707.0	1 204.1	503.0	562.5	1 328.9	60.9	179.9	57.8	113.7	8.4	14 818.5
2017													
1st quarter	2 073.2	300.5	1 772.6	1 242.3	530.3	617.2	1 339.4	59.3	161.9	52.5	115.9	-6.5	15 044.1
2nd quarter	2 095.9	306.7	1 789.2	1 271.9	517.3	614.7	1 359.4	58.0	152.8	48.9	93.3	10.6	15 192.2
3rd quarter	2 153.0	323.7	1 829.3	1 268.3	561.0	611.2	1 372.1	61.9	135.9	46.9	94.1	-5.1	15 402.4
4th quarter	2 193.4	318.3	1 875.1	1 273.9	601.2	606.8	1 394.4	60.2	145.9	46.6	95.4	3.9	15 665.4

¹Includes net transfer payments to the rest of the world, not shown separately.

Table 1-14. Gross and Net Value Added of Domestic Corporate Business

(Billions of dollars, quarterly data are at seasonally adjusted annual rates.)   **NIPA Table 1.14**

Year and quarter	Gross value added of corporate business, total	Consumption of fixed capital	Net value added											Gross value added of financial corporate business
						Net operating surplus								
									Corporate profits with IVA and CCAdj					
											Profits after tax			
			Total	Compensation of employees	Taxes on production and imports less subsidies	Total	Net interest and miscellaneous payments	Business current transfer payments	Total	Taxes on corporate income	Total	Net dividends	Undistributed	
1960	299.9	28.5	271.4	190.7	27.8	52.9	-0.2	1.5	51.5	21.9	29.7	12.3	17.4	17.4
1961	308.7	29.5	279.2	195.6	28.9	54.7	0.4	1.7	52.6	22.2	30.4	12.2	18.2	18.3
1962	336.0	30.8	305.1	211.0	31.2	62.9	0.8	1.9	60.3	23.3	37.0	13.2	23.8	19.1
1963	357.4	32.4	324.9	222.7	33.2	69.1	0.4	2.3	66.4	25.5	40.9	14.4	26.5	19.5
1964	386.0	34.4	351.6	239.2	35.6	76.8	0.8	2.7	73.2	26.6	46.7	16.6	30.1	21.5
1965	423.8	37.1	386.6	259.9	37.8	89.0	1.2	3.1	84.6	29.8	54.8	18.2	36.6	23.0
1966	465.1	40.9	424.2	288.5	38.9	96.8	2.3	2.9	91.6	32.2	59.4	19.5	39.9	25.0
1967	491.2	45.1	446.1	308.4	41.4	96.3	4.0	3.1	89.1	31.0	58.1	20.2	37.9	28.0
1968	542.1	50.0	492.1	340.2	47.8	104.1	4.3	3.7	96.1	37.2	58.9	22.6	36.3	31.2
1969	590.7	55.7	534.9	377.5	52.9	104.6	8.5	4.3	91.8	37.0	54.9	23.4	31.4	36.0
1970	612.1	61.8	550.3	398.0	57.0	95.3	12.5	3.7	79.1	31.3	47.9	23.9	24.0	39.2
1971	660.9	67.6	593.3	421.7	62.8	108.8	12.6	3.4	92.8	34.8	58.0	23.7	34.3	42.8
1972	732.9	73.4	659.5	468.2	67.3	124.0	12.4	3.9	107.7	39.1	68.6	25.2	43.4	47.0
1973	820.2	82.0	738.2	526.1	74.1	138.0	14.7	4.8	118.5	45.6	72.9	27.4	45.4	51.4
1974	889.6	96.0	793.5	577.3	78.6	137.6	23.1	6.3	108.2	47.2	61.0	29.0	32.0	59.5
1975	965.5	113.5	852.0	607.8	84.5	159.7	27.2	8.2	124.2	46.3	78.0	31.8	46.2	67.3
1976	1 087.3	125.0	962.3	682.8	91.4	188.1	22.7	7.6	157.8	59.4	98.4	35.9	62.4	72.6
1977	1 232.5	140.5	1 092.1	771.7	100.0	220.3	27.7	6.0	186.7	68.5	118.2	39.6	78.5	85.1
1978	1 406.9	159.3	1 247.6	884.7	108.7	254.2	30.6	7.9	215.7	77.9	137.8	46.6	91.2	103.0
1979	1 564.3	183.4	1 380.9	1 004.4	115.0	261.5	36.3	10.8	214.4	80.7	133.6	50.8	82.9	114.0
1980	1 702.2	212.1	1 490.1	1 102.0	128.6	259.6	59.4	12.0	188.1	75.5	112.6	59.0	53.6	127.9
1981	1 934.8	244.9	1 689.9	1 220.6	154.4	314.9	82.8	14.3	217.8	70.3	147.5	72.3	75.2	146.1
1982	2 018.4	272.5	1 745.9	1 275.1	161.3	309.4	95.5	16.6	197.3	51.3	146.0	76.5	69.4	163.7
1983	2 172.4	285.9	1 886.5	1 353.0	177.4	356.1	91.9	19.5	244.7	66.4	178.3	85.5	92.7	186.6
1984	2 434.6	303.2	2 131.5	1 501.1	195.6	434.8	106.6	26.9	301.3	81.5	219.8	94.6	125.3	208.8
1985	2 601.3	326.9	2 274.4	1 615.9	209.0	449.5	102.2	30.9	316.4	81.6	234.8	103.5	131.3	232.3
1986	2 706.6	349.9	2 356.7	1 723.4	219.6	413.7	99.5	29.3	284.9	91.9	193.0	106.1	86.9	241.9
1987	2 894.9	371.3	2 523.6	1 847.6	233.4	442.6	99.7	24.9	318.0	112.7	205.3	113.3	91.9	253.2
1988	3 142.4	399.9	2 742.5	2 002.3	252.0	488.2	104.4	26.4	357.5	124.3	233.2	115.4	117.8	268.6
1989	3 320.0	427.1	2 892.8	2 119.3	267.5	506.0	125.2	33.6	347.2	124.4	222.7	148.0	74.7	299.9
1990	3 467.1	454.7	3 012.5	2 234.9	284.5	493.1	117.4	34.0	341.6	121.8	219.8	167.7	52.1	306.6
1991	3 554.4	479.6	3 074.8	2 277.8	307.9	489.1	79.3	33.7	376.1	117.8	258.3	177.0	81.3	323.5
1992	3 741.9	494.3	3 247.6	2 420.5	325.9	501.2	63.2	34.0	404.1	131.9	272.2	178.3	93.9	365.9
1993	3 918.3	517.2	3 401.2	2 515.7	343.8	541.7	62.3	31.8	447.6	155.0	292.6	200.7	91.9	383.9
1994	4 209.4	547.6	3 661.8	2 649.0	376.1	636.7	57.7	32.2	546.8	172.7	374.1	218.3	155.9	393.5
1995	4 473.4	590.4	3 882.9	2 787.9	384.8	710.3	60.2	36.9	613.3	194.4	418.8	249.6	169.2	432.7
1996	4 769.1	626.3	4 142.8	2 953.7	398.4	790.7	59.4	43.7	687.5	211.4	476.1	283.2	192.9	473.8
1997	5 141.8	670.1	4 471.8	3 176.6	416.9	878.3	81.7	34.4	762.2	224.8	537.4	312.9	224.5	533.8
1998	5 473.4	715.0	4 758.4	3 447.5	430.8	880.2	121.6	52.8	705.7	221.8	483.9	341.4	142.5	600.1
1999	5 801.1	769.6	5 031.4	3 684.3	454.0	893.1	126.1	53.8	713.2	227.4	485.8	331.8	154.0	635.1
2000	6 214.4	838.6	5 375.8	4 008.9	479.8	887.1	173.8	72.4	640.9	233.4	407.4	380.8	26.7	706.6
2001	6 199.7	888.6	5 311.1	4 013.8	469.4	827.9	153.2	84.8	589.9	170.1	419.8	357.0	62.8	732.7
2002	6 294.3	914.6	5 379.7	3 972.7	497.5	909.4	92.9	61.6	754.9	160.7	594.3	376.8	217.5	756.4
2003	6 520.7	932.5	5 588.1	4 040.9	524.3	1 023.0	75.3	50.3	897.3	213.8	683.6	423.9	259.7	794.4
2004	6 955.9	973.0	5 982.9	4 240.2	569.4	1 173.3	24.3	54.8	1 094.2	278.5	815.7	519.8	295.8	832.1
2005	7 481.9	1 042.0	6 439.9	4 443.0	616.3	1 380.7	61.2	56.5	1 262.9	379.7	883.2	341.1	542.0	920.5
2006	8 024.9	1 119.3	6 905.6	4 681.2	654.5	1 569.9	115.8	47.6	1 406.5	430.1	976.4	677.2	299.2	1 020.3
2007	8 192.8	1 188.9	7 003.9	4 894.2	676.3	1 433.4	168.4	69.6	1 195.4	391.8	803.6	713.1	90.5	970.4
2008	8 105.0	1 256.6	6 848.4	4 940.3	685.0	1 223.1	231.3	96.2	895.7	255.9	639.7	659.8	-20.1	813.6
2009	7 808.9	1 263.8	6 545.1	4 607.5	655.5	1 282.2	146.1	98.0	1 038.0	203.9	834.1	503.9	330.2	940.0
2010	8 226.5	1 271.2	6 955.3	4 700.8	684.9	1 569.6	126.5	100.1	1 343.0	272.3	1 070.7	521.8	548.9	977.5
2011	8 613.4	1 324.6	7 288.8	4 928.0	718.7	1 642.2	136.6	108.3	1 397.2	280.8	1 116.5	624.2	492.3	994.4
2012	9 171.8	1 392.5	7 779.3	5 182.7	743.2	1 853.5	199.3	62.2	1 592.1	334.6	1 257.5	768.8	488.7	1 111.4
2013	9 469.8	1 450.2	8 019.6	5 352.4	793.1	1 874.1	194.8	67.4	1 611.9	362.6	1 249.2	870.6	378.6	1 091.7
2014	10 045.9	1 527.5	8 518.4	5 645.2	828.3	2 044.9	234.4	95.1	1 715.3	407.1	1 308.3	934.4	373.8	1 260.5
2015	10 471.9	1 588.2	8 883.7	5 944.4	838.1	2 101.2	313.0	122.9	1 665.3	396.3	1 269.0	1 002.1	266.9	1 343.4
2016	10 648.6	1 627.4	9 021.2	6 099.6	853.8	2 067.8	309.1	140.9	1 617.8	376.2	1 241.6	1 003.7	237.9	1 410.5
2017	11 089.1	1 700.8	9 388.3	6 420.3	887.1	2 080.8	334.9	116.0	1 630.0	312.3	1 317.7	1 053.7	263.9	1 425.0
2018	11 735.5	1 780.5	9 954.9	6 768.2	959.0	2 227.8	313.8	130.7	1 783.3	281.5	1 501.7	437.4	1 064.3	1 555.6
2019	12 199.6	1 880.2	10 319.4	7 090.3	997.8	2 231.4	240.6	136.3	1 854.4	302.2	1 552.2	920.1	632.1	1 595.6
2020	11 890.6	1 957.0	9 933.7	7 157.6	531.7	2 244.4	322.6	132.7	1 789.0	275.6	1 513.4	1 086.1	427.3	1 721.9
2018														
1st quarter	11 505.1	1 746.0	9 759.1	6 661.6	937.2	2 160.4	337.8	120.8	1 701.8	256.8	1 445.0	49.3	1 395.6	1 524.1
2nd quarter	11 634.2	1 769.8	9 864.4	6 722.7	951.4	2 190.3	327.1	120.9	1 742.3	282.9	1 459.3	397.3	1 062.0	1 550.7
3rd quarter	11 852.4	1 792.4	10 060.0	6 822.2	965.1	2 272.6	308.5	147.2	1 816.9	287.2	1 529.7	808.7	721.0	1 589.2
4th quarter	11 950.1	1 814.0	10 136.2	6 866.3	982.1	2 287.7	281.7	134.0	1 872.0	299.2	1 572.8	494.3	1 078.5	1 558.5
2019														
1st quarter	12 046.3	1 844.6	10 201.7	7 030.0	980.7	2 190.9	247.0	144.8	1 799.2	297.4	1 501.8	881.3	620.5	1 593.4
2nd quarter	12 157.1	1 872.7	10 284.3	7 065.2	994.0	2 225.2	230.5	136.6	1 858.1	303.8	1 554.2	881.7	672.6	1 594.1
3rd quarter	12 219.1	1 893.8	10 325.3	7 085.8	1 005.5	2 234.0	232.4	142.3	1 859.3	291.5	1 567.8	911.2	656.5	1 572.6
4th quarter	12 375.8	1 909.6	10 466.2	7 180.1	1 010.8	2 275.3	252.6	121.7	1 901.0	316.0	1 585.0	1 006.1	579.0	1 622.3
2020														
1st quarter	12 298.9	1 932.5	10 366.4	7 247.4	1 013.7	2 105.3	291.4	123.5	1 690.4	245.4	1 445.0	963.1	481.9	1 644.6
2nd quarter	10 940.9	1 948.9	8 992.0	6 789.2	224.1	1 978.7	317.4	127.0	1 534.3	241.2	1 293.2	1 103.2	189.9	1 688.7
3rd quarter	11 794.2	1 962.2	9 831.9	7 134.7	240.8	2 456.4	336.0	139.5	1 981.0	300.3	1 680.7	1 107.1	573.6	1 731.7
4th quarter	12 528.6	1 984.3	10 544.3	7 459.2	648.1	2 437.0	345.8	140.7	1 950.5	315.6	1 634.9	1 171.1	463.7	1 822.5

Table 1-15. Gross Value Added of Nonfinancial Domestic Corporate Business in Current and Chained Dollars

(Billions of dollars, quarterly data are at seasonally adjusted annual rates.)   NIPA Table 1.14

Year and quarter	Current-dollar gross value added													Gross value added in billions of chained (2009) dollars
	Total	Consumption of fixed capital	Net value added											
			Total	Compensation of employees	Taxes on production and imports less subsidies	Net operating surplus								
						Total	Net interest and miscellaneous payments	Business current transfer payments	Corporate profits with IVA and CCAdj					
									Total	Taxes on corporate income	Profits after tax			
											Total	Net dividends	Undistributed	
1960	282.5	27.6	254.9	180.4	26.6	47.9	3.3	1.3	43.3	19.1	24.2	10.5	13.7	1 288.2
1961	290.4	28.6	261.9	184.5	27.6	49.7	3.8	1.4	44.5	19.4	25.1	10.6	14.5	1 319.1
1962	316.8	29.8	287.0	199.3	29.9	57.9	4.5	1.6	51.8	20.6	31.2	11.6	19.6	1 430.8
1963	337.8	31.3	306.5	210.1	31.7	64.7	4.8	1.6	58.3	22.8	35.5	12.4	23.1	1 519.0
1964	364.5	33.3	331.3	225.7	33.9	71.7	5.3	1.9	64.6	23.9	40.7	14.0	26.7	1 625.5
1965	400.7	35.8	364.9	245.4	36.0	83.5	6.0	2.1	75.4	27.1	48.3	16.2	32.1	1 762.0
1966	440.1	39.4	400.7	272.9	37.0	90.9	7.2	2.6	81.1	29.5	51.6	16.8	34.8	1 892.2
1967	463.2	43.5	419.7	291.1	39.3	89.4	8.6	2.7	78.1	27.8	50.2	17.3	33.0	1 946.4
1968	510.9	48.1	462.9	320.9	45.5	96.4	10.1	2.9	83.4	33.5	49.8	19.0	30.8	2 072.7
1969	554.6	53.5	501.1	356.1	50.2	94.9	13.5	3.0	78.3	33.3	45.0	19.0	25.9	2 155.6
1970	572.9	59.3	513.6	374.5	54.2	84.9	17.9	3.2	63.9	27.3	36.6	18.3	18.3	2 136.8
1971	618.1	64.7	553.4	396.2	59.5	97.7	18.9	3.6	75.2	30.0	45.2	18.1	27.0	2 221.0
1972	685.9	70.2	615.8	439.9	63.7	112.2	20.0	3.9	88.3	33.8	54.5	19.7	34.8	2 389.1
1973	768.8	78.2	690.7	495.1	70.1	125.5	23.7	4.5	97.2	40.4	56.8	20.8	36.1	2 534.8
1974	830.0	91.4	738.7	542.9	74.4	121.3	30.1	3.7	87.4	42.8	44.6	21.5	23.0	2 496.5
1975	898.3	107.7	790.6	569.0	80.2	141.3	32.4	4.7	104.3	41.9	62.4	24.6	37.8	2 461.9
1976	1 014.7	118.3	896.4	640.0	86.7	169.7	30.0	6.7	133.0	53.5	79.6	27.8	51.8	2 663.6
1977	1 147.4	132.6	1 014.8	723.3	94.6	196.9	33.0	8.7	155.1	60.6	94.6	30.9	63.6	2 860.6
1978	1 303.9	150.2	1 153.8	829.5	102.7	221.6	36.6	9.2	175.8	67.6	108.2	35.9	72.3	3 046.3
1979	1 450.3	172.4	1 277.8	942.4	108.8	226.7	43.6	9.0	174.0	70.6	103.4	37.6	65.8	3 144.1
1980	1 574.4	198.9	1 375.5	1 030.7	121.5	223.3	58.0	9.6	155.7	68.2	87.5	44.7	42.8	3 113.9
1981	1 788.7	229.1	1 559.6	1 139.9	146.7	273.1	72.5	10.7	189.9	66.0	123.9	52.5	71.4	3 240.6
1982	1 854.7	253.9	1 600.8	1 183.3	152.9	264.6	83.2	8.1	173.3	48.8	124.5	54.1	70.5	3 170.0
1983	1 985.8	264.6	1 721.2	1 250.1	168.0	303.1	82.6	10.0	210.5	61.7	148.8	63.2	85.6	3 324.9
1984	2 225.9	279.0	1 946.9	1 388.2	185.0	373.7	93.8	10.9	268.9	75.9	193.0	67.2	125.8	3 621.0
1985	2 369.0	299.0	2 070.0	1 490.1	196.6	383.3	96.9	15.4	271.1	71.1	200.0	72.0	128.0	3 787.4
1986	2 464.7	317.9	2 146.8	1 578.2	204.6	364.1	107.0	26.9	230.2	76.2	154.0	72.9	81.1	3 886.1
1987	2 641.7	334.7	2 307.0	1 685.5	216.8	404.7	115.7	29.7	259.4	94.2	165.1	76.3	88.9	4 092.1
1988	2 873.7	358.2	2 515.5	1 825.3	233.8	456.4	135.4	27.0	294.0	104.0	190.0	82.2	107.8	4 343.6
1989	3 020.0	380.2	2 639.9	1 934.8	248.2	456.9	159.4	23.5	274.0	101.2	172.8	105.4	67.5	4 426.2
1990	3 160.5	402.6	2 757.9	2 037.5	263.5	456.8	169.5	24.9	262.5	98.5	164.0	118.3	45.7	4 490.3
1991	3 231.0	423.6	2 807.4	2 071.1	285.7	450.6	156.4	26.1	268.1	88.6	179.5	125.5	54.0	4 467.0
1992	3 376.1	436.3	2 939.8	2 188.7	302.5	448.6	130.9	30.7	287.1	94.4	192.6	134.3	58.4	4 602.9
1993	3 534.4	455.8	3 078.6	2 271.0	319.3	488.2	117.0	29.5	341.7	108.0	233.7	149.2	84.5	4 716.7
1994	3 815.9	482.3	3 333.5	2 398.7	350.7	584.1	116.3	34.7	433.2	132.4	300.8	158.0	142.9	5 007.3
1995	4 040.6	520.8	3 519.8	2 524.6	358.7	636.6	125.6	30.2	480.8	140.3	340.5	178.0	162.5	5 249.1
1996	4 295.3	554.2	3 741.1	2 667.7	371.7	701.7	118.9	37.3	545.5	152.9	392.6	197.6	195.1	5 556.6
1997	4 608.0	594.6	4 013.4	2 862.6	388.9	762.0	126.6	38.5	596.9	161.4	435.5	215.9	219.6	5 928.1
1998	4 873.1	634.1	4 239.2	3 093.8	402.9	742.5	146.4	34.1	562.0	158.7	403.3	241.0	162.3	6 250.7
1999	5 166.0	679.1	4 486.9	3 310.0	424.6	752.3	156.0	45.6	550.7	166.5	384.3	224.7	159.6	6 565.3
2000	5 507.8	737.5	4 770.4	3 597.3	449.9	723.2	193.3	45.4	484.5	165.1	319.4	251.3	68.1	6 880.2
2001	5 467.0	781.5	4 685.5	3 582.3	441.5	661.7	220.7	55.2	385.8	106.2	279.6	245.4	34.2	6 715.0
2002	5 537.9	802.9	4 735.0	3 540.5	467.0	727.5	198.4	52.0	477.1	91.1	386.0	254.8	131.2	6 781.0
2003	5 726.3	816.1	4 910.1	3 594.3	491.1	824.7	173.4	61.6	589.6	126.5	463.2	293.4	169.8	6 933.3
2004	6 123.7	849.7	5 274.0	3 761.3	531.7	980.9	163.3	62.4	755.3	179.2	576.1	364.5	211.6	7 274.0
2005	6 561.5	911.0	5 650.5	3 928.7	575.7	1 146.1	178.3	79.1	888.7	262.5	626.2	170.8	455.4	7 539.0
2006	7 004.5	981.5	6 023.0	4 127.5	611.8	1 283.7	189.0	68.3	1 026.4	296.1	730.4	471.1	259.3	7 828.0
2007	7 222.4	1 044.0	6 178.5	4 307.1	631.3	1 240.1	252.8	58.8	928.5	277.4	651.1	484.6	166.5	7 899.1
2008	7 291.4	1 105.0	6 186.4	4 094.9	637.4	1 184.7	314.6	46.1	824.0	207.8	616.2	474.2	142.0	7 814.2
2009	6 868.9	1 110.7	5 758.2	4 094.9	608.5	1 054.8	288.3	60.3	706.2	162.1	544.1	351.4	192.7	7 259.7
2010	7 248.9	1 119.8	6 129.2	4 166.6	638.2	1 324.4	288.8	71.6	964.0	203.8	760.2	375.5	384.7	7 574.0
2011	7 619.0	1 169.3	6 449.7	4 372.7	670.8	1 406.1	286.5	79.7	1 039.9	209.0	830.9	441.0	389.9	7 777.8
2012	8 060.4	1 230.6	6 829.8	4 608.3	695.1	1 526.3	292.1	82.1	1 152.1	245.4	906.7	517.9	388.7	8 060.4
2013	8 378.0	1 279.7	7 098.3	4 768.1	742.0	1 588.2	283.8	84.2	1 220.2	263.5	956.7	531.9	424.8	8 265.4
2014	8 785.5	1 349.2	7 436.2	5 026.2	767.6	1 642.4	293.2	79.4	1 269.8	290.7	979.1	597.5	381.5	8 522.2
2015	9 128.5	1 401.7	7 726.8	5 292.6	772.8	1 661.4	304.5	99.3	1 257.7	283.2	974.5	641.1	333.4	8 775.8
2016	9 238.2	1 430.2	7 808.0	5 430.6	785.7	1 591.6	324.1	74.9	1 192.6	261.9	930.8	690.7	240.1	8 819.5
2017	9 664.1	1 492.8	8 171.3	5 705.4	827.0	1 638.9	330.7	95.3	1 212.9	224.9	988.0	720.7	267.3	9 066.4
2018	10 179.9	1 561.2	8 618.7	6 023.8	882.8	1 712.1	279.9	98.5	1 333.7	200.5	1 133.1	226.0	907.1	9 355.0
2019	10 604.0	1 644.8	8 959.1	6 315.2	931.3	1 712.6	273.5	91.6	1 347.5	203.6	1 143.9	695.7	448.2	9 567.6
2020	10 168.8	1 707.6	8 461.2	6 327.5	463.3	1 670.4	254.2	94.1	1 322.0	189.6	1 132.4	796.2	336.2	9 164.2
2018														
1st quarter	9 981.1	1 532.0	8 449.0	5 923.8	862.8	1 662.5	295.6	106.6	1 260.3	182.2	1 078.1	-182.3	1 260.3	9 296.2
2nd quarter	10 083.6	1 552.2	8 531.3	5 979.3	875.9	1 676.1	281.0	99.8	1 295.2	203.1	1 092.2	164.7	927.5	9 275.2
3rd quarter	10 263.2	1 571.4	8 691.7	6 067.4	888.5	1 735.8	272.7	96.7	1 366.4	208.3	1 158.1	584.2	573.9	9 414.4
4th quarter	10 391.6	1 589.3	8 802.3	6 124.5	903.8	1 774.0	270.5	90.8	1 412.7	208.5	1 204.2	337.3	866.9	9 433.9
2019														
1st quarter	10 452.9	1 615.5	8 837.4	6 254.1	915.5	1 667.8	274.4	95.9	1 297.4	202.7	1 094.7	663.8	430.9	9 512.9
2nd quarter	10 563.0	1 638.9	8 924.0	6 293.9	928.1	1 702.1	275.6	82.7	1 343.8	205.6	1 138.2	645.6	492.6	9 550.7
3rd quarter	10 646.5	1 655.9	8 990.6	6 318.9	938.4	1 733.2	274.1	102.9	1 356.2	192.5	1 163.7	731.3	432.4	9 577.2
4th quarter	10 753.5	1 669.0	9 084.5	6 393.9	943.3	1 747.3	269.8	84.9	1 392.6	213.4	1 179.2	742.3	436.9	9 629.6
2020														
1st quarter	10 654.3	1 688.0	8 966.3	6 443.0	928.9	1 594.3	262.9	93.1	1 238.4	162.8	1 075.6	756.5	319.1	9 549.8
2nd quarter	9 252.3	1 701.2	7 551.1	5 965.9	165.4	1 419.9	254.7	96.5	1 068.7	158.7	910.0	789.5	120.4	8 440.6
3rd quarter	10 062.5	1 711.6	8 350.9	6 311.2	181.0	1 858.8	250.5	94.0	1 514.3	214.1	1 300.2	766.3	533.9	9 041.9
4th quarter	10 706.1	1 729.6	8 976.5	6 589.9	578.0	1 808.6	248.9	92.9	1 466.8	222.7	1 244.0	872.5	371.5	9 624.3

Table 1-16. Shares of Income

(Billions of dollars, percent, quarterly data are at seasonally adjusted annual rates.)   **NIPA Tables 1.10, 1.14**

Year and quarter	Gross domestic income, total economy									Net factor income, domestic corporate business				
	Billions of dollars					Percent of total				Billions of dollars			Percent of total	
	Total	Compensation of employees	Taxes on production and imports less subsidies	Net operating surplus	Consumption of fixed capital	Compensation of employees	Taxes on production and imports less subsidies	Net operating surplus	Consumption of fixed capital	Total	Compensation of employees	Net operating surplus	Compensation	Net operating surplus
1959	521.5	285.9	40.0	130.1	65.4	54.8	7.7	24.9	12.5	234.3	180.3	54.0	77.0	23.0
1960	543.7	301.4	43.4	130.9	67.9	55.4	8.0	24.1	12.5	243.6	190.7	52.9	78.3	21.7
1961	563.1	310.6	45.0	137.0	70.6	55.2	8.0	24.3	12.5	250.3	195.6	54.7	78.1	21.9
1962	603.9	332.3	48.1	149.4	74.1	55.0	8.0	24.7	12.3	273.9	211.0	62.9	77.0	23.0
1963	638.9	350.5	51.2	159.3	78.0	54.9	8.0	24.9	12.2	291.8	222.7	69.1	76.3	23.7
1964	684.5	376.0	54.6	171.6	82.4	54.9	8.0	25.1	12.0	316.0	239.2	76.8	75.7	24.3
1965	741.5	405.4	57.7	190.4	88.0	54.7	7.8	25.7	11.9	348.9	259.9	89.0	74.5	25.5
1966	808.3	449.2	59.3	204.5	95.3	55.6	7.3	25.3	11.8	385.3	288.5	96.8	74.9	25.1
1967	856.6	481.8	64.1	207.2	103.6	56.2	7.5	24.2	12.1	404.7	308.4	96.3	76.2	23.8
1968	937.5	530.7	72.2	221.2	113.4	56.6	7.7	23.6	12.1	444.3	340.2	104.1	76.6	23.4
1969	1 016.0	584.4	79.4	227.4	124.9	57.5	7.8	22.4	12.3	482.1	377.5	104.6	78.3	21.7
1970	1 068.0	623.3	86.6	221.2	136.8	58.4	8.1	20.7	12.8	493.3	398.0	95.3	80.7	19.3
1971	1 155.3	665.0	95.8	245.6	148.9	57.6	8.3	21.3	12.9	530.5	421.7	108.8	79.5	20.5
1972	1 271.9	731.3	101.3	278.3	161.0	57.5	8.0	21.9	12.7	592.2	468.2	124.0	79.1	20.9
1973	1 419.2	812.7	112.0	315.9	178.7	57.3	7.9	22.3	12.6	664.1	526.1	138.0	79.2	20.8
1974	1 537.8	887.7	121.6	321.6	206.9	57.7	7.9	20.9	13.5	714.9	577.3	137.6	80.8	19.2
1975	1 671.6	947.3	130.8	355.0	238.5	56.7	7.8	21.2	14.3	767.5	607.8	159.7	79.2	20.8
1976	1 852.8	1 048.4	141.3	402.9	260.2	56.6	7.6	21.7	14.0	870.9	682.8	188.1	78.4	21.6
1977	2 062.4	1 165.9	152.6	454.1	289.8	56.5	7.4	22.0	14.1	992.0	771.7	220.3	77.8	22.2
1978	2 328.3	1 316.9	162.0	522.3	327.2	56.6	7.0	22.4	14.1	1 138.9	884.7	254.2	77.7	22.3
1979	2 582.3	1 477.3	171.6	559.5	373.9	57.2	6.6	21.7	14.5	1 265.9	1 004.4	261.5	79.3	20.7
1980	2 812.9	1 622.3	190.5	571.6	428.4	57.7	6.8	20.3	15.2	1 361.6	1 102.0	259.6	80.9	19.1
1981	3 169.0	1 792.7	224.1	664.9	487.2	56.6	7.1	21.0	15.4	1 535.5	1 220.6	314.9	79.5	20.5
1982	3 335.0	1 893.2	225.9	678.9	537.0	56.8	6.8	20.4	16.1	1 584.5	1 275.1	309.4	80.5	19.5
1983	3 577.1	2 012.7	242.0	759.8	562.6	56.3	6.8	21.2	15.7	1 709.1	1 353.0	356.1	79.2	20.8
1984	3 996.0	2 216.1	268.7	912.8	598.4	55.5	6.7	22.8	15.0	1 935.9	1 501.1	434.8	77.5	22.5
1985	4 284.7	2 387.5	286.7	970.3	640.1	55.7	6.7	22.6	14.9	2 065.4	1 615.9	449.5	78.2	21.8
1986	4 499.6	2 543.8	298.5	972.0	685.3	56.5	6.6	21.6	15.2	2 137.1	1 723.4	413.7	80.6	19.4
1987	4 811.4	2 723.8	317.2	1 040.0	730.4	56.6	6.6	21.6	15.2	2 290.2	1 847.6	442.6	80.7	19.3
1988	5 233.4	2 948.9	345.0	1 155.1	784.5	56.3	6.6	22.1	15.0	2 490.5	2 002.3	488.2	80.4	19.6
1989	5 573.6	3 140.9	371.5	1 223.0	838.3	56.4	6.7	21.9	15.0	2 625.3	2 119.3	506.0	80.7	19.3
1990	5 867.6	3 342.7	398.0	1 238.4	888.5	57.0	6.8	21.1	15.1	2 728.0	2 234.9	493.1	81.9	18.1
1991	6 065.2	3 453.3	429.6	1 249.9	932.4	56.9	7.1	20.6	15.4	2 766.9	2 277.8	489.1	82.3	17.7
1992	6 404.4	3 671.2	453.3	1 319.6	960.2	57.3	7.1	20.6	15.0	2 921.7	2 420.5	501.2	82.8	17.2
1993	6 702.6	3 820.6	466.4	1 412.1	1 003.5	57.0	7.0	21.1	15.0	3 057.4	2 515.7	541.7	82.3	17.7
1994	7 147.3	4 010.2	512.7	1 568.7	1 055.6	56.1	7.2	21.9	14.8	3 285.7	2 649.0	636.7	80.6	19.4
1995	7 546.7	4 202.2	523.1	1 699.1	1 122.4	55.7	6.9	22.5	14.9	3 498.2	2 787.9	710.3	79.7	20.3
1996	8 015.0	4 421.1	545.6	1 873.1	1 175.3	55.2	6.8	23.4	14.7	3 744.4	2 953.7	790.7	78.9	21.1
1997	8 566.0	4 713.2	577.8	2 035.6	1 239.3	55.0	6.7	23.8	14.5	4 054.9	3 176.6	878.3	78.3	21.7
1998	9 118.1	5 075.7	603.1	2 129.5	1 309.7	55.7	6.6	23.4	14.4	4 327.7	3 447.5	880.2	79.7	20.3
1999	9 659.5	5 409.9	628.4	2 222.2	1 398.9	56.0	6.5	23.0	14.5	4 577.4	3 684.3	893.1	80.5	19.5
2000	10 345.2	5 854.6	662.8	2 316.6	1 511.2	56.6	6.4	22.4	14.6	4 896.0	4 008.9	887.1	81.9	18.1
2001	10 695.7	6 046.3	669.0	2 380.9	1 599.5	56.5	6.3	22.3	15.0	4 841.7	4 013.8	827.9	82.9	17.1
2002	11 006.4	6 143.4	718.6	2 486.5	1 658.0	55.8	6.5	22.6	15.1	4 882.1	3 972.7	909.4	81.4	18.6
2003	11 476.3	6 362.3	756.5	2 638.4	1 719.1	55.4	6.6	23.0	15.0	5 063.9	4 040.9	1 023.0	79.8	20.2
2004	12 240.9	6 729.3	821.7	2 868.1	1 821.8	55.0	6.7	23.4	14.9	5 413.5	4 240.2	1 173.3	78.3	21.7
2005	13 091.7	7 077.7	881.5	3 161.4	1 971.0	54.1	6.7	24.1	15.1	5 823.7	4 443.0	1 380.7	76.3	23.7
2006	14 019.9	7 491.3	945.5	3 459.0	2 124.1	53.4	6.7	24.7	15.2	6 251.1	4 681.2	1 569.9	74.9	25.1
2007	14 454.4	7 889.4	982.2	3 330.0	2 252.8	54.6	6.8	23.0	15.6	6 327.6	4 894.2	1 433.4	77.3	22.7
2008	14 572.9	8 068.7	997.1	3 148.2	2 358.8	55.4	6.8	21.6	16.2	6 163.4	4 940.3	1 223.1	80.2	19.8
2009	14 276.0	7 767.2	968.5	3 168.9	2 371.5	54.4	6.8	22.2	16.6	5 889.7	4 607.5	1 282.2	78.2	21.8
2010	14 966.4	7 933.0	1 007.3	3 635.3	2 390.9	53.0	6.7	24.3	16.0	6 270.4	4 700.8	1 569.6	75.0	25.0
2011	15 612.0	8 234.0	1 043.7	3 859.9	2 474.5	52.7	6.7	24.7	15.8	6 570.2	4 928.0	1 642.2	75.0	25.0
2012	16 442.8	8 575.4	1 078.1	4 213.4	2 576.0	52.2	6.6	25.6	15.7	7 036.2	5 182.7	1 853.5	73.7	26.3
2013	16 958.0	8 843.6	1 129.0	4 304.2	2 681.2	52.2	6.7	25.4	15.8	7 226.5	5 352.4	1 874.1	74.1	25.9
2014	17 807.9	9 259.7	1 182.7	4 550.4	2 815.0	52.0	6.6	25.6	15.8	7 690.1	5 645.2	2 044.9	73.4	26.6
2015	18 440.5	9 709.5	1 218.0	4 601.6	2 911.4	52.7	6.6	25.0	15.8	8 045.6	5 944.4	2 101.2	73.9	26.1
2016	18 788.5	9 977.1	1 249.9	4 574.5	2 987.1	53.1	6.7	24.3	15.9	8 167.4	6 099.6	2 067.8	74.7	25.3
2017	19 598.5	10 436.7	1 306.4	4 737.2	3 118.2	53.3	6.7	24.2	15.9	8 501.1	6 420.3	2 080.8	75.5	24.5
2018	20 652.6	10 969.8	1 398.4	5 011.0	3 273.4	53.1	6.8	24.3	15.8	8 996.0	6 768.2	2 227.8	75.2	24.8
2019	21 442.2	11 459.4	1 459.3	5 087.8	3 435.6	53.4	6.8	23.7	16.0	9 321.7	7 090.3	2 231.4	76.1	23.9
2020	21 064.3	11 580.1	773.3	5 135.0	3 575.9	55.0	3.7	24.4	17.0	9 402.0	7 157.6	2 244.4	76.1	23.9
2018														
1st quarter	20 276.4	10 794.3	1 368.5	4 903.8	3 209.7	53.2	6.7	24.2	15.8	8 822.0	6 661.6	2 160.4	75.5	24.5
2nd quarter	20 497.4	10 902.0	1 390.4	4 948.7	3 256.3	53.2	6.8	24.1	15.9	8 913.0	6 722.7	2 190.3	75.4	24.6
3rd quarter	20 823.8	11 054.9	1 411.1	5 062.2	3 295.7	53.1	6.8	24.3	15.8	9 094.8	6 822.2	2 272.6	75.0	25.0
4th quarter	21 012.9	11 128.1	1 423.7	5 129.1	3 332.0	53.0	6.8	24.4	15.9	9 154.0	6 866.3	2 287.7	75.0	25.0
2019														
1st quarter	21 195.6	11 347.4	1 435.8	5 034.4	3 378.0	53.5	6.8	23.8	15.9	9 220.9	7 030.0	2 190.9	76.2	23.8
2nd quarter	21 361.6	11 405.9	1 462.1	5 072.7	3 421.0	53.4	6.8	23.7	16.0	9 290.4	7 065.2	2 225.2	76.0	24.0
3rd quarter	21 481.9	11 465.8	1 466.2	5 092.0	3 457.9	53.4	6.8	23.7	16.1	9 319.8	7 085.8	2 234.0	76.0	24.0
4th quarter	21 729.8	11 618.8	1 473.5	5 152.2	3 485.5	53.5	6.8	23.7	16.0	9 455.4	7 180.1	2 275.3	75.9	24.1
2020														
1st quarter	21 755.9	11 764.8	1 496.2	4 972.6	3 522.3	54.1	6.9	22.9	16.2	9 352.7	7 247.4	2 105.3	77.5	22.5
2nd quarter	19 620.2	11 036.1	336.2	4 696.9	3 550.9	56.2	1.7	23.9	18.1	8 767.9	6 789.2	1 978.7	77.4	22.6
3rd quarter	20 908.5	11 547.2	322.8	5 447.5	3 591.0	55.2	1.5	26.1	17.2	9 591.1	7 134.7	2 456.4	74.4	25.6
4th quarter	21 972.6	11 972.3	937.8	5 423.2	3 639.4	54.5	4.3	24.7	16.6	9 896.2	7 459.2	2 437.0	75.4	24.6

NOTES AND DEFINITIONS, CHAPTER 1

TABLES 1-1 THROUGH 1-16

National Income and Product

SOURCE: U.S. DEPARTMENT OF COMMERCE, BUREAU OF ECONOMIC ANALYSIS (BEA)

The mission of the Bureau of Economic Analysis (BEA) of the Department of Commerce is to promote a better understanding of the U.S. economy by providing timely, relevant, and accurate economic accounts. As such BEA quarterly and annually collect and produce data on how the U.S. economy is functioning. Featured in the NIPAs is gross domestic product (GDP), which measures the value of the goods and services produced by the U.S. economy in a given time period. GDP is one of the most comprehensive and closely watched economic statistics.

The National Income and Product Accounts (NIPA) are a set of economic accounts that provide information on the value and composition of output produced in the United States during a given period and on the types and uses of the income generated by that production. NIPA was created during the Great Depression to try to understand why the U.S. economy was in freefall and how to stop it.

U.S. input – output (I-O) accounts are a primary component of the U.S. economic accounts. I-O analysis is an economic tool that measures the relationships between various industries in the economy. These tables provides a detailed snapshot of the economy. More specifically, I-O tables show the commodity inputs that are used by each industry to produce its outputs; the commodities produced by each industry and the use of commodities by consumers.

NIPA is a snapshot of the economy at a certain time period. Over the past eight decades, new products have been created that use different inputs. To incorporate these changes, BEA conducts comprehensive revisions, called benchmarks, every five years. These comprehensive updates seek to introduce major improvements to maintain and improve the NIPA data.

The 2021 annual update of the National Income and Product Accounts was released on July 29, 2021 The reference year remained 2012. The update of the NIPAs covered the first quarter of 1999 through the first quarter of 2021 and resulted in revisions to gross domestic product (GDP), gross domestic income (GDI), and their components.

Information on COVID-19 and how it impacts data from the BEA can be found at https://www.bea.gov.

The 2018 comprehensive benchmark revision in July 2018 incorporated three major types of revisions: 1) statistical changes to introduce new and improved technologies and newly available source data; 2) changes in definitions to more accurately portray the evolving U.S. economy to more accurately portray the evolving U.S. economy and to provide consistent comparisons with data for other national economies; and 3) changes in presentations to reflect the definitional and statistical changes, where necessary, or to provide additional data or perspective for users. Also output and price measures will be expressed with 2012 equal to 100. The estimates for most tables showing real, or chained-dollar, estimates will begin with 2002.

Major statistical changes to the NIPA data include the 2012 benchmark input-output (I-O) accounts which incorporated the quinquennial economic census. The I-O accounts tracks the flows of detailed inputs and outputs throughout the economy. Another change is the incorporation of the improved methodology for seasonal adjustments over historical time spans and extending back improvements in previous annual updates. Other changes incorporated the handling of issues such as

- fixed investment in software, medical equipment, and communications equipment

- savings institutions and credit unions

- state and local defined benefit pension plans

Major changes in definitions in this comprehensive update are as follows:

- reclassifications of research and development (R & D) for software originals

- recognition of capital services

- reclassification of payments by Federal Reserve banks to the U.S. government

- reclassification of 'other' state and local personal taxes

The above revisions will be incorporated into the presentations produced by BEA.

Currently, BEA has adopted an expansion of the basic concept of production embodied in the accounts and changed the method of accounting for an important category of pension plans. Also, the constant-dollar or "real" estimates were restated to 2012 dollars, so that the levels shown are different even if the indicated rates of change are the same.

Fixed investment, one of the basic building blocks of the estimation of gross domestic product, was expanded in this revision by recognizing expenditures for research and development by business, government, and nonprofit institutions serving households (NPISHs) as investment.

The workers and capital that produce this R&D have always been reported in the labor and capital tabulations, but were treated as if they were costs of producing this year's output only. In the national income accounting as in conventional business accounting, the full costs of the R&D were subtracted from current-year business receipts in calculating business profit.

Now, in the NIPAs, the estimated value of the research over the whole life of the product—for example, from the estimated future sales of a new drug—is added to the value produced this year. However, this R&D will lose value over time and, as with a piece of machinery, its use and obsolescence, called consumption of fixed capital (CFC), is estimated and charged against GDP in each year that this capital is in use. For that reason, this change adds more to gross national product than to net national product and income.

The basic concept of the NIPAs requires equivalence (except for measurement error) between the value of output and the income and other charges against that value. The higher values of production are balanced on the income side of the accounts by the higher capital consumption allowances and by addition, to profits and other operating surplus (nonlabor income) components, of the net R&D investment—the difference between gross investment value and current year's CFC. (This does not change the tax accounting treatment. The firm still gets to charge off the entire expenditure in the year it is made, which is the most favorable treatment possible.)

Similarly, BEA is now capitalizing private spending for certain entertainment, literary, and other artistic originals as fixed investment. This includes movies, books, music, and long-lived TV programs such as situation comedies and drama (but not news, sports, games, or reality shows).

In a third expansion of the GDP investment definition, all ownership transfer costs for residential and nonresidential structures are capitalized (instead of only broker's commissions as in the previous treatment).

The other important conceptual change introduced in this revision was the adoption of accrual instead of cash accounting for defined benefit pension plans. This does not increase income and saving (or dis-saving) overall, but relocates it. Pension benefits are credited to the labor income and saving of employees when earned instead of when paid—matched by an equal and opposite change in the surplus or deficit of the employing government or business.

All the quarterly NIPA data published here, including indexes of quantity and price, are seasonally adjusted; this is not specifically noted on each table. All of the quarterly level values in current and constant dollars are also expressed at annual rates, which means that seasonally adjusted quarterly levels have been multiplied by 4 so that their scale will be comparable with the annual values shown, and this is noted on the pertinent *Business Statistics* tables. Where quarterly percent changes are shown, they are expressed as seasonally adjusted annual rates, which means that the quarter-to-quarter change in the level of GDP is calculated and then raised to the 4th power in order to express what that rate of change would be if continued over an entire year; this is noted in the column headings. For further information on these concepts see "General Notes" at the front of this volume.

Each table is notated, just above the table at the right-hand side, with the numbers of the NIPA tables from which the data are drawn.

All data and references are available on the BEA website, <https://www.bea.gov>.

DEFINITIONS AND NOTES ON THE DATA:

Basic concepts of total output and income (Tables 1-1, 1-11, 1-12, and 1-13)

The NIPAs depict the U.S. economy in several different dimensions. The basic concept, and the measure that is now most frequently cited, is gross domestic product (GDP), which is the market value of all goods and services produced by labor and property located in the United States.

In principle, GDP can be measured by summing the values created by each industry in the economy. However, it can also, and more readily, be measured by summing all the final demands for the economy's output. This final-demand approach also has the advantage of depicting the origins of demand for economic production, whether from consumers, businesses, or government.

Since production for the market necessarily generates incomes equal to its value, there is also an income total that corresponds to the production value total. This income can be measured and its distribution among labor, capital, and other income recipients can be depicted.

The relationships of several of these major concepts are illustrated in Table 1-11. The definitions of these concepts are as follows:

Gross domestic product (GDP), the featured measure of the value of U.S. output, is the market value of the goods and services produced by labor and property located in the United States. Market values represent output valued at the prices paid by the final customer, and therefore include taxes on production and imports, such as sales taxes, customs duties, and taxes on property.

The term "gross" in gross domestic product and gross national product is used to indicate that capital consumption allowances (economic depreciation) have not been deducted.

GDP is primarily measured by summing the values of all of the final demands in the economy, net of the demands met by imports; this is shown in Table 1-1. Specifically, GDP is the sum of personal consumption expenditures (PCE), gross private domestic investment (including change in private inventories and before deduction of charges for consumption of fixed capital), net exports of goods and services, and government consumption expenditures and gross investment. GDP measured in this way excludes duplication involving "intermediate" purchases of goods and services (goods and services purchased by industries and used in production), the value of which is already included in the value of the final products. Production of any intermediate goods that are not used in further production in the current period is captured in the measurement of inventory change.

In concept, GDP is equal to the sum of the economic value added by (also referred to as "gross product originating in") all industries in the United States. This, in turn, also makes it the conceptual equivalent of *gross domestic income (GDI),* a new concept introduced in the 2003 revision. GDI is the sum of the incomes earned in each domestic industry, plus the taxes on production and imports and less the subsidies that account for the difference between output value and factor input value. This derivation is shown in Table 1-12. Since the incomes and taxes can be measured directly, they can be summed to a total that is equivalent to GDP in concept but differs due to imperfections in measurement. The difference between the two is known as the *statistical discrepancy.* It is defined as GDP minus GDI, and is shown in Tables 1-11 and 1-12.

Gross national product (GNP) refers to all goods and services produced by labor and property supplied by U.S. residents—whether located in the United States or abroad—expressed at market prices. It is equal to GDP, plus *income receipts from the rest of the world,* less *income payments to the rest of the world. Domestic* production and income refer to the <u>location</u> of the factors of production, with only factors located in the United States included; *national* production and income refer to the <u>ownership</u> of the factors of production, with only factors owned by United States residents included.

Before the comprehensive NIPA revisions that were made in 1991, GNP was the commonly used measure of U.S. production. However, GDP is clearly preferable to GNP when used in conjunction with indicators such as employment, hours worked, and capital utilized—for example, in the calculation of labor and capital productivity—because it is confined to production taking place within the borders of the United States.

The income-side aggregate corresponding to GNP is *gross national income (GNI),* shown as an addendum to Table 1-11. It consists of gross domestic income plus income receipts from the rest of the world, less income payments to the rest of the world. It is used as the denominator for a national saving-income ratio, presented in Chapter 5. National income is the preferred measure for calculating and comparing saving, since it is the income aggregate from which that saving arises. As with GDP and gross domestic income, the statistical discrepancy indicates the difference between the product-side and income-side measurement of the same concept.

Net national product is the market value, net of depreciation, of goods and services attributable to the labor and property supplied by U.S. residents. It is equal to GNP minus the *consumption of fixed capital (CFC).* CFC relates only to fixed capital located in the United States. (Investment in that capital is measured by private fixed investment and government gross investment.) As of the 2009 comprehensive revision, CFC represents only the normal using-up of capital in the process of production, and no longer includes extraordinary disaster losses such as those caused by Hurricane Katrina and the 9/11 attacks. These losses are still estimated and used to write down the estimates of the capital stock, but they no longer have negative effects on our calculation of current income from production.

National income has been redefined and now includes all net incomes (net of the consumption of fixed capital) earned by U.S. residents, and also includes not only "factor incomes"—net incomes received by labor and capital as a result of their participation in the production process, but also "nonfactor charges"—taxes on production and imports, business transfer payments, and the current surplus of government enterprises, less subsidies. This change has been made to conform with the international guidelines for national accounts, *System of National Accounts (SNA) 1993.* According to *SNA 1993,* these charges cannot be eliminated from the input and output prices.

Since national income now includes the nonfactor charges, it is conceptually equivalent to *net national product* and differs only by the amount of the statistical discrepancy.

The concept formerly known as "national income," which excludes the nonfactor charges, is still included in the accounts as an addendum item, now called "net national factor income." It is shown in Table 1-13. *Net national factor income* consists of compensation of employees, proprietors' income with inventory valuation and capital consumption adjustments (IVA and CCadj, respectively), rental income of persons with capital consumption adjustment, corporate profits with inventory valuation and capital consumption adjustments, and net interest.

By definition, national income and its components exclude all income from capital gains (increases in the value of owned assets). Such increases have no counterpart on the production side of the accounts. This exclusion is partly accomplished by means of the inventory valuation and capital consumption adjustments, which will be described in the definitions of the components of product and income.

DEFINITIONS AND NOTES ON THE DATA:

Imputation

The term *imputation* will appear from time to time in the definitions of product and income components. Imputed values are values estimated by BEA statisticians for certain important product and income components that are not explicitly valued in the source data, usually because a market transaction in money terms is not involved. Imputed values appear on both the product and income side of the accounts; they add equal amounts to income and spending, so that no imputed saving is created.

One important example is the imputed rent on owner-occupied housing. The building of such housing is counted as investment, yet in the monetary accounts of the household sector, there is no income from that investment nor any rental paid for it. In the NIPAs, the rent that each such dwelling would earn if rented is estimated and added to both national and personal income (as part of rental income receipts) and to personal consumption expenditures (as part of expenditures on housing services).

Another important example is imputed interest. For example, many individuals keep monetary balances in a bank or other financial institution, receiving either no interest or below-market interest, but receiving the institution's services, such as clearing checks and otherwise facilitating payments, with little or no charge. In this case, where is the product generated by the institution's workers and capital? In the NIPAs, the depositor is imputed a market-rate-based interest return on his or her balance, which is then imputed as a service charge received by the institution, and therefore included in the value of the institution's output.

DEFINITIONS AND NOTES ON THE DATA:

Components of product (Tables 1-1 through 1-6)

Personal consumption expenditures (PCE) is goods and services purchased by persons residing in the United States. PCE consists mainly of purchases of new goods and services by individuals from businesses. It includes purchases that are financed by insurance, such as government-provided and private medical insurance. In addition, PCE includes purchases of new goods and services by nonprofit institutions, net purchases of used goods ("net" here indicates purchases of used goods from business less sales of used goods to business) by individuals and nonprofit institutions, and purchases abroad of goods and services by U.S. residents traveling or working in foreign countries. PCE also includes purchases for certain goods and services provided by government agencies. (See the notes and definitions for Chapter

4 for additional information.) In the 2009 revision, new detail was provided on the allocation of PCE between the household and nonprofit sectors.

Gross private domestic investment consists of gross private fixed investment and change in private inventories.

Private fixed investment consists of both nonresidential and residential fixed investment. The term "residential" refers to the construction and equipping of living quarters for permanent occupancy. Hotels and motels are included in *nonresidential fixed investment*, as described subsequently in this section.

Private fixed investment consists of purchases of fixed assets, which are commodities that will be used in a production process for more than one year, including replacements and additions to the capital stock, and now also including research and development and other intellectual property. It is measured "gross," before a deduction for consumption of existing fixed capital. It covers all investment by private businesses and nonprofit institutions in the United States, regardless of whether the investment is owned by U.S. residents. The residential component includes investment in owner-occupied housing; the homeowner is treated equivalently to a business in these investment accounts. (However, when GDP by sector is calculated, owner-occupied housing is no longer included in the business sector. It is allocated to the households and institutions sector.) Private fixed investment does not include purchases of the same types of equipment and structures by government agencies, which are included in government gross investment, nor does it include investment by U.S. residents in other countries.

Nonresidential fixed investment is the total of nonresidential structures, nonresidential equipment, and intellectual property.

Nonresidential structures consists of new construction, brokers' commissions and other ownership transfer costs on sales of structures, and net purchases of used structures by private business and by nonprofit institutions from government agencies (that is, purchases of used structures from government minus sales of used structures to government). New construction also includes hotels and motels and mining exploration, shafts, and wells.

Nonresidential equipment consists of private business purchases on capital account of new machinery, equipment, and vehicles; dealers' margins on sales of used equipment; and net purchases of used equipment from government agencies, persons, and the rest of the world (that is, purchases of such equipment minus sales of such equipment). It does not include the estimated personal-use portion of equipment purchased for both business and personal use, which is allocated to PCE.

Intellectual property consists of purchases and in-house production of software; research and development; and private expenditures for specified entertainment, literary, and artistic originals. (See above for further description.)

Residential private fixed investment consists of both residential structures and residential producers' durable equipment (including such equipment as appliances owned by landlords and rented to tenants). Investment in structures consists of new units, improvements to existing units, purchases of manufactured homes, brokers' commissions and other ownership transfer costs on the sale of residential property, and net purchases of used residential structures from government agencies (that is, purchases of such structures from government minus sales of such structures to government). As noted above, it includes investment in owner-occupied housing.

Change in private inventories is the change in the physical volume of inventories held by businesses, with that <u>change</u> being valued at the average price of the period. It differs from the change in the book value of inventories reported by most businesses; an *inventory valuation adjustment (IVA)* converts book value change using historical cost valuations to the change in physical volume, valued at average replacement cost.

Net exports of goods and services is *exports of goods and services* less *imports of goods and services*. It does not include income payments or receipts or transfer payments to and from the rest of the world.

Government consumption expenditures is the estimated value of the services produced by governments (federal, state, and local) for current consumption. Since these are generally not sold, there is no market valuation and they are priced at the cost of inputs. The input costs consist of the compensation of general government employees; the estimated consumption of general government fixed capital including software and R&D (CFC, or economic depreciation); and the cost of goods and services purchased by government less the value of sales to other sectors. The value of investment in equipment and structures produced by government workers and capital is also subtracted, and is instead included in government investment. Government sales to other sectors consist primarily of receipts of tuition payments for higher education and receipts of charges for medical care.

This definition of government consumption expenditures differs in concept—but not in the amount contributed to GDP—from the treatment in existence before the 2003 revision of the NIPAs. In the current definition, goods and services purchased by government are considered to be intermediate output. In the previous definition, they were considered to be final sales. Since their value is added to the other components to yield total government consumption expenditures, the dollar total contributed to GDP is the same. The only practical difference is that the goods purchased disappear from the goods account and appear in the services account instead. In the industry sector accounts, the value added by government is also unchanged. It continues to be measured as the sum of compensation and CFC, or equivalently as gross government output less the value of goods and services purchased.

Gross government investment consists of general government and government enterprise expenditures for fixed assets (structures, equipment, software, and R&D). Government inventory investment is included in government consumption expenditures.

DEFINITIONS AND NOTES ON THE DATA:

Real values, quantity and price indexes (Tables 1-2 through 1-7)

Real, or chained (2012) dollar, estimates are estimates from which the effect of price change has been removed. Prior to the 1996 comprehensive revision, constant-dollar measures were obtained by combining real output measures for different goods and services using the relative prices of a single year as weights for the entire time span of the series. In the recent environment of rapid technological change, which has caused the prices of computers and electronic components to decline rapidly relative to other prices, this method distorts the measurement of economic growth and causes excessive revisions of growth rates at each benchmark revision. The current, chained-dollar measure changes the relative price weights each year, as relative prices shift over time. As a result, recent changes in relative prices do not change historical growth rates.

Chained-dollar estimates, although expressed for continuity's sake as if they had occurred according to the prices of a single year (currently 2009), are usually not additive. This means that because of the changes in price weights each year, the chained (2009) dollar components in any given table for any year other than 2009 usually do not add to the chained (2009) dollar total. The amount of the difference for the major components of GDP is called the *residual* and is shown in Table 1-2. It is specific to each individual BEA tabulation, corresponding to the sum of the lowest level of aggregation <u>on that tabulation.</u> In time periods close to the base year, residuals are usually quite small; over longer periods, the differences become much larger. For this reason, BEA no longer publishes chained-dollar estimates prior to 1999, except for selected aggregate series. For the more detailed components of GDP, historical trends and fluctuations in real volumes are represented by *chain-type quantity indexes,* which are presented in Tables 1-5, 4-3, 5-4, 5-6, 6-6, 6-7, 6-11, 6-16, 7-2, 7-5, and 14-2.

Chain-weighting leads to complexity in estimating the contribution of economic sectors to an overall change in output: it becomes difficult, for someone without access to the complicated statistical methods that BEA uses, to find the correct answers to questions such as "How much are government spending cuts contributing to the drag on GDP growth?" Because of this, BEA is now calculating and publishing estimates of the arithmetic contribution of each major component to the total change in real GDP. *Business Statistics* reproduces these calculations in Table 1-4. (As will be explained later, users of these calculations should, however, bear in mind that imports are treated as a negative contribution to GDP instead of being subtracted from the demand components that give rise to them.) For further information, see J. Steven Landefeld, Brent R. Moulton, and Cindy M. Vojtech, "Chained-Dollar Indexes: Issues, Tips on Their Use, and Upcoming Changes," *Survey of Current Business* (November 2003); and J. Steven Landefeld and Robert P. Parker, "BEA's Chain Indexes, Time Series, and Measures of Long-Term Economic Growth," *Survey of Current Business* (May 1997).

GDP price indexes measure price changes between any two adjacent years (or quarters) for a fixed "market basket" of goods and services consisting of the average quantities purchased in those two years (or quarters). The annual measures are chained together to form an index with prices in 2009 set to equal 100. Using average quantities as weights while changing weights each period eliminates the substitution bias that arises in more conventional indexes, in which weights are taken from a single base period that usually takes place early in the period under measurement. Generally, using a single, early base period leads to an overstatement of price increase. The CPI-U and the CPI-W are examples of such conventional indexes, technically known as "Laspeyres" indexes. See the "General Notes" at the beginning of this volume and the notes and definitions for Chapter 8 for further explanation.

The chain-type formula guarantees that a GDP price index change will differ only trivially from the change in the implicit deflator (ratio of current-dollar to real value, expressed as a percent). Therefore, *Business Statistics* is no longer publishing a separate table of implicit deflators.

DEFINITIONS AND NOTES ON THE DATA:

BEA Aggregates of sales and purchases (Tables 1-1 and 1-5 through 1-7)

Final sales of domestic product is GDP minus change in private inventories. It is the sum of personal consumption expenditures, gross private domestic fixed investment, government consumption expenditures and gross investment, and net exports of goods and services.

Gross domestic purchases is the market value of goods and services purchased by U.S. residents, regardless of where those goods and services were produced. It is GDP minus net exports (that is, minus exports plus imports) of goods and services; equivalently, it is the sum of personal consumption expenditures, gross private domestic investment, and government consumption expenditures and gross investment. The price index for gross domestic purchases is therefore a measure of price change for goods and services purchased by (rather than produced by) U.S. residents.

Final sales to domestic purchasers is gross domestic purchases minus change in private inventories.

DEFINITIONS AND NOTES ON THE DATA:

U.S. Population and per capita product and income estimates (Table 1-3)

In Table 1-3, annual and quarterly measures of product, income, and consumption spending are expressed in per capita terms—the aggregate dollar amount divided by the U.S. population. Population data from 1991 forward reflect the results of the 2000 and 2010 Censuses.

DEFINITIONS AND NOTES ON THE DATA:

Inventory-sales ratios (Table 1-8)

Inventories to sales ratios. The ratios shown in Table 1-8 are based on the inventory estimates underlying the measurement of inventory change in the NIPAs. They include data and estimates for not only the inventories held in manufacturing and trade (which are shown in Chapter 16), but also stocks held by all other businesses in the U.S. economy.

For the current-dollar ratios, inventories at the end of each quarter are valued in the prices that prevailed at the end of that quarter. For the constant-dollar ratios, they are valued in chained (2009) dollars. In both cases, the inventory-sales ratio is the value of the inventories at the end of the quarter divided by quarterly total sales at <u>monthly</u> rates (quarterly totals divided by 3). In other words, they represent how many months' supply businesses had on hand at the end of the period. This makes them comparable in concept and order of magnitude to the ratios shown in Chapter 16. Annual ratios are those for the fourth quarter.

Inventory data consistent with the 2013 revision are only available from 1997 to date. Tables 1-8A and B show the old estimates for earlier years with an overlap period.

DEFINITIONS AND NOTES ON THE DATA:

Shares of aggregate supply and demand (Tables 1-9 and 1-10)

These tables, developed by the editor of *Business Statistics*, are not official NIPA calculations. They are components of current-dollar GDP rearranged in order to highlight relationships that are not always apparent in the official presentation of the NIPAs.

Aggregate supply combines domestic production (GDP) and imports, the two sources that, between them, supply the goods and services demanded by consumers, businesses, and governments in the U.S. economy. In this table the user can observe the growing share of imports that satisfy demands in the U.S. marketplace.

Aggregate final demand is the sum of all final (that is, excluding inventory change) demands for goods and services in the U.S. market—consumption spending, fixed investment, exports, and government consumption and investment. It is different from *final sales of domestic product* (Tables 1-1 and 1-7) because imports are not subtracted; in this table, imports are considered a source of supply, not a negative element of demand. It is different from *gross domestic purchases* (Tables 1-5 and 1-6) because it includes exports, since they are a source of demand for U.S. output, but excludes inventory change. It is like *final sales to domestic purchasers* (Table 1-7) in excluding inventory change, but different because it also includes exports.

Table 1-10 provides alternative data on the question of the relative importance of consumption spending and other final demands to the U.S. economy. NIPA statistics on PCE as a percent of GDP are frequently cited, but there is a problem with this, since PCE includes the value of imports while GDP does not.

DEFINITIONS AND NOTES ON THE DATA:

Components of income (Tables 1-11, 1-12 and 1-13)

There are now two different presentations of aggregate income for the United States: *gross domestic income* (Table 1-12) and *national income* (Table 1-13). As noted above, domestic income refers to income generated from production within the United States, while national income refers to income received by residents of the United States. This means that some of the income components differ between the two tables. Domestic income payments include payments to the rest of the world from domestic industries. National income payments exclude payments to the rest of the world but include payments received by U.S. residents from the rest of the world. These differences are seen in employee compensation, interest, and corporate profits. Taxes on production and imports, taxes on corporate income, business transfer payments, subsidies, proprietors' income, rental income, and the current surplus of government enterprises are the same in both accounts.

All income entries are now calculated on an accrual basis, associating the income with the period in which it was earned rather than when it was paid.

A third important income aggregate is *personal income*. The derivation of this well-known statistic from national income is shown in Table 1-11. See Chapter 4 and its notes and definitions for data and more information.

Compensation of employees is the income accruing to employees as remuneration for their work. It is the sum of wage and salary accruals and supplements to wages and salaries. In the domestic income account, it refers to all payments generated by domestic production, including those to workers residing in the "rest of the world." In the national and personal income accounts, there is a slightly different "compensation of employees," including that received by U.S. residents from the rest of the world but excluding that paid from the domestic production account to workers residing elsewhere.

Wages and salaries consists of the monetary remuneration of employees, including the compensation of corporate officers; corporate directors' fees paid to directors who are also employees of the corporation; commissions, tips, and bonuses; voluntary employee contributions to certain deferred compensation plans, such as 401(k) plans; and receipts-in-kind that represent income. As of the 2003 revision, it also includes judicial fees to jurors and witnesses, compensation of prison inmates, and marriage fees to justices of the peace, all of which were formerly included in "other labor income."

In concept, wages and salaries include the value of the exercise by employees of "nonqualified stock options," in which an employee is allowed to buy stock for less than its current market price. (Actual measurement of these values involves a number of problems, particularly in the short run. Such stock options are not included in the monthly wage data from the Bureau of Labor Statistics, which are the main source for current extrapolations of wages and salaries, and are not consistently reported in corporate financial statements. They are, however, generally included in the unemployment insurance wage data that are used to correct the preliminary wage and salary estimates.) Another form of stock option, the "incentive stock option," leads to a capital gain only and is thus not included in the definition of wages and salaries.

Supplements to wages and salaries consists of *employer contributions for employee pension and insurance funds* and *employer contributions for government social insurance*.

Employer contributions for employee pension and insurance funds consists of employer payments (including payments-in-kind) to private pension and profit-sharing plans, private group health and life insurance plans, privately administered workers' compensation plans, government employee retirement plans, and supplemental unemployment benefit plans. They are now measured in the period in which the employee earns the obligation rather than when the employer makes the cash payment into the fund. This includes the major part of what was once called "other labor income." The remainder of "other labor income" has been reclassified as wages and salaries, as noted above.

Employer contributions for government social insurance consists of employer payments under the following federal, state, and local government programs: old-age, survivors, and disability insurance (Social Security); hospital insurance (Medicare); unemployment insurance; railroad retirement; pension benefit guaranty; veterans' life insurance; publicly administered workers' compensation; military medical insurance; and temporary disability insurance.

Taxes on production and imports is included in the gross domestic income account to make it comparable in concept to gross domestic product. It consists of federal excise taxes and customs duties and of state and local sales taxes, property taxes (including residential real estate taxes), motor vehicle license taxes, severance taxes, special assessments, and other taxes. It is equal to the former "indirect business taxes and nontax liabilities" less most of the nontax liabilities, which have now been reclassified as "business transfer payments."

Subsidies (payments by government to business other than purchases of goods and services) are now presented separately from the current surplus of government enterprises, which is presented as a component of net operating surplus. However, for data representing the years before 1959, subsidies continue to be presented as net of the current surplus of government enterprises, since detailed data to separate the series for this period are not available.

Net operating surplus is a new aggregate introduced in the 2003 NIPA revision—a grouping of the business income components of the gross domestic income account. It represents the net income accruing to business capital. It is equal to gross domestic income minus compensation of employees, taxes on production and imports less subsidies (that is, the taxes are taken out of income and the subsidies are put in), and consumption of fixed capital (CFC). Net operating surplus consists of the surplus for private enterprises and the current surplus of government enterprises. The net operating surplus of private enterprises comprises net interest and miscellaneous payments, business current transfer payments, proprietors' income, rental income of persons, and corporate profits.

Net interest and miscellaneous payments, domestic industries consists of interest paid by domestic private enterprises and of rents and royalties paid by private enterprises to government, less interest received by domestic private enterprises. Interest received does not include interest received by noninsured pension plans, which are recorded as being directly received by persons in personal income. Both interest categories include monetary and imputed interest. In the *national* account, interest paid to the rest of the world is subtracted from the interest paid by domestic industries and interest received from the rest of the world is added. Interest payments on mortgage and home improvement loans and on home equity loans are included as net interest in the private enterprises account.

It should be noted that net interest does not include interest paid by federal, state, or local governments. In fact, government interest does not enter into the national and domestic income accounts, though it does appear as a component of personal income. The NIPAs draw a distinction between interest paid by government and that paid by business.

The reasoning behind this distinction is that interest paid by business is one of the income counterparts of the production side of the account. The value of business production (as measured by its output of goods and services) includes the value added by business capital, and interest paid by business to its lenders is part of the total return to business capital.

However, there is no product flow in the accounts that is a counterpart to the payment of interest by government. The output of government does not have a market value. For purposes of GDP measurement, BEA estimates the government contribution to GDP as the sum of government's compensation of employees, purchases of goods and services, and consumption of government fixed capital. (See above, and also the notes and definitions to Chapter 6.) This implies an estimate (described as "conservative" by BEA) that the net return to government capital is zero—that is, that the gross return is just sufficient to pay down the depreciation. Consequently, this assumption generates no income, imputed or actual, that might correspond to the government's interest payment.

Supporting the distinction between business and government interest payments, it may be noted that most federal government debt was not incurred to finance investment, but rather to finance wars, to avoid tax increases and spending cuts during recessions, or to stimulate the economy. Furthermore, some of the largest and most productive government investments—highways—are typically financed by taxes on a pay-as-you-go basis and not by borrowing.

Business current transfer payments, net consists of payments to persons, government, and the rest of the world by private business for which no current services are performed. Net insurance settlements—actual insured losses (or claims payable) less a normal level of losses—are treated as transfer payments. Payments to government consist of federal deposit insurance premiums, fines, regulatory and inspection fees, tobacco settlements, and other miscellaneous payments previously classified as "nontaxes." Taxes paid by domestic corporations to foreign governments, formerly classified as transfer payments, are now counted as taxes on corporate income.

In the NIPAs, capital income other than interest—corporate profits, proprietors' income, and rental income—is converted from the basis usually shown in the books of business, and reported to the Internal Revenue Service, to a basis that more closely represents income from current production. In the business accounts that provide the source data, depreciation of structures and equipment typically reflects a historical cost basis and a possibly arbitrary service life allowed by law to be used for tax purposes. BEA adjusts these values to reflect the average actual life of the capital goods and the cost of replacing them in the current period's prices. This conversion is done for all three forms of capital income. In addition, corporate and proprietors' incomes also require an adjustment for inventory valuation to exclude any profits or losses that might appear in the books, should the cost of inventory acquisition not be valued in the current period's prices. These two adjustments are called the *capital consumption adjustment (CCAdj)* and the *inventory valuation adjustment (IVA)*. They are described in more detail below.

Proprietors' income with inventory valuation and capital consumption adjustments is the current-production income (including income-in-kind) of sole proprietorships and partnerships and of tax-exempt cooperatives. The imputed net rental income of owner-occupants of farm dwellings is included, but the imputed net rental income of owner-occupants of nonfarm dwellings is included in rental income of persons. Fees paid to outside directors of corporations are included. Proprietors' income excludes dividends and monetary interest received by nonfinancial business and rental incomes received by persons not primarily engaged in the real estate business; these incomes are included in dividends, net interest, and rental income of persons, respectively.

Rental income of persons with capital consumption adjustment is the net current-production income of persons from the rental of real property (except for the income of persons primarily engaged in the real estate business), the imputed net rental income of owner-occupants of nonfarm dwellings, and the royalties received by persons from patents, copyrights, and rights to natural resources. Consistent with the classification of investment in owner-occupied housing as business investment, the homeowner is considered to be paying himself or herself the rental value of the house (classified as PCE for services) and receiving as net income the amount of the rental that remains after paying interest and other costs.

Corporate profits with inventory valuation and capital consumption adjustments, often referred to as "economic profits," is the current-production income, net of economic depreciation, of organizations treated as corporations in the NIPAs. These organizations consist of all entities required to file federal corporate tax returns, including mutual financial institutions and cooperatives subject to federal income tax; private noninsured pension funds; nonprofit institutions that primarily serve business; Federal Reserve Banks, which accrue income stemming from the conduct of monetary policy; and federally sponsored credit agencies. This income is measured as receipts less expenses as defined in federal tax law, except for the following differences: receipts exclude capital gains and dividends received; expenses exclude depletion and capital losses and losses resulting from bad debts; inventory withdrawals are valued at replacement cost;

and depreciation is on a consistent accounting basis and is valued at replacement cost.

Since *national* income is defined as the income of U.S. residents, its profits component includes income earned abroad by U.S. corporations and excludes income earned by the rest of the world within the United States.

Taxes on corporate income consists of taxes on corporate income paid to government and to the rest of the world.

Taxes on corporate income paid to government is the sum of federal, state, and local income taxes on all income subject to taxes. This income includes capital gains and other income excluded from profits before tax. These taxes are measured on an accrual basis, net of applicable tax credits.

Taxes on corporate income paid to the rest of the world consists of nonresident taxes, which are those paid by domestic corporations to foreign governments. These taxes were formerly classified as "business transfer payments to the rest of the world."

Profits after tax is total corporate profits with IVA and CCAdj less taxes on corporate income. It consists of dividends and undistributed corporate profits.

Dividends is payments in cash or other assets, excluding those made using corporations' own stock, that are made by corporations to stockholders. In the domestic account, these are payments by domestic industries to stockholders in the United States and abroad; in the national account, these are dividends received by U.S. residents from domestic and foreign industries. The payments are measured net of dividends received by U.S. corporations. Dividends paid to state and local government social insurance funds and general government are included.

Undistributed profits is corporate profits after tax with IVA and CCAdj less dividends.

The *inventory valuation adjustment (IVA)* is the difference between the cost of inventory withdrawals valued at replacement cost and the cost as valued in the source data used to determine profits before tax, which in many cases charge inventories at acquisition cost. It is calculated separately for corporate profits and for nonfarm proprietors' income. Its behavior is determined by price changes, especially for materials. When prices are rising, which has been typical of much of the postwar period, the business-reported value of inventory change will include a capital gains component, which needs to be removed from reported inventory change on the product side in order to correctly measure the change in the volume of inventories, and from reported profits on the income side of the accounts in order to remove the capital gains element. At such times, the IVA will be a negative figure, which is added to reported profits to yield economic profits. Occasionally, falling prices—especially for petroleum and products—will result in a positive IVA. No adjustment is needed for farm proprietors' income, as farm inventories are measured on a current-market-cost basis.

Consumption of fixed capital (CFC) is a charge for the using-up of private and government fixed capital located in the United States. It is not based on the depreciation schedules allowed in tax law, but instead on studies of prices of used equipment and structures in resale markets and other service life information.

For general government and for nonprofit institutions that primarily serve individuals, CFC on their capital assets is recorded in government consumption expenditures and in personal consumption expenditures, respectively. It is considered to be the value of the current services of the fixed capital assets owned and used by these entities.

Private capital consumption allowances consists of tax-return-based depreciation charges for corporations and nonfarm proprietorships; BEA estimates for R&D and other intellectual property; and historical cost depreciation (calculated by BEA using a geometric pattern of price declines) for farm proprietorships, rental income of persons, and nonprofit institutions.

The *private capital consumption adjustment (CCAdj)* is the difference between private capital consumption allowances and private consumption of fixed capital. The CCAdj has two parts:

- The first component of CCAdj converts tax-return-based depreciation to consistent historical cost accounting based on actual service lives of capital. In the postwar period, this has usually been a large positive number, that is, a net addition to profits and subtraction from reported depreciation. This is the case because U.S. tax law typically allows depreciation periods shorter than actual service lives. Tax depreciation was accelerated even further for 2001 through 2004. This component is a reallocation of gross business saving from depreciation to profits; gross saving is unchanged, with exactly offsetting changes in capital consumption and net saving.

- The second component is analogous to the IVA: it converts reported business capital consumption allowances from the historical cost basis to a replacement cost basis. It is determined by the price behavior of capital goods. These prices have had an upward drift in the postwar period, which has been much more stable than the changes in materials prices. Hence, this component is consistently negative (serving to reduce economic profits relative to the reported data) but less volatile than the IVA.

In 1982 through 2004, positive values for the first component outweighed negative values for the second, resulting in a net positive CCAdj, an addition to profits. However, when the accelerated depreciation expired in 2005, there was a sharp decline

in the consistent-accounting adjustment and it was outweighed by the price adjustment. This led to negative CCAdjs in 2005 through 2007, reducing profits from the reported numbers.

DEFINITIONS AND NOTES ON THE DATA:

Gross value added of domestic corporate business (Tables 1-14 and 1-15)

Gross value added is the term now used for what was formerly called "gross domestic product originating." It represents the share of the GDP that is produced in the specified sector or industry. Tables 1-14 and 1-15 show the current-dollar value of gross value added for all domestic corporate business and its financial and nonfinancial components. For the total and for nonfinancial corporations, consumption of fixed capital and net value added are shown, as is the allocation of net value added among employee compensation, taxes and transfer payments, and capital income. Constant-dollar values are also shown for nonfinancial corporations.

The data for nonfinancial corporations are often considered to be somewhat sturdier than data for the other sectors of the economy, since they exclude sectors whose outputs are difficult to evaluate—households, institutions, general government, and financial business—as well as excluding all noncorporate business, in which the separate contributions of labor and capital are not readily measured.

Data availability and revisions

Annual data are available beginning with 1929. Quarterly data begin with 1946 for current-dollar values and 1947 for quantity and price measures such as real GDP and the GDP price index. Not all data are available for all time periods.

New data are normally released toward the end of each month. The "advance" estimate of GDP for each calendar quarter is released at the end of the month after the quarter's end. The "second" estimate, including more complete product data and the first estimates of corporate profits, is released at the end of the second month after the quarter's end, and a "third" estimate including still more complete data at the end of the third month. Wage and salary and related income-side components may be revised for previous quarters as well.

At the end of each July, there is an "annual" revision, incorporating more complete data and other improvements, affecting at least the previous 3 years. Every five years, there is a "comprehensive" revision, such as the 2013 revision incorporated in this volume, corresponding with updated statistics from the quinquennial benchmark input-output accounts and incorporating a revision of the base year for constant-price and index numbers.

The most recent data are published each month in the *Survey of Current Business*. Current and historical data may be obtained from the BEA Web site at <https://www.bea.gov> and the STAT-USA subscription Web site at <https://www.stat-usa.gov>.

REFERENCES

The 2021 annual revision of the NIPAs is presented and described in a July 29, 2021 release on the BEA Web site.

Other documentation available on the BEA Web site at <https://www.bea.gov> includes the following: "NIPA Handbook: Concepts and Methods of the U.S. National Income and Product Accounts, October 2009"; separate chapters from the Handbook on Personal Consumption Expenditures, Private Fixed Investment, and Change in Private Inventories; "Measuring the Economy: A Primer on GDP and the National Income and Product Accounts";

"An Introduction to the National Income and Product Accounts"; and "Taking the Pulse of the Economy: Measuring GDP," *Journal of Economic Perspectives*, Spring 2008.

-The treatment of employee stock options is discussed in Carol Moylan, "Treatment of Employee Stock Options in the U.S. National Economic Accounts," available on the BEA Web site at <https://www.bea.gov>.

The data for 1929 through 1946 published here have been calculated after the fact and differ from the national income data that were currently available during the 1930s and 1940s. For an article on what was available at that time and the history of the NIPAs during that period, see Rosemary D. Marcuss and Richard E. Kane, "U.S. National Income and Product Statistics: Born of the Great Depression and World War II," *Survey of Current Business,* February 2007, pp. 32-46.

CHAPTER 2: INDUSTRIAL PRODUCTION AND CAPACITY UTILIZATION

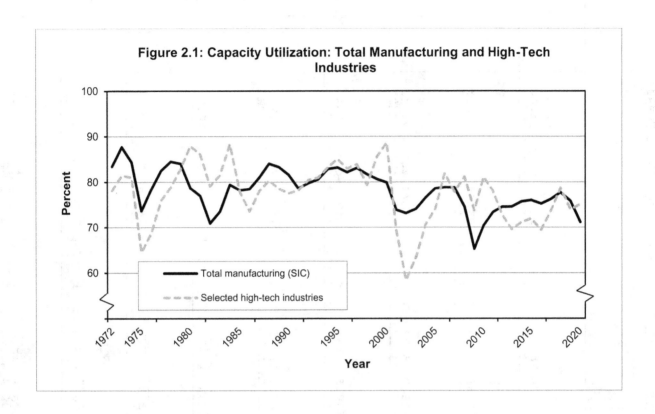

Figure 2.1: Capacity Utilization: Total Manufacturing and High-Tech Industries

- Manufacturing capacity utilization is a key statistic for the U.S. economy, despite being limited to a sector that by some measures has diminished in importance. The Federal Reserve also provides measures of capacity utilization for "total industry"—manufacturing, mining, and utilities. However, mining and utilities are less significant in the context of business cycle analysis, and much of the variation in capacity use by utilities is a result of transitory weather variations, not economic factors. Manufacturing utilization is an important indicator of inflationary pressure and also measures an important element in the demand for new capital goods. (Tables 2-3 and 2-4A)

- In 2020, industrial production decreased for all categories listed in Table 2-2. Total industrial production dropped significantly from 102.3 to 95.0. (Table 2-2)

- Manufacturing capacity utilization plunged in 2008 and 2009 following the Great Recession. In November 2007, capacity utilization reached 80.9 but by June 2009, it collapsed to 66.6. Manufacturing capacity has fluctuated monthly in the years since and it reached a high of 79.2 in December 2018 but it never recovered to its high in 2007. (Table 2-4A)

- Capacity utilization in computer and electronic products peaked in 2000, before the Tech Bubble, at 84.4 but fell over 28 percent by 2002. Capacity utilization has recovered but not to its 2000 level as seen in Figure 2-1. (Tables 2-3 and 2-4A)

Table 2-1. Industrial Production Indexes by Market Groups

(Seasonally adjusted, 2017 = 100.)

Year and month	Total industrial production	Final products and nonindustrial supplies Total	Consumer goods Total	Durable consumer goods Total	Automotive products	Home electronics	Appliances, furniture, and carpeting	Miscellaneous durable goods	Nondurable consumer goods Total
1970	37.6	39.6	51.4	33.6	26.7	0.9	69.8	61.0	60.0
1971	38.2	40.1	54.4	38.1	34.0	1.0	73.7	64.3	61.7
1972	41.8	43.9	58.8	42.7	36.7	1.1	86.5	72.2	65.7
1973	45.3	47.2	61.4	46.0	39.9	1.3	93.5	75.5	67.6
1974	45.1	47.0	59.7	41.8	34.5	1.2	85.3	72.8	67.7
1975	41.1	43.7	57.2	37.9	33.3	1.1	73.4	64.2	66.4
1976	44.4	46.8	61.9	42.8	37.8	1.3	82.7	71.6	70.6
1977	47.8	50.6	65.8	48.2	42.8	1.5	92.9	79.4	73.3
1978	50.4	53.7	67.9	49.4	42.5	1.6	97.9	82.2	75.8
1979	51.9	55.4	66.8	47.5	38.3	1.6	98.4	82.9	75.3
1980	50.5	54.7	64.2	41.4	29.5	1.7	91.7	76.1	75.3
1981	51.2	55.8	64.7	41.9	30.4	1.8	90.5	77.1	75.6
1982	48.5	54.3	64.5	39.5	29.5	1.6	81.8	72.7	76.9
1983	49.9	55.9	66.9	43.9	34.3	2.2	90.3	74.8	77.8
1984	54.3	60.6	70.0	49.1	38.3	2.8	100.4	82.9	79.3
1985	54.9	62.1	70.6	49.1	38.2	2.9	99.8	83.1	80.3
1986	55.5	63.3	73.0	52.2	41.1	3.7	104.7	85.8	82.2
1987	58.4	66.5	76.1	55.4	44.0	3.6	110.4	91.1	85.1
1988	61.4	69.7	79.0	58.0	46.1	4.5	112.4	95.2	88.0
1989	62.0	70.4	79.3	59.4	47.7	5.1	113.4	95.7	87.7
1990	62.6	71.2	79.6	57.6	44.9	5.5	110.5	94.7	89.2
1991	61.7	70.1	79.5	55.0	42.1	6.3	103.0	91.3	90.5
1992	63.5	72.0	82.0	60.4	48.8	7.3	108.9	94.4	91.3
1993	65.6	74.3	84.6	65.3	53.7	9.3	115.0	98.5	92.6
1994	69.0	77.6	88.1	71.1	59.0	12.1	123.1	104.2	94.9
1995	72.2	80.7	90.5	73.8	60.1	17.8	122.6	107.4	97.1
1996	75.5	83.9	92.2	76.1	61.1	21.7	123.8	111.1	98.4
1997	80.9	89.5	95.5	81.3	66.0	30.2	129.6	113.1	100.8
1998	85.7	94.7	99.1	87.2	70.8	39.8	138.2	117.1	103.1
1999	89.4	97.5	101.2	94.2	78.7	50.8	142.6	120.1	103.0
2000	92.9	100.6	103.1	96.9	80.0	58.6	146.6	123.6	104.5
2001	90.0	98.0	102.2	92.4	76.8	60.3	140.3	114.7	105.1
2002	90.2	97.5	104.2	98.4	85.0	61.8	143.6	118.1	105.4
2003	91.4	98.8	105.6	101.4	89.1	68.8	143.8	118.2	106.1
2004	93.8	100.9	106.8	102.8	88.5	80.1	148.2	120.5	107.1
2005	96.9	105.0	109.6	103.3	85.9	91.4	151.1	124.1	110.8
2006	99.1	107.6	110.1	102.7	82.8	110.7	146.5	126.2	111.7
2007	101.7	109.6	110.2	102.3	85.2	118.7	137.4	122.2	111.9
2008	98.1	104.9	104.5	90.3	70.6	132.7	119.6	113.2	108.5
2009	86.9	92.6	96.7	72.9	56.7	115.2	90.9	93.7	104.1
2010	91.7	95.6	97.9	80.0	68.2	77.4	89.9	100.3	103.3
2011	94.6	97.6	98.9	83.0	72.8	81.5	89.5	101.1	103.6
2012	97.4	99.3	97.5	84.9	75.5	90.0	92.1	100.0	101.2
2013	99.3	100.0	98.1	89.6	82.1	95.7	94.1	102.1	100.7
2014	102.3	101.2	99.0	94.0	89.5	92.8	95.6	102.8	100.5
2015	100.9	100.5	100.5	97.9	95.3	99.5	99.9	102.3	101.2
2016	98.7	99.2	101.0	100.2	98.2	100.5	101.3	103.9	101.3
2017	100.0	100.0	100.0	100.0	100.0	100.0	100.0	100.0	100.0
2018	103.2	102.0	100.8	103.2	104.3	116.6	99.1	100.2	100.1
2019	102.3	100.6	100.0	101.5	102.6	131.1	94.8	100.7	99.5
2020	95.0	93.9	96.1	94.2	91.4	142.2	94.5	95.7	96.6
2019									
January	103.3	101.4	100.0	101.2	100.5	131.2	96.4	102.7	99.7
February	102.7	101.2	100.4	101.9	102.6	131.1	94.8	102.0	99.9
March	102.9	101.4	100.7	101.5	102.9	132.0	94.0	100.6	100.5
April	102.3	100.1	99.2	100.9	101.9	128.3	93.3	100.8	98.7
May	102.5	100.4	99.8	102.3	103.7	131.8	95.2	101.2	99.1
June	102.4	100.6	100.3	102.9	105.5	131.6	93.5	100.8	99.6
July	102.1	100.4	100.1	102.9	105.1	131.0	95.3	100.2	99.3
August	102.7	100.8	100.3	103.0	105.1	129.7	95.5	100.7	99.5
September	102.3	100.2	99.4	100.5	100.8	130.7	95.0	100.5	99.1
October	101.5	99.7	99.0	97.2	95.8	130.7	92.8	99.8	99.5
November	102.0	100.8	100.5	102.8	105.4	131.8	95.0	99.4	99.9
December	101.6	100.4	99.7	100.9	101.4	133.4	96.8	99.4	99.4
2020									
January	101.1	99.5	99.0	102.3	102.8	135.5	96.6	101.2	98.1
February	101.3	99.8	99.9	104.0	105.3	138.5	97.2	101.9	98.8
March	97.4	94.9	94.9	88.0	80.1	139.8	93.1	97.1	96.8
April	84.2	81.4	83.9	54.9	33.0	133.8	75.9	82.0	92.2
May	85.8	84.8	87.6	65.7	48.5	131.0	85.4	84.8	93.8
June	91.2	90.6	94.6	90.2	86.6	136.7	93.0	92.4	95.8
July	94.9	94.5	98.6	104.9	110.7	141.5	97.2	94.3	96.8
August	95.9	95.8	99.4	103.8	107.4	143.5	98.7	96.2	98.1
September	95.6	95.2	97.9	102.5	104.6	146.7	97.6	97.3	99.6
October	96.6	96.3	98.2	103.4	104.1	150.6	101.0	99.4	96.7
November	97.2	96.6	98.3	104.9	107.1	153.6	98.4	100.1	96.4
December	98.3	98.0	100.4	105.3	106.8	155.5	100.1	101.3	99.0

Table 2-1. Industrial Production Indexes by Market Groups—*Continued*

(Seasonally adjusted, 2017 = 100.)

Year and month	Consumer goods—*Continued* Nondurable consumer goods—*Continued* Nondurable non-energy consumer goods — Total	Foods and tobacco	Clothing	Chemical products	Paper products	Consumer energy products	Business equipment — Total	Transit	Information processing	Industrial and other	Defense and space equipment	Construction supplies	Business supplies
1970	64.3	58.0	639.3	36.4	96.2	46.5	16.1	42.0	1.0	54.2	53.0	57.4	38.9
1971	65.9	59.8	635.6	38.5	98.2	48.6	15.3	40.7	0.9	51.8	47.6	59.2	40.1
1972	70.2	63.2	691.7	42.1	99.0	51.3	17.5	44.4	1.1	59.0	46.3	67.2	44.1
1973	72.5	64.7	704.9	45.3	102.3	52.0	20.2	52.9	1.3	67.1	50.8	73.0	46.9
1974	72.2	65.3	661.0	47.7	100.6	53.2	21.4	51.6	1.6	69.9	52.5	71.3	46.7
1975	70.3	64.0	643.4	46.0	94.8	54.4	19.1	45.4	1.5	61.2	52.9	60.3	43.0
1976	74.9	68.2	677.4	50.0	98.6	57.4	20.4	46.9	1.8	63.7	51.4	64.9	45.8
1977	77.6	69.6	710.6	52.1	107.8	59.8	23.5	55.7	2.4	69.4	46.0	70.6	49.5
1978	80.6	72.1	727.6	55.3	113.1	60.7	26.5	64.4	3.0	74.2	47.0	74.5	52.3
1979	79.4	71.5	686.9	55.5	114.3	62.2	29.9	75.4	3.7	78.9	50.1	76.5	54.1
1980	80.3	72.6	698.8	55.3	115.7	59.5	30.6	71.1	4.7	76.2	59.5	70.8	52.8
1981	80.9	72.8	698.8	56.1	118.6	59.1	31.5	66.5	5.6	76.0	64.5	69.7	54.0
1982	82.5	75.3	696.9	56.3	121.7	59.5	28.8	50.9	6.3	65.8	77.1	63.2	53.3
1983	83.6	75.4	716.9	56.9	127.1	59.8	29.0	50.3	7.3	60.9	77.5	67.7	55.8
1984	85.0	76.3	719.5	58.2	133.5	61.6	33.2	51.8	9.0	69.5	88.8	73.5	60.7
1985	86.4	78.6	689.3	58.8	140.3	61.4	34.5	53.6	9.7	70.3	99.4	75.3	62.2
1986	88.5	79.9	689.4	63.4	142.2	62.5	34.0	49.0	9.8	70.0	105.6	77.7	64.2
1987	91.7	81.7	696.3	68.3	150.3	64.6	36.3	49.7	11.2	72.5	107.8	82.7	68.0
1988	94.4	84.1	686.1	72.4	154.3	68.3	40.1	55.5	12.6	78.7	108.7	84.6	70.5
1989	93.9	83.5	655.2	73.9	155.0	68.5	41.4	58.3	12.9	81.3	108.8	84.2	71.4
1990	96.1	85.9	643.7	76.7	158.0	67.7	43.0	62.4	14.0	80.7	105.0	83.6	73.1
1991	97.2	86.3	641.5	79.4	158.7	69.8	42.4	64.9	14.2	76.5	97.3	79.1	72.0
1992	98.5	87.7	656.6	79.2	160.7	68.7	44.2	63.4	16.1	77.8	90.3	82.5	73.7
1993	99.3	87.1	668.8	81.3	164.4	71.9	46.4	59.2	17.7	83.0	85.4	86.1	76.0
1994	101.9	90.5	681.0	83.1	162.7	73.0	49.6	57.4	20.2	88.6	80.2	92.4	78.9
1995	104.3	92.8	677.8	86.6	163.7	74.7	54.3	56.8	24.3	94.2	77.4	94.5	82.1
1996	105.0	92.5	659.9	90.9	163.0	78.1	59.7	60.1	29.8	97.5	75.6	98.8	85.3
1997	108.3	94.1	658.2	96.0	177.5	77.3	68.7	70.5	38.0	103.5	74.6	103.5	91.2
1998	111.4	96.7	625.3	100.8	185.8	76.9	76.6	82.9	45.5	106.8	77.9	109.0	96.3
1999	110.6	94.8	599.4	102.5	189.5	79.8	80.7	81.1	55.2	104.4	75.6	111.7	100.3
2000	112.1	96.2	579.8	106.4	188.7	81.2	87.0	72.0	67.2	110.7	67.1	114.1	104.1
2001	112.5	96.2	517.5	112.3	183.4	82.5	81.5	69.3	65.0	100.1	73.7	108.9	100.3
2002	112.0	94.4	396.6	121.6	180.7	85.7	75.9	62.7	56.7	98.4	74.7	108.8	100.4
2003	112.8	95.5	373.6	124.6	174.1	86.4	76.0	59.1	59.7	97.9	79.5	108.5	102.1
2004	113.7	96.7	316.0	127.7	175.1	87.9	80.1	62.4	65.6	100.6	78.0	111.1	104.6
2005	117.5	99.9	303.5	134.4	173.2	91.1	86.1	68.4	72.0	106.0	85.5	116.4	108.5
2006	118.8	100.1	294.3	139.2	172.6	91.1	94.2	79.5	82.4	110.3	85.1	119.3	110.2
2007	117.5	100.0	236.5	140.2	165.4	95.1	99.9	82.2	92.2	114.6	101.3	118.4	111.5
2008	113.0	96.7	191.0	135.3	154.7	94.7	97.6	73.9	95.4	112.2	109.4	107.6	106.6
2009	107.2	95.3	139.7	124.8	136.5	94.9	80.6	59.3	85.7	89.6	105.0	82.8	94.4
2010	105.4	95.6	138.2	119.0	129.0	97.4	86.8	67.0	87.7	97.0	112.9	85.7	97.5
2011	105.7	95.6	135.1	121.0	125.4	98.0	92.0	69.4	87.9	106.5	109.6	87.7	98.3
2012	103.5	95.8	128.4	114.2	121.5	94.7	101.2	83.8	95.1	113.7	111.6	91.4	98.9
2013	100.8	97.2	118.4	103.5	114.3	100.1	101.2	88.9	95.6	110.5	108.0	94.2	100.4
2014	100.5	96.8	113.2	104.4	112.4	100.3	103.2	97.2	93.6	110.8	104.2	97.1	101.1
2015	102.0	98.5	107.6	106.8	108.5	98.6	100.9	101.8	94.9	103.2	101.3	97.8	99.8
2016	101.5	99.3	102.7	104.6	104.8	100.6	95.6	93.5	94.8	97.1	97.7	98.7	99.8
2017	100.0	100.0	100.0	100.0	100.0	100.0	100.0	100.0	100.0	100.0	100.0	100.0	100.0
2018	98.8	99.2	96.4	98.3	95.9	104.0	103.9	101.9	105.2	104.6	102.2	101.7	102.0
2019	98.4	98.6	96.2	98.9	93.0	102.8	99.8	92.2	106.9	101.7	112.3	99.8	99.8
2020	96.2	97.0	88.4	97.1	85.5	97.6	86.2	59.5	111.8	93.5	114.2	96.2	91.6
2019													
January	98.6	99.1	93.0	98.4	94.6	103.0	102.1	94.3	106.9	104.9	107.7	101.8	101.4
February	98.5	98.6	91.6	98.7	95.4	104.2	101.5	95.0	106.7	103.3	107.9	99.8	100.7
March	99.0	98.8	93.8	99.6	95.4	105.2	101.6	95.7	106.3	103.3	109.1	99.9	100.5
April	97.9	97.5	96.7	98.5	95.1	101.4	99.4	91.6	106.2	101.4	109.9	99.3	100.0
May	97.9	98.4	97.1	97.2	93.9	103.0	99.1	89.0	105.9	102.6	110.0	99.7	100.2
June	99.1	100.1	98.3	98.0	93.4	101.0	99.1	90.1	106.4	101.8	112.2	100.1	99.5
July	98.2	97.4	98.0	100.2	92.8	102.9	98.4	90.6	106.3	100.2	112.7	99.5	99.6
August	98.5	97.7	97.8	100.6	92.6	102.6	99.5	91.6	106.3	101.7	113.4	100.0	99.8
September	98.1	97.8	98.5	99.2	92.7	102.5	98.8	91.2	107.6	100.0	114.4	99.9	99.5
October	98.5	98.8	97.3	99.1	90.9	102.5	98.4	90.9	106.6	99.8	115.5	99.1	98.7
November	98.2	98.6	96.0	98.9	89.3	105.1	100.2	95.0	107.9	100.4	116.3	99.0	98.9
December	98.9	100.2	96.2	98.0	90.2	100.5	99.7	91.5	109.5	100.9	117.9	99.8	98.5
2020													
January	98.6	99.3	94.3	98.5	91.5	95.8	95.4	76.8	111.2	101.2	115.5	102.2	98.8
February	98.4	99.2	95.8	98.2	90.7	99.6	93.8	69.0	114.0	102.0	117.6	102.2	99.0
March	97.8	97.7	90.1	100.7	86.5	92.7	87.2	55.5	112.6	97.9	116.5	98.9	94.0
April	90.7	90.7	65.1	94.9	78.9	96.8	65.3	18.7	107.6	79.6	101.3	87.4	82.5
May	92.5	93.9	76.8	93.5	81.1	97.8	72.0	32.2	106.5	84.8	109.2	90.6	83.3
June	94.8	96.7	85.5	94.3	83.1	99.0	81.0	51.2	112.5	88.3	110.5	91.7	86.9
July	95.1	96.0	84.3	96.2	82.6	102.3	87.3	64.5	113.9	91.6	112.7	93.6	89.9
August	97.1	98.2	92.2	97.5	85.6	100.9	89.6	66.6	116.7	93.8	115.5	95.0	91.2
September	95.9	96.2	91.4	97.2	87.5	98.5	89.4	67.8	110.7	94.9	115.6	95.5	91.7
October	96.7	97.4	96.1	97.1	88.0	96.2	90.2	69.1	110.7	95.5	119.0	98.2	93.5
November	97.5	98.8	94.3	97.3	86.1	92.6	91.2	71.2	112.4	95.6	120.0	98.7	93.5
December	98.9	100.2	95.5	99.4	84.6	99.0	91.7	71.4	112.5	96.5	117.4	99.9	94.3

Table 2-1. Industrial Production Indexes by Market Groups—*Continued*

(Seasonally adjusted, 2017 = 100.)

Year and month	Total	Materials — Non-energy materials									Energy materials
		Total	Durable				Nondurable				
			Total	Consumer parts	Equipment parts	Other	Total	Textile	Paper	Chemicals	
1970	34.9	30.2	20.0	43.2	3.4	63.6	61.8	166.5	70.6	45.1	60.6
1971	35.5	30.8	20.1	47.8	3.4	61.3	64.4	174.4	73.7	47.8	61.1
1972	39.1	34.5	22.7	53.2	3.9	69.2	71.0	183.6	78.6	55.6	63.5
1973	42.6	38.2	25.9	61.7	4.6	76.6	74.6	179.0	84.8	61.3	65.3
1974	42.4	38.1	25.6	54.5	4.8	76.4	75.7	167.0	89.2	63.0	65.1
1975	37.8	32.7	21.4	43.9	4.1	64.0	67.7	163.5	77.6	52.8	64.8
1976	41.2	36.4	23.9	56.2	4.4	68.6	75.0	182.6	85.3	60.4	66.3
1977	44.0	39.4	26.0	61.5	5.0	72.6	80.5	194.6	89.1	67.2	68.7
1978	46.2	41.9	28.1	65.1	5.6	77.2	83.5	192.4	93.4	71.3	69.5
1979	47.4	43.0	28.9	61.4	6.2	79.0	85.1	190.8	97.2	74.2	71.3
1980	45.6	40.5	26.8	47.3	6.4	73.2	82.2	186.4	98.0	68.6	71.9
1981	45.9	40.6	26.8	44.9	6.5	73.3	82.9	182.2	99.9	69.2	72.7
1982	42.4	36.5	23.4	38.1	6.0	61.8	78.5	166.5	100.7	62.0	69.7
1983	43.5	39.0	24.9	46.3	6.1	64.6	84.1	186.6	107.0	68.6	67.6
1984	47.6	43.5	28.9	55.1	7.3	71.5	87.8	186.1	113.6	72.9	71.8
1985	47.5	43.5	29.1	57.4	7.3	70.9	87.0	176.1	112.8	71.6	71.6
1986	47.5	44.3	29.4	56.8	7.5	72.2	89.7	183.0	117.6	75.1	69.0
1987	50.1	47.3	31.5	58.4	8.2	77.3	95.0	204.3	123.2	81.6	70.9
1988	52.9	50.3	34.0	63.1	8.9	82.9	98.6	202.3	127.3	86.6	73.6
1989	53.3	50.6	34.2	59.9	9.2	83.3	99.4	206.4	127.2	87.8	74.4
1990	53.8	50.8	34.3	55.7	9.5	84.4	99.7	196.3	127.6	88.7	75.9
1991	53.0	49.7	33.4	52.6	9.5	80.8	98.6	196.2	124.9	87.4	76.2
1992	54.7	52.1	35.6	59.2	10.0	85.0	101.1	207.9	128.0	89.6	75.5
1993	56.5	54.4	37.9	67.0	10.7	88.2	102.2	216.5	128.0	90.0	75.8
1994	60.1	58.8	42.1	77.3	12.1	94.8	105.3	229.6	132.8	92.8	77.1
1995	63.4	62.6	46.3	80.3	14.6	98.4	106.3	225.5	136.2	93.6	78.4
1996	66.7	66.6	51.3	82.5	18.1	101.3	105.3	219.0	131.9	94.1	79.6
1997	71.9	73.5	58.2	88.9	22.9	106.3	110.3	229.2	133.3	100.8	79.4
1998	76.2	78.9	64.5	92.1	28.1	109.4	111.7	227.2	134.6	101.0	79.9
1999	80.9	85.3	72.1	101.1	34.8	111.2	113.0	223.3	136.5	103.9	79.9
2000	84.9	90.1	78.7	101.5	42.7	112.1	112.4	214.4	134.3	104.2	81.3
2001	81.5	85.7	75.4	90.3	43.6	104.3	105.2	189.6	127.3	96.5	80.5
2002	82.6	87.4	76.9	95.1	44.7	104.4	107.1	192.5	127.5	99.9	80.3
2003	83.7	88.9	79.6	94.7	49.7	103.6	106.2	182.7	123.4	100.5	80.2
2004	86.5	93.2	84.8	95.7	56.4	107.4	108.2	174.4	124.8	105.8	80.3
2005	88.6	97.0	89.7	98.1	63.5	109.8	109.5	178.5	124.3	106.9	79.7
2006	90.3	99.3	93.1	97.9	69.0	112.1	109.7	161.8	123.2	108.9	80.6
2007	93.5	103.6	97.1	98.3	78.1	112.1	114.5	148.0	123.2	119.2	82.3
2008	91.2	98.8	94.2	85.5	81.7	107.0	106.1	128.3	117.8	105.7	83.0
2009	81.0	82.2	74.3	61.0	67.3	84.3	95.9	105.2	103.6	93.4	80.6
2010	87.8	91.3	85.2	77.5	77.7	93.3	101.6	116.9	105.7	103.6	84.3
2011	91.6	95.6	92.4	84.4	88.5	97.7	100.8	112.2	105.4	102.5	87.6
2012	95.6	98.2	96.7	94.0	94.3	99.0	100.7	109.8	106.0	101.8	93.2
2013	98.8	100.2	99.2	97.7	96.0	101.6	101.8	114.8	106.2	102.6	98.1
2014	103.7	102.3	103.4	102.6	102.0	104.4	100.5	113.2	104.5	100.0	106.2
2015	101.4	100.6	101.4	104.3	98.6	102.0	99.3	106.2	103.0	97.5	102.8
2016	98.0	99.6	99.4	102.0	96.2	100.3	99.9	103.1	101.6	98.4	95.1
2017	100.0	100.0	100.0	100.0	100.0	100.0	100.0	100.0	100.0	100.0	100.0
2018	104.7	101.5	102.6	100.6	103.3	102.8	99.7	98.8	97.4	99.4	110.2
2019	104.5	98.5	99.7	94.5	103.0	99.8	96.4	93.7	96.6	93.3	115.2
2020	96.2	92.3	91.5	80.5	98.5	91.4	93.6	87.7	89.4	91.4	102.6
2019											
January	105.7	100.3	101.8	98.0	103.5	102.1	98.0	96.1	98.1	96.3	114.9
February	104.7	99.6	101.1	97.0	103.9	100.9	97.3	97.2	96.8	95.0	113.4
March	104.8	99.0	100.7	96.4	103.9	100.4	96.5	97.8	96.4	93.8	114.6
April	105.0	99.0	100.4	95.2	103.2	100.6	96.7	96.5	96.6	93.7	115.5
May	105.1	98.9	100.4	96.2	103.3	100.3	96.5	96.2	96.4	93.4	115.9
June	104.6	98.4	100.2	96.0	103.2	99.9	95.7	96.2	93.7	92.5	115.4
July	104.2	98.2	99.8	96.5	103.0	99.2	95.5	93.7	95.7	92.3	114.6
August	105.1	98.7	100.1	95.0	103.3	100.0	96.5	96.3	97.8	93.3	116.4
September	105.0	98.3	99.1	91.7	102.5	99.8	96.9	94.5	97.1	93.8	116.9
October	103.7	96.8	97.3	87.9	101.9	97.9	96.0	93.6	97.1	92.7	116.0
November	103.4	97.1	98.2	93.1	102.0	97.8	95.3	95.1	97.0	91.2	114.7
December	103.1	97.3	98.1	91.2	102.0	98.3	96.0	95.2	96.3	92.2	113.4
2020											
January	103.2	97.8	98.4	91.7	101.9	98.8	96.9	97.3	97.6	93.4	112.5
February	103.3	98.1	99.0	92.1	102.8	99.2	96.8	97.6	97.5	93.0	112.2
March	100.9	95.2	94.2	76.5	101.0	96.2	96.9	94.8	95.9	94.0	111.1
April	88.0	81.5	77.2	37.7	92.0	82.0	88.5	68.5	88.9	87.1	100.4
May	87.1	83.7	80.6	48.4	94.2	83.8	88.6	76.6	84.2	87.5	92.7
June	91.8	88.0	86.7	75.4	95.3	85.9	90.2	81.2	84.5	87.9	97.9
July	95.2	91.1	91.1	89.5	96.7	88.9	91.1	85.1	84.4	89.3	101.9
August	95.8	92.7	93.0	89.6	97.9	91.5	92.3	88.8	84.8	90.0	100.5
September	95.9	93.2	93.0	89.8	99.3	90.9	93.5	92.6	86.4	90.9	99.7
October	97.0	94.9	94.4	90.6	100.0	92.8	95.6	91.1	89.4	94.2	99.4
November	97.7	95.5	95.1	91.2	100.5	93.5	96.1	88.0	89.9	94.9	100.4
December	98.5	95.9	95.6	93.4	100.6	93.8	96.3	91.1	89.3	95.2	102.0

Table 2-1. Industrial Production Indexes by Market Groups—*Continued*

(Seasonally adjusted, 2017 = 100.)

Year and month	Special aggregates												Total non-energy, excluding high-tech
	Energy						Non-energy						
									Selected high-tech				
	Total	Consumer energy products	Commercial energy products	Oil and gas well drilling	Converted fuels	Primary energy	Total	Total	Computers and peripheral equipment	Communications equipment	Semiconductors and related components	
1970	54.4	46.5	33.4	. . .	61.9	64.9	35.7	0.1	. . .	. . .	. . .	57.5
1971	55.4	48.6	35.1	. . .	63.6	64.5	36.2	0.1	. . .	. . .	. . .	58.6
1972	58.0	51.3	37.0	100.8	67.5	65.5	39.9	0.1	0.0	1.7	0.0	64.4
1973	59.5	52.0	39.0	94.8	70.2	66.7	43.6	0.1	0.1	1.9	0.0	69.9
1974	59.8	53.2	39.1	110.2	69.0	67.4	43.4	0.1	0.1	2.1	0.0	69.1
1975	60.2	54.4	40.4	124.3	66.7	68.4	38.7	0.1	0.1	2.0	0.0	61.6
1976	62.2	57.4	42.4	140.0	70.5	68.5	42.2	0.1	0.1	2.1	0.0	66.8
1977	64.8	59.8	43.8	177.8	73.2	70.8	45.7	0.1	0.2	2.6	0.1	71.8
1978	65.8	60.7	45.0	198.1	72.6	72.6	48.6	0.2	0.3	2.8	0.1	75.8
1979	67.7	62.2	47.5	211.2	75.3	74.0	50.1	0.2	0.4	3.4	0.1	77.1
1980	68.0	59.5	46.5	249.8	74.1	75.6	48.4	0.3	0.5	4.0	0.1	73.5
1981	69.1	59.1	47.2	300.1	73.1	77.2	49.0	0.3	0.7	4.3	0.1	73.7
1982	66.6	59.5	47.9	264.1	67.4	75.2	46.2	0.4	0.8	4.6	0.1	68.6
1983	64.6	59.8	48.7	204.6	67.3	72.0	48.4	0.4	1.2	4.9	0.1	71.1
1984	68.4	61.6	51.4	222.8	71.3	76.5	53.2	0.6	1.7	5.2	0.2	77.3
1985	68.2	61.4	53.0	204.1	71.2	76.3	54.1	0.6	2.0	5.0	0.2	78.4
1986	65.9	62.5	54.5	99.4	68.9	73.4	55.3	0.6	2.1	4.8	0.2	80.1
1987	67.9	64.6	57.3	95.9	72.3	74.3	58.5	0.8	2.8	5.3	0.2	83.8
1988	70.8	68.3	59.2	115.1	75.7	76.8	61.7	0.9	3.4	6.2	0.2	87.7
1989	71.5	68.5	61.3	100.2	78.4	76.5	62.2	1.0	3.6	6.5	0.3	88.1
1990	72.6	67.7	62.8	106.1	78.9	78.7	62.8	1.1	3.8	7.7	0.3	88.2
1991	73.1	69.8	63.6	82.6	79.0	79.1	61.6	1.1	4.0	8.3	0.3	85.9
1992	72.2	68.7	63.2	65.6	80.3	77.1	63.9	1.4	5.0	9.8	0.4	88.3
1993	73.4	71.9	65.0	83.1	82.1	76.6	66.2	1.6	6.2	11.6	0.5	90.6
1994	74.8	73.0	67.7	83.5	83.4	78.0	70.2	2.1	7.7	14.5	0.6	94.6
1995	76.3	74.7	69.9	81.4	84.5	79.4	73.8	2.9	10.7	17.9	0.9	97.0
1996	78.2	78.1	72.3	92.6	86.1	80.5	77.4	4.2	15.3	22.8	1.3	98.4
1997	78.5	77.3	74.9	109.2	87.6	79.5	84.0	6.1	22.0	31.8	2.0	103.4
1998	78.8	76.9	76.0	100.5	89.0	79.5	89.7	8.5	30.6	38.5	2.9	107.2
1999	79.5	79.8	78.9	81.8	90.7	78.5	94.1	12.3	40.6	48.8	4.8	108.5
2000	81.3	81.2	81.8	98.4	93.0	79.6	98.0	17.0	48.7	65.8	7.0	109.3
2001	81.3	82.5	83.0	116.7	90.9	79.2	94.3	17.8	50.4	60.2	8.0	104.1
2002	81.5	85.7	84.1	85.8	92.6	78.1	94.6	17.9	51.6	44.1	9.4	104.3
2003	82.4	86.4	88.8	100.2	92.9	77.9	95.9	21.6	57.0	47.1	12.5	104.4
2004	83.1	87.9	91.6	110.6	95.1	77.2	98.8	25.9	59.4	54.0	16.1	106.4
2005	83.7	91.1	94.1	122.5	96.7	75.7	102.8	30.8	72.4	56.2	19.9	109.7
2006	84.6	91.1	94.6	140.5	96.3	77.1	105.5	37.0	92.9	70.2	22.9	111.3
2007	86.9	95.1	96.8	146.6	100.9	77.9	108.2	44.1	110.4	72.7	29.2	113.0
2008	87.5	94.7	96.9	157.8	98.9	79.3	102.9	51.0	134.4	73.1	34.9	106.2
2009	84.7	94.9	94.4	101.7	93.2	77.8	88.3	45.0	120.1	63.9	30.7	90.9
2010	88.1	97.4	95.7	114.4	98.8	81.0	93.6	55.1	98.9	67.5	45.3	95.7
2011	91.1	98.0	96.6	141.5	97.6	85.4	96.4	62.0	85.4	73.8	54.4	98.1
2012	94.9	94.7	95.3	160.5	101.2	91.6	98.8	68.1	105.7	73.4	60.1	100.2
2013	99.5	100.1	97.5	160.7	100.9	97.6	99.6	75.4	105.9	86.1	66.7	100.6
2014	106.0	100.3	98.7	173.4	102.0	107.5	101.1	83.7	108.4	80.8	80.7	101.7
2015	102.0	98.6	98.1	121.5	102.5	102.7	100.5	86.5	118.1	87.0	81.0	101.0
2016	96.0	100.6	98.4	70.9	101.0	92.4	99.5	91.5	118.0	90.2	87.6	99.7
2017	100.0	100.0	100.0	100.0	100.0	100.0	100.0	100.0	100.0	100.0	100.0	100.0
2018	108.6	104.0	103.4	128.5	106.3	112.0	101.4	109.0	115.0	114.1	106.3	101.2
2019	111.5	102.8	103.9	124.7	105.6	119.2	99.4	113.2	136.5	123.9	106.1	99.0
2020	99.9	97.6	93.5	77.9	99.2	103.6	93.2	121.3	155.8	139.2	110.1	92.4
2019												
January	111.6	103.0	104.5	132.1	107.3	118.0	100.6	110.0	131.5	122.0	102.8	100.3
February	110.7	104.2	102.9	129.5	106.7	116.2	100.1	110.8	132.1	122.4	103.7	99.8
March	111.7	105.2	103.2	128.5	107.5	117.6	100.0	111.1	134.3	122.4	103.8	99.6
April	111.4	101.4	103.5	126.0	104.1	120.3	99.3	111.1	131.0	122.4	104.3	98.9
May	112.0	103.0	103.9	123.5	104.4	120.6	99.3	111.4	133.3	122.6	104.4	99.0
June	111.0	101.0	101.9	124.3	103.6	120.4	99.6	112.5	135.6	123.3	105.4	99.2
July	111.3	102.9	105.1	125.7	105.6	118.4	99.1	113.6	136.3	124.0	106.6	98.6
August	112.3	102.6	104.3	125.1	106.0	120.9	99.6	114.9	141.2	124.3	107.7	99.1
September	112.6	102.5	104.9	122.7	107.7	121.0	99.0	114.4	137.5	124.0	107.6	98.5
October	111.9	102.5	104.1	121.6	104.1	121.2	98.1	114.2	136.2	124.0	107.6	97.7
November	111.6	105.1	104.5	116.9	106.7	118.3	98.9	116.4	144.3	125.5	109.1	98.4
December	109.7	100.5	103.4	120.8	103.4	118.0	99.0	118.4	145.4	129.4	110.6	98.4
2020												
January	108.0	95.8	102.4	124.0	99.3	118.7	98.8	118.6	147.4	134.3	108.9	98.2
February	108.8	99.6	102.6	128.6	101.3	117.3	98.9	118.3	149.7	138.4	106.8	98.3
March	105.9	92.7	96.3	129.8	99.8	116.6	94.8	119.8	153.9	140.5	107.6	94.1
April	98.1	96.8	87.4	95.7	93.5	103.5	80.1	117.6	146.2	140.7	105.5	79.1
May	92.3	97.8	83.8	63.1	90.3	93.4	83.7	117.0	142.0	139.5	105.5	82.8
June	96.1	99.0	89.0	52.5	99.1	96.4	89.4	118.6	149.5	137.8	107.4	88.6
July	99.9	102.3	93.7	50.8	105.2	99.3	93.1	120.6	154.0	136.4	110.3	92.3
August	98.5	100.9	91.9	50.7	103.5	98.1	94.8	120.7	157.4	136.3	109.9	94.0
September	97.5	98.5	92.2	53.6	98.2	99.8	94.7	123.2	163.0	138.1	112.2	93.9
October	97.0	96.2	92.8	58.0	100.8	98.0	96.2	126.0	165.9	140.7	115.1	95.3
November	96.9	92.6	93.4	60.5	97.1	101.4	96.8	127.2	169.8	142.7	115.6	96.0
December	99.9	99.0	96.2	67.2	102.1	101.4	97.4	128.0	171.1	144.7	115.9	96.5

. . . = Not available.

Table 2-2. Industrial Production Indexes by NAICS Industry Groups

(Seasonally adjusted, 2017 = 100.)

Year and month	Total industrial production	Manu-facturing (SIC)	Manufacturing (NAICS)											
			Total	Durable goods manufacturing										
				Total	Wood products	Nonmetallic mineral products	Primary metals	Fabricated metal products	Machinery	Computer and electronic products	Electrical equipment, appliances, and com-ponents	Motor vehicles and parts	Aerospace and miscel-laneous transport equipment
1970	37.6	35.5	...	...	...	...	...	...	...	...	...	...	...	...
1971	38.2	36.1	...	...	...	...	...	...	...	...	...	...	...	...
1972	41.8	39.8	37.5	24.8	84.5	85.6	125.9	70.7	64.0	0.4	80.3	37.1	51.2
1973	45.3	43.4	41.0	27.8	81.8	91.9	146.6	78.1	73.9	0.5	90.3	42.5	58.4
1974	45.1	43.3	40.9	27.7	74.3	90.9	150.1	76.8	77.5	0.6	88.2	36.5	59.3
1975	41.1	38.8	36.5	24.0	68.5	81.4	116.4	66.3	67.5	0.5	70.9	31.8	56.4
1976	44.4	42.3	39.9	26.3	77.2	85.9	123.6	71.1	70.4	0.6	79.9	40.6	52.7
1977	47.8	45.9	43.3	28.8	83.2	91.4	125.1	77.1	76.8	0.8	88.2	46.2	53.2
1978	50.4	48.7	46.0	31.1	84.2	97.5	133.1	80.9	82.7	1.0	93.5	48.2	58.6
1979	51.9	50.2	47.4	32.6	81.2	97.3	136.1	84.5	87.3	1.2	97.4	44.1	68.3
1980	50.5	48.4	45.6	31.2	75.3	87.7	119.3	79.7	83.0	1.5	91.6	32.4	73.5
1981	51.2	48.9	46.0	31.5	73.6	84.0	119.4	79.2	82.2	1.7	90.5	31.6	69.9
1982	48.5	46.2	43.4	28.8	66.1	74.4	83.8	70.9	68.7	1.9	81.5	28.5	65.5
1983	49.9	48.4	45.5	30.3	76.5	79.9	86.3	71.4	62.0	2.2	84.2	36.3	62.5
1984	54.3	53.2	50.1	34.5	82.0	86.3	94.8	77.7	72.3	2.7	94.8	43.5	66.7
1985	54.9	54.0	50.8	35.3	82.8	87.9	87.3	78.8	72.5	2.9	93.3	45.2	71.3
1986	55.5	55.2	51.9	35.9	90.0	91.5	85.5	78.3	71.4	3.0	95.0	45.2	75.0
1987	58.4	58.3	54.9	38.0	98.0	96.5	92.3	79.8	72.8	3.4	96.3	46.9	77.8
1988	61.4	61.4	58.0	40.8	97.8	98.5	103.1	83.8	80.2	3.8	101.0	50.1	81.8
1989	62.0	61.9	58.5	41.3	96.2	97.7	100.8	83.2	83.2	3.9	99.3	49.5	86.8
1990	62.6	62.4	59.0	41.4	95.1	96.2	99.6	82.2	81.2	4.3	96.7	46.6	87.1
1991	61.7	61.2	58.0	40.2	88.9	88.6	93.6	78.5	76.2	4.5	91.7	44.6	84.0
1992	63.5	63.5	60.3	42.3	93.9	92.5	96.2	80.9	76.0	5.0	97.2	50.7	77.7
1993	65.6	65.8	62.5	44.6	95.0	94.4	100.9	84.0	81.6	5.6	103.3	56.0	72.5
1994	69.0	69.6	66.5	48.5	100.7	99.8	108.4	91.3	89.4	6.5	110.8	64.4	65.0
1995	72.2	73.2	70.0	52.5	103.2	102.7	109.7	96.9	95.7	8.4	113.5	66.3	61.8
1996	75.5	76.8	73.7	57.2	106.5	109.3	112.2	100.4	99.0	11.0	116.9	66.8	64.2
1997	80.9	83.2	79.9	64.1	109.4	113.0	116.9	104.9	104.5	14.6	121.3	72.1	71.7
1998	85.7	88.8	85.2	70.8	114.2	118.7	118.9	108.3	107.3	18.8	125.8	75.8	83.1
1999	89.4	93.3	89.6	76.9	118.4	119.8	118.7	109.1	105.0	24.8	127.7	84.0	79.9
2000	92.9	97.1	93.5	82.4	116.9	119.9	114.6	113.4	110.5	32.1	134.2	83.6	70.2
2001	90.0	93.5	90.2	78.9	109.6	115.4	103.7	105.2	97.8	33.2	120.8	76.4	74.6
2002	90.2	93.9	90.8	79.2	114.2	115.5	104.3	102.9	94.2	32.7	111.4	84.0	70.6
2003	91.4	95.1	92.2	81.3	114.1	116.5	102.3	101.8	93.7	37.4	108.6	87.1	67.5
2004	93.8	98.1	95.2	85.1	117.0	120.1	111.2	102.2	97.6	44.0	110.5	87.5	66.4
2005	96.9	102.1	99.3	90.2	124.8	125.2	108.2	107.0	103.6	50.0	112.4	88.0	74.0
2006	99.1	104.7	102.1	94.4	125.8	127.5	111.2	112.8	108.6	57.0	113.1	86.7	78.6
2007	101.7	107.6	105.4	99.1	117.7	126.1	113.5	117.6	113.2	65.8	117.8	86.0	92.3
2008	98.1	102.4	100.5	95.7	100.5	111.4	113.7	113.4	110.2	71.1	113.1	68.8	94.0
2009	86.9	88.3	86.8	77.8	76.8	84.0	84.6	87.2	85.7	63.4	89.1	50.4	85.6
2010	91.7	93.5	92.5	86.2	79.6	86.6	103.8	92.9	95.7	72.2	92.6	66.9	86.8
2011	94.6	96.3	95.5	91.5	79.7	88.0	111.4	99.4	107.8	78.1	97.2	73.2	86.6
2012	97.4	98.8	98.2	96.6	84.5	90.3	109.2	102.4	116.6	84.3	99.5	80.9	95.8
2013	99.3	99.6	99.3	98.7	89.4	95.0	112.7	104.2	111.2	87.1	99.4	86.8	98.6
2014	102.3	100.7	100.5	101.6	91.6	98.5	113.5	106.1	112.7	90.7	101.2	94.7	102.2
2015	100.9	100.2	100.1	100.5	95.3	99.2	105.7	102.6	103.7	91.2	100.7	99.7	102.3
2016	98.7	99.4	99.3	98.3	98.8	100.5	101.0	98.8	95.8	93.2	100.5	101.0	95.3
2017	100.0	100.0	100.0	100.0	100.0	100.0	100.0	100.0	100.0	100.0	100.0	100.0	100.0
2018	103.2	101.3	101.5	103.1	100.4	100.4	103.2	104.6	104.6	104.9	101.6	104.1	99.8
2019	102.3	99.3	99.5	101.0	95.6	98.1	98.8	102.4	101.4	105.8	102.0	101.1	98.8
2020	95.0	92.7	93.2	92.7	93.3	95.2	85.6	94.7	95.2	109.7	96.0	85.2	81.7
2019													
January	103.3	100.6	100.7	102.3	101.1	100.6	101.5	105.3	105.1	105.1	101.8	101.1	98.0
February	102.7	100.0	100.2	101.8	101.9	97.0	100.0	104.1	104.0	105.2	102.7	101.9	98.6
March	102.9	99.9	100.1	101.8	102.5	97.3	100.3	103.8	104.0	104.9	103.1	102.5	98.6
April	102.3	99.2	99.3	100.9	101.4	98.0	100.9	102.9	101.1	104.9	101.9	101.4	96.9
May	102.5	99.2	99.4	101.0	103.3	98.0	99.6	102.2	102.5	104.8	104.0	103.3	95.1
June	102.4	99.4	99.6	101.0	104.8	98.2	97.6	102.2	101.3	105.4	103.3	104.8	96.4
July	102.1	99.0	99.2	100.8	103.6	97.6	97.8	101.4	100.1	105.6	104.0	103.6	97.7
August	102.7	99.5	99.8	101.3	103.4	98.4	99.2	102.1	101.6	105.7	103.5	103.4	98.5
September	102.3	98.9	99.1	100.4	98.2	98.9	98.3	101.8	99.3	106.7	101.5	98.2	100.1
October	101.5	98.2	98.4	99.2	92.3	97.5	96.3	101.4	98.8	106.0	98.9	92.3	101.8
November	102.0	98.9	99.3	101.0	102.2	96.7	96.2	101.2	99.3	107.2	100.1	102.2	102.4
December	101.6	98.9	99.2	100.7	98.0	98.3	97.9	100.9	99.9	108.7	99.6	98.0	101.6
2020													
January	101.1	98.7	99.0	99.9	99.2	101.5	98.5	101.4	100.3	109.4	100.4	99.2	90.3
February	101.3	98.7	99.0	99.9	101.5	101.5	96.0	102.1	101.7	110.7	101.7	101.5	85.9
March	97.4	94.3	94.7	93.2	74.2	96.2	93.1	98.4	98.7	109.9	98.8	74.2	82.5
April	84.2	79.4	79.7	73.4	21.7	81.8	72.9	87.8	80.9	105.4	92.0	21.7	61.2
May	85.8	83.1	83.4	79.0	39.2	89.3	70.5	90.1	85.2	104.4	90.9	39.2	71.3
June	91.2	89.1	89.6	88.3	81.1	93.1	75.3	91.7	89.6	109.1	91.9	81.1	74.7
July	94.9	92.7	93.3	94.4	105.0	95.0	79.5	91.5	93.8	110.6	95.1	105.0	80.1
August	95.9	94.1	94.6	95.5	100.8	95.0	83.5	92.8	96.9	112.0	94.1	100.8	84.3
September	95.6	94.2	94.6	95.6	99.0	93.9	86.9	94.9	97.6	109.9	94.3	99.0	85.5
October	96.6	95.6	96.0	96.9	98.5	96.6	89.1	94.7	99.8	110.8	97.4	98.5	87.9
November	97.2	96.2	96.7	97.9	101.2	97.8	91.5	95.5	98.5	112.1	97.2	101.2	88.7
December	98.3	96.8	97.3	98.3	100.8	100.9	90.3	95.4	99.1	112.3	98.1	100.8	88.2

... = Not available.

Table 2-2. Industrial Production Indexes by NAICS Industry Groups—*Continued*

(Seasonally adjusted, 2017 = 100.)

Year and month	Durable goods manufacturing—*Continued*		Nondurable goods manufacturing									Other manu-facturing (non-NAICS)
	Furniture and related products	Miscel-laneous manu-facturing	Total	Food, beverage, and tobacco products	Textile and product mills	Apparel and leather	Paper	Printing and support	Petroleum and coal products	Chemicals	Plastics and rubber products	
1970	. . .	. . .	. . .	. . .	. . .	. . .	. . .	. . .	. . .	. . .	. . .	. . .
1971	. . .	. . .	. . .	. . .	. . .	. . .	. . .	. . .	. . .	. . .	. . .	. . .
1972	73.4	41.4	64.3	60.8	171.1	632.7	78.9	67.0	63.5	51.8	37.4	138.6
1973	76.9	42.7	67.3	61.4	169.7	643.0	85.3	70.5	62.4	56.6	42.2	143.0
1974	71.1	41.8	67.6	62.5	156.0	605.0	89.1	68.3	67.3	58.9	40.7	143.7
1975	61.0	38.9	62.6	61.2	150.8	590.5	77.2	63.8	66.4	51.7	34.4	136.7
1976	68.0	42.4	68.3	65.4	168.1	620.9	85.1	68.4	73.5	57.9	38.0	141.0
1977	77.9	46.2	73.0	66.7	183.7	650.9	88.9	74.1	78.7	63.0	44.9	154.5
1978	84.0	47.2	75.6	69.1	183.2	665.3	92.9	78.5	79.5	66.2	46.8	159.9
1979	83.8	47.5	76.1	68.7	182.7	624.2	94.3	80.8	84.9	67.7	46.2	163.2
1980	80.9	45.0	73.7	69.8	175.3	636.1	94.0	81.4	75.2	63.9	41.3	168.8
1981	80.2	46.7	74.4	70.5	171.6	636.0	95.3	83.5	71.7	65.0	43.8	172.8
1982	75.6	47.2	73.3	72.6	159.4	632.2	93.7	89.8	68.6	60.8	43.1	174.9
1983	82.9	47.2	76.7	72.7	179.1	650.1	99.8	96.5	69.7	65.0	46.8	179.9
1984	92.8	51.1	80.3	73.7	183.4	649.5	104.7	105.1	71.2	68.9	54.1	188.2
1985	93.8	51.8	80.7	76.0	177.0	621.7	102.5	109.4	70.2	68.3	56.2	195.6
1986	98.0	53.1	83.0	77.0	183.8	619.8	106.6	114.9	69.8	71.4	58.6	199.6
1987	105.0	57.1	87.5	78.6	201.7	627.2	110.0	123.3	73.1	77.0	64.9	211.0
1988	104.0	62.4	90.4	80.8	199.8	616.7	114.3	127.3	75.4	81.4	67.8	210.1
1989	103.6	63.3	91.0	80.4	202.8	590.0	115.5	127.8	74.6	82.9	70.1	207.1
1990	101.5	66.3	92.4	82.6	194.7	578.0	115.4	132.6	74.7	84.8	72.0	204.7
1991	93.8	67.6	92.1	83.3	192.0	574.4	115.7	128.5	73.6	84.6	71.2	196.3
1992	101.2	70.5	94.6	84.5	202.6	590.9	118.5	135.5	73.3	85.9	76.7	192.3
1993	105.5	74.6	95.9	84.3	210.4	602.7	119.9	135.9	73.8	86.9	82.1	193.6
1994	109.0	75.0	99.2	87.0	221.6	610.0	125.0	137.3	75.8	89.1	89.0	191.9
1995	110.7	77.9	100.9	89.5	219.2	605.6	126.8	139.4	77.2	90.6	91.2	191.9
1996	111.7	81.7	101.3	88.8	214.0	591.6	122.9	140.4	79.0	92.5	94.3	190.1
1997	123.7	84.0	105.0	90.8	225.9	591.1	125.4	143.2	81.6	97.9	100.1	206.1
1998	132.5	88.9	106.7	93.7	224.1	562.6	126.5	145.0	80.1	99.5	103.7	218.4
1999	136.8	90.9	107.3	91.9	225.0	535.9	127.4	144.4	83.3	101.6	109.1	224.7
2000	139.2	96.0	107.8	93.2	220.5	516.7	124.1	145.7	82.5	103.0	110.3	224.1
2001	130.5	95.0	104.8	93.1	197.4	454.1	117.1	140.9	82.0	101.3	103.9	209.5
2002	135.0	100.4	106.0	92.2	198.3	357.6	118.5	137.7	86.4	107.1	107.6	202.5
2003	132.9	103.5	106.2	93.8	190.4	332.9	115.7	132.3	85.1	108.9	107.7	196.7
2004	136.7	103.5	107.8	94.1	188.1	292.3	116.6	132.6	90.1	113.2	109.0	197.6
2005	141.7	110.3	110.6	97.5	190.8	285.8	116.2	132.4	92.6	117.0	110.2	197.0
2006	139.7	113.8	111.2	97.7	173.0	279.4	114.9	130.9	94.2	119.9	110.9	194.7
2007	134.5	110.9	112.5	97.9	153.0	227.7	115.4	133.6	96.8	125.8	107.8	183.6
2008	121.4	112.8	105.8	95.2	134.5	183.4	110.5	125.0	92.6	116.4	97.7	167.6
2009	88.1	104.5	97.7	94.5	106.6	135.3	98.6	104.7	91.4	105.1	81.7	140.1
2010	86.9	108.3	99.8	94.8	113.8	136.5	100.6	104.6	90.5	108.6	89.0	129.5
2011	89.8	107.7	100.0	94.6	111.4	134.3	100.6	102.9	92.6	108.6	90.3	123.5
2012	94.6	104.7	100.0	95.0	108.0	126.6	103.3	101.1	92.5	107.1	94.5	116.5
2013	95.3	108.1	100.0	96.5	112.0	117.4	103.6	101.4	96.1	103.5	95.7	110.0
2014	95.8	104.8	99.3	96.5	114.2	112.5	102.6	99.6	92.6	102.4	98.2	108.2
2015	100.6	105.2	99.7	98.6	109.0	107.3	101.9	98.6	90.6	102.0	99.9	103.9
2016	100.8	105.4	100.4	99.7	106.9	102.5	100.9	100.3	96.5	101.5	101.2	100.9
2017	100.0	100.0	100.0	100.0	100.0	100.0	100.0	100.0	100.0	100.0	100.0	100.0
2018	101.1	103.5	99.7	99.8	98.6	96.4	99.1	100.4	99.9	98.6	103.0	96.7
2019	95.3	101.4	97.9	99.5	96.5	95.9	98.4	96.8	99.4	95.4	100.0	92.3
2020	90.2	93.0	93.7	98.1	87.6	88.8	94.2	85.1	86.5	93.0	92.4	78.7
2019												
January	97.4	102.7	99.0	99.7	97.3	93.0	99.7	98.9	101.1	98.4	103.1	94.8
February	95.9	103.4	98.3	99.4	97.5	91.5	98.9	97.0	97.4	98.9	102.3	95.5
March	94.6	103.1	98.3	99.5	99.0	93.5	98.4	96.6	98.6	98.8	101.3	95.0
April	94.8	103.0	97.6	98.6	98.2	96.3	98.4	96.7	98.5	99.4	99.6	94.5
May	95.1	102.3	97.7	99.3	97.3	96.7	98.1	97.2	99.1	99.2	100.6	93.2
June	94.3	101.2	98.0	100.8	97.4	97.9	95.6	96.5	99.8	99.3	101.1	93.8
July	94.5	101.3	97.5	98.5	95.3	97.7	97.6	96.7	100.8	99.8	98.8	92.6
August	94.0	101.2	98.1	98.7	96.1	97.5	99.1	96.9	101.3	98.6	99.9	92.0
September	94.7	100.2	97.8	98.9	95.2	98.0	99.0	96.7	100.6	98.1	98.5	91.3
October	94.9	98.6	97.6	99.7	94.4	96.9	98.6	96.4	98.8	97.6	98.0	89.7
November	96.3	99.8	97.4	99.5	95.3	95.7	98.4	96.6	98.3	98.0	98.8	87.5
December	97.0	99.4	97.7	101.0	95.4	95.9	98.5	94.8	98.6	97.6	98.5	88.0
2020												
January	98.0	99.6	98.1	100.3	97.4	94.2	99.4	96.5	100.8	96.6	99.9	89.0
February	99.1	99.0	98.1	100.3	97.2	95.7	99.1	98.2	99.6	96.6	100.7	87.7
March	94.0	94.4	96.4	99.0	93.3	90.4	99.9	90.0	93.5	96.2	94.1	81.0
April	72.9	77.0	86.6	91.7	70.1	66.4	95.2	68.5	75.9	95.6	76.1	69.5
May	84.0	79.9	88.3	94.7	78.8	77.6	89.5	75.4	76.4	94.9	79.7	70.6
June	88.8	88.3	90.9	97.8	82.7	86.1	89.9	78.8	79.6	94.6	88.3	72.7
July	90.3	94.3	92.0	97.0	84.8	84.7	89.9	82.0	84.0	95.2	91.5	73.6
August	91.2	95.9	93.6	99.1	87.1	92.5	90.2	82.9	84.0	96.0	95.0	78.2
September	91.4	94.3	93.4	97.7	90.7	91.7	92.0	84.6	83.8	95.6	95.3	80.9
October	91.0	96.5	94.9	98.6	90.0	96.0	94.6	88.0	85.8	95.3	96.5	82.5
November	90.1	98.2	95.2	99.9	88.3	94.5	95.4	87.6	85.7	94.6	95.7	80.3
December	91.4	99.0	96.3	101.0	90.7	95.5	94.9	88.2	88.5	94.2	96.6	78.4

. . . = Not available.

Table 2-3. Capacity Utilization by NAICS Industry Groups

(Output as a percent of capacity, seasonally adjusted.)

Year and month	Total industry	Total manufac-turing (SIC)	Manufacturing (NAICS) Total	Durable goods manufacturing Total	Wood products	Nonmetallic mineral products	Primary metals	Fabricated metal products	Machinery	Computer and electronic products	Electrical equipment, appliances, and components	Motor vehicles and parts	Aerospace and miscellaneous transportation equipment
1970	81.3	79.5	. . .	77.7	. . .	73.5	79.4	78.4	79.7	. . .	. . .	66.4	75.4
1971	79.6	78.0	. . .	75.5	. . .	75.0	73.0	78.4	73.7	. . .	. . .	79.2	67.0
1972	84.7	83.4	83.4	82.0	92.2	79.1	82.9	85.1	83.2	80.8	89.8	84.3	65.7
1973	88.3	87.7	87.8	88.6	87.9	84.0	94.7	90.9	92.4	85.2	97.7	91.7	73.6
1974	85.1	84.4	84.4	84.6	77.9	81.6	96.5	86.2	91.9	83.1	91.5	76.7	73.6
1975	75.7	73.7	73.5	71.7	70.0	72.7	75.2	72.3	77.7	68.7	70.8	66.0	70.4
1976	79.8	78.4	78.4	76.5	79.5	77.4	78.6	75.8	79.9	72.2	78.8	81.7	66.2
1977	83.5	82.5	82.5	81.2	86.0	82.4	79.3	79.9	85.5	78.0	85.6	89.8	66.2
1978	85.2	84.5	84.5	83.9	84.8	86.3	84.2	80.7	88.6	80.7	87.7	90.8	72.6
1979	85.0	84.0	84.0	84.0	79.8	84.4	86.1	81.6	90.2	83.7	88.7	81.0	80.9
1980	80.7	78.7	78.4	77.5	72.4	75.0	76.0	75.2	83.6	86.9	81.7	59.8	83.4
1981	79.5	76.9	76.6	75.1	70.6	72.3	77.1	72.8	80.5	84.7	78.7	57.3	76.8
1982	73.6	70.9	70.4	66.5	63.8	64.7	56.5	64.7	66.6	81.3	69.5	50.8	69.8
1983	74.9	73.5	73.0	68.8	75.2	70.2	59.8	66.7	60.5	82.2	72.7	67.4	66.4
1984	80.5	79.4	79.0	77.0	81.1	75.3	69.6	73.7	70.9	87.9	82.3	81.7	69.8
1985	79.3	78.2	77.7	75.9	79.7	75.6	67.9	74.2	70.5	80.7	79.0	83.5	72.5
1986	78.6	78.5	78.0	75.5	83.7	78.0	69.8	73.9	70.0	77.9	80.1	79.2	74.0
1987	81.2	81.0	80.6	77.7	85.7	80.6	78.2	75.5	71.8	80.2	82.4	78.0	75.4
1988	84.3	84.0	83.8	82.1	84.2	81.5	89.3	80.2	80.1	81.6	87.3	82.6	79.7
1989	83.8	83.3	83.2	81.8	82.1	80.7	86.2	79.8	83.8	79.2	86.2	80.9	85.3
1990	82.4	81.6	81.5	79.4	80.2	79.3	84.7	77.6	81.4	79.0	83.8	71.9	84.6
1991	80.0	78.6	78.5	75.5	76.0	73.2	80.1	73.9	76.3	78.6	79.0	64.0	84.6
1992	80.7	79.7	79.7	77.3	78.7	76.9	82.0	76.0	75.1	79.2	82.2	72.4	80.0
1993	81.6	80.6	80.5	78.8	78.8	78.6	85.3	76.9	78.6	78.6	86.6	78.7	75.0
1994	83.6	82.9	82.9	81.7	82.8	81.3	90.7	81.1	83.3	80.5	91.8	86.1	68.4
1995	84.0	83.2	83.2	82.2	80.9	81.5	89.3	83.0	85.5	83.2	91.3	83.4	65.5
1996	83.4	82.2	82.2	81.6	81.2	85.0	88.9	82.4	84.6	81.5	89.8	80.5	67.9
1997	84.1	83.1	83.0	82.4	80.9	84.0	89.9	81.4	85.0	82.0	88.3	81.8	74.1
1998	82.9	81.7	81.4	80.9	81.0	84.5	87.4	79.7	82.0	78.0	85.7	79.2	82.8
1999	81.9	80.6	80.3	80.4	81.4	82.4	86.4	77.8	76.5	81.6	83.1	83.4	77.4
2000	81.6	79.9	79.5	79.9	78.2	79.9	83.1	79.0	77.8	84.4	85.9	81.7	67.0
2001	76.2	73.9	73.4	71.6	72.3	75.1	73.6	73.0	68.3	69.8	76.9	72.8	71.0
2002	75.0	73.1	72.7	70.2	75.0	74.4	76.9	72.1	67.0	60.7	73.4	78.8	67.1
2003	76.0	74.1	73.7	71.3	76.1	74.3	76.0	73.5	68.6	64.3	74.5	78.7	64.0
2004	78.2	76.5	76.2	74.2	79.1	74.8	83.7	75.8	72.6	71.3	77.1	77.2	63.1
2005	80.2	78.6	78.4	76.7	80.7	75.4	81.4	79.6	76.6	73.4	80.9	77.4	69.8
2006	80.5	78.8	78.8	77.8	77.9	73.7	80.7	84.5	79.7	77.7	82.8	72.2	73.1
2007	80.6	78.8	78.9	78.5	73.0	69.0	79.6	86.9	82.4	76.6	87.7	71.7	84.7
2008	77.7	74.5	74.4	74.5	63.3	59.6	77.1	82.0	79.8	77.6	85.6	57.8	84.0
2009	68.4	65.3	65.2	61.3	50.5	45.8	55.1	64.7	62.4	71.2	69.0	43.9	73.8
2010	73.4	70.4	70.7	68.7	56.2	49.3	69.5	71.7	69.8	77.1	74.3	59.3	73.3
2011	76.1	73.3	73.7	72.5	60.5	52.1	75.5	77.6	77.1	77.0	79.5	64.7	71.3
2012	76.9	74.5	75.0	75.0	67.1	54.7	74.6	77.9	82.4	75.8	80.8	70.8	77.1
2013	77.2	74.6	75.0	74.9	71.8	59.1	74.8	78.4	78.2	72.7	80.0	72.5	77.6
2014	78.6	75.7	76.1	76.4	71.8	63.2	72.8	80.3	78.9	72.1	80.9	77.5	82.0
2015	77.0	76.0	76.4	75.9	74.3	66.1	67.8	78.5	73.2	70.8	78.1	81.2	82.7
2016	75.2	75.2	75.5	74.2	77.3	67.3	65.9	76.2	69.6	68.8	76.5	80.7	76.8
2017	76.5	76.2	76.4	75.4	79.3	67.0	67.0	77.1	74.3	73.3	76.9	77.8	79.1
2018	79.2	77.7	77.9	77.5	81.7	68.7	70.6	80.2	78.7	76.2	76.6	78.1	77.0
2019	77.4	75.8	76.0	75.3	78.2	68.6	69.2	78.5	76.8	72.4	75.8	75.0	75.3
2020	71.6	71.1	71.4	69.2	76.1	68.9	61.7	73.3	72.8	72.6	72.7	62.8	61.4
2019													
January	78.7	76.8	77.0	76.4	79.6	69.6	70.1	80.5	79.4	73.8	75.6	75.1	75.3
February	78.1	76.4	76.5	76.0	77.8	67.2	69.2	79.6	78.6	73.5	76.1	75.6	75.6
March	78.1	76.3	76.5	75.9	76.6	67.6	69.6	79.4	78.6	72.9	76.4	76.1	75.5
April	77.5	75.7	75.8	75.3	77.3	68.2	70.2	78.7	76.4	72.5	75.5	75.3	74.2
May	77.6	75.7	75.9	75.3	77.8	68.3	69.5	78.2	77.5	72.0	77.1	76.7	72.7
June	77.4	75.9	76.0	75.3	77.7	68.6	68.3	78.2	76.7	72.1	76.6	77.9	73.6
July	77.1	75.6	75.7	75.1	78.0	68.3	68.6	77.7	75.8	71.9	77.2	76.9	74.4
August	77.5	76.0	76.1	75.4	77.8	69.1	69.8	78.3	77.0	71.6	76.9	76.8	74.9
September	77.2	75.5	75.6	74.8	78.5	69.5	69.4	78.1	75.3	72.0	75.5	72.9	76.0
October	76.5	75.0	75.1	73.8	79.1	68.8	68.2	77.9	75.0	71.3	73.7	68.5	77.1
November	76.8	75.6	75.8	75.2	78.9	68.4	68.3	77.8	75.5	71.9	74.7	75.9	77.4
December	76.5	75.6	75.8	75.0	79.1	69.7	69.7	77.7	76.0	72.7	74.4	72.7	76.7
2020													
January	76.1	75.5	75.6	74.4	80.3	72.2	70.3	78.1	76.4	73.0	75.2	73.5	68.1
February	76.3	75.5	75.7	74.4	79.4	72.5	68.7	78.7	77.5	73.8	76.3	75.2	64.6
March	73.4	72.2	72.4	69.5	76.9	68.9	66.8	75.9	75.3	73.1	74.2	54.9	62.1
April	63.4	60.8	61.0	54.7	67.9	58.8	52.3	67.8	61.7	70.0	69.3	16.0	46.0
May	64.7	63.7	63.9	59.0	70.6	64.3	50.7	69.7	65.1	69.2	68.6	29.0	53.5
June	68.7	68.3	68.6	65.9	73.3	67.4	54.3	71.0	68.5	72.3	69.5	59.9	56.1
July	71.5	71.2	71.5	70.5	76.4	68.9	57.4	71.0	71.8	72.6	72.1	77.4	60.1
August	72.3	72.3	72.6	71.3	75.6	69.1	60.3	72.0	74.3	74.1	71.4	74.2	63.2
September	72.1	72.4	72.6	71.5	75.9	68.5	62.9	73.7	74.9	72.6	71.7	72.8	64.1
October	72.9	73.5	73.7	72.5	77.4	70.6	64.5	73.6	76.6	73.0	74.2	72.4	65.9
November	73.3	74.0	74.2	73.2	78.1	71.7	66.3	74.3	75.7	73.8	74.2	74.4	66.5
December	74.1	74.4	74.7	73.5	80.9	74.1	65.5	74.3	76.3	73.7	75.1	74.1	66.1

. . . = Not available.

Table 2-3. Capacity Utilization by NAICS Industry Groups—*Continued*

(Output as a percent of capacity, seasonally adjusted.)

Year and month	Durable goods manufacturing —Continued		Manufacturing (NAICS)—*Continued* Nondurable goods manufacturing									Other manufac- turing (non- NAICS)
	Furniture and related products	Miscel- laneous manufac- turing	Total	Food, beverage, and tobacco products	Textile and product mills	Apparel and leather	Paper	Printing and support	Petroleum and coal products	Chemicals	Plastics and rubber products	
1970	83.6	. . .	82.2	84.1	. . .	. . .	86.2	. . .	95.9	76.3	79.3	. . .
1971	84.3	. . .	81.8	84.1	. . .	. . .	86.9	. . .	94.6	75.6	79.8	. . .
1972	93.6	80.3	85.3	85.2	88.8	81.6	91.4	92.3	93.1	80.3	88.6	85.5
1973	94.6	79.5	86.6	84.7	86.2	82.2	94.9	94.0	90.3	83.8	92.5	84.8
1974	83.5	74.6	84.2	83.9	76.4	76.3	94.9	88.0	92.5	83.9	84.2	82.7
1975	69.6	67.6	76.1	80.1	72.7	74.6	80.5	79.6	83.7	71.7	70.1	77.2
1976	76.3	72.4	81.2	83.2	81.6	78.3	87.6	82.3	86.0	77.9	77.3	77.6
1977	84.6	77.6	84.4	82.9	89.0	81.6	90.2	86.0	87.7	81.4	88.4	83.1
1978	86.1	78.8	85.3	83.6	88.2	84.5	92.2	87.4	86.5	82.6	88.7	85.0
1979	81.0	78.4	83.9	81.2	87.7	79.7	90.7	86.0	88.5	83.0	83.7	85.5
1980	75.0	73.4	79.8	80.9	83.7	80.5	88.1	83.7	76.4	76.7	74.1	86.7
1981	71.8	75.7	78.9	80.3	80.7	79.3	87.0	81.2	73.1	76.1	77.6	87.4
1982	66.3	73.7	76.4	81.3	74.4	78.3	83.9	82.4	71.2	69.3	74.5	87.3
1983	72.2	70.8	79.4	80.8	84.0	81.6	88.6	84.3	74.3	72.9	81.5	87.8
1984	79.0	75.9	82.1	81.3	85.8	81.7	91.0	87.0	78.4	76.0	91.2	89.4
1985	77.2	73.9	80.5	82.6	81.5	78.3	87.8	84.7	80.0	73.5	87.0	90.1
1986	78.9	73.9	81.8	82.8	84.2	80.2	90.1	85.4	81.8	76.0	85.3	88.7
1987	82.7	77.1	84.8	83.8	91.3	82.5	90.2	89.0	82.4	81.0	89.5	90.3
1988	80.4	81.7	86.2	85.3	88.7	82.6	91.2	90.2	83.3	84.5	89.0	88.4
1989	79.0	79.7	85.0	83.7	88.3	80.7	90.5	88.9	84.3	83.3	87.1	85.5
1990	76.1	79.5	84.2	84.0	83.4	79.5	89.6	88.8	84.7	82.9	83.8	83.6
1991	70.6	78.2	82.4	83.0	81.5	80.7	88.1	84.1	82.6	81.1	78.7	80.7
1992	76.5	77.1	82.8	82.6	85.5	83.3	88.9	86.3	85.3	79.7	82.0	80.1
1993	79.1	77.4	82.8	81.1	87.9	84.3	89.3	84.8	89.0	79.1	86.6	81.3
1994	80.6	77.1	84.6	83.3	90.1	85.4	90.8	84.0	89.0	80.5	91.3	81.4
1995	80.0	79.6	84.5	84.3	86.2	85.0	89.3	83.3	89.6	80.8	89.6	82.2
1996	78.8	81.0	83.2	82.4	82.3	83.7	85.3	83.0	91.7	80.4	88.4	80.5
1997	83.4	79.2	83.8	82.4	84.4	83.5	87.2	81.4	95.3	81.3	89.1	85.5
1998	83.0	79.6	82.2	82.8	81.8	77.8	87.0	79.8	93.0	78.6	87.7	86.7
1999	80.7	77.2	80.1	78.4	81.6	76.4	86.6	77.7	90.7	77.2	86.3	87.1
2000	77.5	76.8	78.9	77.4	79.3	79.3	84.6	77.0	89.4	76.4	82.4	87.4
2001	70.8	73.4	75.7	76.2	71.4	75.6	80.3	74.8	88.5	72.2	76.6	82.8
2002	72.6	74.2	76.0	75.4	73.6	67.3	82.1	74.8	88.9	73.8	78.8	81.5
2003	71.6	75.0	76.8	77.0	72.8	70.0	82.0	75.4	89.9	73.9	79.3	81.5
2004	76.9	75.7	78.8	77.2	74.8	70.7	83.6	77.5	92.9	76.6	83.2	82.4
2005	80.3	78.6	80.4	79.3	78.1	75.8	84.3	77.5	92.1	77.2	84.1	82.0
2006	79.2	77.8	79.9	78.9	75.5	75.9	84.2	77.4	89.2	77.5	82.1	79.6
2007	75.4	73.8	79.4	78.6	73.3	75.8	84.2	76.9	87.3	78.1	78.6	76.6
2008	71.0	74.2	74.2	76.3	69.6	79.0	82.4	69.5	81.3	71.4	69.8	78.0
2009	57.4	69.9	69.7	75.9	57.0	62.8	76.7	59.9	78.3	66.5	59.7	67.4
2010	61.0	75.6	73.1	76.6	63.2	67.4	80.9	62.8	80.4	70.6	68.0	63.5
2011	66.7	77.2	75.0	78.0	65.2	70.6	80.8	63.4	84.6	72.6	69.1	64.0
2012	71.5	75.3	74.9	77.9	66.1	68.7	83.0	63.8	82.9	71.0	74.6	62.7
2013	73.2	77.3	75.2	78.3	70.8	64.4	83.2	66.5	84.2	69.3	79.0	62.4
2014	75.7	76.1	75.7	76.9	73.5	64.0	84.0	68.0	82.0	71.8	81.6	64.7
2015	80.0	79.5	77.0	77.7	70.9	64.1	85.5	70.0	81.9	73.1	84.5	65.5
2016	79.1	82.5	77.1	77.2	71.3	63.5	87.2	73.6	79.1	73.8	84.4	66.7
2017	78.7	79.9	77.6	77.9	69.4	65.9	87.7	75.5	81.4	74.2	82.4	69.6
2018	82.4	83.0	78.4	78.0	70.9	68.0	87.8	75.6	83.8	74.5	85.7	70.4
2019	79.8	80.0	76.8	76.4	70.2	71.6	86.8	75.0	80.3	73.2	83.4	70.6
2020	78.0	73.5	73.9	75.2	63.7	68.8	83.1	68.7	69.3	72.3	77.9	63.9
2019												
January	80.7	81.7	77.7	76.9	70.8	67.8	88.5	74.8	83.5	73.5	85.8	70.8
February	79.6	82.1	77.1	76.6	71.0	67.0	87.7	73.6	80.1	73.6	85.1	71.6
March	78.7	81.7	77.0	76.6	72.1	68.8	87.1	73.6	80.7	73.4	84.3	71.5
April	79.0	81.5	76.5	75.8	71.5	71.2	87.0	74.0	80.2	73.1	82.8	71.5
May	79.4	80.8	76.6	76.3	70.9	71.8	86.7	74.7	80.4	72.6	83.7	70.8
June	78.8	79.8	76.8	77.4	70.9	73.0	84.4	74.6	80.6	72.5	84.2	71.5
July	79.2	79.8	76.4	75.6	69.4	73.2	86.0	75.2	81.1	73.1	82.3	71.0
August	78.9	79.6	76.9	75.7	69.9	73.3	87.3	75.7	81.2	73.8	83.3	70.8
September	79.6	78.8	76.7	75.8	69.2	74.0	87.1	76.0	80.4	73.6	82.2	70.7
October	80.1	77.5	76.6	76.5	68.7	73.4	86.8	76.1	78.8	73.4	81.9	69.7
November	81.5	78.5	76.4	76.3	69.2	72.8	86.5	76.6	78.2	73.1	82.6	68.4
December	82.3	78.2	76.7	77.5	69.3	73.1	86.6	75.5	78.4	72.9	82.4	69.1
2020												
January	83.4	78.4	77.1	76.9	70.8	72.0	87.4	77.1	80.2	73.3	83.7	70.3
February	84.5	77.9	77.1	76.9	70.6	73.4	87.2	78.7	79.2	73.3	84.5	69.6
March	80.4	74.4	75.9	75.9	67.8	69.5	87.9	72.4	74.4	74.2	79.0	64.6
April	62.6	60.7	68.3	70.3	50.9	51.2	83.9	55.2	60.5	69.5	64.0	55.7
May	72.4	63.1	69.6	72.6	57.2	60.0	78.9	60.9	61.0	69.8	67.1	56.9
June	76.8	69.8	71.8	75.0	60.1	66.7	79.3	63.7	63.7	70.2	74.5	58.9
July	78.3	74.7	72.7	74.4	61.6	65.7	79.4	66.4	67.4	71.4	77.2	59.9
August	79.3	75.9	74.0	76.0	63.3	71.9	79.7	67.2	67.5	72.3	80.2	64.0
September	79.7	74.7	73.8	74.9	66.0	71.4	81.3	68.7	67.5	72.3	80.5	66.5
October	79.6	76.4	75.0	75.6	65.5	74.9	83.7	71.5	69.2	73.6	81.6	68.1
November	78.9	77.7	75.3	76.6	64.3	73.9	84.4	71.2	69.3	73.7	80.9	66.6
December	80.2	78.2	76.1	77.3	66.0	74.9	84.0	71.8	71.6	74.3	81.6	65.4

. . . = Not available.

Table 2-4A. Industrial Production and Capacity Utilization, Historical Data, 1955–2020

(Seasonally adjusted.)

Year and month	Production indexes, 2007 = 100										Capacity utilization (output as percent of capacity)	
	Total industry	Manufac-turing (SIC)	Market groups								Total industry	Manufac-turing (SIC)
			Consumer goods			Business equipment	Defense and space equipment	Construction supplies	Business supplies	Materials		
			Total	Durable	Nondurable							
1955	20.6	19.7	28.0	28.0	32.3	7.7	32.4	37.5	19.0	19.7	. . .	87.0
1956	21.6	20.5	29.0	29.0	34.4	8.9	31.7	38.6	20.1	20.2	. . .	86.1
1957	21.8	20.7	29.7	29.7	35.5	9.2	33.1	38.0	20.4	20.2	. . .	83.6
1958	20.4	19.3	29.5	29.5	36.5	7.8	33.2	36.7	20.2	18.2	. . .	75.0
1959	22.9	21.7	32.3	32.3	39.1	8.8	35.0	41.1	22.0	21.0	. . .	81.6
1960	23.4	22.1	33.6	33.6	40.3	9.0	36.0	40.2	22.8	21.3	. . .	80.1
1961	23.5	22.2	34.3	34.3	41.6	8.7	36.6	40.5	23.5	21.3	. . .	77.3
1962	25.5	24.2	36.6	36.6	43.6	9.5	42.3	43.0	24.9	23.2	. . .	81.4
1963	27.0	25.6	38.6	38.6	45.6	9.9	45.7	45.0	26.5	24.7	. . .	83.5
1964	28.8	27.4	40.8	40.8	47.8	11.1	44.2	47.7	28.4	26.7	. . .	85.6
1965	31.7	30.3	44.0	44.0	49.9	12.7	48.9	50.7	30.3	29.7	. . .	89.5
1966	34.5	33.1	46.2	46.2	52.2	14.8	57.5	52.8	32.6	32.4	. . .	91.1
1967	35.2	33.7	47.3	47.3	54.9	15.1	65.6	54.2	34.4	32.1	87.0	87.2
1968	37.2	35.6	50.2	50.2	57.1	15.7	65.7	57.0	36.5	34.2	87.3	87.1
1969	38.9	37.2	52.1	52.1	59.1	16.7	62.6	59.5	38.8	36.2	87.4	86.7
1970	37.6	35.5	51.4	51.4	60.0	16.1	53.0	57.4	38.9	34.9	81.3	79.5
1971	38.2	36.1	54.4	54.4	61.7	15.3	47.6	59.2	40.1	35.5	79.6	78.0
1972	41.8	39.8	58.8	58.8	65.7	17.5	46.3	67.2	44.1	39.1	84.7	83.4
1973	45.3	43.4	61.4	61.4	67.6	20.2	50.8	73.0	46.9	42.6	88.3	87.7
1974	45.1	43.3	59.7	59.7	67.7	21.4	52.5	71.3	46.7	42.4	85.1	84.4
1975	41.1	38.8	57.2	57.2	66.4	19.1	52.9	60.3	43.0	37.8	75.7	73.7
1976	44.4	42.3	61.9	61.9	70.6	20.4	51.4	64.9	45.8	41.2	79.8	78.4
1977	47.8	45.9	65.8	65.8	73.3	23.5	46.0	70.6	49.5	44.0	83.5	82.5
1978	50.4	48.7	67.9	67.9	75.8	26.5	47.0	74.5	52.3	46.2	85.2	84.5
1979	51.9	50.2	66.8	66.8	75.3	29.9	50.1	76.5	54.1	47.4	85.0	84.0
1980	50.5	48.4	64.2	64.2	75.3	30.6	59.5	70.8	52.8	45.6	80.7	78.7
1981	51.2	48.9	64.7	64.7	75.6	31.5	64.5	69.7	54.0	45.9	79.5	76.9
1982	48.5	46.2	64.5	64.5	76.9	28.8	77.1	63.2	53.3	42.4	73.6	70.9
1983	49.9	48.4	66.9	66.9	77.8	29.0	77.5	67.7	55.8	43.5	74.9	73.5
1984	54.3	53.2	70.0	70.0	79.3	33.2	88.8	73.5	60.7	47.6	80.5	79.4
1985	54.9	54.0	70.6	70.6	80.3	34.5	99.4	75.3	62.2	47.5	79.3	78.2
1986	55.5	55.2	73.0	73.0	82.2	34.0	105.6	77.7	64.2	47.5	78.6	78.5
1987	58.4	58.3	76.1	76.1	85.1	36.3	107.8	82.7	68.0	50.1	81.2	81.0
1988	61.4	61.4	79.0	79.0	88.0	40.1	108.7	84.6	70.5	52.9	84.3	84.0
1989	62.0	61.9	79.3	79.3	87.7	41.4	108.8	84.2	71.4	53.3	83.8	83.3
1990	62.6	62.4	79.6	79.6	89.2	43.0	105.0	83.6	73.1	53.8	82.4	81.6
1991	61.7	61.2	79.5	79.5	90.5	42.4	97.3	79.1	72.0	53.0	80.0	78.6
1992	63.5	63.5	82.0	82.0	91.3	44.2	90.3	82.5	73.7	54.7	80.7	79.7
1993	65.6	65.8	84.6	84.6	92.6	46.4	85.4	86.1	76.0	56.5	81.6	80.6
1994	69.0	69.6	88.1	88.1	94.9	49.6	80.2	92.4	78.9	60.1	83.6	82.9
1995	72.2	73.2	90.5	90.5	97.1	54.3	77.4	94.5	82.1	63.4	84.0	83.2
1996	75.5	76.8	92.2	92.2	98.4	59.7	75.6	98.8	85.3	66.7	83.4	82.2
1997	80.9	83.2	95.5	95.5	100.8	68.7	74.6	103.5	91.2	71.9	84.1	83.1
1998	85.7	88.8	99.1	99.1	103.1	76.6	77.9	109.0	96.3	76.2	82.9	81.7
1999	89.4	93.3	101.2	101.2	103.0	80.7	75.6	111.7	100.3	80.9	81.9	80.6
2000	92.9	97.1	103.1	103.1	104.5	87.0	67.1	114.1	104.1	84.9	81.6	79.9
2001	90.0	93.5	102.2	102.2	105.1	81.5	73.7	108.9	100.3	81.5	76.2	73.9
2002	90.2	93.9	104.2	104.2	105.4	75.9	74.7	108.8	100.4	82.6	75.0	73.1
2003	91.4	95.1	105.6	105.6	106.1	76.0	79.5	108.5	102.1	83.7	76.0	74.1
2004	93.8	98.1	106.8	106.8	107.1	80.1	78.0	111.1	104.6	86.5	78.2	76.5
2005	96.9	102.1	109.6	109.6	110.8	86.1	85.5	116.4	108.5	88.6	80.2	78.6
2006	99.1	104.7	110.1	110.1	111.7	94.2	85.1	119.3	110.2	90.3	80.5	78.8
2007	101.7	107.6	110.2	110.2	111.9	99.9	101.3	118.4	111.5	93.5	80.6	78.8
2008	98.1	102.4	104.5	104.5	108.5	97.6	109.4	107.6	106.6	91.2	77.7	74.5
2009	86.9	88.3	96.7	96.7	104.1	80.6	105.0	82.8	94.4	81.0	68.4	65.3
2010	91.7	93.5	97.9	97.9	103.3	86.8	112.9	85.7	97.5	87.8	73.4	70.4
2011	94.6	96.3	98.9	98.9	103.6	92.0	109.6	87.7	98.3	91.6	76.1	73.3
2012	97.4	98.8	97.5	97.5	101.2	101.2	111.6	91.4	98.9	95.6	76.9	74.5
2013	99.3	99.6	98.1	98.1	100.7	101.2	108.0	94.2	100.4	98.8	77.2	74.6
2014	102.3	100.7	99.0	99.0	100.5	103.2	104.2	97.1	101.1	103.7	78.6	75.7
2015	100.9	100.2	100.5	100.5	101.2	100.9	101.3	97.8	99.8	101.4	77.0	76.0
2016	98.7	99.4	101.0	101.0	101.3	95.6	97.7	98.7	99.8	98.0	75.2	75.2
2017	100.0	100.0	100.0	100.0	100.0	100.0	100.0	100.0	100.0	100.0	76.5	76.2
2018	103.2	101.3	100.8	100.8	100.1	103.9	102.2	101.7	102.0	104.7	79.2	77.7
2019	102.3	99.3	100.0	100.0	99.5	99.8	112.3	99.8	99.8	104.5	77.4	75.8
2020	95.0	92.7	96.1	96.1	96.6	86.2	114.2	96.2	91.6	96.2	71.6	71.1
1955												
January	19.4	18.5	26.9	17.8	31.3	7.0	32.9	35.2	18.0	18.1	. . .	83.5
February	19.6	18.7	27.0	18.0	31.3	7.2	32.9	35.7	18.2	18.5	. . .	84.1
March	20.1	19.1	27.5	18.5	31.8	7.2	32.7	36.9	18.7	19.0	. . .	85.8
April	20.3	19.4	27.7	18.8	31.9	7.5	32.7	37.1	18.7	19.4	. . .	86.7
May	20.6	19.7	28.1	19.2	32.2	7.6	32.7	37.3	18.9	19.7	. . .	87.9
June	20.7	19.8	27.9	18.9	32.1	7.7	32.3	37.9	19.1	19.8	. . .	87.6
July	20.8	19.8	27.9	19.1	32.1	7.7	32.3	38.0	19.1	20.0	. . .	87.7
August	20.8	19.8	28.0	19.1	32.1	7.7	32.1	38.0	18.9	20.0	. . .	87.3
September	20.9	19.9	28.2	19.2	32.4	7.8	32.2	38.2	19.3	20.2	. . .	87.5
October	21.3	20.2	28.7	19.3	33.2	8.1	32.0	38.2	19.5	20.5	. . .	88.4
November	21.3	20.3	28.8	19.1	33.5	8.2	32.0	38.7	19.8	20.4	. . .	88.3
December	21.4	20.5	28.9	19.0	33.8	8.3	32.1	38.9	19.7	20.5	. . .	89.0

. . . = Not available.

Table 2-4A. Industrial Production and Capacity Utilization, Historical Data, 1955–2020—*Continued*

(Seasonally adjusted.)

Year and month	Total industry	Manufac-turing (SIC)	Consumer goods			Business equipment	Defense and space equipment	Construction supplies	Business supplies	Materials	Total industry	Manufac-turing (SIC)
			Total	Durable	Nondurable							
1956												
January	21.6	20.4	29.0	18.8	34.0	8.4	31.7	39.5	19.9	20.6	. . .	88.2
February	21.4	20.3	28.9	18.5	34.0	8.5	31.4	39.4	19.9	20.2	. . .	87.4
March	21.4	20.3	28.9	18.5	34.0	8.6	30.7	39.3	20.0	20.1	. . .	87.0
April	21.5	20.6	29.0	18.8	34.0	8.9	30.9	39.1	20.3	20.3	. . .	87.8
May	21.3	20.3	28.8	18.4	34.1	8.8	31.0	38.6	20.1	19.9	. . .	86.3
June	21.2	20.2	28.8	17.9	34.2	8.9	31.0	38.1	20.0	19.6	. . .	85.3
July	20.5	19.4	28.8	17.9	34.4	8.9	31.0	36.1	20.1	18.1	. . .	81.5
August	21.3	20.3	29.0	17.9	34.6	9.0	31.4	38.0	20.2	19.7	. . .	84.9
September	21.8	20.6	28.9	17.7	34.6	9.0	31.7	39.0	20.1	20.8	. . .	86.0
October	22.0	20.8	29.2	17.9	34.9	9.1	32.5	38.7	20.3	21.1	. . .	86.5
November	21.8	20.7	29.0	17.7	34.8	9.2	33.0	38.4	20.3	20.6	. . .	85.8
December	22.2	21.0	29.3	18.4	34.7	9.3	33.8	39.1	20.4	21.0	. . .	86.8
1957												
January	22.1	20.9	29.4	18.4	34.9	9.5	33.9	38.5	20.5	20.6	. . .	86.2
February	22.3	21.2	29.8	18.8	35.2	9.7	34.1	39.7	20.5	20.7	. . .	87.0
March	22.3	21.1	29.9	18.7	35.5	9.6	34.0	39.1	20.4	20.7	. . .	86.4
April	22.0	20.9	29.6	18.1	35.3	9.4	34.1	38.2	20.5	20.4	. . .	85.0
May	21.9	20.7	29.6	18.0	35.4	9.3	33.6	38.0	20.6	20.3	. . .	84.2
June	21.9	20.9	29.8	18.3	35.5	9.3	33.8	38.3	20.4	20.4	. . .	84.6
July	22.1	20.9	29.9	18.2	35.8	9.3	33.4	38.4	20.5	20.5	. . .	84.3
August	22.1	20.9	30.0	18.7	35.7	9.3	33.5	38.1	20.5	20.6	. . .	84.2
September	21.9	20.7	30.0	18.6	35.8	9.2	32.8	37.8	20.5	20.3	. . .	83.2
October	21.6	20.4	29.6	17.9	35.5	9.0	32.0	37.4	20.3	20.0	. . .	81.4
November	21.0	19.9	29.5	17.9	35.3	8.7	30.9	36.9	20.1	19.3	. . .	79.4
December	20.6	19.5	29.3	17.1	35.6	8.5	30.7	36.4	20.0	18.6	. . .	77.5
1958												
January	20.3	19.1	28.9	16.4	35.5	8.3	31.1	35.9	19.9	18.1	. . .	75.7
February	19.8	18.7	28.7	15.8	35.6	8.0	31.3	34.7	19.9	17.5	. . .	73.8
March	19.6	18.5	28.5	15.3	35.6	7.8	31.9	34.6	19.9	17.0	. . .	72.7
April	19.3	18.2	28.2	14.7	35.5	7.7	32.4	34.1	19.8	16.6	. . .	71.3
May	19.5	18.4	28.6	15.2	35.9	7.5	32.8	35.3	19.7	16.8	. . .	71.9
June	20.0	18.9	29.2	15.7	36.5	7.5	33.7	36.7	20.0	17.5	. . .	73.9
July	20.3	19.1	29.6	15.9	36.9	7.5	33.8	36.4	20.0	18.0	. . .	74.3
August	20.7	19.5	29.7	16.2	37.0	7.6	34.1	38.1	20.3	18.5	. . .	75.7
September	20.9	19.7	29.4	15.1	37.1	7.7	34.3	38.2	20.5	19.0	. . .	76.2
October	21.1	19.8	29.6	15.8	37.2	7.8	34.3	38.1	20.8	19.3	. . .	76.4
November	21.7	20.5	31.1	18.5	37.6	8.0	34.5	39.6	21.0	19.8	. . .	79.1
December	21.7	20.6	31.2	18.6	37.6	8.0	34.6	39.1	20.8	19.9	. . .	79.0
1959												
January	22.1	20.9	31.6	18.7	38.1	8.2	34.7	39.9	21.4	20.2	. . .	80.2
February	22.5	21.3	31.8	18.8	38.5	8.3	34.4	41.0	21.6	20.9	. . .	81.4
March	22.8	21.6	31.8	19.1	38.3	8.4	34.5	42.0	21.7	21.4	. . .	82.5
April	23.3	22.1	32.3	19.2	39.0	8.6	34.8	43.2	21.7	22.0	. . .	84.0
May	23.7	22.4	32.5	19.6	39.0	8.9	35.0	43.6	21.8	22.6	. . .	84.9
June	23.7	22.4	32.3	19.8	38.7	9.1	35.1	43.4	22.0	22.4	. . .	84.8
July	23.1	22.0	32.7	20.2	39.0	9.1	35.3	41.7	22.2	21.1	. . .	83.0
August	22.3	21.1	32.8	19.6	39.5	9.0	35.1	39.1	22.2	19.5	. . .	79.5
September	22.3	21.1	32.6	19.0	39.7	9.0	35.3	38.6	22.3	19.5	. . .	79.0
October	22.2	20.9	32.5	19.5	39.2	8.9	35.2	38.7	22.3	19.3	. . .	78.2
November	22.3	21.1	31.8	17.1	39.7	8.7	35.2	40.1	22.2	20.0	. . .	78.5
December	23.7	22.5	32.8	19.2	39.9	8.9	35.4	43.2	22.5	22.2	. . .	83.6
1960												
January	24.3	23.1	33.9	21.4	40.1	9.2	35.7	42.9	22.7	22.8	. . .	85.6
February	24.1	22.9	33.5	21.1	39.6	9.3	35.9	42.4	22.7	22.5	. . .	84.6
March	23.9	22.7	33.5	20.6	40.0	9.3	36.1	41.1	22.7	22.2	. . .	83.2
April	23.7	22.5	33.8	20.6	40.4	9.2	35.9	41.1	23.0	21.6	. . .	82.3
May	23.6	22.4	34.0	20.8	40.6	9.2	36.3	40.7	23.2	21.4	. . .	81.5
June	23.3	22.1	33.7	20.6	40.3	9.1	35.3	40.0	22.9	21.1	. . .	80.2
July	23.3	22.0	33.4	19.8	40.4	9.0	36.2	40.4	22.9	21.1	. . .	79.7
August	23.2	21.9	33.5	20.0	40.4	8.9	36.4	39.4	22.7	21.0	. . .	79.1
September	23.0	21.7	33.3	19.8	40.3	8.8	36.3	39.0	22.6	20.7	. . .	77.9
October	23.0	21.7	33.7	20.0	40.7	8.7	35.9	39.1	22.7	20.6	. . .	77.5
November	22.6	21.3	33.1	19.3	40.3	8.7	36.1	38.7	22.7	20.1	. . .	75.8
December	22.2	20.9	32.8	18.7	40.2	8.5	35.5	38.2	22.3	19.5	. . .	74.3
1961												
January	22.2	20.9	32.6	18.0	40.4	8.6	35.9	37.8	22.7	19.7	. . .	74.1
February	22.2	20.8	32.8	17.9	40.7	8.5	35.6	37.8	22.7	19.6	. . .	73.5
March	22.3	21.0	32.8	17.9	40.7	8.5	35.6	38.6	22.9	19.7	. . .	73.9
April	22.8	21.5	33.5	19.2	41.0	8.6	35.7	39.6	23.1	20.3	. . .	75.4
May	23.2	21.8	33.9	19.8	41.3	8.6	35.7	39.7	23.2	20.9	. . .	76.4
June	23.5	22.1	34.3	20.5	41.5	8.6	35.7	40.6	23.3	21.3	. . .	77.3
July	23.7	22.4	34.6	20.8	41.7	8.7	35.9	41.2	23.6	21.5	. . .	78.1
August	24.0	22.7	34.8	20.9	42.0	8.7	36.1	41.7	23.7	22.0	. . .	79.0
September	23.9	22.6	34.3	19.7	41.8	8.9	36.9	42.1	23.6	22.0	. . .	78.2
October	24.4	23.0	35.2	20.8	42.5	8.8	37.7	42.4	24.0	22.4	. . .	79.6
November	24.8	23.4	35.8	21.7	42.9	9.1	38.6	42.1	24.2	22.7	. . .	80.8
December	25.0	23.7	35.9	22.1	42.9	9.1	39.3	42.4	24.4	23.0	. . .	81.6

. . . = Not available.

Table 2-4A. Industrial Production and Capacity Utilization, Historical Data, 1955–2020—*Continued*

(Seasonally adjusted.)

Year and month	Production indexes, 2007 = 100										Capacity utilization (output as percent of capacity)	
	Total industry	Manufac-turing (SIC)	Consumer goods			Business equipment	Defense and space equipment	Construction supplies	Business supplies	Materials	Total industry	Manufac-turing (SIC)
			Total	Durable	Nondurable							
1962												
January	24.8	23.4	35.6	21.6	42.7	9.1	39.7	40.4	24.4	22.9	. . .	80.2
February	25.2	23.8	35.9	21.8	43.0	9.2	40.4	42.8	24.6	23.2	. . .	81.4
March	25.3	24.0	36.1	22.1	43.3	9.3	41.0	43.3	24.5	23.2	. . .	81.9
April	25.4	24.0	36.4	22.6	43.3	9.4	41.3	42.7	24.5	23.2	. . .	81.7
May	25.3	24.0	36.6	22.8	43.6	9.4	41.6	42.7	25.0	22.9	. . .	81.3
June	25.3	23.9	36.4	22.4	43.5	9.5	42.0	43.0	24.9	22.8	. . .	80.9
July	25.5	24.2	37.0	22.9	44.0	9.6	42.8	42.8	24.9	23.0	. . .	81.5
August	25.6	24.2	36.6	22.6	43.6	9.7	43.4	43.6	25.0	23.1	. . .	81.4
September	25.7	24.4	36.8	22.8	43.9	9.6	43.5	44.1	25.3	23.3	. . .	81.8
October	25.7	24.4	36.7	22.9	43.7	9.7	43.7	43.3	25.2	23.3	. . .	81.4
November	25.9	24.6	37.0	23.0	43.9	9.7	44.1	43.5	25.4	23.5	. . .	81.8
December	25.9	24.6	37.1	23.1	44.1	9.6	44.3	43.9	25.2	23.3	. . .	81.7
1963												
January	26.0	24.7	37.6	23.4	44.7	9.6	46.4	42.8	25.5	23.4	. . .	81.9
February	26.3	24.9	38.0	23.6	45.2	9.7	46.0	42.9	25.7	23.8	. . .	82.4
March	26.5	25.1	38.2	23.7	45.4	9.7	45.8	43.4	25.5	24.1	. . .	82.6
April	26.7	25.4	38.3	23.9	45.6	9.8	45.7	44.9	26.3	24.4	. . .	83.5
May	27.1	25.7	38.4	24.3	45.4	9.7	45.7	45.9	26.5	24.9	. . .	84.0
June	27.2	25.7	38.6	24.7	45.5	9.8	45.7	45.7	26.4	25.0	. . .	83.9
July	27.0	25.6	38.5	24.7	45.3	9.9	45.2	45.5	26.6	24.8	. . .	83.3
August	27.1	25.8	38.8	24.7	45.8	10.1	45.4	45.6	26.8	24.6	. . .	83.5
September	27.4	25.9	38.9	25.1	45.7	10.1	45.6	45.3	27.0	25.0	. . .	83.8
October	27.6	26.2	39.2	25.2	46.0	10.3	45.6	46.0	27.2	25.2	. . .	84.3
November	27.7	26.3	39.2	25.4	46.0	10.4	45.4	46.5	27.5	25.3	. . .	84.3
December	27.6	26.3	39.5	25.5	46.4	10.4	45.5	45.9	27.4	25.2	. . .	84.0
1964												
January	27.9	26.5	39.9	25.5	46.9	10.6	45.1	46.1	27.6	25.4	. . .	84.5
February	28.1	26.6	39.8	25.7	46.7	10.6	44.7	47.3	27.8	25.8	. . .	84.7
March	28.1	26.6	39.6	25.5	46.5	10.7	44.6	47.5	27.9	25.8	. . .	84.4
April	28.5	27.1	40.6	26.2	47.6	11.0	44.5	47.7	28.3	26.1	. . .	85.6
May	28.7	27.2	40.9	26.3	48.1	11.1	43.7	47.9	28.6	26.3	. . .	85.6
June	28.8	27.3	40.8	26.6	47.8	11.1	43.4	47.6	28.6	26.5	. . .	85.4
July	29.0	27.5	41.4	27.0	48.4	11.3	43.3	48.5	28.6	26.5	. . .	85.9
August	29.2	27.7	41.3	27.2	48.1	11.2	43.6	48.0	28.5	27.1	. . .	86.1
September	29.3	27.8	40.9	26.6	47.8	11.3	43.8	47.6	28.5	27.5	. . .	86.2
October	28.9	27.4	40.1	23.8	48.4	11.3	44.2	47.8	28.6	27.0	. . .	84.6
November	29.7	28.2	41.6	27.1	48.6	11.6	44.6	48.9	28.8	27.8	. . .	86.8
December	30.1	28.7	42.4	28.7	48.9	11.8	44.9	48.3	29.1	28.2	. . .	88.0
1965												
January	30.4	29.1	43.0	29.2	49.5	11.8	45.4	48.7	29.3	28.5	. . .	88.6
February	30.6	29.3	43.1	29.6	49.4	12.0	45.9	49.9	29.5	28.6	. . .	88.7
March	31.0	29.6	43.5	30.4	49.5	12.2	46.8	50.3	29.8	29.0	. . .	89.3
April	31.2	29.8	43.4	30.3	49.4	12.3	47.4	49.6	29.8	29.3	. . .	89.3
May	31.4	30.0	43.7	30.5	49.6	12.5	48.4	50.1	30.1	29.4	. . .	89.4
June	31.6	30.2	43.8	30.8	49.7	12.7	49.0	50.1	30.2	29.8	. . .	89.5
July	31.9	30.7	43.8	31.0	49.5	12.9	49.7	51.5	30.2	30.1	. . .	90.3
August	32.1	30.7	43.8	30.7	49.7	12.9	50.1	51.0	30.5	30.3	. . .	89.9
September	32.2	30.8	44.4	31.3	50.3	13.1	50.2	50.6	30.5	30.1	. . .	89.6
October	32.5	31.0	44.7	31.6	50.5	13.3	50.9	51.4	30.8	30.4	. . .	89.8
November	32.6	31.1	44.9	31.8	50.8	13.6	51.3	52.1	31.1	30.3	. . .	89.6
December	33.0	31.6	45.2	32.4	50.7	13.8	51.8	53.2	31.5	30.6	. . .	90.5
1966												
January	33.3	31.9	45.4	32.5	51.0	14.1	52.9	53.1	31.5	31.1	. . .	90.9
February	33.6	32.1	45.5	32.5	51.3	14.1	53.8	52.6	31.9	31.4	. . .	90.9
March	34.0	32.6	45.8	32.7	51.6	14.4	54.2	53.7	32.2	32.0	. . .	91.6
April	34.1	32.8	46.0	33.4	51.5	14.5	55.4	53.7	31.9	31.9	. . .	91.5
May	34.4	33.0	46.0	32.8	51.9	14.7	56.4	53.9	32.4	32.3	. . .	91.6
June	34.6	33.1	46.2	32.8	52.1	14.8	57.2	53.2	32.8	32.5	. . .	91.5
July	34.7	33.3	46.1	32.2	52.5	15.0	58.0	53.7	33.1	32.5	. . .	91.4
August	34.8	33.4	46.0	31.7	52.5	15.1	58.7	52.1	33.0	32.8	. . .	91.1
September	35.1	33.6	46.1	31.9	52.7	15.3	59.5	52.1	33.2	33.1	. . .	91.2
October	35.3	34.0	47.1	33.5	53.1	15.2	60.4	52.1	33.2	33.3	. . .	91.6
November	35.1	33.6	46.9	32.5	53.4	15.0	61.5	52.2	33.3	32.8	. . .	90.1
December	35.2	33.8	46.7	32.2	53.5	15.2	62.2	52.1	33.4	32.8	. . .	90.0
1967												
January	35.3	33.9	47.2	31.4	54.7	15.1	63.2	53.5	34.0	32.7	89.4	89.8
February	34.9	33.5	46.5	30.5	54.3	15.1	64.0	53.0	33.8	32.0	88.0	88.4
March	34.7	33.3	46.7	30.8	54.3	15.1	64.6	53.1	33.8	31.4	87.1	87.5
April	35.1	33.5	47.5	31.0	55.4	15.1	65.3	52.9	34.2	31.7	87.5	87.7
May	34.8	33.3	46.6	30.6	54.2	15.1	65.7	53.8	33.6	31.4	86.4	86.6
June	34.8	33.2	46.7	30.3	54.7	15.1	65.6	54.1	33.8	31.3	86.0	86.1
July	34.7	33.1	46.6	30.7	54.3	14.8	65.9	54.3	33.9	31.3	85.4	85.3
August	35.3	33.7	47.1	31.0	54.8	15.0	66.1	54.9	34.8	32.2	86.6	86.5
September	35.3	33.7	47.2	30.9	55.0	15.0	66.3	55.3	34.9	32.0	86.1	86.1
October	35.6	34.0	47.8	31.5	55.6	14.8	66.8	55.1	35.2	32.4	86.4	86.4
November	36.1	34.6	48.8	33.2	56.1	15.2	66.9	55.4	35.2	32.8	87.3	87.5
December	36.5	35.0	49.6	34.6	56.5	15.4	66.9	55.4	35.2	33.2	87.8	88.0

. . . = Not available.

Table 2-4A. Industrial Production and Capacity Utilization, Historical Data, 1955–2020—*Continued*

(Seasonally adjusted.)

Year and month	Production indexes, 2007 = 100											Capacity utilization (output as percent of capacity)	
	Total industry	Manufac-turing (SIC)	Market groups									Total industry	Manufac-turing (SIC)
			Consumer goods			Business equipment	Defense and space equipment	Construction supplies	Business supplies	Materials			
			Total	Durable	Nondurable								
1968													
January	36.4	34.9	49.0	33.6	56.1	15.4	66.6	55.8	35.3	33.4		87.4	87.4
February	36.6	35.1	49.2	34.1	56.2	15.4	67.4	56.3	35.6	33.4		87.4	87.4
March	36.7	35.1	49.5	34.0	56.7	15.6	66.1	56.4	35.6	33.5		87.3	87.2
April	36.7	35.1	49.4	34.0	56.6	15.5	64.7	56.7	35.9	33.8		87.1	86.9
May	37.1	35.6	49.7	34.5	56.7	15.7	65.6	57.0	36.3	34.3		87.7	87.6
June	37.3	35.7	50.0	34.8	57.0	15.7	66.0	57.0	36.4	34.4		87.7	87.4
July	37.2	35.6	49.9	34.5	57.0	15.6	66.0	57.0	36.4	34.5		87.2	86.7
August	37.3	35.7	50.5	35.0	57.6	15.7	66.1	57.3	36.8	34.2		87.1	86.8
September	37.5	35.8	50.7	35.3	57.7	15.9	66.1	56.9	36.9	34.3		87.1	86.5
October	37.5	36.0	51.0	35.8	57.9	16.0	64.4	56.8	37.1	34.4		86.9	86.6
November	38.0	36.5	51.7	36.6	58.4	16.0	65.0	58.2	37.5	34.9		87.7	87.5
December	38.2	36.5	51.4	36.9	57.7	16.2	64.7	59.2	37.8	35.1		87.7	87.1
1969													
January	38.4	36.7	51.6	36.9	58.1	16.4	64.8	59.6	37.9	35.3		87.9	87.3
February	38.6	37.0	52.1	36.8	58.8	16.4	64.3	60.2	37.8	35.7		88.1	87.7
March	38.9	37.3	52.4	37.0	59.3	16.6	64.6	60.4	39.0	35.8		88.5	88.0
April	38.8	37.1	51.7	36.1	58.7	16.7	64.1	59.8	38.5	35.9		87.8	87.3
May	38.6	37.0	51.3	35.6	58.4	16.6	63.9	59.4	38.8	35.8		87.2	86.6
June	39.0	37.2	51.9	36.8	58.5	16.8	63.0	59.8	39.1	36.3		87.7	86.8
July	39.2	37.5	52.8	36.8	60.0	17.0	62.8	59.2	38.9	36.3		87.9	87.1
August	39.3	37.5	52.7	37.2	59.6	16.9	61.9	59.2	39.1	36.7		87.8	86.9
September	39.3	37.5	52.3	36.8	59.2	17.1	61.5	59.2	39.0	36.8		87.5	86.5
October	39.3	37.5	52.3	37.0	59.1	17.1	60.9	59.4	39.1	36.8		87.2	86.2
November	38.9	37.1	51.8	35.5	59.4	16.7	59.8	59.0	38.9	36.6		86.1	85.0
December	38.8	36.9	51.9	35.3	59.6	16.6	59.1	58.7	39.3	36.4		85.5	84.3
1970													
January	38.1	36.1	51.0	33.4	59.5	16.4	58.3	56.9	39.3	35.6		83.7	82.1
February	38.1	36.1	51.5	33.9	60.0	16.5	57.3	56.7	39.0	35.4		83.4	81.9
March	38.0	36.0	51.5	34.2	59.7	16.5	56.1	57.2	39.2	35.3		83.0	81.4
April	37.9	35.9	51.7	34.2	60.0	16.5	54.8	57.7	39.0	35.0		82.5	80.9
May	37.9	35.8	52.0	34.3	60.4	16.5	53.6	57.8	38.9	34.9		82.2	80.5
June	37.8	35.7	52.1	34.9	60.2	16.4	52.7	57.5	38.9	34.8		81.6	80.0
July	37.9	35.8	52.2	35.0	60.3	16.4	51.8	58.2	39.0	34.9		81.6	80.0
August	37.8	35.6	51.3	33.9	59.6	16.3	51.4	58.0	38.7	35.4		81.2	79.2
September	37.5	35.3	51.1	33.0	60.0	16.0	50.9	57.8	38.9	35.1		80.4	78.3
October	36.8	34.5	50.5	31.0	60.3	15.4	50.2	57.2	38.8	34.2		78.5	76.3
November	36.6	34.3	50.2	31.1	59.7	15.4	49.8	56.5	38.9	34.0		77.8	75.6
December	37.4	35.2	52.3	34.8	60.7	15.5	49.2	57.2	38.9	34.7		79.4	77.3
1971													
January	37.7	35.5	53.1	36.1	61.0	15.2	49.6	57.2	39.1	35.2		79.8	77.8
February	37.6	35.5	53.1	37.0	60.4	15.3	48.4	57.6	39.5	35.0		79.4	77.6
March	37.6	35.4	53.2	37.0	60.6	15.1	48.0	57.4	39.2	35.1		79.1	77.3
April	37.8	35.6	53.7	37.2	61.2	15.0	48.0	57.9	39.6	35.3		79.4	77.5
May	38.0	35.9	53.7	37.8	60.8	14.9	48.6	58.2	39.6	35.7		79.6	77.8
June	38.2	36.0	54.1	38.1	61.3	15.0	47.9	58.8	39.5	35.9		79.7	77.8
July	38.0	36.0	55.0	38.8	62.1	15.0	47.5	59.3	40.5	35.0		79.3	77.7
August	37.8	35.6	54.3	38.5	61.4	15.3	47.5	58.3	40.0	34.8		78.6	76.6
September	38.4	36.3	54.8	38.4	62.2	15.6	47.1	60.5	40.7	35.5		79.7	78.0
October	38.7	36.8	55.6	39.1	63.0	15.8	46.8	61.3	40.9	35.6		80.1	78.9
November	38.9	37.0	56.0	39.5	63.4	15.8	46.4	61.5	41.4	35.7		80.2	79.0
December	39.3	37.3	56.4	39.6	63.9	15.9	45.7	62.6	41.5	36.4		80.9	79.5
1972													
January	40.3	38.3	57.2	40.8	64.5	16.4	45.7	64.3	42.3	37.5		82.7	81.4
February	40.7	38.6	57.6	41.0	64.9	16.7	45.9	64.6	43.0	37.9		83.3	81.8
March	41.0	38.9	57.6	40.7	65.1	16.9	46.2	65.0	43.4	38.3		83.7	82.2
April	41.4	39.3	58.2	41.9	65.3	17.2	46.4	65.7	43.4	38.7		84.4	82.9
May	41.4	39.4	58.0	41.5	65.2	17.2	46.0	66.1	43.7	38.8		84.2	82.8
June	41.5	39.5	58.0	41.6	65.2	17.3	45.8	66.6	44.1	38.8		84.1	82.9
July	41.4	39.5	58.4	42.5	65.2	17.3	45.9	67.6	44.1	38.5		83.8	82.6
August	42.0	40.0	59.1	42.8	66.0	17.6	45.8	68.0	44.6	39.1		84.8	83.5
September	42.3	40.3	59.4	43.3	66.2	17.8	46.2	68.7	44.7	39.5		85.2	83.9
October	42.9	40.9	60.2	44.3	66.9	18.1	46.2	69.7	45.3	39.9		86.0	84.9
November	43.4	41.4	60.7	45.3	66.8	18.4	47.5	70.2	45.5	40.5		86.8	85.7
December	43.9	42.0	61.2	46.2	67.0	18.7	48.3	69.9	45.6	41.1		87.5	86.6
1973													
January	44.2	42.3	61.1	46.1	66.9	19.0	48.9	70.8	46.0	41.5		87.8	87.0
February	44.8	43.0	61.8	46.9	67.6	19.4	49.9	72.1	46.4	42.1		88.8	88.1
March	44.8	43.0	62.0	47.0	67.8	19.5	49.8	72.5	46.5	41.9		88.5	88.0
April	44.8	43.0	61.4	46.3	67.3	19.7	49.5	72.4	46.5	42.0		88.1	87.5
May	45.1	43.2	61.7	46.1	68.0	19.9	49.8	72.7	46.8	42.3		88.4	87.8
June	45.1	43.3	61.3	46.1	67.3	20.1	50.4	72.9	46.9	42.4		88.2	87.5
July	45.3	43.4	61.2	46.0	67.1	20.4	51.4	73.5	47.0	42.6		88.2	87.6
August	45.2	43.3	60.6	44.6	67.2	20.4	51.4	73.5	47.0	42.7		87.8	87.1
September	45.6	43.7	61.5	46.1	67.6	20.8	51.4	73.5	47.0	42.8		88.2	87.4
October	46.0	44.1	61.8	45.8	68.3	21.0	52.7	73.4	47.5	43.2		88.6	88.0
November	46.2	44.4	62.0	45.8	68.6	21.2	52.1	73.9	47.5	43.4		88.7	88.3
December	46.1	44.4	60.9	44.8	67.5	21.3	51.8	74.5	47.2	43.6		88.2	88.1

Table 2-4A. Industrial Production and Capacity Utilization, Historical Data, 1955–2020—*Continued*

(Seasonally adjusted.)

Year and month	Production indexes, 2007 = 100										Capacity utilization (output as percent of capacity)	
	Total industry	Manufac-turing (SIC)	Market groups								Total industry	Manufac-turing (SIC)
			Consumer goods			Business equipment	Defense and space equipment	Construction supplies	Business supplies	Materials		
			Total	Durable	Nondurable							
1974												
January	45.7	44.0	60.1	42.5	67.8	21.2	51.6	74.6	47.3	43.3	87.4	87.1
February	45.6	43.9	59.9	42.4	67.6	21.2	52.1	73.7	47.1	43.2	86.8	86.5
March	45.6	43.8	60.0	42.5	67.7	21.4	52.1	73.9	47.1	43.0	86.6	86.1
April	45.5	43.7	59.8	42.2	67.6	21.1	52.0	73.3	47.1	43.0	86.2	85.6
May	45.8	44.0	60.3	42.3	68.4	21.5	52.2	73.5	47.4	43.3	86.6	85.9
June	45.8	44.0	60.5	42.9	68.3	21.5	51.3	73.1	47.5	43.1	86.2	85.7
July	45.8	44.0	60.5	42.8	68.4	21.5	52.1	71.8	47.2	43.3	86.2	85.5
August	45.3	43.6	60.4	42.7	68.3	21.5	53.0	70.9	46.9	42.5	85.1	84.5
September	45.4	43.6	59.9	42.6	67.5	21.9	53.0	70.4	46.7	42.6	84.9	84.3
October	45.2	43.3	59.9	42.1	67.9	21.9	53.9	69.1	46.5	42.4	84.5	83.5
November	43.7	42.0	58.2	40.1	66.6	21.6	53.6	66.9	45.3	40.6	81.6	80.9
December	42.2	40.1	56.3	36.8	65.8	20.7	52.9	63.8	44.4	39.0	78.5	77.1
1975												
January	41.6	39.3	55.0	35.2	64.8	20.2	53.3	63.5	43.8	38.7	77.3	75.4
February	40.6	38.2	54.3	34.2	64.3	19.5	50.7	61.6	42.9	37.8	75.4	73.1
March	40.2	37.7	54.4	34.6	64.2	19.2	51.2	59.2	42.2	37.2	74.5	72.0
April	40.3	37.7	55.6	36.0	65.1	19.1	50.9	58.8	42.4	37.0	74.5	71.9
May	40.1	37.6	55.8	36.9	64.9	18.8	53.4	58.7	42.2	36.8	74.1	71.7
June	40.4	37.9	56.6	37.3	65.9	18.7	54.0	58.4	42.3	37.0	74.5	72.2
July	40.8	38.5	58.1	39.1	67.0	18.8	53.2	59.2	42.8	37.1	75.1	73.1
August	41.2	38.9	58.4	39.7	67.1	18.7	53.1	59.9	43.1	37.8	75.7	73.7
September	41.7	39.5	59.3	40.5	68.0	19.0	54.6	60.6	43.3	38.3	76.6	74.8
October	41.9	39.7	59.3	40.3	68.2	19.0	54.6	60.9	43.5	38.5	76.8	75.0
November	42.0	39.8	59.5	40.3	68.5	19.0	52.4	61.2	43.5	38.6	76.7	75.0
December	42.6	40.4	60.1	41.0	69.0	19.3	54.0	61.2	44.0	39.2	77.6	75.9
1976												
January	43.1	40.8	60.8	41.7	69.6	19.5	54.0	62.7	44.5	39.8	78.5	76.7
February	43.6	41.4	61.1	42.3	69.7	19.6	53.9	63.8	44.6	40.4	79.1	77.6
March	43.6	41.6	61.0	42.2	69.6	19.8	54.0	62.8	44.9	40.6	79.1	77.7
April	43.9	41.8	61.1	42.2	69.8	19.9	52.8	63.6	45.0	40.8	79.4	78.0
May	44.1	42.0	61.6	42.3	70.5	20.1	52.3	64.3	45.3	40.9	79.5	78.2
June	44.1	42.1	61.4	42.1	70.3	20.2	51.7	64.8	45.0	41.1	79.4	78.1
July	44.4	42.4	61.8	42.3	70.8	20.3	50.3	66.2	45.7	41.2	79.7	78.5
August	44.7	42.6	61.9	42.9	70.6	20.7	50.2	65.6	45.7	41.6	80.1	78.8
September	44.8	42.7	62.0	42.6	70.9	20.6	49.8	66.0	46.7	41.7	80.1	78.8
October	44.8	42.7	62.4	43.2	71.2	20.6	49.8	65.9	47.0	41.4	79.9	78.5
November	45.5	43.3	63.5	44.6	72.0	21.3	49.5	66.2	47.3	42.0	81.0	79.4
December	45.9	43.7	64.2	45.7	72.4	21.6	48.5	66.7	47.7	42.5	81.6	80.0
1977												
January	45.6	43.6	64.0	45.5	72.1	21.7	47.8	65.5	47.4	42.1	80.9	79.5
February	46.4	44.4	64.9	46.1	73.2	22.3	47.7	67.1	48.0	42.7	82.0	80.8
March	47.0	45.0	65.0	47.3	72.4	22.6	46.6	68.4	48.4	43.5	82.8	81.7
April	47.4	45.5	65.4	47.7	72.9	22.9	47.0	70.0	49.0	43.9	83.4	82.4
May	47.8	45.9	65.4	47.9	72.8	23.4	46.8	71.1	49.4	44.2	83.9	82.8
June	48.1	46.3	65.9	48.8	72.9	23.9	46.8	71.6	49.8	44.4	84.3	83.3
July	48.2	46.3	66.0	48.9	73.1	24.1	46.7	71.7	49.9	44.4	84.2	83.1
August	48.2	46.5	66.2	48.9	73.3	24.1	46.4	72.3	50.3	44.3	84.0	83.3
September	48.5	46.6	66.3	49.1	73.3	24.2	46.4	72.0	50.5	44.6	84.1	83.1
October	48.5	46.7	66.8	49.1	74.1	24.1	42.4	71.9	50.5	44.8	84.0	83.1
November	48.6	46.8	66.9	49.1	74.3	24.1	42.1	72.3	50.7	44.9	84.0	83.0
December	48.7	47.3	67.4	49.4	75.0	24.4	45.0	73.0	50.7	44.5	83.8	83.6
1978												
January	48.0	46.6	65.7	46.8	74.0	23.9	45.5	71.6	50.5	44.1	82.4	82.2
February	48.2	46.8	66.8	48.0	74.9	24.6	43.2	71.4	50.7	44.0	82.6	82.3
March	49.2	47.6	68.1	49.4	76.0	25.3	47.1	72.7	51.5	44.7	84.0	83.5
April	50.2	48.3	68.5	50.4	76.1	25.8	46.9	74.3	52.0	46.0	85.4	84.5
May	50.4	48.6	68.2	49.6	76.0	26.0	47.2	74.3	52.3	46.4	85.6	84.7
June	50.7	48.9	68.5	49.9	76.4	26.4	47.6	74.9	52.7	46.6	85.9	85.0
July	50.7	48.8	68.1	49.9	75.8	26.6	47.7	74.8	52.6	46.6	85.5	84.6
August	50.9	49.1	68.0	49.7	75.8	27.1	48.1	74.9	52.6	46.7	85.7	84.8
September	51.0	49.3	68.2	49.4	76.2	27.4	48.1	75.2	52.7	46.8	85.7	84.9
October	51.4	49.7	68.0	49.6	75.9	27.9	47.5	75.9	53.0	47.3	86.1	85.3
November	51.8	50.1	68.3	49.7	76.1	28.4	47.3	76.4	53.3	47.7	86.5	85.8
December	52.0	50.5	68.4	49.9	76.2	28.7	47.9	77.6	53.7	47.8	86.7	86.2
1979												
January	51.7	50.1	68.2	50.2	75.7	29.0	48.1	75.8	53.7	47.3	86.0	85.3
February	52.0	50.3	67.7	49.6	75.4	29.3	49.1	76.3	54.1	47.7	86.2	85.3
March	52.2	50.5	68.0	49.5	75.9	29.6	48.7	77.2	54.4	47.7	86.2	85.5
April	51.6	49.7	66.7	47.0	75.5	29.0	47.4	76.0	54.1	47.4	85.0	83.8
May	52.0	50.4	67.2	48.4	75.3	29.8	48.2	76.5	54.3	47.6	85.5	84.7
June	52.0	50.4	67.0	47.9	75.3	29.9	48.7	76.8	54.1	47.7	85.3	84.6
July	51.9	50.5	66.4	47.3	74.9	30.2	49.5	76.8	54.1	47.5	85.0	84.4
August	51.6	49.9	65.7	45.3	75.0	29.8	50.2	76.1	54.3	47.3	84.2	83.1
September	51.6	49.9	66.1	46.9	74.5	30.6	50.6	76.2	53.6	46.9	84.0	83.0
October	51.9	50.2	66.3	46.6	75.0	30.3	52.4	76.8	54.2	47.4	84.4	83.2
November	51.9	50.0	66.1	45.9	75.3	30.2	53.5	76.6	54.4	47.3	84.1	82.8
December	51.9	50.2	66.1	45.8	75.4	30.5	54.7	76.9	54.4	47.2	84.0	82.8

Table 2-4A. Industrial Production and Capacity Utilization, Historical Data, 1955–2020—*Continued*

(Seasonally adjusted.)

Year and month	Total industry	Manufac-turing (SIC)	Production indexes, 2007 = 100 — Market groups — Consumer goods — Total	Durable	Nondurable	Business equipment	Defense and space equipment	Construction supplies	Business supplies	Materials	Capacity utilization (output as percent of capacity) — Total industry	Manufac-turing (SIC)
1980												
January	52.2	50.4	65.9	44.8	75.6	31.0	55.3	76.7	54.1	47.6	84.3	83.0
February	52.2	50.4	66.1	44.5	76.1	31.2	57.6	75.6	54.1	47.5	84.2	82.8
March	52.0	49.9	65.6	43.8	75.8	30.9	58.2	74.6	53.9	47.5	83.7	81.9
April	51.0	48.9	64.5	41.9	75.4	30.6	58.8	71.2	53.1	46.3	81.9	80.1
May	49.7	47.5	63.2	39.2	75.0	30.1	59.1	68.3	52.0	45.0	79.7	77.5
June	49.1	46.7	62.8	38.5	74.9	29.7	59.5	66.9	51.4	44.2	78.5	76.1
July	48.7	46.2	62.8	38.5	74.9	29.7	59.9	66.3	51.5	43.5	77.8	75.1
August	48.9	46.6	63.0	38.9	75.1	29.7	60.3	67.3	51.7	43.6	77.8	75.5
September	49.7	47.4	63.7	40.7	74.9	30.3	60.1	69.0	52.5	44.5	79.0	76.6
October	50.3	48.2	64.1	41.4	75.1	30.8	61.2	70.5	52.6	45.1	79.8	77.7
November	51.1	49.1	64.4	42.4	74.9	31.3	62.0	71.8	53.2	46.1	80.9	78.9
December	51.5	49.3	64.4	41.8	75.3	31.4	62.2	71.9	53.9	46.6	81.3	79.0
1981												
January	51.2	49.1	64.4	41.6	75.4	31.5	61.9	71.6	53.8	46.1	80.6	78.4
February	51.0	48.8	64.3	41.5	75.3	31.1	61.7	71.0	53.4	45.9	80.0	77.8
March	51.2	49.0	64.3	42.0	74.9	31.4	61.7	71.3	53.4	46.2	80.2	77.8
April	51.0	49.2	64.4	42.6	74.8	31.8	61.8	71.2	53.3	45.6	79.7	78.0
May	51.3	49.5	65.1	43.3	75.4	31.8	62.4	71.2	54.0	45.8	79.9	78.1
June	51.5	49.2	64.6	42.9	74.9	31.6	62.8	70.1	54.3	46.5	80.1	77.6
July	51.9	49.3	65.1	43.1	75.5	31.7	63.7	70.3	54.8	46.8	80.5	77.5
August	51.8	49.3	65.1	42.8	75.7	31.6	64.6	70.1	54.4	46.7	80.2	77.3
September	51.6	49.1	64.6	41.8	75.5	31.7	65.8	69.7	54.6	46.4	79.6	76.8
October	51.2	48.7	65.0	41.6	76.3	31.6	67.5	67.6	54.2	45.7	78.8	75.9
November	50.6	48.1	64.8	40.9	76.6	31.0	69.2	66.5	53.9	44.9	77.7	74.8
December	50.1	47.3	64.2	39.2	76.7	30.6	71.0	65.3	53.8	44.3	76.7	73.4
1982												
January	49.0	46.1	63.0	38.1	75.5	29.4	70.4	63.1	52.9	43.6	75.0	71.4
February	50.0	47.4	64.8	39.5	77.4	30.5	74.3	65.4	54.1	44.1	76.4	73.3
March	49.7	47.1	64.4	39.4	76.9	30.1	75.4	64.0	53.9	43.8	75.7	72.6
April	49.2	46.7	64.4	40.1	76.4	29.7	76.2	63.5	53.6	43.2	74.9	71.9
May	48.9	46.6	64.4	40.1	76.4	29.5	77.6	63.8	53.3	42.7	74.2	71.6
June	48.8	46.5	64.8	40.4	76.9	28.9	77.8	63.3	53.2	42.6	73.9	71.4
July	48.6	46.5	65.0	40.6	77.0	28.8	78.9	63.1	53.2	42.3	73.6	71.2
August	48.2	46.1	64.8	40.0	77.1	28.1	78.6	63.2	53.2	41.9	72.8	70.5
September	48.0	46.0	64.8	39.5	77.5	28.0	79.3	63.3	53.3	41.7	72.5	70.2
October	47.6	45.4	64.8	38.9	77.9	27.4	79.0	62.4	53.1	41.2	71.8	69.3
November	47.4	45.2	64.7	38.9	77.7	27.2	79.3	62.1	53.1	41.0	71.5	68.9
December	47.1	45.0	63.8	38.8	76.4	27.5	78.7	61.6	52.9	40.6	70.9	68.6
1983												
January	48.0	46.1	65.2	40.5	77.5	27.6	78.2	63.8	53.5	41.6	72.2	70.1
February	47.7	46.1	64.4	40.4	76.2	27.5	76.9	63.5	53.4	41.4	71.8	70.1
March	48.1	46.5	64.7	40.9	76.3	27.8	76.9	64.2	54.2	41.8	72.3	70.7
April	48.7	47.0	66.0	41.8	77.7	27.8	76.4	65.1	54.9	42.3	73.2	71.5
May	49.0	47.6	66.2	42.6	77.6	28.2	76.0	66.3	55.0	42.6	73.7	72.3
June	49.3	48.0	66.4	43.4	77.5	28.4	75.5	67.5	55.2	42.9	74.1	72.8
July	50.0	48.6	67.3	44.4	78.2	29.0	76.5	68.9	55.9	43.6	75.1	73.8
August	50.6	49.1	67.9	45.2	78.6	29.3	77.1	69.2	56.5	44.2	76.0	74.5
September	51.3	50.0	68.8	46.0	79.4	30.1	77.7	70.0	57.5	44.8	77.1	75.8
October	51.7	50.5	68.4	46.7	78.4	30.4	78.8	71.2	57.7	45.4	77.6	76.5
November	51.9	50.8	68.5	46.7	78.5	30.7	79.4	71.0	58.0	45.6	77.9	76.8
December	52.2	50.9	68.5	47.8	77.9	31.0	80.2	71.2	58.1	45.8	78.2	76.9
1984												
January	53.2	51.8	69.9	48.9	79.4	31.7	82.3	71.6	59.2	46.8	79.7	78.2
February	53.5	52.4	69.8	49.1	79.1	32.0	84.1	73.2	59.4	47.0	79.9	79.0
March	53.7	52.6	70.1	49.2	79.4	32.3	84.6	72.8	59.9	47.2	80.2	79.2
April	54.0	52.9	70.2	49.1	79.8	32.6	86.6	73.3	59.9	47.5	80.6	79.5
May	54.3	53.0	70.0	48.7	79.7	32.7	87.5	73.4	60.8	47.9	80.8	79.5
June	54.5	53.3	70.0	48.8	79.5	33.1	88.8	74.0	61.1	47.9	81.0	79.7
July	54.7	53.5	69.9	49.3	79.2	33.5	87.7	73.7	61.3	48.1	81.0	79.9
August	54.7	53.6	69.6	49.7	78.4	33.8	90.6	74.0	61.4	48.1	81.0	79.8
September	54.6	53.4	69.4	49.0	78.5	33.9	92.5	74.2	61.3	47.8	80.6	79.4
October	54.6	53.7	70.0	48.6	79.7	34.2	93.5	74.0	61.5	47.4	80.4	79.6
November	54.7	53.8	70.2	49.3	79.6	34.5	92.7	73.8	61.8	47.6	80.4	79.5
December	54.8	54.0	70.5	49.9	79.8	34.7	94.5	74.5	61.4	47.4	80.3	79.5
1985												
January	54.7	53.8	70.1	49.3	79.5	34.6	94.9	73.2	61.4	47.6	80.0	79.1
February	54.9	53.7	70.5	48.8	80.4	34.4	95.8	73.4	62.0	47.7	80.1	78.6
March	55.0	54.1	70.5	49.4	79.9	34.7	97.3	75.3	62.0	47.6	80.0	78.9
April	54.9	53.9	70.1	48.7	79.8	34.5	97.6	75.3	62.3	47.6	79.7	78.5
May	55.0	54.0	70.2	48.7	80.0	34.5	98.2	75.6	62.4	47.6	79.6	78.4
June	54.9	54.0	70.4	48.6	80.4	34.5	99.5	75.9	62.0	47.5	79.3	78.2
July	54.6	53.8	70.2	48.7	80.0	34.4	98.8	75.7	61.7	47.2	78.7	77.7
August	54.8	54.0	70.5	49.2	80.2	34.4	100.4	75.8	62.2	47.3	78.8	77.9
September	55.0	54.1	70.9	49.1	80.8	34.4	100.7	75.8	62.6	47.5	79.0	77.8
October	54.8	54.0	70.8	48.9	80.8	34.3	102.0	75.8	62.2	47.3	78.5	77.5
November	55.0	54.3	71.2	50.1	80.7	34.6	103.5	75.8	62.4	47.3	78.7	77.9
December	55.6	54.5	71.9	50.1	81.7	34.5	104.2	75.6	63.3	48.0	79.3	78.0

Table 2-4A. Industrial Production and Capacity Utilization, Historical Data, 1955–2020—*Continued*

(Seasonally adjusted.)

Year and month	Production indexes, 2007 = 100										Capacity utilization (output as percent of capacity)	
	Total industry	Manufac-turing (SIC)	Market groups								Total industry	Manufac-turing (SIC)
			Consumer goods			Business equipment	Defense and space equipment	Construction supplies	Business supplies	Materials		
			Total	Durable	Nondurable							
1986												
January	55.9	55.2	72.7	51.4	82.3	34.6	105.0	77.2	63.7	48.1	79.6	78.8
February	55.5	54.8	72.1	51.0	81.5	34.2	103.5	76.4	63.2	47.9	79.0	78.3
March	55.1	54.6	71.8	51.0	81.1	34.2	104.5	76.6	62.8	47.3	78.3	78.0
April	55.2	54.9	72.3	51.0	81.9	34.0	104.7	77.4	63.4	47.3	78.3	78.3
May	55.3	55.0	72.7	51.0	82.5	33.9	105.1	77.8	63.9	47.2	78.3	78.3
June	55.0	54.7	72.7	51.6	82.1	33.6	105.2	77.0	64.2	47.0	78.0	77.9
July	55.4	55.0	73.1	52.3	82.4	33.8	106.1	77.4	64.3	47.3	78.4	78.3
August	55.3	55.2	73.1	52.5	82.2	33.8	106.3	78.2	64.4	47.1	78.1	78.4
September	55.4	55.3	73.2	53.0	82.1	33.9	105.9	78.4	64.6	47.3	78.3	78.5
October	55.7	55.5	73.5	53.0	82.5	33.8	106.3	78.3	64.9	47.6	78.5	78.7
November	55.9	55.7	74.0	53.7	82.8	33.8	106.9	78.5	64.9	47.8	78.7	78.8
December	56.4	56.3	74.7	54.8	83.4	34.2	107.1	79.0	65.8	48.2	79.3	79.4
1987												
January	56.2	56.1	73.9	54.4	82.4	34.2	107.6	79.8	65.3	48.1	78.9	78.9
February	57.0	56.9	74.9	55.3	83.3	35.0	108.0	81.4	65.9	48.7	79.8	79.9
March	57.0	57.0	75.1	55.0	83.7	35.0	107.7	81.1	66.3	48.8	79.8	79.8
April	57.4	57.3	75.0	54.6	83.8	35.3	107.9	81.5	67.0	49.2	80.1	80.0
May	57.8	57.7	75.5	55.0	84.5	35.6	107.6	82.1	67.8	49.4	80.5	80.4
June	58.1	57.9	75.8	54.5	85.1	35.8	107.1	82.3	68.1	49.8	80.8	80.5
July	58.5	58.4	76.3	54.4	86.0	36.1	106.8	82.6	68.6	50.2	81.2	80.9
August	58.9	58.7	76.7	54.9	86.3	36.6	107.9	83.2	68.9	50.5	81.6	81.2
September	59.1	59.1	76.4	55.4	85.6	37.2	108.2	83.7	69.1	50.7	81.8	81.5
October	59.9	60.0	77.8	57.2	86.7	37.9	107.9	84.8	69.7	51.4	82.8	82.6
November	60.2	60.3	77.8	57.1	86.8	38.2	108.2	84.8	69.6	51.9	83.1	82.9
December	60.6	60.7	78.0	56.6	87.3	38.6	109.2	85.4	69.8	52.2	83.4	83.3
1988												
January	60.6	60.6	78.3	56.4	87.9	38.7	111.7	84.0	70.0	52.0	83.3	83.1
February	60.9	60.8	78.7	56.4	88.5	39.0	109.9	84.8	70.5	52.2	83.7	83.2
March	61.0	60.9	78.6	56.7	88.1	39.4	109.1	85.1	70.4	52.4	83.8	83.4
April	61.4	61.4	79.2	58.1	88.3	39.8	108.2	84.8	70.5	52.8	84.3	84.1
May	61.2	61.3	78.8	58.1	87.7	40.0	107.8	85.0	69.9	52.7	84.1	83.9
June	61.4	61.4	78.8	58.3	87.5	40.3	107.1	84.3	70.1	53.0	84.3	84.0
July	61.4	61.3	78.7	57.1	88.2	40.0	108.3	84.4	70.4	53.0	84.3	83.9
August	61.7	61.4	79.3	57.5	88.8	40.2	108.1	83.9	71.0	53.3	84.7	84.0
September	61.5	61.6	78.8	58.5	87.4	40.6	108.1	84.1	70.5	53.1	84.4	84.2
October	61.8	61.9	79.4	59.1	88.0	40.8	108.5	84.4	70.8	53.2	84.6	84.5
November	62.0	62.1	79.5	59.8	87.8	40.9	108.4	84.8	70.9	53.4	84.8	84.8
December	62.2	62.4	79.9	60.5	88.0	41.0	108.9	85.0	71.1	53.6	85.1	85.0
1989												
January	62.4	62.9	80.0	61.9	87.3	41.5	108.7	86.4	71.1	53.8	85.2	85.6
February	62.1	62.3	80.0	61.3	87.7	41.3	108.8	84.3	71.3	53.4	84.7	84.7
March	62.3	62.3	80.1	60.4	88.4	41.1	108.1	84.6	72.0	53.6	84.8	84.4
April	62.3	62.3	80.0	60.8	87.9	41.7	109.7	84.5	71.4	53.5	84.7	84.4
May	61.9	61.9	79.2	59.6	87.5	41.2	110.3	83.8	71.2	53.4	84.0	83.6
June	61.9	62.0	79.2	58.9	88.0	41.7	109.8	84.0	71.4	53.1	83.8	83.5
July	61.3	61.2	77.5	56.9	86.4	41.2	110.5	84.0	70.7	52.9	82.8	82.3
August	61.9	61.8	78.8	59.0	87.2	41.8	111.0	84.0	71.2	53.3	83.5	82.8
September	61.7	61.7	78.6	59.0	86.8	41.6	110.5	83.8	71.4	53.0	83.0	82.4
October	61.7	61.5	78.7	57.9	87.7	41.0	106.2	84.1	71.5	53.1	82.7	82.0
November	61.9	61.6	79.0	58.3	88.0	41.3	104.8	84.1	71.8	53.3	82.8	82.0
December	62.2	61.7	80.3	58.9	89.5	41.9	107.2	83.1	72.1	53.2	83.0	81.8
1990												
January	61.9	61.6	78.6	55.7	88.7	41.5	107.7	84.9	72.8	53.2	82.4	81.5
February	62.5	62.4	79.6	59.1	88.3	42.2	107.3	85.3	72.6	53.6	83.0	82.4
March	62.8	62.8	80.1	60.2	88.5	42.9	106.9	85.1	73.1	53.7	83.2	82.6
April	62.6	62.5	79.8	58.8	88.7	42.7	105.9	84.3	73.0	53.8	82.8	82.1
May	62.8	62.7	79.7	59.3	88.4	43.3	105.1	83.8	73.4	53.9	82.9	82.2
June	63.0	62.9	80.5	60.1	89.2	43.3	104.9	84.1	73.3	54.0	83.0	82.2
July	62.9	62.7	79.8	58.4	89.1	43.5	105.3	83.4	73.5	54.0	82.7	81.9
August	63.2	63.0	80.1	58.3	89.6	43.8	103.8	83.3	73.5	54.4	82.9	82.0
September	63.2	62.9	80.7	58.5	90.3	43.8	103.5	83.0	73.4	54.2	82.8	81.7
October	62.8	62.5	79.6	56.6	89.7	43.7	103.9	82.1	73.3	54.0	82.2	81.1
November	62.0	61.7	78.7	53.6	90.0	42.6	101.9	82.1	73.0	53.3	81.0	80.0
December	61.6	61.3	78.1	52.7	89.6	42.3	103.3	81.5	72.5	52.9	80.4	79.3
1991												
January	61.4	60.8	78.5	52.8	90.2	42.1	102.0	78.5	72.3	52.6	80.0	78.6
February	60.9	60.4	77.8	51.6	89.7	41.8	101.0	78.3	71.7	52.3	79.3	78.0
March	60.6	60.0	77.8	51.9	89.7	41.8	100.4	77.3	70.8	51.9	78.8	77.3
April	60.8	60.2	77.9	53.0	89.1	41.8	97.7	78.0	71.2	52.2	79.0	77.6
May	61.4	60.6	79.2	53.9	90.6	42.0	95.9	78.1	71.8	52.7	79.7	78.0
June	61.8	61.2	80.1	55.3	91.3	42.5	96.3	79.4	72.2	53.0	80.2	78.7
July	62.0	61.5	79.9	56.3	90.4	42.7	95.7	79.2	71.8	53.4	80.4	79.0
August	62.0	61.6	79.9	55.5	90.9	42.5	96.2	80.0	72.3	53.4	80.3	79.0
September	62.5	62.2	81.1	57.8	91.4	43.1	95.7	80.3	72.7	53.7	80.9	79.7
October	62.5	62.2	80.9	57.5	91.2	42.8	96.1	79.5	72.5	53.7	80.7	79.5
November	62.4	62.0	81.0	57.7	91.3	42.8	95.6	80.2	72.6	53.5	80.4	79.2
December	62.1	61.9	80.0	57.2	90.0	42.8	94.6	80.2	72.5	53.5	80.0	78.9

Table 2-4A. Industrial Production and Capacity Utilization, Historical Data, 1955–2020—*Continued*

(Seasonally adjusted.)

Year and month	Production indexes, 2007 = 100											Capacity utilization (output as percent of capacity)	
	Total industry	Manufac-turing (SIC)	Market groups									Total industry	Manufac-turing (SIC)
			Consumer goods			Business equipment	Defense and space equipment	Construction supplies	Business supplies	Materials			
			Total	Durable	Nondurable								
1992													
January	61.8	61.5	79.2	54.7	90.2	42.0	93.5	80.3	72.4	53.4		79.4	78.3
February	62.2	62.1	80.0	57.0	90.2	42.9	93.0	81.0	72.4	53.7		79.8	78.8
March	62.7	62.7	80.7	58.2	90.6	43.4	92.3	81.5	72.9	54.1		80.3	79.4
April	63.2	63.1	81.5	59.3	91.2	43.8	90.8	82.1	73.4	54.5		80.7	79.7
May	63.4	63.4	82.0	61.1	91.0	44.2	90.4	82.9	73.6	54.5		80.8	79.9
June	63.4	63.6	81.6	60.3	90.8	44.3	90.3	82.6	73.6	54.8		80.7	80.0
July	64.0	64.2	82.7	61.9	91.6	44.8	89.4	83.1	74.1	55.2		81.3	80.5
August	63.7	63.9	82.7	61.4	91.9	44.5	89.1	83.3	73.9	54.6		80.6	79.9
September	63.9	64.0	82.3	61.2	91.4	44.7	89.1	83.2	74.2	55.0		80.7	79.8
October	64.3	64.4	83.5	62.5	92.5	44.9	88.8	83.3	74.4	55.3		81.1	80.1
November	64.6	64.6	83.6	63.0	92.4	45.2	88.6	83.0	74.6	55.6		81.3	80.2
December	64.6	64.6	83.7	63.7	92.1	45.6	88.7	83.2	75.0	55.6		81.3	80.0
1993													
January	64.9	65.2	84.2	64.7	92.3	45.8	88.1	83.6	75.1	55.8		81.5	80.6
February	65.2	65.4	84.3	64.4	92.6	45.8	87.4	85.1	75.5	56.2		81.7	80.7
March	65.2	65.2	84.3	64.8	92.5	45.9	86.5	84.4	76.1	56.0		81.5	80.4
April	65.4	65.6	84.4	65.1	92.4	46.2	86.5	84.6	76.0	56.3		81.6	80.7
May	65.1	65.5	83.8	65.1	91.5	46.3	85.6	85.6	75.7	56.1		81.2	80.4
June	65.2	65.4	83.9	64.6	92.0	45.9	85.0	85.6	75.8	56.4		81.3	80.2
July	65.4	65.5	84.6	64.4	93.1	45.9	86.0	86.0	75.9	56.3		81.3	80.3
August	65.3	65.4	84.5	63.7	93.3	45.5	84.3	86.3	76.0	56.4		81.1	79.9
September	65.7	65.8	84.8	65.0	93.0	46.3	84.7	86.7	76.2	56.6		81.4	80.3
October	66.2	66.4	85.2	66.7	92.8	47.3	84.0	87.5	76.4	57.0		81.9	80.9
November	66.5	66.7	85.3	67.3	92.7	47.6	83.9	88.3	76.5	57.5		82.1	81.1
December	66.8	67.1	85.5	67.6	92.8	47.9	83.2	89.4	77.0	57.9		82.4	81.4
1994													
January	67.1	67.2	86.1	68.6	93.2	48.1	82.2	89.1	77.4	57.9		82.5	81.3
February	67.1	67.3	86.3	68.5	93.4	47.7	80.9	88.4	77.6	58.2		82.4	81.2
March	67.8	68.1	87.0	69.1	94.2	48.2	81.8	90.0	78.2	58.8		83.0	82.1
April	68.2	68.8	87.2	70.0	94.1	48.6	82.1	91.4	78.4	59.2		83.3	82.5
May	68.5	69.2	87.7	70.2	94.8	48.8	80.8	92.2	78.5	59.6		83.4	82.8
June	69.0	69.4	88.4	70.8	95.4	49.0	79.8	92.3	79.1	60.0		83.7	82.7
July	69.1	69.6	87.9	71.0	94.6	49.6	79.3	93.2	78.9	60.3		83.6	82.8
August	69.5	70.2	89.1	72.2	95.7	49.8	78.2	93.2	79.0	60.7		83.8	83.2
September	69.7	70.5	88.6	72.4	94.9	50.3	78.9	94.0	79.4	61.0		83.8	83.3
October	70.3	71.2	89.4	73.4	95.7	51.2	78.7	94.3	79.9	61.3		84.2	83.7
November	70.7	71.8	89.5	73.3	95.9	51.8	79.7	94.5	80.2	61.9		84.5	84.1
December	71.5	72.5	90.2	73.9	96.5	52.3	79.9	95.5	80.7	62.7		85.1	84.7
1995													
January	71.6	72.7	90.0	74.3	96.1	52.6	79.7	95.6	81.0	62.9		84.9	84.5
February	71.5	72.5	90.2	73.9	96.6	52.6	78.4	94.4	81.0	62.7		84.5	84.0
March	71.6	72.7	90.2	73.8	96.6	53.1	78.6	94.4	81.2	62.8		84.3	83.9
April	71.5	72.5	89.7	73.5	96.1	53.0	78.1	93.6	81.0	62.9		83.9	83.3
May	71.8	72.7	90.0	73.0	96.8	53.7	78.2	93.2	81.5	63.1		84.0	83.2
June	72.1	73.0	90.4	73.4	97.2	54.3	78.5	93.4	81.9	63.2		84.0	83.3
July	71.7	72.5	89.9	71.9	97.2	54.0	77.8	93.1	81.8	62.9		83.3	82.3
August	72.7	73.4	91.3	74.1	98.1	55.1	77.5	94.0	82.8	63.6		84.1	82.9
September	73.0	74.1	91.5	75.0	98.0	55.6	77.2	95.5	82.8	63.9		84.1	83.3
October	72.9	74.0	90.7	74.1	97.2	55.5	76.1	95.4	83.0	64.0		83.6	82.8
November	73.0	74.0	91.0	74.2	97.6	55.7	74.6	95.4	83.3	64.2		83.4	82.4
December	73.3	74.3	91.3	74.7	97.8	56.1	74.6	95.9	83.3	64.4		83.4	82.3
1996													
January	72.9	73.8	90.2	72.7	97.2	55.5	73.7	94.5	83.0	64.4		82.6	81.3
February	74.0	74.8	91.6	74.6	98.3	56.9	75.8	95.5	83.8	65.2		83.4	82.1
March	73.9	74.7	91.1	72.3	98.6	56.8	76.1	96.7	84.0	65.2		82.9	81.4
April	74.6	75.6	91.9	75.7	98.3	58.2	76.0	97.3	84.0	65.8		83.4	82.0
May	75.2	76.2	92.0	76.1	98.2	58.9	76.1	98.2	84.8	66.4		83.6	82.2
June	75.7	76.9	92.7	77.7	98.4	59.8	75.4	99.8	85.0	66.8		83.8	82.5
July	75.7	77.2	92.2	78.0	97.6	60.6	76.1	99.4	85.1	66.8		83.4	82.4
August	76.1	77.6	91.9	77.0	97.6	60.9	76.0	100.2	86.0	67.4		83.5	82.3
September	76.6	78.2	92.9	77.8	98.6	61.6	75.8	100.6	86.3	67.7		83.6	82.6
October	76.6	78.1	92.3	76.1	98.6	61.4	75.6	100.7	86.6	67.8		83.2	82.0
November	77.2	78.8	93.4	77.2	99.7	62.3	75.2	101.4	87.3	68.3		83.6	82.3
December	77.7	79.5	93.6	78.4	99.5	63.5	75.1	100.9	87.8	68.8		83.7	82.6
1997													
January	77.9	79.6	93.4	77.9	99.4	63.8	74.1	100.0	88.4	69.0		83.4	82.2
February	78.8	80.7	93.9	79.2	99.5	64.9	74.6	102.0	89.3	70.0		84.0	82.9
March	79.3	81.5	94.6	80.1	99.9	65.8	74.3	102.9	89.4	70.3		84.1	83.2
April	79.3	81.4	93.6	78.1	99.6	66.4	74.5	102.7	89.8	70.6		83.7	82.6
May	79.8	82.0	94.3	78.9	100.2	67.1	74.3	103.2	90.3	70.8		83.7	82.7
June	80.1	82.5	94.2	80.5	99.3	68.2	74.0	103.1	90.5	71.3		83.7	82.7
July	80.8	83.1	95.1	80.6	100.6	68.6	74.4	103.1	91.2	71.9		83.9	82.8
August	81.6	84.1	96.0	82.2	101.0	70.2	74.8	103.9	91.4	72.6		84.2	83.3
September	82.4	84.9	96.7	82.9	101.7	70.8	74.7	104.4	92.5	73.5		84.5	83.5
October	83.1	85.7	98.2	83.9	103.4	71.8	74.9	105.0	93.6	73.7		84.7	83.6
November	83.8	86.5	98.4	86.0	102.7	73.0	74.5	105.3	93.8	74.5		84.9	83.8
December	84.1	87.0	98.1	85.8	102.3	73.6	75.7	106.7	94.2	75.0		84.7	83.7

Table 2-4A. Industrial Production and Capacity Utilization, Historical Data, 1955–2020—*Continued*

(Seasonally adjusted.)

Year and month	Production indexes, 2007 = 100										Capacity utilization (output as percent of capacity)	
	Total industry	Manufac- turing (SIC)	Market groups								Total industry	Manufac- turing (SIC)
			Consumer goods			Business equipment	Defense and space equipment	Construction supplies	Business supplies	Materials		
			Total	Durable	Nondurable							
1998												
January	84.5	87.6	98.5	86.2	102.8	74.5	76.2	107.4	94.1	75.2	84.5	83.7
February	84.6	87.8	98.4	86.1	102.7	74.8	76.6	108.0	94.5	75.3	84.1	83.2
March	84.7	87.6	98.5	86.3	102.7	75.2	76.1	107.2	94.9	75.2	83.6	82.5
April	85.0	88.0	99.1	86.6	103.5	75.4	76.2	107.7	95.2	75.4	83.4	82.3
May	85.5	88.5	99.5	87.2	103.7	75.9	77.1	109.0	96.0	76.0	83.4	82.1
June	85.0	87.8	98.4	83.2	104.1	75.9	77.4	108.5	96.1	75.4	82.4	80.9
July	84.7	87.4	97.6	79.9	104.4	75.5	78.6	109.2	96.7	75.0	81.6	80.1
August	86.4	89.6	100.3	89.2	104.0	77.8	78.9	109.5	97.2	76.5	82.8	81.5
September	86.3	89.5	99.6	89.2	102.9	77.8	78.4	109.2	97.4	76.7	82.3	81.0
October	87.0	90.3	100.0	90.8	102.8	78.7	80.1	110.2	97.6	77.4	82.5	81.3
November	86.9	90.4	99.3	90.6	101.9	78.7	79.6	110.5	97.9	77.5	82.1	80.9
December	87.3	90.9	99.4	91.3	101.7	78.8	79.1	111.7	97.9	78.1	82.0	81.0
1999												
January	87.6	91.2	100.4	91.4	103.1	78.8	78.8	111.1	98.6	78.4	82.0	80.8
February	88.1	92.0	100.8	92.2	103.4	79.4	79.4	111.3	98.9	78.9	82.1	81.1
March	88.3	92.0	100.6	91.9	103.2	79.4	79.1	110.1	99.3	79.4	81.9	80.7
April	88.5	92.3	100.5	92.9	102.5	79.8	78.0	110.4	99.5	79.8	81.8	80.6
May	89.0	93.0	101.4	93.8	103.5	80.6	77.2	110.7	99.8	80.2	82.0	80.9
June	89.0	92.8	100.5	93.3	102.3	80.4	76.1	110.8	99.9	80.6	81.6	80.3
July	89.5	93.2	100.1	93.7	101.6	81.0	75.9	111.6	100.4	81.6	81.8	80.3
August	89.9	93.8	101.4	95.7	102.5	81.5	75.3	111.5	100.5	81.6	81.9	80.5
September	89.5	93.3	100.6	94.2	102.1	81.2	73.2	111.6	100.5	81.4	81.2	79.8
October	90.7	94.7	102.5	97.4	103.4	81.8	72.7	113.0	101.3	82.4	82.0	80.7
November	91.1	95.4	102.4	96.6	103.7	81.9	71.2	113.7	102.0	83.3	82.1	80.9
December	91.8	96.0	103.5	96.7	105.2	82.6	70.1	114.8	102.7	83.8	82.5	81.1
2000												
January	91.8	96.1	102.2	98.5	102.5	83.9	70.1	115.2	102.9	83.9	82.2	80.8
February	92.1	96.3	103.0	98.2	103.8	84.5	68.5	115.4	103.0	84.1	82.2	80.7
March	92.5	96.9	102.6	97.8	103.4	85.7	67.8	115.5	103.7	84.6	82.2	80.9
April	93.1	97.6	103.4	99.1	104.0	86.6	66.4	116.0	104.7	84.9	82.4	81.0
May	93.3	97.6	103.6	98.7	104.5	87.4	65.7	114.3	104.9	85.3	82.4	80.7
June	93.4	97.7	103.7	98.3	104.8	87.5	66.2	113.8	104.7	85.5	82.2	80.5
July	93.2	97.8	103.3	96.9	104.7	88.0	67.6	114.4	104.7	85.1	81.7	80.3
August	93.0	97.1	102.8	96.6	104.2	87.6	65.8	113.5	104.4	85.1	81.3	79.4
September	93.4	97.6	103.8	96.9	105.5	88.4	63.7	113.7	104.4	85.3	81.3	79.5
October	93.0	97.2	102.7	95.8	104.4	88.5	66.0	113.2	104.0	85.1	80.8	78.9
November	93.0	96.9	103.0	93.8	105.6	88.2	68.1	112.8	104.2	85.0	80.5	78.4
December	92.7	96.4	103.6	92.4	107.0	87.5	68.8	111.3	103.7	84.5	80.0	77.6
2001												
January	92.2	95.9	102.7	90.8	106.5	87.5	70.8	111.9	103.8	83.6	79.3	76.9
February	91.6	95.2	102.0	90.4	105.7	86.9	70.5	110.6	102.2	83.2	78.5	76.1
March	91.4	95.0	102.0	92.6	104.8	86.3	72.5	110.7	101.6	82.9	78.1	75.7
April	91.1	94.7	102.4	92.7	105.2	84.4	73.1	110.5	100.9	82.8	77.6	75.2
May	90.5	94.1	102.4	93.4	105.0	82.9	73.6	109.7	100.4	82.1	76.9	74.5
June	90.0	93.5	102.4	92.9	105.2	81.9	74.8	109.0	100.0	81.4	76.3	73.9
July	89.5	93.0	101.9	93.3	104.3	81.0	75.7	109.0	99.8	80.7	75.6	73.3
August	89.4	92.6	102.1	92.6	104.9	79.5	74.7	107.7	99.5	81.0	75.3	72.9
September	88.9	92.3	101.6	91.7	104.5	78.2	75.3	107.6	99.4	80.7	74.8	72.5
October	88.6	91.9	102.1	90.9	105.5	77.2	75.2	106.5	99.1	80.3	74.4	72.0
November	88.1	91.5	101.9	92.5	104.7	76.5	74.2	106.1	98.3	79.7	73.8	71.6
December	88.1	91.8	102.5	94.6	104.6	75.8	74.4	106.9	98.4	79.5	73.7	71.7
2002												
January	88.7	92.3	103.5	95.0	105.9	75.5	73.7	106.7	98.2	80.4	74.0	72.1
February	88.7	92.3	102.8	95.2	104.8	75.4	73.2	107.1	98.3	80.8	73.9	72.0
March	89.4	93.0	103.7	96.2	105.6	75.7	73.1	108.7	99.1	81.5	74.4	72.4
April	89.8	93.3	103.6	97.6	104.8	75.4	73.2	108.7	99.8	82.4	74.7	72.6
May	90.2	93.7	103.9	98.1	105.1	75.7	73.1	109.2	100.3	82.8	75.0	73.0
June	90.9	94.6	105.0	99.1	106.2	76.2	73.9	109.9	100.7	83.5	75.5	73.7
July	90.9	94.5	105.1	100.4	105.7	76.0	74.2	108.6	100.8	83.5	75.5	73.6
August	90.8	94.6	104.4	99.5	105.2	76.3	74.6	109.0	100.8	83.6	75.4	73.6
September	90.9	94.7	104.5	99.5	105.4	76.4	75.7	109.9	101.4	83.4	75.5	73.7
October	90.6	94.4	104.3	99.0	105.4	76.0	76.4	109.5	101.9	82.9	75.3	73.4
November	91.1	94.9	105.2	101.3	105.5	76.3	76.0	109.5	101.7	83.6	75.7	73.8
December	90.6	94.3	104.2	99.7	104.9	75.5	78.9	108.6	101.5	83.3	75.3	73.4
2003												
January	91.4	95.0	105.5	101.4	106.0	75.7	79.0	109.1	102.6	83.8	75.9	74.0
February	91.5	94.9	106.0	99.8	107.3	75.6	79.9	108.2	102.7	83.8	76.1	73.9
March	91.2	95.0	105.9	100.1	107.1	75.8	79.9	107.7	102.6	83.3	75.9	73.9
April	90.6	94.3	105.1	99.2	106.4	75.1	79.4	106.6	101.6	83.0	75.4	73.4
May	90.6	94.3	104.8	99.2	105.9	75.0	80.0	108.0	101.8	82.9	75.4	73.4
June	90.7	94.7	105.0	100.2	105.8	75.3	80.0	108.4	101.4	83.0	75.5	73.7
July	91.2	95.0	106.1	102.7	106.2	75.6	79.4	107.9	101.9	83.3	75.9	74.0
August	91.0	94.6	105.2	100.7	105.8	75.8	79.8	108.6	101.7	83.3	75.8	73.7
September	91.6	95.4	106.1	103.3	106.0	76.6	80.0	108.4	101.8	83.9	76.3	74.3
October	91.7	95.5	105.4	102.6	105.3	76.4	79.8	109.0	102.3	84.4	76.4	74.4
November	92.4	96.3	106.1	103.8	105.7	77.7	79.1	110.2	102.7	84.9	76.9	75.1
December	92.4	96.3	106.3	103.8	106.0	77.6	77.3	110.1	102.6	85.0	77.0	75.1

Table 2-4A. Industrial Production and Capacity Utilization, Historical Data, 1955–2020—*Continued*

(Seasonally adjusted.)

Year and month	Production indexes, 2007 = 100										Capacity utilization (output as percent of capacity)	
	Total industry	Manufac-turing (SIC)	Market groups									
			Consumer goods			Business equipment	Defense and space equipment	Construction supplies	Business supplies	Materials	Total industry	Manufac-turing (SIC)
			Total	Durable	Nondurable							
2004												
January	92.6	96.2	106.6	104.9	106.0	77.8	75.2	110.1	103.0	85.1	77.1	75.0
February	93.1	96.9	107.1	104.7	106.9	78.8	76.5	110.0	103.8	85.6	77.6	75.6
March	92.7	96.9	106.1	103.8	105.8	78.7	76.8	110.1	103.2	85.4	77.3	75.6
April	93.1	97.2	106.7	103.8	106.7	78.9	76.7	109.9	103.8	85.8	77.7	75.9
May	93.8	97.9	107.2	103.0	107.6	79.6	77.3	111.1	104.5	86.5	78.2	76.5
June	93.1	97.2	105.7	100.7	106.5	79.5	76.4	110.4	104.4	85.9	77.6	76.0
July	93.8	98.1	106.0	101.2	106.8	81.1	77.8	111.6	105.0	86.5	78.2	76.6
August	93.9	98.6	106.5	102.0	107.1	80.8	78.4	111.8	105.0	86.5	78.3	77.0
September	93.9	98.6	106.4	101.3	107.3	81.0	79.5	110.9	104.8	86.7	78.4	76.9
October	94.8	99.5	107.5	103.6	107.9	81.7	79.7	112.7	105.3	87.5	79.1	77.6
November	95.0	99.5	107.3	102.1	108.2	81.4	80.5	112.4	105.8	88.1	79.2	77.5
December	95.7	100.2	108.1	103.1	108.9	82.2	81.4	112.3	106.6	88.7	79.8	78.0
2005												
January	96.1	100.9	108.4	102.3	109.6	83.6	81.3	113.7	107.4	88.7	80.0	78.4
February	96.8	101.8	109.1	104.6	109.6	84.4	84.2	114.5	107.6	89.4	80.5	79.0
March	96.7	101.3	108.5	102.6	109.6	84.4	85.7	113.3	107.6	89.4	80.3	78.5
April	96.9	101.7	108.5	101.7	110.0	85.4	87.2	115.4	108.3	89.3	80.4	78.7
May	97.0	102.0	109.1	101.7	110.7	86.2	86.6	115.5	108.3	89.0	80.4	78.7
June	97.4	102.1	110.1	102.3	111.8	85.9	87.1	114.5	108.7	89.3	80.6	78.7
July	97.0	101.8	109.6	100.4	111.9	85.4	86.6	115.5	108.3	89.0	80.2	78.3
August	97.4	102.3	110.1	103.3	111.5	86.7	87.5	115.9	108.6	89.1	80.4	78.5
September	95.5	101.2	110.2	105.4	110.9	84.0	84.1	117.5	108.7	85.6	78.7	77.5
October	96.6	102.7	110.2	106.4	110.5	88.5	84.7	119.7	109.0	86.7	79.6	78.5
November	97.7	103.6	110.1	105.0	110.8	89.7	85.1	120.5	109.5	88.4	80.3	79.0
December	98.2	103.7	110.8	103.9	112.2	89.0	85.5	121.3	109.8	89.2	80.6	78.9
2006												
January	98.3	104.5	109.9	105.1	110.6	90.6	83.5	122.2	110.1	89.5	80.6	79.4
February	98.3	104.2	109.4	103.3	110.5	91.0	84.3	121.1	110.0	89.8	80.5	79.1
March	98.6	104.2	109.9	104.2	111.0	91.8	82.3	120.9	110.4	89.8	80.6	79.0
April	98.9	104.6	110.3	104.0	111.5	93.3	82.9	120.3	110.4	90.0	80.8	79.1
May	98.9	104.3	110.1	103.4	111.4	93.4	82.4	119.4	110.2	90.2	80.6	78.8
June	99.2	104.6	110.6	104.0	111.9	94.1	83.1	118.8	110.2	90.4	80.7	78.9
July	99.1	104.2	109.6	100.4	111.9	94.7	84.8	119.2	110.2	90.6	80.5	78.5
August	99.6	105.0	110.6	103.1	112.2	95.6	84.8	118.3	110.0	90.8	80.7	78.9
September	99.4	105.1	110.1	101.4	112.2	95.7	85.9	118.2	110.0	90.7	80.4	78.8
October	99.3	104.6	110.0	100.0	112.5	95.9	87.3	116.9	110.1	90.5	80.1	78.2
November	99.2	104.7	110.2	100.5	112.5	96.3	89.1	116.6	109.8	90.3	79.9	78.1
December	100.3	106.2	110.7	102.9	112.4	97.9	91.0	120.0	110.6	91.2	80.5	79.1
2007												
January	99.9	105.8	110.1	100.3	112.5	96.1	93.4	117.9	110.6	91.2	80.0	78.5
February	100.8	106.1	111.3	101.4	113.7	96.8	94.1	118.1	111.4	92.1	80.6	78.6
March	101.0	107.0	110.4	102.0	112.4	98.6	93.3	119.5	111.8	92.5	80.5	79.0
April	101.7	107.8	111.0	103.7	112.5	99.8	95.8	119.0	112.8	93.2	80.9	79.4
May	101.8	107.7	110.6	103.1	112.2	99.9	97.9	118.6	112.3	93.6	80.8	79.1
June	101.8	108.0	110.8	104.4	112.0	99.9	101.4	119.3	111.6	93.4	80.7	79.1
July	101.7	108.0	110.5	103.3	112.0	99.9	102.7	118.8	110.8	93.5	80.5	78.9
August	102.0	107.7	110.3	103.0	111.8	100.1	104.5	118.3	110.9	94.1	80.6	78.5
September	102.2	108.0	110.2	101.7	112.2	101.5	107.0	118.4	111.4	94.1	80.7	78.6
October	101.9	107.8	109.2	101.4	110.9	101.1	107.0	117.7	111.2	94.2	80.5	78.4
November	102.5	108.4	109.1	101.8	110.8	101.9	109.2	117.7	111.6	95.1	80.9	78.7
December	102.5	108.5	108.8	101.8	110.3	102.9	109.9	117.7	111.1	95.1	80.9	78.7
2008												
January	102.3	108.2	108.6	99.2	110.8	103.4	110.7	117.8	111.0	94.8	80.9	78.4
February	101.9	107.5	108.3	98.6	110.8	103.4	110.4	115.4	110.9	94.4	80.6	77.9
March	101.6	107.0	106.8	96.0	109.6	104.1	110.9	113.9	110.3	94.5	80.4	77.6
April	100.9	106.0	106.2	93.9	109.5	102.1	110.7	111.8	109.4	94.1	79.9	76.9
May	100.3	105.3	105.6	92.9	109.0	102.4	110.4	110.6	108.6	93.4	79.5	76.5
June	100.1	104.6	105.3	93.5	108.5	101.8	111.5	109.4	107.7	93.4	79.3	76.0
July	99.6	103.5	104.6	91.3	108.3	99.9	110.0	109.1	106.9	93.3	79.0	75.3
August	98.1	102.2	102.8	87.4	107.2	97.9	110.0	106.9	106.3	91.8	77.7	74.5
September	93.8	98.8	102.1	86.7	106.5	90.2	107.6	104.2	104.8	85.8	74.3	72.1
October	94.7	98.1	102.3	84.6	107.6	87.6	107.5	102.5	103.9	88.2	74.9	71.7
November	93.5	95.7	101.5	81.3	107.5	88.7	106.9	97.4	101.5	86.9	73.9	70.0
December	90.8	92.5	99.5	77.7	106.1	89.5	106.2	91.8	98.0	83.7	71.7	67.7
2009												
January	88.6	89.5	97.2	69.3	106.1	84.2	106.0	87.9	96.5	82.1	69.8	65.7
February	88.0	89.4	97.3	70.8	105.6	83.8	105.1	86.3	95.3	81.6	69.3	65.7
March	86.6	87.7	96.7	70.6	104.9	82.1	103.3	83.4	94.2	80.1	68.1	64.5
April	85.9	87.1	96.4	70.8	104.5	80.5	102.7	81.9	93.7	79.5	67.5	64.2
May	85.1	86.2	95.2	67.9	103.9	78.2	102.7	81.5	93.3	79.0	66.8	63.6
June	84.8	86.0	94.8	67.2	103.5	77.5	103.2	81.6	93.4	78.7	66.6	63.5
July	85.7	87.3	96.0	73.9	102.8	78.7	104.7	81.9	93.3	79.8	67.3	64.6
August	86.7	88.3	96.8	74.7	103.7	79.6	105.6	82.5	93.8	81.0	68.1	65.4
September	87.4	89.1	97.6	77.9	103.5	80.2	106.9	82.2	94.1	81.9	68.7	66.1
October	87.7	89.2	97.9	76.6	104.4	80.5	106.4	80.9	94.8	82.1	69.0	66.3
November	88.0	90.1	97.3	78.0	103.1	80.4	106.9	82.6	95.0	82.9	69.4	67.0
December	88.3	90.0	97.2	77.4	103.2	81.8	107.0	80.6	95.9	83.2	69.7	67.0

Table 2-4A. Industrial Production and Capacity Utilization, Historical Data, 1955–2020—*Continued*

(Seasonally adjusted.)

Year and month	Production indexes, 2007 = 100										Capacity utilization (output as percent of capacity)	
			Market groups									
	Total industry	Manufac-turing (SIC)	Consumer goods			Business equipment	Defense and space equipment	Construction supplies	Business supplies	Materials	Total industry	Manufac-turing (SIC)
			Total	Durable	Nondurable							
2010												
January	89.3	90.9	97.8	78.3	103.8	83.1	109.8	82.3	96.3	84.3	70.6	67.8
February	89.6	90.8	97.0	77.0	103.1	82.6	110.4	82.3	96.3	85.4	71.0	67.8
March	90.2	92.0	97.4	78.0	103.2	84.2	113.2	83.8	96.4	85.9	71.7	68.8
April	90.6	92.7	96.5	78.2	102.0	85.2	114.3	86.3	97.1	86.4	72.1	69.5
May	91.8	93.9	98.3	81.0	103.5	86.9	114.2	86.6	97.9	87.5	73.3	70.5
June	92.0	93.9	98.1	80.3	103.4	87.3	113.9	86.5	97.9	88.0	73.6	70.6
July	92.4	94.4	98.7	83.4	103.2	88.3	115.7	86.1	97.9	88.3	74.1	71.2
August	92.7	94.5	98.5	81.0	103.7	88.3	115.7	86.6	97.8	89.0	74.5	71.4
September	92.9	94.6	98.1	81.0	103.2	88.6	113.6	86.7	97.9	89.6	74.7	71.5
October	92.7	94.6	98.1	81.4	103.1	88.9	112.0	86.8	97.3	89.3	74.7	71.7
November	92.8	94.8	97.6	80.3	102.8	88.8	111.7	87.6	98.3	89.4	74.8	71.9
December	93.6	95.2	98.7	80.0	104.3	89.5	110.9	86.4	98.7	90.6	75.6	72.3
2011												
January	93.5	95.3	98.7	80.8	104.1	90.2	110.6	86.1	98.2	90.2	75.5	72.4
February	93.1	95.4	98.5	82.8	103.1	90.4	109.8	85.5	98.2	89.5	75.1	72.6
March	94.0	96.0	98.7	84.2	103.0	90.2	109.0	86.3	98.4	91.2	75.9	73.1
April	93.7	95.5	98.6	81.0	103.8	89.5	108.8	86.3	98.3	90.8	75.6	72.8
May	93.8	95.5	98.8	81.9	103.7	90.3	108.6	87.4	98.2	90.7	75.7	72.8
June	94.1	95.6	98.7	81.6	103.7	90.3	107.8	87.7	98.0	91.2	75.8	72.9
July	94.6	96.2	99.4	82.8	104.2	91.5	108.5	88.6	98.3	91.5	76.2	73.3
August	95.2	96.6	99.9	83.7	104.7	92.6	109.3	88.4	98.7	92.0	76.5	73.6
September	95.1	96.9	99.3	83.8	103.9	93.1	108.9	88.5	99.0	92.0	76.4	73.8
October	95.7	97.3	99.5	85.3	103.7	94.3	110.1	88.6	98.6	92.8	76.7	74.1
November	95.7	97.2	98.5	83.9	102.9	95.2	111.9	88.6	97.7	93.3	76.6	73.9
December	96.2	97.8	98.4	84.4	102.6	96.7	111.3	89.9	98.2	93.9	76.9	74.4
2012												
January	96.8	98.7	98.3	86.5	101.8	98.3	111.8	90.7	98.6	94.6	77.2	74.9
February	97.1	99.0	98.2	86.0	101.8	98.9	112.8	91.6	98.9	94.9	77.3	75.1
March	96.6	98.5	96.6	85.0	100.0	99.9	112.9	91.4	98.2	94.7	76.8	74.6
April	97.3	99.0	97.4	85.4	100.9	100.9	111.6	92.7	99.0	95.4	77.2	74.9
May	97.5	98.7	97.9	84.7	101.8	101.5	110.2	91.7	99.2	95.4	77.2	74.6
June	97.5	98.9	97.6	84.8	101.4	102.8	109.4	91.0	99.2	95.3	77.0	74.7
July	97.7	98.7	97.7	84.7	101.6	101.7	111.8	90.6	99.2	95.9	77.1	74.4
August	97.3	98.6	97.2	83.8	101.2	102.4	111.9	91.1	98.9	95.3	76.6	74.2
September	97.2	98.4	96.9	82.8	101.1	102.0	111.4	90.9	98.6	95.5	76.5	74.0
October	97.5	98.2	96.9	83.7	100.9	101.1	111.6	90.6	98.6	96.3	76.6	73.8
November	98.0	98.8	97.4	84.7	101.1	102.3	111.9	91.9	99.0	96.6	76.8	74.2
December	98.2	99.5	97.3	86.6	100.5	103.1	111.6	92.3	99.1	96.9	76.9	74.6
2013												
January	98.2	99.2	97.3	86.0	100.7	101.1	110.7	92.7	99.2	97.2	76.7	74.4
February	98.6	99.6	97.8	87.9	100.7	102.0	110.4	94.1	99.3	97.6	77.0	74.6
March	99.1	99.6	98.4	88.9	101.2	102.5	109.8	93.8	99.6	98.0	77.2	74.5
April	99.0	99.3	98.1	88.5	101.0	101.8	109.3	93.4	99.9	98.1	77.1	74.3
May	99.1	99.6	98.0	89.0	100.7	101.3	108.1	93.2	100.4	98.4	77.0	74.5
June	99.2	99.7	98.3	90.1	100.7	101.2	108.2	93.9	100.4	98.4	77.1	74.6
July	98.9	98.9	97.4	88.1	100.2	99.4	107.0	94.0	100.3	98.7	76.8	74.0
August	99.5	99.8	97.9	90.5	100.0	100.9	107.4	94.4	100.8	99.2	77.2	74.6
September	100.1	99.9	98.2	90.9	100.3	101.7	107.1	95.5	101.0	100.0	77.5	74.7
October	99.9	100.0	98.5	91.1	100.7	101.3	107.3	95.3	101.0	99.7	77.3	74.8
November	100.2	100.0	98.5	92.2	100.4	101.1	105.7	96.1	100.9	100.3	77.5	74.8
December	100.4	99.8	99.3	92.1	101.4	100.3	104.6	94.4	101.4	100.5	77.6	74.7
2014												
January	100.0	98.8	97.7	89.4	100.2	100.4	103.7	94.1	100.7	100.8	77.3	74.0
February	100.8	99.7	98.8	92.3	100.7	101.8	103.8	94.7	101.2	101.3	77.8	74.7
March	101.8	100.6	99.5	93.3	101.3	102.9	104.8	96.0	101.6	102.5	78.5	75.4
April	101.8	100.5	99.0	92.4	101.0	102.7	104.3	95.4	101.3	103.0	78.5	75.4
May	102.2	100.8	98.9	94.2	100.3	103.4	104.4	96.9	101.6	103.5	78.7	75.6
June	102.6	101.1	98.9	94.6	100.1	103.0	104.2	97.5	101.4	104.3	78.9	75.9
July	102.8	101.6	99.0	96.9	99.6	104.4	104.8	98.4	101.3	104.4	79.0	76.4
August	102.6	101.0	98.4	94.3	99.7	103.3	103.8	98.4	101.0	104.5	78.8	76.0
September	103.0	101.0	98.9	94.1	100.3	102.9	104.5	98.9	101.0	104.9	78.9	76.0
October	103.0	100.9	98.5	93.8	100.0	103.9	104.5	98.3	100.8	105.0	78.9	76.0
November	103.7	101.6	100.4	96.7	101.5	105.2	103.8	98.2	101.3	105.0	79.3	76.6
December	103.6	101.4	100.1	96.3	101.3	104.1	103.7	98.9	100.5	105.4	79.2	76.5
2015												
January	102.8	100.8	100.3	96.1	101.5	103.5	102.3	98.1	100.5	104.1	78.6	76.2
February	102.2	100.1	99.9	93.7	101.8	102.8	103.9	96.8	100.1	103.7	78.0	75.7
March	101.9	100.4	101.0	96.4	102.4	102.9	103.2	96.3	99.7	102.8	77.8	76.0
April	101.3	100.4	100.1	97.2	101.0	102.1	102.4	97.0	100.0	102.3	77.3	76.1
May	100.8	100.4	100.0	99.4	100.2	102.4	101.8	97.5	99.6	101.5	76.9	76.2
June	100.5	100.0	99.9	96.8	100.8	101.7	101.6	97.8	99.4	101.0	76.6	75.9
July	101.2	100.8	101.4	101.9	101.3	101.7	101.3	97.8	99.5	101.5	77.2	76.6
August	100.9	100.4	101.3	99.3	101.9	101.0	101.3	98.4	99.8	101.0	77.0	76.2
September	100.6	100.0	101.0	98.9	101.6	99.9	100.2	97.5	99.7	100.8	76.7	76.0
October	100.2	100.0	100.7	98.9	101.2	99.1	99.7	98.7	100.0	100.2	76.4	75.9
November	99.4	99.7	100.3	98.1	100.9	97.6	99.0	98.8	100.1	99.1	75.8	75.7
December	98.8	99.4	99.7	98.3	100.1	96.4	99.5	99.0	99.6	98.6	75.4	75.4

Table 2-4A. Industrial Production and Capacity Utilization, Historical Data, 1955–2020—*Continued*

(Seasonally adjusted.)

Year and month	Production indexes, 2007 = 100										Capacity utilization (output as percent of capacity)	
			Market groups									
	Total industry	Manufac-turing (SIC)	Consumer goods			Business equipment	Defense and space equipment	Construction supplies	Business supplies	Materials	Total industry	Manufac-turing (SIC)
			Total	Durable	Nondurable							
2016												
January	99.5	99.9	101.1	99.5	101.6	96.5	98.5	99.3	100.1	99.2	75.9	75.8
February	99.0	99.5	101.0	99.1	101.5	96.2	97.5	98.9	99.9	98.4	75.5	75.5
March	98.2	99.4	100.1	98.7	100.5	95.6	97.0	98.8	99.2	97.7	74.9	75.4
April	98.5	99.3	101.1	99.9	101.5	95.4	96.8	99.1	99.4	97.7	75.1	75.2
May	98.3	99.2	100.8	98.7	101.4	95.3	98.0	98.5	99.6	97.5	74.9	75.1
June	98.7	99.4	101.6	100.5	101.9	95.3	97.1	98.1	99.8	98.0	75.2	75.2
July	98.9	99.6	101.5	101.4	101.6	95.7	97.0	99.0	100.4	98.1	75.4	75.3
August	98.7	99.1	101.6	100.6	101.9	95.1	97.6	98.2	100.2	97.9	75.2	74.9
September	98.6	99.3	101.4	101.1	101.5	94.8	97.4	98.5	100.3	97.7	75.1	75.0
October	98.7	99.4	100.9	101.8	100.7	95.3	98.1	98.8	99.8	98.1	75.1	75.1
November	98.2	99.3	99.9	100.3	99.8	95.3	98.7	99.3	99.7	97.7	74.8	75.1
December	98.9	99.3	101.4	100.7	101.6	96.3	98.7	98.4	99.8	98.0	75.3	75.2
2017												
January	98.7	99.6	100.1	101.2	99.8	96.4	99.2	99.7	99.2	98.3	75.2	75.4
February	98.4	99.5	98.8	100.5	98.3	96.5	98.5	99.9	99.1	98.3	74.9	75.4
March	99.1	99.2	99.5	99.3	99.5	97.3	98.8	99.3	99.6	99.3	75.5	75.3
April	100.0	100.3	100.2	101.5	99.9	100.3	100.0	100.0	99.9	99.9	76.3	76.2
May	100.1	100.2	100.8	100.6	100.9	100.2	100.4	99.7	99.9	99.8	76.5	76.2
June	100.3	100.1	100.2	99.7	100.4	100.1	100.3	99.5	100.1	100.5	76.6	76.3
July	100.2	99.9	100.0	98.0	100.6	100.1	100.4	99.6	100.2	100.3	76.6	76.2
August	99.7	99.6	99.7	98.4	100.1	100.2	101.1	98.8	99.8	99.5	76.3	76.1
September	99.7	99.7	99.7	99.8	99.6	101.5	100.8	100.6	99.5	99.2	76.5	76.2
October	101.0	100.7	100.4	100.7	100.3	102.5	100.5	100.9	100.4	101.1	77.5	77.1
November	101.3	100.7	100.0	99.8	100.1	102.6	100.4	101.1	100.9	101.9	77.8	77.2
December	101.4	100.5	100.5	100.5	100.5	102.2	99.5	101.0	101.3	101.8	77.9	77.0
2018												
January	101.4	100.1	100.8	100.7	100.9	102.6	99.8	99.1	100.9	101.7	77.9	76.8
February	101.6	101.0	100.3	102.2	99.7	103.1	99.6	101.9	101.5	102.1	78.2	77.5
March	102.3	101.2	100.5	104.0	99.5	103.5	99.6	101.3	101.9	103.2	78.7	77.6
April	103.4	101.8	102.1	104.0	101.6	104.6	101.0	102.2	102.6	104.1	79.5	78.1
May	102.5	101.0	99.5	100.1	99.3	102.7	100.4	102.6	102.1	104.2	78.8	77.5
June	103.3	101.5	100.4	102.6	99.8	104.3	101.7	102.2	102.4	104.9	79.4	77.9
July	103.5	101.8	100.3	101.5	100.0	104.5	102.0	102.2	102.6	105.4	79.5	78.0
August	104.2	102.0	101.0	103.8	100.3	105.1	103.4	102.4	102.5	106.1	79.9	78.2
September	104.1	102.0	101.1	105.3	99.9	105.1	104.1	101.8	102.5	106.1	79.8	78.1
October	104.0	101.5	100.9	104.2	100.0	104.6	104.5	101.6	102.4	106.0	79.5	77.7
November	103.9	101.1	101.1	103.9	100.4	103.6	104.1	101.4	101.8	106.1	79.4	77.3
December	103.9	101.3	101.0	106.3	99.5	103.2	106.8	102.1	101.2	106.1	79.2	77.5
2019												
January	103.3	100.6	100.0	101.2	99.7	102.1	107.7	101.8	101.4	105.7	78.7	76.8
February	102.7	100.0	100.4	101.9	99.9	101.5	107.9	99.8	100.7	104.7	78.1	76.4
March	102.9	99.9	100.7	101.5	100.5	101.6	109.1	99.9	100.5	104.8	78.3	76.3
April	102.3	99.2	99.2	100.9	98.7	99.4	109.9	99.3	100.0	105.0	77.5	75.7
May	102.5	99.2	99.8	102.3	99.1	99.1	110.0	99.7	100.2	105.1	77.6	75.7
June	102.4	99.4	100.3	102.9	99.6	99.1	112.2	100.1	99.5	104.6	77.4	75.9
July	102.1	99.0	100.1	102.9	99.3	98.4	112.7	99.5	99.6	104.2	77.1	75.6
August	102.7	99.5	100.3	103.0	99.5	99.5	113.4	100.0	99.8	105.1	77.5	76.0
September	102.3	98.9	99.4	100.5	99.1	98.8	114.4	99.9	99.5	105.0	77.2	75.5
October	101.5	98.2	99.0	97.2	99.5	98.4	115.5	99.1	98.7	103.7	76.5	75.0
November	102.0	98.9	100.5	102.8	99.9	100.2	116.3	99.0	98.9	103.4	76.8	75.6
December	101.6	98.9	99.7	100.9	99.4	99.7	117.9	99.8	98.5	103.1	76.5	75.6
2020												
January	101.1	98.7	99.0	102.3	98.1	95.4	115.5	102.2	98.8	103.2	76.1	75.5
February	101.3	98.7	99.9	104.0	98.8	93.8	117.6	102.2	99.0	103.3	76.3	75.5
March	97.4	94.3	94.9	88.0	96.8	87.2	116.5	98.9	94.0	100.9	73.4	72.2
April	84.2	79.4	83.9	54.9	92.2	65.3	101.3	87.4	82.5	88.0	63.4	60.8
May	85.8	83.1	87.6	65.7	93.8	72.0	109.2	90.6	83.3	87.1	64.7	63.7
June	91.2	89.1	94.6	90.2	95.8	81.0	110.5	91.7	86.9	91.8	68.7	68.3
July	94.9	92.7	98.6	104.9	96.8	87.3	112.7	93.6	89.9	95.2	71.5	71.2
August	95.9	94.1	99.4	103.8	98.1	89.6	115.5	95.0	91.2	95.8	72.3	72.3
September	95.6	94.2	97.9	102.5	96.6	89.4	115.6	95.5	91.7	95.9	72.1	72.4
October	96.6	95.6	98.2	103.4	96.7	90.2	119.0	98.2	93.5	97.0	72.9	73.5
November	97.2	96.2	98.3	104.9	96.4	91.2	120.0	98.7	93.5	97.7	73.3	74.0
December	98.3	96.8	100.4	105.3	99.0	91.7	117.4	99.9	94.3	98.5	74.1	74.4

Table 2-4B. Industrial Production: Historical Data, 1919–1947

(Seasonally adjusted, 2012 = 100.)

Year and month	January	February	March	April	May	June	July	August	September	October	November	December	Annual averages
1919													
Industrial production, total ...	4.93	4.73	4.62	4.71	4.85	5.15	5.32	5.43	5.45	5.43	5.32	4.96	5.07
Manufacturing	4.90	4.82	4.71	4.79	4.82	5.05	5.23	5.44	5.34	5.26	5.47	5.00	5.07
1920													
Industrial production, total ..	5.65	5.68	5.68	5.32	5.65	5.65	5.34	5.45	5.34	5.21	4.71	4.13	5.32
Manufacturing	5.67	5.75	5.75	5.39	5.60	5.54	5.21	5.26	5.23	5.00	4.48	3.89	5.23
1921													
Industrial production, total ..	4.04	3.99	3.88	3.90	4.10	4.04	3.90	4.10	4.21	4.49	4.37	4.01	4.09
Manufacturing	3.86	3.86	3.78	3.83	3.96	3.89	3.78	3.99	4.09	4.35	4.35	3.99	3.98
1922													
Industrial production, total ..	4.37	4.68	4.96	4.73	5.04	5.29	5.15	5.07	5.45	5.87	6.04	5.81	5.21
Manufacturing	4.30	4.51	4.79	4.95	5.26	5.39	5.26	5.13	5.34	5.70	5.91	5.70	5.19
1923													
Industrial production, total ..	5.81	6.01	6.29	6.40	6.56	6.48	6.26	6.29	6.29	6.29	6.12	5.65	6.20
Manufacturing	5.70	5.98	6.32	6.42	6.45	6.32	6.01	6.01	6.17	6.06	5.91	5.57	6.08
1924													
Industrial production, total ...	5.90	6.15	6.15	5.93	5.70	5.43	5.21	5.54	5.90	6.04	5.98	5.81	5.81
Manufacturing	5.78	6.09	6.17	5.98	5.65	5.26	5.03	5.36	5.70	5.88	5.85	5.78	5.71
1925													
Industrial production, total ..	6.15	6.29	6.37	6.40	6.40	6.29	6.29	6.40	6.48	6.70	6.65	6.37	6.40
Manufacturing	6.06	6.32	6.45	6.45	6.32	6.19	6.11	6.22	6.45	6.71	6.66	6.45	6.37
1926													
Industrial production, total ..	6.40	6.62	6.76	6.73	6.73	6.73	6.62	6.95	7.20	7.20	6.95	6.51	6.78
Manufacturing	6.45	6.71	6.81	6.81	6.71	6.63	6.45	6.76	7.05	7.02	6.71	6.32	6.70
1927													
Industrial production, total ..	6.62	6.95	7.09	6.95	6.98	6.92	6.62	6.84	6.92	6.81	6.51	6.17	6.78
Manufacturing	6.42	6.76	6.97	6.97	6.92	6.81	6.50	6.71	6.76	6.66	6.35	6.11	6.66
1928													
Industrial production, total ..	6.45	6.76	6.92	6.92	6.98	6.98	6.87	7.23	7.50	7.64	7.39	6.98	7.05
Manufacturing	6.35	6.76	6.94	6.97	7.02	6.94	6.84	7.20	7.41	7.49	7.28	6.97	7.01
1929													
Industrial production, total ..	7.39	7.70	7.81	8.03	8.22	8.14	7.97	8.11	8.28	8.14	7.39	6.65	7.82
Manufacturing	7.28	7.67	7.95	8.16	8.24	8.16	7.93	8.06	8.16	8.03	7.28	6.45	7.78
1930													
Industrial production, total ..	6.84	7.09	7.03	7.12	7.09	6.81	6.29	6.26	6.37	6.15	5.70	5.32	6.50
Manufacturing	6.74	7.07	7.10	7.20	7.02	6.66	6.11	6.06	6.22	5.91	5.49	5.13	6.39
1931													
Industrial production, total ..	5.34	5.65	5.79	5.93	5.87	5.65	5.43	5.32	5.29	5.04	4.79	4.51	5.38
Manufacturing	5.23	5.57	5.75	5.88	5.78	5.47	5.23	5.13	5.10	4.79	4.56	4.30	5.23
1932													
Industrial production, total ..	4.49	4.57	4.46	4.26	4.13	3.99	3.74	3.88	4.35	4.46	4.26	4.01	4.22
Manufacturing	4.30	4.38	4.25	4.09	3.99	3.83	3.55	3.70	4.15	4.20	4.04	3.78	4.02
1933													
Industrial production, total ..	4.01	4.15	3.88	4.24	4.96	5.68	6.04	5.87	5.76	5.34	4.93	4.79	4.97
Manufacturing	3.83	3.89	3.63	4.15	4.82	5.57	5.91	5.65	5.54	5.13	4.69	4.59	4.78
1934													
Industrial production, total ..	4.96	5.43	5.70	5.81	5.90	5.79	5.26	5.29	5.18	5.26	5.09	5.29	5.41
Manufacturing	4.74	5.23	5.57	5.78	5.80	5.65	5.03	5.10	4.92	5.03	4.92	5.13	5.24
1935													
Industrial production, total ..	5.79	6.12	6.09	6.01	6.01	6.01	5.93	6.26	6.51	6.81	6.81	6.65	6.25
Manufacturing	5.65	5.98	6.01	6.01	5.91	5.80	5.88	6.19	6.45	6.71	6.74	6.61	6.16
1936													
Industrial production, total ..	6.51	6.51	6.62	7.09	7.31	7.34	7.34	7.59	7.89	8.11	8.14	8.14	7.38
Manufacturing	6.40	6.35	6.63	7.10	7.28	7.31	7.28	7.56	7.82	8.06	8.13	8.13	7.34
1937													
Industrial production, total ..	7.92	8.25	8.58	8.64	8.75	8.50	8.36	8.50	8.45	7.92	6.95	6.15	8.08
Manufacturing	7.93	8.26	8.57	8.70	8.78	8.47	8.34	8.42	8.26	7.72	6.71	5.80	8.00
1938													
Industrial production, total ..	5.87	5.93	6.01	5.87	5.81	5.81	6.12	6.59	6.98	7.17	7.31	7.12	6.38
Manufacturing	5.54	5.65	5.78	5.65	5.65	5.57	5.85	6.35	6.81	6.97	7.15	6.94	6.16

Table 2-4B. Industrial Production: Historical Data, 1919–1947—*Continued*

(Seasonally adjusted, 2012 = 100.)

Year and month	January	February	March	April	May	June	July	August	September	October	November	December	Annual averages
1939													
Industrial production, total	7.31	7.31	7.31	7.17	7.20	7.45	7.59	7.70	8.28	8.81	9.05	9.00	7.85
Products	6.84	6.84	6.81	6.66	6.71	6.92	7.05	7.28	7.77	8.32	8.52	8.57	7.36
Consumer goods	12.12	12.08	12.16	12.12	12.16	12.40	12.52	12.56	12.84	13.07	13.35	13.35	12.56
Materials	6.62	6.62	6.62	6.20	6.28	6.67	6.90	6.98	7.96	8.76	8.97	8.86	7.29
Manufacturing	6.84	6.84	6.81	6.66	6.71	6.92	7.05	7.28	7.77	8.32	8.52	8.57	7.36
1940													
Industrial production, total	8.86	8.50	8.28	8.33	8.61	8.97	9.00	9.11	9.41	9.64	9.88	10.16	9.06
Products	8.42	8.06	7.82	7.85	8.21	8.63	8.65	8.81	9.09	9.33	9.51	9.82	8.68
Consumer goods	13.15	12.99	12.76	12.80	12.84	13.15	12.99	13.07	13.51	13.87	14.30	14.66	13.34
Materials	8.68	8.06	7.75	7.75	8.22	8.76	8.92	8.99	9.30	9.46	9.67	9.90	8.79
Manufacturing	8.42	8.06	7.82	7.85	8.21	8.63	8.65	8.81	9.09	9.33	9.51	9.82	8.68
1941													
Industrial production, total	10.38	10.60	10.88	10.83	11.35	11.55	11.57	11.77	11.88	12.04	12.13	12.27	11.44
Products	9.95	10.23	10.47	10.67	11.04	11.24	11.27	11.42	11.48	11.66	11.74	11.84	11.08
Consumer goods	14.74	15.13	15.37	15.57	16.05	16.28	16.24	16.32	16.44	16.52	16.68	16.52	15.99
Materials	10.10	10.23	10.60	10.16	10.91	11.11	11.16	11.27	11.45	11.58	11.68	11.78	11.00
Manufacturing	9.95	10.23	10.47	10.67	11.04	11.24	11.27	11.42	11.48	11.66	11.74	11.84	11.08
1942													
Industrial production, total	12.49	12.65	12.76	12.35	12.40	12.52	12.74	13.18	13.48	13.96	14.29	14.59	13.12
Products	12.02	12.28	12.43	12.02	12.12	12.28	12.54	13.03	13.39	13.94	14.33	14.66	12.92
Consumer goods	16.64	16.36	16.20	13.91	13.79	13.79	14.02	14.26	14.46	14.58	14.74	14.90	14.80
Materials	11.91	12.02	12.15	12.28	12.35	12.38	12.48	12.84	13.08	13.52	13.72	13.75	12.71
Manufacturing	12.02	12.28	12.43	12.02	12.12	12.28	12.54	13.03	13.39	13.94	14.33	14.66	12.92
1943													
Industrial production, total	14.76	15.12	15.28	15.45	15.59	15.59	15.89	16.25	16.59	16.83	17.00	16.75	15.93
Products	14.90	15.21	15.39	15.54	15.72	15.83	16.01	16.37	16.71	17.05	17.25	16.94	16.08
Consumer goods	14.26	14.34	14.26	14.34	14.66	15.05	15.41	15.69	16.01	15.69	15.65	15.17	15.04
Materials	14.16	14.52	14.73	14.81	14.81	14.39	14.73	14.99	15.32	15.66	15.82	15.64	14.97
Manufacturing	14.90	15.21	15.39	15.54	15.72	15.83	16.01	16.37	16.71	17.05	17.25	16.94	16.08
1944													
Industrial production, total	17.08	17.31	17.33	17.33	17.31	17.33	17.33	17.08	17.25	17.00	17.00	16.86	17.14
Products	17.33	17.54	17.62	17.62	17.62	17.56	17.62	17.36	17.54	17.25	17.25	17.10	17.40
Consumer goods	15.13	15.17	15.21	15.25	15.41	15.77	15.93	16.52	16.44	16.24	16.12	15.89	15.76
Materials	16.15	16.38	16.41	16.31	16.10	15.82	15.32	15.38	15.27	15.38	15.43	15.32	15.77
Manufacturing	17.33	17.54	17.62	17.62	17.62	17.56	17.62	17.36	17.54	17.25	17.25	17.10	17.40
1945													
Industrial production, total	16.78	16.83	16.78	16.50	16.14	15.84	15.28	13.65	12.38	11.82	12.27	12.24	14.71
Products	17.02	17.05	16.99	16.66	16.24	15.83	15.21	13.34	11.79	11.27	11.58	11.63	14.55
Consumer goods	15.93	15.81	15.65	15.69	15.81	16.20	16.28	15.81	16.88	16.80	17.15	17.15	16.26
Materials	15.61	15.84	16.00	15.71	15.32	14.86	14.08	12.61	11.60	11.01	11.84	11.73	13.85
Manufacturing	17.02	17.05	16.99	16.66	16.24	15.83	15.21	13.34	11.79	11.27	11.58	11.63	14.55
1946													
Industrial production, total	11.71	11.19	12.38	12.13	11.68	12.49	12.76	13.24	13.48	13.65	13.71	13.68	12.67
Products	12.38	12.26	12.55	12.75	12.61	12.75	13.04	13.47	13.84	14.07	14.21	14.36	13.19
Consumer goods	17.44	18.14	18.02	18.22	18.29	18.33	18.76	19.37	19.76	19.99	20.26	20.38	18.91
Materials	10.11	8.90	11.19	10.45	9.66	11.02	11.66	12.10	12.18	12.45	12.43	12.50	11.22
Manufacturing	10.90	10.20	11.48	11.51	10.97	11.59	11.97	12.51	12.77	13.05	13.20	13.25	11.95
1947													
Industrial production, total	13.96	14.23	14.29	14.01	13.93	14.04	13.24	14.23	14.59	15.01	14.90	14.62	14.25
Products	13.24	13.50	13.57	13.34	13.08	13.24	12.49	13.39	13.78	14.22	14.12	13.81	13.48
Consumer goods	20.01	20.28	20.24	19.65	19.41	20.05	19.41	21.31	21.95	22.38	21.87	21.08	20.64
Materials	13.39	13.59	13.67	13.28	13.26	13.13	12.07	13.02	13.26	13.80	13.90	13.52	13.32
Manufacturing	13.24	13.50	13.57	13.34	13.08	13.24	12.49	13.39	13.78	14.22	14.12	13.81	13.48

NOTES AND DEFINITIONS, CHAPTER 2

TABLES 2-1 THROUGH 2-4

SOURCE: BOARD OF GOVERNORS OF THE FEDERAL RESERVE SYSTEM

Ever since the Federal Reserve was founded in 1913, understanding current business conditions has been a central focus in pursuing its mission of a stable and secure financial system. The index of industrial production is one of the oldest continuous statistical series maintained by the Federal government, and one of the few economic indicators for which monthly data are available before the post-World-War-II period.

The Federal Reserve's monthly index of industrial production and the related capacity indexes and capacity utilization rates cover manufacturing, mining, and electric and gas utilities. The industrial sector, together with construction, accounts for the bulk of the variation in national output over the course of the business cycle. The industrial detail provided by these measures helps illuminate structural developments in the economy.

Around the 15th day of each month, the Federal Reserve issues estimates of industrial production and capacity utilization for the previous month. The production estimates are in the form of index numbers (2012 = 100) that reflect the monthly levels of total output of the nation's factories, mines, and gas and electric utilities expressed as a percent of the monthly average in the 2012 base year. Capacity estimates are expressed as index numbers, 2012 output (not 2012 capacity) = 100, and capacity utilization is measured by the production index as a percent of the capacity index. Since, for each component industry, the bases of those two indexes are the same, this procedure yields production as a percent of capacity. Monthly estimates are subject to revision in subsequent months, as well as to annual and comprehensive revisions in subsequent years.

Definitions and notes on the data

The *industrial production index* measures changes in the physical volume or quantity of output of manufacturing, mining, and electric and gas utilities. *Capacity utilization* is calculated by dividing a seasonally adjusted industrial production index for an industry or group of industries by a related index of productive capacity.

The index of industrial production measures a large portion of the goods output of the national economy on a monthly basis. This portion, together with construction, has also accounted for the bulk of the variation in output over the course of many historical business cycles. The substantial industrial detail included in the index illuminates structural developments in the economy.

The total industrial production index and the indexes for its major components are constructed from individual industry series (312 series for data from 1997 forward) based on the 2012 North American Industry Classification System (NAICS). See the Preface to this volume for information on NAICS.

The Federal Reserve has been able to provide a longer continuous historical series on the NAICS basis than some other government agencies. In a major research effort, the Fed and the Census Bureau's Center for Economic Studies re-coded data from seven Censuses of Manufactures, beginning in 1963, to establish benchmark NAICS data for output, value added, and capacity utilization. The resulting indexes are shown annually for the last 48 years (52 years for aggregate levels) in Tables 2-1 through 2-4.

The Fed's featured indexes for total industry and total manufacturing are on the Standard Industrial Classification (SIC) basis and do not observe the reclassifications under NAICS of the logging industry to the Agriculture sector and the publishing industry to the Information sector. (The reason cited by the Fed was to avoid "changing the scope or historical continuity of these statistics.") One advantage of the SIC index for capacity utilization is that it is a continuous series back to 1949 (shown in Table 2-4A). On the new NAICS basis, production and capacity utilization are shown back to 1970 in Tables 2-2 and 2-3.

The individual series components of the indexes are grouped in two ways: market groups and industry groups.

Market groups. For analyzing market trends and product flows, the individual series are grouped into two major divisions: *final products and nonindustrial supplies* and *materials*. *Final products* consists of products purchased by consumers, businesses, or government for final use. *Nonindustrial supplies* are expected to become inputs in nonindustrial sectors: the two major subgroups are *construction supplies* and *business supplies*. *Materials* comprises industrial output that requires further processing within the industrial sector. This twofold division distinguishes between products that are ready to ship outside the industrial sector and those that will stay within the sector for further processing.

Final products are divided into *consumer goods* and *equipment*, and *equipment* is divided into *business equipment* and *defense and space equipment*. Further subdivisions of each market group are based on type of product and the market destination for the product.

Industry groups are typically groupings by 3-digit NAICS industries and major aggregates of these industries—for example, *durable goods* and *nondurable goods manufacturing*, *mining*, and *utilities*. Indexes are also calculated for *stage-of-process* industry groups—*crude*, *primary and semifinished*, and *finished* processing. The stage-of-process grouping was a new feature in the 2002 revision, replacing the two narrower and less well-defined "primary processing manufacturing" and "advanced processing manufacturing" groups that were previously published. *Crude processing* consists of logging, much of mining, and certain basic manufacturing activities in the chemical, paper, and metals industries. *Primary and semifinished processing* represents industries that produce materials and parts used as inputs by other industries. *Finished processing* includes industries that produce goods in their finished form for use by consumers, business investment, or government.

The indexes of industrial production are constructed using data from a variety of sources. Current monthly estimates of production are based on measures of physical output where possible and appropriate. For a few high-tech industries, the estimated value of nominal output is deflated by a corresponding price index. For industries in which such direct measurement is not possible on a monthly basis, output is inferred from production-worker hours, adjusted for trends in worker productivity derived from annual and benchmark revisions. (Between the 1960s and 1997, electric power consumption was used as a monthly output indicator for some industries instead of hours. However, the coverage of the electric power consumption survey deteriorated, and in the 2005 revision, the decision was made to resume the use of hours in those industries, beginning with the data for 1997.)

In annual and benchmark revisions, the individual indexes are revised using data from the quinquennial Economic Census which includes Manufactures and Mineral Industries, the Annual Survey of Manufactures, and the quarterly Survey of Plant Capacity, prepared by the Census Bureau; deflators from the Producer Price Indexes and other sources; the *Minerals Yearbook*, prepared by the Department of the Interior; publications from the Department of Energy; and other sources.

The weights used in compiling the indexes are based on Census value added—the difference between the value of production and the cost of materials and supplies consumed. Census value added differs in some respects from the economic concept of industry value added used in the national income and product accounts (NIPAs). Industry value added as defined in the NIPAs is not available in sufficient detail for the industrial production indexes. See Chapter 14 for data and a description of NIPA value added (equivalently, gross domestic product) by major industry group.

Before 1972, a linked-Laspeyres formula (base period prices) is used to compute the weighted individual indexes. Beginning with 1972, the index uses a version of the Fisher-ideal index formula—a chain-weighting (continually updated average price) system similar to that in the NIPAs. See the "General Notes" article at the front of this book and the notes and definitions

for Chapter 1 for more information. Chain-weighting keeps the index from being distorted by the use of obsolete relative prices.

For the purpose of these value-added weights, value added per unit of output is based on data from the Censuses of Manufacturing and Mineral Industries, the Census Bureau's Annual Survey of Manufactures, and revenue and expense data reported by the Department of Energy and the American Gas Association, which are projected into recent years by using changes in relevant Producer Price Indexes.

To separate seasonal movements from cyclical patterns and underlying trends, each component of the index is seasonally adjusted by the Census X-12-ARIMA method.

The index does not cover production on farms, in the construction industry, in transportation, or in various trade and service industries. A number of groups and subgroups include data for individual series not published separately.

Capacity utilization is calculated for the manufacturing, mining, and electric and gas utilities industries. Output is measured by seasonally adjusted indexes of industrial production. The capacity indexes attempt to capture the concept of sustainable maximum output, which is defined as the greatest level of output that a plant can maintain within the framework of a realistic work schedule, taking account of normal downtime and assuming sufficient availability of inputs to operate the machinery and equipment in place. The 89 individual industry capacity indexes are based on a variety of data, including capacity data measured in physical units compiled by government agencies and trade associations, Census Bureau surveys of utilization rates and investment, and estimates of growth of the capital stock.

In the "Explanatory Note" to its monthly release, the statistics cover output, capacity, and capacity utilization in the U.S. industrial sector, which is defined by the Federal Reserve to comprise manufacturing, mining, and electric and gas utilities. Mining is defined as all industries in sector 21 of the North American Industry Classification System (NAICS); electric and gas utilities are those in NAICS sectors 2211 and 2212. Manufacturing comprises NAICS manufacturing industries (sector 31-33) plus the logging industry and the newspaper, periodical, book, and directory publishing industries. Logging and publishing are classified elsewhere in NAICS (under agriculture and information respectively), but historically they were considered to be manufacturing and were included in the industrial sector under the Standard Industrial Classification (SIC) system. In December 2002 the Federal Reserve reclassified all its industrial output data from the SIC system to NAICS.

Revisions

Revisions normally occur annual with the newest release on May 28, 2021. The most prominent features of this revision are an update of the base year to 2017 for the indexes, a conversion of the industry group indexes to the 2017 North American Industry Classification System (NAICS), the incorporation of comprehensive annual production data for 2017 to 2019, and the incorporation of new survey utilization rate data for 2019 and 2020.

Data availability

Data are available monthly in Federal Reserve release G.17. Current and historical data and background information are available on the Federal Reserve Web site at <https://www.federalreserve.gov>.

Chain-weighting makes it difficult for the user to analyze in detail the sources of aggregate output change. An "Explanatory Note," included in each month's index release, provides some assistance for the user, including a reference to a an Internet location with the exact contribution of a monthly change in a component index to the monthly change in the total index.

References

The G.17 release each month contains extensive explanatory material, as well as references for further detail.

An earlier detailed description of the industrial production index, together with a history of the index, a glossary of terms, and a bibliography is presented in *Industrial Production—1986 Edition*, available from Publication Services, Mail Stop 127, Board of Governors of the Federal Reserve System, Washington, DC 20551.

CHAPTER 3: INCOME DISTRIBUTION AND POVERTY

SECTION 3A: HOUSEHOLD AND FAMILY INCOME

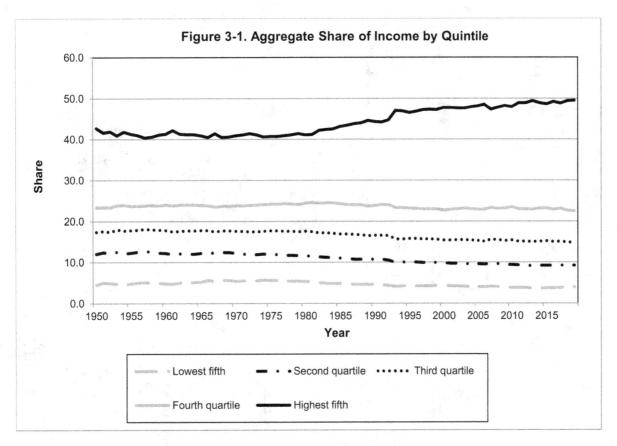

Figure 3-1. Aggregate Share of Income by Quintile

- The Census Bureau collects data on income and poverty in the United States in the Current Population Survey Annual Social and Economic Supplements (CPS ASEC). The most recent report provides estimates for calendar 2019, the last year of the economic expansion spanning from June 2009 through February 2020. The 2020 collection of data occurred during the COVID-19 pandemic. See the Notes Definition section at the end of Chapter 3 for how the pandemic disrupted the collection of this data.

- As stated above, 2019 was the last year of recovery from the Great Recession, thus many of the indicators in this report are positive. For example, median household income rose 8.7 percent to $68,703 for nonfamily households while family income grew at a slower rates. This is the tenth consecutive annual increase in median family household income and seventh consecutive increase for all households. (Tables 3-1 and 3-2)

- In addition, median household income rose for White, Black, Asian and Hispanic households between 2018 and 2019. Asian Americans earned $87,194, the highest among these demographic groups. Black Americans earned the least at $41,361. (See Table 3-1)

- Income inequality is the disparity by the share of aggregate income distributions for five quintiles. Table 3-3 depicts how the gap in U.S. income has widen for the bottom four-fifths of families, with the largest decline in the second quintile, a loss of 2.8 percentage points between 1950 to 2019. (See Figure 3-1)

Table 3-1. Median and Mean Household Income and Median Earnings

(2019 dollars.)

Year	Number of households (thousands)	Average size of household (number of people)	Median household income — All races	White — Total	White — Not Hispanic	Black	Asian [1]	Hispanic (any race)	Mean household income, all races	Median earnings of year-round, full-time workers (2019 dollars) — Male workers	Female workers	Ratio, female to male
1975	72 867	2.89	50 214	52 512	52 908	31 524	...	37 725	58 636	54 291	31 933	0.588
1976	74 142	2.86	51 048	53 474	54 565	31 797	...	38 505	60 045	54 142	32 590	0.602
1977	76 030	2.81	51 371	54 020	55 091	31 878	...	40 299	60 939	55 360	32 620	0.589
1978	77 330	2.78	53 359	55 470	56 515	33 335	...	41 808	62 802	55 718	33 119	0.594
1979	80 776	2.76	53 257	55 839	56 625	32 784	...	42 195	63 264	55 046	32 842	0.597
1980	82 368	2.73	51 528	54 361	55 325	31 318	...	39 718	61 283	54 152	32 578	0.602
1981	83 527	2.72	50 709	53 577	54 351	30 065	...	40 675	60 580	53 862	31 905	0.592
1982	83 918	2.73	50 571	52 943	53 830	30 005	...	38 053	60 946	52 843	32 628	0.617
1983	85 407	2.71	50 216	52 662	...	29 885	...	38 245	61 075	52 611	33 458	0.636
1984	86 789	2.69	51 742	54 586	55 719	31 096	...	39 224	63 397	53 596	34 118	0.637
1985	88 458	2.67	52 709	55 588	56 838	33 072	...	38 977	64 868	53 997	34 869	0.646
1986	89 479	2.66	54 608	57 411	58 716	33 076	...	40 252	67 465	55 395	35 603	0.643
1987	91 124	2.64	55 260	58 222	59 823	33 231	68 332	41 000	68 723	55 016	35 858	0.652
1988	92 830	2.62	55 716	58 900	60 523	33 577	66 034	41 664	69 615	54 551	36 030	0.660
1989	93 347	2.63	56 678	59 619	60 901	35 456	70 787	42 982	71 607	53 590	36 802	0.687
1990	94 312	2.63	55 952	58 359	59 693	34 898	71 848	41 726	69 892	51 720	37 040	0.716
1991	95 669	2.62	54 318	56 920	58 279	33 909	65 718	40 912	68 374	53 047	37 058	0.699
1992	96 426	2.66	53 897	56 665	58 566	32 995	66 502	39 754	68 330	53 125	37 605	0.708
1993	97 107	2.67	53 610	56 560	58 641	33 519	65 804	39 273	71 091	52 119	37 318	0.715
1994	98 990	2.65	54 233	57 198	59 044	35 344	68 047	39 369	72 503	51 863	37 325	0.720
1995	99 627	2.65	55 931	58 705	61 023	36 755	66 662	37 522	73 760	51 696	36 926	0.714
1996	101 018	2.64	56 744	59 413	62 012	37 543	69 189	39 819	75 340	51 391	37 907	0.738
1997	102 528	2.62	57 911	60 990	63 501	39 202	70 813	41 672	77 766	52 698	39 082	0.742
1998	103 874	2.61	60 040	63 170	65 528	39 143	72 010	43 743	80 067	54 574	39 932	0.732
1999	106 434	2.60	61 526	63 989	66 759	42 196	77 044	46 484	82 754	55 018	39 786	0.723
2000	108 209	2.58	61 399	64 216	66 712	43 380	81 530	48 500	83 545	54 471	40 156	0.737
2001	109 297	2.58	60 038	63 293	65 835	41 899	76 256	47 721	82 758	54 418	41 537	0.763
2002	111 278	2.57	59 360	...	...	...	...	46 334	80 975	55 189	42 275	0.766
2003	112 000	2.57	59 286	...	...	...	...	45 160	80 840	55 659	42 049	0.755
2004	113 343	2.57	59 080	...	...	...	...	45 670	80 578	54 365	41 631	0.766
2005	114 384	2.57	59 712	...	...	...	...	46 360	81 647	53 345	41 063	0.770
2006	116 011	2.56	60 178	...	...	...	...	47 169	83 111	52 762	40 594	0.769
2007	116 783	2.56	60 985	...	...	...	...	46 958	82 081	54 769	42 616	0.778
2008	117 181	2.57	58 811	...	...	...	...	44 326	79 997	54 210	41 791	0.771
2009	117 538	2.59	58 400	...	...	...	...	44 628	79 751	55 290	42 562	0.770
2010	119 927	2.56	56 873	...	...	...	...	43 433	77 783	55 344	42 575	0.769
2011	121 084	2.55	56 006	...	...	...	...	43 217	77 962	53 934	41 532	0.770
2012	122 459	2.54	55 900	...	...	...	...	42 738	78 095	54 126	41 408	0.765
2013	122 952	2.55	56 079	...	...	...	...	44 228	78 431	54 021	42 278	0.783
2014	124 587	2.54	56 969	...	...	...	...	45 114	80 413	53 493	42 067	0.786
2015	125 819	2.53	59 901	...	...	...	...	47 852	84 011	54 280	43 183	0.796
2016	126 224	2.54	61 779	...	...	...	...	49 887	87 001	54 036	43 482	0.805
2017	127 586	2.53	62 868	...	...	...	...	51 717	88 322	53 417	43 000	0.805
2018	128 579	2.52	63 179	...	...	...	...	51 450	90 021	55 291	45 097	0.816
2019	128 451	2.52	68 703	...	...	...	...	56 113	98 088	57 456	47 299	0.823
By race												
Race alone												
2004	...	...	...	62 451	65 388	40 573	76 231	...	...	...	...	...
2005	...	...	...	62 177	65 178	40 105	76 631	...	...	...	...	...
2006	...	...	...	62 584	65 458	39 774	78 747	...	...	...	...	...
2007	...	...	...	63 264	65 449	39 913	80 200	...	...	...	...	...
2008	...	...	...	63 270	66 676	41 176	80 252	...	...	...	...	...
2009	...	...	...	61 160	64 923	40 006	76 739	...	...	...	...	...
2010	...	...	...	60 845	63 895	38 228	76 810	...	...	...	...	...
2011	...	...	...	59 682	62 857	37 077	74 167	...	...	...	...	...
2012	...	...	...	58 423	62 001	36 061	72 874	...	...	...	...	...
2013	...	...	...	58 846	62 465	36 510	75 205	...	...	...	...	...
2014	...	...	...	59 661	62 915	37 356	72 411	...	...	...	...	...
2015	...	...	...	60 376	63 976	37 583	78 883	...	...	...	...	...
2016	...	...	...	63 710	66 721	39 108	81 788	...	...	...	...	...
2017	...	...	...	64 729	68 059	41 323	85 210	...	...	...	...	...
2018	...	...	...	66 864	69 806	41 239	83 314	...	...	...	...	...
2019	...	...	...	66 943	70 642	41 361	87 194	...	...	...	...	...
Race alone or in combination												
2004	...	...	...	...	...	40 633	75 632	...	...	...	...	...
2005	...	...	...	...	...	40 292	76 557	...	...	...	...	...
2006	...	...	...	...	...	39 898	78 688	...	...	...	...	...
2007	...	...	...	...	...	40 116	79 778	...	...	...	...	...
2008	...	...	...	...	...	41 388	79 977	...	...	...	...	...
2009	...	...	...	...	...	40 154	76 657	...	...	...	...	...
2010	...	...	...	...	...	38 423	76 345	...	...	...	...	...
2011	...	...	...	...	...	37 114	73 322	...	...	...	...	...
2012	...	...	...	...	...	36 215	72 724	...	...	...	...	...
2013	...	...	...	...	...	36 945	74 707	...	...	...	...	...
2014	...	...	...	...	...	37 547	72 736	...	...	...	...	...
2015	...	...	...	...	...	37 854	79 448	...	...	...	...	...
2016	...	...	...	...	...	39 440	81 359	...	...	...	...	...
2017	...	...	...	...	...	41 924	84 573	...	...	...	...	...
2018	...	...	...	...	...	41 584	82 935	...	...	...	...	...
2019	...	...	...	...	...	41 692	86 815	...	...	...	...	...

[1] For 1987 through 2001, Asian and Pacific Islander.
. . . = Not available.

Table 3-2. Median Family Income by Type of Family

(2019 dollars, except as noted.)

Year	All families	Married couples			Male householder [1]	Female householder [1]	4-person families	Average size of family (number of people)
		Total	Wife in paid labor force	Wife not in paid labor force				
1950	39 929	32 035	35 681	29 549	28 958	17 867	34 164	3.54
1951	40 578	33 058	38 256	30 020	29 741	19 127	35 513	3.54
1952	40 832	34 359	39 751	30 924	30 585	18 910	36 999	3.53
1953	41 202	36 734	43 554	33 175	34 566	20 632	. . .	3.59
1954	41 951	36 092	42 617	32 354	33 435	19 108	. . .	3.59
1955	42 889	38 478	45 101	34 704	35 056	20 674	41 156	3.58
1956	43 497	40 970	47 056	36 692	34 330	22 689	43 821	3.60
1957	43 696	41 136	46 968	36 964	36 541	22 040	43 776	3.64
1958	44 232	41 260	46 253	37 090	33 070	21 278	44 132	3.65
1959	45 111	43 594	49 499	39 252	35 517	21 281	46 735	3.67
1960	45 539	44 491	50 119	40 095	36 817	22 484	47 687	3.70
1961	46 418	45 278	51 691	40 213	38 018	22 448	48 278	3.67
1962	47 059	46 509	53 125	41 041	42 410	23 251	50 170	3.68
1963	47 540	48 293	54 705	42 414	41 825	23 520	52 285	3.70
1964	47 956	50 094	56 610	43 916	41 856	24 989	54 112	3.70
1965	48 509	51 706	58 668	44 985	43 757	25 138	55 514	3.69
1966	49 214	54 246	61 357	47 302	44 516	27 753	57 728	3.67
1967	50 111	56 649	64 066	48 976	45 730	28 818	60 361	3.63
1968	50 823	59 052	66 169	50 868	47 279	28 912	63 508	3.60
1969	51 586	61 829	68 934	52 632	51 560	29 811	65 674	3.58
1970	52 227	61 960	69 353	52 563	53 099	30 008	65 796	3.57
1971	53 296	62 035	69 564	52 737	49 233	28 867	65 625	3.53
1972	54 373	65 233	73 025	55 469	56 475	29 276	70 192	3.48
1973	55 053	67 192	75 350	56 464	55 402	29 898	70 710	3.44
1974	55 698	65 280	72 924	54 986	54 660	30 420	70 185	3.42
1975	56 245	64 412	71 606	52 974	56 302	29 652	68 663	3.39
1976	56 710	66 381	73 579	54 724	52 685	29 542	70 937	3.37
1977	57 215	67 886	74 890	55 658	55 947	29 923	72 152	3.33
1978	57 804	69 746	76 450	55 865	57 579	30 787	73 670	3.31
1979	59 550	70 586	78 520	55 922	55 365	32 544	74 154	3.29
1980	60 309	68 549	76 344	53 886	51 895	30 831	72 077	3.27
1981	61 019	67 843	75 903	52 749	53 833	29 665	71 115	3.25
1982	61 393	66 415	74 261	52 128	51 408	29 313	70 499	3.26
1983	62 015	66 796	75 362	51 380	53 476	28 859	71 442	3.24
1984	62 706	69 594	78 122	53 140	54 818	30 089	73 084	3.23
1985	63 558	70 665	79 370	53 499	51 401	31 038	74 475	3.21
1986	64 491	73 257	82 105	55 248	55 743	30 475	77 524	3.19
1987	65 204	75 298	84 353	55 144	54 420	31 698	80 062	3.17
1988	65 837	75 819	85 323	54 380	55 896	31 974	81 365	3.16
1989	66 090	76 951	86 644	55 025	55 591	32 823	81 375	3.17
1990	66 322	75 899	85 328	55 208	55 259	32 213	78 860	3.18
1991	67 173	75 254	84 783	52 936	52 044	30 641	79 037	3.17
1992	68 216	75 031	85 484	51 821	49 393	30 494	79 260	3.19
1993	68 506	75 134	85 776	50 620	46 240	30 475	78 901	3.20
1994	69 313	76 941	87 475	51 157	47 492	31 208	80 455	3.19
1995	69 597	78 646	89 446	51 875	50 731	32 906	83 032	3.20
1996	70 241	80 911	91 118	52 672	51 437	32 410	83 859	3.19
1997	70 884	82 201	92 685	55 039	52 516	33 496	85 003	3.18
1998	71 551	85 172	96 092	56 013	56 091	34 841	88 129	3.18
1999	73 206	86 969	98 113	56 792	57 474	36 576	91 978	3.15
2000	73 778	87 982	98 829	57 072	56 165	38 284	93 299	3.14
2001	74 340	87 336	98 312	56 602	52 965	37 266	91 596	3.15
2002	75 616	87 114	99 481	54 795	53 780	37 654	89 397	3.13
2003	76 232	86 783	100 431	54 941	52 994	36 995	90 701	3.13
2004	76 866	86 325	99 979	54 918	54 760	36 590	89 577	3.13
2005	77 418	86 489	99 096	55 939	53 950	35 752	92 271	3.13
2006	78 454	88 219	100 900	55 767	53 188	36 645	93 318	3.13
2007	77 908	89 723	102 439	56 092	54 829	37 447	93 538	3.15
2008	78 874	86 588	98 862	55 356	51 864	35 863	91 024	3.15
2009	78 867	85 557	98 437	54 573	49 572	35 560	88 876	3.16
2010	79 559	84 890	98 472	54 908	50 771	34 260	87 838	3.14
2011	80 529	84 060	97 232	55 066	49 063	34 471	86 088	3.13
2012	80 944	84 263	98 170	54 424	47 253	34 232	88 908	3.12
2013	81 217	83 917	99 393	54 639	48 890	34 526	88 333	3.14
2014	81 730	87 357	103 629	56 776	51 451	34 342	90 167	3.14
2015	82 199	90 995	107 295	57 952	53 709	36 826	95 115	3.14
2016	82 854	92 485	108 363	59 956	54 939	39 054	96 678	3.14
2017	83 103	94 019	110 893	61 901	55 223	38 691	98 869	3.14
2018	83 508	95 020	. . .	. . .	55 320	40 962	99 400	3.14
2019	83 698	102 032	. . .	. . .	61 705	43 359	106 567	3.15

[1]No spouse present.
. . . = Not available.

Table 3-3. Shares of Aggregate Income Received by Each Fifth and Top 5 Percent of Households

Year	Money income							Equivalence-adjusted income						
	Share of aggregate income (percent)						Gini coefficient	Share of aggregate income (percent)						Gini coefficient
	Lowest fifth	Second fifth	Third fifth	Fourth fifth	Highest fifth	Top 5 percent		Lowest fifth	Second fifth	Third fifth	Fourth fifth	Highest fifth	Top 5 percent	
1967	4.0	10.8	17.3	24.2	43.6	17.2	0.397	5.6	12.0	17.1	23.2	42.1	. . .	0.362
1968	4.2	11.1	17.6	24.5	42.6	16.3	0.386	5.8	12.3	17.4	23.4	41.1	. . .	0.351
1969	4.1	10.9	17.5	24.5	43.0	16.6	0.391	5.8	12.2	17.3	23.4	41.3	. . .	0.353
1970	4.1	10.8	17.4	24.5	43.3	16.6	0.394	5.7	12.1	17.3	23.4	41.5	. . .	0.357
1971	4.1	10.6	17.3	24.5	43.5	16.7	0.396	5.7	12.0	17.2	23.4	41.7	. . .	0.359
1972	4.1	10.4	17.0	24.5	43.9	17.0	0.401	5.6	11.9	17.2	23.4	41.9	. . .	0.362
1973	4.2	10.4	17.0	24.5	43.9	16.9	0.400	5.6	12.0	17.2	23.5	41.7	. . .	0.360
1974	4.3	10.6	17.0	24.6	43.5	16.5	0.395	5.8	12.1	17.3	23.6	41.2	. . .	0.354
1975	4.3	10.4	17.0	24.7	43.6	16.5	0.397	5.6	11.9	17.3	23.6	41.6	. . .	0.359
1976	4.3	10.3	17.0	24.7	43.7	16.6	0.398	5.6	11.8	17.4	23.8	41.5	. . .	0.359
1977	4.2	10.2	16.9	24.7	44.0	16.8	0.402	5.5	11.7	17.3	23.7	41.7	. . .	0.362
1978	4.2	10.2	16.8	24.7	44.1	16.8	0.402	5.4	11.8	17.3	23.7	41.8	. . .	0.363
1979	4.1	10.2	16.8	24.6	44.2	16.9	0.404	5.3	11.7	17.2	23.8	41.9	. . .	0.366
1980	4.2	10.2	16.8	24.7	44.1	16.5	0.403	5.2	11.6	17.3	24.0	41.9	. . .	0.367
1981	4.1	10.1	16.7	24.8	44.3	16.5	0.406	5.0	11.4	17.2	24.0	42.4	. . .	0.373
1982	4.0	10.0	16.5	24.5	45.0	17.0	0.412	4.7	11.1	17.0	23.9	43.2	. . .	0.384
1983	4.0	9.9	16.4	24.6	45.1	17.0	0.414	4.6	11.0	16.9	24.0	43.5	. . .	0.389
1984	4.0	9.9	16.3	24.6	45.2	17.1	0.415	4.6	11.0	16.8	24.0	43.6	. . .	0.389
1985	3.9	9.8	16.2	24.4	45.6	17.6	0.419	4.6	10.9	16.7	23.7	44.1	. . .	0.394
1986	3.8	9.7	16.2	24.3	46.1	18.0	0.425	4.5	10.8	16.6	23.8	44.3	. . .	0.397
1987	3.8	9.6	16.1	24.3	46.2	18.2	0.426	4.4	10.8	16.7	23.8	44.4	. . .	0.399
1988	3.8	9.6	16.0	24.2	46.3	18.3	0.426	4.4	10.7	16.5	23.7	44.7	. . .	0.402
1989	3.8	9.5	15.8	24.0	46.8	18.9	0.431	4.4	10.5	16.3	23.4	45.4	. . .	0.408
1990	3.8	9.6	15.9	24.0	46.6	18.5	0.428	4.4	10.6	16.3	23.5	45.1	. . .	0.406
1991	3.8	9.6	15.9	24.2	46.5	18.1	0.428	4.3	10.6	16.5	23.7	45.0	. . .	0.406
1992	3.8	9.4	15.8	24.2	46.9	18.6	0.433	4.1	10.3	16.3	23.7	45.5	. . .	0.413
1993	3.6	9.0	15.1	23.5	48.9	21.0	0.454	3.9	9.8	15.6	23.0	47.7	. . .	0.436
1994	3.6	8.9	15.0	23.4	49.1	21.2	0.456	4.0	9.8	15.6	22.8	47.8	. . .	0.436
1995	3.7	9.1	15.2	23.3	48.7	21.0	0.450	4.1	9.9	15.6	22.8	47.6	. . .	0.433
1996	3.6	9.0	15.1	23.3	49.0	21.4	0.455	4.0	9.8	15.5	22.7	47.9	. . .	0.437
1997	3.6	8.9	15.0	23.2	49.4	21.7	0.459	4.0	9.8	15.4	22.6	48.3	. . .	0.440
1998	3.6	9.0	15.0	23.2	49.2	21.4	0.456	4.0	9.8	15.4	22.7	48.1	. . .	0.439
1999	3.6	8.9	14.9	23.2	49.4	21.5	0.458	4.0	9.7	15.3	22.6	48.4	. . .	0.441
2000	3.6	8.9	14.8	23.0	49.8	22.1	0.462	4.1	9.8	15.2	22.3	48.6	. . .	0.442
2001	3.5	8.7	14.6	23.0	50.1	22.4	0.466	4.0	9.6	15.2	22.4	48.8	. . .	0.446
2002	3.5	8.8	14.8	23.3	49.7	21.7	0.462	4.0	9.6	15.2	22.7	48.4	. . .	0.443
2003	3.4	8.7	14.8	23.4	49.8	21.4	0.464	3.9	9.5	15.2	22.8	48.6	. . .	0.445
2004	3.4	8.7	14.7	23.2	50.1	21.8	0.466	3.8	9.6	15.2	22.7	48.7	. . .	0.447
2005	3.4	8.6	14.6	23.0	50.4	22.2	0.469	3.8	9.5	15.1	22.6	49.1	. . .	0.450
2006	3.4	8.6	14.5	22.9	50.5	22.3	0.470	3.8	9.4	14.9	22.5	49.3	. . .	0.452
2007	3.4	8.7	14.8	23.4	49.7	21.2	0.463	3.8	9.5	15.3	22.9	48.5	. . .	0.444
2008	3.4	8.6	14.7	23.3	50.0	21.5	0.466	3.7	9.4	15.1	22.8	48.9	21.4	0.450
2009	3.4	8.6	14.6	23.2	50.3	21.7	0.468	3.6	9.3	15.0	22.9	49.4	21.7	0.456
2010	3.3	8.5	14.6	23.4	50.3	21.3	0.470	3.4	9.2	15.0	23.1	49.2	21.0	0.456
2011	3.2	8.4	14.3	23.0	51.1	22.3	0.477	3.4	9.0	14.8	22.8	50.0	22.1	0.463
2012	3.2	8.3	14.4	23.0	51.0	22.3	0.477	3.4	9.0	14.8	22.9	49.9	22.1	0.463
2013	3.1	8.2	14.3	23.0	51.4	22.2	0.482	3.5	8.8	14.7	22.8	50.3	22.1	0.467
2014	3.1	8.2	14.3	23.2	51.2	21.9	0.480	3.3	9.0	14.8	22.9	50.0	21.8	0.464
2015	3.1	8.2	14.3	23.2	51.1	22.1	0.479	3.4	9.0	14.8	22.9	49.8	21.8	0.462
2016	3.1	8.3	14.2	22.9	51.5	22.6	0.481	3.5	9.1	14.7	22.5	50.2	22.4	0.464
2017	3.1	8.2	14.3	23.0	51.5	22.3	0.482	3.5	9.0	14.7	22.7	50.1	21.8	0.463
2018	3.0	8.1	14.0	22.6	52.3	23.2	0.489	3.4	8.9	14.4	22.4	50.9	22.7	0.471
2019	3.1	8.3	14.1	22.6	52.0	23.1	0.486	3.5	9.1	14.7	22.4	50.3	22.5	0.464
2020	3.1	8.3	14.1	22.7	51.9	23.0	0.484	3.6	9.0	14.6	22.3	50.5	23.0	0.465

. . . = Not available.

Table 3-4. Shares of Aggregate Income Received by Each Fifth and Top 5 Percent of Families

Year	Number of families (thousands)	Share of aggregate income (percent)						Mean family income (2019 dollars)						Gini coefficient
		Lowest fifth	Second fifth	Third fifth	Fourth fifth	Highest fifth	Top 5 percent	Lowest fifth	Second fifth	Third fifth	Fourth fifth	Highest fifth	Top 5 percent	
1950	39 929	4.5	12.0	17.4	23.4	42.7	17.3	...	...	...	...	...	...	0.379
1951	40 578	5.0	12.4	17.6	23.4	41.6	16.8	...	...	...	...	...	...	0.363
1952	40 832	4.9	12.3	17.4	23.4	41.9	17.4	...	...	...	...	...	...	0.368
1953	41 202	4.7	12.5	18.0	23.9	40.9	15.7	...	...	...	...	...	...	0.359
1954	41 951	4.5	12.1	17.7	23.9	41.8	16.3	...	...	...	...	...	...	0.371
1955	42 889	4.8	12.3	17.8	23.7	41.3	16.4	...	...	...	...	...	...	0.363
1956	43 497	5.0	12.5	17.9	23.7	41.0	16.1	...	...	...	...	...	...	0.358
1957	43 696	5.1	12.7	18.1	23.8	40.4	15.6	...	...	...	...	...	...	0.351
1958	44 232	5.0	12.5	18.0	23.9	40.6	15.4	...	...	...	...	...	...	0.354
1959	45 111	4.9	12.3	17.9	23.8	41.1	15.9	...	...	...	...	...	...	0.361
1960	45 539	4.8	12.2	17.8	24.0	41.3	15.9	...	...	...	...	...	...	0.364
1961	46 418	4.7	11.9	17.5	23.8	42.2	16.6	...	...	...	...	...	...	0.374
1962	47 059	5.0	12.1	17.6	24.0	41.3	15.7	...	...	...	...	...	...	0.362
1963	47 540	5.0	12.1	17.7	24.0	41.2	15.8	...	...	...	...	...	...	0.362
1964	47 956	5.1	12.0	17.7	24.0	41.2	15.9	...	...	...	...	...	...	0.361
1965	48 509	5.2	12.2	17.8	23.9	40.9	15.5	...	...	...	...	...	...	0.356
1966	49 214	5.6	12.4	17.8	23.8	40.5	15.6	16 230	36 030	51 554	69 016	117 788	180 865	0.349
1967	50 111	5.4	12.2	17.5	23.5	41.4	16.4	16 483	36 858	52 978	71 052	125 460	198 498	0.358
1968	50 823	5.6	12.4	17.7	23.7	40.5	15.6	17 766	38 748	55 358	74 034	126 505	195 012	0.348
1969	51 586	5.6	12.4	17.7	23.7	40.6	15.6	18 330	40 481	57 928	77 600	132 900	204 126	0.349
1970	52 227	5.4	12.2	17.6	23.8	40.9	15.6	18 053	39 918	57 718	77 857	133 884	203 870	0.353
1971	53 296	5.5	12.0	17.6	23.8	41.1	15.7	18 069	39 332	57 547	77 936	134 236	204 676	0.355
1972	54 373	5.5	11.9	17.5	23.9	41.4	15.9	18 858	41 146	60 437	82 534	143 141	219 444	0.359
1973	55 053	5.5	11.9	17.5	24.0	41.1	15.5	19 351	41 915	61 586	84 166	144 406	217 932	0.356
1974	55 698	5.7	12.0	17.6	24.1	40.6	14.8	19 692	41 570	60 690	83 149	140 107	204 360	0.355
1975	56 245	5.6	11.9	17.7	24.2	40.7	14.9	18 920	39 998	59 473	81 431	137 225	201 300	0.357
1976	56 710	5.6	11.9	17.7	24.2	40.7	14.9	19 378	41 009	61 174	83 584	140 677	205 895	0.358
1977	57 215	5.5	11.7	17.6	24.3	40.9	14.9	19 295	41 245	62 032	85 570	144 157	210 158	0.363
1978	57 804	5.4	11.7	17.6	24.2	41.1	15.1	19 568	42 436	63 720	87 792	148 974	218 305	0.363
1979	59 550	5.4	11.6	17.5	24.1	41.4	15.3	19 757	42 716	64 420	88 690	152 122	225 175	0.365
1980	60 309	5.3	11.6	17.6	24.4	41.1	14.6	18 991	41 341	62 453	86 645	145 884	207 386	0.365
1981	61 019	5.3	11.4	17.5	24.6	41.2	14.4	18 414	40 043	61 244	85 986	144 274	201 599	0.369
1982	61 393	5.0	11.3	17.2	24.4	42.2	15.3	17 370	39 411	60 179	85 370	147 514	211 054	0.380
1983	62 015	4.9	11.2	17.2	24.5	42.4	15.3	17 104	39 354	60 548	86 294	149 626	215 731	0.382
1984	62 706	4.8	11.1	17.1	24.5	42.5	15.4	17 676	40 470	62 440	89 288	155 181	224 363	0.383
1985	63 558	4.8	11.0	16.9	24.3	43.1	16.1	17 880	41 029	63 346	90 801	161 368	241 149	0.389
1986	64 491	4.7	10.9	16.9	24.1	43.4	16.5	18 396	42 476	65 805	94 025	169 354	257 175	0.392
1987	65 204	4.6	10.7	16.8	24.0	43.8	17.2	18 365	42 984	66 747	95 528	174 580	273 295	0.393
1988	65 837	4.6	10.7	16.7	24.0	44.0	17.2	18 533	43 159	67 162	96 454	176 978	276 522	0.395
1989	66 090	4.6	10.6	16.5	23.7	44.6	17.9	18 893	43 954	68 285	98 243	184 982	296 325	0.401
1990	66 322	4.6	10.8	16.6	23.8	44.3	17.4	18 707	43 633	67 199	96 640	179 601	281 802	0.396
1991	67 173	4.5	10.7	16.6	24.1	44.2	17.1	17 869	42 414	65 811	95 450	175 363	271 346	0.397
1992	68 216	4.3	10.5	16.5	24.0	44.7	17.6	17 170	41 413	65 425	95 099	176 969	278 626	0.404
1993	68 506	4.1	9.9	15.7	23.3	47.0	20.3	17 015	40 865	64 758	95 996	193 958	334 765	0.429
1994	69 313	4.2	10.0	15.7	23.3	46.9	20.1	17 776	42 057	66 415	98 174	197 847	339 425	0.426
1995	69 597	4.4	10.1	15.8	23.2	46.5	20.0	18 825	43 374	67 909	99 359	199 619	342 348	0.421
1996	70 241	4.2	10.0	15.8	23.1	46.8	20.3	18 537	43 700	69 126	101 006	204 490	353 801	0.425
1997	70 884	4.2	9.9	15.7	23.0	47.2	20.7	19 211	45 014	71 022	104 144	213 958	374 462	0.429
1998	71 551	4.2	9.9	15.7	23.0	47.3	20.7	19 691	46 346	73 354	107 574	221 413	387 536	0.430
1999	73 206	4.3	9.9	15.6	23.0	47.2	20.3	20 484	47 615	75 157	110 929	227 350	391 993	0.429
2000	73 778	4.3	9.8	15.4	22.7	47.7	21.1	21 024	48 070	75 549	111 344	233 610	413 961	0.433
2001	74 340	4.2	9.7	15.4	22.9	47.7	21.0	20 296	46 995	74 602	110 947	231 088	405 757	0.435
2002	75 616	4.2	9.7	15.5	23.0	47.6	20.8	19 975	46 344	73 916	109 936	227 009	397 292	0.434
2003	76 232	4.1	9.6	15.5	23.2	47.6	20.5	19 328	45 838	73 873	111 073	227 575	392 200	0.436
2004	76 866	4.0	9.6	15.4	23.0	47.9	20.9	19 265	45 854	73 595	109 953	228 835	398 665	0.438
2005	77 418	4.0	9.6	15.3	22.9	48.1	21.1	19 379	46 110	73 787	110 358	231 349	405 024	0.440
2006	78 454	4.0	9.5	15.1	22.9	48.5	21.5	19 752	46 737	74 340	112 358	238 190	421 627	0.444
2007	77 908	4.1	9.7	15.6	23.3	47.3	20.1	19 861	47 346	75 948	113 569	230 559	391 355	0.432
2008	78 874	4.0	9.6	15.5	23.1	47.8	20.5	18 933	45 381	73 303	109 700	226 638	389 151	0.438
2009	78 867	3.9	9.4	15.3	23.2	48.2	20.7	18 262	44 250	71 558	108 652	226 337	388 233	0.443
2010	79 559	3.8	9.4	15.4	23.5	47.9	20.0	17 536	43 374	70 695	107 857	219 884	367 659	0.440
2011	80 529	3.8	9.3	15.1	23.0	48.9	21.3	17 409	42 783	69 527	106 208	225 481	392 484	0.450
2012	80 944	3.8	9.2	15.1	23.0	48.9	21.3	17 329	42 596	69 682	106 507	225 966	393 053	0.451
2013	82 316	3.6	9.1	15.0	22.9	49.4	21.2	17 708	43 437	70 261	106 857	227 205	394 332	0.455
2014	81 730	3.6	9.2	15.1	23.2	48.9	20.8	17 414	43 975	72 315	111 464	234 592	400 049	0.452
2015	82 199	3.7	9.2	15.2	23.2	48.6	20.9	18 741	46 078	76 077	116 022	243 100	417 429	0.448
2016	82 854	3.7	9.2	15.0	22.9	49.2	21.4	19 392	47 881	77 669	118 521	255 140	444 353	0.452
2017	83 103	3.8	9.2	15.1	23.1	48.8	20.7	19 757	48 336	79 096	120 807	255 560	434 528	0.449
2018	83 508	3.8	9.3	14.9	22.6	49.4	21.6	20 747	50 106	80 397	122 076	266 505	465 472	0.452
2019	83 698	3.9	9.2	14.8	22.5	49.5	21.9	22 840	53 823	86 261	131 610	289 141	511 287	0.454

. . . = Not available.

SECTION 3B: POVERTY

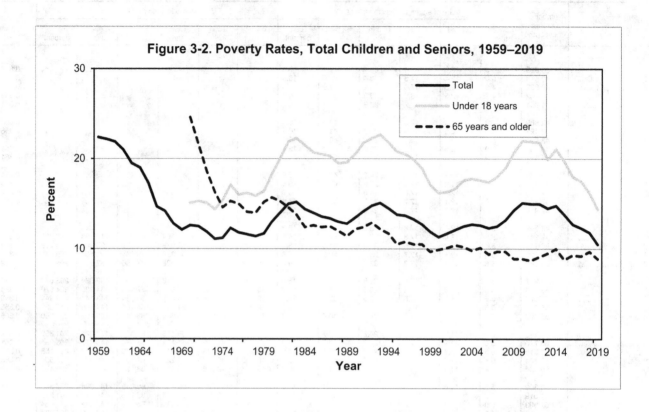

Figure 3-2. Poverty Rates, Total Children and Seniors, 1959–2019

- Poverty measures the ability of families and individuals who cannot earn an income to cover the cost of a minimum standard of living. There is not one poverty amount but rather a range of income depending on age and types and sizes of families. In 2019, an individual aged 65 and over is considered in poverty with an income of $13,300. For a family of three with one child under 18, the poverty threshold was $20,578. (See Table 3-5 and the Notes and Definitions section at the end of Chapter 3 how COVID-19 interrupted the collection of income and poverty data.)

- Figure 3-2 illustrates the growing percentage of employed persons who are classified as working poor. In 2019, over 31 percent of the civilian labor force were identified as working poor. Full time workers are less likely to be working poor. However, women, Blacks, Hispanics, and those without a high school diploma are all more likely to be among the working poor. (See Table 3-9)

- The official poverty rate in 2019 was 10.5 percent, down 1.3 percentage points from 11.8 percent in 2018. This is the fifth consecutive annual decline in poverty. Since 2014, the rate has fallen 4.3 percentage points, from 14.8 percent to 10.5 percent. There were approximately 34 million people in poverty in 2019 down 12.6 million from 2014, the largest number in people in poverty. (Table 3-6)

- Beginning in 2011, the U.S. Census Bureau began publishing the Supplemental Poverty Measure (SPM), which extends the official poverty measure by taking in account many of the government programs designed to assist low-income families and individuals that are not included in the official poverty measure. In 2019, the overall SPM rate was 11.7 percent down 2.2 percentage points from 2019. (See Table 3-10)

Table 3-5. Weighted Average Poverty Thresholds by Family Size

(Dollars.)

Year	Unrelated individuals			Families of 2 people			Families, all ages							CPI-U, all items (1982–1984 = 100)
	All ages	Under 65 years	65 years and older	All ages	Householder under 65 years	Householder 65 years and older	3 people	4 people	5 people	6 people	7 people	8 people	9 people or more	
1959	1 467	1 503	1 397	1 894	1 952	1 761	2 324	2 973	3 506	3 944	...	...	...	29.2
1960	1 490	1 526	1 418	1 924	1 982	1 788	2 359	3 022	3 560	4 002	...	...	...	29.6
1961	1 506	1 545	1 433	1 942	2 005	1 808	2 383	3 054	3 597	4 041	...	...	...	29.9
1962	1 519	1 562	1 451	1 962	2 027	1 828	2 412	3 089	3 639	4 088	...	...	...	30.3
1963	1 539	1 581	1 470	1 988	2 052	1 850	2 442	3 128	3 685	4 135	...	...	...	30.6
1964	1 558	1 601	1 488	2 015	2 079	1 875	2 473	3 169	3 732	4 193	...	...	...	31.0
1965	1 582	1 626	1 512	2 048	2 114	1 906	2 514	3 223	3 797	4 264	...	...	...	31.5
1966	1 628	1 674	1 556	2 107	2 175	1 961	2 588	3 317	3 908	4 388	...	...	...	32.5
1967	1 675	1 722	1 600	2 168	2 238	2 017	2 661	3 410	4 019	4 516	...	...	...	33.4
1968	1 748	1 797	1 667	2 262	2 333	2 102	2 774	3 553	4 188	4 706	...	...	...	34.8
1969	1 840	1 893	1 757	2 383	2 458	2 215	2 924	3 743	4 415	4 958	...	...	...	36.7
1970	1 954	2 010	1 861	2 525	2 604	2 348	3 099	3 968	4 680	5 260	...	...	...	38.8
1971	2 040	2 098	1 940	2 633	2 716	2 448	3 229	4 137	4 880	5 489	...	...	...	40.5
1972	2 109	2 168	2 005	2 724	2 808	2 530	3 339	4 275	5 044	5 673	...	...	...	41.8
1973	2 247	2 307	2 130	2 895	2 984	2 688	3 548	4 540	5 358	6 028	...	...	...	44.4
1974	2 495	2 562	2 364	3 211	3 312	2 982	3 936	5 038	5 950	6 699	...	...	...	49.3
1975	2 724	2 797	2 581	3 506	3 617	3 257	4 293	5 500	6 499	7 316	...	...	...	53.8
1976	2 884	2 959	2 730	3 711	3 826	3 445	4 540	5 815	6 876	7 760	...	...	...	56.9
1977	3 075	3 152	2 906	3 951	4 072	3 666	4 833	6 191	7 320	8 261	...	...	...	60.6
1978	3 311	3 392	3 127	4 249	4 383	3 944	5 201	6 662	7 880	8 891	...	...	...	65.2
1979	3 689	3 778	3 479	4 725	4 878	4 390	5 784	7 412	8 775	9 914	...	...	...	72.6
1980	4 190	4 290	3 949	5 363	5 537	4 983	6 565	8 414	9 966	11 269	12 761	14 199	16 896	82.4
1981	4 620	4 729	4 359	5 917	6 111	5 498	7 250	9 287	11 007	12 449	14 110	15 655	18 572	90.9
1982	4 901	5 019	4 626	6 281	6 487	5 836	7 693	9 862	11 684	13 207	15 036	16 719	19 698	96.5
1983	5 061	5 180	4 775	6 483	6 697	6 023	7 938	10 178	12 049	13 630	15 500	17 170	20 310	99.6
1984	5 278	5 400	4 979	6 762	6 983	6 282	8 277	10 609	12 566	14 207	16 096	17 961	21 247	103.9
1985	5 469	5 593	5 156	6 998	7 231	6 503	8 573	10 989	13 007	14 696	16 656	18 512	22 083	107.6
1986	5 572	5 701	5 255	7 138	7 372	6 630	8 737	11 203	13 259	14 986	17 049	18 791	22 497	109.6
1987	5 778	5 909	5 447	7 397	7 641	6 872	9 056	11 611	13 737	15 509	17 649	19 515	23 105	113.6
1988	6 022	6 155	5 674	7 704	7 958	7 157	9 435	12 092	14 304	16 146	18 232	20 253	24 129	118.3
1989	6 310	6 451	5 947	8 076	8 343	7 501	9 885	12 674	14 990	16 921	19 162	21 328	25 480	124.0
1990	6 652	6 800	6 268	8 509	8 794	7 905	10 419	13 359	15 792	17 839	20 241	22 582	26 848	130.7
1991	6 932	7 086	6 532	8 865	9 165	8 241	10 860	13 924	16 456	18 587	21 058	23 582	27 942	136.2
1992	7 143	7 299	6 729	9 137	9 443	8 487	11 186	14 335	16 952	19 137	21 594	24 053	28 745	140.3
1993	7 363	7 518	6 930	9 414	9 728	8 740	11 522	14 763	17 449	19 718	22 383	24 838	29 529	144.5
1994	7 547	7 710	7 108	9 661	9 976	8 967	11 821	15 141	17 900	20 235	22 923	25 427	30 300	148.2
1995	7 763	7 929	7 309	9 933	10 259	9 219	12 158	15 569	18 408	20 804	23 552	26 237	31 280	152.4
1996	7 995	8 163	7 525	10 233	10 564	9 491	12 516	16 036	18 952	21 389	24 268	27 091	31 971	156.9
1997	8 183	8 350	7 698	10 473	10 805	9 712	12 802	16 400	19 380	21 886	24 802	27 593	32 566	160.5
1998	8 316	8 480	7 818	10 634	10 972	9 862	13 003	16 660	19 680	22 228	25 257	28 166	33 339	163.0
1999	8 499	8 667	7 990	10 864	11 213	10 075	13 289	17 030	20 128	22 730	25 918	28 970	34 436	166.6
2000	8 791	8 959	8 259	11 235	11 589	10 418	13 740	17 604	20 815	23 533	26 750	29 701	35 150	172.2
2001	9 039	9 214	8 494	11 569	11 920	10 715	14 128	18 104	21 405	24 195	27 517	30 627	36 286	177.1
2002	9 183	9 359	8 628	11 756	12 110	10 885	14 348	18 392	21 744	24 576	28 001	30 907	37 062	179.9
2003	9 393	9 573	8 825	12 015	12 384	11 133	14 680	18 810	22 245	25 122	28 544	31 589	37 656	184.0
2004	9 646	9 827	9 060	12 335	12 714	11 430	15 066	19 307	22 830	25 787	29 233	32 641	39 062	188.9
2005	9 973	10 160	9 367	12 755	13 145	11 815	15 577	19 971	23 613	26 683	30 249	33 610	40 288	195.3
2006	10 294	10 488	9 669	13 167	13 569	12 201	16 079	20 614	24 382	27 560	31 205	34 774	41 499	201.6
2007	10 590	10 787	9 944	13 540	13 954	12 550	16 530	21 203	25 080	28 323	32 233	35 816	42 739	207.3
2008	10 991	11 201	10 326	14 051	14 489	13 030	17 163	22 025	26 049	29 456	33 529	37 220	44 346	215.3
2009	10 956	11 161	10 289	13 991	14 439	12 982	17 098	21 954	25 991	29 405	33 372	37 252	44 366	214.5
2010	11 137	11 344	10 458	14 216	14 676	13 194	17 373	22 315	26 442	29 904	34 019	37 953	45 224	218.1
2011	11 484	11 702	10 788	14 657	15 139	13 609	17 916	23 021	27 251	30 847	35 085	39 064	46 572	224.9
2012	11 720	11 945	11 011	14 937	15 400	13 892	18 284	23 492	27 827	31 471	35 743	39 688	47 297	229.6
2013	11 888	12 119	11 173	15 142	15 679	14 095	18 552	23 834	28 265	31 925	36 384	40 484	48 065	233.0
2014	12 071	12 316	11 354	15 379	15 934	14 326	18 850	24 230	28 695	32 473	36 927	40 968	49 021	236.7
2015	12 082	12 331	11 367	15 391	15 952	14 342	18 871	24 257	28 741	32 542	36 998	41 029	49 177	237.0
2016	12 228	12 486	11 511	15 569	16 151	14 522	19 105	24 563	29 111	32 928	37 458	41 781	49 721	240.0
2017	12 488	12 752	11 756	15 877	16 493	14 828	19 515	25 094	29 714	33 618	38 173	42 684	50 681	245.1
2018	12 784	13 064	12 043	16 247	16 889	15 193	19 985	25 701	30 454	34 533	39 194	43 602	51 393	251.1
2019	13 011	13 300	12 261	16 521	17 196	15 468	20 335	26 172	31 021	35 129	40 016	44 461	52 875	255.7

. . . = Not available.

Table 3-6. Poverty Status of People by Race and Hispanic Origin

(Thousands of people, percent of population.)

Year	Number of people, all races	Below poverty level												
		All races		White		White, not Hispanic		Black		Asian [1]		Hispanic (any race)	
		Number	Poverty rate (percent)	Number	Poverty rate (percent)	Number	Poverty rate (percent)	Number	Poverty rate (percent)	Number	Poverty rate (percent)	Number	Poverty rate (percent)
1970	202 183	25 420	12.6	17 484	9.9	. . .	. . .	7 548	33.5	. . .	. . .	. . .	. . .
1971	204 554	25 559	12.5	17 780	9.9	. . .	. . .	7 396	32.5	. . .	. . .	. . .	. . .
1972	206 004	24 460	11.9	16 203	9.0	. . .	. . .	7 710	33.3	. . .	. . .	2 414	22.8
1973	207 621	22 973	11.1	15 142	8.4	12 864	7.5	7 388	31.4	. . .	. . .	2 366	21.9
1974	209 362	23 370	11.2	15 736	8.6	13 217	7.7	7 182	30.3	. . .	. . .	2 575	23.0
1975	210 864	25 877	12.3	17 770	9.7	14 883	8.6	7 545	31.3	. . .	. . .	2 991	26.9
1976	212 303	24 975	11.8	16 713	9.1	14 025	8.1	7 595	31.1	. . .	. . .	2 783	24.7
1977	213 867	24 720	11.6	16 416	8.9	13 802	8.0	7 726	31.3	. . .	. . .	2 700	22.4
1978	215 656	24 497	11.4	16 259	8.7	13 755	7.9	7 625	30.6	. . .	. . .	2 607	21.6
1979	222 903	26 072	11.7	17 214	9.0	14 419	8.1	8 050	31.0	. . .	. . .	2 921	21.8
1980	225 027	29 272	13.0	19 699	10.2	16 365	9.1	8 579	32.5	. . .	. . .	3 491	25.7
1981	227 157	31 822	14.0	21 553	11.1	17 987	9.9	9 173	34.2	. . .	. . .	3 713	26.5
1982	229 412	34 398	15.0	23 517	12.0	19 362	10.6	9 697	35.6	. . .	. . .	4 301	29.9
1983	231 700	35 303	15.2	23 984	12.1	19 538	10.8	9 882	35.7	. . .	. . .	4 633	28.0
1984	233 816	33 700	14.4	22 955	11.5	18 300	10.0	9 490	33.8	. . .	. . .	4 806	28.4
1985	236 594	33 064	14.0	22 860	11.4	17 839	9.7	8 926	31.3	. . .	. . .	5 236	29.0
1986	238 554	32 370	13.6	22 183	11.0	17 244	9.4	8 983	31.1	. . .	. . .	5 117	27.3
1987	240 982	32 221	13.4	21 195	10.4	16 029	8.7	9 520	32.4	1 021	16.1	5 422	28.0
1988	243 530	31 745	13.0	20 715	10.1	15 565	8.4	9 356	31.3	1 117	17.3	5 357	26.7
1989	245 992	31 528	12.8	20 785	10.0	15 599	8.3	9 302	30.7	939	14.1	5 430	26.2
1990	248 644	33 585	13.5	22 326	10.7	16 622	8.8	9 837	31.9	858	12.2	6 006	28.1
1991	251 192	35 708	14.2	23 747	11.3	17 741	9.4	10 242	32.7	996	13.8	6 339	28.7
1992	256 549	38 014	14.8	25 259	11.9	18 202	9.6	10 827	33.4	985	12.7	7 592	29.6
1993	259 278	39 265	15.1	26 226	12.2	18 882	9.9	10 877	33.1	1 134	15.3	8 126	30.6
1994	261 616	38 059	14.5	25 379	11.7	18 110	9.4	10 196	30.6	974	14.6	8 416	30.7
1995	263 733	36 425	13.8	24 423	11.2	16 267	8.5	9 872	29.3	1 411	14.6	8 574	30.3
1996	266 218	36 529	13.7	24 650	11.2	16 462	8.6	9 694	28.4	1 454	14.5	8 697	29.4
1997	268 480	35 574	13.3	24 396	11.0	16 491	8.6	9 116	26.5	1 468	14.0	8 308	27.1
1998	271 059	34 476	12.7	23 454	10.5	15 799	8.2	9 091	26.1	1 360	12.5	8 070	25.6
1999	276 208	32 791	11.9	22 169	9.8	14 735	7.7	8 441	23.6	1 285	10.7	7 876	22.7
2000	278 944	31 581	11.3	21 645	9.5	14 366	7.4	7 982	22.5	1 258	9.9	7 747	21.5
2001	281 475	32 907	11.7	22 739	9.9	15 271	7.8	8 136	22.7	1 275	10.2	7 997	21.4
2002	285 317	34 570	12.1	. . .	. . .	. . .	. . .	. . .	. . .	. . .	. . .	8 555	21.8
2003	287 699	35 861	12.5	. . .	. . .	. . .	. . .	. . .	. . .	. . .	. . .	9 051	22.5
2004	290 617	37 040	12.7	. . .	. . .	. . .	. . .	. . .	. . .	. . .	. . .	9 122	21.9
2005	293 135	36 950	12.6	. . .	. . .	. . .	. . .	. . .	. . .	. . .	. . .	9 368	21.8
2006	296 450	36 460	12.3	. . .	. . .	. . .	. . .	. . .	. . .	. . .	. . .	9 243	20.6
2007	298 699	37 276	12.5	. . .	. . .	. . .	. . .	. . .	. . .	. . .	. . .	9 890	21.5
2008	301 041	39 829	13.2	. . .	. . .	. . .	. . .	. . .	. . .	. . .	. . .	10 987	23.2
2009	303 820	43 569	14.3	. . .	. . .	. . .	. . .	. . .	. . .	. . .	. . .	12 350	25.3
2010	306 130	46 343	15.1	. . .	. . .	. . .	. . .	. . .	. . .	. . .	. . .	13 522	26.5
2011	308 456	46 247	15.0	. . .	. . .	. . .	. . .	. . .	. . .	. . .	. . .	13 244	25.3
2012	310 648	46 496	15.0	. . .	. . .	. . .	. . .	. . .	. . .	. . .	. . .	13 616	25.6
2013	312 965	45 318	14.5	. . .	. . .	. . .	. . .	. . .	. . .	. . .	. . .	12 744	23.5
2014	315 804	46 657	14.8	. . .	. . .	. . .	. . .	. . .	. . .	. . .	. . .	13 104	23.6
2015	318 454	43 123	13.5	. . .	. . .	. . .	. . .	. . .	. . .	. . .	. . .	12 133	21.4
2016	319 911	40 616	12.7	. . .	. . .	. . .	. . .	. . .	. . .	. . .	. . .	11 137	19.4
2017	322 549	39 698	12.3	. . .	. . .	. . .	. . .	. . .	. . .	. . .	. . .	10 790	18.3
2018	323 847	38 146	11.8	. . .	. . .	. . .	. . .	. . .	. . .	. . .	. . .	10 526	17.6
2019	324 754	33 984	10.5	. . .	. . .	. . .	. . .	. . .	. . .	. . .	. . .	9 545	15.7
By race													
Race alone													
2004	. . .	. . .	. . .	25 327	10.8	16 908	8.7	9 014	24.7	. . .	. . .	. . .	. . .
2005	. . .	. . .	. . .	24 872	10.6	16 227	8.3	9 168	24.9	. . .	. . .	. . .	. . .
2006	. . .	. . .	. . .	24 416	10.3	16 013	8.2	9 048	24.3	. . .	. . .	. . .	. . .
2007	. . .	. . .	. . .	25 120	10.5	16 032	8.2	9 237	24.5	. . .	. . .	. . .	. . .
2008	. . .	. . .	. . .	26 990	11.2	17 024	8.6	9 379	24.7	. . .	. . .	. . .	. . .
2009	. . .	. . .	. . .	29 830	12.3	18 530	9.4	9 944	25.8	. . .	. . .	. . .	. . .
2010	. . .	. . .	. . .	31 083	13.0	19 251	9.9	10 746	27.4	. . .	. . .	. . .	. . .
2011	. . .	. . .	. . .	30 849	12.8	19 171	9.8	10 929	27.6	. . .	. . .	. . .	. . .
2012	. . .	. . .	. . .	30 816	12.7	18 940	9.7	10 911	27.2	. . .	. . .	. . .	. . .
2013	. . .	. . .	. . .	31 287	12.9	18 796	9.6	11 041	27.2	. . .	. . .	. . .	. . .
2014	. . .	. . .	. . .	31 089	12.7	19 652	10.1	10 755	26.2	. . .	. . .	. . .	. . .
2015	. . .	. . .	. . .	28 566	11.6	17 786	9.1	10 020	24.1	. . .	. . .	. . .	. . .
2016	. . .	. . .	. . .	27 113	11.0	17 263	8.8	9 234	22.0	. . .	. . .	. . .	. . .
2017	. . .	. . .	. . .	26 436	10.7	16 993	8.7	8 993	21.2	. . .	. . .	. . .	. . .
2018	. . .	. . .	. . .	24 945	10.1	15 725	8.1	8 884	20.8	. . .	. . .	. . .	. . .
2019	. . .	. . .	. . .	22 512	9.1	14 152	7.3	8 073	18.8	. . .	. . .	. . .	. . .
Race alone or in combination													
2010	. . .	. . .	. . .	. . .	. . .	. . .	. . .	11 597	27.4	2 064	12.0	. . .	. . .
2011	. . .	. . .	. . .	. . .	. . .	. . .	. . .	11 730	27.5	2 189	12.3	. . .	. . .
2012	. . .	. . .	. . .	. . .	. . .	. . .	. . .	11 809	27.1	2 072	11.4	. . .	. . .
2013	. . .	. . .	. . .	. . .	. . .	. . .	. . .	11 162	25.3	1 974	10.4	. . .	. . .
2014	. . .	. . .	. . .	. . .	. . .	. . .	. . .	11 581	26.0	2 268	11.5	. . .	. . .
2015	. . .	. . .	. . .	. . .	. . .	. . .	. . .	10 797	23.9	2 234	11.1	. . .	. . .
2016	. . .	. . .	. . .	. . .	. . .	. . .	. . .	9 965	21.8	2 062	9.9	. . .	. . .
2017	. . .	. . .	. . .	. . .	. . .	. . .	. . .	9 820	21.2	2 063	9.6	. . .	. . .
2018	. . .	. . .	. . .	. . .	. . .	. . .	. . .	9 695	20.7	2 166	9.8	. . .	. . .
2019	. . .	. . .	. . .	. . .	. . .	. . .	. . .	8 836	18.7	1 588	7.1	. . .	. . .

[1] For 1987 through 2001, Asian and Pacific Islander.
. . . = Not available.

Table 3-7. Poverty Status of Families by Type of Family

(Thousands of families, percent.)

Year	Married couple families				Families with no spouse present						Unrelated individuals	
	Number of families		Poverty rate (percent)		Male householder			Female householder				
	Total	Total below poverty level	Total	With children under 18 years	Families below poverty level	Poverty rate (percent)		Families below poverty level	Poverty rate (percent)		Below poverty level	Poverty rate
						Total	With children under 18 years		Total	With children under 18 years		
1959	39 335	...	...	...	...	...	...	1 916	42.6	59.9	4 928	46.1
1960	39 624	...	...	...	...	...	...	1 955	42.4	56.3	4 926	45.2
1961	40 405	...	...	...	...	...	...	1 954	42.1	56.0	5 119	45.9
1962	40 923	...	...	...	...	...	...	2 034	42.9	59.7	5 002	45.4
1963	41 311	...	...	...	...	...	...	1 972	40.4	55.7	4 938	44.2
1964	41 648	...	...	...	...	...	...	1 822	36.4	49.7	5 143	42.7
1965	42 107	...	...	...	...	...	...	1 916	38.4	52.2	4 827	39.8
1966	42 553	...	...	...	...	...	...	1 721	33.1	47.1	4 701	38.3
1967	43 292	...	...	...	...	...	...	1 774	33.3	44.5	4 998	38.1
1968	43 842	...	...	...	...	...	...	1 755	32.3	44.6	4 694	34.0
1969	44 436	...	...	...	...	...	...	1 827	32.7	44.9	4 972	34.0
1970	44 739	...	...	...	...	...	...	1 952	32.5	43.8	5 090	32.9
1971	45 752	...	...	...	...	...	...	2 100	33.9	44.9	5 154	31.6
1972	46 314	...	...	...	...	...	...	2 158	32.7	44.5	4 883	29.0
1973	46 812	2 482	5.3	...	154	10.7	...	2 193	32.2	43.2	4 674	25.6
1974	47 069	2 474	5.3	6.0	125	8.9	15.4	2 324	32.1	43.7	4 553	24.1
1975	47 318	2 904	6.1	7.2	116	8.0	11.7	2 430	32.5	44.0	5 088	25.1
1976	47 497	2 606	5.5	6.4	162	10.8	15.4	2 543	33.0	44.1	5 344	24.9
1977	47 385	2 524	5.3	6.3	177	11.1	14.8	2 610	31.7	41.8	5 216	22.6
1978	47 692	2 474	5.2	5.9	152	9.2	14.7	2 654	31.4	42.2	5 435	22.1
1979	49 112	2 640	5.4	6.1	176	10.2	15.5	2 645	30.4	39.6	5 743	21.9
1980	49 294	3 032	6.2	7.7	213	11.0	18.0	2 972	32.7	42.9	6 227	22.9
1981	49 630	3 394	6.8	8.7	205	10.3	14.0	3 252	34.6	44.3	6 490	23.4
1982	49 908	3 789	7.6	9.8	290	14.4	20.6	3 434	36.3	47.8	6 458	23.1
1983	50 081	3 815	7.6	10.1	268	13.2	20.2	3 564	36.0	47.1	6 740	23.1
1984	50 350	3 488	6.9	9.4	292	13.1	18.1	3 498	34.5	45.7	6 609	21.8
1985	50 933	3 438	6.7	8.9	311	12.9	17.1	3 474	34.0	45.4	6 725	21.5
1986	51 537	3 123	6.1	8.0	287	11.4	17.8	3 613	34.6	46.0	6 846	21.6
1987	51 675	3 011	5.8	7.7	340	12.0	16.8	3 654	34.2	45.5	6 857	20.8
1988	52 100	2 897	5.6	7.2	336	11.8	18.0	3 642	33.4	44.7	7 070	20.6
1989	52 317	2 931	5.6	7.3	348	12.1	18.1	3 504	32.2	42.8	6 760	19.2
1990	52 147	2 981	5.7	7.8	349	12.0	18.8	3 768	33.4	44.5	7 446	20.7
1991	52 457	3 158	6.0	8.3	392	13.0	19.6	4 161	35.6	47.1	7 773	21.1
1992	53 090	3 385	6.4	8.6	484	15.8	22.5	4 275	35.4	46.2	8 075	21.9
1993	53 181	3 481	6.5	9.0	488	16.8	22.5	4 424	35.6	46.1	8 388	22.1
1994	53 865	3 272	6.1	8.3	549	17.0	22.6	4 232	34.6	44.0	8 287	21.5
1995	53 570	2 982	5.6	7.5	493	14.0	19.7	4 057	32.4	41.5	8 247	20.9
1996	53 604	3 010	5.6	7.5	531	13.8	20.0	4 167	32.6	41.9	8 452	20.8
1997	54 321	2 821	5.2	7.1	507	13.0	18.7	3 995	31.6	41.0	8 687	20.8
1998	54 778	2 879	5.3	6.9	476	12.0	16.6	3 831	29.9	38.7	8 478	19.9
1999	56 290	2 748	4.9	6.4	485	11.8	16.3	3 559	27.8	35.7	8 400	19.1
2000	56 598	2 637	4.7	6.0	485	11.3	15.3	3 278	25.4	33.0	8 653	19.0
2001	56 755	2 760	4.9	6.1	583	13.1	17.7	3 470	26.4	33.6	9 226	19.9
2002	57 327	3 052	5.3	6.8	564	12.1	16.6	3 613	26.5	33.7	9 618	20.4
2003	57 725	3 115	5.4	7.0	636	13.5	19.1	3 856	28.0	35.5	9 713	20.4
2004	57 983	3 216	5.5	7.0	657	13.4	17.1	3 962	28.3	35.9	9 926	20.4
2005	58 189	2 944	5.1	6.5	669	13.0	17.6	4 044	28.7	36.2	10 425	21.1
2006	58 964	2 910	4.9	6.4	671	13.2	17.9	4 087	28.3	36.5	9 977	20.0
2007	58 395	2 849	4.9	6.7	696	13.6	17.5	4 078	28.3	37.0	10 189	19.7
2008	59 137	3 261	5.5	7.5	723	13.8	17.6	4 163	28.7	37.2	10 710	20.8
2009	58 428	3 409	5.8	8.3	942	16.9	23.7	4 441	29.9	38.5	11 678	22.0
2010	58 667	3 681	6.3	9.0	892	15.8	24.1	4 827	31.7	40.9	12 449	22.9
2011	58 963	3 652	6.2	8.8	950	16.1	21.9	4 894	31.2	40.9	12 416	22.8
2012	59 224	3 705	6.3	8.9	1 023	16.4	22.6	4 793	30.9	40.9	12 558	22.4
2013	59 692	3 476	5.8	7.6	1 008	15.9	19.7	4 646	30.6	39.6	13 181	23.3
2014	60 015	3 735	6.2	8.2	969	15.7	22.0	4 646	30.6	39.8	13 374	23.1
2015	60 258	3 245	5.4	7.5	939	14.9	22.1	4 404	28.2	36.5	12 671	21.5
2016	60 821	3 096	5.1	6.6	847	13.1	17.3	4 136	26.6	35.6	12 336	21.0
2017	61 254	3 005	4.9	6.4	793	12.4	16.2	3 959	25.7	34.4	12 593	20.7
2018	61 971	2 938	4.7	5.8	824	12.7	16.6	3 742	24.9	33.8	12 287	22.6
2019	62 355	2 507	4.0	7.6	746	11.5	16.0	3 300	22.2	36.5	11 300	18.6

... = Not available.

Table 3-8. Poverty Status of People by Sex and Age

(Thousands of people, percent of population.)

Year	Poverty status of people by sex				Poverty status of people by age					
	Males below poverty level		Females below poverty level		Children under 18 years below poverty level		People 18 to 64 years below poverty level		People 65 years and older below poverty level	
	Number (thousands)	Poverty rate (percent)	Number (thousands)	Poverty rate (percent)	Number (thousands)	Poverty rate (percent)	Number (thousands)	Poverty rate (percent)	Number (thousands)	Poverty rate (percent)
1959	. . .	. . .	. . .	. . .	17 552	27.3	16 457	17.0	5 481	35.2
1966	12 225	13.0	16 265	16.3	12 389	17.6	11 007	10.5	5 114	28.5
1967	11 813	12.5	15 951	15.8	11 656	16.6	10 725	10.0	5 388	29.5
1968	10 793	11.3	14 578	14.3	10 954	15.6	9 803	9.0	4 632	25.0
1969	10 292	10.6	13 978	13.6	9 691	14.0	9 669	8.7	4 787	25.3
1970	10 879	11.1	14 632	14.0	10 440	15.1	10 187	9.0	4 793	24.6
1971	10 708	10.8	14 841	14.1	10 551	15.3	10 735	9.3	4 273	21.6
1972	10 190	10.2	14 258	13.4	10 284	15.1	10 438	8.8	3 738	18.6
1973	9 642	9.6	13 316	12.5	9 642	14.4	9 977	8.3	3 354	16.3
1974	9 945	9.8	13 429	12.5	10 156	15.4	10 132	8.3	3 085	14.6
1975	10 908	10.7	14 970	13.8	11 104	17.1	11 456	9.2	3 317	15.3
1976	10 373	10.1	14 603	13.4	10 273	16.0	11 389	9.0	3 313	15.0
1977	10 340	10.0	14 381	13.0	10 288	16.2	11 316	8.8	3 177	14.1
1978	10 017	9.6	14 480	13.0	9 931	15.9	11 332	8.7	3 233	14.0
1979	10 861	10.1	15 211	13.2	10 377	16.4	12 014	8.9	3 682	15.2
1980	12 207	11.2	17 065	14.7	11 543	18.3	13 858	10.1	3 871	15.7
1981	13 360	12.1	18 462	15.8	12 505	20.0	15 464	11.1	3 853	15.3
1982	14 842	13.4	19 556	16.5	13 647	21.9	17 000	12.0	3 751	14.6
1983	15 296	13.6	20 006	16.8	13 911	22.3	17 767	12.4	3 625	13.8
1984	14 537	12.8	19 163	15.9	13 420	21.5	16 952	11.7	3 330	12.4
1985	14 140	12.3	18 923	15.6	13 010	20.7	16 598	11.3	3 456	12.6
1986	13 721	11.8	18 649	15.2	12 876	20.5	16 017	10.8	3 477	12.4
1987	13 781	11.8	18 439	14.9	12 843	20.3	15 815	10.6	3 563	12.5
1988	13 599	11.5	18 146	14.5	12 455	19.5	15 809	10.5	3 481	12.0
1989	13 366	11.2	18 162	14.4	12 590	19.6	15 575	10.2	3 363	11.4
1990	14 211	11.7	19 373	15.2	13 431	20.6	16 496	10.7	3 658	12.2
1991	15 082	12.3	20 626	16.0	14 341	21.8	17 586	11.4	3 781	12.4
1992	16 222	12.9	21 792	16.6	15 294	22.3	18 793	11.9	3 928	12.9
1993	16 900	13.3	22 365	16.9	15 727	22.7	19 781	12.4	3 755	12.2
1994	16 316	12.8	21 744	16.3	15 289	21.8	19 107	11.9	3 663	11.7
1995	15 683	12.2	20 742	15.4	14 665	20.8	18 442	11.4	3 318	10.5
1996	15 611	12.0	20 918	15.4	14 463	20.5	18 638	11.4	3 428	10.8
1997	15 187	11.6	20 387	14.9	14 113	19.9	18 085	10.9	3 376	10.5
1998	14 712	11.1	19 764	14.3	13 467	18.9	17 623	10.5	3 386	10.5
1999	14 079	10.4	18 712	13.2	12 280	17.1	17 289	10.1	3 222	9.7
2000	13 536	9.9	18 045	12.6	11 587	16.2	16 671	9.6	3 323	9.9
2001	14 327	10.4	18 580	12.9	11 733	16.3	17 760	10.1	3 414	10.1
2002	15 162	10.9	19 408	13.3	12 133	16.7	18 861	10.6	3 576	10.4
2003	15 783	11.2	20 078	13.7	12 866	17.6	19 443	10.8	3 552	10.2
2004	16 399	11.5	20 641	13.9	13 041	17.8	20 545	11.3	3 453	9.8
2005	15 950	11.1	21 000	14.1	12 896	17.6	20 450	11.1	3 603	10.1
2006	16 000	11.0	20 460	13.6	12 827	17.4	20 239	10.8	3 394	9.4
2007	16 302	11.1	20 973	13.8	13 324	18.0	20 396	10.9	3 556	9.7
2008	17 698	12.0	22 131	14.4	14 068	19.0	22 105	11.7	3 656	9.7
2009	19 475	13.0	24 094	15.6	15 451	20.7	24 684	12.9	3 433	8.9
2010	20 893	14.0	25 451	16.3	16 286	22.0	26 499	13.8	3 558	8.9
2011	20 501	13.6	25 746	16.3	16 134	21.9	26 492	13.7	3 620	8.7
2012	20 656	13.6	25 840	16.3	16 073	21.8	26 497	13.7	3 926	9.1
2013	20 119	13.1	25 199	15.8	14 659	19.9	26 429	13.6	4 231	9.5
2014	20 708	13.4	25 949	16.1	15 540	21.1	26 527	13.5	4 590	10.0
2015	19 037	12.2	24 086	14.8	14 509	19.7	24 414	12.4	4 201	8.8
2016	17 685	11.3	22 931	14.0	13 253	18.0	22 795	11.6	4 568	9.3
2017	17 365	11.0	22 333	13.6	12 808	17.5	22 209	11.2	4 681	9.2
2018	16 782	10.6	21 363	12.9	11 869	16.2	21 130	10.7	5 146	9.7
2019	14 976	9.4	19 008	11.5	10 466	14.4	18 660	9.4	4 858	8.9

. . . = Not available.

Table 3-9. Working-Age Poor People by Work Experience

(Thousands of people, percent of population [poverty rate], percent of total poor people.)

Year	Total number of working-age poor people	Worked		Worked year-round, full-time			Worked less than year-round or full-time			Did not work		
		Number	Percent of total poor	Number	Poverty rate (percent)	Percent of total poor	Number	Poverty rate (percent)	Percent of total poor	Number	Poverty rate (percent)	Percent of total poor
16 Years and Over												
1978	16 914	6 599	39.0	1 309	. . .	7.7	5 290	. . .	31.3	10 315	. . .	61.0
1979	16 803	6 601	39.3	1 394	. . .	8.3	5 207	. . .	31.0	10 202	. . .	60.7
1980	18 892	7 674	40.6	1 644	. . .	8.7	6 030	. . .	31.9	11 218	. . .	59.4
1981	20 571	8 524	41.4	1 881	. . .	9.1	6 643	. . .	32.3	12 047	. . .	58.6
1982	22 100	9 013	40.8	1 999	. . .	9.0	7 014	. . .	31.7	13 087	. . .	59.2
1983	22 741	9 329	41.0	2 064	. . .	9.1	7 265	. . .	31.9	13 412	. . .	59.0
1984	21 541	8 999	41.8	2 076	. . .	9.6	6 923	. . .	32.1	12 542	. . .	58.2
1985	21 243	9 008	42.4	1 972	. . .	9.3	7 036	. . .	33.1	12 235	. . .	57.6
1986	20 688	8 743	42.3	2 007	. . .	9.7	6 736	. . .	32.6	11 945	. . .	57.7
1987	20 546	8 258	40.2	1 821	2.4	8.9	6 436	12.5	31.3	12 288	21.6	59.8
1988	20 323	8 363	41.2	1 929	2.4	9.5	6 434	12.7	31.7	11 960	21.2	58.8
1989	19 952	8 376	42.0	1 908	2.4	9.6	6 468	12.5	32.4	11 576	20.8	58.0
1990	21 242	8 716	41.0	2 076	2.6	9.8	6 639	12.6	31.3	12 526	22.1	59.0
1991	22 530	9 208	40.9	2 103	2.6	9.3	7 105	13.4	31.5	13 322	22.8	59.1
1992	23 951	9 739	40.6	2 211	2.7	9.2	7 529	14.1	31.4	14 212	23.7	59.3
1993	24 832	10 144	40.8	2 408	2.9	9.7	7 737	14.6	31.2	14 688	24.2	59.1
1994	24 108	9 829	40.8	2 520	2.9	10.5	7 309	13.9	30.3	14 279	23.6	59.2
1995	23 077	9 484	41.1	2 418	2.7	10.5	7 066	13.7	30.6	13 593	22.3	58.9
1996	23 472	9 586	40.8	2 263	2.5	9.6	7 322	14.1	31.2	13 886	22.7	59.2
1997	22 753	9 444	41.5	2 345	2.5	10.3	7 098	13.8	31.2	13 309	21.7	58.5
1998	22 256	9 133	41.0	2 804	2.9	12.6	6 330	12.7	28.4	13 123	21.1	59.0
1999	21 762	9 251	42.5	2 559	2.6	11.8	6 692	13.2	30.8	12 511	19.9	57.5
2000	21 080	8 511	40.4	2 439	2.4	11.6	6 072	12.1	28.8	12 569	19.8	59.6
2001	22 245	8 530	38.3	2 567	2.6	11.5	5 964	11.8	26.8	13 715	20.6	61.7
2002	23 601	8 954	37.9	2 635	2.6	11.2	6 318	12.4	26.8	14 647	21.0	62.1
2003	24 266	8 820	36.3	2 636	2.6	10.9	6 183	12.2	25.5	15 446	21.5	63.7
2004	25 256	9 384	37.2	2 891	2.8	11.4	6 493	12.8	25.7	15 872	21.7	62.8
2005	25 381	9 340	36.8	2 894	2.8	11.4	6 446	12.8	25.4	16 041	21.8	63.2
2006	24 896	9 181	36.9	2 906	2.7	11.7	6 275	12.6	25.2	15 715	21.1	63.1
2007	25 297	9 089	35.9	2 768	2.5	10.9	6 320	12.7	25.0	16 208	21.5	64.1
2008	27 216	10 085	37.1	2 754	2.6	10.1	7 331	13.5	26.9	17 131	22.0	62.9
2009	29 625	10 680	36.1	2 641	2.7	8.9	8 039	14.5	27.1	18 945	22.7	63.9
2010	31 731	10 742	33.9	2 640	2.7	8.3	8 102	15.0	25.5	20 989	23.9	66.1
2011	31 630	10 588	33.5	2 770	2.7	8.8	7 818	14.9	24.7	21 042	23.6	66.5
2012	31 933	10 977	34.4	2 904	2.8	9.1	8 073	15.0	25.3	20 956	23.6	65.6
2013	32 011	11 025	34.4	2 812	2.7	8.8	8 213	15.8	25.7	20 986	23.2	65.6
2014	32 508	10 469	32.2	3 142	2.9	9.7	7 327	14.3	22.5	22 039	24.2	67.8
2015	30 123	9 795	32.5	2 576	2.3	8.8	7 220	13.9	24.0	20 328	22.5	67.5
2016	28 696	9 109	31.7	2 448	2.2	8.5	6 661	13.0	21.6	19 587	21.6	68.3
2017	28 167	8 503	32.2	2 468	2.1	8.8	6 035	12.0	21.4	19 644	21.4	69.7
2018	27 496	8 213	29.9	2 591	2.2	9.4	5 621	11.4	20.4	19 283	20.9	70.1
2019	24 502	7 632	31.1	2 356	2.0	9.6	5 033	12.0	20.5	16 870	18.5	68.9

. . . = Not available.

Table 3-10. Number and Percent of People in Poverty Using the Supplemental Poverty Measure, 2017–2019, and Comparison With Official Measures in 2019

(Numbers in thousands; percent of population.)

Characteristic	SPM 2017		SPM 2018		SPM 2019		Official 2019[1]	
	Number	Percent	Number	Percent	Number	Percent	Number	Percent
All People	44 972	12.7	41 420	13.9	38 163	11.7	34 061	10.5
Sex								
Male	20 717	11.3	19 269	13.1	17 655	11.1	15 009	9.4
Female	24 255	14.0	22 151	14.7	20 508	12.4	19 051	11.5
Age								
Under 18 years	11 521	18.0	10 096	15.6	9 119	12.5	10 542	14.4
18 to 64 years	26 244	11.6	24 151	13.2	22 072	11.2	18 660	9.4
65 years and older	7 207	9.3	7 174	14.1	6 972	12.8	4 858	8.9
Type of Unit								
In married-couple unit	16 879	5.9	15 043	8.7	13 703	6.9	8 977	4.5
In female householder unit	11 408	27.2	10 390	26.9	9 526	23.3	9 378	22.9
In male householder unit	2 382	12.1	2 197	16.3	2 162	14.3	1 484	9.8
Cohabitating	3 558	26.3	3 659	13.3	3 167	12.1	5 789	22.2
Unrelated individuals	10 745	20.8	10 132	23.5	9 603	21.2	8 432	18.6
Race and Hispanic Origin								
White	30 433	11.0	27 820	12.3	26 089	10.5	22 551	9.1
White, not Hispanic	19 249	8.8	16 932	9.8	15 914	8.2	14 179	7.3
Black	9 394	22.0	8 727	22.1	7 907	18.3	8 101	18.8
Asian	2 948	10.1	2 749	15.1	2 327	11.7	1 466	7.3
Hispanic, any race	12 654	19.4	12 216	21.4	11 464	18.9	9 556	15.7
Nativity								
Native born	33 314	12.3	32 540	12.0	30 238	10.8	28 412	10.1
Foreign born	8 761	15.1	8 880	19.3	7 924	17.6	5 648	12.6
Naturalized citizen	3 238	10.0	3 297	14.8	3 109	13.7	2 039	9.0
Not a citizen	5 522	19.5	5 584	23.4	4 815	21.7	3 609	16.3
Educational Attainment								
Total, age 25 and over	25 900	12.9	26 158	11.8	24 319	10.9	19 662	8.8
No high school diploma	6 137	28.2	6 320	27.4	5 563	27.5	4 796	23.7
High school, no college	9 500	16.2	9 272	15.2	8 543	13.9	7 076	11.5
Some college	5 879	11.5	5 599	10.2	5 472	9.5	4 490	7.8
Bachelor's degree or higher	4 474	6.5	4 967	5.8	4 741	5.7	3 300	3.9
Tenure								
Owner/ mortgage	8 588	4.9	7 831	6.4	7 146	5.2	4 843	3.5
Owner/no-mortgage/rent-free	9 967	11.5	10 146	11.7	10 057	11.2	9 012	10.1
Renter	23 521	23.6	23 443	22.4	20 960	21.5	20 206	20.7
Residence								
Inside metropolitan statistical areas	36 790	12.2	36 249	13.1	33 426	11.8	28 406	10.0
Inside principal cities	17 413	15.9	16 818	16.7	15 527	14.8	13 722	13.1
Outside principal cities	19 377	10.0	19 431	11.0	17 898	10.1	14 684	8.3
Outside metropolitan statistical areas	5 285	15.8	5 171	12.3	4 737	11.2	5 655	13.3
Region								
Northeast	7 218	10.8	6 768	12.9	6 431	11.7	5 181	9.4
Midwest	6 874	11.7	6 223	10.2	5 944	8.8	6 530	9.7
South	16 846	14.1	17 219	13.8	15 466	12.4	14 889	12.0
West	11 137	12.8	11 211	14.4	10 321	13.2	7 461	9.6
Health Insurance Coverage								
With private insurance	13 552	5.4	12 747	6.2	12 202	5.5	7 792	3.5
With public, no private insurance	21 107	29.5	21 805	27.6	19 600	25.3	20 753	26.7
Not insured	6 818	23.6	6 868	26.0	6 361	23.7	5 515	20.6
Work Experience								
Total, 18 to 64 years	24 582	11.6	24 151	12.4	22 072	11.2	18 660	9.4
All workers	11 319	5.8	10 959	7.4	10 599	6.9	7 324	4.7
Full-time, year-round	4 925	2.2	4 847	4.5	4 487	4.0	2 291	2.0
Less than full-time, year-round	6 394	14.7	6 112	15.0	6 112	14.6	5 033	12.0
Did not work at least 1 week	13 263	30.5	13 191	29.0	11 473	26.8	11 337	26.4
Disability Status								
Total, 18 to 64 years	24 582	11.6	24 151	12.4	22 072	11.2	18 660	9.4
With a disability	3 429	26.8	3 609	22.7	3 107	21.5	3 252	22.5
With no disability	21 116	10.3	20 500	11.6	18 899	10.4	15 347	8.4

[1]Differs from published official rates because these figures include unrelated individuals under 15 years of age as does the SPM.

SECTION 3C: HEALTH INSURANCE COVERAGE

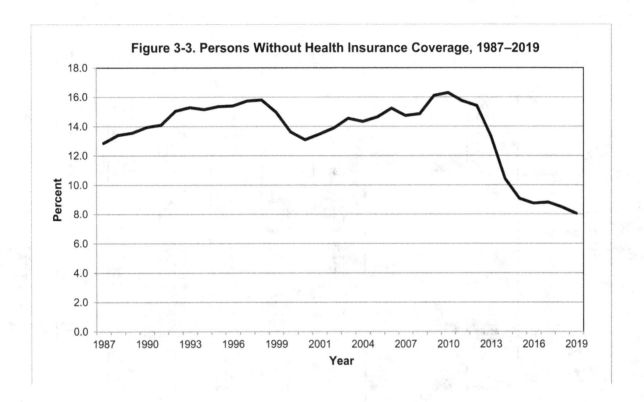

Figure 3-3. Persons Without Health Insurance Coverage, 1987–2019

- Health insurance is a means for financing a person's health care expenses. Over time, changes in the rate of health insurance coverage and the distribution of coverage types may reflect economic trends, shifts in the demographic composition of the populace and policy changes that impact access to care. Such a policy change was the Patient Protection and Affordable Care Act (ACA) in 2010. A new trend began during the COVID-19 in early 2020, when millions of people lost their jobs and their subsequent employer-paid health insurance. See the Notes and Definitions section at the end of this chapter.

- The uninsured rate has steadily fallen from 15.7 percent in 2011 to 8.0 percent in 2019 respectively. In 2010, the percentage of people without health insurance coverage for the entire calendar year was 16.3 percent or 49 million people. By 2019, over 23 million people gained health insurance. (See Tables 3-11 and 3-12)

- Private health insurance coverage continued to be more prevalent than government coverage, at 68.0 percent and 34.1 percent, respectively. Although private health insurance coverage continues to be more prevalent than government insurance, the percentage of people on employer-based insurance has decreased significantly since 1987. (See Table 3-12)

- Immediately following the Great Recession nearly 50 million people were without any type of health insurance coverage. Between 2010 and 2019, the numbers of those without health insurance declined nearly 50 percent. (Table 3-11)

Table 3-11. Health Insurance Coverage

(Number in thousands. People as of March of the following year.)

Year	Total	Total covered	Private health insurance			Government health insurance				Not covered
			Total	Employment	Direct purchase	Total	Medicaid	Medicare	Military	
NUMBER										
1987	241 187	210 161	182 160	149 739	. . .	56 282	20 211	30 458	10 542	31 026
1988	243 685	211 005	182 019	150 940	. . .	56 850	20 728	30 925	10 105	32 680
1989	246 191	212 807	183 610	151 644	. . .	57 382	21 185	31 495	9 870	33 384
1990	248 886	214 167	182 135	150 215	. . .	60 965	24 261	32 260	9 922	34 719
1991	251 447	216 003	181 375	150 077	. . .	63 882	26 880	32 907	9 820	35 444
1992	256 830	218 189	181 466	148 796	. . .	66 244	29 416	33 230	9 510	38 641
1993	259 753	220 040	182 351	148 318	. . .	68 554	31 749	33 097	9 560	39 713
1994	262 105	222 387	184 318	159 634	31 349	70 163	31 645	33 901	11 165	39 718
1995	264 314	223 733	185 881	161 453	30 188	69 776	31 877	34 655	9 375	40 581
1996	266 792	225 699	188 224	164 096	28 419	69 000	31 451	35 227	8 712	41 093
1997	269 094	226 735	189 955	166 419	27 431	66 685	28 956	35 590	8 527	42 359
1998	271 743	228 800	192 507	170 105	26 165	66 087	27 854	35 887	8 747	42 943
1999	550 891	472 175	398 557	349 227	56 608	133 279	55 243	73 056	17 056	78 716
2000	279 517	242 932	205 575	181 862	28 432	68 183	28 062	37 787	8 937	36 585
2001	282 082	244 059	204 142	179 984	28 398	70 330	30 166	37 870	9 580	38 023
2002	285 933	246 157	204 163	179 563	29 287	72 825	31 934	38 359	9 892	39 776
2003	288 280	246 332	201 989	177 362	28 826	76 119	34 326	39 284	10 124	41 948
2004	291 166	249 414	203 014	177 924	29 161	79 480	38 055	39 757	10 584	41 752
2005	293 834	250 799	203 205	178 391	28 980	80 283	38 191	40 167	11 164	43 035
2006	296 824	251 610	203 942	178 880	29 033	80 343	38 370	40 336	10 543	45 214
2007	299 106	255 018	203 903	178 971	28 500	83 147	39 685	41 387	10 955	44 088
2008	301 483	256 702	202 626	177 543	28 513	87 586	42 831	43 031	11 562	44 781
2009	304 280	255 295	196 245	170 762	29 098	93 245	47 847	43 434	12 414	48 985
2010	306 553	256 603	196 147	169 372	30 347	95 525	48 533	44 906	12 927	49 950
2011	308 827	260 214	197 323	170 102	30 244	99 497	50 835	46 922	13 712	48 613
2012	311 116	263 165	198 812	170 877	30 622	101 493	50 903	48 884	13 702	47 951
2013	313 401	271 606	201 038	174 418	35 755	108 287	54 919	49 020	14 016	41 795
2014	316 168	283 200	208 600	175 027	46 165	115 470	61 650	50 546	14 143	32 968
2015	318 868	289 903	214 238	177 540	52 057	118 395	62 384	51 865	14 849	28 966
2016	320 372	292 320	216 203	178 455	51 961	119 361	62 303	53 372	14 638	28 052
2017	323 156	294 613	217 007	181 036	51 821	121 965	62 492	55 623	15 532	28 543
2018	323 668	296 206	217 780	178 350	34 846	111 330	57 819	57 720	11 754	27 462
2019	324 550	298 438	220 848	183 005	33 170	110 687	55 851	58 779	11 755	26 111

. . . = Not available.

Table 3-12.   Percentage of People by Type of Health Insurance by Selected Demographics, 2018–2019

(Number in thousands. Percent. People as of March of the following year.)

Characteristic	Total		Any health insurance		Private health insurance		Government health insurance		Uninsured	
	2018	2019	2018	2019	2018	2019	2018	2019	2018	2019
Total	323 668	324 550	91.5	92.0	67.3	68.0	34.4	34.1	8.5	8.0
Age										
Under age 19	77 333	76 636	94.5	94.8	61.8	63.6	35.7	34.3	5.5	5.2
Aged 19 to 64	193 548	193 217	88.5	88.9	73.5	74.4	17.6	17.2	11.7	11.1
Aged 65 and older	52 788	54 642	99.1	98.9	52.4	51.6	94.1	93.8	0.9	1.1
Marital Status										
Married	101 805	100 795	91.7	92.4	82.3	83.4	12.6	12.2	8.3	7.6
Widowed	3 385	3 319	86.3	86.5	55.6	56.5	34.9	33.5	13.7	13.5
Divorced	18 683	18 290	87.0	88.0	64.7	67.4	25.3	23.6	13.0	12.0
Separated	4 200	3 802	80.1	81.0	52.4	51.8	29.7	31.4	19.9	19.0
Never married	65 475	67 065	84.0	84.3	64.7	65.1	21.6	21.3	16.0	15.7
Disability Status										
With a disability	15 438	15 056	90.4	91.6	44.7	47.3	53.9	52.4	9.6	8.4
With no disability	195 434	194 194	88.5	89.1	74.9	75.8	16.0	15.6	11.5	10.9
Work Experience										
All workers	155 221	157 181	89.3	89.8	805.0	80.8	11.1	11.2	10.7	10.2
Worked full-time, year-round	111 950	112 803	90.5	91.1	85.1	85.8	7.2	7.0	9.5	8.9
Worked less than full-time, year-round	43 271	44 379	86.2	86.6	68.5	68.2	21.3	21.6	13.8	13.4
Did not work at least one week	55 573	53 047	86.9	87.5	51.3	53.1	40.2	39.1	13.1	12.2
Educational Attainment										
Total, 26 to 64 years old	164 250	163 666	88.7	89.4	74.2	75.1	17.5	17.2	11.3	10.6
No high school diploma	15 197	13 733	71.0	71.5	37.0	38.9	36.9	35.9	29.0	28.5
High school graduate (includes equivalency)	44 573	43 630	85.1	85.1	73.8	64.2	24.4	24.2	14.9	14.9
Some college, no degree	24 977	24 315	89.3	89.8	73.8	73.7	19.3	19.7	10.7	10.2
Associate degree	17 735	17 998	91.0	91.6	78.7	79.3	15.8	15.8	9.0	8.4
Bachelor's degree	39 255	40 563	93.8	94.7	87.6	87.6	8.5	9.1	6.2	5.3
Family Status										
In families	261 336	282 991	92.1	92.6	68.7	69.4	32.9	32.8	7.9	7.4
Householder	83 508	83 698	92.4	93.1	72.0	72.4	34.4	34.9	7.6	6.9
Related children under 18	71 750	71 148	94.7	95.0	62.0	63.8	35.6	34.3	5.3	5.0
Related children under 6	22 720	22 439	94.8	95.2	59.7	61.7	38.0	36.6	5.2	4.8
In unrelated subfamilies	1 069	941	86.9	90.6	50.0	58.5	42.4	38.2	13.1	9.4
Unrelated individuals	61 264	60 618	88.0	89.2	61.5	62.4	40.6	39.9	11.1	10.8
Residence										
Inside metropolitan statistical areas	281 369	282 168	91.6	92.1	68.1	68.9	33.2	32.8	8.4	7.9
Inside principal cities	104 716	104 632	90.4	90.4	63.4	63.9	35.3	34.7	9.6	9.6
Outside principal cities	176 653	177 536	92.3	93.1	70.9	71.8	32.0	31.7	7.7	6.9
Outside metropolitan statistical areas	42 300	42 382	90.9	92.1	62.0	62.4	42.4	42.6	9.1	8.8
Race and Hispanic Origin										
White	247 472	247 869	91.8	92.2	69.3	70.1	33.8	33.5	8.2	7.8
White, not Hispanic	194 679	194 518	94.6	94.8	74.8	75.2	33.2	33.0	5.4	5.2
Black	42 758	42 991	90.3	90.4	55.4	55.2	41.2	41.8	9.7	9.6
Asian	19 770	19 905	93.2	93.8	73.1	74.4	26.1	25.2	6.8	6.2
Hispanic (any race)	59 925	60 517	82.2	83.3	49.6	51.6	36.5	35.8	17.8	16.7
Race and Hispanic Origin										
Native born	277 848	279 653	93.2	93.5	69.1	69.7	34.9	34.6	6.8	6.5
Foreign born	45 820	44 897	81.1	82.2	56.0	57.7	31.2	30.8	18.9	17.8
Naturalized citizen	22 296	22 750	91.2	91.3	64.0	64.0	36.4	36.6	8.8	8.7
Not a citizen	23 524	22 147	71.4	72.9	48.4	51.3	26.2	24.9	28.6	27.1

. . . = Not available.

NOTES AND DEFINITIONS, CHAPTER 3

TABLES 3-1 THROUGH 3-12

Income Distribution and Poverty

SOURCE: U.S. DEPARTMENT OF COMMERCE, BUREAU OF THE CENSUS

All data in this chapter are derived from the Current Population Survey (CPS), which is also the source of the data on labor force, employment, and unemployment used in Chapter 10. (See the notes and definitions for Tables 10-1 through 10-5.) In March of each year (with some data also collected in February and April), the households in this monthly survey are asked additional questions concerning earnings and other income in the previous year. This additional information, informally known as the "March Supplement," is now formally known as the Current Population Survey Annual Social and Economic Supplement (CPS-ASEC). It was previously called the Annual Demographic Supplement.

Collected annually, CPS-ASEC is one of the most widely used socioeconomic surveys, and provides detailed information on income, work experience, poverty, health insurance coverage, and living arrangements in the U.S. For the past several years, the Census Bureau has engaged in implementing improvements to the CPS-ASEC, especially to improve data quality, using redesigned income questions. More information on these changes in the section *Notes on the Data*.

Researchers should use caution when comparing results over time. Due to the changes, comparison of variables between 2013 and 2019 are not comparable. The 2014 CPS ASEC included redesigned questions for income and health insurance coverage. All of the approximately 98,000 addresses were eligible to receive the redesigned set of health insurance coverage questions. The redesigned income questions were implemented to a subsample of these 98,000 addresses using a probability split panel design.

The population represented by the income and poverty survey is the civilian noninstitutional population of the United States and members of the armed forces in the United States living off post or with their families on post, but excluding all other members of the armed forces. This is slightly different from the population base for the civilian employment and unemployment data, which excludes those armed forces households. As it is a survey of households, homeless persons are not included.

TABLES 3-1 THROUGH 3-10

Definitions: Racial classification and Hispanic origin

In 2002 and all earlier years, the CPS required respondents to report identification with only one race group. Since 2003, the CPS has allowed respondents to choose more than one race group. Income data for 2002 were collected in early 2003; thus, in the data for 2002 and all subsequent years, an individual could report identification with more than one race group. In the 2010 census, about 2.9 percent of people reported identification with more than one race.

Therefore, data from 2002 onward that are classified by race are not strictly comparable with race-classified data for 2001 and earlier years. As alternative approaches to dealing with this problem, the Census Bureau has tabulated two different race concepts for each racial category in a number of cases. In the case of Blacks, for example, this means there is one income measure for "Black alone," consisting of persons who report Black and no other race, and one for "Black alone or in combination," which includes all the "Black alone" reporters plus those who report Black in combination with any other race. The tables in this volume show both the "alone" and the "alone or in combination" values where available.

The race classifications now used in the CPS are *White, Black, Asian, American Indian and Alaska Native,* and *Native Hawaiian and Other Pacific Islander.* (Native Hawaiians and other Pacific Islanders were included in the "Asian" category in the data for 1987 through 2001.) The last two of these five racial groups are too small to provide reliable data for a single year, but in new Census Bureau tables available on the website, household income and poverty data for all five groups are presented in 2- and 3-year averages. Table 3-1 displays some of these data.

Hispanic origin is a separate question in the survey—not a racial classification—and Hispanics may be of any race. A subgroup of *White non-Hispanic* is shown in some tables. According to the Census 2010 population results, "Being Hispanic was reported by 11.6 percent of White householders who reported only one race, 4.5 percent of Black householders who reported only one race, and 3.5 percent of Asian householders who reported only one race. Data users should exercise caution when interpreting aggregate results for the Hispanic population or for race groups because these populations consist of many distinct groups that differ in socioeconomic characteristics, culture, and recent immigration status." ("Income, and Poverty in the United States: 2017", footnote 2, p. 3 and "Health Insurance Coverage in the United States: 2017" footnote 2, p. 3.

Definitions: General

A *household* consists of all persons who occupy a housing unit. A household includes the related family members and all the unrelated persons, if any (such as lodgers, foster children, wards, or employees), who share the housing unit. A person living alone in a housing unit or a group of unrelated persons sharing a housing unit as partners is also counted as a household. The count of households excludes group quarters.

Earnings includes all income from work, including wages, salaries, armed forces pay, commissions, tips, piece-rate payments, and cash bonuses, before deductions such as taxes, bonds, pensions, and union dues. This category also includes net income from nonfarm self-employment and farm self-employment. Wage and salary supplements that are paid directly by the employer, such as the employer share of Social Security taxes and the cost of employer-provided health insurance, are not included.

Income, in the official definition used in the survey, is money income, including *earnings* from work as defined above; unemployment compensation; workers' compensation; Social Security; Supplemental Security Income; cash public assistance (welfare payments); veterans' payments; survivor benefits; disability benefits; pension or retirement income; interest income; dividends (but not capital gains); rents, royalties, and payments from estates or trusts; educational assistance, such as scholarships or grants; child support; alimony; financial assistance from outside of the household; and other cash income regularly received, such as foster child payments, military family allotments, and foreign government pensions. Receipts not counted as income include capital gains or losses, withdrawals of bank deposits, money borrowed, tax refunds, gifts, and lump-sum inheritances or insurance payments.

A *year-round, full-time worker* is a person who worked 35 or more hours per week and 50 or more weeks during the previous calendar year.

A *family* is a group of two or more persons related by birth, marriage, or adoption who reside together.

Unrelated individuals are persons 15 years old and over who are not living with any relatives. In the official poverty measure, the poverty status of unrelated individuals is determined independently of and is not affected by the incomes of other persons with whom they may share a household.

Median income is the amount of income that divides a ranked income distribution into two equal groups, with half having incomes above the median, and half having incomes below the median. The median income for persons is based on persons 15 years old and over with income. Since median income is updated annually to inflation adjusted current dollars, comparison between editions is not possible.

Mean income is the amount obtained by dividing the total aggregate income of a group by the number of units in that group. In this survey, as in most surveys of incomes, means are higher than medians because of the skewed nature of the income distribution; see the section "Whose standard of living?" in the article at the beginning of this book.

Historical income figures are shown in constant *2018 dollars*. All constant-dollar figures are converted from current-dollar values using the *CPI-U-RS* (the Consumer Price Index, All Urban, Research Series), which measures changes in prices for past periods using the methodologies of the current CPI, and is similar in concept and behavior to the deflators used in the NIPAs for consumer income and spending. See Chapter 8 for CPI-U-RS data and the corresponding notes and definitions.

Definitions: Income distribution

Income distribution is portrayed by dividing the total ranked distribution of families or households into *fifths*, also known as *quintiles,* and also by separately tabulating the top 5 percent (which is included in the highest fifth). The households or families are arrayed from those with the lowest income to those with the highest income, then divided into five groups, with each group containing one-fifth of the total number of households. Within each quintile, incomes are summed and calculated as a share of total income for all quintiles,and are averaged to show the average (mean) income within that quintile.

A statistical measure that summarizes the dispersion of income across the entire income distribution is the *Gini coefficient* (also known as Gini ratio, Gini index, or index of income concentration), which can take values ranging from 0 to 1. A Gini value of 1 indicates "perfect" inequality; that is, one household has all the income and the rest have none. A value of 0 indicates "perfect" equality, a situation in which each household has the same income.

A new "equivalence-adjusted" measure of household income inequality was introduced recently and is displayed in Table 3-3. For a Census-defined household, a given level of money income can have different implications for that household's well-being, depending on the size of the household and how many children, if any, are in the household. Since there have been substantial changes over past decades in the average size and composition of households, some have questioned the pertinence of standard income distribution tables. In response, the Census Bureau now also reports measures of income inequality for households using "equivalence-adjusted" income.

The equivalence adjustment is based on a three-parameter scale reflecting the size of the household and the facts that children consume less than adults; that as family size increases, expenses do not increase at the same rate; and that the increase in expenses is larger for the first child of a single-parent family than the first child of a two-adult family. The same equivalence concept is used in the poverty thresholds for the NAS-based alternative poverty estimates shown in Tables 3-11 and described later in these Notes.

As can be seen in Table 3-3, the equivalence-adjusted measures generally show somewhat less inequality than the raw money income measures, but they show a greater rise in inequality over the period 1967-2018.

Definitions: Poverty

The *number of people below poverty level,* or the number of poor people, is the number of people with family or individual incomes below a specified level that is intended to measure the cost of a minimum standard of living. These minimum levels vary by size and composition of family and are known as *poverty thresholds.*

The official poverty thresholds are based on a definition developed in 1964 by Mollie Orshansky of the Social Security Administration. She calculated food budgets for families of various sizes and compositions, using an "economy food plan" developed by the U.S. Department of Agriculture (the cheapest of four plans developed). Reflecting a 1955 Department of Agriculture survey that found that families of three or more persons spent about one-third of their after-tax incomes on food, Orshansky multiplied the costs of the food plan by 3 to arrive at a set of thresholds for poverty income for families of three or larger. For 2-person families, the multiplier was 3.7; for 1-person families, the threshold was 80 percent of the two-person threshold.

These poverty thresholds have been adjusted each year for price increases, using the percent change in the Consumer Price Index for All Urban Consumers (CPI-U). See Chapter 8 for additional information on the Consumer Price Index.

For more information on the Orshansky thresholds (the description of which has been simplified here), see Gordon Fisher, "The Development of the Orshansky Thresholds and Their Subsequent History as the Official U.S. Poverty Measure" (May 1992), available on the Census Bureau Web site at https://www.census.gov/library/working-papers/1997/demo/fisher-02.html.

The *poverty rate* for a demographic group is the number of poor people or poor families in that group expressed as a percentage of the total number of people or families in the group.

Average poverty thresholds. The thresholds used to calculate the official poverty rates vary not only with the size of the family but with the number of children in the family. For example, the threshold for a three-person family in 2019 was $19,998 if there were no children in the family but $20,598 if the family consisted of 1 adults and 2 children. There are 48 different threshold values depending on size of household, number of children, and whether the householder is 65 years old or over (with lower thresholds for the older householders). To give a general sense of the "poverty line," the Census Bureau also publishes the average threshold for each size family, based on the actual mix of family types in that year. These are the values shown in Table 3-5 to represent the history of poverty thresholds.

A person with *work experience* (Table 3-9) is one who, during the preceding calendar year and on a part-time or full-time basis, did any work for pay or profit or worked without pay on a family-operated farm or business at any time during the year). A *year-round* worker is one who worked for 50 weeks or more during the preceding calendar year. A person is classified as having worked *full time* if he or she worked 35 hours or more per week during a majority of the weeks worked. A *year-round, full-time worker* is a person who worked 35 or more hours per week and 50 or more weeks during the previous calendar year.

Working poor: Those workers employed full- or -part time whose income still falls below the poverty thresholds of their family size.

Toward better measures of income and poverty

The definition of the official poverty rate is established by the Office of Management of Budget in the Executive Office of the President and has not been substantially changed since 1969. Criticisms of the current definition are legion. In response to these criticisms, the Census Bureau has published extensive research work illustrating the effects of various ways of modifying income definitions and poverty thresholds. Some of the results of this work are published here in Tables 3-10 and 3-11 and explained in the notes and definitions below.

Improving the Income Concept

One type of criticism accepted the general concept of the Orshansky threshold but recommended making the income definition more realistic by including some or all of the following: capital gains; taxes and tax credits; noncash food, housing, and health benefits provided by government and employers; and the value of homeownership. There is debate about whether it is appropriate to use income data augmented in this way in conjunction with the official thresholds. The original 1964 thresholds made no allowance for health insurance or other health expenses—in effect, they assumed that the poor would get free medical care, or at least that the poverty calculation was not required to allow for medical needs—and because of the imprecision of Orshansky's multiplier it is not clear to what extent they include housing expenses in a way that is comparable with the inclusion of a homeownership component in income. Nevertheless, the Census Bureau has calculated and published income and poverty figures based on broadened income definitions and either the official thresholds or thresholds that are closely related to the official ones. Some of these calculations are presented in Table 3-10 and 3-11 and described below.

Still accepting the validity of the basic Orshansky threshold concept, some critics have also argued that use of the CPI-U in the official measure to update the thresholds each year has overstated the price increase, and that an inflator such as the CPI-U-RS should be used instead. (See the notes and definitions for Chapter 8.) Use of the CPI-U-RS leads to lower poverty thresholds beginning in the late 1970s, when the CPI began to be distorted by housing and other biases subsequently corrected by new methods; these newer methods were not carried backward to revise the official CPI-U. Use of the CPI-U-RS, which does carry current methods back and thereby revises the CPI time series, eliminates a presumed upward bias in the poverty rate relative to the poverty rates estimated before the bias emerged. This is a bias in the behavior of the time series given the concept of the Orshansky threshold, not necessarily a bias in the current level of poverty, since all the other criticisms of the Orshansky thresholds need to be considered when assessing the general adequacy of today's poverty measurements.

Improving the concepts of income and poverty together

Another type of criticism argues that the official thresholds are also no longer relevant to today's needs, and that the concepts of income (or "resources") and of the threshold level that depicts a minimum adequate standard of living need to be rethought together. These critics cite the availability of more up-to-date and detailed information about consumer spending at various income levels. The Consumer Expenditure Survey (CEX), originally designed to provide the weights for the Consumer Price Index, is now conducted quarterly and provides extensive data on consumer spending patterns. To give just one example of the information available now that was not available to Mollie Orshansky, the CEX indicates that food now accounts for one-sixth, not one-third, of total family expenditures, even among low-income families. (For data from, and notes on, the Consumer Expenditure Survey, see Bernan Press, *Handbook of U.S. Labor Statistics.*)

A special panel of the National Academy of Sciences (NAS) undertook a study that reconsidered both resources and thresholds. The Census Bureau has calculated and published experimental poverty rates for 1999 through 2015, developed following NAS recommendations, which are presented in Table 3-10. Beginning in November 2011 the Bureau has issued "The Research Supplemental Poverty Measure" or SPM for the most recent two years, a further refinement of the NAS recommendations; SPM measures are presented in Tables 3-10.

Supplemental Poverty Measure—Tables 3-10

In March of 2010, an Interagency Technical Working Group produced suggestions for a Supplemental Poverty Measure (SPM), which were first implemented in the "Research Supplemental Poverty Measure: 2010" issued by the Census Bureau in November 2011. The SPM goes beyond the experimental measures just described, and takes advantage of new data from questions introduced in the CPS-ASEC in recent years. In the new SPM:

- The measurement unit now covers not just the family but "all related individuals who live at the same address, including

any co-resident unrelated children who are cared for by the family (such as foster children) and any co-habitors and their children." This redefinition adds unrelated individuals under the age of 15 to the universe measured by the official rate. The "official" measures shown in Table 3-10 have been adjusted to include these individuals, and are therefore slightly higher than the regular published official rates shown in Tables 3-6 through 3-9.

- The SPM thresholds are calculated separately for three housing status groups: owners with mortgages, owners without mortgages, and renters. For each of these three groups the basic threshold represents the 33rd percentile of expenditures on food, clothing, shelter, and utilities (FCSU), averaged over a five-year period, by consumer units with two children, multiplied by 1.2 to allow for other needs. (Before averaging, the expenditures are converted to their dollar values in the prices of the threshold year using the CPI-U.) The consumer units selected for calculating the threshold include not only two-adult two-child families but also other types with two children, such as single-parent families. But they are adjusted to a four-person basis, using the equivalence scales, before averaging them to determine the basic threshold appropriate to a two-adult two-child household. Then that threshold is used as the basis for calculating thresholds for other size measurement units, again using the three-parameter equivalence scales for family size and composition, and for geographic differences.

- The thresholds are updated each year, using an updated five-year moving average of FCSU at the 33rd percentile, expressed in the prices of the new threshold year. Thus the thresholds are adjusted for inflation, but in addition, the "real" (constant-dollar) purchasing power of the poverty threshold will change (gradually) over time as the real standard of FCSU spending in the 33rd percentile changes. The real value of the threshold will likely change more slowly and gradually than in the "experimental" measures described above, because of using five instead of three years in the average.

- Family resources include cash income, plus in-kind benefits that families can use to meet their FCSU needs (for example, the Supplemental Nutrition Assistance Program [SNAP] formerly known as food stamps), minus income and payroll taxes, plus tax credits, minus childcare and other work-related expenses, minus child support payments to another household, and minus out-of-pocket medical expenses.

The SPM is not intended to replace the official poverty measure and is not to be used in calculations affecting program eligibility and funding distribution. According to the report referenced above, it is "designed to provide information on aggregate levels of economic need at a national level or within large subpopulations or areas…providing further understanding of economic conditions and trends." Census Bureau presentation of the SPM has focused on the different distribution of the poverty population indicated by the new measures, as shown in Table 3-10.

Notes on the data

The following are the principal changes that may affect year-to-year comparability of all income and poverty data from the CPS.

- Beginning in 1952, the estimates are based on 1950 census population controls. Earlier figures were based on 1940 census population controls.

- Beginning in 1962, 1960 census–based sample design and population controls are fully implemented.

- With 1971 and 1972 data, 1970 census–based sample design and population controls were introduced.

- With 1983–1985 data, 1980 census–based sample design was introduced; 1980 population controls were introduced; and these were extended back to 1979 data.

- With 1993 data, there was a major redesign of the CPS, including the introduction of computer-assisted interviewing. The limits used to "code" reported income amounts were changed, resulting in reporting of higher income values for the highest-income families and, consequently, an exaggerated year-to-year increase in income inequality. (It is possible that this jump actually reflects in one year an increase that had emerged more gradually, so that the distribution measures for 1993 and later years may be properly comparable with data for decades earlier even if they should not be directly compared with 1992.) In addition, 1990 census–based population controls were introduced, and these were extended back to the 1992 data.

- With 1995 data, the 1990 census–based sample design was implemented and the sample was reduced by 7,000 households.

- Data for 2001 implemented population controls based on the 2000 census, which were carried back to 2000 and 1999 data as well. Data from 2000 forward also incorporate results from a 28,000-household sample expansion.

- Beginning with the data for 2010 presented here, population controls based on the 2010 census were implemented. (This resulted in some revision of CPS data initially published for 2010.)

- In 2014, the Census Bureau introduced redesigned income and health insurance questions in the CPS-ASEC. The second phase of the implementation in 2019, updated the processing system that imputes missing data, determines family relationships and constructs key health insurance measures.

For more information on these and other changes that could affect comparability, see "Current Population Survey Technical Paper 63RV: Design and Methodology" (March 2002) and footnotes to CPS historical income tables, both available on the Census Bureau Web site at www.census.gov/hhes/income.

Data availability

Data embodying the official definitions of income and poverty are published annually in late summer or early fall by the Census Bureau, as part of a series with the general title *Current Population Reports: Consumer Income, P60*. Most of the data up to 2012 in this chapter were derived from report P60-245, "Income, Poverty, and Health Insurance Coverage in the United States: 2012" (September 2013), and from the "Historical Income Tables" and "Historical Poverty Tables" on the Census Web site (see below for the address). In 2013, the Census Bureau split the previous report in two. Health insurance coverage is now published separately from income and poverty. The historical tables can be found in the "CPS-ASEC" section under the "Data" category.

The SPM data in Tables 3-10 are from reports entitled "The Research Supplemental Poverty Measure." Reports for 2012, 2011, and 2010 respectively are numbered P60-247, P60-244, and P60-241, and are available on the Census Web site.

All these reports and related data, including historical tabulations, used in *Business Statistics* are available on the Census Bureau Web site at <https://www.census.gov>, under the general headings of "Income" and "Poverty."

References

Definitions and descriptions of the concepts and data of all series are provided in the source documents listed above and in the references contained therein.

TABLES 3-11 AND 3-12

Health Insurance Coverage

SOURCE: U.S. DEPARTMENT COMMERCE, BUREAU OF THE CENSUS

The Current Population Survey Annual Social and Economic Supplement (CPS ASEC) and the American Community Survey (ACS) is used to produce official estimates of income and poverty, and it serves as the most widely-cited source of estimates on health insurance coverage.

Due to questions of the validity of the health insurance data in previous reports, the Census Bureau implemented changes in 2014 to CPS ACS, including a complete redesign of the health insurance questions that replaced the existing questions in the CPS ASEC. Due the differences in measurement, health insurance estimates from calendar year 2013 are different from estimates in previous years.

Health insurance coverage in the CPS ASEC refers to comprehensive coverage during the calendar year. The American Community Survey (ACS) health insurance coverage status is at the time the individual is interviewed. Therefore, two uninsured measures are reported.

Since the passage of the Patient Protection and Affordable Care Act (ACA) in 2010, several provisions of the ACA have gone into effect at different times. For example, in 2010, the Young Adult Provision enabled adults under age 26 to remain as dependents on their parents' health insurance plans. In 2014 policy changes associated with the ACA provide the option for states to expand Medicaid to people whose income-to-poverty ratio full under a particular threshold. The decreases in the uninsured rates in 2013 and 2014 are consistent with what some of the provisions of the ACA intended.

Definitions

Health insurance coverage refers to comprehensive coverage during the calendar year for the civilian, noninstitutionalized population.

Private coverage is a plan provided through market forces.

Employment-based provided by an employer or union.

Direct-purchase: Coverage purchased directly from an insurance company or a federal or state marketplace or exchange.

TRICARE: Coverage through TRICARE, formerly known as Civilian Health and Medical Program of the Uniformed Services (e.g. healthcare.gov).

Government health insurance: Coverage provided by the federal government.

Medicare: Federal program that helps to pay health care costs for people aged 65 years and older and for certain people under age 65 with long-term disabilities.

Medicaid: Medicaid, the Children's Health Insurance Program (CHIP), and individual state health plans.

CHAMPVA or *VA*: Civilian Health and Medical Program of the Department of Veterans Affairs, as well as care provided by the Department of Veterans Affairs and the military.

Uninsured are people if, for an entire year, they were not covered by any type of health insurance. Additionally, people were considered uninsured if they only had coverage through the Indian Health Service (IHS).

Data availability

Detailed health insurance questions have been asked in the CPS since 1988 as part of a mandate to collect data on non-cash basis. However, as noted, comparing older results with newer ones is uncertain due to the changes in questions in 2013, 2014 and 2018.

CHAPTER 4: CONSUMER INCOME AND SPENDING

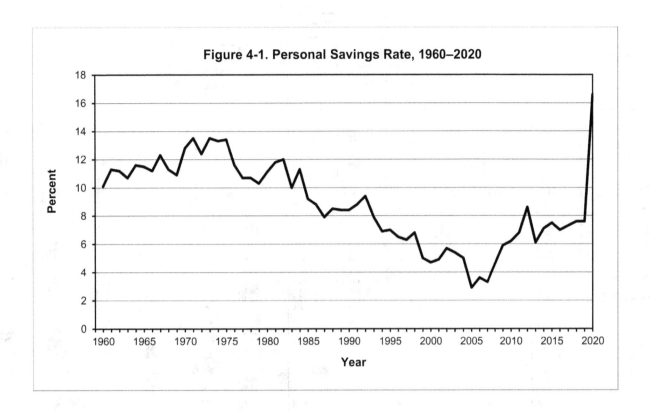

Figure 4-1. Personal Savings Rate, 1960–2020

- The personal saving rate—now defined to include saving in individual pension plans as the earned benefits rather than the employer contributions—got as high as 13 percent in the early 1970s. (Benefits from social insurance systems such as Social Security, unlike those in private and government employee retirement plans, do not figure in personal saving; any excess of receipts over payments is counted as government saving.) Since then, the personal saving rate entered a downtrend for many years, and hit the lowest rates since the Great Depression in the real estate bubble years 2005 through 2007, saving as a percent of disposable personal income has increased. In 2020, however, the personal savings rate skyrocketed to a high of 16.6 percent, more than double the 7.6 percent in 2019. (Tables 4-1A and B)

- It should be noted that personal income does not, by definition, include any capital gains. Despite that, taxes on realized capital gains are deducted (along with all other income taxes) from personal income to get after-tax income. Capital gains, both realized and unrealized, can be a source of spending power in addition to current disposable income; during the housing price bubble they were converted into cash by asset sales, refinancing, and home equity loans, all of which were reflected in low saving rates. (Table 12-7)

- Government social benefits were 5.8 percent of personal income in 1960, rising to 14.1 percent in the high-employment year 2007. In the recession they rose further, to 18.1 percent in 2010, and increased to 21.3 percent in 2020 due in large part to government related COVID-19 assistance specifically unemployment insurance. It should be understood that this category counts as income all spending financed by government health insurance programs such as Medicare and Medicaid, simultaneously counting that spending as personal consumption expenditures rather than direct government spending in the NIPAs. (Table 4-1)

Table 4-1A. Personal Income and Its Disposition: Recent Data

(Billions of current dollars, except as noted; quarterly data are at seasonally adjusted annual rates.)   **NIPA Table 2.1**

Year and quarter	Personal income											
					Personal income receipts on assets		Personal current transfer receipts					
								Government social benefits to persons				
	Total	Compensation of employees	Proprietors' income with IVA and CCAdj	Rental income of persons with CCAdj	Personal interest income	Personal dividend income	Total	Social Security and Medicare	Government unemployment insurance	Veterans	Medicaid	Other government benefits to persons
1960	422.1	301.3	50.6	16.5	31.1	13.4	24.4	11.1	3.1	4.5	. . .	5.7
1961	440.6	310.4	53.2	17.2	33.4	13.9	28.1	12.6	4.4	4.9	. . .	6.2
1962	468.8	332.2	55.2	18.0	37.1	15.0	28.8	14.3	3.2	4.6	. . .	6.8
1963	492.8	350.4	56.4	18.7	40.5	16.2	30.3	15.2	3.1	4.8	. . .	7.3
1964	528.2	376.0	59.1	18.8	44.9	18.2	31.3	16.0	2.8	4.6	. . .	7.9
1965	570.7	405.4	63.7	19.3	49.3	20.2	33.9	18.1	2.4	4.8	. . .	8.6
1966	620.3	449.2	67.9	19.9	54.3	20.7	37.5	20.8	1.9	4.8	1.9	8.1
1967	665.7	481.8	69.5	20.3	59.5	21.5	45.8	25.8	2.2	5.5	2.7	9.4
1968	730.9	530.8	73.8	20.1	65.3	23.5	53.3	30.5	2.2	5.9	4.0	10.8
1969	800.3	584.5	77.0	20.3	76.1	24.2	59.0	33.1	2.3	6.6	4.6	12.4
1970	865.0	623.3	77.8	20.7	90.6	24.3	71.7	38.7	4.2	7.5	5.5	16.0
1971	932.8	665.0	83.9	21.8	100.1	25.0	85.4	44.6	6.2	8.4	6.7	19.4
1972	1 024.5	731.3	95.1	22.7	109.8	26.8	94.8	49.7	6.0	9.4	8.2	21.4
1973	1 140.8	812.7	112.5	23.1	125.5	29.9	108.6	60.9	4.6	10.2	9.6	23.3
1974	1 251.8	887.7	112.2	23.2	147.4	33.2	128.6	70.3	7.0	11.6	11.2	28.4
1975	1 369.4	947.2	118.2	22.3	168.0	32.9	163.1	81.5	18.1	14.0	13.9	35.7
1976	1 502.6	1 048.3	131.0	20.3	181.0	39.0	177.6	93.3	16.4	13.8	15.5	38.7
1977	1 659.2	1 165.8	144.5	15.9	206.9	44.7	189.5	105.3	13.1	13.3	16.7	40.9
1978	1 863.7	1 316.8	166.0	16.5	235.1	50.7	203.4	116.9	9.4	13.6	18.6	44.9
1979	2 082.7	1 477.2	179.4	16.1	269.7	57.4	227.3	132.5	9.7	14.2	21.1	49.9
1980	2 323.6	1 622.2	171.6	19.0	332.9	64.0	271.5	154.8	16.1	14.7	23.9	62.1
1981	2 605.1	1 792.5	179.7	23.8	412.2	73.6	307.8	182.1	15.9	15.8	27.7	66.3
1982	2 791.6	1 893.0	171.2	23.8	479.5	77.6	343.1	204.6	25.2	16.3	30.2	66.8
1983	2 981.1	2 012.5	186.3	24.4	516.3	83.3	370.5	222.2	26.4	16.4	33.9	71.5
1984	3 292.7	2 215.9	228.2	24.7	590.1	90.6	380.9	237.7	16.0	16.3	36.6	74.3
1985	3 524.9	2 387.3	241.1	26.2	628.9	97.4	403.1	253.0	15.9	16.6	39.7	78.0
1986	3 733.1	2 542.1	256.5	18.3	662.1	106.0	428.6	268.9	16.5	16.6	43.6	83.0
1987	3 961.6	2 722.4	286.5	16.6	679.0	112.2	447.9	282.6	14.6	16.5	47.8	86.4
1988	4 283.4	2 948.0	325.5	22.5	721.7	129.7	476.9	300.2	13.3	16.7	53.0	93.6
1989	4 625.6	3 139.6	341.1	21.5	806.5	157.8	521.1	325.6	14.4	17.2	60.8	103.1
1990	4 913.8	3 340.4	353.2	28.2	836.5	168.8	574.7	351.7	18.2	17.7	73.1	113.9
1991	5 084.9	3 450.5	354.2	38.6	823.5	180.2	650.5	381.7	26.8	18.1	96.9	127.0
1992	5 420.9	3 668.2	400.2	60.6	809.8	189.1	731.8	414.4	39.6	18.6	116.2	142.9
1993	5 657.9	3 817.3	428.0	90.1	802.3	204.7	778.9	444.7	34.8	19.3	130.1	150.0
1994	5 947.1	4 006.2	456.6	113.7	814.6	235.2	815.7	476.6	23.9	19.7	139.4	156.1
1995	6 291.4	4 198.1	481.2	124.9	878.6	258.0	864.7	508.9	21.7	20.5	149.6	164.0
1996	6 678.5	4 416.9	543.8	142.5	899.0	302.2	906.3	536.9	22.3	21.4	158.2	167.6
1997	7 092.5	4 708.8	584.0	147.1	947.1	337.9	935.4	563.5	20.1	22.3	163.1	166.4
1998	7 606.7	5 071.1	640.2	165.2	1 015.5	355.4	957.9	574.8	19.7	23.3	170.2	170.0
1999	8 006.8	5 402.7	696.4	178.5	1 017.7	346.6	992.2	588.6	20.5	24.1	184.6	174.4
2000	8 655.9	5 847.1	753.9	183.5	1 106.5	383.5	1 044.9	620.5	20.7	25.0	199.5	179.1
2001	9 012.8	6 038.3	831.0	202.4	1 112.3	369.3	1 145.8	667.7	31.9	26.6	227.3	192.4
2002	9 160.9	6 135.1	870.0	208.4	1 014.8	398.8	1 251.0	706.6	53.5	29.5	250.0	211.3
2003	9 498.5	6 353.6	897.5	227.1	1 020.2	432.1	1 321.0	740.2	53.2	31.8	264.5	231.2
2004	10 044.3	6 719.5	962.9	242.8	965.4	561.7	1 404.5	789.9	36.4	34.1	289.8	254.3
2005	10 604.9	7 066.1	979.1	221.1	1 117.4	577.8	1 490.9	844.8	31.8	36.4	304.4	273.5
2006	11 384.7	7 479.7	1 050.9	181.1	1 258.9	722.8	1 593.0	943.2	30.4	38.9	299.1	281.5
2007	12 021.4	7 878.5	995.5	186.3	1 379.2	815.3	1 697.3	1 003.9	32.7	41.7	324.2	294.9
2008	12 477.6	8 056.8	959.7	290.3	1 399.4	804.6	1 919.3	1 067.1	51.1	45.0	338.3	417.7
2009	12 080.4	7 759.0	937.6	347.6	1 300.7	553.0	2 107.7	1 157.5	131.2	51.5	369.6	398.0
2010	12 594.5	7 925.4	1 107.3	433.7	1 242.9	543.9	2 281.4	1 203.6	138.9	58.0	396.9	484.2
2011	13 339.3	8 226.2	1 227.4	506.5	1 255.6	681.5	2 310.1	1 248.9	107.2	63.3	406.0	484.8
2012	14 014.3	8 567.4	1 346.4	534.5	1 318.6	835.1	2 322.6	1 316.8	83.6	70.1	417.5	434.4
2013	14 193.6	8 835.0	1 402.2	577.4	1 265.6	793.3	2 385.9	1 371.8	62.5	79.1	440.0	432.5
2014	14 976.6	9 250.2	1 445.6	602.7	1 336.8	953.2	2 498.6	1 434.6	35.5	84.2	490.9	453.5
2015	15 685.2	9 699.4	1 420.8	609.5	1 441.8	1 033.1	2 635.1	1 506.7	32.5	92.6	535.9	467.4
2016	16 096.9	9 966.1	1 423.3	626.6	1 465.2	1 077.4	2 717.3	1 558.6	32.0	96.8	562.8	467.1
2017	16 850.2	10 426.1	1 505.8	652.7	1 553.4	1 154.5	2 807.6	1 618.6	30.2	111.4	573.8	473.6
2018	17 706.0	10 959.5	1 580.4	681.9	1 615.0	1 253.3	2 926.1	1 707.3	27.7	119.7	589.8	481.5
2019	18 424.4	11 447.7	1 598.9	692.1	1 652.0	1 316.0	3 083.1	1 816.4	27.6	130.9	614.0	494.2
2020	19 627.6	11 572.2	1 650.0	711.6	1 614.4	1 297.8	4 181.3	1 897.1	536.6	145.5	657.3	944.7
2018												
1st quarter	17 406.1	10 784.1	1 567.0	671.8	1 581.8	1 204.2	2 892.6	1 677.8	29.0	117.0	581.9	486.9
2nd quarter	17 598.5	10 891.8	1 572.1	677.3	1 605.1	1 237.3	2 918.5	1 696.3	27.6	118.5	592.6	483.4
3rd quarter	17 821.1	11 044.3	1 581.3	689.8	1 620.0	1 264.4	2 939.4	1 717.1	27.2	120.5	595.1	479.5
4th quarter	17 998.3	11 118.0	1 601.4	688.6	1 653.1	1 307.3	2 954.0	1 738.2	27.1	122.8	589.5	476.3
2019												
1st quarter	18 238.9	11 336.1	1 585.5	687.0	1 647.4	1 296.9	3 039.6	1 787.7	28.4	125.6	598.8	499.0
2nd quarter	18 345.4	11 394.1	1 572.8	691.0	1 660.5	1 312.0	3 074.1	1 807.5	27.8	128.9	614.5	495.4
3rd quarter	18 464.7	11 453.9	1 610.6	691.5	1 646.2	1 327.0	3 101.0	1 826.3	27.4	132.5	622.4	492.4
4th quarter	18 648.5	11 606.8	1 626.8	699.0	1 654.0	1 328.0	3 117.9	1 844.2	26.8	136.6	620.5	489.8
2020												
1st quarter	18 842.2	11 755.5	1 638.3	712.2	1 638.2	1 338.1	3 173.8	1 876.4	39.5	140.8	606.2	511.0
2nd quarter	20 348.7	11 029.2	1 471.1	709.5	1 611.3	1 299.6	5 570.5	1 896.4	1 039.4	144.4	654.2	1 836.1
3rd quarter	19 777.4	11 539.7	1 760.7	714.5	1 597.6	1 254.2	4 310.5	1 906.0	767.8	147.4	690.4	799.0
4th quarter	19 542.0	11 964.2	1 730.0	710.0	1 610.3	1 299.2	3 670.2	1 909.8	299.9	149.5	678.3	632.7

. . . = Not available.

Table 4-1A. Personal Income and Its Disposition: Recent Data—*Continued*

(Billions of current dollars, except as noted; quarterly data are at seasonally adjusted annual rates.)   NIPA Table 2.1

Year and quarter	Personal income—Continued		Less: Personal current taxes	Equals: Disposable personal income	Less: Personal outlays						Equals: Personal saving		Billions of chained (2009) dollars	
	Personal current transfer receipts—Continued: From business, net	Less: Contributions for government social insurance, domestic			Total	Personal consumption expenditures	Personal interest payments	Personal current transfer payments			Billions of dollars	Percent of disposable personal income	Percent income excluding current transfers	Disposable personal income
								Total	To government	To the rest of the world, net				
1960	1.3	16.4	46.1	376.1	338.2	331.2	6.2	0.8	0.3	0.5	37.9	10.1	2 411.0	2 287.4
1961	1.4	17.0	47.3	393.3	348.9	341.5	6.5	1.0	0.5	0.5	44.4	11.3	2 474.9	2 367.8
1962	1.5	19.1	51.6	417.3	370.6	362.6	6.9	1.1	0.5	0.6	46.7	11.2	2 608.8	2 482.9
1963	1.9	21.7	54.6	438.2	391.1	382.0	7.9	1.2	0.5	0.7	47.1	10.7	2 708.0	2 576.7
1964	2.2	22.4	52.1	476.1	420.8	410.6	8.9	1.3	0.6	0.7	55.3	11.6	2 867.2	2 759.6
1965	2.3	23.4	57.7	513.0	454.2	443.0	9.9	1.4	0.6	0.8	58.8	11.5	3 053.8	2 931.0
1966	2.1	31.3	66.4	554.0	492.1	479.9	10.6	1.6	0.8	0.8	61.9	11.2	3 236.2	3 087.1
1967	2.3	34.9	73.0	592.8	519.8	506.7	11.1	2.0	1.0	1.0	73.0	12.3	3 358.0	3 222.4
1968	2.8	38.7	87.0	643.9	571.0	556.9	12.1	2.0	1.0	1.0	72.9	11.3	3 530.3	3 368.7
1969	3.3	44.1	104.5	695.8	619.8	603.6	13.9	2.2	1.1	1.1	76.1	10.9	3 694.6	3 483.3
1970	2.9	46.4	103.1	762.0	664.4	646.7	15.1	2.6	1.3	1.3	97.6	12.8	3 779.9	3 644.1
1971	2.7	51.2	101.7	831.1	719.2	699.9	16.4	2.8	1.5	1.4	111.9	13.5	3 875.0	3 812.6
1972	3.1	59.2	123.6	900.8	789.3	768.2	18.0	3.2	1.8	1.4	111.5	12.4	4 110.3	3 996.2
1973	3.9	75.5	132.4	1 008.4	872.6	849.6	19.6	3.4	1.8	1.6	135.8	13.5	4 328.3	4 244.8
1974	4.7	85.2	151.0	1 100.8	954.5	930.2	20.9	3.4	2.1	1.4	146.3	13.3	4 264.5	4 196.8
1975	6.8	89.3	147.6	1 221.8	1 057.8	1 030.5	23.4	3.8	2.5	1.3	164.0	13.4	4 221.1	4 299.8
1976	6.7	101.3	172.7	1 330.0	1 175.6	1 147.7	23.5	4.4	3.0	1.4	154.4	11.6	4 398.2	4 437.1
1977	5.1	113.1	197.9	1 461.4	1 305.4	1 274.0	26.6	4.8	3.5	1.4	155.9	10.7	4 588.1	4 577.7
1978	6.5	131.3	229.6	1 634.1	1 459.0	1 422.3	31.3	5.4	3.9	1.6	175.1	10.7	4 843.6	4 785.8
1979	8.2	152.7	268.9	1 813.8	1 627.0	1 585.4	35.5	6.0	4.3	1.7	186.8	10.3	4 968.3	4 878.6
1980	8.6	166.2	299.5	2 024.1	1 800.1	1 750.7	42.5	6.9	5.0	2.0	224.1	11.1	4 962.2	4 915.1
1981	11.2	195.7	345.8	2 259.3	1 993.9	1 934.0	48.4	11.5	6.0	5.6	265.5	11.8	5 094.9	5 035.2
1982	12.4	208.9	354.7	2 436.9	2 143.5	2 071.3	58.5	13.8	7.1	6.7	293.3	12.0	5 143.5	5 145.0
1983	13.8	226.0	352.9	2 628.2	2 364.2	2 281.6	67.4	15.1	8.1	7.0	264.0	10.0	5 258.9	5 322.6
1984	19.7	257.5	377.9	2 914.8	2 584.5	2 492.3	75.0	17.1	9.2	7.9	330.3	11.3	5 643.9	5 688.2
1985	22.3	281.4	417.8	3 107.1	2 822.1	2 712.8	90.6	18.8	10.4	8.3	284.9	9.2	5 844.8	5 859.0
1986	22.9	303.4	437.8	3 295.3	3 004.7	2 886.3	97.3	21.1	12.0	9.1	290.6	8.8	6 056.2	6 081.6
1987	20.2	323.1	489.6	3 472.0	3 196.6	3 076.3	97.1	23.2	13.2	10.0	275.4	7.9	6 254.5	6 216.1
1988	20.6	361.5	505.9	3 777.5	3 457.0	3 330.0	101.3	25.6	14.8	10.8	320.5	8.5	6 523.2	6 508.6
1989	23.2	385.2	567.7	4 057.8	3 717.9	3 576.8	113.1	28.0	16.5	11.6	340.0	8.4	6 738.0	6 699.2
1990	22.2	410.1	594.7	4 319.1	3 958.0	3 809.0	118.4	30.6	18.4	12.2	361.1	8.4	6 827.2	6 830.7
1991	17.6	430.2	588.9	4 496.0	4 100.0	3 943.4	119.9	36.7	22.6	14.1	396.0	8.8	6 759.1	6 880.4
1992	16.3	455.0	612.8	4 808.1	4 354.2	4 197.6	116.1	40.5	26.0	14.5	453.9	9.4	6 965.3	7 166.9
1993	14.1	477.4	648.8	5 009.2	4 611.5	4 452.0	113.9	45.6	28.6	17.1	397.7	7.9	7 075.4	7 285.2
1994	13.3	508.2	693.1	5 254.0	4 890.6	4 721.0	119.9	49.8	30.9	18.9	363.4	6.9	7 291.5	7 485.1
1995	18.7	532.8	748.4	5 543.0	5 155.9	4 962.6	140.4	52.9	32.6	20.3	387.1	7.0	7 545.5	7 733.9
1996	22.9	555.1	837.1	5 841.4	5 459.2	5 244.6	157.0	57.6	34.9	22.6	382.3	6.5	7 853.9	7 979.7
1997	19.4	587.2	931.8	6 160.7	5 770.4	5 536.8	169.7	63.9	38.2	25.7	390.3	6.3	8 240.9	8 271.8
1998	26.0	624.7	1 032.4	6 574.2	6 127.7	5 877.2	180.9	69.5	39.9	29.7	446.5	6.8	8 822.1	8 757.4
1999	34.0	661.3	1 111.9	6 894.9	6 550.9	6 283.8	190.8	76.3	44.1	32.3	344.0	5.0	9 165.2	9 052.7
2000	42.4	705.8	1 236.3	7 419.6	7 068.1	6 767.2	217.7	83.2	48.8	34.5	351.4	4.7	9 692.1	9 501.3
2001	46.8	733.2	1 239.0	7 773.8	7 390.9	7 073.8	225.6	91.5	52.9	38.6	382.8	4.9	9 817.5	9 759.2
2002	34.2	751.5	1 052.2	8 108.8	7 646.3	7 348.9	200.6	96.7	56.4	40.4	462.5	5.7	9 759.0	10 047.8
2003	26.3	779.3	1 003.5	8 495.0	8 038.3	7 740.7	196.5	101.1	60.5	40.6	456.7	5.4	9 892.6	10 309.7
2004	16.8	829.2	1 048.7	8 995.5	8 550.1	8 232.0	207.3	110.9	66.9	44.0	445.4	5.0	10 211.7	10 652.8
2005	25.8	873.3	1 212.5	9 392.5	9 124.5	8 769.1	237.3	118.1	71.6	46.5	268.0	2.9	10 461.1	10 811.4
2006	20.8	922.5	1 357.0	10 027.7	9 669.1	9 277.2	266.9	124.9	75.3	49.6	358.7	3.6	10 938.9	11 226.5
2007	30.8	961.4	1 492.5	10 528.9	10 176.2	9 746.6	291.2	138.4	79.2	59.2	352.7	3.3	11 235.4	11 492.6
2008	35.8	988.4	1 507.5	10 970.1	10 466.7	10 050.1	272.0	144.6	81.0	63.7	503.4	4.6	11 155.5	11 630.0
2009	39.0	964.3	1 152.4	10 928.0	10 288.4	9 891.2	252.8	144.3	80.1	64.3	639.7	5.9	10 560.7	11 617.9
2010	43.7	983.7	1 237.6	11 356.9	10 647.6	10 260.3	242.3	145.0	79.4	65.6	709.3	6.2	10 725.5	11 861.4
2011	48.5	916.7	1 453.7	11 885.6	11 079.6	10 698.9	229.9	150.8	82.2	68.6	806.0	6.8	11 185.3	12 107.2
2012	40.4	950.5	1 509.5	12 504.8	11 431.8	11 047.4	229.6	154.8	86.3	68.5	1 073.1	8.6	11 651.3	12 504.8
2013	38.4	1 104.3	1 676.4	12 517.3	11 751.3	11 363.5	229.5	158.3	87.5	70.8	766.0	6.1	11 612.1	12 350.0
2014	42.9	1 153.6	1 784.6	13 192.0	12 261.1	11 847.7	243.7	169.6	93.4	76.3	930.9	7.1	12 086.1	12 821.9
2015	50.3	1 204.7	1 939.9	13 745.3	12 710.4	12 263.5	263.5	183.5	100.9	82.5	1 034.9	7.5	12 607.0	13 330.0
2016	59.7	1 238.8	1 958.2	14 138.7	13 150.8	12 693.3	272.8	184.8	103.4	81.4	987.8	7.0	12 789.3	13 575.5
2017	48.7	1 298.8	2 049.0	14 801.2	13 724.8	13 239.1	291.6	194.1	107.5	86.7	1 076.4	7.3	13 195.3	13 956.6
2018	50.2	1 360.5	2 076.3	15 629.7	14 438.8	13 913.5	321.0	204.3	113.9	90.3	1 190.9	7.6	13 598.5	14 429.4
2019	56.0	1 421.4	2 205.1	16 219.3	14 981.5	14 428.7	340.4	212.4	118.6	93.9	1 237.8	7.6	13 905.6	14 755.2
2020	59.9	1 459.5	2 195.6	17 432.0	14 544.5	14 047.6	285.4	211.5	114.6	96.9	2 887.5	16.6	13 833.7	15 672.8
2018														
1st quarter	48.0	1 343.4	2 076.2	15 329.8	14 176.5	13 667.4	309.3	199.8	111.5	88.3	1 153.3	7.5	13 449.7	14 253.3
2nd quarter	49.4	1 352.9	2 049.8	15 548.7	14 383.7	13 864.8	315.6	203.3	113.1	90.2	1 165.0	7.5	13 524.3	14 373.0
3rd quarter	50.9	1 369.0	2 091.3	15 729.7	14 536.1	14 002.6	327.5	206.0	114.7	91.3	1 193.7	7.6	13 663.6	14 491.8
4th quarter	52.5	1 376.6	2 087.7	15 910.6	14 658.8	14 119.3	331.5	207.9	116.4	91.5	1 251.8	7.9	13 756.1	14 599.1
2019														
1st quarter	54.2	1 407.6	2 169.3	16 069.6	14 692.9	14 155.6	330.6	206.8	117.6	89.1	1 376.7	8.6	13 882.2	14 729.6
2nd quarter	55.6	1 414.6	2 222.8	16 122.6	14 928.3	14 375.7	339.3	213.2	118.7	94.5	1 194.4	7.4	13 853.6	14 679.3
3rd quarter	56.7	1 422.0	2 205.2	16 259.6	15 087.9	14 529.5	346.6	211.8	119.1	92.7	1 171.7	7.2	13 898.3	14 763.1
4th quarter	57.5	1 441.4	2 223.2	16 425.3	15 216.9	14 653.9	345.0	217.9	118.8	99.1	1 208.4	7.4	13 989.7	14 850.5
2020														
1st quarter	58.0	1 472.0	2 241.6	16 600.6	14 989.2	14 439.1	337.8	212.3	114.9	97.5	1 611.4	9.7	14 070.2	14 962.7
2nd quarter	63.3	1 405.9	2 099.0	18 249.6	13 477.7	12 989.7	273.6	214.4	114.4	100.0	4 772.0	26.1	13 317.7	16 516.9
3rd quarter	58.9	1 458.7	2 181.8	17 595.7	14 774.3	14 293.8	274.4	206.1	114.3	91.8	2 821.3	16.0	13 820.2	15 782.4
4th quarter	59.2	1 501.3	2 259.8	17 282.2	14 936.8	14 467.6	255.9	213.2	114.8	98.4	2 345.5	13.6	14 129.7	15 443.0

Table 4-1B. Personal Income and Its Disposition: Historical Data

(Billions of current dollars, except as noted; quarterly data are at seasonally adjusted annual rates.)　　　**NIPA Table 2.1**

| Year and quarter | Personal income | | | | | | | Less: Personal current taxes | Equals: Disposable personal income | Less: Personal outlays | Equals: Personal saving | | Billions of chained (2009) dollars | |
	Total	Compensation of employees	Proprietors' income with IVA and CCAdj	Rental income of persons with CCAdj	Personal income receipts on assets	Personal current transfer receipts	Less: Contributions for government social insurance, domestic				Billions of dollars	Percent of disposable personal income	Personal income excluding current transfers	Disposable personal income
1929	85.3	51.4	14.0	6.1	12.7	1.2	0.1	1.7	83.6	79.6	4.0	4.7	904.7	898.9
1930	76.5	47.2	10.9	5.4	12.0	1.2	0.1	1.6	75.0	71.6	3.3	4.5	846.0	842.1
1931	65.7	40.1	8.3	4.4	10.6	2.3	0.1	1.0	64.7	61.8	2.8	4.4	796.6	813.5
1932	50.3	31.3	5.0	3.6	8.7	1.7	0.1	0.7	49.6	49.7	-0.1	-0.2	692.5	707.1
1933	47.2	29.8	5.3	2.9	7.7	1.7	0.1	0.8	46.4	46.8	-0.3	-0.7	673.6	686.6
1934	54.1	34.6	7.0	2.5	8.3	1.8	0.1	0.9	53.2	52.3	0.9	1.7	740.5	752.6
1935	60.8	37.7	10.1	2.6	8.6	2.0	0.1	1.1	59.8	56.8	3.0	5.1	812.9	825.4
1936	69.2	43.3	10.4	2.7	10.1	3.1	0.3	1.3	67.9	63.1	4.8	7.1	905.0	929.4
1937	74.7	48.3	12.5	3.0	10.4	2.0	1.5	1.9	72.8	67.9	4.9	6.7	960.2	960.9
1938	69.1	45.4	10.6	3.5	8.8	2.4	1.6	1.9	67.2	65.3	2.0	2.9	900.9	908.2
1939	73.6	48.6	11.1	3.7	9.5	2.5	1.8	1.5	72.1	68.2	3.9	5.4	970.1	984.2
1940	79.4	52.7	12.2	3.8	9.8	2.7	1.9	1.7	77.7	72.4	5.3	6.8	1 037.9	1 051.3
1941	97.9	66.2	16.7	4.4	10.3	2.7	2.3	2.3	95.6	82.3	13.3	13.9	1 212.7	1 217.1
1942	126.7	88.0	23.3	5.5	10.1	2.7	2.9	4.9	121.8	90.0	31.9	26.2	1 405.0	1 379.8
1943	156.2	112.7	28.2	6.0	10.5	2.5	3.8	16.7	139.5	100.8	38.6	27.7	1 594.0	1 446.2
1944	169.7	124.3	29.3	6.3	11.0	3.1	4.3	17.7	152.1	109.7	42.4	27.9	1 634.0	1 491.2
1945	175.8	126.3	30.8	6.6	11.8	5.6	5.3	19.4	156.3	121.2	35.2	22.5	1 604.5	1 474.4
1946	182.5	122.5	35.7	6.9	13.5	10.5	6.6	17.2	165.3	145.8	19.6	11.8	1 516.3	1 457.6
1947	194.5	132.4	34.6	6.9	15.4	10.8	5.6	19.8	174.7	163.7	11.0	6.3	1 470.2	1 398.4
1948	213.5	144.3	39.3	7.5	16.8	10.3	4.6	19.2	194.3	177.1	17.2	8.8	1 539.8	1 472.0
1949	211.1	144.3	34.7	7.8	17.9	11.2	4.9	16.7	194.3	180.7	13.6	7.0	1 526.1	1 483.9
1950	233.7	158.3	37.5	8.8	20.7	14.0	5.5	18.9	214.8	194.8	20.0	9.3	1 658.3	1 621.1
1951	264.2	185.7	42.6	9.7	21.4	11.4	6.6	27.1	237.2	211.3	25.9	10.9	1 786.2	1 675.6
1952	282.5	201.1	43.0	10.8	22.6	11.9	6.9	32.0	250.5	222.6	27.8	11.1	1 873.2	1 733.9
1953	299.2	215.2	42.0	12.0	24.5	12.5	7.1	33.2	266.0	236.8	29.2	11.0	1 959.1	1 817.5
1954	302.2	214.1	42.3	13.1	26.5	14.3	8.1	30.2	272.1	243.9	28.1	10.3	1 950.8	1 843.5
1955														
1st quarter	313.5	221.9	43.7	13.3	28.2	15.3	8.9	31.4	282.1	255.9	26.2	9.3	2 019.8	1 910.6
2nd quarter	321.1	228.1	44.3	13.4	28.7	15.6	9.0	32.4	288.6	261.2	27.5	9.5	2 066.7	1 952.9
3rd quarter	328.5	233.9	44.6	13.4	29.8	15.9	9.2	33.4	295.1	265.6	29.5	10.0	2 106.8	1 988.9
4th quarter	333.6	238.4	44.5	13.5	30.4	16.0	9.3	34.2	299.4	269.8	29.6	9.9	2 134.9	2 012.1
1956														
1st quarter	339.0	242.8	44.9	13.6	31.2	16.3	9.9	35.4	303.6	271.6	32.1	10.6	2 159.8	2 032.4
2nd quarter	344.8	247.5	45.3	13.6	31.8	16.6	10.0	36.2	308.6	274.3	34.2	11.1	2 182.4	2 051.7
3rd quarter	350.1	250.4	46.4	13.7	32.5	17.1	10.0	36.9	313.2	277.6	35.5	11.3	2 192.9	2 062.3
4th quarter	357.8	256.4	46.8	13.8	33.6	17.3	10.1	37.9	319.9	283.1	36.8	11.5	2 228.6	2 094.2
1957														
1st quarter	362.4	260.2	46.9	13.9	34.5	18.2	11.4	38.6	323.8	287.7	36.1	11.1	2 233.0	2 100.8
2nd quarter	367.1	262.1	47.7	14.0	35.4	19.4	11.4	39.0	328.1	290.1	38.1	11.6	2 241.5	2 115.6
3rd quarter	371.7	264.7	48.8	14.1	35.9	19.6	11.5	39.2	332.5	294.7	37.8	11.4	2 251.4	2 126.3
4th quarter	370.8	263.3	47.7	14.3	36.0	20.8	11.3	38.8	332.0	296.4	35.6	10.7	2 226.5	2 112.1
1958														
1st quarter	371.3	259.8	50.3	14.6	35.9	22.1	11.3	38.2	333.1	295.9	37.2	11.2	2 194.4	2 093.4
2nd quarter	373.7	259.4	50.3	14.8	36.6	23.9	11.3	37.7	336.0	298.8	37.2	11.1	2 194.5	2 108.0
3rd quarter	382.6	267.2	50.1	14.9	37.6	24.2	11.4	38.9	343.7	303.8	39.9	11.6	2 246.8	2 154.3
4th quarter	388.2	272.3	49.9	15.0	38.9	23.7	11.5	39.4	348.8	307.8	41.0	11.8	2 286.0	2 187.4
1959														
1st quarter	394.0	279.7	50.1	15.0	38.8	24.0	13.7	40.8	353.2	315.4	37.9	10.7	2 304.4	2 200.1
2nd quarter	402.4	286.5	50.3	15.4	40.1	23.9	13.9	42.0	360.4	321.6	38.8	10.8	2 347.5	2 235.6
3rd quarter	404.7	286.9	50.4	15.8	41.4	24.2	13.9	42.7	362.1	327.1	35.0	9.7	2 346.6	2 232.5
4th quarter	410.4	290.2	50.6	16.0	42.6	24.8	13.9	43.7	366.6	329.4	37.2	10.2	2 364.3	2 248.4
1960														
1st quarter	416.7	298.7	49.7	16.2	43.7	24.6	16.4	45.3	371.4	333.1	38.3	10.3	2 400.9	2 274.4
2nd quarter	421.7	301.7	50.7	16.4	44.1	25.3	16.5	46.0	375.7	339.2	36.5	9.7	2 415.5	2 289.1
3rd quarter	424.4	302.6	50.9	16.5	44.9	26.0	16.5	46.5	377.8	339.3	38.6	10.2	2 417.8	2 293.5
4th quarter	425.8	302.1	51.0	16.7	45.3	27.0	16.4	46.4	379.4	341.3	38.0	10.0	2 409.8	2 292.5
1961														
1st quarter	430.2	303.1	52.3	16.9	45.7	28.8	16.7	46.5	383.7	341.9	41.7	10.9	2 420.8	2 314.2
2nd quarter	436.4	307.3	52.6	17.1	46.6	29.7	16.9	46.9	389.4	346.8	42.6	10.9	2 453.4	2 349.3
3rd quarter	443.4	312.3	53.3	17.3	47.7	29.9	17.1	47.4	396.0	349.8	46.2	11.7	2 485.9	2 380.6
4th quarter	452.3	318.9	54.5	17.5	49.3	29.4	17.3	48.1	404.2	357.2	47.0	11.6	2 539.5	2 427.0
1962														
1st quarter	459.3	325.5	55.3	17.7	49.7	30.0	18.9	49.4	409.9	362.5	47.4	11.6	2 566.9	2 450.9
2nd quarter	466.8	331.4	55.0	18.0	51.5	30.0	19.1	50.9	415.8	368.4	47.5	11.4	2 602.1	2 477.4
3rd quarter	471.5	334.2	54.9	18.2	53.0	30.4	19.2	52.3	419.2	372.5	46.7	11.1	2 620.8	2 490.7
4th quarter	477.8	337.7	55.8	18.3	54.1	31.2	19.3	53.6	424.2	379.0	45.2	10.7	2 645.6	2 512.8
1963														
1st quarter	483.2	342.7	56.0	18.5	54.7	32.6	21.3	54.1	429.1	382.9	46.2	10.8	2 661.4	2 534.6
2nd quarter	488.1	347.6	55.8	18.7	55.9	31.7	21.5	54.3	433.7	387.3	46.4	10.7	2 691.4	2 558.0
3rd quarter	495.2	352.6	56.2	18.8	57.3	32.0	21.8	54.6	440.6	394.7	45.9	10.4	2 718.8	2 586.0
4th quarter	504.6	358.8	57.6	18.8	58.9	32.5	22.0	55.2	449.4	399.6	49.8	11.1	2 760.6	2 628.1

Table 4-1B. Personal Income and Its Disposition: Historical Data—*Continued*

(Billions of current dollars, except as noted; quarterly data are at seasonally adjusted annual rates.)   NIPA Table 2.1

| Year and quarter | Personal income | | | | | | | Less: Personal current taxes | Equals: Disposable personal income | Less: Personal outlays | Equals: Personal saving | | Billions of chained (2009) dollars | |
	Total	Compensation of employees	Proprietors' income with IVA and CCAdj	Rental income of persons with CCAdj	Personal income receipts on assets	Personal current transfer receipts	Less: Contributions for government social insurance, domestic				Billions of dollars	Percent of disposable personal income	Personal income excluding current transfers	Disposable personal income
1964														
1st quarter	514.1	365.2	57.9	18.8	60.7	33.6	22.0	53.8	460.4	409.3	51.1	11.1	2 797.0	2 679.5
2nd quarter ...	523.6	372.6	58.8	18.8	62.4	33.2	22.3	49.7	473.8	417.6	56.3	11.9	2 847.6	2 751.7
3rd quarter	533.2	380.0	59.3	18.9	64.0	33.5	22.5	51.6	481.6	426.8	54.7	11.4	2 892.2	2 787.6
4th quarter	541.9	386.1	60.5	18.8	65.4	33.7	22.7	53.2	488.7	429.6	59.0	12.1	2 931.8	2 819.3
1965														
1st quarter	553.0	392.9	61.9	19.1	66.9	35.0	22.9	57.0	496.0	440.5	55.5	11.2	2 978.7	2 852.5
2nd quarter ...	562.6	399.9	63.2	19.3	68.7	34.6	23.2	58.4	504.1	447.9	56.3	11.2	3 020.8	2 884.7
3rd quarter	576.9	408.3	64.0	19.5	70.5	38.1	23.6	57.0	519.9	457.3	62.6	12.0	3 071.1	2 963.6
4th quarter	590.2	420.5	65.6	19.5	71.8	36.9	24.0	58.3	532.0	471.4	60.6	11.4	3 144.7	3 023.3
1966														
1st quarter	602.9	433.1	69.2	19.8	73.3	37.8	30.4	61.5	541.4	481.9	59.5	11.0	3 186.7	3 053.2
2nd quarter ...	612.8	444.4	67.2	19.8	74.4	37.9	30.8	65.6	547.2	487.3	59.9	11.0	3 216.1	3 061.3
3rd quarter	626.0	455.7	67.2	20.0	75.5	39.6	31.9	67.9	558.2	496.6	61.6	11.0	3 255.5	3 098.7
4th quarter	639.6	463.8	68.1	20.0	76.7	43.1	32.2	70.6	569.1	502.6	66.5	11.7	3 286.0	3 135.0
1967														
1st quarter	650.5	470.0	68.9	20.3	78.9	46.1	33.6	71.2	579.3	507.1	72.2	12.5	3 320.1	3 182.2
2nd quarter ...	657.6	475.6	68.5	20.4	80.5	47.2	34.6	70.9	586.7	516.8	69.9	11.9	3 337.2	3 207.5
3rd quarter	671.6	485.3	70.5	20.4	81.9	48.7	35.2	73.8	597.8	523.8	74.0	12.4	3 374.1	3 238.0
4th quarter	683.2	496.2	70.0	20.3	82.6	50.0	36.0	75.9	607.3	531.4	75.9	12.5	3 400.5	3 261.6
1968														
1st quarter	702.5	510.9	71.7	20.1	85.1	52.4	37.6	78.6	624.0	549.8	74.2	11.9	3 454.9	3 316.0
2nd quarter ...	722.4	524.0	73.2	20.1	87.6	55.9	38.4	81.7	640.7	563.9	76.8	12.0	3 506.0	3 370.6
3rd quarter	741.3	537.8	75.0	20.2	90.0	57.3	39.1	91.9	649.4	580.6	68.8	10.6	3 561.1	3 381.4
4th quarter	757.5	550.3	75.5	20.0	92.7	58.7	39.7	95.9	661.7	589.8	71.9	10.9	3 598.9	3 407.5
1969														
1st quarter	772.4	562.8	75.6	20.2	96.2	60.4	42.9	102.6	669.8	602.3	67.4	10.1	3 631.0	3 416.0
2nd quarter ...	790.6	576.7	77.1	20.3	98.7	61.5	43.7	105.7	685.0	614.3	70.6	10.3	3 671.6	3 449.4
3rd quarter	811.6	593.4	78.0	20.4	101.5	62.9	44.6	104.1	707.5	625.0	82.5	11.7	3 724.9	3 519.7
4th quarter	826.8	604.9	77.3	20.4	105.0	64.3	45.3	105.6	721.1	637.4	83.7	11.6	3 749.7	3 546.6
1970														
1st quarter	841.7	615.0	77.1	20.4	109.2	66.1	46.0	104.6	737.2	648.9	88.3	12.0	3 770.9	3 583.9
2nd quarter ...	860.0	620.2	76.7	20.2	113.1	76.1	46.3	105.5	754.5	659.1	95.4	12.6	3 769.6	3 628.1
3rd quarter	874.7	628.2	78.5	20.9	117.5	76.3	46.7	100.7	774.0	671.3	102.7	13.3	3 801.8	3 686.1
4th quarter	883.7	630.0	78.9	21.2	120.0	80.1	46.5	101.5	782.2	678.2	103.9	13.3	3 777.9	3 677.2
1971														
1st quarter	903.7	647.9	80.3	21.1	122.8	82.0	50.5	98.3	805.3	697.6	107.7	13.4	3 826.6	3 750.6
2nd quarter ...	927.1	659.8	82.8	21.7	124.2	89.6	51.0	100.7	826.4	712.1	114.2	13.8	3 856.5	3 805.2
3rd quarter	941.1	670.1	84.6	22.0	126.1	89.6	51.3	102.3	838.8	725.1	113.7	13.6	3 883.2	3 825.1
4th quarter	959.3	682.2	87.9	22.5	127.4	91.3	51.9	105.5	853.8	741.8	112.1	13.1	3 934.1	3 869.7
1972														
1st quarter	986.5	708.4	87.9	23.1	131.0	94.3	58.1	119.8	866.8	759.4	107.4	12.4	4 001.5	3 887.4
2nd quarter ...	1 004.2	722.5	91.3	20.2	134.1	94.9	58.8	123.4	880.8	778.4	102.4	11.6	4 054.8	3 927.8
3rd quarter	1 030.1	735.7	95.5	23.9	138.4	96.0	59.5	124.3	905.8	797.2	108.7	12.0	4 129.0	4 004.2
4th quarter	1 077.0	758.8	105.6	23.8	142.8	106.4	60.4	127.1	949.9	822.2	127.6	13.4	4 255.6	4 164.7
1973														
1st quarter	1 095.1	785.4	104.1	23.5	146.6	109.1	73.6	126.4	968.7	847.0	121.7	12.6	4 271.4	4 196.3
2nd quarter ...	1 124.9	803.2	109.9	23.3	151.6	111.5	74.7	129.2	995.7	863.0	132.7	13.3	4 307.1	4 231.7
3rd quarter	1 152.5	820.4	113.8	22.3	158.8	113.3	76.1	134.1	1 018.4	881.8	136.6	13.4	4 337.6	4 250.8
4th quarter	1 190.7	841.7	122.2	23.3	164.6	116.5	77.6	140.0	1 050.7	898.4	152.3	14.5	4 393.4	4 297.4
1974														
1st quarter	1 206.8	858.3	115.7	23.5	170.5	121.9	83.1	142.8	1 064.0	915.3	148.7	14.0	4 309.1	4 226.0
2nd quarter ...	1 232.9	878.5	108.6	22.9	177.6	129.9	84.7	148.9	1 084.0	944.4	139.6	12.9	4 260.1	4 186.7
3rd quarter	1 269.1	900.2	111.0	23.3	183.9	137.1	86.4	154.9	1 114.2	973.9	140.2	12.6	4 257.4	4 190.5
4th quarter	1 298.5	913.8	113.5	23.0	190.4	144.3	86.6	157.6	1 140.9	984.3	156.5	13.7	4 233.7	4 184.9
1975														
1st quarter	1 318.4	918.4	112.7	22.7	196.4	155.9	87.6	158.0	1 160.4	1 011.8	148.6	12.8	4 186.1	4 178.6
2nd quarter ...	1 350.0	931.2	114.3	22.4	198.5	171.5	88.0	121.1	1 228.9	1 040.4	188.5	15.3	4 192.3	4 371.9
3rd quarter	1 386.5	956.0	120.7	22.2	202.5	174.8	89.8	152.8	1 233.6	1 074.8	158.9	12.9	4 231.5	4 308.3
4th quarter	1 422.7	983.4	125.2	21.9	206.5	177.6	91.8	158.5	1 264.2	1 104.0	160.1	12.7	4 276.4	4 342.0
1976														
1st quarter	1 456.1	1 014.7	126.4	21.6	210.5	181.8	98.9	162.5	1 293.6	1 137.3	156.3	12.1	4 329.0	4 394.4
2nd quarter ...	1 481.2	1 035.5	128.6	20.5	217.1	180.0	100.4	169.3	1 311.9	1 157.1	154.8	11.8	4 383.4	4 419.4
3rd quarter	1 518.4	1 058.4	132.7	20.0	222.8	186.7	102.2	176.1	1 342.3	1 186.9	155.4	11.6	4 418.7	4 453.9
4th quarter	1 554.9	1 084.8	136.2	19.1	229.7	188.8	103.8	182.7	1 372.1	1 221.1	151.0	11.0	4 462.2	4 482.1
1977														
1st quarter	1 588.8	1 113.3	138.6	16.4	238.8	191.0	109.3	188.8	1 400.0	1 258.2	141.9	10.1	4 485.3	4 492.2
2nd quarter ...	1 633.0	1 150.3	140.5	16.3	246.6	191.4	112.1	195.7	1 437.3	1 287.0	150.4	10.5	4 547.9	4 534.4
3rd quarter	1 677.7	1 182.1	142.4	15.6	255.4	196.6	114.3	198.6	1 479.2	1 318.8	160.4	10.8	4 603.6	4 597.4
4th quarter	1 737.4	1 217.6	156.5	15.1	265.5	199.3	116.7	208.5	1 528.9	1 357.8	171.1	11.2	4 713.3	4 685.3

Table 4-1B. Personal Income and Its Disposition: Historical Data—*Continued*

(Billions of current dollars, except as noted; quarterly data are at seasonally adjusted annual rates.)   **NIPA Table 2.1**

Year and quarter	Personal income							Less: Personal current taxes	Equals: Disposable personal income	Less: Personal outlays	Equals: Personal saving		Billions of chained (2009) dollars	
	Total	Compensation of employees	Proprietors' income with IVA and CCAdj	Rental income of persons with CCAdj	Personal income receipts on assets	Personal current transfer receipts	Less: Contributions for government social insurance, domestic				Billions of dollars	Percent of disposable personal income	Personal income excluding current transfers	Disposable personal income
1978														
1st quarter	1 778.1	1 250.9	158.5	15.9	273.3	203.3	123.9	212.0	1 566.1	1 388.5	177.6	11.3	4 748.1	4 722.1
2nd quarter	1 838.2	1 299.1	166.1	15.6	281.3	205.1	129.0	223.1	1 615.1	1 447.5	167.6	10.4	4 825.1	4 772.0
3rd quarter	1 892.6	1 336.9	168.3	17.1	289.8	213.9	133.4	236.3	1 656.3	1 479.8	176.5	10.7	4 874.2	4 809.1
4th quarter	1 946.0	1 380.2	170.9	17.5	298.9	217.2	138.8	247.2	1 698.7	1 520.2	178.5	10.5	4 926.3	4 840.8
1979														
1st quarter	2 005.4	1 422.5	180.1	17.3	308.8	222.7	146.0	253.6	1 751.8	1 556.7	195.0	11.1	4 985.8	4 899.4
2nd quarter	2 045.4	1 454.7	179.2	15.6	318.8	227.4	150.3	262.0	1 783.4	1 598.3	185.1	10.4	4 949.3	4 855.1
3rd quarter	2 110.9	1 496.7	180.7	15.4	330.4	243.0	155.4	274.8	1 836.0	1 653.9	182.1	9.9	4 961.7	4 877.1
4th quarter	2 169.0	1 534.9	177.8	16.1	350.4	249.1	159.4	285.2	1 883.8	1 698.9	184.9	9.8	4 979.2	4 885.7
1980														
1st quarter	2 231.9	1 573.6	167.6	15.8	377.5	259.4	161.9	284.8	1 947.1	1 751.3	195.8	10.1	4 966.6	4 902.6
2nd quarter	2 269.4	1 599.2	160.3	17.1	391.2	264.6	162.9	292.2	1 977.3	1 753.6	223.6	11.3	4 927.4	4 859.5
3rd quarter	2 348.5	1 628.6	173.4	19.9	397.0	296.6	167.0	302.2	2 046.3	1 812.2	234.1	11.4	4 927.6	4 914.1
4th quarter	2 444.7	1 687.6	185.0	23.2	421.9	300.0	173.0	318.9	2 125.8	1 883.0	242.9	11.4	5 026.0	4 981.8
1981														
1st quarter	2 508.9	1 739.6	188.2	24.0	440.5	306.5	189.9	330.9	2 178.0	1 941.4	236.6	10.9	5 030.6	4 974.8
2nd quarter	2 559.8	1 774.8	176.4	23.3	469.0	309.9	193.6	342.7	2 217.1	1 975.7	241.4	10.9	5 054.1	4 980.6
3rd quarter	2 659.1	1 815.1	182.3	23.1	508.5	328.5	198.4	356.9	2 302.2	2 019.6	282.6	12.3	5 150.8	5 088.0
4th quarter	2 692.7	1 840.7	171.8	24.7	525.4	331.1	201.0	352.7	2 340.0	2 038.8	301.2	12.9	5 140.6	5 093.6
1982														
1st quarter	2 727.8	1 864.7	165.2	23.5	544.1	336.3	206.0	352.5	2 375.3	2 082.1	293.2	12.3	5 140.7	5 105.9
2nd quarter	2 772.3	1 884.4	169.4	21.1	559.9	345.5	208.0	359.7	2 412.5	2 110.9	301.6	12.5	5 166.9	5 136.7
3rd quarter	2 812.5	1 904.8	170.7	24.4	560.8	362.1	210.3	350.1	2 462.3	2 159.3	303.0	12.3	5 136.2	5 161.3
4th quarter	2 853.8	1 918.1	179.5	26.3	563.2	377.9	211.2	356.6	2 497.2	2 221.7	275.5	11.0	5 133.3	5 177.5
1983														
1st quarter	2 892.4	1 947.2	183.3	25.8	574.3	380.7	218.9	350.9	2 541.5	2 263.2	278.4	11.0	5 165.0	5 226.4
2nd quarter	2 942.1	1 986.3	182.6	24.7	584.4	386.9	222.9	359.6	2 582.5	2 330.6	251.9	9.8	5 206.9	5 262.6
3rd quarter	3 001.2	2 029.6	183.8	23.7	609.2	382.5	227.7	345.4	2 655.8	2 403.9	251.8	9.5	5 267.1	5 341.6
4th quarter	3 088.6	2 086.8	195.3	23.5	630.2	387.0	234.3	355.7	2 732.9	2 458.9	274.0	10.0	5 397.8	5 460.6
1984														
1st quarter	3 178.9	2 143.8	221.9	23.2	645.6	393.9	249.5	361.2	2 817.8	2 506.0	311.8	11.1	5 505.0	5 569.6
2nd quarter	3 262.9	2 195.2	231.8	21.7	671.4	398.3	255.5	370.4	2 892.4	2 566.5	325.9	11.3	5 607.7	5 662.2
3rd quarter	3 337.4	2 241.6	232.4	24.4	698.4	401.0	260.5	384.1	2 953.3	2 607.2	346.1	11.7	5 704.1	5 736.9
4th quarter	3 391.7	2 282.9	226.9	29.3	707.7	409.4	264.5	395.9	2 995.7	2 658.1	337.6	11.3	5 757.8	5 783.7
1985														
1st quarter	3 455.4	2 323.5	240.7	26.9	718.6	420.0	274.3	432.3	3 023.1	2 740.5	282.7	9.3	5 792.0	5 768.6
2nd quarter ...	3 495.5	2 363.6	238.5	25.3	723.8	422.6	278.3	388.5	3 107.0	2 789.6	317.3	10.2	5 816.4	5 881.0
3rd quarter	3 543.1	2 406.4	240.7	27.1	724.1	427.9	283.2	421.5	3 121.5	2 865.2	256.4	8.2	5 850.5	5 862.6
4th quarter	3 605.5	2 455.7	244.3	25.6	738.7	430.9	289.6	428.9	3 176.6	2 893.3	283.3	8.9	5 920.9	5 924.6
1986														
1st quarter	3 667.6	2 491.1	245.6	22.0	762.3	443.2	296.7	426.3	3 241.3	2 940.1	301.2	9.3	5 971.1	6 002.5
2nd quarter	3 708.8	2 517.2	251.6	21.1	770.2	449.1	300.4	429.4	3 279.4	2 969.3	310.0	9.5	6 042.8	6 079.3
3rd quarter	3 757.1	2 555.2	264.4	16.6	770.3	456.1	305.5	439.5	3 317.7	3 036.0	281.7	8.5	6 087.4	6 118.0
4th quarter	3 798.8	2 604.7	264.2	13.4	769.8	457.8	311.1	456.0	3 342.8	3 073.2	269.5	8.1	6 124.0	6 127.3
1987														
1st quarter	3 856.0	2 647.8	275.4	14.5	771.1	463.1	315.9	450.7	3 405.3	3 102.2	303.0	8.9	6 161.2	6 183.8
2nd quarter ...	3 917.5	2 692.0	282.3	14.1	781.0	468.1	320.0	511.7	3 405.8	3 172.7	233.2	6.8	6 204.3	6 125.9
3rd quarter	3 988.5	2 740.3	289.5	17.5	796.9	469.2	324.8	489.0	3 499.6	3 238.6	260.9	7.5	6 270.8	6 235.5
4th quarter	4 084.3	2 809.6	298.6	20.3	815.4	472.2	331.7	507.0	3 577.4	3 273.0	304.4	8.5	6 381.1	6 319.6
1988														
1st quarter	4 160.6	2 857.6	319.2	21.1	824.0	489.9	351.1	502.1	3 658.5	3 355.5	303.0	8.3	6 433.6	6 412.3
2nd quarter	4 234.8	2 923.1	322.5	20.3	833.7	493.5	358.3	497.8	3 737.0	3 417.4	319.6	8.6	6 485.8	6 478.3
3rd quarter	4 326.3	2 975.8	333.6	21.2	860.5	499.6	364.5	506.7	3 819.6	3 489.6	330.0	8.6	6 553.1	6 541.0
4th quarter	4 411.9	3 035.4	326.8	27.4	887.5	506.8	372.0	517.2	3 894.7	3 565.3	329.4	8.5	6 620.4	6 602.7
1989														
1st quarter	4 537.2	3 079.1	348.1	23.1	933.6	531.4	378.0	552.9	3 984.4	3 626.3	358.0	9.0	6 713.8	6 677.8
2nd quarter	4 592.9	3 114.6	339.5	21.2	961.5	538.8	382.6	566.7	4 026.2	3 693.9	332.3	8.3	6 704.3	6 658.2
3rd quarter	4 648.5	3 155.0	337.2	20.0	975.6	547.9	387.2	571.6	4 076.9	3 751.7	325.2	8.0	6 741.4	6 702.4
4th quarter	4 723.7	3 209.7	339.7	21.8	986.6	558.8	393.1	579.8	4 143.9	3 799.5	344.4	8.3	6 793.3	6 759.1
1990														
1st quarter	4 818.9	3 272.8	345.6	23.1	999.5	579.5	401.6	582.5	4 236.3	3 884.5	351.9	8.3	6 815.9	6 811.0
2nd quarter	4 899.2	3 334.7	351.1	26.7	1 003.1	590.5	406.9	594.6	4 304.6	3 930.6	374.0	8.7	6 865.0	6 858.4
3rd quarter	4 958.5	3 372.5	358.9	31.6	1 010.0	600.0	414.6	600.7	4 357.8	3 997.1	360.7	8.3	6 857.1	6 856.0
4th quarter	4 978.6	3 381.5	357.0	31.3	1 008.7	617.5	417.4	600.8	4 377.8	4 019.8	357.9	8.2	6 771.6	6 797.5
1991														
1st quarter	4 992.5	3 387.5	347.5	33.0	1 003.9	641.6	421.0	580.8	4 411.7	4 028.3	383.4	8.7	6 720.5	6 814.5
2nd quarter	5 054.1	3 427.6	353.0	35.5	1 004.2	661.4	427.7	585.9	4 468.2	4 083.2	384.9	8.6	6 748.4	6 864.4
3rd quarter	5 107.1	3 469.9	353.6	39.4	1 006.8	670.8	433.5	590.2	4 516.8	4 130.5	386.3	8.6	6 769.5	6 892.4
4th quarter	5 186.0	3 517.0	362.6	46.4	999.9	698.8	438.6	598.7	4 587.4	4 158.2	429.1	9.4	6 798.1	6 949.7

Table 4-1B. Personal Income and Its Disposition: Historical Data—*Continued*

(Billions of current dollars, except as noted; quarterly data are at seasonally adjusted annual rates.) NIPA Table 2.1

| Year and quarter | Personal income | | | | | | Less: Contributions for government social insurance, domestic | Less: Personal current taxes | Equals: Disposable personal income | Less: Personal outlays | Equals: Personal saving | | Billions of chained (2009) dollars | |
	Total	Compen-sation of employees	Pro-prietors' income with IVA and CCAdj	Rental income of persons with CCAdj	Personal income receipts on assets	Personal current transfer receipts					Billions of dollars	Percent of disposable personal income	Personal income excluding current transfers	Disposable personal income
1992														
1st quarter	5 297.8	3 595.7	378.7	50.0	996.8	727.0	450.4	588.9	4 708.9	4 255.1	453.8	9.6	6 881.6	7 089.6
2nd quarter ...	5 394.4	3 651.9	395.2	57.3	1 000.4	745.6	456.0	607.2	4 787.2	4 311.2	476.0	9.9	6 952.8	7 159.9
3rd quarter	5 456.3	3 688.5	407.9	64.3	997.1	757.6	459.1	616.2	4 840.1	4 388.0	452.1	9.3	6 982.9	7 193.1
4th quarter	5 535.0	3 736.9	418.8	70.7	1 000.9	762.0	454.4	638.9	4 896.1	4 462.5	433.5	8.9	7 044.3	7 225.8
1993														
1st quarter	5 560.7	3 745.6	418.9	80.7	1 007.7	781.6	473.8	617.0	4 943.7	4 508.3	435.4	8.8	7 011.4	7 252.9
2nd quarter ...	5 635.8	3 800.2	429.6	86.9	1 007.4	786.0	474.2	643.5	4 992.3	4 578.0	414.3	8.3	7 067.6	7 275.3
3rd quarter	5 677.6	3 834.1	423.4	92.5	1 006.4	799.9	478.8	659.2	5 018.4	4 646.1	372.3	7.4	7 077.4	7 281.7
4th quarter	5 757.7	3 889.3	440.0	100.2	1 006.7	804.3	482.9	675.3	5 082.4	4 713.7	368.7	7.3	7 146.1	7 332.3
1994														
1st quarter	5 807.9	3 913.4	450.2	109.0	1 015.2	818.1	498.0	673.7	5 134.3	4 783.9	350.4	6.8	7 173.0	7 380.7
2nd quarter ...	5 912.7	3 991.5	454.1	113.5	1 035.9	822.9	505.1	697.8	5 214.9	4 850.1	364.8	7.0	7 276.3	7 455.0
3rd quarter	5 978.4	4 031.8	456.8	116.3	1 057.7	826.9	511.0	695.4	5 283.0	4 925.8	357.2	6.8	7 311.8	7 498.5
4th quarter	6 089.4	4 088.1	465.5	115.9	1 090.4	848.0	518.5	705.4	5 384.0	5 002.8	381.2	7.1	7 404.7	7 606.1
1995														
1st quarter	6 181.2	4 134.4	467.4	118.3	1 112.7	874.0	525.5	724.6	5 456.6	5 042.6	414.0	7.6	7 461.1	7 671.1
2nd quarter ...	6 250.7	4 172.9	472.0	121.6	1 130.9	883.5	530.0	746.8	5 503.9	5 124.1	379.9	6.9	7 501.8	7 692.8
3rd quarter	6 329.3	4 219.7	484.5	125.7	1 144.3	890.4	535.4	752.2	5 577.0	5 195.4	381.6	6.8	7 571.0	7 763.3
4th quarter	6 404.3	4 265.3	501.0	134.0	1 158.4	886.0	540.3	770.0	5 634.3	5 261.6	372.7	6.6	7 647.9	7 808.7
1996														
1st quarter	6 521.0	4 314.5	523.3	139.5	1 170.8	916.0	543.2	801.7	5 719.2	5 337.7	381.5	6.7	7 725.1	7 882.6
2nd quarter ...	6 649.8	4 387.5	547.5	141.6	1 188.5	936.4	551.6	839.6	5 810.3	5 432.5	377.8	6.5	7 822.4	7 954.9
3rd quarter	6 725.9	4 451.2	547.5	143.7	1 210.7	931.8	559.0	843.5	5 882.3	5 492.0	390.4	6.6	7 899.0	8 019.3
4th quarter	6 817.5	4 514.5	556.8	145.3	1 234.7	932.6	566.5	863.5	5 954.0	5 574.5	379.4	6.4	7 968.5	8 062.0
1997														
1st quarter	6 939.4	4 592.4	575.6	144.2	1 251.4	950.2	574.4	902.1	6 037.2	5 658.1	379.1	6.3	8 074.0	8 138.8
2nd quarter ...	7 022.3	4 660.0	575.1	144.6	1 274.5	950.0	581.9	916.2	6 106.0	5 702.5	403.6	6.6	8 165.6	8 211.0
3rd quarter	7 135.3	4 738.9	588.5	147.4	1 294.9	956.2	590.5	941.1	6 194.2	5 815.8	378.4	6.1	8 287.4	8 307.6
4th quarter	7 273.0	4 844.0	596.6	152.1	1 319.4	963.1	602.2	967.8	6 305.2	5 905.2	400.0	6.3	8 436.3	8 429.9
1998														
1st quarter	7 434.6	4 942.0	617.4	156.8	1 353.9	974.7	610.3	996.1	6 438.4	5 961.5	476.9	7.4	8 636.1	8 607.4
2nd quarter ...	7 561.1	5 028.3	629.6	162.6	1 379.1	981.1	619.7	1 022.4	6 538.7	6 082.6	456.1	7.0	8 780.8	8 725.8
3rd quarter	7 668.1	5 114.9	645.0	168.0	1 385.2	984.5	629.5	1 043.2	6 624.9	6 181.1	443.8	6.7	8 891.8	8 813.7
4th quarter	7 762.9	5 199.4	668.7	173.4	1 365.3	995.4	639.2	1 068.0	6 694.9	6 285.6	409.3	6.1	8 979.8	8 883.4
1999														
1st quarter	7 859.1	5 287.0	681.9	176.1	1 349.7	1 014.6	650.2	1 077.9	6 781.2	6 358.1	423.1	6.2	9 064.4	8 980.4
2nd quarter ...	7 922.9	5 343.9	690.1	179.6	1 347.3	1 017.8	655.7	1 095.2	6 827.8	6 496.9	330.8	4.8	9 092.9	8 991.1
3rd quarter	8 038.3	5 424.0	699.8	179.4	1 367.2	1 030.9	663.0	1 120.6	6 917.7	6 604.6	313.1	4.5	9 177.2	9 059.7
4th quarter	8 206.9	5 555.9	713.9	178.9	1 393.0	1 041.4	676.2	1 154.0	7 052.9	6 743.8	309.1	4.4	9 327.5	9 181.0
2000														
1st quarter	8 443.3	5 749.2	720.9	179.8	1 432.6	1 056.7	696.0	1 208.8	7 234.6	6 902.9	331.7	4.6	9 537.8	9 341.5
2nd quarter ...	8 586.0	5 791.7	751.3	180.2	1 477.5	1 083.7	698.4	1 230.2	7 355.9	7 004.5	351.4	4.8	9 641.2	9 453.0
3rd quarter	8 746.9	5 903.9	760.8	182.9	1 512.9	1 098.0	711.6	1 247.7	7 499.2	7 127.7	371.5	5.0	9 766.5	9 575.4
4th quarter	8 847.4	5 943.7	782.4	191.0	1 536.8	1 110.8	717.3	1 258.7	7 588.7	7 237.5	351.2	4.6	9 822.7	9 634.9
2001														
1st quarter	9 009.2	6 050.1	809.8	197.1	1 528.9	1 155.6	732.3	1 301.9	7 707.3	7 315.0	392.3	5.1	9 897.7	9 713.4
2nd quarter ...	9 032.4	6 040.9	827.7	202.6	1 507.0	1 187.4	733.1	1 308.9	7 723.6	7 361.9	361.7	4.7	9 840.8	9 688.4
3rd quarter	9 009.7	6 024.6	845.6	204.8	1 474.9	1 192.2	732.4	1 113.6	7 896.1	7 389.1	507.0	6.4	9 801.2	9 899.7
4th quarter	8 999.9	6 037.8	840.9	205.1	1 416.0	1 235.2	735.0	1 231.8	7 768.1	7 497.9	270.2	3.5	9 731.1	9 735.3
2002														
1st quarter	9 041.5	6 060.7	859.5	207.3	1 397.0	1 260.0	743.1	1 075.2	7 966.4	7 520.6	445.7	5.6	9 732.7	9 963.9
2nd quarter ...	9 141.3	6 129.1	864.5	208.9	1 408.1	1 282.3	751.5	1 051.0	8 090.3	7 606.2	484.2	6.0	9 757.4	10 044.6
3rd quarter	9 188.4	6 156.9	872.9	207.7	1 413.1	1 292.1	754.3	1 044.1	8 144.2	7 691.0	453.2	5.6	9 753.2	10 059.5
4th quarter	9 272.6	6 193.7	883.3	209.9	1 436.3	1 306.4	757.0	1 038.4	8 234.2	7 767.3	466.8	5.7	9 793.9	10 123.4
2003														
1st quarter	9 313.6	6 213.2	876.3	218.7	1 444.5	1 324.2	763.3	1 021.3	8 292.3	7 859.7	432.6	5.2	9 748.0	10 117.5
2nd quarter ...	9 425.6	6 307.3	892.4	223.2	1 436.1	1 340.6	773.9	1 020.8	8 404.8	7 957.7	447.1	5.3	9 854.8	10 244.6
3rd quarter	9 559.0	6 393.7	905.3	227.5	1 455.3	1 361.0	783.8	950.7	8 608.3	8 117.1	491.2	5.7	9 927.1	10 424.0
4th quarter	9 695.8	6 500.2	916.1	239.0	1 473.4	1 363.2	796.1	1 021.3	8 674.5	8 218.8	455.7	5.3	10 040.8	10 452.8
2004														
1st quarter	9 792.4	6 541.3	946.5	243.0	1 473.6	1 397.1	809.2	1 012.3	8 780.1	8 356.6	423.5	4.8	10 039.0	10 499.2
2nd quarter ...	9 957.8	6 668.5	963.0	243.4	1 490.5	1 416.0	823.6	1 026.8	8 931.0	8 460.5	470.5	5.3	10 146.0	10 608.3
3rd quarter	10 103.6	6 803.7	964.2	241.8	1 507.5	1 425.5	839.2	1 064.4	9 039.2	8 603.8	435.4	4.8	10 257.4	10 684.3
4th quarter	10 323.3	6 864.5	977.8	242.9	1 636.7	1 446.3	844.9	1 091.6	9 231.7	8 779.3	452.4	4.9	10 403.6	10 819.3
2005														
1st quarter	10 345.2	6 926.3	957.1	233.7	1 598.1	1 488.1	858.1	1 172.3	9 172.9	8 891.0	281.9	3.1	10 320.2	10 688.3
2nd quarter ...	10 516.8	7 005.6	964.1	231.2	1 669.6	1 512.6	866.3	1 196.3	9 320.5	9 054.8	265.6	2.9	10 425.7	10 792.0
3rd quarter	10 686.1	7 122.6	988.1	213.6	1 713.0	1 528.3	879.5	1 225.5	9 460.6	9 229.1	231.4	2.4	10 490.4	10 837.2
4th quarter	10 871.7	7 209.9	1 007.2	206.0	1 800.1	1 537.9	889.5	1 255.8	9 615.9	9 322.9	293.0	3.0	10 607.4	10 928.0

Table 4-1B. Personal Income and Its Disposition: Historical Data—*Continued*

(Billions of current dollars, except as noted; quarterly data are at seasonally adjusted annual rates.) **NIPA Table 2.1**

| Year and quarter | Personal income | | | | | | | Less: Personal current taxes | Equals: Disposable personal income | Less: Personal outlays | Equals: Personal saving | | Billions of chained (2009) dollars | |
	Total	Compensation of employees	Proprietors' income with IVA and CCAdj	Rental income of persons with CCAdj	Personal income receipts on assets	Personal current transfer receipts	Less: Contributions for government social insurance, domestic				Billions of dollars	Percent of disposable personal income	Personal income excluding current transfers	Disposable personal income
2006														
1st quarter	11 181.1	7 379.7	1 049.1	194.5	1 882.7	1 588.3	913.2	1 320.5	9 860.6	9 474.0	386.6	3.9	10 845.1	11 147.9
2nd quarter	11 336.3	7 428.0	1 052.1	183.4	1 988.0	1 602.8	918.1	1 351.3	9 985.0	9 612.8	372.3	3.7	10 908.4	11 190.4
3rd quarter	11 435.7	7 487.3	1 049.0	177.8	2 015.8	1 628.3	922.6	1 358.6	10 077.1	9 750.4	326.6	3.2	10 912.7	11 212.8
4th quarter	11 585.7	7 623.6	1 053.3	168.7	2 040.4	1 635.9	936.2	1 397.5	10 188.3	9 839.1	349.1	3.4	11 089.6	11 355.3
2007														
1st quarter	11 824.1	7 806.0	1 017.5	162.5	2 087.1	1 706.7	955.7	1 466.5	10 357.5	9 988.2	369.3	3.6	11 174.3	11 439.5
2nd quarter	11 988.7	7 845.2	997.9	180.3	2 212.3	1 710.4	957.3	1 495.9	10 492.8	10 109.8	383.0	3.6	11 256.5	11 491.3
3rd quarter	12 069.2	7 885.2	986.8	193.6	2 231.6	1 732.7	960.6	1 498.9	10 570.4	10 232.7	337.6	3.2	11 256.6	11 511.2
4th quarter	12 203.4	7 977.5	979.8	208.7	2 246.9	1 762.7	972.1	1 508.6	10 694.8	10 374.1	320.7	3.0	11 255.5	11 529.3
2008														
1st quarter	12 335.3	8 054.9	964.1	249.2	2 248.2	1 802.9	984.0	1 535.1	10 800.2	10 433.3	366.9	3.4	11 262.4	11 548.8
2nd quarter	12 669.4	8 054.9	967.2	280.9	2 204.2	2 148.4	986.2	1 552.5	11 117.0	10 549.4	567.5	5.1	11 141.6	11 772.7
3rd quarter	12 508.6	8 074.4	956.6	305.3	2 222.5	1 941.4	991.5	1 497.5	11 011.1	10 578.1	433.0	3.9	11 072.3	11 537.5
4th quarter	12 396.9	8 043.2	950.7	325.7	2 141.3	1 927.8	991.7	1 444.9	10 951.9	10 306.0	646.0	5.9	11 147.5	11 661.6
2009														
1st quarter	12 057.0	7 730.4	913.2	326.6	2 006.9	2 039.7	959.8	1 202.4	10 854.7	10 214.0	640.7	5.9	10 739.0	11 636.7
2nd quarter	12 087.3	7 762.0	901.5	335.9	1 875.6	2 178.6	966.3	1 131.1	10 956.2	10 203.1	753.2	6.9	10 580.6	11 699.1
3rd quarter	12 033.3	7 746.5	934.5	355.8	1 783.9	2 176.3	963.8	1 135.3	10 898.0	10 335.7	562.2	5.2	10 453.3	11 557.3
4th quarter	12 144.0	7 797.2	1 001.3	372.0	1 748.4	2 192.3	967.2	1 140.7	11 003.3	10 400.7	602.6	5.5	10 473.1	11 579.7
2010														
1st quarter	12 321.2	7 767.6	1 055.8	404.9	1 763.3	2 303.2	973.6	1 191.8	11 129.4	10 495.1	634.3	5.7	10 502.3	11 667.4
2nd quarter	12 544.7	7 910.6	1 102.7	428.9	1 775.8	2 311.1	984.5	1 213.2	11 331.4	10 596.1	735.4	6.5	10 711.7	11 860.9
3rd quarter	12 682.0	7 982.2	1 128.0	442.6	1 780.5	2 336.1	987.4	1 256.3	11 425.7	10 685.3	740.5	6.5	10 808.5	11 936.6
4th quarter	12 830.2	8 041.0	1 142.7	458.3	1 827.5	2 350.1	989.5	1 289.1	11 541.1	10 813.9	727.2	6.3	10 879.0	11 980.4
2011														
1st quarter	13 175.9	8 170.1	1 179.0	489.1	1 887.8	2 361.8	911.8	1 426.6	11 749.3	10 937.9	811.4	6.9	11 132.1	12 094.8
2nd quarter	13 280.6	8 206.4	1 210.2	501.4	1 915.4	2 361.6	914.5	1 445.9	11 834.7	11 054.1	780.7	6.6	11 130.6	12 064.1
3rd quarter	13 413.8	8 287.3	1 251.6	510.1	1 935.6	2 352.1	922.9	1 471.4	11 942.3	11 135.2	807.1	6.8	11 224.2	12 117.7
4th quarter	13 486.9	8 240.9	1 268.9	525.6	2 009.8	2 359.3	917.4	1 470.9	12 016.0	11 191.2	824.8	6.9	11 253.9	12 152.3
2012														
1st quarter	13 786.3	8 456.4	1 321.8	526.7	2 081.4	2 340.4	940.3	1 468.3	12 317.9	11 342.4	975.5	7.9	11 499.6	12 375.7
2nd quarter	13 945.9	8 503.8	1 355.6	532.4	2 136.0	2 362.8	944.7	1 487.7	12 458.2	11 390.1	1 068.1	8.6	11 609.3	12 486.5
3rd quarter	13 922.7	8 546.1	1 344.9	536.1	2 078.6	2 364.7	947.6	1 510.0	12 412.6	11 441.9	970.7	7.8	11 550.6	12 404.8
4th quarter	14 402.6	8 763.2	1 363.2	542.8	2 318.7	2 384.2	969.4	1 572.0	12 830.5	11 552.6	1 278.0	10.0	11 943.8	12 750.9
2013														
1st quarter	14 019.5	8 732.6	1 387.2	560.8	2 026.1	2 403.5	1 090.6	1 650.0	12 369.5	11 651.9	717.6	5.8	11 502.5	12 248.6
2nd quarter	14 153.0	8 819.6	1 410.6	573.1	2 036.5	2 416.2	1 103.1	1 682.5	12 470.5	11 678.0	792.5	6.4	11 613.8	12 339.8
3rd quarter	14 244.1	8 845.6	1 411.0	585.1	2 074.2	2 434.5	1 106.3	1 674.9	12 569.2	11 766.6	802.6	6.4	11 638.6	12 387.2
4th quarter	14 358.0	8 942.5	1 400.0	590.7	2 099.0	2 443.2	1 117.2	1 698.1	12 659.9	11 908.6	751.3	5.9	11 693.4	12 424.6
2014														
1st quarter	14 625.1	9 114.2	1 411.4	598.1	2 167.0	2 474.1	1 139.8	1 744.8	12 880.3	12 019.9	860.4	6.7	11 868.1	12 580.4
2nd quarter	14 874.6	9 172.4	1 450.6	602.6	2 266.7	2 526.8	1 144.5	1 758.4	13 116.2	12 192.4	923.8	7.0	12 000.3	12 747.1
3rd quarter	15 099.5	9 280.6	1 466.2	604.6	2 336.0	2 568.2	1 156.1	1 798.6	13 300.9	12 350.2	950.7	7.1	12 144.2	12 890.1
4th quarter	15 307.1	9 433.5	1 454.4	605.5	2 390.4	2 597.1	1 173.8	1 836.5	13 470.6	12 481.9	988.7	7.3	12 331.6	13 069.5
2015														
1st quarter	15 497.7	9 563.8	1 434.9	596.2	2 447.6	2 644.1	1 188.9	1 904.6	13 593.2	12 518.3	1 074.9	7.9	12 522.9	13 243.4
2nd quarter	15 639.9	9 666.2	1 411.3	611.3	2 469.7	2 682.3	1 200.9	1 943.0	13 696.9	12 669.2	1 027.7	7.5	12 563.2	13 280.1
3rd quarter	15 757.0	9 751.7	1 423.2	614.9	2 478.9	2 699.1	1 210.9	1 947.3	13 809.6	12 799.7	1 009.9	7.3	12 629.8	13 357.0
4th quarter	15 846.4	9 816.0	1 413.8	615.6	2 503.2	2 716.1	1 218.3	1 964.9	13 881.4	12 854.5	1 027.0	7.4	12 712.6	13 439.8
2016														
1st quarter	15 918.6	9 851.7	1 410.1	619.8	2 517.0	2 745.4	1 225.3	1 924.6	13 994.0	12 947.8	1 046.2	7.5	12 747.4	13 541.6
2nd quarter	16 002.1	9 905.2	1 409.6	626.7	2 524.3	2 767.7	1 231.4	1 943.4	14 058.7	13 089.1	969.6	6.9	12 726.7	13 519.5
3rd quarter	16 151.6	9 998.5	1 431.0	627.6	2 549.9	2 787.1	1 242.5	1 972.0	14 179.6	13 218.4	961.2	6.8	12 803.9	13 584.8
4th quarter	16 315.3	10 109.1	1 442.5	632.5	2 579.4	2 807.9	1 256.0	1 992.9	14 322.4	13 348.0	974.3	6.8	12 879.8	13 656.9
2017														
1st quarter	16 552.0	10 225.4	1 484.4	643.9	2 643.2	2 832.1	1 277.0	2 005.0	14 547.0	13 515.0	1 032.0	7.1	13 010.9	13 795.2
2nd quarter	16 739.7	10 337.9	1 498.5	645.1	2 708.8	2 838.9	1 289.6	2 007.2	14 732.5	13 627.2	1 105.3	7.5	13 145.3	13 931.9
3rd quarter	16 932.4	10 480.5	1 502.9	654.9	2 728.2	2 870.8	1 304.8	2 056.1	14 876.2	13 758.5	1 117.7	7.5	13 248.0	14 015.4
4th quarter	17 176.7	10 660.7	1 537.5	667.0	2 751.6	2 883.6	1 323.7	2 127.6	15 049.1	13 998.4	1 050.7	7.0	13 376.6	14 084.1
2018														
1st quarter	17 406.1	10 784.1	1 567.0	671.8	2 786.0	2 940.6	1 343.4	2 076.2	15 329.8	14 176.5	1 153.3	7.5	13 449.7	14 253.3
2nd quarter	17 598.5	10 891.8	1 572.1	677.3	2 842.4	2 967.9	1 352.9	2 049.8	15 548.7	14 383.7	1 165.0	7.5	13 524.3	14 373.0
3rd quarter	17 821.1	11 044.3	1 581.3	689.8	2 884.4	2 990.3	1 369.0	2 091.3	15 729.7	14 536.1	1 193.7	7.6	13 663.6	14 491.8
4th quarter	17 998.3	11 118.0	1 601.4	688.6	2 960.5	3 006.5	1 376.6	2 087.7	15 910.6	14 658.8	1 251.8	7.9	13 756.1	14 599.1
2019														
1st quarter	18 238.9	11 336.1	1 585.5	687.0	2 944.3	3 093.8	1 407.6	2 169.3	16 069.6	14 692.9	1 376.7	8.6	13 882.2	14 729.6
2nd quarter	18 345.4	11 394.1	1 572.8	691.0	2 972.5	3 129.6	1 414.6	2 222.8	16 122.6	14 928.3	1 194.4	7.4	13 853.6	14 679.3
3rd quarter	18 464.7	11 453.9	1 610.6	691.5	2 973.2	3 157.7	1 422.0	2 205.2	16 259.6	15 087.9	1 171.7	7.2	13 898.3	14 763.1
4th quarter	18 648.5	11 606.8	1 626.8	699.0	2 982.1	3 175.3	1 441.4	2 223.2	16 425.3	15 216.9	1 208.4	7.4	13 989.7	14 850.5

Table 4-2. Personal Consumption Expenditures by Major Type of Product

(Billions of dollars, quarterly data are at seasonally adjusted rates.)   NIPA Table 2.3.5

Year and quarter	Personal consumption expenditures, total	Goods										
		Total goods	Durable goods					Nondurable goods				
			Durable goods, total	Motor vehicles and parts	Furnishings and household equipment	Recreational goods and vehicles	Other durable goods	Nondurable goods, total	Food and beverages off-premises	Clothing and footwear	Gasoline and other energy goods	Other nondurable goods
1960	331.2	177.0	45.6	19.6	15.4	6.4	4.3	131.4	62.6	25.9	15.8	27.1
1961	341.5	178.8	44.2	17.7	15.6	6.6	4.3	134.6	63.7	26.6	15.7	28.6
1962	362.6	189.0	49.5	21.4	16.4	6.9	4.7	139.5	64.7	27.9	16.3	30.7
1963	382.0	198.2	54.2	24.2	17.5	7.6	4.9	143.9	65.9	28.6	16.9	32.5
1964	410.6	212.3	59.6	25.8	19.5	8.8	5.5	152.7	69.5	31.1	17.7	34.5
1965	443.0	229.7	66.4	29.6	20.7	10.1	6.0	163.3	74.4	32.7	19.1	37.1
1966	479.9	249.6	71.7	29.9	22.6	12.3	6.9	177.9	80.6	35.8	20.7	40.8
1967	506.7	259.0	74.0	29.6	23.7	13.6	7.1	185.0	82.6	37.5	21.9	43.0
1968	556.9	284.6	84.8	35.4	26.1	15.3	8.0	199.8	88.8	41.3	23.2	46.5
1969	603.6	304.7	90.5	37.4	27.6	16.7	8.7	214.2	95.4	44.3	25.0	49.5
1970	646.7	318.8	90.0	34.5	28.2	17.9	9.4	228.8	103.5	45.5	26.3	53.6
1971	699.9	342.1	102.4	43.2	29.9	19.2	10.1	239.7	107.1	49.0	27.6	55.9
1972	768.2	373.8	116.4	49.4	33.5	22.6	11.0	257.4	114.5	53.5	29.4	60.0
1973	849.6	416.6	130.5	54.4	38.0	25.3	12.9	286.1	126.7	59.2	34.3	65.8
1974	930.2	451.5	130.2	48.2	40.9	26.6	14.5	321.4	143.0	62.4	43.8	72.1
1975	1 030.5	491.3	142.2	52.6	42.6	30.4	16.5	349.2	156.6	66.9	48.0	77.7
1976	1 147.7	546.3	168.6	68.2	47.2	34.2	19.1	377.7	167.3	72.2	53.0	85.2
1977	1 274.0	600.4	192.0	79.8	53.4	37.7	21.1	408.4	179.8	79.3	57.8	91.5
1978	1 422.3	663.6	213.3	89.2	59.0	41.7	23.5	450.2	196.1	89.3	61.5	103.3
1979	1 585.4	737.9	226.3	90.2	65.3	45.8	25.1	511.6	218.4	96.4	80.4	116.5
1980	1 750.7	799.8	226.4	84.4	67.8	46.5	27.6	573.4	239.2	103.0	101.9	129.3
1981	1 934.0	869.4	243.9	93.0	71.5	49.9	29.6	625.4	255.3	113.2	113.4	143.5
1982	2 071.3	899.3	253.0	100.0	71.8	51.3	29.9	646.3	267.1	116.7	108.4	154.0
1983	2 281.6	973.8	295.0	122.9	79.8	58.7	33.7	678.8	277.0	126.4	106.5	168.8
1984	2 492.3	1 063.7	342.2	147.2	88.8	67.8	38.3	721.5	291.1	137.6	108.2	184.6
1985	2 712.8	1 137.6	380.4	170.1	94.6	74.1	41.6	757.2	303.0	146.8	110.5	196.9
1986	2 886.3	1 195.6	421.4	187.5	103.5	83.0	47.5	774.2	316.4	157.2	91.2	209.4
1987	3 076.3	1 256.3	442.0	188.2	109.5	91.8	52.5	814.3	324.3	167.7	96.4	225.9
1988	3 330.0	1 337.3	475.1	202.2	115.2	99.9	57.8	862.3	342.8	178.2	99.9	241.4
1989	3 576.8	1 423.8	494.3	207.8	121.4	103.9	61.3	929.5	365.4	190.4	110.4	263.3
1990	3 809.0	1 491.3	497.1	205.1	120.9	105.6	65.5	994.2	391.2	195.2	124.2	283.6
1991	3 943.4	1 497.4	477.2	185.7	118.8	107.7	64.9	1 020.3	403.0	199.1	121.1	297.1
1992	4 197.6	1 563.3	508.1	204.8	124.3	111.0	68.0	1 055.2	404.5	211.2	125.0	314.5
1993	4 452.0	1 642.3	551.5	224.7	131.4	123.5	72.0	1 090.8	413.5	219.1	126.9	331.4
1994	4 721.0	1 746.6	607.2	249.8	140.5	140.3	76.5	1 139.4	432.1	227.4	129.2	350.6
1995	4 962.6	1 815.5	635.7	255.7	146.7	153.7	79.6	1 179.8	443.7	231.2	133.4	371.4
1996	5 244.6	1 917.7	676.3	273.5	153.5	164.9	84.3	1 241.4	461.9	239.5	144.7	395.2
1997	5 536.8	2 006.5	715.5	293.1	160.5	174.6	87.3	1 291.0	474.8	247.5	147.7	421.0
1998	5 877.2	2 108.4	779.3	320.2	173.6	191.4	94.2	1 329.1	487.4	257.8	132.4	451.5
1999	6 283.8	2 287.1	855.6	350.7	191.2	210.9	102.7	1 431.5	515.5	271.1	146.5	498.3
2000	6 767.2	2 453.2	912.6	363.2	208.1	230.9	110.4	1 540.6	540.6	280.8	184.5	534.7
2001	7 073.8	2 525.6	941.5	383.3	214.9	234.9	108.4	1 584.1	564.0	277.9	178.0	564.2
2002	7 348.9	2 598.8	985.4	401.3	225.9	244.8	113.4	1 613.4	575.1	278.8	167.9	591.7
2003	7 740.7	2 722.6	1 017.8	401.5	235.2	259.5	121.7	1 704.8	599.6	285.3	196.4	623.5
2004	8 232.0	2 902.0	1 080.6	409.3	254.3	284.8	132.1	1 821.4	632.6	297.4	232.7	658.7
2005	8 769.1	3 082.9	1 128.6	410.0	271.3	306.4	141.0	1 954.3	668.2	310.5	283.8	691.8
2006	9 277.2	3 239.7	1 158.3	394.9	283.6	326.3	153.5	2 081.3	700.3	320.0	319.7	741.4
2007	9 746.6	3 367.0	1 188.0	400.6	283.5	339.2	164.8	2 179.0	737.3	323.5	345.5	772.6
2008	10 050.1	3 363.2	1 098.8	343.3	264.3	328.1	163.0	2 264.5	769.1	317.4	391.1	786.9
2009	9 891.2	3 180.0	1 012.1	318.6	238.3	297.5	157.7	2 167.9	772.9	304.0	287.0	803.9
2010	10 260.3	3 317.8	1 049.0	344.5	240.9	298.6	165.0	2 268.9	786.9	316.6	336.7	828.7
2011	10 698.9	3 518.1	1 093.5	365.2	246.9	305.4	176.1	2 424.6	819.5	332.6	413.8	858.7
2012	11 047.4	3 637.7	1 144.2	396.6	253.9	311.8	181.9	2 493.5	846.2	345.2	421.9	880.2
2013	11 363.5	3 730.0	1 189.4	417.5	263.6	321.6	186.7	2 540.6	864.0	350.5	418.2	907.8
2014	11 847.7	3 863.0	1 242.1	442.0	276.2	329.9	194.0	2 620.9	896.9	360.8	403.3	959.9
2015	12 263.5	3 923.0	1 307.6	475.3	294.2	336.5	201.6	2 615.4	921.0	368.7	309.4	1 016.3
2016	12 693.3	3 991.8	1 345.2	484.3	308.5	349.4	203.0	2 646.7	940.6	375.7	275.7	1 054.6
2017	13 239.1	4 158.6	1 396.6	501.3	322.7	366.4	206.2	2 761.9	973.1	381.0	309.9	1 097.9
2018	13 913.5	4 353.7	1 469.2	519.5	345.5	391.1	213.1	2 884.5	1 000.3	392.0	350.4	1 141.8
2019	14 428.7	4 478.9	1 513.3	514.5	360.2	420.9	217.6	2 965.6	1 030.9	398.2	337.6	1 198.9
2020	14 047.6	4 653.8	1 616.4	541.3	390.4	476.2	208.5	3 037.4	1 146.7	362.4	246.8	1 281.5
2018												
1st quarter	13 667.4	4 298.4	1 449.4	514.7	338.9	383.8	211.9	2 849.1	992.8	387.3	343.2	1 125.8
2nd quarter	13 864.8	4 354.4	1 471.3	519.4	347.0	389.7	215.1	2 883.2	997.7	394.1	352.9	1 138.5
3rd quarter	14 002.6	4 373.2	1 478.2	522.8	348.5	394.5	212.5	2 895.0	1 002.3	393.7	354.2	1 144.8
4th quarter	14 119.3	4 388.8	1 477.8	521.0	347.7	396.4	212.8	2 911.0	1 008.6	392.8	351.3	1 158.3
2019												
1st quarter	14 155.6	4 382.8	1 473.3	500.1	351.8	406.8	214.6	2 909.5	1 013.4	393.4	323.9	1 178.9
2nd quarter	14 375.7	4 479.4	1 509.2	512.6	360.0	419.5	217.2	2 970.1	1 027.4	398.3	350.1	1 194.4
3rd quarter	14 529.5	4 512.7	1 531.4	519.0	364.5	428.6	219.4	2 981.3	1 041.3	400.0	332.8	1 207.1
4th quarter	14 653.9	4 540.8	1 539.2	526.6	364.5	428.8	219.3	3 001.6	1 041.5	401.0	343.7	1 215.4
2020												
1st quarter	14 439.1	4 530.9	1 484.9	482.0	365.7	428.7	208.5	3 046.0	1 125.1	366.3	305.2	1 249.5
2nd quarter	12 989.7	4 349.9	1 468.3	485.2	361.2	458.0	163.9	2 881.7	1 152.1	293.6	188.5	1 247.4
3rd quarter	14 293.8	4 867.2	1 753.3	595.8	419.3	509.5	228.8	3 113.9	1 159.5	394.2	245.4	1 314.7
4th quarter	14 467.6	4 867.3	1 759.2	602.1	415.4	508.7	233.1	3 108.1	1 150.0	395.6	247.9	1 314.6

Table 4-2. Personal Consumption Expenditures by Major Type of Product—*Continued*

(Billions of dollars, quarterly data are at seasonally adjusted rates.) NIPA Table 2.3.5

						Services							
Year and quarter		Household consumption expenditures for services									Nonprofit institutions serving households (NPISHs)		
	Services	Household services, total	Housing and utilities	Health care	Transportation services	Recreation services	Food services and accommodations	Financial services and insurance	Other services	Final consumption expenditures	Gross output	Less: receipts from sales of goods and services
1960	154.2	149.1	56.7	16.0	9.2	6.5	20.5	13.2	27.1	5.1	14.8	9.8
1961	162.7	157.4	60.3	17.1	9.6	6.9	21.0	14.3	28.3	5.2	15.8	10.5
1962	173.6	168.1	64.5	19.1	10.1	7.5	22.3	14.8	29.9	5.5	16.9	11.5
1963	183.9	178.1	68.2	21.0	10.6	7.9	23.3	15.5	31.6	5.8	18.3	12.6
1964	198.4	191.9	72.1	24.1	11.4	8.5	24.9	17.2	33.8	6.4	20.3	13.8
1965	213.3	206.3	76.6	26.0	12.1	9.0	27.2	18.8	36.6	7.0	22.1	15.1
1966	230.3	222.8	81.2	28.7	13.1	9.8	29.6	20.6	39.9	7.5	24.3	16.9
1967	247.7	239.6	86.3	31.9	14.3	10.5	31.0	22.1	43.6	8.1	27.0	18.9
1968	272.2	263.4	92.7	36.6	15.9	11.7	34.6	25.2	46.8	8.8	30.3	21.6
1969	299.0	289.5	101.0	42.1	18.0	12.9	37.5	27.7	50.5	9.4	34.0	24.6
1970	327.9	317.5	109.4	47.7	20.0	14.0	41.6	30.1	54.6	10.5	38.1	27.6
1971	357.8	346.1	120.0	53.7	22.4	15.1	43.8	33.1	58.1	11.7	42.8	31.1
1972	394.3	381.5	131.2	59.8	24.5	16.3	48.9	37.1	63.7	12.8	47.4	34.5
1973	432.9	419.2	143.5	67.2	26.1	18.3	54.8	39.9	69.3	13.8	51.8	38.1
1974	478.6	463.1	158.6	76.1	28.5	20.9	60.6	44.1	74.4	15.5	58.8	43.3
1975	539.2	522.2	176.5	89.0	32.0	23.7	68.8	51.8	80.3	17.0	67.2	50.2
1976	601.4	582.4	194.7	101.8	36.2	26.5	77.8	56.8	88.6	19.0	76.3	57.3
1977	673.6	653.0	217.8	115.7	41.4	29.6	85.7	65.1	97.7	20.6	85.2	64.5
1978	758.7	735.7	244.3	131.2	45.2	32.9	97.1	76.7	108.3	23.0	96.7	73.6
1979	847.5	821.4	273.4	148.8	50.7	36.7	110.9	83.6	117.2	26.1	109.4	83.2
1980	950.9	920.8	312.5	171.7	55.4	40.8	121.7	91.7	127.1	30.0	126.1	96.1
1981	1 064.6	1 030.4	352.1	201.9	59.8	47.1	133.9	98.5	137.2	34.1	145.7	111.5
1982	1 172.0	1 134.0	387.5	225.2	61.7	52.5	142.5	113.7	150.9	38.0	163.8	125.8
1983	1 307.8	1 267.1	421.2	253.1	68.9	59.4	153.6	141.0	169.9	40.8	179.2	138.5
1984	1 428.6	1 383.3	457.5	276.5	80.0	66.1	164.9	150.8	187.5	45.4	194.4	149.0
1985	1 575.2	1 527.3	500.6	302.2	90.1	74.0	174.3	178.2	207.9	47.9	209.3	161.4
1986	1 690.7	1 638.0	537.0	330.2	95.0	80.4	186.7	187.7	221.2	52.6	227.3	174.7
1987	1 820.0	1 764.3	571.6	366.0	103.1	87.3	204.4	189.5	242.4	55.7	246.9	191.2
1988	1 992.7	1 929.4	614.4	410.1	114.2	99.2	225.8	202.9	262.8	63.3	275.5	212.2
1989	2 153.0	2 084.9	655.2	451.2	121.8	110.7	242.6	222.3	281.1	68.0	301.2	233.2
1990	2 317.7	2 241.8	696.5	506.2	126.4	121.8	262.7	230.8	297.5	75.9	334.4	258.6
1991	2 446.0	2 365.9	735.2	555.8	123.7	127.2	273.4	250.1	300.5	80.1	362.9	282.8
1992	2 634.3	2 546.4	771.1	612.8	133.6	139.8	286.3	277.0	325.7	87.9	396.4	308.5
1993	2 809.6	2 719.6	814.9	648.8	145.7	153.4	298.4	314.0	344.3	90.1	418.7	328.7
1994	2 974.4	2 876.6	863.3	680.5	161.0	164.7	308.3	327.9	371.0	97.8	440.1	342.3
1995	3 147.1	3 044.7	913.7	719.9	176.4	181.1	316.1	347.0	390.6	102.3	458.5	356.2
1996	3 326.9	3 216.9	962.4	752.1	192.7	195.6	326.6	372.1	415.5	110.0	483.1	373.1
1997	3 530.3	3 424.7	1 009.8	790.9	211.8	208.3	343.4	408.9	451.5	105.6	502.6	397.0
1998	3 768.8	3 645.0	1 065.5	832.0	225.2	220.2	361.8	446.1	494.2	123.8	542.5	418.7
1999	3 996.7	3 858.5	1 123.1	863.6	241.3	238.1	380.3	484.6	527.4	138.2	576.3	438.1
2000	4 314.0	4 156.0	1 198.6	918.4	261.3	254.4	408.8	541.9	572.6	158.0	621.6	463.6
2001	4 548.2	4 369.1	1 287.5	996.6	259.8	262.3	419.7	529.3	614.0	179.1	676.4	497.4
2002	4 750.1	4 551.8	1 329.5	1 082.9	251.9	271.4	436.3	539.0	640.8	198.3	737.1	538.7
2003	5 018.2	4 812.6	1 391.1	1 154.0	259.6	288.9	462.7	574.2	682.1	205.5	774.6	569.1
2004	5 329.9	5 123.6	1 466.6	1 238.9	271.2	311.5	498.2	619.3	717.9	206.4	819.0	612.6
2005	5 686.1	5 475.9	1 580.1	1 320.5	283.9	328.1	533.6	676.8	752.8	210.3	868.5	658.2
2006	6 037.6	5 798.4	1 665.7	1 391.9	297.1	351.3	570.6	719.5	802.3	239.2	932.2	693.0
2007	6 379.6	6 130.8	1 759.6	1 478.2	307.6	375.6	601.5	762.7	845.7	248.8	983.1	734.4
2008	6 686.9	6 399.6	1 872.7	1 555.3	312.7	389.1	620.2	777.5	872.1	287.3	1 047.4	760.1
2009	6 711.2	6 422.0	1 900.0	1 632.7	297.4	388.4	612.7	720.5	870.3	289.2	1 088.3	799.1
2010	6 942.4	6 648.0	1 947.9	1 699.6	305.2	403.7	635.7	768.0	887.9	294.4	1 128.6	834.2
2011	7 180.7	6 868.9	1 983.3	1 757.1	328.4	409.0	669.5	811.1	910.6	311.9	1 173.5	861.7
2012	7 409.6	7 068.1	2 014.7	1 821.3	341.1	430.8	704.9	830.9	924.4	341.5	1 236.5	895.0
2013	7 633.6	7 281.0	2 083.5	1 858.2	359.9	447.1	732.3	869.3	930.7	352.6	1 271.7	919.1
2014	7 984.8	7 619.2	2 151.4	1 940.5	383.0	466.6	776.9	922.9	977.7	365.6	1 322.4	956.8
2015	8 340.5	7 968.9	2 206.6	2 057.3	398.7	491.7	832.9	974.4	1 007.3	371.6	1 383.3	1 011.7
2016	8 701.4	8 300.0	2 280.8	2 159.4	419.7	518.6	873.2	996.1	1 052.1	401.4	1 460.1	1 058.7
2017	9 080.6	8 662.6	2 363.2	2 238.8	440.9	542.3	913.5	1 069.0	1 095.0	417.9	1 510.2	1 092.3
2018	9 559.8	9 115.1	2 472.1	2 339.6	469.4	564.7	960.8	1 151.9	1 156.7	444.7	1 587.8	1 143.1
2019	9 949.8	9 509.9	2 571.5	2 458.2	495.3	583.3	1 008.3	1 171.6	1 221.8	439.9	1 643.6	1 203.7
2020	9 393.7	8 872.9	2 668.1	2 308.4	363.4	416.5	801.5	1 196.3	1 118.5	520.9	1 644.8	1 123.9
2018												
1st quarter	9 369.0	8 940.9	2 431.8	2 300.2	467.2	558.2	940.5	1 128.5	1 114.5	428.1	1 544.5	1 116.4
2nd quarter	9 510.3	9 071.4	2 460.2	2 326.3	468.0	560.5	954.3	1 147.2	1 154.9	438.9	1 580.7	1 141.8
3rd quarter	9 629.4	9 184.8	2 479.4	2 364.4	467.6	568.5	973.9	1 161.3	1 169.7	444.6	1 608.6	1 164.0
4th quarter	9 730.5	9 263.5	2 517.0	2 367.4	474.7	571.5	974.6	1 170.5	1 187.8	467.0	1 617.3	1 150.3
2019												
1st quarter	9 772.7	9 336.7	2 534.7	2 408.7	479.6	573.7	986.9	1 156.3	1 196.7	436.1	1 625.1	1 189.0
2nd quarter	9 896.3	9 459.1	2 554.1	2 449.7	492.2	582.5	1 006.8	1 166.6	1 207.2	437.3	1 637.8	1 200.5
3rd quarter	10 016.0	9 571.5	2 585.3	2 469.9	502.2	582.8	1 019.4	1 177.0	1 234.9	445.3	1 650.4	1 205.1
4th quarter	10 113.0	9 672.3	2 611.8	2 504.3	507.3	594.0	1 020.0	1 186.5	1 248.4	440.9	1 661.1	1 220.2
2020												
1st quarter	9 908.2	9 387.7	2 622.6	2 406.9	467.3	541.7	933.6	1 193.9	1 221.7	520.5	1 668.1	1 147.6
2nd quarter	8 639.8	8 062.8	2 667.7	2 000.3	291.2	303.7	616.8	1 168.7	1 014.4	577.0	1 585.3	1 008.3
3rd quarter	9 426.6	8 932.1	2 682.6	2 369.2	342.5	405.7	829.8	1 200.5	1 102.0	494.6	1 640.2	1 145.6
4th quarter	9 600.4	9 109.0	2 699.7	2 457.2	352.8	415.0	826.1	1 222.0	1 136.1	491.4	1 685.5	1 194.1

Table 4-3. Chain-Type Quantity Indexes for Personal Consumption Expenditures by Major Type of Product

(Index numbers, 2012 = 100.)   NIPA Table 2.3.3

Year and quarter	Personal consumption expend- itures, total	Total goods	Goods									
			Durable goods					Nondurable goods				
			Durable goods, total	Motor vehicles and parts	Furnishings and household equipment	Recreational goods and vehicles	Other durable goods	Nondurable goods, total	Food and beverages off-premises	Clothing and footwear	Gasoline and other energy goods	Other nondurable goods
1960	18.2	18.3	7.0	16.7	12.2	0.8	7.9	29.2	44.7	14.5	53.2	18.5
1961	18.6	18.4	6.8	15.0	12.2	0.8	8.0	29.8	45.4	14.8	52.9	19.5
1962	19.5	19.3	7.5	17.8	12.9	0.9	8.8	30.7	45.7	15.5	54.6	20.9
1963	20.3	20.1	8.2	20.1	13.8	0.9	9.1	31.3	46.0	15.7	56.5	21.8
1964	21.5	21.3	9.0	21.2	15.3	1.1	9.9	32.8	47.6	16.9	59.5	22.8
1965	22.9	22.8	10.1	24.5	16.3	1.3	10.9	34.5	50.0	17.6	62.3	24.2
1966	24.2	24.3	11.0	24.9	17.7	1.6	12.6	36.4	51.9	18.8	65.7	26.1
1967	24.9	24.7	11.1	24.3	18.1	1.7	12.7	37.2	53.1	19.0	67.4	26.8
1968	26.4	26.3	12.4	28.1	19.2	1.9	13.9	38.7	55.5	19.7	70.2	27.9
1969	27.4	27.1	12.8	29.2	19.6	2.0	14.4	39.8	57.0	20.1	73.3	28.7
1970	28.0	27.3	12.5	26.1	19.6	2.2	15.1	40.7	58.6	19.9	76.1	29.7
1971	29.1	28.4	13.7	31.2	20.5	2.2	15.8	41.4	59.3	20.7	78.7	29.8
1972	30.8	30.3	15.5	35.5	22.6	2.6	16.7	43.1	60.5	22.2	82.7	31.2
1973	32.4	31.9	17.1	38.9	25.0	2.9	19.0	44.4	59.4	23.8	87.5	33.3
1974	32.1	30.7	16.0	32.5	24.9	2.9	19.9	43.3	58.2	23.3	80.4	33.2
1975	32.8	30.9	16.0	32.3	23.6	3.1	21.1	43.7	59.3	23.9	82.2	32.1
1976	34.7	33.1	18.0	38.9	25.1	3.4	23.2	45.7	62.2	25.0	86.6	33.5
1977	36.1	34.5	19.6	43.0	27.4	3.6	24.5	46.8	63.1	26.4	88.2	34.0
1978	37.7	35.9	20.7	44.9	28.8	3.9	25.8	48.5	62.8	29.1	89.6	36.4
1979	38.6	36.5	20.5	42.2	30.0	4.1	25.5	49.7	63.7	30.8	87.0	38.5
1980	38.5	35.6	18.9	36.8	28.8	3.9	23.3	49.6	64.4	31.8	79.3	39.2
1981	39.0	36.0	19.1	37.7	28.3	4.0	23.7	50.3	64.1	33.8	78.3	40.1
1982	39.6	36.2	19.1	38.7	27.0	4.0	23.7	50.8	65.4	34.4	78.4	40.0
1983	41.8	38.6	21.8	46.1	29.3	4.7	25.9	52.4	67.0	36.7	80.2	41.0
1984	44.0	41.3	24.9	53.6	32.3	5.5	28.8	54.6	68.4	39.8	82.3	43.2
1985	46.3	43.5	27.4	60.6	34.0	6.1	31.0	56.2	70.4	41.5	83.9	44.4
1986	48.2	45.9	30.0	65.0	36.8	7.0	34.5	58.2	71.8	44.6	88.2	45.4
1987	49.9	46.8	30.6	62.4	38.3	7.9	35.7	59.2	71.4	46.3	89.9	47.1
1988	51.9	48.5	32.4	66.0	39.7	8.6	36.9	60.8	73.3	47.7	92.4	48.1
1989	53.5	49.7	33.1	65.9	41.8	9.0	37.4	62.4	74.2	50.2	93.9	49.7
1990	54.5	50.0	32.9	64.8	41.2	9.2	37.6	63.2	75.7	49.8	92.2	51.0
1991	54.6	49.0	31.2	57.1	40.2	9.5	36.0	63.0	75.6	49.9	91.5	50.7
1992	56.6	50.6	32.9	61.8	41.6	10.1	36.7	64.2	75.3	52.5	95.1	51.8
1993	58.6	52.7	35.4	65.2	43.7	11.7	38.5	65.8	75.9	54.8	97.5	53.6
1994	60.9	55.5	38.2	69.3	46.1	13.6	40.3	68.4	78.1	57.8	99.1	56.3
1995	62.7	57.1	39.7	68.2	48.2	15.5	41.2	70.1	78.5	60.2	100.9	58.7
1996	64.9	59.7	42.7	71.5	50.3	17.9	44.0	72.1	79.2	63.1	102.5	61.3
1997	67.3	62.5	46.2	76.3	52.6	20.7	46.2	74.2	79.9	65.2	104.6	64.6
1998	70.9	66.7	51.8	84.3	57.0	24.8	50.7	77.0	81.0	69.2	107.5	68.0
1999	74.7	72.0	58.4	92.1	63.6	29.9	56.8	80.9	84.3	73.7	110.0	72.2
2000	78.4	75.7	63.4	95.0	69.7	34.9	61.8	83.5	86.4	77.3	107.1	75.8
2001	80.4	78.0	66.8	99.9	73.3	38.2	60.5	85.0	87.6	78.0	107.0	78.2
2002	82.4	81.0	71.7	105.1	78.6	42.5	64.4	86.5	88.0	80.4	107.9	80.5
2003	85.0	85.0	76.8	108.2	84.2	48.1	70.7	89.6	90.0	84.4	108.0	84.6
2004	88.2	89.3	83.2	111.2	92.2	55.5	77.1	92.5	92.1	88.2	108.9	88.3
2005	91.4	93.0	87.8	109.7	98.3	63.2	83.1	95.6	95.6	92.9	108.4	91.4
2006	94.0	96.5	91.7	105.6	103.3	71.6	89.7	98.7	98.6	96.2	108.1	95.9
2007	96.3	99.2	96.1	107.7	104.1	79.9	94.5	100.4	99.9	98.1	107.9	98.5
2008	96.4	96.2	90.6	94.1	97.8	81.3	91.2	98.8	98.2	97.0	103.7	98.0
2009	95.2	93.2	85.0	87.4	88.5	78.3	88.0	97.2	97.5	92.2	104.3	95.8
2010	97.0	95.8	89.8	90.8	93.4	84.5	92.4	98.7	99.0	96.6	103.8	97.0
2011	98.7	97.9	94.4	93.3	97.2	92.4	96.1	99.6	99.1	99.8	101.4	99.0
2012	100.0	100.0	100.0	100.0	100.0	100.0	100.0	100.0	100.0	100.0	100.0	100.0
2013	101.5	103.1	106.1	104.7	105.8	108.9	104.9	101.8	101.1	100.5	101.9	103.0
2014	104.2	107.4	113.8	110.8	114.8	116.9	113.5	104.5	103.0	103.2	101.9	107.6
2015	107.7	112.5	122.4	119.2	125.4	124.2	122.3	108.0	104.6	106.7	106.6	112.6
2016	110.3	116.3	129.0	122.8	135.0	135.5	124.1	110.7	107.9	109.1	107.4	115.4
2017	113.0	120.8	137.1	128.7	145.2	147.9	127.7	113.7	111.8	111.3	106.8	118.8
2018	116.3	125.6	146.7	133.9	157.2	164.1	134.5	116.4	114.3	114.4	106.2	122.8
2019	118.8	129.8	152.9	132.3	162.7	184.1	140.5	119.8	116.6	117.8	106.1	128.5
2020	114.3	135.9	164.7	136.6	175.0	217.6	138.5	123.5	125.5	113.0	91.6	135.9
2018												
1st quarter	115.0	124.0	144.0	133.1	154.4	158.8	131.7	115.3	113.7	112.7	105.8	121.1
2nd quarter	116.0	125.3	146.5	134.3	157.1	162.9	134.6	116.1	114.2	113.5	106.6	122.3
3rd quarter	116.8	126.2	147.9	134.4	159.3	166.3	134.7	116.8	114.4	115.8	106.1	123.2
4th quarter	117.3	126.9	148.3	134.0	158.0	168.4	137.1	117.6	114.9	115.6	106.4	124.8
2019												
1st quarter	117.5	127.3	148.0	129.0	158.2	174.0	139.0	118.3	114.7	115.5	106.4	126.9
2nd quarter	118.5	129.5	151.8	131.6	162.2	182.4	138.9	119.7	116.4	117.6	106.8	128.2
3rd quarter	119.4	131.0	155.0	133.3	164.4	188.9	141.8	120.6	117.9	117.8	106.2	129.4
4th quarter	119.9	131.6	156.8	135.5	166.1	191.2	142.3	120.7	117.6	120.2	105.0	129.3
2020												
1st quarter	117.8	131.7	151.9	124.3	165.6	193.6	136.4	122.8	126.1	109.4	98.1	132.7
2nd quarter	106.4	128.3	151.3	125.7	163.5	210.2	108.3	118.3	124.8	93.5	81.0	132.3
3rd quarter	116.1	141.8	177.5	147.9	186.8	233.1	152.1	126.7	126.1	124.1	95.1	139.0
4th quarter	117.0	141.7	178.0	148.7	184.1	233.4	157.1	126.4	125.0	125.1	92.0	139.6

Table 4-3. Chain-Type Quantity Indexes for Personal Consumption Expenditures by Major Type of Product—*Continued*

(Index numbers, 2012 = 100.)   NIPA Table 2.3.3

		Services											
		Household consumption expenditures for services									Nonprofit institutions serving households (NPISHs)		
Year and quarter	Services	Household services, total	Housing and utilities	Health care	Transportation services	Recreation services	Food services and accommodations	Financial services and insurance	Other services	Final consumption expenditures	Gross output	Less: receipts from sales of goods and services
1960	17.6	18.8	20.8	14.0	20.6	10.3	26.4	12.1	25.0	2.9	12.6	19.3
1961	18.3	19.5	21.8	14.7	20.9	10.7	26.5	12.8	25.8	2.9	13.1	20.4
1962	19.2	20.5	23.1	16.0	21.7	11.3	27.5	12.7	26.8	3.0	13.8	21.7
1963	20.0	21.3	24.2	17.0	22.6	11.7	28.2	13.2	27.8	3.1	14.6	23.1
1964	21.2	22.6	25.3	19.0	23.8	12.2	29.6	14.1	29.1	3.5	15.7	24.6
1965	22.3	23.8	26.7	19.8	25.1	12.7	31.7	15.1	30.7	3.7	16.7	26.1
1966	23.4	25.0	27.9	20.9	26.5	13.4	33.3	15.6	32.5	3.8	17.8	28.2
1967	24.4	26.0	29.2	21.9	27.9	13.9	33.0	16.4	34.4	4.0	18.8	30.1
1968	25.7	27.4	30.6	23.6	29.7	14.7	35.0	17.3	35.4	4.2	20.1	32.4
1969	26.8	28.7	32.3	25.3	31.7	15.6	35.8	17.5	36.4	4.2	21.2	34.6
1970	27.9	29.8	33.5	26.7	32.8	16.2	37.0	18.1	37.6	4.5	22.2	36.2
1971	28.9	30.8	35.0	28.6	34.2	16.7	37.0	18.8	37.7	4.8	23.8	39.0
1972	30.5	32.6	36.9	30.6	36.1	17.6	39.8	19.9	39.4	5.0	25.2	41.3
1973	32.0	34.1	38.6	32.8	36.8	19.1	41.8	21.0	40.5	5.0	25.9	42.8
1974	32.6	34.8	40.4	33.9	37.0	20.4	41.4	21.5	39.2	5.0	26.2	43.8
1975	33.8	36.2	41.7	35.7	37.5	21.5	43.1	23.6	39.5	5.0	27.2	45.9
1976	35.2	37.7	42.9	37.2	39.3	22.9	45.7	24.8	41.0	5.3	28.7	48.3
1977	36.7	39.3	44.1	39.0	42.1	24.4	46.9	26.4	43.0	5.4	29.8	50.5
1978	38.4	41.1	46.2	40.8	43.1	25.6	48.9	27.6	45.3	5.6	31.4	53.4
1979	39.6	42.4	47.8	42.2	44.4	26.8	50.4	28.5	45.7	5.8	32.3	54.8
1980	40.2	43.0	49.5	43.4	41.8	27.7	50.5	28.9	45.5	6.1	33.3	56.1
1981	40.8	43.6	50.2	45.5	40.3	30.1	51.0	28.7	44.5	6.6	34.7	57.7
1982	41.7	44.3	50.6	45.6	39.4	31.8	51.3	31.2	45.4	7.8	36.2	58.1
1983	43.8	46.4	51.6	47.0	42.3	34.5	53.0	35.5	48.4	9.0	37.6	58.4
1984	45.5	48.0	53.4	47.7	47.3	36.8	54.4	35.7	50.8	10.5	38.9	58.3
1985	47.8	50.4	55.5	49.2	52.3	39.4	55.2	39.2	54.4	11.4	40.2	59.6
1986	49.3	51.8	56.8	50.7	54.5	41.2	56.8	40.6	55.0	12.9	42.2	61.1
1987	51.5	54.1	58.4	52.8	56.8	43.1	59.7	43.0	58.8	13.9	43.9	62.8
1988	53.9	56.4	60.4	54.9	60.1	47.2	63.3	43.8	61.2	16.0	46.3	64.6
1989	55.6	58.0	61.9	55.5	61.4	50.2	65.0	46.3	63.1	18.4	47.9	64.9
1990	57.2	59.3	63.0	57.4	61.3	52.3	67.4	47.0	64.1	22.4	50.8	66.1
1991	58.1	60.0	64.4	58.5	58.4	52.0	67.4	50.9	61.8	25.6	52.7	66.6
1992	60.4	62.1	65.7	60.3	61.4	55.4	69.1	54.3	64.3	30.9	55.5	67.6
1993	62.3	63.9	67.5	60.6	64.7	58.9	70.6	58.4	65.7	33.4	56.9	68.2
1994	64.2	65.8	69.7	61.0	70.7	61.9	71.7	59.8	68.2	36.4	58.1	68.5
1995	66.1	67.6	71.8	62.3	75.8	66.6	71.9	61.7	69.5	38.1	58.9	68.8
1996	68.0	69.5	73.5	63.6	82.0	69.6	72.3	63.8	71.9	40.3	60.4	69.9
1997	70.2	72.0	75.1	65.6	88.0	71.8	73.8	67.2	76.0	37.1	61.3	72.9
1998	73.3	75.2	77.4	67.7	92.0	74.1	75.7	73.1	81.5	40.7	64.2	75.4
1999	76.3	78.1	79.7	68.8	97.3	77.6	77.6	80.1	84.9	43.9	66.4	76.9
2000	80.0	81.9	82.1	71.1	102.2	79.8	81.1	88.5	90.5	47.5	68.9	78.7
2001	81.8	83.4	84.3	74.7	101.2	79.7	81.0	86.0	94.0	51.5	72.2	81.6
2002	83.3	84.7	84.7	79.1	98.1	80.2	82.2	85.5	94.3	56.7	76.5	85.2
2003	85.1	86.4	85.9	81.2	99.0	82.8	85.4	85.6	96.5	60.9	78.3	85.6
2004	87.7	89.0	88.1	84.1	102.1	87.0	89.0	88.6	98.1	61.9	80.3	88.1
2005	90.5	92.0	91.6	86.9	103.1	89.1	92.3	93.3	99.4	61.7	82.3	91.0
2006	92.8	94.0	92.7	88.9	103.5	92.3	95.5	95.1	102.3	69.3	85.4	92.0
2007	94.8	96.0	94.6	91.0	104.9	96.0	96.9	97.4	104.4	71.3	87.4	94.0
2008	96.6	97.3	97.3	93.2	101.0	96.5	96.5	96.2	103.2	81.7	90.7	94.3
2009	96.2	96.7	97.6	95.3	93.8	95.2	92.9	92.9	100.6	84.7	93.0	96.2
2010	97.6	98.1	99.8	96.7	94.1	98.0	95.1	98.7	100.1	87.5	94.9	97.7
2011	99.0	99.4	100.2	98.2	98.2	97.6	97.7	101.3	100.7	91.7	96.7	98.6
2012	100.0	100.0	100.0	100.0	100.0	100.0	100.0	100.0	100.0	100.0	100.0	100.0
2013	100.7	100.7	100.9	100.6	104.5	102.0	101.7	99.4	98.4	101.2	100.7	100.5
2014	102.7	102.8	101.2	103.9	109.8	104.6	105.2	99.7	102.0	101.1	102.4	102.9
2015	105.4	105.7	101.2	109.5	113.8	108.5	109.7	102.2	104.3	99.1	105.0	107.3
2016	107.5	107.7	101.7	113.7	119.1	111.7	112.1	100.0	107.8	103.6	108.6	110.6
2017	109.5	109.7	101.9	116.1	123.6	113.6	114.9	101.9	111.7	104.0	109.6	111.8
2018	112.1	112.3	103.4	119.1	128.8	115.9	118.1	103.4	115.7	108.2	112.6	114.2
2019	114.0	114.5	104.3	123.0	133.2	117.4	120.5	102.2	120.5	103.7	113.7	117.7
2020	105.4	104.6	105.4	112.7	98.8	82.1	94.1	102.5	108.6	120.4	110.7	106.6
2018												
1st quarter	111.0	111.3	102.8	118.0	129.9	115.4	116.7	103.2	112.3	105.3	110.5	112.5
2nd quarter	111.8	112.1	103.2	118.6	129.0	115.4	117.3	103.5	115.9	107.2	112.4	114.4
3rd quarter	112.6	112.8	103.3	120.2	127.8	116.3	119.4	103.5	116.6	108.0	113.8	116.1
4th quarter	113.0	113.0	104.0	119.7	128.4	116.5	118.9	103.4	118.0	112.4	113.6	114.0
2019												
1st quarter	113.1	113.5	104.0	121.4	130.0	116.3	119.2	102.6	118.5	104.9	113.7	117.2
2nd quarter	113.6	114.1	104.0	122.9	132.4	117.5	120.4	101.9	119.5	103.5	113.6	117.7
3rd quarter	114.3	114.9	104.5	123.4	135.0	117.3	121.3	101.9	121.6	103.6	113.6	117.6
4th quarter	114.8	115.4	104.8	124.3	135.4	118.4	121.2	102.4	122.5	102.6	113.7	118.2
2020												
1st quarter	111.8	111.3	104.5	118.9	125.8	107.5	110.4	102.0	119.1	120.5	113.4	110.4
2nd quarter	97.4	95.5	105.7	97.9	79.9	59.9	73.0	101.3	98.8	134.9	107.3	95.9
3rd quarter	105.5	105.0	105.8	115.0	94.2	79.9	97.1	102.6	106.7	114.1	109.9	108.0
4th quarter	106.8	106.6	105.8	118.8	95.5	81.0	95.9	104.1	109.9	112.2	112.3	112.1

Table 4-4. Chain-Type Price Indexes for Personal Consumption Expenditures by Major Type of Product

(Index numbers, 2012 =1000.)   NIPA Table 2.3.4

Year and quarter	Personal consumption expend- itures, total	Total goods	Goods									
			Durable goods					Nondurable goods				
			Durable goods, total	Motor vehicles and parts	Furnishings and household equipment	Recreational goods and vehicles	Other durable goods	Nondurable goods, total	Food and beverages off-premises	Clothing and footwear	Gasoline and other energy goods	Other nondurable goods
1960	16.4	26.6	56.9	29.6	50.0	266.2	29.7	18.1	16.5	51.7	7.0	16.6
1961	16.6	26.7	57.0	29.8	50.2	264.8	29.6	18.1	16.6	52.0	7.1	16.6
1962	16.8	26.9	57.3	30.2	50.1	261.9	29.5	18.2	16.7	52.2	7.1	16.7
1963	17.0	27.1	57.5	30.5	50.1	261.3	29.6	18.4	16.9	52.6	7.1	16.9
1964	17.3	27.4	57.8	30.7	50.2	258.2	30.4	18.7	17.3	53.1	7.0	17.2
1965	17.5	27.7	57.3	30.5	49.8	254.6	30.2	19.0	17.6	53.6	7.3	17.4
1966	17.9	28.3	57.2	30.3	50.3	251.8	30.2	19.6	18.3	55.1	7.5	17.8
1967	18.4	28.8	58.1	30.7	51.4	253.3	30.9	20.0	18.4	57.4	7.7	18.2
1968	19.1	29.8	59.9	31.7	53.4	258.3	31.6	20.7	18.9	60.6	7.8	18.9
1969	20.0	30.9	61.6	32.4	55.3	264.2	33.2	21.6	19.8	63.9	8.1	19.6
1970	20.9	32.1	63.0	33.4	56.5	264.6	34.0	22.6	20.9	66.3	8.2	20.5
1971	21.8	33.1	65.1	35.0	57.5	274.0	35.0	23.2	21.4	68.6	8.3	21.3
1972	22.5	33.9	65.9	35.1	58.4	278.0	36.1	23.9	22.4	69.9	8.4	21.8
1973	23.8	35.9	66.8	35.2	59.7	282.2	37.3	25.9	25.2	72.2	9.3	22.4
1974	26.2	40.4	71.2	37.4	64.6	294.7	40.2	29.8	29.0	77.5	12.9	24.6
1975	28.4	43.7	77.6	41.1	71.0	314.2	43.2	32.1	31.2	81.0	13.8	27.5
1976	30.0	45.4	81.8	44.2	74.1	325.1	45.3	33.1	31.8	83.6	14.5	28.9
1977	31.9	47.8	85.5	46.8	76.8	334.4	47.3	35.0	33.7	87.2	15.5	30.6
1978	34.1	50.8	90.3	50.1	80.7	346.4	49.9	37.3	36.9	88.8	16.3	32.2
1979	37.2	55.6	96.3	53.8	85.7	361.8	54.1	41.3	40.5	90.6	21.9	34.3
1980	41.2	61.8	104.6	57.8	92.7	381.9	65.1	46.3	43.9	93.9	30.4	37.5
1981	44.9	66.4	111.6	62.3	99.6	399.0	68.7	49.9	47.1	97.0	34.3	40.6
1982	47.4	68.2	116.0	65.2	104.7	408.2	69.4	51.0	48.3	98.4	32.7	43.8
1983	49.4	69.4	118.3	67.3	107.1	403.3	71.6	51.9	48.8	99.7	31.5	46.8
1984	51.2	70.7	120.1	69.2	108.4	397.6	73.1	53.0	50.3	100.3	31.1	48.5
1985	53.0	71.9	121.4	70.8	109.6	390.6	73.9	54.0	50.9	102.4	31.2	50.4
1986	54.2	71.5	122.7	72.7	110.8	378.3	75.7	53.3	52.1	102.0	24.5	52.4
1987	55.9	73.8	126.2	76.1	112.5	373.5	80.8	55.1	53.7	104.9	25.4	54.5
1988	58.0	75.8	128.3	77.3	114.1	371.1	86.1	56.9	55.3	108.3	25.6	57.0
1989	60.6	78.7	130.6	79.6	114.5	370.1	90.1	59.7	58.2	109.9	27.9	60.1
1990	63.2	81.9	131.9	79.8	115.6	367.1	95.8	63.1	61.1	113.5	31.9	63.2
1991	65.3	83.9	133.9	82.1	116.3	362.4	99.3	65.0	63.0	115.6	31.4	66.5
1992	67.1	84.9	134.8	83.6	117.7	351.3	101.9	65.9	63.5	116.5	31.1	69.0
1993	68.8	85.7	136.1	86.9	118.3	338.7	102.7	66.4	64.3	115.9	30.8	70.2
1994	70.2	86.6	138.8	90.9	120.1	331.6	104.4	66.8	65.4	113.9	30.9	70.7
1995	71.7	87.4	139.8	94.5	119.9	317.7	106.1	67.5	66.8	111.3	31.3	71.9
1996	73.2	88.3	138.4	96.4	120.3	295.2	105.5	69.0	68.9	109.9	33.5	73.3
1997	74.5	88.2	135.4	96.8	120.1	270.5	104.0	69.7	70.2	110.0	33.5	74.1
1998	75.1	86.9	131.5	95.7	120.0	247.6	102.1	69.2	71.1	108.0	29.2	75.5
1999	76.2	87.3	128.0	96.0	118.4	226.1	99.5	70.9	72.2	106.5	31.6	78.4
2000	78.1	89.1	125.7	96.4	117.6	211.9	98.2	74.0	73.9	105.3	40.8	80.1
2001	79.7	89.0	123.3	96.8	115.5	197.5	98.5	74.8	76.1	103.2	39.4	82.0
2002	80.7	88.2	120.1	96.3	113.2	184.7	96.9	74.8	77.2	100.5	36.9	83.5
2003	82.4	88.1	115.8	93.5	110.0	173.0	94.7	76.3	78.7	98.0	43.1	83.7
2004	84.4	89.3	113.5	92.8	108.6	164.5	94.2	79.0	81.2	97.6	50.7	84.7
2005	86.9	91.1	112.3	94.2	108.6	155.6	93.3	82.0	82.6	96.8	62.0	86.0
2006	89.3	92.3	110.4	94.3	108.1	146.2	94.1	84.6	84.0	96.4	70.1	87.8
2007	91.6	93.3	108.0	93.8	107.2	136.2	95.9	87.0	87.2	95.5	75.9	89.1
2008	94.3	96.1	106.0	92.0	106.5	129.4	98.3	91.9	92.6	94.7	89.4	91.2
2009	94.1	93.8	104.0	91.9	106.1	121.8	98.6	89.5	93.7	95.6	65.2	95.3
2010	95.7	95.2	102.1	95.7	101.5	113.4	98.2	92.2	93.9	94.9	76.9	97.0
2011	98.2	98.8	101.3	98.7	100.0	106.0	100.8	97.7	97.7	96.5	96.7	98.5
2012	100.0	100.0	100.0	100.0	100.0	100.0	100.0	100.0	100.0	100.0	100.0	100.0
2013	101.4	99.4	98.0	100.5	98.1	94.7	97.9	100.1	101.0	101.0	97.3	100.2
2014	102.9	98.9	95.4	100.6	96.7	90.5	94.0	100.6	102.9	101.3	93.8	101.3
2015	103.1	95.9	93.4	100.5	92.4	86.9	90.6	97.1	104.1	100.1	68.8	102.5
2016	104.1	94.3	91.1	99.4	90.0	82.7	89.9	95.9	103.0	99.8	60.9	103.8
2017	106.1	94.6	89.1	98.2	87.5	79.4	88.7	97.5	102.9	99.2	68.8	105.0
2018	108.3	95.3	87.5	97.8	86.6	76.4	87.1	99.3	103.4	99.3	78.2	105.6
2019	109.9	94.8	86.5	98.0	87.2	73.3	85.2	99.2	104.4	97.9	75.4	106.0
2020	111.2	94.2	85.8	99.9	87.8	70.2	82.8	98.6	108.0	92.9	63.9	107.1
2018												
1st quarter	107.6	95.3	88.0	97.5	86.4	77.5	88.5	99.1	103.2	99.6	76.9	105.6
2nd quarter	108.2	95.5	87.8	97.6	87.0	76.7	87.9	99.6	103.3	100.6	78.5	105.8
3rd quarter	108.5	95.2	87.4	98.1	86.1	76.1	86.8	99.4	103.5	98.5	79.1	105.6
4th quarter	109.0	95.1	87.1	98.0	86.7	75.5	85.4	99.3	103.7	98.4	78.2	105.5
2019												
1st quarter	109.1	94.6	87.0	97.7	87.6	74.9	84.9	98.7	104.4	98.6	72.1	105.5
2nd quarter	109.8	95.1	86.8	98.2	87.4	73.7	86.0	99.5	104.3	98.1	77.6	105.8
3rd quarter	110.1	94.7	86.4	98.2	87.3	72.7	85.1	99.1	104.4	98.4	74.3	106.0
4th quarter	110.6	94.9	85.8	98.0	86.4	71.9	84.7	99.7	104.7	96.6	77.7	106.8
2020												
1st quarter	111.0	94.6	85.5	97.9	87.0	71.0	84.0	99.5	105.5	97.0	74.0	107.0
2nd quarter	110.5	93.2	84.8	97.5	87.0	69.8	83.2	97.7	109.1	91.0	55.5	107.1
3rd quarter	111.5	94.4	86.4	101.8	88.5	70.1	82.6	98.6	108.7	92.0	61.6	107.4
4th quarter	111.9	94.4	86.5	102.3	88.9	69.9	81.5	98.6	108.7	91.6	64.4	107.0

Table 4-4. Chain-Type Price Indexes for Personal Consumption Expenditures by Major Type of Product—*Continued*

(Index numbers, 2012 =1000.)   NIPA Table 2.3.4

Year and quarter	Services	Household consumption expenditures for services								Nonprofit institutions serving households (NPISHs)		
		Household services, total	Housing and utilities	Health care	Transportation services	Recreation services	Food services and accommodations	Financial services and insurance	Other services	Final consumption expenditures	Gross output	Less: receipts from sales of goods and services
1960	11.8	11.2	13.5	6.3	13.0	14.6	11.0	13.1	11.7	51.5	9.6	5.7
1961	12.0	11.4	13.7	6.4	13.4	15.0	11.2	13.5	11.8	52.1	9.7	5.8
1962	12.2	11.6	13.9	6.6	13.7	15.4	11.5	14.0	12.0	52.8	9.9	5.9
1963	12.4	11.8	14.0	6.8	13.8	15.7	11.7	14.1	12.3	53.7	10.2	6.1
1964	12.7	12.0	14.1	7.0	14.0	16.1	11.9	14.7	12.6	53.9	10.4	6.3
1965	12.9	12.3	14.3	7.2	14.2	16.5	12.2	15.0	12.9	55.4	10.7	6.5
1966	13.3	12.6	14.4	7.5	14.5	16.9	12.6	15.9	13.3	57.4	11.1	6.7
1967	13.7	13.0	14.7	8.0	15.0	17.5	13.3	16.2	13.7	59.3	11.6	7.0
1968	14.3	13.6	15.0	8.5	15.7	18.4	14.0	17.5	14.3	61.5	12.2	7.4
1969	15.0	14.3	15.5	9.1	16.6	19.2	14.9	19.0	15.0	65.4	13.0	7.9
1970	15.9	15.1	16.2	9.8	17.9	20.1	16.0	20.0	15.7	68.3	13.9	8.5
1971	16.7	15.9	17.0	10.3	19.2	21.0	16.8	21.2	16.6	72.1	14.5	8.9
1972	17.4	16.6	17.7	10.7	19.9	21.5	17.4	22.4	17.5	75.1	15.2	9.4
1973	18.3	17.4	18.5	11.3	20.8	22.3	18.6	22.9	18.5	79.9	16.2	10.0
1974	19.8	18.8	19.5	12.3	22.6	23.8	20.8	24.7	20.5	91.5	18.1	11.1
1975	21.5	20.4	21.0	13.7	25.1	25.6	22.6	26.5	22.0	99.9	19.9	12.2
1976	23.0	21.8	22.5	15.0	26.9	26.9	24.1	27.5	23.4	105.1	21.5	13.3
1977	24.8	23.5	24.5	16.3	28.8	28.1	25.9	29.7	24.6	112.2	23.1	14.3
1978	26.7	25.3	26.3	17.7	30.7	29.8	28.2	33.4	25.9	119.6	24.9	15.4
1979	28.9	27.4	28.4	19.4	33.5	31.8	31.2	35.3	27.7	131.3	27.4	17.0
1980	31.9	30.3	31.4	21.7	38.8	34.2	34.2	38.2	30.3	143.5	30.6	19.1
1981	35.2	33.5	34.8	24.4	43.5	36.4	37.3	41.2	33.4	150.6	34.0	21.6
1982	37.9	36.2	38.0	27.1	46.0	38.4	39.4	43.9	36.0	142.8	36.6	24.2
1983	40.3	38.6	40.5	29.6	47.7	40.0	41.1	47.8	38.0	132.1	38.6	26.5
1984	42.4	40.8	42.5	31.8	49.6	41.8	43.0	50.8	39.9	126.3	40.5	28.6
1985	44.5	42.9	44.8	33.7	50.6	43.6	44.8	54.7	41.4	123.5	42.1	30.3
1986	46.3	44.7	46.9	35.7	51.1	45.2	46.7	55.6	43.5	119.5	43.6	32.0
1987	47.7	46.1	48.6	38.0	53.2	47.0	48.5	53.0	44.6	117.2	45.5	34.0
1988	49.9	48.4	50.5	41.0	55.7	48.8	50.6	55.7	46.5	115.8	48.2	36.7
1989	52.3	50.9	52.6	44.6	58.2	51.2	52.9	57.8	48.2	108.3	50.8	40.2
1990	54.7	53.5	54.8	48.4	60.4	54.0	55.3	59.1	50.2	99.2	53.2	43.7
1991	56.8	55.8	56.7	52.2	62.1	56.8	57.5	59.2	52.6	91.7	55.7	47.4
1992	58.9	58.0	58.2	55.8	63.8	58.6	58.8	61.4	54.8	83.3	57.7	51.0
1993	60.9	60.2	59.9	58.8	66.1	60.5	59.9	64.7	56.7	78.9	59.5	53.8
1994	62.5	61.9	61.5	61.2	66.8	61.8	61.0	66.0	58.8	78.7	61.2	55.8
1995	64.3	63.7	63.1	63.4	68.2	63.1	62.4	67.7	60.8	78.7	62.9	57.9
1996	66.1	65.4	65.0	64.9	68.9	65.2	64.1	70.2	62.5	80.0	64.7	59.6
1997	67.9	67.3	66.8	66.2	70.5	67.3	66.0	73.2	64.3	83.4	66.3	60.9
1998	69.4	68.6	68.3	67.5	71.8	69.0	67.8	73.5	65.6	89.1	68.3	62.1
1999	70.7	69.9	70.0	69.0	72.7	71.2	69.5	72.8	67.2	92.3	70.2	63.6
2000	72.7	71.8	72.4	70.9	75.0	74.0	71.5	73.7	68.4	97.4	72.9	65.8
2001	75.1	74.1	75.8	73.3	75.4	76.4	73.5	74.1	70.7	101.9	75.7	68.1
2002	77.0	76.1	78.0	75.2	75.3	78.6	75.3	75.9	73.5	102.3	77.9	70.7
2003	79.6	78.8	80.4	78.0	76.9	81.0	76.9	80.7	76.5	98.7	80.0	74.3
2004	82.0	81.4	82.7	80.9	77.8	83.1	79.4	84.1	79.1	97.6	82.5	77.7
2005	84.8	84.2	85.6	83.5	80.7	85.5	82.0	87.3	81.9	99.7	85.4	80.8
2006	87.8	87.3	89.2	86.0	84.1	88.4	84.8	91.0	84.8	101.0	88.3	84.1
2007	90.8	90.3	92.3	89.2	86.0	90.8	88.0	94.2	87.6	102.2	91.0	87.2
2008	93.5	93.1	95.6	91.6	90.8	93.6	91.5	93.7	91.4	102.9	93.3	90.1
2009	94.2	93.9	96.6	94.1	93.0	94.7	93.5	87.7	93.6	99.9	94.6	92.8
2010	96.0	95.9	96.8	96.5	95.1	95.7	94.8	93.7	95.9	98.5	96.2	95.4
2011	97.9	97.8	98.2	98.2	98.1	97.3	97.2	96.4	97.8	99.6	98.1	97.6
2012	100.0	100.0	100.0	100.0	100.0	100.0	100.0	100.0	100.0	100.0	100.0	100.0
2013	102.3	102.3	102.5	101.4	101.0	101.7	102.1	105.2	102.3	102.0	102.1	102.2
2014	104.9	104.8	105.5	102.5	102.5	103.6	103.6	111.4	103.7	105.9	104.4	103.9
2015	106.8	106.7	108.2	103.1	102.7	105.2	107.7	114.8	104.5	109.8	106.5	105.3
2016	109.2	109.0	111.3	104.3	103.3	107.8	110.5	119.9	105.5	113.5	108.7	107.0
2017	112.0	111.7	115.1	105.9	104.6	110.8	112.8	126.3	106.0	117.7	111.4	109.1
2018	115.1	114.9	118.7	107.8	106.9	113.1	115.4	134.1	108.2	120.3	114.1	111.8
2019	117.8	117.5	122.3	109.7	109.0	115.3	118.7	138.0	109.6	124.3	116.9	114.3
2020	120.3	120.0	125.6	112.5	107.8	117.8	120.9	140.5	111.4	126.6	120.1	117.8
2018												
1st quarter	113.9	113.7	117.4	107.1	105.4	112.3	114.4	131.7	107.4	119.1	113.1	110.9
2nd quarter	114.8	114.5	118.3	107.7	106.3	112.8	115.4	133.4	107.8	119.8	113.8	111.5
3rd quarter	115.5	115.2	119.1	108.0	107.3	113.5	115.7	135.0	108.5	120.5	114.3	112.1
4th quarter	116.2	116.0	120.1	108.6	108.4	113.9	116.3	136.3	108.9	121.7	115.2	112.8
2019												
1st quarter	116.7	116.4	120.9	108.9	108.1	114.5	117.5	135.6	109.2	121.8	115.6	113.4
2nd quarter	117.5	117.3	121.9	109.4	109.0	115.1	118.7	137.8	109.2	123.7	116.6	114.0
3rd quarter	118.3	117.9	122.8	109.9	109.1	115.3	119.2	139.0	109.9	125.8	117.5	114.5
4th quarter	118.9	118.6	123.7	110.7	109.9	116.4	119.4	139.4	110.2	125.8	118.1	115.4
2020												
1st quarter	119.6	119.3	124.6	111.1	109.0	117.0	120.0	140.9	111.0	126.4	118.9	116.1
2nd quarter	119.7	119.5	125.3	112.2	107.0	117.7	119.9	138.8	111.1	125.2	119.5	117.5
3rd quarter	120.6	120.3	125.9	113.1	106.8	117.8	121.3	140.8	111.7	126.8	120.7	118.5
4th quarter	121.3	120.9	126.6	113.5	108.5	118.8	122.2	141.3	111.9	128.2	121.4	119.0

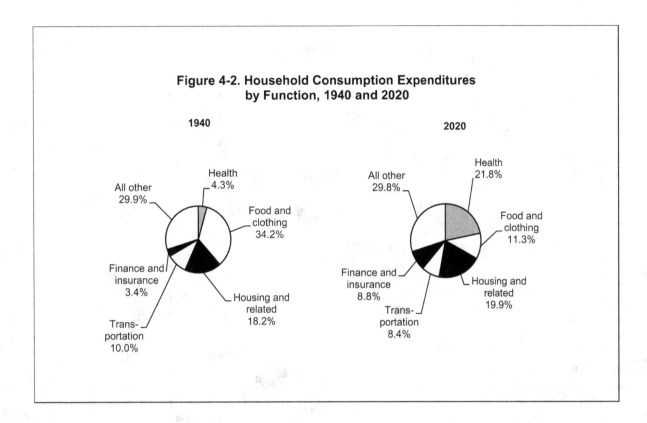

Figure 4-2. Household Consumption Expenditures by Function, 1940 and 2020

- Figure 4-2 compares the composition of household consumer spending (excluding the net spending of nonprofit institutions) in 1940 and 2020, the latest available data at the time this edition of *Business Statistics* was compiled. (Table 4-5)

- Household spending on health in 2020 made up 21.8 percent of all household consumption spending—more than five times the percentage in 1940. It is important to recognize that household consumption spending, as presented in these data, includes (in health spending and in the total) medical care payments made by government and private insurance on behalf of individuals as well as out-of-pocket consumer payments. (Table 4-5)

- In 2020, a much smaller share was required for food and clothing than in 1940, (11.3 percent vs 34.2 percent respectively) as seen in Figure 4-2. The shares of housing-related spending and transportation were similar in the two years. The share of finance and insurance spending nearly tripled, and households also spent a larger share on the remaining category, here labeled "all other," which includes communication, recreation, education, food services, accommodations, and other miscellaneous goods and services. (Table 4-5)

Table 4-5. Household Consumption Expenditures by Function

(Billions of dollars.)   NIPA Table 2.5.5

Year	Household consumption expenditures, total	Food and beverages off-premises	Clothing, footwear, and related services	Housing, utilities, and fuels	Furnishings, household equipment, and mainte-nance	Health	Transpor-tation	Commun-ication	Recreation	Education	Food services and accommo-dations	Financial services and insurance	Other goods and services	Foreign travel and expend-itures, net
1940	70.2	15.9	8.1	12.8	6.0	3.0	7.0	0.7	3.9	0.6	4.4	2.4	5.3	0.1
1941	80.0	18.2	9.5	13.7	7.1	3.2	8.3	0.8	4.5	0.6	5.3	2.5	6.0	0.1
1942	87.7	21.6	11.8	14.8	7.4	3.6	5.4	1.0	4.9	0.7	6.9	2.6	6.8	0.2
1943	98.4	24.3	14.4	15.5	7.4	4.0	5.4	1.2	5.3	0.8	9.1	2.8	8.0	0.3
1944	107.0	26.0	15.7	16.2	8.0	4.5	5.7	1.3	5.8	0.9	10.9	3.0	8.5	0.6
1945	118.2	28.2	17.6	16.9	8.9	4.8	6.6	1.4	6.5	0.9	12.7	3.2	9.3	1.2
1946	142.2	34.9	19.7	18.8	12.7	5.9	12.1	1.6	9.0	1.0	12.7	3.7	10.3	-0.1
1947	159.7	40.2	20.4	21.2	15.5	6.6	15.4	1.7	9.8	1.2	12.5	4.1	11.1	0.0
1948	172.6	41.8	21.8	23.9	16.8	7.6	18.0	1.9	10.3	1.3	12.6	4.6	11.7	0.3
1949	176.0	40.4	21.1	25.6	16.3	7.9	21.2	2.1	10.6	1.4	12.4	4.8	11.8	0.6
1950	189.6	41.4	21.4	28.4	18.7	8.5	24.6	2.3	11.7	1.5	12.7	5.4	12.2	0.7
1951	205.7	46.0	23.1	31.6	19.7	9.3	24.2	2.6	12.3	1.6	15.0	6.2	13.3	0.9
1952	216.4	48.4	23.9	34.6	19.3	10.1	24.4	2.9	13.0	1.7	16.0	6.6	14.3	1.1
1953	229.7	49.3	24.2	37.9	20.0	11.0	28.0	3.2	13.8	1.8	16.5	7.5	15.0	1.5
1954	236.4	50.6	24.3	40.9	19.9	11.9	27.4	3.3	14.3	1.9	16.6	8.3	15.4	1.5
1955	254.9	52.0	25.4	43.8	22.3	12.8	33.4	3.6	15.4	2.1	17.0	9.2	16.3	1.6
1956	267.3	54.2	26.5	46.8	23.6	14.1	32.7	3.9	16.4	2.4	17.7	10.0	17.5	1.7
1957	282.3	57.1	26.8	50.0	23.9	15.5	35.7	4.3	16.8	2.6	18.5	10.6	18.8	1.7
1958	291.3	59.8	27.1	53.3	24.1	17.1	33.7	4.5	17.3	2.9	18.7	11.2	19.9	1.9
1959	312.3	61.6	28.6	56.9	25.6	18.8	38.8	4.8	18.8	3.1	19.7	12.1	21.4	2.0
1960	326.1	62.6	29.3	60.5	26.2	20.4	40.8	5.2	19.7	3.4	20.5	13.2	22.4	2.1
1961	336.2	63.7	29.9	64.0	26.8	21.8	39.3	5.6	20.5	3.6	21.0	14.3	23.7	2.0
1962	357.1	64.7	31.3	68.2	28.3	24.3	44.1	5.9	22.1	4.0	22.3	14.8	24.9	2.3
1963	376.3	65.9	32.1	72.2	29.8	26.4	47.8	6.4	23.9	4.3	23.3	15.5	26.2	2.5
1964	404.2	69.5	34.7	76.2	32.7	29.8	50.7	6.9	26.3	4.8	24.9	17.2	27.8	2.6
1965	436.0	74.4	36.5	81.0	34.7	32.0	56.5	7.5	28.9	5.5	27.2	18.8	30.2	2.9
1966	472.5	80.6	39.8	85.8	37.8	35.0	59.0	8.1	33.4	6.2	29.6	20.6	33.3	3.1
1967	498.6	82.6	41.7	91.1	39.7	38.4	61.0	8.9	35.8	6.9	31.0	22.1	35.8	3.8
1968	548.1	88.8	45.6	97.4	43.2	43.8	69.8	9.7	39.9	7.7	34.6	25.2	38.6	3.7
1969	594.2	95.4	48.8	105.5	45.4	50.0	75.9	10.7	43.7	8.7	37.5	27.7	41.0	4.0
1970	636.3	103.5	49.9	113.8	46.6	56.8	76.5	11.6	47.0	9.9	41.6	30.1	44.3	4.5
1971	688.2	107.1	53.4	124.5	48.8	63.4	88.7	12.8	50.1	10.9	43.8	33.1	47.0	4.8
1972	755.3	114.5	58.0	136.2	53.5	70.4	98.3	14.4	56.2	11.7	48.9	37.1	51.0	5.2
1973	835.8	126.7	63.7	149.7	59.9	78.7	108.6	16.1	63.0	13.0	54.8	39.9	56.9	4.7
1974	914.7	143.0	66.9	166.3	64.6	88.7	112.8	17.7	68.9	14.2	60.6	44.1	62.2	4.7
1975	1 013.5	156.6	71.4	184.8	67.8	102.7	124.4	20.0	77.1	15.9	68.8	51.8	67.8	4.4
1976	1 128.7	167.3	76.9	204.6	75.0	116.8	147.4	22.4	86.2	17.4	77.8	56.8	76.3	3.8
1977	1 253.3	179.8	84.3	228.7	84.0	131.6	168.1	24.3	94.9	18.8	85.7	65.1	83.8	4.3
1978	1 399.2	196.1	94.6	255.6	93.6	149.4	184.5	27.0	106.3	20.9	97.1	76.7	93.2	4.3
1979	1 559.3	218.4	101.9	287.5	104.3	169.9	207.1	29.4	118.9	22.9	110.9	83.6	100.4	4.1
1980	1 720.6	239.2	108.8	327.7	110.7	195.5	226.5	31.8	127.4	25.4	121.7	91.7	110.7	3.5
1981	1 899.8	255.3	119.1	367.6	118.3	228.9	250.7	36.0	141.6	28.3	133.9	98.5	121.2	0.4
1982	2 033.3	267.1	122.7	401.7	121.0	254.9	255.9	41.1	151.4	31.0	142.5	113.7	127.8	2.5
1983	2 240.8	277.0	132.9	434.6	132.3	287.1	284.9	44.8	169.3	34.3	153.6	141.0	143.4	5.4
1984	2 447.0	291.1	144.7	471.1	147.1	315.2	321.8	48.4	190.0	37.7	164.9	150.8	157.7	6.6
1985	2 664.9	303.0	154.3	513.9	156.0	345.3	357.4	53.1	207.2	41.2	174.3	178.2	173.3	7.7
1986	2 833.7	316.4	165.1	548.1	168.7	378.4	362.6	56.9	225.4	44.5	186.7	187.7	190.0	3.3
1987	3 020.6	324.3	176.4	582.6	176.9	419.9	376.6	60.0	247.0	48.8	204.4	189.5	208.2	6.1
1988	3 266.7	342.8	188.1	625.9	186.6	470.7	404.8	63.1	273.4	54.4	225.8	202.9	225.4	2.8
1989	3 508.7	365.4	201.2	666.9	197.5	519.0	428.3	67.3	295.7	60.6	242.6	222.3	245.7	-3.7
1990	3 733.1	391.2	206.5	709.3	200.6	583.7	442.9	70.1	314.7	66.0	262.7	230.8	262.3	-7.7
1991	3 863.3	403.0	210.1	747.5	199.1	638.4	418.3	73.9	326.3	70.6	273.4	250.1	268.0	-15.2
1992	4 109.6	404.5	223.0	783.3	209.4	700.4	451.3	81.1	346.8	76.4	286.3	277.0	290.1	-20.0
1993	4 361.9	413.5	231.1	827.3	221.9	741.7	485.0	85.8	378.4	81.1	298.4	314.0	304.5	-20.7
1994	4 623.2	432.1	240.1	876.1	238.6	779.9	527.3	93.3	414.0	86.4	308.3	327.9	316.9	-17.6
1995	4 860.3	443.7	244.7	926.7	251.7	826.0	552.5	98.9	449.8	92.3	316.1	347.0	332.7	-21.9
1996	5 134.6	461.9	253.5	976.7	263.7	868.3	596.7	108.3	481.5	99.6	326.6	372.1	350.8	-25.2
1997	5 431.2	474.8	262.0	1 023.1	277.3	919.9	639.3	120.1	509.5	107.1	343.4	408.9	368.4	-22.5
1998	5 753.4	487.4	273.1	1 077.0	297.3	979.7	666.2	128.8	544.3	115.2	361.8	446.1	393.7	-17.3
1999	6 145.5	515.5	287.2	1 135.5	320.6	1 033.3	726.3	140.2	589.9	123.9	380.3	484.6	429.4	-21.2
2000	6 609.1	540.6	297.5	1 214.5	344.0	1 109.6	793.1	153.8	633.7	134.3	408.8	541.9	458.5	-21.1
2001	6 894.7	564.0	294.6	1 303.0	353.2	1 209.4	805.6	159.1	647.0	143.6	419.7	529.3	477.9	-11.6
2002	7 150.6	575.1	295.2	1 343.8	366.3	1 317.1	806.8	161.1	669.3	149.5	436.3	539.0	496.8	-5.8
2003	7 535.2	599.6	301.4	1 408.5	381.1	1 410.7	840.1	165.1	704.3	159.5	462.7	574.2	526.5	1.5
2004	8 025.6	632.6	313.4	1 486.0	406.6	1 514.9	893.8	171.2	758.8	169.0	498.2	619.3	559.1	2.6
2005	8 558.8	668.2	326.4	1 602.4	430.1	1 612.3	955.3	177.3	805.2	180.5	533.6	676.8	589.5	1.1
2006	9 038.1	700.3	336.2	1 689.4	448.7	1 715.0	987.9	190.5	855.7	193.1	570.6	719.5	624.5	6.7
2007	9 497.8	737.3	339.5	1 785.2	455.0	1 823.2	1 028.0	203.0	897.0	206.0	601.5	762.7	657.6	1.7
2008	9 762.8	769.1	333.1	1 902.8	438.7	1 909.3	1 017.0	214.0	900.0	216.4	620.2	777.5	667.9	-3.2
2009	9 602.0	772.9	319.1	1 923.2	405.9	1 999.3	879.7	212.8	863.4	226.1	612.7	720.5	666.4	0.0
2010	9 965.8	786.9	331.7	1 972.5	410.7	2 078.1	961.8	220.7	884.4	240.3	635.7	768.0	687.2	-12.1
2011	10 387.0	819.5	347.1	2 010.3	423.7	2 153.2	1 080.3	228.1	901.6	248.2	669.5	811.1	712.1	-17.7
2012	10 705.8	846.2	359.5	2 038.9	438.6	2 230.7	1 135.5	232.5	934.4	250.6	704.9	830.9	725.4	-22.2
2013	11 010.9	864.0	365.3	2 108.7	454.3	2 288.3	1 170.5	237.5	967.4	256.7	732.3	869.3	740.1	-43.3
2014	11 482.1	896.9	376.0	2 177.7	476.6	2 409.1	1 202.0	254.0	1 004.5	263.3	776.9	922.9	766.2	-44.1
2015	11 891.9	921.0	384.1	2 226.4	500.1	2 564.8	1 163.7	259.8	1 045.6	271.9	832.9	974.4	797.9	-50.7
2016	12 291.8	940.6	391.3	2 297.4	519.1	2 690.1	1 163.1	268.1	1 094.1	281.7	873.2	996.1	822.1	-45.2
2017	12 821.2	973.1	397.0	2 382.1	540.2	2 796.0	1 233.2	266.4	1 143.6	288.8	913.5	1 069.0	855.5	-37.2
2018	13 468.9	1 000.3	408.4	2 494.1	575.7	2 919.5	1 317.3	273.3	1 200.1	297.9	960.8	1 151.9	891.2	-21.7
2019	13 988.8	1 030.9	414.9	2 592.5	601.2	3 073.9	1 326.5	276.7	1 261.5	308.4	1 008.3	1 171.6	927.0	-4.5
2020	13 526.7	1 146.7	377.0	2 686.2	645.2	2 954.1	1 133.4	274.5	1 176.9	293.2	801.5	1 196.3	851.3	-9.5

NOTES AND DEFINITIONS, CHAPTER 4

TABLES 4-1 THROUGH Table 4-5

SOURCE: U.S. DEPARTMENT OF COMMERCE, BUREAU OF ECONOMIC ANALYSIS (BEA)

All personal income and personal consumption expenditure series are from the national income and product accounts (NIPAs). All quarterly series are shown at seasonally adjusted annual rates. Current and constant dollar values are in billions of dollars. Indexes of price and quantity are based on the average for the year 2012, which equals 100.

Tables 4-1 through 4-4 cover all income and spending by the personal sector, which includes nonprofit institutions serving households (NPISHs). In a new feature introduced in the 2009 comprehensive revision of the NIPAs, Tables 4-2, 4-3, and 4-4 show the services component of personal consumption expenditures broken down into separate aggregates for "household consumption expenditures for services" and "final consumption expenditures" by NPISHs.

The last table gives further details of the separate accounts for households and NPISHs that are only available annually. Table 4-5 shows a more detailed functional breakdown of household consumption expenditures, not including NPISHs.

In several cases, the notes and definitions below will refer to *imputations* or *imputed values*. See the notes and definitions to Chapter 1 for an explanation of imputation and the role it plays in national and personal income measurement.

TABLES 4-1 THROUGH 4-4

Sources and Disposition of Personal Income; Personal Consumption Expenditures by Major Type of Product

Definitions

Personal income is the income received by persons residing in the United States from participation in production, from government and business transfer payments, and from government interest, which is treated similarly to a transfer payment rather than as income from participation in production. *Persons* denotes the total for individuals, *nonprofit institutions that primarily serve households (NPISHs),* private noninsured welfare funds, and private trust funds. Personal income, outlays, and saving excluding NPISHs are referred to as *household* income, outlays, and saving. All proprietors' income is treated as received by individuals. Life insurance carriers and private noninsured pension funds are not counted as persons, but their saving is credited to persons.

Income from the sale of illegal goods and services is excluded by definition from national and personal income, and the value of purchases of illegal goods and services is not included in personal consumption expenditures.

Personal income is the sum of compensation received by employees, proprietors' income with inventory valuation and capital consumption adjustments (IVA and CCAdj), rental income of persons with capital consumption adjustment, personal receipts on assets, and personal current transfer receipts, less contributions for social insurance.

Personal income differs from national income in that it includes current transfer payments and interest received by persons, regardless of source, while it excludes the following national income components: employee and employer contributions for social insurance; business transfer payments, interest payments, and other payments on assets other than to persons; taxes on production and imports less subsidies; the current surplus of government enterprises; and undistributed corporate profits with IVA and CCAdj. The relationships of GDP, gross and net national product, national income, and personal income are displayed in Table 1-11.

Compensation of employees is the sum of wages and salaries and supplements to wages and salaries, as defined in the *national* income account (see Table 1-13 and the notes and definitions to Chapter 1).

As in *national* income, the *compensation of employees* component of personal income refers to compensation received by residents of the United States, including compensation from the rest of the world, but excludes compensation from domestic industries to workers residing in the rest of the world.

Wages and salaries consists of the monetary remuneration of employees, including wages and salaries as conventionally defined; the compensation of corporate officers; corporate directors' fees paid to directors who are also employees of the corporation; the value of employee exercise of "nonqualified stock options"; commissions, tips, and bonuses; voluntary employee contributions to certain deferred-compensation plans, such as 401(k) plans; and receipts in kind that represent income. This category also now includes judicial fees to jurors and witnesses, compensation of prison inmates, and marriage fees to justices of the peace, which earlier were classified as "other labor income". As of the 2013 revision, wages and salaries are now measured on an accrual basis, that is to say when earned rather than when paid, consistent with the treatment in the gross domestic income and national income tables.

Supplements to wages and salaries consists of employer contributions to employee pension and insurance funds and to government social insurance funds. In a substantial change introduced in the 2013 revision, defined benefit pension plan transactions are now recorded on an accrual basis instead of a cash transactions basis: employees are now credited with defined pension benefits, based on actuarial estimates of pension costs, at the time they earn them. (This was already the case with defined contribution plans.)

The following two categories, *proprietors' income* and *rental income,* are both measured net of depreciation of the capital (structures, equipment, and intellectual property products) involved. BEA calculates normal depreciation, based on the estimated life of the capital, and subtracts it from the estimated value of receipts to yield net income.

Proprietors' income with inventory valuation and capital consumption adjustments is the current production income (including income-in-kind) of sole proprietors and partnerships and of taxexempt cooperatives. The imputed net rental income of owner occupants of farm dwellings is included. Dividends and monetary interest received by proprietors of nonfinancial business and rental incomes received by persons not primarily engaged in the real estate business are excluded. These incomes are included in personal income receipts on assets and rental income of persons, respectively. Fees paid to outside directors of corporations are included. The two valuation adjustments are designed to obtain income measures that exclude any element of capital gains: inventory withdrawals are valued at replacement cost, rather than historical cost, and charges for depreciation are on an economically consistent accounting basis and are valued at replacement cost.

Rental income of persons with capital consumption adjustment consists of the net currentproduction income of persons from the rental of real property (other than the incomes of persons primarily engaged in the real estate business), the imputed net rental income of owneroccupants of nonfarm dwellings, and the royalties received by persons from patents, copyrights, and rights to natural resources. The capital consumption adjustment converts charges for depreciation to an economically consistent accounting basis valued at replacement cost. Rental income is net of interest and other expenses, and hence is affected by changing indebtedness and interest payments on owner-occupied and other housing.

Personal income receipts on assets consists of personal interest income and personal dividend income.

Personal interest income is the interest income (monetary and imputed) of persons from all sources, including interest paid by government to government employee retirement plans as well as government interest paid directly to persons.

Personal dividend income is the dividend income of persons from all sources, excluding capital gains distributions. It equals net

dividends paid by corporations (dividends paid by corporations minus dividends received by corporations) less a small amount of corporate dividends received by general government. Dividends received by government employee retirement systems are included in personal dividend income.

Personal current transfer receipts is income payments to persons for which no current services are performed. It consists of government social benefits to persons and net receipts from business.

Government social benefits to persons consists of benefits from the following categories of programs:

- *Social Security and Medicare,* consisting of federal oldage, survivors, disability, and health insurance benefits distributed from the Social Security and Medicare trust funds;

- *Medicaid,* the federal-state means-tested program covering medical expenses for lower-income children and adults as well as nursing care expenses;

- *Unemployment insurance*;

- *Veterans' benefits;*

- *Other government benefits to persons*, which includes pension benefit guaranty; workers' compensation; military medical insurance; temporary disability insurance; food stamps; Black Lung benefits; supplemental security income; family assistance, which consists of aid to families with dependent children and (beginning in 1996) assistance programs operating under the Personal Responsibility and Work Opportunity Reconciliation Act of 1996; educational assistance; and the earned income credit. Government payments to nonprofit institutions, other than for work under research and development contracts, also are included. Payments from government employee retirement plans are not included.

Note that the value of Medicare and Medicaid spending, though in practice it is usually paid directly from the government to the health care provider, is treated as if it were cash income to the consumer which is then expended in personal consumption expenditures; this value is not treated in the national accounts as a government purchase of medical services but as a government benefit paid to persons, which then finances personal consumption spending.

Contributions for government social insurance, domestic, which is subtracted to arrive at personal income, includes payments by U.S. employers, employees, self-employed, and other individuals who participate in the following programs: oldage, survivors, and disability insurance (Social Security); hospital insurance and supplementary medical insurance (Medicare); unemployment insurance; railroad retirement; veterans' life insurance; and temporary disability insurance. Contributions to government employee retirement plans are not included in this item.

In the 2009 comprehensive revision, most transactions between the U.S. government and economic agents in Guam, the U.S. Virgin Islands, American Samoa, Puerto Rico, and the Northern Mariana Islands are treated as government transactions with the rest of the world. Since the NIPAs only cover the 50 states and the District of Columbia, the *domestic* contributions to government social insurance funds are the only ones that need to be subtracted from NIPA payroll data to calculate personal income. The social insurance receipts of governments, shown in Chapter 6, will be somewhat larger than this personal income entry because they will include contributions from residents of those territories and commonwealths.

Personal current taxes is tax payments (net of refunds) by persons residing in the United States that are not chargeable to business expenses, including taxes on income, on realized net capital gains, and on personal property. As of the 1999 revisions, estate and gift taxes are classified as capital transfers and are not included in personal current taxes.

Disposable personal income is personal income minus personal current taxes. It is the income from current production that is available to persons for spending or saving. However, it is not the cash flow available, since it excludes realized capital gains. Disposable personal income in chained (2009) dollars represents the inflation-adjusted value of disposable personal income, using the implicit price deflator for personal consumption expenditures.

Personal income excluding current transfer receipts, also shown in chained (2009) dollars using the implicit price deflator for personal consumption expenditures, is an important business cycle indicator, to which particular attention is paid because it is calculated monthly as well as quarterly and annually, and thus can help establish monthly cycle turning point dates. As a pre-income-tax measure which excludes transfer payments, it is a better measure of income generated by the economy than alternative monthly income indicators such as total or disposable personal income, which are more oriented toward purchasing power.

Personal outlays is the sum of *personal consumption expenditures* (defined below), *personal interest payments,* and *personal current transfer payments.*

Personal interest payments is nonmortgage interest paid by households. As noted above in the definition of rental income, mortgage interest has been subtracted from gross rental or imputed rental receipts of persons to yield a net rental income estimate; hence, it is not included as an interest outlay in this category.

Personal current transfer payments to government includes donations, fees, and fines paid to federal, state, and local governments.

Personal current transfer payments to the rest of the world (net) is personal remittances in cash and in kind to the rest of the world less such remittances from the rest of the world.

Personal saving is derived by subtracting personal outlays from disposable personal income. It is the current net saving of individuals (including proprietors), nonprofit institutions that primarily serve individuals, life insurance carriers, retirement funds (including those of government employees), private noninsured welfare funds, and private trust funds. Conceptually, personal saving may also be viewed as the sum of the net acquisition of financial assets and the change in physical assets less the sum of net borrowing and consumption of fixed capital. In either case, it is defined to exclude both realized and unrealized capital gains.

Note that in the context of national income accounting, the term just defined is *saving,* not "savings." *Saving* refers to a flow of income during a particular time span (such as a year or a quarter) that is not consumed. It is therefore available to finance a commensurate flow of investment during that time span. Strictly defined, "savings" denotes an accumulated stock of monetary funds—possibly the cumulative effects of successive periods of *saving*—available to the owner in asset form, such as in a bank savings account.

Personal consumption expenditures (PCE) is goods and services purchased by persons residing in the United States. Persons are defined as individuals and nonprofit institutions that primarily serve individuals. PCE mostly consists of purchases of new goods and services by individuals from business, including purchases financed by insurance (such as both private and government medical insurance). In addition, PCE includes purchases of new goods and services by nonprofit institutions, net purchases of used goods by individuals and nonprofit institutions, and purchases abroad of goods and services by U.S. residents traveling or working in foreign countries. PCE also includes purchases for certain goods and services provided by the government, primarily tuition payments for higher education, charges for medical care, and charges for water and sanitary services. Finally, PCE includes imputed purchases that keep PCE invariant to changes in the way that certain activities are carried out. For example, to take account of the value of the services provided by owner-occupied housing, PCE includes an imputation equal to what (estimated) rent homeowners would pay if they rented their houses from themselves. (See the discussion of imputation in the notes and definitions to Chapter 1.) Actual purchases of residential structures by individuals are classified as gross private domestic investment.

In the 2009 comprehensive revision, the classification system used for breakdowns of PCE was revised, and new calculations were introduced separating the consumption spending of the household sector proper from that of nonprofit institutions serving households.

Goods is the sum of *Durable* and *Nondurable goods*.

The PCE category *Durable goods* is subdivided into *Motor vehicles and parts, Furnishings and household equipment* (which includes appliances), *Recreational goods and vehicles* (which includes video, audio, photographic, and information processing equipment and media), and *Other durable goods*.

Nondurable goods encompasses *Food and beverages off-premises, Clothing and footwear, Gasoline and other energy goods,* and *Other nondurable goods*. This food and beverages category no longer includes meals and beverages purchased for consumption on the premises, which are now included in services, since they have a high service component and since their prices are much more stable than those of off-premises food and beverages.

Services, total is subdivided into *Household services* and *Final consumption expenditures of nonprofit institutions serving households (NPISHs)*. The latter is the difference between the *gross output* of NPISHs and the amounts that they receive from sales of goods and services to households—for example, payments for services of a nonprofit hospital. Such sales of goods and services appear in the appropriate category of household expenditures—for example, *Health* in the case of the hospital services.

The components of *Household services* are *Housing and utilities, Health care, Transportation services, Recreation services, Food services and accommodations* (which includes meals and beverages purchased for consumption on premises, as well as payments for hotels and similar accommodations), *Financial services and insurance,* and *Other services*.

These are the categories used in the quarterly data presented in Tables 4-2, 4-3, and 4-4. This classification system is not particularly helpful with respect to the objective of spending. For example, the *Health care* component of services does not include drugs and medicines, which are included instead in nondurable goods. For a more precise classification of consumption spending by objective, see Table 4-5, Household Consumption Expenditures by Function, described in more detail below. This classification by type of expenditure is only available on an annual basis, and later than the principal quarterly NIPA data.

Data availability

Monthly data on personal income and spending are made available in a BEA press release, usually distributed the first business day following the monthly release of the latest quarterly national income and product account (NIPA) estimates. Monthly and quarterly data are subsequently published each month in the BEA's *Survey of Current Business*. Current and historical data are available on the BEA Web site at <https://www.bea.gov>.

References

References can be found in the notes and definitions to Chapter 1. A discussion of monthly estimates of personal income and its disposition appears in the November 1979 edition of the *Survey of Current Business*. Additional and more recent information can be found in the articles listed in the notes and definitions for Chapter 1.

TABLE 4-5

Household Consumption Expenditures by Function

SOURCE: BUREAU OF ECONOMIC ANALYSIS (BEA)

In this table, also derived from the NIPAs, annual estimates of the current-dollar value of PCE by households—excluding the "final" consumption expenditures of nonprofit institutions serving households (NPISHs); see definition above--are presented by function.

Definitions

Food and beverages includes food and beverages (including alcoholic beverages) purchased for home consumption and food produced and consumed on farms.

Clothing, footwear, and related services includes purchases, rental, cleaning, and repair of clothing and footwear.

Housing, utilities, and fuels includes rents paid for rental housing, imputed rent of owner-occupied dwellings, and purchase of fuels and utility services.

Furnishings, household equipment, and routine household maintenance includes furniture, floor coverings, household textiles, appliances, tableware etc., tools, and other supplies and services.

Health includes drugs, other medical products and equipment, and outpatient, hospital, and nursing home services.

Transportation includes the purchase and operation of motor vehicles and public transportation services.

Communication includes telephone equipment, postal and delivery services, telecommunication services, and Internet access.

Recreation includes video and audio equipment, computers, and related services; sports vehicles and other sports goods and services; memberships and admissions; magazines, newspapers, books, and stationery; pets and related goods and services; photo goods and services; tour services; and legal gambling. (As noted earlier, purchases of goods and services that are illegal and the incomes from such purchases are outside the scope of the national income and product accounts.)

Education includes educational services and books.

Food services and accommodations includes meals and beverages purchased for consumption on the premises, food furnished to employees, and hotel and other accommodations including housing at schools.

Financial services and insurance consists of financial services and life, household, medical care, motor vehicle, and other insurance.

Other goods and services includes personal goods (such as cosmetics, jewelry, and luggage) and services, social services and religious activities, professional and other services, and tobacco.

Foreign travel and expenditures, net consists of foreign travel spending and other expenditures abroad by U.S. residents <u>minus</u> expenditures in the United States by nonresidents. A negative figure indicates that foreigners spent more here than U.S. residents spent abroad. Positive values for this foreign travel category, indicating that U.S. residents spent more abroad than foreigners spent here, appear in the 1980s when the dollar was strong against other major currencies. (The international value of the dollar is shown in Table 13-2.) Negative values in subsequent years have resulted in part from the weakening of the dollar, which discouraged U.S. residents' travel abroad and encouraged tourism by foreigners in the United States. The negative sign does not indicate a drain on GDP—these effects of a weaker dollar are in fact positive for real GDP—but rather reflects the fact that the goods and services purchased by foreigners in the United States must be subtracted from the total consumer purchases recorded in the other columns of this table in order to be added to other exports and classified in the category of exports rather than in the consumption spending of U.S. residents.

Data availability and revisions

Data are updated once a year, after the general midyear revision of the NIPAs, and are available on the BEA Web site at <https://www.bea.gov>.

CHAPTER 5: SAVING AND INVESTMENT

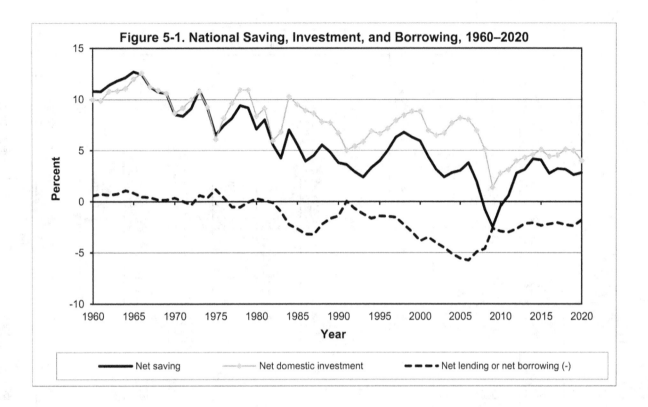

Figure 5-1. National Saving, Investment, and Borrowing, 1960–2020

- Net national saving—the middle line in Figure 5-1—averaged a much lower rate of gross national income (GNI) in the years 1984 through 2000, than in the rates seen in the 1950s and 1960s. Net saving is gross saving by U.S. persons, businesses, and governments, <u>less</u> the consumption of fixed capital. Thus, it represents saving available for investment over and above the replacement of the existing capital stock. (Tables 5-1A and B)

- In the recession that began at the end of 2007, net national saving fell into negative territory, for the first time since the depression years 1931 through 1934. Government deficits soared as the Great Recession cut deeply into tax revenues and called forth both automatic and discretionary anti-recession spending such as unemployment compensation, food stamps (Supplemental Nutrition Assistance Program – SNAP), and temporary assistance for needy families - TANF. In one year, 2008 to 2009, the budget deficit doubled. (Tables 5-1A and B and Table 6-14B) In 2020, the deficit more than tripled from 2019, due in large part to the global pandemic.

- Net saving is currently much lower than it was in the 1960s and 1970s. In 1965, net saving got as high as 12.7 percent. It gradually declined through the 1980 and 1990s. In 2020, the national saving rate declined for the second consecutive year, to its lowest level since 2011.   (Table 5-1A)

Table 5-1A. Saving and Investment: Recent Data

(Billions of dollars, except as noted; quarterly data are at seasonally adjusted annual rates.)   **NIPA Tables 1.7.5, 5.1**

Year and quarter	Total	Net saving Total	Private Total	Personal saving	Domestic corporate business	Government Federal	Government State and local	Consumption of fixed capital Total	Private Total	Domestic business	House-holds and institutions	Government Federal	Government State and local
1960	127.0	59.1	56.4	37.9	18.5	0.2	2.5	67.9	48.2	40.0	8.2	15.2	4.5
1961	131.6	61.0	63.5	44.4	19.2	-4.7	2.2	70.6	49.8	41.3	8.5	16.0	4.8
1962	143.4	69.3	71.6	46.7	24.9	-5.4	3.1	74.1	51.8	42.9	8.8	17.2	5.1
1963	154.1	76.1	75.0	47.1	27.9	-2.2	3.3	78.0	54.2	44.9	9.3	18.4	5.5
1964	166.1	83.7	86.6	55.3	31.4	-6.9	3.9	82.4	57.3	47.4	9.9	19.2	5.9
1965	182.9	94.9	96.8	58.8	38.0	-5.5	3.7	88.0	61.6	50.9	10.7	20.0	6.4
1966	196.5	101.2	103.4	61.9	41.6	-7.0	4.7	95.3	67.2	55.6	11.5	21.0	7.1
1967	200.5	96.9	112.5	73.0	39.5	-19.5	4.0	103.6	73.3	60.9	12.4	22.5	7.8
1968	214.6	101.2	111.5	72.9	38.6	-13.8	3.5	113.4	80.6	67.0	13.6	24.2	8.6
1969	233.1	108.2	110.3	76.1	34.2	-5.1	3.1	124.9	89.4	74.2	15.2	25.8	9.6
1970	228.2	91.4	124.8	97.6	27.2	-34.8	1.4	136.8	98.3	81.8	16.5	27.6	10.9
1971	246.1	97.2	149.4	111.9	37.5	-50.9	-1.3	148.9	107.6	89.4	18.2	29.1	12.2
1972	277.6	116.6	159.6	111.5	48.0	-49.0	6.1	161.0	117.5	97.2	20.3	30.2	13.3
1973	335.3	156.6	189.3	135.8	53.5	-38.3	5.6	178.7	131.5	108.2	23.3	32.4	14.8
1974	349.2	142.3	186.0	146.3	39.7	-41.3	-2.3	206.9	153.2	126.1	27.0	35.4	18.4
1975	348.1	109.6	218.3	164.0	54.3	-97.9	-10.7	238.5	178.8	147.9	30.9	38.7	21.0
1976	399.3	139.1	224.4	154.4	70.0	-80.9	-4.4	260.2	196.5	162.2	34.3	41.7	22.0
1977	459.4	169.6	242.5	155.9	86.6	-73.4	0.5	289.8	221.1	181.5	39.6	45.3	23.4
1978	548.0	220.8	278.0	175.1	102.9	-62.0	4.9	327.2	252.1	205.5	46.6	49.7	25.4
1979	613.5	239.6	288.2	186.8	101.4	-47.4	-1.2	373.9	290.7	236.4	54.4	54.6	28.6
1980	630.1	201.7	296.4	224.1	72.3	-88.8	-5.9	428.4	335.0	272.8	62.2	60.4	33.1
1981	743.9	256.6	354.9	265.5	89.4	-88.1	-10.2	487.2	381.9	313.5	68.5	67.5	37.8
1982	725.8	188.9	379.0	293.3	85.6	-167.4	-22.8	537.0	420.4	347.5	72.9	75.4	41.2
1983	716.7	154.1	379.7	264.0	115.7	-207.2	-18.4	562.6	438.8	362.8	76.0	81.1	42.7
1984	881.6	283.2	479.9	330.3	149.5	-196.5	-0.2	598.4	463.5	382.7	80.9	90.6	44.3
1985	881.0	240.8	442.5	284.9	157.5	-199.2	-2.4	640.1	496.4	410.3	86.2	97.0	46.8
1986	864.5	179.2	399.1	290.6	108.5	-215.9	-4.0	685.3	531.6	438.1	93.4	103.6	50.1
1987	948.9	218.5	398.6	275.4	123.2	-165.7	-14.4	730.4	566.3	464.5	101.8	110.1	54.0
1988	1 076.6	292.1	463.4	320.5	142.9	-160.0	-11.3	784.5	607.9	499.2	108.8	118.9	57.7
1989	1 109.8	271.5	450.2	340.0	110.3	-159.4	-19.3	838.3	649.6	532.6	117.0	126.9	61.8
1990	1 113.4	224.8	464.4	361.1	103.2	-203.3	-36.2	888.5	688.4	564.6	123.8	133.5	66.6
1991	1 153.4	221.0	529.5	396.0	133.5	-248.4	-60.1	932.4	721.5	592.3	129.2	140.1	70.8
1992	1 147.6	187.4	592.8	453.9	139.0	-334.5	-71.0	960.2	742.9	608.2	134.7	143.3	74.1
1993	1 163.4	159.9	545.9	397.7	148.2	-313.5	-72.5	1 003.5	778.2	634.2	144.0	147.0	78.3
1994	1 295.1	239.5	559.0	363.4	195.7	-255.6	-63.9	1 055.6	822.5	669.0	153.5	150.3	82.8
1995	1 426.3	303.9	616.5	387.1	229.4	-242.1	-70.4	1 122.4	880.7	717.8	162.9	153.5	88.1
1996	1 578.9	403.6	638.8	382.3	254.5	-179.4	-53.8	1 175.3	929.1	758.5	170.6	153.7	92.5
1997	1 780.5	541.2	675.1	390.3	284.9	-92.0	-42.0	1 239.3	987.8	807.9	179.9	154.3	97.3
1998	1 930.6	620.8	649.5	446.5	203.0	1.4	-30.1	1 309.7	1 052.2	860.1	192.1	155.4	102.2
1999	2 007.2	608.3	578.1	344.0	234.0	69.1	-38.9	1 398.9	1 132.2	924.0	208.2	158.2	108.6
2000	2 124.6	613.4	494.3	351.4	142.9	159.7	-40.6	1 511.2	1 231.5	1 004.6	227.0	163.1	116.6
2001	2 069.1	469.6	573.5	382.8	190.7	15.0	-119.0	1 599.5	1 311.7	1 064.9	246.8	164.4	123.4
2002	1 996.0	338.0	788.7	462.5	326.2	-267.8	-182.9	1 658.0	1 361.8	1 098.8	263.0	166.8	129.3
2003	1 983.5	264.5	843.1	456.7	386.5	-397.4	-181.3	1 719.1	1 411.9	1 125.4	286.6	172.2	134.9
2004	2 153.4	331.6	874.1	445.4	428.6	-393.5	-149.0	1 821.8	1 497.1	1 178.8	318.3	180.5	144.2
2005	2 349.4	378.3	774.9	268.0	506.9	-293.8	-102.8	1 971.0	1 622.6	1 266.4	356.2	190.5	157.9
2006	2 636.9	512.8	819.7	358.7	461.1	-221.9	-85.0	2 124.1	1 751.8	1 362.6	389.2	201.3	171.0
2007	2 504.4	251.6	640.5	352.7	287.9	-259.7	-129.3	2 252.8	1 852.5	1 446.7	405.8	212.8	187.5
2008	2 206.0	-152.8	693.0	503.4	189.6	-624.9	-220.9	2 358.8	1 931.8	1 524.9	407.0	225.9	201.2
2009	1 987.4	-384.1	1 200.5	639.7	560.8	-1 243.2	-341.3	2 371.5	1 928.7	1 531.2	397.5	233.6	209.1
2010	2 287.7	-103.3	1 522.6	709.3	813.3	-1 318.4	-307.5	2 390.9	1 933.8	1 537.1	396.7	243.7	213.4
2011	2 521.2	46.7	1 555.9	806.0	749.9	-1 234.1	-275.1	2 474.5	1 997.3	1 595.1	402.2	254.9	222.2
2012	3 007.7	431.7	1 787.2	1 073.1	714.1	-1 072.7	-282.8	2 576.0	2 082.4	1 670.4	412.0	261.6	232.0
2013	3 189.2	507.9	1 405.0	766.0	639.1	-631.8	-265.3	2 681.2	2 176.6	1 738.8	437.8	265.9	238.8
2014	3 527.8	712.7	1 548.0	930.9	617.1	-597.4	-237.9	2 815.0	2 298.5	1 831.2	467.3	270.2	246.3
2015	3 669.6	758.2	1 534.2	1 034.9	499.3	-560.2	-215.8	2 911.4	2 388.5	1 903.1	485.4	271.5	251.4
2016	3 534.7	547.7	1 460.0	987.8	472.1	-667.6	-244.7	2 987.1	2 459.9	1 950.9	509.0	270.7	256.4
2017	3 795.8	677.6	1 628.9	1 076.4	552.5	-720.7	-230.6	3 118.2	2 576.1	2 037.6	538.4	275.9	266.2
2018	4 025.6	752.1	1 876.0	1 190.9	685.0	-928.1	-195.8	3 273.4	2 708.1	2 133.3	574.8	284.9	280.5
2019	4 156.1	720.5	1 917.0	1 237.8	679.2	-1 047.5	-149.0	3 435.6	2 848.6	2 248.3	600.3	293.3	293.7
2020	4 002.9	426.9	3 460.8	2 887.5	573.3	-3 110.0	76.1	3 575.9	2 969.6	2 338.6	631.0	303.5	302.8
2018													
1st quarter	3 980.7	771.0	1 848.1	1 153.3	694.7	-909.7	-167.4	3 209.7	2 654.6	2 092.2	562.4	281.0	274.1
2nd quarter	3 938.5	682.1	1 831.9	1 165.0	666.9	-928.8	-221.0	3 256.3	2 693.0	2 120.7	572.3	284.2	279.1
3rd quarter	4 065.6	769.9	1 871.0	1 193.7	677.3	-901.4	-199.7	3 295.7	2 726.9	2 147.4	579.5	286.3	282.4
4th quarter	4 117.5	785.4	1 952.9	1 251.8	701.1	-972.5	-195.0	3 332.0	2 757.7	2 172.6	585.1	288.1	286.2
2019													
1st quarter	4 203.4	825.4	2 009.0	1 376.7	632.3	-1 015.4	-168.2	3 378.0	2 798.1	2 207.4	590.6	291.3	288.7
2nd quarter	4 147.3	726.3	1 883.9	1 194.4	689.5	-1 033.2	-124.4	3 421.0	2 836.1	2 239.5	596.5	291.9	293.1
3rd quarter	4 101.4	643.5	1 874.9	1 171.7	703.2	-1 080.9	-150.5	3 457.9	2 867.9	2 264.0	604.0	294.2	295.7
4th quarter	4 172.2	686.8	1 900.2	1 208.4	691.8	-1 060.4	-153.0	3 485.5	2 892.5	2 282.4	610.1	295.8	297.2
2020													
1st quarter	4 347.5	825.2	2 117.7	1 611.4	506.3	-1 158.0	-134.6	3 522.3	2 924.5	2 308.7	615.9	298.2	299.6
2nd quarter	3 556.7	5.8	5 077.8	4 772.0	305.8	-5 625.6	553.6	3 550.9	2 949.0	2 327.5	621.5	301.6	300.3
3rd quarter	3 596.3	5.2	3 587.9	2 821.3	766.5	-3 516.3	-66.3	3 591.0	2 981.5	2 345.3	636.2	305.1	304.5
4th quarter	4 511.0	871.6	3 059.8	2 345.5	714.4	-2 140.1	-48.2	3 639.4	3 023.3	2 372.9	650.4	309.2	306.9

Table 5-1A. Saving and Investment: Recent Data—*Continued*

(Billions of dollars, except as noted; quarterly data are at seasonally adjusted annual rates.) **NIPA Tables 1.7.5, 5.1**

| Year and quarter | Gross domestic investment, capital account transactions, and net lending, NIPAs | | | | | | Statistical discrepancy | Net domestic investment | Gross national income | Gross saving as a percent of gross national income | Net saving as a percent of gross national income |
| | Total | Gross domestic investment | | | Capital account transactions, net | Net lending or net borrowing (-), NIPAs | | | | | |
		Total	Private	Government							
1960	125.7	122.5	86.5	36.0	. . .	3.2	-1.3	54.6	546.8	23.2	10.8
1961	130.7	126.5	86.6	39.9	. . .	4.2	-0.9	55.9	566.6	23.2	10.8
1962	143.4	139.6	97.0	42.6	. . .	3.8	0.0	65.5	608.0	23.6	11.4
1963	152.7	147.7	103.3	44.4	. . .	4.9	-1.5	69.7	643.4	24.0	11.8
1964	166.0	158.5	112.2	46.4	. . .	7.5	0.0	76.2	689.4	24.1	12.1
1965	183.7	177.5	129.6	47.9	. . .	6.2	0.7	89.5	746.8	24.5	12.7
1966	201.6	197.8	144.2	53.6	. . .	3.8	5.1	102.4	813.4	24.2	12.4
1967	203.9	200.4	142.7	57.7	. . .	3.5	3.4	96.8	862.0	23.3	11.2
1968	217.7	216.2	156.9	59.2	. . .	1.5	3.1	102.8	943.6	22.7	10.7
1969	234.7	233.1	173.6	59.5	0.0	1.6	1.6	108.2	1 022.1	22.8	10.6
1970	233.6	229.8	170.0	59.8	0.0	3.7	5.3	93.0	1 074.4	21.2	8.5
1971	255.6	255.3	196.8	58.5	0.0	0.3	9.5	106.4	1 162.9	21.2	8.4
1972	284.8	288.8	228.1	60.7	0.0	-4.1	7.2	127.8	1 280.5	21.7	9.1
1973	341.4	332.6	266.9	65.6	0.0	8.8	6.1	153.9	1 431.8	23.4	10.9
1974	356.6	350.7	274.5	76.2	0.0	5.9	7.4	143.8	1 553.3	22.5	9.2
1975	361.5	341.7	257.3	84.4	0.1	19.8	13.3	103.1	1 684.6	20.7	6.5
1976	420.0	412.9	323.2	89.6	0.1	7.0	20.7	152.6	1 869.6	21.4	7.4
1977	478.9	489.8	396.6	93.2	0.1	-11.0	19.4	199.9	2 082.7	22.1	8.1
1978	571.3	583.9	478.4	105.6	0.1	-12.7	23.3	256.7	2 349.9	23.3	9.4
1979	658.6	659.8	539.7	120.1	0.1	-1.3	45.1	285.9	2 614.2	23.5	9.2
1980	674.6	666.0	530.1	135.9	0.1	8.4	44.4	237.6	2 847.1	22.1	7.1
1981	781.9	778.6	631.2	147.3	0.1	3.3	38.1	291.3	3 201.9	23.2	8.0
1982	734.7	738.0	581.0	156.9	0.1	-3.4	8.8	201.0	3 371.4	21.5	5.6
1983	773.6	808.7	637.5	171.2	0.1	-35.2	57.0	246.1	3 614.2	19.8	4.3
1984	923.2	1 013.3	820.1	193.2	0.1	-90.2	41.6	414.9	4 032.3	21.9	7.0
1985	935.2	1 049.5	829.7	219.9	0.1	-114.5	54.3	409.4	4 310.1	20.4	5.6
1986	944.6	1 087.2	849.1	238.1	0.1	-142.8	80.1	401.9	4 516.5	19.1	4.0
1987	992.7	1 146.8	892.2	254.6	0.1	-154.2	43.8	416.4	4 828.9	19.7	4.5
1988	1 079.6	1 195.4	937.0	258.4	0.1	-115.9	3.0	410.9	5 256.1	20.5	5.6
1989	1 177.8	1 270.1	999.7	270.4	0.3	-92.7	68.0	431.9	5 598.4	19.8	4.9
1990	1 208.9	1 283.8	993.4	290.4	7.4	-82.3	95.5	395.3	5 902.3	18.9	3.8
1991	1 246.3	1 238.4	944.3	294.1	5.3	2.6	93.0	306.0	6 096.8	18.9	3.6
1992	1 263.6	1 309.1	1 013.0	296.1	-1.3	-44.3	115.9	348.9	6 435.5	17.8	2.9
1993	1 319.3	1 398.7	1 106.8	291.9	0.9	-80.2	156.0	395.2	6 733.8	17.3	2.4
1994	1 435.1	1 550.7	1 256.5	294.2	1.3	-116.9	140.0	495.0	7 170.3	18.1	3.3
1995	1 519.3	1 625.2	1 317.5	307.7	0.4	-106.3	93.0	502.8	7 574.7	18.8	4.0
1996	1 637.0	1 752.0	1 432.1	320.0	0.2	-115.2	58.1	576.7	8 045.9	19.6	5.0
1997	1 792.1	1 922.2	1 595.6	326.6	0.5	-130.6	11.6	682.9	8 589.3	20.7	6.3
1998	1 875.3	2 080.7	1 736.7	344.0	0.2	-205.6	-55.2	770.9	9 135.5	21.1	6.8
1999	1 978.9	2 255.5	1 887.1	368.5	6.7	-283.3	-28.3	856.6	9 690.4	20.7	6.3
2000	2 030.4	2 427.3	2 038.4	388.9	4.6	-401.4	-94.2	916.0	10 383.7	20.5	5.9
2001	1 955.3	2 346.7	1 934.8	411.9	-11.9	-379.5	-113.8	747.2	10 746.1	19.3	4.4
2002	1 918.7	2 374.1	1 930.4	443.7	4.2	-459.6	-77.3	716.1	11 052.2	18.1	3.1
2003	1 963.6	2 491.3	2 027.1	464.2	8.8	-536.4	-19.9	772.2	11 534.8	17.2	2.3
2004	2 129.7	2 767.5	2 281.3	486.2	4.6	-642.4	-23.7	945.6	12 317.6	17.5	2.7
2005	2 296.8	3 048.0	2 534.7	513.3	-0.7	-750.5	-52.5	1 077.0	13 166.5	17.8	2.9
2006	2 432.5	3 251.8	2 701.0	550.9	7.7	-827.0	-204.3	1 127.7	14 066.4	18.7	3.6
2007	2 524.2	3 265.0	2 673.0	592.0	6.4	-747.2	19.8	1 012.2	14 550.1	17.2	1.7
2008	2 403.0	3 107.2	2 477.6	629.6	0.8	-705.0	197.0	748.4	14 718.1	15.0	-1.0
2009	2 189.5	2 572.6	1 929.7	642.9	6.3	-389.4	202.0	201.1	14 426.3	13.8	-2.7
2010	2 370.2	2 810.0	2 165.5	644.5	7.4	-447.2	82.5	419.1	15 172.1	15.1	-0.7
2011	2 508.8	2 969.2	2 332.6	636.6	9.5	-469.8	-12.3	494.7	15 850.0	15.9	0.3
2012	2 818.8	3 242.8	2 621.8	621.0	-0.5	-423.4	-188.9	666.8	16 675.6	18.0	2.6
2013	3 074.3	3 426.4	2 826.0	600.4	7.0	-359.0	-114.8	745.2	17 188.3	18.6	3.0
2014	3 270.6	3 646.7	3 044.2	602.6	6.9	-383.0	-257.2	831.7	18 043.1	19.6	4.0
2015	3 435.1	3 859.8	3 237.2	622.6	8.3	-433.0	-234.5	948.4	18 660.9	19.7	4.1
2016	3 441.3	3 845.0	3 205.0	639.9	7.0	-410.7	-93.4	857.9	19 020.5	18.6	2.9
2017	3 676.9	4 049.8	3 381.4	668.4	16.0	-388.9	-118.9	931.6	19 893.1	19.1	3.4
2018	3 900.1	4 340.4	3 637.8	702.6	4.7	-445.0	-125.5	1 067.0	20 946.8	19.2	3.6
2019	4 086.4	4 566.3	3 826.3	740.0	6.9	-486.7	-69.7	1 130.7	21 708.7	19.1	3.3
2020	3 832.3	4 419.4	3 637.8	781.5	5.9	-593.0	-170.6	843.5	21 286.6	18.8	2.0
2018											
1st quarter	3 848.1	4 241.9	3 550.8	691.0	5.8	-399.6	-132.7	1 032.1	20 593.0	19.3	3.7
2nd quarter	3 933.6	4 308.8	3 603.2	705.6	12.2	-387.4	-4.9	1 052.5	20 798.1	18.9	3.3
3rd quarter	3 900.9	4 388.0	3 679.6	708.4	2.2	-489.3	-164.7	1 092.3	21 095.4	19.3	3.6
4th quarter	3 917.9	4 422.9	3 717.5	705.4	-1.5	-503.6	-199.6	1 090.9	21 300.7	19.3	3.7
2019											
1st quarter	4 009.4	4 526.8	3 801.9	724.8	11.4	-528.7	-194.0	1 148.7	21 448.4	19.6	3.8
2nd quarter	4 075.0	4 581.1	3 843.0	738.1	3.9	-510.0	-72.3	1 160.0	21 637.3	19.2	3.4
3rd quarter	4 124.5	4 601.2	3 858.2	743.0	4.0	-480.7	23.1	1 143.3	21 757.6	18.9	3.0
4th quarter	4 136.8	4 556.0	3 801.9	754.1	8.2	-427.4	-35.4	1 070.6	21 991.4	19.0	3.1
2020											
1st quarter	4 073.0	4 525.1	3 752.4	772.7	11.9	-463.9	-274.5	1 002.7	21 995.8	19.8	3.8
2nd quarter	3 413.9	3 941.7	3 167.0	774.7	4.2	-532.0	-142.8	390.8	19 792.2	18.0	0.0
3rd quarter	3 826.3	4 491.1	3 708.8	782.3	2.7	-667.4	230.0	900.0	21 135.4	17.0	0.0
4th quarter	4 016.0	4 719.7	3 923.2	796.5	4.9	-708.7	-495.0	1 080.3	22 223.2	20.3	3.9

. . . = Not available.

Table 5-1B. Saving and Investment: Historical Data

(Billions of dollars, except as noted; quarterly data are at seasonally adjusted annual rates.) **NIPA Tables 1.7.5, 5.1**

Year and quarter	Gross saving								Gross domestic investment and net lending, NIPAs				Net domestic invest-ment	Gross national income	Net saving as a percent-age of gross national income
	Total	Net saving			Consumption of fixed capital				Gross domestic investment			Net lending or net borrow-ing (-), NIPAs			
		Private	Government		Total	Private	Government		Total	Private	Govern-ment				
			Federal	State and local			Federal	State and local							
1929	20.1	7.6	0.8	1.3	10.4	9.4	0.2	0.8	20.1	17.2	2.9	0.8	9.7	104.6	...
1930	15.8	4.5	0.0	1.1	10.2	9.2	0.2	0.8	14.7	11.4	3.3	0.7	4.5	93.3	...
1931	9.1	1.2	-2.4	0.7	9.5	8.6	0.2	0.7	9.6	6.5	3.1	0.2	0.1	77.2	...
1932	4.0	-3.2	-1.6	0.4	8.3	7.5	0.2	0.7	4.1	1.8	2.3	0.2	-4.3	59.6	...
1933	3.9	-3.1	-1.2	0.2	8.0	7.0	0.2	0.7	4.3	2.3	2.0	0.2	-3.7	56.9	...
1934	7.0	0.1	-2.6	1.0	8.4	7.3	0.3	0.9	7.0	4.3	2.7	0.4	-1.5	66.7	...
1935	10.4	3.2	-2.3	1.0	8.5	7.3	0.3	0.9	10.2	7.4	2.9	-0.1	1.7	74.8	...
1936	12.3	5.1	-3.6	2.1	8.8	7.5	0.4	0.9	13.6	9.4	4.2	-0.1	4.8	83.9	...
1937	17.1	5.8	-0.2	1.8	9.8	8.4	0.4	1.0	16.9	13.0	3.9	0.2	7.1	93.4	...
1938	12.7	2.8	-1.8	1.7	10.0	8.6	0.4	1.0	12.2	7.9	4.3	1.2	2.2	87.1	...
1939	14.6	5.3	-2.6	1.7	10.1	8.6	0.5	1.1	14.8	10.2	4.6	1.0	4.7	92.5	...
1940	19.5	8.3	-1.0	1.6	10.6	9.0	0.5	1.1	19.0	14.6	4.4	1.5	8.4	102.1	...
1941	31.1	16.9	0.6	1.5	12.1	10.0	0.9	1.2	30.2	19.4	10.8	1.3	18.1	129.4	...
1942	41.6	37.0	-11.4	1.1	14.9	11.2	2.2	1.4	40.7	11.8	29.0	-0.1	25.8	167.3	...
1943	47.0	45.0	-17.1	1.0	18.0	11.5	5.0	1.5	47.3	7.4	39.9	-2.1	29.3	205.2	...
1944	42.8	49.8	-29.4	1.1	21.3	12.0	7.8	1.5	47.3	9.2	38.2	-2.0	26.0	222.2	...
1945	32.6	40.4	-32.0	1.1	23.1	12.5	9.2	1.4	37.7	12.4	25.3	-1.3	14.6	224.4	...
1946	41.5	23.1	-8.1	0.8	25.7	14.2	9.9	1.6	37.8	33.1	4.7	4.9	12.1	227.0	...
1947	49.2	17.6	2.5	0.1	29.1	17.7	9.5	1.9	42.8	37.1	5.7	9.3	13.7	247.9	...
1948	61.5	29.1	1.0	0.1	31.3	20.8	8.4	2.1	58.8	50.3	8.5	2.4	27.5	276.2	...
1949	49.6	25.2	-8.5	0.5	32.3	22.6	7.5	2.2	50.4	39.1	11.3	0.9	18.1	272.0	...
1950	64.9	29.3	1.9	0.3	33.4	24.3	6.9	2.2	68.0	56.5	11.5	-1.8	34.6	300.0	...
1951	79.8	35.9	4.5	1.6	37.7	27.7	7.4	2.6	82.3	62.8	19.6	0.9	44.6	345.4	...
1952	79.9	39.5	-2.1	1.9	40.6	29.5	8.3	2.8	81.9	57.3	24.6	0.6	41.3	366.7	...
1953	82.0	40.3	-4.2	2.3	43.5	31.3	9.3	2.9	87.1	60.4	26.7	-1.3	43.6	387.3	...
1954	80.7	40.7	-8.0	2.0	46.0	33.0	10.1	3.0	83.5	58.1	25.4	0.2	37.5	389.7	...
1947															
1st quarter	47.1	16.5	2.5	0.1	28.1	16.3	10.0	1.8	40.8	35.9	4.9	9.4	12.7	241.1	7.9
2nd quarter	46.7	15.7	2.1	0.2	28.7	17.3	9.6	1.8	39.6	34.5	5.1	9.9	10.9	244.3	7.4
3rd quarter	49.1	19.9	-0.4	0.0	29.5	18.2	9.4	1.9	41.0	34.9	6.1	10.1	11.5	248.7	7.9
4th quarter	54.0	18.3	5.6	-0.1	30.2	19.1	9.1	2.0	49.8	43.3	6.6	7.8	19.6	257.4	9.3
1948															
1st quarter	59.0	23.6	5.1	-0.3	30.6	19.9	8.7	2.0	54.7	47.2	7.5	4.9	24.1	266.5	10.6
2nd quarter	62.7	29.0	2.6	0.1	31.1	20.6	8.4	2.1	58.6	50.3	8.2	3.0	27.5	275.1	11.5
3rd quarter	62.0	31.4	-1.1	0.1	31.7	21.2	8.3	2.2	61.3	52.5	8.8	0.9	29.6	280.4	10.8
4th quarter	62.4	32.6	-2.7	0.5	32.0	21.7	8.1	2.2	60.7	51.3	9.4	0.8	28.7	282.7	10.8
1949															
1st quarter	54.7	27.9	-6.0	0.6	32.2	22.1	8.0	2.2	53.4	43.1	10.3	2.2	21.1	275.6	8.2
2nd quarter	48.6	24.9	-9.1	0.4	32.3	22.4	7.6	2.2	47.5	36.2	11.3	1.7	15.3	272.0	6.0
3rd quarter	50.1	26.6	-9.4	0.6	32.3	22.8	7.3	2.2	51.5	39.5	11.9	0.6	19.2	272.1	6.6
4th quarter	44.8	21.5	-9.4	0.3	32.4	23.1	7.1	2.2	49.3	37.5	11.8	-1.0	16.9	268.4	4.6
1950															
1st quarter	53.2	32.3	-11.5	0.0	32.4	23.4	6.9	2.1	57.4	46.7	10.7	-1.0	25.0	278.7	7.4
2nd quarter	61.7	29.8	-0.6	-0.3	32.8	23.9	6.8	2.1	63.4	52.3	11.1	-1.2	30.6	291.3	9.9
3rd quarter	67.1	23.1	9.6	0.8	33.6	24.6	6.8	2.2	70.4	58.6	11.7	-2.7	36.8	309.1	10.8
4th quarter	77.6	32.0	10.0	0.8	34.8	25.5	7.0	2.3	80.8	68.4	12.3	-2.5	45.9	320.9	13.3
1951															
1st quarter	74.3	23.6	12.7	1.7	36.3	26.6	7.2	2.5	79.5	64.6	14.9	-1.7	43.2	334.1	11.4
2nd quarter	82.5	38.5	5.1	1.5	37.3	27.5	7.2	2.6	85.6	67.4	18.2	0.4	48.3	342.5	13.2
3rd quarter	80.7	41.6	-0.5	1.4	38.3	28.2	7.4	2.7	83.1	62.0	21.1	2.2	44.9	348.8	12.2
4th quarter	81.5	40.1	0.7	1.7	39.0	28.7	7.6	2.7	81.2	57.1	24.1	2.7	42.1	356.0	11.9
1952															
1st quarter	82.0	39.4	1.2	1.8	39.5	29.0	7.9	2.7	82.2	58.1	24.1	3.5	42.7	358.1	11.9
2nd quarter	76.0	36.9	-2.4	1.3	40.2	29.3	8.1	2.8	77.3	53.0	24.3	1.1	37.1	360.6	9.9
3rd quarter	79.3	40.9	-4.8	2.1	41.0	29.7	8.4	2.9	82.1	57.2	24.8	-1.1	41.1	368.0	10.4
4th quarter	82.3	40.8	-2.5	2.3	41.7	30.2	8.7	2.8	86.0	60.7	25.3	-1.2	44.3	380.2	10.7
1953															
1st quarter	84.0	41.2	-1.5	1.7	42.5	30.7	8.9	2.9	88.2	61.7	26.5	-1.3	45.7	387.0	10.7
2nd quarter	84.2	41.4	-3.3	2.8	43.3	31.1	9.2	2.9	89.3	62.1	27.2	-1.8	46.0	390.6	10.5
3rd quarter	83.7	40.2	-2.6	2.3	43.8	31.6	9.3	2.9	88.5	61.4	27.0	-1.2	44.6	389.4	10.2
4th quarter	76.0	38.4	-9.2	2.4	44.4	32.0	9.5	2.9	82.4	56.4	25.9	-0.9	38.0	382.4	8.3
1954															
1st quarter	78.9	41.2	-9.7	2.4	44.9	32.4	9.7	2.8	82.1	55.7	26.4	-0.5	37.2	384.6	8.8
2nd quarter	79.2	39.8	-8.4	2.1	45.7	32.8	10.0	3.0	81.4	55.4	25.9	0.3	35.7	385.6	8.7
3rd quarter	80.2	39.7	-7.6	1.8	46.3	33.2	10.2	3.0	83.7	59.0	24.7	-0.1	37.4	389.6	8.7
4th quarter	84.7	42.1	-6.3	1.9	47.0	33.5	10.4	3.0	86.6	62.1	24.5	0.9	39.6	399.2	9.4
1955															
1st quarter	89.9	43.7	-2.9	1.7	47.5	34.0	10.5	3.0	92.8	68.7	24.1	0.5	45.4	412.1	10.3
2nd quarter	95.4	45.8	-0.5	2.0	48.2	34.5	10.6	3.1	97.4	72.7	24.8	-0.2	49.3	422.1	11.2
3rd quarter	97.8	46.8	-0.7	2.5	49.3	35.3	10.8	3.2	99.0	74.7	24.3	0.8	49.7	430.7	11.3
4th quarter	102.3	47.2	1.9	2.6	50.6	36.2	11.1	3.3	103.2	78.9	24.3	0.4	52.5	438.3	11.8
1956															
1st quarter	105.6	48.3	2.3	2.9	52.1	37.3	11.4	3.5	103.9	78.3	25.6	0.9	51.7	443.4	12.1
2nd quarter	107.5	50.2	0.7	3.1	53.5	38.4	11.6	3.6	103.6	77.0	26.6	2.2	50.1	450.5	12.0
3rd quarter	111.6	52.5	1.2	3.1	54.8	39.3	11.8	3.7	106.0	78.3	27.8	3.0	51.2	456.7	12.4
4th quarter	113.4	53.1	1.4	2.9	56.0	40.2	12.0	3.8	105.8	77.1	28.7	4.5	49.8	466.1	12.3

. . . = Not available.

Table 5-1B. Saving and Investment: Historical Data—*Continued*

(Billions of dollars, except as noted; quarterly data are at seasonally adjusted annual rates.)   NIPA Tables 1.7.5, 5.1

Year and quarter	Gross saving Total	Net saving Private	Net saving Government Federal	Net saving Government State and local	Consumption of fixed capital Total	Consumption of fixed capital Private	Consumption of fixed capital Government Federal	Consumption of fixed capital Government State and local	Gross domestic investment Total	Gross domestic investment Private	Gross domestic investment Government	Net lending or net borrowing (-), NIPAs	Net domestic investment	Gross national income	Net saving as a percentage of gross national income
1957															
1st quarter	114.3	53.3	0.4	3.4	57.3	41.1	12.4	3.8	107.5	77.7	29.8	5.6	50.2	474.2	12.0
2nd quarter	114.4	54.7	-1.6	2.8	58.4	41.9	12.6	4.0	107.6	77.9	29.7	4.8	49.2	477.3	11.7
3rd quarter	114.2	53.8	-1.6	2.5	59.5	42.7	12.8	4.0	109.9	79.3	30.6	4.9	50.5	482.1	11.3
4th quarter	104.3	49.6	-7.7	1.9	60.4	43.4	13.1	4.0	101.9	71.0	30.8	3.6	41.4	476.2	9.2
1958															
1st quarter	100.1	48.2	-10.2	1.0	61.1	44.0	13.1	4.0	98.0	66.7	31.3	1.5	36.9	470.8	8.3
2nd quarter	96.8	48.9	-15.0	0.9	62.0	44.7	13.3	4.1	97.0	65.1	32.0	0.8	35.0	473.6	7.3
3rd quarter	105.0	53.6	-12.5	0.9	62.9	45.2	13.5	4.2	104.9	72.0	32.9	1.0	42.0	487.4	8.6
4th quarter	113.1	57.9	-10.6	1.9	63.8	45.7	13.8	4.2	114.3	80.0	34.3	-0.1	50.5	501.0	9.8
1959															
1st quarter	117.8	56.6	-4.6	1.3	64.5	46.2	14.0	4.3	119.4	83.2	36.2	-1.4	54.9	512.7	10.4
2nd quarter	124.9	59.7	-1.8	2.0	65.1	46.6	14.2	4.3	125.5	89.4	36.2	-2.9	60.4	527.5	11.3
3rd quarter	117.3	53.3	-4.3	2.5	65.8	47.0	14.4	4.3	119.7	83.6	36.1	0.0	54.0	525.4	9.8
4th quarter	120.3	56.2	-5.0	2.6	66.4	47.4	14.6	4.4	121.5	86.5	34.9	-0.8	55.1	531.2	10.1
1960															
1st quarter	132.9	58.6	4.7	2.6	67.0	47.7	14.9	4.4	131.6	96.5	35.1	1.9	64.6	545.1	12.1
2nd quarter	126.3	55.0	1.2	2.5	67.6	48.0	15.1	4.5	122.3	87.1	35.2	1.7	54.7	546.4	10.8
3rd quarter	127.1	56.8	-0.4	2.5	68.2	48.4	15.3	4.6	123.2	86.4	36.8	4.2	55.0	548.5	10.7
4th quarter	121.5	55.1	-4.9	2.5	68.8	48.7	15.5	4.6	112.8	76.0	36.9	4.9	44.0	547.3	9.6
1961															
1st quarter	124.6	57.8	-4.7	2.1	69.5	49.1	15.7	4.7	118.0	78.4	39.6	5.4	48.5	549.8	10.0
2nd quarter	127.0	61.3	-6.4	1.9	70.2	49.5	15.9	4.8	122.6	84.1	38.5	3.2	52.4	560.1	10.1
3rd quarter	134.6	66.1	-4.9	2.4	71.0	50.0	16.2	4.8	130.8	90.9	39.9	4.3	59.8	570.7	11.1
4th quarter	140.2	68.9	-2.9	2.5	71.8	50.5	16.4	4.9	134.5	92.9	41.6	3.9	62.8	586.0	11.7
1962															
1st quarter	141.6	71.5	-5.4	2.8	72.7	51.0	16.7	5.0	140.0	98.1	42.0	3.1	67.3	596.1	11.6
2nd quarter	142.0	71.3	-5.7	2.8	73.5	51.5	16.9	5.1	138.6	96.7	41.9	3.7	65.0	604.1	11.3
3rd quarter	144.4	71.4	-4.9	3.4	74.5	52.1	17.3	5.2	141.3	98.2	43.1	4.8	66.7	611.5	11.4
4th quarter	145.5	72.3	-5.5	3.2	75.6	52.6	17.7	5.3	138.4	95.0	43.5	3.6	62.8	620.5	11.3
1963															
1st quarter	149.1	73.1	-3.5	3.0	76.5	53.2	18.0	5.4	142.9	99.7	43.3	4.0	66.4	628.4	11.5
2nd quarter	153.8	74.3	-1.1	3.1	77.5	53.8	18.3	5.5	145.2	101.7	43.6	4.3	67.7	638.4	12.0
3rd quarter	154.7	74.3	-1.7	3.6	78.5	54.5	18.5	5.5	150.4	104.6	45.8	5.2	71.9	647.9	11.8
4th quarter	158.9	78.4	-2.4	3.4	79.5	55.2	18.7	5.7	152.3	107.2	45.1	6.3	72.8	658.9	12.1
1964															
1st quarter	161.9	82.8	-5.5	4.1	80.6	55.9	18.9	5.8	156.3	110.5	45.8	8.2	75.6	672.4	12.1
2nd quarter	163.0	87.6	-10.2	3.9	81.8	56.8	19.1	5.9	157.0	110.5	46.5	6.0	75.3	683.6	11.9
3rd quarter	166.4	86.2	-6.7	4.0	82.9	57.7	19.3	6.0	159.2	112.6	46.6	8.1	76.3	696.1	12.0
4th quarter	172.9	90.0	-5.1	3.7	84.2	58.7	19.5	6.1	161.7	115.0	46.7	7.6	77.5	705.6	12.6
1965															
1st quarter	180.8	92.6	-1.0	3.5	85.6	59.7	19.7	6.2	172.7	126.5	46.2	5.7	87.1	725.6	13.1
2nd quarter	182.7	93.9	-2.0	3.7	87.1	60.9	19.9	6.4	174.0	127.1	46.9	6.3	86.8	738.3	12.9
3rd quarter	183.3	100.2	-9.4	3.7	88.8	62.1	20.1	6.5	180.1	131.2	48.9	6.6	91.3	751.2	12.6
4th quarter	185.0	100.3	-9.6	3.8	90.5	63.5	20.4	6.6	183.2	133.8	49.5	6.1	92.7	772.2	12.2
1966															
1st quarter	194.3	101.4	-4.1	4.7	92.3	65.0	20.6	6.8	196.1	144.2	51.9	4.6	103.8	794.3	12.8
2nd quarter	194.9	101.2	-5.7	5.0	94.3	66.4	20.9	7.0	195.4	143.5	51.9	3.3	101.1	806.1	12.5
3rd quarter	195.3	102.0	-7.9	4.9	96.3	67.9	21.2	7.2	197.4	143.2	54.2	3.2	101.1	819.4	12.1
4th quarter	201.4	109.1	-10.3	4.3	98.3	69.4	21.5	7.4	202.1	145.9	56.2	4.1	103.8	833.8	12.4
1967															
1st quarter	197.6	112.0	-19.3	4.6	100.3	70.9	21.8	7.5	200.7	142.8	57.9	4.3	100.4	842.0	11.6
2nd quarter	194.0	108.2	-20.5	4.0	102.4	72.5	22.2	7.6	194.1	137.5	56.6	3.3	91.7	850.8	10.8
3rd quarter	201.9	112.6	-18.8	3.5	104.6	74.1	22.7	7.9	200.8	142.8	57.9	3.6	96.1	868.5	11.2
4th quarter	208.5	117.0	-19.5	4.0	107.0	75.8	23.1	8.1	206.0	147.7	58.3	2.8	99.0	886.7	11.4
1968															
1st quarter	207.0	111.0	-17.0	3.5	109.5	77.6	23.6	8.3	210.6	152.3	58.4	1.6	101.1	909.9	10.7
2nd quarter	213.6	116.0	-18.7	4.3	111.9	79.5	23.9	8.5	218.5	158.9	59.5	2.0	106.5	933.5	10.9
3rd quarter	215.5	107.8	-10.1	3.2	114.5	81.6	24.3	8.6	215.2	155.7	59.5	1.8	100.7	955.5	10.6
4th quarter	222.1	111.2	-9.3	2.8	117.5	83.7	24.8	8.9	220.3	160.8	59.6	0.7	102.9	975.5	10.7
1969															
1st quarter	231.0	105.5	2.2	2.8	120.5	86.1	25.2	9.2	233.9	172.4	61.5	1.7	113.4	995.1	11.1
2nd quarter	231.3	106.4	-1.6	3.0	123.5	88.3	25.6	9.5	232.4	172.7	59.7	0.5	108.9	1 013.6	10.6
3rd quarter	237.7	116.5	-8.7	3.6	126.3	90.6	26.0	9.8	237.5	177.6	59.9	1.7	111.2	1 034.4	10.8
4th quarter	232.5	112.7	-12.6	3.2	129.3	92.8	26.4	10.1	228.6	171.6	57.0	2.5	99.3	1 045.6	9.9
1970															
1st quarter	226.9	113.9	-22.3	3.0	132.2	94.9	27.0	10.4	227.1	168.1	59.0	3.9	94.9	1 053.4	9.0
2nd quarter	229.8	125.0	-32.7	2.3	135.3	97.1	27.4	10.8	230.3	171.5	58.8	5.0	95.0	1 068.5	8.8
3rd quarter	231.3	131.2	-39.6	1.4	138.3	99.4	27.9	11.1	234.1	173.9	60.2	3.7	95.8	1 086.1	8.6
4th quarter	224.9	129.0	-44.7	-0.9	141.5	101.7	28.3	11.5	227.9	166.8	61.1	2.2	86.3	1 089.5	7.7
1971															
1st quarter	238.7	141.4	-45.6	-1.8	144.6	104.1	28.7	11.8	247.5	189.5	58.1	4.5	102.9	1 129.3	8.3
2nd quarter	243.2	149.4	-52.5	-1.3	147.6	106.5	29.0	12.1	255.7	197.3	58.3	-0.2	108.1	1 152.0	8.3
3rd quarter	249.0	152.1	-51.8	-1.7	150.4	108.8	29.2	12.3	261.2	202.1	59.2	0.0	110.9	1 172.7	8.4
4th quarter	253.6	154.6	-53.7	-0.4	153.1	111.1	29.3	12.7	256.9	198.4	58.5	-3.1	103.8	1 197.8	8.4

Table 5-1B. Saving and Investment: Historical Data—*Continued*

(Billions of dollars, except as noted; quarterly data are at seasonally adjusted annual rates.)   **NIPA Tables 1.7.5, 5.1**

Year and quarter	Gross saving Total	Net saving Private	Net saving Government Federal	Net saving Government State and local	Consumption of fixed capital Total	Consumption of fixed capital Private	Consumption of fixed capital Government Federal	Consumption of fixed capital Government State and local	Gross domestic investment Total	Gross domestic investment Private	Gross domestic investment Government	Net lending or net borrowing (-), NIPAs	Net domestic investment	Gross national income	Net saving as a percentage of gross national income
1972															
1st quarter	263.0	152.4	-45.8	0.4	155.9	113.4	29.6	12.9	273.0	213.0	60.0	-5.1	117.0	1 233.8	8.7
2nd quarter	265.7	148.8	-51.1	9.1	159.0	116.0	29.9	13.1	287.7	226.8	60.9	-4.8	128.8	1 257.2	8.5
3rd quarter	279.8	157.8	-40.9	0.2	162.7	118.8	30.5	13.4	292.3	233.1	59.2	-3.6	129.6	1 290.6	9.1
4th quarter	302.1	179.3	-58.3	14.7	166.4	121.8	30.8	13.8	302.3	239.7	62.6	-2.8	135.9	1 340.5	10.1
1973															
1st quarter	316.0	177.1	-40.5	9.0	170.5	125.2	31.2	14.2	320.5	254.3	66.2	2.2	150.0	1 381.5	10.5
2nd quarter	324.8	184.4	-40.8	5.8	175.4	129.0	31.8	14.6	333.7	268.2	65.5	5.4	158.3	1 411.1	10.6
3rd quarter	339.0	190.7	-37.3	4.4	181.2	133.4	32.8	15.0	329.0	264.3	64.6	12.4	147.7	1 445.2	10.9
4th quarter	361.4	205.2	-34.5	3.1	187.6	138.3	33.7	15.6	347.1	280.9	66.2	15.3	159.5	1 489.5	11.7
1974															
1st quarter	355.8	196.7	-36.1	0.9	194.3	143.8	34.0	16.5	339.3	268.4	71.0	16.5	145.0	1 508.2	10.7
2nd quarter	346.4	183.1	-38.1	-0.7	202.1	149.7	34.6	17.8	353.4	277.4	76.0	2.6	151.3	1 536.8	9.4
3rd quarter	345.9	173.6	-37.0	-1.9	211.2	156.1	36.0	19.1	349.2	271.0	78.2	0.3	138.0	1 571.7	8.6
4th quarter	348.7	190.5	-54.2	-7.6	220.0	163.0	36.9	20.0	360.8	281.3	79.5	4.4	140.9	1 596.5	8.1
1975															
1st quarter	329.8	189.7	-76.2	-12.3	228.7	170.3	37.8	20.6	327.3	244.3	83.0	17.8	98.6	1 612.1	6.3
2nd quarter	330.0	237.9	-132.9	-10.8	235.8	176.6	38.3	20.9	322.4	243.3	79.2	21.4	86.7	1 649.6	5.7
3rd quarter	360.1	218.6	-90.9	-9.7	242.1	182.0	39.1	21.1	350.7	265.2	85.5	18.3	108.6	1 713.8	6.9
4th quarter	372.6	226.9	-91.7	-10.0	247.4	186.3	39.8	21.4	366.1	276.2	89.9	21.6	118.7	1 762.7	7.1
1976															
1st quarter	392.0	228.6	-81.9	-6.6	251.9	189.6	40.7	21.7	397.5	304.6	92.9	13.1	145.6	1 817.5	7.7
2nd quarter	399.3	224.7	-76.8	-5.3	256.7	193.7	41.1	22.0	411.3	322.3	89.0	8.9	154.6	1 848.0	7.7
3rd quarter	402.1	225.3	-80.8	-5.2	262.7	198.6	42.0	22.1	417.0	328.3	88.7	2.4	154.3	1 886.3	7.4
4th quarter	403.8	219.1	-84.2	-0.7	269.6	204.2	42.9	22.4	425.6	337.7	88.0	3.8	156.1	1 926.5	7.0
1977															
1st quarter	416.0	214.5	-73.5	-2.5	277.5	210.7	44.0	22.8	451.7	360.3	91.4	-8.1	174.2	1 981.7	7.0
2nd quarter	454.4	237.0	-67.6	-0.7	285.7	217.5	45.0	23.2	483.9	389.7	94.2	-8.9	198.3	2 056.0	8.2
3rd quarter	479.3	257.7	-75.1	2.9	293.8	224.5	45.6	23.6	507.8	414.1	93.6	-7.9	214.0	2 118.8	8.8
4th quarter	488.0	260.9	-77.7	2.4	302.4	231.8	46.5	24.0	515.7	422.3	93.4	-19.0	213.3	2 174.3	8.5
1978															
1st quarter	500.5	266.8	-81.6	3.7	311.6	239.4	47.7	24.5	528.3	434.8	93.5	-25.1	216.7	2 222.1	8.5
2nd quarter	540.6	271.3	-62.3	9.6	322.0	247.5	49.4	25.1	575.5	470.6	105.0	-12.9	253.5	2 328.3	9.4
3rd quarter	561.5	283.5	-56.0	2.0	332.0	256.2	50.1	25.7	602.0	492.4	109.7	-11.5	270.1	2 386.7	9.6
4th quarter	589.4	290.3	-48.3	4.1	343.2	265.4	51.4	26.3	629.9	515.8	114.1	-1.4	286.7	2 462.3	10.0
1979															
1st quarter	608.8	299.2	-45.1	-0.1	354.8	275.2	52.5	27.1	635.5	525.8	109.7	-1.9	280.8	2 527.4	10.1
2nd quarter	612.5	289.4	-42.6	-1.6	367.2	285.3	53.9	28.0	656.2	539.3	116.9	-2.8	289.0	2 579.7	9.5
3rd quarter	615.0	283.5	-48.5	-0.3	380.3	295.8	55.5	29.0	671.0	545.6	125.4	2.3	290.7	2 645.2	8.9
4th quarter	617.8	280.8	-53.3	-2.9	393.2	306.6	56.6	30.1	676.2	547.9	128.4	-2.7	283.0	2 704.5	8.3
1980															
1st quarter	611.5	274.4	-66.2	-3.5	406.8	317.7	57.9	31.2	690.3	554.6	135.7	-10.8	283.5	2 759.7	7.4
2nd quarter	607.9	289.2	-93.3	-9.0	421.0	329.0	59.6	32.4	654.0	519.3	134.7	9.7	233.0	2 777.2	6.7
3rd quarter	624.8	300.8	-104.1	-7.3	435.4	340.7	61.0	33.7	629.4	495.1	134.4	28.0	194.1	2 858.1	6.6
4th quarter	676.3	321.1	-91.5	-3.9	450.6	352.5	63.1	35.0	690.5	551.5	139.0	6.6	239.9	2 993.2	7.5
1981															
1st quarter	707.9	321.1	-74.3	-4.5	465.5	364.7	64.7	36.2	765.8	619.4	146.4	1.5	300.2	3 096.0	7.8
2nd quarter	719.4	326.9	-78.7	-9.2	480.4	376.4	66.7	37.3	755.1	609.8	145.3	0.1	274.7	3 156.7	7.6
3rd quarter	775.7	378.4	-86.8	-10.5	494.5	387.8	68.4	38.3	798.0	652.3	145.7	7.0	303.5	3 263.9	8.6
4th quarter	772.5	393.0	-112.4	-16.5	508.4	398.8	70.4	39.3	795.4	643.4	152.0	4.5	287.0	3 291.0	8.0
1982															
1st quarter	736.9	371.6	-136.7	-20.0	521.9	409.4	72.5	40.1	738.6	588.3	150.2	0.5	216.6	3 308.0	6.5
2nd quarter	762.0	392.9	-143.3	-21.5	533.9	418.0	74.9	41.0	750.0	593.6	156.4	17.3	216.1	3 367.5	6.8
3rd quarter	730.6	390.9	-179.3	-23.7	542.7	424.7	76.4	41.7	750.4	593.0	157.4	-14.1	207.6	3 395.7	5.5
4th quarter	673.7	360.5	-210.2	-25.9	549.3	429.5	77.8	42.0	713.0	549.2	163.8	-17.4	163.7	3 414.7	3.6
1983															
1st quarter	691.6	377.7	-208.6	-29.8	552.3	432.3	77.7	42.3	730.2	565.5	164.7	-8.0	177.9	3 476.7	4.0
2nd quarter	700.9	365.3	-203.2	-20.2	559.1	436.0	80.5	42.5	780.8	613.8	167.1	-27.7	221.8	3 563.3	4.0
3rd quarter	703.1	370.5	-219.8	-13.7	566.2	440.6	82.7	42.8	826.8	652.3	174.5	-48.0	260.6	3 651.3	3.8
4th quarter	771.1	405.3	-197.1	-10.1	572.9	446.2	83.6	43.1	896.9	718.5	178.4	-56.9	324.0	3 765.3	5.3
1984															
1st quarter	854.4	455.9	-182.3	-1.5	582.2	452.6	86.1	43.5	975.0	790.9	184.1	-78.6	392.7	3 903.1	7.0
2nd quarter	873.6	470.4	-191.0	2.7	591.5	459.5	87.9	44.0	1 008.4	818.9	189.5	-88.0	416.9	4 000.3	7.1
3rd quarter	898.1	497.5	-199.6	-3.0	603.2	467.0	91.6	44.6	1 032.6	838.9	193.8	-90.5	429.4	4 077.5	7.2
4th quarter	900.3	495.7	-213.1	1.0	616.7	474.9	96.7	45.0	1 037.1	831.7	205.4	-103.5	420.5	4 148.3	6.8
1985															
1st quarter	889.6	436.4	-171.0	0.6	623.6	483.4	94.5	45.8	1 018.1	809.9	208.3	-89.5	394.5	4 216.8	6.3
2nd quarter	887.3	474.9	-221.4	-0.7	634.6	492.0	96.2	46.4	1 045.4	827.0	218.4	-111.5	410.9	4 275.8	5.9
3rd quarter	865.9	424.7	-200.6	-3.3	645.2	500.7	97.4	47.1	1 048.4	822.2	226.3	-121.4	403.2	4 348.0	5.1
4th quarter	880.9	433.9	-203.9	-6.2	657.2	509.6	99.7	47.8	1 086.1	859.5	226.6	-135.3	428.9	4 399.7	5.1
1986															
1st quarter	895.5	432.0	-206.5	1.8	668.2	518.6	100.9	48.6	1 092.5	863.5	229.0	-128.4	424.3	4 461.4	5.1
2nd quarter	871.0	423.9	-228.0	-4.8	679.9	527.4	102.9	49.6	1 089.7	855.2	234.4	-142.0	409.8	4 484.0	4.3
3rd quarter	838.6	382.5	-232.3	-2.4	691.0	536.0	104.4	50.6	1 081.5	835.8	245.7	-150.3	390.6	4 533.2	3.3
4th quarter	852.8	358.1	-196.9	-10.4	702.1	544.3	106.1	51.7	1 085.3	842.1	243.2	-150.4	383.2	4 587.5	3.3

Table 5-1B. Saving and Investment: Historical Data—*Continued*

(Billions of dollars, except as noted; quarterly data are at seasonally adjusted annual rates.)   NIPA Tables 1.7.5, 5.1

Year and quarter	Gross saving Total	Net saving Private	Net saving Government Federal	Net saving Government State and local	Consumption of fixed capital Total	Consumption of fixed capital Private	Consumption of fixed capital Government Federal	Consumption of fixed capital Government State and local	Gross domestic investment Total	Gross domestic investment Private	Gross domestic investment Government	Net lending or net borrowing (-), NIPAs	Net domestic investment	Gross national income	Net saving as a percentage of gross national income
1987															
1st quarter	897.9	401.3	-197.6	-18.4	712.6	552.3	107.7	52.6	1 118.8	871.2	247.7	-151.1	406.2	4 666.5	4.0
2nd quarter	926.6	353.4	-144.0	-6.6	723.8	561.2	109.1	53.5	1 128.0	874.6	253.5	-154.5	404.3	4 777.3	4.2
3rd quarter	961.2	396.1	-155.6	-15.4	736.1	570.7	110.9	54.5	1 134.8	876.5	258.3	-154.2	398.7	4 882.7	4.6
4th quarter	1 009.8	443.6	-165.8	-17.1	749.1	581.0	112.8	55.3	1 205.6	946.5	259.1	-157.2	456.5	4 989.0	5.2
1988															
1st quarter	1 029.9	446.1	-166.6	-13.4	763.8	591.9	115.6	56.3	1 162.1	908.6	253.5	-127.0	398.3	5 093.1	5.2
2nd quarter	1 069.0	465.1	-158.7	-15.1	777.7	602.6	117.9	57.2	1 192.7	934.5	258.2	-110.1	415.0	5 199.1	5.6
3rd quarter	1 096.4	465.8	-153.3	-7.5	791.4	613.3	119.9	58.1	1 200.1	942.0	258.1	-106.6	408.7	5 305.7	5.7
4th quarter	1 111.3	476.6	-161.3	-9.1	805.1	623.9	122.2	59.1	1 226.5	962.7	263.8	-119.7	421.4	5 426.5	5.6
1989															
1st quarter	1 145.0	475.4	-140.1	-8.7	818.4	634.4	124.0	60.1	1 269.3	1 005.5	263.8	-106.8	450.9	5 516.1	5.9
2nd quarter	1 104.7	447.4	-161.5	-12.9	831.7	644.7	125.8	61.2	1 268.3	1 001.0	267.2	-93.7	436.6	5 564.1	4.9
3rd quarter	1 100.5	440.3	-165.6	-19.1	844.9	654.8	127.8	62.3	1 271.5	996.5	275.0	-81.8	426.6	5 630.3	4.5
4th quarter	1 089.0	437.8	-170.3	-36.6	858.0	664.6	129.9	63.5	1 271.5	995.8	275.6	-88.5	413.4	5 683.0	4.1
1990															
1st quarter	1 102.7	456.3	-198.6	-24.9	870.0	674.3	131.0	64.7	1 297.7	1 010.8	286.8	-90.9	427.7	5 797.3	4.0
2nd quarter	1 134.9	493.1	-208.0	-32.4	882.2	683.8	132.4	66.0	1 303.0	1 014.7	288.3	-73.0	420.8	5 896.4	4.3
3rd quarter	1 105.6	448.6	-199.6	-38.4	895.0	693.1	134.4	67.4	1 292.4	1 000.8	291.6	-82.5	397.3	5 937.9	3.5
4th quarter	1 110.2	459.5	-206.9	-49.3	906.9	702.3	136.1	68.4	1 242.2	947.5	294.7	-82.7	335.3	5 977.5	3.4
1991															
1st quarter	1 199.7	521.6	-185.8	-55.0	919.0	711.4	138.2	69.4	1 215.7	924.6	291.1	42.1	296.7	6 012.1	4.7
2nd quarter	1 144.5	520.7	-244.6	-60.4	928.9	719.0	139.5	70.5	1 222.6	926.5	296.0	14.2	293.6	6 062.6	3.6
3rd quarter	1 122.7	516.5	-273.3	-58.3	937.8	725.3	141.1	71.4	1 243.5	947.5	296.0	-29.0	305.7	6 123.3	3.0
4th quarter	1 146.4	559.1	-290.0	-66.6	943.9	730.2	141.6	72.1	1 272.0	978.8	293.2	-17.0	328.1	6 189.0	3.3
1992															
1st quarter	1 156.0	598.7	-325.6	-65.2	948.2	733.7	141.8	72.7	1 256.3	956.8	299.5	-22.0	308.2	6 317.3	3.3
2nd quarter	1 175.0	617.7	-328.7	-69.2	955.2	738.8	142.7	73.7	1 310.2	1 013.1	297.1	-39.8	355.0	6 407.0	3.4
3rd quarter	1 125.4	582.3	-344.2	-76.0	963.4	745.4	143.4	74.5	1 318.3	1 024.2	294.1	-46.8	354.9	6 455.7	2.5
4th quarter	1 134.0	572.7	-339.5	-73.4	974.3	753.6	145.1	75.5	1 351.7	1 058.0	293.7	-68.6	377.4	6 561.9	2.4
1993															
1st quarter	1 131.0	564.3	-337.5	-82.0	986.2	763.4	146.1	76.8	1 372.3	1 083.8	288.5	-60.0	386.2	6 582.6	2.2
2nd quarter	1 168.0	555.1	-308.8	-75.8	997.5	773.2	146.5	77.9	1 387.7	1 094.5	293.2	-74.7	390.1	6 694.4	2.5
3rd quarter	1 143.8	528.8	-318.9	-74.8	1 008.7	783.1	146.9	78.7	1 386.5	1 095.9	290.7	-77.9	377.8	6 752.9	2.0
4th quarter	1 210.9	535.4	-289.0	-57.1	1 021.6	793.2	148.7	79.7	1 448.3	1 153.1	295.2	-108.5	426.7	6 905.2	2.7
1994															
1st quarter	1 232.5	534.6	-269.1	-66.3	1 033.3	803.3	149.0	81.0	1 485.4	1 201.7	283.7	-93.1	452.1	6 983.1	2.9
2nd quarter	1 297.0	554.7	-238.6	-66.1	1 047.0	815.0	149.9	82.0	1 555.2	1 264.9	290.3	-112.8	508.3	7 120.7	3.5
3rd quarter	1 305.9	557.5	-256.8	-57.1	1 062.3	828.4	150.5	83.4	1 553.8	1 251.7	302.1	-122.8	491.5	7 226.2	3.4
4th quarter	1 345.0	589.4	-258.0	-66.3	1 079.9	843.3	151.9	84.7	1 608.2	1 307.6	300.6	-138.8	528.3	7 351.0	3.6
1995															
1st quarter	1 394.2	616.4	-254.4	-66.9	1 099.2	859.8	153.1	86.2	1 634.6	1 327.6	307.0	-119.5	535.4	7 431.0	4.0
2nd quarter	1 394.1	604.2	-243.0	-82.9	1 115.8	874.8	153.4	87.6	1 614.4	1 304.0	310.4	-119.1	498.6	7 512.7	3.7
3rd quarter	1 437.0	624.6	-247.0	-71.3	1 130.8	888.2	153.8	88.8	1 610.4	1 303.2	307.1	-101.8	479.6	7 628.4	4.0
4th quarter	1 479.9	620.6	-224.0	-60.6	1 143.9	900.1	153.8	90.0	1 641.4	1 335.1	306.3	-84.8	497.5	7 726.6	4.3
1996															
1st quarter	1 520.1	645.9	-224.8	-56.6	1 155.6	910.4	154.0	91.1	1 672.2	1 355.4	316.8	-103.1	516.6	7 856.6	4.6
2nd quarter	1 559.9	630.4	-180.2	-57.9	1 167.6	922.0	153.6	91.9	1 736.1	1 418.4	317.8	-109.5	568.6	7 995.0	4.9
3rd quarter	1 596.2	636.8	-170.6	-51.9	1 181.9	934.9	153.9	93.0	1 795.4	1 474.4	321.0	-133.7	613.5	8 091.5	5.1
4th quarter	1 639.4	633.9	-141.9	-48.8	1 196.2	949.0	153.1	94.1	1 804.4	1 480.1	324.2	-114.5	608.2	8 240.5	5.4
1997															
1st quarter	1 696.4	652.3	-121.5	-47.8	1 213.3	964.4	153.6	95.3	1 841.7	1 522.4	319.3	-132.2	628.4	8 372.4	5.8
2nd quarter	1 767.8	686.5	-104.0	-45.9	1 231.2	979.9	154.6	96.7	1 914.2	1 590.2	324.0	-102.5	683.0	8 505.0	6.3
3rd quarter	1 818.3	676.4	-68.5	-37.4	1 247.8	995.5	154.5	97.8	1 956.7	1 625.3	331.5	-123.5	708.9	8 670.3	6.6
4th quarter	1 839.6	685.3	-73.8	-36.8	1 265.0	1 011.2	154.6	99.2	1 976.2	1 644.5	331.7	-164.1	711.2	8 809.4	6.5
1998															
1st quarter	1 910.1	683.9	-24.5	-30.7	1 281.3	1 027.0	154.2	100.2	2 043.6	1 712.3	331.2	-165.1	762.2	8 923.2	7.0
2nd quarter	1 915.7	660.1	-10.4	-34.1	1 300.0	1 043.3	155.5	101.2	2 036.8	1 695.8	341.1	-196.3	736.8	9 067.1	6.8
3rd quarter	1 958.0	650.8	19.9	-31.5	1 318.6	1 060.4	155.6	102.8	2 095.8	1 741.6	354.2	-224.9	777.0	9 217.4	6.9
4th quarter	1 938.5	603.3	20.6	-24.2	1 338.8	1 078.0	156.4	104.4	2 146.5	1 797.0	349.5	-236.0	807.7	9 334.1	6.4
1999															
1st quarter	2 046.3	674.9	48.0	-35.3	1 358.7	1 096.3	156.6	105.9	2 210.1	1 853.1	357.1	-235.6	851.4	9 508.0	7.2
2nd quarter	1 988.2	580.9	68.2	-44.2	1 383.2	1 117.9	157.5	107.7	2 210.9	1 848.3	362.5	-263.9	827.6	9 596.7	6.3
3rd quarter	1 979.9	537.0	71.7	-39.6	1 410.7	1 143.1	158.3	109.3	2 263.8	1 893.7	370.0	-295.0	853.1	9 724.7	5.9
4th quarter	2 014.5	519.3	88.6	-36.6	1 443.2	1 171.6	160.2	111.4	2 337.4	1 953.1	384.3	-338.8	894.2	9 932.1	5.8
2000															
1st quarter	2 123.9	496.3	175.5	-26.9	1 479.0	1 203.5	162.0	113.4	2 339.8	1 950.7	389.2	-372.9	860.8	10 189.8	6.3
2nd quarter	2 122.2	495.8	147.6	-27.4	1 506.1	1 227.5	162.8	115.8	2 461.6	2 075.8	385.8	-381.3	955.5	10 323.5	6.0
3rd quarter	2 151.8	513.9	157.7	-44.7	1 525.0	1 243.5	163.7	117.7	2 446.2	2 060.0	386.2	-420.4	921.2	10 471.1	6.0
4th quarter	2 100.6	471.3	158.0	-63.6	1 534.8	1 251.5	163.9	119.5	2 461.5	2 067.2	394.2	-431.1	926.6	10 550.3	5.4
2001															
1st quarter	2 162.6	547.5	128.4	-79.8	1 566.4	1 281.2	164.0	121.2	2 372.7	1 971.3	400.9	-424.2	805.8	10 724.3	5.6
2nd quarter	2 142.6	560.5	94.8	-106.7	1 594.0	1 307.1	164.3	122.7	2 392.0	1 973.0	418.9	-379.8	797.9	10 777.2	5.1
3rd quarter	2 049.6	697.2	-130.0	-129.2	1 611.6	1 322.8	164.8	124.0	2 348.4	1 944.9	403.5	-361.0	736.8	10 736.4	4.1
4th quarter	1 921.5	488.8	-33.0	-160.3	1 626.0	1 335.7	164.8	125.5	2 274.3	1 850.1	424.3	-353.0	648.4	10 746.3	2.7

Table 5-1B. Saving and Investment: Historical Data—Continued

(Billions of dollars, except as noted; quarterly data are at seasonally adjusted annual rates.)   **NIPA Tables 1.7.5, 5.1**

Year and quarter	Gross saving								Gross domestic investment and net lending, NIPAs				Net domestic invest- ment	Gross national income	Net saving as a percent- age of gross national income
		Net saving			Consumption of fixed capital				Gross domestic investment			Net lending or net borrow- ing (-), NIPAs			
			Government				Government								
	Total	Private	Federal	State and local	Total	Private	Federal	State and local	Total	Private	Govern- ment				
2002															
1st quarter	1 983.5	738.6	-225.8	-165.6	1 636.3	1 343.8	165.5	127.1	2 347.4	1 912.7	434.7	-413.4	711.1	10 873.7	3.2
2nd quarter	1 991.1	789.4	-262.2	-185.1	1 648.9	1 354.0	166.2	128.7	2 371.7	1 933.3	438.4	-458.2	722.9	10 994.2	3.1
3rd quarter	1 981.4	777.8	-278.7	-183.0	1 665.2	1 367.8	167.2	130.1	2 380.3	1 933.2	447.1	-463.5	715.0	11 090.3	2.9
4th quarter	2 027.9	848.8	-304.6	-197.8	1 681.5	1 381.7	168.4	131.4	2 397.0	1 942.5	454.5	-503.4	715.5	11 250.7	3.1
2003															
1st quarter	1 938.2	786.0	-330.4	-212.8	1 695.5	1 392.7	169.7	133.0	2 417.3	1 960.2	457.1	-554.3	721.9	11 285.0	2.2
2nd quarter	1 965.0	839.9	-387.3	-196.1	1 708.5	1 403.1	171.2	134.2	2 430.7	1 972.4	458.3	-538.0	722.2	11 429.5	2.2
3rd quarter	1 981.0	891.5	-469.4	-167.2	1 726.1	1 417.5	173.0	135.5	2 513.4	2 044.3	469.1	-536.6	787.3	11 615.4	2.2
4th quarter	2 050.0	855.2	-402.4	-149.1	1 746.3	1 434.4	175.1	136.8	2 603.7	2 131.3	472.4	-516.9	857.4	11 809.5	2.6
2004															
1st quarter	2 069.1	881.8	-429.0	-157.8	1 774.1	1 458.2	177.3	138.5	2 628.4	2 154.1	474.3	-560.7	854.3	12 011.1	2.5
2nd quarter	2 153.4	910.2	-396.9	-163.4	1 803.5	1 482.3	179.4	141.8	2 745.9	2 262.6	483.3	-629.2	942.4	12 217.7	2.9
3rd quarter	2 225.0	905.9	-366.0	-150.7	1 835.8	1 508.4	181.2	146.2	2 808.4	2 318.3	490.1	-642.4	972.6	12 452.8	3.1
4th quarter	2 166.2	798.4	-382.1	-124.0	1 873.9	1 539.5	184.0	150.4	2 887.2	2 390.1	497.1	-737.1	1 013.3	12 589.0	2.3
2005															
1st quarter	2 276.0	773.0	-305.2	-103.3	1 911.5	1 572.4	186.7	152.5	2 987.6	2 486.1	501.6	-713.5	1 076.1	12 831.5	2.8
2nd quarter	2 301.7	766.6	-306.7	-106.7	1 948.5	1 603.4	189.1	156.0	2 986.7	2 476.5	510.2	-730.2	1 038.2	13 034.2	2.7
3rd quarter	2 328.0	745.8	-300.6	-107.1	1 989.9	1 638.1	191.7	160.1	3 048.4	2 531.1	517.3	-703.0	1 058.6	13 259.9	2.5
4th quarter	2 491.7	814.1	-262.5	-94.1	2 034.2	1 676.6	194.7	163.0	3 169.3	2 645.3	524.0	-855.2	1 135.1	13 540.5	3.4
2006															
1st quarter	2 640.2	880.8	-245.3	-66.0	2 070.7	1 708.4	197.4	164.9	3 249.4	2 709.7	539.7	-812.1	1 178.7	13 847.5	4.1
2nd quarter	2 646.4	835.6	-230.6	-65.9	2 107.2	1 737.9	200.0	169.3	3 261.1	2 709.3	551.8	-836.4	1 153.8	14 016.9	3.8
3rd quarter	2 632.6	798.4	-212.9	-93.8	2 140.9	1 765.7	202.7	172.5	3 259.5	2 709.4	550.1	-881.8	1 118.6	14 155.6	3.5
4th quarter	2 628.3	764.1	-199.1	-114.4	2 177.7	1 795.2	205.1	177.4	3 237.4	2 675.4	562.0	-777.8	1 059.7	14 245.5	3.2
2007															
1st quarter	2 553.1	659.2	-209.8	-111.2	2 214.9	1 823.9	208.4	182.6	3 238.6	2 664.3	574.3	-818.1	1 023.7	14 378.6	2.4
2nd quarter	2 610.4	703.8	-231.0	-103.8	2 241.3	1 844.2	211.2	185.9	3 288.9	2 699.2	589.6	-780.3	1 047.5	14 563.5	2.5
3rd quarter	2 465.6	619.0	-279.0	-139.4	2 265.0	1 861.7	214.3	189.0	3 281.9	2 686.0	596.0	-713.0	1 016.9	14 574.3	1.4
4th quarter	2 388.5	580.2	-318.9	-162.8	2 290.0	1 880.2	217.3	192.6	3 250.8	2 642.6	608.2	-677.5	960.8	14 684.0	0.7
2008															
1st quarter	2 301.5	554.3	-404.6	-168.2	2 319.9	1 903.0	221.0	196.0	3 175.3	2 563.7	611.6	-747.4	855.4	14 719.1	-0.1
2nd quarter	2 184.7	780.4	-776.4	-166.5	2 347.3	1 923.9	224.5	198.9	3 168.2	2 540.6	627.6	-735.2	820.9	14 771.0	-1.1
3rd quarter	2 223.3	714.2	-619.5	-247.4	2 376.0	1 945.7	227.7	202.6	3 136.0	2 498.2	637.7	-698.8	759.9	14 882.0	-1.0
4th quarter	2 114.5	723.0	-699.2	-301.4	2 392.1	1 954.7	230.3	207.1	2 949.3	2 307.9	641.4	-638.6	557.2	14 500.3	-1.9
2009															
1st quarter	1 976.2	1 020.9	-1 100.3	-331.1	2 386.7	1 946.0	231.3	209.3	2 654.9	2 014.9	640.0	-407.4	268.3	14 276.0	-2.9
2nd quarter	1 954.4	1 220.8	-1 300.8	-335.0	2 369.5	1 927.9	232.5	209.0	2 510.2	1 863.7	646.5	-364.1	140.7	14 302.7	-2.9
3rd quarter	1 924.0	1 228.2	-1 307.4	-355.8	2 359.1	1 916.4	234.0	208.7	2 486.4	1 841.4	644.9	-372.5	127.3	14 435.6	-3.0
4th quarter	2 095.1	1 331.9	-1 264.1	-343.5	2 370.7	1 924.5	236.7	209.5	2 638.8	1 998.7	640.1	-413.6	268.1	14 690.7	-1.9
2010															
1st quarter	2 124.1	1 426.7	-1 344.4	-333.7	2 375.6	1 925.3	239.3	211.0	2 671.3	2 038.2	633.2	-434.7	295.8	14 843.2	-1.7
2nd quarter	2 225.1	1 500.9	-1 325.0	-333.8	2 383.1	1 927.8	242.5	212.7	2 796.8	2 148.8	648.0	-449.0	413.7	15 059.5	-1.0
3rd quarter	2 395.7	1 602.4	-1 309.1	-290.1	2 392.6	1 933.5	244.9	214.2	2 885.9	2 236.5	649.4	-477.9	493.3	15 322.2	0.0
4th quarter	2 405.7	1 560.3	-1 294.8	-272.3	2 412.5	1 948.5	248.2	215.8	2 885.8	2 238.4	647.4	-427.2	473.4	15 463.4	0.0
2011															
1st quarter	2 361.5	1 448.7	-1 244.4	-279.1	2 436.4	1 966.7	251.8	217.9	2 845.3	2 206.0	639.4	-483.9	408.9	15 567.2	-0.5
2nd quarter	2 457.2	1 526.3	-1 274.4	-256.8	2 462.2	1 987.2	254.2	220.7	2 933.6	2 297.4	636.3	-494.8	471.4	15 781.5	0.0
3rd quarter	2 563.6	1 581.7	-1 218.5	-287.6	2 487.9	2 007.7	256.4	223.8	2 958.0	2 322.8	635.1	-443.0	470.0	15 935.5	0.5
4th quarter	2 702.3	1 667.0	-1 199.3	-276.8	2 511.4	2 027.6	257.3	226.5	3 139.8	2 504.1	635.7	-457.6	628.5	16 115.7	1.2
2012															
1st quarter	2 948.1	1 801.5	-1 110.4	-279.6	2 536.5	2 047.9	259.7	228.9	3 194.6	2 567.8	626.8	-475.8	658.1	16 535.8	2.5
2nd quarter	3 028.5	1 838.6	-1 093.1	-281.5	2 564.4	2 071.8	261.2	231.4	3 264.0	2 636.9	627.1	-453.3	699.5	16 645.5	2.8
3rd quarter	2 924.4	1 707.6	-1 086.7	-287.5	2 591.0	2 095.2	262.6	233.2	3 263.5	2 644.1	619.4	-404.4	672.5	16 607.5	2.0
4th quarter	3 130.0	1 801.1	-1 000.5	-282.7	2 612.0	2 114.6	263.0	234.4	3 249.0	2 638.3	610.8	-360.2	637.0	16 913.7	3.1
2013															
1st quarter	3 069.0	1 469.6	-774.0	-261.6	2 635.0	2 135.5	263.6	235.9	3 336.9	2 738.2	598.7	-389.1	701.9	16 959.1	2.6
2nd quarter	3 196.4	1 307.8	-528.5	-247.1	2 664.2	2 161.3	265.1	237.7	3 373.7	2 775.3	598.5	-385.6	709.5	17 128.9	3.1
3rd quarter	3 208.6	1 490.6	-699.2	-277.0	2 694.2	2 188.4	266.2	239.6	3 483.2	2 880.0	603.2	-359.6	789.0	17 230.3	3.0
4th quarter	3 282.7	1 352.3	-525.3	-275.6	2 731.4	2 221.0	268.5	241.9	3 511.8	2 910.5	601.3	-301.9	780.4	17 435.0	3.2
2014															
1st quarter	3 330.0	1 371.7	-558.9	-253.5	2 770.8	2 257.1	269.8	243.9	3 488.0	2 899.2	588.7	-382.5	717.2	17 596.6	3.2
2nd quarter	3 533.6	1 543.1	-582.4	-224.4	2 797.3	2 281.9	269.9	245.6	3 633.1	3 030.4	602.7	-351.8	835.8	17 938.0	4.1
3rd quarter	3 607.1	1 638.3	-631.3	-232.8	2 832.9	2 315.1	270.4	247.4	3 714.1	3 107.6	606.5	-362.3	881.2	18 245.3	4.2
4th quarter	3 640.3	1 638.9	-616.8	-240.9	2 859.1	2 339.9	270.7	248.5	3 751.8	3 139.5	612.3	-435.5	892.7	18 392.5	4.2
2015															
1st quarter	3 717.0	1 632.4	-582.5	-225.7	2 892.8	2 371.8	271.8	249.2	3 853.0	3 245.1	608.0	-431.6	960.3	18 497.4	4.5
2nd quarter	3 711.7	1 587.3	-546.9	-231.7	2 903.0	2 380.7	271.3	251.0	3 872.2	3 245.8	626.4	-409.9	969.2	18 649.9	4.3
3rd quarter	3 630.9	1 528.5	-568.3	-249.5	2 920.2	2 396.0	271.8	252.5	3 882.2	3 251.7	630.5	-468.0	961.9	18 728.0	3.8
4th quarter	3 618.6	1 388.5	-543.2	-156.2	2 929.5	2 405.5	271.1	253.0	3 831.6	3 206.1	625.5	-422.6	902.1	18 768.4	3.7
2016															
1st quarter	3 588.7	1 534.4	-642.5	-243.2	2 940.0	2 417.9	269.0	253.1	3 814.3	3 174.4	639.9	-439.5	874.3	18 845.1	3.4
2nd quarter	3 475.0	1 415.6	-653.4	-262.2	2 975.0	2 448.7	270.3	256.0	3 815.7	3 178.5	637.2	-403.6	840.7	18 886.1	2.6
3rd quarter	3 486.9	1 412.5	-682.1	-243.2	2 999.8	2 471.5	271.1	257.2	3 822.8	3 185.7	637.0	-401.9	823.0	19 056.0	2.6
4th quarter	3 588.3	1 477.3	-692.4	-230.1	3 033.5	2 501.6	272.6	259.3	3 927.1	3 281.5	645.6	-397.7	893.6	19 294.7	2.9
2017															
1st quarter	3 700.5	1 562.2	-683.8	-243.5	3 065.5	2 530.1	273.4	262.1	3 940.4	3 283.5	656.9	-366.7	874.9	19 545.4	3.2
2nd quarter	3 746.0	1 622.6	-708.0	-271.6	3 103.0	2 563.4	275.0	264.5	4 022.1	3 357.4	664.8	-442.0	919.2	19 742.7	3.3
3rd quarter	3 850.3	1 678.7	-729.4	-236.3	3 137.3	2 593.0	276.6	267.8	4 080.1	3 413.3	666.8	-384.2	942.7	19 978.9	3.6
4th quarter	3 886.3	1 651.9	-761.5	-170.9	3 166.8	2 617.9	278.6	270.4	4 156.4	3 471.4	685.0	-362.7	989.6	20 305.3	3.5

Table 5-2. Gross Private Fixed Investment by Type

(Billions of dollars, quarterly data are at seasonally adjusted annual rates.)   NIPA Table 5.3.5

Year and quarter	Total gross private fixed investment	Nonresidential Total	Structures Total	Commercial and health care	Manufacturing	Power and communication	Mining exploration, shafts, and wells	Other nonresidential structures	Equipment Total	Information processing equipment Total	Computers and peripheral equipment	Other information processing	Industrial equipment
1960	83.2	56.4	19.6	4.8	2.9	4.4	2.3	5.2	29.7	4.7	0.2	4.6	9.4
1961	83.6	56.6	19.7	5.5	2.8	4.1	2.3	5.0	28.9	5.1	0.3	4.8	8.8
1962	90.9	61.2	20.8	6.2	2.8	4.1	2.5	5.2	32.1	5.5	0.3	5.1	9.3
1963	97.7	64.8	21.2	6.1	2.9	4.4	2.3	5.6	34.4	6.1	0.7	5.4	10.0
1964	107.3	72.2	23.7	6.8	3.6	4.8	2.4	6.2	38.7	6.8	0.9	5.9	11.4
1965	120.4	85.2	28.3	8.2	5.1	5.4	2.4	7.2	45.8	7.8	1.2	6.7	13.7
1966	130.6	97.2	31.3	8.3	6.6	6.3	2.5	7.8	53.0	9.7	1.7	8.0	16.2
1967	132.8	99.2	31.5	8.2	6.0	7.1	2.4	7.8	53.7	10.1	1.9	8.2	16.9
1968	147.9	107.7	33.6	9.4	6.0	8.3	2.6	7.3	58.5	10.6	1.9	8.7	17.3
1969	164.4	120.0	37.7	11.7	6.8	8.7	2.8	7.8	65.2	12.8	2.4	10.4	19.1
1970	168.0	124.6	40.3	12.5	7.0	10.2	2.8	7.8	66.4	14.3	2.7	11.6	20.3
1971	188.6	130.4	42.7	14.9	6.3	11.0	2.7	7.9	69.1	14.9	2.8	12.2	19.5
1972	219.0	146.6	47.2	17.6	5.9	12.1	3.1	8.6	78.9	16.7	3.5	13.2	21.4
1973	251.0	172.7	55.0	19.8	7.9	13.8	3.5	9.9	95.1	19.9	3.5	16.3	26.0
1974	260.5	191.1	61.2	20.6	10.0	15.1	5.2	10.3	104.3	23.1	3.9	19.2	30.7
1975	263.5	196.8	61.4	17.7	10.6	15.7	7.4	10.1	107.6	23.8	3.6	20.2	31.3
1976	306.1	219.3	65.9	18.1	10.1	18.2	8.6	11.0	121.2	27.5	4.4	23.1	34.1
1977	374.3	259.1	74.6	20.3	11.1	19.3	11.5	12.5	148.7	33.7	5.7	28.0	39.4
1978	452.6	314.6	93.6	25.3	16.2	21.4	15.4	15.2	180.6	42.3	7.6	34.8	47.7
1979	521.7	373.8	117.7	33.5	22.0	24.6	19.0	18.5	208.1	50.3	10.2	40.2	56.2
1980	536.4	406.9	136.2	41.0	20.5	27.3	27.4	20.0	216.4	58.9	12.5	46.4	60.7
1981	601.4	472.9	167.3	48.3	25.4	30.0	42.5	21.2	240.9	69.6	17.1	52.5	65.5
1982	595.9	485.1	177.6	55.8	26.1	29.6	44.8	21.3	234.9	74.2	18.9	55.3	62.7
1983	643.3	482.2	154.3	55.8	19.5	25.8	30.0	23.3	246.5	83.7	23.9	59.8	58.9
1984	754.7	564.3	177.4	70.6	20.9	26.5	31.3	28.1	291.9	101.2	31.6	69.6	68.1
1985	807.8	607.8	194.5	84.1	24.1	26.5	27.9	31.8	307.9	106.6	33.7	72.9	72.5
1986	842.6	607.8	176.5	80.9	21.0	28.3	15.7	30.7	317.7	111.1	33.4	77.7	75.4
1987	865.0	615.2	174.2	80.8	21.2	25.4	13.1	33.7	320.9	112.2	35.8	76.4	76.7
1988	918.5	662.3	182.8	86.3	23.2	25.0	15.7	32.5	346.8	120.8	38.0	82.8	84.2
1989	972.0	716.0	193.7	88.3	28.8	27.5	14.9	34.3	372.2	130.7	43.1	87.6	93.3
1990	978.9	739.2	202.9	87.5	33.6	26.3	17.9	37.6	371.9	129.6	38.6	90.9	92.1
1991	944.7	723.6	183.6	68.9	31.4	31.6	18.5	33.2	360.8	129.2	37.7	91.5	89.3
1992	996.7	741.9	172.6	64.5	29.0	33.9	14.2	31.0	381.7	142.1	44.0	98.1	93.0
1993	1 086.0	799.2	177.2	69.4	23.6	33.2	16.6	34.5	425.1	153.3	47.9	105.4	102.2
1994	1 192.7	868.9	186.8	75.4	28.9	31.2	16.4	34.9	476.4	167.0	52.4	114.6	113.6
1995	1 286.3	962.2	207.3	83.1	35.5	33.1	15.0	40.6	528.1	188.4	66.1	122.3	129.0
1996	1 401.3	1 043.2	224.6	91.5	38.2	29.2	16.8	48.9	565.3	204.7	72.8	131.9	136.5
1997	1 524.7	1 149.1	250.3	104.3	37.6	28.8	22.4	57.2	610.9	222.8	81.4	141.4	140.4
1998	1 673.0	1 254.1	276.0	116.0	40.5	34.2	22.3	63.1	660.0	240.1	87.9	152.2	147.4
1999	1 826.2	1 364.5	285.7	125.4	35.1	40.4	18.3	66.4	713.6	259.8	97.2	162.5	149.1
2000	1 983.9	1 498.4	321.0	139.3	37.6	48.1	23.7	72.2	766.1	293.8	103.2	190.6	162.9
2001	1 973.1	1 460.1	333.5	137.3	37.8	51.1	34.6	72.7	711.5	265.9	87.6	178.4	151.9
2002	1 910.4	1 352.8	287.0	119.4	22.7	51.0	30.2	63.6	659.6	236.7	79.7	157.0	141.7
2003	2 013.0	1 375.9	286.6	115.0	21.4	48.1	38.5	63.6	670.6	242.7	79.9	162.8	143.4
2004	2 217.2	1 467.4	307.7	125.3	23.2	43.1	47.3	68.8	721.9	255.8	84.2	171.6	144.2
2005	2 477.2	1 621.0	353.0	135.9	28.4	48.1	69.4	71.2	794.9	267.0	84.2	182.8	162.4
2006	2 632.0	1 793.8	425.2	156.3	32.3	55.8	96.0	84.7	862.3	288.5	92.6	195.9	181.6
2007	2 639.1	1 948.6	510.3	181.8	40.2	81.6	102.2	104.5	893.4	310.9	95.4	215.5	194.1
2008	2 506.9	1 990.9	571.1	181.9	53.0	95.6	120.3	120.3	845.4	306.3	93.9	212.4	194.3
2009	2 080.4	1 690.4	455.8	126.8	56.8	95.8	79.2	97.3	670.3	275.6	88.9	186.7	153.7
2010	2 111.6	1 735.0	379.8	92.1	40.3	83.8	93.5	70.1	777.0	307.5	99.6	207.9	155.2
2011	2 286.3	1 907.5	404.5	93.4	39.6	81.8	124.7	65.0	881.3	313.3	95.6	217.7	191.5
2012	2 550.5	2 118.5	479.4	103.8	46.8	102.4	152.9	73.6	983.4	331.2	103.5	227.7	211.2
2013	2 721.5	2 211.5	492.5	109.8	49.9	98.9	155.6	78.3	1 027.0	341.7	102.1	239.6	209.3
2014	2 960.2	2 400.1	577.6	127.4	58.1	115.3	188.3	88.4	1 091.9	346.0	101.9	244.1	218.8
2015	3 100.4	2 466.6	584.4	145.4	79.6	121.1	137.1	101.1	1 119.5	352.8	101.3	251.5	218.2
2016	3 168.8	2 469.3	560.4	172.1	76.3	124.3	75.8	111.9	1 087.8	353.0	99.4	253.6	213.9
2017	3 351.9	2 591.6	599.3	181.6	67.6	121.3	108.5	120.2	1 117.4	369.2	104.7	264.5	225.0
2018	3 579.1	2 780.6	633.3	191.2	69.6	118.6	126.6	127.3	1 190.5	390.2	119.3	270.9	242.7
2019	3 752.6	2 938.7	672.6	203.2	77.9	132.5	127.3	131.8	1 231.3	393.9	119.1	274.8	251.9
2020	3 697.4	2 799.6	597.2	204.7	69.4	130.3	75.6	117.2	1 123.9	413.9	128.1	285.8	241.7
2018													
1st quarter	3 505.0	2 716.0	627.2	191.2	67.7	121.9	119.7	126.6	1 166.4	389.5	117.0	272.5	237.0
2nd quarter	3 579.0	2 770.1	641.6	192.8	68.5	124.4	127.5	128.4	1 175.7	388.1	120.1	268.0	240.1
3rd quarter	3 602.5	2 798.1	638.2	192.2	70.5	116.0	131.9	127.6	1 195.7	392.6	121.0	271.6	243.7
4th quarter	3 629.9	2 838.1	626.1	188.5	71.7	112.2	127.1	126.7	1 224.2	390.6	119.2	271.4	250.1
2019													
1st quarter	3 683.4	2 886.9	639.9	194.5	77.8	110.2	126.7	130.7	1 240.2	396.6	120.0	276.6	249.5
2nd quarter	3 754.5	2 946.1	669.4	197.7	78.6	129.3	133.2	130.5	1 247.4	397.6	121.8	275.8	254.2
3rd quarter	3 791.2	2 969.3	696.0	208.3	77.8	142.4	133.9	133.5	1 227.4	391.0	115.6	275.4	256.0
4th quarter	3 781.4	2 952.6	685.3	212.2	77.1	148.1	115.3	132.6	1 210.3	390.2	118.9	271.3	247.8
2020													
1st quarter	3 773.0	2 900.1	687.1	218.7	74.1	145.3	119.4	129.6	1 141.9	379.1	113.5	265.6	242.8
2nd quarter	3 456.9	2 659.1	585.9	208.0	69.3	129.5	60.6	118.8	1 020.6	397.0	126.0	270.9	229.1
3rd quarter	3 693.8	2 776.6	563.5	198.9	69.0	126.0	56.8	112.8	1 135.5	432.2	133.9	298.3	241.5
4th quarter	3 865.9	2 862.7	552.3	193.0	65.6	120.3	65.7	107.6	1 197.5	447.3	138.9	308.5	253.4

Table 5-2. Gross Private Fixed Investment by Type—*Continued*

(Billions of dollars, quarterly data are at seasonally adjusted annual rates.)   NIPA Table 5.3.5

Year and quarter	Nonresidential—*Continued*						Residential						
	Equipment—*Continued*		Intellectual property				Total	Residential structures					Residential equipment
	Transportation equipment	Other nonresidential equipment	Total	Software [1]	Research and development [2]	Entertainment, literary, and artistic originals		Total	Permanent site			Other residential structures	
									Total	Single family	Multifamily		
1960	8.5	7.1	7.1	0.1	4.9	2.1	26.9	26.3	17.5	14.9	2.6	8.8	0.5
1961	8.0	7.0	8.0	0.2	5.2	2.7	27.0	26.5	17.4	14.1	3.3	9.1	0.5
1962	9.8	7.5	8.4	0.2	5.6	2.6	29.6	29.1	19.9	15.1	4.8	9.2	0.5
1963	9.4	8.8	9.2	0.4	6.0	2.8	32.9	32.3	22.4	16.0	6.4	9.8	0.6
1964	10.6	9.9	9.8	0.5	6.5	2.8	35.1	34.5	24.1	17.6	6.4	10.4	0.6
1965	13.2	11.0	11.1	0.7	7.2	3.2	35.2	34.5	23.8	17.8	6.0	10.6	0.7
1966	14.5	12.7	12.8	1.0	8.1	3.7	33.4	32.7	21.8	16.6	5.2	10.9	0.7
1967	14.3	12.4	14.0	1.2	9.0	3.8	33.6	32.9	21.5	16.8	4.7	11.4	0.7
1968	17.6	13.0	15.6	1.3	9.9	4.3	40.2	39.3	26.7	19.5	7.2	12.6	0.9
1969	18.9	14.4	17.2	1.8	11.0	4.4	44.4	43.4	29.2	19.7	9.5	14.1	1.0
1970	16.2	15.6	17.9	2.3	11.5	4.1	43.4	42.3	27.1	17.5	9.5	15.2	1.1
1971	18.4	16.3	18.7	2.4	11.9	4.4	58.2	56.9	38.7	25.8	12.9	18.2	1.3
1972	21.8	19.0	20.6	2.8	12.9	4.9	72.4	70.9	50.1	32.8	17.2	20.8	1.5
1973	26.6	22.6	22.7	3.2	14.6	4.9	78.3	76.6	54.6	35.2	19.4	22.0	1.7
1974	26.3	24.3	25.5	3.9	16.4	5.2	69.5	67.6	43.4	29.7	13.7	24.2	1.9
1975	25.2	27.4	27.8	4.8	17.5	5.5	66.7	64.8	36.3	29.6	6.7	28.5	1.9
1976	30.0	29.6	32.2	5.2	19.6	7.4	86.8	84.6	50.8	43.9	6.9	33.9	2.1
1977	39.3	36.3	35.8	5.5	21.8	8.6	115.2	112.8	72.2	62.2	10.0	40.6	2.4
1978	47.3	43.2	40.4	6.3	24.9	9.1	138.0	135.3	85.6	72.8	12.8	49.7	2.7
1979	53.6	47.9	48.1	8.1	29.1	10.9	147.8	144.7	89.3	72.3	17.0	55.4	3.2
1980	48.4	48.3	54.4	9.8	34.2	10.3	129.5	126.1	69.6	52.9	16.7	56.5	3.4
1981	50.6	55.2	64.8	11.8	39.7	13.2	128.5	124.9	69.4	52.0	17.5	55.4	3.6
1982	46.8	51.2	72.7	14.0	44.8	13.9	110.8	107.2	57.0	41.5	15.5	50.2	3.7
1983	53.5	50.4	81.3	16.4	49.6	15.3	161.1	156.9	95.0	72.5	22.4	61.9	4.2
1984	64.4	58.2	95.0	20.4	56.9	17.8	190.4	185.6	114.6	86.4	28.2	71.0	4.7
1985	69.0	59.9	105.3	23.8	63.0	18.6	200.1	195.0	115.9	87.4	28.5	79.1	5.1
1986	70.5	60.7	113.5	25.6	66.5	21.4	234.8	229.3	135.2	104.1	31.0	94.1	5.5
1987	68.1	64.0	120.1	29.0	69.2	21.9	249.8	244.0	142.7	117.2	25.5	101.3	5.8
1988	72.9	69.0	132.7	33.3	76.4	23.0	256.2	250.1	142.4	120.1	22.3	107.7	6.1
1989	67.9	80.2	150.1	40.6	84.1	25.4	256.0	249.9	143.2	120.9	22.3	106.6	6.1
1990	70.0	80.2	164.4	45.4	91.5	27.5	239.7	233.7	132.1	112.9	19.3	101.5	6.0
1991	71.5	70.8	179.1	48.7	101.0	29.4	221.2	215.4	114.6	99.4	15.1	100.8	5.7
1992	74.7	72.0	187.7	51.1	105.4	31.2	254.7	248.8	135.1	122.0	13.1	113.8	5.9
1993	89.4	80.2	196.9	57.2	106.3	33.4	286.8	280.7	150.9	140.1	10.8	129.8	6.1
1994	107.7	88.1	205.7	60.4	109.2	36.1	323.8	317.6	176.4	162.3	14.1	141.2	6.2
1995	116.1	94.7	226.8	65.5	121.2	40.2	324.1	317.7	171.4	153.5	17.9	146.3	6.3
1996	123.2	101.0	253.3	74.5	134.5	44.3	358.1	351.7	191.1	170.8	20.3	160.6	6.3
1997	135.5	112.1	288.0	93.8	148.1	46.1	375.6	369.3	198.1	175.2	22.9	171.3	6.3
1998	147.1	125.4	318.1	109.2	160.6	48.3	418.8	412.1	224.0	199.4	24.6	188.2	6.7
1999	174.4	130.4	365.1	136.6	177.5	51.0	461.8	454.5	251.3	223.8	27.4	203.2	7.3
2000	170.8	138.6	411.3	156.8	199.0	55.6	485.4	477.7	265.0	236.8	28.3	212.7	7.7
2001	154.2	139.5	415.0	157.7	202.7	54.7	513.1	505.2	279.4	249.1	30.3	225.8	7.8
2002	141.6	139.6	406.2	152.5	196.1	57.6	557.6	549.6	298.8	265.9	33.0	250.7	8.0
2003	134.1	150.5	418.7	155.0	201.0	62.7	637.1	628.8	345.7	310.6	35.1	283.1	8.3
2004	159.2	162.7	437.8	166.3	207.4	64.1	749.8	740.8	417.5	377.6	39.9	323.3	9.0
2005	179.6	186.0	473.1	178.6	224.7	69.8	856.2	846.6	480.8	433.5	47.3	365.8	9.6
2006	194.3	198.0	506.3	189.5	245.6	71.2	838.2	828.1	468.8	416.0	52.8	359.3	10.0
2007	188.8	199.6	544.8	206.4	268.0	70.4	690.5	680.6	354.1	305.2	49.0	326.5	9.9
2008	148.7	196.1	574.4	223.8	284.2	66.4	516.0	506.4	230.1	185.8	44.3	276.3	9.6
2009	74.9	166.1	564.4	226.0	274.6	63.7	390.0	381.2	133.9	105.3	28.5	247.3	8.8
2010	135.8	178.5	578.2	226.4	282.4	69.4	376.6	367.4	127.3	112.6	14.7	240.2	9.2
2011	177.8	198.7	621.7	249.8	303.4	68.6	378.8	369.1	123.2	108.2	15.0	245.9	9.8
2012	215.3	225.7	655.7	272.1	313.4	70.2	432.0	421.5	154.5	132.0	22.5	267.0	10.5
2013	242.5	233.6	691.9	283.7	337.9	70.3	510.0	499.0	202.3	170.8	31.5	296.7	11.0
2014	272.8	254.4	730.5	297.5	359.5	73.4	560.2	548.8	235.2	193.6	41.6	313.7	11.3
2015	306.3	242.2	762.7	307.1	378.3	77.3	633.8	622.1	273.6	221.1	52.5	348.5	11.8
2016	292.3	228.5	821.2	334.8	404.4	82.0	699.4	687.3	304.4	242.5	61.9	383.0	12.1
2017	294.0	229.1	875.0	365.7	423.5	85.8	760.3	747.9	332.6	270.2	62.5	415.3	12.4
2018	309.5	248.1	956.7	401.3	465.6	89.8	798.5	785.6	355.0	289.6	65.5	430.6	12.9
2019	320.3	265.3	1 034.8	427.7	514.4	92.7	813.9	800.8	349.4	280.0	69.4	451.4	13.1
2020	206.0	262.3	1 078.5	453.4	537.7	87.4	897.8	883.4	381.9	309.4	72.5	501.5	14.3
2018													
1st quarter	303.0	237.0	922.3	386.9	447.2	88.2	789.0	776.3	350.7	287.1	63.6	425.6	12.7
2nd quarter	300.6	246.9	952.7	400.2	463.1	89.5	808.9	795.9	361.6	297.0	64.6	434.3	13.0
3rd quarter	309.2	250.2	964.2	405.5	468.3	90.4	804.3	791.3	358.9	293.8	65.1	432.5	13.0
4th quarter	325.2	258.3	987.7	412.8	483.7	91.2	791.8	779.0	349.0	280.4	68.6	430.0	12.8
2019													
1st quarter	333.0	261.1	1 006.7	415.5	499.7	91.6	796.5	783.6	343.2	271.8	71.3	440.4	13.0
2nd quarter	328.3	267.3	1 029.3	423.5	513.4	92.4	808.5	795.3	346.6	276.5	70.1	448.7	13.2
3rd quarter	312.5	267.8	1 046.0	432.7	520.2	93.1	821.9	808.6	351.4	283.0	68.5	457.2	13.3
4th quarter	307.4	264.8	1 057.0	439.1	524.3	93.6	828.8	815.7	356.3	288.6	67.7	459.4	13.1
2020													
1st quarter	260.2	259.8	1 071.1	449.2	529.8	92.2	872.9	859.7	376.2	306.3	70.0	483.4	13.2
2nd quarter	155.5	239.1	1 052.6	444.9	519.9	87.9	797.8	784.1	347.1	279.4	67.7	437.0	13.7
3rd quarter	191.2	270.7	1 077.6	453.6	539.9	84.1	917.2	901.8	373.6	298.9	74.7	528.2	15.4
4th quarter	217.1	279.7	1 112.9	466.0	561.3	85.6	1 003.2	988.2	430.7	353.0	77.7	557.4	15.0

[1]Excludes software "embedded," or bundled, in computers and other equipment. Includes software development expenditures.
[2]Excludes software development.

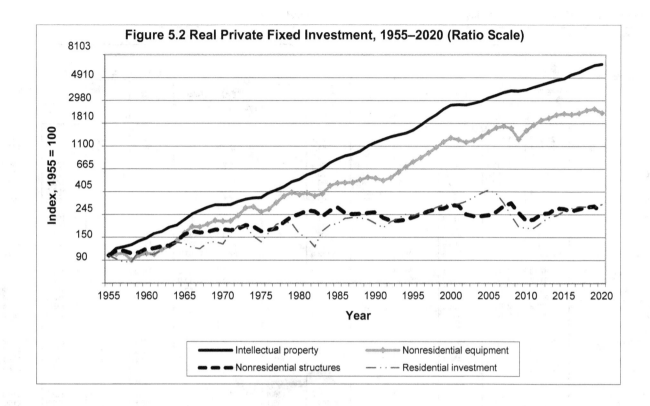

- Between 1955 and 2006, which was the recent high point for total real (constant-dollar) investment, the quantity of real gross private fixed investment increased eightfold, with an average annual growth rate of 4.2 percent. Every major type of investment grew in real terms between those two years, but as Figure 5-2 indicates, by far the fastest-growing major category has been "intellectual property products." Computer software is the main driver of growth in this category, but it also includes research and development and "entertainment, literary, and artistic originals." (Table 5-3)

- Between 2008 and 2009, overall gross investment fell 16.0 percent in real terms—a collapse unprecedented in the postwar period. (Table 5-3) By 2019, gross investment surpassed the 2006 level by 27.4 percent, achieving a new all-time high but it fell again in 2020. (Table 5-4)

- Intellectual property investment barely hesitated in 2009 and went on to new record peaks in each year through 2020. Equipment purchases continued to increase and went on to a new record in 2019 before declining again in 2020. On the other hand, residential investment dropped 40.6 percent between 2007 and 2009. Residential investment increased steadily from 2012 to 2017 declined in 2018 and 2019 and increased again in 2020. (Table 5-4)

Table 5-3. Real Gross Private Fixed Investment by Type

(Billions of chained [2012] dollars, quarterly data are at seasonally adjusted annual rates.) **NIPA Table 5.3.6**

Year and quarter	Total gross private fixed investment	Nonresidential Total	Structures Total	Commercial and health care	Manufacturing	Power and communication	Mining exploration, shafts, and wells	Other nonresidential structures	Equipment Total	Information processing equipment Total	Computers and peripheral equipment[1]	Other information processing	Industrial equipment
2003	2 280.6	1 509.4	456.6	161.7	29.9	76.7	97.6	79.7	634.3	150.4	40.2	111.1	182.2
2004	2 440.7	1 594.0	456.3	165.7	30.7	64.0	103.6	82.0	688.6	169.4	45.7	124.7	178.8
2005	2 618.7	1 716.4	466.1	164.3	34.9	66.4	113.4	79.7	760.0	187.6	51.8	136.5	194.2
2006	2 686.8	1 854.2	501.7	174.2	37.2	70.4	122.5	89.1	832.6	217.0	64.7	152.4	210.6
2007	2 653.5	1 982.1	568.6	191.6	44.0	98.1	120.5	105.0	865.8	247.2	73.9	173.3	217.3
2008	2 499.4	1 994.2	605.4	184.6	55.1	107.8	129.4	118.9	824.4	260.6	79.7	180.9	208.3
2009	2 099.8	1 704.3	492.2	128.0	57.9	109.3	92.4	98.1	649.7	247.5	81.1	166.5	162.7
2010	2 164.2	1 781.0	412.8	96.2	42.2	91.7	108.3	72.6	781.2	289.1	94.1	195.1	162.5
2011	2 317.8	1 935.4	424.1	95.8	40.6	84.6	136.7	66.5	886.2	303.2	93.9	209.3	194.9
2012	2 550.5	2 118.5	479.4	103.8	46.8	102.4	152.9	73.6	983.4	331.2	103.5	227.7	211.2
2013	2 692.1	2 206.0	485.5	107.5	48.7	97.8	155.4	76.1	1 029.2	351.8	103.0	248.8	208.4
2014	2 869.2	2 365.3	538.8	121.3	55.0	112.5	167.8	82.4	1 101.1	370.2	102.9	267.7	216.5
2015	2 979.0	2 420.3	534.1	136.0	74.0	116.4	119.9	91.0	1 134.6	393.3	103.4	291.0	216.7
2016	3 041.0	2 442.0	511.0	158.8	70.4	118.9	69.7	97.5	1 114.6	410.5	103.0	309.3	213.4
2017	3 164.3	2 541.4	532.5	163.8	61.0	113.5	96.9	101.4	1 145.5	438.6	108.9	331.9	222.5
2018	3 316.2	2 704.4	553.6	166.0	59.9	107.0	123.0	102.8	1 218.8	472.0	123.7	349.2	235.4
2019	3 421.3	2 822.0	565.0	168.5	63.2	114.9	121.0	102.3	1 258.8	489.6	127.6	363.0	240.6
2020	3 329.4	2 671.1	494.2	166.2	54.7	109.5	75.6	88.2	1 154.0	523.0	140.7	382.5	228.8
2011													
1st quarter	2 216.2	1 842.7	387.8	90.5	34.3	77.5	122.8	62.7	846.3	292.9	87.8	205.1	182.8
2nd quarter	2 268.0	1 890.4	414.8	95.0	39.0	83.7	130.5	66.4	858.0	302.1	93.6	208.5	185.4
3rd quarter	2 363.3	1 978.9	439.4	98.2	43.6	88.7	141.1	67.7	909.7	308.2	97.5	210.7	199.1
4th quarter	2 423.7	2 029.4	454.5	99.2	45.5	88.3	152.4	69.3	930.7	309.6	96.8	212.8	212.1
2012													
1st quarter	2 499.4	2 081.3	476.0	101.7	44.5	102.0	156.4	71.4	959.6	327.3	105.3	222.0	210.3
2nd quarter	2 549.8	2 128.0	487.4	104.0	46.6	104.8	158.1	73.9	986.7	333.5	104.6	228.9	215.0
3rd quarter	2 553.6	2 120.9	481.8	105.2	47.4	103.2	151.1	74.8	983.8	327.3	100.6	226.7	207.5
4th quarter	2 599.4	2 144.0	472.5	104.1	48.6	99.4	145.9	74.4	1 003.4	336.8	103.6	233.2	212.1
2013													
1st quarter	2 643.9	2 171.6	462.1	106.3	47.0	81.9	153.3	73.4	1 021.1	349.9	105.9	244.0	210.1
2nd quarter	2 665.3	2 177.5	475.8	103.4	46.2	91.3	159.3	75.4	1 019.0	348.6	100.2	248.5	207.7
3rd quarter	2 711.3	2 214.7	499.8	106.9	51.0	104.2	159.9	77.7	1 019.0	352.1	101.2	251.0	209.2
4th quarter	2 748.0	2 260.0	504.2	113.2	50.7	113.9	148.9	77.7	1 057.9	356.5	104.8	251.8	206.4
2014													
1st quarter	2 775.6	2 291.7	521.9	113.1	49.6	126.1	155.5	78.5	1 066.9	358.9	101.3	257.9	211.4
2nd quarter	2 852.8	2 353.3	540.3	119.2	50.4	119.0	170.9	81.2	1 093.6	372.1	103.5	269.0	217.1
3rd quarter	2 907.3	2 400.8	542.2	124.2	54.6	109.4	171.7	82.4	1 127.0	370.6	102.3	268.7	222.0
4th quarter	2 941.2	2 415.5	551.0	128.8	65.6	95.5	173.1	87.4	1 116.9	379.3	104.7	275.1	215.3
2015													
1st quarter	2 949.5	2 412.6	545.1	129.4	72.4	106.6	152.1	85.8	1 126.0	381.8	103.0	279.5	215.8
2nd quarter	2 974.2	2 423.6	549.1	138.1	76.8	122.9	122.7	92.1	1 130.3	388.4	103.5	285.7	217.6
3rd quarter	2 999.8	2 432.4	531.8	137.1	74.7	121.3	108.1	94.5	1 148.3	399.2	105.6	294.5	216.0
4th quarter	2 991.8	2 412.8	510.6	139.6	72.1	114.6	96.6	91.5	1 133.6	403.8	101.3	304.3	217.4
2016													
1st quarter	3 009.2	2 410.4	491.9	148.7	70.3	110.4	74.4	92.1	1 127.6	406.5	104.7	303.2	212.7
2nd quarter	3 025.5	2 426.1	501.5	154.5	72.8	114.5	64.7	99.0	1 113.4	406.9	103.5	305.0	215.1
3rd quarter	3 052.8	2 457.8	521.4	164.4	71.1	121.8	69.2	99.4	1 108.3	411.5	101.0	312.7	212.1
4th quarter	3 076.5	2 473.6	529.0	167.3	67.5	128.8	70.5	99.7	1 109.0	417.2	102.9	316.4	213.8
2017													
1st quarter	3 124.7	2 505.1	538.3	165.5	63.2	124.9	89.1	100.4	1 115.7	423.0	103.4	322.0	216.2
2nd quarter	3 154.2	2 531.0	538.6	165.5	62.8	115.2	97.0	102.2	1 138.6	437.0	107.5	331.8	222.4
3rd quarter	3 158.1	2 538.7	523.8	161.4	58.7	108.3	97.5	101.5	1 147.4	439.0	112.6	327.9	223.3
4th quarter	3 220.3	2 590.5	529.3	162.9	59.1	105.5	104.0	101.4	1 180.4	455.4	112.0	345.9	227.9
2018													
1st quarter	3 273.2	2 654.0	554.2	168.9	59.4	112.2	113.9	104.0	1 196.6	467.2	121.1	347.2	231.6
2nd quarter	3 321.2	2 698.0	563.7	168.3	59.4	112.9	124.2	104.1	1 205.4	468.4	124.5	344.4	233.3
3rd quarter	3 327.9	2 716.7	557.7	166.4	60.7	103.7	130.1	102.6	1 221.3	475.5	125.3	350.9	235.6
4th quarter	3 342.6	2 749.0	538.9	160.4	59.9	99.3	123.8	100.7	1 251.7	477.1	123.9	354.4	241.0
2019													
1st quarter	3 372.8	2 780.7	544.7	164.2	64.5	96.8	120.8	102.8	1 265.2	487.0	125.7	362.8	239.2
2nd quarter	3 423.2	2 826.0	563.2	164.5	63.9	112.8	125.4	102.0	1 273.1	492.6	129.9	363.5	243.1
3rd quarter	3 449.3	2 846.5	582.0	171.5	62.8	123.2	127.4	103.1	1 256.4	487.8	124.7	364.8	244.1
4th quarter	3 439.9	2 834.7	570.0	173.8	61.8	126.8	110.4	101.4	1 240.6	490.8	130.3	361.1	235.8
2020													
1st quarter	3 419.6	2 775.5	568.8	177.9	59.0	123.1	115.9	98.2	1 168.3	478.0	125.1	353.8	230.2
2nd quarter	3 123.0	2 535.7	485.8	169.0	54.0	109.1	61.0	89.6	1 044.0	501.7	138.1	363.0	217.4
3rd quarter	3 318.5	2 646.9	466.0	161.4	54.0	105.6	57.9	84.6	1 166.6	545.9	146.6	399.5	228.5
4th quarter	3 456.6	2 726.2	456.1	156.6	51.5	100.1	67.6	80.4	1 237.1	566.5	152.9	413.7	238.8

[1]See notes and definitions.

Table 5-3. Real Gross Private Fixed Investment by Type—Continued

(Billions of chained [2012] dollars, quarterly data are at seasonally adjusted annual rates.)   **NIPA Table 5.3.6**

Year and quarter	Nonresidential—Continued						Residential						
	Equipment—Continued		Intellectual property				Total	Residential structures					Residential equipment
	Transportation equipment	Other nonresidential equipment	Total	Software²	Research and development³	Entertainment, literary, and artistic originals		Total	Permanent site			Other residential structures	
									Total	Single family	Multifamily		
2003	150.3	180.2	437.7	133.5	246.1	64.6	755.5	747.7	416.1	362.0	49.6	329.2	8.1
2004	171.2	193.3	459.2	149.3	248.1	65.6	830.9	822.1	464.3	405.4	53.4	355.4	9.1
2005	192.1	211.9	493.1	163.4	261.6	71.0	885.4	876.3	497.0	432.8	58.7	376.7	9.5
2006	206.4	220.7	521.5	173.5	279.6	71.8	818.9	809.5	453.6	390.4	59.1	353.5	9.7
2007	197.7	218.0	554.3	191.1	296.1	70.0	665.8	656.6	337.7	283.5	52.3	317.7	9.4
2008	155.0	207.4	575.3	206.7	304.8	66.0	504.6	495.7	224.2	178.1	46.0	270.9	9.1
2009	72.5	165.3	572.4	212.9	297.4	63.4	395.3	386.9	134.5	105.3	29.3	252.3	8.4
2010	141.5	186.2	588.1	220.9	298.5	69.5	383.0	373.8	129.1	114.3	14.7	244.7	9.3
2011	181.8	206.2	624.8	245.2	311.0	69.8	382.5	372.4	124.5	109.1	15.4	247.9	10.0
2012	215.3	225.7	655.7	272.1	313.4	70.2	432.0	421.5	154.5	132.0	22.5	267.0	10.5
2013	238.5	230.6	691.4	287.2	333.8	70.3	485.5	474.1	192.4	161.8	30.6	281.7	11.4
2014	265.0	248.9	724.8	305.3	346.9	72.7	504.1	491.8	210.4	171.8	38.8	281.4	12.4
2015	292.8	232.4	752.4	320.2	357.1	75.5	555.4	542.0	235.2	191.5	44.0	306.8	13.4
2016	276.3	218.9	818.8	354.0	387.1	78.5	592.1	577.7	250.5	201.3	49.3	327.1	14.5
2017	273.5	219.0	865.2	392.6	394.7	81.0	615.9	600.6	261.6	214.8	47.2	338.9	15.5
2018	287.0	234.0	935.5	437.1	419.9	83.7	612.3	596.9	266.4	220.7	46.2	330.2	15.7
2019	295.0	244.1	1 002.9	467.8	454.8	85.5	606.7	591.3	254.7	206.8	48.2	336.5	15.8
2020	191.3	240.2	1 031.3	502.3	458.8	79.6	648.0	631.6	269.7	219.7	50.2	361.9	16.9
2011													
1st quarter	172.0	198.5	607.4	232.1	306.5	69.3	373.4	363.6	122.1	108.2	14.0	241.5	9.8
2nd quarter	170.2	199.8	617.4	240.2	309.2	68.3	377.6	367.7	121.7	107.2	14.5	246.0	10.0
3rd quarter	188.0	214.3	629.9	249.8	311.7	68.5	384.4	374.4	125.5	109.4	16.0	248.9	10.1
4th quarter	197.1	212.0	644.3	258.5	316.5	69.5	394.4	384.1	128.7	111.7	17.0	255.4	10.3
2012													
1st quarter	205.6	216.5	645.7	263.1	312.3	70.3	418.3	407.8	139.3	120.5	18.8	268.5	10.4
2nd quarter	215.6	222.7	653.9	272.1	311.5	70.2	421.9	411.5	147.6	126.2	21.4	263.9	10.4
3rd quarter	216.1	232.9	655.2	272.8	312.4	70.1	432.7	422.1	158.1	134.5	23.6	264.1	10.6
4th quarter	223.9	230.6	668.0	280.2	317.6	70.2	455.2	444.5	173.1	146.9	26.2	271.4	10.7
2013													
1st quarter	232.2	229.0	688.6	288.3	330.1	70.2	471.8	460.7	184.3	156.0	28.2	276.4	11.1
2nd quarter	236.6	226.2	682.9	280.2	331.9	70.8	486.8	475.5	192.6	163.0	29.5	282.9	11.3
3rd quarter	237.2	220.7	695.8	288.3	337.1	70.3	495.5	483.9	196.5	165.7	30.8	287.4	11.6
4th quarter	248.2	246.4	698.1	292.1	336.1	70.0	487.7	476.2	196.3	162.6	33.8	279.9	11.5
2014													
1st quarter	252.4	243.8	702.5	296.2	335.3	71.2	484.3	472.6	199.9	165.0	35.0	272.8	11.7
2nd quarter	260.5	243.8	718.5	303.3	343.3	72.1	499.8	487.5	207.6	169.5	38.3	279.9	12.4
3rd quarter	275.6	257.5	731.4	309.8	348.7	73.2	507.1	494.7	209.9	169.9	40.3	284.8	12.6
4th quarter	271.6	250.5	746.6	311.9	360.2	74.4	525.2	512.4	224.1	182.8	41.6	288.3	12.8
2015													
1st quarter	286.6	241.4	741.1	315.2	351.5	74.7	535.5	522.5	227.4	185.4	42.3	295.0	13.0
2nd quarter	292.4	232.1	743.6	318.2	350.9	75.0	548.9	535.6	229.6	187.3	42.5	306.0	13.4
3rd quarter	302.8	230.9	753.6	320.3	357.8	75.8	563.7	550.1	239.0	194.4	44.8	311.1	13.6
4th quarter	289.4	225.2	771.3	327.1	368.1	76.3	573.6	559.9	244.8	198.7	46.3	315.0	13.7
2016													
1st quarter	286.8	224.4	795.1	339.6	378.8	77.2	591.2	577.0	252.6	203.7	49.1	324.3	14.3
2nd quarter	274.6	220.9	814.3	348.9	388.6	77.4	592.0	577.7	252.4	202.9	49.6	325.2	14.3
3rd quarter	272.7	216.9	829.4	359.2	391.8	79.3	588.9	574.4	246.4	196.8	49.8	328.1	14.7
4th quarter	270.9	213.2	836.3	368.2	389.4	80.2	596.3	581.6	250.6	201.9	48.9	331.0	14.8
2017													
1st quarter	267.3	216.1	851.2	378.1	394.5	80.5	611.8	596.7	254.1	206.7	47.6	342.8	15.2
2nd quarter	269.0	218.4	854.7	387.0	390.0	80.6	615.7	600.5	261.2	214.0	47.6	339.2	15.3
3rd quarter	275.1	218.0	870.4	398.2	394.8	80.9	612.7	597.4	264.0	218.0	46.4	333.2	15.5
4th quarter	282.6	223.4	884.6	406.9	399.7	81.8	623.2	607.6	267.0	220.4	47.0	340.5	15.9
2018													
1st quarter	281.9	226.1	905.2	420.1	407.1	82.5	616.5	600.9	267.9	222.7	45.8	332.7	16.0
2nd quarter	279.2	234.5	930.3	434.5	417.6	83.2	621.5	605.8	271.8	226.7	45.8	333.7	15.9
3rd quarter	285.6	235.0	940.8	441.4	421.0	83.8	612.2	596.8	267.7	222.7	45.5	328.9	15.6
4th quarter	301.3	240.5	965.8	452.2	433.8	85.1	599.0	584.0	258.1	210.8	47.7	325.7	15.2
2019													
1st quarter	307.7	240.7	978.5	454.8	443.4	85.1	599.1	584.0	251.3	201.9	49.5	332.6	15.4
2nd quarter	301.2	246.3	995.7	461.4	453.8	85.1	605.2	589.8	253.9	205.5	48.6	335.9	15.7
3rd quarter	288.5	246.2	1 010.5	471.2	458.7	85.7	610.6	595.0	255.9	208.6	47.6	339.0	16.0
4th quarter	282.7	243.1	1 027.1	483.8	463.4	86.0	612.2	596.4	257.8	211.1	47.1	338.5	16.2
2020													
1st quarter	237.1	238.2	1 036.6	497.4	463.0	84.2	641.2	625.2	269.9	221.8	48.5	355.1	16.3
2nd quarter	140.9	218.7	1 008.0	492.2	446.1	79.2	584.9	569.2	247.8	201.1	46.9	321.3	16.6
3rd quarter	178.5	247.7	1 027.7	503.5	457.1	77.0	657.8	640.6	262.0	210.5	51.7	378.9	17.8
4th quarter	208.7	256.1	1 053.0	516.1	469.0	78.0	708.2	691.3	299.0	245.6	53.7	392.2	16.8

²Excludes software "embedded," or bundled, in computers and other equipment.
³Excludes software development.

Table 5-4. Chain-Type Quantity Indexes for Private Fixed Investment by Type

(Index numbers, 2012 = 100, quarterly data are seasonally adjusted.)   NIPA Table 5.3.3

Year and quarter	Total gross private fixed investment	Nonresidential Total	Structures Total	Commercial and health care	Manufacturing	Power and communication	Mining exploration, shafts, and wells	Other nonresidential structures	Equipment Total	Information processing equipment Total	Computers and peripheral equipment[1]	Other information processing	Industrial equipment
1960	13.9	8.8	46.3	47.3	60.9	36.1	42.0	62.1	5.4	0.2	0.0	2.3	28.7
1961	13.9	8.8	46.9	54.0	59.6	33.8	42.8	60.6	5.3	0.2	0.0	2.5	27.2
1962	15.1	9.5	49.1	60.2	60.2	34.0	44.9	61.9	5.9	0.3	0.0	2.7	28.6
1963	16.3	10.1	49.7	58.3	60.4	36.3	42.1	65.5	6.4	0.3	0.0	2.8	30.9
1964	17.8	11.2	54.8	63.4	72.6	39.5	45.1	71.8	7.2	0.3	0.0	3.0	34.9
1965	19.7	13.0	63.6	74.3	100.4	43.7	44.6	80.7	8.5	0.4	0.0	3.4	41.1
1966	20.9	14.6	67.9	72.5	124.8	49.8	42.2	83.8	9.8	0.5	0.0	4.0	47.3
1967	20.7	14.6	66.2	69.7	109.8	54.5	40.4	82.0	9.7	0.6	0.0	4.0	47.5
1968	22.1	15.3	67.1	76.3	105.7	60.6	40.6	72.4	10.3	0.6	0.0	4.1	46.5
1969	23.4	16.4	70.7	88.0	111.2	60.6	42.3	71.8	11.1	0.7	0.0	4.8	49.6
1970	23.0	16.2	70.9	89.2	107.3	66.3	39.8	67.5	10.9	0.8	0.0	5.2	50.3
1971	24.5	16.2	69.8	97.5	88.6	66.9	36.9	63.3	11.0	0.8	0.0	5.2	46.2
1972	27.3	17.6	72.0	106.5	77.4	69.7	39.5	64.0	12.4	1.0	0.0	5.5	49.9
1973	29.7	19.9	77.8	111.2	95.9	74.2	42.2	69.0	14.7	1.1	0.0	6.7	58.9
1974	28.0	20.1	76.2	104.3	109.3	69.5	50.2	63.1	15.0	1.3	0.0	7.4	63.5
1975	25.3	18.3	68.2	81.3	104.8	64.0	58.6	55.6	13.4	1.3	0.0	7.1	53.8
1976	27.8	19.3	69.8	80.2	96.8	69.8	63.2	58.4	14.3	1.4	0.0	7.8	54.1
1977	31.5	21.4	72.7	84.4	99.4	68.7	71.4	61.6	16.5	1.8	0.0	9.4	57.3
1978	35.2	24.4	83.2	96.2	132.6	72.0	81.4	70.0	19.0	2.3	0.1	11.2	63.8
1979	37.2	26.8	93.7	114.7	162.9	74.7	86.7	76.9	20.5	2.8	0.1	12.6	68.3
1980	35.0	26.8	99.2	126.1	136.2	75.4	121.9	74.7	19.6	3.3	0.1	13.5	65.4
1981	35.9	28.5	107.2	136.5	154.7	77.4	141.7	72.3	20.3	3.8	0.2	14.3	64.4
1982	33.7	27.6	105.4	148.7	149.3	73.1	131.0	68.2	19.0	4.0	0.3	14.4	58.8
1983	36.3	27.5	94.0	144.3	108.0	62.8	108.4	72.0	19.9	4.6	0.4	15.1	54.1
1984	42.1	32.1	107.1	175.6	111.8	64.2	123.3	84.4	23.8	5.9	0.7	17.2	61.9
1985	44.4	34.2	114.7	202.8	125.0	63.5	109.8	92.8	25.1	6.5	0.9	17.8	64.8
1986	45.2	33.6	102.2	188.4	105.0	67.8	64.4	87.2	25.4	7.0	1.0	18.5	64.5
1987	45.5	33.6	99.2	181.5	102.4	60.3	62.9	92.4	25.5	7.3	1.3	17.7	62.9
1988	47.0	35.3	99.9	187.0	108.0	56.8	69.0	86.2	27.2	7.9	1.4	19.0	66.1
1989	48.5	37.3	101.9	184.6	129.4	59.0	62.4	87.9	28.6	8.7	1.7	19.8	70.7
1990	47.8	37.7	103.4	177.3	146.6	54.9	72.1	93.3	28.0	8.8	1.7	20.3	66.6
1991	45.3	36.2	91.9	137.7	135.0	65.2	70.5	81.0	26.7	9.0	1.9	20.2	62.3
1992	47.8	37.3	86.3	128.0	124.0	69.2	58.4	75.0	28.3	10.3	2.6	21.4	63.4
1993	51.5	40.1	86.1	133.2	97.4	66.0	67.8	81.0	31.9	11.7	3.3	23.1	68.8
1994	55.7	43.2	87.7	139.4	115.3	59.8	65.9	79.2	35.8	13.3	4.1	25.2	75.0
1995	59.1	47.4	93.2	147.6	135.9	61.0	56.0	88.7	40.1	16.1	6.1	27.1	82.3
1996	64.3	51.7	98.5	159.0	142.9	52.5	59.6	104.3	44.0	19.4	8.9	29.7	85.3
1997	69.8	57.3	105.8	175.7	136.5	50.6	70.2	118.3	48.9	23.4	12.9	32.3	87.2
1998	77.0	63.5	111.5	186.7	141.1	59.4	61.4	126.5	55.3	28.9	18.7	36.3	91.0
1999	84.0	69.8	112.0	193.5	117.7	70.1	51.9	128.4	62.1	35.3	26.5	40.5	91.5
2000	89.9	76.3	121.1	206.4	121.4	80.8	64.8	134.1	68.2	42.6	32.2	48.8	99.4
2001	88.7	74.6	119.6	196.4	118.0	83.4	76.4	129.5	65.3	42.1	33.0	47.3	92.1
2002	85.6	69.5	98.8	166.4	68.9	81.3	55.9	110.9	61.8	40.3	34.6	43.2	85.9
2003	89.4	71.2	95.2	155.8	63.8	74.9	63.9	108.2	64.5	45.4	38.9	48.8	86.3
2004	95.7	75.2	95.2	159.7	65.7	62.6	67.8	111.4	70.0	51.2	44.1	54.8	84.7
2005	102.7	81.0	97.2	158.3	74.6	64.8	74.2	108.3	77.3	56.6	50.0	60.0	91.9
2006	105.3	87.5	104.6	167.9	79.6	68.8	80.1	121.0	84.7	65.5	62.5	66.9	99.7
2007	104.0	93.6	118.6	184.6	94.1	95.8	78.8	142.6	88.0	74.6	71.4	76.1	102.9
2008	98.0	94.1	126.3	177.9	117.9	105.4	84.6	161.4	83.8	78.7	77.0	79.4	98.6
2009	82.3	80.5	102.7	123.3	123.9	106.8	60.4	133.2	66.1	74.7	78.3	73.1	77.0
2010	84.9	84.1	86.1	92.7	90.2	89.6	70.8	98.6	79.4	87.3	90.9	85.7	76.9
2011	90.9	91.4	88.5	92.3	86.8	82.6	89.4	90.4	90.1	91.5	90.7	91.9	92.3
2012	100.0	100.0	100.0	100.0	100.0	100.0	100.0	100.0	100.0	100.0	100.0	100.0	100.0
2013	105.6	104.1	101.3	103.6	104.2	95.6	101.6	103.3	104.7	106.2	99.5	109.3	98.6
2014	112.5	111.6	112.4	116.9	117.7	109.9	109.7	111.9	112.0	111.8	99.4	117.6	102.5
2015	116.8	114.2	111.4	131.1	158.2	113.7	78.4	123.6	115.4	118.7	99.8	127.8	102.6
2016	119.2	115.3	106.6	153.0	150.6	116.1	45.6	132.5	113.3	123.9	99.5	135.8	101.0
2017	124.1	120.0	111.1	157.9	130.3	110.8	63.4	137.7	116.5	132.4	105.2	145.7	105.3
2018	130.0	127.7	115.5	160.0	128.0	104.5	80.4	139.7	123.9	142.5	119.5	153.4	111.4
2019	134.1	133.2	117.8	162.4	135.2	112.3	79.1	139.0	128.0	147.8	123.3	159.4	113.9
2020	130.5	126.1	103.1	160.2	117.0	107.0	49.4	119.8	117.3	157.9	135.9	168.0	108.3
2018													
1st quarter	128.3	125.3	115.6	162.8	127.1	109.6	74.5	141.2	121.7	141.0	117.0	152.5	109.7
2nd quarter	130.2	127.4	117.6	162.2	127.1	110.3	81.2	141.4	122.6	141.4	120.2	151.2	110.5
3rd quarter	130.5	128.2	116.3	160.4	129.7	101.3	85.1	139.3	124.2	143.6	121.0	154.1	111.5
4th quarter	131.1	129.8	112.4	154.5	128.2	97.0	80.9	136.8	127.3	144.0	119.7	155.6	114.1
2019													
1st quarter	132.2	131.3	113.6	158.2	137.8	94.6	79.0	139.7	128.7	147.0	121.4	159.3	113.2
2nd quarter	134.2	133.4	117.5	158.5	136.6	110.2	82.0	138.5	129.5	148.7	125.4	159.6	115.1
3rd quarter	135.2	134.4	121.4	165.3	134.2	120.4	83.3	140.0	127.8	147.3	120.4	160.2	115.6
4th quarter	134.9	133.8	118.9	167.5	132.1	123.9	72.2	137.8	126.2	148.2	125.8	158.6	111.7
2020													
1st quarter	134.1	131.0	118.6	171.4	126.0	120.3	75.8	133.4	118.8	144.3	120.8	155.4	109.0
2nd quarter	122.4	119.7	101.3	162.9	116.4	106.6	39.9	121.7	106.2	151.5	133.4	159.4	102.9
3rd quarter	130.1	124.9	97.2	155.5	115.5	103.2	37.9	114.9	118.6	164.8	141.6	175.5	108.2
4th quarter	135.5	128.7	95.1	150.9	110.1	97.8	44.2	109.3	125.8	171.0	147.7	181.7	113.1

[1]See notes and definitions.

Table 5-4. Chain-Type Quantity Indexes for Private Fixed Investment by Type—*Continued*

(Index numbers, 2012 = 100, quarterly data are seasonally adjusted.)   **NIPA Table 5.3.3**

Year and quarter	Nonresidential—*Continued*		Intellectual property				Residential						
	Equipment—*Continued*						Total	Residential structures					Residential equipment
								Total	Permanent site			Other residential structures	
	Transportation equipment	Other nonresidential equipment	Total	Software [2]	Research and development [3]	Entertainment, literary, and artistic originals			Total	Single family	Multifamily		
1960	16.5	18.9	3.5	0.0	8.0	17.5	49.9	51.7	97.3	92.6	114.5	25.8	8.6
1961	15.6	18.7	3.9	0.0	8.5	21.1	50.1	51.9	96.8	87.7	144.3	26.4	8.6
1962	19.2	20.0	4.0	0.0	9.2	20.2	54.9	56.9	110.4	93.5	209.8	26.7	9.1
1963	18.6	23.2	4.4	0.1	9.9	21.7	61.3	63.6	125.2	99.9	281.6	28.8	10.2
1964	21.0	25.8	4.6	0.1	10.6	20.6	65.0	67.4	133.7	109.6	279.7	30.0	10.9
1965	26.3	28.6	5.2	0.1	11.9	22.9	63.4	65.5	127.8	107.1	251.4	30.3	12.2
1966	29.0	32.2	5.9	0.2	13.3	25.0	58.0	59.9	112.1	95.4	210.8	30.2	12.5
1967	28.0	30.4	6.4	0.3	14.7	24.8	56.5	58.3	106.9	93.5	183.1	30.6	12.8
1968	33.7	30.8	6.9	0.3	15.9	25.9	64.2	66.1	125.6	102.7	264.5	32.3	15.3
1969	35.0	32.8	7.2	0.4	16.9	24.5	66.2	68.0	129.2	97.6	329.1	33.3	17.4
1970	28.7	34.3	7.2	0.5	17.0	21.4	62.7	64.2	116.9	84.8	322.1	34.1	18.9
1971	31.0	34.2	7.2	0.6	16.9	21.1	79.4	81.6	157.5	117.7	409.9	38.6	21.3
1972	36.1	38.7	7.8	0.7	17.7	22.8	93.2	95.7	190.6	139.9	513.2	42.3	25.5
1973	43.4	45.2	8.1	0.7	18.9	21.8	92.6	94.8	189.7	136.8	527.6	41.4	28.6
1974	39.2	44.7	8.4	0.9	19.0	22.1	74.5	75.8	137.3	105.0	339.7	40.8	29.2
1975	33.8	41.3	8.5	1.0	18.7	21.4	65.5	66.5	105.1	95.9	151.5	44.1	27.2
1976	37.6	41.7	9.4	1.1	19.9	27.2	80.0	81.6	138.1	133.5	146.8	49.1	28.6
1977	45.7	46.9	10.0	1.1	20.9	30.3	96.4	98.5	178.2	171.5	194.6	53.2	31.3
1978	50.5	51.7	10.7	1.4	22.6	29.8	102.8	105.0	186.4	177.1	219.2	58.7	34.0
1979	52.7	52.7	11.9	1.7	24.2	34.2	98.9	100.8	174.4	157.0	267.8	58.7	37.3
1980	43.0	47.3	12.5	2.0	25.9	31.0	78.2	79.3	122.5	103.2	239.7	54.1	37.3
1981	41.8	48.6	13.9	2.3	27.5	37.4	71.8	72.6	113.0	93.9	230.6	49.1	37.3
1982	37.1	42.1	14.8	2.7	29.0	37.7	58.8	59.1	88.1	72.0	187.9	42.2	35.8
1983	41.8	40.5	15.9	3.2	30.6	39.7	83.5	84.6	143.9	125.0	257.3	50.6	40.0
1984	49.7	45.9	18.1	4.0	33.7	44.3	95.8	97.1	169.1	145.1	314.5	56.1	44.3
1985	51.7	46.3	19.7	4.7	36.6	44.1	98.0	99.2	166.9	143.8	306.4	60.4	47.8
1986	49.7	45.5	21.1	5.3	38.1	48.7	110.1	111.6	186.3	164.6	315.4	68.7	51.7
1987	47.3	46.8	21.9	6.1	38.8	47.9	112.3	113.8	188.8	177.9	248.9	70.6	53.8
1988	50.0	49.0	23.5	7.0	40.9	48.4	111.3	112.7	182.1	175.7	212.4	72.5	55.7
1989	45.1	54.7	26.2	9.0	43.7	50.6	107.7	108.9	177.6	170.7	211.8	69.3	56.0
1990	44.5	52.7	28.4	10.5	46.5	52.4	98.6	99.5	160.4	155.1	184.8	64.3	54.3
1991	43.3	45.0	30.3	11.3	49.9	52.9	89.8	90.5	138.1	135.9	142.4	62.5	52.2
1992	44.3	44.8	32.0	13.0	50.8	55.5	102.2	103.3	161.0	165.1	121.0	69.5	53.8
1993	52.8	49.0	33.4	14.7	50.6	58.5	110.5	111.8	171.9	180.8	97.6	76.6	54.8
1994	61.8	53.0	34.7	16.1	50.9	61.6	120.4	122.1	192.4	200.1	126.1	81.1	55.2
1995	66.5	55.8	37.1	17.6	53.7	66.7	116.3	117.8	179.7	181.6	156.3	81.5	55.9
1996	68.7	57.9	41.3	20.6	58.8	71.5	125.9	127.7	196.6	198.4	172.8	87.2	55.6
1997	73.7	63.5	46.7	26.9	62.8	73.6	128.9	130.8	197.7	197.8	186.1	91.4	55.2
1998	79.7	70.0	51.8	32.6	67.1	77.1	140.0	142.2	216.5	219.4	184.1	98.5	59.1
1999	94.0	71.9	58.6	40.6	72.4	79.4	148.8	151.0	232.5	235.6	198.7	103.2	65.3
2000	92.1	75.9	64.1	45.8	78.3	84.1	149.8	151.9	234.4	238.2	195.3	103.4	69.4
2001	83.4	75.3	64.8	46.3	79.9	81.5	151.2	153.2	235.8	238.5	203.8	104.7	70.7
2002	75.4	74.7	64.3	46.1	77.9	85.6	160.3	162.6	245.3	247.8	214.5	113.8	72.8
2003	69.8	79.8	66.8	49.1	78.5	92.0	174.9	177.4	269.3	274.2	220.2	123.3	77.3
2004	79.5	85.6	70.0	54.9	79.2	93.4	192.3	195.1	300.5	307.1	237.3	133.1	86.2
2005	89.2	93.9	75.2	60.1	83.5	101.2	204.9	207.9	321.7	327.8	260.9	141.1	90.0
2006	95.9	97.8	79.5	63.8	89.2	102.3	189.5	192.1	293.6	295.8	262.6	132.4	91.7
2007	91.8	96.6	84.5	70.2	94.5	99.8	154.1	155.8	218.5	214.7	232.6	119.0	89.1
2008	72.0	91.9	87.7	76.0	97.2	94.1	116.8	117.6	145.1	134.9	204.5	101.5	86.3
2009	33.7	73.3	87.3	78.2	94.9	90.4	91.5	91.8	87.0	79.7	130.1	94.5	80.1
2010	65.7	82.5	89.7	81.2	95.2	99.0	88.7	88.7	83.5	86.6	65.3	91.7	87.9
2011	84.5	91.4	95.3	90.1	99.2	98.2	88.5	88.4	80.6	82.6	68.2	92.9	95.4
2012	100.0	100.0	100.0	100.0	100.0	100.0	100.0	100.0	100.0	100.0	100.0	100.0	100.0
2013	110.8	102.2	105.4	105.6	106.5	100.2	112.4	112.5	124.5	122.6	136.0	105.5	107.9
2014	123.1	110.3	110.5	112.2	110.7	103.6	116.7	116.7	136.1	130.1	172.3	105.4	117.3
2015	136.0	103.0	114.7	117.7	113.9	107.5	128.6	128.6	152.2	145.0	195.4	114.9	127.5
2016	128.3	97.0	124.9	130.1	123.5	111.9	137.1	137.1	162.1	152.5	219.2	122.5	137.9
2017	127.1	97.0	132.0	144.3	125.9	115.4	142.6	142.5	169.3	162.7	209.5	127.0	147.0
2018	133.3	103.7	142.7	160.7	134.0	119.2	141.7	141.6	172.4	167.2	205.3	123.7	149.2
2019	137.0	108.2	153.0	171.9	145.1	121.8	140.4	140.3	164.9	156.6	214.0	126.1	150.4
2020	88.9	106.4	157.3	184.6	146.4	113.4	150.0	149.8	174.5	166.4	223.1	135.6	160.4
2018													
1st quarter	131.0	100.2	138.1	154.4	129.9	117.5	142.7	142.6	173.4	168.7	203.7	124.6	152.3
2nd quarter	129.7	103.9	141.9	159.7	133.2	118.6	143.9	143.7	175.9	171.7	203.4	125.0	151.2
3rd quarter	132.6	104.1	143.5	162.3	134.3	119.5	141.7	141.6	173.2	168.7	202.3	123.2	148.5
4th quarter	139.9	106.6	147.3	166.2	138.4	121.3	138.6	138.6	167.0	159.7	211.7	122.0	144.6
2019													
1st quarter	142.9	106.7	149.2	167.2	141.5	121.3	138.7	138.6	162.7	153.0	219.8	124.6	146.1
2nd quarter	139.9	109.1	151.9	169.6	144.8	121.2	140.1	139.9	164.3	155.7	215.8	125.8	149.2
3rd quarter	134.0	109.1	154.1	173.2	146.3	122.1	141.3	141.2	165.6	158.0	211.4	127.0	152.3
4th quarter	131.3	107.7	156.6	177.8	147.8	122.6	141.7	141.5	166.9	159.9	209.1	126.8	154.0
2020													
1st quarter	110.1	105.6	158.1	182.8	147.7	120.0	148.4	148.3	174.7	168.0	215.5	133.0	154.5
2nd quarter	65.4	96.9	153.7	180.9	142.3	112.8	135.4	135.1	160.3	152.3	208.4	120.4	157.9
3rd quarter	82.9	109.8	156.7	185.1	145.8	109.7	152.3	152.0	169.6	159.4	229.8	141.9	169.3
4th quarter	97.0	113.5	160.6	189.7	149.6	111.2	163.9	164.0	193.5	186.0	238.7	146.9	159.7

[2]Excludes software "embedded," or bundled, in computers and other equipment.
[3]Excludes software development.

Table 5-5A. Current-Cost Net Stock of Fixed Assets: Recent Data

(Billions of dollars, year-end estimates.)

Year	Total	Private Total	Private Nonresidential Total	Equip-ment	Struc-tures	Intellec-tual property products	Resi-dential	Government Total	Government Nonresidential Total	Equip-ment	Struc-tures	Intellec-tual property products	Resi-dential	Federal	State and local
1955	1 197.2	888.8	457.0	141.2	296.3	19.6	431.7	308.4	301.1	68.3	219.5	13.3	7.3	158.3	150.0
1956	1 301.6	958.5	505.5	158.6	324.9	22.1	452.9	343.1	334.5	72.4	246.2	15.9	8.6	173.1	170.0
1957	1 369.5	1 008.9	540.6	172.9	343.3	24.4	468.3	360.6	351.6	74.7	257.9	19.0	9.0	182.4	178.2
1958	1 415.1	1 034.0	551.3	178.0	346.9	26.4	482.6	381.1	371.3	76.2	273.0	22.1	9.8	191.4	189.7
1959	1 471.2	1 078.1	573.9	186.6	358.4	29.0	504.1	393.1	382.4	80.5	277.0	25.0	10.7	198.0	195.1
1960	1 520.5	1 111.0	586.9	192.7	363.0	31.1	524.1	409.6	398.2	83.5	286.7	28.1	11.3	205.2	204.4
1961	1 580.2	1 147.6	604.3	196.1	374.6	33.7	543.3	432.6	420.5	87.5	301.4	31.6	12.1	215.7	216.8
1962	1 652.8	1 190.4	626.8	203.7	387.2	35.9	563.6	462.4	449.5	94.6	319.6	35.3	12.9	230.3	232.2
1963	1 717.5	1 228.7	650.6	212.3	399.5	38.9	578.1	488.8	475.6	96.7	338.3	40.6	13.2	240.7	248.1
1964	1 829.7	1 314.0	689.3	224.9	422.5	41.9	624.6	515.7	501.8	98.9	356.6	46.3	14.0	251.0	264.8
1965	1 954.3	1 402.9	738.8	242.5	450.6	45.8	664.0	551.5	536.8	100.6	384.0	52.2	14.7	263.0	288.5
1966	2 119.9	1 522.1	804.3	270.0	483.7	50.5	717.8	597.8	582.0	104.3	418.6	59.1	15.7	278.9	318.9
1967	2 285.4	1 636.6	871.2	296.2	518.7	56.3	765.3	648.8	632.3	110.2	455.6	66.6	16.5	299.8	349.0
1968	2 511.4	1 804.7	957.9	326.5	568.5	62.8	846.9	706.6	688.1	114.1	499.0	75.1	18.5	319.6	387.1
1969	2 744.0	1 962.9	1 055.8	360.1	625.2	70.5	907.1	781.1	760.5	117.7	558.0	84.8	20.6	343.0	438.0
1970	2 990.8	2 121.0	1 161.7	394.8	689.4	77.5	959.3	869.8	847.8	123.2	629.9	94.7	21.9	370.2	499.6
1971	3 294.5	2 352.7	1 275.1	422.5	770.1	82.5	1 077.6	941.9	917.3	123.3	691.3	102.6	24.6	391.2	550.7
1972	3 621.8	2 594.0	1 385.7	455.1	841.9	88.7	1 208.2	1 027.9	1 000.3	127.7	761.8	110.8	27.5	424.7	603.1
1973	4 110.6	2 946.9	1 560.5	507.1	955.0	98.4	1 386.4	1 163.7	1 132.6	135.9	872.9	123.8	31.1	470.8	692.9
1974	4 887.7	3 468.3	1 893.8	625.5	1 156.4	111.9	1 574.5	1 419.4	1 384.7	149.1	1 096.7	138.9	34.7	539.7	879.7
1975	5 277.3	3 786.4	2 083.8	716.2	1 246.2	121.5	1 702.6	1 490.9	1 452.8	165.0	1 138.2	149.6	38.0	572.1	918.8
1976	5 747.3	4 168.9	2 280.1	792.5	1 354.7	132.9	1 888.7	1 578.5	1 536.0	180.7	1 194.5	160.8	42.5	619.5	958.9
1977	6 415.5	4 735.7	2 532.5	891.6	1 495.1	145.8	2 203.2	1 679.7	1 630.9	198.3	1 258.6	174.1	48.9	656.0	1 023.7
1978	7 261.1	5 412.9	2 870.3	1 018.0	1 689.2	163.2	2 542.5	1 848.2	1 791.7	222.5	1 378.7	190.6	56.5	722.1	1 126.1
1979	8 360.7	6 264.5	3 313.9	1 181.9	1 945.2	186.8	2 950.5	2 096.2	2 028.9	236.7	1 578.9	213.3	67.3	800.2	1 296.0
1980	9 512.5	7 118.0	3 800.4	1 369.9	2 216.6	213.8	3 317.6	2 394.5	2 320.8	260.3	1 819.6	240.9	73.7	888.6	1 505.9
1981	10 490.4	7 860.3	4 300.0	1 528.5	2 526.7	244.9	3 560.2	2 630.1	2 549.3	286.7	1 992.5	270.1	80.8	960.0	1 670.1
1982	11 083.9	8 297.0	4 588.9	1 619.9	2 694.9	274.1	3 708.0	2 787.0	2 701.3	315.1	2 092.4	293.8	85.7	1 024.5	1 762.5
1983	11 468.9	8 599.6	4 744.7	1 670.5	2 770.2	304.1	3 854.8	2 869.3	2 773.3	345.2	2 110.8	317.3	96.0	1 084.6	1 784.7
1984	12 140.1	9 112.5	5 041.0	1 758.8	2 943.8	338.5	4 071.5	3 027.5	2 928.0	404.3	2 182.7	341.0	99.5	1 182.2	1 845.4
1985	12 759.0	9 619.0	5 332.4	1 858.0	3 101.8	372.6	4 286.6	3 140.0	3 039.6	400.2	2 274.6	364.7	100.4	1 210.4	1 929.6
1986	13 548.2	10 230.6	5 603.6	1 964.7	3 232.5	406.4	4 627.0	3 317.6	3 213.7	413.1	2 415.0	385.6	103.9	1 260.1	2 057.5
1987	14 342.5	10 843.5	5 919.1	2 055.3	3 415.1	448.7	4 924.4	3 499.0	3 385.6	431.0	2 538.2	416.3	113.4	1 318.2	2 180.8
1988	15 228.3	11 536.2	6 311.3	2 178.1	3 641.8	491.5	5 224.9	3 692.1	3 563.5	466.3	2 648.8	448.4	128.6	1 405.8	2 286.3
1989	16 093.7	12 203.1	6 699.8	2 300.6	3 858.7	540.5	5 503.2	3 890.7	3 753.2	498.4	2 780.9	474.0	137.4	1 477.7	2 413.0
1990	16 856.4	12 773.6	7 071.3	2 423.7	4 055.4	592.3	5 702.3	4 082.8	3 940.9	534.7	2 907.9	498.2	141.9	1 541.0	2 541.8
1991	17 273.0	13 058.9	7 242.6	2 482.2	4 116.7	643.6	5 816.3	4 214.1	4 071.3	559.1	2 994.6	517.6	142.8	1 592.5	2 621.5
1992	17 999.5	13 608.9	7 487.0	2 544.3	4 251.0	691.7	6 121.9	4 390.6	4 239.5	585.5	3 120.0	534.0	151.1	1 652.1	2 738.4
1993	18 900.8	14 321.2	7 837.6	2 642.4	4 458.5	736.6	6 483.7	4 579.6	4 417.8	608.9	3 262.5	546.4	161.8	1 704.8	2 874.8
1994	20 027.3	15 202.7	8 272.9	2 784.9	4 696.8	791.2	6 929.8	4 824.5	4 652.0	634.4	3 452.8	564.8	172.6	1 770.4	3 054.1
1995	20 999.8	15 951.3	8 723.3	2 959.2	4 913.2	851.0	7 228.0	5 048.5	4 869.7	641.7	3 648.7	579.2	178.8	1 811.0	3 237.5
1996	22 001.5	16 767.8	9 152.3	3 104.1	5 136.2	912.1	7 615.4	5 233.7	5 047.1	633.9	3 826.7	586.4	186.6	1 833.8	3 399.9
1997	23 170.1	17 703.7	9 674.8	3 235.2	5 445.7	993.8	8 029.0	5 466.3	5 271.2	629.5	4 043.3	598.5	195.1	1 864.3	3 602.0
1998	24 472.3	18 775.2	10 226.6	3 384.7	5 759.2	1 082.7	8 548.6	5 697.1	5 492.1	639.3	4 240.2	612.6	205.0	1 902.5	3 794.6
1999	26 042.8	20 027.0	10 849.4	3 578.7	6 063.8	1 206.8	9 177.6	6 015.7	5 798.0	660.8	4 503.0	634.2	217.8	1 967.3	4 048.4
2000	27 759.9	21 418.9	11 608.8	3 805.2	6 468.4	1 335.1	9 810.2	6 341.0	6 111.4	655.2	4 799.9	656.3	229.6	2 003.8	4 337.2
2001	29 310.4	22 706.4	12 189.4	3 913.4	6 880.7	1 395.2	10 517.0	6 604.0	6 359.8	650.9	5 040.4	668.5	244.2	2 026.4	4 577.6
2002	30 737.0	23 838.3	12 615.9	3 959.3	7 212.5	1 444.0	11 222.4	6 898.7	6 641.1	666.8	5 285.2	689.1	257.6	2 077.6	4 821.1
2003	32 394.9	25 197.2	13 036.2	4 000.4	7 514.3	1 521.6	12 161.0	7 197.7	6 922.0	685.7	5 510.1	726.2	275.7	2 149.8	5 047.9
2004	35 711.1	27 734.8	14 150.5	4 225.9	8 334.0	1 590.6	13 584.3	7 976.3	7 673.3	711.2	6 199.5	762.6	303.0	2 289.1	5 687.2
2005	39 293.0	30 580.2	15 429.8	4 423.0	9 311.4	1 695.4	15 150.4	8 712.8	8 380.8	735.3	6 842.1	803.4	332.0	2 432.9	6 279.9
2006	42 509.6	32 900.5	16 707.3	4 729.2	10 180.9	1 797.2	16 193.2	9 609.2	9 262.1	768.0	7 654.8	839.3	347.0	2 579.5	7 029.7
2007	44 415.9	34 061.0	17 653.8	4 952.1	10 772.1	1 929.6	16 407.2	10 354.9	10 010.1	803.6	8 316.4	890.1	344.8	2 709.8	7 645.1
2008	45 920.8	34 882.8	18 787.1	5 200.2	11 557.2	2 029.7	16 095.7	11 038.0	10 702.1	855.2	8 919.1	927.8	335.9	2 828.7	8 209.3
2009	45 085.8	33 995.6	18 237.6	5 120.2	11 029.7	2 087.7	15 758.0	11 090.2	10 760.4	885.7	8 918.4	956.4	329.8	2 838.4	8 251.8
2010	45 984.7	34 467.5	18 684.5	5 224.0	11 286.3	2 174.2	15 783.0	11 517.2	11 184.7	923.4	9 249.1	1 012.2	332.5	2 955.8	8 561.4
2011	47 576.5	35 444.0	19 551.3	5 459.7	11 799.6	2 292.0	15 892.7	12 132.5	11 795.5	954.8	9 800.5	1 040.2	337.0	3 061.3	9 071.2
2012	49 092.1	36 569.3	20 216.9	5 699.6	12 126.7	2 390.6	16 352.4	12 522.8	12 175.1	969.0	10 142.0	1 064.1	347.6	3 126.7	9 396.0
2013	51 510.7	38 567.6	21 073.3	5 897.2	12 641.7	2 534.5	17 494.3	12 943.2	12 572.0	979.9	10 492.1	1 100.0	371.1	3 204.8	9 738.4
2014	53 585.1	40 346.1	22 037.1	6 138.8	13 245.0	2 653.3	18 309.0	13 238.9	12 854.9	992.4	10 747.2	1 115.3	384.0	3 248.7	9 990.2
2015	54 879.1	41 443.7	22 487.0	6 307.0	13 442.6	2 737.3	18 956.7	13 435.5	13 044.2	990.7	10 935.0	1 118.5	391.3	3 250.9	10 184.5
2016	57 162.3	43 335.0	23 118.3	6 461.5	13 765.4	2 891.4	20 216.7	13 827.3	13 414.9	1 001.1	11 266.1	1 147.7	412.5	3 315.6	10 511.7
2017	59 547.7	45 167.4	24 000.9	6 678.7	14 248.1	3 074.0	21 166.6	14 380.3	13 954.3	1 016.8	11 745.2	1 192.4	426.0	3 406.2	10 974.1
2018	62 701.2	47 573.4	25 220.0	6 992.0	14 950.8	3 277.2	22 353.4	15 127.8	14 681.9	1 055.0	12 393.8	1 233.1	445.9	3 521.7	11 606.1
2019	64 992.0	49 310.2	26 209.2	7 227.5	15 497.2	3 484.6	23 101.0	15 681.8	15 225.6	1 082.2	12 867.4	1 276.1	456.1	3 603.7	12 078.0

Table 5-5B. Current-Cost Net Stock of Fixed Assets: Historical Data

(Billions of dollars, year-end estimates.)

Year	Total	Private						Government							
		Total	Nonresidential				Resi-dential	Total	Nonresidential				Resi-dential	Federal	State and local
			Total	Equip-ment	Struc-tures	Intellect-ual property products			Total	Equip-ment	Struc-tures	Intellect-ual property products			
1925	261.7	223.4	127.0	31.1	94.0	1.9	96.4	38.3	38.3	2.6	35.6	0.1	0.0	8.9	29.4
1926	270.5	231.6	131.5	32.8	96.7	2.0	100.0	38.9	38.9	2.6	36.2	0.1	0.0	8.8	30.1
1927	277.2	236.9	134.2	33.5	98.5	2.1	102.7	40.3	40.3	2.6	37.7	0.1	0.0	8.6	31.7
1928	289.2	248.6	137.8	34.2	101.3	2.3	110.8	40.7	40.7	2.5	38.0	0.1	0.0	8.3	32.4
1929	294.4	251.7	137.1	34.3	100.3	2.5	114.6	42.7	42.7	2.5	40.0	0.2	0.0	8.9	33.8
1930	281.7	239.4	130.2	32.7	95.0	2.5	109.2	42.3	42.3	2.4	39.7	0.2	0.0	8.4	33.9
1931	245.5	205.4	116.2	29.7	84.0	2.5	89.2	40.0	40.0	2.4	37.4	0.3	0.0	7.8	32.3
1932	222.3	187.6	107.6	26.7	78.6	2.4	79.9	34.7	34.7	2.3	32.1	0.3	0.0	7.5	27.2
1933	236.3	196.5	109.3	26.4	80.5	2.4	87.2	39.8	39.8	2.3	37.1	0.4	0.0	8.5	31.3
1934	246.0	198.6	110.6	26.5	81.6	2.6	87.9	47.4	47.4	2.5	44.5	0.4	0.0	9.4	38.0
1935	247.3	199.5	110.3	25.9	81.6	2.8	89.2	47.7	47.7	2.6	44.6	0.4	0.0	10.5	37.2
1936	275.1	220.4	121.4	27.8	90.4	3.1	99.1	54.7	54.5	2.7	51.3	0.5	0.1	12.1	42.5
1937	289.9	231.7	126.5	29.9	93.1	3.4	105.2	58.1	57.9	3.0	54.4	0.5	0.3	13.4	44.7
1938	292.7	232.0	125.2	29.9	91.6	3.7	106.8	60.7	60.4	3.1	56.7	0.6	0.3	14.2	46.5
1939	298.2	235.6	125.5	30.5	91.0	4.0	110.1	62.6	62.2	3.3	58.3	0.6	0.4	14.8	47.7
1940	320.5	254.4	133.6	32.8	96.5	4.3	120.8	66.1	65.6	3.7	61.3	0.6	0.6	16.8	49.3
1941	365.5	282.8	151.0	37.6	108.2	5.1	131.9	82.7	81.6	7.1	73.6	0.9	1.1	27.1	55.6
1942	424.9	302.3	160.5	38.5	115.9	6.0	141.8	122.5	120.6	21.0	98.3	1.3	1.9	57.5	65.0
1943	478.7	317.1	163.3	38.9	117.6	6.8	153.8	161.6	158.6	46.5	109.9	2.2	3.0	92.5	69.1
1944	513.4	329.3	165.2	38.8	119.0	7.5	164.1	184.0	180.7	67.4	109.8	3.5	3.3	117.0	67.1
1945	554.9	353.0	180.2	44.2	127.9	8.1	172.8	201.9	198.3	78.5	115.5	4.3	3.6	135.7	66.2
1946	639.7	434.0	221.0	53.3	158.6	9.1	213.0	205.7	201.4	70.7	125.7	5.0	4.3	132.7	73.0
1947	734.2	516.6	265.7	65.5	189.6	10.6	250.9	217.6	212.0	60.0	146.4	5.5	5.6	124.2	93.3
1948	780.0	562.2	291.6	80.3	199.9	11.3	270.6	217.9	212.9	50.2	156.6	6.2	5.0	116.2	101.7
1949	785.1	581.1	296.7	84.6	200.4	11.7	284.4	204.0	198.9	42.4	149.7	6.8	5.1	106.7	97.2

Table 5-6A.　Chain-Type Quantity Indexes for Net Stock of Fixed Assets: Recent Data

(Index numbers, 2012 = 100.)

Year	Total	Private						Government							
		Total	Nonresidential				Resi-dential	Total	Nonresidential				Resi-dential	Federal	State and local
			Total	Equip-ment	Struc-tures	Intellect-ual property products			Total	Equip-ment	Struc-tures	Intellect-ual property products			
1950	17.3	16.4	14.5	8.3	24.0	3.1	18.9	20.5	20.6	28.2	22.3	4.7	17.1	34.7	14.5
1951	18.0	17.0	15.0	8.8	24.6	3.2	19.6	21.4	21.4	30.3	23.0	5.0	18.3	36.2	15.1
1952	18.7	17.5	15.5	9.2	25.1	3.4	20.4	22.5	22.6	34.2	23.8	5.4	19.7	38.9	15.6
1953	19.4	18.2	16.0	9.7	25.8	3.7	21.1	23.8	23.9	38.4	24.7	5.9	20.9	41.7	16.2
1954	20.2	18.8	16.5	10.0	26.5	4.0	21.9	24.9	25.0	40.5	25.7	6.4	21.5	43.5	17.0
1955	21.0	19.6	17.1	10.5	27.2	4.3	22.9	25.8	25.9	41.3	26.8	7.1	21.9	44.5	17.9
1956	21.8	20.3	17.8	11.0	28.1	4.6	23.8	26.8	26.9	41.8	27.8	8.3	22.5	45.7	18.8
1957	22.5	21.0	18.4	11.4	28.9	5.0	24.5	27.8	27.9	42.5	28.8	9.6	23.5	46.9	19.7
1958	23.2	21.6	18.8	11.6	29.6	5.3	25.3	29.0	29.1	43.2	30.0	10.8	25.4	48.4	20.8
1959	24.1	22.3	19.3	11.9	30.4	5.6	26.3	30.3	30.4	45.0	31.2	12.1	27.5	50.3	21.9
1960	24.9	23.0	19.9	12.2	31.2	6.0	27.3	31.5	31.6	46.3	32.4	13.5	29.1	52.0	23.0
1961	25.8	23.7	20.5	12.5	32.0	6.4	28.2	33.0	33.1	48.3	33.7	15.0	31.0	54.1	24.1
1962	26.7	24.5	21.1	12.9	32.9	6.8	29.2	34.5	34.6	50.4	35.0	16.8	33.1	56.5	25.3
1963	27.8	25.4	21.8	13.4	33.8	7.2	30.3	36.1	36.1	51.6	36.4	19.2	34.2	58.5	26.7
1964	28.9	26.4	22.7	14.1	34.9	7.6	31.6	37.6	37.7	52.4	37.9	21.8	35.3	60.4	28.1
1965	30.1	27.5	23.8	15.1	36.2	8.2	32.7	39.2	39.2	52.5	39.4	24.4	36.6	62.0	29.6
1966	31.5	28.7	25.2	16.4	37.6	8.8	33.7	40.9	41.0	53.2	41.1	27.5	37.9	64.1	31.3
1967	32.7	29.8	26.4	17.4	39.0	9.5	34.6	42.8	42.8	54.4	42.8	30.5	39.4	66.1	33.0
1968	34.0	31.0	27.6	18.6	40.3	10.1	35.7	44.4	44.5	54.4	44.5	33.4	40.9	67.4	34.8
1969	35.3	32.3	28.9	19.8	41.7	10.8	36.8	45.8	45.9	53.9	46.0	36.0	42.7	68.3	36.5
1970	36.4	33.4	30.0	20.8	43.1	11.3	37.8	47.0	47.0	53.2	47.3	37.8	44.6	68.7	38.0
1971	37.5	34.5	31.1	21.6	44.4	11.6	39.3	47.9	47.9	51.0	48.6	39.3	46.4	68.3	39.3
1972	38.8	36.0	32.3	22.8	45.7	12.0	41.0	48.7	48.7	49.2	49.7	40.8	48.0	68.1	40.6
1973	40.2	37.5	33.7	24.4	47.2	12.5	42.7	49.5	49.5	47.7	50.8	42.1	49.5	68.0	41.8
1974	41.3	38.8	35.1	25.9	48.6	12.9	43.8	50.4	50.3	47.2	51.9	42.9	50.9	68.0	43.0
1975	42.2	39.7	36.0	26.8	49.6	13.2	44.7	51.2	51.1	46.8	52.8	43.7	52.6	68.0	44.1
1976	43.2	40.8	36.9	27.7	50.7	13.8	45.9	52.0	52.0	46.7	53.8	44.6	53.9	68.3	45.2
1977	44.5	42.2	38.2	29.1	51.8	14.4	47.6	52.8	52.7	46.7	54.6	45.7	55.1	68.6	46.2
1978	46.0	43.8	39.8	31.0	53.2	15.1	49.3	53.7	53.6	46.5	55.6	47.0	56.2	69.0	47.3
1979	47.6	45.6	41.6	33.0	54.9	16.1	50.9	54.7	54.6	46.9	56.7	48.4	57.2	69.6	48.5
1980	48.9	46.9	43.2	34.4	56.8	17.0	51.9	55.7	55.6	47.4	57.7	49.9	58.4	70.3	49.6
1981	50.1	48.3	44.9	35.8	59.0	18.2	52.7	56.6	56.5	48.2	58.5	51.5	59.9	71.2	50.5
1982	51.1	49.3	46.3	36.5	61.0	19.4	53.2	57.5	57.3	49.3	59.2	53.0	61.3	72.3	51.3
1983	52.2	50.4	47.5	37.2	62.5	20.6	54.3	58.4	58.3	51.1	59.8	54.7	63.0	73.7	52.0
1984	53.7	52.1	49.3	38.7	64.5	22.3	55.8	59.6	59.4	53.2	60.6	56.8	64.4	75.3	53.0
1985	55.4	53.8	51.2	40.2	66.8	24.1	57.2	61.0	60.9	56.0	61.6	59.5	66.2	77.4	54.2
1986	57.0	55.5	52.8	41.3	68.6	25.8	58.9	62.6	62.5	59.6	62.6	62.1	68.0	79.9	55.4
1987	58.6	57.0	54.2	42.2	70.3	27.5	60.7	64.3	64.1	63.3	63.8	64.9	70.0	82.5	56.7
1988	60.2	58.7	55.8	43.3	71.9	28.9	62.4	65.8	65.6	65.9	64.9	67.1	71.7	84.2	58.1
1989	61.7	60.2	57.4	44.5	73.5	31.0	63.8	67.2	67.0	68.7	66.0	68.8	73.3	85.6	59.5
1990	63.1	61.6	58.9	45.4	75.3	33.1	65.1	68.7	68.5	71.6	67.2	70.4	74.9	87.0	61.1
1991	64.2	62.6	59.9	45.9	76.5	35.2	66.0	70.1	69.9	73.7	68.5	71.3	76.4	87.9	62.7
1992	65.3	63.6	60.9	46.5	77.3	37.3	67.2	71.4	71.1	75.4	69.8	72.0	77.9	88.5	64.2
1993	66.6	65.0	62.2	47.9	78.2	39.2	68.6	72.4	72.2	76.1	71.1	72.3	79.3	88.7	65.7
1994	68.0	66.5	63.7	49.8	79.1	41.0	70.3	73.3	73.1	76.0	72.3	72.4	80.4	88.4	67.1
1995	69.6	68.3	65.5	52.1	80.2	43.0	71.8	74.4	74.1	76.0	73.6	72.4	81.8	88.2	68.7
1996	71.4	70.3	67.7	54.8	81.6	45.7	73.6	75.5	75.3	76.0	75.1	72.5	83.2	88.4	70.3
1997	73.3	72.5	70.2	57.8	83.2	49.0	75.4	76.6	76.3	75.5	76.6	72.8	84.6	87.9	72.0
1998	75.5	74.9	73.0	61.4	84.9	52.7	77.5	77.8	77.5	75.4	78.1	73.3	85.9	87.5	73.9
1999	77.9	77.6	76.0	65.5	86.6	57.1	79.7	79.2	78.9	75.8	79.7	73.9	87.1	87.3	75.9
2000	80.4	80.4	79.3	69.8	88.6	61.8	81.9	80.6	80.3	76.1	81.3	74.7	88.2	87.1	78.0
2001	82.5	82.7	81.7	72.6	90.3	65.3	84.0	82.1	81.8	76.4	83.1	76.0	89.3	87.0	80.2
2002	84.4	84.6	83.3	74.4	91.3	67.9	86.3	83.9	83.7	77.6	85.0	77.9	90.6	87.6	82.5
2003	86.4	86.6	84.7	76.3	92.2	70.5	89.0	85.8	85.6	78.7	86.9	80.2	91.7	88.5	84.8
2004	88.5	88.8	86.3	78.8	92.9	73.2	91.8	87.6	87.4	80.3	88.7	82.7	92.9	89.6	86.9
2005	90.6	91.1	88.1	82.0	93.6	76.4	94.6	89.2	89.0	82.3	90.1	85.4	93.8	90.7	88.6
2006	92.9	93.6	90.4	86.0	94.7	79.9	97.3	90.9	90.8	84.8	91.7	88.1	94.7	92.0	90.6
2007	95.0	95.7	93.0	90.0	96.3	83.9	99.1	92.7	92.6	87.8	93.3	90.6	95.5	93.3	92.5
2008	96.5	97.2	95.2	92.6	98.0	87.6	99.7	94.5	94.4	91.4	94.9	92.9	96.6	94.8	94.4
2009	97.2	97.6	95.8	91.9	98.8	90.4	99.8	96.2	96.1	94.5	96.4	95.0	97.6	96.4	96.1
2010	98.0	98.1	96.7	93.3	99.0	93.1	99.8	97.8	97.7	97.1	97.9	97.0	98.8	98.1	97.7
2011	98.9	98.9	98.1	96.1	99.4	96.5	99.8	99.1	99.1	98.8	99.1	98.7	99.7	99.3	99.0
2012	100.0	100.0	100.0	100.0	100.0	100.0	100.0	100.0	100.0	100.0	100.0	100.0	100.0	100.0	100.0
2013	101.2	101.4	102.0	104.0	100.8	103.9	100.7	100.7	100.8	100.2	100.8	101.0	100.0	100.0	101.0
2014	102.6	103.1	104.4	108.5	101.9	107.8	101.4	101.4	101.4	100.2	101.5	101.5	100.0	99.8	101.9
2015	104.1	104.8	106.7	112.8	103.0	111.9	102.5	102.1	102.2	100.0	102.4	102.1	100.0	99.6	103.0
2016	105.6	106.4	108.7	116.2	103.9	116.9	103.7	103.0	103.0	100.4	103.3	102.9	99.9	99.5	104.1
2017	106.9	107.9	110.6	119.4	104.7	121.7	104.7	103.9	104.0	101.4	104.2	104.0	99.9	99.7	105.3
2018	108.5	109.7	113.1	123.7	105.9	127.4	105.8	104.8	104.9	103.1	105.1	105.1	99.8	99.8	106.4
2019	110.2	111.6	115.6	127.8	107.1	133.6	107.0	105.9	106.1	105.4	106.1	106.9	99.7	100.6	107.7

Table 5-6B. Chain-Type Quantity Indexes for Net Stock of Fixed Assets: Historical Data

(Index numbers, 2012 = 100.)

Year	Total	Private						Government							
		Total	Nonresidential				Residential	Total	Nonresidential				Residential	Federal	State and local
			Total	Equipment	Structures	Intellectual property products			Total	Equipment	Structures	Intellectual property products			
1925	10.6	11.5	10.6	4.8	19.8	0.7	13.1	5.5	5.7	2.5	8.0	0.10	0.00	4.5	6.7
1926	11.0	12.0	10.9	5.0	20.4	0.7	13.7	5.8	6.0	2.4	8.3	0.10	0.00	4.4	7.0
1927	11.4	12.4	11.2	5.1	21.0	0.8	14.2	6.0	6.2	2.4	8.7	0.10	0.00	4.3	7.5
1928	11.8	12.8	11.5	5.2	21.6	0.8	14.7	6.3	6.5	2.4	9.2	0.10	0.00	4.3	7.9
1929	12.1	13.2	11.9	5.4	22.2	0.9	15.0	6.6	6.8	2.5	9.6	0.10	0.00	4.3	8.4
1930	12.4	13.3	12.1	5.4	22.7	1.0	15.0	7.0	7.2	2.4	10.2	0.20	0.00	4.3	9.0
1931	12.5	13.3	12.0	5.2	22.8	1.1	15.1	7.3	7.6	2.5	10.7	0.30	0.10	4.4	9.6
1932	12.4	13.2	11.8	4.9	22.6	1.1	15.0	7.6	7.9	2.4	11.2	0.30	0.10	4.6	10.0
1933	12.4	13.0	11.6	4.7	22.4	1.2	14.9	7.9	8.1	2.4	11.5	0.40	0.10	4.8	10.2
1934	12.4	12.9	11.4	4.5	22.2	1.2	14.8	8.1	8.4	2.4	11.9	0.40	0.10	5.1	10.4
1935	12.4	12.9	11.3	4.5	22.0	1.3	14.8	8.4	8.7	2.6	12.3	0.40	0.20	5.6	10.7
1936	12.6	12.9	11.4	4.6	22.0	1.4	14.8	8.9	9.2	2.6	13.1	0.50	0.70	6.1	11.2
1937	12.8	13.0	11.6	4.8	22.1	1.5	14.9	9.3	9.6	2.7	13.6	0.50	1.30	6.5	11.6
1938	12.9	13.1	11.6	4.7	22.0	1.7	15.0	10.0	10.2	2.9	14.3	0.50	1.50	6.9	12.1
1939	13.2	13.2	11.6	4.8	22.0	1.8	15.2	10.3	10.5	3.1	15.0	0.60	1.90	7.3	12.8
1940	13.4	13.3	11.8	5.0	22.1	1.9	15.4	10.8	11.0	3.2	15.7	0.60	2.80	7.9	13.2
1941	13.9	13.6	12.0	5.2	22.2	2.1	15.7	12.3	12.5	6.1	17.0	0.90	5.20	11.9	13.5
1942	14.6	13.5	11.9	5.2	22.0	2.2	15.7	16.3	16.5	19.2	19.8	1.20	8.10	24.0	13.5
1943	15.2	13.4	11.8	5.1	21.8	2.3	15.6	20.8	21.0	45.0	20.9	1.70	12.00	38.7	13.4
1944	15.8	13.4	11.8	5.1	21.6	2.4	15.6	24.4	24.8	70.1	21.2	2.40	13.00	51.0	13.2
1945	16.1	13.5	12.0	5.4	21.6	2.5	15.5	25.8	26.2	79.2	21.4	3.00	13.40	55.8	13.1
1946	16.1	13.9	12.4	5.9	22.1	2.6	15.9	23.9	24.2	64.6	21.2	3.40	14.90	49.7	13.1
1947	16.2	14.5	13.0	6.7	22.5	2.8	16.5	22.3	22.5	50.9	21.1	3.70	15.30	43.8	13.3
1948	16.5	15.1	13.6	7.4	23.0	2.9	17.3	21.1	21.3	39.7	21.3	4.00	15.50	39.2	13.5
1949	16.8	15.7	14.0	7.8	23.4	3.0	17.9	20.8	20.9	33.9	21.8	4.30	16.40	36.9	14.0

Table 5-7. Capital Expenditures

(Millions of dollars, except totals are shown in billions.)

Capital expenditures	All companies												
	2007	2008	2009	2010	2011	2012	2013	2014	2015	2016	2017	2018	2019
TOTAL (billions)	1 354.7	1 374.2	1 090.7	1 105.7	1 243.0	1 424.2	1 491.3	1 597.9	1 642.0	1 574.8	1 678.8	. . .	1 919.2
Structures	525 273	562 381	449 545	428 713	471 779	570 489	581 836	643 590	642 859	599 707	665 642	. . .	770
New	480 839	522 999	422 780	394 517	442 745	534 696	549 359	606 980	589 689	543 758	616 850	. . .	703
Used	44 434	39 382	26 765	34 196	29 034	35 793	32 477	36 610	53 171	55 948	48 792	. . .	67
Equipment	829 455	811 779	641 149	676 989	771 177	853 661	909 477	954 261	999 122	975 138	101 318	. . .	1 150
New	790 407	765 279	606 576	639 214	730 033	800 519	856 012	898 581	941 297	924 954	956 582	. . .	1 077
Used	39 048	46 501	34 572	37 775	41 144	53 142	53 466	55 680	57 825	50 184	56 607	. . .	73

Capital expenditures	Companies with employees												
	2007	2008	2009	2010	2011	2012	2013	2014	2015	2016	2017	2018	2019
TOTAL (billions)	1 270.5	1 294.5	1 015.3	1 036.2	1 169.6	1 334.9	1 400.9	1 506.6	1 548.1	1 479.4	1 577.8	1 699.1	1 807.8
Structures	490 779	529 393	414 051	395 531	440 893	533 115	546 056	608 698	600 766	552 637	612 025	648	710
New	457 233	500 474	395 022	366 853	414 958	501 420	518 430	577 743	557 641	508 523	576 460	613	658
Used	33 546	28 919	19 030	28 678	25 935	31 695	27 625	30 955	43 126	44 114	35 565	36	53
Equipment	779 744	765 098	601 270	640 631	728 710	801 820	854 827	897 885	947 291	926 802	965 760	1 051	1 097
New	750 353	728 322	577 051	612 441	697 766	759 632	813 972	853 888	900 519	887 884	920 780	998	1 039
Used	29 391	36 776	24 219	28 190	30 944	42 189	40 855	43 996	46 772	38 918	44 981	53	58

Capital expenditures	Companies without employees												
	2007	2008	2009	2010	2011	2012	2013	2014	2015	2016	2017	2018	2019
TOTAL (billions)	84.2	79.7	75.4	69.5	73.4	89.2	90.4	91.3	93.9	95.4	101.0	. . .	111.4
Structures	34 494	32 988	35 493	33 182	30 886	37 374	35 780	34 892	42 093	47 070	53 617	. . .	59
New	23 606	22 525	27 758	27 664	27 787	33 276	30 929	29 237	32 048	35 236	40 390	. . .	45
Used	10 888	10 463	7 735	5 518	3 099	4 098	4 851	5 655	10 045	11 834	13 227	. . .	14
Equipment	49 711	46 681	39 878	36 357	42 467	51 840	54 650	56 376	51 831	48 336	47 429	. . .	52
New	40 054	36 957	29 525	26 773	32 267	40 887	42 040	44 693	40 778	37 070	35 802	. . .	37
Used	9 657	9 724	10 353	9 585	10 200	10 953	12 610	11 684	11 053	11 266	11 627	. . .	15

. . . = Not available.

Table 5-8. Capital Expenditures for Structures and Equipment for Companies with Employees by Major Industry Sector

(Millions of dollars.)

Year and type of expenditure	Total	Forestry, fishing, and agricultural services (113–115)	Mining (21)	Utilities (22)	Construction (23)	Manufacturing (31–33) Total	Durable goods industries (321, 327, 33)	Nondurable goods industries (31, 322–326)	Wholesale trade (42)	Retail trade (44–45)	Transportation and warehousing (48–49)	Information (51)
2010												
Total expenditures	1 036 153	3 255	115 749	94 462	17 856	160 798	86 570	74 227	31 075	65 252	58 952	97 150
Structures, total	396 398	679	85 221	43 896	2 633	31 166	14 099	17 068	6 879	29 169	23 401	21 771
Equipment, total	639 755	2 576	30 528	50 566	15 223	129 631	72 472	57 160	24 196	36 084	35 551	75 379
2011												
Total expenditures	1 169 604	3 063	165 693	98 047	21 778	192 441	110 151	82 290	35 745	68 131	72 722	100 057
Structures, total	440 893	529	124 508	46 729	2 867	36 339	17 394	18 946	7 988	27 332	29 026	20 152
Equipment, total	728 710	2 534	41 185	51 319	18 910	156 102	92 758	63 344	27 757	40 799	43 696	79 905
2012												
Total expenditures	1 334 421	3 149	196 653	124 958	23 555	203 119	113 299	89 820	40 852	77 567	81 792	106 537
Structures, total	533 042	496	150 653	70 940	1 975	43 080	20 181	22 900	9 367	33 443	32 397	23 263
Equipment, total	801 378	2 653	46 000	54 017	21 580	160 039	93 118	66 921	31 485	44 124	49 395	83 274
2013												
Total expenditures	1 400 883	2 965	202 213	111 310	27 562	221 345	121 494	99 850	37 505	77 520	92 616	123 881
Structures, total	546 056	492	152 441	58 051	2 545	46 594	20 303	26 291	9 659	33 865	37 645	33 297
Equipment, total	854 827	2 473	49 773	53 260	25 018	174 751	101 191	73 560	27 846	43 655	54 971	90 584
2014												
Total expenditures	1 506 582	3 985	230 776	118 895	30 277	231 089	124 797	106 292	44 758	82 402	111 010	132 049
Structures, total	608 698	952	187 348	63 844	3 815	50 481	19 520	30 962	12 288	35 564	40 557	33 315
Equipment, total	897 885	3 033	43 428	55 052	26 462	180 608	105 277	75 331	32 470	46 838	70 453	98 734
2015												
Total expenditures	1 548 057	3 322	174 069	130 514	33 276	245 123	127 714	117 409	42 378	85 963	116 633	132 671
Structures, total	600 766	598	135 552	71 277	2 600	54 716	22 845	31 871	12 624	37 005	42 490	30 161
Equipment, total	947 291	2 724	38 517	59 237	30 676	190 407	104 869	85 537	29 754	48 959	74 144	102 510
2016												
Total expenditures	1 479 439	4 561	92 641	133 455	35 979	243 595	122 898	120 698	43 768	86 931	109 650	142 911
Structures, total	552 637	559	75 865	73 533	4 302	57 171	22 759	34 412	13 290	39 098	35 717	32 303
Equipment, total	926 802	4 002	16 776	59 922	31 676	186 425	100 139	86 286	30 478	47 833	73 933	110 608
2017												
Total expenditures	1 577 785	4 497	134 380	133 888	34 989	247 013	129 121	117 891	43 977	90 493	108 538	158 888
Structures, total	612 025	750	108 370	66 586	3 251	57 732	24 206	33 526	14 000	38 739	40 439	34 432
Equipment, total	965 760	3 747	26 011	67 302	31 738	189 281	104 915	84 366	29 977	51 754	68 098	124 456
2018												
Total expenditures	1 699 123	4 653	153 370	151 043	38 979	258 073	137 785	120 288	42 799	89 233	122 356	175 084
Structures, total	648 379	716	114 089	78 323	4 045	58 915	26 336	32 579	12 762	38 864	44 618	43 490
Equipment, total	1 050 744	3 937	39 281	72 720	34 935	199 159	111 449	87 710	30 036	50 368	77 738	131 594
2019												
Total expenditures	1 807 827	4 057	158 054	172 646	50 355	272 878	141 393	131 485	40 573	98 594	128 515	176 763
Structures, total	710 339	840	114 635	90 664	7 676	65 494	27 592	37 902	10 121	42 823	52 651	51 438
Equipment, total	1 097 488	3 216	43 419	81 982	42 678	207 383	113 801	93 583	30 453	55 771	75 865	125 325

Table 5-8. Capital Expenditures for Structures and Equipment for Companies with Employees by Major Industry Sector—*Continued*

(Millions of dollars.)

Year and type of expenditure	Finance and insurance (52)	Real estate and rental and leasing (53)	Professional, scientific, and technical services (54)	Management of companies and enterprises (55)	Administrative and support and waste management (56)	Educational services (61)	Health care and social assistance (62)	Arts, entertainment, and recreation (71)	Accommodation and food services (72)	Other services, except public administration (81)	Structure and equipment expenditures serving multiple industries
2010											
Total expenditures	103 093	81 282	28 203	4 946	16 873	23 368	78 381	12 121	19 915	20 951	2 471
Structures, total	16 209	32 375	5 706	1 567	3 552	17 673	42 861	7 709	9 765	13 605	562
Equipment, total	86 884	48 908	22 497	3 379	13 321	5 695	35 520	4 412	10 151	7 346	1 909
2011											
Total expenditures	109 229	91 124	28 109	5 449	18 423	21 019	83 114	11 430	24 833	16 064	3 133
Structures, total	14 405	33 540	6 733	1 368	3 536	15 037	42 910	6 589	12 021	8 675	608
Equipment, total	94 823	57 583	21 376	4 081	14 887	5 982	40 204	4 841	12 811	7 389	2 524
2012											
Total expenditures	130 168	115 652	31 605	6 916	18 811	21 629	88 860	13 296	28 802	16 789	3 711
Structures, total	17 749	42 034	7 536	2 555	3 578	15 721	45 981	8 055	14 154	9 078	988
Equipment, total	112 419	73 618	24 069	4 361	15 233	5 908	42 879	5 241	14 649	7 711	2 722
2013											
Total expenditures	137 824	114 181	35 655	6 147	21 760	22 619	94 181	14 981	34 532	18 615	3 472
Structures, total	15 458	39 359	8 571	1 577	4 123	16 583	49 364	8 263	16 304	10 999	868
Equipment, total	122 366	74 821	27 084	4 570	17 637	6 036	44 817	6 718	18 228	7 616	2 604
2014											
Total expenditures	153 260	121 919	30 383	5 366	22 568	25 823	89 011	19 550	29 836	20 304	3 321
Structures, total	17 843	44 677	7 228	1 237	4 112	19 710	47 481	12 153	14 181	11 075	837
Equipment, total	135 417	77 241	23 156	4 128	18 456	6 114	41 531	7 397	15 654	9 230	2 484
2015											
Total expenditures	164 594	151 875	33 327	5 180	26 183	33 176	93 755	16 142	33 066	23 195	3 613
Structures, total	19 787	62 188	8 393	1 047	6 547	25 906	49 234	8 822	17 331	13 092	1 395
Equipment, total	144 807	89 688	24 933	4 133	19 636	7 270	44 521	7 321	15 734	10 103	2 218
2016											
Total expenditures	161 653	150 686	31 728	6 161	27 672	30 424	93 588	22 544	29 855	27 249	4 389
Structures, total	19 485	62 906	8 736	1 618	6 867	23 999	48 238	13 534	16 795	16 794	1 827
Equipment, total	142 168	87 779	22 992	4 543	20 805	6 425	45 350	9 010	13 059	10 456	2 562
2017											
Total expenditures	163 038	161 396	37 213	6 918	26 505	36 951	104 628	22 448	35 828	21 667	4 530
Structures, total	22 742	73 028	11 569	1 674	4 948	30 171	56 711	13 972	18 295	13 178	1 439
Equipment, total	140 297	88 368	25 643	5 244	21 557	6 781	47 917	8 476	17 533	8 489	3 091
2018											
Total expenditures	181 508	173 879	41 995	6 879	29 386	35 496	108 552	24 740	35 396	22 210	3 493
Structures, total	25 555	70 473	13 579	1 749	6 960	29 118	59 881	14 760	17 385	12 374	722
Equipment, total	155 953	103 406	28 416	5 130	22 426	6 378	48 671	9 979	18 011	9 836	2 770
2019											
Total expenditures	195 328	181 150	43 522	7 305	31 654	31 796	116 735	24 544	44 708	25 313	3 337
Structures, total	31 812	72 575	13 050	1 732	7 480	25 029	69 319	15 225	22 002	15 199	572
Equipment, total	163 516	108 575	30 473	5 573	24 174	6 767	47 415	9 318	22 706	10 113	2 766

NOTES AND DEFINITIONS, CHAPTER 5

TABLES 5-1 THROUGH 5-4

Gross Saving and Investment Accounts

SOURCE: U.S. DEPARTMENT OF COMMERCE, BUREAU OF ECONOMIC ANALYSIS (BEA)

All of the data in these tables are from the July 29, 2021 National Income and Product Accounts (NIPA), publication. Explanation of NIPA data are described in the Notes and Definitions to Chapter 1. All quarterly series are shown at seasonally adjusted annual rates. Current and constant dollar values are in billions of dollars. Constant dollar values are in 2009 dollars. Indexes of quantity are based on the average for the year 2009, set to equal 100.

The 2013 revision included a major expansion of the investment accounts. Expenditures for research and development are now recognized as fixed investment. Before 2013, they were treated as if they were costs of producing this year's output. R&D spending by business, government, and nonprofit institutions serving households (NPISHs) is now counted as fixed investment. It is depreciated (with the estimated depreciation added to capital consumption allowances), so that there can be either positive or negative net investment in R&D. A similar treatment is now given to expenditures by private enterprises for the creation of entertainment, literary, and artistic originals. Finally, an expanded set of ownership transfer costs for residential fixed assets is recognized as fixed investment.

Results from the 2017 Annual Update of NIPA slightly revised the average growth rates of GDP between 2013 and 2016. Other revisions were incorporated include the Census Bureau's annual retail sales, construction, manufacturing plus others.

Definitions: Table 5-1

Gross saving is saving before the deduction of allowances for the consumption of fixed capital. It represents the amount of saving available to finance gross investment. *Net saving* is gross saving less allowances for fixed capital consumption. It represents the amount of saving available for financing expansion of the capital stock, and comprises net private saving (the sum of personal saving, undistributed corporate profits, and wage accruals less disbursements) and the net saving of federal, state, and local governments.

Personal saving is derived by subtracting personal outlays from disposable personal income. (See Chapter 4 for more information.) It is the current net saving of individuals (including proprietors of unincorporated businesses), nonprofit institutions that primarily serve individuals, life insurance carriers, retirement funds, private noninsured welfare funds, and private trust funds. Conceptually, personal saving may also be viewed as the sum for all persons (including institutions as previously defined) of the net acquisition of financial assets and the change in physical assets, less the sum of net borrowing and consumption of fixed capital. In either case, it is defined to exclude capital gains. That is, it excludes profits on the increase in the value of homes, securities, and other property—whether realized or unrealized—and therefore includes the noncorporate inventory valuation adjustment and the capital consumption adjustment (IVA and CCAdj, respectively). (See notes and definitions to Chapter 1.)

The net saving of *Domestic corporate business* is corporate profits after tax less dividends plus the corporate IVA and corporate CCAdj. (See notes and definitions for Chapter 1.)

Government net saving was formerly called "current surplus or deficit (-) of general government." (See Chapter 6 for further detail from the government accounts.) Where current receipts of government exceed current expenditures, government has a current surplus (indicated by a positive value) and saving is made available to finance investment by government or other sectors—for example, by the repayment of debt, which can free up funds for private investment. Where current expenditures exceed current receipts, there is a government deficit (indicated by a negative value) and government must borrow, drawing on funds that would otherwise be available for private investment. In these accounts, current expenditures are defined to include a charge for the consumption of fixed capital.

Consumption of fixed capital is an accounting charge for the using-up of private and government fixed capital, including software, located in the United States. It is based on studies of prices of used equipment and structures in resale markets. As of the 2013 revision, it also includes estimated charges for the using-up of the research and development and other intellectual property capital now defined as investment spending.

For general government and nonprofit institutions that primarily serve individuals, consumption of fixed capital is recorded in government consumption expenditures and in personal consumption expenditures (PCE), respectively, and taken to be the value of the current services of the fixed capital assets owned and used by these entities and the estimated using-up of R&D and other intellectual property.

Private consumption of fixed capital consists of tax-return-based depreciation charges for corporations and nonfarm proprietorships and historical-cost depreciation (calculated by the Bureau of Economic Analysis [BEA] using a geometric pattern of price declines) for farm proprietorships, rental income of persons, and nonprofit institutions, minus the capital consumption adjustments. (In other words, in the NIPA treatment of saving, the amount of the CCAdj is taken out of book depreciation and added to income and profits—a reallocation from one form of gross saving to another.) It also includes the charges for the using-up of private R&D and other intellectual property, as described above.

Gross private domestic investment consists of gross private fixed investment and change in private inventories. (See the notes and definitions for Chapter 1.)

Gross government investment consists of federal, state, and local general government and government enterprise expenditures for fixed assets (structures, equipment, and intellectual property). Government inventory investment is included in government consumption expenditures. For further detail, see Chapter 6.

Capital account transactions, net are the net cash or in-kind transfers between the United States and the rest of the world that are linked to the acquisition or disposition of assets rather than the purchase or sale of currently-produced goods and services. When positive, it represents a net transfer from the United States to the rest of the world; when negative, it represents a net transfer to the United States from the rest of the world. This is a definitional category that was introduced in the 1999 revision of the NIPAs. Estimates are available only from 1982 forward. With the new treatment of disaster losses and disaster insurance introduced in the 2009 revision, this line will include disaster-related insurance payouts to the rest of the world less what is received from the rest of the world.

Net lending or net borrowing (-), NIPAs is equal to the international balance on current account as measured in the NIPAs (see Chapter 7) less capital account transactions, net. When positive, this represents net investment by the United States in the rest of the world; when negative, it represents net borrowing by the United States from the rest of the world. For data before 1982, net lending or net borrowing equals the NIPA balance on current account, because estimates of capital account transactions are not available.

By definition, gross national saving must equal the sum of gross domestic investment, capital account transactions, and net international lending (where net international borrowing appears as negative lending). In practice, due to differences in measurement, these two aggregates differ by the *statistical discrepancy* calculated in the product and income accounts. (See Chapter 1.) Gross saving is therefore equal to the sum of gross domestic investment, capital account transactions, and net international lending minus the statistical discrepancy. Where the statistical discrepancy is negative, it means that the sum of measured investment, capital transactions, and net international lending has fallen short of measured saving.

Net domestic investment is gross domestic investment minus consumption of fixed capital, calculated by the editors from the data shown in the table.

Gross national income is national income plus the consumption of fixed capital. (See Chapter 1 for further information.) This is a new concept introduced in the 2003 revision. It is conceptually equal to gross national product, but differs by the statistical discrepancy. Gross national income is an appropriate denominator for the national saving ratios. Saving was previously shown as a percentage of gross national product; in the revision, it is instead shown as a percentage of the income-side equivalent of gross national product. Since saving is measured as a residual from income, it is appropriate to involve consistent measurements—and consistent imperfections in those measurements—in both the numerator and the denominator of the fraction.

Definitions: Tables 5-2 through 5-4

Gross private fixed investment comprises both nonresidential and residential fixed investment. It consists of purchases of fixed assets, which are commodities that will be used in a production process for more than one year, including replacements and additions to the capital stock, and intellectual property, including software, research and development, and entertainment, literary, and artistic originals. It is "gross" in the sense that it is measured before a deduction for consumption of fixed capital. It covers investment by private businesses and nonprofit institutions in the United States, regardless of whether the investment is owned by U.S. residents. It does not include purchases of the same types of equipment, structures, or intellectual property by government agencies, which are included in government gross investment. It also does not include investment by U.S. residents in other countries.

Gross nonresidential fixed investment consists of structures, equipment, and intellectual property that are not related to personal residences.

Nonresidential structures consists of new construction, brokers' commissions on sales of structures, and net purchases (purchases less sales) of used structures by private business and by nonprofit institutions from government agencies. New construction includes hotels, motels, and mining exploration, shafts, and wells.

Other nonresidential structures consists primarily of religious, educational, vocational, lodging, railroads, farm, and amusement and recreational structures, net purchases of used structures, and brokers' commissions on the sale of structures.

Nonresidential equipment consists of private business purchases—on capital account—of new machinery, equipment, and vehicles; dealers' margins on sales of used equipment; and net purchases (purchases less sales) of used equipment from government agencies, persons, and the rest of the world. (However, it does not include the personal-use portion of equipment purchased for both business and personal use. This is included in PCE.)

Computers have displayed phenomenal growth in numbers and power not easily represented by index numbers or constant-dollar estimates at the scale shown in these tables. Zero entries shown in the quantity indexes for early years actually represent very small quantities. Because of rapid growth in computing power and declines in its price, constant-dollar measures are deemed not meaningful and are not calculated by BEA.

Other information processing includes communication equipment, nonmedical instruments, medical equipment and instruments, photocopy and related equipment, and office and accounting equipment.

Other nonresidential equipment consists primarily of furniture and fixtures, agricultural machinery, construction machinery, mining and oilfield machinery, service industry machinery, and electrical equipment not elsewhere classified.

Intellectual property comprises information processing software, research and development, and entertainment, literary, and artistic originals.

Software excludes the value of software "embedded," or bundled, in computers and other equipment, which is instead included in the value of that equipment.

Research and development consists of expenditures for both purchased and own-account R&D by businesses, NPISHs, and general governments. Government R&D expenditures are treated as investment regardless of whether the R&D is protected or made freely available to the public. Investment is measured as the sum of production costs.

Entertainment, literary, and other artistic originals include theatrical movies, long-lived television programs, books, music, and other miscellaneous entertainment.

Residential private fixed investment consists of both *structures* and residential producers' durable *equipment*—that is, equipment owned by landlords and rented to tenants. Investment in *structures* consists of new units, improvements to existing units, manufactured homes, brokers' commissions and other ownership transfer costs on the sale of residential property, and net purchases (purchases less sales) of used structures from government agencies.

Other residential structures consists primarily of manufactured homes, improvements, dormitories, net purchases of used structures, and brokers' commissions on the sale of residential structures.

Real gross private investment (Table 5-3) and *chain-type quantity indexes for private fixed investment* (Table 5-4) are defined and explained in the notes and definitions to Chapter 1. The chained-dollar (2012) estimates in Table 5-3 are constructed by applying

the changes in the chain-type quantity indexes, as shown in Table 5-4, to the 2012 current-dollar values. Thus, they do not contain any information about time trends that is not already present in the quantity indexes.

In Table 5-4, the user may wish to distinguish between the use of the "not available" symbol (...) and the publication of zero values (0.0). The "not available" values shown for computers and software mean that BEA has no separate estimates of their values; they are included in total "information processing equipment and software." The zeroes indicate quantities so small relative to the 2009 base that they round to zero, but they do exist and are included in the higher-level aggregates.

As the quantity indexes are chain-weighted at the basic level of aggregation, chained constant-dollar components generally do not add to the chained constant-dollar totals. For this reason, BEA only makes available year-2009-dollar estimates back to 1999 (except for the very highest levels of aggregation of gross domestic product [GDP]), since the addition problem is less severe for years close to the base year. However, the addition problem is so severe for computers that BEA does not even publish recent year-2012-dollar values for this component. BEA notes that "The quantity index for computers can be used to accurately measure the real growth rate of this component. However, because computers exhibit rapid changes in prices relative to other prices in the economy, the chained-dollar estimates should not be used to measure the component's relative importance or its contribution to the growth rate of more aggregate series." (Footnote to BEA Table 5.3.6, *Survey of Current Business*, available on the BEA Web site at <https://www.bea.gov>.) Accurate estimates of these contributions are shown in BEA Table 5.3.2, which is published in the *Survey of Current Business* and can be found on the BEA Web site.

Data availability, revisions, and references

See the information on the NIPAs at the end of the notes and definitions to Chapter 1. All current and historical data are available on the BEA Web site at <https://www.bea.gov>.

Tables 5-5 and 5-6

Current-Cost Net Stock of Fixed Assets; Chain-Type Quantity Indexes for Net Stock of Fixed Assets

SOURCE: U.S. DEPARTMENT OF COMMERCE, BUREAU OF ECONOMIC ANALYSIS (BEA)

The Bureau of Economic Analysis (BEA) calculates annual, end-of-year measurements, integrated with the national income and product accounts (NIPAs), of the level of the stock of fixed assets in the U.S. economy, or what is commonly called the "capital stock." (The fixed investment component of the GDP is a <u>flow</u>, or the increment of new capital goods into the capital stock.) Data on consumer stocks of durable goods are also included in the accounts, but are not shown here. Historical data are available back to 1901, with detailed estimates of net stocks, depreciation, and investment by type and by NAICS (North American Industry Classification System) industry. From this data system, *Business Statistics* presents time series data on the net stock of fixed assets valued in current dollars and also as constant-dollar quantity indexes.

The expanded definition of investment introduced in the 2013 comprehensive revision of the NIPAs, explained at the beginning of the Notes and Definitions to this chapter, was not incorporated in the fixed assets accounts until October 2013, so this edition of *Business Statistics* now publishes for the first time fixed assets data including the new NIPA categories.

Definitions and methods

The definitions of capital stock categories are now the same as the fixed investment categories listed earlier in these Notes and Definitions.

The values of fixed capital and depreciation typically reported by businesses are inadequate for economic analysis and are not typically used in these measures. In business reports, capital is generally valued at historical costs—each year's capital acquisition in the prices of the year acquired—and the totals thus represent a mixture of pricing bases. Reported depreciation is generally based on historical cost and on depreciation rates allowable by federal income tax law, rather than on a realistic rate of economic depreciation.

In these data, the *net stock of fixed assets* is measured by a perpetual inventory method. In other words, net stock at any given time is the cumulative value of past gross investment less the cumulative value of past depreciation (measured by "consumption of fixed capital," the component of the NIPAs that is subtracted from GDP in order to yield net domestic product) and also less damages from disasters and war losses that exceed normal depreciation (such as Hurricane Katrina and the terrorist attacks of September 11, 2001).

The initial calculations using this perpetual inventory method are performed in real terms for each type of asset. They are then aggregated to higher levels using an annual-weighted Fisher-type index. (See the definition of *real or chained-dollar estimates* in the notes and definitions for Chapter 1.) This provides the *chain-type quantity indexes* shown in Table 5-6. Growth rates in these indexes measure real growth in the capital stock.

The real values are then converted to a *current-cost* basis to yield the values shown in Table 5-5. They are converted by multiplying the real values by the appropriate price index for the period under consideration. A major use of the current-cost net stock figures is comparison with the value of output in that year; for example, the current-cost net stock of fixed assets for the total economy divided by the current-dollar value of GDP yields a capital-output ratio for the entire economy. Growth rates in current-cost values will reflect both the real growth measured by the quantity indexes and the increase in the value at current prices of the existing stock.

Data availability and references

The 2017 Capital Spending Report: U.S.: Capital Spending Patterns, 2006 – 2015 was released on May 3, 2017. Full historical data are available on the BEA website at www.bea.gov (select Surveys and Programs.

Tables 5-7 and 5-8

Annual Capital Expenditures

SOURCE: U.S. DEPARTMENT OF COMMERCE, CENSUS BUREAU

These data are from the Census Bureau's Annual Capital Expenditures Survey (ACES). The survey provides detailed information on capital investment in new and used structures and equipment by nonfarm businesses.

The survey is based on a stratified random sample of approximately 45,000 companies with employees and 30,000 non-employer businesses (businesses with an owner but no employees). For companies with employees, the Census Bureau reports data for 132 separate industry categories from the North American Industry Classification System (NAICS). Major exclusions are foreign operations of U.S. businesses, businesses in U.S. territories, government operations (including the U.S. Postal Service, agricultural production companies and private households.

Table 5-8 shows these data for the major NAICS sectors. Total capital expenditures, with no industry detail, are reported for the nonemployer businesses and are shown in Table 5-7, where they can be compared with the totals for companies with employees. The 1999 ACES was the first to use NAICS, providing data for the years 1998 forward on that basis.

Definitions

Capital expenditures include all capitalized costs during the year for both new and used structures and equipment, including software, that were chargeable to fixed asset accounts for which depreciation or amortization accounts are ordinarily maintained. For projects lasting longer than one year, this definition includes gross additions to construction-in-progress accounts, even if the asset was not in use and not yet depreciated. For *capital leases*, the company using the asset (lessee) is asked to include the cost or present value of the leased assets in the year in which the lease was entered. Also included in capital expenditures are capitalized leasehold improvements and capitalized interest charges on loans used to finance capital projects.

Structures consist of the capitalized costs of buildings and other structures and all necessary expenditures to acquire, construct, and prepare the structures. The costs of any machinery and equipment that is integral to or built-in features of the structures are classified as structures. Also included are major additions and alterations to existing structures and capitalized repairs and improvements to buildings.

New structures include new buildings and other structures not previously owned, as well as buildings and other structures that have been previously owned but not used or occupied.

Used structures are buildings and other structures that have been previously owned and occupied.

Equipment includes machinery, furniture and fixtures, computers, and vehicles used in the production and distribution of goods and services. Expenditures for machinery and equipment that is housed in structures and can be removed or replaced without significantly altering the structure are classified as equipment.

New equipment consists of machinery and equipment purchased new, as well as equipment produced in the company for the company's own use.

Used equipment is secondhand machinery and equipment.

Capital leases consist of new assets acquired under capital lease arrangements entered into during the year. Capital leases are defined by the criteria in the Financial Accounting Standards (FASB) Number 13.

Capitalized computer software consists of costs of materials and services directly related to the development or acquisition of software; payroll and payroll-related costs for employees directly associated with software development; and interest cost incurred while developing the software. Capitalized computer software is defined by the criteria in Statement of Position 98-1, Accounting for the Costs of Computer Software Developed or Obtained for Internal Use.

Prepackaged software is purchased off-the-shelf through retailers or other mass-market outlets for internal use by the company and includes the cost of licensing fees and service/maintenance agreements.

Vendor-customized software is externally developed by vendors and customized for the company's use.

Internally-developed software is developed by the company's employees for internal use and includes loaded payroll (salaries, wages, benefits, and bonuses related to all software development activities).

Data availability and references

Current and historical data and references are available on the Census Bureau Web site at https://www.census.gov/programs-surveys/aces.html.

CHAPTER 6: GOVERNMENT

SECTION 6A: FEDERAL GOVERNMENT IN THE NATIONAL INCOME AND PRODUCT ACCOUNTS

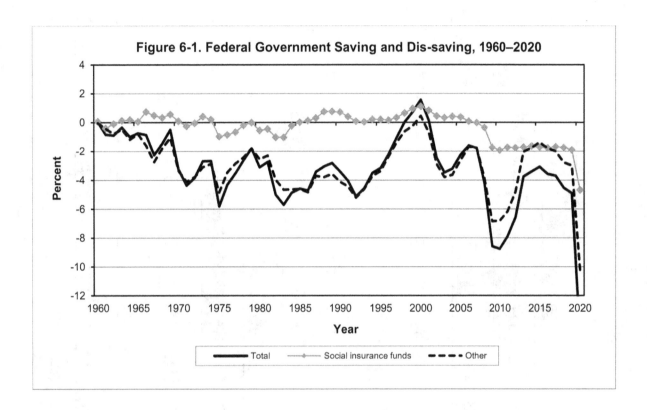

Figure 6-1. Federal Government Saving and Dis-saving, 1960–2020

- In the recovery and economic expansion of the early 2000s, the federal budget never got back to a surplus such as those achieved in 1999 and 2000. With the onset of the most severe recession of the postwar period beginning in December 2007, deficits grew rapidly, due both to the "automatic stabilizers"; such as unemployment insurance, built into the budget structure and to anti-recession programs, such as the American Recovery and Reinvestment Act of 2009. (Table 6-1)

- In calendar 2009, the NIPA budget deficit peaked at 10.7 percent of GDP, including $251.7 billion deficit in social insurance funds. This was not as great as World War II deficits but exceeded in scale the deficits of the 1930s. By 2015, the deficit shrank to less than a third from its peak and was 2.6 percent of GDP, the smallest since 2007. However, since 2015 the deficit has increased each year and ballooned to 15.0 percent of GDP in 2020. (Tables 6-1, 1-1, and 6-14B)

- The main contributors to the rise in the deficit from 2007 to 2010 were increasing social benefits to persons, such as Social Security and unemployment insurance, and a drop in non-social-insurance tax receipts. Federal consumption spending and grants to state and local governments also rose. The deficit shrinkage from 2010 to 2015 was powered mainly by a resurgence in non-social-insurance tax receipts while the increase in the deficit in 2018 and 2019 was due to tax cuts. The deficit, as a percent of GDP, more than tripled in 2020 as a result of COVID-19. (Table 6-1)

- Total federal government current expenditures have increased from 17.2 percent of gross domestic product (GDP) in 1960 to 24.1 percent in 2009, decreasing again to 21.8 percent in 2017 and then increasing to 32.5 percent in 2020. The composition of current expenditures changed significantly over the last several decades. As a percent of GDP, "Consumption" spending on defense and nondefense programs fell significantly while benefits to persons, such as Social Security and Medicare, increased significantly. (Tables 6-1, 1-1 and 6-3)

Table 6-1. Federal Government Current Receipts and Expenditures

(National income and product accounts, calendar years, billions of dollars, quarterly data are at seasonally adjusted annual rates.)

NIPA Table 3.2

Year and quarter	Total current receipts	Total tax receipts [1]	Personal current taxes	Excise taxes	Customs duties	Federal Reserve banks	Other corporate taxes	Taxes from the rest of the world	Contributions for government social insurance	Interest receipts	Non-federal reserve bank dividends	Rents and royalties	Current transfer receipts	Current surplus of government enterprises
1960	93.6	75.6	41.8	12.0	1.1	0.9	20.6	0.1	16.0	1.3	...	0.2	0.3	-0.7
1961	95.1	76.8	42.7	12.1	1.0	0.7	20.8	0.1	16.6	1.4	...	0.2	0.4	-0.9
1962	103.2	82.5	46.5	12.9	1.2	0.8	21.7	0.1	18.6	1.6	...	0.2	0.4	-0.9
1963	111.3	87.7	49.1	13.5	1.2	0.9	23.7	0.2	21.1	1.7	...	0.2	0.5	-0.7
1964	111.3	86.2	46.0	14.1	1.3	1.6	24.6	0.2	21.8	1.7	...	0.2	0.6	-0.8
1965	120.4	94.3	51.1	13.8	1.6	1.3	27.6	0.2	22.7	1.8	...	0.2	0.9	-0.9
1966	137.4	103.1	58.6	12.6	1.9	1.6	29.8	0.2	30.6	2.0	...	0.2	1.0	-1.2
1967	146.3	107.9	64.4	13.3	1.9	1.9	28.1	0.2	34.1	2.3	...	0.3	1.0	-1.3
1968	170.6	127.2	76.4	14.6	2.3	2.5	33.6	0.3	37.9	2.7	...	0.3	1.0	-1.0
1969	191.8	143.0	91.7	15.4	2.4	3.0	33.0	0.4	43.3	2.5	...	0.3	1.0	-1.3
1970	185.1	134.4	88.9	15.6	2.5	3.5	27.1	0.4	45.5	2.8	...	0.4	1.0	-2.5
1971	190.7	135.3	85.8	15.9	3.1	3.4	30.1	0.4	50.3	3.1	...	0.5	0.9	-2.8
1972	219.0	155.0	102.8	15.5	3.0	3.2	33.4	0.4	58.3	3.3	...	0.5	1.1	-2.4
1973	249.2	168.7	109.6	16.5	3.3	4.3	38.9	0.4	74.5	3.4	...	0.7	1.0	-3.4
1974	278.5	186.5	126.5	16.4	3.7	5.6	39.6	0.4	84.1	3.6	...	0.9	1.1	-3.2
1975	276.8	181.5	120.7	16.2	5.9	5.4	38.2	0.5	88.1	4.3	...	1.0	1.1	-4.4
1976	322.6	212.4	141.6	16.8	4.6	5.9	48.7	0.7	99.8	5.2	...	1.1	1.2	-2.9
1977	363.9	241.6	162.5	17.3	5.4	5.9	55.7	0.7	111.1	5.8	...	1.3	1.6	-3.4
1978	423.8	279.8	189.2	18.2	7.1	7.0	64.4	1.0	128.7	7.4	...	1.5	2.2	-2.9
1979	487.0	316.9	224.9	18.2	7.5	9.3	65.1	1.1	149.8	9.2	...	2.1	2.5	-2.7
1980	533.7	344.5	250.6	26.5	7.2	11.7	58.6	1.6	163.6	11.3	...	3.0	3.1	-3.6
1981	621.1	394.3	291.2	41.3	8.6	14.0	51.7	1.5	193.0	14.8	...	4.4	3.1	-2.6
1982	618.7	371.8	295.6	32.3	8.6	15.2	33.8	1.4	206.0	18.3	...	5.1	4.4	-2.1
1983	644.8	379.5	286.8	35.3	9.1	14.2	47.1	1.2	223.1	20.4	...	4.3	5.2	-1.9
1984	711.2	409.7	301.9	35.4	11.9	16.1	59.2	1.3	254.1	22.8	...	4.9	6.3	-2.7
1985	775.7	442.9	336.5	33.9	12.2	17.8	58.5	1.9	277.9	25.6	...	4.6	8.6	-1.6
1986	817.9	462.0	350.6	30.0	13.7	17.8	66.0	1.7	298.9	28.8	...	3.3	7.6	-0.6
1987	899.5	526.4	393.0	30.4	15.5	17.7	85.4	2.0	317.4	25.1	...	3.1	10.2	-0.5
1988	962.4	549.8	403.8	33.4	16.4	17.4	93.8	2.4	354.8	27.4	...	2.8	9.6	0.7
1989	1 042.5	601.1	453.1	32.3	17.5	21.6	95.6	2.7	378.0	25.9	...	3.0	11.8	1.1
1990	1 087.6	620.6	472.1	33.4	17.5	23.6	94.5	3.0	402.0	26.9	...	3.5	13.3	-2.3
1991	1 107.8	617.1	463.6	44.9	16.8	20.8	89.2	2.6	420.6	26.2	...	3.8	17.2	2.1
1992	1 154.4	645.4	477.5	45.0	18.3	16.8	102.0	2.6	444.0	22.2	...	3.5	18.4	4.1
1993	1 231.0	699.3	507.7	46.5	19.8	16.0	122.5	2.7	465.5	22.9	...	3.8	20.2	3.5
1994	1 329.3	763.5	545.1	57.5	21.4	20.5	136.3	3.1	496.2	20.1	...	3.6	21.6	4.0
1995	1 417.4	825.7	590.3	55.7	19.8	23.4	155.9	3.9	521.9	20.9	...	3.0	17.5	5.0
1996	1 536.3	917.0	668.4	53.6	19.2	20.1	170.5	5.2	545.4	22.6	...	4.1	22.7	4.5
1997	1 667.4	1 015.1	749.8	58.2	19.6	20.7	182.3	5.1	579.4	21.0	...	4.5	20.1	6.6
1998	1 789.8	1 095.3	831.2	60.2	19.6	26.6	177.7	5.7	617.4	17.4	...	4.2	21.5	7.6
1999	1 906.0	1 174.5	897.4	63.3	19.2	25.4	187.6	6.1	654.8	16.5	...	4.0	23.4	7.2
2000	2 067.8	1 288.5	999.6	65.1	21.1	25.3	194.1	7.6	698.6	18.8	...	6.3	24.9	5.3
2001	2 032.4	1 226.8	996.0	63.7	20.6	27.1	137.6	7.9	723.3	18.3	...	8.4	25.7	2.8
2002	1 870.9	1 053.2	832.3	65.9	19.9	24.5	126.0	8.1	739.4	15.5	...	6.5	25.0	6.8
2003	1 896.1	1 053.9	778.6	67.7	21.5	22.0	175.8	9.2	763.3	17.1	...	7.0	26.2	6.6
2004	2 028.1	1 140.6	803.0	70.9	23.3	18.1	232.2	10.1	809.0	17.0	0.1	8.7	29.8	4.8
2005	2 304.7	1 367.8	937.2	72.7	25.3	21.5	319.5	11.7	853.4	17.5	0.2	9.7	33.7	0.9
2006	2 538.8	1 534.8	1 055.8	71.5	26.7	29.1	366.0	13.7	905.7	19.1	0.3	9.9	38.1	1.9
2007	2 668.3	1 607.7	1 170.9	64.8	28.8	34.6	328.2	13.9	947.3	22.6	0.2	11.1	42.7	2.1
2008	2 582.1	1 489.5	1 176.6	63.7	29.2	31.7	202.0	16.9	974.5	21.2	0.6	13.8	49.7	1.1
2009	2 242.1	1 123.7	866.6	67.3	23.1	47.4	153.0	12.8	950.7	26.4	18.7	7.0	67.2	0.9
2010	2 446.3	1 273.6	943.6	67.2	28.6	79.3	219.4	13.9	970.9	31.7	17.0	8.0	68.1	-2.4
2011	2 573.6	1 478.4	1 130.8	75.7	31.9	75.4	224.0	15.1	903.2	27.1	18.8	9.9	67.1	-6.3
2012	2 700.8	1 573.0	1 166.4	80.6	33.5	88.4	274.7	16.7	938.0	21.8	21.1	10.2	56.1	-7.8
2013	3 139.6	1 744.9	1 302.9	89.0	35.5	79.6	298.4	18.1	1 091.8	23.5	131.3	9.3	69.3	-10.1
2014	3 293.0	1 900.1	1 403.7	97.8	37.4	96.9	339.6	20.4	1 140.1	24.8	40.7	10.3	87.3	-7.1
2015	3 449.0	2 024.2	1 532.6	101.0	38.1	110.4	329.1	22.2	1 190.8	28.0	16.0	6.7	76.2	-3.2
2016	3 463.8	2 020.4	1 547.9	97.8	37.5	91.5	311.9	24.1	1 224.4	29.7	14.8	4.8	79.7	-1.4
2017	3 525.2	2 015.5	1 613.6	91.9	38.5	80.6	245.4	24.9	1 284.2	29.8	23.2	6.1	85.0	1.0
2018	3 569.0	2 014.6	1 616.5	109.1	53.3	65.3	208.8	25.7	1 345.4	36.4	13.7	7.8	86.3	-0.6
2019	3 713.7	2 127.6	1 708.6	95.7	77.8	54.9	217.0	27.2	1 406.2	37.7	8.9	8.4	72.5	-2.6
2020	3 684.5	2 057.8	1 679.6	88.1	68.6	90.7	192.7	27.4	1 444.6	23.5	0.1	5.5	62.9	-0.6
2018														
1st quarter	3 494.3	1 962.2	1 597.2	107.8	41.9	78.3	189.2	24.9	1 328.5	34.3	0.2	7.3	83.0	0.6
2nd quarter	3 536.8	2 000.7	1 607.4	108.6	47.6	67.1	210.3	25.7	1 338.0	36.0	3.9	7.7	83.5	-0.1
3rd quarter	3 619.9	2 028.4	1 627.1	108.9	52.3	60.7	213.3	25.5	1 353.9	37.5	24.4	8.0	108.0	-1.0
4th quarter	3 625.1	2 067.3	1 634.1	111.2	71.3	55.2	222.5	27.0	1 361.4	38.0	26.3	8.3	70.6	-2.0
2019														
1st quarter	3 676.4	2 107.7	1 696.4	96.3	75.9	44.9	211.3	26.6	1 392.4	37.1	19.1	8.4	69.3	-2.4
2nd quarter	3 706.0	2 120.4	1 701.9	97.3	73.6	58.8	218.9	27.4	1 399.3	37.3	16.3	8.5	68.4	-2.9
3rd quarter	3 708.9	2 117.1	1 707.8	95.1	79.0	53.4	206.5	27.5	1 406.9	38.0	0.2	8.4	87.8	-2.8
4th quarter	3 763.4	2 165.3	1 728.6	94.2	82.5	62.4	231.4	27.4	1 426.4	38.5	0.2	8.3	64.5	-2.2
2020														
1st quarter	3 751.2	2 119.0	1 737.9	103.9	80.7	73.1	166.7	28.6	1 457.1	35.0	0.2	8.2	59.5	-0.9
2nd quarter	3 481.1	1 913.3	1 581.5	78.3	58.7	89.7	167.4	26.1	1 391.6	19.1	0.2	5.1	62.7	-0.6
3rd quarter	3 690.5	2 051.8	1 662.2	85.1	65.0	108.4	211.7	26.6	1 443.8	19.5	0.1	4.3	62.6	-0.2
4th quarter	3 815.1	2 147.0	1 736.9	85.2	70.1	91.5	225.1	28.3	1 486.0	20.3	0.1	4.4	66.6	-0.8

[1] Does not include "contributions for government social insurance" (the taxes that fund Social Security, Medicare, and unemployment insurance), which are shown separately in column 9.
. . . = Not available.

Table 6-1. Federal Government Current Receipts and Expenditures—*Continued*

(National income and product accounts, calendar years, billions of dollars, quarterly data are at seasonally adjusted annual rates.)

NIPA Table 3.2

Year and quarter	Total current expenditures	Consumption expenditures	Government social benefits — Benefits to persons	Government social benefits — Benefits to the rest of the world	Other current transfer payments — Grants-in-aid to state and local governments	Other current transfer payments — Payments to the rest of the world (net)	Interest payments — Total	Interest payments — To persons and business	Interest payments — To the rest of the world	Subsidies	Net federal government saving, NIPA (surplus + / deficit -) — Total	Net federal government saving, NIPA — Social insurance funds	Net federal government saving, NIPA — Other
1960	93.4	51.0	19.9	0.2	3.8	3.5	13.9	13.5	0.3	1.1	0.2	0.4	-0.2
1961	99.8	52.7	23.1	0.3	4.3	3.5	13.9	13.6	0.3	2.0	-4.7	-2.3	-2.4
1962	108.6	59.0	23.5	0.3	4.7	3.6	15.1	14.8	0.3	2.3	-5.4	-0.6	-4.8
1963	113.5	61.2	24.6	0.3	5.2	3.6	16.3	15.9	0.4	2.2	-2.2	0.8	-3.0
1964	118.2	63.1	25.2	0.3	6.0	3.4	17.5	17.0	0.5	2.7	-6.9	1.2	-8.1
1965	125.9	66.5	27.3	0.5	6.6	3.6	18.6	18.1	0.5	3.0	-5.5	0.4	-5.9
1966	144.4	76.5	29.9	0.5	9.4	4.0	20.3	19.7	0.5	3.9	-7.0	6.0	-13.0
1967	165.8	88.1	36.5	0.6	10.9	4.0	21.9	21.3	0.6	3.8	-19.5	4.1	-23.6
1968	184.3	96.8	41.9	0.6	11.8	4.5	24.6	23.9	0.7	4.1	-13.8	3.2	-16.9
1969	197.0	100.5	45.8	0.6	13.7	4.5	27.5	26.7	0.8	4.5	-5.1	5.7	-10.8
1970	219.9	102.3	55.6	0.7	18.3	4.8	33.3	32.4	0.9	4.8	-34.8	1.0	-35.8
1971	241.6	106.7	66.1	0.8	22.1	6.0	35.2	33.5	1.8	4.6	-50.9	-3.0	-47.9
1972	268.0	112.3	72.9	1.0	30.5	7.2	37.6	35.1	2.6	6.6	-49.0	-0.6	-48.4
1973	287.6	114.5	84.5	1.2	33.5	5.4	43.3	39.6	3.7	5.1	-38.3	5.9	-44.2
1974	319.8	123.2	103.3	1.3	34.9	6.0	48.0	43.9	4.0	3.2	-41.3	3.2	-44.5
1975	374.8	133.9	132.3	2.0	43.6	6.1	52.5	48.1	4.3	4.3	-97.9	-16.3	-81.6
1976	403.5	140.0	143.5	2.5	49.1	4.5	58.9	54.6	4.3	4.9	-80.9	-16.0	-64.9
1977	437.3	151.1	152.4	2.6	54.8	4.2	65.3	60.0	5.2	6.9	-73.4	-14.1	-59.4
1978	485.9	162.4	162.7	2.7	63.5	5.0	79.1	70.9	8.2	8.7	-62.0	-4.7	-57.3
1979	534.4	178.8	183.0	3.0	64.0	5.8	91.5	80.9	10.6	8.2	-47.4	-0.1	-47.3
1980	622.5	204.6	220.3	3.5	69.7	7.3	107.5	95.7	11.9	9.4	-88.8	-15.8	-73.0
1981	709.1	233.6	250.7	4.3	69.4	6.7	133.4	117.2	16.3	11.1	-88.1	-14.3	-73.8
1982	786.0	258.4	281.9	4.1	66.3	8.1	152.7	134.7	18.0	14.6	-167.4	-34.4	-132.9
1983	851.9	280.0	303.6	3.6	67.9	8.9	167.0	148.9	18.1	20.9	-207.2	-37.9	-169.3
1984	907.7	296.2	309.7	3.7	72.3	11.2	193.8	173.7	20.2	20.7	-196.5	-9.4	-187.1
1985	975.0	320.4	325.9	4.0	76.2	13.8	213.7	191.6	22.2	21.0	-199.2	0.8	-200.1
1986	1 033.8	339.8	344.3	4.4	82.4	14.2	224.2	200.9	23.3	24.6	-215.9	5.6	-221.5
1987	1 065.2	350.3	357.2	4.3	78.4	12.7	232.3	208.2	24.1	30.0	-165.7	14.4	-180.2
1988	1 122.4	363.5	378.4	4.6	85.7	13.2	247.9	219.2	28.8	29.2	-160.0	39.0	-198.9
1989	1 201.8	382.9	411.7	5.1	91.8	13.5	269.7	235.1	34.5	27.1	-159.4	42.6	-201.9
1990	1 290.9	404.2	447.0	6.2	104.4	13.5	289.0	253.0	36.1	26.6	-203.3	42.3	-245.6
1991	1 356.2	426.1	494.0	6.3	124.0	-25.6	304.4	268.3	36.1	27.1	-248.4	24.6	-273.0
1992	1 488.9	432.1	551.8	6.2	141.7	20.6	306.9	272.6	34.3	29.7	-334.5	5.3	-339.8
1993	1 544.6	429.5	583.7	6.2	155.7	21.7	311.4	277.3	34.2	36.3	-313.5	2.8	-316.3
1994	1 585.0	429.3	609.0	6.8	166.8	19.9	320.8	284.5	36.4	32.2	-255.6	15.3	-270.9
1995	1 659.5	429.0	647.1	6.8	174.5	15.4	352.3	305.2	47.1	34.5	-242.1	15.5	-257.6
1996	1 715.7	429.4	682.1	7.6	181.5	20.4	360.0	303.2	56.8	34.9	-179.4	12.8	-192.2
1997	1 759.4	439.6	707.9	7.9	188.1	17.0	365.6	295.9	69.7	33.4	-92.0	28.8	-120.8
1998	1 788.4	437.8	722.1	8.2	200.8	18.0	365.6	293.5	72.1	35.9	1.4	58.2	-56.8
1999	1 836.8	455.9	739.9	8.7	219.2	16.3	352.2	285.1	67.1	44.8	69.1	92.2	-23.1
2000	1 908.1	475.7	773.4	8.9	233.1	17.9	353.7	288.6	65.1	45.3	159.7	114.0	45.7
2001	2 017.3	506.4	840.8	9.8	261.3	16.9	331.2	273.6	57.6	51.1	15.0	87.7	-72.6
2002	2 138.7	560.9	918.0	9.9	288.7	19.4	301.3	251.3	50.0	40.5	-267.8	48.8	-316.6
2003	2 293.5	631.6	967.5	10.4	321.7	21.7	291.7	243.5	48.2	49.0	-397.4	37.5	-434.9
2004	2 421.6	683.7	1 019.5	11.0	332.3	23.0	306.0	249.4	56.7	46.0	-393.5	50.8	-444.3
2005	2 598.5	725.8	1 084.4	11.6	343.5	28.3	344.4	272.6	71.8	60.5	-293.8	48.0	-341.7
2006	2 760.7	765.5	1 189.1	12.4	341.0	29.3	372.2	285.0	87.2	51.1	-221.9	11.8	-233.7
2007	2 928.0	801.0	1 263.3	13.3	359.1	35.9	408.0	305.0	102.9	47.5	-259.7	-3.2	-256.5
2008	3 207.0	880.3	1 463.2	15.4	371.2	38.9	388.4	286.3	102.1	49.6	-624.9	-53.6	-571.3
2009	3 485.2	938.2	1 614.5	16.0	458.1	46.9	354.5	265.9	88.7	56.9	-1 243.2	-251.7	-991.5
2010	3 764.6	1 002.9	1 757.5	16.5	505.2	46.8	381.5	286.9	94.6	54.2	-1 318.4	-290.6	-1 027.8
2011	3 807.8	1 004.1	1 779.5	17.0	472.5	49.8	425.4	320.7	104.7	59.5	-1 234.1	-271.5	-962.7
2012	3 773.5	999.7	1 781.8	18.0	444.4	49.3	422.6	320.6	102.0	57.6	-1 072.7	-287.7	-785.0
2013	3 771.3	957.5	1 821.5	18.9	450.1	47.7	416.3	316.4	100.0	59.2	-631.8	-288.6	-343.1
2014	3 890.4	952.2	1 881.1	19.5	495.0	45.8	439.1	338.5	100.6	57.6	-597.4	-287.2	-310.1
2015	4 009.2	955.1	1 969.9	20.4	533.1	44.8	429.3	334.3	95.0	56.7	-560.2	-310.9	-249.4
2016	4 131.4	965.7	2 024.2	20.9	556.7	48.2	454.3	348.8	105.5	61.2	-667.6	-330.4	-337.2
2017	4 245.9	982.7	2 098.8	21.8	560.5	46.0	476.8	360.2	116.6	59.3	-720.7	-330.3	-390.4
2018	4 497.1	1 039.4	2 196.4	22.8	582.5	51.5	541.8	404.4	137.4	62.7	-928.1	-357.9	-570.1
2019	4 761.1	1 097.4	2 324.4	24.0	609.2	50.3	583.5	438.1	145.4	72.4	-1 047.5	-409.5	-638.0
2020	6 794.5	1 161.4	3 373.0	33.1	880.5	51.4	534.2	411.9	122.3	760.8	-3 110.0	-977.2	-2 132.8
2018													
1st quarter	4 404.0	1 014.8	2 172.9	22.4	582.7	44.4	508.7	377.5	131.2	58.1	-909.7	-346.0	-563.7
2nd quarter	4 465.6	1 036.2	2 186.8	22.8	575.7	53.4	533.1	397.5	135.6	57.7	-928.8	-354.5	-574.3
3rd quarter	4 521.3	1 049.0	2 203.5	23.1	582.7	52.6	553.2	413.3	139.9	57.3	-901.4	-359.2	-542.2
4th quarter	4 597.5	1 057.8	2 222.3	23.0	588.9	55.5	572.2	429.2	143.0	77.9	-972.5	-372.2	-600.3
2019													
1st quarter	4 691.8	1 075.5	2 298.1	23.5	593.8	52.1	580.5	433.8	146.7	68.4	-1 015.4	-392.2	-623.2
2nd quarter	4 739.1	1 095.7	2 315.5	23.7	610.5	46.3	589.2	441.1	148.1	58.2	-1 033.2	-405.4	-627.8
3rd quarter	4 789.8	1 105.1	2 333.2	24.3	610.4	50.7	585.6	439.2	146.4	80.6	-1 080.9	-419.2	-661.7
4th quarter	4 823.8	1 113.3	2 350.8	24.5	622.4	51.9	578.7	438.2	140.5	82.2	-1 060.4	-421.2	-639.2
2020													
1st quarter	4 909.2	1 124.7	2 417.9	25.2	640.6	54.2	566.4	434.2	132.2	80.3	-1 158.0	-440.6	-717.4
2nd quarter	9 106.7	1 187.6	4 766.7	44.1	1 400.0	47.3	537.3	416.4	120.9	1 123.6	-5 625.6	-1 542.1	-4 083.5
3rd quarter	7 206.8	1 169.4	3 468.3	35.0	738.5	53.6	521.5	403.8	117.6	1 220.5	-3 516.3	-1 222.0	-2 294.3
4th quarter	5 955.2	1 164.1	2 839.1	28.2	743.0	50.5	511.7	393.1	118.5	618.6	-2 140.1	-704.0	-1 436.1

Table 6-2. Federal Government Consumption Expenditures and Gross Investment

(National income and product accounts, calendar years, billions of dollars, quarterly data are at seasonally adjusted annual rates.)

NIPA Tables 3.9.5, 3.10.5

Year and quarter	Total	Consumption expenditures					Gross investment						
		Total	Compensation of general government employees	Consumption of general government fixed capital	Intermediate goods and services purchased [1]	Less: Own-account investment and sales to other sectors	Total	National defense			Nondefense		
								Structures	Equipment	Intellectual property	Structures	Equipment	Intellectual property
1960	72.9	51.0	26.6	15.0	12.0	2.7	21.9	2.2	10.1	5.9	1.7	0.3	1.7
1961	77.4	52.7	27.7	15.9	11.9	2.8	24.6	2.4	11.5	6.5	1.9	0.3	2.1
1962	85.5	59.0	29.5	17.0	15.6	3.1	26.5	2.0	12.5	6.7	2.1	0.3	2.9
1963	87.9	61.2	30.8	18.2	15.6	3.4	26.7	1.6	10.9	6.9	2.3	0.4	4.5
1964	90.3	63.1	33.0	19.0	14.9	3.8	27.1	1.3	10.1	6.9	2.5	0.6	5.7
1965	93.2	66.5	34.8	19.8	16.0	4.2	26.7	1.1	8.9	6.7	2.8	0.5	6.8
1966	106.6	76.5	39.8	20.8	20.6	4.7	30.1	1.3	10.4	7.0	2.8	0.6	7.9
1967	120.0	88.1	43.8	22.2	26.5	4.5	31.9	1.2	12.2	7.9	2.2	0.6	7.8
1968	128.0	96.8	48.3	23.9	29.3	4.6	31.1	1.2	10.8	7.9	2.1	0.5	8.6
1969	131.2	100.5	51.4	25.5	28.7	5.1	30.7	1.5	9.7	8.2	1.9	0.6	8.8
1970	132.8	102.3	55.2	27.3	25.3	5.4	30.5	1.3	9.6	8.1	2.1	0.7	8.8
1971	134.5	106.7	58.8	28.7	25.0	5.8	27.8	1.8	5.5	8.4	2.5	0.8	8.9
1972	141.6	112.3	62.6	29.7	26.9	6.9	29.3	1.8	5.3	9.2	2.7	1.1	9.2
1973	146.2	114.5	64.6	31.8	25.8	7.7	31.7	2.1	6.0	9.7	3.1	1.1	9.6
1974	158.8	123.2	67.8	34.7	29.2	8.6	35.7	2.2	8.2	10.0	3.4	1.5	10.4
1975	173.7	133.9	72.5	38.0	31.8	8.4	39.9	2.3	9.9	10.5	4.1	1.7	11.5
1976	184.8	140.0	76.5	40.8	31.3	8.5	44.8	2.1	12.1	11.3	4.6	1.8	12.7
1977	200.3	151.1	80.9	44.3	35.6	9.7	49.2	2.4	13.3	12.3	5.0	2.3	14.0
1978	218.9	164.2	87.1	48.6	39.3	10.8	54.7	2.5	14.3	13.3	6.1	2.7	15.9
1979	240.6	178.8	92.0	53.4	45.8	12.4	61.7	2.5	17.5	14.9	6.3	2.7	17.9
1980	274.9	204.6	100.8	59.1	58.4	13.6	70.2	3.2	19.8	17.2	7.1	3.2	19.8
1981	314.0	233.6	112.2	66.0	69.6	14.3	80.4	3.2	24.1	20.9	7.7	3.3	21.2
1982	348.3	258.4	122.0	73.7	77.6	14.9	90.0	4.0	29.1	25.2	6.8	3.9	21.1
1983	382.4	280.0	127.7	79.4	88.8	15.9	102.3	4.8	35.2	29.8	6.7	4.3	21.6
1984	411.8	296.2	136.5	88.7	88.3	17.4	115.6	4.9	41.1	35.0	7.0	4.7	22.8
1985	452.9	320.4	145.0	95.0	99.1	18.7	132.5	6.2	47.9	41.3	7.3	5.1	24.6
1986	481.7	339.8	149.1	101.5	108.7	19.6	141.9	6.8	52.7	43.9	8.0	4.8	25.7
1987	502.8	350.3	153.1	108.0	110.2	20.9	152.4	7.7	55.0	48.1	9.0	5.2	27.4
1988	511.4	363.5	161.9	116.6	107.4	22.5	148.0	7.4	49.6	48.5	6.8	6.1	29.6
1989	534.1	382.9	168.5	124.3	114.0	23.9	151.2	6.4	51.5	47.3	6.9	7.2	31.9
1990	562.4	404.2	176.0	130.7	123.1	25.6	158.2	6.1	54.6	46.6	8.0	8.1	34.8
1991	582.9	426.1	186.5	137.0	129.4	26.8	156.8	4.6	53.4	43.3	9.2	8.9	37.4
1992	588.5	432.1	189.6	140.0	129.4	26.9	156.4	5.2	50.7	41.3	10.3	10.0	38.9
1993	580.2	429.5	188.0	143.4	125.1	27.2	150.7	5.3	44.7	39.2	11.2	9.9	40.4
1994	574.7	429.3	186.1	146.6	126.1	29.3	145.4	5.8	41.9	38.1	10.2	7.5	41.9
1995	576.7	429.0	183.3	149.6	123.2	27.3	147.7	6.7	39.8	38.4	10.8	8.6	43.4
1996	579.2	429.4	182.2	149.6	125.2	27.6	149.8	6.3	39.9	38.9	11.3	9.7	43.8
1997	583.3	439.6	183.5	150.1	131.6	25.6	143.7	6.1	33.6	39.2	9.9	10.0	44.9
1998	585.5	437.8	185.8	150.9	127.7	26.6	147.7	5.8	34.1	39.4	10.8	10.2	47.5
1999	610.7	455.9	191.7	153.3	136.4	25.6	154.9	5.4	36.8	39.3	10.7	11.9	50.7
2000	633.1	475.7	202.4	157.9	143.6	28.2	157.4	5.4	37.8	40.2	8.4	10.8	54.8
2001	670.2	506.4	211.2	159.1	165.7	29.6	163.8	5.3	39.9	42.5	8.1	10.0	58.1
2002	743.1	560.9	236.3	161.5	194.5	31.5	182.2	6.1	46.4	47.9	10.0	11.9	59.8
2003	826.8	631.6	267.7	167.0	230.4	33.5	195.2	7.1	50.0	53.0	10.3	12.3	62.5
2004	892.1	683.7	284.3	175.1	259.0	34.6	208.4	6.9	55.7	58.3	9.6	13.3	64.5
2005	947.8	725.8	303.5	184.9	276.6	39.2	222.0	7.2	61.4	62.9	8.1	15.2	67.3
2006	1 001.2	765.5	314.5	195.4	295.7	40.0	235.6	7.8	66.0	65.7	9.4	17.4	69.2
2007	1 051.0	801.0	329.1	206.7	305.4	40.1	250.0	10.0	71.8	69.4	11.4	16.1	71.4
2008	1 152.0	880.3	349.6	219.5	353.6	42.3	271.7	13.7	82.6	70.8	11.4	17.5	75.7
2009	1 220.8	938.2	375.8	227.2	378.8	43.6	282.6	17.1	86.6	69.6	12.0	17.8	79.5
2010	1 300.2	1 002.9	402.8	237.2	409.4	46.5	297.2	16.7	89.3	70.2	16.0	19.2	85.9
2011	1 299.8	1 004.1	411.6	248.1	395.2	50.9	295.7	13.3	87.3	71.3	16.7	18.4	88.5
2012	1 287.0	999.7	409.1	254.6	383.0	47.0	287.3	8.1	85.2	70.5	14.5	18.7	90.2
2013	1 227.2	957.5	399.8	258.6	346.0	46.9	269.6	6.5	78.8	67.7	11.6	16.2	88.8
2014	1 216.0	952.2	404.2	262.7	334.4	49.0	263.8	5.3	74.7	64.8	12.0	17.4	89.6
2015	1 221.8	955.1	409.9	263.7	330.9	49.4	266.6	5.0	72.6	65.3	12.7	18.8	92.2
2016	1 234.5	965.7	421.1	262.8	333.3	51.5	268.8	4.8	72.3	61.8	12.3	18.9	98.6
2017	1 262.8	982.7	431.7	267.5	335.7	52.2	280.0	5.6	77.4	61.7	10.2	19.0	106.2
2018	1 339.0	1 039.4	449.9	276.1	367.3	53.8	299.6	6.0	84.2	64.8	12.1	19.7	112.7
2019	1 414.9	1 097.4	465.5	284.0	404.7	56.8	317.5	7.4	93.6	66.0	15.3	20.0	115.2
2020	1 501.8	1 161.4	488.6	293.9	436.5	57.6	340.3	10.0	97.2	73.7	17.6	20.6	121.3
2018													
1st quarter	1 305.8	1 014.8	442.8	272.4	351.4	51.8	291.0	5.5	80.9	63.9	10.4	19.6	110.7
2nd quarter	1 331.7	1 036.2	447.4	275.5	367.1	53.8	295.6	5.7	81.1	64.8	11.8	19.7	112.5
3rd quarter	1 350.8	1 049.0	452.8	277.4	372.0	53.2	301.8	6.3	83.9	65.2	13.0	19.9	113.5
4th quarter	1 367.7	1 057.8	456.7	279.0	378.7	56.7	309.9	6.6	90.9	65.2	13.2	19.6	114.3
2019													
1st quarter	1 387.0	1 075.5	459.6	282.1	388.0	54.3	311.5	7.4	90.9	64.7	15.2	19.3	114.0
2nd quarter	1 406.9	1 095.7	463.1	282.6	406.7	56.8	311.2	7.3	88.8	65.2	15.0	20.2	114.8
3rd quarter	1 424.1	1 105.1	467.7	284.8	409.3	56.7	319.0	7.0	94.6	66.3	15.3	20.2	115.6
4th quarter	1 441.7	1 113.3	471.5	286.3	414.9	59.4	328.4	8.0	100.0	67.9	15.8	20.3	116.3
2020													
1st quarter	1 454.7	1 124.7	476.9	288.7	416.4	57.3	330.0	8.8	95.2	70.3	17.8	20.3	117.5
2nd quarter	1 525.0	1 187.6	484.7	292.0	467.3	56.5	337.4	9.6	99.0	72.3	18.8	20.5	117.2
3rd quarter	1 515.1	1 169.4	496.7	295.4	434.8	57.5	345.7	10.7	95.3	74.8	18.4	20.4	126.1
4th quarter	1 512.3	1 164.1	496.0	299.5	427.6	59.1	348.2	10.7	99.2	77.3	15.3	21.1	124.5

[1] Includes general government intermediate inputs for goods and services sold to other sectors and for own-account investment.

Table 6-3. Federal Government Defense and Nondefense Consumption Expenditures by Type

(National income and product accounts, calendar years, billions of dollars, quarterly data are at seasonally adjusted annual rates.)

NIPA Table 3.10.5

Year and quarter	Defense consumption expenditures [1]						Nondefense consumption expenditures [1]					
	Total	Compensation of general government employees	Consumption of general government fixed capital	Intermediate goods and services purchased [2]			Total	Compensation of general government employees	Consumption of general government fixed capital	Intermediate goods and services purchased [2]		
				Durable goods	Nondurable goods	Services				Durable goods	Nondurable goods	Services
1960	42.6	21.1	13.8	4.4	1.7	3.5	8.4	5.6	1.3	0.0	0.5	1.9
1961	44.2	21.7	14.5	3.6	2.2	4.0	8.6	6.1	1.4	0.1	-0.3	2.3
1962	48.6	22.9	15.4	4.6	2.8	4.7	10.5	6.5	1.6	0.1	1.1	2.4
1963	50.5	23.6	16.3	4.7	2.5	5.2	10.7	7.2	1.9	0.1	0.6	2.6
1964	51.4	25.2	16.7	4.0	2.8	4.7	11.7	7.8	2.3	0.1	0.3	3.0
1965	53.9	26.4	17.1	4.2	3.2	5.1	12.6	8.3	2.8	0.1	0.4	3.1
1966	63.8	30.8	17.5	6.1	4.7	7.0	12.7	9.0	3.3	0.1	-0.7	3.3
1967	73.7	34.2	18.4	6.2	7.3	9.7	14.3	9.7	3.9	0.1	0.1	3.1
1968	81.4	37.6	19.4	7.4	8.4	10.5	15.4	10.7	4.5	0.1	0.8	2.0
1969	82.6	40.0	20.3	6.4	7.6	10.5	17.9	11.5	5.2	0.1	1.4	2.6
1970	81.8	41.9	21.3	6.1	5.4	9.6	20.6	13.3	6.0	0.1	0.5	3.6
1971	82.3	43.4	21.9	4.6	4.4	10.6	24.3	15.5	6.7	0.1	0.9	4.4
1972	84.4	45.6	22.4	5.5	4.7	9.5	27.9	17.0	7.4	0.2	1.2	5.8
1973	84.9	46.1	23.6	5.3	4.3	9.3	29.7	18.4	8.2	0.2	1.0	5.8
1974	89.5	47.7	25.3	5.0	5.2	10.7	33.6	20.1	9.4	0.3	1.4	6.7
1975	95.3	50.2	27.3	5.8	5.1	10.9	38.5	22.3	10.6	0.3	2.1	7.6
1976	99.3	51.8	29.2	5.7	4.4	11.7	40.7	24.7	11.6	0.3	2.1	7.1
1977	106.5	53.9	31.5	7.6	4.5	12.7	44.7	27.0	12.8	0.4	2.5	7.8
1978	115.1	57.6	34.4	9.0	4.9	13.3	49.0	29.5	14.3	0.5	3.2	8.4
1979	125.7	60.9	37.3	10.8	6.2	14.9	53.1	31.1	16.1	0.6	3.3	10.0
1980	143.2	66.7	40.6	12.3	10.0	18.7	61.4	34.0	18.5	0.8	5.5	11.2
1981	165.1	76.3	45.0	15.7	11.8	22.0	68.4	35.9	21.1	0.8	8.7	10.5
1982	187.2	84.8	50.4	19.1	11.5	28.1	71.2	37.2	23.3	0.8	7.5	10.7
1983	202.3	89.3	55.2	24.6	11.3	28.9	77.7	38.4	24.2	0.8	10.1	13.1
1984	217.7	95.9	62.3	26.6	10.4	30.7	78.5	40.7	26.4	0.9	5.8	13.9
1985	234.1	102.4	67.2	29.0	9.9	34.7	86.3	42.6	27.8	0.9	8.9	15.7
1986	249.0	106.2	72.6	31.7	10.2	38.3	90.8	42.9	28.9	0.9	11.7	16.1
1987	261.6	109.5	77.7	33.6	10.2	40.9	88.7	43.6	30.2	1.0	6.2	18.3
1988	276.6	113.8	84.4	33.4	10.6	45.4	86.8	48.1	32.2	1.1	-0.8	17.7
1989	286.1	117.9	90.1	32.0	10.8	46.5	96.8	50.6	34.2	1.2	5.1	18.2
1990	297.7	121.2	94.5	31.6	11.0	51.8	106.5	54.8	36.2	1.4	5.0	22.2
1991	312.7	126.8	98.5	31.0	10.7	58.1	113.4	59.7	38.6	1.5	5.9	22.3
1992	309.3	126.8	99.8	28.4	9.4	57.6	122.8	62.8	40.2	1.6	6.5	25.9
1993	302.4	121.0	101.3	26.4	8.5	58.1	127.1	67.1	42.1	1.6	7.6	23.0
1994	296.3	117.4	102.7	22.9	7.6	60.2	133.0	68.7	43.9	1.5	6.1	27.7
1995	292.2	114.1	103.3	20.9	6.3	59.8	136.8	69.2	46.4	1.4	7.5	27.3
1996	292.3	112.0	101.7	20.8	7.6	62.5	137.1	70.2	47.9	1.5	6.6	26.0
1997	293.0	111.4	100.4	20.9	7.6	64.6	146.6	72.0	49.7	1.6	8.5	28.5
1998	289.5	110.8	99.7	20.9	7.0	62.6	148.3	75.1	51.3	1.5	9.4	26.3
1999	301.8	112.7	99.4	22.2	8.2	70.9	154.1	79.0	53.9	1.7	7.2	26.3
2000	309.2	116.9	100.7	22.1	10.4	71.4	166.5	85.5	57.2	1.8	9.3	28.5
2001	325.5	123.2	99.8	22.3	10.3	84.2	180.9	88.0	59.3	1.9	12.2	34.8
2002	358.5	139.3	100.4	23.4	11.4	100.0	202.4	97.0	61.1	2.2	12.6	44.8
2003	411.2	160.8	103.5	26.0	13.5	124.6	220.4	106.9	63.5	2.2	15.4	48.7
2004	448.9	172.2	108.8	28.5	17.1	139.8	234.8	112.1	66.3	2.5	17.1	54.0
2005	478.0	186.0	115.2	29.8	21.0	145.3	247.8	117.5	69.7	2.7	19.0	58.9
2006	501.3	193.0	122.1	32.8	22.3	152.5	264.3	121.5	73.3	3.0	20.3	64.9
2007	528.1	201.5	129.6	37.0	24.0	157.9	272.9	127.6	77.1	3.0	20.2	63.3
2008	583.2	214.3	138.3	43.2	30.3	180.0	297.1	135.2	81.2	3.3	23.6	73.3
2009	614.3	229.2	143.5	47.1	24.5	193.0	323.9	146.6	83.7	3.5	26.6	84.0
2010	651.8	244.0	149.5	47.4	26.8	207.8	351.1	158.8	87.7	3.9	28.4	94.9
2011	662.0	250.8	156.3	46.2	33.0	201.8	342.1	160.8	91.8	3.7	24.8	85.8
2012	650.3	248.0	159.6	45.2	31.9	191.6	349.4	161.1	95.0	3.7	24.0	86.7
2013	611.2	239.6	160.5	39.9	28.2	169.4	346.3	160.2	98.1	3.5	22.6	82.5
2014	598.7	239.1	160.9	36.5	26.0	162.8	353.5	165.0	101.8	3.6	22.0	83.5
2015	586.8	238.7	159.7	35.7	21.0	158.2	368.3	171.3	104.0	3.8	23.0	89.2
2016	588.9	242.2	157.0	36.2	20.5	158.9	376.8	179.0	105.8	3.9	22.7	91.1
2017	601.8	246.6	157.3	38.5	22.9	161.8	380.9	185.1	110.2	3.7	22.2	86.5
2018	637.8	257.9	160.0	41.5	26.0	178.9	401.7	192.0	116.1	3.9	24.3	92.7
2019	680.5	268.2	162.7	45.3	24.7	207.4	416.9	197.2	121.3	4.1	26.1	97.0
2020	700.5	280.1	167.5	47.9	22.1	212.3	461.0	208.5	126.4	8.5	25.9	119.9
2018												
1st quarter	617.2	253.3	158.6	38.8	25.9	166.7	397.6	189.5	113.8	3.9	24.0	92.2
2nd quarter	636.5	256.3	160.0	41.7	25.8	179.0	399.7	191.1	115.5	3.9	24.1	92.5
3rd quarter	643.9	259.9	160.6	43.6	26.3	180.1	405.0	192.8	116.8	4.0	24.5	93.4
4th quarter	653.5	262.3	160.9	41.7	25.9	189.8	404.3	194.5	118.1	4.0	24.7	92.7
2019												
1st quarter	666.3	264.3	162.1	43.1	24.9	199.3	409.1	195.3	120.0	3.9	24.9	91.9
2nd quarter	679.1	266.7	162.0	43.7	25.1	209.3	416.6	196.4	120.6	4.1	27.0	97.5
3rd quarter	684.5	269.5	162.9	45.2	24.5	210.5	420.6	198.2	121.9	4.1	26.5	98.4
4th quarter	692.0	272.5	163.7	49.4	24.4	210.4	421.3	199.1	122.6	4.2	26.2	100.3
2020												
1st quarter	693.9	274.6	164.9	45.5	24.0	213.7	430.8	202.3	123.8	6.2	25.6	101.4
2nd quarter	691.5	279.6	166.4	50.0	20.0	204.7	496.1	205.1	125.7	10.7	25.6	156.4
3rd quarter	703.0	282.1	168.2	48.5	22.0	212.0	466.4	214.7	127.3	10.7	25.8	115.9
4th quarter	713.5	284.3	170.5	47.6	22.5	218.8	450.6	211.8	128.9	6.3	26.5	105.9

[1]Excludes government sales to other sectors and government own-account investment (construction and software).
[2]Includes general government intermediate inputs for goods and services sold to other sectors and for own-account investment.

Table 6-4. National Defense Consumption Expenditures and Gross Investment: Selected Detail

(National income and product accounts, calendar years, billions of dollars, quarterly data are at seasonally adjusted annual rates.)

NIPA Table 3.11.5

Year and quarter	Defense consumption expenditures								Defense gross investment				
	Compensation of general government employees		Intermediate goods and services purchased [1]						Aircraft	Missiles	Ships	Software	Research and development
			Durable goods	Nondurable goods		Services							
	Military	Civilian	Aircraft	Petroleum products	Ammunition	Installation support	Weapons support	Personnel support					
1980	41.5	25.2	5.6	6.8	1.4	8.3	3.9	2.3	6.1	2.3	4.1	1.0	16.2
1981	48.8	27.6	7.7	7.7	1.6	9.6	4.8	2.9	7.5	2.8	5.1	1.3	19.6
1982	54.9	29.9	10.2	6.8	2.1	12.6	6.3	3.6	8.4	3.4	6.2	1.4	23.7
1983	57.8	31.5	13.6	6.4	2.5	12.4	7.0	3.9	10.1	4.6	7.1	1.7	28.1
1984	62.0	33.9	14.0	5.9	2.2	13.8	7.2	3.7	10.9	5.7	8.0	2.2	32.8
1985	66.2	36.1	15.4	5.8	1.3	15.1	8.4	5.0	13.4	6.6	9.0	2.7	38.6
1986	69.4	36.8	17.2	3.6	3.6	16.0	9.4	6.2	17.9	7.9	8.9	3.2	40.7
1987	72.2	37.3	18.2	3.9	2.8	17.7	9.2	6.8	17.6	8.7	8.8	3.6	44.5
1988	74.8	39.0	17.9	3.5	3.5	18.3	10.3	9.5	13.5	7.8	8.6	4.3	44.3
1989	76.5	41.4	16.4	4.2	3.1	18.0	10.5	10.2	12.2	8.8	10.0	4.8	42.5
1990	78.5	42.7	14.8	5.3	2.8	21.4	11.6	10.1	12.0	11.2	10.8	5.2	41.4
1991	82.4	44.4	13.6	4.7	2.7	22.9	10.0	9.5	9.2	10.8	10.2	5.4	37.9
1992	80.9	45.9	12.2	3.5	2.6	23.1	9.4	13.7	8.3	10.6	10.1	5.6	35.6
1993	75.1	45.9	10.7	3.2	2.5	25.2	8.8	14.7	9.3	7.9	8.7	5.4	33.7
1994	71.7	45.7	9.2	3.0	1.8	26.2	9.4	16.3	10.5	5.7	8.1	5.3	32.8
1995	69.5	44.6	8.9	2.8	1.2	24.9	9.5	17.0	9.0	4.7	8.0	5.3	33.1
1996	67.7	44.3	8.8	3.4	1.4	25.6	9.0	19.3	9.2	4.1	6.8	5.5	33.4
1997	67.8	43.6	9.4	2.9	1.7	24.7	10.5	21.3	5.8	2.9	6.1	5.6	33.6
1998	68.0	42.8	9.9	2.1	1.9	23.5	10.0	20.6	5.8	3.3	6.4	5.9	33.5
1999	69.8	42.9	10.5	2.6	1.9	24.5	11.3	26.0	7.0	2.9	6.7	5.9	33.3
2000	72.9	44.1	9.8	4.1	1.8	24.7	11.7	26.1	7.8	2.7	6.6	6.0	34.2
2001	78.4	44.8	9.8	4.2	2.1	27.1	14.8	32.4	8.5	3.3	7.2	5.8	36.7
2002	89.7	49.6	9.8	4.6	2.4	30.6	18.0	41.3	9.6	3.3	8.4	5.6	42.3
2003	107.4	53.4	11.4	5.3	2.7	35.8	22.6	49.5	9.2	3.5	9.3	5.7	47.3
2004	113.9	58.3	12.0	7.0	3.6	36.8	23.8	62.4	11.1	4.0	9.8	5.8	52.5
2005	123.3	62.7	10.8	10.1	4.0	36.0	26.5	66.9	13.5	4.0	9.6	6.1	56.8
2006	128.1	64.9	11.1	11.4	4.1	38.3	27.8	71.4	13.6	4.5	10.5	6.4	59.3
2007	133.4	68.1	11.5	12.2	4.2	38.4	29.0	70.7	12.9	4.3	10.3	6.8	62.5
2008	143.0	71.3	12.9	17.6	4.3	41.6	31.3	86.5	13.5	4.3	11.0	7.4	63.4
2009	152.5	76.8	14.9	10.5	4.2	44.2	32.8	93.4	13.8	5.1	11.1	7.5	62.1
2010	159.1	84.9	16.2	13.7	4.2	46.5	37.4	99.3	16.7	5.6	11.8	8.1	62.1
2011	160.9	89.9	18.0	19.2	4.2	44.5	35.6	97.1	20.2	5.1	11.7	8.7	62.6
2012	159.1	88.9	19.3	18.3	4.3	41.9	33.6	97.3	20.2	6.9	12.0	9.0	61.5
2013	153.2	86.3	17.9	15.0	3.6	35.5	28.9	89.9	21.7	6.4	12.5	9.1	58.5
2014	150.0	89.1	16.3	13.3	3.1	39.2	31.1	78.0	19.2	6.6	13.3	9.4	55.4
2015	147.5	91.2	15.8	8.4	2.8	36.5	32.3	75.8	17.6	6.6	13.5	9.4	55.9
2016	148.2	94.0	15.8	6.7	3.1	37.9	33.5	73.3	16.4	4.8	14.4	10.3	51.6
2017	149.0	97.5	16.8	7.9	3.7	39.3	35.7	72.3	18.7	4.7	14.1	11.1	50.6
2018	155.8	102.1	17.1	10.3	4.7	40.4	39.4	83.9	19.7	4.6	15.5	12.3	52.5
2019	162.7	105.6	17.9	8.8	5.5	40.5	44.3	106.5	23.3	5.1	17.2	13.0	53.0
2020	169.6	110.5	18.8	6.0	5.4	45.0	46.3	108.5	21.8	6.8	18.6	13.4	60.3
2014													
1st quarter	151.3	87.6	17.2	14.7	3.3	37.8	30.3	79.1	17.3	6.1	12.4	9.2	55.9
2nd quarter	150.7	88.7	16.7	13.5	3.2	39.2	30.4	74.1	20.6	6.4	14.0	9.3	55.2
3rd quarter	149.6	89.6	15.2	13.2	3.0	40.8	33.0	87.2	19.3	6.6	13.6	9.5	55.1
4th quarter	148.5	90.6	16.1	11.7	2.9	39.0	30.9	71.4	19.5	7.4	13.0	9.4	55.4
2015													
1st quarter	147.5	90.6	16.0	9.1	2.8	37.3	31.7	77.4	15.6	6.5	13.8	9.4	56.3
2nd quarter	147.2	90.8	15.3	8.9	2.8	37.0	32.8	76.8	19.2	6.3	13.1	9.4	56.5
3rd quarter	147.4	91.4	15.7	8.1	2.8	35.5	32.1	74.5	18.1	5.8	13.6	9.4	56.0
4th quarter	147.9	92.0	16.2	7.4	2.9	36.2	32.8	74.3	17.6	7.7	13.6	9.5	54.9
2016													
1st quarter	148.2	92.5	16.3	6.1	2.9	37.2	33.2	73.5	18.7	5.1	14.4	9.9	53.2
2nd quarter	148.3	93.5	14.6	6.5	3.0	37.3	32.5	69.2	16.6	5.6	13.8	10.1	51.9
3rd quarter	148.3	94.5	15.7	7.0	3.1	38.1	34.2	75.4	15.2	5.0	14.7	10.4	50.9
4th quarter	147.9	95.4	16.5	7.2	3.2	38.9	34.1	75.2	15.3	3.7	14.6	10.6	50.4
2017													
1st quarter	148.1	96.4	16.7	8.1	3.4	38.3	33.3	67.5	17.6	5.1	12.3	10.8	50.2
2nd quarter	148.1	96.8	18.2	7.2	3.6	39.2	35.3	75.0	18.4	4.8	14.4	11.1	50.3
3rd quarter	149.2	97.9	15.6	7.6	3.8	39.8	36.8	72.4	18.1	4.7	14.4	11.3	50.6
4th quarter	150.7	99.1	16.8	8.7	4.0	40.0	37.3	74.3	20.5	4.2	15.3	11.5	51.2
2018													
1st quarter	153.0	100.3	15.5	10.3	4.3	39.9	37.3	74.6	17.8	4.7	15.4	11.8	52.1
2nd quarter	154.7	101.7	17.4	10.3	4.5	40.9	39.7	83.3	17.4	4.1	15.7	12.2	52.6
3rd quarter	157.0	102.9	19.3	10.5	4.8	40.3	39.6	84.9	19.7	4.2	15.2	12.4	52.8
4th quarter	158.7	103.6	16.3	10.0	5.1	40.5	41.0	92.7	24.1	5.3	15.8	12.6	52.6
2019													
1st quarter	160.2	104.1	16.9	9.1	5.4	39.8	42.4	101.2	23.7	4.8	16.1	12.7	52.1
2nd quarter	161.6	105.1	17.1	9.2	5.5	40.0	44.1	109.1	20.9	4.0	16.7	12.9	52.3
3rd quarter	163.7	105.8	17.6	8.5	5.6	40.6	44.9	108.9	22.8	4.9	17.9	13.2	53.1
4th quarter	165.2	107.3	20.0	8.5	5.5	41.6	45.7	107.0	25.8	6.7	18.0	13.3	54.6
2020													
1st quarter	165.7	108.9	17.1	8.0	5.5	43.6	46.0	109.3	20.2	6.1	18.5	13.5	56.8
2nd quarter	170.0	109.6	20.3	3.9	5.4	43.9	45.3	104.9	22.8	7.4	18.5	13.2	59.1
3rd quarter	170.8	111.3	19.1	5.8	5.3	45.8	46.4	107.4	20.1	7.0	18.3	13.4	61.4
4th quarter	171.9	112.3	18.7	6.3	5.2	46.6	47.4	112.3	24.1	6.8	18.8	13.6	63.8

[1] Includes general government intermediate inputs for goods and services sold to other sectors and for own-account investment.

Table 6-5. Federal Government Output, Lending and Borrowing, and Net Investment

(National income and product accounts, calendar years, billions of dollars, quarterly data are at seasonally adjusted annual rates.)

NIPA Tables 3.2, 3.10.5

Year and quarter	Output						Net lending (net borrowing -)							Net investment
	Gross		Value added		Intermediate goods and services purchased [1]		Net saving, current (surplus +, deficit -)	Plus: capital transfer receipts	Minus			Plus: Consumption of fixed capital	Equals: Net lending (borrowing -)	
	Defense	Non-defense	Defense	Non-defense	Defense	Non-defense			Gross investment	Capital transfer payments	Net purchases of non-produced assets			
1960	44.4	9.3	34.8	6.8	9.6	2.4	0.2	1.8	21.9	2.6	0.5	15.2	-7.9	6.7
1961	46.0	9.6	36.2	7.5	9.8	2.1	-4.7	2.0	24.6	2.9	0.5	16.0	-14.7	8.6
1962	50.4	11.7	38.3	8.2	12.1	3.5	-5.4	2.1	26.5	3.1	0.6	17.2	-16.3	9.3
1963	52.3	12.3	39.9	9.1	12.4	3.2	-2.2	2.2	26.7	3.6	0.5	18.4	-12.3	8.3
1964	53.3	13.6	41.9	10.1	11.4	3.5	-6.9	2.6	27.1	4.1	0.6	19.2	-16.9	7.9
1965	55.9	14.7	43.5	11.1	12.4	3.6	-5.5	2.8	26.7	4.0	0.5	20.0	-13.9	6.7
1966	66.1	15.1	48.3	12.4	17.9	2.7	-7.0	3.0	30.1	4.4	0.6	21.0	-18.0	9.1
1967	75.7	16.8	52.5	13.5	23.2	3.3	-19.5	3.1	31.9	4.3	-0.2	22.5	-30.0	9.4
1968	83.4	18.0	57.0	15.1	26.4	2.9	-13.8	3.1	31.1	6.0	-0.9	24.2	-22.7	6.9
1969	84.9	20.7	60.3	16.6	24.6	4.1	-5.1	3.6	30.7	5.9	0.1	25.8	-12.5	4.9
1970	84.2	23.5	63.2	19.3	21.0	4.3	-34.8	3.7	30.5	5.3	-0.3	27.6	-39.0	2.9
1971	84.9	27.6	65.3	22.2	19.6	5.4	-50.9	4.6	27.8	5.9	-0.4	29.1	-50.6	-1.3
1972	87.6	31.6	68.0	24.4	19.7	7.2	-49.0	5.4	29.3	6.1	-0.7	30.2	-48.1	-0.9
1973	88.6	33.6	69.7	26.6	18.9	6.9	-38.3	5.1	31.7	6.0	-3.2	32.4	-35.3	-0.7
1974	93.8	37.8	73.0	29.5	20.8	8.3	-41.3	4.8	35.7	7.9	-5.7	35.4	-39.1	0.3
1975	99.4	42.9	77.6	32.9	21.8	10.0	-97.9	4.9	39.9	9.7	-0.4	38.7	-103.4	1.2
1976	102.8	45.8	81.0	36.2	21.8	9.5	-80.9	5.6	44.8	10.6	-2.4	41.7	-86.6	3.1
1977	110.3	50.5	85.4	39.8	24.8	10.8	-73.4	7.2	49.2	11.2	-1.4	45.3	-80.0	3.9
1978	119.2	55.8	92.0	43.8	27.2	12.1	-62.0	5.2	54.7	12.0	-0.6	49.7	-73.2	5.0
1979	130.1	61.1	98.2	47.2	31.9	13.9	-47.4	5.5	61.7	14.5	-2.8	54.6	-60.7	7.1
1980	148.2	70.0	107.3	52.5	40.9	17.5	-88.8	6.5	70.2	16.7	-4.1	60.4	-104.8	9.8
1981	170.9	77.0	121.3	57.0	49.6	20.1	-88.1	6.9	80.4	15.7	-5.5	67.5	-104.3	12.9
1982	193.9	79.5	135.2	60.5	58.7	19.0	-167.4	7.5	90.0	14.7	-3.7	75.4	-185.4	14.6
1983	209.3	86.6	144.4	62.6	64.8	24.0	-207.2	5.8	102.3	15.6	-4.9	81.1	-233.3	21.2
1984	225.9	87.6	158.2	67.1	67.7	20.5	-196.5	6.0	115.6	17.8	-4.0	90.6	-229.4	25.0
1985	243.2	95.8	169.6	70.4	73.6	25.4	-199.2	6.4	132.5	19.6	-1.2	97.0	-246.8	35.5
1986	258.9	100.4	178.8	71.8	80.1	28.6	-215.9	7.0	141.9	20.1	-3.0	103.6	-264.3	38.3
1987	272.0	99.3	187.2	73.8	84.8	25.5	-165.7	7.2	152.4	19.1	-0.4	110.1	-219.5	42.3
1988	287.6	98.3	198.2	80.3	89.4	18.0	-160.0	7.6	148.0	19.8	-0.2	118.9	-201.0	29.1
1989	297.4	109.3	208.0	84.8	89.4	24.5	-159.4	8.9	151.2	20.2	-0.7	126.9	-194.3	24.3
1990	310.1	119.6	215.7	91.0	94.5	28.6	-203.3	11.6	158.2	28.2	-0.8	133.5	-243.8	24.7
1991	324.9	128.0	225.2	98.3	99.7	29.7	-248.4	11.0	156.8	26.5	0.1	140.1	-280.8	16.7
1992	322.0	137.0	226.6	103.0	95.4	34.0	-334.5	11.3	156.4	22.6	0.2	143.3	-359.2	13.1
1993	315.3	141.3	222.3	109.2	92.9	32.2	-313.5	12.9	150.7	24.3	0.2	147.0	-328.7	3.7
1994	310.8	147.9	220.0	112.6	90.7	35.3	-255.6	15.1	145.4	26.0	0.1	150.3	-261.7	-4.9
1995	304.4	151.8	217.4	115.6	87.0	36.2	-242.1	14.9	147.7	27.9	-7.9	153.5	-241.3	-5.8
1996	304.7	152.2	213.7	118.1	91.0	34.2	-179.4	17.5	149.8	28.4	-4.8	153.7	-181.7	-3.9
1997	304.9	160.3	211.8	121.7	93.0	38.6	-92.0	20.6	143.7	29.2	-8.8	154.3	-81.2	-10.6
1998	301.0	163.5	210.4	126.4	90.5	37.2	1.4	25.2	147.7	28.9	-6.0	155.4	11.4	-7.7
1999	313.3	168.1	212.0	133.0	101.3	35.2	69.1	28.8	154.9	38.8	-1.2	158.2	63.6	-3.3
2000	321.6	182.4	217.6	142.7	104.0	39.6	159.7	28.1	157.4	41.2	-0.6	163.1	152.9	-5.7
2001	339.8	196.2	223.0	147.3	116.8	48.9	15.0	28.0	163.8	43.6	-1.5	164.4	1.5	-0.6
2002	374.6	217.8	239.7	158.1	134.9	59.7	-267.8	25.3	182.2	53.4	-0.3	166.8	-310.9	15.4
2003	428.3	236.8	264.3	170.4	164.1	66.4	-397.4	22.0	195.2	69.8	-0.8	172.2	-467.2	23.0
2004	466.3	252.0	281.0	178.4	185.4	73.6	-393.5	24.6	208.4	71.4	-0.6	180.5	-467.5	27.9
2005	497.2	267.8	301.2	187.2	196.0	80.7	-293.8	25.0	222.0	97.5	-1.8	190.5	-396.0	31.5
2006	522.6	283.0	315.1	194.8	207.5	88.2	-221.9	27.8	235.6	76.7	-14.2	201.3	-290.9	34.3
2007	550.0	291.1	331.1	204.6	218.9	86.5	-259.7	26.5	250.0	85.9	-3.3	212.8	-353.0	37.2
2008	606.1	316.5	352.6	216.4	253.5	100.1	-624.9	28.3	271.7	152.1	-20.4	225.9	-774.2	45.8
2009	637.3	344.4	372.7	230.3	264.6	114.1	-1 243.2	20.6	282.6	212.6	-8.9	233.6	-1 475.3	49.0
2010	675.6	373.8	393.5	246.5	282.1	127.3	-1 318.4	15.1	297.2	148.1	-1.0	243.7	-1 504.0	53.5
2011	688.1	366.9	407.1	252.6	281.0	114.2	-1 234.1	9.6	295.7	131.2	-0.9	254.9	-1 395.6	40.8
2012	676.3	370.4	407.6	256.1	268.7	114.3	-1 072.7	14.1	287.3	105.0	-2.0	261.6	-1 187.3	25.7
2013	637.6	366.8	400.1	258.3	237.5	108.5	-631.8	20.9	269.6	85.1	-2.5	265.9	-697.3	3.7
2014	625.3	375.9	400.0	266.8	225.3	109.1	-597.4	18.8	263.8	83.7	-2.6	270.2	-653.2	-6.4
2015	613.3	391.3	398.4	275.3	214.9	116.0	-560.2	20.2	266.6	80.1	-30.9	271.5	-584.4	-4.9
2016	614.7	402.5	399.1	284.8	215.6	117.7	-667.6	20.1	268.8	80.6	-8.9	270.7	-717.3	-1.9
2017	627.2	407.8	403.9	295.3	223.3	112.4	-720.7	273.2	280.0	91.2	-2.2	275.9	-540.7	4.1
2018	664.3	429.0	418.0	308.0	246.3	121.0	-928.1	22.7	299.6	82.2	-0.8	284.9	-1 001.5	14.7
2019	708.4	445.8	430.9	318.5	277.5	127.3	-1 047.5	16.2	317.5	93.9	-2.6	293.3	-1 146.9	24.2
2020	729.9	489.1	447.6	334.9	282.3	154.2	-3 110.0	19.1	340.3	91.8	-2.9	303.5	-3 216.5	36.8
2018														
1st quarter	643.1	423.4	411.8	303.3	231.3	120.1	-909.7	24.1	291.0	77.9	-0.3	281.0	-973.2	10.0
2nd quarter	662.8	427.2	416.3	306.6	246.5	120.6	-928.8	23.7	295.6	85.3	-0.4	284.2	-1 001.2	11.4
3rd quarter	670.7	431.5	420.5	309.6	250.1	121.9	-901.4	22.5	301.8	84.4	-0.4	286.3	-978.3	15.5
4th quarter	680.6	434.0	423.2	312.6	257.4	121.4	-972.5	20.4	309.9	81.4	-2.0	288.1	-1 053.3	21.8
2019														
1st quarter	693.7	436.0	426.4	315.3	267.3	120.7	-1 015.4	17.7	311.5	84.5	-6.3	291.3	-1 096.1	20.2
2nd quarter	706.8	445.6	428.8	316.9	278.1	128.6	-1 033.2	15.5	311.2	77.9	-1.8	291.9	-1 113.1	19.3
3rd quarter	712.6	449.2	432.4	320.2	280.2	129.0	-1 080.9	15.5	319.0	81.0	-1.7	294.2	-1 169.5	24.8
4th quarter	720.4	452.3	436.2	321.7	284.2	130.7	-1 060.4	16.0	328.4	132.3	-0.4	295.8	-1 208.9	32.6
2020														
1st quarter	722.7	459.3	439.5	326.1	283.2	133.2	-1 158.0	17.8	330.0	92.5	-0.3	298.2	-1 264.1	31.8
2nd quarter	720.7	523.4	446.0	330.8	274.7	192.7	-5 625.6	19.3	337.4	92.0	-0.1	301.6	-5 733.9	35.8
3rd quarter	732.7	494.3	450.2	341.9	282.4	152.4	-3 516.3	19.7	345.7	92.1	-11.1	305.1	-3 618.2	40.6
4th quarter	743.7	479.5	454.8	340.7	288.9	138.7	-2 140.1	19.6	348.2	90.4	-0.2	309.2	-2 249.7	39.0

[1] Includes general government intermediate inputs for goods and services sold to other sectors and for own-account investment.

Table 6-6. Chain-Type Quantity Indexes for Federal Government Defense and Nondefense Consumption Expenditures and Gross Investment

(Seasonally adjusted, 2012 = 100.)   NIPA Tables 3.9.3, 3.10.3

Year and quarter	Defense consumption expenditures[1]						Defense gross investment	Nondefense consumption expenditures[1]						Non-defense gross investment
	Total	Compensation of general government employees	Consumption of general government fixed capital	Intermediate goods and services purchased[2]				Total	Compensation of general government employees	Consumption of general government fixed capital	Intermediate goods and services purchased[2]			
				Durable goods	Non-durable goods	Services					Durable goods	Non-durable goods excluding CCC inventory change	Services	
1965	67.1	124.2	59.0	35.1	123.2	20.9	40.4	26.1	57.5	13.4	4.7	16.8	21.7	33.8
1966	76.2	136.9	59.8	51.0	175.7	26.8	44.9	25.3	59.8	15.9	5.0	17.0	22.4	37.8
1967	85.7	149.0	61.4	50.4	269.3	34.2	50.4	28.0	62.8	18.2	4.9	19.0	20.4	34.8
1968	89.6	151.0	63.0	58.3	309.3	35.4	46.0	28.2	64.2	20.5	3.2	12.6	12.5	35.5
1969	86.5	151.2	63.3	48.6	274.6	33.1	42.9	30.9	64.8	22.6	3.2	13.1	15.2	34.2
1970	79.4	140.2	62.9	43.5	191.2	30.7	39.2	32.1	65.7	24.4	3.9	16.5	20.9	32.8
1971	73.5	129.5	61.2	31.4	156.4	31.2	30.7	34.9	67.8	26.0	4.8	20.3	24.3	32.7
1972	68.8	119.7	59.0	38.3	159.1	26.8	27.6	38.1	69.8	27.3	7.9	24.8	32.0	33.8
1973	64.1	113.6	57.2	35.0	118.3	24.7	28.8	38.1	70.0	28.7	7.2	23.8	30.4	34.0
1974	62.3	111.9	55.9	30.4	102.4	26.0	31.0	40.6	73.5	30.0	7.7	25.1	31.4	34.1
1975	60.9	110.4	54.9	32.2	84.8	23.9	32.3	42.4	74.8	31.2	8.1	22.8	31.8	35.1
1976	59.5	108.2	54.3	29.1	67.5	23.9	34.4	42.2	78.5	32.6	8.5	22.6	26.6	37.4
1977	59.8	107.2	54.1	36.5	64.5	23.8	35.4	43.9	80.2	34.1	11.1	22.3	29.0	39.5
1978	60.2	108.0	53.9	40.1	65.4	23.0	35.7	45.6	82.3	35.9	12.8	32.9	29.8	43.6
1979	60.6	107.1	53.9	43.7	67.4	23.5	39.1	46.4	82.2	37.8	15.0	32.3	32.5	44.1
1980	62.1	107.7	54.4	46.0	73.7	26.0	41.9	49.6	84.4	39.7	16.9	31.4	33.2	45.2
1981	65.1	111.1	55.5	54.1	78.4	28.1	46.5	50.8	81.9	41.4	15.8	58.7	28.2	44.5
1982	68.6	113.6	57.3	59.4	78.1	33.7	52.5	49.8	80.4	42.8	14.6	43.8	26.7	41.3
1983	71.5	115.4	60.1	70.9	81.4	34.0	60.5	53.3	81.6	44.1	15.6	54.8	32.2	41.2
1984	73.2	117.0	63.7	72.0	77.0	35.5	68.1	51.6	81.6	45.4	16.9	57.0	33.1	42.4
1985	76.8	119.2	68.5	77.7	75.4	39.1	80.4	54.6	81.8	46.6	17.4	49.6	35.9	44.7
1986	80.8	119.6	73.9	83.7	95.8	41.7	89.5	56.4	80.5	47.9	17.2	42.3	35.7	45.8
1987	83.6	120.7	79.3	88.9	93.9	42.6	97.0	54.9	82.0	49.3	19.6	49.0	40.2	48.8
1988	85.3	119.2	83.8	91.2	91.2	44.8	90.6	51.8	84.1	50.7	20.7	48.8	37.9	48.2
1989	85.8	119.2	86.9	87.7	88.2	44.8	88.3	56.1	84.5	52.2	23.4	43.6	37.5	50.6
1990	86.1	118.5	89.1	84.5	78.3	47.5	88.3	60.1	88.7	53.8	26.7	46.4	44.5	54.5
1991	87.4	118.0	90.1	81.1	79.4	51.2	81.7	60.4	88.5	55.7	28.4	40.6	44.1	58.1
1992	83.6	111.3	90.0	72.8	73.6	49.5	77.0	64.0	90.1	57.3	30.9	50.5	49.7	61.6
1993	80.8	106.5	88.9	65.9	67.6	48.9	68.9	63.4	90.0	58.9	30.1	55.0	42.5	62.7
1994	77.2	101.0	87.1	56.5	61.5	49.4	64.4	64.1	87.5	60.3	28.3	46.2	50.0	59.7
1995	74.1	95.5	85.0	51.5	50.3	47.6	61.8	63.5	84.0	61.7	27.6	52.1	48.2	61.0
1996	72.7	91.4	83.0	51.1	55.5	48.7	61.3	62.2	81.8	63.3	31.4	45.0	45.5	62.9
1997	71.6	88.1	81.2	51.3	56.0	49.4	57.0	64.9	81.3	65.0	33.8	54.9	48.4	62.4
1998	69.7	85.3	79.4	51.7	57.8	47.0	57.1	64.5	82.2	66.8	34.0	59.7	44.3	65.9
1999	70.7	83.2	77.9	55.0	64.2	52.1	57.7	65.1	82.4	69.1	38.1	44.4	43.9	69.9
2000	69.7	82.6	76.7	54.4	67.3	51.1	58.3	67.7	84.9	71.5	41.9	50.5	46.1	69.0
2001	71.6	83.1	75.7	54.7	69.6	58.0	61.6	71.9	84.9	73.5	45.1	67.1	54.2	70.6
2002	75.5	85.3	75.7	57.3	80.0	67.4	70.8	77.1	86.4	75.6	54.9	73.3	67.8	75.8
2003	81.7	88.2	76.9	62.9	87.3	81.0	76.6	80.4	88.6	77.5	56.5	88.0	71.9	78.3
2004	85.7	89.9	78.9	68.3	97.9	88.0	83.0	82.2	87.8	79.5	62.6	98.5	77.2	79.2
2005	86.7	90.2	81.5	70.0	99.0	88.8	88.5	83.5	87.7	81.7	68.9	99.7	81.4	80.4
2006	87.4	88.9	84.5	75.4	96.3	90.3	92.6	86.3	87.8	84.4	77.2	98.4	86.8	84.2
2007	89.0	88.6	87.6	84.8	98.3	90.8	98.6	86.3	88.4	87.1	79.0	95.6	81.9	85.4
2008	94.8	91.9	91.2	97.9	100.1	100.2	106.6	91.4	91.7	89.6	88.6	106.3	91.6	88.5
2009	100.8	97.8	94.5	106.1	105.9	107.1	110.4	98.8	96.5	92.3	96.7	123.2	105.1	92.6
2010	104.4	101.0	97.3	106.7	102.3	113.4	111.1	103.8	100.7	94.8	106.5	129.8	115.1	100.6
2011	102.9	102.0	99.2	103.0	104.3	106.7	105.9	98.6	99.5	97.5	99.8	106.9	100.5	101.0
2012	100.0	100.0	100.0	100.0	100.0	100.0	100.0	100.0	100.0	100.0	100.0	100.0	100.0	100.0
2013	93.4	96.5	99.7	87.6	88.9	87.2	93.0	97.5	97.1	102.3	94.7	92.3	94.0	93.7
2014	90.1	94.5	98.5	79.7	83.3	82.4	86.9	97.3	97.0	104.3	97.9	90.2	93.4	94.1
2015	88.0	92.2	97.0	77.5	84.6	80.0	85.8	100.2	98.1	106.2	102.7	95.9	100.1	97.9
2016	88.0	92.1	95.6	78.7	90.4	79.6	83.6	101.4	100.1	108.3	104.4	96.3	101.2	102.6
2017	88.3	92.2	94.6	83.6	93.0	79.5	86.4	99.8	99.9	111.1	100.2	91.8	94.0	105.5
2018	90.8	93.1	94.2	89.4	94.7	85.8	91.2	101.6	99.2	114.2	104.4	95.5	98.2	110.1
2019	95.3	94.6	94.5	96.9	93.0	97.5	97.1	103.1	99.1	117.2	106.2	101.7	100.4	112.6
2020	97.1	96.8	95.5	101.8	94.9	98.8	103.8	112.8	104.0	120.1	217.2	101.0	122.8	117.4
2018														
1st quarter	88.8	92.5	94.2	83.9	96.3	80.6	89.1	101.9	99.4	113.0	104.6	96.0	98.8	108.2
2nd quarter	90.8	93.0	94.2	90.0	93.7	86.1	89.3	101.7	99.7	113.8	104.3	94.8	98.2	109.9
3rd quarter	91.3	93.4	94.2	94.1	94.8	86.2	91.3	102.4	99.8	114.6	104.9	95.2	98.6	111.2
4th quarter	92.3	93.5	94.2	89.6	94.2	90.4	95.2	100.6	97.9	115.3	104.0	95.9	97.2	111.3
2019														
1st quarter	93.8	94.1	94.3	92.3	93.7	94.3	94.9	99.3	93.8	116.1	101.5	97.0	96.0	111.1
2nd quarter	95.2	94.3	94.4	93.4	93.0	98.6	94.0	104.0	100.6	116.8	107.2	104.2	101.2	112.6
3rd quarter	95.7	94.8	94.5	96.5	92.7	98.9	97.6	104.7	101.3	117.6	107.8	103.9	101.5	112.9
4th quarter	96.4	95.4	94.7	105.4	92.3	98.3	102.0	104.3	100.9	118.3	108.5	101.9	102.9	113.9
2020														
1st quarter	96.4	95.8	95.0	96.8	93.6	99.5	100.8	106.2	101.8	119.0	159.9	100.2	103.9	115.9
2nd quarter	96.5	97.2	95.3	106.4	94.1	95.7	104.3	121.8	102.7	119.7	273.9	101.5	160.5	115.5
3rd quarter	97.2	97.0	95.7	102.9	95.2	98.6	103.7	113.9	107.0	120.5	272.7	98.3	118.6	121.1
4th quarter	98.1	97.2	96.1	101.1	96.6	101.4	106.6	109.4	104.4	121.2	162.3	103.9	108.0	117.3

[1]Excludes government sales to other sectors and government own-account investment (construction and software).
[2]Includes general government intermediate inputs for goods and services sold to other sectors and for own-account investment.

Table 6-7. Chain-Type Quantity Indexes for National Defense Consumption Expenditures and Gross Investment: Selected Detail

(Seasonally adjusted, 2012 = 100.)

NIPA Table 3.11.3

| Year and quarter | Compensation of general government employees | | Intermediate goods and services purchased [1] | | | | | | Defense gross investment | | | | |
| | | | Durable goods | Nondurable goods | | Services | | | | | | | Research and develop- ment |
	Military	Civilian	Aircraft	Petroleum products	Ammu- nition	Installation support	Weapons support	Personnel support	Aircraft	Missiles	Ships	Software	
1980	103.8	113.6	49.9	118.3	65.8	51.4	30.8	8.6	31.9	32.0	84.7	11.7	61.4
1981	107.2	116.8	64.3	116.3	74.3	55.8	33.6	9.6	36.9	37.1	96.5	14.0	68.2
1982	109.1	120.6	75.0	109.6	91.6	68.1	41.4	11.3	37.1	47.9	112.6	15.3	76.8
1983	111.0	122.1	91.4	117.2	107.4	65.1	43.3	12.4	42.1	60.6	125.1	17.8	87.1
1984	112.3	124.2	86.5	116.9	90.9	70.5	43.9	11.5	45.3	72.9	132.5	23.5	97.5
1985	114.0	127.5	92.9	119.1	54.2	74.7	49.5	14.9	61.8	83.1	145.6	28.7	112.3
1986	115.0	126.8	102.7	119.6	145.9	74.7	54.5	17.5	94.2	105.3	140.5	34.1	116.6
1987	116.4	127.2	109.9	122.0	110.7	79.4	52.6	17.7	108.1	119.8	136.5	38.1	125.4
1988	115.5	124.4	113.7	103.4	127.8	79.0	56.6	21.0	88.9	109.1	129.5	44.2	119.5
1989	115.0	125.6	107.2	113.2	106.9	77.0	55.3	21.3	81.3	124.9	143.7	50.6	111.1
1990	115.3	122.7	94.2	111.9	96.4	87.4	59.3	19.6	75.0	162.2	151.6	54.8	105.8
1991	116.6	118.8	84.2	110.6	90.9	92.0	48.7	17.5	53.9	163.1	136.0	56.3	93.8
1992	106.7	118.2	73.4	92.4	86.3	90.5	43.7	24.0	47.2	161.3	131.4	60.8	86.2
1993	101.2	115.0	63.7	89.0	85.7	98.1	39.3	25.0	50.8	117.2	110.9	58.0	80.1
1994	96.4	108.3	54.0	91.6	59.0	99.0	41.0	26.8	50.8	86.0	99.8	57.1	76.1
1995	91.4	101.9	51.5	83.0	37.8	91.1	40.7	27.0	41.1	72.5	93.9	56.0	73.6
1996	88.1	96.5	51.1	83.7	44.2	92.7	37.8	29.5	40.0	64.9	79.3	58.9	73.1
1997	85.7	91.6	54.6	75.4	54.3	89.1	42.7	32.0	27.8	48.0	70.4	60.5	71.9
1998	83.8	87.4	57.9	73.5	61.5	83.7	40.5	30.2	28.0	54.1	74.4	64.6	70.7
1999	82.3	84.3	61.2	79.7	62.6	85.8	44.7	36.9	29.1	49.0	78.8	64.4	68.9
2000	83.0	81.5	57.0	73.5	59.5	85.3	44.9	35.5	33.9	46.2	75.0	63.6	68.6
2001	84.7	80.2	56.2	87.0	68.0	90.7	55.5	42.4	39.6	58.0	82.2	60.2	73.4
2002	87.8	80.7	56.6	103.2	80.5	100.3	66.9	52.5	47.3	58.0	95.1	58.7	84.3
2003	92.6	80.5	64.3	99.5	87.4	112.2	82.3	61.2	45.0	59.8	103.3	60.4	92.8
2004	93.7	83.2	66.2	103.0	110.7	110.3	84.4	75.3	55.4	67.9	105.0	62.6	100.8
2005	93.1	85.0	58.5	100.5	117.7	103.1	91.3	78.8	69.5	65.8	100.0	65.8	106.5
2006	91.0	85.2	58.9	99.2	112.9	105.7	93.6	81.9	70.7	74.1	105.7	68.9	109.0
2007	90.2	85.7	61.0	98.3	111.0	102.0	95.7	78.3	67.4	70.3	99.4	73.3	112.1
2008	94.2	87.8	68.0	99.0	105.1	106.6	100.7	94.1	68.2	68.1	102.3	78.6	110.6
2009	101.5	91.3	78.2	99.8	107.2	114.2	103.5	100.2	69.1	79.1	101.1	80.3	108.5
2010	103.1	97.2	85.0	102.0	105.3	116.7	116.3	105.2	82.7	85.6	104.6	88.6	106.1
2011	102.7	100.7	94.2	104.8	99.7	106.9	108.0	101.2	97.5	75.4	98.7	95.5	103.6
2012	100.0	100.0	100.0	100.0	100.0	100.0	100.0	100.0	100.0	100.0	100.0	100.0	100.0
2013	97.5	94.7	92.6	83.8	82.7	83.5	84.8	91.2	110.1	92.8	104.7	101.6	94.3
2014	94.4	94.6	83.8	77.5	70.7	90.2	89.8	78.0	97.5	96.5	108.7	104.9	87.3
2015	91.0	94.2	80.8	80.4	64.9	85.6	91.9	74.8	93.5	95.5	110.8	106.7	87.3
2016	90.4	94.8	80.7	82.2	71.4	88.4	94.0	71.3	87.2	71.0	117.9	117.2	80.8
2017	90.5	94.9	85.9	77.1	85.5	89.6	98.7	68.9	100.7	70.8	114.6	128.4	77.6
2018	91.6	95.6	87.1	75.9	108.8	89.4	106.9	78.2	106.9	69.3	125.0	142.8	78.1
2019	93.0	97.3	90.6	71.7	127.2	87.9	118.1	97.5	126.3	76.9	137.3	151.5	77.0
2020	95.3	99.3	94.6	75.1	124.2	95.9	121.5	97.8	118.0	105.4	147.1	158.0	84.4
2014													
1st quarter	96.0	94.7	88.6	81.2	75.1	87.4	87.9	79.6	86.4	88.1	101.9	102.6	88.2
2nd quarter	95.2	94.6	86.0	75.2	72.4	90.0	87.8	74.3	104.4	93.2	114.9	104.3	87.2
3rd quarter	93.8	94.4	78.0	75.4	68.9	93.3	94.9	87.1	98.5	96.4	111.6	106.8	86.7
4th quarter	92.5	94.5	82.5	78.2	66.6	90.3	88.4	71.0	100.9	108.3	106.4	106.0	87.3
2015													
1st quarter	91.6	94.5	81.8	82.0	64.5	87.6	90.1	76.9	80.7	94.5	113.3	106.2	87.8
2nd quarter	90.9	94.1	78.0	77.1	63.6	86.7	93.3	76.0	102.9	91.9	107.5	106.2	87.8
3rd quarter	90.7	94.1	80.6	79.5	64.7	83.2	91.3	73.4	96.2	85.8	111.3	106.4	87.3
4th quarter	90.7	94.2	82.9	82.8	66.8	85.0	92.9	73.1	94.3	110.0	111.2	108.1	86.1
2016													
1st quarter	90.7	94.4	83.4	85.9	68.4	87.5	93.7	72.0	99.5	75.9	118.2	112.7	84.1
2nd quarter	90.5	94.7	74.5	80.9	70.0	87.3	91.4	67.4	88.8	80.4	113.3	115.6	81.4
3rd quarter	90.4	95.0	80.4	82.0	72.0	88.6	95.8	73.1	79.9	72.6	120.3	118.9	79.7
4th quarter	90.2	95.1	84.3	79.8	74.9	90.0	95.2	72.7	80.7	54.9	119.8	121.7	78.1
2017													
1st quarter	90.1	95.1	85.4	78.2	78.5	88.3	92.8	64.7	94.3	76.1	99.8	124.1	77.7
2nd quarter	90.1	94.8	92.4	76.9	82.7	89.6	97.8	71.7	99.7	72.3	117.6	126.8	77.4
3rd quarter	90.6	94.9	79.8	76.3	87.6	90.3	101.7	69.0	98.2	71.8	117.0	129.7	77.5
4th quarter	91.2	94.9	85.9	76.9	93.0	90.0	102.5	70.3	110.4	63.1	124.2	133.1	77.9
2018													
1st quarter	91.2	94.7	78.8	79.7	99.0	89.0	102.1	70.1	97.5	70.8	124.5	137.2	78.4
2nd quarter	91.4	95.7	88.7	75.0	105.2	90.7	108.0	77.9	94.8	60.2	126.9	142.0	78.3
3rd quarter	91.8	96.1	98.2	75.1	111.9	89.0	107.2	79.0	106.6	64.9	121.6	144.3	78.2
4th quarter	92.0	96.0	82.8	73.7	119.1	89.0	110.5	85.9	128.6	81.4	126.9	147.6	77.6
2019													
1st quarter	92.6	96.6	85.9	73.8	124.2	86.9	113.7	93.1	126.6	72.2	129.4	147.2	76.3
2nd quarter	92.6	97.1	86.6	71.9	127.6	87.1	118.0	100.0	113.6	62.2	134.2	150.2	76.1
3rd quarter	93.1	97.5	89.1	70.9	128.9	88.0	119.5	99.5	125.2	72.9	142.5	153.0	76.7
4th quarter	93.8	98.1	101.0	70.3	128.3	89.7	121.2	97.3	139.6	100.4	143.0	155.8	78.7
2020													
1st quarter	93.9	98.8	86.1	72.3	127.3	93.6	121.7	98.7	110.4	91.3	147.2	158.5	81.0
2nd quarter	96.2	98.9	102.7	73.5	125.6	94.1	119.2	95.0	126.7	108.7	147.2	155.9	83.1
3rd quarter	95.5	99.6	95.7	75.2	123.5	97.5	121.4	96.9	108.4	111.2	145.1	157.8	85.6
4th quarter	95.7	99.8	94.0	79.5	120.6	98.5	123.6	100.7	126.5	110.3	148.9	160.0	88.0

[1] Includes general government intermediate inputs for goods and services sold to other sectors and for own-account investment.

SECTION 6B: STATE AND LOCAL GOVERNMENT IN THE NATIONAL INCOME AND PRODUCT ACCOUNTS

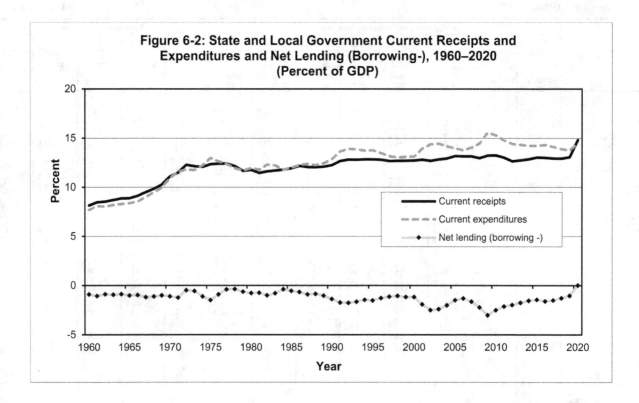

Figure 6-2: State and Local Government Current Receipts and Expenditures and Net Lending (Borrowing-), 1960–2020 (Percent of GDP)

- Both current receipts and current spending of state and local governments have increased as a share of gross domestic product (GDP) over the postwar period, but the growth slowed markedly after the early 1970s. (Tables 6-8 and 1-1)

- State and local governments have consistently been net borrowers in capital markets, as can be seen by the negative values in Figure 6-2. Although they are usually constrained to balance their statutory budgets, they have consistently made net investments and been able to borrow for that purpose. In addition, as revealed by the accrual accounting adopted in the NIPA accounts last year, they have often incurred hidden deficits by failing to fund commitments for public employee retirement benefits. (Table 6-10)

- A larger gap between current expenditures and current receipts appeared during the slow-growth years 2001–2003, and a still-greater one during the Great Recession beginning in late 2007. Generally, in both of those periods of rising deficits, receipts barely kept pace with the economy, while general ("consumption") expenditures, social benefits, and interest payments all fueled higher spending. (Table 6-8)

- Net lending by state and local government reached a high of $-437 billion in 2009 but declined to $220.7 billion in 2019 and was a positive $3.1 billion in 2020. (Table 6-8)

Table 6-8. State and Local Government Current Receipts and Expenditures

(National income and product accounts, calendar years, billions of dollars, quarterly data are at seasonally adjusted annual rates.)

NIPA Table 3.3

Year and quarter	Total current receipts	Current receipts											
		Current tax receipts						Taxes on corporate income	Contribu-tions for govern-ment social insurance	Income receipts on assets		
		Total tax receipts	Personal current taxes		Taxes on production and imports					Interest receipts	Dividends	Rents and royalties
			Income taxes	Other personal taxes	Sales taxes	Property taxes	Other taxes on prod. and imports					
1960	44.2	37.0	2.5	1.7	5.3	16.2	3.1	1.2	0.5	1.0	. . .	0.3
1961	47.7	39.7	2.8	1.8	5.8	17.6	3.2	1.3	0.5	1.1	. . .	0.4
1962	51.6	42.8	3.2	1.8	6.4	19.0	3.3	1.5	0.5	1.1	. . .	0.4
1963	55.5	45.8	3.4	2.0	6.9	20.2	3.5	1.7	0.6	1.2	. . .	0.4
1964	60.7	49.8	4.0	2.1	7.7	21.7	3.7	1.8	0.7	1.5	. . .	0.4
1965	65.9	53.9	4.4	2.2	8.6	23.2	3.9	2.0	0.8	1.8	. . .	0.4
1966	74.2	58.8	5.4	2.4	9.8	24.5	4.3	2.2	0.8	2.1	. . .	0.5
1967	81.7	64.0	6.1	2.5	10.7	27.0	4.4	2.6	0.9	2.4	. . .	0.6
1968	92.6	73.4	7.8	2.7	13.1	29.9	4.6	3.3	0.9	2.8	. . .	0.7
1969	104.5	82.5	9.8	3.0	15.1	32.8	4.7	3.6	1.0	3.6	. . .	0.8
1970	119.1	91.3	10.9	3.3	17.0	36.7	5.0	3.7	1.1	4.3	. . .	0.8
1971	133.7	101.7	12.4	3.5	19.1	40.4	5.7	4.3	1.2	4.6	. . .	0.9
1972	157.1	115.6	17.2	3.7	21.8	43.2	6.4	5.3	1.3	4.9	. . .	1.0
1973	173.0	126.3	18.9	4.0	24.5	46.4	7.0	6.0	1.5	6.6	0.0	1.1
1974	186.6	136.0	20.4	4.2	28.0	49.0	7.7	6.7	1.7	8.9	0.0	1.3
1975	208.0	147.4	22.5	4.4	30.3	53.4	8.1	7.3	1.8	9.8	0.0	1.3
1976	232.2	165.7	26.3	4.8	34.4	58.2	9.0	9.6	2.2	9.0	0.0	1.3
1977	258.3	183.7	30.4	5.0	39.0	63.2	9.7	11.4	2.8	10.4	0.0	1.3
1978	285.8	198.2	35.0	5.5	44.2	63.7	10.9	12.1	3.4	13.3	0.1	1.3
1979	306.3	212.0	38.2	5.8	49.5	64.4	12.7	13.6	3.9	18.1	0.1	1.9
1980	335.9	230.0	42.6	6.3	53.6	68.8	15.0	14.5	3.6	23.1	0.1	3.1
1981	367.5	255.8	47.9	6.7	58.8	77.1	17.9	15.4	3.9	28.5	0.1	3.3
1982	388.5	273.2	51.9	7.3	62.0	85.3	18.5	14.0	4.0	33.1	0.2	3.5
1983	425.3	300.9	58.3	7.8	70.4	91.9	19.4	15.9	4.1	37.0	0.2	4.3
1984	476.1	337.3	67.5	8.6	80.6	99.7	21.8	18.8	4.7	42.6	0.2	4.9
1985	517.5	363.7	72.1	9.2	87.9	107.5	23.5	20.2	4.9	50.1	0.2	5.4
1986	557.4	389.5	77.4	9.8	93.7	116.2	23.7	22.7	6.0	52.6	0.2	6.2
1987	585.5	422.1	86.0	10.6	100.9	126.4	24.9	23.9	7.2	53.0	0.2	5.3
1988	630.4	452.8	90.6	11.5	110.0	136.5	25.7	26.0	8.4	56.6	0.2	4.4
1989	681.4	488.0	102.3	12.4	117.4	149.9	26.9	24.2	9.0	62.3	0.2	4.1
1990	730.1	519.1	109.6	13.0	125.6	161.5	28.2	22.5	10.0	64.1	0.2	4.2
1991	779.9	544.3	111.7	13.6	128.0	176.1	28.6	23.6	11.6	62.4	0.3	4.5
1992	836.1	579.8	120.4	14.9	136.0	184.7	31.1	24.4	13.1	58.8	0.5	4.8
1993	878.0	604.7	126.2	14.8	143.7	187.3	33.1	26.9	14.1	56.2	0.6	4.5
1994	935.1	644.2	132.2	15.8	155.4	199.4	35.4	30.0	14.5	58.4	0.8	4.5
1995	981.0	672.1	141.7	16.4	164.4	202.6	37.0	31.7	13.6	63.8	1.0	4.5
1996	1 033.7	709.6	152.3	16.3	174.4	212.4	39.3	33.0	12.5	68.0	1.4	4.6
1997	1 086.7	749.9	164.7	17.3	184.2	223.5	41.6	34.1	10.8	72.0	1.5	4.8
1998	1 149.6	794.9	183.0	18.2	194.9	231.0	43.9	34.9	10.4	75.2	1.6	4.6
1999	1 222.9	840.4	195.5	19.0	208.6	242.8	45.8	35.8	9.8	79.0	1.5	5.1
2000	1 304.3	893.2	217.4	19.4	221.4	254.7	49.8	35.2	10.8	86.8	1.4	6.3
2001	1 354.1	914.3	223.3	19.7	223.1	268.0	52.6	28.9	13.7	82.2	1.4	6.5
2002	1 386.9	923.9	199.3	20.6	222.5	289.2	56.3	30.9	15.8	71.4	1.6	6.6
2003	1 470.9	974.3	202.8	22.1	233.3	306.9	63.0	34.0	19.9	63.7	1.8	7.6
2004	1 579.2	1 060.3	221.4	24.3	252.0	326.1	77.4	41.7	24.7	65.7	2.3	8.5
2005	1 717.5	1 173.2	249.1	26.2	272.8	351.2	91.7	54.9	24.6	76.3	2.5	9.8
2006	1 815.3	1 258.2	274.2	26.9	293.9	375.2	92.1	59.2	21.5	94.2	3.0	10.5
2007	1 901.4	1 321.7	294.3	27.3	301.4	403.7	92.9	57.9	18.8	103.9	3.4	11.7
2008	1 915.3	1 334.1	304.1	26.8	301.1	415.7	94.7	47.4	18.7	91.1	3.4	12.2
2009	1 915.5	1 265.8	258.9	26.9	279.6	439.6	72.3	44.5	18.6	73.8	2.9	11.2
2010	1 993.1	1 306.4	265.8	28.3	295.1	438.6	77.8	46.1	17.8	67.8	3.0	11.4
2011	2 029.1	1 366.4	294.1	28.8	311.3	439.2	83.9	48.4	17.9	65.9	3.4	12.2
2012	2 055.2	1 414.7	313.1	30.0	324.4	443.3	86.7	50.7	17.2	64.3	4.1	12.5
2013	2 144.9	1 490.6	343.1	30.4	343.9	456.8	91.6	53.9	17.7	64.3	4.7	12.5
2014	2 256.4	1 541.9	349.4	31.5	361.7	475.0	93.0	56.5	18.7	65.3	5.3	12.7
2015	2 372.6	1 598.4	374.5	32.9	374.2	490.4	89.0	56.2	19.2	64.9	5.4	11.2
2016	2 429.1	1 638.8	375.9	34.4	384.8	511.6	91.8	53.4	20.0	66.6	5.7	10.9
2017	2 517.6	1 724.7	399.8	35.6	405.6	536.0	97.1	54.6	19.8	71.4	5.9	10.9
2018	2 650.6	1 818.4	421.8	38.0	426.9	555.1	107.4	60.5	20.4	77.4	6.1	10.9
2019	2 793.1	1 927.0	457.1	39.4	443.9	599.6	108.9	72.9	20.4	78.2	6.6	12.0
2020	3 096.6	1 963.6	476.1	39.8	448.9	615.3	109.8	71.0	19.9	76.8	6.3	13.3
2018												
1st quarter	2 636.5	1 810.9	441.0	38.1	420.0	543.9	105.2	55.6	20.2	75.6	5.9	10.7
2nd quarter	2 616.9	1 793.9	404.5	37.9	424.8	549.1	106.8	60.3	20.4	77.1	6.2	10.7
3rd quarter	2 665.9	1 832.3	426.3	37.9	431.4	557.7	108.6	61.7	20.5	78.1	6.3	10.9
4th quarter	2 683.2	1 836.4	415.4	38.2	431.7	569.7	108.9	64.3	20.5	78.8	5.9	11.1
2019												
1st quarter	2 725.8	1 877.5	434.1	38.9	434.2	585.2	106.9	73.2	20.6	78.6	6.7	11.5
2nd quarter	2 811.4	1 942.4	481.7	39.2	437.8	597.1	108.6	72.8	20.5	78.3	6.6	11.8
3rd quarter	2 810.2	1 942.6	457.8	39.6	452.7	605.6	109.1	73.1	20.3	78.0	6.4	12.2
4th quarter	2 824.8	1 945.5	454.9	39.8	451.0	610.5	111.1	72.4	20.2	77.7	6.8	12.6
2020												
1st quarter	2 856.3	1 961.6	463.9	39.9	457.0	612.0	115.0	66.5	20.1	76.8	6.3	13.0
2nd quarter	3 550.7	1 901.6	480.2	37.3	419.3	613.9	101.0	61.9	19.1	76.8	6.2	13.2
3rd quarter	2 979.2	1 989.1	478.7	40.9	457.2	616.3	111.0	76.8	19.9	76.7	5.9	13.4
4th quarter	3 000.2	2 002.0	481.8	41.1	462.0	619.1	112.2	78.8	20.5	77.1	6.7	13.5

. . . = Not available.

Table 6-9. State and Local Government Consumption Expenditures and Gross Investment

(National income and product accounts, calendar years, billions of dollars, quarterly data are at seasonally adjusted annual rates.)

NIPA Tables 3.9.5, 3.10.5

Year and quarter	Total	Consumption expenditures [1]								Gross investment			
		Total	Compensation of general government employees	Consumption of general government fixed capital	Intermediate goods and services purchased [2]	Less: Own-account investment	Less: Sales to other sectors — Total [3]	Tuition and related educational charges	Health and hospital charges	Total	Structures	Equipment	Intellectual property
1960	47.6	33.5	25.9	3.6	8.9	0.9	3.9	0.4	1.0	14.1	12.7	1.2	0.2
1961	51.9	36.6	28.5	3.8	9.6	1.0	4.3	0.5	1.0	15.3	13.8	1.2	0.2
1962	54.8	38.7	30.6	4.1	10.1	1.1	4.9	0.6	1.3	16.1	14.5	1.3	0.2
1963	59.3	41.5	33.2	4.4	10.8	1.3	5.6	0.7	1.3	17.8	16.0	1.5	0.3
1964	64.5	45.2	36.2	4.7	11.9	1.3	6.3	0.8	1.5	19.3	17.2	1.7	0.3
1965	70.9	49.7	39.8	5.1	13.4	1.4	7.2	1.0	1.8	21.2	19.0	1.8	0.4
1966	78.9	55.4	44.6	5.7	14.9	1.5	8.2	1.2	2.1	23.5	21.0	2.0	0.4
1967	87.0	61.3	49.5	6.2	16.4	1.6	9.3	1.4	2.5	25.7	23.0	2.2	0.5
1968	97.6	69.4	56.3	6.9	18.6	1.8	10.7	1.6	3.1	28.1	25.2	2.3	0.6
1969	107.8	79.0	63.2	7.8	21.8	1.9	11.8	1.9	3.5	28.8	25.6	2.6	0.7
1970	119.8	90.4	71.5	8.8	25.3	2.1	13.1	2.4	3.8	29.3	25.8	2.8	0.8
1971	133.0	102.3	80.5	9.8	29.1	2.2	14.9	2.9	4.6	30.7	27.0	2.9	0.8
1972	144.5	113.2	89.5	10.7	32.0	2.3	16.7	3.2	5.6	31.3	27.1	3.3	0.9
1973	158.6	124.6	98.5	11.9	35.3	2.4	18.7	3.7	6.6	34.0	29.1	3.8	1.0
1974	182.5	142.0	108.1	14.7	42.6	2.8	20.5	4.0	7.4	40.5	34.7	4.6	1.2
1975	207.4	162.8	121.3	16.7	50.5	3.0	22.6	4.3	8.5	44.6	38.1	5.1	1.3
1976	219.4	174.5	130.6	17.4	55.0	3.0	25.6	4.7	9.9	44.9	38.1	5.3	1.5
1977	234.0	190.0	142.1	18.4	60.8	3.1	28.3	5.2	10.9	44.0	36.9	5.4	1.6
1978	257.4	206.6	155.7	19.9	66.6	3.5	32.0	5.8	12.7	50.8	42.8	6.1	1.9
1979	284.2	225.9	170.6	22.2	73.9	4.3	36.6	6.4	15.2	58.4	49.0	7.1	2.2
1980	314.7	249.0	187.9	25.7	81.6	4.9	41.2	7.2	17.3	65.7	55.1	8.1	2.6
1981	340.4	273.5	205.9	29.3	91.2	5.3	47.6	8.3	21.0	66.9	55.4	8.5	3.0
1982	363.1	296.1	223.6	32.0	100.0	5.7	53.8	9.4	24.5	67.0	54.2	9.4	3.4
1983	384.2	315.4	239.6	33.0	109.0	6.1	60.1	10.6	27.8	68.8	54.2	10.8	3.8
1984	416.1	338.5	257.8	34.1	118.4	7.0	64.7	11.7	29.4	77.6	60.5	12.7	4.4
1985	457.6	370.3	281.7	35.9	131.4	7.9	70.8	12.7	32.0	87.3	67.6	14.8	5.0
1986	494.4	398.2	304.2	38.6	141.7	8.8	77.4	13.8	34.8	96.2	74.2	16.4	5.6
1987	528.7	426.6	327.8	41.6	150.0	9.5	83.4	15.0	37.0	102.2	78.8	17.2	6.2
1988	567.4	457.0	354.4	44.5	159.8	10.4	91.2	16.6	40.3	110.4	84.8	18.6	7.0
1989	617.8	498.5	388.4	47.7	175.8	11.9	101.4	18.4	45.0	119.2	88.7	21.9	8.6
1990	676.2	544.0	426.5	51.6	190.5	13.1	111.6	20.3	50.0	132.2	98.5	23.9	9.7
1991	716.0	578.7	457.2	55.1	204.7	14.1	124.1	22.6	57.0	137.3	103.2	23.5	10.6
1992	756.0	616.3	492.6	57.6	218.9	14.4	138.4	25.4	65.3	139.7	104.2	24.0	11.4
1993	784.8	643.6	516.1	60.8	234.0	14.8	152.5	27.4	73.1	141.2	104.5	24.9	11.9
1994	827.6	678.8	541.9	64.3	251.5	15.4	163.5	29.3	78.8	148.8	108.7	28.1	12.0
1995	872.7	712.8	565.4	68.6	270.6	16.1	175.6	31.1	85.0	160.0	117.3	30.5	12.3
1996	913.7	743.5	586.6	72.0	285.8	16.8	184.0	32.9	86.6	170.2	126.8	30.5	12.8
1997	963.8	781.0	613.5	75.8	304.2	18.3	194.3	35.4	89.9	182.9	136.6	32.0	14.3
1998	1 026.1	829.8	646.3	79.9	326.7	19.4	203.7	37.9	93.4	196.3	146.1	34.7	15.5
1999	1 109.2	895.6	688.1	85.1	357.5	20.7	214.4	40.5	96.7	213.6	159.7	37.4	16.5
2000	1 193.4	961.9	732.5	91.5	392.3	22.6	231.8	43.6	104.0	231.5	174.6	38.8	18.1
2001	1 279.8	1 031.8	785.4	96.9	425.8	25.0	251.4	46.1	116.2	248.0	190.6	38.4	19.1
2002	1 346.4	1 084.9	829.1	101.4	444.9	26.0	264.6	49.3	120.7	261.5	204.1	38.0	19.4
2003	1 383.8	1 114.8	864.9	105.2	449.9	26.7	278.6	53.4	124.8	269.1	211.1	37.6	20.4
2004	1 446.0	1 168.2	907.6	111.8	471.2	27.8	294.4	56.7	130.9	277.8	219.1	37.2	21.5
2005	1 527.5	1 236.3	944.9	122.1	506.7	29.7	307.8	60.9	132.3	291.3	231.5	37.1	22.7
2006	1 622.7	1 307.4	989.8	132.2	541.7	32.2	324.2	64.0	141.0	315.3	251.4	39.1	24.7
2007	1 739.5	1 397.5	1 045.8	145.4	577.5	34.3	336.9	65.9	149.3	342.0	271.4	44.0	26.6
2008	1 831.1	1 473.2	1 095.9	156.2	605.0	36.1	347.8	67.8	158.4	357.9	284.5	45.1	28.3
2009	1 855.6	1 495.3	1 117.9	162.6	610.7	36.3	359.7	69.7	168.7	360.3	288.9	43.1	28.3
2010	1 855.4	1 508.1	1 141.1	165.0	610.8	35.6	373.1	71.6	176.1	347.3	279.8	39.6	27.9
2011	1 848.2	1 507.2	1 141.9	171.2	615.6	35.9	385.6	73.6	182.4	341.0	273.4	38.6	29.0
2012	1 849.5	1 515.7	1 147.1	178.4	621.6	35.8	395.5	76.1	188.5	333.7	265.0	39.2	29.6
2013	1 905.9	1 575.1	1 197.8	183.2	638.9	36.4	408.4	78.9	197.6	330.8	259.3	39.9	31.5
2014	1 952.8	1 614.1	1 232.5	188.7	656.0	37.3	425.8	81.3	209.0	338.8	266.1	39.9	32.8
2015	2 009.8	1 653.8	1 275.3	192.0	673.5	39.2	447.7	85.8	220.1	356.0	281.4	40.3	34.2
2016	2 068.5	1 697.4	1 303.3	195.3	706.2	40.8	466.6	90.0	229.1	371.1	292.5	42.8	35.9
2017	2 136.5	1 748.0	1 338.7	202.4	736.6	42.8	487.0	92.4	240.9	388.3	304.1	45.8	38.5
2018	2 233.0	1 830.0	1 392.9	213.2	778.7	45.0	509.8	94.8	254.0	403.0	314.1	47.7	41.3
2019	2 299.0	1 876.5	1 433.3	222.7	791.7	46.0	525.3	97.7	261.4	422.5	330.9	48.8	42.7
2020	2 357.8	1 916.5	1 459.8	229.6	768.8	47.7	493.9	97.4	250.9	441.2	345.5	50.4	45.4
2018													
1st quarter	2 199.7	1 799.7	1 373.1	208.5	764.0	44.5	501.5	93.7	250.1	400.0	313.0	46.7	40.4
2nd quarter	2 232.6	1 822.6	1 386.6	212.2	775.3	45.0	506.6	94.2	253.0	410.0	321.0	47.8	41.2
3rd quarter	2 250.1	1 843.5	1 402.5	214.6	784.0	45.2	512.4	95.0	255.5	406.6	316.8	48.3	41.6
4th quarter	2 249.7	1 854.2	1 409.3	217.4	791.5	45.3	518.7	96.1	257.5	395.5	305.7	48.0	41.9
2019													
1st quarter	2 263.5	1 850.2	1 412.5	219.0	787.0	45.4	522.8	97.1	258.5	413.3	322.0	49.3	42.0
2nd quarter	2 296.0	1 869.1	1 420.8	222.4	797.4	45.7	525.8	97.8	260.2	426.9	335.1	49.5	42.3
3rd quarter	2 307.2	1 883.2	1 440.5	224.3	790.7	46.1	526.1	97.9	261.8	424.0	332.8	48.2	43.0
4th quarter	2 329.2	1 903.5	1 459.6	225.3	791.8	46.7	526.3	98.1	265.0	425.7	333.7	48.3	43.7
2020													
1st quarter	2 376.9	1 934.3	1 486.0	227.1	784.7	47.3	516.2	97.5	260.5	442.7	349.1	48.6	45.0
2nd quarter	2 334.6	1 897.3	1 438.4	227.7	733.2	46.6	455.5	97.5	222.8	437.3	346.2	47.7	43.4
3rd quarter	2 346.5	1 909.9	1 458.6	231.0	767.6	48.1	499.1	97.3	257.7	436.6	338.7	52.1	45.8
4th quarter	2 373.0	1 924.7	1 456.0	232.7	789.7	48.8	504.9	97.3	262.7	448.3	348.0	53.1	47.3

[1]Excludes government sales to other sectors and government own-account investment (construction and software).
[2]Includes general government intermediate inputs for goods and services sold to other sectors and for own-account investment.
[3]Includes components not shown separately.

Table 6-10. State and Local Government Output, Lending and Borrowing, and Net Investment

(National income and product accounts, calendar years, billions of dollars, quarterly data are at seasonally adjusted annual rates.)

NIPA Tables 3.3, 3.10.5

| Year and quarter | Output | | | Net lending (net borrowing -) | | | | | | | Net investment |
| | Gross | Value added | Intermediate goods and services purchased [1] | Net saving, current (surplus +, deficit -) | Plus: Capital transfer receipts | Minus | | | Plus: consumption of fixed capital | Equals: Net lending (borrowing -) | |
						Gross investment	Capital transfer payments	Net purchases of nonproduced assets			
1960	38.4	29.5	8.9	2.5	3.0	14.1	...	0.9	4.5	-4.9	9.6
1961	41.9	32.3	9.6	2.2	3.3	15.3	...	1.0	4.8	-6.0	10.5
1962	44.7	34.6	10.1	3.1	3.5	16.1	...	1.1	5.1	-5.4	11.0
1963	48.4	37.6	10.8	3.3	4.1	17.8	...	1.2	5.5	-6.0	12.3
1964	52.8	40.9	11.9	3.9	4.7	19.3	...	1.3	5.9	-6.0	13.4
1965	58.3	44.9	13.4	3.7	4.7	21.2	...	1.3	6.4	-7.6	14.8
1966	65.1	50.2	14.9	4.7	5.1	23.5	...	1.4	7.1	-7.9	16.4
1967	72.2	55.8	16.4	4.0	5.1	25.7	...	1.4	7.8	-10.2	17.9
1968	81.9	63.3	18.6	3.5	6.8	28.1	...	1.4	8.6	-10.6	19.5
1969	92.7	70.9	21.8	3.1	6.8	28.8	...	1.0	9.6	-10.2	19.2
1970	105.6	80.3	25.3	1.4	6.2	29.3	...	1.1	10.9	-11.8	18.4
1971	119.4	90.3	29.1	-1.3	7.0	30.7	...	1.6	12.2	-14.4	18.5
1972	132.2	100.2	32.0	6.1	7.3	31.3	...	1.7	13.3	-6.3	18.0
1973	145.7	110.4	35.3	5.6	7.3	34.0	...	1.7	14.8	-8.0	19.2
1974	165.3	122.8	42.6	-2.3	9.2	40.5	...	1.9	18.4	-17.2	22.1
1975	188.5	138.0	50.5	-10.7	11.0	44.6	...	1.9	21.0	-25.3	23.6
1976	203.0	148.0	55.0	-4.4	12.0	44.9	...	1.7	22.0	-17.0	22.9
1977	221.4	160.6	60.8	0.5	13.1	44.0	...	1.6	23.4	-8.5	20.6
1978	242.1	175.5	66.6	4.9	13.7	50.8	...	1.8	25.4	-8.6	25.4
1979	266.7	192.8	73.9	-1.2	16.2	58.4	...	2.0	28.6	-16.8	29.8
1980	295.1	213.5	81.6	-5.9	18.6	65.7	...	2.2	33.1	-22.1	32.6
1981	326.4	235.2	91.2	-10.2	17.8	66.9	...	2.2	37.8	-23.8	29.1
1982	355.6	255.6	100.0	-22.8	16.9	67.0	...	2.2	41.2	-33.8	25.8
1983	381.6	272.6	109.0	-18.4	18.0	68.8	...	2.2	42.7	-28.8	26.1
1984	410.2	291.9	118.4	-0.2	20.1	77.6	...	2.6	44.3	-16.0	33.3
1985	449.0	317.6	131.4	-2.4	22.0	87.3	...	3.1	46.8	-24.1	40.5
1986	484.4	342.7	141.7	-4.0	23.0	96.2	...	3.7	50.1	-30.7	46.1
1987	519.5	369.4	150.0	-14.4	22.3	102.2	...	4.2	54.0	-44.4	48.2
1988	558.6	398.8	159.8	-11.3	23.1	110.4	...	4.3	57.7	-45.3	52.7
1989	611.8	436.1	175.8	-19.3	23.4	119.2	0.0	4.9	61.8	-58.3	57.4
1990	668.7	478.2	190.5	-36.2	25.0	132.2	0.0	5.7	66.6	-82.5	65.6
1991	716.9	512.2	204.7	-60.1	25.8	137.3	0.0	5.8	70.8	-106.6	66.5
1992	769.2	550.2	218.9	-71.0	26.9	139.7	0.0	5.9	74.1	-115.5	65.6
1993	810.9	576.9	234.0	-72.5	28.2	141.2	0.0	5.9	78.3	-113.1	62.9
1994	857.7	606.2	251.5	-63.9	29.9	148.8	0.0	6.2	82.8	-106.3	66.0
1995	904.5	633.9	270.6	-70.4	32.4	160.0	0.0	6.6	88.1	-116.5	71.9
1996	944.4	658.6	285.8	-53.8	33.8	170.2	0.0	6.0	92.5	-103.6	77.7
1997	993.5	689.3	304.2	-42.0	35.2	182.9	0.0	5.8	97.3	-98.2	85.6
1998	1 052.9	726.2	326.7	-30.1	35.9	196.3	0.0	7.6	102.2	-95.9	94.1
1999	1 130.6	773.1	357.5	-38.9	40.0	213.6	0.0	8.6	108.6	-112.6	105.0
2000	1 216.3	824.0	392.3	-40.6	44.2	231.5	0.0	8.6	116.6	-119.9	114.9
2001	1 308.1	882.3	425.8	-119.0	51.7	248.0	0.0	10.1	123.4	-202.1	124.6
2002	1 375.5	930.6	444.9	-182.9	52.9	261.5	0.0	11.2	129.3	-273.3	132.2
2003	1 420.0	970.1	449.9	-181.3	52.3	269.1	0.0	11.4	134.9	-274.6	134.2
2004	1 490.5	1 019.3	471.2	-149.0	52.5	277.8	4.5	11.3	144.2	-245.8	133.6
2005	1 573.8	1 067.0	506.7	-102.8	56.9	291.3	6.4	10.0	157.9	-195.7	133.4
2006	1 663.8	1 122.1	541.7	-85.0	57.9	315.3	0.0	11.2	171.0	-182.5	144.3
2007	1 768.7	1 191.2	577.5	-129.3	59.8	342.0	0.0	13.9	187.5	-237.9	154.5
2008	1 857.1	1 252.1	605.0	-220.9	63.1	357.9	0.0	13.3	201.2	-327.8	156.7
2009	1 891.3	1 280.5	610.7	-341.3	68.0	360.3	0.0	12.6	209.1	-437.1	151.2
2010	1 916.9	1 306.1	610.8	-307.5	76.9	347.3	0.0	12.0	213.4	-376.4	133.9
2011	1 928.7	1 313.1	615.6	-275.1	74.1	341.0	0.0	11.5	222.2	-331.2	118.8
2012	1 947.1	1 325.5	621.6	-282.8	74.4	333.7	0.0	10.9	232.0	-321.1	101.7
2013	2 019.9	1 380.9	638.9	-265.3	71.6	330.8	0.0	10.4	238.8	-296.0	92.0
2014	2 077.1	1 421.1	656.0	-237.9	70.6	338.8	0.0	10.6	246.3	-270.3	92.5
2015	2 140.8	1 467.3	673.5	-215.8	69.8	356.0	0.0	11.9	251.4	-262.4	104.6
2016	2 204.9	1 498.6	706.2	-244.7	72.6	371.1	0.0	12.9	256.4	-299.7	114.7
2017	2 277.8	1 541.2	736.6	-230.6	73.2	388.3	1.2	14.3	266.2	-295.0	122.1
2018	2 384.8	1 606.1	778.7	-195.8	72.2	403.0	0.0	16.1	280.5	-262.2	122.5
2019	2 447.8	1 656.1	791.7	-149.0	73.9	422.5	0.0	16.8	293.7	-220.7	128.8
2020	2 458.2	1 689.4	768.8	76.1	82.7	441.2	0.0	17.3	302.8	3.1	138.4
2018											
1st quarter	2 345.6	1 581.6	764.0	-167.4	69.6	400.0	0.0	15.5	274.1	-239.3	125.9
2nd quarter	2 374.2	1 598.9	775.3	-221.0	70.6	410.0	0.0	16.0	279.1	-297.3	130.9
3rd quarter	2 401.1	1 617.1	784.0	-199.7	78.2	406.6	0.0	16.3	282.4	-262.0	124.2
4th quarter	2 418.2	1 626.7	791.5	-195.0	70.4	395.5	0.0	16.5	286.2	-250.4	109.3
2019											
1st quarter	2 418.4	1 631.4	787.0	-168.2	71.6	413.3	0.0	16.6	288.7	-237.9	124.6
2nd quarter	2 440.6	1 643.2	797.4	-124.4	72.4	426.9	0.0	16.7	293.1	-202.5	133.8
3rd quarter	2 455.5	1 664.8	790.7	-150.5	75.2	424.0	0.0	16.8	295.7	-220.4	128.3
4th quarter	2 476.6	1 684.8	791.8	-153.0	76.5	425.7	0.0	16.9	297.2	-222.0	128.5
2020											
1st quarter	2 497.8	1 713.1	784.7	-134.6	78.4	442.7	0.0	17.0	299.6	-216.2	143.1
2nd quarter	2 399.3	1 666.2	733.2	553.6	85.0	437.3	0.0	17.2	300.3	484.4	137.0
3rd quarter	2 457.2	1 689.6	767.6	-66.3	84.5	436.6	0.0	17.4	304.5	-131.3	132.1
4th quarter	2 478.4	1 688.7	789.7	-48.2	82.8	448.3	0.0	17.7	306.9	-124.5	141.4

[1] Includes general government intermediate inputs for goods and services sold to other sectors and for own-account investment.
. . . = Not available.

Table 6-11. Chain-Type Quantity Indexes for State and Local Government Consumption Expenditures and Gross Investment

(Seasonally adjusted, 2012 = 100.)   NIPA Tables 3.9.3, 3.10.3

Year and quarter	Total	Consumption expenditures [1]					Less			Gross investment			
		Total	Compensation of general government employees	Consumption of general government fixed capital	Intermediate goods and services purchased [2]	Own-account investment	Sales to other sectors			Total	Structures	Equipment	Intellectual property
							Total [3]	Tuition and related educational charges	Health and hospital charges				
1965	36.5	33.2	43.8	18.5	16.6	29.2	23.0	32.3	15.4	47.3	72.0	9.0	4.4
1966	38.7	35.2	46.4	19.7	17.9	31.2	25.1	36.6	17.6	50.4	76.5	9.8	5.2
1967	40.7	36.8	48.2	21.0	19.4	31.4	27.7	40.8	20.0	53.6	81.3	10.2	5.8
1968	43.1	39.2	51.1	22.3	21.3	33.2	30.1	45.9	23.3	56.0	85.0	10.6	6.2
1969	44.6	41.7	53.3	23.6	23.7	33.7	31.3	50.5	24.1	53.8	80.5	11.4	6.9
1970	45.9	44.3	55.7	24.8	26.1	34.6	32.6	58.8	24.6	50.5	74.4	11.8	7.6
1971	47.3	46.5	57.9	25.9	28.5	35.1	35.4	66.2	28.6	49.1	72.0	11.9	7.9
1972	48.4	48.2	59.9	26.8	30.3	34.7	37.9	70.3	32.8	47.6	68.5	13.3	8.3
1973	49.7	49.9	62.0	27.8	31.2	34.6	39.5	75.8	36.4	47.9	67.9	14.9	8.8
1974	51.5	52.1	64.3	28.8	32.6	36.2	39.3	75.6	37.5	48.2	67.6	16.2	9.1
1975	53.4	54.7	66.2	29.8	35.3	35.1	39.9	75.7	38.6	47.9	67.1	15.7	9.8
1976	53.9	55.5	67.0	30.7	36.4	32.9	42.2	78.1	41.0	47.2	66.1	15.4	10.4
1977	54.1	56.6	67.9	31.4	37.7	31.5	43.6	81.3	41.7	44.5	61.7	15.0	10.8
1978	55.9	57.7	69.5	32.2	38.7	33.9	45.8	85.8	44.6	48.6	67.7	15.7	12.0
1979	56.7	58.0	70.7	33.0	38.7	38.0	48.0	88.2	48.4	51.0	70.6	17.0	13.2
1980	56.6	57.8	71.6	33.9	37.3	39.6	48.8	91.1	48.8	51.2	70.2	18.1	14.0
1981	55.4	57.6	71.3	34.7	37.5	38.7	50.7	93.1	51.9	47.0	63.2	17.7	14.9
1982	55.5	58.5	71.7	35.4	39.1	39.4	51.9	92.9	53.4	44.2	58.0	18.6	15.9
1983	56.2	59.2	71.2	36.1	41.8	39.8	53.8	95.7	54.8	44.9	57.4	21.2	17.3
1984	58.4	60.5	71.4	37.1	44.0	43.3	53.9	95.6	53.5	50.3	63.9	24.8	19.1
1985	61.7	63.2	73.4	38.4	47.7	47.1	55.8	95.5	54.8	55.8	70.1	28.7	21.5
1986	64.8	66.1	75.5	40.0	51.6	51.4	57.8	96.3	56.2	59.7	74.4	31.5	23.8
1987	66.2	67.4	76.7	41.6	52.8	53.5	59.0	96.9	56.2	61.3	76.0	32.7	25.6
1988	68.7	69.8	79.3	43.4	54.4	56.0	60.2	99.9	56.2	64.5	79.3	34.9	28.4
1989	71.4	72.3	81.6	45.6	57.0	60.9	61.9	102.9	56.7	67.9	80.9	40.3	33.7
1990	74.4	74.7	83.8	48.1	58.9	63.9	63.2	105.2	57.3	73.1	86.9	43.3	37.5
1991	76.0	76.3	84.5	50.4	61.9	66.4	65.3	106.9	59.7	74.8	89.7	41.8	40.3
1992	77.6	78.0	85.7	52.6	64.9	65.8	68.2	108.9	63.2	75.8	90.1	42.6	43.8
1993	78.6	79.4	86.6	54.7	67.8	65.7	71.4	107.6	66.9	75.2	88.1	44.0	44.8
1994	80.8	81.6	87.9	56.7	71.6	66.7	73.8	107.7	69.6	77.5	89.1	49.6	45.2
1995	83.0	83.5	89.5	58.7	74.5	67.5	76.3	108.1	72.7	80.8	92.1	54.4	45.0
1996	84.9	85.1	90.6	60.9	76.5	69.3	77.8	108.4	72.4	84.3	96.5	55.7	47.4
1997	87.6	87.4	92.2	63.4	80.3	74.1	80.4	110.9	74.1	89.0	100.3	60.9	53.0
1998	91.5	90.9	93.9	66.3	86.6	77.7	82.8	114.0	76.3	94.3	104.1	69.4	58.1
1999	95.3	94.1	95.1	69.5	92.9	80.6	85.0	117.4	77.6	100.4	109.6	77.8	61.6
2000	97.8	96.1	96.8	72.8	96.6	84.9	89.3	121.4	81.4	105.4	114.7	82.2	65.9
2001	101.4	99.4	98.8	76.0	103.4	91.7	94.1	122.1	88.2	110.6	121.1	83.9	68.8
2002	104.3	102.0	100.6	78.9	107.4	93.9	96.2	122.2	88.6	114.7	126.1	85.6	70.2
2003	103.8	101.1	100.9	81.2	104.1	94.2	96.8	122.1	87.3	116.3	127.5	86.4	74.1
2004	103.7	101.2	101.0	83.6	104.2	95.2	97.6	118.3	87.6	115.0	125.1	86.3	78.3
2005	103.7	101.8	101.4	86.0	104.6	98.3	98.1	118.3	85.6	112.2	120.4	87.7	82.2
2006	104.9	102.8	102.1	88.4	106.2	103.6	99.2	116.6	87.7	114.2	120.5	95.5	88.6
2007	106.7	104.7	103.3	91.2	107.8	106.9	99.0	112.9	89.9	115.5	118.9	109.5	94.1
2008	106.9	105.0	104.4	93.9	105.0	108.4	98.1	109.3	92.7	115.9	118.3	113.3	97.7
2009	109.0	107.7	104.5	96.0	111.5	108.2	98.7	106.1	96.0	114.7	117.5	109.0	98.0
2010	106.0	105.0	103.2	97.6	106.8	104.0	99.5	103.6	97.5	110.4	113.4	101.4	96.1
2011	102.2	101.5	101.7	98.9	101.1	102.5	100.1	101.3	99.0	105.5	107.1	99.5	98.7
2012	100.0	100.0	100.0	100.0	100.0	100.0	100.0	100.0	100.0	100.0	100.0	100.0	100.0
2013	99.7	100.3	99.7	101.1	101.4	99.3	100.8	99.5	102.8	97.3	95.7	101.7	105.6
2014	99.9	100.4	99.6	102.1	103.0	99.7	103.0	98.9	107.4	97.5	95.8	100.3	109.3
2015	102.9	103.1	100.3	103.2	111.4	105.0	106.9	100.8	112.1	101.5	100.1	101.0	115.6
2016	105.8	105.9	101.4	104.6	118.3	108.5	109.9	102.9	115.3	105.1	103.0	107.4	121.3
2017	106.4	106.2	102.3	106.2	118.7	111.4	112.6	103.6	119.2	107.5	104.2	114.4	129.1
2018	106.9	106.7	103.0	108.0	119.8	113.5	115.1	104.0	122.8	107.8	103.2	118.1	137.0
2019	108.2	107.9	104.0	109.8	121.1	113.9	116.0	104.2	123.9	109.7	104.8	120.7	140.7
2020	109.2	108.4	102.0	111.8	119.4	116.3	106.5	102.5	115.3	113.1	107.7	124.9	148.5
2018													
1st quarter	106.8	106.4	102.7	107.3	119.1	113.4	114.2	103.9	121.7	108.7	104.8	116.2	134.6
2nd quarter	107.2	106.6	103.0	107.8	119.5	113.8	114.8	104.3	122.6	109.9	105.8	118.8	136.9
3rd quarter	107.1	106.8	103.2	108.2	120.0	113.5	115.5	103.9	123.4	108.2	103.6	119.3	137.7
4th quarter	106.4	106.9	103.1	108.7	120.6	113.2	116.0	103.9	123.7	104.2	98.7	117.9	138.8
2019													
1st quarter	107.3	107.1	103.1	109.1	121.2	112.9	116.3	104.2	123.5	108.5	103.6	121.1	138.3
2nd quarter	108.1	107.5	103.4	109.6	121.4	113.4	116.4	104.3	123.7	110.8	106.2	122.2	139.1
3rd quarter	108.4	108.1	104.2	110.1	121.1	114.1	116.1	104.3	124.0	109.5	104.8	119.4	141.0
4th quarter	109.1	108.9	105.3	110.5	120.4	115.4	115.4	104.0	124.4	109.8	104.8	120.2	144.3
2020													
1st quarter	110.3	109.5	105.1	111.0	120.4	116.5	112.5	102.8	121.6	113.9	109.1	121.2	148.7
2nd quarter	108.7	107.8	99.8	111.5	116.9	114.0	98.3	102.4	102.7	112.8	108.8	118.2	142.3
3rd quarter	108.8	108.1	102.1	112.0	119.2	117.1	107.1	102.3	117.6	111.5	105.3	128.7	149.8
4th quarter	109.1	108.0	101.2	112.5	121.1	117.6	108.0	102.5	119.4	114.1	107.7	131.5	153.3

[1] Excludes government sales to other sectors and government own-account investment (construction and software).
[2] Includes general government intermediate inputs for goods and services sold to other sectors and for own-account investment.
[3] Includes components not shown separately.

Table 6-12. State Government Current Receipts and Expenditures

(National income and product accounts, calendar years, billions of dollars.)   **NIPA Table 3.20**

Year	Total [1]	Total	Personal current taxes Total [1]	Income taxes	Total	Sales taxes	Property taxes	Other	Taxes on corporate income	Contributions for government social insurance	Total [1]	Interest receipts	Rents and royalties
1959	21.6	16.7	3.1	2.0	12.5	10.0	0.5	2.0	1.1	0.4	0.5	0.3	0.2
1960	23.3	18.1	3.4	2.3	13.5	10.8	0.5	2.2	1.2	0.5	0.5	0.4	0.2
1961	25.0	19.3	3.7	2.5	14.4	11.6	0.5	2.3	1.3	0.5	0.6	0.4	0.2
1962	27.1	21.0	4.0	2.8	15.4	12.6	0.6	2.3	1.5	0.5	0.6	0.4	0.2
1963	29.1	22.4	4.3	3.1	16.4	13.4	0.6	2.4	1.6	0.6	0.6	0.4	0.2
1964	31.8	24.5	4.9	3.6	17.7	14.5	0.6	2.6	1.8	0.7	0.7	0.4	0.2
1965	35.1	26.9	5.4	3.9	19.6	16.1	0.7	2.8	1.9	0.8	0.8	0.5	0.3
1966	41.5	30.2	6.4	4.8	21.7	18.0	0.7	3.0	2.2	0.8	0.9	0.6	0.3
1967	45.6	32.7	7.0	5.3	23.3	19.4	0.7	3.1	2.5	0.9	1.1	0.8	0.3
1968	53.8	38.6	8.8	6.9	26.7	22.8	0.8	3.2	3.1	0.9	1.7	1.4	0.3
1969	61.6	44.0	10.8	8.6	29.9	25.7	0.9	3.3	3.4	1.0	2.1	1.8	0.3
1970	69.1	48.1	12.0	9.6	32.7	28.2	0.9	3.6	3.5	1.1	2.5	2.2	0.3
1971	78.2	53.8	13.4	11.0	36.3	31.4	1.0	3.9	4.0	1.2	2.7	2.3	0.4
1972	95.0	63.5	17.9	15.2	40.7	35.2	1.1	4.4	5.0	1.3	2.9	2.5	0.4
1973	103.1	70.2	19.8	16.8	44.7	38.8	1.2	4.7	5.7	1.5	3.9	3.3	0.5
1974	112.1	75.9	21.1	18.0	48.4	42.0	1.1	5.3	6.3	1.7	5.0	4.4	0.6
1975	125.8	81.9	23.2	19.9	51.8	44.7	1.4	5.6	6.9	1.8	5.6	5.0	0.6
1976	141.7	93.8	27.0	23.4	57.7	49.9	1.5	6.3	9.1	2.2	5.3	4.7	0.6
1977	158.1	105.1	30.9	27.2	63.4	55.0	1.5	6.9	10.8	2.8	6.1	5.4	0.6
1978	177.2	117.4	35.6	31.6	70.3	60.8	1.9	7.6	11.5	3.4	7.4	6.7	0.6
1979	194.8	128.9	38.9	34.6	77.1	65.7	2.3	9.0	12.9	3.9	10.3	9.2	1.1
1980	216.0	140.9	43.7	39.1	83.4	70.0	2.6	10.8	13.7	3.6	13.4	11.2	2.0
1981	236.4	155.6	48.5	43.6	92.7	76.5	2.7	13.6	14.5	3.9	15.6	13.2	2.2
1982	244.7	162.3	52.3	47.0	97.0	80.3	2.8	13.9	13.1	4.0	17.5	15.3	2.1
1983	269.3	180.5	58.9	53.2	106.8	90.0	3.0	13.8	14.9	4.1	19.5	17.2	2.2
1984	303.7	205.4	68.2	61.9	119.7	100.9	3.4	15.5	17.4	4.7	22.4	19.8	2.5
1985	328.6	220.9	73.2	66.1	129.0	109.0	3.5	16.5	18.7	4.9	26.1	23.4	2.6
1986	354.0	234.0	78.3	70.7	134.9	115.8	3.6	15.6	20.7	6.0	27.5	24.6	2.7
1987	375.0	253.7	87.5	79.1	144.3	124.6	3.7	16.0	21.8	7.2	28.4	25.6	2.6
1988	403.1	269.4	90.4	81.5	155.2	135.1	3.8	16.3	23.8	8.4	30.8	28.0	2.7
1989	435.2	288.4	102.4	92.9	163.5	142.3	4.3	17.0	22.4	9.0	32.8	30.2	2.4
1990	469.2	305.6	109.6	99.6	175.4	152.5	4.6	18.3	20.5	10.0	33.9	31.4	2.3
1991	504.1	314.2	111.8	101.4	180.8	157.5	4.9	18.3	21.6	11.6	34.1	31.2	2.6
1992	551.4	338.8	120.6	109.0	195.9	169.7	6.1	20.1	22.2	13.1	33.6	30.4	2.7
1993	584.8	357.1	126.3	114.9	206.3	179.4	5.9	21.0	24.5	14.1	32.4	29.4	2.5
1994	621.6	380.4	132.1	120.2	220.8	191.7	7.0	22.1	27.5	14.5	33.9	30.6	2.5
1995	653.2	401.5	140.9	128.4	231.3	200.5	7.2	23.6	29.2	13.6	36.9	33.4	2.6
1996	686.2	425.9	150.9	138.6	245.0	211.8	8.2	25.0	29.9	12.5	39.4	35.3	2.7
1997	719.6	449.1	162.7	149.7	255.4	221.3	8.1	26.0	31.0	10.8	41.8	37.5	2.7
1998	764.1	480.7	180.4	166.8	268.8	233.3	8.5	27.0	31.6	10.4	43.3	39.2	2.4
1999	812.5	507.9	192.6	178.4	283.0	245.9	9.1	27.9	32.3	9.8	46.6	42.5	2.6
2000	867.7	540.1	213.5	199.2	294.8	255.5	7.8	31.6	31.7	10.8	49.3	44.3	3.6
2001	904.5	546.8	220.1	205.7	300.8	259.9	8.1	32.8	25.9	13.7	46.5	41.4	3.7
2002	917.8	533.7	199.1	184.3	309.6	268.0	7.7	33.9	25.0	15.8	42.4	37.2	3.7
2003	970.5	558.8	202.4	186.4	328.9	282.0	9.1	37.8	27.5	19.9	42.0	35.9	4.4
2004	1 048.7	606.4	220.3	203.4	352.3	300.5	8.3	43.5	33.8	24.7	44.4	37.4	5.1
2005	1 136.5	676.3	246.5	229.0	385.3	325.6	9.1	50.6	44.5	24.6	50.6	42.7	6.0
2006	1 193.9	728.1	271.0	252.5	409.1	346.6	9.7	52.7	48.0	21.5	59.2	50.7	6.5
2007	1 247.9	759.7	288.9	269.8	424.0	359.0	9.8	55.2	46.9	18.9	65.0	55.3	7.5
2008	1 264.0	763.6	299.8	280.9	425.4	354.3	9.7	61.3	38.4	18.7	60.1	49.6	7.9
2009	1 267.1	688.2	256.6	236.3	393.2	335.6	10.4	47.2	38.4	18.6	52.2	43.0	7.0
2010	1 336.1	720.0	264.7	242.2	415.5	354.7	10.7	50.1	39.8	18.1	51.3	42.4	6.6
2011	1 357.8	773.2	293.2	270.5	437.6	369.9	9.8	57.9	42.4	18.3	50.7	41.8	6.7
2012	1 372.3	804.9	313.8	290.4	448.3	379.2	9.7	59.3	42.9	17.5	50.1	40.8	6.9

[1] Includes components not shown separately.

Table 6-12. State Government Current Receipts and Expenditures—*Continued*

(National income and product accounts, calendar years, billions of dollars.)   **NIPA Table 3.20**

Year	Current receipts—*Continued*					Current expenditures					Net state government saving, NIPA (surplus + / deficit -)		
	Current transfer receipts					Total [1]	Consumption expenditures	Government social benefits to persons	Grants-in-aid to local governments	Interest payments	Total	Social insurance funds	Other
	Total	Federal grants-in-aid	Local grants-in-aid	From business, net	From persons								
1959	3.6	3.2	0.2	0.0	0.1	20.9	8.2	3.6	7.8	1.2	0.7	0.0	0.7
1960	3.7	3.3	0.2	0.0	0.1	22.9	8.9	3.8	8.8	1.3	0.4	0.0	0.4
1961	4.2	3.7	0.3	0.0	0.1	25.0	9.6	4.1	9.8	1.5	0.0	0.0	0.0
1962	4.6	4.1	0.3	0.1	0.2	27.0	10.2	4.4	10.8	1.6	0.1	0.0	0.1
1963	5.0	4.5	0.3	0.1	0.2	29.4	11.0	4.7	11.9	1.7	-0.3	0.0	-0.3
1964	5.5	4.9	0.3	0.1	0.2	31.9	11.8	5.1	13.0	1.8	-0.1	0.0	-0.1
1965	6.1	5.5	0.3	0.1	0.3	35.6	13.0	5.5	15.0	2.0	-0.4	0.1	-0.5
1966	8.9	8.2	0.4	0.1	0.3	40.7	14.6	6.4	17.4	2.2	0.8	0.1	0.6
1967	10.3	9.4	0.5	0.1	0.3	46.8	16.7	7.7	19.9	2.3	-1.2	0.1	-1.3
1968	11.8	10.7	0.6	0.1	0.3	54.6	19.2	9.5	23.0	2.7	-0.8	0.1	-1.0
1969	13.7	12.4	0.8	0.1	0.4	62.8	22.4	10.8	26.4	2.9	-1.2	0.2	-1.3
1970	16.6	15.2	0.9	0.1	0.4	72.8	25.8	12.9	30.4	3.4	-3.7	0.2	-3.9
1971	19.9	18.4	1.0	0.1	0.4	82.9	28.8	15.3	34.3	4.2	-4.7	0.2	-5.0
1972	26.4	24.6	1.1	0.2	0.5	92.9	31.5	17.5	38.5	5.0	2.2	0.3	1.9
1973	26.6	24.5	1.2	0.2	0.7	103.3	35.3	19.4	42.6	5.4	-0.1	0.3	-0.4
1974	28.6	26.3	1.3	0.2	0.8	116.5	42.1	19.9	47.3	6.4	-4.4	0.4	-4.8
1975	35.4	32.4	1.7	0.2	1.0	134.8	49.1	24.2	52.8	7.5	-9.0	0.5	-9.5
1976	39.1	35.4	2.3	0.3	1.2	145.6	52.8	26.9	57.0	7.7	-4.0	0.6	-4.6
1977	42.8	38.8	2.4	0.3	1.4	158.0	57.5	29.1	61.6	8.5	0.1	1.0	-0.9
1978	47.4	43.1	2.5	0.3	1.5	174.2	63.1	32.0	68.2	9.3	3.0	1.5	1.5
1979	50.1	45.9	2.2	0.4	1.6	193.8	70.0	35.4	76.3	10.3	1.0	1.8	-0.8
1980	56.5	52.1	2.3	0.4	1.7	217.8	78.8	41.3	84.6	11.1	-1.8	1.3	-3.2
1981	59.7	54.6	2.7	0.5	2.0	239.8	86.9	46.7	91.3	12.6	-3.4	1.3	-4.7
1982	58.7	52.7	3.1	0.6	2.3	257.0	93.7	51.0	95.3	14.6	-12.4	1.2	-13.6
1983	62.4	55.0	4.2	0.6	2.6	274.7	99.5	55.9	99.9	16.7	-5.5	1.2	-6.7
1984	67.7	59.0	5.0	0.8	3.0	297.5	106.9	59.8	109.8	17.9	6.2	1.4	4.8
1985	72.2	62.6	5.2	0.9	3.6	327.9	117.4	65.2	121.2	20.8	0.6	1.3	-0.7
1986	81.5	69.3	5.3	2.8	4.1	352.3	124.9	71.4	130.1	22.2	1.7	1.9	-0.1
1987	80.3	69.4	5.5	0.9	4.5	374.8	132.7	77.4	139.5	20.9	0.2	2.2	-2.0
1988	88.0	76.2	5.6	1.1	5.2	402.7	142.4	84.4	149.8	21.2	0.4	2.5	-2.1
1989	98.1	85.1	5.8	1.3	5.9	440.8	153.9	94.4	162.6	24.7	-5.6	2.3	-7.9
1990	112.4	97.6	6.2	1.6	6.9	480.7	167.2	111.0	173.1	23.8	-11.5	2.0	-13.4
1991	136.7	117.1	7.6	2.0	10.0	532.2	175.4	137.6	186.1	27.3	-28.1	2.4	-30.5
1992	158.0	134.3	9.0	2.6	12.1	580.8	183.9	159.5	201.0	30.4	-29.4	3.1	-32.6
1993	172.7	147.6	10.1	2.9	12.1	614.6	193.1	173.6	212.9	29.1	-29.8	4.2	-34.0
1994	183.7	156.9	11.0	3.4	12.4	649.8	204.5	184.4	226.2	28.4	-28.1	4.6	-32.8
1995	191.3	164.0	11.1	4.1	12.2	685.0	213.6	194.8	239.0	30.8	-31.8	4.0	-35.8
1996	197.9	168.9	12.0	5.0	12.0	708.1	219.7	202.5	250.3	27.9	-21.8	2.8	-24.7
1997	207.2	174.1	13.5	6.6	13.0	735.5	231.4	206.8	263.0	25.7	-15.9	1.2	-17.1
1998	219.3	182.9	13.3	9.8	13.2	774.0	248.3	214.6	282.4	19.8	-9.9	1.7	-11.6
1999	238.2	199.1	12.9	11.4	14.9	836.1	272.6	230.3	306.6	17.1	-23.6	1.7	-25.3
2000	258.8	212.6	14.0	15.0	17.2	896.0	292.8	248.4	331.0	13.5	-28.4	2.0	-30.3
2001	289.7	238.9	14.9	16.1	19.8	984.0	314.4	281.0	350.7	20.2	-79.5	2.6	-82.1
2002	317.7	263.5	15.5	17.2	21.5	1 037.5	320.3	307.2	367.5	31.5	-119.7	1.4	-121.1
2003	340.5	285.1	16.4	16.6	22.3	1 086.6	319.2	326.2	383.5	47.5	-116.1	3.2	-119.4
2004	363.4	303.4	17.6	17.7	24.6	1 139.7	327.1	355.8	401.6	44.5	-91.0	7.3	-98.3
2005	374.1	312.2	16.6	18.4	26.9	1 195.2	347.4	375.2	413.9	46.8	-58.7	7.2	-65.9
2006	375.4	314.2	15.6	18.2	28.0	1 239.7	361.2	371.3	441.7	52.3	-45.8	4.6	-50.5
2007	397.4	332.2	17.7	19.0	29.0	1 324.9	384.6	398.5	469.2	51.8	-77.0	2.7	-79.7
2008	415.6	346.6	17.7	21.1	30.7	1 383.9	407.7	418.6	486.1	54.1	-119.9	1.7	-121.6
2009	501.2	432.8	16.5	21.7	30.7	1 455.0	411.7	453.0	486.3	87.3	-187.9	2.2	-190.1
2010	539.5	473.3	16.6	20.1	30.1	1 487.1	411.2	481.5	488.8	88.4	-151.0	3.2	-154.2
2011	507.6	441.0	16.6	19.7	31.3	1 515.1	425.5	489.9	494.6	88.4	-157.2	4.2	-161.4
2012	491.2	424.0	16.8	18.8	32.4	1 579.2	459.7	501.9	502.8	97.8	-206.9	3.9	-210.9

[1]Includes components not shown separately.

Table 6-13. Local Government Current Receipts and Expenditures

(National income and product accounts, calendar years, billions of dollars.) NIPA Table 3.21

Year	Total 1	Current tax receipts Total	Personal current taxes Total 1	Income taxes	Taxes on production and imports Total	Sales taxes	Property taxes	Other	Taxes on corporate income	Contributions for government social insurance	Income receipts on assets Total 1	Interest receipts	Rents and royalties
1959	27.0	17.1	0.8	0.2	16.4	1.2	14.3	0.9	0.0	...	0.7	0.5	0.1
1960	30.0	18.8	0.8	0.3	18.0	1.3	15.7	0.9	0.0	...	0.8	0.7	0.1
1961	32.9	20.3	0.9	0.3	19.4	1.4	17.0	1.0	0.0	...	0.9	0.7	0.2
1962	35.6	21.8	1.0	0.3	20.8	1.5	18.4	1.0	0.0	...	1.0	0.8	0.2
1963	38.7	23.4	1.1	0.4	22.3	1.6	19.7	1.0	0.0	...	1.0	0.9	0.2
1964	42.3	25.3	1.2	0.5	24.1	1.9	21.1	1.1	0.0	...	1.3	1.1	0.2
1965	46.1	27.0	1.2	0.5	25.7	2.1	22.5	1.1	0.0	...	1.4	1.2	0.2
1966	50.5	28.5	1.4	0.6	27.1	2.0	23.8	1.3	0.0	...	1.7	1.4	0.3
1967	56.5	31.3	1.6	0.8	29.5	1.9	26.2	1.3	0.2	...	2.0	1.6	0.3
1968	62.6	34.8	1.7	0.9	32.8	2.3	29.1	1.4	0.3	...	1.7	1.4	0.4
1969	70.1	38.4	2.0	1.1	36.1	2.9	31.9	1.4	0.3	...	2.2	1.8	0.4
1970	81.4	43.2	2.3	1.3	40.6	3.5	35.7	1.5	0.2	...	2.6	2.2	0.5
1971	90.9	47.9	2.5	1.5	45.2	4.0	39.5	1.8	0.3	...	2.8	2.3	0.5
1972	101.9	52.0	3.0	2.0	48.8	4.6	42.2	2.0	0.3	...	3.0	2.4	0.6
1973	114.0	56.1	3.0	2.0	52.7	5.2	45.2	2.3	0.3	...	3.9	3.3	0.6
1974	123.8	60.2	3.4	2.3	56.4	6.1	47.9	2.4	0.3	...	5.2	4.5	0.7
1975	137.7	65.5	3.7	2.5	61.4	7.0	51.9	2.5	0.4	...	5.6	4.9	0.7
1976	150.8	71.9	4.1	2.8	67.3	7.9	56.7	2.7	0.5	...	5.1	4.4	0.7
1977	165.3	78.6	4.5	3.2	73.6	9.0	61.7	2.9	0.6	...	5.6	4.9	0.7
1978	180.5	80.8	4.9	3.4	75.3	10.2	61.8	3.3	0.6	...	7.2	6.5	0.7
1979	191.3	83.1	5.1	3.6	77.3	11.5	62.1	3.7	0.6	...	9.8	8.9	0.9
1980	208.3	89.1	5.1	3.5	83.3	12.8	66.2	4.2	0.7	...	12.9	11.8	1.1
1981	226.9	100.2	6.2	4.3	93.0	14.3	74.4	4.3	1.0	...	16.4	15.3	1.1
1982	244.4	110.8	6.9	4.9	103.0	15.9	82.5	4.6	1.0	...	19.2	17.8	1.4
1983	262.5	120.4	7.2	5.1	112.1	17.7	88.9	5.5	1.0	...	21.9	19.8	2.1
1984	289.9	131.9	7.8	5.6	122.7	20.1	96.3	6.3	1.4	...	25.2	22.8	2.4
1985	318.4	142.8	8.2	6.0	133.1	22.1	104.0	7.0	1.5	...	29.5	26.7	2.7
1986	342.5	155.6	8.9	6.8	144.7	24.1	112.6	8.1	2.0	...	31.4	27.9	3.5
1987	360.1	168.5	9.1	6.8	157.3	25.7	122.7	8.9	2.1	...	30.1	27.4	2.7
1988	387.9	183.3	11.7	9.1	169.4	27.2	132.7	9.4	2.3	...	30.4	28.6	1.7
1989	420.0	199.6	12.3	9.4	185.6	30.1	145.6	10.0	1.8	...	33.8	32.1	1.7
1990	446.2	213.6	12.9	10.0	198.7	31.8	157.0	9.9	2.0	...	34.5	32.7	1.8
1991	475.9	230.1	13.5	10.3	214.5	33.2	171.1	10.2	2.1	...	33.2	31.2	1.9
1992	501.1	241.0	14.7	11.4	224.2	34.6	178.6	11.0	2.1	...	30.4	28.4	2.0
1993	522.2	247.7	14.8	11.3	230.5	37.0	181.3	12.1	2.4	...	28.7	26.6	2.1
1994	556.9	263.8	15.9	12.0	245.4	39.7	192.4	13.3	2.5	...	29.6	27.6	2.0
1995	584.6	270.7	17.2	13.3	251.0	42.2	195.3	13.4	2.5	...	32.2	30.3	2.0
1996	617.4	283.7	17.8	13.7	262.9	44.4	204.2	14.4	3.1	...	34.3	32.4	2.0
1997	652.4	300.8	19.3	14.9	278.4	47.4	215.5	15.6	3.1	...	36.3	34.3	2.1
1998	690.4	314.2	20.9	16.2	290.0	50.6	222.5	16.9	3.4	...	38.0	35.8	2.2
1999	739.5	332.5	21.9	17.1	307.1	55.6	233.7	17.8	3.5	...	38.6	36.1	2.5
2000	791.8	353.1	23.2	18.1	326.5	61.3	246.9	18.3	3.5	...	44.6	42.0	2.7
2001	825.4	367.5	22.9	17.6	341.6	61.9	260.0	19.8	3.0	...	42.6	39.8	2.8
2002	865.1	394.8	22.7	17.1	366.2	63.1	281.6	21.5	5.9	...	36.2	33.2	2.9
2003	915.7	419.8	24.4	18.3	389.0	66.8	297.9	24.2	6.5	...	31.9	28.6	3.2
2004	957.8	451.5	27.1	20.3	416.4	70.5	317.9	28.0	7.9	...	32.4	29.0	3.4
2005	1 016.4	490.2	30.0	22.5	449.8	76.8	342.3	30.7	10.4	...	38.0	34.2	3.8
2006	1 089.2	526.4	31.5	23.6	483.6	85.2	365.3	33.1	11.3	...	48.0	44.0	3.9
2007	1 154.8	561.6	34.6	26.5	516.0	90.0	394.1	32.0	11.0	...	52.9	48.9	4.0
2008	1 164.4	565.3	33.8	26.1	522.6	90.4	404.0	28.1	9.0	...	45.6	41.4	4.2
2009	1 171.2	580.0	31.2	23.3	541.6	88.3	424.7	28.6	7.2	...	35.7	31.4	4.2
2010	1 184.5	585.7	33.0	25.0	544.9	91.2	424.4	29.3	7.8	...	31.3	26.7	4.6
2011	1 200.4	593.1	33.8	25.7	550.9	93.8	427.1	30.1	8.4	...	29.3	24.5	4.8
2012	1 204.4	600.3	35.1	26.9	556.7	95.7	430.3	30.7	8.5	...	28.4	23.4	5.0

1Includes components not shown separately.
. . . = Not available.

Table 6-13. Local Government Current Receipts and Expenditures—*Continued*

(National income and product accounts, calendar years, billions of dollars.)   **NIPA Table 3.21**

Year	Current receipts—*Continued*					Current expenditures					Net local government saving, NIPA (surplus + / deficit -)		
	Current transfer receipts												
	Total	Federal grants-in-aid	State grants-in-aid	From business, net	From persons	Total [1]	Consumption expenditures	Government social benefits to persons	Grants-in-aid to state governments	Interest payments	Total	Social insurance funds	Other
1959	8.4	0.4	7.8	0.1	0.1	25.5	23.0	0.7	0.2	1.5	1.5	...	1.5
1960	9.6	0.5	8.8	0.1	0.2	27.9	25.2	0.8	0.2	1.7	2.2	...	2.2
1961	10.8	0.6	9.8	0.2	0.3	30.7	27.7	0.9	0.3	1.8	2.2	...	2.2
1962	11.9	0.6	10.8	0.2	0.3	32.3	29.1	0.9	0.3	1.9	3.3	...	3.3
1963	13.1	0.8	11.9	0.2	0.3	34.7	31.3	1.0	0.3	2.1	4.0	...	4.0
1964	14.6	1.1	13.0	0.2	0.3	37.9	34.2	1.0	0.3	2.3	4.4	...	4.4
1965	16.6	1.1	15.0	0.3	0.3	41.6	37.6	1.1	0.3	2.5	4.5	...	4.5
1966	19.3	1.2	17.4	0.2	0.4	46.1	41.7	1.3	0.4	2.7	4.4	...	4.4
1967	22.4	1.5	19.9	0.4	0.6	50.6	45.6	1.6	0.5	2.9	5.9	...	5.9
1968	25.2	1.1	23.0	0.4	0.7	57.5	51.5	2.0	0.6	3.3	5.1	...	5.1
1969	28.8	1.3	26.4	0.4	0.7	64.9	58.1	2.4	0.8	3.6	5.3	...	5.3
1970	34.8	3.2	30.4	0.4	0.8	74.7	66.3	3.2	0.9	4.3	6.7	...	6.7
1971	39.5	3.8	34.3	0.5	0.9	85.6	75.4	4.0	1.0	5.2	5.3	...	5.3
1972	46.0	5.9	38.5	0.5	1.1	95.6	83.9	4.5	1.1	6.1	6.3	...	6.3
1973	53.2	8.9	42.6	0.7	1.0	104.3	91.5	4.7	1.2	6.8	9.8	...	9.8
1974	57.9	8.7	47.3	0.9	1.1	117.0	102.4	5.4	1.3	7.9	6.8	...	6.8
1975	66.4	11.2	52.8	1.0	1.4	134.3	116.5	6.6	1.7	9.2	3.5	...	3.5
1976	73.5	13.6	57.0	1.1	1.7	144.0	124.4	7.3	2.3	9.8	6.8	...	6.8
1977	80.9	16.0	61.6	1.3	1.9	156.9	135.5	8.0	2.4	10.7	8.4	...	8.4
1978	92.3	20.4	68.2	1.5	2.2	170.1	146.8	8.7	2.5	11.7	10.4	...	10.4
1979	98.8	18.1	76.3	1.8	2.6	184.0	159.4	8.9	2.2	13.2	7.2	...	7.2
1980	107.3	17.6	84.6	2.0	3.0	201.1	174.0	9.9	2.3	14.5	7.2	...	7.2
1981	112.2	14.8	91.3	2.4	3.7	219.4	189.2	10.4	2.7	16.7	7.5	...	7.5
1982	115.6	13.5	95.3	2.7	4.1	237.1	203.7	10.2	3.1	19.6	7.3	...	7.3
1983	120.4	13.0	99.9	3.0	4.5	255.8	217.2	11.0	4.2	22.8	6.7	...	6.7
1984	131.7	13.3	109.8	3.4	5.2	275.2	233.0	11.4	5.0	25.3	14.7	...	14.7
1985	144.0	13.6	121.2	3.5	5.7	298.8	254.4	12.1	5.2	26.4	19.6	...	19.6
1986	153.7	13.2	130.1	3.9	6.5	323.8	275.0	12.9	5.3	29.6	18.7	...	18.7
1987	159.2	9.0	139.5	4.0	6.7	348.3	295.6	13.4	5.5	32.6	11.9	...	11.9
1988	170.5	9.5	149.8	4.3	6.9	371.3	316.5	14.1	5.6	33.8	16.6	...	16.6
1989	181.9	6.8	162.6	5.1	7.5	407.0	347.4	15.0	5.8	37.6	13.0	...	13.0
1990	193.4	6.7	173.1	5.5	8.0	441.2	379.0	16.6	6.2	38.0	5.0	...	5.0
1991	207.7	7.0	186.1	5.9	8.7	472.9	404.7	18.9	7.6	40.3	3.0	...	3.0
1992	224.8	7.4	201.0	6.7	9.8	509.2	435.2	20.5	9.0	43.2	-8.1	...	-8.1
1993	240.0	8.1	212.9	7.7	11.4	529.6	453.4	21.6	10.1	43.1	-7.4	...	-7.4
1994	257.6	9.9	226.2	8.6	12.9	555.8	477.7	22.4	11.0	43.3	1.2	...	1.2
1995	273.2	10.5	239.0	9.4	14.3	584.3	503.2	22.9	11.1	45.8	0.3	...	0.3
1996	288.7	12.6	250.3	10.2	15.7	608.0	528.4	21.8	12.0	44.5	9.4	...	9.4
1997	305.4	14.0	263.0	11.1	17.3	634.8	554.5	20.8	13.5	44.5	17.6	...	17.6
1998	330.0	17.9	282.4	11.8	17.9	665.1	587.4	21.1	13.3	41.7	25.3	...	25.3
1999	358.7	20.1	306.6	12.7	19.3	706.6	629.4	22.1	12.9	40.7	32.9	...	32.9
2000	385.8	20.5	331.0	13.5	20.8	753.6	676.3	23.0	14.0	38.6	38.3	...	38.3
2001	409.1	22.4	350.7	13.7	22.3	811.2	725.4	24.0	14.9	45.3	14.2	...	14.2
2002	430.7	23.7	367.5	15.4	24.1	866.4	770.8	25.8	15.5	52.8	-1.2	...	-1.2
2003	464.4	36.6	383.5	17.2	27.1	921.0	808.0	27.3	16.4	67.7	-5.3	...	-5.3
2004	478.3	28.8	401.6	18.8	29.1	975.2	860.5	29.2	17.6	65.9	-17.4	...	-17.4
2005	492.8	31.1	413.9	18.1	29.6	1 024.3	909.2	31.4	16.6	65.0	-7.9	...	-7.9
2006	520.8	26.6	441.7	20.6	31.3	1 082.8	964.8	32.6	15.6	67.8	6.4	...	6.4
2007	550.4	26.8	469.2	21.5	32.5	1 150.6	1 026.8	34.8	17.7	69.7	4.3	...	4.3
2008	566.0	24.4	486.1	22.4	32.6	1 209.6	1 081.0	36.8	17.7	73.0	-45.2	...	-45.2
2009	567.7	25.3	486.3	22.3	33.3	1 255.2	1 096.7	39.6	16.5	101.4	-84.0	...	-84.0
2010	577.8	31.9	488.8	23.3	33.1	1 270.8	1 107.1	42.3	16.6	103.7	-86.3	...	-86.3
2011	585.4	31.4	494.6	24.4	33.9	1 256.2	1 092.0	42.1	16.6	104.5	-55.9	...	-55.9
2012	581.0	19.2	502.8	23.1	35.1	1 250.2	1 076.7	42.4	16.8	113.2	-45.8	...	-45.8

[1]Includes components not shown separately.
. . . = Not available.

SECTION 6C: FEDERAL GOVERNMENT BUDGET ACCOUNTS

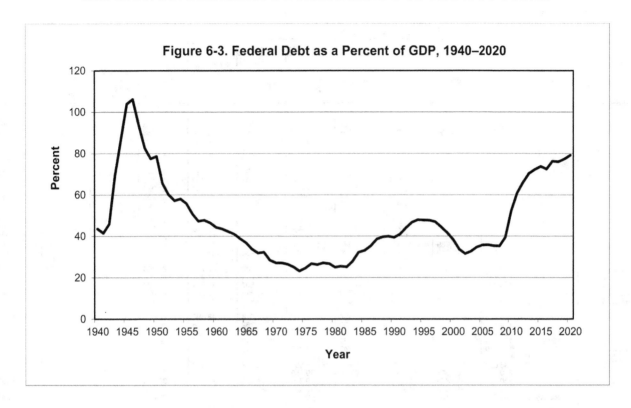

Figure 6-3. Federal Debt as a Percent of GDP, 1940–2020

- The "debt held by the public" is generally thought to be a more significant measure of the burden of the federal debt on credit markets than the gross debt, because it nets out the intragovernmental debt of the Social Security and other U.S. government trust funds. The ratio of debt held by the public to GDP was reduced in the late 1990s, began to creep back upward after 2001, and then rose rapidly beginning in 2008, as the recession reduced revenues and increased spending, and taxes were reduced further. The spending increases were a result of both automatic stabilizer programs, such as unemployment insurance, and an unprecedented level of spending for stimulus and financial rescue programs. At the end of fiscal year 2020, the debt held by the public was 79.2 percent of GDP, an increase from 73.7 percent five years earlier in 2015. This represented the highest debt/GDP ratio since 1948. (Tables 6-14 and 6-15)

- At the end of 2020, foreign residents—including central banks—held nearly $7.1 trillion of Treasury debt, 42.1 percent of the nearly $16.8 trillion total debt held by the public. (Table 6-15)

Table 6-14A. Federal Government Receipts and Outlays by Fiscal Year [1]

(Budget accounts, millions of dollars.)

Year	Total receipts, net	Total outlays, net	Budget surplus or deficit (-)			Sources of financing, total		Individual income taxes	Corporate income taxes	Social insurance taxes and contributions		
			Total	On-budget	Off-budget	Borrowing from the public	Other financing			Employment taxes and contributions	Unemployment insurance	Other retirement contributions
1945	45 159	92 712	-47 553	-48 720	1 167	50 386	-2 833	18 372	15 988	1 592	1 568	291
1946	39 296	55 232	-15 936	-16 964	1 028	6 679	9 257	16 098	11 883	1 517	1 316	282
1947	38 514	34 496	4 018	2 861	1 157	-17 522	13 504	17 935	8 615	1 835	1 329	259
1948	41 560	29 764	11 796	10 548	1 248	-8 069	-3 727	19 315	9 678	2 168	1 343	239
1949	39 415	38 835	580	-684	1 263	-1 948	1 368	15 552	11 192	2 246	1 205	330
1950	39 443	42 562	-3 119	-4 702	1 583	4 701	-1 582	15 755	10 449	2 648	1 332	358
1951	51 616	45 514	6 102	4 259	1 843	-4 697	-1 405	21 616	14 101	3 688	1 609	377
1952	66 167	67 686	-1 519	-3 383	1 864	432	1 087	27 934	21 226	4 315	1 712	418
1953	69 608	76 101	-6 493	-8 259	1 766	3 625	2 868	29 816	21 238	4 722	1 675	423
1954	69 701	70 855	-1 154	-2 831	1 677	6 116	-4 962	29 542	21 101	5 192	1 561	455
1955	65 451	68 444	-2 993	-4 091	1 098	2 117	876	28 747	17 861	5 981	1 449	431
1956	74 587	70 640	3 947	2 494	1 452	-4 460	513	32 188	20 880	7 059	1 690	571
1957	79 990	76 578	3 412	2 639	773	-2 836	-576	35 620	21 167	7 405	1 950	642
1958	79 636	82 405	-2 769	-3 315	546	7 016	-4 247	34 724	20 074	8 624	1 933	682
1959	79 249	92 098	-12 849	-12 149	-700	8 365	4 484	36 719	17 309	8 821	2 131	770
1960	92 492	92 191	301	510	-209	2 139	-2 440	40 715	21 494	11 248	2 667	768
1961	94 388	97 723	-3 335	-3 766	431	1 517	1 818	41 338	20 954	12 679	2 903	857
1962	99 676	106 821	-7 146	-5 881	-1 265	9 653	-2 507	45 571	20 523	12 835	3 337	875
1963	106 560	111 316	-4 756	-3 966	-789	5 968	-1 212	47 588	21 579	14 746	4 112	946
1964	112 613	118 528	-5 915	-6 546	632	2 871	3 044	48 697	23 493	16 959	3 997	1 007
1965	116 817	118 228	-1 411	-1 605	194	3 929	-2 518	48 792	25 461	17 358	3 803	1 081
1966	130 835	134 532	-3 698	-3 068	-630	2 936	762	55 446	30 073	20 662	3 755	1 129
1967	148 822	157 464	-8 643	-12 620	3 978	2 912	5 731	61 526	33 971	27 823	3 575	1 221
1968	152 973	178 134	-25 161	-27 742	2 581	22 919	2 242	68 726	28 665	29 224	3 346	1 354
1969	186 882	183 640	3 242	-507	3 749	-11 437	8 195	87 249	36 678	34 236	3 328	1 451
1970	192 807	195 649	-2 842	-8 694	5 852	5 090	-2 248	90 412	32 829	39 133	3 464	1 765
1971	187 139	210 172	-23 033	-26 052	3 019	19 839	3 194	86 230	26 785	41 699	3 674	1 952
1972	207 309	230 681	-23 373	-26 068	2 695	19 340	4 033	94 737	32 166	46 120	4 357	2 097
1973	230 799	245 707	-14 908	-15 246	338	18 533	-3 625	103 246	36 153	54 876	6 051	2 187
1974	263 224	269 359	-6 135	-7 198	1 063	2 789	3 346	118 952	38 620	65 888	6 837	2 347
1975	279 090	332 332	-53 242	-54 148	906	51 001	2 241	122 386	40 621	75 199	6 771	2 565
1976	298 060	371 792	-73 732	-69 427	-4 306	82 704	-8 972	131 603	41 409	79 901	8 054	2 814
1977	81 232	95 975	-14 744	-14 065	-679	18 105	-3 361	38 801	8 460	21 801	2 698	720
1978	355 559	409 218	-53 659	-49 933	-3 726	53 595	64	157 626	54 892	92 199	11 312	2 974
1979	399 561	458 746	-59 185	-55 416	-3 770	58 022	1 163	180 988	59 952	10 388	13 850	3 237
1980	463 302	504 028	-40 726	-39 633	-1 093	33 180	7 546	217 841	65 677	12 005	15 387	3 494
1981	517 112	590 941	-73 830	-73 141	-689	71 617	2 213	244 069	64 600	13 874	15 336	3 719
1982	599 272	678 241	-78 968	-73 859	-5 109	77 487	1 481	285 917	61 137	16 297	15 763	3 984
1983	617 766	745 743	-127 977	-120 593	-7 384	135 165	-7 188	297 744	49 207	18 068	16 600	4 212
1984	600 562	808 364	-207 802	-207 692	-110	212 693	-4 891	288 938	37 022	18 576	18 799	4 429
1985	666 438	851 805	-185 367	-185 269	-98	169 707	15 660	298 415	56 893	20 965	25 138	4 580
1986	734 037	946 344	-212 308	-221 529	9 222	200 285	12 023	334 531	61 331	23 464	25 758	4 759
1987	769 155	990 382	-221 227	-237 915	16 688	233 363	-12 136	348 959	63 143	25 506	24 098	4 742
1988	854 287	1 004 017	-149 730	-168 357	18 627	149 130	600	392 557	83 926	27 302	25 575	4 715
1989	909 238	1 064 416	-155 178	-192 265	37 087	161 863	-6 685	401 181	94 508	30 509	24 584	4 658
1990	991 104	1 143 743	-152 639	-205 393	52 754	139 100	13 539	445 690	10 329	33 285	22 011	4 546
1991	1 031 958	1 252 993	-221 036	-277 626	56 590	220 842	194	466 884	93 507	35 389	21 635	4 522
1992	1 054 988	1 324 226	-269 238	-321 435	52 198	277 441	-8 203	467 827	98 086	37 052	20 922	4 568
1993	1 091 208	1 381 529	-290 321	-340 408	50 087	310 738	-20 417	475 964	10 027	38 549	23 410	4 788
1994	1 154 334	1 409 386	-255 051	-300 398	45 347	248 659	6 392	509 680	11 752	39 693	26 556	4 805
1995	1 258 566	1 461 752	-203 186	-258 840	55 654	184 669	18 517	543 055	14 038	42 881	28 004	4 661
1996	1 351 790	1 515 742	-163 952	-226 367	62 415	171 313	-7 361	590 244	15 700	45 104	28 878	4 550
1997	1 453 053	1 560 484	-107 431	-174 019	66 588	129 695	-22 264	656 417	17 182	47 636	28 584	4 469
1998	1 579 232	1 601 116	-21 884	-103 248	81 364	38 271	-16 387	737 466	18 229	50 675	28 202	4 418
1999	1 721 728	1 652 458	69 270	-29 925	99 195	-51 245	-18 025	828 586	18 867	54 001	27 484	4 333
2000	1 827 452	1 701 842	125 610	1 920	123 690	-88 736	-36 874	879 480	18 468	58 088	26 480	4 473
2001	2 025 191	1 788 950	236 241	86 422	149 819	-222 559	-13 682	100 446	20 728	62 045	27 640	4 761
2002	1 991 082	1 862 846	128 236	-32 445	160 681	-90 189	-38 047	994 339	15 107	66 144	27 812	4 713
2003	1 853 136	2 010 894	-157 758	-317 417	159 659	220 812	-63 054	858 345	14 804	66 854	27 619	4 594
2004	1 782 314	2 159 899	-377 585	-538 418	160 833	373 016	4 569	793 699	131 778	674 981	33 366	4 631
2005	1 880 114	2 292 841	-412 727	-567 961	155 234	382 101	30 626	808 959	189 371	689 360	39 453	4 594
2006	2 153 611	2 471 957	-318 346	-493 611	175 265	296 668	21 678	927 222	278 282	747 664	42 002	4 459
2007	2 406 869	2 655 050	-248 181	-434 494	186 313	236 760	11 421	1 043 908	353 915	790 043	43 420	4 358
2008	2 567 985	2 728 686	-160 701	-342 153	181 452	206 157	-45 456	1 163 472	370 243	824 258	41 091	4 258
2009	2 523 991	2 982 544	-458 553	-641 848	183 295	767 921	-309 368	1 145 747	304 346	856 459	39 527	4 169
2010	2 104 989	3 517 677	-1 412 688	-1 549 681	136 993	1 741 657	-328 969	915 308	138 229	848 885	37 889	4 143
2011	2 162 706	3 457 079	-1 294 373	-1 371 378	77 005	1 474 175	-179 802	898 549	191 437	815 894	44 823	4 097
2012	2 303 466	3 603 065	-1 299 599	-1 366 781	67 182	1 109 305	190 294	1 091 473	181 085	758 516	56 241	4 035
2013	2 449 990	3 526 563	-1 076 573	-1 138 486	61 913	1 152 944	-76 371	1 132 206	242 289	774 927	66 647	3 740
2014	2 775 106	3 454 881	-679 775	-719 238	39 463	701 582	-21 807	1 316 405	273 506	887 445	56 811	3 564
2015	3 021 491	3 506 284	-484 793	-514 305	29 512	797 186	-312 393	1 394 568	320 731	965 029	54 957	3 472
2016	3 249 890	3 691 850	-441 960	-469 255	27 295	336 793	105 167	1 540 802	343 797	101 042	51 178	3 652
2017	3 267 965	3 852 616	-584 651	-620 158	35 507	1 050 932	-466 281	1 546 075	299 571	106 230	48 856	3 904
2018	3 316 184	3 981 630	-665 446	-714 863	49 417	497 815	167 631	1 587 120	297 048	111 189	45 808	4 192
2019	3 329 907	4 109 044	-779 137	-785 312	6 175	1 084 128	-304 991	1 683 538	204 733	112 115	45 042	4 504
2020	3 464 161	4 448 316	-984 155	-991 841	7 686	1 051 179	-67 024	1 717 857	230 245	119 739	41 193	4 786

[1]Fiscal years through 1976 are from July 1 through June 30. Beginning with October 1976 (fiscal year 1977), fiscal years are from October 1 through September 30. The period from July 1 through September 30, 1976, is a separate fiscal period known as the transition quarter (TQ) and is not included in any fiscal year.
. . . = Not available.

Table 6-14A. Federal Government Receipts and Outlays by Fiscal Year ¹—Continued

(Budget accounts, millions of dollars.)

Year	Receipts by source—Continued					Outlays by function						
	Excise taxes	Estate and gift taxes	Customs duties and fees	Federal reserve deposits	All other	National defense	International affairs	General science, space, and technology	Energy	Natural resources and environment	Agriculture	Commerce and housing credit
1945	6 265	637	341	...	105	82 965	1 913	111	25	455	1 635	-2 630
1946	6 998	668	424	...	109	42 681	1 935	34	41	482	610	-1 857
1947	7 211	771	477	15	69	12 808	5 791	5	18	700	814	-923
1948	7 356	890	403	100	68	9 105	4 566	1	292	780	69	306
1949	7 502	780	367	187	54	13 150	6 052	48	341	1 080	1 924	800
1950	7 550	698	407	192	55	13 724	4 673	55	327	1 308	2 049	1 035
1951	8 648	708	609	189	72	23 566	3 647	51	383	1 310	-323	1 228
1952	8 852	818	533	278	81	46 089	2 691	49	474	1 233	176	1 278
1953	9 877	881	596	298	81	52 802	2 119	49	425	1 289	2 253	910
1954	9 945	934	542	341	88	49 266	1 596	46	432	1 007	1 817	-184
1955	9 131	924	585	251	90	42 729	2 223	74	325	940	3 514	92
1956	9 929	1 161	682	287	140	42 523	2 414	79	174	870	3 486	506
1957	10 534	1 365	735	434	139	45 430	3 147	122	240	1 098	2 288	1 424
1958	10 638	1 393	782	664	123	46 815	3 364	141	348	1 407	2 411	930
1959	10 578	1 333	925	491	171	49 015	3 144	294	382	1 632	4 509	1 933
1960	11 676	1 606	1 105	1 093	119	48 130	2 988	599	464	1 559	2 623	1 618
1961	11 860	1 896	982	788	130	49 601	3 184	1 042	510	1 779	2 641	1 203
1962	12 534	2 016	1 142	718	125	52 345	5 639	1 723	604	2 044	3 562	1 424
1963	13 194	2 167	1 205	828	194	53 400	5 308	3 051	530	2 251	4 384	62
1964	13 731	2 394	1 252	947	139	54 757	4 945	4 897	572	2 364	4 609	418
1965	14 570	2 716	1 442	1 372	222	50 620	5 273	5 823	699	2 531	3 954	1 157
1966	13 062	3 066	1 767	1 713	163	58 111	5 580	6 717	612	2 719	2 447	3 245
1967	13 719	2 978	1 901	1 805	302	71 417	5 566	6 233	782	2 869	2 990	3 979
1968	14 079	3 051	2 038	2 091	400	81 926	5 301	5 524	1 037	2 988	4 544	4 280
1969	15 222	3 491	2 319	2 662	247	82 497	4 600	5 020	1 010	2 900	5 826	-119
1970	15 705	3 644	2 430	3 266	158	81 692	4 330	4 511	997	3 065	5 166	2 112
1971	16 614	3 735	2 591	3 533	325	78 872	4 159	4 182	1 035	3 915	4 290	2 366
1972	15 477	5 436	3 287	3 252	380	79 174	4 781	4 175	1 296	4 241	5 227	2 222
1973	16 260	4 917	3 188	3 495	425	76 681	4 149	4 032	1 237	4 775	4 821	931
1974	16 844	5 035	3 334	4 845	523	79 347	5 710	3 980	1 303	5 697	2 194	4 705
1975	16 551	4 611	3 676	5 777	935	86 509	7 097	3 991	2 916	7 346	2 997	9 947
1976	16 963	5 216	4 074	5 451	2 576	89 619	6 433	4 373	4 204	8 184	3 109	7 619
1977	4 473	1 455	1 212	1 500	111	22 269	2 458	1 162	1 129	2 524	972	931
1978	17 548	7 327	5 150	5 908	623	97 241	6 353	4 736	5 770	10 032	6 734	3 093
1979	18 376	5 285	6 573	6 641	778	10 449	7 482	4 926	7 991	10 983	11 301	6 254
1980	18 745	5 411	7 439	8 327	925	11 634	7 459	5 234	9 179	12 135	11 176	4 686
1981	24 329	6 389	7 174	11 767	981	13 399	12 714	5 831	10 156	13 858	8 774	9 390
1982	40 839	6 787	8 083	12 834	956	15 751	13 104	6 468	15 166	13 568	11 241	8 206
1983	36 311	7 991	8 854	15 186	975	18 530	12 300	7 199	13 527	12 998	15 866	6 256
1984	35 300	6 053	8 655	14 492	1 108	20 990	11 848	7 934	9 353	12 672	22 807	6 681
1985	37 361	6 010	11 370	15 684	1 328	22 741	15 869	8 311	7 073	12 586	13 477	6 959
1986	35 992	6 422	12 079	17 059	1 460	25 274	16 169	8 622	5 608	13 345	25 427	4 337
1987	32 919	6 958	13 327	18 374	1 574	27 337	14 146	8 962	4 690	13 628	31 319	5 058
1988	32 457	7 493	15 085	16 817	2 635	28 199	11 645	9 200	4 072	13 355	26 466	6 434
1989	35 227	7 594	16 198	17 163	3 031	29 036	10 466	10 820	2 296	14 601	17 088	19 163
1990	34 386	8 745	16 334	19 604	3 639	30 355	9 583	12 821	2 705	16 169	16 698	29 709
1991	35 345	11 500	16 707	24 319	3 647	29 932	13 758	14 426	3 341	17 055	11 637	67 599
1992	42 402	11 138	15 949	19 158	4 412	27 328	15 846	16 092	2 436	18 544	14 886	76 270
1993	45 569	11 143	17 359	22 920	4 293	29 834	16 090	16 389	4 499	20 001	14 922	10 918
1994	48 057	12 577	18 802	14 908	4 491	29 108	17 218	17 006	4 319	20 224	20 081	-2 185
1995	55 225	15 225	20 099	18 023	5 081	28 164	17 067	16 189	5 218	21 000	14 795	-4 228
1996	57 484	14 763	19 301	23 378	5 143	27 206	16 429	16 692	4 936	21 889	9 671	-1 780
1997	54 014	17 189	18 670	20 477	5 048	26 574	13 487	16 684	2 839	21 503	9 035	-1 047
1998	56 924	19 845	17 928	19 636	5 769	27 050	15 173	17 136	1 475	21 201	8 889	-1 464
1999	57 673	24 076	18 297	24 540	8 048	26 819	13 054	18 172	1 270	22 278	12 077	1 007
2000	70 414	27 782	18 336	25 917	9 010	27 476	15 239	18 084	911	23 943	22 879	2 641
2001	68 865	29 010	19 914	32 293	10 506	29 436	17 213	18 594	-761	25 003	36 458	3 207
2002	66 232	28 400	19 369	26 124	11 576	30 473	16 485	19 753	9	25 532	26 252	5 731
2003	66 989	26 507	18 602	23 683	10 206	34 845	22 315	20 734	475	29 426	21 965	-407
2004	67 524	21 959	19 862	21 878	12 636	40 473	21 199	20 831	-725	29 667	22 496	727
2005	69 855	24 831	21 083	19 652	12 956	45 581	26 870	23 029	-147	30 694	15 439	5 265
2006	73 094	24 764	23 379	19 297	13 448	495 294	34 565	23 597	440	27 983	26 565	7 566
2007	73 961	27 877	24 810	29 945	14 632	521 820	29 499	23 584	785	33 025	25 969	6 187
2008	65 069	26 044	26 010	32 043	15 497	551 258	28 482	24 407	-852	31 721	17 662	487
2009	67 334	28 844	27 568	33 598	16 399	616 066	28 857	26 773	631	31 820	18 387	27 870
2010	62 483	23 482	22 453	34 318	17 799	661 012	37 529	28 417	4 755	35 573	22 237	291 535
2011	66 909	18 885	25 298	75 845	20 969	693 485	45 195	30 100	11 618	43 667	21 356	-82 316
2012	72 381	7 399	29 519	82 546	20 271	705 554	45 685	29 466	12 174	45 473	20 662	-12 564
2013	79 061	13 973	30 307	81 957	24 883	677 852	36 802	29 060	14 858	41 631	17 791	40 647
2014	84 007	18 912	31 815	75 767	26 874	633 446	46 464	28 908	11 042	38 145	29 678	-83 198
2015	93 368	19 300	33 926	99 235	36 905	603 457	46 879	28 570	5 270	36 171	24 386	-94 861
2016	98 279	19 232	35 041	96 468	51 014	589 659	52 040	29 412	6 841	36 033	18 500	-37 905
2017	95 026	21 354	34 838	115 672	40 364	593 372	45 306	30 174	3 721	39 082	18 344	-34 077
2018	83 823	22 768	34 574	81 287	47 667	598 722	46 309	30 394	3 856	37 896	18 872	-26 685
2019	94 986	22 983	41 299	70 750	40 917	631 130	48 996	31 534	2 169	39 140	21 789	-9 470
2020	99 452	16 672	70 784	52 793	32 986	686 003	52 739	32 410	5 041	37 844	38 257	-25 715

¹Fiscal years through 1976 are from July 1 through June 30. Beginning with October 1976 (fiscal year 1977), fiscal years are from October 1 through September 30. The period from July 1 through September 30, 1976, is a separate fiscal period known as the transition quarter (TQ) and is not included in any fiscal year.
... = Not available.

Table 6-14A. Federal Government Receipts and Outlays by Fiscal Year [1]—*Continued*

(Budget accounts, millions of dollars.)

Year	Outlays by function—*Continued*										
	Transportation	Community and regional development	Education, employment, and social services	Health	Medicare	Income security	Social Security	Veterans benefits and services	Administration of justice	General government	Net interest
1945	3 654	243	134	211	0	1 137	267	110	178	581	3 112
1946	1 970	200	85	201	0	2 384	358	2 465	176	825	4 111
1947	1 130	302	102	177	0	2 820	466	6 344	176	1 114	4 204
1948	787	78	191	162	0	2 499	558	6 457	170	1 045	4 341
1949	916	-33	178	197	0	3 174	657	6 599	184	824	4 523
1950	967	30	241	268	0	4 097	781	8 834	193	986	4 812
1951	956	47	235	323	0	3 352	1 565	5 526	218	1 097	4 665
1952	1 124	73	339	347	0	3 655	2 063	5 341	267	1 163	4 701
1953	1 264	117	441	336	0	3 823	2 717	4 519	243	1 209	5 156
1954	1 229	100	370	307	0	4 434	3 352	4 613	257	799	4 811
1955	1 246	129	445	291	0	5 071	4 427	4 675	256	651	4 850
1956	1 450	92	591	359	0	4 734	5 478	4 891	302	1 201	5 079
1957	1 662	135	590	479	0	5 427	6 661	5 005	303	1 360	5 354
1958	2 334	169	643	541	0	7 535	8 219	5 350	325	655	5 604
1959	3 655	211	789	685	0	8 239	9 737	5 443	356	926	5 762
1960	4 126	224	968	795	0	7 378	11 602	5 441	366	1 184	6 947
1961	3 987	275	1 063	913	0	9 683	12 474	5 705	400	1 354	6 716
1962	4 290	469	1 241	1 198	0	9 198	14 365	5 628	429	1 049	6 889
1963	4 596	574	1 458	1 451	0	9 304	15 788	5 521	465	1 230	7 740
1964	5 242	933	1 555	1 788	0	9 650	16 620	5 682	489	1 518	8 199
1965	5 763	1 114	2 140	1 791	0	9 462	17 460	5 723	536	1 499	8 591
1966	5 730	1 105	4 363	2 543	64	9 671	20 694	5 923	564	1 603	9 386
1967	5 936	1 108	6 453	3 351	2 748	10 253	21 725	6 743	618	1 719	10 268
1968	6 316	1 382	7 634	4 390	4 649	11 806	23 854	7 042	659	1 757	11 090
1969	6 526	1 552	7 548	5 162	5 695	13 066	27 298	7 642	766	1 939	12 699
1970	7 008	2 392	8 634	5 907	6 213	15 645	30 270	8 679	959	2 320	14 380
1971	8 052	2 917	9 849	6 843	6 622	22 936	35 872	9 778	1 307	2 442	14 841
1972	8 392	3 423	12 529	8 674	7 479	27 638	40 157	10 732	1 684	2 960	15 478
1973	9 066	4 605	12 744	9 356	8 052	28 265	49 090	12 015	2 174	9 774	17 349
1974	9 172	4 229	12 455	10 733	9 639	33 700	55 867	13 388	2 505	10 032	21 449
1975	10 918	4 322	16 022	12 930	12 875	50 161	64 658	16 599	3 028	10 374	23 244
1976	13 739	5 442	18 910	15 734	15 834	60 784	73 899	18 433	3 430	9 706	26 727
1977	3 358	1 569	5 169	3 924	4 264	14 981	19 763	3 963	918	3 878	6 949
1978	14 829	7 021	21 104	17 302	19 345	61 045	85 061	18 038	3 701	12 791	29 901
1979	15 521	11 841	26 706	18 524	22 768	61 492	93 861	18 978	3 923	11 961	35 458
1980	18 079	10 480	30 218	20 494	26 495	66 364	10 407	19 931	4 286	12 241	42 633
1981	21 329	11 252	31 835	23 169	32 090	86 548	11 854	21 185	4 702	12 975	52 533
1982	23 379	10 568	33 146	26 866	39 149	10 028	13 958	22 991	4 908	11 373	68 766
1983	20 625	8 347	26 609	27 445	46 567	10 813	15 596	23 958	4 842	10 861	85 032
1984	21 334	7 564	26 192	28 643	52 588	12 301	17 072	24 846	5 246	11 181	89 808
1985	23 669	7 673	26 913	30 420	57 540	11 337	17 822	25 601	5 811	11 746	11 110
1986	25 838	7 676	28 584	33 546	65 822	12 900	18 862	26 281	6 426	11 515	12 947
1987	28 113	7 233	29 771	35 935	70 164	12 065	19 875	26 343	6 735	12 491	13 601
1988	26 222	5 049	28 915	39 967	75 120	12 410	20 735	26 761	7 715	7 487	13 861
1989	27 272	5 293	30 939	44 471	78 878	13 038	21 934	29 409	9 397	9 399	15 180
1990	27 608	5 362	35 314	48 390	84 964	13 755	23 254	30 038	9 644	9 317	16 898
1991	29 485	8 531	37 167	57 700	98 102	14 878	24 862	29 088	10 185	10 462	18 434
1992	31 099	6 810	41 260	71 139	10 448	17 258	26 901	31 319	12 486	11 568	19 444
1993	33 332	6 836	42 807	89 415	11 902	19 965	28 758	34 112	14 650	12 883	19 934
1994	35 004	9 146	47 455	99 321	13 055	21 008	30 458	35 690	15 193	12 944	19 871
1995	38 066	10 620	43 337	10 705	14 474	21 723	31 956	37 617	15 516	11 159	20 293
1996	39 350	10 746	51 067	11 535	15 985	22 375	33 584	37 910	16 508	13 799	23 213
1997	39 565	10 741	48 334	11 934	17 422	22 969	34 967	37 003	17 898	11 755	24 105
1998	40 767	11 049	49 014	12 379	19 001	23 498	36 525	39 332	20 617	12 547	24 398
1999	40 343	9 771	50 534	13 140	19 282	23 769	37 921	41 793	23 359	15 544	24 111
2000	42 532	11 865	50 608	14 104	19 044	24 241	39 003	43 216	26 536	15 363	22 975
2001	46 853	10 623	53 766	15 450	19 711	25 367	40 942	47 040	28 499	13 013	22 294
2002	54 447	11 773	57 089	17 223	21 738	26 972	43 295	45 024	30 201	14 358	20 616
2003	61 833	12 981	70 592	19 647	23 085	31 267	45 598	50 979	35 061	16 951	17 094
2004	67 069	18 850	82 733	219 605	249 433	334 574	474 680	56 832	35 340	23 164	15 307
2005	64 627	15 820	87 997	240 148	269 360	333 027	495 548	59 729	45 576	22 338	16 024
2006	67 894	26 262	97 553	250 605	298 638	345 800	523 305	70 112	40 019	16 997	18 398
2007	70 244	54 465	118 473	252 779	329 868	352 425	548 549	69 832	41 016	18 177	22 660
2008	72 905	29 567	91 647	266 425	375 407	365 931	586 153	72 828	42 362	17 425	23 710
2009	77 616	23 952	91 304	280 626	390 758	431 211	617 027	84 711	48 097	20 323	25 275
2010	84 289	27 676	79 744	334 368	430 093	533 080	682 963	95 545	52 581	22 017	18 690
2011	91 972	23 894	128 595	369 081	451 636	622 106	706 737	108 478	54 383	23 014	19 619
2012	92 966	23 883	101 256	372 481	485 653	597 269	730 811	127 269	56 056	27 476	22 996
2013	93 019	25 132	90 822	346 755	471 793	541 248	773 290	124 679	56 277	28 035	22 040
2014	91 673	32 335	72 860	358 264	497 826	536 411	813 551	139 038	52 601	27 737	22 088
2015	91 915	20 670	90 610	409 497	511 688	513 596	850 533	149 621	50 457	26 913	22 895
2016	89 533	20 669	122 035	482 257	546 202	508 800	887 753	159 781	51 906	20 956	22 318
2017	92 566	20 140	109 709	511 325	594 536	514 098	916 067	174 557	55 768	23 146	24 003
2018	93 552	24 907	143 953	533 152	597 307	503 443	944 878	176 584	57 944	23 821	26 255
2019	92 785	42 159	95 503	551 219	588 706	495 289	987 791	178 895	60 418	23 885	324 975
2020	97 116	26 876	136 752	584 816	650 996	514 787	104 440	199 843	65 740	23 436	375 158

[1]Fiscal years through 1976 are from July 1 through June 30. Beginning with October 1976 (fiscal year 1977), fiscal years are from October 1 through September 30. The period from July 1 through September 30, 1976, is a separate fiscal period known as the transition quarter (TQ) and is not included in any fiscal year.
. . . = Not available.

Table 6-14B. The Federal Budget and GDP

(Billions of dollars; percent.)

Year	Fiscal year GDP	Billions of dollars						Percent of GDP					
		Receipts			Outlays		Total budget surplus or deficit	Receipts			Outlays		Total budget surplus or deficit
		Total	Individual income taxes	Corporate income taxes	Total	National defense		Total	Individual income taxes	Corporate income taxes	Total	National defense	
1950	278.7	39.4	15.8	10.4	42.6	13.7	-3.1	14.2	5.7	3.7	15.1	4.9	-1.7
1951	327.1	51.6	21.6	14.1	45.5	23.6	6.1	15.8	6.6	4.3	13.5	7.2	1.3
1952	357.1	66.2	27.9	21.2	67.7	46.1	-1.5	18.5	7.8	5.9	18.5	12.9	-0.9
1953	382.1	69.6	29.8	21.2	76.1	52.8	-6.5	18.2	7.8	5.6	19.3	13.8	-2.2
1954	387.2	69.7	29.5	21.1	70.9	49.3	-1.2	18.0	7.6	5.5	17.5	12.7	-0.7
1955	406.3	65.5	28.7	17.9	68.4	42.7	-3.0	16.1	7.1	4.4	15.9	10.5	-1.0
1956	438.3	74.6	32.2	20.9	70.6	42.5	3.9	17.0	7.3	4.8	15.0	9.7	0.6
1957	463.4	80.0	35.6	21.2	76.6	45.4	3.4	17.3	7.7	4.6	15.2	9.8	0.6
1958	473.5	79.6	34.7	20.1	82.4	46.8	-2.8	16.8	7.3	4.2	15.8	9.9	-0.7
1959	504.6	79.2	36.7	17.3	92.1	49.0	-12.8	15.7	7.3	3.4	16.5	9.7	-2.4
1960	534.3	92.5	40.7	21.5	92.2	48.1	0.3	17.3	7.6	4.0	15.2	9.0	0.1
1961	546.6	94.4	41.3	21.0	97.7	49.6	-3.3	17.3	7.6	3.8	15.7	9.1	-0.7
1962	585.7	99.7	45.6	20.5	106.8	52.3	-7.1	17.0	7.8	3.5	15.9	8.9	-1.0
1963	618.2	106.6	47.6	21.6	111.3	53.4	-4.8	17.2	7.7	3.5	15.6	8.6	-0.6
1964	661.7	112.6	48.7	23.5	118.5	54.8	-5.9	17.0	7.4	3.6	15.5	8.3	-1.0
1965	709.3	116.8	48.8	25.5	118.2	50.6	-1.4	16.5	6.9	3.6	14.3	7.1	-0.2
1966	780.5	130.8	55.4	30.1	134.5	58.1	-3.7	16.8	7.1	3.9	14.7	7.4	-0.4
1967	836.5	148.8	61.5	34.0	157.5	71.4	-8.6	17.8	7.4	4.1	16.4	8.5	-1.5
1968	897.6	153.0	68.7	28.7	178.1	81.9	-25.2	17.0	7.7	3.2	17.4	9.1	-3.1
1969	980.3	186.9	87.2	36.7	183.6	82.5	3.2	19.1	8.9	3.7	16.2	8.4	-0.1
1970	1 046.7	192.8	90.4	32.8	195.6	81.7	-2.8	18.4	8.6	3.1	16.1	7.8	-0.8
1971	1 116.6	187.1	86.2	26.8	210.2	78.9	-23.0	16.8	7.7	2.4	15.9	7.1	-2.3
1972	1 216.3	207.3	94.7	32.2	230.7	79.2	-23.4	17.0	7.8	2.6	15.9	6.5	-2.1
1973	1 352.7	230.8	103.2	36.2	245.7	76.7	-14.9	17.1	7.6	2.7	14.8	5.7	-1.1
1974	1 482.9	263.2	119.0	38.6	269.4	79.3	-6.1	17.8	8.0	2.6	14.6	5.4	-0.5
1975	1 606.9	279.1	122.4	40.6	332.3	86.5	-53.2	17.4	7.6	2.5	16.9	5.4	-3.4
1976	1 786.1	298.1	131.6	41.4	371.8	89.6	-73.7	16.7	7.4	2.3	16.9	5.0	-3.9
1977	2 024.3	355.6	157.6	54.9	409.2	97.2	-53.7	17.6	7.8	2.7	16.2	4.8	-2.5
1978	2 273.5	399.6	181.0	60.0	458.7	104.5	-59.2	17.6	8.0	2.6	16.3	4.6	-2.4
1979	2 565.6	463.3	217.8	65.7	504.0	116.3	-40.7	18.1	8.5	2.6	15.8	4.5	-1.5
1980	2 791.9	517.1	244.1	64.6	590.9	134.0	-73.8	18.5	8.7	2.3	17.1	4.8	-2.6
1981	3 133.2	599.3	285.9	61.1	678.2	157.5	-79.0	19.1	9.1	2.0	17.3	5.0	-2.4
1982	3 313.4	617.8	297.7	49.2	745.7	185.3	-128.0	18.6	9.0	1.5	18.0	5.6	-3.6
1983	3 536.0	600.6	288.9	37.0	808.4	209.9	-207.8	17.0	8.2	1.0	18.7	5.9	-5.9
1984	3 949.2	666.4	298.4	56.9	851.8	227.4	-185.4	16.9	7.6	1.4	17.4	5.8	-4.7
1985	4 265.1	734.0	334.5	61.3	946.3	252.7	-212.3	17.2	7.8	1.4	18.0	5.9	-5.2
1986	4 526.3	769.2	349.0	63.1	990.4	273.4	-221.2	17.0	7.7	1.4	17.8	6.0	-5.3
1987	4 767.7	854.3	392.6	83.9	1 004.0	282.0	-149.7	17.9	8.2	1.8	17.0	5.9	-3.5
1988	5 138.6	909.2	401.2	94.5	1 064.4	290.4	-155.2	17.7	7.8	1.8	16.7	5.7	-3.7
1989	5 554.7	991.1	445.7	103.3	1 143.7	303.6	-152.6	17.8	8.0	1.9	16.8	5.5	-3.7
1990	5 898.8	1 032.0	466.9	93.5	1 253.0	299.3	-221.0	17.5	7.9	1.6	17.4	5.1	-4.7
1991	6 093.2	1 055.0	467.8	98.1	1 324.2	273.3	-269.2	17.3	7.7	1.6	17.8	4.5	-5.3
1992	6 416.3	1 091.2	476.0	100.3	1 381.5	298.3	-290.3	17.0	7.4	1.6	17.6	4.6	-5.3
1993	6 775.3	1 154.3	509.7	117.5	1 409.4	291.1	-255.1	17.0	7.5	1.7	16.9	4.3	-4.4
1994	7 176.9	1 258.6	543.1	140.4	1 461.8	281.6	-203.2	17.5	7.6	2.0	16.5	3.9	-3.6
1995	7 560.4	1 351.8	590.2	157.0	1 515.7	272.1	-164.0	17.9	7.8	2.1	16.2	3.6	-3.0
1996	7 951.3	1 453.1	656.4	171.8	1 560.5	265.7	-107.4	18.3	8.3	2.2	15.8	3.3	-2.2
1997	8 451.0	1 579.2	737.5	182.3	1 601.1	270.5	-21.9	18.7	8.7	2.2	15.3	3.2	-1.2
1998	8 930.8	1 721.7	828.6	188.7	1 652.5	268.2	69.3	19.3	9.3	2.1	15.0	3.0	-0.3
1999	9 479.4	1 827.5	879.5	184.7	1 701.8	274.8	125.6	19.3	9.3	1.9	14.6	2.9	. . .
2000	10 117.5	2 025.2	1 004.5	207.3	1 789.0	294.4	236.2	20.0	9.9	2.0	14.4	2.9	0.9
2001	10 526.5	1 991.1	994.3	151.1	1 862.8	304.7	128.2	18.9	9.4	1.4	14.4	2.9	-0.3
2002	10 833.7	1 853.1	858.3	148.0	2 010.9	348.5	-157.8	17.1	7.9	1.4	15.3	3.2	-2.9
2003	11 283.8	1 782.3	793.7	131.8	2 159.9	404.7	-377.6	15.8	7.0	1.2	15.9	3.6	-4.8
2004	12 025.5	1 880.1	809.0	189.4	2 292.8	455.8	-412.7	15.6	6.7	1.6	15.9	3.8	-4.7
2005	12 834.2	2 153.6	927.2	278.3	2 472.0	495.3	-318.3	16.8	7.2	2.2	16.1	3.9	-3.8
2006	13 638.4	2 406.9	1 043.9	353.9	2 655.1	521.8	-248.2	17.6	7.7	2.6	16.4	3.8	-3.2
2007	14 290.8	2 568.0	1 163.5	370.2	2 728.7	551.3	-160.7	18.0	8.1	2.6	15.9	3.9	-2.4
2008	14 743.3	2 524.0	1 145.7	304.3	2 982.5	616.1	-458.6	17.1	7.8	2.1	17.0	4.2	-4.4
2009	14 431.8	2 105.0	915.3	138.2	3 517.7	661.0	-1 412.7	14.6	6.3	1.0	20.8	4.6	-10.7
2010	14 838.9	2 162.7	898.5	191.4	3 457.1	693.5	-1 294.4	14.6	6.1	1.3	19.6	4.7	-9.2
2011	15 403.7	2 303.5	1 091.5	181.1	3 603.1	705.6	-1 299.6	15.0	7.1	1.2	20.2	4.6	-8.9
2012	16 056.5	2 450.0	1 132.2	242.3	3 526.6	677.9	-1 076.6	15.3	7.1	1.5	18.8	4.2	-7.1
2013	16 603.8	2 775.1	1 316.4	273.5	3 454.9	633.4	-679.8	16.7	7.9	1.6	17.0	3.8	-4.3
2014	17 335.6	3 021.5	1 394.6	320.7	3 506.3	603.5	-484.8	17.4	8.0	1.9	16.2	3.5	-3.0
2015	18 106.1	3 249.9	1 540.8	343.8	3 691.9	589.7	-442.0	17.9	8.5	1.9	16.3	3.3	-2.6
2016	18 581.7	3 268.0	1 546.1	299.6	3 852.6	593.4	-584.7	17.6	8.3	1.6	16.6	3.2	-3.3
2017	19 316.6	3 316.2	1 587.1	297.0	3 981.6	598.7	-665.4	17.2	8.2	1.5	16.5	3.1	-3.7
2018	20 368.9	3 329.9	1 683.5	204.7	4 109.0	631.1	-779.1	16.3	8.3	1.0	16.0	3.1	-3.9
2019	21 223.9	3 463.4	1 717.9	230.2	4 447.0	686.0	-983.6	16.3	8.1	1.1	16.7	3.2	-4.7
2020	20 999.7	3 421.2	1 608.7	211.8	6 550.4	724.6	-3 129.2	16.3	7.7	1.0	26.7	3.5	-15.0

. . . = Not available.

Table 6-15. Federal Government Debt by Fiscal Year

(Billions of dollars, except as noted.)

| Year | Federal government debt held by the public at end of fiscal year | | Gross federal debt at end of fiscal year held by: | | | | | | |
| | Debt held by the public | Debt/GDP ratio (percent) | Total | Social Security funds [1] | Other U.S. government accounts | Federal Reserve System | Private investors | | |
							Total	Foreign residents	Domestic investors
1940	43	43.6	51	2	6	2	40	...	...
1941	48	41.5	58	2	7	2	46	...	...
1942	68	45.9	79	3	8	3	65	...	...
1943	128	69.2	143	4	11	7	121	...	...
1944	185	86.4	204	5	14	15	170	...	...
1945	235	103.9	260	7	18	22	213	...	...
1946	242	106.1	271	8	21	24	218	...	...
1947	224	93.9	257	9	24	22	202	...	...
1948	216	82.6	252	10	26	21	195	...	...
1949	214	77.5	253	11	27	19	195	...	...
1950	219	78.6	257	13	25	18	201	...	...
1951	214	65.5	255	15	26	23	191	...	...
1952	215	60.1	259	17	28	23	192	...	...
1953	218	57.2	266	18	29	25	194	...	...
1954	224	58.0	271	20	26	25	199	...	...
1955	227	55.8	274	21	27	24	203	...	...
1956	222	50.7	273	23	28	24	198	...	...
1957	219	47.3	272	23	30	23	196	...	...
1958	226	47.8	280	24	29	25	201	...	...
1959	235	46.5	287	23	30	26	209	...	...
1960	237	44.3	291	23	31	27	210	...	...
1961	238	43.6	293	23	31	27	211	...	...
1962	248	42.3	303	22	33	30	218	...	...
1963	254	41.1	310	21	35	32	222	...	...
1964	257	38.8	316	22	37	35	222	...	...
1965	261	36.8	322	22	39	39	222	12	210
1966	264	33.8	328	22	43	42	222	12	210
1967	267	31.9	340	26	48	47	220	11	209
1968	290	32.3	369	28	51	52	237	11	226
1969	278	28.4	366	32	56	54	224	10	214
1970	283	27.1	381	38	60	58	225	14	211
1971	303	27.1	408	41	64	66	238	32	206
1972	322	26.5	436	44	70	71	251	49	202
1973	341	25.2	466	44	81	75	266	59	207
1974	344	23.2	484	46	94	81	263	57	206
1975	395	24.6	542	48	99	85	310	66	244
1976	477	26.7	629	45	107	95	383	70	313
1977	496	26.3	644	44	105	97	399	96	303
1978	549	27.1	706	40	118	105	444	121	323
1979	607	26.7	777	35	134	115	492	120	372
1980	640	25.0	829	33	156	116	525	122	403
1981	712	25.5	909	32	165	121	591	131	460
1982	789	25.2	995	27	178	124	665	141	524
1983	925	27.9	1 137	19	193	134	790	160	630
1984	1 137	32.2	1 372	32	202	156	982	176	806
1985	1 307	33.1	1 565	32	225	155	1 152	223	929
1986	1 507	35.3	1 817	40	270	170	1 337	266	1 071
1987	1 741	38.5	2 121	46	334	191	1 550	280	1 270
1988	1 890	39.6	2 346	65	391	212	1 678	346	1 332
1989	2 052	39.9	2 601	104	445	229	1 822	395	1 427
1990	2 191	39.4	2 868	157	520	220	1 971	464	1 507
1991	2 412	40.9	3 206	215	580	234	2 177	506	1 671
1992	2 689	44.1	3 598	268	641	259	2 430	563	1 867
1993	3 000	46.8	4 002	319	683	296	2 703	619	2 084
1994	3 248	47.9	4 351	366	737	326	2 923	682	2 241
1995	3 433	47.8	4 643	423	788	355	3 078	820	2 258
1996	3 604	47.7	4 921	483	833	374	3 230	993	2 237
1997	3 734	47.0	5 181	550	898	391	3 343	1 231	2 112
1998	3 772	44.6	5 369	631	966	425	3 348	1 224	2 124
1999	3 721	41.7	5 478	730	1 027	458	3 263	1 281	1 982
2000	3 632	38.3	5 606	855	1 118	497	3 136	1 039	2 097
2001	3 410	33.7	5 629	1 007	1 212	511	2 898	1 006	1 892
2002	3 320	31.5	5 770	1 170	1 280	534	2 785	1 201	1 584
2003	3 540	32.7	6 198	1 329	1 329	604	2 936	1 454	1 482
2004	3 913	34.7	6 760	1 485	1 362	656	3 257	1 799	1 458
2005	4 296	35.7	7 355	1 635	1 424	700	3 595	1 930	1 665
2006	4 592	35.8	7 905	1 809	1 504	736	3 856	2 025	1 831
2007	4 829	35.4	8 451	1 994	1 628	769	4 060	2 235	1 825
2008	5 035	35.2	8 951	2 181	1 735	780	4 255	2 802	1 453
2009	5 803	39.4	9 986	2 366	1 817	491	5 312	3 571	1 741
2010	7 545	52.3	11 876	2 504	1 827	769	6 776	4 324	2 452
2011	9 019	60.8	13 529	2 585	1 924	812	8 207	4 912	3 295
2012	10 128	65.8	14 764	2 653	1 983	1 665	8 464	5 476	2 988
2013	11 281	70.3	16 051	2 718	2 052	1 645	9 636	5 652	3 984
2014	11 983	72.2	16 719	2 756	1 981	2 072	9 910	6 069	3 841
2015	12 780	73.7	17 794	2 783	2 232	2 452	10 328	6 105	4 223
2016	13 117	72.4	18 120	2 808	2 195	2 462	10 655	6 155	4 500
2017	14 168	76.2	19 539	2 842	2 529	2 463	11 704	6 301	5 403
2018	14 665	75.9	20 206	2 890	2 651	2 465	12 200	6 225	5 975
2019	15 750	77.3	21 462	2 894	2 819	2 313	13 436	6 923	6 513
2020	16 801	79.2	22 669	2 901	2 968	2 113	14 687	7 069	7 618

[1]Sum of old age and survivors insurance fund and disability insurance trust fund.
. . . = Not available.

SECTION 6D: GOVERNMENT OUTPUT AND EMPLOYMENT

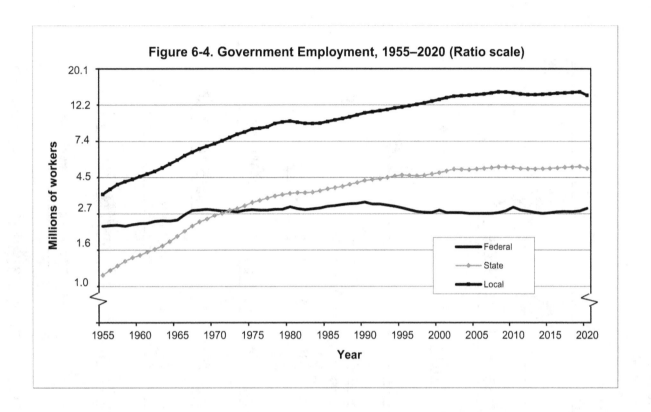

Figure 6-4. Government Employment, 1955–2020 (Ratio scale)

- From 1955 to 2020, total reported employment of civilians by all levels of government has increased 212 percent. Federal employment rose 27.6 percent; state government employment rose 334.4 percent, with 53.0 percent of this increase due to education. However, budget cuts hit all levels of government employment. For example, the Department of Defense lost nearly 25 percent of its employees between 1955 and 2020. (Tables 6-17)

- Contracting and outsourcing of federal government spending can be seen in comparisons between government purchases and government value added. From 1960 to 2020, the volume (measured by the quantity index) of "intermediate" goods and services purchased for nondefense purposes rose 1,010 percent, compared with the 320.7 percent rise in nondefense value added by government itself in such activities. (Real value added comprises the input of government employees and government-owned capital, valued in constant dollars). For defense, government value added rose 15.6 percent over that period, while purchases of goods and services rose 248.2 percent in real terms. (Table 6-16)

- A similar process has occurred at state and local governments, where real value added increased 235.4 percent while goods and services purchased rose 929.3 percent. (Table 6-16)

Table 6-16. Chain-Type Quantity Indexes for Government Output

(Seasonally adjusted, 2012 = 100.)

NIPA Table 3.10.3

Year and quarter	Federal government									State and local government		
	Gross output of general government			Value added			Intermediate goods and services purchased [1]			Gross output of general government	Value added	Intermediate goods and services purchased [1]
	Total	Defense	Nondefense	Total	Defense	Nondefense	Total	Defense	Nondefense			
1960	45.1	59.3	21.2	60.6	83.4	26.1	22.3	28.4	10.9	23.7	30.8	11.6
1961	46.0	60.8	21.1	62.6	86.1	27.1	21.8	28.6	9.4	25.0	32.4	12.4
1962	50.7	65.9	25.1	65.7	90.1	28.9	28.0	34.7	15.2	26.0	33.5	12.9
1963	51.1	66.1	25.8	67.0	90.6	31.2	27.3	34.5	13.9	27.4	35.3	13.8
1964	50.8	64.9	27.1	68.2	91.5	33.0	25.2	30.9	14.2	29.2	37.4	15.1
1965	51.9	66.0	28.3	69.3	92.0	34.9	26.3	32.6	14.4	31.3	39.7	16.6
1966	57.4	74.9	27.9	74.0	98.2	37.5	32.3	44.8	10.4	33.3	42.0	17.9
1967	63.8	83.5	30.7	79.1	104.7	40.4	40.0	55.8	12.4	35.0	43.8	19.4
1968	66.2	87.2	30.9	81.0	106.5	42.4	42.8	61.6	10.3	37.4	46.5	21.3
1969	65.4	84.4	33.5	81.8	106.8	44.0	40.1	54.9	13.8	39.7	48.6	23.7
1970	61.7	77.6	34.6	79.2	101.4	45.5	34.9	46.5	14.0	42.0	50.7	26.1
1971	59.1	71.9	37.2	76.3	95.3	47.4	32.9	41.0	17.3	44.2	52.8	28.5
1972	58.0	68.0	40.6	73.4	89.3	49.1	34.6	40.1	23.0	46.0	54.7	30.3
1973	55.3	63.8	40.5	71.4	85.4	49.9	30.7	35.1	21.4	47.6	56.6	31.2
1974	55.2	62.3	42.9	71.4	83.9	52.3	30.5	33.5	23.7	49.5	58.7	32.6
1975	54.8	60.5	44.6	71.1	82.6	53.6	29.7	31.1	25.6	51.6	60.4	35.3
1976	53.7	58.8	44.7	71.3	81.2	56.2	26.9	28.9	22.1	52.5	61.2	36.4
1977	54.6	59.1	46.7	71.6	80.6	57.9	28.7	30.4	24.2	53.6	62.2	37.7
1978	55.6	59.5	48.7	72.6	80.9	59.9	29.7	30.9	26.0	54.9	63.7	38.7
1979	56.3	59.9	50.0	72.7	80.5	60.9	31.2	32.3	27.6	55.7	64.8	38.7
1980	58.3	61.5	52.6	73.9	81.1	63.0	34.1	35.1	30.7	55.7	65.7	37.3
1981	60.5	64.5	53.2	75.1	83.3	62.8	37.3	38.8	32.6	55.7	65.7	37.5
1982	62.3	67.9	52.0	76.5	85.5	62.8	39.5	43.5	29.5	56.7	66.2	39.1
1983	65.3	70.8	55.5	78.4	87.8	64.1	43.8	46.8	35.9	57.6	65.9	41.8
1984	66.1	72.7	53.9	80.5	90.7	64.8	42.7	47.5	30.9	58.7	66.3	44.0
1985	69.5	76.4	56.8	83.0	94.3	65.6	47.1	51.1	36.9	61.3	68.2	47.7
1986	72.7	80.4	58.8	85.0	97.4	65.7	51.9	55.9	41.5	64.1	70.2	51.6
1987	74.2	83.2	57.8	87.7	100.9	67.2	51.7	57.8	36.7	65.4	71.6	52.8
1988	74.4	84.9	55.1	89.4	102.5	69.0	49.8	59.6	27.0	67.6	74.1	54.4
1989	76.2	85.3	59.4	90.8	104.1	70.0	52.0	58.5	36.9	70.0	76.3	57.0
1990	77.8	85.9	63.2	92.4	104.8	73.0	53.7	58.7	41.9	72.1	78.6	58.9
1991	78.8	86.8	64.1	92.9	105.2	73.9	55.3	60.5	42.8	73.8	79.7	61.9
1992	77.5	83.3	67.0	91.4	101.7	75.5	54.3	57.0	48.1	75.8	81.0	64.9
1993	75.4	80.5	66.1	89.8	98.7	76.3	51.4	54.5	44.1	77.5	82.1	67.8
1994	73.6	77.4	66.9	87.4	95.1	75.6	50.8	52.2	47.4	79.7	83.6	71.6
1995	71.0	73.8	66.1	84.6	91.2	74.5	48.6	49.0	47.6	81.7	85.2	74.5
1996	69.7	72.5	64.8	82.5	88.2	74.1	48.4	50.1	44.4	83.3	86.5	76.5
1997	69.6	71.2	66.6	81.2	85.6	74.6	50.1	50.6	48.9	85.7	88.2	80.3
1998	68.4	69.3	66.9	80.3	83.2	75.9	48.5	49.2	47.0	89.0	90.1	86.6
1999	69.0	70.2	66.7	79.7	81.4	77.1	51.0	54.0	43.9	92.0	91.6	92.9
2000	69.5	69.4	69.7	80.1	80.5	79.6	51.7	53.3	47.8	94.5	93.6	96.6
2001	72.2	71.5	73.3	80.3	80.3	80.4	58.3	58.6	57.4	98.1	95.8	103.4
2002	76.5	75.6	78.0	81.8	81.5	82.2	67.3	66.7	68.7	100.7	97.7	107.4
2003	81.5	81.6	81.3	83.9	83.7	84.3	77.2	78.4	74.5	100.1	98.3	104.1
2004	84.6	85.5	83.2	85.1	85.5	84.6	83.8	85.4	79.9	100.4	98.6	104.2
2005	86.1	86.6	85.0	86.2	86.7	85.4	85.7	86.4	84.2	101.0	99.4	104.6
2006	87.4	87.6	87.2	86.9	87.1	86.5	88.4	88.2	88.8	102.1	100.2	106.2
2007	88.3	89.1	86.9	88.1	88.2	87.9	88.7	90.5	84.6	103.6	101.6	107.8
2008	93.8	94.8	91.9	91.4	91.6	91.0	98.1	99.7	94.2	103.6	103.0	105.0
2009	100.1	100.6	99.1	95.9	96.5	94.9	107.3	106.7	108.7	105.9	103.4	111.5
2010	104.2	104.1	104.4	99.2	99.6	98.5	113.0	111.0	117.8	103.9	102.5	106.8
2011	101.7	102.9	99.7	100.1	100.9	98.8	104.6	105.8	101.8	101.2	101.3	101.1
2012	100.0	100.0	100.0	100.0	100.0	100.0	100.0	100.0	100.0	100.0	100.0	100.0
2013	95.0	93.7	97.4	98.2	97.8	99.0	89.4	87.5	93.8	100.4	99.9	101.4
2014	93.0	90.5	97.6	97.5	96.1	99.7	85.3	82.1	92.8	100.9	99.9	103.0
2015	92.8	88.5	100.5	96.8	94.1	101.1	85.8	80.0	99.4	103.9	100.7	111.4
2016	93.3	88.3	102.2	97.3	93.5	103.1	86.4	80.5	100.2	106.8	101.8	118.3
2017	92.9	88.5	100.9	97.4	93.1	104.0	85.1	81.5	93.7	107.6	102.8	118.7
2018	95.1	91.0	102.5	97.9	93.6	104.6	90.4	87.3	97.9	108.5	103.7	119.8
2019	98.5	95.4	104.1	98.9	94.6	105.6	98.1	97.0	100.8	109.7	104.8	121.1
2020	102.9	97.2	113.0	101.6	96.4	109.8	105.6	98.9	121.0	108.1	103.3	119.4
2018												
1st quarter	93.8	89.0	102.4	97.5	93.2	104.3	87.4	82.7	98.3	108.1	103.3	119.1
2nd quarter	95.1	91.0	102.6	97.9	93.5	104.8	90.5	87.5	97.7	108.4	103.6	119.5
3rd quarter	95.6	91.5	103.0	98.2	93.7	105.1	91.3	88.4	98.2	108.7	103.8	120.0
4th quarter	95.8	92.4	102.0	97.8	93.8	104.1	92.5	90.6	97.2	108.9	103.8	120.6
2019												
1st quarter	96.0	93.9	100.0	97.1	94.2	101.6	94.6	94.0	96.4	109.1	103.9	121.2
2nd quarter	98.8	95.3	105.1	99.1	94.4	106.4	98.6	97.3	102.0	109.4	104.2	121.4
3rd quarter	99.3	95.8	105.6	99.6	94.7	107.2	99.1	97.9	102.0	109.8	105.0	121.1
4th quarter	99.8	96.5	105.8	99.9	95.2	107.1	100.0	98.9	102.8	110.4	106.0	120.4
2020												
1st quarter	100.2	96.5	106.9	100.4	95.5	108.0	100.3	98.6	104.7	110.2	105.8	120.4
2nd quarter	105.6	96.7	121.3	101.3	96.5	108.8	113.9	97.3	151.6	106.0	101.3	116.9
3rd quarter	103.3	97.3	113.9	102.6	96.6	111.9	105.0	99.0	119.0	108.1	103.3	119.2
4th quarter	102.4	98.2	109.8	102.2	96.8	110.4	103.2	100.9	108.8	108.2	102.7	121.1

[1] Includes general government intermediate inputs for goods and services sold to other sectors and for own-account investment.

Table 6-17. Government Employment

(Calendar years, payroll employment in thousands.)

Year and month	Total government employment	Federal			State			Local		
		Total	Department of Defense	Postal Service	Total	Education	State government hospitals	Total	Education	Local government hospitals
1950	6 120	2 023	533	516	. . .	. . .	. . .	. . .	. . .	. . .
1951	6 502	2 415	797	521	. . .	. . .	. . .	. . .	. . .	. . .
1952	6 727	2 539	868	542	. . .	. . .	. . .	. . .	. . .	. . .
1953	6 758	2 418	818	530	. . .	. . .	. . .	. . .	. . .	. . .
1954	6 858	2 295	744	533	. . .	. . .	. . .	. . .	. . .	. . .
1955	7 021	2 295	744	534	1 168	308	. . .	3 558	1 751	. . .
1956	7 386	2 318	749	539	1 249	334	. . .	3 819	1 884	. . .
1957	7 724	2 326	729	555	1 328	363	. . .	4 071	2 026	. . .
1958	7 946	2 298	695	567	1 415	389	. . .	4 232	2 115	. . .
1959	8 192	2 342	699	578	1 484	420	. . .	4 366	2 198	. . .
1960	8 464	2 381	681	591	1 536	448	. . .	4 547	2 314	. . .
1961	8 706	2 391	683	601	1 607	474	. . .	4 708	2 411	. . .
1962	9 004	2 455	697	601	1 669	511	. . .	4 881	2 522	. . .
1963	9 341	2 473	687	603	1 747	557	. . .	5 121	2 674	. . .
1964	9 711	2 463	676	604	1 856	609	. . .	5 392	2 839	. . .
1965	10 191	2 495	679	619	1 996	679	. . .	5 700	3 031	. . .
1966	10 910	2 690	741	686	2 141	775	. . .	6 080	3 297	. . .
1967	11 525	2 852	802	719	2 302	873	. . .	6 371	3 490	. . .
1968	11 972	2 871	801	729	2 442	958	. . .	6 660	3 649	. . .
1969	12 330	2 893	815	737	2 533	1 042	. . .	6 904	3 785	. . .
1970	12 687	2 865	756	741	2 664	1 104	. . .	7 158	3 912	. . .
1971	13 012	2 828	731	731	2 747	1 149	. . .	7 437	4 091	. . .
1972	13 465	2 815	720	703	2 859	1 188	459	7 790	4 262	467
1973	13 862	2 794	696	698	2 923	1 205	472	8 146	4 433	477
1974	14 303	2 858	698	710	3 039	1 267	483	8 407	4 584	483
1975	14 820	2 882	704	699	3 179	1 323	503	8 758	4 722	489
1976	15 001	2 863	693	676	3 273	1 371	518	8 865	4 786	492
1977	15 258	2 859	676	657	3 377	1 385	538	9 023	4 859	494
1978	15 812	2 893	661	660	3 474	1 367	541	9 446	4 958	535
1979	16 068	2 894	649	673	3 541	1 378	538	9 633	4 989	571
1980	16 375	3 000	645	673	3 610	1 398	530	9 765	5 090	604
1981	16 180	2 922	655	675	3 640	1 420	515	9 619	5 095	622
1982	15 982	2 884	690	684	3 640	1 433	494	9 458	5 049	635
1983	16 011	2 915	699	685	3 662	1 450	471	9 434	5 020	644
1984	16 159	2 943	716	706	3 734	1 488	459	9 482	5 076	623
1985	16 533	3 014	738	750	3 832	1 540	449	9 687	5 221	608
1986	16 838	3 044	736	792	3 893	1 561	438	9 901	5 358	601
1987	17 156	3 089	736	815	3 967	1 586	439	10 100	5 469	606
1988	17 540	3 124	719	835	4 076	1 621	446	10 339	5 590	619
1989	17 927	3 136	735	838	4 182	1 668	442	10 609	5 740	632
1990	18 415	3 196	722	825	4 305	1 730	426	10 914	5 902	646
1991	18 545	3 110	702	813	4 355	1 768	417	11 081	5 994	653
1992	18 787	3 111	702	800	4 408	1 799	419	11 267	6 076	665
1993	18 989	3 063	670	793	4 488	1 834	414	11 438	6 206	673
1994	19 275	3 018	657	821	4 576	1 882	407	11 682	6 329	673
1995	19 432	2 949	627	850	4 635	1 919	395	11 849	6 453	669
1996	19 539	2 877	597	867	4 606	1 911	376	12 056	6 592	648
1997	19 664	2 806	588	866	4 582	1 904	360	12 276	6 759	632
1998	19 909	2 772	550	881	4 612	1 922	346	12 525	6 921	630
1999	20 307	2 769	525	890	4 709	1 983	344	12 829	7 120	626
2000	20 790	2 865	510	880	4 786	2 031	343	13 139	7 294	622
2001	21 118	2 764	504	873	4 905	2 113	345	13 449	7 479	628
2002	21 513	2 766	499	842	5 029	2 243	349	13 718	7 654	642
2003	21 583	2 761	486	809	5 002	2 255	348	13 820	7 709	651
2004	21 621	2 730	473	782	4 982	2 238	348	13 909	7 765	656
2005	21 804	2 732	488	774	5 032	2 260	350	14 041	7 856	655
2006	21 974	2 732	493	770	5 075	2 293	357	14 167	7 913	647
2007	22 218	2 734	491	769	5 122	2 318	360	14 362	7 987	654
2008	22 509	2 762	496	747	5 177	2 354	361	14 571	8 084	659
2009	22 555	2 832	519	703	5 169	2 360	359	14 554	8 079	661
2010	22 490	2 977	545	659	5 137	2 373	354	14 376	8 013	650
2011	22 086	2 859	559	631	5 078	2 374	348	14 150	7 873	648
2012	21 920	2 820	552	611	5 055	2 389	349	14 045	7 778	647
2013	21 853	2 769	537	595	5 046	2 393	350	14 037	7 777	646
2014	21 882	2 733	524	593	5 050	2 389	347	14 098	7 815	642
2015	22 029	2 757	526	597	5 077	2 401	354	14 195	7 871	648
2016	22 224	2 795	529	609	5 110	2 429	367	14 319	7 905	658
2017	22 350	2 805	527	615	5 165	2 479	376	14 379	7 922	667
2018	22 455	2 800	530	608	5 173	2 487	381	14 481	7 963	674
2019	22 613	2 831	544	607	5 206	2 515	387	14 576	8 001	682
2020	21 909	2 929	560	602	5 074	2 380	397	13 906	7 574	683

. . . = Not available.

NOTES AND DEFINITIONS, CHAPTER 6

TABLES 6-1 THROUGH 6-11 AND 6-16

Federal, State, and Local Government in the National Income and Product Accounts

SOURCE: U.S. DEPARTMENT OF COMMERCE, BUREAU OF ECONOMIC ANALYSIS (BEA)

These data are from the national income and product accounts (NIPAs), as redefined in the 2018 comprehensive NIPA revision and updated in the 2021 annual revision. For general information about the NIPAs see the notes and definitions for Chapter 1.

The 2021 annual update of the National Income and Product Accounts was released on July 29, 2021. The reference year remained 2012.

The framework for the government accounts

In an earlier major revision in 2003, a new framework was introduced for government consumption expenditures—federal, state, and local—that explicitly recognizes the services produced by general government. Governments serve several functions in the economy. Three of these functions are recognized in the NIPAs: the production of nonmarket services; the consumption of these services, as the value of services provided to the general public is treated as government consumption expenditures; and the provision of transfer payments. These functions are financed through taxation, through contributions to social insurance funds, and by borrowing in the world's capital markets.

In this framework, the value of the government services produced and consumed (most of which are not sold in the market) is measured as the sum of the costs of the three major inputs: compensation of government employees, consumption of fixed capital (CFC), and intermediate goods and services purchased. The purchase from the private sector of goods and services by government, classified as final sales to government before the 2003 revision, was reclassified as intermediate purchases.

The value of government final purchases of consumption expenditures and gross investment, which constitutes the contribution of government demand to the gross domestic product (GDP), was not changed by this reclassification, since the previous definition of that contribution was the sum of compensation, CFC, and goods and services purchased. However, the distribution of GDP by type of product was changed—final sales of goods were reduced by the amount of goods purchased by government, and final sales of services were increased by the same amount.

In addition to this change in the conceptual framework, a number of the categories of government receipts and expenditures were redefined to make more precise distinctions. For example, items that used to be called "nontax payments" and included with taxes are now classified as transfer or fee payments and not included in taxes.

Finally, the concept previously known as "current surplus or deficit (-), national income and product accounts" was renamed "net government saving." This recognizes, in part, the role of government in the capital markets. When government runs a current surplus, net government saving is positive and funds are made available (for example, by retiring outstanding government debt) to finance investment—both private-sector capital spending and government investment. By the same token, when government runs a current deficit, or "dis-saves," it must borrow funds that would otherwise be available to finance investment.

However, this definition of net government saving does not give a complete picture of governments' role in capital markets, because it is based on current receipts and expenditures alone and does not include government investment activity.

In the NIPAs, the capital spending of all levels of government is treated the same way as the accounts treat private investment spending. A depreciation, or more precisely "consumption of fixed capital" (CFC), entry for existing capital is calculated, using estimated replacement costs and realistic depreciation rates. In the government accounts this CFC value is entered as one element of current expenditures and output. Capital spending is excluded from government current expenditures but appears in the account for "net lending or borrowing (-)."

The basic concept expressed in the net lending section of the NIPAs is that when CFC exceeds actual investment expenditures, governments have a positive net cash flow and can lend (or repay debt); if gross investment exceeds CFC, government must borrow to finance the difference, indicating negative net cash flow and requiring borrowing. (As will be seen below in the definitions, capital transfer and purchase accounts also enter into the calculation of net lending.)

The federal *budget* accounts (see Tables 6-1 and 6-2) do not draw a distinction between current and capital spending. The budget accounts of individual state and local governments typically separate capital from current spending and allow capital spending to be financed by borrowing—even when deficit financing of current spending is constitutionally forbidden. However, neither federal nor state and local government budget accounts typically show depreciation as a current expense in the way that is standard to private-sector accounting or in the way adopted in the NIPAs.

Notes on the data

Government receipts and expenditures data are derived from the U.S. government accounts and from Census Bureau censuses and surveys of the finances of state and local governments. However, BEA makes a number of adjustments to the data to convert them from fiscal year to calendar year and quarter bases and to agree with the concepts of national income accounting. Data are converted from the cash basis usually found in financial statements to the timing bases required for the NIPAs. In the NIPAs, receipts from businesses are generally on an accrual basis, purchases of goods and services are recorded when delivered, and receipts from and transfer payments to persons are on a cash basis. The federal receipts and expenditure data from the NIPAs in Table 6-1 therefore differ from the federal receipts and outlay data in Table 6-14. Among other differences, the latter are by fiscal year and are on a modified cash basis.

The NIPA data on government receipts and expenditures record transactions of governments (federal, state, and local) with other U.S. residents and foreigners. Each entry in the government receipts and expenditures account has a corresponding entry elsewhere in the NIPAs. Thus, for example, the sum of personal current taxes received by federal and state and local governments (Tables 6-1 and 6-8) is equal to personal current taxes paid, as shown in personal income (Table 4-1).

Definitions: general

In the 2003 revision of the NIPAs, several items appear separately that were previously treated as "negative expenditures" and netted against other items on the expenditures side. This grossing-up of the accounts raises both receipts and outlays and has no effect on net saving. Grossing-up has been applied to taxes from the rest of the world, interest receipts (back to 1960 for the federal government and back to 1946 for state and local governments), dividends, and subsidies and the current surplus of government enterprises (back to 1959).

Definitions: current receipts

Current tax receipts includes personal current taxes, taxes on production and imports, taxes on corporate income and (for the federal government only) taxes from the rest of the world. The category *total tax receipts* does not include *contributions for government social insurance*, which are the taxes levied to finance Social Security, unemployment insurance, and Medicare, and are included in *receipts* in the budget accounts (Table 6-14). Analysts using NIPA data to analyze tax burdens as they are usually understood should add *contributions for government social insurance* to *tax receipts* for this purpose.

Personal current taxes is personal tax payments from residents of the United States that are not chargeable to business expense. Personal taxes consist of taxes on income, including on realized net capital gains, and on personal property. Personal contributions for social insurance are not included in this category. As of the 1999 revisions, estate and gift taxes are classified as capital transfers and are no longer included in personal current taxes. However, estate and gift taxes continue to be included in federal government receipts in Table 6-14.

Taxes on production and imports in the case of the federal government consists of *excise taxes* and *customs duties*. In the case of state and local governments, these taxes include *sales taxes*, *property taxes* (including residential real estate taxes), and *Other* taxes such as motor vehicle licenses, severance taxes, and special assessments. Before the 2003 revision, all of these taxes were components of "indirect business tax and nontax liabilities."

Taxes on corporate income covers federal, state, and local government taxes on all corporate income subject to taxes. This taxable income includes capital gains and other income excluded from NIPA profits. The taxes are measured on an accrual basis, net of applicable tax credits. Federal corporate income tax receipts in the NIPAs include, but show separately, receipts from *Federal Reserve Banks* that represent the return of the surplus earnings of the Federal Reserve system. (In the budget accounts in Table 6-14, these are classified not as corporate taxes but as the major component of "Miscellaneous receipts.")

Contributions for social insurance includes employer and personal contributions for Social Security, Medicare, unemployment insurance, and other government social insurance programs. As of the 1999 revisions, contributions to government employee retirement plans are no longer included in this category; these plans are now treated the same as private pension plans.

Income receipts on assets consists of *interest*, *dividends* and *rents and royalties*.

Interest receipts (1960 to the present for federal government; 1946 to the present for state and local governments) consists of monetary and imputed interest received on loans and investments. In the NIPAs, this no longer includes interest received by government employee retirement plans, which is now credited to personal income. However, such interest received is still deducted from interest paid in the budget accounts that are shown in Table 6-14. Before the indicated years, receipts are deducted from aggregate interest payments in the NIPAs. Hence, they are not shown as receipts, and net interest is presented on the expenditure side. In the federal budget accounts in Table 6-14, net interest (total interest expenditures minus interest receipts) is the interest "expenditure" concept used throughout the period covered.

Current transfer receipts include receipts in categories other than those specified above from persons and business. In the case of state and local government accounts (Table 6-8), it also includes *federal grants-in-aid,* a component of federal expenditures. Receipts from *business* and *persons* were previously included with income taxes in "tax and nontax payments." They consist of federal deposit insurance premiums and other nontaxes (largely fines and regulatory and inspection fees), state and local fines and other nontaxes (largely donations and tobacco settlements), and net insurance settlements paid to governments as policyholders.

The *current surplus of government enterprises* is the current operating revenue and subsidies received from other levels of government by such enterprises less their current expenses. No deduction is made for depreciation charges or net interest paid. Before 1959, this category of receipts is treated as a deduction from subsidies. In the federal NIPA accounts before 1959, there is no entry shown for the current surplus on the receipts side, and on the expenditure side, there is an entry for subsidies, which is net of the current surplus. (Subsidies are usually a larger amount than the enterprise surplus in the federal accounts.) In the state and local NIPA accounts before 1959, there is an entry for the surplus on the receipts side, which is net of subsidies. (Subsidies are typically smaller than the enterprise surplus in state and local finance.)

Definitions: consumption expenditures, saving, and gross investment

Government consumption expenditures is expenditures by governments (federal or state and local) on services for current consumption. It includes *compensation of general government employees* (including employer contributions to government employee retirement plans, as of the 1999 revision); an allowance for *consumption of general government fixed capital (CFC),* including R&D and software (depreciation); and *intermediate goods and services purchased.* (See the general discussion above for an explanation.) The estimated value of *own-account investment*—investment goods, including R&D and software, produced by government resources and purchased inputs—is subtracted here, and added to *government gross investment. Sales to other sectors*—primarily tuition payments received from individuals for higher education and charges for medical care to individuals—are also deducted, since these are counted elsewhere in the accounts, as (for example) personal consumption expenditures for those categories.

Government social benefits consists of payments to individuals for which the individuals do not render current services. Examples are Social Security benefits, Medicare, Medicaid, unemployment benefits, and public assistance. Retirement payments to retired government employees from their pension plans are no longer included in this category.

Government social benefits to persons consists of payments to persons residing in the United States (with a corresponding entry of an equal amount in the personal income receipts accounts). Government social benefits to the *rest of the world* appear only in the federal government account, and are transfers, mainly retirement benefits, to former residents of the United States.

Other current transfer payments (federal account only) includes *grants-in-aid to state and local governments* and *grants to the rest of the world*—military and nonmilitary grants to foreign governments.

Federal grants-in-aid comprises net payments from federal to state and local governments that are made to help finance programs such as health (Medicaid), public assistance (the old Aid to Families with Dependent Children and the new Temporary Assistance for Needy Families), and education. Investment grants to state and local governments for highways, transit, air transportation, and water treatment plants are now classified as capital transfers and are no longer included in this category. However, such investment grants continue to be included as federal government outlays in Table 6-14.

Interest payments is monetary interest paid to U.S. and foreign persons and businesses and to foreign governments for public debt and other financial obligations. As noted above, from 1960 forward for the federal government and from 1946 forward for state and local governments, this represents gross total (not net) interest payments. Before those dates in the NIPAs, and throughout the federal budget accounts presented in Table 6-14, net instead of aggregate interest is shown; that is, gross total interest paid less interest received.

Subsidies are monetary grants paid by government to business, including to government enterprises at another level of government. Subsidies no longer include federal maritime construction subsidies, which are now classified as a capital transfer. For years prior to 1959, subsidies continue to be presented net of the *current surplus of government enterprises,* because detailed data to separate the series are not available for this period. See the entry for *current surplus of government enterprises,* described above, for explanation of the pre-1959 treatment of this item in the federal accounts in *Business Statistics,* which differs from the treatment in the state and local accounts.

Net saving, NIPA (surplus+/deficit-), is the sum of current receipts less the sum of current expenditures. This is shown separately for *social insurance funds* (which, in the case of the federal government, include Social Security and other trust funds) and *other* (all other government).

Gross government investment consists of general government and government enterprise expenditures for fixed assets—*structures, equipment*, and *intellectual property* (R&D and software). The expenditures include the compensation of government employees producing the assets and the purchase of goods and services as intermediate inputs to be incorporated in the assets. Government inventory investment is included in government consumption expenditures.

Capital consumption. Consumption of fixed capital (CFC; economic depreciation) is included in government consumption expenditures as a partial measure of the value of the services of general government fixed assets, including structures, equipment, R&D, and software.

Definitions: output, lending and borrowing, and net investment

In Tables 6-5 and 6-10, current-dollar values of gross output and value added of government are presented, as described in the general discussion above. *Gross output* of government is the sum of the *intermediate goods and services purchased* by government and the value added by government as a producing industry. *Value added* consists of compensation of general government employees and consumption of general government fixed capital. Since this depreciation allowance is the only entry on the product side of the accounts measuring the output associated with such capital, a zero <u>net</u> return on these assets is implicitly assumed.

Gross output minus own-account investment and sales to other sectors (see the previous description) yields *government consumption expenditures*, which represents the contribution of government consumption spending to final demands in GDP.

Net lending (net borrowing -) consists of current *net saving* as defined above, plus the *consumption of fixed capital* (CFC, from the current expenditure account), minus *gross investment*, plus *capital transfer receipts*, and minus *capital transfer payments* and *net purchases of non-produced assets*. (If this definition sounds somehow counter-intuitive, it should be remembered that "subtraction" in this context means "increasing the deficit [negative value] which must be financed.)

Capital transfer receipts and *payments* include grants between levels of government, or between government and the private sector, associated with acquisition or disposal of assets rather than with current consumption expenditures. Examples are federal grants to state and local government for highways, transit, air transportation, and water treatment plants; federal shipbuilding subsidies and other subsidies to businesses; and lump-sum payments to amortize the unfunded liability of the Uniformed Services Retiree Health Care Fund. Government capital transfer receipts include estate and gift taxes, which are

no longer included in personal tax receipts. (Federal estate and gift taxes are shown in Table 6-14, where they are reported on a fiscal year basis, and are similar in order of magnitude to the calendar year values for federal capital transfer receipts in Table 6-5.)

Non-produced assets are land and radio spectrum. Unusually large negative entries for net purchases of non-produced assets in some recent years result from the negative purchase–that is, the sale–of spectrum.

The values of *net investment* shown in these tables are calculated by the editor, as gross investment minus the consumption of fixed capital.

Definitions: chain-type quantity indexes

Chain-type quantity indexes represent changes over time in real values, removing the effects of inflation. Indexes for key categories in the government expenditure accounts, as well as for government gross output, value added, and intermediate goods and services purchased, use the chain formula described in the notes and definitions for Chapter 1 and are expressed as index numbers, with the average for the year 2012 equal to 100.

Data availability

The most recent data are published each month in the *Survey of Current Business.* Current and historical data may be obtained from the BEA Web site at <https://www.bea.gov>.

References

See the references regarding the 2018 comprehensive revision of the NIPAs in the notes and definitions for Chapter 1. NIPA concepts and their differences from the budget estimates are discussed in "NIPA Estimates of the Federal Sector and the Federal Budget Estimates," *Survey of Current Business,* March 2007, p. 11.

For information about the classification of government expenditures into current consumption and gross investment, first undertaken in the 1996 comprehensive revisions, see the *Survey of Current Business* article, "Preview of the Comprehensive Revision of the National Income and Product Accounts: Recognition of Government Investment and Incorporation of a New Methodology for Calculating Depreciation" September 1995. Other sources of information about the NIPAs are listed in the notes and definitions for Chapter 1.

Tables 6-12 and 6-13

State Government Current Receipts and Expenditures; Local Government Current Receipts and Expenditures

SOURCE: BUREAU OF ECONOMIC ANALYSIS (BEA)

In the standard presentation of the state and local sector of the national income and product accounts (NIPAs) such as in Tables 6-8 through 6-11 above, state and local governments are combined. Annual measures for aggregate state governments and aggregate local governments are also available on the BEA Web site. These measures are shown in Tables 6-12 and 6-13. The definitions are the same as in the other NIPA tables described above.

The data shown here now reflect the 2013 comprehensive revision, affecting some concepts, that has been incorporated in the quarterly and annual data elsewhere in this chapter and this volume.

Two categories not shown in Table 6-8 appear in each table, detailing inter-governmental flows that are consolidated in Table 6-8. State government receipts include not only *federal grants-in-aid* but also *local grants-in-aid*, and state government expenditures include *grants-in-aid to local governments*. Local government receipts include not only *federal grants-in-aid* but also *state grants-in-aid*, and local government expenditures include *grants-in-aid to state governments*. To make room for these columns, the components *current surplus of government enterprises* and *subsidies* are not shown, though they are included in total current receipts and total current expenditures respectively.

These measures are described in "Receipts and Expenditures of State Governments and of Local Governments," *Survey of Current Business*, October 2005. Data back to 1959 are available on the BEA Web site at <https://www.bea.gov>.

Tables 6-14A and 6-14B

Federal Government Receipts and Outlays by Fiscal Year; The Federal Budget and GDP

SOURCE: U.S. OFFICE OF MANAGEMENT AND BUDGET

These data on federal government receipts and outlays are on a modified cash basis and are from the *Budget of the United States Government: Historical Tables*. The data are by federal fiscal years, which are defined as July 1 through June 30 through 1976 and October 1 through September 30 for 1977 and subsequent years. They are identified by the year of the final fiscal quarter—i.e., the year from July 1, 1975, through June 30, 1976, is identified as Fiscal 1976, and the year from October 1, 1976, through June 30, 1977, is identified as Fiscal Year 1977. The period July 1 through September 30, 1976, is a separate fiscal period known as the transition quarter (TQ) and is not included in any fiscal year.

There are numerous differences in both timing and definition between these estimates and the NIPA estimates in Tables 6-1 through 6-7. See the notes and definitions for those tables for the definitional differences that were introduced with the 1999 comprehensive revision of the NIPAs.

Definitions

The definitions for these tables are not affected by the 2013, 2003, or 1999 changes in the government sectors of the NIPAs.

Table references will be given indicating the source of each item in the *Historical Tables*; for example, "HT Table 1.1."

Receipts consist of gifts and of taxes or other compulsory payments to the government. Other types of payments to the government are netted against outlays. (HT Table 1.1)

Outlays occur when the federal government liquidates an obligation through a cash payment or when interest accrues on public debt issues. Beginning with the data for 1992, outlays include the subsidy cost of direct and guaranteed loans made. Before 1992, the costs and repayments associated with such loans are recorded on a cash basis. As noted previously, various types of nontax receipts are netted against cash outlays. These accounts do not distinguish between investment outlays and current consumption and do not include allowances for depreciation. (HT Table 1.1)

The *total budget surplus (deficit-)* is receipts minus outlays. It is sometimes presented, including in Table 6-14, as composed of two components, *on-budget and off-budget*. By law, two government programs that are included in the federal receipts and outlays totals are "off-budget"—old-age, survivors, and disability insurance (Social Security) and the Postal Service. The former accounts for nearly all of the off-budget activity. The *surplus (deficit-)* not accounted for by these two programs is the on-budget surplus or deficit. The *on-budget deficit* is based on an arbitrary distinction and is not customarily referred to as the *budget deficit,* a term reserved in customary use for the total deficit. (HT Table 1.1)

Sources of financing is the means by which the total deficit is financed or the surplus is distributed. By definition, sources of financing sum to the total deficit or surplus with the sign reversed. The principal source is *borrowing from the public*, shown as a positive number, that is, the increase in the debt held by the public. (This entry is calculated by the editors as the change in the debt held by the public as shown in HT Table 7.1.) When there is a budget surplus, as in fiscal years 1998 to 2001, this provides resources for debt reduction, which is indicated by a minus sign in this column. *Other financing* includes drawdown (or buildup, shown here with a minus sign) in Treasury cash balances, seigniorage on coins, direct and guaranteed loan account cash transactions, and miscellaneous other transactions. Large negative "other financing" in 2008 through 2010 resulted from direct loans and asset purchases under TARP and other emergency financial procedures; in other words, the government borrowed from the public to undertake these loans and asset purchases, but they are not included in budget expenditures or the budget deficit. *Other financing* is calculated by the editors, by reversing the sign of the surplus/deficit—so that the deficit becomes a positive number—and subtracting the value of borrowing from the public.

Some of the categories of *receipts by source* are self-explanatory. *Employment taxes and contributions* includes taxes for old-age, survivors, and disability insurance (Social Security), hospital insurance (Medicare), and railroad retirement funds. *Other retirement contributions* includes the employee share of payments for retirement pensions, mainly those for federal employees. *Excise taxes* includes federal taxes on alcohol, tobacco, telephone service, and transportation fuels, as well as taxes funding smaller programs such as black lung disability and vaccine injury compensation. *Miscellaneous receipts* includes deposits of earnings by the Federal Reserve system and all other receipts. (HT Tables 2.1, 2.4, and 2.5)

Outlays by function presents outlays according to the major purpose of the spending. Functional classifications cut across departmental and agency lines. Most categories of offsetting receipts are netted against cash outlays in the appropriate function, which explains how recorded outlays in *energy* and *commerce and housing credit* (which, as its name suggests, includes loan programs) can be negative. There is also a category of "undistributed offsetting receipts" (not shown), always with a negative sign, that includes proceeds from the sale or lease of assets and payments from federal agencies to federal retirement funds and to the Social Security and Medicare trust funds. Note that *Social Security* is recorded separately from other *income security* outlays, and *Medicare* separately from other *health* outlays. (HT Table 3.1) For further explanation, consult the *Budget of the United States Government.*

In order to provide authoritative comparisons of these budget values with the overall size of the economy, a special calculation of gross domestic product by fiscal year is supplied to the Office of Management and Budget by the BEA, and is shown in Table 6-14B. That table also displays selected budget aggregates in dollar values and as a percent of GDP. (HT Tables 1.2, 1.3, 2.3, and 3.1)

Data availability and references

Definitions, budget concepts, and historical data are from *Budget of the United States Government for Fiscal Year 2015: Historical Tables*, available on the Office of Management and Budget Web site at <https://www.whitehouse.gov/omb/Budget/historicals>

Similarly defined data for the latest month, the year-ago month, and the current and year-ago fiscal year to date are published in the *Monthly Treasury Statement* prepared by the Financial Management Service, U.S. Department of the Treasury.

Table 6-15

Federal Government Debt by Fiscal Year

SOURCE: U.S. OFFICE OF MANAGEMENT AND BUDGET

Debt outstanding at the end of each fiscal year is from the *Budget of the United States Government*. Most securities are recorded at sales price plus amortized discount or less amortized premium.

Definitions

Federal government debt held by the public consists of all federal debt held outside the federal government accounts—by individuals, financial institutions (including the Federal Reserve Banks), and foreign individuals, businesses, and central banks. It does not include federal debt held by federal government trust funds such as the Social Security trust fund. The level and change of the ratio of this debt to the value of gross domestic product (GDP) provide proportional measures of the impact of federal borrowing on credit markets. (HT Table 7.1) This measure of debt held by the public is very similar in concept and scope to the total federal government credit market debt outstanding in the flow-of-funds accounts, shown in *Business Statistics* in Table 12-5; however, it is not identical, being priced somewhat differently, and is shown here in Chapter 6 on a fiscal year rather than calendar year basis.

Gross federal debt—total. This is the total debt owed by the U.S. Treasury. It includes a small amount of matured debt. (HT Table 7.1)

Debt held by Social Security funds is the sum of the end-year trust fund balances for old age and survivors insurance and disability insurance. The separate disability trust fund begins in 1957. (HT Table 13.1)

Debt held by other U.S. government accounts is calculated by the editors by subtracting the Social Security debt holdings from the total debt held by federal government accounts, which is shown in HT Table 7.1. It includes the balances in all the other trust funds, including the Medicare funds, federal employee retirement funds, and the highway trust fund.

Debt held by the Federal Reserve System is the total value of Treasury securities held by the 12 Federal Reserve Banks, which are acquired in open market operations that carry out monetary policy. (HT Table 7.1)

Debt held by private investors is calculated by subtracting the Federal Reserve debt from the total debt held by the public, and is shown as "Debt Held by the Public: Other" in HT Table 7.1.

Debt held by foreign residents is based on surveys by the Treasury Department. (Table 5-7, *Budget of the United States for Fiscal Year 2015: Analytical Perspectives.*)

Debt held by domestic investors is calculated by the editors by subtracting the foreign-held debt from the total debt held by private investors.

The "debt subject to statutory limitation," not shown here, is close to the gross federal debt in concept and size, but there are some relatively minor definitional differences specified by law. The debt limit can only be changed by an Act of Congress. For information about the debt subject to limit and other debt subjects, see the latest *Budget of the United States Government: Historical Statistics* and *Analytical Perspectives.*

Data availability and references

For the end-of-fiscal-year data, see *Historical Tables* and *Analytical Perspectives* in the *Budget of the United States Government*, which is available on the OMB Web site at <https://www.whitehouse.gov/omb/Budget>. In the *Analytical Perspectives,* debt analysis and data are included in the "Economic and Budget Analysis" section.

Recent quarterly data, measured on a somewhat different basis, are found in the *Treasury Bulletin* in the chapter on "Ownership of Federal Securities (OFS)," in Tables OFS-1 and OFS-2. Holdings by Social Security funds are also available in the *Bulletin* in the chapter on "Federal Debt," Table FD-3. The Disability Fund is listed separately from the Old-Age and Survivors Fund.

Table 6-17

Government Employment

SOURCE: U.S. DEPARTMENT OF LABOR, BUREAU OF LABOR STATISTICS (SEE NOTES AND DEFINITIONS FOR TABLE 10-8).

Government payroll employment includes federal, state, and local activities such as legislative, executive, and judicial functions, as well as all governmentowned and governmentoperated business enterprises, establishments, and institutions (arsenals, navy yards, hospitals, etc.), and government force account construction. The figures relate to civilian employment only. The Bureau of Labor Statistics (BLS) considers regular fulltime teachers (private and governmental) to be employed during the summer vacation period, regardless of whether they are specifically paid in those months.

Employment in federal government establishments reflects employee counts as of the pay period containing the 12th of the month. Federal government employment excludes employees of the Central Intelligence Agency and the National Security Agency.

CHAPTER 7: U.S. FOREIGN TRADE AND FINANCE

SECTION 7A: FOREIGN TRANSACTIONS IN THE NATIONAL INCOME AND PRODUCT ACCOUNTS

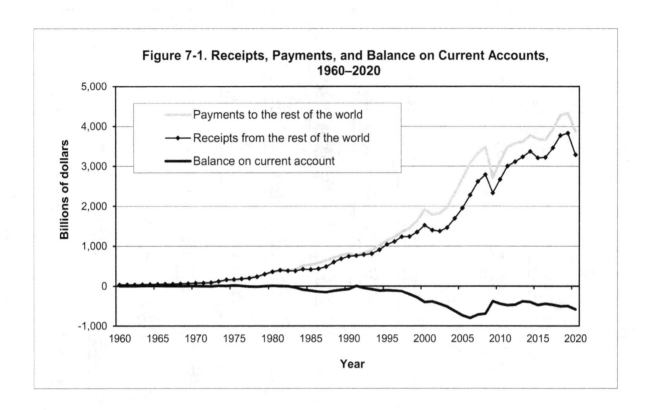

Figure 7-1. Receipts, Payments, and Balance on Current Accounts, 1960–2020

- During the pandemic in 2020, the U.S. economy almost came to a total stop. Stay-at-home orders, closure of businesses, work-from-home options, and closed schools all led to few outside activities. Between 2019 and 2020 total exports and imports of goods and services fell, 15.7 percent and 11 percent respectively. Automobile exports fell 21.4 percent while travel services dropped 63.5 percent due to restricted traveling because of COVID-19. Imports of petroleum and products declined 39.6 percent between 2019 and 2020. Imports of travel services, which includes foreign persons traveling to the U.S. declined by 73.1 percent. (See Table 7-4.)

- Beginning in 1983, chronic current-account deficits in U.S. transactions with the rest of the world have emerged and increased, requiring increasing net capital inflows from abroad to finance them. The only current-account surplus since then occurred in 1991, when payments from other countries financed most of the cost of the first Gulf War.

- Table 7-4 lists the exports and imports of major categories for goods and services. In 2020, the largest exports of goods were capital goods, except automotive ($460.5 billion) and industrial supplies and materials ($450.4 billion).

- The term "services" refers to an expanding range of economic activities, such as audiovisual, computer and related services, express delivery, telecommunications, e-commerce, financial, professional (such as accounting and legal services), retail and wholesaling, transportation, and tourism. (Table 7-4)

Table 7-1. Foreign Transactions in the National Income and Product Accounts

(Billions of dollars, quarterly data are at seasonally adjusted annual rates.)

NIPA Table 4.1

	Current receipts from the rest of the world					Current payments to the rest of the world						Balance on current account, NIPAs	Net lending or net borrowing (-), NIPAs
Year and quarter	Total	Exports of goods and services			Income receipts	Total	Imports of goods and services			Income payments	Current taxes and transfer payments, net		
		Goods [1]		Services [1]			Goods [1]		Services [1]				
		Durable	Nondurable				Durable	Nondurable					
1960	31.9	11.3	9.2	6.6	4.9	28.8	6.4	8.9	7.6	1.8	4.1	3.2	3.2
1961	32.9	11.5	9.4	6.7	5.3	28.7	6.0	9.0	7.6	1.8	4.2	4.2	4.2
1962	35.0	12.0	9.7	7.4	5.9	31.2	6.9	9.9	8.1	1.8	4.4	3.8	3.8
1963	37.6	12.7	10.7	7.7	6.5	32.7	7.4	10.3	8.4	2.1	4.5	4.9	4.9
1964	42.3	14.7	12.1	8.3	7.2	34.8	8.4	11.0	8.7	2.3	4.4	7.5	7.5
1965	45.0	15.8	12.1	9.2	7.9	38.9	10.4	11.8	9.3	2.6	4.7	6.2	6.2
1966	49.0	17.7	13.4	9.8	8.1	45.2	13.3	13.1	10.7	3.0	5.1	3.8	3.8
1967	52.2	18.6	13.9	10.9	8.7	48.7	14.5	13.2	12.2	3.3	5.5	3.5	3.5
1968	58.0	21.2	14.5	12.2	10.1	56.5	18.8	15.1	12.6	4.0	5.9	1.5	1.5
1969	63.7	23.9	14.8	13.2	11.8	62.1	20.8	16.1	13.7	5.7	5.9	1.6	1.6
1970	72.5	27.4	17.7	14.7	12.8	68.8	22.8	18.1	14.9	6.4	6.6	3.7	3.7
1971	77.0	27.9	18.3	16.8	14.0	76.7	26.6	19.9	15.8	6.4	7.9	0.3	0.3
1972	87.1	31.4	21.2	18.3	16.3	91.2	33.3	23.6	17.3	7.7	9.2	-4.0	-4.1
1973	118.8	42.3	33.5	19.5	23.5	109.9	40.8	31.0	19.3	10.9	7.9	8.9	8.8
1974	156.5	57.7	45.8	23.2	29.8	150.5	50.3	54.2	22.9	14.3	8.7	6.0	5.9
1975	166.7	65.2	47.3	26.2	28.0	146.9	45.6	53.4	23.7	15.0	9.1	19.8	19.8
1976	181.9	70.9	50.6	28.0	32.4	174.8	56.8	67.8	26.5	15.5	8.1	7.1	7.0
1977	196.5	74.4	54.0	30.9	37.2	207.5	69.2	83.4	29.8	16.9	8.1	-10.9	-11.0
1978	233.1	87.5	62.4	37.0	46.3	245.8	89.0	88.4	34.8	24.7	8.8	-12.6	-12.7
1979	298.5	109.6	77.6	42.9	68.3	299.6	100.4	112.3	39.9	36.4	10.6	-1.2	-1.3
1980	359.9	135.7	94.8	50.3	79.1	351.4	111.9	136.6	45.3	44.9	12.6	8.5	8.4
1981	397.3	143.2	102.0	60.0	92.0	393.9	126.0	141.8	49.9	59.1	17.0	3.4	3.3
1982	384.2	128.4	94.1	60.7	101.0	387.5	125.1	125.4	52.6	64.5	19.8	-3.3	-3.4
1983	378.9	123.8	90.3	62.9	101.9	413.9	147.3	125.4	56.0	64.8	20.5	-35.1	-35.2
1984	424.2	135.2	96.1	71.1	121.9	514.3	192.4	143.9	68.8	85.6	23.6	-90.1	-90.2
1985	415.9	139.9	87.6	75.7	112.7	530.2	204.2	139.1	73.9	87.3	25.7	-114.3	-114.5
1986	432.3	145.3	86.1	89.6	111.3	575.0	238.8	131.2	82.9	94.4	27.8	-142.7	-142.8
1987	487.2	166.9	98.6	98.4	123.3	641.3	264.2	150.6	93.9	105.8	26.8	-154.1	-154.2
1988	596.7	211.9	120.1	112.5	152.1	712.4	294.8	157.3	101.9	129.5	29.0	-115.7	-115.9
1989	682.0	242.5	132.2	129.5	177.7	774.3	310.3	174.5	106.2	152.9	30.4	-92.4	-92.7
1990	740.7	265.3	138.0	148.6	188.8	815.6	314.5	193.5	121.7	154.2	31.7	-74.9	-82.3
1991	763.3	285.6	144.6	164.8	168.4	755.4	315.5	185.2	122.8	136.8	-4.9	7.9	2.6
1992	785.1	304.2	151.1	177.7	152.1	830.7	346.7	198.2	122.9	121.0	41.9	-45.6	-44.3
1993	810.4	317.9	149.9	187.1	155.6	889.8	386.4	206.4	127.2	124.4	45.4	-79.4	-80.2
1994	905.5	353.8	164.6	202.6	184.5	1 021.1	454.0	222.8	136.6	161.6	46.1	-115.6	-116.9
1995	1 042.6	398.6	193.8	220.4	229.8	1 148.5	510.8	246.7	145.1	201.9	44.1	-105.9	-106.3
1996	1 114.0	426.4	202.4	238.8	246.4	1 229.0	533.4	274.1	156.5	215.5	49.5	-115.0	-115.2
1997	1 233.9	488.4	211.5	253.9	280.1	1 364.0	588.5	297.1	170.1	256.8	51.4	-130.1	-130.6
1998	1 239.8	492.4	200.2	260.4	286.8	1 445.1	637.7	293.0	184.9	269.4	60.0	-205.3	-205.6
1999	1 355.2	508.7	203.0	281.2	324.6	1 631.9	715.8	335.4	201.3	293.7	85.7	-276.6	-283.3
2000	1 527.8	572.3	222.8	301.1	390.6	1 924.7	822.8	428.4	226.0	352.2	95.4	-396.9	-401.4
2001	1 411.6	523.2	216.4	287.2	339.6	1 803.0	757.4	418.8	227.4	289.3	110.2	-391.4	-379.5
2002	1 390.6	489.5	217.1	291.4	335.8	1 846.0	774.0	424.9	238.9	290.0	118.3	-455.4	-459.6
2003	1 478.5	498.0	235.8	301.3	377.4	2 006.2	807.8	491.3	258.1	318.9	130.1	-527.6	-536.4
2004	1 705.6	562.5	265.5	348.4	464.7	2 343.4	937.7	576.0	296.9	388.0	144.9	-637.8	-642.4
2005	1 940.9	626.2	293.2	382.2	569.3	2 692.0	1 027.5	695.2	318.7	494.5	156.1	-751.2	-750.5
2006	2 247.7	711.8	331.3	427.1	702.6	3 067.0	1 131.9	768.7	356.0	656.2	154.2	-819.3	-827.0
2007	2 584.4	779.6	380.2	499.6	850.2	3 325.2	1 175.9	826.8	392.5	754.5	175.5	-740.9	-747.2
2008	2 779.9	825.3	465.7	544.3	855.2	3 484.1	1 162.8	985.9	427.5	710.0	198.0	-704.2	-705.0
2009	2 362.1	667.8	389.6	525.4	689.3	2 745.3	892.7	695.4	413.8	539.0	204.3	-383.1	-389.4
2010	2 714.1	798.1	474.8	584.3	760.0	3 153.8	1 105.6	841.4	442.5	554.3	209.9	-439.8	-447.2
2011	3 049.8	894.8	573.7	647.4	827.9	3 510.1	1 231.9	999.2	464.3	589.9	224.7	-460.3	-469.8
2012	3 161.8	941.7	587.9	688.1	827.4	3 585.8	1 322.3	971.0	476.1	594.7	221.8	-423.9	-423.4
2013	3 265.2	957.7	606.1	723.1	847.2	3 617.2	1 356.4	937.5	472.5	616.9	233.9	-352.1	-359.0
2014	3 404.8	994.0	623.0	760.5	881.6	3 781.0	1 449.2	940.1	498.1	646.4	247.2	-376.2	-383.0
2015	3 267.5	955.2	541.5	772.0	860.8	3 692.2	1 489.7	799.9	505.3	640.4	257.0	-424.7	-433.0
2016	3 272.2	927.3	520.3	784.5	893.5	3 675.9	1 463.7	755.0	519.7	661.5	276.0	-403.7	-410.7
2017	3 582.2	962.5	584.1	837.1	1 032.7	3 955.1	1 562.3	807.6	553.8	738.2	293.3	-372.9	-388.9
2018	3 829.6	1 008.8	660.5	864.2	1 142.1	4 269.9	1 657.3	901.7	570.6	847.9	292.3	-440.3	-445.0
2019	3 844.4	982.6	659.1	878.0	1 160.3	4 324.2	1 629.3	888.6	598.1	893.9	314.3	-479.8	-486.7
2020	3 287.7	825.7	590.9	706.8	992.9	3 874.8	1 506.2	803.0	465.4	770.6	329.6	-587.1	-593.0
2018													
1st quarter	3 763.3	1 636.4	624.9	868.0	1 113.5	4 157.1	1 645.8	882.6	556.1	796.9	275.7	-393.8	-399.6
2nd quarter	3 872.3	1 706.1	686.0	862.2	1 151.1	4 247.5	1 643.5	896.1	568.5	850.4	289.1	-375.2	-387.4
3rd quarter	3 829.7	1 670.4	671.6	863.8	1 134.5	4 316.8	1 666.9	919.7	571.6	863.0	295.6	-487.1	-489.3
4th quarter	3 853.1	1 664.3	659.6	862.8	1 169.3	4 358.2	1 673.1	908.5	586.4	881.5	308.6	-505.0	-503.6
2019													
1st quarter	3 824.1	1 659.2	651.4	865.5	1 140.8	4 341.5	1 665.6	878.6	586.8	888.1	322.4	-517.4	-528.7
2nd quarter	3 878.2	1 648.4	668.5	885.1	1 184.4	4 384.2	1 646.2	917.1	602.5	908.8	309.8	-506.1	-510.0
3rd quarter	3 854.1	1 634.8	660.8	877.4	1 168.8	4 330.7	1 630.5	891.9	603.7	893.0	311.6	-476.6	-480.7
4th quarter	3 821.2	1 624.6	655.9	884.1	1 147.3	4 240.4	1 574.8	867.0	599.3	885.8	313.6	-419.2	-427.4
2020													
1st quarter	3 606.6	1 586.2	649.6	799.3	1 048.9	4 058.6	1 529.7	855.3	542.2	809.0	322.3	-452.0	-463.9
2nd quarter	2 858.7	1 146.3	507.3	661.5	883.5	3 386.5	1 211.4	730.7	404.6	711.5	328.3	-527.8	-532.0
3rd quarter	3 252.4	1 413.0	576.7	666.6	996.1	3 917.1	1 570.5	798.2	436.5	769.2	342.6	-664.8	-667.4
4th quarter	3 433.3	1 520.8	629.8	699.9	1 043.2	4 137.0	1 713.0	827.8	478.3	792.5	325.4	-703.7	-708.7

[1]Exports and imports of certain goods, primarily military equipment purchased and sold by the federal government, are included in services. Beginning with 1986, repairs and alterations of equipment are reclassified from goods to services.

Table 7-2. Chain-Type Quantity Indexes for Exports and Imports of Goods and Services

(Index numbers, 2012 = 100; quarterly indexes are seasonally adjusted.)   **NIPA Table 4.2.3**

Year and quarter	Exports of goods and services					Imports of goods and services				
	Total	Goods [1]			Services [1]	Total	Goods [1]			Services [1]
		Total	Durable	Nondurable			Total	Durable	Nondurable	
1975	12.65	12.74	9.79	21.80	12.30	10.78	9.88	4.85	24.69	15.91
1976	13.20	13.40	9.97	23.97	12.43	12.89	12.11	5.94	30.30	17.00
1977	13.52	13.65	10.00	24.97	12.99	14.30	13.59	6.72	33.74	17.85
1978	14.94	15.07	11.08	27.42	14.45	15.54	14.81	7.76	34.84	19.13
1979	16.42	16.67	12.49	29.51	15.48	15.80	15.06	7.94	35.25	19.39
1980	18.19	18.71	13.97	33.33	16.12	14.75	13.94	8.00	30.34	18.96
1981	18.41	18.59	13.53	34.35	17.69	15.13	14.23	8.67	29.43	20.05
1982	17.00	17.02	11.83	33.48	16.91	14.94	13.87	8.76	27.71	21.11
1983	16.56	16.46	11.54	32.01	16.88	16.83	15.75	10.56	29.51	22.82
1984	17.91	17.63	12.70	33.01	18.87	20.92	19.56	14.05	33.61	28.54
1985	18.51	18.25	13.69	32.15	19.40	22.28	20.79	15.46	34.02	30.71
1986	19.93	19.23	14.51	33.55	22.18	24.18	22.91	16.89	38.03	31.06
1987	22.11	21.58	16.70	36.08	23.86	25.62	23.98	17.64	39.95	34.72
1988	25.70	25.41	20.55	39.39	26.70	26.62	24.96	18.38	41.47	35.89
1989	28.67	28.32	23.36	42.35	29.90	27.79	26.03	19.19	43.16	37.63
1990	31.20	30.75	25.88	44.26	32.75	28.79	26.79	19.70	44.62	40.09
1991	33.26	32.81	27.77	46.72	34.83	28.74	26.91	19.81	44.75	39.05
1992	35.57	35.28	29.99	49.82	36.70	30.76	29.45	21.88	48.16	37.99
1993	36.73	36.43	31.54	49.51	37.92	33.42	32.39	24.48	51.41	39.01
1994	39.97	39.91	35.31	51.80	40.57	37.41	36.72	28.52	55.23	41.08
1995	44.08	44.56	40.32	55.15	43.32	40.40	40.03	31.79	57.49	42.32
1996	47.69	48.52	44.96	57.13	46.03	43.91	43.78	35.20	61.34	44.53
1997	53.37	55.55	53.10	61.06	48.45	49.83	50.09	41.00	67.72	48.41
1998	54.61	56.76	54.79	60.95	49.80	55.65	56.02	46.41	73.91	53.67
1999	57.33	59.14	57.35	62.79	53.30	62.10	63.20	53.10	80.86	56.66
2000	62.10	64.94	64.27	65.50	55.73	70.17	71.45	61.16	88.09	63.84
2001	58.63	60.76	58.80	64.80	53.87	68.45	69.11	57.31	90.39	65.12
2002	57.48	58.66	55.57	65.75	54.89	70.96	71.68	59.74	92.90	67.35
2003	58.69	60.35	57.41	67.02	55.01	74.59	76.05	63.30	98.76	67.59
2004	64.35	65.77	64.02	69.58	61.19	82.79	84.58	72.30	105.16	74.23
2005	68.81	70.78	70.30	71.73	64.46	88.16	90.52	78.82	109.37	77.02
2006	75.33	77.89	78.43	76.67	69.66	93.82	96.02	86.18	110.93	83.41
2007	81.93	83.34	84.52	80.79	78.78	96.23	97.87	88.59	111.70	88.35
2008	86.66	88.22	88.60	87.13	83.19	94.16	94.67	85.77	107.90	91.66
2009	79.47	77.75	73.70	84.93	83.22	82.29	80.02	68.38	98.02	92.71
2010	89.71	89.53	86.92	93.90	90.12	93.13	92.33	84.49	103.46	96.94
2011	96.14	96.20	95.24	97.75	96.01	97.61	97.42	92.47	104.22	98.54
2012	100.00	100.00	100.00	100.00	100.00	100.00	100.00	100.00	100.00	100.00
2013	102.97	102.94	102.21	104.11	103.04	101.21	102.01	104.70	98.34	97.46
2014	106.97	107.53	106.45	109.26	105.79	106.44	107.69	113.99	99.15	100.60
2015	107.26	107.15	104.10	112.35	107.43	111.96	113.92	121.58	103.44	103.06
2016	107.70	107.82	102.97	116.56	107.40	113.58	115.18	123.06	104.38	106.13
2017	112.09	112.28	106.26	123.27	111.68	118.63	120.33	131.70	104.08	110.72
2018	115.24	117.00	109.98	129.86	111.93	123.49	126.42	139.07	108.32	110.68
2019	115.16	116.93	107.10	134.93	111.85	124.91	127.10	139.48	109.36	114.98
2020	99.54	105.05	89.87	133.75	89.70	113.76	119.93	129.42	106.49	89.02
2014										
1st quarter	104.83	104.71	103.82	106.13	105.07	103.86	104.67	108.74	99.11	100.04
2nd quarter	107.10	107.46	106.22	109.44	106.32	106.23	107.60	114.05	98.90	99.83
3rd quarter	107.53	108.52	107.86	109.56	105.45	106.43	107.87	114.86	98.41	99.74
4th quarter	108.42	109.42	107.90	111.90	106.32	109.22	110.61	118.30	100.16	102.78
2015										
1st quarter	107.54	107.30	104.46	112.15	107.94	110.80	112.99	120.28	103.12	100.97
2nd quarter	107.82	108.04	104.98	113.26	107.35	111.62	113.78	121.30	103.54	101.90
3rd quarter	106.92	106.92	104.02	111.86	106.87	112.58	114.61	122.57	103.67	103.42
4th quarter	106.76	106.32	102.94	112.15	107.56	112.82	114.28	122.18	103.43	105.96
2016										
1st quarter	106.45	106.84	101.87	115.89	105.67	112.66	114.23	121.53	104.38	105.36
2nd quarter	107.26	106.83	102.57	114.38	107.98	112.78	114.31	121.90	103.99	105.59
3rd quarter	108.92	108.76	103.35	118.58	109.15	113.60	114.90	123.13	103.52	107.32
4th quarter	108.16	108.85	104.10	117.38	106.81	115.28	117.27	125.66	105.64	106.25
2017										
1st quarter	110.73	111.06	103.95	124.17	110.05	116.95	118.61	128.37	104.81	109.23
2nd quarter	111.17	111.04	104.90	122.26	111.35	118.20	119.64	131.22	103.05	111.32
3rd quarter	111.91	111.60	106.96	119.95	112.44	118.16	119.33	131.08	102.46	112.34
4th quarter	114.54	115.42	109.23	126.72	112.87	121.20	123.74	136.11	105.99	109.98
2018										
1st quarter	115.06	115.88	110.68	125.39	113.48	121.98	125.06	137.62	107.07	108.60
2nd quarter	116.47	119.01	110.92	133.78	111.71	122.42	125.15	137.33	107.71	110.40
3rd quarter	114.65	116.32	108.71	130.25	111.49	124.20	127.36	139.97	109.31	110.48
4th quarter	114.78	116.81	109.59	130.00	111.02	125.38	128.13	141.36	109.19	113.25
2019										
1st quarter	115.68	117.98	109.77	132.97	111.41	125.37	128.14	141.44	109.06	113.24
2nd quarter	115.04	116.44	106.59	134.49	112.41	125.90	128.14	140.71	110.12	115.78
3rd quarter	114.80	116.76	106.16	136.20	111.13	125.57	127.65	139.86	110.17	116.02
4th quarter	115.13	116.53	105.88	136.06	112.44	122.81	124.45	135.93	108.09	114.90
2020										
1st quarter	110.12	115.12	102.06	139.34	101.05	118.58	122.05	131.84	108.26	103.79
2nd quarter	87.61	88.55	70.02	125.07	85.57	98.14	103.05	104.86	101.44	78.29
3rd quarter	97.68	105.17	90.85	131.83	84.49	115.10	123.11	134.62	106.48	83.55
4th quarter	102.77	111.34	96.55	138.78	87.69	123.20	131.49	146.35	109.77	90.47

[1]Exports and imports of certain goods, primarily military equipment purchased and sold by the federal government, are included in services. Beginning with 1986, repairs and alterations of equipment are reclassified from goods to services.

Table 7-3. Chain-Type Price Indexes for Exports and Imports of Goods and Services

(Index numbers, 2012 = 100; quarterly indexes are seasonally adjusted.) NIPA Table 4.2.4

Year and quarter	Exports of goods and services					Imports of goods and services				
	Total	Goods [1]			Services [1]	Total	Goods [1]			Services [1]
		Total	Durable	Nondurable			Total	Durable	Nondurable	
1975	49.39	57.70	31.30	28.79	30.88	41.23	43.88	30.16	15.43	31.29
1976	51.01	59.27	31.27	28.75	32.67	42.47	45.05	29.82	16.12	32.71
1977	53.09	61.47	32.55	29.94	34.50	46.21	49.18	32.56	17.46	35.03
1978	56.32	65.00	34.05	31.33	37.08	49.47	52.45	34.98	17.77	38.22
1979	63.10	73.43	41.28	37.94	40.13	57.93	61.85	41.76	23.94	43.16
1980	69.50	80.46	46.38	42.62	45.24	72.17	78.06	50.46	36.47	50.09
1981	74.65	86.18	48.09	44.20	49.18	76.07	82.43	51.15	40.08	52.26
1982	75.01	85.47	46.62	42.87	51.97	73.51	79.11	49.25	37.26	52.30
1983	75.31	84.98	45.31	41.64	54.04	70.75	75.80	46.63	34.01	51.44
1984	76.02	85.74	46.72	42.94	54.60	70.14	75.28	46.12	33.82	50.56
1985	73.75	81.46	44.85	40.84	56.57	67.84	72.32	43.75	31.76	50.50
1986	72.52	78.67	45.60	37.81	58.50	67.83	70.70	44.98	21.80	55.97
1987	74.12	80.43	49.70	42.55	59.75	71.94	75.73	48.64	24.68	56.76
1988	77.92	85.38	55.83	46.82	61.08	75.38	79.34	57.70	23.42	59.53
1989	79.21	86.48	57.30	47.50	62.77	77.02	81.56	60.98	26.25	59.22
1990	79.66	85.71	57.02	48.31	65.75	79.23	83.06	58.40	29.35	63.66
1991	80.55	85.67	56.51	46.73	68.56	78.57	81.49	56.70	26.37	65.98
1992	80.15	84.34	57.43	44.34	70.17	78.64	81.04	56.77	25.48	67.84
1993	80.28	83.91	60.97	43.24	71.46	78.03	80.13	56.81	24.06	68.41
1994	81.21	84.87	63.22	46.82	72.32	78.77	80.72	58.83	23.49	69.75
1995	83.03	86.89	67.71	54.68	73.68	80.92	82.87	63.38	25.98	71.93
1996	81.92	84.68	65.37	51.82	75.14	79.51	80.77	62.48	28.29	73.73
1997	80.48	82.34	64.78	51.75	75.90	76.75	77.43	63.60	27.22	73.72
1998	78.57	79.74	62.12	48.62	75.74	72.62	72.76	60.61	21.76	72.28
1999	77.97	78.66	60.50	48.31	76.33	73.02	72.80	60.73	24.61	74.54
2000	79.47	80.02	61.99	53.72	78.16	76.22	76.64	64.11	34.93	74.26
2001	78.84	79.56	60.96	51.82	77.11	74.22	74.46	61.96	31.85	73.21
2002	78.20	78.73	61.12	50.18	76.95	73.24	73.10	59.65	30.87	74.27
2003	79.40	79.51	63.82	54.57	79.17	75.45	74.69	61.17	36.57	79.87
2004	82.28	82.32	72.10	60.65	82.24	79.06	78.23	71.96	43.29	83.82
2005	85.13	84.93	78.57	68.84	85.63	83.70	83.18	75.90	55.60	86.72
2006	87.84	87.59	88.36	74.56	88.49	86.91	86.53	83.18	64.09	89.13
2007	91.14	91.00	94.11	80.56	91.50	89.92	89.43	89.50	70.07	92.77
2008	95.41	95.71	97.00	92.74	94.75	98.96	99.23	98.81	95.73	97.80
2009	89.69	88.92	82.75	73.38	91.39	87.99	86.63	83.50	62.43	94.51
2010	93.35	92.97	92.26	85.13	94.20	92.78	92.05	95.39	77.82	96.42
2011	99.24	99.79	102.08	102.30	98.00	99.83	99.91	104.84	98.81	99.39
2012	100.00	100.00	100.00	100.00	100.00	100.00	100.00	100.00	100.00	100.00
2013	100.17	99.31	96.95	98.35	102.10	98.64	98.05	97.83	96.30	101.58
2014	100.17	98.32	95.52	96.50	104.34	97.78	96.72	97.33	93.46	103.20
2015	95.15	91.28	89.75	76.78	103.84	89.73	87.46	88.74	60.91	101.50
2016	93.25	87.82	86.35	68.31	105.40	86.53	83.77	84.71	50.61	100.92
2017	95.92	90.49	89.76	75.95	108.08	88.51	85.76	92.34	58.90	102.84
2018	99.10	93.19	93.02	84.92	112.39	91.18	88.15	98.98	69.56	107.03
2019	98.75	91.82	92.10	79.33	114.39	89.99	86.39	96.95	64.91	108.77
2020	96.19	88.16	93.46	66.48	114.52	88.08	83.96	102.75	52.37	109.82
2014										
1st quarter	100.74	99.48	96.17	101.25	103.57	99.30	98.56	97.03	100.87	103.06
2nd quarter	100.77	99.20	95.89	98.11	104.29	98.45	97.50	97.05	96.53	103.28
3rd quarter	100.52	98.56	95.85	97.03	104.93	97.69	96.56	98.45	92.67	103.49
4th quarter	98.66	96.05	94.15	89.62	104.56	95.66	94.24	96.80	83.76	102.95
2015										
1st quarter	96.17	92.84	92.25	79.25	103.67	91.68	89.71	93.62	66.54	101.87
2nd quarter	95.97	92.37	91.03	80.52	104.07	90.48	88.26	90.06	63.21	101.98
3rd quarter	94.97	90.90	88.80	76.44	104.11	89.36	87.05	86.89	60.64	101.37
4th quarter	93.48	89.00	86.93	70.93	103.50	87.40	84.83	84.39	53.24	100.77
2016										
1st quarter	92.12	86.57	85.28	63.76	104.50	85.90	83.06	82.47	47.01	100.73
2nd quarter	93.07	87.76	86.04	67.43	104.97	86.22	83.36	84.11	48.89	101.07
3rd quarter	93.61	88.26	86.59	69.63	105.59	86.88	84.18	86.11	52.28	100.95
4th quarter	94.19	88.69	87.47	72.42	106.52	87.12	84.47	86.13	54.27	100.93
2017										
1st quarter	95.07	89.72	89.27	74.38	107.05	88.10	85.58	89.54	59.95	101.21
2nd quarter	95.14	89.61	89.15	73.47	107.50	88.09	85.40	91.21	57.49	102.12
3rd quarter	96.03	90.68	89.45	76.40	108.00	88.31	85.40	92.85	56.33	103.46
4th quarter	97.46	91.94	91.18	79.55	109.79	89.55	86.67	95.76	61.82	104.55
2018										
1st quarter	98.13	92.24	92.85	81.88	111.35	91.12	88.21	98.35	68.87	106.36
2nd quarter	99.36	93.58	94.29	85.22	112.32	91.25	88.25	100.17	69.16	106.94
3rd quarter	99.64	93.80	92.81	87.50	112.75	91.38	88.34	99.27	70.88	107.29
4th quarter	99.28	93.13	92.12	85.07	113.14	90.97	87.82	98.14	69.34	107.51
2019										
1st quarter	98.55	92.00	93.53	92.00	113.32	90.29	86.82	97.33	64.80	108.41
2nd quarter	99.34	92.55	93.87	92.83	114.65	90.49	86.99	96.02	67.37	108.77
3rd quarter	98.76	91.56	94.07	93.45	115.02	89.75	86.09	96.73	63.67	108.87
4th quarter	98.35	91.18	93.66	93.36	114.55	89.43	85.68	97.73	63.78	109.03
2020										
1st quarter	97.78	90.22	92.11	73.10	114.98	89.19	85.27	99.85	60.35	109.75
2nd quarter	93.18	84.82	90.41	58.50	112.38	86.42	82.25	96.10	45.22	108.61
3rd quarter	96.16	88.06	94.55	66.08	114.69	88.10	83.98	104.55	51.16	109.80
4th quarter	97.62	89.55	96.75	68.22	116.02	88.59	84.35	110.51	52.75	111.11

[1] Exports and imports of certain goods, primarily military equipment purchased and sold by the federal government, are included in services. Beginning with 1986, repairs and alterations of equipment are reclassified from goods to services.

Table 7-4. Exports and Imports of Selected NIPA Types of Product

(Billions of dollars, quarterly data are at seasonally adjusted annual rates.)   NIPA Table 4.2.5

| | Exports | | | | | | | Imports | | | | | | | |
| | Goods | | | | | Services | | Goods | | | | | | Services | |
Year and quarter	Foods, feeds, and beverages	Industrial supplies and materials	Capital goods, except auto-motive	Auto-motive vehicles, engines, and parts	Consumer goods, except food and auto-motive	Travel	Other business services	Foods, feeds, and beverages	Industrial supplies and materials, except petroleum and products	Petroleum and products	Capital goods, except auto-motive	Auto-motive vehicles, engines, and parts	Consumer goods, except food and auto-motive	Travel	Other business services
1975	19.2	29.3	36.6	10.8	6.6	4.7	3.7	9.6	50.6	27.0	10.2	12.1	13.2	6.4	2.3
1976	19.8	31.6	39.1	12.2	8.0	5.7	4.5	11.5	63.1	34.6	12.3	16.8	17.2	6.9	2.9
1977	19.7	33.2	39.8	13.5	8.9	6.2	4.9	14.0	78.4	45.0	14.0	19.4	21.8	7.5	3.2
1978	25.7	38.4	47.5	15.2	11.4	7.2	6.2	15.8	81.9	42.6	19.3	25.0	29.4	8.5	3.9
1979	30.5	53.3	60.2	17.9	14.0	8.4	7.3	18.0	105.4	60.4	24.6	26.6	31.3	9.4	4.6
1980	36.3	68.0	76.3	17.4	17.8	10.6	8.6	18.6	126.9	79.5	31.6	28.3	34.3	10.4	5.1
1981	38.8	65.7	84.2	19.7	17.7	15.6	10.5	18.6	130.4	78.4	37.1	31.0	38.4	11.8	6.0
1982	32.2	61.8	76.5	17.2	16.1	15.5	13.8	17.5	107.3	62.0	38.4	34.3	39.7	12.8	7.0
1983	32.1	57.1	71.7	18.5	14.9	14.5	14.1	18.8	106.2	55.1	43.7	43.0	47.3	13.6	6.8
1984	32.2	61.9	77.0	22.4	15.1	21.3	14.5	21.9	120.7	58.1	60.4	56.5	61.1	23.4	7.7
1985	24.6	59.4	79.3	24.9	14.6	22.4	14.8	21.8	110.6	51.4	61.3	64.9	66.3	25.1	8.8
1986	23.5	59.0	82.8	25.1	16.7	25.5	23.3	24.4	96.7	34.3	72.0	78.1	79.4	26.5	13.3
1987	25.2	67.4	92.7	27.6	20.3	29.0	24.2	24.8	109.0	42.9	85.1	85.2	88.8	29.9	16.7
1988	33.8	84.2	119.1	33.4	27.0	35.2	25.7	24.9	116.3	39.6	102.2	87.9	96.4	32.8	17.8
1989	36.3	95.4	136.9	35.1	35.9	43.0	30.3	24.9	129.7	50.9	112.3	87.4	103.6	34.2	19.2
1990	35.1	101.9	153.0	36.2	43.5	50.9	32.7	26.4	140.5	62.3	116.4	88.2	105.0	38.2	22.4
1991	35.7	106.2	166.6	39.9	46.6	56.7	39.9	26.2	127.4	51.7	121.1	85.5	107.7	36.2	25.9
1992	40.3	105.2	176.4	46.9	51.2	64.0	41.1	27.6	134.0	51.6	134.8	91.5	122.4	39.6	24.3
1993	40.5	102.9	182.7	51.6	54.5	67.9	43.5	27.9	140.2	51.5	153.2	102.1	133.7	41.9	26.6
1994	42.4	115.4	205.7	57.5	59.7	69.4	49.9	31.0	156.2	51.3	185.0	118.1	145.9	45.1	30.3
1995	50.8	141.0	234.4	61.4	64.2	74.9	53.6	33.2	175.6	56.0	222.1	123.7	159.7	46.4	33.7
1996	56.0	141.3	254.0	64.4	69.3	81.8	61.3	35.7	197.3	72.7	228.4	128.7	172.5	49.7	38.1
1997	52.0	153.0	295.8	73.4	77.0	86.2	71.2	39.7	206.5	71.8	253.6	139.4	195.2	53.8	41.4
1998	46.8	143.3	299.8	72.5	79.4	85.1	78.1	41.3	193.1	50.9	269.8	148.6	218.5	58.5	45.6
1999	46.0	145.7	311.2	75.3	80.9	89.1	94.4	44.1	221.9	72.1	296.1	178.2	243.7	58.9	60.9
2000	47.9	171.1	357.0	80.4	89.3	96.9	99.1	46.5	301.3	126.1	347.7	195.0	284.6	64.2	67.6
2001	49.4	159.5	321.7	75.4	88.3	86.4	102.5	47.2	276.8	109.4	299.2	188.7	287.1	60.5	73.4
2002	49.6	157.3	290.4	78.9	84.3	79.6	110.0	50.3	270.6	109.3	284.9	202.8	311.3	59.0	80.7
2003	55.0	173.3	293.7	80.6	89.9	77.0	117.7	56.5	317.8	140.4	297.6	209.2	338.4	61.2	87.7
2004	56.6	206.3	327.5	89.2	103.2	85.6	135.5	63.0	418.3	189.9	346.1	227.3	378.1	70.3	99.2
2005	59.0	236.8	358.4	98.4	115.2	93.4	146.6	69.1	531.4	263.2	382.8	238.7	412.7	74.1	107.7
2006	66.0	279.1	404.0	107.3	129.0	96.1	172.7	76.1	610.1	316.7	422.6	256.0	447.6	78.4	138.2
2007	84.3	316.3	433.0	121.3	145.9	106.9	212.5	83.0	644.5	346.7	449.1	258.5	479.8	82.6	163.9
2008	108.3	386.9	457.7	121.5	161.2	117.0	236.8	90.4	794.6	476.1	458.7	233.2	485.7	84.3	186.9
2009	93.9	293.5	391.5	81.7	149.3	110.8	239.6	82.9	464.4	267.7	374.1	159.2	429.9	82.5	188.4
2010	107.7	388.6	447.8	112.0	164.9	130.3	261.2	92.5	603.2	353.6	450.4	225.6	485.1	85.2	199.8
2011	126.2	485.3	494.2	133.0	174.7	142.2	291.0	108.3	755.0	462.1	513.4	255.2	515.9	86.6	212.3
2012	133.0	483.2	527.5	146.2	181.0	153.9	312.6	111.1	723.2	434.3	551.8	298.5	518.8	90.3	217.0
2013	136.2	492.4	534.8	152.7	188.1	171.0	322.8	116.0	679.0	387.8	559.0	309.6	532.9	91.1	219.5
2014	143.7	500.7	551.8	159.8	198.4	180.3	350.0	126.8	669.9	353.6	598.8	329.5	558.7	96.2	233.2
2015	127.7	418.1	539.8	151.9	197.3	192.6	360.4	128.8	488.1	197.2	607.2	350.0	596.4	102.7	239.3
2016	130.5	387.6	520.0	150.4	193.3	192.9	374.5	131.0	437.4	159.6	593.6	350.8	584.9	109.2	247.6
2017	132.8	459.4	533.7	157.9	197.2	196.5	412.9	138.8	503.1	197.4	642.9	359.1	603.5	117.9	266.3
2018	133.1	536.9	563.4	158.8	205.5	200.7	430.9	148.3	574.2	238.9	694.2	372.0	647.7	126.1	261.6
2019	131.0	526.4	548.0	162.8	205.0	199.4	447.9	151.6	519.1	207.4	679.1	376.0	655.5	133.3	279.3
2020	139.3	450.4	460.5	127.9	174.0	72.8	440.7	155.4	424.4	125.2	648.5	311.3	641.1	35.8	284.5
2015															
1st quarter	136.2	436.4	548.9	148.2	200.0	187.8	363.6	128.9	533.8	224.5	617.4	335.1	592.8	98.6	233.8
2nd quarter	129.4	439.0	545.4	151.8	196.3	193.4	358.6	130.2	499.8	205.8	612.7	354.1	595.4	102.7	237.1
3rd quarter	122.7	413.6	535.1	154.7	196.4	194.9	356.4	129.0	482.8	196.4	601.5	357.4	603.1	103.9	242.3
4th quarter	122.6	383.6	529.8	153.0	196.5	194.3	362.9	126.9	436.1	162.3	597.1	353.6	594.3	105.5	243.9
2016															
1st quarter	121.3	369.2	522.2	147.0	190.9	191.7	362.9	129.7	403.7	137.3	585.1	349.8	585.7	107.2	245.2
2nd quarter	121.1	384.0	520.7	151.6	191.8	192.4	372.5	128.8	422.7	150.6	596.8	347.4	580.7	108.4	244.2
3rd quarter	143.9	394.4	515.8	152.5	195.5	194.5	379.8	130.4	453.8	170.6	593.0	350.6	582.4	109.6	246.7
4th quarter	135.8	402.8	521.3	150.6	194.8	192.9	383.0	135.1	469.4	179.8	599.5	355.6	590.9	111.5	254.3
2017															
1st quarter	134.8	448.0	522.2	156.7	195.5	191.3	402.3	134.3	506.4	212.8	616.0	360.6	591.0	114.0	258.9
2nd quarter	130.7	441.5	523.7	156.3	198.1	195.1	410.7	137.3	494.5	188.5	633.6	358.6	601.1	116.6	264.6
3rd quarter	132.9	448.7	541.4	155.6	195.2	198.2	417.6	140.2	486.4	180.2	649.7	356.0	589.4	119.7	272.5
4th quarter	132.6	499.3	547.5	162.8	200.0	201.3	421.0	143.4	525.3	208.1	672.2	361.2	632.4	121.4	269.2
2018															
1st quarter	131.4	508.9	555.7	165.6	204.1	203.2	430.0	147.0	559.9	230.9	684.2	370.7	649.7	123.1	256.2
2nd quarter	146.0	549.5	567.8	161.2	205.7	203.6	423.8	148.0	577.8	242.2	697.4	361.1	632.0	125.1	260.3
3rd quarter	133.7	548.2	563.1	154.6	203.7	198.4	432.0	147.8	597.4	260.6	701.9	371.7	642.6	127.2	262.3
4th quarter	121.5	540.9	567.1	153.8	208.5	197.7	438.0	150.3	561.6	221.8	693.5	384.5	666.3	129.1	267.7
2019															
1st quarter	129.7	522.8	565.5	164.5	210.6	201.8	435.0	149.9	525.1	197.7	689.7	383.1	668.1	132.3	274.0
2nd quarter	135.5	535.0	543.8	162.4	205.3	199.7	453.6	153.9	539.7	228.6	684.2	385.1	663.5	132.3	280.3
3rd quarter	133.1	521.8	541.8	164.7	204.6	194.3	451.7	152.3	516.4	205.8	676.3	378.6	663.3	134.0	283.8
4th quarter	125.6	526.1	540.7	159.4	199.4	201.7	451.3	150.1	495.4	197.3	666.3	357.3	627.3	134.5	279.1
2020															
1st quarter	133.4	518.5	525.8	151.1	187.4	145.6	437.3	154.6	479.7	180.0	649.6	353.3	612.2	88.7	282.5
2nd quarter	129.3	370.2	398.3	61.3	134.1	55.7	432.9	147.8	356.7	82.5	588.6	165.0	570.5	9.5	276.1
3rd quarter	139.0	434.9	448.0	145.8	179.3	42.1	437.7	158.9	408.9	113.3	661.1	340.6	670.4	14.7	283.8
4th quarter	155.7	477.9	469.8	153.5	195.1	47.9	454.8	160.4	452.5	125.0	694.6	386.4	711.1	30.2	295.9

Table 7-5. Chain-Type Quantity Indexes for Exports and Imports of Selected NIPA Types of Product

(Index numbers, 2012 = 100; quarterly indexes are seasonally adjusted.)   NIPA Table 4.2.3

Year and quarter	Exports Goods: Foods, feeds, and beverages	Exports Goods: Industrial supplies and materials	Exports Goods: Capital goods, except automotive	Exports Goods: Automotive vehicles, engines, and parts	Exports Goods: Consumer goods, except food and automotive	Exports Services: Travel	Exports Services: Other business services	Imports Goods: Foods, feeds, and beverages	Imports Goods: Industrial supplies and materials, except petroleum and products	Imports Goods: Petroleum and products	Imports Goods: Capital goods, except automotive	Imports Goods: Automotive vehicles, engines, and parts	Imports Goods: Consumer goods, except food and automotive	Imports Services: Travel	Imports Services: Other business services
1975	33.04	20.42	5.71	24.41	8.73	14.12	3.14	26.37	38.82	53.59	0.86	14.20	4.67	17.59	2.24
1976	37.49	22.05	5.63	25.52	9.85	16.08	3.63	30.01	47.02	64.61	1.05	18.81	6.02	18.70	2.69
1977	37.46	22.24	5.54	25.70	10.65	16.12	3.74	29.71	53.87	77.73	1.12	19.93	7.27	19.27	2.82
1978	46.28	24.58	6.32	26.39	12.30	17.31	4.43	33.36	54.44	73.49	1.44	21.56	8.93	19.91	3.29
1979	49.09	28.14	7.59	26.55	12.93	18.56	4.94	34.24	53.80	74.34	1.77	20.85	9.00	19.42	3.73
1980	55.34	31.94	8.86	22.36	15.67	20.73	5.28	29.80	44.81	60.04	2.08	20.66	9.07	19.40	3.81
1981	56.50	29.79	8.90	22.11	15.02	27.59	6.03	31.01	42.66	52.60	2.45	19.99	9.93	21.14	4.23
1982	53.09	28.89	7.87	18.12	13.52	25.46	7.47	31.61	37.47	45.24	2.67	21.40	10.38	25.08	4.78
1983	50.75	27.49	7.59	18.74	12.37	22.61	7.26	34.30	40.27	44.78	3.23	26.19	12.49	28.41	4.43
1984	49.38	28.89	8.40	22.12	12.30	31.42	7.24	38.86	46.09	47.30	4.82	33.65	15.77	51.35	4.95
1985	42.73	29.06	9.24	24.07	11.94	31.45	7.12	40.54	44.88	44.41	5.43	37.71	17.21	56.65	5.53
1986	44.08	30.36	10.08	23.67	13.21	34.69	10.89	41.50	50.46	54.91	6.17	40.82	19.07	52.72	8.05
1987	47.18	31.11	11.64	25.51	15.54	37.63	10.90	42.54	51.02	57.35	7.04	41.89	19.69	62.40	9.23
1988	51.85	35.08	14.79	30.28	19.85	43.89	11.54	40.85	53.31	63.44	8.12	40.84	19.98	64.19	9.84
1989	53.93	39.01	17.16	31.13	25.45	51.86	13.47	41.77	54.07	68.60	9.18	39.80	20.91	66.21	11.51
1990	55.64	41.31	19.85	31.17	29.86	58.22	14.02	43.37	54.80	69.33	9.92	39.85	20.54	70.73	12.49
1991	56.70	44.12	21.72	33.43	30.93	60.95	16.48	41.40	54.13	69.08	10.66	37.16	20.89	64.24	13.94
1992	64.27	44.94	23.79	38.54	33.32	67.09	16.66	43.71	58.33	72.20	12.35	39.07	23.07	66.25	12.98
1993	63.95	43.75	25.35	42.02	35.01	70.21	17.42	44.23	63.52	79.09	14.41	42.93	24.98	69.55	13.76
1994	64.61	46.02	29.25	46.44	38.25	71.06	19.84	45.24	71.13	84.44	17.67	48.14	27.07	72.08	15.54
1995	71.38	49.64	34.86	48.95	40.54	75.52	20.94	46.38	72.95	82.91	21.75	48.97	29.20	72.86	17.11
1996	70.24	52.16	40.40	50.76	43.24	80.41	23.59	51.01	77.78	89.90	25.56	50.63	31.44	75.76	18.76
1997	70.68	56.71	49.52	57.46	47.69	82.71	27.14	56.17	83.04	93.62	32.08	54.73	36.01	82.34	20.10
1998	69.96	56.08	51.63	56.67	49.14	80.46	29.96	60.29	91.15	100.07	36.90	58.26	40.87	93.17	22.42
1999	72.00	57.85	54.48	58.46	50.24	85.03	31.51	66.60	96.94	107.56	42.35	69.39	45.90	93.93	27.67
2000	75.60	62.97	62.68	61.74	55.25	88.07	33.71	70.95	102.23	111.48	50.88	75.06	54.04	107.08	31.55
2001	77.63	60.41	56.46	57.70	54.82	75.56	38.00	74.14	101.22	114.76	45.10	72.60	54.92	98.64	36.55
2002	76.26	60.79	51.87	60.10	52.62	71.19	42.25	78.05	102.32	112.09	44.42	77.79	60.21	93.33	40.82
2003	77.57	62.43	54.51	60.95	55.77	67.77	44.97	84.10	105.76	119.57	48.60	79.81	65.88	86.11	43.31
2004	72.50	66.50	61.35	66.91	63.44	74.63	51.18	89.09	117.79	127.47	57.57	85.29	73.49	94.41	48.23
2005	76.76	68.21	67.34	72.98	70.06	78.18	53.87	92.32	122.99	130.04	64.35	88.62	80.03	97.54	50.55
2006	82.83	73.24	76.12	78.59	77.46	77.37	61.73	98.02	124.14	127.59	72.12	94.66	87.15	98.67	66.03
2007	90.10	77.21	81.21	87.83	85.76	84.29	73.32	99.29	120.43	124.57	77.01	94.64	92.96	96.36	76.79
2008	95.64	85.26	85.93	86.90	92.77	90.34	79.35	97.91	114.04	120.29	78.95	83.26	92.48	92.04	88.35
2009	91.84	79.71	73.86	58.17	85.76	83.02	85.57	92.50	96.93	110.55	66.16	56.41	82.93	84.47	92.10
2010	101.26	92.13	85.10	79.30	93.71	91.70	90.14	94.59	102.84	111.09	81.19	79.41	94.51	88.22	94.56
2011	100.79	98.23	93.82	92.63	97.97	96.05	96.73	96.41	104.38	108.99	92.74	87.15	99.34	89.09	99.61
2012	100.00	100.00	100.00	100.00	100.00	100.00	100.00	100.00	100.00	100.00	100.00	100.00	100.00	100.00	100.00
2013	102.11	104.03	101.31	103.88	105.07	108.45	105.63	103.93	97.16	94.12	102.76	104.12	105.19	96.37	102.51
2014	110.23	107.68	104.89	108.12	112.28	114.97	111.28	109.31	98.19	90.49	111.50	111.49	112.75	103.00	104.63
2015	112.39	107.67	103.69	102.88	114.08	124.95	112.87	113.69	99.63	91.58	116.17	120.85	123.89	116.07	106.33
2016	118.73	109.46	101.25	102.61	114.26	123.89	112.37	115.34	102.52	96.56	116.72	122.12	124.53	127.59	106.18
2017	119.45	118.27	102.44	107.35	118.15	123.78	118.13	117.94	104.25	96.18	127.39	125.68	130.14	137.76	109.42
2018	119.24	126.54	108.89	107.34	121.99	123.26	117.81	127.12	104.10	91.41	139.63	130.29	139.00	146.97	105.85
2019	117.80	131.41	105.46	109.59	121.24	118.30	116.54	130.55	98.39	85.20	138.40	132.26	143.39	148.33	112.07
2020	123.61	127.64	88.40	86.34	102.63	43.46	113.87	134.89	90.28	74.60	133.09	108.68	142.85	39.90	113.07
2015															
1st quarter	112.60	107.44	104.45	100.99	115.39	122.54	115.71	111.53	100.58	91.85	116.37	115.36	122.09	112.23	105.13
2nd quarter	115.84	109.97	104.81	102.86	113.07	125.69	117.44	114.93	99.28	91.21	116.54	122.17	123.48	114.75	104.94
3rd quarter	110.94	107.87	103.04	104.99	113.72	125.44	110.26	114.14	99.90	92.13	115.71	123.17	125.62	116.29	107.81
4th quarter	110.17	105.40	102.44	102.68	114.12	126.14	114.01	114.14	98.74	91.14	116.04	122.72	124.39	121.01	107.43
2016															
1st quarter	108.69	108.29	101.19	101.19	113.31	125.59	109.78	117.70	100.13	94.54	114.03	122.06	123.94	125.52	106.75
2nd quarter	110.58	110.30	101.19	103.36	112.91	122.79	111.84	116.95	101.70	95.86	116.77	120.36	122.92	124.23	105.51
3rd quarter	134.60	110.30	100.52	104.28	115.40	124.19	113.53	112.24	103.51	98.53	117.10	122.25	124.46	127.15	105.44
4th quarter	121.03	108.94	102.10	101.61	115.44	123.01	114.34	114.45	104.74	97.32	118.98	123.82	126.80	133.47	107.02
2017															
1st quarter	118.03	115.75	100.61	108.39	119.07	122.55	117.20	116.69	104.84	100.94	121.95	126.07	128.10	137.02	107.26
2nd quarter	122.38	117.47	100.75	106.87	118.24	123.59	116.78	117.28	104.42	96.96	125.29	124.91	128.60	137.26	108.90
3rd quarter	122.90	115.66	103.61	106.36	116.62	124.77	119.07	117.91	103.37	93.58	128.95	124.95	127.75	135.91	111.78
4th quarter	114.51	124.20	104.77	108.29	118.69	124.21	119.45	119.87	104.37	93.25	133.38	126.79	136.12	140.86	133.23
2018															
1st quarter	113.85	123.04	108.08	113.11	121.53	126.22	117.62	123.88	102.83	90.54	136.47	128.66	139.32	141.91	105.59
2nd quarter	130.80	128.17	109.52	109.06	121.59	123.79	116.39	126.91	104.45	93.00	139.40	126.79	134.95	142.20	104.60
3rd quarter	123.89	125.98	108.24	104.95	121.36	121.26	118.64	129.84	105.72	94.39	141.60	131.42	138.03	145.14	106.16
4th quarter	108.43	128.98	109.73	102.23	123.47	121.74	118.58	127.83	103.39	87.71	141.04	134.29	143.69	150.61	107.03
2019															
1st quarter	116.45	130.79	109.18	110.27	125.13	110.51	133.16	128.93	100.51	85.16	139.42	133.90	144.57	132.92	116.42
2nd quarter	120.96	128.71	104.18	108.51	121.12	109.86	136.73	128.90	99.53	87.21	138.27	135.30	144.23	139.00	120.60
3rd quarter	119.17	130.95	103.72	111.27	121.22	107.25	136.45	132.35	99.02	85.50	138.03	134.34	146.05	133.15	122.43
4th quarter	114.41	135.61	104.20	107.50	117.62	108.35	138.06	131.93	95.92	84.36	137.70	126.41	139.11	135.00	123.21
2020															
1st quarter	118.72	137.82	100.92	101.86	110.56	86.04	112.55	133.57	94.77	83.20	133.67	123.79	135.79	98.19	112.26
2nd quarter	119.62	116.57	76.40	41.36	79.57	33.60	114.56	128.24	85.24	67.47	120.71	57.50	127.11	11.25	110.96
3rd quarter	125.53	123.91	85.86	98.65	105.53	25.37	112.86	137.21	87.83	72.39	135.46	118.76	149.20	16.83	112.64
4th quarter	130.57	132.27	90.41	103.50	114.86	28.84	115.50	140.54	93.29	75.32	142.52	134.68	159.29	33.32	116.41

SECTION 7B: U.S. INTERNATIONAL TRANSACTIONS ACCOUNTS

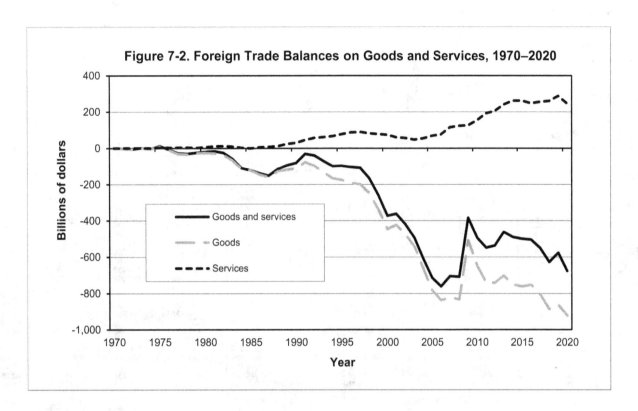

Figure 7-2. Foreign Trade Balances on Goods and Services, 1970–2020

- As noted in other chapters, the COVID-19 pandemic impacted all sectors of the economy, both in the U.S. and globally. As indicated by tables in this chapter, trade between the U.S. and partners has declined.

- The U.S. current-account international balance is also recorded in the International Transactions Accounts (ITAs). The definitional differences between this balance and the balance in the NIPAs are minor, and the trends in the two measures are similar. The ITAs measure the current account surplus or deficit (commonly known as the "balance of payments") and directly measure the financial flows required to finance it. (Table 7-6)

- U.S. imports from Canada and Mexico in 2020 amounted to $595.5 billion, more than the $415.5 billion imported from the European Union and the $554.2 billion from China and Japan. (Table 7-11)

- Through the early 1980s, the United States was still a net creditor with the world, meaning that the value of stock of U.S. owed assets abroad exceeded the value of U.S. liabilities to the rest of the word. Since then, persistent borrowing to finance current-account deficits has accumulated, resulting in a growing net debtor status. (Table 7-6)

Table 7-6. U.S. Exports and Imports of Goods and Services

(Balance of payments basis; millions of dollars, seasonally adjusted.)

Year and month	Goods and services			Goods			Services		
	Exports	Imports	Balance	Exports	Imports	Balance	Exports	Imports	Balance
1970	56 640	54 386	2 254	42 469	39 866	2 603	14 171	14 520	-349
1971	59 677	60 979	-1 302	43 319	45 579	-2 260	16 358	15 400	958
1972	67 222	72 665	-5 443	49 381	55 797	-6 416	17 841	16 868	973
1973	91 242	89 342	1 900	71 410	70 499	911	19 832	18 843	989
1974	120 897	125 190	-4 293	98 306	103 811	-5 505	22 591	21 379	1 212
1975	132 585	120 181	12 404	107 088	98 185	8 903	25 497	21 996	3 501
1976	142 716	148 798	-6 082	114 745	124 228	-9 483	27 971	24 570	3 401
1977	152 301	179 547	-27 246	120 816	151 907	-31 091	31 485	27 640	3 845
1978	178 428	208 191	-29 763	142 075	176 002	-33 927	36 353	32 189	4 164
1979	224 131	248 696	-24 565	184 439	212 007	-27 568	39 692	36 689	3 003
1980	271 834	291 241	-19 407	224 250	249 750	-25 500	47 584	41 491	6 093
1981	294 398	310 570	-16 172	237 044	265 067	-28 023	57 354	45 503	11 851
1982	275 236	299 391	-24 156	211 157	247 642	-36 485	64 079	51 749	12 329
1983	266 106	323 874	-57 767	201 799	268 901	-67 102	64 307	54 973	9 335
1984	291 094	400 166	-109 072	219 926	332 418	-112 492	71 168	67 748	3 420
1985	289 070	410 950	-121 880	215 915	338 088	-122 173	73 155	72 862	294
1986	310 033	448 572	-138 538	223 344	368 425	-145 081	86 689	80 147	6 543
1987	348 869	500 552	-151 684	250 208	409 765	-159 557	98 661	90 787	7 874
1988	431 149	545 715	-114 566	320 230	447 189	-126 959	110 919	98 526	12 393
1989	487 003	580 144	-93 141	359 916	477 665	-117 749	127 087	102 479	24 607
1990	535 233	616 097	-80 864	387 401	498 438	-111 037	147 832	117 659	30 173
1991	578 344	609 479	-31 135	414 083	491 020	-76 937	164 261	118 459	45 802
1992	616 882	656 094	-39 212	439 631	536 528	-96 897	177 251	119 566	57 685
1993	642 863	713 174	-70 311	456 943	589 394	-132 451	185 920	123 780	62 141
1994	703 254	801 747	-98 493	502 859	668 690	-165 831	200 395	133 057	67 338
1995	794 387	890 771	-96 384	575 204	749 374	-174 170	219 183	141 397	77 786
1996	851 602	955 667	-104 065	612 113	803 113	-191 000	239 489	152 554	86 935
1997	934 453	1 042 726	-108 273	678 366	876 794	-198 428	256 087	165 932	90 155
1998	933 174	1 099 314	-166 140	670 416	918 637	-248 221	262 758	180 677	82 081
1999	969 867	1 228 485	-258 617	698 524	1 035 592	-337 068	271 343	192 893	78 450
2000	1 075 321	1 447 837	-372 517	784 940	1 231 722	-446 783	290 381	216 115	74 266
2001	1 005 654	1 367 165	-361 511	731 331	1 153 701	-422 370	274 323	213 465	60 858
2002	978 706	1 397 660	-418 955	698 036	1 173 281	-475 245	280 670	224 379	56 290
2003	1 020 418	1 514 308	-493 890	730 446	1 272 089	-541 643	289 972	242 219	47 754
2004	1 161 549	1 771 433	-609 883	823 584	1 488 349	-664 766	337 966	283 083	54 882
2005	1 286 022	2 000 267	-714 245	913 016	1 695 820	-782 804	373 006	304 448	68 558
2006	1 457 642	2 219 358	-761 716	1 040 905	1 878 194	-837 289	416 738	341 165	75 573
2007	1 653 548	2 358 922	-705 375	1 165 151	1 986 347	-821 196	488 396	372 575	115 821
2008	1 841 612	2 550 339	-708 726	1 308 795	2 141 287	-832 492	532 817	409 052	123 765
2009	1 583 053	1 966 827	-383 774	1 070 331	1 580 025	-509 694	512 722	386 801	125 920
2010	1 853 606	2 348 263	-494 658	1 290 273	1 938 950	-648 678	563 333	409 313	154 020
2011	2 127 021	2 675 646	-548 625	1 499 240	2 239 886	-740 646	627 781	435 761	192 020
2012	2 218 989	2 755 762	-536 773	1 562 578	2 303 749	-741 171	656 411	452 013	204 398
2013	2 293 457	2 755 334	-461 876	1 592 002	2 294 247	-702 244	701 455	461 087	240 368
2014	2 375 905	2 866 241	-490 336	1 633 986	2 385 480	-751 494	741 919	480 761	261 157
2015	2 263 907	2 764 352	-500 445	1 510 757	2 272 612	-761 855	753 150	491 740	261 410
2016	2 208 072	2 712 866	-504 794	1 455 704	2 208 211	-752 507	752 368	504 654	247 714
2017	2 352 546	2 902 669	-550 123	1 553 589	2 358 789	-805 200	798 957	543 880	255 077
2018	2 501 310	3 128 989	-627 679	1 674 330	2 561 667	-887 337	826 980	567 322	259 658
2019	2 528 262	3 105 127	-576 865	1 652 437	2 516 767	-864 331	875 825	588 359	287 466
2020	2 134 441	2 811 125	-676 684	1 428 798	2 350 825	-922 026	705 643	460 301	245 342
2019									
January	210 243	259 267	-49 023	138 878	211 247	-72 369	71 366	211 247	23 346
February	210 809	258 109	-47 300	139 190	210 222	-71 032	71 619	210 222	23 732
March	213 157	262 072	-48 914	140 980	213 712	-72 732	72 177	213 712	23 817
April	209 288	258 491	-49 203	136 436	209 748	-73 312	72 852	209 748	24 109
May	212 852	264 110	-51 258	139 091	215 053	-75 962	73 761	215 053	24 704
June	209 254	261 003	-51 749	135 542	210 839	-75 298	73 712	210 839	23 549
July	210 462	261 503	-51 041	137 465	212 071	-74 606	72 997	212 071	23 565
August	210 517	261 295	-50 778	137 358	211 956	-74 598	73 159	211 956	23 820
September	209 210	257 049	-47 839	136 108	208 032	-71 925	73 102	208 032	24 085
October	210 403	253 432	-43 029	136 851	203 982	-67 131	73 552	203 982	24 102
November	210 571	251 625	-41 054	136 888	202 280	-65 391	73 682	202 280	24 337
December	211 496	257 171	-45 676	137 651	207 625	-69 975	73 845	207 625	24 299
2020									
January	205 091	250 543	-45 452	135 567	203 406	-67 839	69 524	47 137	22 387
February	204 819	246 458	-41 639	135 701	199 403	-63 702	69 118	47 055	22 063
March	187 490	234 647	-47 157	126 875	195 594	-68 718	60 615	39 053	21 561
April	150 074	203 033	-52 959	95 025	169 641	-74 616	55 049	33 392	21 657
May	146 108	201 023	-54 915	91 051	167 703	-76 652	55 056	33 320	21 736
June	158 805	209 480	-50 675	103 702	175 706	-72 004	55 103	33 774	21 329
July	170 908	231 651	-60 743	115 880	196 672	-80 792	55 028	34 979	20 049
August	174 287	238 020	-63 733	118 981	201 947	-82 966	55 306	36 073	19 233
September	178 063	240 689	-62 625	121 965	203 577	-81 613	56 099	37 111	18 987
October	182 732	246 410	-63 678	125 761	207 888	-82 127	56 971	38 522	18 450
November	185 186	252 494	-67 307	126 789	213 017	-86 227	58 397	39 477	18 920
December	190 877	256 678	-65 802	131 500	216 270	-84 770	59 377	40 408	18 969

Table 7-7. U.S. Exports of Goods by End-Use and Advanced Technology Categories

(Census basis, except as noted; billions of dollars; seasonally adjusted, except as noted.)

Year and month	Total exports of goods — Total, balance of payments basis	Net adjustments	Total, Census basis	Foods, feeds, and beverages	Industrial supplies and materials — Total	Industrial supplies and materials — Petroleum and products	Capital goods, except automotive	Automotive vehicles, engines, and parts	Consumer goods, except automotive	Other goods	Advanced technology products [1]
1980	224.25	3.55	220.70	36.28	72.09	3.57	76.28	17.44	17.75	...	...
1981	237.04	3.31	233.74	38.84	70.19	4.56	84.17	19.69	17.70	...	...
1982	211.16	-1.12	212.28	32.20	64.05	6.87	76.50	17.23	16.13	...	...
1983	201.80	0.09	201.71	32.09	58.94	5.59	71.66	18.46	14.93	...	...
1984	219.93	1.18	218.74	32.20	64.12	5.43	77.01	22.42	15.09	...	...
1985	215.92	3.29	212.62	24.57	61.16	5.71	79.32	24.95	14.59	...	...
1986	223.34	-3.13	226.47	23.52	64.72	4.43	82.82	25.10	16.73	...	...
1987	250.21	-3.70	253.90	25.23	70.05	4.63	92.71	27.58	20.31	...	...
1988	320.23	-3.11	323.34	33.77	90.02	4.48	119.10	33.40	26.98	...	...
1989	359.92	-3.08	363.00	36.34	98.36	6.46	136.94	35.05	36.01	...	...
1990	387.40	-5.57	392.97	35.18	105.55	8.36	153.07	36.07	43.60	20.73	...
1991	414.08	-7.77	421.85	35.79	109.69	8.40	166.72	39.72	46.65	23.66	...
1992	439.63	-8.54	448.16	40.27	109.14	7.62	175.92	47.03	51.42	24.39	...
1993	456.94	-7.92	465.09	40.63	111.81	7.50	181.70	52.40	54.66	23.89	...
1994	502.86	-9.77	512.63	41.96	121.40	6.97	205.02	57.78	59.98	26.50	...
1995	575.20	-9.54	584.74	50.47	146.25	8.10	233.05	61.83	64.43	28.72	...
1996	612.11	-12.96	625.08	55.53	147.65	9.63	252.98	65.02	70.06	33.84	...
1997	678.37	-10.82	689.18	51.51	158.23	10.42	294.55	74.03	77.37	33.51	...
1998	670.42	-11.72	682.14	46.40	148.27	8.08	299.35	72.39	80.29	35.44	...
1999	698.52	-11.83	695.80	45.98	147.52	8.62	310.79	75.26	80.92	35.32	...
2000	784.94	-9.92	781.92	47.87	172.62	12.01	356.93	80.36	89.38	34.77	227.39
2001	731.33	-10.39	729.10	49.41	160.10	10.64	321.71	75.44	88.33	34.11	199.63
2002	698.04	-10.68	693.10	49.62	156.81	10.34	290.44	78.94	84.36	32.94	178.57
2003	730.45	-11.36	724.77	55.03	173.04	12.69	293.67	80.63	89.91	32.49	180.21
2004	823.58	-11.26	814.88	56.57	203.91	17.08	327.54	89.21	103.24	34.40	201.42
2005	913.02	-11.35	901.08	58.96	233.05	22.66	358.43	98.41	115.29	36.96	216.06
2006	1 040.91	-10.16	1 025.97	65.96	276.05	31.57	404.03	107.26	129.08	43.59	252.71
2007	1 165.15	-9.82	1 148.20	84.26	316.38	37.76	433.02	121.26	145.98	47.30	264.88
2008	1 308.80	20.06	1 287.44	108.35	388.03	67.18	457.66	121.45	161.28	50.67	270.13
2009	1 070.33	13.69	1 056.04	93.91	296.51	49.18	391.24	81.72	149.46	43.22	244.71
2010	1 290.28	10.30	1 278.50	107.72	391.66	70.83	447.54	112.01	165.23	54.34	273.31
2011	1 498.89	15.56	1 482.51	126.25	501.08	113.71	493.96	133.04	175.30	52.89	287.72
2012	1 562.63	15.99	1 545.82	133.05	501.18	123.46	527.18	146.16	181.68	56.58	305.01
2013	1 593.71	13.19	1 578.52	136.16	508.21	137.42	534.41	152.66	188.82	58.25	319.79
2014	1 635.56	29.12	1 621.87	143.72	505.81	145.24	551.49	159.81	199.00	62.04	336.48
2015	1 511.38	24.43	1 503.33	127.72	427.02	98.09	539.54	151.89	197.75	59.40	343.13
2016	1 457.34	20.41	1 451.46	130.52	397.27	88.85	519.74	150.40	193.66	59.88	345.52
2017	1 557.00	16.75	1 547.20	132.76	465.16	125.64	533.42	157.87	197.71	60.27	353.80
2018	1 676.91	11.13	1 665.79	133.14	541.24	174.78	563.20	158.83	206.02	63.35	368.58
2019	1 652.07	9.25	1 642.82	130.99	529.46	179.25	547.71	162.75	205.63	66.27	364.01
2020	1 428.80	3.86	1 424.94	139.34	465.92	130.73	460.30	127.92	174.77	56.70	300.78
2018											
January	134.15	0.88	133.27	10.58	41.35	12.05	45.41	13.54	17.56	4.82	27.45
February	136.65	0.90	135.75	10.97	43.45	12.43	45.79	13.96	16.56	5.02	26.02
March	140.86	0.88	139.98	11.30	44.73	13.74	47.67	13.91	17.09	5.30	34.91
April	141.71	1.03	140.68	11.77	46.28	14.83	46.48	13.85	17.13	5.17	28.53
May	144.28	1.11	143.17	12.49	45.50	15.18	48.16	13.45	17.57	6.01	32.28
June	142.07	0.97	141.10	12.24	46.28	15.45	47.25	13.01	16.83	5.50	32.88
July	140.20	0.96	139.24	11.75	46.94	15.97	46.65	12.92	16.08	4.90	28.14
August	139.19	0.94	138.25	11.13	44.98	14.64	46.77	12.66	17.51	5.21	29.89
September	140.90	0.92	139.98	10.56	46.56	15.15	47.29	13.07	17.48	5.03	31.47
October	142.15	0.93	141.22	10.26	47.31	16.67	47.30	12.96	17.87	5.53	32.37
November	138.68	0.82	137.85	10.14	44.76	14.95	47.71	12.72	17.19	5.33	32.04
December	136.08	0.78	135.30	9.97	43.11	13.71	46.72	12.78	17.18	5.54	32.67
2019											
January	137.72	0.59	137.13	10.70	43.79	13.95	46.29	13.57	17.44	5.34	28.17
February	138.26	0.78	137.48	10.65	43.05	14.14	47.39	13.58	17.63	5.18	28.75
March	141.18	0.84	140.34	11.08	44.46	15.03	47.64	13.97	17.75	5.44	34.18
April	137.28	0.97	136.32	11.34	44.59	15.52	44.97	13.27	17.15	5.00	27.72
May	139.99	0.85	139.14	11.18	44.62	15.33	46.13	13.79	17.91	5.51	29.99
June	136.74	0.85	135.90	11.37	44.39	14.83	44.79	13.55	16.38	5.43	30.71
July	138.53	0.83	137.70	11.35	43.34	14.22	46.14	13.75	17.58	5.56	29.73
August	137.43	0.82	136.62	11.55	44.15	14.82	44.39	13.96	16.79	5.78	29.55
September	135.81	0.76	135.05	10.37	43.84	14.67	44.86	13.47	16.94	5.56	30.66
October	136.30	0.67	135.63	10.39	44.71	15.65	44.72	13.28	16.66	5.88	31.83
November	136.13	0.64	135.48	10.54	43.77	14.85	45.15	13.65	16.91	5.46	29.73
December	136.70	0.66	136.04	10.48	44.76	16.24	45.23	12.93	16.51	6.14	32.99
2020											
January	135.57	0.72	134.85	10.98	44.80	15.95	44.29	13.20	16.37	5.20	27.53
February	135.70	0.65	135.05	11.29	44.39	15.21	44.40	13.31	16.00	5.66	27.58
March	126.88	0.39	126.48	11.08	41.63	13.06	42.71	11.27	14.72	5.08	29.49
April	95.03	0.10	94.93	11.23	32.90	8.30	32.37	3.71	10.37	4.35	21.24
May	91.05	0.07	90.98	10.71	30.42	6.63	31.79	3.35	10.99	3.72	20.20
June	103.70	0.24	103.47	10.38	32.96	8.25	35.38	8.27	12.34	4.13	23.45
July	115.88	0.27	115.61	10.69	35.53	10.25	37.76	11.98	14.84	4.80	24.41
August	118.98	0.31	118.67	11.57	39.02	10.63	36.53	12.02	14.98	4.55	23.15
September	121.97	0.24	121.73	12.48	39.31	10.41	37.65	12.44	15.18	4.67	24.30
October	125.76	0.29	125.47	12.56	40.58	10.23	38.98	12.61	16.03	4.71	26.87
November	126.79	0.25	126.54	12.75	41.38	9.86	38.71	12.55	16.39	4.76	25.04
December	131.50	0.33	131.17	13.61	43.00	11.97	39.71	13.22	16.55	5.07	27.53

[1]Not seasonally adjusted.
. . . = Not available.

Table 7-8. U.S. Imports of Goods by End-Use and Advanced Technology Categories

(Census basis, except as noted; billions of dollars; seasonally adjusted, except as noted.)

Year and month	Total imports of goods			Principal end-use category							Advanced technology products [1]
	Total, balance of payments basis	Net adjustments	Total, Census basis	Foods, feeds, and beverages	Industrial supplies and materials		Capital goods, except automotive	Automotive vehicles, engines, and parts	Consumer goods, except automotive	Other goods	
					Total	Petroleum and products					
1980	249.75	4.23	245.52	18.55	124.96	. . .	30.72	28.13	34.22	. . .	. . .
1981	265.07	3.76	261.31	18.53	131.10	. . .	36.86	30.80	38.30	. . .	. . .
1982	247.64	3.70	243.94	17.47	107.82	. . .	38.22	34.26	39.66	. . .	. . .
1983	268.90	7.18	261.72	18.56	105.63	. . .	42.61	42.04	46.59	. . .	. . .
1984	332.42	1.91	330.51	21.92	122.72	. . .	60.15	56.77	61.19	. . .	. . .
1985	338.09	1.71	336.38	21.89	112.48	. . .	60.81	65.21	66.43	. . .	. . .
1986	368.43	2.75	365.67	24.40	101.37	. . .	71.86	78.25	79.43	. . .	. . .
1987	409.77	3.48	406.28	24.81	110.67	. . .	84.77	85.17	88.82	. . .	. . .
1988	447.19	5.26	441.93	24.93	118.06	. . .	101.79	87.95	96.42	. . .	. . .
1989	477.37	3.72	473.65	25.08	132.40	. . .	112.45	87.38	102.26	. . .	. . .
1990	498.34	2.36	495.98	26.65	143.41	62.16	116.04	87.69	105.29	16.09	. . .
1991	490.98	2.53	488.45	26.21	131.38	51.78	120.80	84.94	107.78	15.94	. . .
1992	536.53	3.80	532.66	27.61	138.64	51.60	134.25	91.79	122.66	17.71	. . .
1993	589.39	8.78	580.66	27.87	145.61	51.50	152.37	102.42	134.02	18.39	. . .
1994	668.69	5.33	663.26	30.96	162.11	51.28	184.37	118.27	146.27	21.27	. . .
1995	749.37	6.03	743.54	33.18	181.85	56.16	221.43	123.80	159.91	23.39	. . .
1996	803.11	8.04	795.29	35.71	204.48	72.75	228.07	128.94	171.98	26.10	. . .
1997	876.79	6.66	869.70	39.69	213.77	71.77	253.28	139.81	193.81	29.34	. . .
1998	918.64	5.28	911.90	41.24	200.14	50.90	269.45	148.68	217.00	35.39	. . .
1999	1 035.59	5.37	1 024.62	43.60	221.39	67.81	295.72	178.96	241.91	43.04	. . .
2000	1 231.72	6.40	1 218.02	45.98	298.98	120.28	347.03	195.88	281.83	48.33	222.08
2001	1 153.70	4.90	1 141.00	46.64	273.87	103.59	297.99	189.78	284.29	48.42	195.18
2002	1 173.28	3.35	1 161.37	49.69	267.69	103.51	283.32	203.74	307.84	49.08	195.15
2003	1 272.09	3.60	1 257.12	55.83	313.82	133.10	295.87	210.14	333.88	47.59	207.03
2004	1 488.35	7.39	1 469.70	62.14	412.77	180.46	343.58	228.16	372.94	50.11	238.28
2005	1 695.82	8.33	1 673.46	68.09	523.77	251.86	379.33	239.45	407.24	55.57	290.76
2006	1 878.19	7.44	1 853.94	74.94	601.99	302.43	418.26	256.63	442.64	59.49	290.76
2007	1 986.35	12.41	1 956.96	81.68	634.75	330.98	444.51	256.67	474.55	64.81	326.81
2008	2 141.29	33.97	2 103.64	89.00	779.48	453.28	453.74	231.24	481.64	68.54	331.18
2009	1 580.03	15.87	1 559.63	81.62	462.38	253.69	370.48	157.65	427.33	60.17	300.89
2010	1 938.95	25.09	1 913.86	91.75	603.10	336.11	449.39	225.10	483.23	61.30	354.25
2011	2 239.89	31.93	2 207.95	107.48	755.78	439.34	510.80	254.62	514.11	65.17	386.44
2012	2 303.75	27.48	2 276.27	110.27	730.64	415.17	548.71	297.78	516.92	71.95	396.23
2013	2 294.25	26.13	2 267.99	115.13	681.53	369.68	555.65	308.80	531.67	75.20	401.08
2014	2 385.48	29.12	2 356.36	125.88	667.02	334.00	594.14	328.64	557.09	83.59	422 101.00
2015	2 273.25	24.44	2 248.81	127.80	485.97	181.98	602.45	349.16	594.18	89.25	434.99
2016	2 207.19	20.41	2 186.79	130.01	443.27	146.61	589.68	349.92	583.10	90.80	464.47
2017	2 356.35	18.92	2 339.59	137.83	507.00	186.50	639.83	358.23	601.42	95.28	496.01
2018	2 555.66	19.52	2 536.15	147.26	574.63	225.28	690.91	371.11	645.37	106.87	496.06
2019	2 513.59	19.85	2 493.74	150.51	520.84	193.74	675.58	375.15	653.22	118.44	495.99
2020	2 350.82	14.83	2 335.99	154.33	479.52	116.76	645.26	310.60	639.90	106.38	491.96
2018											
January	207.93	1.57	206.36	11.86	46.32	18.21	55.67	30.68	53.35	8.49	38.94
February	211.79	1.50	210.29	12.40	47.02	18.13	57.48	30.79	54.65	7.95	33.88
March	211.04	1.52	209.52	12.20	47.09	18.17	57.12	31.00	53.90	8.22	40.73
April	211.57	1.71	209.87	12.23	47.75	18.64	57.58	30.36	52.82	9.13	37.96
May	210.79	1.82	208.97	12.32	47.82	18.73	58.34	29.74	52.10	8.66	42.37
June	211.31	1.61	209.70	12.17	48.85	19.67	57.62	29.96	52.42	8.69	41.41
July	214.37	1.64	212.73	12.37	49.69	20.49	58.18	30.43	52.97	9.10	41.36
August	213.98	1.78	212.20	12.29	49.77	20.53	57.29	31.22	52.54	9.08	42.21
September	217.13	1.57	215.56	12.07	49.57	20.59	59.15	31.04	54.62	9.10	44.02
October	218.13	1.69	216.45	12.33	49.45	19.89	56.50	31.76	56.54	9.86	46.65
November	212.48	1.66	210.82	12.34	46.15	16.94	57.20	32.07	53.59	9.48	44.59
December	215.13	1.45	213.68	12.67	45.16	15.29	58.78	32.06	55.88	9.13	41.95
2019											
January	210.14	1.47	208.66	12.36	43.25	14.18	56.70	31.94	55.49	8.93	38.62
February	210.09	1.61	208.48	11.94	42.61	15.17	57.21	31.56	55.61	9.55	34.88
March	214.54	1.60	212.94	12.89	45.25	16.99	57.75	32.07	55.37	9.61	41.07
April	210.94	1.76	209.18	12.80	44.82	17.62	56.12	31.14	55.26	9.04	38.89
May	216.42	1.88	214.54	12.70	46.39	19.31	57.18	32.77	55.75	9.76	41.32
June	211.03	1.67	209.36	12.68	43.07	16.61	56.80	32.13	54.21	10.46	41.10
July	211.77	1.78	209.99	12.67	44.41	16.91	55.78	32.15	54.96	10.02	41.06
August	211.19	1.90	209.29	12.59	42.77	15.79	56.72	31.60	55.91	9.70	43.04
September	207.18	1.62	205.57	12.61	42.20	15.20	55.51	30.67	54.34	10.25	43.22
October	203.34	1.63	201.71	12.46	41.63	15.10	55.67	29.04	52.38	10.52	47.24
November	201.07	1.45	199.62	12.34	40.86	14.55	55.00	30.14	51.35	9.93	42.67
December	205.89	1.49	204.40	12.47	43.58	16.30	55.14	29.93	52.60	10.67	42.88
2020											
January	203.41	1.42	201.98	12.96	41.64	15.04	55.27	29.42	52.98	9.72	39.14
February	199.40	1.81	197.60	12.53	40.79	15.09	52.30	30.59	51.57	9.82	32.83
March	195.59	1.29	194.31	12.87	41.38	11.88	54.03	28.13	48.02	9.88	40.02
April	169.64	1.09	168.55	12.14	41.60	6.04	48.57	13.53	45.19	7.54	35.05
May	167.70	0.77	166.93	12.13	43.87	5.95	48.01	9.02	46.55	7.34	37.19
June	175.71	1.07	174.64	12.40	35.73	7.02	49.97	18.62	50.73	7.19	42.37
July	196.67	1.09	195.58	12.70	39.87	8.05	54.33	26.07	53.99	8.62	41.48
August	201.95	1.09	200.86	13.39	38.25	9.21	54.54	27.84	57.29	9.55	42.16
September	203.58	1.61	201.97	13.40	37.05	9.22	55.29	31.01	56.18	9.04	43.01
October	207.89	1.28	206.61	13.30	38.23	9.50	56.77	32.05	57.52	8.75	46.26
November	213.02	1.08	211.94	13.42	39.40	9.53	57.84	31.28	60.55	9.46	46.94
December	216.27	1.25	215.03	13.11	41.71	10.23	58.33	33.05	59.36	9.47	45.51

[1]Not seasonally adjusted.
. . . = Not available.

Table 7-9. U.S. Exports and Imports of Goods by Principal End-Use Category in Constant Dollars

(Census basis; billions of 2012 chain-weighted dollars, except as noted; seasonally adjusted.)

Year and month	Exports							Imports						
	Total	Foods, feeds, and beverages	Industrial supplies and materials	Capital goods, except auto-motive	Auto-motive vehicles, engines, and parts	Consumer goods, except automotive	Other goods	Total	Foods, feeds, and beverages	Industrial supplies and materials	Capital goods, except auto-motive	Auto-motive vehicles, engines, and parts	Consumer goods, except automotive	Other goods
1995	712.38	101.87	253.24	196.62	70.95	76.73	42.73	928.46	50.57	551.80	132.86	144.68	166.43	28.41
1996	787.89	98.62	268.78	233.39	73.84	82.35	49.89	1 025.33	55.99	585.42	160.26	149.62	178.25	31.71
1997	893.07	98.34	290.85	285.92	83.32	90.44	49.54	1 167.72	61.36	625.78	200.68	161.75	202.94	35.87
1998	914.15	97.73	289.74	298.56	81.32	93.97	53.65	1 305.30	66.02	685.91	230.18	171.86	230.06	44.21
1999	943.54	101.08	291.84	314.72	84.21	94.63	53.61	1 462.44	72.10	696.85	264.02	205.26	258.33	53.94
2000	1 047.54	106.71	321.11	364.20	89.05	103.87	51.60	1 656.42	76.78	740.31	316.80	223.15	303.86	59.66
2001	982.79	109.54	306.65	328.47	83.25	102.71	50.69	1 601.50	79.75	736.67	279.63	216.30	308.87	60.23
2002	909.96	107.07	301.64	280.75	86.77	98.41	47.18	1 631.30	85.02	737.94	258.51	231.54	337.43	60.92
2003	933.89	108.87	314.83	286.68	88.18	103.78	45.28	1 718.52	92.87	767.45	274.39	237.52	366.47	58.04
2004	1 016.04	100.50	336.09	322.28	96.86	118.15	45.95	1 921.28	98.59	862.16	323.53	254.00	406.44	59.42
2005	1 088.65	105.18	346.06	352.41	105.73	130.19	47.33	2 058.36	102.24	906.53	360.64	263.89	439.58	63.74
2006	1 198.66	112.76	372.59	396.62	114.04	143.15	53.39	2 182.04	108.21	910.77	403.10	281.53	474.87	66.65
2007	1 293.52	119.92	397.85	426.95	127.59	157.91	55.12	2 223.92	109.13	883.13	429.06	278.75	501.57	70.64
2008	1 385.46	126.88	445.88	453.35	126.38	170.78	55.79	2 158.81	106.70	842.41	438.11	245.30	495.69	70.96
2009	1 198.93	123.67	396.47	388.40	84.63	157.41	50.08	1 820.18	99.87	705.51	363.71	166.20	441.00	64.98
2010	1 379.61	135.65	454.60	445.18	115.49	170.24	59.44	2 091.57	103.66	746.18	447.24	235.88	498.29	64.38
2011	1 486.80	132.97	494.94	493.40	135.10	177.18	53.20	2 221.30	106.79	758.64	508.41	259.44	521.70	65.37
2012	1 545.82	133.05	501.18	527.18	146.16	181.68	56.58	2 276.27	110.27	730.64	548.71	297.78	516.92	71.95
2013	1 589.07	132.72	523.08	533.01	151.88	190.81	58.61	2 301.79	113.99	706.16	563.42	309.75	532.57	75.79
2014	1 648.01	141.65	532.96	550.17	158.11	204.04	63.00	2 405.34	119.40	707.10	607.34	331.35	555.61	84.01
2015	1 638.63	144.56	532.17	541.37	150.43	207.29	64.85	2 521.14	123.52	710.76	630.17	358.85	597.30	92.49
2016	1 639.76	156.98	533.51	528.67	150.13	207.18	67.61	2 541.56	125.27	737.80	633.48	362.40	588.27	95.64
2017	1 710.83	158.61	581.79	540.33	157.24	214.02	66.43	2 643.15	128.13	745.30	688.08	372.34	606.68	99.14
2018	1 782.25	158.39	620.36	566.86	156.98	220.51	67.30	2 782.08	137.38	748.45	738.85	385.60	648.57	109.85
2019	1 781.28	155.64	636.11	549.31	160.28	218.28	71.19	2 776.50	140.22	709.18	730.57	392.35	659.11	122.51
2020	1 611.99	164.44	633.90	461.28	126.27	184.35	63.59	2 655.52	145.26	720.55	698.29	322.41	646.81	109.29
2018														
January	144.12	12.64	48.74	45.78	13.44	18.83	5.19	227.94	10.94	61.96	59.63	31.78	53.90	8.74
February	146.41	13.05	50.83	46.25	13.82	17.72	5.39	230.86	11.26	61.94	61.41	31.89	55.03	8.17
March	150.75	13.04	52.47	48.19	13.75	18.27	5.67	230.23	11.22	62.18	60.95	32.17	54.21	8.44
April	150.78	13.65	53.69	46.81	13.70	18.30	5.51	230.71	11.33	63.15	61.42	31.51	53.07	9.37
May	152.21	14.43	51.65	48.46	13.28	18.77	6.34	228.52	11.39	61.82	62.28	30.91	52.28	8.88
June	149.79	14.31	52.15	47.49	12.85	18.02	5.80	229.32	11.60	62.39	61.60	31.16	52.70	8.93
July	148.32	14.40	52.78	46.90	12.77	17.20	5.18	232.56	11.95	63.32	62.22	31.64	53.11	9.36
August	147.20	13.45	50.69	47.02	12.51	18.74	5.50	232.38	11.83	63.85	61.32	32.48	52.69	9.35
September	149.06	12.89	52.36	47.54	12.90	18.72	5.31	235.47	11.36	63.25	63.30	32.29	54.80	9.36
October	149.39	12.60	52.16	47.53	12.79	19.13	5.80	236.08	11.23	63.16	60.43	33.04	56.81	10.12
November	147.65	12.31	51.28	47.94	12.57	18.41	5.66	231.12	11.47	59.84	61.26	33.38	53.85	9.75
December	146.59	11.64	51.58	46.94	12.62	18.41	5.96	236.89	11.80	61.58	63.03	33.35	56.14	9.39
2019														
January	149.68	12.76	53.33	46.47	13.40	18.71	5.79	234.05	11.52	61.98	60.80	33.26	55.93	9.22
February	148.94	12.69	51.42	47.58	13.35	18.83	5.56	231.82	11.09	58.69	61.36	32.88	55.99	9.84
March	150.83	13.06	52.00	47.82	13.73	18.95	5.79	234.84	12.04	59.63	62.03	33.45	55.78	9.89
April	146.17	13.52	51.72	45.16	13.02	18.23	5.31	230.53	11.45	58.99	60.54	32.58	55.77	9.32
May	149.65	13.55	51.96	46.36	13.55	19.03	5.87	236.06	11.47	60.32	61.69	34.28	56.33	10.08
June	147.33	13.43	53.41	44.95	13.30	17.37	5.82	232.32	11.65	57.84	61.39	33.60	54.80	10.84
July	148.81	13.29	51.83	46.30	13.51	18.56	5.95	233.85	11.67	60.59	60.36	33.66	55.48	10.38
August	148.55	13.71	53.66	44.49	13.74	17.71	6.22	233.89	11.74	59.03	61.48	33.10	56.38	10.05
September	147.32	12.49	53.61	44.90	13.28	17.91	6.01	229.96	12.01	57.98	60.28	32.14	54.81	10.63
October	147.88	12.43	54.62	44.76	13.11	17.63	6.35	226.15	11.91	57.51	60.59	30.45	52.87	10.92
November	147.67	12.41	53.59	45.23	13.48	17.88	5.89	223.98	11.84	56.44	59.98	31.57	51.88	10.30
December	148.46	12.33	54.97	45.30	12.80	17.46	6.63	229.06	11.82	60.20	60.08	31.36	53.09	11.05
2020														
January	146.11	12.64	54.33	44.28	13.03	17.32	5.57	225.77	12.27	57.08	60.18	30.65	53.50	10.05
February	148.83	13.38	56.36	44.25	13.12	16.89	6.18	221.30	11.62	56.84	56.90	31.88	52.11	10.14
March	141.21	13.31	54.75	42.49	11.11	15.57	5.63	220.80	12.11	61.52	58.68	29.28	48.65	10.22
April	112.17	13.81	50.06	32.39	3.66	11.01	5.11	196.25	11.63	68.76	52.65	14.02	45.77	7.84
May	107.83	13.30	46.44	31.83	3.31	11.69	4.39	194.66	11.30	73.58	51.99	9.36	47.19	7.62
June	119.93	12.78	47.27	35.46	8.17	13.12	4.75	201.75	11.50	57.89	54.02	19.31	51.35	7.43
July	132.47	12.88	49.64	37.82	11.85	15.69	5.46	224.41	11.93	62.32	58.71	27.06	54.61	8.89
August	135.53	14.09	53.82	36.60	11.89	15.80	5.15	227.78	12.51	56.76	58.86	28.88	57.87	9.77
September	138.16	14.73	53.86	37.73	12.30	15.92	5.25	227.76	12.42	53.76	59.66	32.10	56.71	9.18
October	142.16	14.38	55.65	39.30	12.44	16.77	5.27	233.67	12.34	56.20	61.29	33.20	58.08	8.89
November	142.44	14.16	56.05	39.07	12.36	17.24	5.29	239.65	12.91	57.17	62.41	32.43	61.12	9.64
December	145.16	14.97	55.67	40.06	13.02	17.35	5.54	241.74	12.73	58.68	62.95	34.25	59.85	9.62

Table 7-10. U.S. Exports of Goods by Selected Regions and Countries

(Census f.a.s. basis; millions of dollars, not seasonally adjusted.)

Year and month	Total, all countries	Selected regions [1]			Selected countries				
		European Union, 15 countries	European Union, 28 countries	OPEC	Brazil	Canada	China	Japan	Mexico
1985	...	48 994	...	12 478	3 140	47 251	3 856	22 631	13 635
1986	...	53 154	...	10 844	3 885	45 333	3 106	26 882	12 392
1987	254 122	60 575	...	11 057	4 040	59 814	3 497	28 249	14 582
1988	322 426	75 755	...	13 994	4 266	71 622	5 022	37 725	20 629
1989	363 812	86 331	...	13 196	4 804	78 809	5 755	44 494	24 982
1990	393 592	98 027	...	13 703	5 048	83 674	4 806	48 580	28 279
1991	421 730	103 123	...	19 054	6 148	85 150	6 278	48 125	33 277
1992	448 165	102 958	...	21 960	5 751	90 594	7 419	47 813	40 592
1993	465 090	96 973	...	19 500	6 058	100 444	8 763	47 892	41 581
1994	512 625	102 818	...	17 868	8 102	114 439	9 282	53 488	50 844
1995	584 740	123 671	...	19 533	11 439	127 226	11 754	64 343	46 292
1996	625 073	127 710	...	22 275	12 718	134 210	11 993	67 607	56 792
1997	689 180	140 773	143 931	25 525	15 915	151 767	12 862	65 549	71 389
1998	682 139	149 035	151 967	25 154	15 142	156 604	14 241	57 831	78 773
1999	695 797	151 814	154 825	20 166	13 203	166 600	13 111	57 466	86 909
2000	781 918	165 065	168 181	19 078	15 321	178 941	16 185	64 924	111 349
2001	729 101	158 768	161 931	20 052	15 879	163 424	19 182	57 452	101 297
2002	693 101	143 691	146 621	18 812	12 376	160 923	22 128	51 449	97 470
2003	724 771	151 731	155 170	17 279	11 211	169 924	28 368	52 004	97 412
2004	814 875	168 572	171 230	22 256	13 886	189 880	34 428	53 569	110 731
2005	901 082	...	185 166	31 641	15 372	211 899	41 192	54 681	120 248
2006	1 025 967	...	211 887	38 658	18 887	230 656	53 673	58 459	133 722
2007	1 148 199	...	244 166	48 485	24 172	248 888	62 937	61 160	135 918
2008	1 287 442	...	271 810	64 880	32 299	261 150	69 733	65 142	151 220
2009	1 056 043	...	220 599	49 857	26 095	204 658	69 497	51 134	128 892
2010	1 278 495	...	239 591	54 226	35 418	249 256	91 911	60 472	163 665
2011	1 482 508	...	269 069	64 809	43 019	281 292	104 122	65 800	198 289
2012	1 545 821	...	265 373	81 727	43 771	292 651	110 517	69 976	215 875
2013	1 578 517	...	262 095	84 730	44 106	300 755	121 746	65 237	225 954
2014	1 621 874	...	276 274	82 533	42 432	312 817	123 657	66 892	241 007
2015	1 503 328	...	271 911	72 878	31 641	280 855	115 873	62 388	236 460
2016	1 451 460	...	269 650	71 053	30 193	266 734	115 595	63 247	230 229
2017	1 547 195	...	283 291	59 337	37 331	282 774	129 997	67 603	243 609
2018	1 665 787	...	318 490	59 282	39 400	299 732	120 281	75 164	265 968
2019	1 642 820	...	336 487	51 318	42 866	292 820	106 448	74 497	256 316
2020	1 424 935	...	231 223	...	34 595	255 392	124 485	63 756	211 481
2018									
January	125 038	...	23 421	3 538	3 031	22 641	9 909	5 675	21 434
February	128 219	...	24 935	4 191	2 909	23 675	9 743	5 389	20 369
March	149 562	...	30 005	5 216	3 276	27 267	12 653	6 496	21 958
April	138 230	...	26 825	4 494	3 200	25 834	10 510	5 840	22 532
May	145 528	...	28 006	5 771	3 243	27 066	10 398	6 129	23 043
June	145 499	...	28 155	5 187	3 337	26 349	10 856	6 396	22 243
July	133 808	...	23 916	4 173	3 385	23 708	10 152	6 392	22 917
August	140 218	...	25 634	5 241	3 679	25 608	9 278	6 325	22 570
September	139 389	...	27 053	4 986	3 342	24 586	9 733	6 452	21 664
October	147 082	...	28 001	5 151	3 863	26 194	9 189	6 551	24 753
November	139 278	...	26 828	5 777	2 942	24 490	8 650	6 748	22 958
December	133 936	...	25 710	5 555	3 194	22 314	9 210	6 772	19 528
2019									
January	129 662	...	27 717	4 343	3 351	22 683	7 104	6 385	21 986
February	129 916	...	28 472	3 926	2 964	23 191	8 083	5 420	20 215
March	148 306	...	30 577	5 003	3 674	26 448	10 577	6 426	21 722
April	134 814	...	27 259	3 793	3 271	25 334	7 884	5 666	22 268
May	142 241	...	28 240	4 469	3 538	26 158	9 070	6 635	22 645
June	138 008	...	27 465	4 043	3 883	24 887	9 167	6 136	20 683
July	133 201	...	25 816	3 585	3 588	23 465	8 699	6 596	22 213
August	138 316	...	27 902	4 205	3 715	25 309	9 409	6 156	21 941
September	134 043	...	27 718	4 610	3 525	24 307	8 600	5 811	20 617
October	142 272	...	30 169	4 725	3 851	25 267	8 854	6 502	22 272
November	136 820	...	28 235	4 010	4 048	23 430	10 103	5 977	20 802
December	135 221	...	26 918	4 608	3 459	22 340	8 899	6 786	18 951
2020									
January	128 767	...	21 522	...	3 547	22 551	7 154	5 470	20 754
February	130 553	...	22 516	...	3 166	23 210	6 828	6 064	19 171
March	132 921	...	23 701	...	3 426	23 575	7 900	6 496	19 685
April	94 471	...	15 746	...	2 297	14 736	8 624	5 442	12 414
May	90 738	...	15 454	...	2 233	14 830	9 672	4 834	10 404
June	104 669	...	16 246	...	2 171	20 116	9 237	4 759	15 712
July	112 711	...	18 411	...	2 595	21 265	9 088	4 791	18 472
August	117 833	...	18 550	...	2 768	22 841	10 962	5 208	16 999
September	121 115	...	19 676	...	2 877	23 336	11 498	4 780	18 715
October	132 348	...	20 642	...	3 087	23 616	14 773	5 362	20 443
November	126 614	...	19 454	...	3 064	22 431	14 220	4 951	19 257
December	132 194	...	19 305	...	3 365	22 884	14 530	5 599	19 456

[1]See notes and definitions for definitions of regions.
. . . = Not available.

Table 7-11. U.S. Imports of Goods by Selected Regions and Countries

(Census Customs basis; millions of dollars, not seasonally adjusted.)

| Year and month | Total, all countries | Selected regions [1] | | | Selected countries | | | | |
		European Union, 15 countries	European Union, 28 countries	OPEC	Brazil	Canada	China	Japan	Mexico
1985	. . .	67 822	. . .	22 801	7 526	69 006	3 862	68 783	19 132
1986	. . .	75 736	. . .	19 751	6 813	68 253	4 771	81 911	17 302
1987	406 241	81 188	. . .	23 952	7 865	71 085	6 294	84 575	20 271
1988	440 952	84 939	. . .	22 962	9 294	81 398	8 511	89 519	23 260
1989	473 211	85 153	. . .	30 611	8 410	87 953	11 990	93 553	27 162
1990	495 311	91 868	. . .	38 052	7 898	91 380	15 237	89 684	30 157
1991	488 453	86 481	. . .	32 644	6 717	91 064	18 969	91 511	31 130
1992	532 662	93 993	. . .	33 200	7 609	98 630	25 728	97 414	35 211
1993	580 656	97 941	. . .	31 739	7 479	111 216	31 540	107 246	39 918
1994	663 252	110 875	. . .	31 685	8 683	128 406	38 787	119 156	49 494
1995	743 545	131 871	. . .	35 606	8 833	144 370	45 543	123 479	62 100
1996	795 287	142 947	. . .	44 285	8 773	155 893	51 513	115 187	74 297
1997	869 703	157 528	160 896	44 025	9 625	167 234	62 558	121 663	85 938
1998	911 897	176 380	180 550	33 925	10 102	173 256	71 169	121 845	94 629
1999	1 024 616	195 227	200 053	41 977	11 314	198 711	81 788	130 864	109 721
2000	1 218 023	220 019	226 901	67 090	13 853	230 838	100 018	146 479	135 926
2001	1 140 998	220 057	226 568	59 754	14 466	216 268	102 278	126 473	131 338
2002	1 161 366	225 771	232 313	53 245	15 781	209 088	125 193	121 429	134 616
2003	1 257 121	244 826	253 042	68 344	17 910	221 595	152 436	118 037	138 060
2004	1 469 705	272 439	281 959	92 099	21 160	256 360	196 682	129 805	155 902
2005	1 673 454	298 879	309 628	127 169	24 436	290 384	243 470	138 004	170 109
2006	1 853 938	319 590	330 482	150 758	26 367	302 438	287 774	148 181	198 253
2007	1 956 961	. . .	354 409	165 651	25 644	317 057	321 443	145 463	210 714
2008	2 103 641	. . .	367 617	242 579	30 453	339 491	337 773	139 262	215 942
2009	1 559 625	. . .	281 801	111 602	20 070	226 248	296 374	95 804	176 654
2010	1 913 857	. . .	319 264	149 893	23 958	277 637	364 953	120 552	229 986
2011	2 207 954	. . .	368 464	191 470	31 737	315 325	399 371	128 928	262 874
2012	2 276 267	. . .	381 755	180 752	32 123	324 263	425 619	146 432	277 594
2013	2 267 987	. . .	387 510	152 688	27 541	332 504	440 430	138 575	280 556
2014	2 356 356	. . .	420 609	132 370	30 021	349 286	468 475	134 505	295 730
2015	2 248 811	. . .	427 810	66 241	27 474	296 305	483 202	131 445	296 433
2016	2 186 786	. . .	416 331	77 551	26 043	277 720	462 420	132 000	293 501
2017	2 339 591	. . .	434 866	72 165	29 462	299 065	505 165	136 411	312 667
2018	2 536 145	. . .	486 895	80 237	31 203	318 575	538 514	142 228	343 681
2019	2 493 738	. . .	515 079	45 640	30 934	318 778	450 760	143 586	356 157
2020	2 335 991	. . .	415 473	. . .	23 397	270 313	434 749	119 499	325 212
2018									
January	203 029	. . .	36 894	6 480	2 750	26 184	45 681	11 270	25 788
February	186 770	. . .	36 940	5 577	2 013	23 997	38 956	10 809	25 777
March	207 985	. . .	41 769	6 050	2 341	26 954	38 274	12 839	29 754
April	205 084	. . .	41 433	7 689	2 568	26 533	38 228	12 061	27 895
May	216 027	. . .	40 990	6 493	2 381	28 164	43 867	11 642	29 209
June	211 253	. . .	39 990	6 884	2 645	28 040	44 524	11 523	29 350
July	216 854	. . .	41 672	7 674	2 752	26 835	47 010	11 861	27 999
August	221 897	. . .	41 152	6 560	3 261	27 959	47 796	12 316	30 886
September	211 317	. . .	37 652	6 857	2 619	26 297	49 938	10 302	28 985
October	235 858	. . .	45 473	7 535	3 103	28 055	52 081	12 775	31 637
November	213 493	. . .	41 938	6 604	2 336	25 627	46 345	12 567	29 465
December	206 578	. . .	40 992	5 833	2 435	23 929	45 815	12 263	26 935
2019									
January	204 061	. . .	39 371	5 325	2 547	23 351	41 369	11 537	27 561
February	185 513	. . .	37 750	3 494	2 289	22 961	33 101	11 428	27 507
March	207 645	. . .	44 754	3 887	2 579	27 572	31 187	13 059	31 102
April	208 881	. . .	45 227	3 916	2 477	26 733	34 625	12 981	30 235
May	220 308	. . .	45 459	4 639	3 097	29 197	39 104	11 999	31 919
June	206 685	. . .	41 406	4 189	2 611	27 646	38 871	11 913	30 198
July	218 473	. . .	45 924	3 640	3 096	26 762	41 377	12 884	29 961
August	215 385	. . .	43 173	3 757	2 410	26 636	41 080	12 422	30 891
September	206 362	. . .	41 546	3 459	2 439	26 853	40 061	10 819	29 285
October	219 158	. . .	46 749	2 999	2 390	28 537	40 000	11 573	30 940
November	199 187	. . .	41 208	3 025	2 400	25 242	36 398	11 445	29 048
December	202 080	. . .	42 512	3 310	2 600	27 286	33 586	11 525	27 507
2020									
January	196 142	. . .	35 034	. . .	2 093	25 321	33 173	10 458	28 300
February	178 487	. . .	32 835	. . .	1 554	24 361	22 721	10 669	29 037
March	194 562	. . .	41 638	. . .	2 122	25 099	19 789	12 175	30 081
April	165 725	. . .	31 485	. . .	1 678	14 955	30 923	9 859	15 817
May	163 789	. . .	27 177	. . .	1 763	15 850	36 552	7 382	14 914
June	179 478	. . .	30 328	. . .	1 909	20 335	37 495	6 647	25 807
July	200 450	. . .	34 116	. . .	1 926	22 340	40 658	8 272	29 070
August	203 342	. . .	34 154	. . .	1 703	23 762	40 792	9 695	29 772
September	206 457	. . .	35 677	. . .	1 800	24 606	41 194	9 937	29 857
October	219 513	. . .	36 850	. . .	2 302	24 878	44 779	11 240	33 113
November	212 675	. . .	36 718	. . .	1 948	24 087	44 839	11 726	29 865
December	215 373	. . .	39 463	. . .	2 599	24 719	41 834	11 438	29 580

[1]See notes and definitions for definitions of regions.
. . . = Not available.

Table 7-12A. U.S. Exports of Services: Recent Data

(Balance of payments basis, millions of dollars, seasonally adjusted.)

Year and month	Total services	Maintenance and repair services, n.i.e.	Transport	Travel for all purposes including education	Construction services	Insurance services	Financial services	Charges for the use of intellectual property n.i.e	Telecommunications, computer and information services	Other business services	Personal, cultural, and recreational services	Government goods and services, n.i.e.
1999	278 001	3 656	46 302	89 146	3 974	3 052	25 998	39 913	12 320	36 415	9 007	8 218
2000	298 023	4 423	49 462	96 872	1 993	3 631	29 192	43 476	12 250	38 217	9 351	9 156
2001	284 035	5 191	45 965	86 408	2 608	3 424	27 500	41 005	12 862	41 250	9 631	8 191
2002	288 059	5 368	45 954	79 625	3 128	4 415	29 903	44 815	12 487	44 625	10 089	7 653
2003	297 740	5 073	46 701	76 983	2 377	5 974	33 499	47 308	14 099	46 171	10 522	9 033
2004	344 536	5 181	54 419	85 648	2 253	7 314	42 767	56 943	15 009	51 609	11 409	11 985
2005	378 487	6 652	58 377	93 423	1 489	7 566	47 405	64 466	15 568	56 846	11 114	15 582
2006	423 086	7 106	64 026	96 148	1 856	9 445	56 522	70 999	17 242	65 990	14 532	19 222
2007	495 664	8 899	70 837	106 918	2 774	10 867	73 980	84 498	20 339	79 366	16 265	20 921
2008	540 791	9 362	78 237	117 030	4 072	13 491	79 897	89 672	23 892	89 975	16 080	19 084
2009	522 461	11 573	65 806	110 757	4 260	14 594	73 844	85 730	24 925	93 508	16 926	20 538
2010	582 041	13 111	76 357	130 315	2 951	14 854	86 512	94 968	26 556	99 595	17 612	19 210
2011	644 665	14 739	82 930	142 197	3 187	14 673	101 077	107 053	29 376	108 423	19 538	21 470
2012	684 823	14 944	88 238	153 921	3 234	15 978	105 419	107 869	33 522	118 451	21 098	22 148
2013	719 529	15 720	89 999	170 979	2 213	15 768	109 794	113 824	36 325	122 166	20 888	21 852
2014	756 705	17 978	90 687	180 265	2 070	16 277	119 933	116 380	38 629	132 240	22 551	19 693
2015	768 362	19 847	84 434	192 602	2 759	15 464	114 951	111 151	41 427	141 421	24 220	20 087
2016	780 530	21 587	81 779	192 868	1 690	16 249	114 762	112 981	43 122	153 089	23 626	18 777
2017	830 388	23 239	86 342	193 834	2 053	18 223	128 035	118 147	47 657	167 270	25 664	19 924
2018	862 433	27 948	93 251	196 465	2 948	17 904	132 420	118 875	49 653	177 261	23 759	21 949
2019	875 825	27 868	91 092	193 315	3 189	16 238	135 698	117 401	55 657	189 441	23 372	22 555
2020	705 643	13 278	56 706	72 813	2 349	20 431	144 343	113 779	56 682	183 180	20 442	21 642
2018												
January	72 249	2 108	7 638	16 672	206	1 526	11 014	10 363	4 205	14 652	2 168	1 696
February	72 531	2 185	7 779	16 679	216	1 500	11 002	10 267	4 226	14 736	2 209	1 731
March	72 579	2 275	7 825	16 869	224	1 479	11 032	10 130	4 231	14 611	2 109	1 793
April	71 130	2 278	7 711	16 219	230	1 461	11 029	9 952	4 219	14 278	1 871	1 882
May	71 306	2 283	7 854	16 472	235	1 464	11 142	9 850	4 174	14 163	1 752	1 918
June	71 180	2 266	7 797	16 315	237	1 487	11 238	9 825	4 096	14 266	1 753	1 901
July	71 451	2 321	7 797	16 319	237	1 530	11 095	9 876	3 985	14 587	1 873	1 832
August	71 812	2 409	7 836	16 177	243	1 544	11 146	9 872	3 955	14 864	1 961	1 804
September	72 023	2 442	7 805	16 240	257	1 531	10 999	9 813	4 006	15 097	2 017	1 817
October	72 031	2 492	7 789	16 045	277	1 491	10 902	9 698	4 137	15 286	2 041	1 872
November	72 080	2 464	7 719	16 167	290	1 458	10 875	9 628	4 206	15 370	2 028	1 875
December	72 059	2 424	7 700	16 290	295	1 433	10 947	9 602	4 214	15 350	1 976	1 828
2019												
January	71 366	2 295	7 795	15 956	291	1 417	11 038	9 619	4 160	15 224	1 887	1 683
February	71 619	2 190	7 711	16 242	283	1 395	11 132	9 646	4 215	15 241	1 851	1 713
March	72 177	2 212	7 631	16 320	271	1 368	11 313	9 683	4 381	15 399	1 870	1 730
April	72 852	2 123	7 722	16 158	253	1 336	11 450	9 730	4 655	15 701	1 942	1 782
May	73 761	2 225	7 647	16 448	249	1 335	11 547	9 750	4 815	15 914	1 981	1 851
June	73 712	2 304	7 560	16 253	258	1 365	11 432	9 743	4 858	16 039	1 988	1 913
July	72 997	2 323	7 383	15 899	281	1 426	11 184	9 708	4 786	16 077	1 963	1 967
August	73 159	2 365	7 518	15 903	288	1 437	11 152	9 728	4 745	16 075	1 953	1 995
September	73 102	2 399	7 432	15 919	280	1 396	11 147	9 801	4 736	16 035	1 959	1 997
October	73 552	2 470	7 543	15 997	257	1 305	11 385	9 927	4 757	15 956	1 981	1 973
November	73 682	2 492	7 521	16 082	242	1 244	11 452	10 012	4 771	15 903	1 995	1 968
December	73 845	2 469	7 628	16 140	235	1 213	11 466	10 054	4 778	15 877	2 002	1 982
2020												
January	69 524	1 645	7 516	13 954	211	1 675	11 713	9 440	4 669	15 149	1 688	1 865
February	69 118	1 336	7 351	14 165	207	1 692	11 831	9 255	4 646	15 099	1 636	1 901
March	60 615	1 204	5 344	8 285	206	1 661	11 745	9 023	4 642	15 201	1 483	1 820
April	55 049	1 156	3 616	4 828	208	1 582	11 631	8 888	4 634	15 455	1 360	1 691
May	55 056	1 161	3 590	4 722	208	1 568	11 665	8 964	4 580	15 542	1 373	1 684
June	55 103	1 123	3 797	4 364	208	1 620	11 810	9 108	4 505	15 462	1 387	1 720
July	55 028	993	3 938	3 799	206	1 737	11 814	9 362	4 403	15 215	1 746	1 815
August	55 306	896	4 076	3 405	200	1 802	11 971	9 593	4 451	15 093	1 962	1 858
September	56 099	944	4 178	3 323	190	1 815	12 219	9 802	4 647	15 094	2 032	1 855
October	56 971	909	4 215	3 553	176	1 776	12 383	9 988	4 989	15 220	1 954	1 809
November	58 397	945	4 462	4 005	167	1 754	12 710	10 130	5 208	15 304	1 913	1 799
December	59 377	966	4 624	4 410	162	1 751	12 850	10 225	5 308	15 346	1 910	1 825

n.i.e = Not included elsewhere.

Table 7-12B. U.S. Exports of Services: Historical Data

(Balance of payments basis, millions of dollars, seasonally adjusted.)

Year	Total	Travel	Passenger fares	Other transportation	Royalties and license fees	Other private services (financial, professional, etc.)	Transfers under U.S. military sales contracts [1]	U.S. government miscellaneous services
1960	6 290	919	175	1 607	837	570	2 030	153
1961	6 295	947	183	1 620	906	607	1 867	164
1962	6 941	957	191	1 764	1 056	585	2 193	195
1963	7 348	1 015	205	1 898	1 162	613	2 219	236
1964	7 840	1 207	241	2 076	1 314	651	2 086	265
1965	8 824	1 380	271	2 175	1 534	714	2 465	285
1966	9 616	1 590	317	2 333	1 516	814	2 721	326
1967	10 667	1 646	371	2 426	1 747	951	3 191	336
1968	11 917	1 775	411	2 548	1 867	1 024	3 939	353
1969	12 806	2 043	450	2 652	2 019	1 160	4 138	343
1970	14 171	2 331	544	3 125	2 331	1 294	4 214	332
1971	16 358	2 534	615	3 299	2 545	1 546	5 472	347
1972	17 841	2 817	699	3 579	2 770	1 764	5 856	357
1973	19 832	3 412	975	4 465	3 225	1 985	5 369	401
1974	22 591	4 032	1 104	5 697	3 821	2 321	5 197	419
1975	25 497	4 697	1 039	5 840	4 300	2 920	6 256	446
1976	27 971	5 742	1 229	6 747	4 353	3 584	5 826	489
1977	31 485	6 150	1 366	7 090	4 920	3 848	7 554	557
1978	36 353	7 183	1 603	8 136	5 885	4 717	8 209	620
1979	39 692	8 441	2 156	9 971	6 184	5 439	6 981	520
1980	47 584	10 588	2 591	11 618	7 085	6 276	9 029	398
1981	57 354	12 913	3 111	12 560	7 284	10 250	10 720	517
1982	64 079	12 393	3 174	12 317	5 603	17 444	12 572	576
1983	64 307	10 947	3 610	12 590	5 778	18 192	12 524	666
1984	71 168	17 177	4 067	13 809	6 177	19 255	9 969	714
1985	73 155	17 762	4 411	14 674	6 678	20 035	8 718	878
1986	86 689	20 385	5 582	15 438	8 113	28 027	8 549	595
1987	98 661	23 563	7 003	17 027	10 174	29 263	11 106	526
1988	110 919	29 434	8 976	19 311	12 139	31 111	9 284	664
1989	127 087	36 205	10 657	20 526	13 818	36 729	8 564	587
1990	147 832	43 007	15 298	22 042	16 634	40 251	9 932	668
1991	164 261	48 385	15 854	22 631	17 819	47 748	11 135	690
1992	177 252	54 742	16 618	21 531	20 841	50 292	12 387	841
1993	185 920	57 875	16 528	21 958	21 695	53 510	13 471	883
1994	200 395	58 417	16 997	23 754	26 712	60 841	12 787	887
1995	219 183	63 395	18 909	26 081	30 289	65 048	14 643	818
1996	239 489	69 809	20 422	26 074	32 470	73 340	16 446	928
1997	256 087	73 426	20 868	27 006	33 228	83 929	16 675	955
1998	262 758	71 325	20 098	25 604	35 626	91 774	17 405	926
1999	268 790	75 161	19 425	23 792	47 731	96 812	5 211	657

Note: The category "Royalties and license fees" is the earlier terminology for the category called "Charges for the use of intellectual property n.i.e" in the revised and updated data shown in Tables 7-15A/7-16A. Other categories differ in both title and content; see the Notes and Definitions.

[1]Contains goods that cannot be separately identified.

Table 7-13A. U.S. Imports of Services: Recent Data

(Balance of payments basis, millions of dollars, seasonally adjusted.)

Year and month	Total services	Maintenance and repair services, n.i.e.	Transport	Travel for all purposes including education	Construction services	Insurance services	Financial services	Charges for the use of intellectual property n.i.e	Telecommunications, computer and information services	Other business services	Personal, cultural, and recreational services	Government goods and services, n.i.e.
1999	196 742	1 193	49 892	58 864	1 524	9 389	12 489	12 845	14 664	19 999	1 670	14 212
2000	220 927	2 316	58 526	64 174	1 447	11 284	16 445	16 139	14 128	20 306	1 645	14 516
2001	222 039	1 821	56 571	60 525	1 870	16 706	15 982	16 207	14 012	21 204	1 820	15 322
2002	233 480	2 016	55 398	59 017	2 616	21 927	15 214	18 981	13 214	24 027	1 719	19 353
2003	252 340	2 043	61 084	61 244	1 974	25 233	15 766	18 653	14 928	25 748	2 049	23 619
2004	290 609	2 181	71 954	70 332	2 303	29 089	19 043	22 818	16 382	28 026	2 183	26 296
2005	312 225	2 730	78 796	74 112	1 295	28 710	21 971	24 127	18 404	32 076	2 550	27 454
2006	349 329	4 091	82 348	78 375	1 650	39 382	27 005	23 076	20 850	41 378	3 822	27 353
2007	385 464	4 590	86 097	82 606	2 570	47 166	33 768	24 615	23 660	48 455	3 678	28 260
2008	420 650	5 128	92 837	84 317	3 526	58 444	29 519	27 764	26 138	59 675	4 421	28 880
2009	407 538	5 257	75 784	82 512	3 667	63 965	24 900	29 421	26 038	59 517	5 016	31 460
2010	436 456	5 857	88 394	85 166	2 578	63 452	27 215	31 116	29 421	65 903	5 393	31 960
2011	458 188	7 168	95 027	86 623	3 025	58 277	30 312	32 911	32 832	74 082	6 636	31 293
2012	469 610	7 078	99 323	90 340	3 340	58 747	28 736	35 061	33 285	78 678	7 160	27 861
2013	465 819	6 674	94 434	91 119	2 583	52 993	29 284	35 295	35 868	84 024	8 205	25 341
2014	490 932	6 732	99 810	96 248	2 314	52 760	32 770	37 562	38 461	90 716	9 323	24 236
2015	497 755	8 084	99 557	102 664	3 012	49 842	32 594	35 178	38 815	95 119	11 358	21 531
2016	511 898	7 595	92 391	109 155	1 768	52 070	32 672	41 974	39 720	100 505	12 544	21 503
2017	544 836	6 796	96 515	117 972	1 950	50 889	36 649	44 405	43 091	106 991	17 530	22 047
2018	562 069	7 133	106 303	126 008	3 151	43 735	39 249	43 933	42 558	107 834	19 190	22 975
2019	588 359	7 823	107 458	134 594	1 327	51 547	40 350	42 733	43 720	113 584	21 140	24 083
2020	460 301	6 090	72 411	35 808	1 131	55 617	42 256	42 984	38 594	117 673	23 185	24 553
2018												
January	45 680	575	8 360	10 161	220	3 612	3 214	3 673	3 583	8 908	1 504	1 869
February	46 637	569	8 606	10 283	242	3 434	3 201	4 457	3 567	8 864	1 526	1 887
March	45 993	549	8 685	10 583	251	3 393	3 217	3 413	3 574	8 853	1 578	1 898
April	46 313	514	8 861	10 420	246	3 488	3 314	3 430	3 605	8 875	1 658	1 903
May	46 255	514	8 711	10 332	244	3 559	3 342	3 440	3 604	8 911	1 687	1 910
June	46 474	545	8 718	10 242	244	3 606	3 310	3 691	3 572	8 961	1 664	1 921
July	46 886	612	8 939	10 492	246	3 630	3 224	3 685	3 509	9 026	1 590	1 934
August	46 842	662	8 854	10 588	261	3 680	3 293	3 469	3 478	9 066	1 553	1 939
September	47 082	666	8 952	10 582	287	3 755	3 245	3 541	3 481	9 082	1 553	1 935
October	47 814	659	9 324	10 603	326	3 857	3 287	3 654	3 516	9 074	1 592	1 923
November	47 830	604	9 045	10 798	319	3 884	3 285	3 725	3 534	9 088	1 627	1 922
December	48 263	664	9 249	10 925	265	3 837	3 318	3 754	3 534	9 125	1 658	1 933
2019												
January	48 020	626	9 305	10 877	164	3 716	3 351	3 743	3 517	9 134	1 685	1 901
February	47 887	632	9 007	11 056	103	3 726	3 246	3 700	3 530	9 178	1 711	1 997
March	48 360	712	9 017	11 124	82	3 867	3 380	3 625	3 574	9 242	1 734	2 004
April	48 743	648	8 858	11 406	100	4 139	3 369	3 517	3 648	9 326	1 755	1 977
May	49 057	646	9 059	11 144	111	4 323	3 443	3 465	3 688	9 430	1 764	1 985
June	50 164	670	8 975	12 118	115	4 418	3 393	3 466	3 694	9 555	1 759	2 000
July	49 432	663	8 983	11 186	112	4 426	3 409	3 521	3 666	9 700	1 741	2 024
August	49 339	636	8 874	11 116	110	4 459	3 402	3 552	3 655	9 754	1 743	2 038
September	49 017	642	8 811	10 849	108	4 518	3 345	3 558	3 661	9 717	1 764	2 043
October	49 449	636	8 861	11 278	107	4 604	3 307	3 539	3 683	9 588	1 805	2 040
November	49 345	653	8 758	11 247	107	4 661	3 322	3 527	3 699	9 502	1 832	2 037
December	49 546	660	8 950	11 191	107	4 689	3 381	3 521	3 706	9 459	1 846	2 036
2020												
January	47 137	577	8 555	9 380	113	4 482	3 508	3 676	3 366	9 638	1 823	2 020
February	47 055	555	8 765	8 899	112	4 497	3 514	3 801	3 259	9 772	1 858	2 024
March	39 053	494	6 201	3 900	106	4 474	3 714	3 380	3 174	9 716	1 862	2 032
April	33 392	447	4 588	874	96	4 415	3 475	2 918	3 146	9 549	1 839	2 044
May	33 320	474	4 541	775	87	4 435	3 490	2 975	3 134	9 517	1 841	2 052
June	33 774	472	4 805	734	79	4 534	3 481	3 111	3 097	9 542	1 868	2 051
July	34 979	502	5 050	1 062	73	4 711	3 403	3 476	3 048	9 647	1 962	2 044
August	36 073	506	5 451	1 215	73	4 818	3 347	3 761	3 066	9 774	2 021	2 042
September	37 111	500	5 726	1 410	81	4 853	3 454	3 928	3 149	9 921	2 043	2 047
October	38 522	515	5 946	2 166	96	4 817	3 570	3 936	3 298	10 091	2 030	2 057
November	39 477	519	6 264	2 454	106	4 795	3 665	3 972	3 401	10 215	2 021	2 066
December	40 408	528	6 519	2 938	111	4 788	3 634	4 050	3 458	10 291	2 017	2 074

n.i.e = Not included elsewhere.

Table 7-13B. U.S. Imports of Services: Historical Data

(Balance of payments basis, millions of dollars, seasonally adjusted.)

Year	Total	Travel	Passenger fares	Other transportation	Royalties and license fees	Other private services (financial, professional, etc.)	Direct defense expenditures [1]	U.S. government miscellaneous services
1960	7 674	1 750	513	1 402	74	593	3 087	254
1961	7 671	1 785	506	1 437	89	588	2 998	268
1962	8 092	1 939	567	1 558	100	528	3 105	296
1963	8 362	2 114	612	1 701	112	493	2 961	370
1964	8 619	2 211	642	1 817	127	527	2 880	415
1965	9 111	2 438	717	1 951	135	461	2 952	457
1966	10 494	2 657	753	2 161	140	506	3 764	513
1967	11 863	3 207	829	2 157	166	565	4 378	561
1968	12 302	3 030	885	2 367	186	668	4 535	631
1969	13 322	3 373	1 080	2 455	221	751	4 856	586
1970	14 520	3 980	1 215	2 843	224	827	4 855	576
1971	15 400	4 373	1 290	3 130	241	956	4 819	592
1972	16 868	5 042	1 596	3 520	294	1 043	4 784	589
1973	18 843	5 526	1 790	4 694	385	1 180	4 629	640
1974	21 379	5 980	2 095	5 942	346	1 262	5 032	722
1975	21 996	6 417	2 263	5 708	472	1 551	4 795	789
1976	24 570	6 856	2 568	6 852	482	2 006	4 895	911
1977	27 640	7 451	2 748	7 972	504	2 190	5 823	951
1978	32 189	8 475	2 896	9 124	671	2 573	7 352	1 099
1979	36 689	9 413	3 184	10 906	831	2 822	8 294	1 239
1980	41 491	10 397	3 607	11 790	724	2 909	10 851	1 214
1981	45 503	11 479	4 487	12 474	650	3 562	11 564	1 287
1982	51 749	12 394	4 772	11 710	795	8 159	12 460	1 460
1983	54 973	13 149	6 003	12 222	943	8 001	13 087	1 568
1984	67 748	22 913	5 735	14 843	1 168	9 040	12 516	1 534
1985	72 862	24 558	6 444	15 643	1 170	10 203	13 108	1 735
1986	80 147	25 913	6 505	17 766	1 401	13 146	13 730	1 686
1987	90 787	29 310	7 283	19 010	1 857	16 485	14 950	1 893
1988	98 526	32 114	7 729	20 891	2 601	17 667	15 604	1 921
1989	102 479	33 416	8 249	22 172	2 528	18 930	15 313	1 871
1990	117 659	37 349	10 531	24 966	3 135	22 229	17 531	1 919
1991	118 459	35 322	10 012	24 975	4 035	25 590	16 409	2 116
1992	119 566	38 552	10 603	23 767	5 161	25 386	13 835	2 263
1993	123 779	40 713	11 410	24 524	5 032	27 760	12 086	2 255
1994	133 057	43 782	13 062	26 019	5 852	31 565	10 217	2 560
1995	141 397	44 916	14 663	27 034	6 919	35 199	10 043	2 623
1996	152 554	48 078	15 809	27 403	7 837	39 679	11 061	2 687
1997	165 932	52 051	18 138	28 959	9 161	43 154	11 707	2 762
1998	180 677	56 483	19 971	30 363	11 235	47 591	12 185	2 849
1999	195 172	59 332	20 946	31 494	13 302	55 885	11 849	2 364

Note: The category "Royalties and license fees" is the earlier terminology for the category called "Charges for the use of intellectual property n.i.e" in the revised and updated data shown in Tables 7-15A/7-16A. Other categories differ in both title and content; see the Notes and Definitions.

[1]Contains goods that cannot be separately identified.

Table 7-14. U.S. Export and Import Price Indexes by End-Use Category

(2000 = 100, not seasonally adjusted.)

Year and month	Exports			Imports		
	All commodities	Agricultural	Nonagricultural	All commodities	Petroleum [1]	Nonpetroleum
1990	95.5	105.1	94.4	94.0	75.5	97.1
1991	96.3	103.4	95.4	94.2	67.3	98.7
1992	96.3	102.5	95.7	94.9	62.9	100.0
1993	96.9	104.4	96.2	94.6	57.7	100.6
1994	98.9	109.4	98.0	96.2	54.3	103.2
1995	103.9	119.0	102.5	100.6	59.8	107.2
1996	104.5	132.6	101.6	101.6	71.1	106.4
1997	103.1	120.6	101.3	99.1	66.0	104.1
1998	99.7	108.8	98.8	93.1	44.8	100.4
1999	98.4	101.1	98.2	93.9	60.1	99.0
2000	100.0	100.0	100.0	100.0	100.0	100.0
2001	99.2	101.2	99.0	96.5	82.8	98.5
2002	98.2	103.2	97.8	94.1	85.3	96.2
2003	99.7	112.3	98.8	96.9	103.2	97.3
2004	103.6	123.4	102.1	102.3	134.6	99.8
2005	106.9	121.0	105.9	110.0	185.1	102.5
2006	110.7	125.8	109.6	115.4	223.3	104.2
2007	116.1	150.9	113.6	120.2	249.1	107.0
2008	123.1	183.5	118.8	134.1	343.2	112.7
2009	117.4	160.0	114.3	118.6	219.9	108.0
2010	123.1	172.6	119.6	126.8	282.2	111.0
2011	133.0	211.0	127.5	140.6	385.1	115.9
2012	133.5	216.1	127.6	141.0	384.0	116.3
2013	133.0	219.7	126.7	139.5	374.2	115.6
2014	132.3	213.8	126.3	138.0	353.2	115.7
2015	123.9	185.4	119.3	123.9	190.8	112.5
2016	119.9	175.5	115.7	119.8	153.1	110.8
2017	122.8	178.2	118.6	123.3	193.9	112.0
2018	126.9	179.3	122.9	127.1	236.6	113.5
2019	125.9	178.5	121.8	125.5	230.4	112.3
2020	122.4	178.0	118.1	122.4	162.7	112.6
2017						
January	121.6	175.8	117.4	122.3	192.0	111.2
February	122.0	178.3	117.7	122.7	193.6	111.5
March	122.1	180.2	117.7	122.5	188.6	111.6
April	122.4	180.3	118.0	122.8	187.2	111.9
May	121.7	177.4	117.5	122.7	185.8	111.9
June	121.6	174.9	117.5	122.4	178.7	112.0
July	122.2	178.1	117.9	122.2	177.6	111.9
August	122.9	178.1	118.7	122.9	185.7	112.1
September	123.9	176.9	119.8	123.9	197.7	112.5
October	124.0	180.4	119.7	124.1	198.6	112.5
November	124.6	179.1	120.5	125.3	217.5	112.7
December	124.7	178.5	120.5	125.5	223.6	112.6
2018						
January	125.6	178.5	121.5	126.5	229.6	113.3
February	125.8	179.5	121.7	126.8	227.1	113.7
March	126.3	185.2	121.8	126.5	221.6	113.7
April	126.9	183.1	122.6	127.1	231.2	113.8
May	127.8	186.0	123.3	128.2	248.4	113.9
June	128.0	184.2	123.7	128.2	255.4	113.5
July	127.4	174.7	123.8	128.1	256.8	113.4
August	127.3	175.4	123.6	127.6	251.5	113.1
September	127.3	173.2	123.8	127.7	251.5	113.2
October	127.9	173.0	124.4	128.3	258.9	113.4
November	126.9	176.0	123.1	126.2	220.2	113.5
December	126.1	182.6	121.7	124.4	186.4	113.7
2019						
January	125.3	178.7	121.2	124.6	200.9	113.0
February	126.1	179.0	122.1	125.9	221.3	113.2
March	127.0	180.7	122.9	126.6	235.5	113.2
April	127.1	178.1	123.2	126.8	246.3	112.7
May	126.7	176.2	122.9	127.0	255.7	112.4
June	126.0	180.5	121.8	125.6	236.6	112.0
July	126.2	180.8	122.0	125.6	237.3	111.9
August	125.5	176.5	121.6	124.9	226.7	111.8
September	125.1	173.6	121.4	125.0	228.8	111.8
October	125.1	176.5	121.1	124.5	223.4	111.7
November	125.2	180.7	121.0	124.7	225.3	111.8
December	125.0	180.5	120.7	125.0	227.0	112.0
2020						
January	125.8	184.2	121.4	125.2	227.9	112.1
February	124.3	178.8	120.1	124.3	207.5	112.3
March	122.5	176.3	118.4	121.3	151.3	112.1
April	118.2	170.4	114.3	118.2	102.3	111.5
May	118.2	169.7	114.3	119.0	117.1	111.6
June	120.3	172.4	116.3	120.6	142.6	111.9
July	121.5	175.2	117.4	122.1	166.1	112.1
August	122.1	171.3	118.4	123.2	171.7	113.0
September	122.8	176.1	118.7	123.4	161.2	113.7
October	123.0	182.2	118.5	123.3	160.9	113.6
November	124.0	188.5	119.1	123.4	165.0	113.6
December	125.5	190.3	120.6	124.6	179.0	114.1

[1]Petroleum and petroleum products.

NOTES AND DEFINITIONS, CHAPTER 7

This chapter presents data from two different data systems on international flows of goods, services, income payments, and financial transactions as they affect the U.S. economy. Tables 7-1 through 7-5 present data on the value, quantities, and prices of foreign transactions in the national income and product accounts (NIPAs). The Census Bureau source data for exports and imports of goods and services are presented in greater detail in Tables 7-6 through 7-14.

Due to a few differences in concept, scope, and definitions, the aggregate values of international transactions in the NIPAs (shown in Tables 7-1 and 7-4) are not exactly equal to the values for similar concepts in the ITAs or the Census values that serve as their sources, shown in Tables 7-6 through 7-16. The principal sources of differences are as follows:

- The NIPAs cover only the 50 states and the District of Columbia. The ITAs include the U.S. territories and Puerto Rico as part of the U.S. economy.

- Gold is treated differently.

- Services without payment by financial intermediaries except life insurance carriers (imputed interest) is treated differently.

A reconciliation of the two sets of international accounts is published from time to time in the *Survey of Current Business*.

The conventions of presentation no longer differ between the two sets of international accounts. In all the tables that follow, as in their source documents, values of imports of goods and services and of all other transactions that result in a payment to the rest of the world—income payments to foreigners, net transfers to foreigners, and net acquisition of assets from abroad—are presented normally as positive.

TABLES 7-1 AND 7-4

Foreign Transactions in the National Income and Product Accounts

SOURCE: U.S. DEPARTMENT OF COMMERCE, BUREAU OF ECONOMIC ANALYSIS

See the notes and definitions to Chapter 1 for an overview of the national income and product accounts (NIPAs).

Definitions

In accordance with the split between current and capital account, there are now two NIPA measures of the balance of international transactions.

The *balance on current account, national income and product accounts* is *current receipts from the rest of the world* minus *current payments to the rest of the world*. A negative value indicates that current payments exceed current receipts.

Net lending or net borrowing (-), national income and product accounts is equal to the balance on current account less capital account transactions with the rest of the world (net). Capital account transactions with the rest of the world (net) is not shown separately in Table 7-1 (for space reasons) but can be calculated from that table as the difference between net lending/ borrowing and the current account balance. (A similar measure, a component of the ITAs, is shown explicitly in Table 7-6.) Capital account transactions with the rest of the world are cash or in-kind transfers linked to the acquisition or disposition of an existing, nonproduced, nonfinancial asset. In contrast, the current account is limited to flows associated with current production of goods and services.

Net lending or net borrowing provides an indirect measure of the net acquisition of foreign assets by U.S. residents less the net acquisition of U.S. assets by foreign residents. These asset flows are measured directly in the ITAs. See Table 7-6 and its notes and definitions for a more extensive discussion of the relationship between the balances on current and capital account and international asset flows.

Current receipts from the rest of the world is *exports of goods and services* plus *income receipts*.

Current payments to the rest of the world is *imports of goods and services* plus *income payments* plus *current taxes and transfer payments (net)*.

Exports and imports of goods and services. Goods, in general, are products that can be stored or inventoried. *Services*, in general, are products that cannot be stored and are consumed at the place and time of their purchase. Goods imports include expenditures abroad by U.S. residents, except for travel. Services include foreign travel by U.S. residents, expenditures in the United States by foreign travelers, and exports and imports of certain goods— primarily military equipment purchased and sold by the federal government. See the following paragraph for the definition of *travel*.

Table 7-4 shows values for selected components of total goods and services; the components shown will not add to the total because of omitted items. In the case of goods, a miscellaneous "other" category is not shown. In the case of services, only two components are shown in this table. One is *travel* (for all purposes including education), which does not include passenger fares but includes as exports spending by foreign tourists and students in the United States, and includes as imports all other spending abroad by tourists and students from the United States. The other component shown here is a category called *other business services*, which includes the professional and financial services (for example, computer services) that have accounted for a large part of the long-term growth in the service category. The remaining components of total services are transport (of both persons and goods), charges for the use of intellectual property not elsewhere classified, government goods and services not elsewhere classified, and a miscellaneous, smaller *other* category.

Income receipts and payments. Income receipts—receipts from abroad of factor (labor or capital) income by U.S. residents—are analogous to exports and are combined with them to yield total *current receipts from the rest of the world. Income payments* by U.S. entities of factor income to entities abroad are analogous to imports.

Current taxes and transfer payments (net) consists of net payments between the United States and abroad that do not involve payment for the services of the labor or capital factors of production, purchase of currently-produced goods and services, or transfer of an existing asset. It includes net flows from persons, government, and business. The types of payments included are personal remittances from U.S. residents to the rest of the world, net of remittances from foreigners to U.S. residents; government grants; and transfer payments from businesses. Only the net payment to the rest of the world is shown. It usually appears in these accounts as a positive value, with transfers from the United States to abroad exceeding the reverse flow. An exception came in 1991, when U.S. allies in the Gulf War reimbursed the United States for the cost of the war, causing the only current-account surplus since 1981. This resulted in net payments to the United States from the rest of the world and appears as a negative entry in the net transfer payments column of the NIPA accounts.

Tables 7-2, 7-3 and 7-5

Chain-Type Quantity and Price Indexes for NIPA Foreign Transactions

These indexes represent the separation of the current-dollar values in Tables 7-1 and 7-4 into their real quantity and price trends components. (See the notes and definitions to Chapter 1 for a general explanation of chained-dollar estimates of real output and prices.) As those notes explain, quantity indexes are shown instead of constant-dollar estimates, because BEA no longer publishes its real output estimates before 1999 in any detail in the constant-dollar form. Therefore, quantity indexes are the only comprehensive source of information about longer-term trends in real volumes.

Table 7-6 through 7-13

Exports and Imports of Goods and Services

SOURCES: U.S. DEPARTMENT OF COMMERCE, CENSUS BUREAU AND BUREAU OF ECONOMIC ANALYSIS

These tables present the source data used to build up the aggregate measures of goods and services flows shown in Tables 7-1 through 7-5. These data are compiled and published monthly, making trends evident before the publication of the quarterly aggregate estimates. They also provide more detail than the quarterly aggregates.

Monthly and annual data on exports and imports of *goods* are compiled by the Census Bureau from documents collected by the U.S. Customs Service. The Bureau of Economic Analysis (BEA) makes certain adjustments to these data (as described below) to place the estimates on a *balance of payments* basis—a basis consistent with the national and international accounts.

Data on exports and imports of *services* are prepared by BEA from a variety of sources. Monthly data on services are available from January 1992. Annual and quarterly data for earlier years are available as part of the international transactions accounts. Current data on goods and services are available each month in a joint Census Bureau-BEA press release.

In the case of some of the detailed breakdowns of exports and imports, such as by end-use categories, monthly data may not sum exactly to annual totals. This is due to later revisions, which are made only to annual data and are not allocated to monthly data. Also, the constant-dollar figures expressed in 2009 dollars are now calculated using chain weights. Therefore, the 2009-dollar detail will not add to the 2009-dollar totals.

In addition, monthly and annual data on exports and imports of goods for individual countries and various country groupings do not reflect subsequent revisions of annual total data. These country data are compiled by the Census Bureau for all countries, although this volume includes only a selection of the most significant countries and areas. The full set of data can be accessed on the Census Web site at <https://www.census.gov>.

Definitions: Goods

Goods: Census basis. The Census basis goods data are compiled from documents collected by the U.S. Customs Service. They reflect the movement of goods between foreign countries and the 50 states, the District of Columbia, Puerto Rico, the U.S. Virgin Islands, and U.S. Foreign Trade Zones. They include government and nongovernment shipments of goods, and exclude shipments between the United States and its territories and possessions; transactions with U.S. military, diplomatic, and consular installations abroad; U.S. goods returned to the United States by its armed forces; personal and household effects of travelers; and intransit shipments. The general import values reflect the total arrival of merchandise from foreign countries that immediately enters consumption channels, warehouses, or Foreign Trade Zones.

For *imports,* the value reported is the U.S. Customs Service appraised value of merchandise (generally, the price paid for merchandise for export to the United States). Import duties, freight, insurance, and other charges incurred in bringing merchandise to the United States are excluded.

Exports are valued at the f.a.s. (free alongside ship) value of merchandise at the U.S. port of export, based on the transaction price including inland freight, insurance, and other charges incurred in placing the merchandise alongside the carrier at the U.S. port of exportation.

Goods: balance of payments (BOP) basis. Goods on a Census basis are adjusted by BEA to goods on a BOP basis to bring the data in line with the concepts and definitions used to prepare the international and national accounts. In general, the adjustments include changes in ownership that occur without goods passing into or out of the customs territory of the United States. These adjustments are necessary to supplement coverage of the Census basis data, to eliminate duplication of transactions recorded elsewhere in the international accounts, and to value transactions according to a standard definition. With the June 4, 2013 release, improved BOP adjustments involving U.S. military transactions were introduced for data beginning with 1999.

The *export* adjustments include the following: (1) The deduction of *U.S. military sales contracts.* The Census Bureau has included these contracts in the goods data, but BEA includes them in the service category "Transfers Under U.S. Military Sales Contracts." BEA's source material for these contracts is more comprehensive but does not distinguish between goods and services. (2) The addition of *private gift parcels* mailed to foreigners by individuals through the U.S. Postal Service. Only commercial shipments are covered in Census goods exports. (3) The addition to *nonmonetary gold exports* of gold purchased by foreign official agencies from private dealers in the United States and held at the Federal Reserve Bank of New York. The Census data include only gold that leaves the customs territory. (4) *Smaller adjustments* includes deductions for repairs of goods, exposed motion picture film, and military grant aid, and additions for sales of fish in U.S. territorial waters, exports of electricity to Mexico, and vessels and oil rigs that change ownership without export documents being filed.

The *import* adjustments include the following: (1) On *inland freight in Canada*, the customs value for imports for certain Canadian goods is the point of origin in Canada. BEA makes an addition for the inland freight charges of transporting these Canadian goods to the U.S. border. (2) An addition is made to *nonmonetary gold imports* for gold sold by foreign official agencies to private purchasers out of stock held at the Federal Reserve Bank of New York. The Census Bureau data include only gold that enters the customs territory. (3) A deduction is made for *imports by U.S. military agencies.* The Census Bureau has included these contracts in the goods data, but BEA includes them in the service category "Direct Defense Expenditures." BEA's source material is more comprehensive but does not distinguish between goods and services. (4) *Smaller adjustments* includes deductions for repairs of goods and for exposed motion picture film and additions for imported electricity from Mexico, conversion of vessels for commercial use, and repairs to U.S. vessels abroad.

Definitions: Services

These statistics are estimates of service transactions between foreign countries and the 50 states, the District of Columbia, Puerto Rico, the U.S. Virgin Islands, and other U.S. territories and possessions. Transactions with U.S. military, diplomatic, and consular installations abroad are excluded because they are considered to be part of the U.S. economy.

In the 2014 comprehensive revision of the ITAs, new categories have been introduced in the services reports, beginning with January 1999. The 9 new categories, shown in Tables 7-12 and 7-13, are as follows:

Maintenance and repair services n.i.e. (not included elsewhere) were previously included in "other private services."

Transport includes the previous categories of "passenger fares" and "other transportation."

Travel for all purposes including education is broader than the previous "travel" category and now includes business travel, expenditures by border, seasonal, and other short-term workers, and personal travel including that related to health and education. As before, it consists of expenditures for food, lodging, recreation, gifts, and other items incidental to a foreign visit but not the actual transportation expenses.

Insurance services and *financial services* were previously included in other private services.

Charges for the use of intellectual property n.i.e. was previously named "royalties and license fees."

Telecommunications, computer, and information services and *other business services* were previously included in "other private services."

Government goods and services n.i.e. replaces the government categories in the previous system.

Earlier services definitions

Before 1999, services are classified in the broad categories described below. For six of these categories, the definitions are the same for imports and exports. For the seventh, the export category is "Transfers under U.S. Military Sales Contracts," while for imports, the category is "Direct Defense Expenditures."

Travel includes purchases of services and goods by U.S. travelers abroad and by foreign visitors to the United States. A traveler is defined as a person who stays for a period of less than one year in a country where the person is not a resident. Included are expenditures for food, lodging, recreation, gifts, and other items incidental to a foreign visit. Not included are the international costs of the travel itself, which are covered in *passenger fares* (see below).

Passenger fares consists of fares paid by residents of one country to residents in other countries. Receipts consist of fares received by U.S. carriers from foreign residents for travel between the United States and foreign countries and between two foreign points. Payments consist of fares paid by U.S. residents to foreign carriers for travel between the United States and foreign countries.

Other transportation includes charges for the transportation of goods by ocean, air, waterway, pipeline, and rail carriers to and from the United States. Included are freight charges, operating expenses that transportation companies incur in foreign ports, and payments for vessel charter and aircraft and freight car rentals.

Royalties and license fees consists of transactions with foreign residents involving intangible assets and proprietary rights, such as the use of patents, techniques, processes, formulas, designs, knowhow, trademarks, copyrights, franchises, and manufacturing rights. The term *royalties* generally refers to payments for the utilization of copyrights or trademarks, and the term *license fees* generally refers to payments for the use of patents or industrial processes.

Other private services includes transactions with "affiliated" foreigners for which no identification by type is available and transactions with unaffiliated foreigners.

The term "affiliated" refers to a direct investment relationship, which exists when a U.S. person has ownership or control (directly or indirectly) of 10 percent or more of a foreign business enterprise, or when a foreign person has a similar interest in a U.S. enterprise.

Transactions with "unaffiliated" foreigners in this "other private services" category consist of education services, financial services, insurance services, telecommunications services, and business,

professional, and technical services. Included in the last group are advertising services; computer and data processing services; database and other information services; research, development, and testing services; management, consulting, and public relations services; legal services; construction, engineering, architectural, and mining services; industrial engineering services; installation, maintenance, and repair of equipment; and other services, including medical services and film and tape rental.

The insurance component of "other private services" was measured before the July 2003 revision as premiums less actual losses paid or recovered. Furthermore, catastrophic losses were entered immediately when the loss occurred, rather than when the insurance claim was actually paid out. This led to sharp swings for any month in which catastrophic losses occurred, such as Hurricane Katrina in August 2005 or the September 11, 2001, terror attacks. In the accounts as revised in July 2003 and presented here, insurance services are now measured as premiums less "normal" losses. Normal losses consist of a measure of expected regularly occurring losses based on six years of past experience plus an additional allowance for catastrophic loss. Catastrophic losses, when they occur, are added in equal increments to the estimate of regularly occurring losses over the 20 years following the occurrence. As adoption of this methodology introduces a difference between actual and normal losses, an amount equal to the difference is entered in the international accounts as a capital account transaction.

Transfers under U.S. military sales contracts (exports only) includes exports in which U.S. government military agencies participate. This category has included both goods, such as equipment, and services, such as repair services and training, that could not be separately identified. In the 2010 and 2013 annual revisions, more precise breakdowns between goods and services in this category were introduced and incorporated as revised estimates of services and of the BOP goods adjustment, beginning with the data for 2007. Transfers of goods and services under U.S. military grant programs are included.

Direct defense expenditures (imports only) consists of expenditures incurred by U.S. military agencies abroad, including expenditures by U.S. personnel, payments of wages to foreign residents, construction expenditures, payments for foreign contractual services, and procurement of foreign goods. Improved breakdowns between goods and services are now incorporated beginning with statistics for 1999.

U.S. government miscellaneous services includes transactions of U.S. government nonmilitary agencies with foreign residents. Most of these transactions involve the provision of services to, or purchases of services from, foreigners. Transfers of some goods are also included.

Services estimates are based on quarterly, annual, and benchmark surveys and partial information generated from monthly reports.

Service transactions are estimated at market prices. Estimates are seasonally adjusted when statistically significant seasonal patterns are present.

Definitions: Area groupings

The Census trade statistics for groups of countries present "groups as they were at the time of reporting", which means that as multinational organizations such as the European Union expand, the statistics for trade with that group include the added country only beginning with the year it entered the group. The European Union was expanded from 15 to 28 nations as of July 1, 2013, and data for that year are available for both the new and the old group; to provide historical perspective, they are both shown here, along with the historical data back to 1974 for the original group.

The *European Union* (EU) now includes 27 countries: Austria, Belgium, Bulgaria, Croatia, Cyprus, Czech Republic, Denmark, Estonia, Finland, France, Germany, Greece, Hungary, Ireland, Italy, Latvia, Lithuania, Luxembourg, Malta, Netherlands, Poland, Portugal, Romania, Slovakia, Slovenia, Spain, and Sweden. The United Kingdom withdrew from the European Union in late 2020.

In a referendum on June 23, 2016, a majority of British voters supported leaving the EU. On March 29, 2017, the United Kingdom government invoked Article 50 of the Treaty on European Union. The European Union (Withdrawal) Act 2018 declares "exit day" to be March 29, 2019.

The *Euro area* now includes Austria, Belgium, Cyprus, Estonia, Finland, France, Germany, Greece, Ireland, Italy, Luxembourg, Malta, the Netherlands, Portugal, Slovakia, Slovenia, and Spain. See the notes and definitions in Table 13-2 for further information about the euro.

With the June 3, 2016 International Trade and Services Annual Revision for 2015, the area grouping *Asian Newly Industrialized Countries (NICS)* has been removed from all relevant exhibits and publications and are listed separately as Hong Kong, South Korea, Singapore, and Taiwan. This group was initially called the *Four Asian Tigers*.

The *Organization of Petroleum Exporting Countries (OPEC)* currently consists of Algeria, Angola, Ecuador, Equatorial Guinea, Iran, Iraq, Kuwait, Libya, Nigeria, Qatar, Saudi Arabia, the United Arab Emirates, and Venezuela.

Notes on the data

U.S./Canada data exchange and substitution. The data for U.S. exports to Canada are derived from import data compiled by Canada. The use of Canada's import data to produce U.S. export data requires several alignments in order to compare the two series.

- *Coverage*: Canadian imports are based on country of origin. U.S. goods shipped from a third country are included, but U.S. exports exclude these foreign shipments. U.S. export coverage also excludes certain Canadian postal shipments.

- *Valuation*: Canadian imports are valued at their point of origin in the United States. However, U.S. exports are valued at the port of exit in the United States and include inland freight charges, making the U.S. export value slightly larger. Canada requires inland freight to be reported.

- *Re-exports*: U.S. exports include re-exports of foreign goods. Again, the aggregate U.S. export figure is slightly larger.

- *Exchange Rate*: Average monthly exchange rates are applied to convert the published data to U.S. currency.

End-use categories and seasonal adjustment of trade in goods. Goods are initially classified under the Harmonized System, which describes and measures the characteristics of goods traded. Combining trade into approximately 140 export and 140 import enduse categories makes it possible to examine goods according to their principal uses. These categories are used as the basis for computing the seasonal and working-day adjusted data. Adjusted data are then summed to the six end-use aggregates for publication.

The seasonal adjustment procedure is based on a model that estimates the monthly movements as percentages above or below the general level of each end-use commodity series (unlike other methods that redistribute the actual series values over the calendar year). Imports of petroleum and petroleum products are adjusted for the length of the month.

Data availability

Data are released monthly in a joint Census Bureau-BEA press release (FT-900), which is published about six weeks after the end of the month to which the data pertain. The release and historical data are available on the Census Bureau Web site at <https://www.census.gov/foreign-trade/index.html >.

Revisions

Data for recent years are normally revised annually. In some cases, revisions to annual totals are not distributed to monthly data; therefore, monthly data may not sum to the revised total shown. Data on trade in services may be subject to extensive revision as part of BEA's annual revision of the international transactions accounts (ITAs), usually released in July.

References

See the references for Table 7-6.

Table 7-14

Export and Import Price Indexes

SOURCE: U.S. DEPARTMENT OF LABOR, BUREAU OF LABOR STATISTICS

The International Price Program of the Bureau of Labor Statistics (BLS) collects price data for nonmilitary goods traded between the United States and the rest of the world and for selected transportation services in international markets. BLS aggregates the goods price data into export and import price indexes. Summary values of these price indexes for goods are presented in *Business Statistics*. For product and locality detail on international prices for both goods and services, see the *Handbook of U.S. Labor Statistics,* also published by Bernan Press.

Definitions

The *export* price index provides a measure of price change for all goods sold by U.S. residents (businesses and individuals located within the geographic boundaries of the United States, whether or not owned by U.S. citizens) to foreign buyers.

The *import* price index provides a measure of price change for goods purchased from other countries by U.S. residents.

Notes on the data

Published index series use a base year of 2000 = 100 whenever possible.

The product universe for both the import and export indexes includes raw materials, agricultural products, and manufactures. Price data are primarily collected by mail questionnaire, and directly from the exporter or importer in all but a few cases.

To the greatest extent possible, the data refer to prices at the U.S. border for exports and at either the foreign border or the U.S. border for imports. For nearly all products, the prices refer to transactions completed during the first week of the month and

represent the actual price for which the product was bought or sold, including discounts, allowances, and rebates.

For the export price indexes, the preferred pricing basis is f.a.s. (free alongside ship) U.S. port of exportation. Where necessary, adjustments are made to reported prices to place them on this basis. An attempt is made to collect two prices for imports: f.o.b. (free on board) at the port of exportation and c.i.f. (cost, insurance, and freight) at the U.S. port of importation. Adjustments are made to account for changes in product characteristics in order to obtain a pure measure of price change.

The indexes are weighted indexes of the Laspeyres type. (See "General Notes" at the beginning of this volume for further explanation.) The values assigned to each weight category are based on trade value figures compiled by the Census Bureau. They are reweighted annually, with a two-year lag (as concurrent value data are not available) in revisions.

The merchandise price indexes are published using three different classification systems: the Harmonized System, the Bureau of Economic Analysis End-Use System, and the Standard International Trade Classification (SITC) system. The aggregate indexes shown here are from the End-Use System.

Data availability

Indexes are published monthly in a press release and a more detailed report. Indexes are published for detailed product categories, as well as for all commodities. Aggregate import indexes by country or region of origin also are available, as are indexes for selected categories of internationally traded services. Additional information is available from the Division of International Prices in the Bureau of Labor Statistics. Complete historical data are available on the BLS Web site at <https://www.bls.gov>.

References

The indexes are described in "BLS to Produce Monthly Indexes of Export and Import Prices," *Monthly Labor Review* (December 1988), and Chapter 15, "International Price Indexes," *BLS Handbook of Methods* Bulletin 2490 (April 1997).

CHAPTER 8: PRICES

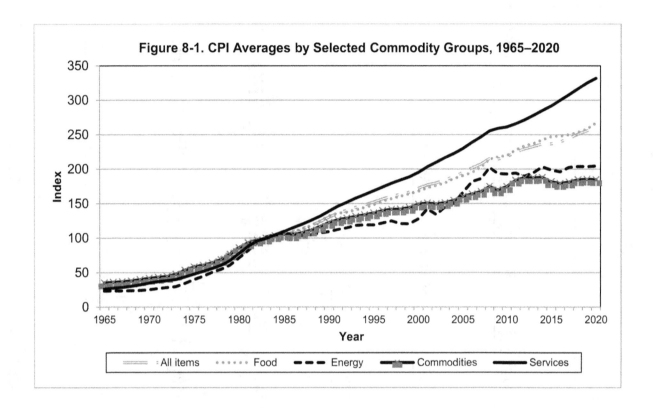

Figure 8-1. CPI Averages by Selected Commodity Groups, 1965–2020

- The Bureau of Labor Statistics (BLS) collects prices for more than 200 categories arranged in eight major groups called the market basket. (See Notes and Definitions for more information.) The Consumer Price Index for All Urban Consumers (CPI-U) represents all goods and services purchased for consumption for day-to-day living expenditures. Inflation refers to an increase in prices. Recent U.S. tariffs imposed on goods from China, Canada and the European Union will drive prices up. See Chapter 7 for more information.

- Deflation—a reduction in prices—occurred during the Great Depression from October 1931 to March 1933. (Table 8-1C). Congress amended the Social Security Act of 1935 with public law 92-336 in 1973. Part of that amendment called for automatic annual cost of living increases to be made to Social Security payments based on the CPI. With CPI negative in 2009 and 2015, Social Security payments should have decreased. However, the action taken was to hold the amount stable. In 2021, prices are increasing significantly as demand increases but supply chain issues continue due to the pandemic.

- With the release of the Consumer Price Index (CPI) each month, the Bureau of Labor Statistics (BLS) also publishes average retail prices for various goods and commodities as shown in Figure 8-1 and Table 8-1. Average prices are what consumers pay for a good or service. As shown, energy prices typically are among the most volatile while food prices rise more steadily.

Table 8-1A. Summary Consumer Price Indexes: Recent Data

(Seasonally adjusted.)

Year and month	Urban wage earners and clerical workers (CPI-W), all items	Consumer Price Index, 1982–1984 = 100					
		All urban consumers (CPI-U)					
		All items	Food	Energy	All items less food and energy	Commod-ities	Services
1965	31.7	31.5	32.2	22.9	32.7	35.2	26.6
1966	32.6	32.4	33.8	23.3	33.5	36.1	27.6
1967	33.6	33.4	34.1	23.8	34.7	36.8	28.8
1968	35.0	34.8	35.3	24.2	36.3	38.1	30.3
1969	36.9	36.7	37.1	24.8	38.4	39.9	32.4
1970	39.0	38.8	39.2	25.5	40.8	41.7	35.0
1971	40.7	40.5	40.4	26.5	42.7	43.2	37.0
1972	42.1	41.8	42.1	27.2	44.0	44.5	38.4
1973	44.7	44.4	48.2	29.4	45.6	47.8	40.1
1974	49.6	49.3	55.1	38.1	49.4	53.5	43.8
1975	54.1	53.8	59.8	42.1	53.9	58.2	48.0
1976	57.2	56.9	61.6	45.1	57.4	60.7	52.0
1977	60.9	60.6	65.5	49.4	61.0	64.2	56.0
1978	65.6	65.2	72.0	52.5	65.5	68.8	60.8
1979	73.1	72.6	79.9	65.7	71.9	76.6	67.5
1980	82.9	82.4	86.8	86.0	80.8	86.0	77.9
1981	91.4	90.9	93.6	97.7	89.2	93.2	88.1
1982	96.9	96.5	97.4	99.2	95.8	97.0	96.0
1983	99.8	99.6	99.4	99.9	99.6	99.8	99.4
1984	103.3	103.9	103.2	100.9	104.6	103.2	104.6
1985	106.9	107.6	105.6	101.6	109.1	105.4	109.9
1986	108.6	109.6	109.0	88.2	113.5	104.4	115.4
1987	112.5	113.6	113.5	88.6	118.2	107.7	120.2
1988	117.0	118.3	118.2	89.3	123.4	111.5	125.7
1989	122.6	124.0	125.1	94.3	129.0	116.7	131.9
1990	129.0	130.7	132.4	102.1	135.5	122.8	139.2
1991	134.3	136.2	136.3	102.5	142.1	126.6	146.3
1992	138.2	140.3	137.9	103.0	147.3	129.1	152.0
1993	142.1	144.5	140.9	104.2	152.2	131.5	157.9
1994	145.6	148.2	144.3	104.6	156.5	133.8	163.1
1995	149.8	152.4	148.4	105.2	161.2	136.4	168.7
1996	154.1	156.9	153.3	110.1	165.6	139.9	174.1
1997	157.6	160.5	157.3	111.5	169.5	141.8	179.4
1998	159.7	163.0	160.7	102.9	173.4	141.9	184.2
1999	163.2	166.6	164.1	106.6	177.0	144.4	188.8
2000	168.9	172.2	167.8	124.6	181.3	149.2	195.3
2001	173.5	177.1	173.1	129.3	186.1	150.7	203.4
2002	175.9	179.9	176.2	121.7	190.5	149.7	209.8
2003	179.8	184.0	180.0	136.5	193.2	151.2	216.5
2004	184.5	188.9	186.2	151.4	196.6	154.7	222.8
2005	191.0	195.3	190.7	177.1	200.9	160.2	230.1
2006	197.1	201.6	195.2	196.9	205.9	164.0	238.9
2007	202.8	207.3	202.9	207.7	210.7	167.5	246.8
2008	211.1	215.3	214.1	236.7	215.6	174.8	255.5
2009	209.6	214.5	218.0	193.1	219.2	169.7	259.2
2010	214.0	218.1	219.6	211.4	221.3	174.6	261.3
2011	221.6	224.9	227.8	243.9	225.0	183.9	265.8
2012	226.2	229.6	233.8	246.1	229.8	187.6	271.4
2013	229.3	233.0	237.0	244.4	233.8	187.7	277.9
2014	232.8	236.7	242.7	243.6	237.9	187.9	285.1
2015	231.8	237.0	247.2	202.9	242.2	181.7	291.7
2016	234.1	240.0	247.9	189.5	247.6	179.2	299.9
2017	239.1	245.1	250.1	204.5	252.2	181.2	308.1
2018	245.1	251.1	253.6	219.9	257.6	184.6	316.6
2019	249.2	255.7	258.3	215.3	263.2	185.3	325.1
2020	243.0	248.8	252.0	217.7	255.1	183.9	312.8
2019							
January	243.6	249.5	252.1	221.0	255.6	184.3	313.6
February	243.4	249.4	252.3	215.7	256.1	183.5	314.3
March	244.0	250.0	253.0	217.2	256.5	184.1	314.9
April	244.7	250.6	253.1	219.8	257.1	184.6	315.7
May	245.3	251.2	253.5	222.0	257.4	185.1	316.3
June	245.5	251.5	253.9	220.8	257.9	185.0	317.0
July	246.0	251.9	254.1	223.7	258.1	185.2	317.6
August	246.3	252.3	254.3	222.7	258.6	185.4	318.2
September	246.9	252.8	254.1	225.5	259.0	185.7	318.9
October	246.6	252.7	254.7	219.2	259.5	184.8	319.5
November	246.3	252.7	255.6	213.5	260.0	183.8	320.5
December	246.0	252.6	256.1	206.6	260.6	183.1	321.1
2020							
January	246.8	253.2	257.0	209.4	260.9	183.8	321.7
February	247.7	254.1	257.6	215.1	261.3	184.8	322.4
March	248.7	254.9	257.5	220.4	261.8	185.7	323.3
April	248.8	255.2	258.1	218.8	262.2	185.6	323.7
May	248.9	255.4	258.3	214.9	262.9	185.4	324.5
June	249.7	256.1	258.4	216.8	263.6	185.8	325.4
July	249.8	256.3	258.5	213.9	264.2	185.5	326.2
August	250.0	256.6	258.9	212.2	264.7	185.3	326.9
September	250.8	257.2	259.5	215.9	265.0	185.6	327.9
October	251.3	257.8	259.8	217.6	265.5	185.9	328.8
November	252.0	258.4	260.2	221.1	265.8	186.6	329.3

Table 8-1B. Summary Consumer Price Indexes: Historical Data, 1946 to Date

(Seasonally adjusted.)

Year and month	Urban wage earners and clerical workers (CPI-W), all items	Consumer Price Index, 1982–1984 = 100					
		All urban consumers (CPI-U)					
		All items	Food	Energy	All items less food and energy	Commod- ities	Services
1946	19.6	19.5	19.8	. . .	. . .	22.9	14.1
1947	22.5	22.3	24.1	. . .	. . .	27.6	14.7
1948	24.2	24.1	26.1	. . .	. . .	29.6	15.6
1949	24.0	23.8	25.0	. . .	. . .	28.8	16.4
1950	24.2	24.1	25.4	. . .	. . .	29.0	16.9
1951	26.1	26.0	28.2	. . .	. . .	31.6	17.8
1952	26.7	26.5	28.7	. . .	. . .	32.0	18.6
1953	26.9	26.7	28.3	. . .	. . .	31.9	19.4
1954	27.0	26.9	28.2	. . .	. . .	31.6	20.0
1955	26.9	26.8	27.8	. . .	. . .	31.3	20.4
1956	27.3	27.2	28.0	. . .	. . .	31.6	20.9
1957	28.3	28.1	28.9	21.5	28.9	32.6	21.8
1958	29.1	28.9	30.2	21.5	29.6	33.3	22.6
1959	29.3	29.1	29.7	21.9	30.2	33.3	23.3
1960	29.8	29.6	30.0	22.4	30.6	33.6	24.1
1961	30.1	29.9	30.4	22.5	31.0	33.8	24.5
1962	30.4	30.2	30.6	22.6	31.4	34.1	25.0
1963	30.8	30.6	31.1	22.6	31.8	34.4	25.5
1964	31.2	31.0	31.5	22.5	32.3	34.8	26.0
1949							
January	24.2	24.0	25.4	. . .	. . .	. . .	. . .
February	24.1	23.9	25.3	. . .	. . .	. . .	. . .
March	24.0	23.9	25.3	. . .	. . .	. . .	. . .
April	24.1	23.9	25.3	. . .	. . .	. . .	. . .
May	24.0	23.9	25.2	. . .	. . .	. . .	. . .
June	24.1	23.9	25.3	. . .	. . .	. . .	. . .
July	23.8	23.7	24.8	. . .	. . .	. . .	. . .
August	23.8	23.7	24.8	. . .	. . .	. . .	. . .
September	23.9	23.8	25.0	. . .	. . .	. . .	. . .
October	23.8	23.7	24.8	. . .	. . .	. . .	. . .
November	23.8	23.7	24.8	. . .	. . .	. . .	. . .
December	23.8	23.6	24.5	. . .	. . .	. . .	. . .
1950							
January	23.6	23.5	24.3	. . .	. . .	. . .	. . .
February	23.7	23.6	24.7	. . .	. . .	. . .	. . .
March	23.8	23.6	24.6	. . .	. . .	. . .	. . .
April	23.8	23.7	24.6	. . .	. . .	. . .	. . .
May	23.9	23.8	24.8	. . .	. . .	. . .	. . .
June	24.0	23.9	25.1	. . .	. . .	. . .	. . .
July	24.2	24.1	25.6	. . .	. . .	. . .	. . .
August	24.3	24.2	25.8	. . .	. . .	. . .	. . .
September	24.5	24.3	25.8	. . .	. . .	. . .	. . .
October	24.6	24.5	26.0	. . .	. . .	. . .	. . .
November	24.7	24.6	26.1	. . .	. . .	. . .	. . .
December	25.1	25.0	26.9	. . .	. . .	. . .	. . .
1951							
January	25.5	25.4	27.6	. . .	. . .	. . .	. . .
February	26.0	25.8	28.5	. . .	. . .	. . .	. . .
March	26.0	25.9	28.4	. . .	. . .	. . .	. . .
April	26.1	25.9	28.2	. . .	. . .	. . .	. . .
May	26.1	26.0	28.3	. . .	. . .	. . .	. . .
June	26.1	25.9	28.0	. . .	. . .	. . .	. . .
July	26.1	25.9	27.9	. . .	. . .	. . .	. . .
August	26.0	25.9	27.8	. . .	. . .	. . .	. . .
September	26.2	26.0	27.9	. . .	. . .	. . .	. . .
October	26.3	26.2	28.4	. . .	. . .	. . .	. . .
November	26.5	26.3	28.6	. . .	. . .	. . .	. . .
December	26.6	26.5	28.9	. . .	. . .	. . .	. . .
1952							
January	26.6	26.5	28.9	. . .	. . .	. . .	. . .
February	26.6	26.4	28.6	. . .	. . .	. . .	. . .
March	26.5	26.4	28.5	. . .	. . .	. . .	. . .
April	26.6	26.5	28.7	. . .	. . .	. . .	. . .
May	26.6	26.5	28.7	. . .	. . .	. . .	. . .
June	26.7	26.5	28.6	. . .	. . .	. . .	. . .
July	26.8	26.7	28.9	. . .	. . .	. . .	. . .
August	26.8	26.7	28.9	. . .	. . .	. . .	. . .
September	26.8	26.6	28.7	. . .	. . .	. . .	. . .
October	26.8	26.7	28.8	. . .	. . .	. . .	. . .
November	26.8	26.7	28.8	. . .	. . .	. . .	. . .
December	26.9	26.7	28.6	. . .	. . .	. . .	. . .

. . . = Not available.

Table 8-1B. Summary Consumer Price Indexes: Historical Data, 1946 to Date—*Continued*

(Seasonally adjusted.)

Year and month	Consumer Price Index, 1982–1984 = 100						
	Urban wage earners and clerical workers (CPI-W), all items	All urban consumers (CPI-U)					
		All items	Food	Energy	All items less food and energy	Commod-ities	Services
1953							
January	26.8	26.6	28.4	. . .	. . .	. . .	. . .
February	26.7	26.6	28.3	. . .	. . .	. . .	. . .
March	26.8	26.6	28.3	. . .	. . .	. . .	. . .
April	26.8	26.7	28.1	. . .	. . .	. . .	. . .
May	26.9	26.7	28.2	. . .	. . .	. . .	. . .
June	26.9	26.8	28.4	. . .	. . .	. . .	. . .
July	26.9	26.8	28.2	. . .	. . .	. . .	. . .
August	27.0	26.9	28.3	. . .	. . .	. . .	. . .
September	27.0	26.9	28.4	. . .	. . .	. . .	. . .
October	27.1	27.0	28.4	. . .	. . .	. . .	. . .
November	27.0	26.9	28.1	. . .	. . .	. . .	. . .
December	27.0	26.9	28.3	. . .	. . .	. . .	. . .
1954							
January	27.1	26.9	28.5	. . .	. . .	. . .	. . .
February	27.1	27.0	28.5	. . .	. . .	. . .	. . .
March	27.1	26.9	28.4	. . .	. . .	. . .	. . .
April	27.0	26.9	28.4	. . .	. . .	. . .	. . .
May	27.1	26.9	28.4	. . .	. . .	. . .	. . .
June	27.1	26.9	28.4	. . .	. . .	. . .	. . .
July	27.0	26.9	28.4	. . .	. . .	. . .	. . .
August	27.0	26.9	28.3	. . .	. . .	. . .	. . .
September	27.0	26.8	28.0	. . .	. . .	. . .	. . .
October	26.9	26.7	27.9	. . .	. . .	. . .	. . .
November	26.9	26.8	27.9	. . .	. . .	. . .	. . .
December	26.9	26.8	27.8	. . .	. . .	. . .	. . .
1955							
January	26.9	26.8	27.8	. . .	. . .	. . .	. . .
February	27.0	26.8	28.0	. . .	. . .	. . .	. . .
March	26.9	26.8	28.0	. . .	. . .	. . .	. . .
April	26.9	26.8	28.0	. . .	. . .	. . .	. . .
May	26.9	26.8	27.9	. . .	. . .	. . .	. . .
June	26.9	26.7	27.7	. . .	. . .	. . .	. . .
July	26.9	26.8	27.7	. . .	. . .	. . .	. . .
August	26.9	26.7	27.6	. . .	. . .	. . .	. . .
September	27.0	26.9	27.8	. . .	. . .	. . .	. . .
October	27.0	26.8	27.7	. . .	. . .	. . .	. . .
November	27.0	26.9	27.6	. . .	. . .	. . .	. . .
December	27.0	26.9	27.6	. . .	. . .	. . .	. . .
1956							
January	27.0	26.8	27.5	. . .	. . .	31.2	20.7
February	27.0	26.9	27.5	. . .	. . .	31.1	20.7
March	27.1	26.9	27.5	. . .	. . .	31.2	20.7
April	27.1	26.9	27.6	. . .	. . .	31.3	20.8
May	27.2	27.0	27.8	. . .	. . .	31.4	20.8
June	27.3	27.2	28.1	. . .	. . .	31.5	20.9
July	27.4	27.3	28.4	. . .	. . .	31.8	20.9
August	27.5	27.3	28.2	. . .	. . .	31.7	21.0
September	27.5	27.4	28.2	. . .	. . .	31.8	21.1
October	27.7	27.5	28.3	. . .	. . .	32.0	21.1
November	27.7	27.5	28.4	. . .	. . .	32.0	21.2
December	27.8	27.6	28.5	. . .	. . .	32.1	21.3
1957							
January	27.8	27.7	28.4	21.3	28.5	32.1	21.4
February	28.0	27.8	28.7	21.4	28.6	32.3	21.4
March	28.0	27.9	28.6	21.5	28.7	32.3	21.6
April	28.1	27.9	28.6	21.6	28.8	32.4	21.6
May	28.2	28.0	28.7	21.6	28.8	32.4	21.7
June	28.3	28.1	28.9	21.6	28.9	32.5	21.8
July	28.4	28.2	29.1	21.5	29.0	32.6	21.8
August	28.4	28.3	29.4	21.4	29.0	32.8	21.9
September	28.5	28.3	29.2	21.4	29.1	32.8	22.0
October	28.5	28.3	29.2	21.4	29.2	32.7	22.1
November	28.6	28.4	29.2	21.5	29.3	32.8	22.2
December	28.6	28.5	29.2	21.5	29.3	32.9	22.2
1958							
January	28.8	28.6	29.8	21.6	29.3	33.1	22.3
February	28.9	28.7	29.9	21.3	29.4	33.2	22.4
March	29.0	28.9	30.5	21.4	29.5	33.4	22.4
April	29.1	28.9	30.6	21.4	29.5	33.5	22.5
May	29.1	28.9	30.5	21.5	29.5	33.5	22.6
June	29.1	28.9	30.3	21.5	29.6	33.4	22.6
July	29.1	28.9	30.2	21.6	29.6	33.3	22.7
August	29.1	28.9	30.1	21.7	29.6	33.3	22.7
September	29.1	28.9	30.0	21.7	29.7	33.3	22.8
October	29.1	28.9	30.0	21.7	29.7	33.2	22.8
November	29.1	29.0	30.0	21.4	29.8	33.3	22.8
December	29.1	29.0	29.9	21.4	29.9	33.3	22.8

. . . = Not available.

Table 8-1B. Summary Consumer Price Indexes: Historical Data, 1946 to Date—*Continued*

(Seasonally adjusted.)

Year and month	Urban wage earners and clerical workers (CPI-W), all items	Consumer Price Index, 1982–1984 = 100					
		All urban consumers (CPI-U)					
		All items	Food	Energy	All items less food and energy	Commod-ities	Services
1959							
January	29.2	29.0	30.0	21.4	29.9	33.3	22.9
February	29.2	29.0	29.8	21.6	29.9	33.3	23.0
March	29.1	29.0	29.7	21.7	30.0	33.2	23.0
April	29.1	29.0	29.5	21.8	30.0	33.2	23.1
May	29.2	29.0	29.5	21.8	30.1	33.3	23.2
June	29.3	29.1	29.7	21.9	30.2	33.3	23.2
July	29.3	29.2	29.6	21.8	30.2	33.3	23.3
August	29.3	29.2	29.6	21.9	30.2	33.3	23.4
September	29.4	29.3	29.7	21.9	30.3	33.5	23.5
October	29.5	29.4	29.7	22.2	30.4	33.5	23.6
November	29.5	29.4	29.7	22.2	30.4	33.5	23.6
December	29.6	29.4	29.6	22.3	30.5	33.5	23.7
1960							
January	29.5	29.4	29.6	22.3	30.5	33.5	23.7
February	29.6	29.4	29.5	22.2	30.6	33.4	23.8
March	29.6	29.4	29.6	22.3	30.6	33.5	23.9
April	29.7	29.5	30.0	22.4	30.6	33.6	23.9
May	29.7	29.6	30.0	22.3	30.6	33.6	24.0
June	29.8	29.6	30.0	22.4	30.7	33.6	24.0
July	29.7	29.6	29.9	22.5	30.6	33.5	24.1
August	29.8	29.6	30.0	22.5	30.6	33.6	24.1
September	29.8	29.6	30.1	22.6	30.6	33.6	24.2
October	29.9	29.8	30.3	22.5	30.8	33.7	24.2
November	30.0	29.8	30.5	22.7	30.8	33.8	24.3
December	30.0	29.8	30.5	22.6	30.7	33.9	24.3
1961							
January	30.0	29.8	30.5	22.7	30.8	33.8	24.4
February	30.0	29.8	30.5	22.6	30.8	33.8	24.4
March	30.0	29.8	30.5	22.6	30.9	33.8	24.4
April	30.0	29.8	30.4	22.2	30.9	33.8	24.5
May	30.0	29.8	30.3	22.4	30.9	33.8	24.5
June	30.0	29.8	30.2	22.5	31.0	33.8	24.5
July	30.1	29.9	30.3	22.5	31.0	33.9	24.5
August	30.1	29.9	30.3	22.5	31.1	33.9	24.6
September	30.2	30.0	30.3	22.6	31.1	33.9	24.6
October	30.2	30.0	30.3	22.4	31.1	33.9	24.7
November	30.2	30.0	30.3	22.5	31.2	33.8	24.7
December	30.2	30.0	30.3	22.4	31.2	33.9	24.8
1962							
January	30.2	30.0	30.4	22.4	31.2	33.9	24.8
February	30.3	30.1	30.5	22.6	31.2	34.0	24.8
March	30.4	30.2	30.6	22.4	31.3	34.0	24.9
April	30.4	30.2	30.7	22.7	31.3	34.1	24.9
May	30.4	30.2	30.6	22.7	31.4	34.1	25.0
June	30.4	30.2	30.5	22.5	31.4	34.1	25.0
July	30.4	30.2	30.4	22.3	31.4	34.0	25.1
August	30.5	30.3	30.6	22.4	31.5	34.1	25.1
September	30.6	30.4	30.9	22.8	31.5	34.3	25.1
October	30.6	30.4	30.8	22.7	31.5	34.2	25.1
November	30.6	30.4	30.9	22.7	31.5	34.3	25.2
December	30.6	30.4	30.7	22.8	31.6	34.2	25.2
1963							
January	30.6	30.4	31.0	22.8	31.5	34.3	25.3
February	30.7	30.5	31.1	22.7	31.6	34.3	25.3
March	30.7	30.5	31.0	22.7	31.7	34.3	25.3
April	30.7	30.5	30.9	22.6	31.7	34.3	25.4
May	30.7	30.5	30.9	22.6	31.7	34.3	25.4
June	30.8	30.6	31.0	22.5	31.8	34.4	25.5
July	30.9	30.7	31.2	22.7	31.8	34.5	25.5
August	30.9	30.8	31.2	22.6	31.9	34.6	25.6
September	30.9	30.7	31.1	22.5	31.9	34.5	25.6
October	30.9	30.8	31.0	22.7	32.0	34.5	25.6
November	31.0	30.8	31.2	22.6	32.0	34.6	25.7
December	31.1	30.9	31.3	22.6	32.1	34.7	25.8
1964							
January	31.1	30.9	31.4	22.8	32.2	34.7	25.8
February	31.1	30.9	31.4	22.2	32.2	34.7	25.8
March	31.1	30.9	31.4	22.6	32.2	34.7	25.8
April	31.1	31.0	31.4	22.5	32.2	34.7	25.9
May	31.2	31.0	31.4	22.5	32.2	34.7	25.9
June	31.2	31.0	31.4	22.6	32.3	34.7	26.0
July	31.2	31.0	31.5	22.5	32.3	34.7	26.0
August	31.2	31.1	31.4	22.6	32.3	34.7	26.0
September	31.3	31.1	31.6	22.5	32.3	34.8	26.0
October	31.3	31.1	31.6	22.5	32.4	34.8	26.1
November	31.4	31.2	31.7	22.5	32.5	34.9	26.2
December	31.4	31.3	31.7	22.6	32.5	35.0	26.2

Table 8-1B. Summary Consumer Price Indexes: Historical Data, 1946 to Date—*Continued*

(Seasonally adjusted.)

Year and month	Consumer Price Index, 1982–1984 = 100						
	Urban wage earners and clerical workers (CPI-W), all items	All urban consumers (CPI-U)					
		All items	Food	Energy	All items less food and energy	Commod-ities	Services
1965							
January	31.5	31.3	31.6	22.8	32.6	35.0	26.3
February	31.5	31.3	31.5	22.7	32.6	34.9	26.4
March	31.5	31.3	31.7	22.6	32.6	35.0	26.4
April	31.6	31.4	31.8	22.9	32.7	35.0	26.5
May	31.7	31.5	32.1	23.0	32.7	35.1	26.5
June	31.8	31.6	32.6	23.1	32.7	35.3	26.5
July	31.8	31.6	32.5	23.0	32.7	35.3	26.6
August	31.7	31.6	32.4	23.0	32.7	35.2	26.6
September	31.8	31.6	32.3	23.1	32.8	35.2	26.7
October	31.8	31.7	32.5	23.0	32.8	35.3	26.8
November	31.9	31.8	32.6	23.1	32.9	35.4	26.9
December	32.0	31.9	32.8	23.1	33.0	35.5	26.9
1966							
January	32.1	31.9	33.0	23.1	33.0	35.6	27.0
February	32.3	32.1	33.5	23.2	33.1	35.8	27.0
March	32.4	32.2	33.8	23.2	33.1	35.9	27.1
April	32.5	32.3	33.8	23.2	33.3	36.0	27.3
May	32.5	32.4	33.7	23.2	33.4	36.0	27.4
June	32.6	32.4	33.7	23.3	33.5	36.0	27.5
July	32.6	32.5	33.5	23.4	33.6	36.1	27.7
August	32.8	32.7	34.0	23.3	33.7	36.2	27.7
September	32.9	32.8	34.1	23.4	33.8	36.4	27.9
October	33.0	32.9	34.2	23.4	34.0	36.4	28.0
November	33.1	32.9	34.1	23.5	34.0	36.4	28.2
December	33.1	32.9	34.0	23.5	34.1	36.4	28.2
1967							
January	33.1	32.9	33.9	23.6	34.2	36.4	28.3
February	33.2	33.0	33.8	23.7	34.2	36.4	28.4
March	33.2	33.0	33.8	23.6	34.3	36.4	28.5
April	33.3	33.1	33.7	23.9	34.4	36.4	28.6
May	33.3	33.1	33.7	23.9	34.5	36.5	28.6
June	33.5	33.3	34.0	23.8	34.6	36.6	28.8
July	33.6	33.4	34.1	23.8	34.7	36.8	28.8
August	33.7	33.5	34.3	23.9	34.9	37.0	28.9
September	33.8	33.6	34.3	24.0	35.0	37.0	29.0
October	33.9	33.7	34.4	23.9	35.1	37.1	29.2
November	34.0	33.9	34.5	24.0	35.2	37.2	29.2
December	34.1	34.0	34.6	23.9	35.4	37.4	29.4
1968							
January	34.3	34.1	34.6	24.0	35.5	37.5	29.5
February	34.4	34.2	34.8	24.1	35.7	37.6	29.6
March	34.5	34.3	34.9	24.1	35.8	37.7	29.8
April	34.6	34.4	35.0	24.0	35.9	37.8	29.9
May	34.7	34.5	35.1	24.1	36.0	37.8	30.0
June	34.9	34.7	35.2	24.2	36.2	38.0	30.2
July	35.0	34.9	35.3	24.2	36.4	38.1	30.4
August	35.2	35.0	35.4	24.3	36.5	38.3	30.6
September	35.3	35.1	35.6	24.3	36.7	38.4	30.7
October	35.5	35.3	35.9	24.3	36.9	38.6	30.9
November	35.6	35.4	35.9	24.4	37.1	38.7	31.0
December	35.8	35.6	36.0	24.3	37.2	38.8	31.2
1969							
January	35.9	35.7	36.1	24.4	37.3	38.9	31.4
February	36.0	35.8	36.1	24.4	37.6	39.0	31.5
March	36.3	36.1	36.2	24.7	37.8	39.3	31.8
April	36.5	36.3	36.4	24.9	38.1	39.4	32.0
May	36.6	36.4	36.6	24.8	38.1	39.5	32.2
June	36.8	36.6	37.0	25.0	38.3	39.8	32.3
July	37.0	36.8	37.3	24.9	38.5	39.9	32.5
August	37.1	36.9	37.5	24.9	38.7	40.1	32.7
September	37.3	37.1	37.7	25.0	38.9	40.2	33.0
October	37.5	37.3	37.8	25.0	39.1	40.4	33.1
November	37.7	37.5	38.2	25.0	39.2	40.6	33.3
December	37.9	37.7	38.6	25.1	39.4	40.8	33.5
1970							
January	38.1	37.9	38.7	25.1	39.6	41.0	33.8
February	38.3	38.1	38.9	25.1	39.8	41.2	34.0
March	38.5	38.3	38.9	25.0	40.1	41.2	34.4
April	38.7	38.5	39.0	25.5	40.4	41.4	34.6
May	38.8	38.6	39.2	25.4	40.5	41.5	34.8
June	39.0	38.8	39.2	25.3	40.8	41.6	35.0
July	39.1	38.9	39.2	25.5	40.9	41.7	35.2
August	39.2	39.0	39.2	25.4	41.1	41.8	35.4
September	39.4	39.2	39.4	25.6	41.3	42.0	35.6
October	39.6	39.4	39.5	25.9	41.5	42.2	35.8
November	39.8	39.6	39.5	26.0	41.8	42.3	36.0
December	40.0	39.8	39.5	26.2	42.0	42.5	36.2

Table 8-1B. Summary Consumer Price Indexes: Historical Data, 1946 to Date—*Continued*

(Seasonally adjusted.)

Year and month	Urban wage earners and clerical workers (CPI-W), all items	Consumer Price Index, 1982–1984 = 100					
		All urban consumers (CPI-U)					
		All items	Food	Energy	All items less food and energy	Commodities	Services
1971							
January	40.1	39.9	39.4	26.3	42.1	42.5	36.4
February	40.2	39.9	39.5	26.2	42.2	42.6	36.5
March	40.2	40.0	39.8	26.2	42.2	42.7	36.5
April	40.4	40.1	40.1	26.1	42.4	42.9	36.6
May	40.5	40.3	40.3	26.2	42.6	43.1	36.7
June	40.7	40.5	40.5	26.3	42.8	43.2	37.0
July	40.9	40.6	40.6	26.3	42.9	43.3	37.1
August	41.0	40.7	40.6	26.8	43.0	43.4	37.3
September	41.0	40.8	40.6	26.9	43.0	43.4	37.4
October	41.1	40.9	40.7	27.0	43.1	43.5	37.5
November	41.2	41.0	40.9	26.9	43.2	43.5	37.6
December	41.4	41.1	41.3	27.0	43.3	43.8	37.7
1972							
January	41.5	41.2	41.1	27.0	43.5	43.8	37.9
February	41.6	41.4	41.7	26.8	43.6	44.0	38.0
March	41.7	41.4	41.6	26.9	43.6	44.0	38.1
April	41.7	41.5	41.6	26.9	43.8	44.1	38.2
May	41.8	41.6	41.7	27.0	43.9	44.2	38.3
June	41.9	41.7	41.9	27.0	44.0	44.3	38.4
July	42.1	41.8	42.1	27.1	44.1	44.5	38.5
August	42.2	41.9	42.2	27.3	44.3	44.5	38.6
September	42.3	42.1	42.5	27.6	44.3	44.8	38.7
October	42.5	42.2	42.8	27.7	44.4	44.9	38.8
November	42.6	42.4	43.0	27.9	44.4	45.1	38.9
December	42.8	42.5	43.2	27.8	44.6	45.2	39.0
1973							
January	43.0	42.7	44.0	27.9	44.6	45.5	39.1
February	43.2	43.0	44.6	28.2	44.8	45.9	39.2
March	43.6	43.4	45.8	28.3	45.0	46.4	39.4
April	43.9	43.7	46.5	28.6	45.1	46.8	39.5
May	44.2	43.9	47.1	28.8	45.3	47.2	39.6
June	44.4	44.2	47.6	29.2	45.4	47.5	39.8
July	44.5	44.2	47.7	29.2	45.5	47.5	39.9
August	45.3	45.0	50.5	29.4	45.7	48.7	40.2
September	45.4	45.2	50.4	29.4	46.0	48.7	40.5
October	45.8	45.6	50.7	30.3	46.3	49.0	41.0
November	46.2	45.9	51.4	31.5	46.5	49.5	41.3
December	46.5	46.3	51.9	32.5	46.7	49.9	41.5
1974							
January	47.0	46.8	52.5	34.1	46.9	50.5	41.8
February	47.6	47.3	53.6	35.4	47.2	51.3	42.0
March	48.1	47.8	54.2	36.9	47.6	51.9	42.4
April	48.3	48.1	54.1	37.6	47.9	52.1	42.6
May	48.8	48.6	54.5	38.3	48.5	52.7	43.1
June	49.2	49.0	54.5	38.6	49.0	53.1	43.5
July	49.6	49.3	54.3	38.9	49.5	53.3	44.0
August	50.2	49.9	55.1	39.2	50.2	54.1	44.5
September	50.9	50.6	56.2	39.3	50.7	54.8	45.0
October	51.3	51.0	56.8	39.2	51.2	55.3	45.4
November	51.8	51.5	57.5	39.4	51.6	55.8	45.8
December	52.2	51.9	58.2	39.6	52.0	56.3	46.2
1975							
January	52.6	52.3	58.4	40.0	52.3	56.7	46.5
February	52.9	52.6	58.5	40.3	52.8	56.9	46.9
March	53.1	52.8	58.4	40.6	53.0	57.1	47.0
April	53.3	53.0	58.3	41.0	53.3	57.2	47.3
May	53.4	53.1	58.6	41.3	53.5	57.5	47.5
June	53.8	53.5	59.2	41.7	53.8	57.9	47.8
July	54.3	54.0	60.3	42.5	54.0	58.6	48.0
August	54.5	54.2	60.3	42.8	54.2	58.7	48.3
September	54.9	54.6	60.7	43.2	54.5	59.0	48.7
October	55.2	54.9	61.3	43.5	54.8	59.4	49.0
November	55.6	55.3	61.7	43.9	55.2	59.7	49.6
December	55.9	55.6	62.1	44.1	55.5	59.9	49.9
1976							
January	56.2	55.8	61.9	44.5	55.9	60.0	50.5
February	56.2	55.9	61.3	44.4	56.2	59.9	50.8
March	56.3	56.0	60.9	44.1	56.5	59.8	51.1
April	56.5	56.1	60.9	43.9	56.7	59.9	51.3
May	56.7	56.4	61.1	44.1	57.0	60.2	51.4
June	57.0	56.7	61.3	44.4	57.2	60.4	51.7
July	57.3	57.0	61.6	44.8	57.6	60.7	52.1
August	57.6	57.3	61.8	45.2	57.9	61.0	52.4
September	57.9	57.6	62.1	45.7	58.2	61.3	52.8
October	58.2	57.9	62.4	46.1	58.5	61.6	53.1
November	58.4	58.1	62.3	46.8	58.7	61.7	53.4
December	58.7	58.4	62.5	47.5	58.9	62.0	53.7

Table 8-1B. Summary Consumer Price Indexes: Historical Data, 1946 to Date—*Continued*

(Seasonally adjusted.)

Year and month	Urban wage earners and clerical workers (CPI-W), all items	Consumer Price Index, 1982–1984 = 100 — All urban consumers (CPI-U) All items	Food	Energy	All items less food and energy	Commod- ities	Services
1977							
January	59.1	58.7	62.7	48.1	59.3	62.3	54.1
February	59.6	59.3	63.9	48.1	59.7	63.0	54.4
March	59.9	59.6	64.2	48.4	60.0	63.2	54.8
April	60.3	60.0	65.0	48.6	60.3	63.7	55.2
May	60.6	60.2	65.3	48.9	60.6	63.9	55.4
June	60.9	60.5	65.7	48.9	61.0	64.2	55.8
July	61.2	60.8	65.9	49.1	61.2	64.4	56.3
August	61.4	61.1	66.2	49.5	61.5	64.6	56.6
September	61.7	61.3	66.4	49.8	61.8	64.8	56.9
October	61.9	61.6	66.6	50.5	62.0	65.0	57.2
November	62.3	62.0	67.1	51.3	62.3	65.5	57.6
December	62.6	62.3	67.4	51.6	62.7	65.7	57.9
1978							
January	63.0	62.7	67.9	51.1	63.1	66.1	58.3
February	63.3	63.0	68.6	50.6	63.4	66.4	58.7
March	63.8	63.4	69.5	51.0	63.8	66.8	59.1
April	64.2	63.9	70.6	51.4	64.3	67.4	59.6
May	64.8	64.5	71.6	51.7	64.7	68.0	60.0
June	65.3	65.0	72.7	51.9	65.2	68.6	60.5
July	65.8	65.5	73.0	52.1	65.6	69.1	61.0
August	66.2	65.9	73.3	52.6	66.1	69.4	61.5
September	66.7	66.5	73.6	53.2	66.7	70.0	62.1
October	67.4	67.1	74.2	54.1	67.2	70.6	62.6
November	67.8	67.5	74.7	54.9	67.6	71.1	63.1
December	68.3	67.9	75.1	55.9	68.0	71.6	63.3
1979							
January	68.8	68.5	76.4	55.8	68.5	72.2	63.8
February	69.6	69.2	77.7	55.9	69.2	72.9	64.4
March	70.3	69.9	78.4	57.4	69.8	73.8	64.9
April	71.1	70.6	79.0	59.5	70.3	74.7	65.5
May	71.9	71.4	79.7	62.0	70.8	75.6	66.2
June	72.7	72.2	80.0	64.7	71.3	76.4	66.8
July	73.5	73.0	80.5	67.3	71.9	77.2	67.6
August	74.2	73.7	80.4	69.7	72.7	77.9	68.5
September	75.0	74.4	80.9	71.9	73.3	78.6	69.2
October	75.7	75.2	81.5	73.5	74.0	79.3	70.1
November	76.5	76.0	82.0	74.8	74.8	80.0	71.1
December	77.3	76.9	82.8	76.8	75.7	80.8	72.0
1980							
January	78.5	78.0	83.3	79.1	76.7	82.0	73.1
February	79.4	79.0	83.4	81.9	77.5	82.8	74.1
March	80.6	80.1	84.1	84.5	78.6	83.9	75.4
April	81.4	80.9	84.7	85.4	79.5	84.4	76.6
May	82.2	81.7	85.2	86.4	80.1	84.9	77.6
June	83.0	82.5	85.7	86.5	81.0	85.3	79.0
July	83.1	82.6	86.6	86.7	80.8	85.9	78.5
August	83.7	83.2	88.0	87.2	81.3	86.9	78.5
September	84.4	83.9	89.1	87.5	82.1	87.8	79.0
October	85.3	84.7	89.8	88.0	83.0	88.5	80.0
November	86.2	85.6	90.8	88.8	83.9	89.2	81.1
December	87.0	86.4	91.3	90.7	84.9	89.7	82.2
1981							
January	87.7	87.2	91.6	92.1	85.4	90.4	83.0
February	88.6	88.0	92.1	95.2	85.9	91.4	83.7
March	89.1	88.6	92.6	97.4	86.4	91.9	84.4
April	89.6	89.1	92.8	97.6	87.0	92.0	85.3
May	90.2	89.7	92.8	97.9	87.8	92.4	86.4
June	90.9	90.5	93.2	97.3	88.6	92.9	87.5
July	92.0	91.5	93.9	97.3	89.8	93.6	88.9
August	92.7	92.2	94.4	97.8	90.7	94.0	89.9
September	93.5	93.1	94.8	98.6	91.8	94.6	91.2
October	93.8	93.4	95.0	99.2	92.1	94.7	91.7
November	94.2	93.8	95.1	100.5	92.5	94.9	92.5
December	94.5	94.1	95.3	101.5	93.0	95.1	93.0
1982							
January	94.8	94.4	95.6	100.6	93.3	95.2	93.5
February	95.1	94.7	96.3	98.0	93.8	95.4	93.9
March	95.0	94.7	96.2	96.6	93.9	95.3	94.0
April	95.3	95.0	96.4	94.2	94.7	95.1	94.9
May	96.1	95.9	97.2	95.7	95.4	96.0	95.7
June	97.3	97.0	98.1	98.4	96.1	97.4	96.5
July	97.8	97.5	98.2	99.3	96.7	97.9	97.0
August	98.1	97.7	98.0	99.8	97.1	97.9	97.6
September	98.1	97.7	98.2	100.3	97.2	97.8	97.6
October	98.5	98.1	98.2	101.7	97.5	98.2	97.9
November	98.4	98.0	98.2	102.5	97.3	98.3	97.7
December	98.1	97.7	98.2	102.8	97.2	98.3	96.9

Table 8-1B. Summary Consumer Price Indexes: Historical Data, 1946 to Date—*Continued*

(Seasonally adjusted.)

Year and month	Urban wage earners and clerical workers (CPI-W), all items	Consumer Price Index, 1982–1984 = 100 — All urban consumers (CPI-U)					
		All items	Food	Energy	All items less food and energy	Commodities	Services
1983							
January	98.2	97.9	98.1	99.6	97.6	98.3	97.5
February	98.2	98.0	98.2	97.7	98.0	98.1	97.9
March	98.5	98.1	98.8	96.8	98.2	98.2	98.1
April	99.1	98.8	99.2	98.9	98.6	98.9	98.7
May	99.5	99.2	99.5	100.4	98.9	99.5	98.9
June	99.7	99.4	99.6	100.6	99.2	99.8	99.2
July	100.0	99.8	99.6	100.9	99.8	100.2	99.6
August	100.5	100.1	99.7	101.2	100.1	100.5	99.8
September	100.7	100.4	100.0	101.0	100.5	100.7	100.2
October	101.0	100.8	100.3	100.8	101.0	101.0	100.7
November	101.2	101.1	100.3	100.5	101.5	101.1	101.3
December	101.3	101.4	100.6	100.0	101.8	101.2	101.6
1984							
January	101.8	102.1	102.0	100.2	102.5	101.9	102.1
February	102.0	102.6	102.7	101.4	102.8	102.4	102.6
March	102.0	102.9	102.9	101.4	103.2	102.6	103.0
April	102.2	103.3	102.9	101.7	103.7	102.9	103.5
May	102.5	103.5	102.7	101.6	104.1	103.0	103.9
June	102.7	103.7	103.1	100.8	104.5	103.1	104.2
July	103.2	104.1	103.3	100.5	105.0	103.2	104.9
August	104.1	104.4	103.9	100.1	105.4	103.4	105.4
September	104.5	104.7	103.8	100.6	105.8	103.6	105.9
October	104.7	105.1	104.0	104.0	106.2	103.9	106.3
November	104.8	105.3	104.1	100.8	106.4	103.9	106.7
December	104.9	105.5	104.5	100.1	106.8	103.9	107.1
1985							
January	105.2	105.7	104.7	100.3	107.1	104.1	107.4
February	105.7	106.3	105.2	100.3	107.7	104.7	107.9
March	106.1	106.8	105.5	101.3	108.1	105.1	108.4
April	106.4	107.0	105.4	102.3	108.4	105.4	108.7
May	106.6	107.2	105.2	102.2	108.8	105.2	109.4
June	106.9	107.5	105.5	102.2	109.1	105.3	109.8
July	107.0	107.7	105.5	102.2	109.4	105.3	110.3
August	107.1	107.9	105.6	101.2	109.8	105.2	110.7
September	107.3	108.1	105.8	101.2	110.0	105.4	111.0
October	107.7	108.5	105.8	101.2	110.5	105.6	111.5
November	108.2	109.0	106.5	101.8	111.1	106.1	112.1
December	108.7	109.5	107.3	102.4	111.4	106.6	112.5
1986							
January	109.1	109.9	107.5	102.6	111.9	106.9	113.1
February	108.8	109.7	107.3	99.5	112.2	106.0	113.5
March	108.1	109.1	107.5	92.6	112.5	104.5	114.1
April	107.7	108.7	107.7	87.2	112.9	103.3	114.6
May	107.8	109.0	108.2	87.2	113.1	103.5	114.8
June	108.3	109.4	108.3	88.8	113.4	103.8	115.5
July	108.3	109.5	109.1	85.6	113.8	103.7	115.7
August	108.4	109.6	110.1	83.6	114.2	103.6	116.1
September	108.8	110.0	110.2	84.4	114.6	104.0	116.5
October	108.9	110.2	110.5	82.8	115.0	104.0	116.9
November	109.2	110.4	111.1	82.1	115.3	104.2	117.2
December	109.5	110.8	111.4	82.5	115.6	104.5	117.5
1987							
January	110.2	111.4	111.8	85.4	115.9	105.5	117.9
February	110.7	111.8	112.2	87.4	116.2	106.1	118.3
March	111.1	112.2	112.4	87.6	116.6	106.5	118.6
April	111.6	112.7	112.6	87.6	117.3	106.9	119.2
May	111.9	113.0	113.2	87.1	117.7	107.2	119.6
June	112.4	113.5	113.9	88.5	117.9	107.7	120.0
July	112.7	113.8	113.7	89.2	118.3	108.0	120.3
August	113.2	114.3	113.9	90.5	118.7	108.5	120.9
September	113.6	114.7	114.3	90.3	119.2	108.8	121.4
October	113.9	115.0	114.5	89.6	119.8	109.0	121.8
November	114.2	115.4	114.5	90.0	120.1	109.3	122.2
December	114.4	115.6	115.1	89.5	120.4	109.3	122.6
1988							
January	114.7	116.0	115.6	88.8	120.9	109.5	123.0
February	114.9	116.2	115.6	88.7	121.2	109.5	123.5
March	115.2	116.5	115.8	88.4	121.7	109.8	123.9
April	115.8	117.2	116.4	88.8	122.3	110.5	124.4
May	116.2	117.5	116.9	88.5	122.7	110.7	124.8
June	116.6	118.0	117.6	88.9	123.2	111.2	125.4
July	117.3	118.5	118.8	89.4	123.6	111.9	125.8
August	117.7	119.0	119.4	90.1	124.0	112.2	126.4
September	118.2	119.5	120.1	89.8	124.7	112.8	126.9
October	118.6	119.9	120.3	89.8	125.2	113.0	127.5
November	118.9	120.3	120.5	89.8	125.6	113.3	127.9
December	119.3	120.7	121.1	89.6	126.0	113.5	128.4

Table 8-1B. Summary Consumer Price Indexes: Historical Data, 1946 to Date—*Continued*

(Seasonally adjusted.)

Year and month	Urban wage earners and clerical workers (CPI-W), all items	Consumer Price Index, 1982–1984 = 100					
		All urban consumers (CPI-U)					
		All items	Food	Energy	All items less food and energy	Commod-ities	Services
1989							
January	119.9	121.2	121.6	90.3	126.5	114.1	128.9
February	120.3	121.6	122.5	90.8	126.9	114.5	129.4
March	120.9	122.2	123.2	91.8	127.4	115.1	130.0
April	121.9	123.1	123.9	96.6	127.8	116.5	130.5
May	122.5	123.7	124.7	97.4	128.3	117.1	131.1
June	122.8	124.1	125.1	96.9	128.8	117.2	131.6
July	123.2	124.5	125.6	96.7	129.2	117.3	132.3
August	123.2	124.5	125.9	94.9	129.5	117.0	132.8
September	123.4	124.8	126.3	93.8	129.9	117.2	133.1
October	123.9	125.4	126.8	94.4	130.6	117.8	133.7
November	124.4	125.9	127.4	93.9	131.1	118.1	134.3
December	124.9	126.3	127.8	94.2	131.6	118.4	134.9
1990							
January	126.1	127.5	129.7	98.9	132.1	120.2	135.4
February	126.6	128.0	130.8	98.2	132.7	120.7	136.0
March	127.0	128.6	131.0	97.6	133.5	120.9	136.8
April	127.3	128.9	130.8	97.5	134.0	121.0	137.4
May	127.5	129.1	131.1	96.7	134.4	121.0	137.9
June	128.2	129.9	132.1	97.3	135.1	121.6	138.8
July	128.8	130.5	132.8	97.1	135.8	122.0	139.6
August	129.9	131.6	133.2	101.6	136.6	123.2	140.6
September	130.9	132.5	133.6	106.5	137.1	124.5	141.1
October	131.7	133.4	134.1	110.8	137.6	125.8	141.6
November	132.1	133.7	134.5	111.2	138.0	126.0	142.2
December	132.5	134.2	134.6	111.0	138.6	126.3	142.7
1991							
January	132.9	134.7	135.0	108.5	139.5	126.3	143.7
February	132.9	134.8	135.1	104.5	140.2	125.9	144.4
March	133.0	134.8	135.3	101.9	140.5	125.5	144.7
April	133.3	135.1	136.1	101.2	140.9	126.0	144.9
May	133.8	135.6	136.6	102.1	141.3	126.4	145.4
June	134.1	136.0	137.4	101.1	141.8	126.7	145.9
July	134.3	136.2	136.7	100.7	142.3	126.6	146.5
August	134.6	136.6	136.2	101.1	142.9	126.8	146.9
September	135.0	137.0	136.4	101.5	143.4	127.0	147.6
October	135.2	137.2	136.2	101.6	143.7	127.0	148.0
November	135.8	137.8	136.7	102.4	144.2	127.6	148.5
December	136.2	138.2	137.0	103.1	144.7	127.9	149.2
1992							
January	136.2	138.3	136.6	101.5	145.1	127.6	149.6
February	136.5	138.6	137.1	101.2	145.4	127.8	149.9
March	136.9	139.1	137.6	101.2	145.9	128.2	150.4
April	137.2	139.4	137.5	101.4	146.3	128.3	150.9
May	137.5	139.7	137.2	102.0	146.8	128.6	151.3
June	138.0	140.1	137.6	103.3	147.1	129.1	151.7
July	138.4	140.5	137.4	103.7	147.6	129.3	152.2
August	138.7	140.8	138.4	103.5	147.9	129.6	152.6
September	139.0	141.1	138.9	103.6	148.1	129.9	152.9
October	139.5	141.7	138.9	104.3	148.8	130.2	153.7
November	139.8	142.1	138.7	105.1	149.2	130.3	154.3
December	140.1	142.3	138.8	105.3	149.6	130.5	154.7
1993							
January	140.5	142.8	139.1	105.0	150.1	130.7	155.3
February	140.8	143.1	139.6	104.3	150.6	131.1	155.6
March	141.0	143.3	139.6	104.9	150.8	131.1	156.0
April	141.4	143.8	140.0	104.9	151.4	131.4	156.7
May	141.8	144.2	141.0	104.3	151.8	131.6	157.3
June	142.0	144.3	140.6	103.9	152.1	131.3	157.8
July	142.1	144.5	140.6	103.4	152.3	131.3	158.1
August	142.4	144.8	141.1	103.4	152.8	131.6	158.6
September	142.5	145.0	141.4	103.0	152.9	131.3	159.0
October	143.2	145.6	142.0	105.3	153.4	132.2	159.4
November	143.4	146.0	142.3	104.4	153.9	132.4	159.9
December	143.7	146.3	142.8	103.7	154.3	132.4	160.5
1994							
January	143.8	146.3	142.9	102.8	154.5	132.3	160.8
February	144.0	146.7	142.7	104.1	154.8	132.4	161.4
March	144.3	147.1	142.7	104.3	155.3	132.5	162.0
April	144.5	147.2	143.0	103.7	155.5	132.6	162.2
May	144.8	147.5	143.3	102.8	155.9	132.9	162.4
June	145.3	147.9	143.8	103.1	156.4	133.5	162.8
July	145.9	148.4	144.6	104.5	156.7	134.1	163.1
August	146.5	149.0	145.1	106.7	157.1	134.7	163.8
September	146.8	149.3	145.3	106.1	157.5	134.8	164.1
October	146.9	149.4	145.3	105.7	157.8	134.8	164.5
November	147.3	149.8	145.6	106.1	158.2	135.0	165.0
December	147.6	150.1	146.8	105.9	158.3	135.4	165.2

Table 8-1B. Summary Consumer Price Indexes: Historical Data, 1946 to Date—*Continued*

(Seasonally adjusted.)

Year and month	Urban wage earners and clerical workers (CPI-W), all items	Consumer Price Index, 1982–1984 = 100 — All urban consumers (CPI-U)					
		All items	Food	Energy	All items less food and energy	Commodities	Services
1995							
January	148.0	150.5	146.7	105.7	159.0	135.4	166.0
February	148.4	150.9	147.3	105.8	159.4	135.6	166.5
March	148.6	151.2	147.1	105.5	159.9	135.6	167.1
April	149.2	151.8	148.1	105.6	160.4	136.2	167.7
May	149.5	152.1	148.2	105.8	160.7	136.4	168.1
June	149.8	152.4	148.3	106.7	161.1	136.6	168.5
July	149.9	152.6	148.5	105.8	161.4	136.6	168.9
August	150.2	152.9	148.6	105.6	161.8	136.8	169.3
September	150.4	153.1	149.1	104.1	162.2	136.8	169.7
October	150.8	153.5	149.5	104.4	162.7	137.1	170.3
November	150.9	153.7	149.6	103.4	163.0	137.0	170.7
December	151.3	153.9	149.9	104.4	163.1	137.3	170.9
1996							
January	152.0	154.7	150.4	106.9	163.7	138.2	171.5
February	152.3	155.0	150.8	107.1	164.0	138.3	172.0
March	152.9	155.5	151.4	108.3	164.4	139.0	172.4
April	153.4	156.1	152.0	111.2	164.6	139.6	172.8
May	153.8	156.4	151.9	112.0	165.0	139.7	173.4
June	154.0	156.7	152.9	110.3	165.4	139.8	173.8
July	154.3	157.0	153.4	110.1	165.7	139.8	174.4
August	154.5	157.2	153.9	109.7	166.0	139.8	174.9
September	154.9	157.7	154.6	109.8	166.5	140.3	175.4
October	155.4	158.2	155.5	110.5	166.8	140.8	175.8
November	155.9	158.7	156.1	111.8	167.2	141.4	176.3
December	156.3	159.1	156.3	113.9	167.4	141.7	176.7
1997							
January	156.6	159.4	155.9	115.2	167.8	141.8	177.3
February	156.9	159.7	156.5	115.0	168.1	142.1	177.6
March	156.9	159.8	156.6	113.0	168.4	141.8	178.0
April	157.0	159.9	156.5	111.0	168.9	141.6	178.4
May	157.0	159.9	156.6	108.8	169.2	141.4	178.7
June	157.3	160.2	156.9	110.0	169.4	141.5	179.2
July	157.4	160.4	157.2	109.1	169.7	141.4	179.7
August	157.8	160.8	157.7	110.9	169.8	141.9	179.9
September	158.2	161.2	158.0	112.4	170.2	142.2	180.4
October	158.4	161.5	158.3	111.8	170.6	142.2	180.9
November	158.6	161.7	158.6	111.4	170.8	142.1	181.4
December	158.6	161.8	158.7	109.8	171.2	142.1	181.7
1998							
January	158.8	162.0	159.5	107.5	171.6	142.0	182.1
February	158.7	162.0	159.4	105.1	171.9	141.8	182.3
March	158.7	162.0	159.7	103.3	172.2	141.4	182.8
April	158.8	162.2	159.7	102.4	172.5	141.3	183.3
May	159.3	162.6	160.3	103.2	172.9	141.7	183.7
June	159.5	162.8	160.2	103.6	173.2	141.8	184.0
July	159.8	163.2	160.6	103.3	173.5	142.1	184.3
August	160.0	163.4	161.0	102.1	174.0	142.2	184.7
September	160.1	163.5	161.1	101.3	174.2	142.0	185.1
October	160.5	163.9	162.0	101.5	174.4	142.3	185.5
November	160.7	164.1	162.2	101.1	174.8	142.2	186.0
December	161.1	164.4	162.4	100.1	175.4	142.5	186.4
1999							
January	161.4	164.7	163.0	99.7	175.6	142.8	186.6
February	161.3	164.7	163.3	99.2	175.6	142.4	186.9
March	161.4	164.8	163.3	100.4	175.7	142.4	187.4
April	162.4	165.9	163.5	105.5	176.3	144.0	187.9
May	162.6	166.0	163.8	104.9	176.5	143.9	188.1
June	162.6	166.0	163.7	104.5	176.6	143.8	188.3
July	163.3	166.7	163.9	106.7	177.1	144.5	188.9
August	163.8	167.1	164.2	109.5	177.3	145.0	189.3
September	164.6	167.8	164.6	111.8	177.8	145.9	189.8
October	164.9	168.1	165.0	112.0	178.1	146.1	190.2
November	165.1	168.4	165.3	111.5	178.4	145.9	190.9
December	165.6	168.8	165.5	113.8	178.7	146.5	191.2
2000							
January	166.0	169.3	165.6	115.0	179.3	146.7	192.0
February	166.7	170.0	166.2	118.8	179.4	147.6	192.5
March	167.8	171.0	166.5	124.3	180.0	149.1	193.1
April	167.6	170.9	166.7	120.9	180.3	148.5	193.5
May	167.9	171.2	167.3	120.0	180.7	148.5	194.0
June	169.0	172.2	167.4	126.8	181.1	149.6	194.9
July	169.5	172.7	168.3	127.3	181.5	149.8	195.7
August	169.3	172.7	168.7	123.8	181.9	149.2	196.3
September	170.3	173.6	168.9	129.2	182.3	150.4	196.9
October	170.5	173.9	169.0	129.6	182.6	150.1	197.7
November	170.8	174.2	169.2	129.2	183.1	150.3	198.1
December	171.2	174.6	170.0	130.1	183.3	150.4	198.8

Table 8-1B. Summary Consumer Price Indexes: Historical Data, 1946 to Date—*Continued*

(Seasonally adjusted.)

Year and month	Urban wage earners and clerical workers (CPI-W), all items	Consumer Price Index, 1982–1984 = 100					
		All urban consumers (CPI-U)					
		All items	Food	Energy	All items less food and energy	Commod-ities	Services
2001							
January	172.2	175.6	170.3	135.0	183.9	150.6	200.6
February	172.5	176.0	171.2	134.1	184.4	150.8	201.2
March	172.6	176.1	171.7	131.7	184.7	150.5	201.6
April	173.0	176.4	172.1	132.3	185.1	150.9	202.0
May	174.0	177.3	172.4	138.4	185.3	151.9	202.7
June	174.2	177.7	173.1	136.9	186.0	151.9	203.5
July	173.8	177.4	173.6	129.6	186.4	150.9	203.8
August	173.8	177.4	174.0	127.3	186.7	150.4	204.4
September	174.7	178.1	174.2	130.9	187.1	151.6	204.5
October	173.9	177.6	174.8	122.9	187.4	150.3	204.8
November	173.7	177.5	174.9	116.9	188.1	149.2	205.6
December	173.4	177.4	174.7	113.9	188.4	148.3	206.1
2002							
January	173.7	177.7	175.3	114.2	188.7	148.3	206.8
February	173.9	178.0	175.7	113.5	189.1	148.3	207.5
March	174.5	178.5	176.1	117.6	189.2	149.0	207.9
April	175.4	179.3	176.4	121.5	189.7	150.0	208.5
May	175.5	179.5	175.8	121.9	190.0	149.7	209.0
June	175.7	179.6	175.9	121.6	190.2	149.7	209.3
July	176.1	180.0	176.1	122.4	190.5	149.9	209.9
August	176.6	180.5	176.1	123.1	191.1	150.2	210.6
September	176.8	180.8	176.5	123.7	191.3	150.2	211.1
October	177.2	181.2	176.4	126.9	191.5	150.5	211.7
November	177.5	181.5	176.9	126.7	191.9	150.5	212.4
December	177.7	181.8	177.1	127.1	192.1	150.3	213.0
2003							
January	178.6	182.6	177.1	133.5	192.4	151.3	213.7
February	179.7	183.6	178.1	140.8	192.5	152.7	214.2
March	180.1	183.9	178.4	143.9	192.5	152.6	215.0
April	179.2	183.2	178.5	136.5	192.5	151.1	215.1
May	178.7	182.9	178.8	129.4	192.9	149.4	216.0
June	178.9	183.1	179.7	129.8	193.0	149.7	216.2
July	179.4	183.7	179.8	132.2	193.4	150.3	216.8
August	180.3	184.5	180.5	137.8	193.6	151.4	217.2
September	180.9	185.1	180.9	142.9	193.7	152.1	217.8
October	180.6	184.9	181.6	137.8	194.0	151.1	218.4
November	180.6	185.0	182.6	136.9	194.0	151.1	218.6
December	181.0	185.5	183.5	138.8	194.2	151.6	219.0
2004							
January	181.9	186.3	183.4	143.9	194.6	152.5	219.7
February	182.4	186.7	183.9	145.8	194.9	153.1	220.1
March	182.7	187.1	184.2	145.1	195.5	153.3	220.8
April	182.8	187.4	184.6	143.4	195.9	153.0	221.4
May	183.8	188.2	186.1	147.6	196.2	154.2	221.9
June	184.4	188.9	186.4	151.5	196.6	154.9	222.7
July	184.6	189.1	186.8	151.1	196.8	154.6	223.2
August	184.7	189.2	187.0	151.5	196.9	154.4	223.7
September	185.3	189.8	186.9	152.9	197.5	154.9	224.2
October	186.4	190.8	187.8	158.6	197.9	156.7	224.6
November	187.4	191.7	188.4	163.8	198.3	157.8	225.4
December	187.4	191.7	188.4	162.3	198.6	157.4	225.8
2005							
January	187.2	191.6	188.7	157.2	199.0	156.8	226.2
February	188.0	192.4	188.6	161.8	199.4	157.5	226.9
March	188.6	193.1	189.1	163.5	200.1	157.9	228.0
April	189.3	193.7	190.4	166.7	200.2	158.6	228.5
May	189.1	193.6	190.6	163.3	200.5	158.1	228.9
June	189.3	193.7	190.5	163.7	200.6	158.0	229.1
July	190.6	194.9	190.9	172.8	200.9	159.6	229.9
August	192.0	196.1	191.1	183.5	201.1	161.5	230.4
September	195.1	198.8	191.5	208.2	201.3	166.0	231.4
October	195.2	199.1	192.0	205.9	202.0	164.8	233.1
November	193.7	198.1	192.6	191.0	202.5	161.8	234.2
December	193.7	198.1	192.9	187.6	202.8	161.5	234.4
2006							
January	195.1	199.3	193.6	196.6	203.2	162.9	235.5
February	195.0	199.4	193.7	194.1	203.6	162.5	235.9
March	195.3	199.7	194.0	192.0	204.3	162.6	236.5
April	196.4	200.7	193.8	198.5	204.8	164.1	237.1
May	197.0	201.3	194.1	199.8	205.4	164.6	237.8
June	197.4	201.8	194.7	199.8	205.9	164.8	238.5
July	198.6	202.9	195.2	207.9	206.3	166.4	239.2
August	199.5	203.8	195.7	211.9	206.8	167.2	239.9
September	198.3	202.8	196.3	198.1	207.2	164.6	240.7
October	197.1	201.9	196.9	184.1	207.6	162.5	241.0
November	197.2	202.0	197.0	184.1	207.8	162.0	241.7
December	198.4	203.1	197.1	192.7	208.1	163.4	242.4

Table 8-1B. Summary Consumer Price Indexes: Historical Data, 1946 to Date—*Continued*

(Seasonally adjusted.)

Year and month	Urban wage earners and clerical workers (CPI-W), all items	Consumer Price Index, 1982–1984 = 100					
		All urban consumers (CPI-U)					
		All items	Food	Energy	All items less food and energy	Commod-ities	Services
2007							
January	198.6	203.4	198.4	190.3	208.6	163.3	243.2
February	199.4	204.2	199.7	192.3	209.1	164.1	244.1
March	200.7	205.3	200.4	200.2	209.4	165.6	244.7
April	201.3	205.9	201.0	203.3	209.7	166.2	245.3
May	202.3	206.8	201.7	208.6	210.1	167.3	245.9
June	202.7	207.2	202.6	209.8	210.4	167.5	246.6
July	203.0	207.6	203.2	209.6	210.8	167.8	247.1
August	203.0	207.7	204.0	206.4	211.1	167.5	247.5
September	204.0	208.5	205.0	210.7	211.6	168.5	248.2
October	204.7	209.2	205.7	212.4	212.1	169.0	249.1
November	206.5	210.8	206.5	223.8	212.7	171.5	249.8
December	207.1	211.4	206.9	225.6	213.2	172.0	250.5
2008							
January	207.9	212.2	208.1	226.8	213.8	172.7	251.3
February	208.4	212.6	208.9	229.7	213.9	173.0	251.8
March	209.2	213.4	209.3	233.3	214.4	173.7	252.9
April	209.8	214.0	211.1	234.8	214.6	174.1	253.6
May	211.1	215.2	212.0	243.9	214.9	175.5	254.7
June	213.7	217.5	213.3	262.1	215.4	178.8	255.8
July	215.5	219.1	215.4	271.1	216.0	180.7	257.1
August	215.0	218.7	216.5	262.6	216.4	179.6	257.6
September	215.1	218.9	217.8	260.1	216.7	179.8	257.6
October	212.7	217.0	218.7	238.1	216.8	175.8	257.7
November	207.9	213.1	219.1	195.2	216.9	168.0	257.8
December	205.9	211.4	219.1	176.6	216.9	164.5	258.0
2009							
January	206.5	212.0	219.2	178.8	217.3	165.3	258.4
February	207.4	212.8	219.0	184.9	217.8	166.8	258.7
March	207.1	212.6	218.5	178.8	218.3	166.2	258.7
April	207.4	212.7	218.2	177.1	218.7	166.5	258.7
May	207.8	213.0	217.8	179.7	218.9	167.2	258.6
June	209.9	214.7	217.8	196.9	219.2	170.7	258.7
July	210.0	214.7	217.4	195.6	219.3	170.5	258.7
August	210.9	215.5	217.4	201.5	219.5	171.3	259.3
September	211.3	215.9	217.3	202.8	219.9	171.9	259.6
October	211.9	216.5	217.5	204.6	220.5	172.7	260.0
November	212.7	217.1	217.6	210.3	220.6	173.8	260.2
December	213.0	217.3	217.9	210.3	220.8	174.2	260.3
2010							
January	213.4	217.5	218.5	212.8	220.6	174.9	259.8
February	213.3	217.3	218.6	209.6	220.7	174.3	260.0
March	213.3	217.4	219.0	209.3	220.8	174.1	260.3
April	213.2	217.4	219.2	209.2	220.8	173.9	260.7
May	212.9	217.3	219.3	206.6	221.0	173.4	260.9
June	212.9	217.2	219.3	203.8	221.2	172.9	261.2
July	213.5	217.6	219.2	206.9	221.4	173.4	261.5
August	213.9	217.9	219.5	208.8	221.5	173.8	261.7
September	214.3	218.3	220.2	209.8	221.7	174.4	261.9
October	215.1	219.0	220.5	216.7	221.8	175.7	262.1
November	215.5	219.6	220.9	219.5	222.1	176.5	262.4
December	216.9	220.5	221.2	227.1	222.3	177.9	262.7
2011							
January	217.5	221.2	222.5	229.3	222.8	178.9	263.2
February	218.2	221.9	223.5	232.1	223.2	179.8	263.7
March	219.5	223.0	225.2	240.1	223.5	181.8	264.1
April	220.8	224.1	226.1	248.0	223.7	183.5	264.5
May	221.6	224.8	226.9	250.7	224.2	184.5	264.9
June	221.5	224.8	227.5	245.5	224.7	184.1	265.3
July	222.1	225.4	228.5	246.2	225.2	184.6	266.0
August	222.8	226.1	229.6	246.9	225.9	185.3	266.7
September	223.4	226.6	230.7	248.6	226.1	185.8	267.1
October	223.5	226.8	230.9	246.7	226.5	185.7	267.5
November	224.0	227.2	231.1	247.6	226.9	186.2	267.8
December	223.9	227.2	231.6	243.4	227.4	185.7	268.5
2012							
January	224.5	227.8	232.2	244.9	227.9	186.5	268.9
February	225.1	228.3	232.1	248.9	228.0	187.4	269.0
March	225.7	228.8	232.6	249.7	228.5	187.9	269.6
April	226.0	229.2	233.0	249.7	228.9	188.1	270.1
May	225.4	228.7	233.2	241.8	229.2	186.8	270.4
June	225.0	228.5	233.7	235.9	229.6	185.8	271.0
July	224.9	228.6	233.8	233.6	230.0	185.5	271.4
August	226.4	229.9	234.2	245.0	230.2	187.5	272.1
September	227.7	231.0	234.4	253.0	230.7	189.1	272.7
October	228.4	231.6	234.8	256.0	231.0	189.8	273.2
November	227.8	231.2	235.3	248.8	231.3	188.5	273.8
December	227.7	231.2	235.7	244.7	231.7	187.7	274.4

Table 8-1B. Summary Consumer Price Indexes: Historical Data, 1946 to Date—*Continued*

(Seasonally adjusted.)

Year and month	Urban wage earners and clerical workers (CPI-W), all items	Consumer Price Index, 1982–1984 = 100					
		All urban consumers (CPI-U)					
		All items	Food	Energy	All items less food and energy	Commod-ities	Services
2013							
January	228.1	231.7	236.0	245.0	232.2	188.0	275.1
February	229.6	232.9	236.0	255.7	232.6	189.9	275.8
March	228.8	232.3	236.2	246.6	232.8	188.1	276.2
April	228.1	231.8	236.7	240.5	232.8	186.8	276.5
May	228.3	231.9	236.5	240.5	233.0	186.5	277.0
June	228.8	232.4	237.0	242.7	233.4	187.1	277.4
July	229.2	232.9	237.2	243.0	233.9	187.3	278.1
August	229.8	233.5	237.5	244.8	234.3	187.8	278.7
September	229.8	233.5	237.5	242.7	234.7	187.4	279.4
October	229.9	233.7	237.8	242.0	234.9	187.2	279.8
November	230.4	234.1	237.9	242.7	235.4	187.5	280.3
December	231.0	234.7	238.2	245.7	235.8	188.2	280.9
2014							
January	231.6	235.3	238.5	250.3	236.0	188.5	281.7
February	231.9	235.5	239.4	249.9	236.2	188.4	282.3
March	232.3	236.0	240.4	250.0	236.6	188.1	283.5
April	232.8	236.5	241.2	249.9	237.1	188.8	283.8
May	233.1	236.9	242.4	249.2	237.5	188.8	284.7
June	233.4	237.2	242.6	249.7	237.8	189.0	285.1
July	233.6	237.5	243.2	248.7	238.2	188.9	285.7
August	233.5	237.5	243.8	245.7	238.4	188.5	286.0
September	233.4	237.5	244.5	241.6	238.8	188.1	286.4
October	233.2	237.4	244.9	237.1	239.2	187.5	286.9
November	232.6	237.0	245.4	229.0	239.5	186.1	287.4
December	231.5	236.3	246.2	218.5	239.6	184.0	288.0
2015							
January	229.5	234.7	246.2	199.9	239.8	180.3	288.6
February	230.3	235.3	246.5	203.0	240.2	181.1	288.9
March	230.9	236.0	246.1	205.8	240.8	181.9	289.5
April	231.1	236.2	246.0	203.6	241.3	181.6	290.2
May	232.0	237.0	246.2	209.0	241.7	182.9	290.5
June	232.7	237.7	246.9	212.0	242.1	183.4	291.3
July	233.0	238.0	247.2	211.6	242.6	183.4	292.0
August	233.0	238.0	247.7	208.6	242.8	182.9	292.5
September	232.1	237.5	248.5	197.2	243.3	181.2	293.1
October	232.3	237.7	248.8	195.6	243.8	180.9	293.9
November	232.5	238.0	248.5	195.1	244.2	180.7	294.6
December	232.1	237.8	248.2	190.1	244.5	179.7	295.0
2016							
January	231.9	237.7	248.4	185.2	245.0	178.8	295.8
February	231.3	237.3	248.6	176.4	245.5	177.5	296.4
March	232.2	238.1	248.0	182.2	245.9	178.3	297.1
April	233.2	239.0	248.2	186.7	246.6	179.3	297.9
May	233.7	239.6	247.9	188.6	247.1	179.5	298.9
June	234.4	240.2	247.7	192.9	247.5	179.9	299.7
July	234.1	240.1	247.7	189.0	247.8	178.9	300.5
August	234.5	240.5	247.7	188.8	248.4	178.8	301.4
September	235.2	241.2	247.8	192.2	248.8	179.5	302.0
October	235.8	241.7	247.8	196.0	249.1	180.1	302.5
November	236.0	242.0	247.7	196.4	249.5	179.8	303.3
December	236.7	242.6	247.7	199.5	249.9	180.3	304.0
2017							
January	237.7	243.6	248.0	205.5	250.5	181.6	304.8
February	237.9	243.9	248.7	203.5	250.9	181.2	305.7
March	237.7	243.8	249.1	202.2	250.8	181.1	305.6
April	238.2	244.3	249.5	203.8	251.3	181.4	306.3
May	237.9	244.1	249.9	198.7	251.5	180.3	306.9
June	238.0	244.2	249.8	197.7	251.8	179.9	307.6
July	238.0	244.3	250.3	195.7	252.0	179.5	308.1
August	239.0	245.2	250.5	201.1	252.6	180.4	309.0
September	240.6	246.6	250.9	211.9	253.0	182.5	309.7
October	240.6	246.7	251.2	208.4	253.5	181.9	310.5
November	241.5	247.4	251.3	214.7	253.7	182.8	311.0
December	241.8	247.7	251.7	213.1	254.3	182.7	311.8
2018							
January	242.9	248.7	252.2	217.3	255.0	183.9	312.6
February	243.4	249.3	252.2	219.8	255.5	184.2	313.5
March	243.5	249.5	252.3	216.5	256.1	183.8	314.3
April	244.3	250.3	252.9	219.4	256.7	184.6	315.0
May	244.8	250.8	252.9	220.8	257.2	184.8	315.8
June	245.3	251.2	253.3	221.1	257.5	184.9	316.5
July	245.4	251.3	253.8	219.2	257.9	184.7	317.1
August	245.8	251.7	254.1	221.8	258.1	184.8	317.6
September	246.2	252.2	254.4	222.4	258.5	185.1	318.2
October	247.1	252.9	254.2	226.7	259.0	185.9	318.9
November	246.8	252.8	254.9	221.3	259.4	185.2	319.4
December	246.1	252.5	255.7	212.4	259.9	183.5	320.4

Table 8-1C. Consumer and Producer Price Indexes: Historical Data, 1913–1949

(Not seasonally adjusted.)

| Year and month | Consumer price indexes, 1982–1984 =100 | | | | Producer Price Indexes for goods, 1982 = 100 | | | |
| | All urban consumers (CPI-U) | | Urban wage earners and clerical workers (CPI-W) | | All commodities | | Farm products | Industrial commodities |
	Index	Percent change	Index	Percent change	Index	Percent change		
1913	9.9	. . .	10.0	. . .	12.0	. . .	18.0	11.9
1914	10.0	1.0	10.1	1.0	11.8	-1.7	17.9	11.3
1915	10.1	1.0	10.2	1.0	12.0	1.7	18.0	11.6
1916	10.9	7.9	11.0	7.8	14.7	22.5	21.3	15.0
1917	12.8	17.4	12.9	17.3	20.2	37.4	32.6	19.5
1918	15.1	18.0	15.1	17.1	22.6	11.9	37.4	21.1
1919	17.3	14.6	17.4	15.2	23.9	5.8	39.8	22.0
1920	20.0	15.6	20.1	15.5	26.6	11.3	38.0	27.4
1921	17.9	-10.5	18.0	-10.4	16.8	-36.8	22.3	17.8
1922	16.8	-6.1	16.9	-6.1	16.7	-0.6	23.7	17.4
1923	17.1	1.8	17.2	1.8	17.3	3.6	24.9	17.8
1924	17.1	0.0	17.2	0.0	16.9	-2.3	25.2	17.0
1925	17.5	2.3	17.6	2.3	17.8	5.3	27.7	17.5
1926	17.7	1.1	17.8	1.1	17.2	-3.4	25.3	17.0
1927	17.4	-1.7	17.5	-1.7	16.5	-4.1	25.1	16.0
1928	17.1	-1.7	17.2	-1.7	16.7	1.2	26.7	15.8
1929	17.1	0.0	17.2	0.0	16.4	-1.8	26.4	15.6
1930	16.7	-2.3	16.8	-2.3	14.9	-9.1	22.4	14.5
1931	15.2	-9.0	15.3	-8.9	12.6	-15.4	16.4	12.8
1932	13.7	-9.9	13.7	-10.5	11.2	-11.1	12.2	11.9
1933	13.0	-5.1	13.0	-5.1	11.4	1.8	13.0	12.1
1934	13.4	3.1	13.5	3.8	12.9	13.2	16.5	13.3
1935	13.7	2.2	13.8	2.2	13.8	7.0	19.8	13.3
1936	13.9	1.5	13.9	0.7	13.9	0.7	20.4	13.5
1937	14.4	3.6	14.4	3.6	14.9	7.2	21.8	14.5
1938	14.1	-2.1	14.2	-1.4	13.5	-9.4	17.3	13.9
1939	13.9	-1.4	14.0	-1.4	13.3	-1.5	16.5	13.9
1940	14.0	0.7	14.1	0.7	13.5	1.5	17.1	14.1
1941	14.7	5.0	14.8	5.0	15.1	11.9	20.8	15.1
1942	16.3	10.9	16.4	10.8	17.0	12.6	26.7	16.2
1943	17.3	6.1	17.4	6.1	17.8	4.7	30.9	16.5
1944	17.6	1.7	17.7	1.7	17.9	0.6	31.2	16.7
1945	18.0	2.3	18.1	2.3	18.2	1.7	32.4	17.0
1946	19.5	8.3	19.6	8.3	20.8	14.3	37.5	18.6
1947	22.3	14.4	22.5	14.8	25.6	23.1	45.1	22.7
1948	24.1	8.1	24.2	7.6	27.7	8.2	48.5	24.6
1949	23.8	-1.2	24.0	-0.8	26.3	-5.1	41.9	24.1
1913								
January	9.8	. . .	9.9	. . .	12.1	. . .	17.6	12.3
February	9.8	0.0	9.8	-1.0	12.0	-0.8	17.5	12.2
March	9.8	0.0	9.8	0.0	12.0	0.0	17.6	12.1
April	9.8	0.0	9.9	1.0	12.0	0.0	17.5	12.0
May	9.7	-1.0	9.8	-1.0	11.9	-0.8	17.4	11.9
June	9.8	1.0	9.8	0.0	11.9	0.0	17.6	11.8
July	9.9	1.0	9.9	1.0	12.0	0.8	18.1	11.8
August	9.9	0.0	10.0	1.0	12.0	0.0	18.2	11.7
September	10.0	1.0	10.0	0.0	12.2	1.7	18.8	11.8
October	10.0	0.0	10.1	1.0	12.2	0.0	18.8	11.8
November	10.1	1.0	10.1	0.0	12.1	-0.8	18.9	11.7
December	10.0	-1.0	10.1	0.0	11.9	-1.7	18.5	11.6
1914								
January	10.0	0.0	10.1	0.0	11.8	-0.8	18.4	11.5
February	9.9	-1.0	10.0	-1.0	11.8	0.0	18.3	11.5
March	9.9	0.0	10.0	0.0	11.7	-0.8	18.2	11.5
April	9.8	-1.0	9.9	-1.0	11.7	0.0	18.0	11.5
May	9.9	1.0	9.9	0.0	11.6	-0.9	18.0	11.4
June	9.9	0.0	10.0	1.0	11.6	0.0	18.1	11.3
July	10.0	1.0	10.1	1.0	11.6	0.0	18.0	11.2
August	10.2	2.0	10.2	1.0	12.0	3.4	18.3	11.2
September	10.2	0.0	10.3	1.0	12.1	0.8	17.9	11.3
October	10.1	-1.0	10.2	-1.0	11.7	-3.3	17.2	11.0
November	10.2	1.0	10.2	0.0	11.7	0.0	17.6	11.0
December	10.1	-1.0	10.2	0.0	11.6	-0.9	17.4	11.0
1915								
January	10.1	0.0	10.2	0.0	11.8	1.7	18.1	11.1
February	10.0	-1.0	10.1	-1.0	11.8	0.0	18.4	11.0
March	9.9	-1.0	10.0	-1.0	11.8	0.0	17.9	11.0
April	10.0	1.0	10.1	1.0	11.8	0.0	18.2	11.1
May	10.1	1.0	10.1	0.0	11.9	0.8	18.2	11.2
June	10.1	0.0	10.2	1.0	11.8	-0.8	17.7	11.4
July	10.1	0.0	10.2	0.0	11.9	0.8	18.1	11.5
August	10.1	0.0	10.2	0.0	11.8	-0.8	17.9	11.5
September	10.1	0.0	10.2	0.0	11.8	0.0	17.5	11.7
October	10.2	1.0	10.3	1.0	12.1	2.5	18.1	11.9
November	10.3	1.0	10.4	1.0	12.3	1.7	18.0	12.3
December	10.3	0.0	10.4	0.0	12.8	4.1	18.4	12.9

. . . = Not available.

Table 8-1C. Consumer and Producer Price Indexes: Historical Data, 1913–1949—*Continued*

(Not seasonally adjusted.)

Year and month	Consumer price indexes, 1982–1984 =100				Producer Price Indexes for goods, 1982 = 100			
	All urban consumers (CPI-U)		Urban wage earners and clerical workers (CPI-W)		All commodities		Farm products	Industrial commodities
	Index	Percent change	Index	Percent change	Index	Percent change		
1916								
January	10.4	1.0	10.5	1.0	13.3	3.9	19.4	13.6
February	10.4	0.0	10.5	0.0	13.5	1.5	19.4	14.0
March	10.5	1.0	10.6	1.0	13.9	3.0	19.4	14.4
April	10.6	1.0	10.7	0.9	14.1	1.4	19.6	14.6
May	10.7	0.9	10.7	0.0	14.2	0.7	19.8	14.7
June	10.8	0.9	10.9	1.9	14.3	0.7	19.7	14.8
July	10.8	0.0	10.9	0.0	14.4	0.7	20.3	14.6
August	10.9	0.9	11.0	0.9	14.7	2.1	21.7	14.6
September	11.1	1.8	11.2	1.8	15.0	2.0	22.6	14.8
October	11.3	1.8	11.3	0.9	15.7	4.7	23.7	15.5
November	11.5	1.8	11.5	1.8	16.8	7.0	25.3	16.8
December	11.6	0.9	11.6	0.9	17.1	1.8	25.0	17.7
1917								
January	11.7	0.9	11.8	1.7	17.6	2.9	26.2	18.3
February	12.0	2.6	12.0	1.7	18.0	2.3	27.2	18.6
March	12.0	0.0	12.1	0.8	18.5	2.8	28.6	18.8
April	12.6	5.0	12.6	4.1	19.7	6.5	31.6	19.0
May	12.8	1.6	12.9	2.4	20.8	5.6	33.6	19.8
June	13.0	1.6	13.0	0.8	21.0	1.0	33.8	20.4
July	12.8	-1.5	12.9	-0.8	21.2	1.0	34.0	20.7
August	13.0	1.6	13.1	1.6	21.5	1.4	34.6	20.7
September	13.3	2.3	13.3	1.5	21.3	-0.9	34.3	20.1
October	13.5	1.5	13.6	2.3	21.1	-0.9	35.2	19.1
November	13.5	0.0	13.6	0.0	21.2	0.5	36.0	19.2
December	13.7	1.5	13.8	1.5	21.2	0.0	35.6	19.5
1918								
January	14.0	2.2	14.0	1.4	21.6	1.9	37.0	19.9
February	14.1	0.7	14.2	1.4	21.1	-2.3	37.1	19.0
March	14.0	-0.7	14.1	-0.7	21.8	3.3	37.3	20.2
April	14.2	1.4	14.3	1.4	22.1	1.4	36.6	20.7
May	14.5	2.1	14.5	1.4	22.1	0.0	35.4	21.0
June	14.7	1.4	14.8	2.1	22.2	0.5	35.4	21.3
July	15.1	2.7	15.2	2.7	22.7	2.3	37.0	21.5
August	15.4	2.0	15.4	1.3	23.2	2.2	38.6	21.7
September	15.7	1.9	15.8	2.6	23.7	2.2	39.6	22.1
October	16.0	1.9	16.1	1.9	23.5	-0.8	38.2	22.1
November	16.3	1.9	16.3	1.2	23.5	0.0	38.0	22.1
December	16.5	1.2	16.6	1.8	23.5	0.0	38.1	21.8
1919								
January	16.5	0.0	16.6	0.0	23.2	-1.3	38.9	21.1
February	16.2	-1.8	16.2	-2.4	22.4	-3.4	37.5	20.6
March	16.4	1.2	16.5	1.9	22.6	0.9	38.5	20.1
April	16.7	1.8	16.8	1.8	22.9	1.3	40.0	20.0
May	16.9	1.2	17.0	1.2	23.3	1.7	40.9	20.2
June	16.9	0.0	17.0	0.0	23.4	0.4	39.6	21.1
July	17.4	3.0	17.5	2.9	24.3	3.8	41.5	22.1
August	17.7	1.7	17.8	1.7	24.9	2.5	41.3	23.1
September	17.8	0.6	17.9	0.6	24.3	-2.4	38.7	23.2
October	18.1	1.7	18.2	1.7	24.4	0.4	38.5	23.5
November	18.5	2.2	18.6	2.2	24.9	2.0	40.3	23.8
December	18.9	2.2	19.0	2.2	26.0	4.4	41.8	24.7
1920								
January	19.3	2.1	19.4	2.1	27.2	4.6	43.0	26.1
February	19.5	1.0	19.6	1.0	27.1	-0.4	41.2	27.1
March	19.7	1.0	19.8	1.0	27.3	0.7	41.5	27.7
April	20.3	3.0	20.4	3.0	28.5	4.4	42.5	28.7
May	20.6	1.5	20.7	1.5	28.8	1.1	42.8	29.0
June	20.9	1.5	21.0	1.4	28.7	-0.3	42.3	29.0
July	20.8	-0.5	20.9	-0.5	28.6	-0.3	40.5	29.5
August	20.3	-2.4	20.4	-2.4	27.8	-2.8	37.8	29.7
September	20.0	-1.5	20.1	-1.5	26.8	-3.6	36.4	28.5
October	19.9	-0.5	20.0	-0.5	24.9	-7.1	32.2	26.9
November	19.8	-0.5	19.9	-0.5	23.0	-7.6	30.0	24.5
December	19.4	-2.0	19.5	-2.0	20.8	-9.6	26.4	22.7
1921								
January	19.0	-2.1	19.1	-2.1	19.6	-5.8	25.6	21.1
February	18.4	-3.2	18.5	-3.1	18.1	-7.7	23.4	19.4
March	18.3	-0.5	18.4	-0.5	17.7	-2.2	22.7	18.7
April	18.1	-1.1	18.2	-1.1	17.0	-4.0	20.9	18.4
May	17.7	-2.2	17.8	-2.2	16.6	-2.4	21.0	17.9
June	17.6	-0.6	17.7	-0.6	16.1	-3.0	20.3	17.4
July	17.7	0.6	17.8	0.6	16.1	0.0	21.8	16.9
August	17.7	0.0	17.8	0.0	16.1	0.0	22.5	16.5
September	17.5	-1.1	17.6	-1.1	16.1	0.0	22.7	16.5
October	17.5	0.0	17.6	0.0	16.2	0.6	22.7	17.0
November	17.4	-0.6	17.5	-0.6	16.2	0.0	22.1	17.3
December	17.3	-0.6	17.4	-0.6	16.0	-1.2	22.2	17.0

Table 8-1C. Consumer and Producer Price Indexes: Historical Data, 1913–1949—*Continued*

(Not seasonally adjusted.)

Year and month	Consumer price indexes, 1982–1984 =100				Producer Price Indexes for goods, 1982 = 100			
	All urban consumers (CPI-U)		Urban wage earners and clerical workers (CPI-W)		All commodities		Farm products	Industrial commodities
	Index	Percent change	Index	Percent change	Index	Percent change		
1922								
January	16.9	-2.3	17.0	-2.3	15.7	-1.9	22.2	16.7
February	16.9	0.0	17.0	0.0	16.0	1.9	24.0	16.6
March	16.7	-1.2	16.8	-1.2	16.0	0.0	23.6	16.5
April	16.7	0.0	16.8	0.0	16.1	0.6	23.4	16.6
May	16.7	0.0	16.8	0.0	16.6	3.1	23.8	17.4
June	16.7	0.0	16.8	0.0	16.6	0.0	23.4	17.4
July	16.8	0.6	16.9	0.6	17.1	3.0	24.1	18.1
August	16.6	-1.2	16.7	-1.2	17.0	-0.6	23.0	18.2
September	16.6	0.0	16.7	0.0	17.1	0.6	23.3	18.2
October	16.7	0.6	16.8	0.6	17.2	0.6	23.8	17.9
November	16.8	0.6	16.9	0.6	17.3	0.6	24.7	17.7
December	16.9	0.6	17.0	0.6	17.3	0.0	25.0	17.7
1923								
January	16.8	-0.6	16.9	-0.6	17.6	1.7	25.1	18.2
February	16.8	0.0	16.9	0.0	17.8	1.1	25.3	18.6
March	16.8	0.0	16.9	0.0	18.0	1.1	25.3	18.8
April	16.9	0.6	17.0	0.6	17.9	-0.6	24.8	18.7
May	16.9	0.0	17.0	0.0	17.5	-2.2	24.4	18.3
June	17.0	0.6	17.1	0.6	17.3	-1.1	24.2	17.9
July	17.2	1.2	17.3	1.2	17.0	-1.7	23.7	17.6
August	17.1	-0.6	17.2	-0.6	16.9	-0.6	24.2	17.4
September	17.2	0.6	17.3	0.6	17.2	1.8	25.3	17.3
October	17.3	0.6	17.4	0.6	17.1	-0.6	25.4	17.1
November	17.3	0.0	17.4	0.0	17.0	-0.6	25.7	16.9
December	17.3	0.0	17.4	0.0	16.9	-0.6	25.5	16.9
1924								
January	17.3	0.0	17.4	0.0	17.2	1.8	25.6	17.4
February	17.2	-0.6	17.3	-0.6	17.2	0.0	25.0	17.6
March	17.1	-0.6	17.2	-0.6	17.0	-1.2	24.2	17.5
April	17.0	-0.6	17.1	-0.6	16.7	-1.8	24.6	17.3
May	17.0	0.0	17.1	0.0	16.5	-1.2	24.0	17.0
June	17.0	0.0	17.1	0.0	16.4	-0.6	23.8	16.7
July	17.1	0.6	17.2	0.6	16.5	0.6	24.9	16.6
August	17.0	-0.6	17.1	-0.6	16.7	1.2	25.7	16.6
September	17.1	0.6	17.2	0.6	16.7	0.0	25.3	16.6
October	17.2	0.6	17.3	0.6	16.9	1.2	26.0	16.6
November	17.2	0.0	17.3	0.0	17.1	1.2	26.2	16.8
December	17.3	0.6	17.4	0.6	17.5	2.3	27.3	17.1
1925								
January	17.3	0.0	17.4	0.0	17.7	1.1	28.7	17.3
February	17.2	-0.6	17.3	-0.6	17.9	1.1	28.4	17.7
March	17.3	0.6	17.4	0.6	17.9	0.0	28.5	17.5
April	17.2	-0.6	17.3	-0.6	17.5	-2.2	27.1	17.2
May	17.3	0.6	17.4	0.6	17.5	0.0	27.1	17.3
June	17.5	1.2	17.6	1.1	17.7	1.1	27.6	17.5
July	17.7	1.1	17.8	1.1	18.0	1.7	28.3	17.6
August	17.7	0.0	17.8	0.0	17.9	-0.6	28.1	17.4
September	17.7	0.0	17.8	0.0	17.8	-0.6	27.7	17.4
October	17.7	0.0	17.8	0.0	17.8	0.0	27.0	17.5
November	18.0	1.7	18.1	1.7	18.0	1.1	27.3	17.6
December	17.9	-0.6	18.0	-0.6	17.8	-1.1	26.6	17.6
1926								
January	17.9	0.0	18.0	0.0	17.8	0.0	27.1	17.5
February	17.9	0.0	18.0	0.0	17.6	-1.1	26.5	17.3
March	17.8	-0.6	17.9	-0.6	17.3	-1.7	25.7	17.1
April	17.9	0.6	18.0	0.6	17.3	0.0	26.0	17.0
May	17.8	-0.6	17.9	-0.6	17.3	0.0	25.8	17.0
June	17.7	-0.6	17.8	-0.6	17.3	0.0	25.5	17.0
July	17.5	-1.1	17.6	-1.1	17.1	-1.2	24.9	16.9
August	17.4	-0.6	17.5	-0.6	17.1	0.0	24.6	16.9
September	17.5	0.6	17.6	0.6	17.2	0.6	25.1	16.9
October	17.6	0.6	17.7	0.6	17.1	-0.6	24.7	16.9
November	17.7	0.6	17.8	0.6	17.0	-0.6	23.9	16.9
December	17.7	0.0	17.8	0.0	16.9	-0.6	24.0	16.7
1927								
January	17.5	-1.1	17.6	-1.1	16.4	-3.0	24.3	16.4
February	17.4	-0.6	17.5	-0.6	16.6	1.2	24.1	16.3
March	17.3	-0.6	17.4	-0.6	16.5	-0.6	23.8	16.1
April	17.3	0.0	17.4	0.0	16.3	-1.2	23.8	15.9
May	17.4	0.6	17.5	0.6	16.2	-0.6	24.3	15.9
June	17.6	1.1	17.7	1.1	16.2	0.0	24.3	15.9
July	17.3	-1.7	17.4	-1.7	16.2	0.0	24.6	15.9
August	17.2	-0.6	17.3	-0.6	16.4	1.2	25.8	15.9
September	17.3	0.6	17.4	0.6	16.6	1.2	26.7	16.0
October	17.4	0.6	17.5	0.6	16.7	0.6	26.5	15.9
November	17.3	-0.6	17.4	-0.6	16.6	-0.6	26.3	15.8
December	17.3	0.0	17.4	0.0	16.6	0.0	26.3	15.9

Table 8-1C. Consumer and Producer Price Indexes: Historical Data, 1913–1949—*Continued*

(Not seasonally adjusted.)

Year and month	Consumer price indexes, 1982–1984 =100				Producer Price Indexes for goods, 1982 = 100			
	All urban consumers (CPI-U)		Urban wage earners and clerical workers (CPI-W)		All commodities		Farm products	Industrial commodities
	Index	Percent change	Index	Percent change	Index	Percent change		
1928								
January	17.3	0.0	17.4	0.0	16.6	0.0	26.8	15.8
February	17.1	-1.2	17.2	-1.1	16.5	-0.6	26.4	15.8
March	17.1	0.0	17.2	0.0	16.5	0.0	26.1	15.8
April	17.1	0.0	17.2	0.0	16.7	1.2	27.1	15.8
May	17.2	0.6	17.3	0.6	16.8	0.6	27.7	15.8
June	17.1	-0.6	17.2	-0.6	16.7	-0.6	26.9	15.8
July	17.1	0.0	17.2	0.0	16.8	0.6	27.4	15.8
August	17.1	0.0	17.2	0.0	16.8	0.0	27.0	15.8
September	17.3	1.2	17.4	1.2	17.0	1.2	27.5	15.8
October	17.2	-0.6	17.3	-0.6	16.7	-1.8	26.1	15.8
November	17.2	0.0	17.3	0.0	16.5	-1.2	25.7	15.8
December	17.1	-0.6	17.2	-0.6	16.5	0.0	26.2	15.8
1929								
January	17.1	0.0	17.2	0.0	16.5	0.0	26.7	15.7
February	17.1	0.0	17.2	0.0	16.4	-0.6	26.6	15.6
March	17.0	-0.6	17.1	-0.6	16.6	1.2	27.1	15.7
April	16.9	-0.6	17.0	-0.6	16.5	-0.6	26.5	15.6
May	17.0	0.6	17.1	0.6	16.3	-1.2	25.8	15.6
June	17.1	0.6	17.2	0.6	16.4	0.6	26.1	15.6
July	17.3	1.2	17.4	1.2	16.6	1.2	27.1	15.6
August	17.3	0.0	17.4	0.0	16.6	0.0	27.1	15.5
September	17.3	0.0	17.4	0.0	16.6	0.0	26.9	15.6
October	17.3	0.0	17.4	0.0	16.4	-1.2	26.2	15.6
November	17.3	0.0	17.4	0.0	16.1	-1.8	25.5	15.5
December	17.2	-0.6	17.3	-0.6	16.1	0.0	25.7	15.4
1930								
January	17.1	-0.6	17.2	-0.6	15.9	-1.2	25.5	15.2
February	17.0	-0.6	17.1	-0.6	15.7	-1.3	24.7	15.1
March	16.9	-0.6	17.0	-0.6	15.5	-1.3	23.9	15.0
April	17.0	0.6	17.1	0.6	15.5	0.0	24.2	15.0
May	16.9	-0.6	17.0	-0.6	15.3	-1.3	23.5	14.9
June	16.8	-0.6	16.9	-0.6	15.0	-2.0	22.5	14.6
July	16.6	-1.2	16.7	-1.2	14.5	-3.3	21.0	14.4
August	16.5	-0.6	16.6	-0.6	14.5	0.0	21.4	14.2
September	16.6	0.6	16.7	0.6	14.5	0.0	21.5	14.2
October	16.5	-0.6	16.6	-0.6	14.3	-1.4	20.8	14.0
November	16.4	-0.6	16.5	-0.6	14.0	-2.1	20.0	13.8
December	16.1	-1.8	16.2	-1.8	13.7	-2.1	19.0	13.6
1931								
January	15.9	-1.2	16.0	-1.2	13.5	-1.5	18.4	13.4
February	15.7	-1.3	15.7	-1.9	13.2	-2.2	17.7	13.3
March	15.6	-0.6	15.6	-0.6	13.1	-0.8	17.8	13.1
April	15.5	-0.6	15.5	-0.6	12.9	-1.5	17.7	12.9
May	15.3	-1.3	15.4	-0.6	12.6	-2.3	16.9	12.8
June	15.1	-1.3	15.2	-1.3	12.4	-1.6	16.5	12.6
July	15.1	0.0	15.2	0.0	12.4	0.0	16.4	12.6
August	15.1	0.0	15.1	-0.7	12.4	0.0	16.1	12.6
September	15.0	-0.7	15.1	0.0	12.3	-0.8	15.3	12.6
October	14.9	-0.7	15.0	-0.7	12.1	-1.6	14.8	12.4
November	14.7	-1.3	14.8	-1.3	12.1	0.0	14.8	12.5
December	14.6	-0.7	14.7	-0.7	11.8	-2.5	14.1	12.3
1932								
January	14.3	-2.1	14.4	-2.0	11.6	-1.7	13.3	12.2
February	14.1	-1.4	14.2	-1.4	11.4	-1.7	12.8	12.1
March	14.0	-0.7	14.1	-0.7	11.4	0.0	12.7	12.0
April	13.9	-0.7	14.0	-0.7	11.3	-0.9	12.4	12.0
May	13.7	-1.4	13.8	-1.4	11.1	-1.8	11.8	11.9
June	13.6	-0.7	13.7	-0.7	11.0	-0.9	11.6	11.9
July	13.6	0.0	13.7	0.0	11.1	0.9	12.1	11.8
August	13.5	-0.7	13.5	-1.5	11.2	0.9	12.4	11.9
September	13.4	-0.7	13.5	0.0	11.3	0.9	12.4	11.9
October	13.3	-0.7	13.4	-0.7	11.1	-1.8	11.8	11.9
November	13.2	-0.8	13.3	-0.7	11.0	-0.9	11.8	11.9
December	13.1	-0.8	13.2	-0.8	10.8	-1.8	11.1	11.7
1933								
January	12.9	-1.5	13.0	-1.5	10.5	-2.8	10.8	11.4
February	12.7	-1.6	12.8	-1.5	10.3	-1.9	10.3	11.2
March	12.6	-0.8	12.7	-0.8	10.4	1.0	10.8	11.2
April	12.6	0.0	12.6	-0.8	10.4	0.0	11.2	11.1
May	12.6	0.0	12.7	0.8	10.8	3.8	12.7	11.3
June	12.7	0.8	12.8	0.8	11.2	3.7	13.4	11.7
July	13.1	3.1	13.2	3.1	11.9	6.3	15.2	12.3
August	13.2	0.8	13.3	0.8	12.0	0.8	14.6	12.6
September	13.2	0.0	13.3	0.0	12.2	1.7	14.4	13.0
October	13.2	0.0	13.3	0.0	12.3	0.8	14.1	13.1
November	13.2	0.0	13.3	0.0	12.3	0.0	14.3	13.1
December	13.2	0.0	13.2	-0.8	12.2	-0.8	14.0	13.2

Table 8-1C. Consumer and Producer Price Indexes: Historical Data, 1913–1949—*Continued*

(Not seasonally adjusted.)

Year and month	Consumer price indexes, 1982–1984 =100				Producer Price Indexes for goods, 1982 = 100			
	All urban consumers (CPI-U)		Urban wage earners and clerical workers (CPI-W)		All commodities		Farm products	Industrial commodities
	Index	Percent change	Index	Percent change	Index	Percent change		
1934								
January	13.2	0.0	13.3	0.8	12.4	1.6	14.8	13.3
February	13.3	0.8	13.4	0.8	12.7	2.4	15.5	13.4
March	13.3	0.0	13.4	0.0	12.7	0.0	15.5	13.4
April	13.3	0.0	13.4	0.0	12.7	0.0	15.1	13.4
May	13.3	0.0	13.4	0.0	12.7	0.0	15.1	13.4
June	13.4	0.8	13.4	0.0	12.9	1.6	16.0	13.3
July	13.4	0.0	13.4	0.0	12.9	0.0	16.3	13.3
August	13.4	0.0	13.5	0.7	13.2	2.3	17.6	13.3
September	13.6	1.5	13.7	1.5	13.4	1.5	18.5	13.3
October	13.5	-0.7	13.6	-0.7	13.2	-1.5	17.8	13.3
November	13.5	0.0	13.5	-0.7	13.2	0.0	17.8	13.3
December	13.4	-0.7	13.5	0.0	13.3	0.8	18.2	13.3
1935								
January	13.6	1.5	13.7	1.5	13.6	2.3	19.6	13.2
February	13.7	0.7	13.8	0.7	13.7	0.7	20.0	13.2
March	13.7	0.0	13.8	0.0	13.7	0.0	19.7	13.2
April	13.8	0.7	13.9	0.7	13.8	0.7	20.3	13.1
May	13.8	0.0	13.8	-0.7	13.8	0.0	20.3	13.2
June	13.7	-0.7	13.8	0.0	13.8	0.0	19.8	13.3
July	13.7	0.0	13.7	-0.7	13.7	-0.7	19.5	13.3
August	13.7	0.0	13.7	0.0	13.9	1.5	20.0	13.3
September	13.7	0.0	13.8	0.7	13.9	0.0	20.1	13.2
October	13.7	0.0	13.8	0.0	13.9	0.0	19.7	13.3
November	13.8	0.7	13.9	0.7	13.9	0.0	19.6	13.4
December	13.8	0.0	13.9	0.0	14.0	0.7	19.8	13.4
1936								
January	13.8	0.0	13.9	0.0	13.9	-0.7	19.7	13.4
February	13.8	0.0	13.8	-0.7	13.9	0.0	20.1	13.4
March	13.7	-0.7	13.8	0.0	13.7	-1.4	19.3	13.4
April	13.7	0.0	13.8	0.0	13.7	0.0	19.4	13.4
May	13.7	0.0	13.8	0.0	13.5	-1.5	19.0	13.4
June	13.8	0.7	13.9	0.7	13.7	1.5	19.7	13.4
July	13.9	0.7	14.0	0.7	13.9	1.5	20.5	13.5
August	14.0	0.7	14.1	0.7	14.0	0.7	21.2	13.5
September	14.0	0.0	14.1	0.0	14.0	0.0	21.2	13.5
October	14.0	0.0	14.1	0.0	14.0	0.0	21.2	13.6
November	14.0	0.0	14.1	0.0	14.2	1.4	21.5	13.8
December	14.0	0.0	14.1	0.0	14.5	2.1	22.4	14.0
1937								
January	14.1	0.7	14.2	0.7	14.8	2.1	23.1	14.2
February	14.1	0.0	14.2	0.0	14.9	0.7	23.1	14.3
March	14.2	0.7	14.3	0.7	15.1	1.3	23.8	14.5
April	14.3	0.7	14.4	0.7	15.2	0.7	23.3	14.7
May	14.4	0.7	14.4	0.0	15.1	-0.7	22.7	14.7
June	14.4	0.0	14.5	0.7	15.0	-0.7	22.3	14.6
July	14.5	0.7	14.5	0.0	15.2	1.3	22.6	14.7
August	14.5	0.0	14.6	0.7	15.1	-0.7	21.8	14.6
September	14.6	0.7	14.7	0.7	15.1	0.0	21.7	14.6
October	14.6	0.0	14.6	-0.7	14.7	-2.6	20.3	14.5
November	14.5	-0.7	14.5	-0.7	14.4	-2.0	19.1	14.3
December	14.4	-0.7	14.5	0.0	14.1	-2.1	18.4	14.2
1938								
January	14.2	-1.4	14.3	-1.4	14.0	-0.7	18.1	14.2
February	14.1	-0.7	14.2	-0.7	13.8	-1.4	17.6	14.1
March	14.1	0.0	14.2	0.0	13.7	-0.7	17.7	14.1
April	14.2	0.7	14.2	0.0	13.5	-1.5	17.2	14.0
May	14.1	-0.7	14.2	0.0	13.5	0.0	17.0	13.9
June	14.1	0.0	14.2	0.0	13.5	0.0	17.3	13.8
July	14.1	0.0	14.2	0.0	13.6	0.7	17.5	13.9
August	14.1	0.0	14.2	0.0	13.4	-1.5	17.0	13.9
September	14.1	0.0	14.2	0.0	13.5	0.7	17.2	13.9
October	14.0	-0.7	14.1	-0.7	13.4	-0.7	16.8	13.8
November	14.0	0.0	14.1	0.0	13.4	0.0	17.1	13.7
December	14.0	0.0	14.1	0.0	13.3	-0.7	17.0	13.6
1939								
January	14.0	0.0	14.0	-0.7	13.3	0.0	17.0	13.6
February	13.9	-0.7	14.0	0.0	13.3	0.0	16.9	13.6
March	13.9	0.0	13.9	-0.7	13.2	-0.8	16.6	13.7
April	13.8	-0.7	13.9	0.0	13.1	-0.8	16.1	13.7
May	13.8	0.0	13.9	0.0	13.1	0.0	16.1	13.7
June	13.8	0.0	13.9	0.0	13.0	-0.8	15.7	13.6
July	13.8	0.0	13.9	0.0	13.0	0.0	15.8	13.6
August	13.8	0.0	13.9	0.0	12.9	-0.8	15.4	13.6
September	14.1	2.2	14.2	2.2	13.6	5.4	17.3	14.0
October	14.0	-0.7	14.1	-0.7	13.7	0.7	16.9	14.2
November	14.0	0.0	14.1	0.0	13.6	-0.7	17.0	14.3
December	14.0	0.0	14.0	-0.7	13.7	0.7	17.1	14.3

Table 8-1C. Consumer and Producer Price Indexes: Historical Data, 1913–1949—*Continued*

(Not seasonally adjusted.)

Year and month	Consumer price indexes, 1982–1984 =100				Producer Price Indexes for goods, 1982 = 100			
	All urban consumers (CPI-U)		Urban wage earners and clerical workers (CPI-W)		All commodities		Farm products	Industrial commodities
	Index	Percent change	Index	Percent change	Index	Percent change		
1940								
January	13.9	-0.7	14.0	0.0	13.7	0.0	17.4	14.3
February	14.0	0.7	14.1	0.7	13.6	-0.7	17.3	14.2
March	14.0	0.0	14.1	0.0	13.5	-0.7	17.1	14.1
April	14.0	0.0	14.1	0.0	13.5	0.0	17.5	14.0
May	14.0	0.0	14.1	0.0	13.5	0.0	17.1	14.0
June	14.1	0.7	14.1	0.0	13.4	-0.7	16.7	14.0
July	14.0	-0.7	14.1	0.0	13.4	0.0	16.8	14.0
August	14.0	0.0	14.1	0.0	13.4	0.0	16.5	14.0
September	14.0	0.0	14.1	0.0	13.4	0.0	16.7	14.0
October	14.0	0.0	14.1	0.0	13.6	1.5	16.8	14.2
November	14.0	0.0	14.1	0.0	13.7	0.7	17.2	14.3
December	14.1	0.7	14.2	0.7	13.8	0.7	17.6	14.3
1941								
January	14.1	0.0	14.2	0.0	13.9	0.7	18.1	14.3
February	14.1	0.0	14.2	0.0	13.9	0.0	17.7	14.3
March	14.2	0.7	14.2	0.0	14.0	0.7	18.1	14.4
April	14.3	0.7	14.4	1.4	14.4	2.9	18.8	14.6
May	14.4	0.7	14.5	0.7	14.6	1.4	19.3	14.9
June	14.7	2.1	14.7	1.4	15.0	2.7	20.7	15.1
July	14.7	0.0	14.8	0.7	15.3	2.0	21.7	15.2
August	14.9	1.4	14.9	0.7	15.6	2.0	22.1	15.5
September	15.1	1.3	15.2	2.0	15.8	1.3	23.0	15.6
October	15.3	1.3	15.4	1.3	15.9	0.6	22.7	15.9
November	15.4	0.7	15.5	0.6	15.9	0.0	22.9	15.9
December	15.5	0.6	15.5	0.0	16.2	1.9	23.9	15.9
1942								
January	15.7	1.3	15.7	1.3	16.5	1.9	25.5	16.1
February	15.8	0.6	15.9	1.3	16.7	1.2	25.6	16.1
March	16.0	1.3	16.1	1.3	16.8	0.6	26.0	16.2
April	16.1	0.6	16.2	0.6	17.0	1.2	26.4	16.2
May	16.3	1.2	16.3	0.6	17.0	0.0	26.3	16.3
June	16.3	0.0	16.4	0.6	17.0	0.0	26.3	16.3
July	16.4	0.6	16.5	0.6	17.0	0.0	26.6	16.3
August	16.5	0.6	16.6	0.6	17.1	0.6	26.8	16.2
September	16.5	0.0	16.6	0.0	17.2	0.6	27.2	16.2
October	16.7	1.2	16.8	1.2	17.2	0.0	27.5	16.2
November	16.8	0.6	16.9	0.6	17.3	0.6	27.9	16.3
December	16.9	0.6	17.0	0.6	17.4	0.6	28.7	16.3
1943								
January	16.9	0.0	17.0	0.0	17.5	0.6	29.5	16.4
February	16.9	0.0	17.0	0.0	17.7	1.1	30.0	16.4
March	17.2	1.8	17.3	1.8	17.8	0.6	31.0	16.4
April	17.4	1.2	17.5	1.2	17.9	0.6	31.2	16.5
May	17.5	0.6	17.6	0.6	17.9	0.0	31.7	16.5
June	17.5	0.0	17.6	0.0	17.9	0.0	31.9	16.5
July	17.4	-0.6	17.5	-0.6	17.8	-0.6	31.5	16.5
August	17.3	-0.6	17.4	-0.6	17.8	0.0	31.2	16.5
September	17.4	0.6	17.5	0.6	17.8	0.0	31.0	16.5
October	17.4	0.0	17.5	0.0	17.8	0.0	30.9	16.5
November	17.4	0.0	17.5	0.0	17.7	-0.6	30.6	16.6
December	17.4	0.0	17.5	0.0	17.8	0.6	30.7	16.6
1944								
January	17.4	0.0	17.5	0.0	17.8	0.0	30.7	16.6
February	17.4	0.0	17.5	0.0	17.8	0.0	30.9	16.7
March	17.4	0.0	17.5	0.0	17.9	0.6	31.2	16.7
April	17.5	0.6	17.6	0.6	17.9	0.0	31.1	16.7
May	17.5	0.0	17.6	0.0	17.9	0.0	31.0	16.7
June	17.6	0.6	17.7	0.6	18.0	0.6	31.5	16.7
July	17.7	0.6	17.8	0.6	17.9	-0.6	31.3	16.7
August	17.7	0.0	17.8	0.0	17.9	0.0	30.9	16.8
September	17.7	0.0	17.8	0.0	17.9	0.0	31.0	16.8
October	17.7	0.0	17.8	0.0	17.9	0.0	31.2	16.8
November	17.7	0.0	17.8	0.0	18.0	0.6	31.4	16.8
December	17.8	0.6	17.9	0.6	18.0	0.0	31.6	16.8
1945								
January	17.8	0.0	17.9	0.0	18.1	0.6	31.9	16.8
February	17.8	0.0	17.9	0.0	18.1	0.0	32.1	16.9
March	17.8	0.0	17.9	0.0	18.1	0.0	32.1	16.9
April	17.8	0.0	17.9	0.0	18.2	0.6	32.5	16.9
May	17.9	0.6	18.0	0.6	18.3	0.5	32.8	16.9
June	18.1	1.1	18.2	1.1	18.3	0.0	32.9	16.9
July	18.1	0.0	18.2	0.0	18.3	0.0	32.5	17.0
August	18.1	0.0	18.2	0.0	18.2	-0.5	32.0	17.0
September	18.1	0.0	18.2	0.0	18.1	-0.5	31.4	17.0
October	18.1	0.0	18.2	0.0	18.2	0.6	32.1	17.0
November	18.1	0.0	18.2	0.0	18.4	1.1	33.1	17.0
December	18.2	0.6	18.3	0.5	18.4	0.0	33.2	17.1

Table 8-1C. Consumer and Producer Price Indexes: Historical Data, 1913–1949—*Continued*

(Not seasonally adjusted.)

Year and month	Consumer price indexes, 1982–1984 =100				Producer Price Indexes for goods, 1982 = 100			
	All urban consumers (CPI-U)		Urban wage earners and clerical workers (CPI-W)		All commodities		Farm products	Industrial commodities
	Index	Percent change	Index	Percent change	Index	Percent change		
1946								
January	18.2	0.0	18.3	0.0	18.4	0.0	32.7	17.1
February	18.1	-0.5	18.2	-0.5	18.5	0.5	33.0	17.2
March	18.3	1.1	18.4	1.1	18.8	1.6	33.6	17.4
April	18.4	0.5	18.5	0.5	19.0	1.1	34.1	17.5
May	18.5	0.5	18.6	0.5	19.1	0.5	34.7	17.7
June	18.7	1.1	18.8	1.1	19.4	1.6	35.4	18.0
July	19.8	5.9	19.9	5.9	21.5	10.8	39.6	18.6
August	20.2	2.0	20.3	2.0	22.2	3.3	40.6	19.0
September	20.4	1.0	20.5	1.0	21.4	-3.6	39.0	19.1
October	20.8	2.0	20.9	2.0	23.1	7.9	41.7	19.7
November	21.3	2.4	21.5	2.9	24.1	4.3	42.8	20.6
December	21.5	0.9	21.6	0.5	24.3	0.8	42.4	21.2
1947								
January	21.5	0.0	21.6	0.0	24.5	0.8	41.6	21.8
February	21.5	0.0	21.6	0.0	24.7	0.8	42.6	22.0
March	21.9	1.9	22.1	2.3	25.3	2.4	45.5	22.3
April	21.9	0.0	22.1	0.0	25.1	-0.8	44.0	22.4
May	21.9	0.0	22.0	-0.5	25.0	-0.4	43.6	22.3
June	22.0	0.5	22.2	0.9	25.0	0.0	43.8	22.4
July	22.2	0.9	22.4	0.9	25.3	1.2	44.3	22.5
August	22.5	1.4	22.6	0.9	25.6	1.2	44.8	22.8
September	23.0	2.2	23.1	2.2	26.1	2.0	46.6	23.1
October	23.0	0.0	23.1	0.0	26.4	1.1	47.4	23.3
November	23.1	0.4	23.3	0.9	26.7	1.1	47.7	23.6
December	23.4	1.3	23.6	1.3	27.2	1.9	50.1	23.9
1948								
January	23.7	1.3	23.8	0.8	27.7	1.8	51.2	24.3
February	23.5	-0.8	23.6	-0.8	27.2	-1.8	47.7	24.1
March	23.4	-0.4	23.6	0.0	27.2	0.0	47.6	24.1
April	23.8	1.7	23.9	1.3	27.4	0.7	48.3	24.3
May	23.9	0.4	24.1	0.8	27.5	0.4	49.4	24.3
June	24.1	0.8	24.2	0.4	27.7	0.7	50.4	24.4
July	24.4	1.2	24.5	1.2	28.0	1.1	50.2	24.6
August	24.5	0.4	24.6	0.4	28.2	0.7	49.6	24.9
September	24.5	0.0	24.6	0.0	28.1	-0.4	48.8	25.0
October	24.4	-0.4	24.5	-0.4	27.8	-1.1	46.9	25.0
November	24.2	-0.8	24.4	-0.4	27.8	0.0	46.3	25.1
December	24.1	-0.4	24.2	-0.8	27.6	-0.7	45.2	25.1
1949								
January	24.0	-0.4	24.2	0.0	27.3	-1.1	43.8	24.9
February	23.8	-0.8	23.9	-1.2	26.8	-1.8	42.0	24.7
March	23.8	0.0	24.0	0.4	26.8	0.0	42.7	24.6
April	23.9	0.4	24.0	0.0	26.5	-1.1	42.7	24.3
May	23.8	-0.4	24.0	0.0	26.3	-0.8	42.7	24.0
June	23.9	0.4	24.0	0.0	26.0	-1.1	41.8	23.8
July	23.7	-0.8	23.8	-0.8	26.0	0.0	41.7	23.7
August	23.8	0.4	23.9	0.4	26.0	0.0	41.7	23.8
September	23.9	0.4	24.0	0.4	26.1	0.4	41.8	23.8
October	23.7	-0.8	23.9	-0.4	26.0	-0.4	41.0	23.8
November	23.8	0.4	23.9	0.0	26.0	0.0	40.9	23.8
December	23.6	-0.8	23.8	-0.4	25.9	-0.4	40.3	23.8

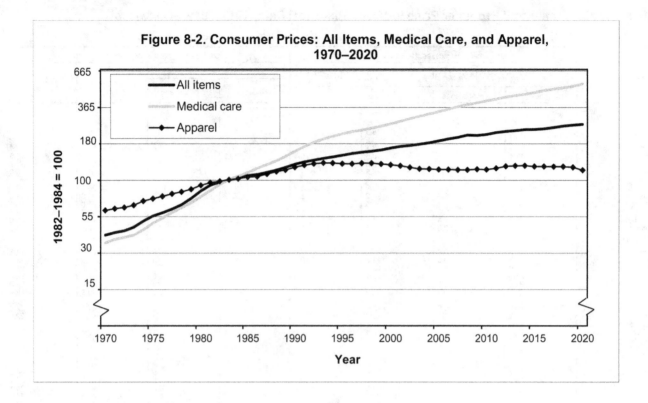

Figure 8-2. Consumer Prices: All Items, Medical Care, and Apparel, 1970–2020

- Figure 8-2 charts two components of the Consumer Price Index for All Urban Consumers (CPI-U) along with the total for all items. Apparel is one of the commodity groups most subject to international competition. It has grown far less rapidly than prices in general.

- Medical care, on the other hand, has little price competition from producers in other countries. It is often paid for by third-party insurers, both government and private, rather than directly by consumers. Furthermore, it is characterized by trend growth in demand, due to rising income and expectations and to technological progress. All of these economic factors cause medical care prices to rise faster than the general price level.

- During the pandemic, demand fell as states and counties issued stay-at-home orders. Now that economies are opening, supply has not been able to keep up with demand. Hence, prices have spiked.

- A broader system of Producer Price Indexes including services and construction as well as goods was introduced in 2014, featuring a more detailed representation by stages of production as well. These new measures only go back to November 2009—not enough time yet to determine what kind of signals about future inflation they will contain. (Tables 8-5 and 8-6)

Table 8-2. Consumer Price Indexes and Purchasing Power of the Dollar

(1982–1984 = 100, seasonally adjusted, except as noted.)

Year and month	CPI-U, All items			CPI-U, Food and beverages										
	Not seasonally adjusted	Seasonally adjusted		Total	Total food	Food at home							Food away from home [1]	Alcoholic beverages
		Index	Percent change from previous period			Total	Cereals and bakery products	Meats, poultry, fish, and eggs	Dairy and related products [1]	Fruits and vegetables	Non-alcoholic beverages	Other food at home		
1970	38.8	38.8	5.7	40.1	39.2	39.9	37.1	44.6	44.7	37.8	27.1	32.9	37.5	52.1
1971	40.5	40.5	4.4	41.4	40.4	40.9	38.8	44.1	46.1	39.7	28.1	34.3	39.4	54.2
1972	41.8	41.8	3.2	43.1	42.1	42.7	39.0	48.0	46.8	41.6	28.0	34.6	41.0	55.4
1973	44.4	44.4	6.2	48.8	48.2	49.7	43.5	60.9	51.2	47.4	30.1	36.7	44.2	56.8
1974	49.3	49.3	11.0	55.5	55.1	57.1	56.5	62.2	60.7	55.2	35.9	47.8	49.8	61.1
1975	53.8	53.8	9.1	60.2	59.8	61.8	62.9	67.0	62.6	56.9	41.3	55.4	54.5	65.9
1976	56.9	56.9	5.8	62.1	61.6	63.1	61.5	68.0	67.7	58.4	49.4	56.4	58.2	68.1
1977	60.6	60.6	6.5	65.8	65.5	66.8	62.5	67.4	69.5	63.8	74.4	68.4	62.6	70.0
1978	65.2	65.2	7.6	72.2	72.0	73.8	68.1	77.6	74.2	70.9	78.7	73.6	68.3	74.1
1979	72.6	72.6	11.3	79.9	79.9	81.8	74.9	89.0	82.8	76.6	82.6	79.0	75.9	79.9
1980	82.4	82.4	13.5	86.7	86.8	88.4	83.9	92.0	90.9	82.1	91.4	88.4	83.4	86.4
1981	90.9	90.9	10.3	93.5	93.6	94.8	92.3	96.0	97.4	92.0	95.3	94.9	90.9	92.5
1982	96.5	96.5	6.2	97.3	97.4	98.1	96.5	99.6	98.8	97.0	97.9	97.3	95.8	96.7
1983	99.6	99.6	3.2	99.5	99.4	99.1	99.6	99.2	100.0	97.3	99.8	99.5	100.0	100.4
1984	103.9	103.9	4.3	103.2	103.2	102.8	103.9	101.3	101.3	105.7	102.3	103.1	104.2	103.0
1985	107.6	107.6	3.6	105.6	105.6	104.3	107.9	100.1	103.2	108.4	104.3	105.7	108.3	106.4
1986	109.6	109.6	1.9	109.1	109.0	107.3	110.9	104.5	103.3	109.4	110.4	109.4	112.5	111.1
1987	113.6	113.6	3.6	113.5	113.5	111.9	114.8	110.5	105.9	119.1	107.5	110.5	117.0	114.1
1988	118.3	118.3	4.1	118.2	118.2	116.6	122.1	114.3	108.4	128.1	107.5	113.1	121.8	118.6
1989	124.0	124.0	4.8	124.9	125.1	124.2	132.4	121.3	115.6	138.0	111.3	119.1	127.4	123.5
1990	130.7	130.7	5.4	132.1	132.4	132.3	140.0	130.0	126.5	149.0	113.5	123.4	133.4	129.3
1991	136.2	136.2	4.2	136.8	136.3	135.8	145.8	132.6	125.1	155.8	114.1	127.3	137.9	142.8
1992	140.3	140.3	3.0	138.7	137.9	136.8	151.5	130.9	128.5	155.4	114.3	128.8	140.7	147.3
1993	144.5	144.5	3.0	141.6	140.9	140.1	156.6	135.5	129.4	159.0	114.6	130.5	143.2	149.6
1994	148.2	148.2	2.6	144.9	144.3	144.1	163.0	137.2	131.7	165.0	123.2	135.6	145.7	151.5
1995	152.4	152.4	2.8	148.9	148.4	148.8	167.5	138.8	132.8	177.7	131.7	140.8	149.0	153.9
1996	156.9	156.9	3.0	153.7	153.3	154.3	174.0	144.8	142.1	183.9	128.6	142.9	152.7	158.5
1997	160.5	160.5	2.3	157.7	157.3	158.1	177.6	148.5	145.5	187.5	133.4	147.3	157.0	162.8
1998	163.0	163.0	1.6	161.1	160.7	161.1	181.1	147.3	150.8	198.2	133.0	150.8	161.1	165.7
1999	166.6	166.6	2.2	164.6	164.1	164.2	185.0	147.9	159.6	203.1	134.3	153.5	165.1	169.7
2000	172.2	172.2	3.4	168.4	167.8	167.9	188.3	154.5	160.7	204.6	137.8	155.6	169.0	174.7
2001	177.1	177.1	2.8	173.6	173.1	173.4	193.8	161.3	167.1	212.2	139.2	159.6	173.9	179.3
2002	179.9	179.9	1.6	176.8	176.2	175.6	198.0	162.1	168.1	220.9	139.2	160.8	178.3	183.6
2003	184.0	184.0	2.3	180.5	180.0	179.4	202.8	169.3	167.9	225.9	139.8	162.6	182.1	187.2
2004	188.9	188.9	2.7	186.6	186.2	186.2	206.0	181.7	180.2	232.7	140.4	164.9	187.5	192.1
2005	195.3	195.3	3.4	191.2	190.7	189.8	209.0	184.7	182.4	241.4	144.4	167.0	193.4	195.9
2006	201.6	201.6	3.2	195.7	195.2	193.1	212.8	186.6	181.4	252.9	147.4	169.6	199.4	200.7
2007	207.3	207.3	2.8	203.3	202.9	201.2	222.1	195.6	194.8	262.6	153.4	173.3	206.7	207.0
2008	215.3	215.3	3.8	214.2	214.1	214.1	244.9	204.7	210.4	278.9	160.0	184.2	215.8	214.5
2009	214.5	214.5	-0.4	218.2	218.0	215.1	252.6	203.8	197.0	272.9	163.0	191.2	223.3	220.8
2010	218.1	218.1	1.6	220.0	219.6	215.8	250.4	207.7	199.2	273.5	161.6	191.1	226.1	223.3
2011	224.9	224.9	3.2	227.9	227.8	226.2	260.3	223.2	212.7	284.7	166.8	197.4	231.4	226.7
2012	229.6	229.6	2.1	233.7	233.8	231.8	267.7	231.0	217.3	282.8	168.6	204.8	238.0	230.8
2013	233.0	233.0	1.5	237.0	237.0	233.9	270.4	236.0	217.6	290.0	166.9	204.8	243.1	234.6
2014	236.7	236.7	1.6	242.4	242.7	239.5	271.1	253.0	225.3	294.4	166.0	206.2	249.0	237.3
2015	237.0	237.0	0.1	246.8	247.2	242.3	274.1	260.3	222.4	293.8	167.9	209.3	256.1	239.5
2016	240.0	240.0	1.3	247.7	247.9	239.1	273.1	247.7	217.3	296.3	167.3	209.5	262.7	242.5
2017	245.1	245.1	2.1	249.8	250.1	238.6	271.7	245.8	217.5	295.7	167.6	209.9	268.8	245.4
2018	251.1	251.1	2.4	253.3	253.6	239.7	272.8	248.9	216.5	297.8	167.6	210.2	275.9	249.1
2019	255.7	255.7	1.8	258.0	258.3	241.8	276.6	249.8	218.7	300.9	170.8	211.1	284.4	252.5
2020	258.8	258.8	1.2	266.6	267.2	250.2	282.6	265.2	228.3	304.9	176.9	217.3	293.9	257.2
2019														
January	251.7	252.4	1.5	256.1	256.3	241.2	274.9	249.8	215.7	301.1	170.6	210.9	280.4	251.7
February	252.8	253.0	1.5	256.9	257.2	242.0	276.2	250.4	216.0	303.4	171.2	211.1	281.4	252.1
March	254.2	254.1	1.9	257.3	257.6	242.3	276.6	249.5	216.9	306.3	170.6	211.3	281.9	251.8
April	255.5	255.3	2.0	257.0	257.3	241.3	276.4	248.4	217.4	303.2	170.1	210.2	282.8	251.3
May	256.1	255.4	1.8	257.6	257.9	241.7	277.6	249.2	218.5	301.3	171.5	210.4	283.4	252.2
June	256.1	255.4	1.7	257.7	258.0	241.3	275.8	247.7	218.8	300.3	170.5	211.6	284.3	252.6
July	256.6	255.9	1.8	258.0	258.2	241.3	276.9	248.5	219.2	300.6	170.4	210.3	284.9	253.7
August	256.6	256.1	1.7	258.2	258.4	241.1	276.5	247.9	219.2	299.7	170.5	210.8	285.5	253.7
September	256.8	256.5	1.7	258.7	259.0	241.7	277.2	249.5	219.8	298.3	170.9	211.6	286.2	253.4
October	257.3	257.4	1.8	259.2	259.6	242.2	276.8	251.0	220.2	299.8	170.7	211.8	286.8	253.0
November	257.2	258.0	2.0	259.6	260.0	242.7	277.5	251.7	221.4	298.8	172.0	211.9	287.3	252.2
December	257.0	258.2	2.3	260.0	260.4	242.7	276.3	254.6	221.2	297.8	171.3	211.2	288.1	252.9
2020														
January	258.0	258.7	2.5	260.6	261.0	243.0	275.9	254.6	221.7	298.4	171.5	211.7	289.1	253.7
February	258.7	258.8	2.3	261.4	261.8	244.0	276.9	255.3	223.8	298.6	171.9	213.1	289.8	254.3
March	258.1	258.0	1.5	262.1	262.5	244.9	276.9	255.2	225.0	300.4	172.9	214.3	290.2	255.3
April	256.4	256.2	0.3	265.7	266.3	251.0	284.8	265.1	228.6	304.3	178.6	218.3	290.6	256.0
May	256.4	255.9	0.2	267.5	268.1	253.2	284.7	273.5	230.8	305.7	178.4	218.6	291.7	257.8
June	257.8	257.3	0.7	268.8	269.5	254.7	284.9	278.8	229.8	306.9	179.3	218.8	293.2	258.1
July	259.1	258.6	1.0	268.0	268.7	252.3	284.6	269.1	228.8	307.1	178.9	218.6	294.6	257.5
August	259.9	259.5	1.3	268.4	269.0	252.3	284.4	265.7	231.7	307.7	179.1	219.5	295.4	258.0
September	260.3	260.1	1.4	268.6	269.3	251.6	284.3	265.3	230.8	307.4	178.2	218.5	297.1	257.8
October	260.4	260.5	1.2	269.2	269.8	251.9	285.1	266.5	228.7	307.7	178.3	219.1	297.9	258.8
November	260.2	260.9	1.1	269.2	269.7	251.6	284.2	266.8	229.4	307.9	177.3	218.0	298.3	259.7
December	260.5	261.6	1.3	270.0	270.7	252.3	285.0	266.4	231.0	307.3	178.8	219.4	299.4	260.0

[1]Not seasonally adjusted.

Table 8-2. Consumer Price Indexes and Purchasing Power of the Dollar—*Continued*

(1982–1984 = 100, seasonally adjusted, except as noted.)

Year and month	CPI-U, Housing													
	Total	Shelter						Fuels and utilities				Household furnishings and operations	
		Total	Rent of shelter [2]	Rent of primary residence	Lodging away from home [3]	Owners' equivalent rent of primary residence [2]	Tenants' and household insurance [1,3]	Total	Fuels		Water and sewer and trash collection services [3]	Total	Household operations [1,3]
									Fuel oil and other fuels	Energy services			
1970	36.4	35.5	. . .	46.5	. . .	. . .	. . .	29.1	17.0	25.4	. . .	46.8	. . .
1971	38.0	37.0	. . .	48.7	. . .	. . .	. . .	31.1	18.2	27.1	. . .	48.6	. . .
1972	39.4	38.7	. . .	50.4	. . .	. . .	. . .	32.5	18.3	28.5	. . .	49.7	. . .
1973	41.2	40.5	. . .	52.5	. . .	. . .	. . .	34.3	21.1	29.9	. . .	51.1	. . .
1974	45.8	44.4	. . .	55.2	. . .	. . .	. . .	40.7	33.2	34.5	. . .	56.8	. . .
1975	50.7	48.8	. . .	58.0	. . .	. . .	. . .	45.4	36.4	40.1	. . .	63.4	. . .
1976	53.8	51.5	. . .	61.1	. . .	. . .	. . .	49.4	38.8	44.7	. . .	67.3	. . .
1977	57.4	54.9	. . .	64.8	. . .	. . .	. . .	54.7	43.9	50.5	. . .	70.4	. . .
1978	62.4	60.5	. . .	69.3	. . .	. . .	. . .	58.5	46.2	55.0	. . .	74.7	. . .
1979	70.1	68.9	. . .	74.3	. . .	. . .	. . .	64.8	62.4	61.0	. . .	79.9	. . .
1980	81.1	81.0	. . .	80.9	. . .	. . .	. . .	75.4	86.1	71.4	. . .	86.3	. . .
1981	90.4	90.5	. . .	87.9	. . .	. . .	. . .	86.4	104.6	81.9	. . .	93.0	. . .
1982	96.9	96.9	. . .	94.6	. . .	. . .	. . .	94.9	103.4	93.2	. . .	98.0	. . .
1983	99.5	99.1	102.7	100.1	. . .	102.5	. . .	100.2	97.2	101.5	. . .	100.2	. . .
1984	103.6	104.0	107.7	105.3	. . .	107.3	. . .	104.8	99.4	105.4	. . .	101.9	. . .
1985	107.7	109.8	113.9	111.8	. . .	113.2	. . .	106.5	95.9	107.1	. . .	103.8	. . .
1986	110.9	115.8	120.2	118.3	. . .	119.4	. . .	104.1	77.6	105.7	. . .	105.2	. . .
1987	114.2	121.3	125.9	123.1	. . .	124.8	. . .	103.0	77.9	103.8	. . .	107.1	. . .
1988	118.5	127.1	132.0	127.8	. . .	131.1	. . .	104.4	78.1	104.6	. . .	109.4	. . .
1989	123.0	132.8	138.0	132.8	. . .	137.4	. . .	107.8	81.7	107.5	. . .	111.2	. . .
1990	128.5	140.0	145.5	138.4	. . .	144.8	. . .	111.6	99.3	109.3	. . .	113.3	. . .
1991	133.6	146.3	152.1	143.3	. . .	150.4	. . .	115.3	94.6	112.6	. . .	116.0	. . .
1992	137.5	151.2	157.3	146.9	. . .	155.5	. . .	117.8	90.7	114.8	. . .	118.0	. . .
1993	141.2	155.7	162.0	150.3	. . .	160.5	. . .	121.3	90.3	118.5	. . .	119.3	. . .
1994	144.8	160.5	167.0	154.0	. . .	165.8	. . .	122.8	88.8	119.2	. . .	121.0	. . .
1995	148.5	165.7	172.4	157.8	. . .	171.3	. . .	123.7	88.1	119.2	. . .	123.0	. . .
1996	152.8	171.0	178.0	162.0	. . .	176.8	. . .	127.5	99.2	122.1	. . .	124.7	. . .
1997	156.8	176.3	183.4	166.7	. . .	181.9	. . .	130.8	99.8	125.1	. . .	125.4	. . .
1998	160.4	182.1	189.6	172.1	109.0	187.8	99.8	128.5	90.0	121.2	101.6	126.6	101.5
1999	163.9	187.3	195.0	177.5	112.3	192.9	101.3	128.8	91.4	120.9	104.0	126.7	104.5
2000	169.6	193.4	201.3	183.9	117.5	198.7	103.7	137.9	129.7	128.0	106.5	128.2	110.5
2001	176.4	200.6	208.9	192.1	118.6	206.3	106.2	150.2	129.3	142.4	109.6	129.1	115.6
2002	180.3	208.1	216.7	199.7	118.3	214.7	108.7	143.6	115.5	134.4	113.0	128.3	119.0
2003	184.8	213.1	221.9	205.5	119.3	219.9	114.8	154.5	139.5	145.0	117.2	126.1	121.8
2004	189.5	218.8	227.9	211.0	125.9	224.9	116.2	161.9	160.5	150.6	124.0	125.5	125.0
2005	195.7	224.4	233.7	217.3	130.3	230.2	117.6	179.0	208.6	166.5	130.3	126.1	130.3
2006	203.2	232.1	241.9	225.1	136.0	238.2	116.5	194.7	234.9	182.1	136.8	127.0	136.6
2007	209.6	240.6	250.8	234.7	142.8	246.2	117.0	200.6	251.5	186.3	143.7	126.9	140.6
2008	216.3	246.7	257.2	243.3	143.7	252.4	118.8	220.0	334.4	202.2	152.1	127.8	147.5
2009	217.1	249.4	259.9	248.8	134.2	256.6	121.5	210.7	239.8	193.6	161.1	128.7	150.3
2010	216.3	248.4	258.8	249.4	133.7	256.6	125.7	214.2	275.1	192.9	170.9	125.5	150.3
2011	219.1	251.6	262.2	253.6	137.4	259.6	127.4	220.4	337.1	194.4	179.6	124.9	151.8
2012	222.7	257.1	267.8	260.4	140.5	264.8	131.3	219.0	335.9	189.7	189.3	125.7	155.2
2013	227.4	263.1	274.0	267.7	142.4	270.7	135.4	225.2	332.0	194.8	197.6	124.8	157.6
2014	233.2	270.5	281.8	276.2	148.5	277.8	141.9	234.6	338.9	203.4	204.9	123.1	161.6
2015	238.1	278.8	290.4	286.0	153.0	285.9	146.4	230.1	256.2	198.7	214.0	122.6	166.9
2016	244.0	288.2	300.3	296.8	158.1	295.4	147.7	228.9	226.3	196.1	221.7	121.6	171.6
2017	251.2	297.8	310.3	308.1	159.4	305.1	148.8	237.3	254.4	202.7	229.1	120.7	176.3
2018	258.5	307.7	320.7	319.3	161.1	315.2	150.7	241.6	293.0	203.8	237.1	121.6	186.0
2019	266.0	318.1	331.6	331.1	165.9	325.6	151.8	242.6	280.8	203.5	244.7	123.8	194.5
2020	271.8	325.9	339.9	341.5	148.9	334.8	151.1	243.9	237.6	204.5	252.5	125.9	200.6
2019													
January	262.4	312.9	326.2	325.4	162.0	320.6	151.6	242.5	266.7	204.8	241.4	123.2	191.6
February	263.0	313.9	327.3	326.3	163.1	321.6	151.7	242.0	279.5	203.6	241.8	123.3	191.0
March	263.9	315.0	328.4	327.6	165.6	322.5	151.5	242.8	286.1	204.1	242.4	123.4	190.7
April	264.6	316.2	329.7	328.9	168.7	323.6	151.4	242.9	288.3	203.8	243.2	123.2	191.8
May	265.1	317.0	330.6	329.6	169.2	324.4	151.6	242.5	289.7	203.2	243.8	123.1	190.6
June	265.9	318.0	331.6	330.9	168.8	325.4	152.2	241.9	281.2	202.6	244.5	123.9	195.9
July	266.5	318.8	332.4	331.8	168.8	326.2	152.2	242.3	280.2	203.0	245.1	124.1	197.1
August	266.8	319.4	333.0	332.7	165.7	327.0	151.8	242.1	279.0	202.7	245.4	124.1	196.9
September	267.6	320.4	334.2	333.9	167.9	327.9	151.8	241.8	277.8	202.3	246.0	124.5	196.4
October	268.0	320.8	334.6	334.6	164.3	328.6	151.9	243.4	280.6	203.7	247.0	124.4	197.0
November	268.6	321.7	335.4	335.5	164.0	329.5	151.8	243.7	280.6	204.0	247.4	124.3	197.3
December	268.9	322.3	336.1	336.5	161.2	330.3	151.7	243.5	280.3	203.6	247.7	124.1	197.5
2020													
January	269.6	323.3	337.1	337.6	161.4	331.3	151.3	243.6	273.6	203.8	248.6	124.0	197.8
February	270.2	324.3	338.2	338.6	164.1	332.1	151.7	243.2	265.8	203.4	249.6	124.2	199.1
March	270.3	324.5	338.4	339.5	154.8	332.9	150.8	242.4	245.7	203.0	250.2	124.2	199.3
April	270.4	324.5	338.4	340.3	145.3	333.5	151.2	241.9	221.7	203.3	250.5	124.8	199.3
May	270.8	325.2	339.1	341.1	143.8	334.3	150.4	241.6	215.3	203.0	251.0	125.2	199.2
June	271.3	325.6	339.5	341.5	145.7	334.7	150.4	242.2	225.7	203.1	251.7	125.6	199.4
July	271.9	326.3	340.2	342.1	146.4	335.3	150.9	242.5	229.7	203.1	252.5	126.0	200.1
August	272.5	326.7	340.7	342.5	146.9	335.8	150.8	242.7	235.0	202.7	253.8	127.3	201.0
September	272.9	327.0	341.1	343.0	145.9	336.1	150.8	244.8	229.1	205.3	254.4	127.2	201.7
October	273.2	327.4	341.5	343.5	142.0	336.8	151.2	245.9	229.8	206.4	255.0	126.9	202.4
November	273.9	327.8	342.0	343.8	146.0	337.0	151.6	247.8	233.2	208.3	255.6	127.7	201.7
December	274.3	328.2	342.3	344.2	145.6	337.5	151.8	248.7	242.2	208.7	256.6	128.0	205.7

[1] Not seasonally adjusted.
[2] December 1982 = 100.
[3] December 1997 = 100.
. . . = Not available.

Table 8-3. Alternative Measures of Total and Core Consumer Prices: Index Levels

(Various bases; monthly data seasonally adjusted, except as noted.)

Year and month	CPIs, all items					CPIs, all items less food and energy		
	CPI-U, 1982–1984 = 100	CPI-W, 1982–1984 = 100	CPI-U-X1, 1982–1984 = 100	CPI-U-RS, Dec. 1977 = 100, not seasonally adjusted	C-CPI-U, Dec. 1999 = 100, not seasonally adjusted	CPI-U, 1982–1984 = 100	CPI-U-RS, Dec. 1977 = 100, not seasonally adjusted	C-CPI-U, Dec. 1999 = 100, not seasonally adjusted
1975	53.8	54.1	56.2	. . .	. . .	53.9	. . .	. . .
1976	56.9	57.2	59.4	. . .	. . .	57.4	. . .	. . .
1977	60.6	60.9	63.2	. . .	. . .	61.0	. . .	. . .
1978	65.2	65.6	67.5	104.4	. . .	65.5	103.6	. . .
1979	72.6	73.1	74.0	114.3	. . .	71.9	111.0	. . .
1980	82.4	82.9	82.3	127.1	. . .	80.8	120.9	. . .
1981	90.9	91.4	90.1	139.1	. . .	89.2	132.2	. . .
1982	96.5	96.9	95.6	147.5	. . .	95.8	142.4	. . .
1983	99.6	99.8	99.6	153.8	. . .	99.6	150.4	. . .
1984	103.9	103.3	103.9	160.2	. . .	104.6	157.9	. . .
1985	107.6	106.9	107.6	165.7	. . .	109.1	164.8	. . .
1986	109.6	108.6	109.6	168.6	. . .	113.5	171.4	. . .
1987	113.6	112.5	113.6	174.4	. . .	118.2	178.1	. . .
1988	118.3	117.0	118.3	180.7	. . .	123.4	185.2	. . .
1989	124.0	122.6	124.0	188.6	. . .	129.0	192.6	. . .
1990	130.7	129.0	130.7	197.9	. . .	135.5	201.4	. . .
1991	136.2	134.3	136.2	205.1	. . .	142.1	209.9	. . .
1992	140.3	138.2	140.3	210.2	. . .	147.3	216.4	. . .
1993	144.5	142.1	144.5	215.5	. . .	152.2	222.5	. . .
1994	148.2	145.6	148.2	220.0	. . .	156.5	227.7	. . .
1995	152.4	149.8	152.4	225.3	. . .	161.2	233.4	. . .
1996	156.9	154.1	156.9	231.3	. . .	165.6	239.1	. . .
1997	160.5	157.6	160.5	236.3	. . .	169.5	244.4	. . .
1998	163.0	159.7	163.0	239.5	. . .	173.4	249.6	. . .
1999	166.6	163.2	166.6	244.6	. . .	177.0	254.6	. . .
2000	172.2	168.9	172.2	252.9	102.0	181.3	260.9	101.4
2001	177.1	173.5	177.1	260.1	104.3	186.1	267.9	103.5
2002	179.9	175.9	179.9	264.2	105.6	190.5	274.1	105.4
2003	184.0	179.8	184.0	270.2	107.8	193.2	278.1	106.6
2004	188.9	184.5	188.9	277.5	110.5	196.6	283.1	108.4
2005	195.3	191.0	195.3	286.9	113.7	200.9	289.2	110.4
2006	201.6	197.1	201.6	296.2	117.0	205.9	296.5	112.9
2007	207.3	202.8	207.3	304.6	120.0	210.7	303.4	115.0
2008	215.3	211.1	215.3	316.3	124.4	215.6	310.3	117.3
2009	214.5	209.6	214.5	315.2	123.9	219.2	315.6	119.1
2010	218.1	214.0	218.1	320.4	125.6	221.3	318.7	120.0
2011	224.9	221.6	224.9	330.5	129.5	225.0	324.0	121.9
2012	229.6	226.2	229.6	337.5	132.0	229.8	331.0	124.3
2013	233.0	229.3	233.0	342.5	. . .	233.8	337.0	. . .
2014	236.7	232.8	236.7	348.3	. . .	237.9	343.1	. . .
2015	237.0	231.8	237.0	348.9	. . .	242.2	349.7	. . .
2016	240.0	234.1	240.0	353.4	. . .	247.6	357.5	. . .
2017	245.1	239.1	245.1	361.0	. . .	252.2	364.2	. . .
2018	251.1	245.1	251.1	369.8	. . .	257.6	372.0	. . .
2019	255.7	249.2	255.7	376.5	. . .	263.2	380.1	. . .
2020	258.8	252.2	258.8	381.2	. . .	267.7	386.6	. . .
2019								
January	252.4	246.0	252.4	370.7	142.0	260.4	375.7	137.4
February	253.0	246.5	253.0	372.2	142.6	260.7	377.1	137.9
March	254.1	247.8	254.1	374.3	143.3	261.3	378.1	138.2
April	255.3	249.1	255.3	376.3	143.9	262.1	378.8	138.4
May	255.4	249.0	255.4	377.1	144.2	262.4	379.2	138.6
June	255.4	248.9	255.4	377.2	144.2	263.1	380.0	138.8
July	255.9	249.5	255.9	377.8	144.4	263.6	380.6	139.0
August	256.1	249.6	256.1	377.8	144.4	264.2	381.5	139.2
September	256.5	250.0	256.5	378.1	144.4	264.6	382.0	139.3
October	257.4	251.0	257.4	379.0	144.6	265.0	382.8	139.5
November	258.0	251.5	258.0	378.8	144.5	265.4	382.9	139.4
December	258.2	251.8	258.2	378.5	144.3	265.7	382.6	139.2
2020								
January	258.7	252.2	258.7	379.9	144.8	266.3	384.2	139.7
February	258.8	252.2	258.8	381.0	145.2	[1]266.9	386.0	140.3
March	258.0	251.3	258.0	380.1	144.9	[1]266.8	386.0	140.4
April	256.2	249.3	256.2	377.6	144.1	[1]265.8	384.3	139.8
May	255.9	249.0	255.9	377.6	144.0	[1]265.6	383.9	139.5
June	257.3	250.5	257.3	379.7	144.8	[1]266.2	384.6	139.8
July	258.6	252.1	258.6	381.6	145.6	[1]267.7	386.6	140.5
August	259.5	253.1	259.5	382.8	146.1	268.7	388.1	141.1
September	260.1	253.8	260.1	383.3	146.3	269.2	388.5	141.2
October	260.5	254.2	260.5	383.5	146.3	269.4	388.9	141.4
November	260.9	254.6	260.9	383.2	146.2	269.8	389.1	141.5
December	261.6	255.3	261.6	383.6	146.3	269.9	388.8	141.3

[1]Interim values.
. . . = Not available.

Table 8-4. Alternative Measures of Total and Core Consumer Prices: Inflation Rates

(Percent changes from year earlier, except as noted; monthly data seasonally adjusted, except as noted.)

Year and month	CPIs, all items					CPIs, all items less food and energy		
	CPI-U, 1982–1984 = 100	CPI-W, 1982–1984 = 100	CPI-U-X1, 1982–1984 = 100	CPI-U-RS, Dec. 1977 = 100, not seasonally adjusted	C-CPI-U, Dec. 1999 = 100, not seasonally adjusted	CPI-U, 1982–1984 = 100	CPI-U-RS, Dec. 1977 = 100, not seasonally adjusted	C-CPI-U, Dec. 1999 = 100, not seasonally adjusted
1975	9.1	9.1	8.3	. . .	. . .	9.1	. . .	. . .
1976	5.8	5.7	5.7	. . .	. . .	6.5	. . .	. . .
1977	6.5	6.5	6.4	. . .	. . .	6.3	. . .	. . .
1978	7.6	7.7	6.8	. . .	. . .	7.4	. . .	. . .
1979	11.3	11.4	9.6	9.5	. . .	9.8	7.1	. . .
1980	13.5	13.4	11.2	11.2	. . .	12.4	8.9	. . .
1981	10.3	10.3	9.5	9.4	. . .	10.4	9.3	. . .
1982	6.2	6.0	6.1	6.0	. . .	7.4	7.7	. . .
1983	3.2	3.0	4.2	4.3	. . .	4.0	5.6	. . .
1984	4.3	3.5	4.3	4.2	. . .	5.0	5.0	. . .
1985	3.6	3.5	3.6	3.4	. . .	4.3	4.4	. . .
1986	1.9	1.6	1.9	1.8	. . .	4.0	4.0	. . .
1987	3.6	3.6	3.6	3.4	. . .	4.1	3.9	. . .
1988	4.1	4.0	4.1	3.6	. . .	4.4	4.0	. . .
1989	4.8	4.8	4.8	4.4	. . .	4.5	4.0	. . .
1990	5.4	5.2	5.4	4.9	. . .	5.0	4.6	. . .
1991	4.2	4.1	4.2	3.6	. . .	4.9	4.2	. . .
1992	3.0	2.9	3.0	2.5	. . .	3.7	3.1	. . .
1993	3.0	2.8	3.0	2.5	. . .	3.3	2.8	. . .
1994	2.6	2.5	2.6	2.1	. . .	2.8	2.3	. . .
1995	2.8	2.9	2.8	2.4	. . .	3.0	2.5	. . .
1996	3.0	2.9	3.0	2.7	. . .	2.7	2.4	. . .
1997	2.3	2.3	2.3	2.2	. . .	2.4	2.2	. . .
1998	1.6	1.3	1.6	1.4	. . .	2.3	2.1	. . .
1999	2.2	2.2	2.2	2.1	. . .	2.1	2.0	. . .
2000	3.4	3.5	3.4	3.4	. . .	2.4	2.5	. . .
2001	2.8	2.7	2.8	2.8	. . .	2.6	2.7	2.1
2002	1.6	1.4	1.6	1.6	. . .	2.4	2.3	1.8
2003	2.3	2.2	2.3	2.3	. . .	1.4	1.5	1.1
2004	2.7	2.6	2.7	2.7	. . .	1.8	1.8	1.7
2005	3.4	3.5	3.4	3.4	2.3	2.2	2.2	1.8
2006	3.2	3.2	3.2	3.2	1.2	2.5	2.5	2.3
2007	2.8	2.9	2.8	2.8	2.1	2.3	2.3	1.8
2008	3.8	4.1	3.8	3.8	2.5	2.3	2.3	2.0
2009	-0.4	-0.7	-0.4	-0.3	2.9	1.7	1.7	1.5
2010	1.6	2.1	1.6	1.6	2.9	1.0	1.0	0.7
2011	3.2	3.6	3.2	3.2	2.5	1.7	1.7	1.6
2012	2.1	2.1	2.1	2.1	3.7	2.1	2.2	2.0
2013	1.5	1.4	1.5	1.5	-0.5	1.8	1.8	. . .
2014	1.6	1.5	1.6	1.7	1.4	1.7	1.8	. . .
2015	0.1	-0.4	0.1	0.2	3.1	1.8	1.9	. . .
2016	1.3	1.0	1.3	1.3	1.9	2.2	2.2	. . .
2017	2.1	2.1	2.1	2.2	. . .	1.8	1.9	. . .
2018	2.4	2.5	2.4	2.4	. . .	2.1	2.1	. . .
2019	1.8	1.7	1.8	1.8	. . .	2.2	2.2	. . .
2020	1.2	1.2	1.2	1.2	. . .	1.7	1.7	. . .
2020								
January	2.5	2.5	2.5	2.5	1.6	2.3	2.3	1.3
February	2.3	2.3	2.3	2.4	1.3	2.4	2.4	1.5
March	1.5	1.4	1.5	1.5	0.7	2.1	2.1	1.4
April	0.3	0.1	0.3	0.3	0.0	1.4	1.5	0.9
May	0.2	0.0	0.2	0.1	-0.2	1.2	1.2	0.5
June	0.7	0.6	0.7	0.7	0.3	1.2	1.2	0.6
July	1.0	1.0	1.0	1.0	0.8	1.6	1.6	0.9
August	1.3	1.4	1.3	1.3	1.1	[1]1.7	1.7	1.3
September	1.4	1.6	1.4	1.4	1.1	[1]1.7	1.7	1.3
October	1.2	1.3	1.2	1.2	1.2	[1]1.6	1.6	1.4
November	1.1	1.2	1.1	1.2	1.4	[1]1.7	1.6	1.7
December	1.3	1.4	1.3	1.3	1.0	[1]1.6	1.6	1.1

[1]Interim values.
. . . = Not available.

Table 8-5. Producer Price Indexes for Goods and Services: Final Demand

(November 2009 =100, except as noted.)

Year and month	Final demand	Final demand goods	Final demand foods	Final demand energy goods	Final demand goods less food and energy Total	Finished goods less foods and energy (1982=100) Total	Private capital equipment	Final demand services	Final demand trade services	Final demand transportation and warehousing services	Final demand services less trade, transportation, and warehousing	Final demand construction	Final demand less food and energy (April 2010=100)
NOT SEASONALLY ADJUSTED													
2010	101.8	102.8	103.7	107.2	101.4	173.6	157.3	101.3	101.7	103.2	100.9	100.3	. . .
2011	105.7	109.9	112.5	126.2	104.9	177.8	159.7	103.4	104.0	110.0	102.5	102.5	102.7
2012	107.7	111.7	115.9	126.3	106.8	182.4	162.8	105.4	106.7	114.2	103.9	105.5	104.7
2013	109.1	112.6	117.8	125.3	107.9	185.1	164.2	107.1	108.2	115.3	105.8	107.5	106.2
2014	110.9	114.0	121.6	124.2	109.5	188.6	166.4	109.0	110.2	117.7	107.5	110.6	108.1
2015	109.9	109.1	118.4	98.6	109.9	192.3	168.5	110.0	111.6	115.3	108.7	112.7	108.9
2016	110.4	107.6	115.1	90.4	110.7	195.3	169.3	111.5	113.1	113.5	110.6	114.0	110.2
2017	113.0	111.2	116.5	99.8	113.2	198.9	170.9	113.5	114.8	115.9	112.8	116.5	112.3
2018	116.2	115.0	116.7	110.0	116.0	203.4	173.6	116.5	116.9	122.0	115.8	121.2	115.3
2019	118.2	115.5	118.9	105.0	117.6	207.8	177.4	119.1	119.7	125.5	118.2	127.2	117.7
2020	118.4	113.8	120.4	91.5	118.5	210.2	179.3	120.2	121.7	121.2	119.5	130.2	118.7
2017													
January	111.6	109.7	113.9	96.8	112.3	197.8	170.4	112.3	113.6	115.2	111.5	114.9	111.2
February	111.8	110.1	114.8	97.6	112.5	197.9	170.6	112.3	112.9	115.4	111.8	114.9	111.3
March	112.1	110.4	115.8	97.2	112.8	198.1	170.8	112.7	114.0	114.9	111.9	115.0	111.6
April	112.7	111.1	117.5	98.7	113.1	198.6	170.9	113.2	114.5	115.6	112.4	115.5	112.1
May	112.7	110.7	117.1	97.3	113.0	198.4	170.6	113.4	115.1	115.0	112.5	115.7	112.2
June	112.9	111.1	118.2	98.1	113.1	198.7	170.7	113.5	114.4	116.1	112.9	115.8	112.3
July	113.0	111.0	117.8	98.2	113.0	198.6	170.5	113.7	114.5	115.7	113.2	117.3	112.4
August	113.2	111.4	117.0	100.6	113.1	198.6	170.5	113.9	115.0	115.6	113.2	117.4	112.6
September	113.5	112.0	116.6	104.3	113.1	198.4	170.5	113.9	115.3	115.6	113.1	117.3	112.6
October	114.1	112.0	116.4	102.0	113.8	200.2	171.4	114.8	116.9	116.9	113.6	118.0	113.4
November	114.1	112.5	116.5	103.7	114.0	200.5	171.7	114.6	116.0	117.9	113.6	117.9	113.3
December	113.8	112.5	116.2	103.4	114.1	200.6	171.8	114.2	115.0	117.3	113.5	118.0	113.1
2018													
January	114.5	113.2	116.1	105.2	114.7	201.4	171.9	114.8	115.2	117.9	114.4	119.0	113.7
February	114.9	113.5	115.5	106.4	115.0	201.8	172.2	115.3	115.8	119.0	114.8	119.0	114.1
March	115.4	114.0	118.0	105.6	115.4	202.1	172.5	115.8	116.0	120.5	115.3	119.1	114.6
April	115.7	114.4	116.8	108.0	115.6	202.4	172.6	116.0	116.5	120.8	115.2	120.4	114.8
May	116.2	115.5	117.8	112.8	115.8	202.6	172.9	116.1	116.7	120.7	115.4	120.5	114.9
June	116.6	116.0	116.9	115.3	116.0	202.9	173.2	116.6	117.2	122.6	115.7	120.7	115.3
July	116.8	115.9	116.3	114.9	116.2	203.3	173.5	116.8	116.8	122.9	116.3	121.2	115.5
August	116.6	115.8	115.7	114.6	116.3	203.7	174.0	116.7	116.4	122.3	116.3	121.4	115.5
September	116.6	115.8	115.2	114.7	116.3	203.9	174.3	116.7	116.3	122.7	116.3	121.4	115.5
October	117.6	116.3	115.7	114.9	116.9	205.2	175.3	117.8	118.8	124.6	116.7	123.8	116.5
November	117.1	115.4	117.0	108.0	117.1	205.7	175.6	117.6	118.3	125.4	116.5	124.0	116.4
December	116.8	114.3	119.4	100.2	117.1	205.8	175.7	117.6	118.6	124.9	116.4	124.1	116.4
2019													
January	116.7	113.9	117.6	97.4	117.6	207.2	176.8	117.8	118.1	125.5	116.8	125.0	116.6
February	117.1	114.3	117.4	99.5	117.7	207.3	177.0	118.1	118.6	124.3	117.3	125.0	116.9
March	117.7	115.4	118.0	104.7	117.8	207.5	176.9	118.5	119.1	124.8	117.6	125.2	117.2
April	118.5	116.3	118.2	109.3	117.8	207.5	177.0	119.1	120.3	125.5	117.9	126.9	117.7
May	118.6	116.4	118.5	110.3	117.6	207.6	177.2	119.2	119.8	125.4	118.3	127.1	117.7
June	118.5	116.0	119.6	107.5	117.5	207.6	177.2	119.3	119.8	126.4	118.4	127.1	117.8
July	118.7	116.2	119.3	108.8	117.6	207.8	177.3	119.5	119.9	126.5	118.7	128.0	118.0
August	118.8	115.7	118.4	106.9	117.5	207.7	177.2	119.9	120.9	125.3	118.9	128.1	118.2
September	118.3	115.2	118.3	105.1	117.3	207.7	177.3	119.4	120.0	124.1	118.6	128.2	117.8
October	118.8	115.6	119.4	104.8	117.7	208.6	178.0	120.0	121.4	125.7	118.8	128.6	118.4
November	118.3	115.6	121.0	103.2	117.8	208.9	178.2	119.2	119.3	125.5	118.6	128.7	117.8
December	118.4	115.5	120.8	102.6	117.8	208.8	178.2	119.3	119.5	127.6	118.5	128.9	117.9
2020													
January	119.0	116.0	120.9	103.6	118.3	209.3	178.6	120.0	119.9	126.4	119.4	129.6	118.5
February	118.4	115.0	118.7	99.6	118.4	209.8	179.0	119.7	119.4	125.6	119.3	129.7	118.3
March	118.1	113.4	118.8	91.5	118.3	209.7	178.9	120.0	120.8	122.5	119.4	129.6	118.5
April	116.7	110.3	118.6	75.7	118.0	210.1	179.1	119.5	122.3	118.3	118.3	130.3	118.1
May	117.3	112.2	126.2	80.0	117.8	209.9	179.0	119.4	121.6	119.3	118.4	130.2	118.0
June	117.7	113.0	120.3	89.0	117.9	209.8	178.8	119.6	121.2	121.5	118.7	130.1	118.2
July	118.4	113.7	118.8	93.3	118.2	210.0	179.1	120.3	122.2	120.5	119.4	130.8	118.7
August	118.5	113.8	118.3	93.8	118.4	210.2	179.2	120.3	122.2	118.8	119.7	130.5	118.8
September	118.7	114.1	119.8	92.8	118.6	210.2	179.4	120.5	122.0	118.9	120.0	130.4	119.0
October	119.5	114.4	122.0	91.6	118.9	210.9	179.9	121.6	124.4	121.4	120.3	130.2	119.8
November	119.3	114.7	122.1	91.8	119.3	211.4	180.2	121.1	123.0	120.7	120.3	130.4	119.6
December	119.4	115.5	120.6	95.6	119.8	211.6	180.5	120.8	121.8	120.1	120.5	130.4	119.5

. . . = Not available.

Table 8-5. Producer Price Indexes for Goods and Services: Final Demand—*Continued*

(November 2009 =100, except as noted.)

Year and month	Final demand	Final demand goods						Final demand services				Final demand construction	Final demand less food and energy (April 2010 =100)
		Final demand goods	Final demand foods	Final demand energy goods	Final demand goods less food and energy			Final demand services	Final demand trade services	Final demand transportation and warehousing services	Final demand services less trade, transportation, and warehousing		
					Total	Finished goods less foods and energy (1982 =100)							
						Total	Private capital equipment						
SEASONALLY ADJUSTED													
2017													
January	111.9	110.1	114.5	99.3	112.1	197.2	170.1	112.6	114.2	115.1	111.6	114.9	111.3
February	111.9	110.5	115.4	100.2	112.3	197.3	170.2	112.3	113.0	115.5	111.7	114.9	111.2
March	112.1	110.7	116.1	99.0	112.7	197.8	170.6	112.5	113.7	114.3	111.8	115.0	111.4
April	112.6	111.1	117.6	99.2	113.0	198.4	170.8	113.0	114.0	115.1	112.4	115.5	111.9
May	112.6	110.4	116.5	96.1	113.0	198.5	170.7	113.4	114.9	115.2	112.6	115.7	112.1
June	112.6	110.4	117.0	95.5	113.1	198.8	170.9	113.5	114.6	115.5	112.8	115.8	112.2
July	112.7	110.4	117.1	95.6	113.1	198.9	170.9	113.6	114.8	115.2	112.9	117.3	112.4
August	113.1	111.0	116.5	98.4	113.3	199.2	171.0	113.9	115.4	115.7	113.0	117.4	112.6
September	113.5	111.8	116.6	102.0	113.4	199.1	171.0	114.0	115.3	116.7	113.2	117.3	112.7
October	113.9	112.1	116.8	102.0	113.8	200.0	171.2	114.5	116.2	117.1	113.5	118.0	113.2
November	114.3	112.9	117.0	105.5	114.1	200.5	171.5	114.7	115.9	118.2	113.8	117.9	113.4
December	114.3	113.1	116.6	106.4	114.2	200.6	171.5	114.5	115.4	117.5	113.9	118.0	113.3
2018													
January	114.8	113.6	116.6	107.7	114.5	200.9	171.6	115.1	115.7	117.8	114.5	119.0	113.8
February	115.1	114.1	116.1	109.8	114.8	201.3	171.9	115.3	115.8	119.2	114.7	119.0	114.1
March	115.4	114.3	118.3	107.5	115.2	201.8	172.3	115.6	115.8	119.9	115.1	119.1	114.4
April	115.5	114.4	117.0	108.5	115.5	202.2	172.5	115.7	116.0	120.2	115.2	120.4	114.6
May	116.0	115.1	117.3	110.9	115.7	202.7	172.9	116.1	116.6	120.8	115.4	120.5	114.9
June	116.4	115.3	115.8	112.2	116.0	203.1	173.4	116.6	117.4	121.9	115.7	120.7	115.3
July	116.5	115.3	115.7	111.5	116.3	203.7	173.8	116.7	117.0	122.4	116.0	121.2	115.5
August	116.5	115.4	115.4	111.9	116.5	204.1	174.4	116.7	116.7	122.6	116.1	121.4	115.5
September	116.6	115.5	115.2	112.3	116.6	204.5	174.8	116.8	116.3	124.0	116.4	121.4	115.6
October	117.5	116.4	116.1	114.8	116.9	205.2	175.1	117.6	118.2	124.6	116.7	123.8	116.3
November	117.3	115.8	117.5	109.7	117.1	205.6	175.4	117.7	118.3	125.5	116.7	124.0	116.5
December	117.2	114.9	119.7	102.9	117.2	205.8	175.6	118.0	119.0	125.2	116.8	124.1	116.7
2019													
January	117.0	114.2	118.0	99.3	117.4	206.7	176.5	118.0	118.6	125.5	116.9	125.0	116.8
February	117.3	114.8	117.9	102.5	117.5	206.9	176.7	118.1	118.5	124.6	117.3	125.0	116.9
March	117.7	115.7	118.3	106.5	117.6	207.2	176.8	118.3	118.8	124.2	117.5	125.2	117.0
April	118.3	116.3	118.3	110.0	117.6	207.3	176.8	118.9	119.8	124.8	117.9	126.9	117.5
May	118.4	115.9	118.0	108.4	117.6	207.7	177.2	119.2	119.7	125.5	118.3	127.1	117.7
June	118.3	115.4	118.5	104.9	117.5	207.8	177.3	119.3	120.0	125.7	118.3	127.1	117.8
July	118.5	115.6	118.6	105.5	117.7	208.1	177.6	119.5	120.1	126.1	118.5	128.0	117.9
August	118.6	115.2	118.1	104.3	117.6	208.2	177.6	119.9	121.3	125.8	118.7	128.1	118.3
September	118.3	115.0	118.5	103.0	117.6	208.3	177.8	119.5	120.0	125.2	118.7	128.2	118.0
October	118.7	115.6	119.8	104.8	117.7	208.5	177.8	119.8	120.9	125.6	118.7	128.6	118.2
November	118.5	116.0	121.5	104.9	117.8	208.8	178.0	119.3	119.3	125.4	118.8	128.7	117.9
December	118.8	116.1	121.0	105.5	117.8	208.8	178.1	119.7	119.9	127.9	118.8	128.9	118.2
2020													
January	119.2	116.4	121.3	105.9	118.1	208.8	178.3	120.2	120.3	126.5	119.5	129.6	118.6
February	118.6	115.6	119.2	103.1	118.2	209.4	178.6	119.6	119.3	126.0	119.2	129.7	118.2
March	118.0	113.6	119.1	92.6	118.2	209.4	178.7	119.8	120.5	122.0	119.3	129.6	118.3
April	116.7	110.4	118.7	76.6	117.9	209.9	179.0	119.3	121.8	117.8	118.3	130.3	117.9
May	117.2	112.0	125.5	79.4	117.8	209.9	179.0	119.4	121.5	119.4	118.4	130.2	117.9
June	117.6	112.5	119.3	87.0	117.9	209.9	179.0	119.6	121.4	120.9	118.7	130.1	118.2
July	118.2	113.1	118.2	90.6	118.3	210.4	179.3	120.2	122.5	120.2	119.2	130.8	118.7
August	118.4	113.5	117.9	91.5	118.6	210.7	179.6	120.4	122.4	119.2	119.6	130.5	118.9
September	118.7	113.9	119.9	91.2	118.9	210.8	179.9	120.6	122.0	119.9	120.1	130.4	119.1
October	119.4	114.5	122.4	91.7	118.9	210.8	179.8	121.4	123.8	121.2	120.2	130.2	119.7
November	119.4	115.0	122.6	93.3	119.3	211.4	180.0	121.2	122.9	120.6	120.4	130.4	119.6
December	119.8	116.0	120.9	97.9	119.9	211.6	180.3	121.2	122.1	120.4	120.9	130.4	119.8

Table 8-6. Producer Price Indexes for Goods and Services: Intermediate Demand

(November 2009 = 100, except as noted.)

Year and month	Intermediate demand by commodity type						Intermediate demand by production flow (Prices of inputs to indicated stage of production)			
	Processed goods (1982=100)	Unprocessed goods (1982=100)	Services	Construction	Processed materials less foods and energy (1982=100)	Unprocessed nonfood materials less energy (1982 =100)	Stage 4 intermediate demand	Stage 3 intermediate demand	Stage 2 intermediate demand	Stage 1 intermediate demand
NOT SEASONALLY ADJUSTED										
2010	183.4	212.2	101.1	101.1	180.8	329.1	102.0	104.2	103.5	106.2
2011	199.9	249.4	103.2	102.3	192.0	390.4	106.9	111.7	112.9	115.7
2012	200.7	241.4	105.3	103.8	192.6	369.6	108.6	112.7	110.7	114.7
2013	200.8	246.7	107.2	105.7	193.8	351.2	109.9	114.1	112.8	114.8
2014	201.9	249.3	108.9	108.0	195.2	345.7	111.2	116.9	112.2	116.1
2015	188.0	189.1	110.2	110.1	189.4	296.0	109.9	110.5	98.9	106.8
2016	182.2	173.4	112.1	111.7	186.9	288.0	109.8	107.3	98.3	104.2
2017	190.7	190.8	115.0	114.1	193.3	324.1	113.0	111.9	103.4	110.4
2018	200.9	200.1	118.6	116.2	201.8	340.7	117.0	116.9	108.5	116.7
2019	198.1	185.9	121.4	119.3	201.1	323.4	118.9	117.2	106.0	114.6
2020	192.5	167.6	121.9	119.8	198.9	346.0	119.4	113.5	102.0	111.0
2017										
January	186.7	193.4	113.4	113.5	189.8	314.4	111.2	109.7	103.2	107.8
February	188.0	192.8	114.0	113.5	191.3	318.4	111.8	110.6	103.2	108.7
March	188.3	188.3	114.0	113.7	192.3	325.3	111.8	111.1	101.8	109.1
April	189.4	191.9	114.6	113.8	193.2	323.5	112.5	111.4	103.2	109.6
May	189.9	191.6	114.6	114.0	193.2	321.6	112.7	111.8	102.7	109.5
June	190.8	191.8	115.2	114.2	193.3	323.4	113.2	112.4	102.8	110.1
July	190.8	192.0	115.1	114.3	193.0	325.5	113.2	112.2	102.9	110.3
August	191.5	187.6	115.5	114.3	193.5	328.2	113.5	112.1	102.9	111.1
September	192.7	186.8	115.3	114.4	194.0	332.5	113.6	112.3	103.3	111.4
October	192.9	186.2	116.0	114.6	194.8	323.7	113.8	112.5	104.0	111.6
November	193.5	192.0	116.3	114.6	195.7	323.1	114.1	113.5	104.9	112.3
December	193.9	194.7	116.1	114.7	195.8	329.8	114.1	113.5	105.5	112.6
2018										
January	195.4	199.7	117.0	115.3	197.0	341.9	114.9	114.4	106.7	114.0
February	197.0	203.0	117.5	115.3	198.2	342.8	115.4	115.4	107.7	114.7
March	197.3	198.2	117.7	115.5	199.5	347.2	115.8	115.7	106.5	115.0
April	198.5	199.9	118.0	115.6	200.1	349.6	116.2	116.1	107.4	115.7
May	201.7	205.7	118.2	115.9	201.6	349.3	116.9	117.7	108.9	117.0
June	203.4	204.2	118.6	116.0	202.5	350.8	117.5	118.5	108.8	118.0
July	203.6	204.8	119.0	116.1	203.1	342.4	117.7	118.4	109.7	118.2
August	203.8	194.6	119.0	116.5	203.7	332.3	117.6	117.3	109.0	117.8
September	204.3	194.8	119.1	116.5	204.4	328.2	117.7	117.5	109.4	117.8
October	204.6	200.3	119.8	117.0	204.7	330.6	118.1	118.7	110.2	118.6
November	202.2	194.4	119.9	117.2	204.0	333.5	117.8	117.6	108.4	117.7
December	199.4	202.0	119.7	117.4	202.7	339.2	117.6	115.8	109.3	116.1
2019										
January	197.8	193.6	120.3	117.9	202.9	333.4	117.7	116.0	107.4	114.9
February	198.2	189.4	120.5	118.7	202.6	334.3	118.0	116.2	106.6	115.1
March	199.6	190.6	120.9	118.8	202.6	339.6	118.6	117.3	106.9	116.2
April	200.2	193.4	121.6	119.0	202.4	332.9	119.2	118.9	107.3	116.4
May	200.2	188.8	121.5	119.4	202.0	321.3	119.2	118.9	106.8	115.6
June	198.8	183.8	121.7	118.9	201.3	319.3	119.2	117.9	105.4	114.5
July	198.9	184.9	121.7	119.6	200.8	321.5	119.4	117.7	105.7	114.7
August	197.7	179.7	122.2	119.8	200.0	318.5	119.5	117.3	105.1	114.2
September	197.2	177.4	122.1	119.8	199.6	314.2	119.4	116.4	105.2	113.7
October	196.8	177.9	121.5	119.9	200.1	311.6	118.9	116.8	104.5	113.2
November	196.4	184.4	121.4	120.0	199.7	311.9	118.9	116.7	105.5	113.1
December	196.0	187.2	121.7	120.0	199.1	322.3	119.2	116.7	105.8	113.6
2020										
January	195.8	186.5	122.3	120.9	199.5	339.4	119.6	117.2	105.4	113.8
February	194.2	174.6	122.1	121.0	199.3	336.0	119.1	115.6	103.4	112.4
March	191.7	160.9	122.2	119.6	199.2	339.9	118.8	114.0	100.7	111.0
April	185.0	138.1	120.2	119.4	196.3	328.0	116.8	107.9	96.2	106.3
May	185.8	150.8	119.7	119.4	195.2	329.8	117.1	109.3	97.6	105.6
June	188.8	158.5	120.1	119.4	196.0	332.7	117.9	111.2	99.4	107.9
July	191.6	159.2	120.6	119.5	197.1	333.8	118.8	112.4	100.1	109.5
August	193.2	163.4	121.7	119.5	198.6	342.5	119.7	113.1	101.5	110.8
September	194.1	170.1	122.8	119.6	200.2	356.2	120.6	113.6	103.0	112.0
October	195.0	173.7	123.6	119.6	200.7	357.8	120.9	114.9	103.6	112.5
November	196.1	185.5	123.6	119.7	201.0	367.7	121.0	115.7	105.5	113.6
December	198.9	189.6	124.2	119.8	203.7	388.4	122.1	116.6	107.3	116.6

Table 8-6. Producer Price Indexes for Goods and Services: Intermediate Demand—*Continued*

(November 2009 = 100, except as noted.)

Year and month	Intermediate demand by commodity type						Intermediate demand by production flow (Prices of inputs to indicated stage of production)			
	Processed goods (1982=100)	Unprocessed goods (1982=100)	Services	Construction	Processed materials less foods and energy (1982=100)	Unprocessed nonfood materials less energy (1982 =100)	Stage 4 intermediate demand	Stage 3 intermediate demand	Stage 2 intermediate demand	Stage 1 intermediate demand
SEASONALLY ADJUSTED										
2016										
January	187.4	193.5	113.4	113.5	189.9	314.3	111.3	110.1	103.2	108.1
February	188.8	192.9	113.8	113.5	191.3	317.6	111.8	111.0	103.1	109.0
March	188.9	186.6	113.9	113.7	192.1	324.2	112.0	111.1	101.6	109.3
April	189.9	190.5	114.4	113.8	193.0	321.9	112.5	111.2	103.0	109.7
May	189.5	189.1	114.6	114.0	192.9	319.6	112.5	111.2	102.6	109.4
June	189.6	189.1	115.0	114.2	193.1	321.5	112.8	111.5	102.6	109.5
July	189.6	189.8	115.1	114.3	192.9	324.5	112.8	111.5	102.7	109.7
August	190.6	189.1	115.4	114.3	193.5	329.4	113.2	111.9	102.9	110.6
September	192.0	189.8	115.5	114.4	194.1	334.7	113.4	112.5	103.5	111.3
October	193.1	188.9	116.2	114.6	195.0	325.7	114.0	113.0	104.2	111.9
November	194.4	194.0	116.4	114.6	195.9	325.2	114.5	114.1	105.1	112.6
December	194.9	196.3	116.6	114.7	196.2	330.9	114.6	114.4	105.8	113.2
2017										
January	196.3	199.5	116.9	115.3	197.2	342.0	115.1	114.8	106.7	114.4
February	198.1	202.6	117.3	115.3	198.2	341.8	115.5	115.8	107.6	115.1
March	198.1	196.4	117.6	115.5	199.3	345.9	115.9	115.7	106.3	115.2
April	199.2	198.6	117.9	115.6	199.9	347.9	116.3	116.0	107.2	115.9
May	201.1	203.3	118.2	115.9	201.4	347.1	116.8	116.9	108.7	116.8
June	202.1	201.7	118.4	116.0	202.3	348.9	117.1	117.6	108.6	117.3
July	202.3	203.1	119.0	116.1	203.0	341.4	117.4	117.6	109.6	117.5
August	202.7	196.1	118.9	116.5	203.7	333.7	117.4	117.2	109.0	117.3
September	203.3	197.8	119.2	116.5	204.4	330.4	117.6	117.7	109.7	117.5
October	204.7	202.8	119.9	117.0	204.8	332.7	118.3	119.1	110.4	118.7
November	203.0	196.2	120.0	117.2	204.1	335.7	118.1	118.1	108.7	118.0
December	200.2	203.1	120.1	117.4	203.1	340.2	118.0	116.6	109.6	116.6
2018										
January	198.5	192.8	120.3	117.9	203.0	333.3	117.8	116.1	107.4	115.2
February	199.2	188.5	120.3	118.7	202.6	333.2	118.1	116.5	106.5	115.5
March	200.3	188.9	120.8	118.8	202.4	338.4	118.7	117.3	106.7	116.5
April	200.9	192.8	121.4	119.0	202.2	331.3	119.2	118.9	107.1	116.6
May	199.7	186.9	121.5	119.4	201.8	319.4	119.0	118.3	106.6	115.3
June	197.6	181.9	121.5	118.9	201.1	317.3	118.8	117.2	105.2	113.9
July	197.6	183.5	121.7	119.6	200.7	320.3	119.1	117.0	105.6	114.0
August	196.6	181.1	122.2	119.8	200.0	319.9	119.2	117.1	105.2	113.8
September	196.4	180.6	122.3	119.8	199.7	316.7	119.3	116.7	105.4	113.5
October	196.8	180.1	121.6	119.9	200.2	313.6	119.0	117.1	104.7	113.3
November	197.2	185.7	121.5	120.0	199.8	314.0	119.1	117.1	105.8	113.4
December	196.9	188.0	122.1	120.0	199.4	323.3	119.6	117.5	106.1	114.0
2019										
January	196.6	185.6	122.2	120.9	199.6	339.2	119.7	117.3	105.4	114.2
February	195.3	173.6	121.9	121.0	199.4	334.9	119.2	116.0	103.3	112.8
March	192.2	159.5	122.0	119.6	199.0	338.9	118.8	113.9	100.4	111.2
April	185.5	137.7	120.0	119.4	196.1	326.7	116.9	108.0	96.0	106.4
May	185.5	149.3	119.6	119.4	195.0	328.3	117.0	108.9	97.4	105.5
June	187.8	157.4	120.0	119.4	195.9	331.1	117.6	110.8	99.2	107.4
July	190.4	158.4	120.6	119.5	197.1	332.8	118.5	112.0	100.0	109.0
August	192.2	164.8	121.6	119.5	198.6	343.7	119.5	113.0	101.5	110.4
September	193.4	173.3	122.9	119.6	200.2	358.6	120.5	114.0	103.3	111.8
October	195.1	175.5	123.7	119.6	200.8	359.7	121.0	115.2	103.8	112.6
November	196.9	186.6	123.7	119.7	201.2	369.9	121.3	116.0	105.7	113.8
December	199.7	190.5	124.6	119.8	204.1	389.5	122.4	117.3	107.6	117.0

Table 8-7. Producer Price Indexes by Major Commodity Groups

(1982 = 100.)

Year and month	All commodities	Farm products	Processed foods and feeds	Industrial commodities													
				Total	Textile products and apparel	Hides, leather, and related products	Fuels and related products and power	Chemicals and allied products	Rubber and plastics products	Lumber and wood products	Pulp, paper, and allied products	Metals and metal products	Machinery and equipment	Furniture and household durables	Nonmetallic mineral products	Transportation equipment	Miscellaneous products
1950	27.3	44.0	33.2	25.0	50.2	32.9	12.6	30.4	35.6	31.4	25.7	22.0	22.6	40.9	23.5	. . .	28.6
1951	30.4	51.2	36.9	27.6	56.0	37.7	13.0	34.8	43.7	34.1	30.5	24.5	25.3	44.4	25.0	. . .	30.3
1952	29.6	48.4	36.4	26.9	50.5	30.5	13.0	33.0	39.6	33.2	29.7	24.5	25.3	43.5	25.0	. . .	30.2
1953	29.2	43.8	34.8	27.2	49.3	31.0	13.4	33.4	36.9	33.1	29.6	25.3	25.9	44.4	26.0	. . .	31.0
1954	29.3	43.2	35.4	27.2	48.2	29.5	13.2	33.8	37.5	32.5	29.6	25.5	26.3	44.9	26.6	. . .	31.3
1955	29.3	40.5	33.8	27.8	48.2	29.4	13.2	33.7	42.4	34.1	30.4	27.2	27.2	45.1	27.3	. . .	31.3
1956	30.3	40.0	33.8	29.1	48.2	31.2	13.6	33.9	43.0	34.6	32.4	29.6	29.3	46.3	28.5	. . .	31.7
1957	31.2	41.1	34.8	29.9	48.3	31.2	14.3	34.6	42.8	32.8	33.0	30.2	31.4	47.5	29.6	. . .	32.6
1958	31.6	42.9	36.5	30.0	47.4	31.6	13.7	34.9	42.8	32.5	33.4	30.0	32.1	47.9	29.9	. . .	33.3
1959	31.7	40.2	35.6	30.5	48.1	35.9	13.7	34.8	42.6	34.7	33.7	30.6	32.8	48.0	30.3	. . .	33.4
1960	31.7	40.1	35.6	30.5	48.6	34.6	13.9	34.8	42.7	33.5	34.0	30.6	33.0	47.8	30.4	. . .	33.6
1961	31.6	39.7	36.2	30.4	47.8	34.9	14.0	34.5	41.1	32.0	33.0	30.5	33.0	47.5	30.5	. . .	33.7
1962	31.7	40.4	36.5	30.4	48.2	35.3	14.0	33.9	39.9	32.2	33.4	30.2	33.0	47.2	30.5	. . .	33.9
1963	31.6	39.6	36.8	30.3	48.2	34.3	13.9	33.5	40.1	32.8	33.1	30.3	33.1	46.9	30.3	. . .	34.2
1964	31.6	39.0	36.7	30.5	48.5	34.4	13.5	33.6	39.6	33.5	33.0	31.1	33.3	47.1	30.4	. . .	34.4
1965	32.3	40.7	38.0	30.9	48.8	35.9	13.8	33.9	39.7	33.7	33.3	32.0	33.7	46.8	30.4	. . .	34.7
1966	33.3	43.7	40.2	31.5	48.9	39.4	14.1	34.0	40.5	35.2	34.2	32.8	34.7	47.4	30.7	. . .	35.3
1967	33.4	41.3	39.8	32.0	48.9	38.1	14.4	34.2	41.4	35.1	34.6	33.2	35.9	48.3	31.2	. . .	36.2
1968	34.2	42.3	40.6	32.8	50.7	39.3	14.3	34.1	42.8	39.8	35.0	34.0	37.0	49.7	32.4	. . .	37.0
1969	35.6	45.0	42.7	33.9	51.8	41.5	14.6	34.2	43.6	44.0	36.0	36.0	38.2	50.7	33.6	40.4	38.1
1970	36.9	45.8	44.6	35.2	52.4	42.0	15.3	35.0	44.9	39.9	37.5	38.7	40.0	51.9	35.3	41.9	39.8
1971	38.1	46.6	45.5	36.5	53.3	43.4	16.6	35.6	45.2	44.7	38.1	39.4	41.4	53.1	38.2	44.2	40.8
1972	39.8	51.6	48.0	37.8	55.5	50.0	17.1	35.6	45.3	50.7	39.3	40.9	42.3	53.8	39.4	45.5	41.5
1973	45.0	72.7	58.9	40.3	60.5	54.5	19.4	37.6	46.6	62.2	42.3	44.0	43.7	55.7	40.7	46.1	43.3
1974	53.5	77.4	68.0	49.2	68.0	55.2	30.1	50.2	56.4	64.5	52.5	57.0	50.0	61.8	47.8	50.3	48.1
1975	58.4	77.0	72.6	54.9	67.4	56.5	35.4	62.0	62.2	62.1	59.0	61.5	57.9	67.5	54.4	56.7	53.4
1976	61.1	78.8	70.8	58.4	72.4	63.9	38.3	64.0	66.0	72.2	62.1	65.0	61.3	70.3	58.2	60.5	55.6
1977	64.9	79.4	74.0	62.5	75.3	68.3	43.6	65.9	69.4	83.0	64.6	69.3	65.2	73.2	62.6	64.6	59.4
1978	69.9	87.7	80.6	67.0	78.1	76.1	46.5	68.0	72.4	96.9	67.7	75.3	70.3	77.5	69.6	69.5	66.7
1979	78.7	99.6	88.5	75.7	82.5	96.1	58.9	76.0	80.5	105.5	75.9	86.0	76.7	82.8	77.6	75.3	75.5
1980	89.8	102.9	95.9	88.0	89.7	94.7	82.8	89.0	90.1	101.5	86.3	95.0	86.0	90.7	88.4	82.9	93.6
1981	98.0	105.2	98.9	97.4	97.6	99.3	100.2	98.4	96.4	102.8	94.8	99.6	94.4	95.9	96.7	94.3	96.1
1982	100.0	100.0	100.0	100.0	100.0	100.0	100.0	100.0	100.0	100.0	100.0	100.0	100.0	100.0	100.0	100.0	100.0
1983	101.3	102.4	101.8	101.1	100.3	103.2	95.9	100.3	100.8	107.9	103.3	101.8	102.7	103.4	101.6	102.8	104.8
1984	103.7	105.5	105.4	103.3	102.7	109.0	94.8	102.9	102.3	108.0	110.3	104.8	105.1	105.7	105.4	105.2	107.0
1985	103.2	95.1	103.5	103.7	102.9	108.9	91.4	103.7	101.9	106.6	113.3	104.4	107.2	107.1	108.6	107.9	109.4
1986	100.2	92.9	105.4	100.0	103.2	113.0	69.8	102.6	101.9	107.2	116.1	103.2	108.8	108.2	110.0	110.5	111.6
1987	102.8	95.5	107.9	102.6	105.1	120.4	70.2	106.4	103.0	112.8	121.8	107.1	110.4	109.9	110.0	112.5	114.9
1988	106.9	104.9	112.7	106.3	109.2	131.4	66.7	116.3	109.3	118.9	130.4	118.7	113.2	113.1	111.2	114.3	120.2
1989	112.2	110.9	117.8	111.6	112.3	136.3	72.9	123.0	112.6	126.7	137.8	124.1	117.4	116.9	112.6	117.7	126.5
1990	116.3	112.2	121.9	115.8	115.0	141.7	82.3	123.6	113.6	129.7	141.2	122.9	120.7	119.2	114.7	121.5	134.2
1991	116.5	105.7	121.9	116.5	116.3	138.9	81.2	125.6	115.1	132.1	142.9	120.2	123.0	121.2	117.2	126.4	140.8
1992	117.2	103.6	122.1	117.4	117.8	140.4	80.4	125.9	115.1	146.6	145.2	119.2	123.4	122.2	117.3	130.4	145.3
1993	118.9	107.1	124.0	119.0	118.0	143.7	80.0	128.2	116.0	174.0	147.3	119.2	124.0	123.7	120.0	133.7	145.4
1994	120.4	106.3	125.5	120.7	118.3	148.5	77.8	132.1	117.6	180.0	152.5	124.8	125.1	126.1	124.2	137.2	141.9
1995	124.7	107.4	127.0	125.5	120.8	153.7	78.0	142.5	124.3	178.1	172.2	134.5	126.6	128.2	129.0	139.7	145.4
1996	127.7	122.4	133.3	127.3	122.4	150.5	85.8	142.1	123.8	176.1	168.7	131.0	126.5	130.4	131.0	141.7	147.7
1997	127.6	112.9	134.0	127.7	122.6	154.2	86.1	143.6	123.2	183.8	167.9	131.8	125.9	130.8	133.2	141.6	150.9
1998	124.4	104.6	131.6	124.8	122.9	148.0	75.3	143.9	122.6	179.1	171.7	127.8	124.9	131.3	135.4	141.2	156.0
1999	125.5	98.4	131.1	126.5	121.1	146.0	80.5	144.2	122.5	183.6	174.1	124.6	124.3	131.7	138.9	141.8	166.6
2000	132.7	99.5	133.1	134.8	121.4	151.5	103.5	151.0	125.5	178.2	183.7	128.1	124.0	132.6	142.5	143.8	170.8
2001	134.2	103.8	137.3	135.7	121.3	158.4	105.3	151.8	127.2	174.4	184.8	125.4	123.7	133.2	144.3	145.2	181.3
2002	131.1	99.0	136.2	132.4	119.9	157.6	93.2	151.9	126.8	173.3	185.9	125.9	122.9	133.5	146.2	144.6	182.4
2003	138.1	111.5	143.4	139.1	119.8	162.3	112.9	161.8	130.1	177.4	190.0	129.2	121.9	133.8	148.2	145.7	179.6
2004	146.7	123.3	151.2	147.6	121.0	164.5	126.9	174.4	133.8	195.6	195.7	149.6	121.1	135.1	153.2	148.6	183.2
2005	157.4	118.5	153.1	160.2	122.8	165.4	156.4	192.0	143.8	196.5	202.6	160.8	123.7	139.4	164.2	151.0	195.1
2006	164.7	117.0	153.8	168.8	124.5	168.4	166.7	205.8	153.8	194.4	209.8	181.6	126.2	142.6	179.9	152.6	205.6
2007	172.6	143.4	165.1	175.1	125.8	173.6	177.6	214.8	155.0	192.4	216.9	193.5	127.3	144.7	186.2	155.0	210.3
2008	189.6	161.3	180.5	192.3	128.9	173.1	214.6	245.5	165.9	191.3	226.8	213.0	129.7	148.9	197.1	158.6	216.6
2009	172.9	134.6	176.2	174.8	129.5	157.0	158.7	229.4	165.2	182.8	225.6	186.8	131.3	153.1	202.4	162.2	217.5
2010	184.7	151.0	182.3	187.0	131.7	181.4	185.8	246.6	170.7	192.7	236.9	207.6	131.1	153.2	201.8	163.4	221.5
2011	201.0	186.7	197.5	202.0	141.7	199.9	215.9	275.1	182.7	194.7	245.1	225.9	132.7	156.4	205.0	166.1	229.2
2012	202.2	192.5	205.2	202.1	142.2	202.3	212.1	276.6	186.9	201.6	244.2	219.9	134.2	160.6	211.0	169.8	235.6
2013	203.4	195.3	208.3	203.0	143.4	217.9	211.8	279.2	189.0	214.9	248.8	213.5	135.2	161.1	216.9	171.8	239.5
2014	205.3	197.4	216.5	204.1	145.5	229.1	209.8	280.9	190.2	224.2	250.5	215.0	136.2	163.2	223.7	174.1	243.0
2015	190.4	173.8	209.1	188.8	144.1	210.4	160.5	266.0	187.0	221.9	248.8	200.3	136.9	164.7	228.9	176.5	247.4
2016	185.4	157.0	203.5	184.6	143.3	195.1	145.9	265.1	184.6	222.7	247.7	194.3	136.9	165.1	233.3	177.4	252.1
2017	193.5	161.8	205.4	193.7	145.1	192.1	163.7	280.8	189.0	230.4	254.6	207.8	137.9	166.9	238.6	179.0	257.6
2018	202.0	160.9	206.1	203.7	149.3	180.4	181.6	295.1	195.1	243.9	260.0	223.6	140.3	171.6	247.3	181.2	264.0
2019	199.8	161.5	209.1	200.7	150.7	165.9	168.7	289.1	196.0	236.7	259.4	221.3	143.3	176.4	253.2	182.9	274.2
2020	194.4	157.9	212.0	193.9	149.4	157.1	144.0	279.8	194.2	254.5	259.9	219.9	144.9	179.1	257.5	183.8	281.6

. . . = Not available.

NOTES AND DEFINITIONS

CHAPTER 8: PRICE INDEXES

This chapter presents price indexes (Consumer and Producer) from two major price collection systems, both conducted by the U.S. Bureau of Labor Statistics. Effective on February 26, 2015, the Bureau of Labor Statistics began utilizing a new estimation system for the Consumer Price Index. The new estimation system, the first major improvement to the existing system in over 25 years. This system is redesigned, state-of-the-art with improved flexibility and review capabilities.

In 2014 the Producer Price Index system was expanded to include services and construction as well as goods. A new index for "Final Demand" for goods, services and construction, with more than double the scope, is now presented alongside the familiar Finished Goods index. The expanded system is only available beginning in November 2009, and the historical Producer Price Indexes for goods—with data going back to 1913—are also maintained and carried forward. See the Notes and Definitions for Tables 8-5 through 8-7, below, for further information.

Tables 8-1 through 8-4

Average Price Data

SOURCES: U.S. DEPARTMENT OF LABOR, BUREAU OF LABOR STATISTICS (BLS) AND U.S. DEPARTMENT OF COMMERCE, BUREAU OF ECONOMIC ANALYSIS (BEA)

With the release of the Consumer Price Index (CPI) each month, the Bureau of Labor Statistics (BLS) also publishes average retail prices for select utility, automotive fuel, and food items. Although average prices are calculated from the price observations collected for the CPI, they serve a different purpose. The CPI measures price change while average prices provide estimates of price levels. Specifically, average prices are estimates of the average price paid by the consumer for a good or service.

At the U.S. level, the BLS publishes approximately 70 average prices for food items, 6 for utility gas (natural gas) and electricity, and 5 for automotive fuels. Average prices are estimates of the average price paid by the consumer, not estimates of price change. They provide an estimate of the price levels in a given month which cannot be determined from an index. Average prices can be used for comparing price levels of different items in the same month.

Consumer Price Indexes

The Consumer Price Index (CPI), which is compiled by the Bureau of Labor Statistics (BLS), was originally conceived as a

statistical measure of the average change in the cost to consumers of a market basket of goods and services purchased by urban wage earners and clerical workers. In 1978, its scope was broadened to also provide a measure of the change in the cost of the average market basket for all urban consumers. There was still a demand for a wage-earner index, so both versions have been calculated and published since then. The most commonly cited measure in this system is the Consumer Price Index for All Urban Consumers (CPI-U). The wage-earner alternative, used according to law for calculating cost of living adjustments in many government programs, including Social Security, and also used by choice of the contracting parties in wage agreements, is called the Consumer Price Index for Urban Wage Earners and Clerical Workers (CPI-W). Both are presented by the BLS back to 1913, and reproduced in *Business Statistics*; however, the movements (percent changes) in the two indexes before 1978 are identical and are based on the wage-earner market basket. (The pre-1978 levels of the two indexes differ because of differences between 1978 and the reference base period.)

These CPIs have typically been called "cost-of-living" indexes, even though the original fixed market basket concept does not correspond to economists' definition of a cost-of- living index, which is the cost of maintaining a constant standard of living or level of satisfaction. In recent years, the concept measured in practice in the CPI has developed into something intended to be closer to the theoretical definition of a cost-of-living index. In addition, a new variation of the CPI—the Chained Consumer Price Index for All Urban Consumers (C-CPI-U)—is intended to provide an even closer approximation.

The reference base for the total BLS Consumer Price Index and most of its components is currently 1982–1984 = 100. However, new products that have been introduced into the index since January 1982 are shown on later reference bases, as is the entire C-CPI-U.

Price indexes for personal consumption expenditures (PCE) are calculated and published by the Bureau of Economic Analysis (BEA) as a part of the national income and product accounts (NIPAs). (See Chapters 1 and 4 and their notes and definitions.) Monthly, quarterly, and annual values are all available. The reference base for these indexes is the average in the NIPA base year, 2009. These indexes differ in a number of other respects from the CPIs, and are often emphasized by the Federal Reserve in its analyses of the nation's economy. The Federal Reserve is mandated to maximize employment (see Chapter 10) and maintain price stability as measured by the Consumer Price Index (CPI). The target inflation rate is 2 percent. Four important NIPA aggregate price indexes are shown in Tables 8-3 and 8-4 for convenient comparison with the CPIs. See the definitions for those tables for more information.

The CPI-U and the CPI-W

The *CPI-U*, which is displayed in Tables 8-1 through 8-4 and also provides all of the component category sub-indexes shown in Table 8-2, uses the consumption patterns for all urban consumers, who currently comprise about 89 percent of the population.

A slightly different index that is widely used for adjusting wages and government benefits is the *CPI-W*, of which the all-items total is shown in each of Tables 8-1 through 8-4. It represents the buying habits of only urban wage earners and clerical workers, who currently comprise about 28 percent of the population. The weights are derived from the same Consumer Expenditure Surveys (CES) used for the CPI-U weights, and are changed on the same schedule. However, they include only consumers from the specified categories instead of all urban consumers.

Beginning with February 2020, the weights in both indexes are based on consumer expenditures in the 2018-2019 period In February 2016, the weights in both indexes are based on consumer expenditures in the 2014-2015 period. In January 2012, the weights in both indexes are based on consumer expenditures in the 2009–2010 period. From January 2010 to December 2011, 2007–2008 weights were used; from January 2008 to December 2009, 2005–2006 weights; from January 2006 to December 2007, 2003–2004 weights; from January 2004 to December 2005, 2001–2002 weights; from January 2002 to December 2003, 1999–2000 weights; and from January 1998 to December 2001, 1993–1995 weights. The weights will continue to be updated at two-year intervals, with new weights introduced in the January indexes of each even-numbered year. Previously, new weights were introduced only at the time of a major revision, which translated into a lag of a decade or more.

Specifically, the CPI weights for 1964 through 1977 were derived from reported expenditures of a sample of wageearner and clericalworker families and individuals in 1960–1961 and adjusted for price changes between the survey dates and 1963. Weights for the 1978–1986 period were derived from a survey undertaken during the 1972–1974 period and adjusted for price change between the survey dates and December 1977. For 1987 through 1997, the spending patterns reflected in the CPI were derived from a survey undertaken during the 1982–1984 period. The reported expenditures were adjusted for price change between the survey dates and December 1986.

The CPI was overhauled and updated in the latest major revision, which took effect in January 1998. In addition, new products and improved methods are regularly introduced into the index, usually in January.

The latest change in methods was the introduction of a geometric mean formula for calculating many of the basic components of the index. Beginning with the index for January 1999, this formula is used for categories comprising approximately 61 percent of total consumer spending. The new formula allows for the possibility that some consumers may react to changing relative prices within a category by substituting items whose relative prices have declined for products whose relative prices have risen, while maintaining their overall level of satisfaction. The geometric mean formula is not used for a few categories in which consumer substitution in the short term is not feasible, currently housing rent and utilities.

The CPI-U was introduced in 1978. Before that time, only CPI-W data were available. The movements of the CPI-U before 1978 are therefore based on the changes in the CPI-W. However, the index levels are different because the two indexes differed in the 1982–1984 base period.

Because the official CPI-U and CPI-W are so widely used in "escalation"—the calculation of cost-of-living adjustments for wages and other private contracts, and for government payments and tax parameters—these price indexes are not retrospectively revised to incorporate new information and methods. (An exception is occasionally made for outright error, which happened in September 2000 and affected the data for January through August of that year.) Instead, the new information and methods of calculation are introduced in the current index and affect future index changes only. In Tables 8-3 and 8-4, PCE indexes, which are subject to routine revision, and special CPI indexes that have been retrospectively revised are presented. These indexes can be used by researchers to provide more consistent historical information.

Notes on the CPI data

The CPI is based on prices of food, clothing, shelter, fuel, utilities, transportation, medical care, and other goods and services that people buy for daytoday living. The quantity and quality of these priced items are kept essentially constant between revisions to ensure that only price changes will be measured. All taxes directly associated with the purchase and use of these items, such as sales and property taxes, are included in the index; the effects of income and payroll tax changes are not included.

Data are collected on about 83,400 individually defined goods and services from about 22,000 retail and service establishments and about 6,000 housing units in 75 urban areas across the country. These data are used to develop the U.S. city average.

Periodic major revisions of the indexes update the content and weights of the market basket of goods and services; update the statistical sample of urban areas, outlets, and unique items used in calculating the CPI; and improve the statistical methods used. In addition, retail outlets and items are resampled on a rotating 5-year basis. Adjustments for changing quality are made at times of major product changes, such as the annual auto model changeover. Other methodological changes are introduced from time to time.

The Consumer Expenditure Survey (CES) provides the weights—that is, the relative importance—used to combine the individual price changes into subtotals and totals. This survey is composed of two separate surveys: an interview survey and a diary survey, both of which are conducted by the Census Bureau for BLS. Each expenditure reported in the two surveys is classified into a series of detailed categories, which are then combined into expenditure classes and ultimately into major expenditure groups. CPI data as of 1998 are grouped into eight such categories: (1) food and beverages, (2) housing, (3) apparel, (4) transportation, (5) medical care, (6) entertainment (7) education and communication, and (8) other goods and services.

Seasonally adjusted national CPI indexes are published for selected series for which there is a significant seasonal pattern of price change. The factors currently in use were derived by the X13ARIMA-SEATS seasonal adjustment method. Some series with extreme or sharp movements are seasonally adjusted using Intervention Analysis Seasonal Adjustment. Seasonally adjusted indexes and seasonal factors for the preceding five years are updated annually based on data through the previous December. Due to these revisions, BLS advises against the use of seasonally adjusted data for escalation. Detailed descriptions of seasonal adjustment procedures are available upon request from BLS.

BLS estimates the "standard error"—the error due to collecting data from a sample instead of the universe—of the one-month percent change in the not-seasonally-adjusted U.S. all-items index in 2013 was 0.03 percentage point. This means that for the 2013 median 0.12 percent change in the All Items CPI-U, BLS is 95 percent confident that the actual percent change based on all retail prices would fall between 0.06 and 0.18 percent. Monthly percent changes in the seasonally adjusted indexes, in contrast, may be revised by 0.1 percentage point when reviewed at the end of the year, and occasionally by even more.

CPI Definitions

Definitions of the major CPI groupings were modified beginning with the data for January 1998. These modifications were carried back to 1993. The following definitions are the current definitions currently used for the CPI components.

The *food and beverage index* includes both food at home and food away from home (restaurant meals and other food bought and eaten away from home).

The *housing index* measures changes in rental costs and expenses connected with the acquisition and operation of a home. The CPIU, beginning with data for January 1983, and the CPIW, beginning with data for January 1985, reflect a change in the methodology used to compute the homeownership component. A rental equivalence measure replaced an assetprice approach, which included purchase prices and interest costs. The intent of the change was to separate shelter costs from the investment component of homeownership, so that the index would only reflect the cost of the shelter services provided by owner-occupied

homes. In addition to measures of the cost of shelter, the housing category includes insurance, fuel, utilities, and household furnishings and operations.

The *apparel index* includes the purchase of apparel and footwear.

The *private transportation index* includes prices paid by urban consumers for such items as new and used automobiles and other vehicles, gasoline, motor oil, tires, repairs and maintenance, insurance, registration fees, driver's licenses, parking fees, and the like. Auto finance charges, like mortgage interest payments, are considered to be a cost of asset acquisition, not of current consumption. Therefore, they are no longer included in the CPI. City bus, streetcar, subway, taxicab, intercity bus, airplane, and railroad coach fares are some of the components of the *public transportation index*.

The *medical care index* includes prices for professional medical services, hospital and related services, prescription and nonprescription drugs, and other medical care commodities. The weight for the portion of health insurance premiums that is used to cover the costs of these medical goods and services is distributed among the items; the weight for the portion of health insurance costs attributable to administrative expenses and profits of insurance providers constitutes a separate health insurance item. Effective with the January 1997 data, the method of calculating the hospital cost component was changed from the pricing of individual commodities and services to a more comprehensive cost-of-treatment approach.

Recreation includes components formerly listed in housing, apparel, entertainment, and "other goods and services."

Education and communication is a new group including components formerly categorized in housing and "other goods and services," such as college tuition and books, telephone and internet services, and computers.

Other goods and services now includes tobacco, personal care, and miscellaneous.

Table 8-2

Purchasing Power of the Dollar

SOURCE: U.S. DEPARTMENT OF LABOR, BUREAU OF LABOR STATISTICS (BLS)

The purchasing power of the dollar measures changes in the quantity of goods and services a dollar will buy at a particular date compared with a selected base date. It must be defined in terms of the following: (1) the specific commodities and services that are to be purchased with the dollar; (2) the market level (producer, retail, etc.) at which they are purchased; and (3) the dates for which the comparison is to be made. Thus, the purchasing power of the dollar for a selected period, compared with another period, may be measured in terms of a single commodity or a large group of commodities such as all goods and services purchased by consumers at retail.

The purchasing power of the dollar is computed by dividing the price index number for the base period by the price index number for the comparison date and expressing the result in dollars and cents. The base period is the period in which the price index equals 100; the average purchasing power in that base period—1982–1984 in the case of the measure shown here—is therefore $1.00.

Purchasing power estimates in terms of both the CPI-U and the CPI-W are calculated by BLS, based on indexes not adjusted for seasonal variation, and published in the CPI press release. The CPI-U version is shown here.

Alternative price measures in Tables 8-3 and 8-4

Table 8-3 shows the all-items CPI-U and CPI-W, along with a number of other indexes that various analysts of price trends have preferred as measures of the price level. Table 8-4 shows the inflation rates (percent changes in price levels) implied by each of the indexes in Table 8-3.

As food and energy prices are volatile and frequently determined by forces separate from monetary aggregate demand pressures, many analysts prefer an index of prices excluding those components. Indexes *excluding food and energy* are known as *core* indexes, and inflation rates calculated from them are known as *core inflation rates.*

The *CPI-U-X1* is a special experimental version of the CPI that researchers have used to provide a more historically consistent series. As explained above, the official CPI-U treated homeownership on an asset-price basis until January 1983. It then changed to a rental equivalence method. The CPI-U-X1 incorporates a rental equivalence approach to homeowners' costs for the years 1967–1982 as well. It is rebased to the December 1982 value of the CPI-U (1982–1984 = 100); thus, it is identical to the CPI-U in December 1982 and all subsequent periods, as can be seen in Table 8-3. For this reason, it is not updated or published in the CPI news release or on the BLS Web site. We continue to present it here because it provides the only available data before 1978 on changes in an improved and more consistent CPI.

The *CPI-E* is an experimental re-weighting of components of the CPI-U to represent price change for the goods and services purchased by Americans age 62 years and over, who accounted for 16.5 percent of the total number of urban consumer units in the 2001–2002 CES.

BLS does not consider the CPI-E to be an ideal measure of price change for older Americans. Because the sample is small, the sampling error in the weights is greater than the error in the all-urban index. The products and outlets sampled are those characteristic of the general urban population rather than older residents. In addition, senior discounts are not included in the prices collected. Such discounts are included—appropriately—in the weights, which are based on the expenditures reported by the older consumers' households. Therefore, such discounts are only a problem if they do not move proportionately to general prices.

The *CPI-U-RS* is a "research series" CPI that retroactively incorporates estimates of the effects of most of the methodological changes implemented since 1978, including the rental equivalence method, new or improved quality adjustments, and improvement of formulas to eliminate bias and allow for some consumer substitution within categories. This index is calculated from 1977 onward. Its reference base is December 1977 = 100. Thus, although it generally shows less increase than the official index, its current levels are considerably higher because the earlier reference base period had lower prices. Unlike the official CPIs and the CPI-U-X1, its historical values will be revised each time a significant change is made in the calculation of the current index. This index is not seasonally adjusted and is not included in the CPI news release. It is available on the BLS Web site, along with an explanation and background material. The CPI-U-RS is used by BLS in the calculation of historical trends in real compensation per hour in its Productivity and Costs system; see Table 9-3 and its notes and definitions. It is also now used by the Census Bureau to convert household incomes into constant dollars, as seen in Chapter 3. And it is used by the editor in some analytical calculations in this volume.

The *C-CPI-U* (Chained Consumer Price Index for All Urban Consumers) is a new, supplemental index that has been published in the monthly CPI news release since August 2002. It is available only from December 1999 to date and is calculated with the base December 1999 = 100; it is not seasonally adjusted. It is designed to be a still-closer approximation to a true cost-of-living index than the CPI-U and the CPI-W, in that it assumes that consumers substitute between as well as within categories as relative prices change, in order to maintain a fixed basket of "consumer satisfaction."

The C-CPI-U is technically a "superlative" index, using a method known as the "Tornqvist formula" to incorporate the composition of consumer spending in the current period as well as in the earlier base period. (All of the other Consumer Price Indexes use a "Laspeyres" formula; see the General Notes at the beginning of this volume.) As it requires consumer expenditure data for the current as well as the earlier period, its final version can only be calculated after the expenditure data become available—about two years later—and is approximated in more recent periods by making more extensive use of the geometric mean formula (see above). With the release of January 2014 data, the indexes for 2012 were revised to their final form, and the initial indexes for 2013 were revised to "interim" levels, shown in Tables 8-3 and 8-4.

Personal consumption expenditure (PCE) chain-type price indexes are calculated by the Bureau of Economic Analysis (BEA) in the framework of the national income and product accounts (NIPAs). (See the notes and definitions for Chapters 1 and 4.) The scope of NIPA PCE is broader than the scope of the CPI. PCE includes the rural as well as the urban population and also covers the consumption spending of nonprofit entities. The CPI includes only consumer out-of-pocket cash spending, whereas PCE includes some imputed servi and includes expenditures financed by government and private insurance, particularly in the medical care area. For this reason, there is a large difference between the relatively small weight of medical care spending in the CPI and the markedly greater percentage of PCE that is accounted for by total medical care spending. Housing, on the other hand, has a somewhat smaller weight in PCE while all non-housing components have a higher weight. The reason for this is that the CES—the survey on which the CPI weights are based—tends to report housing expenditures accurately and somewhat underestimate other spending. This suggests that the weight of housing relative to all other products may be overestimated in the CPI but measured more correctly in the PCE price index.

PCE chain-type indexes use the expenditure weights of both the earlier and the later period to determine the aggregate price change between the two periods. (See the notes and definitions for Chapter 1, as well as the General Notes on index number formulas.) Thus, they are subject to revision as improved data on the composition of consumption spending become available, and in this respect resemble the C-CPI-U.

For a large share of PCE, the price movements for basic individual spending categories are determined by CPI components. Hence, the differences between the rates of change in the aggregate CPI and PCE indexes are largely the result of the different weights, but also reflect some alternative methodologies and the previously mentioned differences in scope.

Market-based PCE indexes are based on household expenditures for which there are observable price measures. They exclude most implicit prices (for example, the services furnished without payment by financial intermediaries) and they exclude items not deflated by a detailed component of either the Consumer Price Index (CPI) or the Producer Price Index (PPI). This means that the price observations that make up these new aggregate measures are all based on observed market transactions, making them "market-based price indexes." The imputed rent for owner-occupied housing is included in the market-based price index, since it is based on observed rentals of comparable homes. Household insurance premiums are also included in the market-based index, since they are deflated by the CPI for tenants' and household insurance. Excluded are services furnished without payment by financial intermediaries, most insurance purchases, expenses of NPISHs (nonprofit institutions serving households), legal gambling (illegal gambling is excluded from all measures), margins on used light motor vehicles, and expenditures by U.S. residents working and traveling abroad. Also excluded are medical, hospitalization, and income loss insurance; expense of handling life insurance; motor vehicle insurance; and workers' compensation.

The *inflation rates* shown in Table 8-4 are percent changes in the price indexes introduced in Table 8-3. For annual indexes, the rate is the percent change from the previous year. For monthly indexes, the rate is the percent change from the same month a year earlier. To give an indication of the longer-run implications of these different price indicators, comparisons of compound annual inflation rates, calculated by the editor, are also shown for the 1978–2013, 1983–2013, 2000–2013 and 2013-2015 periods, using the growth rate formula presented in the article at the beginning of this volume.

Data availability and references

The CPI-U, CPI-W, and C-CPI-U are initially issued in a press release two to three weeks after the end of the month for which the data were collected. This release and detailed and complete current and historical data on the CPI and its variants and components, along with extensive documentation, are available on the BLS Web site at <https://www.bls.gov/cpi>. Seasonal factors and seasonally adjusted indexes are revised once a year with the issuance of the January index.

Information available on the BLS Web site includes "Common Misconceptions about the Consumer Price Index: Questions and Answers;" another fact sheet on frequently asked questions; a fact sheet on seasonal adjustment; Chapter 17 of the *BLS Handbook of Methods*, entitled "The Consumer Price Index"; a section entitled "Note on Chained Consumer Price Index for All Urban Consumers"; and a number of explanatory CPI fact sheets on specific subjects.

As previously indicated, the CPI-U-X1 is not currently published because its recent values are identical to the CPI-U. The CPI-E is presented in articles in the CPI section of the BLS Web site, the most recent of which is "Experimental Consumer Price Index for Americans 62 Years of Age and Older, 1998-2005"; recent values are available by request from BLS. The CPI-U-RS is updated each month in a report entitled "CPI Research Series Using Current Methods" on the site. In both cases, the reports describe the indexes and provide references.

The monthly PCE indexes are included in the personal income report issued by BEA, which is published near the end of the following month. These indexes are revised month-by-month to reflect new information and annually to reflect the annual and quinquennial benchmarking of the NIPAs. The complete historical record can be found on the BEA Web site at <https://www.bea.gov> in the Personal Income and Outlays section of the NIPA tables, in tables entitled "Price Indexes for Personal Consumption Expenditures by Major Type of Product."

Two special editions of the *Monthly Labor Review* were devoted to CPI issues. The December 1996 issue describes the subsequently implemented 1997 and 1998 revisions in a series of articles, and the December 1993 issue, entitled *The Anatomy of Price Change*, includes the following articles: "The Consumer Price Index: Underlying Concepts and Caveats"; "Basic Components of the CPI: Estimation of Price Changes"; "The Commodity Substitution Effect in CPI Data, 1982–1991"; and "Quality Adjustment of Price Indexes."

The new formula for calculating basic components is described in "Incorporating a Geometric Mean Formula into the CPI," *Monthly Labor Review* (October 1998). For a detailed discussion of the treatment of homeownership, see "Changing the Homeownership Component of the Consumer Price Index to Rental Equivalence," *CPI Detailed Report* (January 1983).

For a comprehensive professional review of CPI concepts and methodology, see Charles Schultze and Christopher Mackie, ed., *At What Price? Conceptualizing and Measuring Cost-of-Living and Price Indexes* (Washington, DC: National Academy Press, 2001). Earlier references include: "Using Survey Data to Assess Bias in the Consumer Price Index," *Monthly Labor Review* (April 1998); Joel Popkin, "Improving the CPI: The Record and Suggested Next Steps," *Business Economics*, Vol. XXXII, No. 3 (July 1997), pages 42–47; *Measurement Issues in the Consumer Price Index* (Bureau of Labor Statistics, U.S. Department of Labor, June 1997); *Toward a More Accurate Measure of the Cost of Living* (Final Report to the Senate Finance Committee from the Advisory Commission to Study the Consumer Price Index, December 4, 1996)—also known as the "Boskin Commission" report; and *Government Price Statistics* (U.S. Congress Joint Economic Committee, 87th Congress, 1st Session, January 24, 1961)—also known as the "Stigler Committee" report.

For an explanation of the differences between the CPI-U and the PCE index, see Clinton P. McCully, Brian C. Moyer, and Kenneth J. Stewart, "Comparing the Consumer Price Index and the Personal Consumption Expenditures Price Index," *Survey of Current Business,* November 2007, pp. 26-33.

TABLES 8-1 AND 8-5 THROUGH 8-7

Producer Price Indexes

SOURCE: U.S. DEPARTMENT OF LABOR, BUREAU OF LABOR STATISTICS (BLS)

The Bureau of Labor Statistics first compiled and published a "Wholesale Price Index," measuring prices of various goods from the perspective of the seller, in 1902; it covered the years 1890-1901. Over the years this index was broadened and refined. In a major revamping in 1978, it was structured into an input-output format, differentiated between stages of processing, and renamed the Producer Price Index. The index for "Finished Goods," from the stage-of-processing system, became the featured "headline" number. Still, this index only covered goods.

New FD-ID system (Tables 8-5 and 8-6)

Over subsequent years the Bureau instituted collection of an increasing number of prices for services as well. All prices are collected within an industry input-output structure, with one of the most important purposes being to measure real output quantities by deflating industry outputs and inputs. In the new aggregation system introduced in February 2014, prices for goods, services, and construction have been integrated into a set of Final Demand-Intermediate Demand (FD-ID) indexes, organized by class of buyer, degree of fabrication, and stage of production. Its principal components are calculated beginning in November 2009 with that month as the reference base (i.e. November 2009 = 100). Components of the previous goods PPI system continue to be calculated on the base 1982 = 100 as well.

> In the new FD-ID system, all products, including services and construction, are referred to as "commodities." In the old PPI system and in the CPI system, the term "commodities" refers to goods only; note, for example, how the CPI components are aggregated into summary measures of "commodities" [goods] and services, displaying different trends and behaviors. Unless and until these terminologies are reconciled, users need to be mindful of which system they are operating in.

More that 100,000 producer price quotations from over 25,000 establishment are collected each month; more than 10,000 indexes for individual products and groups of products are released each month. The prices are organized into three sets of PPIs: the FD-ID indexes; commodity indexes; and indexes for the net output of industries and their products.

Final demand. The final demand portion of the FD-ID structure measures price change for commodities sold for personal consumption, capital investment, government, and export. *Final demand trade services* measures changes in margins received by wholesalers and retailers. The other main components are *final demand goods, final demand transportation and warehousing services, other final demand services,* and *final demand construction.* The total index for final demand is now featured by BLS in its press release as its "headline number," replacing the previously featured Finished Goods index.

Intermediate demand. This portion of the system tracks price changes for goods, services, and construction products sold to businesses as inputs to production and not as capital investment. There are two parallel treatments.

The first treatment organizes intermediate demand commodities by type, including the distinction between *processed goods* and *unprocessed goods,* which is carried over from the older PPI goods system.

The second system organizes intermediate demand commodities into production stages, with the explicit goal of developing a forward-flow model of production and price change. For each production stage, the intermediate demand index measures the prices of inputs to the included industries. Many commodities, for example energy products, are sold to both final demand and various intermediate stages of production; their weight is allocated proportionately to all the consuming stages of production and their price movements are proportionately represented in each stage.

Industries assigned to *Stage 4* primarily produce final demand commodities. The intermediate demand index for Stage 4 measures inputs to those industries, such as motor vehicle parts, beef and veal, and long distance motor carrying.

Industries assigned to *Stage 3* produce the output sold to Stage 4, and therefore include motor vehicle parts and slaughtering. Examples of inputs to Stage 3 included in their intermediate demand index include slaughter steers and heifers, industrial electric power, steel plates, and temporary help services.

Industries assigned to *Stage 2* include petroleum refining, electricity, and insurance agencies. The goods and services that they purchase and that are included in their intermediate demand index include crude oil and business loans.

Industries assigned to *Stage 1* include oil and gas extraction, paper mills, and advertising services. Inputs to those industries include electric power and solid waste collection. According to BLS, "It should be noted that all inputs purchased by stage 1 industries are by definition produced either within stage 1 or by later stages of processing, leaving stage 1 less useful for price transmission analysis."

Commodity indexes

Aggregation by *commodity* organizes the price measures by similarity of product or end use, disregarding industry of origin. For the original Wholesale Price Index (goods only), this was the principal means of aggregation; in Table 8-1C, producer price indexes are shown for *farm products, industrial commodities,* and "*all commodities*" back to the year 1913. Table 8-7 shows 16 goods commodity groups from 1950 to date. Whatever their imperfections, these measures provide the longest historical perspective for producer prices.

The major goods commodity groups—particularly the totals for all commodities and industrial commodities—came under criticism in the energy price crisis of the early 1970s, for aggregating successive stages of processing of the same product (e.g. crude oil) and thus exaggerating price trends. As a result, the stage-of-processing grouping was introduced in 1978, and the finished goods components, in total and minus food and energy, became the headline Producer Price Indexes.

Stage of processing indexes

In the PPI for goods as reconstructed in 1978 and shown in Table 8-1B, the three major indexes are: (1) *finished goods*, or goods that will not undergo further processing and are ready for sale to the ultimate user (such as automobiles, meats, apparel, and machine tools, and also unprocessed foods such as eggs and fresh vegetables, that are ready for the consumer); (2) *processed goods for intermediate demand* (formerly *intermediate materials, supplies, and components*), or goods that have been processed but require further processing before they become finished goods (such as steel mill products, cotton yarns, lumber, and flour), as well as physically complete goods that are purchased by business firms as inputs for their operations (such as diesel fuel and paper boxes); and (3) *unprocessed goods for intermediate demand* (formerly *crude materials for further processing*), or goods entering the market for the first time that have not been manufactured or fabricated and are not sold directly to consumers (such as ores, scrap metals, crude petroleum, raw cotton, and livestock).

Notes on the data

The probability sample used for calculating the PPI provides more than 100,000 price quotations per month. To the greatest extent possible, prices used in calculating the PPI represent prices received by domestic producers in the first important commercial transaction for each commodity. These indexes attempt to measure only price changes (changes in receipts per unit of measurement not influenced by changes in quality, quantity sold, terms of sale, or level of distribution). Transaction prices are sought instead of list or book prices. Price data are collected monthly via Internet, mail, and fax. Prices are obtained directly from producing companies on a voluntary and confidential basis. Prices are generally reported for the Tuesday of the week containing the 13th day of the month. Samples are updated regularly.

The BLS revises the PPI weighting structure when data from economic censuses become available. Beginning with data for January 2012, the weights used to construct the PPI reflect 2007 shipments values as measured by the 2007 Economic Censuses. Data for January 2007 through December 2011 used 2002 values; 2002 through 2006, 1997 shipments values; 1996 through 2001, 1992 values; 1992 through 1995, 1987 values; 1987 through 1991, 1982 values; 1976 through 1986, 1972 values; and 1967 through 1975, 1963 values.

Price indexes are available in unadjusted form and are also adjusted for seasonal variation using the X-12-ARIMA method. Since January 1988, BLS has also used X-12-ARIMA Intervention Analysis Seasonal Adjustment for a small number of series to remove unusual values that might distort seasonal patterns before calculating the seasonal adjustment factors. Seasonal factors for the PPI are revised annually to take into account the most recent 12 months of data. Seasonally adjusted data for the previous 5 years are subject to these annual revisions.

The newer FD-ID indexes are only available beginning in November 2009. Hence, they only regard, so far, the recovery and expansion phase of a particularly severe business cycle; the editor suggests that up to now, both seasonal adjustments and broader inferences about relative price behavior are necessarily based on a short and possibly unrepresentative time period. Partly for that reason, we present both unadjusted and seasonally adjusted indexes in Tables 8-5 and 8-6.

Data availability and references

The indexes are initially issued in a press release two to three weeks after the end of the month for which the data were collected. Data are subsequently published in greater detail in a monthly BLS publication, *PPI Detailed Report*. Each month, data for the fourth previous month (both unadjusted and seasonally adjusted) are revised to reflect late reports and corrections.

The press release, the *PPI Detailed Report*, detailed and complete current and historical data, and extensive documentation are available at <https://www.bls.gov/ppi>. The items available on this Web site include Chapter 14 of the *BLS Handbook of Methods*, "Producer Price Indexes"; a selection of *Monthly Labor Review* articles on the PPI; and fact sheets on a number of issues and index components.

CHAPTER 9: EMPLOYMENT COSTS, PRODUCTIVITY, AND PROFITS

SECTION 9A: EMPLOYMENT COST INDEXES

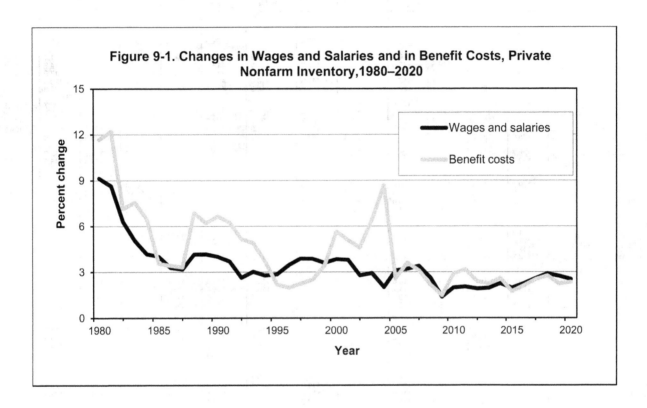

Figure 9-1. Changes in Wages and Salaries and in Benefit Costs, Private Nonfarm Inventory,1980–2020

- The Employment Cost Index (ECI) measures the change in the cost of labor, free from the influence of employment shifts among occupations and industries. This cost of labor includes not only wages and salaries but also benefits. These benefits include vacations and sick leave, overtime, health insurance, and retirement. (See Chapter 8.)

- Analogous to the ECI is the Consumer Price Index (CPI), which holds the market basket constant in any individual time period so as to reflect only an aggregate of price changes affecting individual defined products.

- SIC industrial classification began in 1930 when the U.S. was manufacturing-based. Changes to the economy to serviced-based could not be accommodated by SIC. Table 9-1 presents the ECI by the North American Industrial Classification (NAICS) while Table 9-2 presents the data for Standard Industrial Code (SIC). The NAICS system began with the North American Free Trade Agreement (NAFTA), instituted in 1994 with Canada and Mexico.

- From 2008 to 2020, total compensation for all civilian workers rose 30 percent. During this period, wages and salaries grew slightly less at 28.9 percent while total benefits grew more rapidly at 32.4 percent. Much of this increase was due to medical care costs. (Table 9-1)

Table 9-1. Employment Cost Indexes, NAICS Basis

(December 2005 [not seasonally adjusted] = 100; annual values are for December, not seasonally adjusted; quarterly values, seasonally adjusted, except as noted.)

Year and month	All civilian workers [1]	State and local government workers	Private industry workers										
				By occupational group					By industry				
			All private industry workers	Management, professional, and related	Sales and office	Natural resources, construction, and maintenance	Production, transportation, and material moving	Service occupations	Goods-producing industries		Service-providing	Union [2]	Non-union [2]
									Total	Manufacturing			
TOTAL COMPENSATION													
2008	109.5	111.6	108.9	109.9	107.9	109.6	106.9	109.8	107.5	105.9	109.4	108.0	109.1
2009	111.0	114.2	110.2	110.7	109.2	111.2	108.9	111.8	108.6	107.0	110.8	111.1	110.1
2010	113.2	116.2	112.5	113.0	111.6	113.3	111.5	113.5	111.1	110.0	113.0	114.8	112.1
2011	115.5	117.7	115.0	115.4	114.2	115.8	114.2	115.4	113.8	113.1	115.3	117.9	114.5
2012	117.7	119.9	117.1	117.7	116.3	117.8	116.0	117.4	115.6	114.9	117.6	120.5	116.6
2013	120.0	122.2	119.4	120.2	119.0	120.1	118.0	119.0	117.7	117.0	120.0	122.6	119.0
2014	122.7	124.7	122.2	123.0	121.9	123.2	120.6	121.1	120.3	119.8	122.8	126.7	121.5
2015	125.1	127.8	124.5	125.3	123.9	124.9	123.7	123.2	123.2	122.8	124.9	128.7	123.8
2016	127.9	130.9	127.2	127.4	126.8	127.7	127.0	127.2	125.8	125.5	127.7	130.6	126.6
2017	131.2	134.2	130.5	130.5	130.1	131.2	131.0	130.9	128.9	128.9	131.0	134.5	129.9
2018	135.0	137.7	134.4	133.8	135.0	134.5	134.7	135.6	131.9	131.6	135.2	138.8	133.7
2019	138.7	141.7	138.0	136.8	138.8	137.9	139.2	140.6	135.8	135.3	138.7	142.3	137.3
2020	142.2	144.9	141.6	139.5	143.2	141.3	143.8	145.6	138.9	138.5	142.4	146.3	140.9
2009													
March	109.9	112.4	109.3	110.2	108.1	109.9	107.7	110.6	107.9	106.4	109.8	109.1	109.4
June	110.2	113.2	109.5	110.4	108.2	110.3	108.1	111.0	108.1	106.6	110.0	109.8	109.6
September	110.7	113.5	109.9	110.6	108.8	110.7	108.6	111.6	108.3	106.8	110.5	110.5	109.9
December	111.1	114.1	110.4	111.0	109.3	111.3	109.0	112.0	108.8	107.3	110.9	111.1	110.1
2010													
March	111.8	114.5	111.1	111.7	109.9	112.3	109.9	112.3	109.7	108.4	111.5	112.8	110.9
June	112.3	115.1	111.6	112.1	110.6	112.6	110.4	112.6	110.2	109.0	112.1	113.7	111.4
September	112.8	115.5	112.1	112.7	111.1	112.9	111.2	113.3	110.9	109.9	112.5	114.6	111.8
December	113.3	116.1	112.6	113.3	111.7	113.4	111.6	113.6	111.2	110.2	113.1	114.8	112.1
2011													
March	114.0	116.7	113.3	114.0	112.2	113.9	112.2	114.5	112.0	111.3	113.8	115.6	113.0
June	114.7	117.0	114.2	114.7	113.2	114.8	113.5	114.7	113.2	112.6	114.5	117.1	113.8
September	115.1	117.3	114.6	115.1	113.7	115.4	113.7	115.0	113.3	112.8	115.0	117.4	114.2
December	115.6	117.7	115.1	115.7	114.3	115.9	114.3	115.5	113.9	113.3	115.5	117.9	114.5
2012													
March	116.3	118.3	115.7	116.3	115.1	116.4	114.5	116.0	114.1	113.4	116.3	118.3	115.3
June	116.8	118.9	116.3	117.0	115.7	116.9	115.0	116.5	114.6	113.9	116.9	119.3	116.0
September	117.3	119.5	116.8	117.3	116.2	117.5	115.6	116.8	115.2	114.6	117.3	120.2	116.3
December	117.8	119.9	117.2	118.0	116.5	118.0	116.1	117.4	115.7	115.1	117.7	120.5	116.6
2013													
March	118.4	120.5	117.9	118.5	117.3	118.7	116.7	117.8	116.4	115.7	118.3	121.5	117.3
June	119.0	121.0	118.5	119.3	117.7	119.0	117.1	118.3	116.9	116.2	119.0	122.1	118.0
September	119.5	121.4	119.0	119.9	118.4	119.7	117.5	118.4	117.4	116.7	119.5	122.5	118.5
December	120.1	122.2	119.6	120.4	119.2	120.3	118.1	119.1	117.8	117.2	120.2	122.6	119.0
2014													
March	120.5	122.8	119.9	120.7	119.3	120.9	118.8	119.0	118.6	118.0	120.4	123.5	119.4
June	121.4	123.5	120.9	121.9	120.3	121.9	119.5	119.6	119.1	118.6	121.5	125.0	120.4
September	122.2	124.1	121.7	122.7	121.1	122.6	120.2	120.5	119.8	119.3	122.3	125.8	121.1
December	122.8	124.7	122.4	123.1	122.1	123.4	120.8	121.2	120.4	120.0	123.0	126.7	121.5
2015													
March	123.6	125.4	123.2	123.8	123.3	123.7	121.6	121.8	121.0	120.8	123.8	127.4	122.5
June	123.8	126.2	123.2	124.0	122.6	124.0	122.4	122.1	121.8	121.6	123.7	127.5	122.7
September	124.6	126.9	124.0	124.8	123.5	124.5	123.0	122.6	122.4	122.1	124.5	128.0	123.4
December	125.3	127.8	124.6	125.5	124.3	125.1	123.9	123.3	123.3	123.0	125.1	128.7	123.8
2016													
March	126.0	128.5	125.3	126.0	125.0	125.8	124.6	124.2	123.8	123.6	125.8	129.6	124.7
June	126.7	129.2	126.1	126.3	126.5	126.5	125.5	125.5	124.6	124.4	126.6	130.0	125.7
September	127.4	130.2	126.7	127.0	126.7	126.9	126.3	126.5	125.1	125.1	127.3	130.4	126.3
December	128.1	130.9	127.4	127.6	127.1	127.8	127.2	127.3	125.8	125.7	127.9	130.6	126.6
2017													
March	128.9	131.8	128.2	128.4	128.1	128.6	128.1	128.4	126.5	126.3	128.8	131.9	127.8
June	129.7	132.5	129.0	129.4	128.6	129.6	129.0	129.2	127.2	127.0	129.6	132.7	128.6
September	130.6	133.3	130.0	130.0	129.9	130.5	130.4	130.0	128.3	128.4	130.5	133.7	129.5
December	131.4	134.2	130.7	130.7	130.3	131.3	131.2	131.1	129.0	129.0	131.3	134.5	129.9
2018													
March	132.4	134.8	131.8	131.7	131.9	131.9	132.3	132.4	129.9	129.9	132.4	135.4	131.4
June	133.4	135.7	132.8	132.5	133.1	133.2	133.2	133.4	130.8	130.7	133.4	137.4	132.2
September	134.3	136.8	133.7	133.3	134.4	133.8	134.1	134.6	131.2	130.9	134.5	137.8	133.2
December	135.2	137.8	134.6	134.1	135.3	134.6	134.9	135.8	132.0	131.7	135.4	138.8	133.7
2019													
March	136.1	138.8	135.4	134.7	136.3	135.4	136.2	137.0	133.1	132.9	136.2	140.0	134.9
June	137.0	139.7	136.3	135.5	137.0	136.0	137.2	138.4	134.0	133.7	137.0	140.8	135.8
September	138.0	140.9	137.3	136.3	138.4	137.2	138.1	139.3	135.1	134.6	138.0	141.4	136.8
December	138.9	141.8	138.2	137.1	139.0	138.0	139.4	140.7	135.9	135.4	138.9	142.3	137.3
2020													
March	139.9	142.8	139.2	137.9	140.5	139.4	140.4	141.9	136.7	136.2	140.0	143.1	138.8
June	140.7	143.6	139.9	138.3	141.3	139.7	141.7	143.1	137.6	137.1	140.6	144.7	139.4
September	141.4	144.3	140.7	139.0	141.9	140.5	142.7	144.4	138.1	137.7	141.4	145.6	140.1
December	142.4	145.1	141.8	139.7	143.4	141.4	144.0	145.7	139.0	138.6	142.6	146.3	140.9

[1]Excludes farm workers, private household workers, and federal government employees.
[2]Not seasonally adjusted.

Table 9-1. Employment Cost Indexes, NAICS Basis—*Continued*

(December 2005 [not seasonally adjusted] = 100; annual values are for December, not seasonally adjusted; quarterly values, seasonally adjusted, except as noted.)

Year and month	All civilian workers [1]	State and local government workers	Private industry workers										
			All private industry workers	By occupational group					By industry			Union [2]	Non-union [2]
				Management, professional, and related	Sales and office	Natural resources, construction, and maintenance	Production, transportation, and material moving	Service occupations	Goods-producing industries		Service-providing		
									Total	Manufacturing			
WAGES AND SALARIES													
2008	109.6	110.4	109.4	110.5	108.0	110.5	107.8	110.1	109.0	107.7	109.6	108.1	109.6
2009	111.2	112.5	110.8	111.5	109.4	112.0	109.6	112.3	110.0	108.9	111.1	110.9	110.9
2010	113.0	113.8	112.8	113.7	111.5	113.3	111.3	113.5	111.6	110.7	113.1	112.9	112.7
2011	114.6	114.9	114.6	115.5	113.6	115.4	112.8	115.1	113.5	112.7	114.9	114.9	114.6
2012	116.5	116.2	116.6	117.7	115.8	116.7	115.1	116.8	115.4	114.8	117.0	117.4	116.5
2013	118.7	117.5	119.0	120.2	118.4	118.8	117.2	118.3	117.6	117.2	119.4	119.8	118.9
2014	121.2	119.4	121.6	122.8	121.3	121.4	119.9	120.7	120.1	119.8	122.1	123.1	121.5
2015	123.7	121.6	124.2	125.6	123.5	123.5	122.8	122.8	123.2	123.0	124.5	125.5	124.0
2016	126.6	124.1	127.1	128.1	126.2	126.7	126.6	127.1	126.2	126.2	127.4	127.3	127.1
2017	129.8	126.7	130.6	131.1	129.8	130.4	130.7	131.3	129.3	129.3	131.0	130.9	130.6
2018	133.8	129.7	134.7	134.6	135.0	133.4	135.1	136.4	133.0	132.9	135.2	134.6	134.7
2019	137.7	133.0	138.7	137.7	139.2	137.4	140.5	142.2	137.5	137.1	139.1	139.2	138.7
2020	141.3	135.4	142.6	140.4	144.1	141.2	145.5	147.6	141.0	140.7	143.1	143.0	142.6
2009													
March	110.0	111.0	109.8	110.9	108.1	110.7	108.3	110.9	109.2	108.0	110.0	108.8	110.0
June	110.4	111.7	110.1	111.1	108.2	111.1	108.8	111.3	109.4	108.3	110.2	109.6	110.2
September	110.8	111.9	110.5	111.3	108.9	111.5	109.3	112.0	109.7	108.6	110.7	110.2	110.6
December	111.2	112.4	111.0	111.8	109.5	112.1	109.7	112.4	110.2	109.1	111.2	110.9	110.9
2010													
March	111.7	112.8	111.4	112.3	109.8	112.6	109.9	112.5	110.5	109.3	111.7	111.5	111.4
June	112.1	113.2	111.9	112.8	110.5	112.8	110.3	112.8	110.9	109.9	112.2	112.1	111.9
September	112.5	113.3	112.3	113.4	110.8	113.0	111.0	113.2	111.4	110.5	112.6	112.7	112.4
December	113.0	113.8	112.9	113.9	111.5	113.3	111.3	113.5	111.7	110.9	113.2	112.9	112.7
2011													
March	113.4	114.1	113.2	114.4	111.8	113.8	111.6	114.2	112.2	111.5	113.6	113.6	113.2
June	113.9	114.4	113.7	114.8	112.5	114.5	112.0	114.3	112.7	111.9	114.1	114.0	113.8
September	114.3	114.5	114.2	115.2	113.1	115.0	112.4	114.6	113.1	112.5	114.6	114.6	114.3
December	114.7	114.8	114.7	115.7	113.7	115.4	112.9	115.1	113.6	113.0	115.0	114.9	114.6
2012													
March	115.3	115.2	115.3	116.3	114.5	115.7	113.7	115.4	114.0	113.5	115.7	115.6	115.2
June	115.8	115.6	115.8	116.9	115.0	116.0	114.0	115.9	114.4	113.9	116.2	116.2	115.9
September	116.2	115.8	116.3	117.2	115.7	116.4	114.6	116.2	115.0	114.5	116.7	116.9	116.3
December	116.6	116.1	116.7	117.8	115.9	116.8	115.2	116.8	115.5	115.0	117.1	117.4	116.5
2013													
March	117.2	116.4	117.4	118.5	116.7	117.3	115.8	117.2	116.1	115.6	117.7	118.4	117.2
June	117.7	116.7	118.0	119.3	117.1	117.6	116.2	117.7	116.7	116.3	118.3	119.0	117.9
September	118.2	116.9	118.4	119.7	117.7	118.4	116.6	117.6	117.3	116.8	118.8	119.6	118.4
December	118.8	117.4	119.1	120.3	118.6	118.9	117.3	118.3	117.7	117.4	119.5	119.8	118.9
2014													
March	119.1	117.8	119.4	120.6	118.6	119.5	118.0	118.4	118.2	118.0	119.7	120.5	119.2
June	119.8	118.2	120.2	121.7	119.5	120.0	118.7	119.0	118.9	118.6	120.6	121.2	120.2
September	120.7	118.8	121.1	122.5	120.3	120.7	119.5	120.1	119.5	119.3	121.5	122.1	121.0
December	121.3	119.4	121.8	122.8	121.5	121.5	120.0	120.8	120.2	120.0	122.2	123.1	121.5
2015													
March	122.1	120.0	122.6	123.5	123.2	121.8	120.7	121.5	120.9	120.8	123.1	123.7	122.4
June	122.4	120.6	122.8	124.1	122.1	122.6	121.5	121.6	121.7	121.6	123.2	124.5	122.7
September	123.1	121.0	123.6	125.0	123.0	123.0	122.1	122.2	122.4	122.3	124.0	124.8	123.6
December	123.8	121.5	124.3	125.7	123.8	123.6	123.0	122.9	123.3	123.2	124.6	125.5	124.0
2016													
March	124.5	122.1	125.1	126.5	124.4	124.5	123.8	123.8	124.0	123.9	125.4	126.4	125.0
June	125.4	122.7	126.0	126.8	126.2	125.4	124.9	125.2	124.8	124.8	126.4	126.8	126.0
September	126.0	123.4	126.6	127.6	126.2	125.8	125.8	126.4	125.4	125.7	127.0	127.2	126.6
December	126.7	124.0	127.3	128.2	126.4	126.8	126.8	127.3	126.3	126.4	127.6	127.3	127.1
2017													
March	127.5	124.8	128.2	129.0	127.6	127.7	127.8	128.4	127.1	127.0	128.5	128.6	128.2
June	128.3	125.3	129.0	130.0	128.1	128.6	128.7	129.3	127.8	127.8	129.4	129.2	129.1
September	129.2	125.9	129.9	130.4	129.5	129.6	130.1	130.3	128.7	128.7	130.3	129.9	130.0
December	130.0	126.6	130.8	131.3	130.0	130.5	131.0	131.5	129.5	129.5	131.2	130.9	130.6
2018													
March	131.0	127.1	131.9	132.3	131.7	131.1	132.2	132.7	130.4	130.3	132.4	131.6	132.1
June	131.9	127.8	132.8	132.9	132.8	131.9	133.2	134.0	131.4	131.2	133.2	132.7	132.9
September	133.0	128.7	134.0	134.0	134.3	132.5	134.4	135.3	132.2	132.1	134.5	133.5	134.1
December	133.9	129.6	134.9	134.8	135.1	133.4	135.3	136.6	133.1	133.0	135.4	134.6	134.7
2019													
March	134.8	130.3	135.8	135.4	136.3	134.2	136.9	138.0	134.2	134.1	136.3	135.7	136.0
June	135.7	131.0	136.8	136.3	137.0	135.3	137.9	139.7	135.2	135.1	137.2	137.0	136.9
September	136.9	132.3	137.9	137.2	138.8	136.5	139.2	140.6	136.5	136.2	138.4	138.1	138.0
December	137.8	132.9	138.9	137.9	139.4	137.5	140.7	142.3	137.6	137.3	139.3	139.2	138.7
2020													
March	139.0	133.7	140.2	139.0	141.3	139.2	141.8	143.6	138.5	138.2	140.7	140.2	140.4
June	139.6	134.4	140.8	139.2	142.1	139.3	143.1	144.9	139.5	139.1	141.2	141.2	140.9
September	140.3	134.7	141.6	139.9	142.6	140.3	144.3	146.3	140.1	139.9	142.0	142.2	141.6
December	141.4	135.3	142.8	140.7	144.3	141.2	145.7	147.7	141.1	140.8	143.3	143.0	142.6

[1]Excludes farm workers, private household workers, and federal government employees.
[2]Not seasonally adjusted.

Table 9-2. Employment Cost Indexes, SIC Basis

(Not seasonally adjusted, December 2005 = 100; annual values are for December.)

Year	All civilian workers [1,2]	State and local government workers [2]	All private industry workers [2]	Private industry workers excluding sales occupations	Private industry workers — By occupational group — Production and nonsupervisory occupations	White-collar occupations	Blue-collar occupations	Service occupations [2]	By industry division — Goods-producing industries — Total [2]	Construction [2]	Manufacturing [2]	Service-providing industries — Total [2]	Transportation and utilities	Wholesale trade	Retail trade	Finance, insurance, and real estate [2]	Services
TOTAL COMPENSATION																	
1979	...	...	32.8	32.5	...	31.2	35.0	33.9	33.7	...	33.1	32.0	...	...	...	...	...
1980	...	...	35.9	35.9	...	34.2	38.5	37.1	37.0	...	36.4	35.1	...	...	...	...	...
1981	39.0	36.8	39.5	39.4	40.1	37.6	42.2	40.5	40.7	...	40.0	38.6	...	...	...	...	...
1982	41.5	39.4	42.0	42.0	42.8	40.1	44.7	43.9	43.2	...	42.4	41.1	...	...	...	...	...
1983	43.9	41.8	44.4	44.4	45.2	42.7	47.0	46.3	45.3	...	44.6	43.8	...	...	...	...	...
1984	46.2	44.6	46.6	46.7	47.3	44.8	49.0	49.4	47.4	...	46.9	46.0	...	...	...	...	...
1985	48.2	47.1	48.4	48.3	49.1	47.0	50.5	50.9	49.0	50.8	48.4	48.1	50.6	...	52.4	44.7	46.1
1986	49.9	49.6	49.9	49.9	50.5	48.6	51.9	52.4	50.5	52.3	50.0	49.6	51.8	48.5	53.5	46.1	48.1
1987	51.7	51.8	51.6	51.7	52.2	50.4	53.5	53.7	52.1	54.2	51.5	51.4	53.3	50.4	54.8	47.0	50.5
1988	54.2	54.7	54.1	54.1	54.8	52.9	55.9	56.5	54.4	56.5	53.8	54.0	54.9	52.5	58.0	50.0	53.5
1989	56.9	58.1	56.7	56.5	57.6	55.7	58.2	59.0	56.7	59.0	56.3	56.8	56.9	57.1	59.9	52.7	56.4
1990	59.7	61.5	59.3	59.3	60.1	58.4	60.7	61.8	59.4	60.9	59.1	59.4	59.1	58.2	62.5	54.9	59.9
1991	62.3	63.7	61.9	62.0	62.7	61.0	63.4	64.7	62.1	63.3	61.9	61.9	61.7	60.7	65.2	57.2	62.5
1992	64.4	66.0	64.1	64.2	64.9	63.1	65.6	66.7	64.5	65.6	64.3	63.9	63.9	62.5	66.9	57.9	65.2
1993	66.7	67.9	66.4	66.6	67.3	65.4	68.1	68.8	67.0	67.1	66.9	66.2	66.1	64.4	68.9	60.5	67.5
1994	68.7	69.9	68.5	68.6	69.2	67.5	70.0	70.8	69.0	69.6	69.0	68.1	68.7	66.4	70.8	61.8	69.4
1995	70.6	72.0	70.2	70.4	71.0	69.4	71.7	72.1	70.7	71.1	70.8	70.0	71.2	69.4	72.3	64.0	70.9
1996	72.6	73.9	72.4	72.4	73.1	71.7	73.6	74.2	72.7	72.9	72.9	72.3	73.4	71.5	75.1	65.5	73.1
1997	75.0	75.6	74.9	74.9	75.4	74.4	75.5	77.2	74.5	74.8	74.6	75.1	75.5	73.8	77.7	69.9	75.9
1998	77.6	77.8	77.5	77.2	78.1	77.3	77.6	79.4	76.5	77.4	76.6	78.0	78.4	78.0	80.0	74.1	78.2
1999	80.2	80.5	80.2	80.0	80.4	79.9	80.2	82.1	79.1	79.9	79.2	80.6	80.1	81.1	83.0	77.1	80.9
2000	83.6	82.9	83.6	83.6	84.0	83.6	83.6	85.3	82.6	84.6	82.3	84.2	83.5	84.4	86.4	81.0	84.5
2001	87.0	86.4	87.1	87.0	87.4	87.1	86.7	89.1	85.7	88.2	85.3	87.8	87.5	87.2	90.3	83.9	88.3
2002	90.0	89.9	90.0	89.9	90.2	89.9	89.8	92.0	88.9	91.0	88.5	90.5	91.0	91.1	91.9	87.6	90.7
2003	93.5	92.9	93.6	93.6	93.6	93.6	93.4	94.9	92.4	94.1	92.2	94.2	94.0	94.0	94.9	94.1	94.0
2004	96.9	96.1	97.1	97.2	97.2	96.9	97.5	97.7	96.8	96.4	96.7	97.3	97.6	96.5	97.1	96.7	97.5
2005	100.0	100.0	100.0	100.0	100.0	100.0	100.0	100.0	100.0	100.0	100.0	100.0	100.0	100.0	100.0	100.0	100.0
WAGES AND SALARIES																	
1979	...	...	36.1	36.1	36.8	34.1	39.4	37.9	38.2	41.4	37.5	34.9	39.1	33.7	39.7	32.8	31.7
1980	...	...	39.4	39.3	40.3	37.1	43.1	41.0	41.8	45.0	41.0	38.0	43.5	37.1	42.5	35.2	34.5
1981	42.3	40.1	42.8	42.9	43.9	40.4	46.8	44.4	45.4	49.0	44.5	41.4	47.1	40.0	45.6	38.8	38.1
1982	45.0	42.7	45.5	45.6	46.7	43.1	49.4	48.2	48.0	51.5	47.0	44.2	50.5	42.5	47.5	41.3	41.2
1983	47.3	45.0	47.8	47.9	48.9	45.7	51.3	50.4	49.9	53.0	49.0	46.7	53.0	45.1	49.5	44.3	43.9
1984	49.4	47.7	49.8	50.1	50.8	47.6	53.1	53.5	51.8	53.7	51.2	48.7	54.8	47.6	52.0	43.9	46.7
1985	51.5	50.3	51.8	51.9	52.9	50.0	55.0	54.8	53.6	55.3	53.0	51.0	56.9	49.7	54.5	47.9	48.4
1986	53.3	53.0	53.5	53.6	54.3	51.7	56.4	56.2	55.3	56.7	54.8	52.5	57.9	51.5	55.7	49.2	50.3
1987	55.2	55.2	55.2	55.5	56.0	53.6	58.1	57.6	57.1	57.6	56.6	54.3	59.1	53.6	57.2	49.8	53.0
1988	57.5	57.9	57.5	57.5	58.4	56.1	59.9	60.1	58.9	60.7	58.3	56.9	60.6	55.6	60.1	52.9	55.6
1989	60.1	61.0	59.9	59.8	61.0	58.7	62.0	62.3	61.2	62.8	60.6	59.5	62.2	60.7	62.0	55.7	58.3
1990	62.6	64.2	62.3	62.4	63.2	61.2	64.2	64.8	63.4	64.1	63.1	61.8	64.3	61.2	64.2	57.6	61.6
1991	64.9	66.4	64.6	64.7	65.4	63.5	66.4	67.4	65.8	66.0	65.6	64.1	66.6	63.6	66.6	59.6	63.8
1992	66.6	68.4	66.3	66.5	67.2	65.2	68.1	68.8	67.6	67.3	67.6	65.7	68.7	65.5	68.2	59.5	66.0
1993	68.7	70.2	68.3	68.5	69.2	67.4	70.0	70.3	69.6	68.6	69.7	67.8	70.9	67.1	70.2	62.1	68.0
1994	70.6	72.4	70.2	70.5	71.1	69.3	72.0	72.4	71.7	70.8	71.8	69.6	73.5	69.1	71.9	62.8	70.0
1995	72.7	74.7	72.2	72.5	73.0	71.3	74.1	74.0	73.7	72.5	73.9	71.7	76.0	72.4	73.6	65.1	71.7
1996	75.1	76.8	74.7	74.9	75.5	73.8	76.3	76.6	76.0	74.6	76.3	74.2	78.1	74.7	76.8	67.2	74.2
1997	77.9	78.9	77.6	77.7	78.3	77.0	78.8	79.9	78.3	77.1	78.6	77.4	80.7	77.0	79.7	71.8	77.5
1998	80.8	81.3	80.6	80.4	81.4	80.3	81.3	82.4	81.1	79.9	81.3	80.5	83.0	81.5	82.2	76.9	80.1
1999	83.6	84.2	83.5	83.4	83.8	83.1	84.0	85.1	83.8	82.5	84.1	83.4	84.8	84.5	85.2	79.8	83.0
2000	86.7	87.0	86.7	86.7	87.1	86.4	87.1	88.3	87.1	86.9	87.1	86.6	87.5	87.4	88.6	83.4	86.3
2001	90.0	90.2	90.0	90.0	90.4	89.6	90.5	91.8	90.2	90.4	90.2	89.9	91.7	89.3	91.9	85.8	90.0
2002	92.6	93.1	92.4	92.5	92.6	92.0	93.0	94.1	92.9	92.8	93.0	92.3	94.7	92.8	93.2	89.4	92.0
2003	95.2	95.0	95.2	95.4	95.1	95.2	95.2	96.2	95.1	95.1	95.2	95.3	96.2	95.3	95.5	95.9	94.8
2004	97.5	97.0	97.5	97.8	97.5	97.5	97.6	97.9	97.4	97.0	97.5	97.7	98.6	96.6	97.2	97.7	97.8
2005	100.0	100.0	100.0	100.0	100.0	100.0	100.0	100.0	100.0	100.0	100.0	100.0	100.0	100.0	100.0	100.0	100.0

[1]Excludes farm workers, private household workers, and federal government employees.
[2]Roughly continuous and comparable with new NAICS-based series. See notes and definitions for more information.
. . . = Not available.

Table 9-2. Employment Cost Indexes, SIC Basis—*Continued*

(Not seasonally adjusted, December 2005 = 100; annual values are for December.)

Year	All civilian workers [1,2]	State and local government workers [2]	All private industry workers [2]	Private industry workers excluding sales occupations	Production and nonsupervisory occupations	White-collar occupations	Blue-collar occupations	Service occupations [2]	Total [2]	Construction [2]	Manufacturing [2]	Total [2]	Transportation and utilities	Wholesale trade	Retail trade	Finance, insurance, and real estate [2]	Services
									Goods-producing industries			Service-providing industries					
TOTAL BENEFITS																	
1979	...	...	25.7	...	...	24.7	27.4	...	26.0	...	25.8	25.4	...	...	...	...	...
1980	...	...	28.7	...	...	27.7	30.4	...	28.8	...	28.5	28.6	...	...	...	...	...
1981	31.8	...	32.2	...	...	31.1	34.0	...	32.4	...	32.1	31.9	...	...	...	...	...
1982	34.2	...	34.5	...	...	33.3	36.5	...	34.8	...	34.4	34.1	...	...	...	...	...
1983	36.8	...	37.1	...	...	35.8	39.1	...	37.2	...	36.9	36.8	...	...	...	...	...
1984	39.3	...	39.5	...	...	38.3	41.4	...	39.6	...	39.3	39.4	...	...	...	...	...
1985	40.8	...	40.9	...	...	40.0	42.5	41.2	40.8	...	40.4	40.9	...	...	...	...	...
1986	42.4	...	42.3	...	...	41.4	43.8	42.9	42.0	...	41.6	42.5	...	...	...	...	...
1987	44.0	...	43.7	...	...	42.9	45.3	43.9	43.2	...	42.7	44.2	...	...	...	...	...
1988	47.0	...	46.7	...	...	45.6	48.6	47.4	46.3	...	46.0	47.1	...	...	...	...	...
1989	50.1	52.2	49.6	...	...	48.6	51.2	50.5	48.8	...	48.7	50.2	...	...	...	...	...
1990	53.5	55.8	52.9	...	...	52.0	54.4	53.8	52.3	...	52.1	53.4	...	...	...	...	...
1991	56.5	58.0	56.2	...	...	55.2	57.8	57.7	55.5	...	55.2	56.7	...	...	...	...	...
1992	59.5	61.1	59.1	...	...	57.8	61.0	61.0	58.7	...	58.3	59.4	...	...	...	...	...
1993	62.2	62.9	62.0	...	...	60.5	64.4	64.4	62.0	...	61.8	62.0	...	...	...	...	...
1994	64.4	64.6	64.3	...	...	63.2	66.2	66.0	64.1	...	63.9	64.4	...	...	...	...	...
1995	65.8	66.3	65.7	...	...	64.8	67.2	66.6	65.2	...	65.0	66.0	...	...	...	...	...
1996	67.1	67.8	67.0	...	...	66.2	68.4	67.3	66.4	...	66.5	67.3	...	...	...	...	...
1997	68.5	68.6	68.5	...	...	68.0	69.4	69.6	67.3	...	67.4	69.2	...	...	...	...	...
1998	70.3	70.7	70.2	...	...	69.9	70.7	70.9	68.1	...	67.9	71.4	...	...	...	...	...
1999	72.6	72.7	72.6	...	...	72.3	73.0	73.4	70.5	...	70.3	73.8	...	...	...	...	...
2000	76.2	74.4	76.7	...	...	76.5	76.9	76.6	74.3	...	73.6	78.1	...	...	...	...	...
2001	80.2	78.5	80.6	...	...	81.1	79.5	81.3	77.3	...	76.3	82.5	...	...	...	...	...
2002	84.2	83.3	84.4	...	...	84.6	83.8	85.7	81.3	...	80.4	86.1	...	...	...	...	...
2003	89.5	88.4	89.8	...	...	89.7	89.8	91.3	87.4	...	86.7	91.2	...	...	...	...	...
2004	95.7	94.3	96.0	...	...	95.3	97.3	97.1	95.7	...	95.3	96.2	...	...	...	...	...
2005	100.0	100.0	100.0	...	...	100.0	100.0	100.0	100.0	...	100.0	100.0	...	...	...	...	...

[1]Excludes farm workers, private household workers, and federal government employees.
[2]Roughly continuous and comparable with new NAICS-based series. See notes and definitions for more information.
. . . = Not available.

SECTION 9B: PRODUCTIVITY AND RELATED DATA

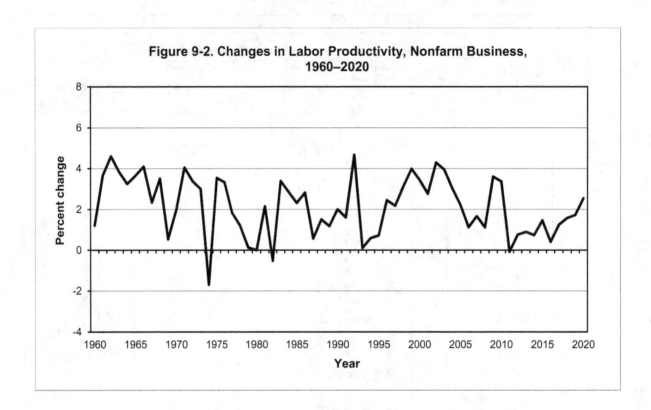

Figure 9-2. Changes in Labor Productivity, Nonfarm Business, 1960–2020

- As Figure 9-2 demonstrates, the rate of change in U.S. nonfarm labor productivity has often been quite variable from year to year. Up through the 1980s, productivity tended to decline (growth rates were less than zero) in recession years but rebound sharply in recovery. Firms often expected these declines in demand to be temporary so they therefore held on to their experienced workers in order to be prepared for the recovery. In 2020, many businesses shut down due to COVID-19. Openings were staggered with restrictions changing by geography. As expected, production fell sharply but rebounded slowly. (Table 9-3A and B)

- As the U.S. economy has become more service-oriented and less dependent on manufacturing, labor has become less dominant. The lag between compensation and productivity mainly reflects a decline to unprecedented levels in the labor share of the total value of sector output. (Table 9-3A)

- Corporate profits are one of the most closely watched U.S. economic indicators. Profitability provides a summary measure of corporate financial health and thus serves as an essential indicator of economic performance. The estimates of corporate profits are an integral part of the national income and product accounts (NIPAs), a set of accounts prepared by the Bureau of Economic Analysis (BEA) that provides a logical and consistent framework for presenting statistics on U.S. economic activity. See Chapter 1 for in-depth information on NIPA accounting. (Table 9-4).

Table 9-3A. Productivity and Related Data: Recent Data

(2012 = 100, seasonally adjusted.)

Year and quarter	Output per hour of all persons	Output	Hours of all persons	Employment	Average weekly hours	Unit labor costs	Compensation per hour	Real hourly compensation	Labor share	Unit nonlabor payments	Implicit price deflator	Current dollar output	Compensation	Nonlabor payments	Output per job
						Business sector									
1960	31.0	17.6	56.7	50.2	112.9	23.0	7.1	50.5	115.7	15.9	19.9	3.5	4.0	2.8	35.0
1961	32.1	17.9	55.8	49.7	112.4	23.1	7.4	52.0	115.1	16.2	20.1	3.6	4.1	2.9	36.1
1962	33.6	19.1	56.8	50.3	113.0	23.0	7.7	53.7	113.8	16.7	20.2	3.9	4.4	3.2	38.0
1963	34.9	20.0	57.2	50.6	113.2	23.0	8.0	54.9	112.8	17.0	20.4	4.1	4.6	3.4	39.5
1964	36.0	21.2	58.9	51.5	114.4	23.1	8.3	56.2	112.0	17.4	20.6	4.4	4.9	3.7	41.2
1965	37.3	22.7	60.9	53.0	114.9	23.1	8.6	57.4	110.4	18.1	20.9	4.8	5.3	4.1	42.9
1966	38.9	24.3	62.5	54.6	114.5	23.7	9.2	59.5	110.4	18.6	21.4	5.2	5.8	4.5	44.5
1967	39.8	24.8	62.3	55.3	112.7	24.5	9.7	61.0	111.1	18.9	22.0	5.5	6.1	4.7	44.8
1968	41.2	26.0	63.3	56.4	112.1	25.5	10.5	63.1	111.3	19.5	22.9	6.0	6.6	5.1	46.2
1969	41.4	26.8	64.9	58.2	111.5	27.1	11.2	64.1	113.4	19.8	23.9	6.4	7.3	5.3	46.1
1970	42.2	26.8	63.6	58.0	109.6	28.6	12.1	65.2	114.6	20.3	24.9	6.7	7.7	5.4	46.3
1971	43.9	27.9	63.4	58.1	109.1	29.1	12.8	66.2	112.0	22.0	26.0	7.2	8.1	6.1	47.9
1972	45.4	29.7	65.4	59.8	109.2	30.0	13.6	68.2	111.4	23.0	26.9	8.0	8.9	6.8	49.6
1973	46.8	31.7	67.9	62.4	108.7	31.4	14.7	69.3	111.0	24.3	28.3	9.0	10.0	7.7	50.8
1974	46.0	31.2	68.0	63.4	107.3	34.9	16.0	68.2	112.4	26.1	31.1	9.7	10.9	8.2	49.3
1975	47.6	31.0	65.0	61.5	105.8	37.3	17.8	69.2	109.6	29.9	34.1	10.5	11.6	9.2	50.4
1976	49.2	33.0	67.2	63.4	106.0	39.0	19.2	70.7	108.8	31.8	35.8	11.8	12.9	10.5	52.1
1977	50.1	34.9	69.8	66.1	105.5	41.4	20.7	71.7	109.0	33.6	38.0	13.3	14.5	11.7	52.8
1978	50.7	37.2	73.4	69.8	105.2	44.3	22.5	72.6	109.2	35.8	40.6	15.1	16.5	13.3	53.3
1979	50.7	38.5	75.9	72.5	104.7	48.6	24.6	72.7	110.4	38.1	44.0	16.9	18.7	14.7	53.1
1980	50.7	38.1	75.2	72.6	103.5	53.8	27.3	72.4	112.3	40.3	47.9	18.3	20.5	15.4	52.5
1981	51.8	39.2	75.7	73.4	103.2	57.6	29.8	72.4	110.1	45.5	52.3	20.5	22.6	17.9	53.5
1982	51.5	38.1	74.0	72.2	102.5	62.2	32.1	73.4	112.6	46.4	55.3	21.1	23.7	17.7	52.8
1983	53.3	40.1	75.3	72.8	103.4	62.8	33.5	73.5	109.7	50.1	57.3	23.0	25.2	20.1	55.1
1984	54.8	43.7	79.7	76.5	104.2	63.8	35.0	73.7	108.3	52.6	58.9	25.7	27.9	23.0	57.1
1985	56.1	45.7	81.6	78.4	104.0	65.5	36.8	74.9	108.4	53.9	60.4	27.6	30.0	24.6	58.3
1986	57.7	47.4	82.2	79.7	103.2	67.3	38.8	77.7	109.9	53.4	61.3	29.0	31.9	25.3	59.5
1987	58.0	49.1	84.7	81.8	103.4	69.5	40.3	78.0	111.3	53.3	62.4	30.6	34.1	26.2	60.0
1988	58.9	51.2	87.0	84.3	103.1	72.1	42.4	79.3	111.9	54.5	64.4	33.0	36.9	27.9	60.7
1989	59.6	53.2	89.3	86.2	103.6	73.4	43.7	78.2	110.0	58.2	66.8	35.5	39.0	31.0	61.7
1990	60.7	54.0	88.9	86.7	102.5	76.5	46.5	79.2	110.9	59.3	69.0	37.3	41.3	32.1	62.3
1991	61.7	53.7	87.0	85.4	101.9	78.8	48.6	80.0	111.0	61.0	71.0	38.1	42.3	32.7	62.9
1992	64.6	56.0	86.6	84.9	102.0	79.9	51.6	82.9	110.8	62.2	72.1	40.4	44.7	34.8	65.9
1993	64.7	57.6	89.0	86.7	102.6	81.0	52.4	82.0	109.8	64.6	73.8	42.5	46.6	37.2	66.4
1994	65.0	60.3	92.8	89.7	103.4	81.1	52.7	80.9	108.0	67.4	75.1	45.3	48.9	40.7	67.3
1995	65.5	62.2	94.9	92.2	103.0	82.5	54.0	80.9	107.9	68.7	76.5	47.5	51.3	42.7	67.4
1996	67.1	65.1	97.0	94.2	102.9	83.4	56.0	81.7	107.4	70.3	77.7	50.5	54.3	45.7	69.0
1997	68.6	68.5	99.9	96.8	103.2	84.9	58.2	83.1	107.7	71.0	78.8	54.0	58.1	48.6	70.8
1998	70.7	72.0	101.9	98.8	103.1	87.2	61.7	86.9	110.0	69.1	79.3	57.1	62.8	49.7	72.9
1999	73.5	76.1	103.5	100.4	103.1	87.9	64.6	89.2	110.2	69.3	79.8	60.7	66.9	52.7	75.8
2000	76.1	79.8	104.9	102.1	102.7	90.9	69.1	92.3	112.3	68.2	81.0	64.6	72.5	54.4	78.1
2001	78.2	80.4	102.8	101.4	101.4	92.5	72.3	93.8	112.4	69.2	82.3	66.1	74.3	55.6	79.3
2002	81.5	81.8	100.3	99.2	101.1	90.7	73.9	94.4	109.4	72.9	82.9	67.8	74.1	59.6	82.5
2003	84.7	84.5	99.7	99.0	100.7	90.5	76.7	95.8	107.8	75.5	83.9	70.9	76.5	63.8	85.3
2004	87.3	88.1	100.9	100.3	100.6	92.0	80.3	97.6	106.8	78.5	86.1	75.8	81.0	69.1	87.8
2005	89.2	91.5	102.6	102.1	100.4	93.2	83.2	97.9	105.1	82.9	88.7	81.2	85.3	75.9	89.6
2006	90.2	94.6	104.9	104.1	100.7	95.7	86.4	98.4	105.1	85.2	91.1	86.2	90.6	80.6	90.9
2007	91.7	96.8	105.5	105.0	100.5	98.4	90.3	100.0	105.6	86.6	93.2	90.2	95.2	83.8	92.2
2008	92.8	95.8	103.3	103.5	99.8	100.0	92.8	99.0	105.6	87.8	94.7	90.7	95.8	84.1	92.6
2009	96.1	92.3	96.0	97.7	98.3	97.4	93.6	100.2	102.6	91.7	94.9	87.5	89.8	84.6	94.5
2010	99.3	95.2	95.9	96.5	99.3	95.9	95.3	100.3	100.3	99.9	96.1	96.0	91.4	91.3	91.5	98.7
2011	99.3	97.1	97.8	98.1	99.7	98.0	97.3	99.4	99.9	98.3	98.2	95.3	95.1	95.4	99.0
2012	100.0	100.0	100.0	100.0	100.0	100.0	100.0	100.0	100.0	100.0	100.0	100.0	100.0	100.0	100.0
2013	100.9	102.4	101.5	101.7	99.9	100.6	101.4	100.0	99.1	102.6	101.5	103.9	103.0	105.1	100.8
2014	101.6	105.6	104.0	103.8	100.1	102.5	104.1	100.9	99.3	104.0	103.1	109.0	108.2	109.9	101.7
2015	103.1	109.6	106.3	106.3	100.1	103.9	107.2	103.7	100.3	103.1	103.6	113.6	113.9	113.0	103.2
2016	103.5	111.6	107.9	108.1	99.7	104.7	108.3	103.5	100.2	104.1	104.4	116.6	116.9	116.3	103.2
2017	104.8	114.7	109.4	109.8	99.7	107.1	112.2	104.9	100.8	105.2	106.3	121.9	122.8	120.6	104.5
2018	106.4	118.7	111.5	111.8	99.8	109.0	116.0	105.9	100.4	108.0	108.6	128.9	129.4	128.2	106.2
2019	108.3	121.6	112.3	113.1	99.3	111.1	120.3	107.8	100.8	109.1	110.2	134.0	135.0	132.6	107.5
2020	111.0	116.6	105.0	106.0	99.1	115.8	128.5	113.8	104.4	104.6	110.9	129.3	135.0	121.9	110.0
2018															
1st quarter	106.1	117.6	110.9	111.1	99.8	108.4	115.0	105.7	100.7	106.6	107.6	126.5	127.5	125.4	105.8
2nd quarter	106.4	118.5	111.4	111.5	99.9	108.4	115.3	105.4	99.9	108.7	108.5	128.6	128.4	128.8	106.2
3rd quarter	106.6	119.1	111.8	112.0	99.9	109.4	116.6	106.2	100.5	108.1	108.9	129.7	130.4	128.8	106.4
4th quarter	106.7	119.6	112.0	112.5	99.6	109.7	117.1	106.2	100.4	108.7	109.3	130.6	131.2	130.0	106.3
2019															
1st quarter	107.7	120.6	112.0	112.6	99.5	111.2	119.7	108.4	101.7	107.0	109.4	131.9	134.1	129.1	107.1
2nd quarter	108.3	121.0	111.8	112.7	99.2	111.0	120.1	107.8	100.7	109.1	110.2	133.3	134.3	132.1	107.4
3rd quarter	108.3	121.9	112.5	113.4	99.2	110.8	120.1	107.4	100.3	110.0	110.4	134.6	135.1	134.0	107.5
4th quarter	108.7	122.7	112.9	113.7	99.3	111.3	121.1	107.6	100.5	110.1	110.8	136.0	136.7	135.1	107.9
2020															
1st quarter	108.6	120.8	111.2	112.6	98.8	113.8	123.7	109.6	102.6	107.4	111.0	134.1	137.6	129.7	107.3
2nd quarter	111.3	107.7	96.8	98.9	97.9	117.2	130.4	116.5	106.7	100.3	109.8	118.3	126.2	108.1	109.0
3rd quarter	112.8	118.1	104.7	105.4	99.3	114.2	128.8	113.8	102.9	106.9	111.0	131.1	134.8	126.3	112.0
4th quarter	111.5	119.7	107.4	107.2	100.2	118.0	131.6	115.5	105.8	103.2	111.5	133.6	141.3	123.6	111.7

Table 9-3A. Productivity and Related Data: Recent Data—*Continued*

(2012 = 100, seasonally adjusted.)

Year and quarter	Nonfarm business sector														
	Output per hour of all persons	Output	Hours of all persons	Employ-ment	Average weekly hours	Unit labor costs	Compen-sation per hour	Real hourly compen-sation	Labor share	Unit nonlabor payments	Implicit price deflator	Current dollar output	Compen-sation	Nonlabor payments	Output per job
1960	33.0	17.3	52.5	45.9	114.4	22.6	7.5	52.9	115.9	15.5	19.5	3.4	3.9	2.7	37.8
1961	34.1	17.7	52.0	45.5	114.1	22.6	7.7	54.2	115.0	15.8	19.7	3.5	4.0	2.8	38.9
1962	35.7	18.9	53.1	46.4	114.5	22.5	8.0	55.8	113.4	16.4	19.9	3.8	4.3	3.1	40.8
1963	36.9	19.8	53.7	46.9	114.5	22.5	8.3	56.9	112.5	16.8	20.0	4.0	4.5	3.3	42.2
1964	37.9	21.1	55.7	48.1	115.9	22.6	8.6	57.9	111.3	17.3	20.3	4.3	4.8	3.7	44.0
1965	39.1	22.6	57.9	49.8	116.3	22.6	8.8	58.9	110.0	17.9	20.5	4.7	5.1	4.0	45.5
1966	40.5	24.3	59.9	51.7	115.8	23.1	9.4	60.6	110.0	18.3	21.0	5.1	5.6	4.4	46.9
1967	41.3	24.7	59.9	52.6	113.8	24.0	9.9	62.2	110.8	18.6	21.7	5.4	5.9	4.6	47.0
1968	42.8	26.0	60.9	53.8	113.2	24.9	10.7	64.2	110.8	19.3	22.5	5.9	6.5	5.0	48.4
1969	42.8	26.8	62.7	55.7	112.4	26.6	11.4	65.1	113.1	19.5	23.5	6.3	7.1	5.2	48.2
1970	43.5	26.8	61.7	55.8	110.6	28.0	12.2	65.8	114.2	20.0	24.5	6.6	7.5	5.4	48.1
1971	45.2	27.8	61.6	55.9	110.0	28.6	12.9	67.0	111.8	21.7	25.6	7.1	8.0	6.0	49.7
1972	46.8	29.7	63.5	57.6	110.1	29.5	13.8	69.1	111.7	22.4	26.4	7.8	8.7	6.6	51.5
1973	48.2	31.8	66.1	60.2	109.7	30.8	14.8	70.0	112.6	22.8	27.3	8.7	9.8	7.3	52.9
1974	47.4	31.4	66.2	61.2	108.1	34.2	16.2	69.0	113.5	24.8	30.2	9.5	10.7	7.8	51.3
1975	48.7	30.9	63.3	59.4	106.6	36.8	17.9	69.9	110.4	28.9	33.4	10.3	11.4	8.9	51.9
1976	50.4	33.1	65.6	61.4	106.7	38.3	19.3	71.2	109.0	31.0	35.2	11.6	12.7	10.3	53.8
1977	51.3	35.0	68.2	64.2	106.1	40.8	20.9	72.4	109.2	32.9	37.4	13.1	14.3	11.5	54.4
1978	52.0	37.3	71.7	67.8	105.8	43.7	22.7	73.4	109.7	34.8	39.8	14.8	16.3	13.0	55.0
1979	51.9	38.6	74.3	70.7	105.1	47.9	24.9	73.4	111.1	36.9	43.1	16.6	18.5	14.2	54.5
1980	51.9	38.2	73.7	70.9	103.9	53.1	27.6	73.2	112.4	39.6	47.2	18.1	20.3	15.1	53.9
1981	52.6	39.1	74.3	71.7	103.6	57.4	30.2	73.3	110.8	44.5	51.8	20.2	22.4	17.4	54.5
1982	52.2	37.9	72.6	70.6	102.8	62.1	32.4	74.2	112.9	45.7	55.0	20.8	23.5	17.3	53.7
1983	54.4	40.3	74.0	71.3	103.9	62.3	33.9	74.3	109.5	49.8	56.9	22.9	25.1	20.1	56.5
1984	55.6	43.7	78.6	75.1	104.6	63.6	35.3	74.4	108.7	51.8	58.5	25.5	27.7	22.6	58.1
1985	56.6	45.6	80.6	77.2	104.3	65.5	37.0	75.5	108.8	53.4	60.2	27.5	29.9	24.3	59.0
1986	58.2	47.3	81.2	78.6	103.3	67.3	39.2	78.4	110.1	53.0	61.1	28.9	31.8	25.1	60.2
1987	58.6	49.0	83.7	80.8	103.6	69.4	40.7	78.7	111.6	52.9	62.2	30.5	34.0	25.9	60.7
1988	59.5	51.3	86.1	83.4	103.3	71.8	42.8	79.9	112.0	54.1	64.1	32.9	36.8	27.7	61.5
1989	60.1	53.1	88.5	85.3	103.7	73.2	44.0	78.7	110.2	57.7	66.5	35.3	38.9	30.6	62.3
1990	61.1	53.9	88.3	85.9	102.8	76.3	46.6	79.6	111.1	58.9	68.7	37.1	41.2	31.7	62.8
1991	62.1	53.6	86.3	84.5	102.2	78.7	48.9	80.4	111.0	60.7	70.9	38.0	42.2	32.6	63.5
1992	64.9	55.8	85.9	84.0	102.3	80.0	51.9	83.3	111.0	61.8	72.1	40.2	44.6	34.5	66.4
1993	65.0	57.5	88.5	86.0	102.9	80.9	52.5	82.3	109.7	64.5	73.8	42.4	46.5	37.1	66.8
1994	65.4	60.1	91.9	88.8	103.5	81.1	53.1	81.4	108.0	67.3	75.1	45.2	48.8	40.5	67.7
1995	66.1	62.2	94.1	91.4	103.0	82.2	54.4	81.5	107.5	69.0	76.5	47.6	51.1	42.9	68.1
1996	67.5	65.0	96.3	93.5	102.9	83.3	56.3	82.1	107.5	70.0	77.5	50.4	54.2	45.5	69.5
1997	68.8	68.4	99.3	96.2	103.3	84.9	58.5	83.5	107.7	71.0	78.9	53.9	58.0	48.5	71.1
1998	71.0	72.0	101.4	98.3	103.2	87.2	61.8	87.2	109.8	69.3	79.4	57.1	62.7	49.9	73.2
1999	73.7	76.1	103.3	100.1	103.1	87.9	64.7	89.3	109.8	69.8	80.0	60.9	66.8	53.1	76.0
2000	76.1	79.7	104.7	101.9	102.7	91.0	69.3	92.4	111.9	68.7	81.3	64.8	72.5	54.7	78.2
2001	78.2	80.3	102.7	101.3	101.4	92.5	72.3	93.8	112.0	69.7	82.6	66.3	74.2	56.0	79.3
2002	81.6	81.7	100.1	99.0	101.1	90.7	74.0	94.5	108.9	73.7	83.3	68.0	74.1	60.2	82.5
2003	84.7	84.3	99.6	98.9	100.6	90.6	76.7	95.8	107.6	75.9	84.2	71.0	76.4	64.0	85.2
2004	87.1	87.9	100.9	100.3	100.6	92.1	80.2	97.6	106.8	78.6	86.2	75.8	80.9	69.0	87.6
2005	89.0	91.3	102.6	102.1	100.4	93.4	83.1	97.8	104.8	83.5	89.1	81.3	85.3	76.2	89.4
2006	90.0	94.4	104.9	104.2	100.8	95.9	86.3	98.4	104.8	85.9	91.6	86.5	90.6	81.1	90.7
2007	91.6	96.7	105.6	105.1	100.5	98.4	90.1	99.8	105.3	86.9	93.4	90.4	95.2	84.1	92.0
2008	92.6	95.7	103.4	103.6	99.8	100.1	92.7	98.9	105.5	88.1	94.9	90.8	95.8	84.4	92.4
2009	95.9	92.0	96.0	97.7	98.3	97.6	93.5	100.1	102.3	92.5	95.4	87.8	89.8	85.1	94.2
2010	99.2	95.0	95.8	96.5	99.3	96.1	95.3	100.4	99.8	96.6	96.3	91.5	91.3	91.8	98.5
2011	99.2	96.9	97.8	98.0	99.7	98.2	97.4	99.5	100.0	98.1	98.2	95.2	95.2	95.1	98.9
2012	100.0	100.0	100.0	100.0	100.0	100.0	100.0	100.0	100.0	100.0	100.0	100.0	100.0	100.0	100.0
2013	100.5	102.2	101.7	101.8	99.9	100.8	101.3	99.8	99.3	102.3	101.5	103.7	103.0	104.6	100.4
2014	101.4	105.4	104.0	103.9	100.1	102.7	104.1	100.9	99.5	104.0	103.3	108.9	108.3	109.7	101.5
2015	102.9	109.4	106.2	106.2	100.0	104.3	107.4	103.9	100.3	103.6	104.0	113.7	114.1	113.3	103.0
2016	103.3	111.3	107.8	108.1	99.7	105.1	108.6	103.7	100.0	105.0	105.0	116.9	117.0	116.9	103.0
2017	104.6	114.4	109.4	109.8	99.6	107.5	112.4	105.1	100.6	105.9	106.8	122.2	123.0	121.2	104.2
2018	106.1	118.4	111.6	111.9	99.8	109.5	116.1	106.0	100.3	108.8	109.2	129.3	129.6	128.9	105.9
2019	108.0	121.3	112.4	113.2	99.3	111.5	120.4	107.9	100.6	110.0	110.8	134.5	135.3	133.4	107.2
2020	110.7	116.2	105.0	106.0	99.0	116.3	128.8	114.0	104.2	105.5	111.6	129.7	135.2	122.6	109.6
2018															
1st quarter	105.8	117.3	110.9	111.2	99.7	108.8	115.1	105.8	100.6	107.4	108.2	126.9	127.7	126.0	105.5
2nd quarter	106.0	118.2	111.5	111.7	99.9	108.9	115.4	105.5	99.8	109.5	109.1	129.0	128.7	129.4	105.8
3rd quarter	106.3	118.9	111.8	112.0	99.8	109.9	116.8	106.4	100.4	109.0	109.5	130.2	130.7	129.6	106.1
4th quarter	106.4	119.3	112.1	112.6	99.6	110.2	117.3	106.3	100.3	109.5	109.9	131.1	131.5	130.6	106.0
2019															
1st quarter	107.4	120.4	112.1	112.7	99.5	111.6	119.9	108.5	101.5	107.9	110.0	132.5	134.4	129.9	106.8
2nd quarter	107.9	120.8	111.9	112.8	99.2	111.4	120.3	107.9	100.5	110.1	110.8	133.9	134.6	132.9	107.1
3rd quarter	108.1	121.6	112.6	113.5	99.2	111.3	120.2	107.5	100.1	110.9	111.1	135.1	135.3	134.9	107.2
4th quarter	108.5	122.5	112.9	113.8	99.2	111.8	121.2	107.8	100.3	111.0	111.4	136.5	136.9	136.0	107.6
2020															
1st quarter	108.3	120.5	111.3	112.7	98.8	114.4	123.9	109.8	102.5	108.1	111.7	134.6	137.9	130.2	107.0
2nd quarter	111.2	107.4	96.6	98.7	97.9	117.7	130.8	116.9	106.4	101.5	110.6	118.9	126.4	109.0	108.8
3rd quarter	112.3	117.7	104.8	105.5	99.3	114.7	128.9	113.9	102.6	108.0	111.8	131.6	135.0	127.1	111.6
4th quarter	111.3	119.4	107.3	107.2	100.1	118.6	131.9	115.8	105.7	103.9	112.2	133.9	141.5	124.0	111.4

Table 9-3B. Productivity and Related Data: Historical Data

(2012 = 100, seasonally adjusted.)

Year and quarter	Business sector								Nonfarm business sector							
	Output per hour of all persons	Output	Hours of all persons	Compensation per hour	Real compensation per hour	Unit labor costs	Unit nonlabor payments	Implicit price deflator	Output per hour of all persons	Output	Hours of all persons	Compensation per hour	Real compensation per hour	Unit labor costs	Unit nonlabor payments	Implicit price deflator
1947	20.4	11.2	54.7	3.6	33.9	17.7	11.8	15.1	20.4	11.2	54.7	3.6	33.9	16.4	11.3	14.2
1948	21.3	11.7	55.1	3.9	34.0	18.4	13.0	16.0	21.3	11.7	55.1	3.9	34.0	17.4	12.2	15.1
1949	21.8	11.6	53.3	4.0	34.9	18.2	12.9	15.9	21.8	11.6	53.3	4.0	34.9	17.3	12.5	15.2
1950	23.6	12.7	54.1	4.2	36.9	18.0	13.5	16.1	23.6	12.7	54.1	4.2	36.9	17.2	13.1	15.4
1951	24.3	13.6	55.8	4.7	37.5	19.2	14.9	17.3	24.3	13.6	55.8	4.7	37.5	18.2	14.1	16.4
1952	25.0	14.0	55.9	4.9	39.1	19.7	14.6	17.5	25.0	14.0	55.9	4.9	39.1	18.9	14.0	16.8
1953	25.9	14.7	56.6	5.3	41.2	20.2	14.3	17.6	25.9	14.7	56.6	5.3	41.2	19.5	14.0	17.1
1954	26.5	14.5	54.7	5.4	42.3	20.4	14.2	17.7	26.5	14.5	54.7	5.4	42.3	19.7	14.0	17.2
1955	27.6	15.7	56.8	5.6	43.5	20.1	15.2	18.0	27.6	15.7	56.8	5.6	43.5	19.6	14.9	17.5
1956	27.7	16.0	57.6	5.9	45.7	21.4	14.9	18.5	27.7	16.0	57.6	5.9	45.7	20.9	14.6	18.2
1957	28.6	16.3	56.8	6.3	47.1	22.1	15.4	19.1	28.6	16.3	56.8	6.3	47.1	21.5	15.1	18.7
1958	29.4	16.0	54.3	6.6	47.8	22.4	15.7	19.5	29.4	16.0	54.3	6.6	47.8	21.9	15.3	19.0
1959	30.5	17.2	56.5	6.9	49.4	22.5	16.1	19.7	30.5	17.2	56.5	6.9	49.4	22.0	15.9	19.3
1947																
1st quarter	20.4	10.8	46.3	3.7	35.9	16.0	11.6	14.6	23.3	10.8	46.3	3.7	35.9	16.0	10.8	13.7
2nd quarter	20.5	11.0	46.3	3.8	36.2	16.0	11.5	14.8	23.8	11.0	46.3	3.8	36.2	16.0	11.2	13.9
3rd quarter	20.3	10.7	46.4	3.9	36.5	17.0	11.8	15.2	23.1	10.7	46.4	3.9	36.5	17.0	11.4	14.5
4th quarter	20.5	11.3	46.9	4.0	36.3	16.7	12.3	15.7	24.0	11.3	46.9	4.0	36.3	16.7	11.7	14.5
1948																
1st quarter	21.0	11.4	47.2	4.1	36.4	17.0	12.8	15.8	24.1	11.4	47.2	4.1	36.4	17.0	11.8	14.7
2nd quarter	21.4	11.3	47.1	4.2	36.3	17.3	13.2	15.9	24.1	11.3	47.1	4.2	36.3	17.3	12.0	15.0
3rd quarter	21.3	11.4	47.5	4.2	36.4	17.6	13.2	16.2	24.1	11.4	47.5	4.2	36.4	17.6	12.3	15.3
4th quarter	21.5	11.4	47.0	4.3	37.1	17.7	12.9	16.2	24.2	11.4	47.0	4.3	37.1	17.7	12.6	15.5
1949																
1st quarter	21.4	11.3	46.2	4.3	37.7	17.6	13.0	16.1	24.5	11.3	46.2	4.3	37.7	17.6	12.5	15.4
2nd quarter	21.5	11.2	45.5	4.3	37.8	17.5	12.8	15.9	24.7	11.2	45.5	4.3	37.8	17.5	12.3	15.2
3rd quarter	22.1	11.4	45.0	4.3	38.2	17.1	13.0	15.8	25.3	11.4	45.0	4.3	38.2	17.1	12.7	15.2
4th quarter	22.1	11.3	44.8	4.3	38.2	17.1	12.7	15.8	25.2	11.3	44.8	4.3	38.2	17.1	12.5	15.1
1950																
1st quarter	23.1	11.7	45.1	4.4	39.3	17.0	12.9	15.7	26.0	11.7	45.1	4.4	39.3	17.0	12.8	15.2
2nd quarter	23.4	12.2	46.3	4.5	39.9	17.2	13.0	15.8	26.3	12.2	46.3	4.5	39.9	17.2	12.8	15.2
3rd quarter	23.8	12.8	47.7	4.6	39.9	17.1	13.8	16.2	26.9	12.8	47.7	4.6	39.9	17.1	13.2	15.4
4th quarter	23.9	13.0	48.2	4.7	40.1	17.5	14.3	16.5	27.0	13.0	48.2	4.7	40.1	17.5	13.4	15.7
1951																
1st quarter	23.9	13.2	49.0	4.8	39.4	17.9	14.9	17.1	27.0	13.2	49.0	4.8	39.4	17.9	13.9	16.2
2nd quarter	24.0	13.3	49.4	4.9	39.9	18.4	14.7	17.3	26.9	13.3	49.4	4.9	39.9	18.4	13.8	16.4
3rd quarter	24.7	13.4	48.9	5.0	40.4	18.2	15.0	17.3	27.5	13.4	48.9	5.0	40.4	18.2	14.3	16.5
4th quarter	24.6	13.5	48.9	5.1	40.6	18.5	15.0	17.5	27.6	13.5	48.9	5.1	40.6	18.5	14.2	16.6
1952																
1st quarter	24.7	13.6	49.2	5.1	40.8	18.6	14.8	17.4	27.7	13.6	49.2	5.1	40.8	18.6	14.1	16.6
2nd quarter	24.9	13.6	49.0	5.2	41.0	18.7	14.5	17.4	27.7	13.6	49.0	5.2	41.0	18.7	13.9	16.6
3rd quarter	25.0	13.6	49.4	5.3	41.3	19.1	14.6	17.6	27.5	13.6	49.4	5.3	41.3	19.1	13.9	16.8
4th quarter	25.4	14.3	50.7	5.4	42.2	19.1	14.5	17.6	28.1	14.3	50.7	5.4	42.2	19.1	14.1	16.9
1953																
1st quarter	25.8	14.5	51.2	5.4	42.9	19.2	14.4	17.6	28.4	14.5	51.2	5.4	42.9	19.2	14.0	17.0
2nd quarter	26.0	14.6	51.3	5.5	43.2	19.4	14.4	17.6	28.4	14.6	51.3	5.5	43.2	19.4	14.1	17.1
3rd quarter	26.0	14.5	50.8	5.6	43.5	19.5	14.2	17.7	28.5	14.5	50.8	5.6	43.5	19.5	14.1	17.1
4th quarter	25.9	14.2	50.0	5.6	43.8	19.8	14.2	17.7	28.4	14.2	50.0	5.6	43.8	19.8	13.8	17.1
1954																
1st quarter	25.9	14.1	49.3	5.7	44.1	19.9	14.1	17.7	28.5	14.1	49.3	5.7	44.1	19.9	13.7	17.2
2nd quarter	26.3	14.1	49.0	5.7	44.2	19.8	14.0	17.7	28.7	14.1	49.0	5.7	44.2	19.8	13.9	17.2
3rd quarter	26.7	14.3	48.8	5.7	44.7	19.6	14.4	17.7	29.2	14.3	48.8	5.7	44.7	19.6	14.1	17.2
4th quarter	27.1	14.6	49.4	5.8	45.3	19.5	14.4	17.7	29.6	14.6	49.4	5.8	45.3	19.5	14.3	17.3
1955																
1st quarter	27.5	15.1	50.2	5.8	45.5	19.3	15.2	17.8	30.1	15.1	50.2	5.8	45.5	19.3	14.8	17.4
2nd quarter	27.8	15.4	50.8	5.9	45.9	19.4	15.1	17.8	30.2	15.4	50.8	5.9	45.9	19.4	14.8	17.4
3rd quarter	27.7	15.6	51.4	6.0	46.7	19.7	15.2	18.0	30.4	15.6	51.4	6.0	46.7	19.7	14.9	17.6
4th quarter	27.5	15.7	52.0	6.0	47.0	19.9	15.3	18.2	30.2	15.7	52.0	6.0	47.0	19.9	15.0	17.8
1956																
1st quarter	27.4	15.6	52.3	6.1	47.7	20.5	14.9	18.3	29.9	15.6	52.3	6.1	47.7	20.5	14.6	17.9
2nd quarter	27.6	15.7	52.4	6.2	48.3	20.8	14.7	18.4	30.0	15.7	52.4	6.2	48.3	20.8	14.5	18.0
3rd quarter	27.6	15.7	52.2	6.3	48.6	21.1	15.0	18.7	30.0	15.7	52.2	6.3	48.6	21.1	14.6	18.3
4th quarter	28.2	15.9	52.5	6.4	49.0	21.2	15.1	18.7	30.3	15.9	52.5	6.4	49.0	21.2	14.7	18.4
1957																
1st quarter	28.4	16.1	52.5	6.5	49.3	21.3	15.3	19.0	30.7	16.1	52.5	6.5	49.3	21.3	15.1	18.6
2nd quarter	28.4	16.0	52.4	6.6	49.3	21.6	15.3	19.1	30.6	16.0	52.4	6.6	49.3	21.6	15.0	18.7
3rd quarter	28.7	16.2	52.2	6.7	49.6	21.6	15.6	19.2	31.0	16.2	52.2	6.7	49.6	21.6	15.2	18.8
4th quarter	29.0	15.9	51.1	6.8	50.0	21.8	15.3	19.2	31.1	15.9	51.1	6.8	50.0	21.8	15.0	18.8
1958																
1st quarter	28.8	15.3	49.9	6.8	49.4	22.1	15.3	19.4	30.7	15.3	49.9	6.8	49.4	22.1	14.8	18.9
2nd quarter	29.2	15.4	49.2	6.8	49.5	21.9	15.7	19.5	31.3	15.4	49.2	6.8	49.5	21.9	15.2	18.9
3rd quarter	29.7	15.9	49.8	7.0	50.7	22.0	15.7	19.5	31.9	15.9	49.8	7.0	50.7	22.0	15.3	19.0
4th quarter	30.0	16.4	50.5	7.0	50.9	21.7	16.2	19.6	32.4	16.4	50.5	7.0	50.9	21.7	15.8	19.1
1959																
1st quarter	30.3	16.7	51.5	7.1	51.3	21.9	16.0	19.6	32.4	16.7	51.5	7.1	51.3	21.9	15.8	19.2
2nd quarter	30.4	17.2	52.5	7.1	51.6	21.8	16.2	19.6	32.7	17.2	52.5	7.1	51.6	21.8	15.9	19.3
3rd quarter	30.6	17.2	52.3	7.2	51.6	21.9	16.2	19.7	32.8	17.2	52.3	7.2	51.6	21.9	16.0	19.3
4th quarter	30.6	17.1	52.4	7.3	51.8	22.2	16.0	19.8	32.7	17.1	52.4	7.3	51.8	22.2	15.8	19.4

Table 9-3B. Productivity and Related Data: Historical Data—*Continued*

(2012 = 100, seasonally adjusted.)

Year and quarter	Business sector								Nonfarm business sector							
	Output per hour of all persons	Output	Hours of all persons	Compensation per hour	Real compensation per hour	Unit labor costs	Unit nonlabor payments	Implicit price deflator	Output per hour of all persons	Output	Hours of all persons	Compensation per hour	Real compensation per hour	Unit labor costs	Unit nonlabor payments	Implicit price deflator
1960																
1st quarter	31.5	17.6	52.7	7.4	52.9	22.2	16.2	19.8	33.5	17.6	52.7	7.4	52.9	22.2	15.9	19.5
2nd quarter	30.8	17.4	52.8	7.5	52.9	22.7	15.8	19.9	32.9	17.4	52.8	7.5	52.9	22.7	15.4	19.5
3rd quarter	31.0	17.4	52.5	7.5	53.2	22.7	16.0	19.9	33.1	17.4	52.5	7.5	53.2	22.7	15.5	19.6
4th quarter	30.7	17.0	52.0	7.5	53.1	23.1	15.6	20.0	32.7	17.0	52.0	7.5	53.1	23.1	15.2	19.6
1961																
1st quarter	31.1	17.1	51.7	7.6	53.5	23.0	15.7	20.0	33.1	17.1	51.7	7.6	53.5	23.0	15.3	19.7
2nd quarter	32.1	17.5	51.6	7.7	54.2	22.7	16.1	20.0	34.0	17.5	51.6	7.7	54.2	22.7	15.8	19.7
3rd quarter	32.5	17.9	51.9	7.8	54.4	22.5	16.4	20.1	34.6	17.9	51.9	7.8	54.4	22.5	16.1	19.7
4th quarter	32.8	18.3	52.5	7.8	54.7	22.5	16.5	20.1	34.9	18.3	52.5	7.8	54.7	22.5	16.1	19.7
1962																
1st quarter	33.2	18.7	52.7	8.0	55.4	22.4	16.7	20.2	35.4	18.7	52.7	8.0	55.4	22.4	16.4	19.8
2nd quarter	33.3	18.8	53.4	8.0	55.5	22.7	16.5	20.2	35.3	18.8	53.4	8.0	55.5	22.7	16.2	19.9
3rd quarter	33.9	19.1	53.2	8.1	55.8	22.5	16.8	20.3	35.9	19.1	53.2	8.1	55.8	22.5	16.5	19.9
4th quarter	34.2	19.1	52.9	8.1	56.1	22.5	16.7	20.3	36.1	19.1	52.9	8.1	56.1	22.5	16.5	19.9
1963																
1st quarter	34.3	19.3	53.2	8.2	56.5	22.7	16.8	20.3	36.3	19.3	53.2	8.2	56.5	22.7	16.5	20.0
2nd quarter	34.5	19.6	53.6	8.3	56.7	22.6	16.9	20.3	36.5	19.6	53.6	8.3	56.7	22.6	16.6	20.0
3rd quarter	35.4	20.1	53.7	8.3	56.9	22.3	17.2	20.4	37.4	20.1	53.7	8.3	56.9	22.3	17.0	20.0
4th quarter	35.4	20.2	54.1	8.4	57.4	22.6	17.3	20.5	37.4	20.2	54.1	8.4	57.4	22.6	16.9	20.1
1964																
1st quarter	35.8	20.8	55.2	8.4	57.1	22.4	17.5	20.5	37.7	20.8	55.2	8.4	57.1	22.4	17.3	20.2
2nd quarter	35.9	21.0	55.4	8.5	57.7	22.5	17.4	20.6	37.9	21.0	55.4	8.5	57.7	22.5	17.3	20.2
3rd quarter	36.3	21.4	55.8	8.6	58.3	22.5	17.5	20.6	38.3	21.4	55.8	8.6	58.3	22.5	17.4	20.3
4th quarter	36.1	21.4	56.3	8.7	58.4	22.9	17.3	20.7	37.9	21.4	56.3	8.7	58.4	22.9	17.1	20.4
1965																
1st quarter	36.7	22.0	57.2	8.7	58.5	22.7	17.8	20.8	38.5	22.0	57.2	8.7	58.5	22.7	17.6	20.5
2nd quarter	36.7	22.3	57.8	8.8	58.5	22.7	17.8	20.9	38.6	22.3	57.8	8.8	58.5	22.7	17.6	20.5
3rd quarter	37.7	22.8	57.9	8.9	58.9	22.5	18.3	20.9	39.4	22.8	57.9	8.9	58.9	22.5	18.0	20.6
4th quarter	38.2	23.4	58.4	9.0	59.5	22.5	18.6	21.1	40.1	23.4	58.4	9.0	59.5	22.5	18.3	20.7
1966																
1st quarter	38.9	24.1	59.3	9.2	60.0	22.6	18.7	21.2	40.7	24.1	59.3	9.2	60.0	22.6	18.3	20.7
2nd quarter	38.7	24.2	59.9	9.3	60.4	23.1	18.4	21.3	40.4	24.2	59.9	9.3	60.4	23.1	18.1	20.9
3rd quarter	38.8	24.4	60.2	9.4	60.7	23.3	18.5	21.5	40.5	24.4	60.2	9.4	60.7	23.3	18.2	21.1
4th quarter	39.1	24.5	60.0	9.6	61.0	23.5	18.7	21.7	40.8	24.5	60.0	9.6	61.0	23.5	18.5	21.3
1967																
1st quarter	39.5	24.6	59.9	9.7	61.7	23.6	18.8	21.8	41.1	24.6	59.9	9.7	61.7	23.6	18.6	21.4
2nd quarter	39.8	24.6	59.6	9.9	62.3	23.9	18.7	21.9	41.2	24.6	59.6	9.9	62.3	23.9	18.5	21.6
3rd quarter	39.9	24.8	59.8	10.0	62.6	24.1	18.9	22.1	41.5	24.8	59.8	10.0	62.6	24.1	18.6	21.7
4th quarter	40.0	25.0	60.0	10.1	62.7	24.4	19.1	22.3	41.6	25.0	60.0	10.1	62.7	24.4	18.8	21.9
1968																
1st quarter	40.9	25.6	60.1	10.4	63.8	24.5	19.4	22.5	42.5	25.6	60.1	10.4	63.8	24.5	19.2	22.2
2nd quarter	41.3	26.0	60.7	10.6	64.2	24.6	19.7	22.8	42.9	26.0	60.7	10.6	64.2	24.6	19.5	22.4
3rd quarter	41.3	26.2	61.1	10.7	64.4	25.0	19.5	22.9	42.9	26.2	61.1	10.7	64.4	25.0	19.3	22.6
4th quarter	41.3	26.3	61.5	11.0	64.8	25.6	19.5	23.3	42.8	26.3	61.5	11.0	64.8	25.6	19.3	22.9
1969																
1st quarter	41.4	26.8	62.1	11.1	64.9	25.7	20.0	23.5	43.2	26.8	62.1	11.1	64.9	25.7	19.8	23.1
2nd quarter	41.4	26.8	62.7	11.3	65.0	26.4	19.8	23.8	42.8	26.8	62.7	11.3	65.0	26.4	19.5	23.4
3rd quarter	41.5	27.0	63.0	11.5	65.2	26.8	19.8	24.0	42.9	27.0	63.0	11.5	65.2	26.8	19.5	23.6
4th quarter	41.4	26.8	62.8	11.7	65.5	27.5	19.6	24.3	42.7	26.8	62.8	11.7	65.5	27.5	19.2	23.9
1970																
1st quarter	41.6	26.8	62.5	11.9	65.6	27.9	19.6	24.6	42.8	26.8	62.5	11.9	65.6	27.9	19.3	24.1
2nd quarter	42.0	26.8	61.7	12.1	65.7	27.9	20.3	24.9	43.4	26.8	61.7	12.1	65.7	27.9	20.0	24.5
3rd quarter	42.8	27.1	61.4	12.3	66.1	27.9	20.6	25.0	44.1	27.1	61.4	12.3	66.1	27.9	20.3	24.6
4th quarter	42.5	26.6	60.9	12.4	65.8	28.5	20.6	25.3	43.7	26.6	60.9	12.4	65.8	28.5	20.4	25.0
1971																
1st quarter	43.7	27.5	61.2	12.7	66.6	28.2	21.6	25.6	45.0	27.5	61.2	12.7	66.6	28.2	21.3	25.2
2nd quarter	43.8	27.7	61.4	12.9	67.0	28.5	21.9	25.9	45.1	27.7	61.4	12.9	67.0	28.5	21.6	25.5
3rd quarter	44.3	28.0	61.4	13.1	67.3	28.7	22.3	26.1	45.6	28.0	61.4	13.1	67.3	28.7	22.0	25.8
4th quarter	43.9	28.0	62.1	13.1	67.2	29.1	22.0	26.3	45.2	28.0	62.1	13.1	67.2	29.1	21.6	25.9
1972																
1st quarter	44.4	28.8	62.8	13.5	68.5	29.5	22.2	26.6	45.9	28.8	62.8	13.5	68.5	29.5	21.9	26.2
2nd quarter	45.5	29.6	63.2	13.7	68.9	29.2	22.9	26.7	46.8	29.6	63.2	13.7	68.9	29.2	22.5	26.3
3rd quarter	45.6	29.9	63.6	13.9	69.2	29.4	23.2	27.0	47.0	29.9	63.6	13.9	69.2	29.4	22.5	26.4
4th quarter	46.1	30.5	64.2	14.1	69.8	29.7	23.5	27.3	47.4	30.5	64.2	14.1	69.8	29.7	22.5	26.6
1973																
1st quarter	47.0	31.6	65.2	14.5	70.6	29.8	23.7	27.5	48.5	31.6	65.2	14.5	70.6	29.8	22.7	26.8
2nd quarter	47.1	32.0	65.9	14.7	70.1	30.3	24.2	27.9	48.5	32.0	65.9	14.7	70.1	30.3	22.9	27.1
3rd quarter	46.4	31.9	66.3	14.9	69.9	31.1	24.3	28.5	48.1	31.9	66.3	14.9	69.9	31.1	22.6	27.4
4th quarter	46.6	31.9	66.7	15.2	69.6	31.9	25.0	29.1	47.8	31.9	66.7	15.2	69.6	31.9	23.0	28.0
1974																
1st quarter	46.0	31.6	66.4	15.6	69.1	32.7	25.1	29.8	47.7	31.6	66.4	15.6	69.1	32.7	23.5	28.7
2nd quarter	46.1	31.6	66.6	16.0	69.0	34.3	25.7	30.5	47.5	31.6	66.6	16.0	69.0	33.7	24.6	29.7
3rd quarter	45.7	31.2	66.3	16.5	69.2	35.0	26.1	31.5	47.1	31.2	66.3	16.5	69.2	35.0	25.0	30.7
4th quarter	46.1	31.0	65.2	16.9	68.9	35.6	27.6	32.5	47.5	31.0	65.2	16.9	68.9	35.6	26.3	31.6

Table 9-3B. Productivity and Related Data: Historical Data—*Continued*

(2012 = 100, seasonally adjusted.)

Year and quarter	Business sector								Nonfarm business sector							
	Output per hour of all persons	Output	Hours of all persons	Compensation per hour	Real compensation per hour	Unit labor costs	Unit nonlabor payments	Implicit price deflator	Output per hour of all persons	Output	Hours of all persons	Compensation per hour	Real compensation per hour	Unit labor costs	Unit nonlabor payments	Implicit price deflator
1975																
1st quarter	46.8	30.2	63.2	17.4	69.6	36.4	28.5	33.3	47.9	30.2	63.2	17.4	69.6	36.4	27.6	32.6
2nd quarter	47.5	30.4	62.6	17.8	70.2	36.6	29.3	33.7	48.6	30.4	62.6	17.8	70.2	36.6	28.5	33.1
3rd quarter	48.0	31.1	63.2	18.1	70.0	36.8	30.6	34.3	49.2	31.1	63.2	18.1	70.0	36.8	29.4	33.6
4th quarter	48.2	31.7	64.2	18.4	69.9	37.4	31.0	34.9	49.3	31.7	64.2	18.4	69.9	37.4	29.8	34.1
1976																
1st quarter	48.8	32.6	65.3	18.8	70.4	37.6	31.3	35.2	50.0	32.6	65.3	18.8	70.4	37.6	30.5	34.5
2nd quarter	49.2	33.0	65.3	19.1	71.1	37.9	31.6	35.5	50.5	33.0	65.3	19.1	71.1	37.9	30.9	34.9
3rd quarter	49.2	33.2	65.6	19.5	71.5	38.6	31.8	36.0	50.6	33.2	65.6	19.5	71.5	38.6	31.1	35.3
4th quarter	49.5	33.5	65.9	19.9	71.9	39.3	32.3	36.6	50.7	33.5	65.9	19.9	71.9	39.3	31.7	36.0
1977																
1st quarter	49.8	34.0	66.6	20.3	72.0	39.8	32.9	37.2	51.1	34.0	66.6	20.3	72.0	39.8	32.2	36.5
2nd quarter	49.9	34.8	67.9	20.7	72.2	40.5	33.3	37.7	51.3	34.8	67.9	20.7	72.2	40.5	32.7	37.1
3rd quarter	50.6	35.6	68.6	21.1	72.6	40.8	33.8	38.1	51.8	35.6	68.6	21.1	72.6	40.8	33.4	37.6
4th quarter	50.0	35.4	69.3	21.5	72.8	42.1	34.1	38.9	51.1	35.4	69.3	21.5	72.8	42.1	33.3	38.2
1978																
1st quarter	49.8	35.6	69.6	22.1	73.6	43.2	33.8	39.4	51.2	35.6	69.6	22.1	73.6	43.2	32.9	38.7
2nd quarter	50.8	37.4	71.7	22.5	73.2	43.0	35.7	40.2	52.2	37.4	71.7	22.5	73.2	43.0	34.6	39.4
3rd quarter	51.0	37.7	72.3	22.9	73.3	43.8	36.3	40.9	52.2	37.7	72.3	22.9	73.3	43.8	35.3	40.1
4th quarter	51.1	38.4	73.1	23.5	73.7	44.6	37.1	41.7	52.5	38.4	73.1	23.5	73.7	44.6	36.1	40.9
1979																
1st quarter	50.9	38.4	73.7	24.1	73.9	46.2	36.9	42.5	52.1	38.4	73.7	24.1	73.9	46.2	35.6	41.6
2nd quarter	50.8	38.4	73.9	24.6	73.6	47.4	38.0	43.6	52.0	38.4	73.9	24.6	73.6	47.4	36.8	42.8
3rd quarter	50.8	38.7	74.6	25.2	73.3	48.5	38.6	44.5	51.9	38.7	74.6	25.2	73.3	48.5	37.4	43.7
4th quarter	50.7	38.8	74.7	25.8	73.3	49.7	38.8	45.3	51.8	38.8	74.7	25.8	73.3	49.7	37.7	44.5
1980																
1st quarter	51.0	38.8	74.6	26.5	73.0	50.9	39.5	46.3	52.1	38.8	74.6	26.5	73.0	50.9	38.8	45.6
2nd quarter	50.5	37.7	73.2	27.2	73.2	52.8	39.4	47.3	51.6	37.7	73.2	27.2	73.2	52.8	39.3	46.9
3rd quarter	50.6	37.7	72.8	27.9	73.3	54.0	40.3	48.4	51.8	37.7	72.8	27.9	73.3	54.0	39.5	47.7
4th quarter	51.1	38.6	73.8	28.7	73.5	54.8	42.0	49.6	52.3	38.6	73.8	28.7	73.5	54.8	40.8	48.7
1981																
1st quarter	52.0	39.4	74.3	29.4	73.4	55.4	44.6	50.9	53.1	39.4	74.3	29.4	73.4	55.4	43.6	50.2
2nd quarter	51.6	39.0	74.3	29.9	73.2	57.1	44.8	51.9	52.4	39.0	74.3	29.9	73.2	57.1	43.7	51.3
3rd quarter	52.3	39.3	74.3	30.6	73.4	57.8	46.4	52.8	52.9	39.3	74.3	30.6	73.4	57.8	45.2	52.3
4th quarter	51.7	38.7	73.9	31.1	73.3	59.4	46.1	53.6	52.4	38.7	73.9	31.1	73.3	59.4	45.4	53.3
1982																
1st quarter	51.4	37.9	72.7	31.9	74.4	61.2	45.2	54.3	52.1	37.9	72.7	31.9	74.4	61.2	44.5	53.9
2nd quarter	51.5	38.1	73.0	32.2	74.2	61.7	46.1	54.9	52.1	38.1	73.0	32.2	74.2	61.7	45.5	54.6
3rd quarter	51.5	37.9	72.5	32.7	74.1	62.5	46.7	55.7	52.2	37.9	72.5	32.7	74.1	62.5	45.9	55.3
4th quarter	52.0	37.8	71.8	33.1	74.3	62.9	47.4	56.2	52.7	37.8	71.8	33.1	74.3	62.9	46.9	55.9
1983																
1st quarter	52.4	38.5	72.2	33.5	74.7	62.7	48.4	56.6	53.4	38.5	72.2	33.5	74.7	62.7	47.6	56.2
2nd quarter	53.3	39.8	73.1	33.8	74.5	62.0	49.7	57.0	54.5	39.8	73.1	33.8	74.5	62.0	49.2	56.4
3rd quarter	53.6	40.8	74.6	34.0	74.2	62.1	50.9	57.5	54.8	40.8	74.6	34.0	74.2	62.1	51.0	57.3
4th quarter	54.0	41.8	76.0	34.4	74.3	62.4	51.3	57.9	55.0	41.8	76.0	34.4	74.3	62.4	51.3	57.6
1984																
1st quarter	54.3	42.8	77.4	34.8	74.2	62.9	51.9	58.3	55.3	42.8	77.4	34.8	74.2	62.9	51.0	57.7
2nd quarter	54.8	43.6	78.4	35.1	74.2	63.2	52.6	58.7	55.6	43.6	78.4	35.1	74.2	63.2	51.8	58.3
3rd quarter	55.1	44.0	78.8	35.6	74.7	63.8	52.8	59.1	55.8	44.0	78.8	35.6	74.7	63.8	52.1	58.7
4th quarter	55.2	44.3	79.3	35.9	74.7	64.3	53.0	59.4	55.9	44.3	79.3	35.9	74.7	64.3	52.2	59.0
1985																
1st quarter	55.5	44.8	79.9	36.4	75.0	64.9	53.7	60.0	56.1	44.8	79.9	36.4	75.0	64.9	53.0	59.7
2nd quarter	55.7	45.2	80.4	36.7	75.1	65.3	53.8	60.3	56.2	45.2	80.4	36.7	75.1	65.3	53.3	60.1
3rd quarter	56.6	45.9	80.7	37.3	75.7	65.4	54.4	60.6	57.0	45.9	80.7	37.3	75.7	65.4	54.1	60.5
4th quarter	56.8	46.4	81.1	38.0	76.4	66.4	53.6	60.8	57.2	46.4	81.1	38.0	76.4	66.4	53.1	60.6
1986																
1st quarter	57.3	46.8	80.9	38.5	77.1	66.6	53.9	61.0	57.9	46.8	80.9	38.5	77.1	66.6	53.6	61.0
2nd quarter	57.7	47.1	80.7	39.0	78.4	66.8	53.7	61.2	58.3	47.1	80.7	39.0	78.4	66.8	53.4	61.0
3rd quarter	58.0	47.5	81.1	39.5	78.9	67.4	53.5	61.3	58.6	47.5	81.1	39.5	78.9	67.4	52.9	61.1
4th quarter	57.9	47.8	81.7	40.0	79.5	68.4	52.6	61.5	58.5	47.8	81.7	40.0	79.5	68.4	52.1	61.3
1987																
1st quarter	57.6	48.2	82.7	40.2	78.9	69.0	52.6	61.8	58.2	48.2	82.7	40.2	78.9	69.0	52.1	61.7
2nd quarter	58.0	48.8	83.2	40.5	78.7	69.1	53.3	62.2	58.6	48.8	83.2	40.5	78.7	69.1	52.8	62.0
3rd quarter	58.1	49.1	83.8	40.9	78.7	69.8	53.5	62.7	58.6	49.1	83.8	40.9	78.7	69.8	53.1	62.5
4th quarter	58.6	50.1	84.7	41.4	79.0	69.9	53.8	62.9	59.2	50.1	84.7	41.4	79.0	69.9	53.3	62.7
1988																
1st quarter	58.7	50.3	84.7	42.1	79.8	70.9	53.7	63.5	59.4	50.3	84.7	42.1	79.8	70.9	53.1	63.1
2nd quarter	58.8	51.2	85.9	42.6	80.0	71.5	53.9	64.0	59.5	51.2	85.9	42.6	80.0	71.5	53.5	63.7
3rd quarter	59.0	51.4	86.2	43.1	80.0	72.2	54.8	64.8	59.7	51.4	86.2	43.1	80.0	72.2	54.3	64.5
4th quarter	59.1	52.1	87.1	43.4	79.9	72.6	55.5	65.3	59.8	52.1	87.1	43.4	79.9	72.6	55.6	65.2
1989																
1st quarter	59.3	52.7	88.0	43.6	79.3	72.8	56.9	65.9	59.9	52.7	88.0	43.6	79.3	72.8	56.1	65.5
2nd quarter	59.6	53.0	88.3	43.7	78.5	72.9	58.4	66.6	60.1	53.0	88.3	43.7	78.5	72.9	57.9	66.3
3rd quarter	59.8	53.4	88.5	44.1	78.6	73.2	58.9	67.0	60.3	53.4	88.5	44.1	78.6	73.2	58.6	66.8
4th quarter	59.9	53.4	88.5	44.8	79.0	74.2	58.5	67.4	60.4	53.4	88.5	44.8	79.0	74.2	58.0	67.2

Table 9-3B. Productivity and Related Data: Historical Data—*Continued*

(2012 = 100, seasonally adjusted.)

Year and quarter	Business sector								Nonfarm business sector							
	Output per hour of all persons	Output	Hours of all persons	Compensation per hour	Real compensation per hour	Unit labor costs	Unit nonlabor payments	Implicit price deflator	Output per hour of all persons	Output	Hours of all persons	Compensation per hour	Real compensation per hour	Unit labor costs	Unit nonlabor payments	Implicit price deflator
1990																
1st quarter	60.5	54.1	88.8	45.6	79.3	74.9	59.2	68.1	60.9	54.1	88.8	45.6	79.3	74.9	58.5	67.8
2nd quarter	60.9	54.2	88.4	46.5	80.1	75.9	59.3	68.8	61.3	54.2	88.4	46.5	80.1	75.9	58.8	68.5
3rd quarter	61.3	54.1	87.9	47.2	79.9	76.6	59.7	69.3	61.5	54.1	87.9	47.2	79.9	76.6	59.2	69.0
4th quarter	60.6	53.3	87.5	47.5	79.3	78.0	59.1	69.8	60.9	53.3	87.5	47.5	79.3	78.0	58.8	69.7
1991																
1st quarter	60.7	53.0	86.7	47.8	79.3	78.2	60.2	70.4	61.1	53.0	86.7	47.8	79.3	78.2	60.0	70.3
2nd quarter	61.7	53.5	86.2	48.7	80.5	78.5	60.8	70.8	62.1	53.5	86.2	48.7	80.5	78.5	60.6	70.7
3rd quarter	62.2	53.9	86.1	49.3	80.9	78.7	61.4	71.2	62.6	53.9	86.1	49.3	80.9	78.7	61.3	71.2
4th quarter	62.5	54.0	85.9	50.0	81.4	79.4	61.3	71.5	62.9	54.0	85.9	50.0	81.4	79.4	61.0	71.4
1992																
1st quarter	63.9	54.8	85.4	51.2	83.1	79.9	61.1	71.6	64.2	54.8	85.4	51.2	83.1	79.9	60.7	71.5
2nd quarter	64.4	55.5	85.7	51.7	83.3	79.9	61.8	71.9	64.7	55.5	85.7	51.7	83.3	79.9	61.3	71.8
3rd quarter	65.0	56.1	85.9	52.3	83.7	80.1	62.3	72.2	65.3	56.1	85.9	52.3	83.7	80.1	61.8	72.2
4th quarter	65.4	56.8	86.4	52.6	83.6	80.1	63.4	72.7	65.7	56.8	86.4	52.6	83.6	80.1	63.2	72.7
1993																
1st quarter	63.9	56.8	87.2	52.2	82.5	80.2	64.1	73.2	65.1	56.8	87.2	52.2	82.5	80.2	64.2	73.2
2nd quarter	64.4	57.1	88.2	52.6	82.5	81.3	63.8	73.6	64.7	57.1	88.2	52.6	82.5	81.3	63.8	73.7
3rd quarter	65.0	57.7	88.7	52.6	82.3	80.9	64.7	74.0	65.0	57.7	88.7	52.6	82.3	80.9	64.7	73.9
4th quarter	65.4	58.4	89.5	53.0	82.3	81.2	65.5	74.4	65.3	58.4	89.5	53.0	82.3	81.2	65.2	74.3
1994																
1st quarter	65.2	59.0	90.1	52.7	81.6	80.5	67.0	74.6	65.5	59.0	90.1	52.7	81.6	80.5	66.8	74.5
2nd quarter	65.1	60.0	91.6	53.1	81.8	81.1	66.9	74.9	65.5	60.0	91.6	53.1	81.8	81.1	66.8	74.9
3rd quarter	64.8	60.4	92.6	53.1	81.2	81.5	67.3	75.3	65.1	60.4	92.6	53.1	81.2	81.5	67.3	75.3
4th quarter	65.4	61.2	93.0	53.5	81.4	81.3	68.3	75.6	65.8	61.2	93.0	53.5	81.4	81.3	68.5	75.7
1995																
1st quarter	65.3	61.6	93.5	53.9	81.4	81.7	68.2	76.0	65.9	61.6	93.5	53.9	81.4	81.7	68.6	76.0
2nd quarter	65.5	61.8	93.3	54.3	81.5	82.0	68.6	76.3	66.2	61.8	93.3	54.3	81.5	82.0	69.0	76.4
3rd quarter	65.5	62.5	94.4	54.6	81.5	82.5	68.8	76.6	66.2	62.5	94.4	54.6	81.5	82.5	69.0	76.6
4th quarter	66.0	63.0	94.6	55.0	81.8	82.7	69.1	76.9	66.6	63.0	94.6	55.0	81.8	82.7	69.1	76.8
1996																
1st quarter	66.5	63.5	94.8	55.6	82.1	83.1	69.5	77.2	67.0	63.5	94.8	55.6	82.1	83.1	69.2	77.0
2nd quarter	67.2	64.7	95.7	56.2	82.1	83.0	70.5	77.6	67.6	64.7	95.7	56.2	82.1	83.0	69.9	77.3
3rd quarter	67.5	65.5	96.5	56.6	82.4	83.4	70.3	77.7	67.9	65.5	96.5	56.6	82.4	83.4	70.1	77.6
4th quarter	67.6	66.3	97.6	56.9	82.2	83.8	70.7	78.1	67.9	66.3	97.6	56.9	82.2	83.8	70.5	78.0
1997																
1st quarter	67.4	66.7	98.4	57.6	82.6	84.9	70.4	78.6	67.8	66.7	98.4	57.6	82.6	84.9	70.1	78.5
2nd quarter	68.5	68.0	98.9	58.1	83.2	84.5	71.2	78.6	68.8	68.0	98.9	58.1	83.2	84.5	71.3	78.7
3rd quarter	69.1	69.0	99.5	58.7	83.7	84.6	71.7	78.9	69.4	69.0	99.5	58.7	83.7	84.6	71.8	79.0
4th quarter	69.5	69.7	99.9	59.7	84.7	85.7	70.6	79.1	69.7	69.7	99.9	59.7	84.7	85.7	70.7	79.2
1998																
1st quarter	69.9	70.5	100.6	60.7	86.0	86.6	69.5	79.1	70.1	70.5	100.6	60.7	86.0	86.6	69.6	79.2
2nd quarter	70.2	71.3	101.1	61.5	86.9	87.2	68.7	79.2	70.5	71.3	101.1	61.5	86.9	87.2	69.0	79.3
3rd quarter	71.2	72.3	101.2	62.5	87.9	87.5	68.9	79.4	71.5	72.3	101.2	62.5	87.9	87.5	69.2	79.5
4th quarter	71.8	73.8	102.5	62.9	88.1	87.3	69.1	79.4	72.0	73.8	102.5	62.9	88.1	87.3	69.3	79.5
1999																
1st quarter	72.9	74.6	102.3	64.0	89.3	87.7	68.9	79.5	73.0	74.6	102.3	64.0	89.3	87.7	69.2	79.6
2nd quarter	73.0	75.3	102.9	64.2	89.0	87.8	69.0	79.6	73.1	75.3	102.9	64.2	89.0	87.8	69.5	79.9
3rd quarter	73.7	76.5	103.5	64.8	89.1	87.8	69.4	79.8	73.8	76.5	103.5	64.8	89.1	87.8	70.1	80.1
4th quarter	74.8	77.9	104.0	66.1	90.2	88.2	69.7	80.1	75.0	77.9	104.0	66.1	90.2	88.2	70.4	80.5
2000																
1st quarter	74.7	78.4	104.9	68.2	92.1	91.3	66.4	80.4	74.8	78.2	104.6	68.4	92.4	91.4	66.9	80.7
2nd quarter	76.2	80.1	105.1	68.4	91.7	89.8	69.2	80.8	76.3	80.0	104.9	68.5	91.9	89.9	69.7	81.1
3rd quarter	76.2	80.1	105.1	69.7	92.6	91.5	67.9	81.2	76.3	80.0	104.8	69.9	92.8	91.6	68.5	81.5
4th quarter	77.1	80.7	104.6	70.2	92.6	91.0	69.2	81.5	77.1	80.5	104.5	70.3	92.7	91.1	69.7	81.8
2001																
1st quarter	76.8	80.2	104.5	71.8	93.8	93.6	66.9	81.9	76.7	80.1	104.4	71.9	93.9	93.6	67.4	82.2
2nd quarter	78.0	80.7	103.5	72.2	93.6	92.5	69.2	82.3	78.0	80.7	103.4	72.1	93.6	92.4	69.7	82.6
3rd quarter	78.5	80.2	102.2	72.3	93.5	92.2	70.0	82.5	78.5	80.1	102.1	72.2	93.4	92.0	70.5	82.7
4th quarter	79.5	80.4	101.1	72.9	94.4	91.7	70.6	82.5	79.5	80.2	101.0	72.9	94.4	91.7	71.3	82.9
2002																
1st quarter	80.9	81.2	100.3	73.2	94.4	90.4	72.5	82.6	81.2	81.3	100.1	73.2	94.5	90.2	73.2	82.8
2nd quarter	81.3	81.7	100.5	73.8	94.5	90.9	72.3	82.7	81.3	81.6	100.3	73.9	94.6	90.9	73.2	83.2
3rd quarter	82.0	82.1	100.1	74.2	94.5	90.5	73.3	83.0	81.9	81.9	100.0	74.3	94.6	90.6	74.0	83.4
4th quarter	81.9	82.2	100.3	74.4	94.2	90.8	73.7	83.3	81.9	82.0	100.1	74.4	94.3	90.9	74.3	83.7
2003																
1st quarter	82.8	82.6	99.8	74.9	93.8	90.4	74.8	83.6	82.7	82.4	99.6	74.9	93.9	90.5	75.5	84.0
2nd quarter	84.1	83.5	99.2	76.3	95.8	90.8	74.6	83.7	83.8	83.2	99.3	76.2	95.7	90.9	75.2	84.1
3rd quarter	85.7	85.3	99.6	77.3	96.3	90.2	76.1	84.1	85.7	85.2	99.5	77.3	96.4	90.3	76.5	84.3
4th quarter	86.4	86.5	100.1	78.3	97.2	90.7	76.3	84.4	86.5	86.5	100.0	78.4	97.3	90.7	76.5	84.5
2004																
1st quarter	86.4	86.8	100.4	78.3	96.4	90.6	78.3	85.2	86.2	86.5	100.4	78.3	96.3	90.8	78.3	85.4
2nd quarter	87.1	87.5	100.5	79.8	97.4	91.7	78.3	85.8	87.0	87.4	100.4	79.8	97.4	91.7	78.2	85.8
3rd quarter	87.5	88.5	101.2	81.2	98.5	92.8	77.8	86.2	87.4	88.3	101.1	81.2	98.5	92.9	77.9	86.4
4th quarter	88.2	89.5	101.4	81.8	98.2	92.7	79.6	87.0	87.8	89.2	101.6	81.6	97.9	92.9	79.8	87.2

Table 9-3B. Productivity and Related Data: Historical Data—*Continued*

(2012 = 100, seasonally adjusted.)

Year and quarter	Business sector								Nonfarm business sector							
	Output per hour of all persons	Output	Hours of all persons	Compensation per hour	Real compensation per hour	Unit labor costs	Unit nonlabor payments	Implicit price deflator	Output per hour of all persons	Output	Hours of all persons	Compensation per hour	Real compensation per hour	Unit labor costs	Unit nonlabor payments	Implicit price deflator
2005																
1st quarter	89.1	90.6	101.7	82.3	98.2	92.3	81.6	87.6	88.8	90.4	101.8	82.1	98.1	92.5	82.0	87.9
2nd quarter	88.7	91.0	102.5	82.6	97.9	93.0	82.2	88.3	88.6	90.8	102.4	82.6	98.0	93.2	82.6	88.6
3rd quarter	89.5	91.9	102.8	83.6	97.7	93.5	83.5	89.1	89.3	91.7	102.7	83.6	97.8	93.7	84.0	89.5
4th quarter	89.7	92.6	103.2	84.3	97.5	93.9	84.5	89.8	89.4	92.4	103.3	84.2	97.4	94.2	85.1	90.2
2006																
1st quarter	90.3	94.1	104.2	86.0	99.0	95.2	84.1	90.3	90.0	93.9	104.4	85.8	98.9	95.4	84.8	90.8
2nd quarter	90.2	94.3	104.6	85.9	98.1	95.3	85.5	91.0	89.9	94.1	104.7	85.9	98.0	95.6	86.2	91.5
3rd quarter	89.9	94.5	105.1	86.1	97.3	95.8	86.0	91.5	89.6	94.3	105.2	86.0	97.3	96.0	86.7	92.0
4th quarter	90.6	95.5	105.5	87.5	99.4	96.7	85.2	91.6	90.4	95.4	105.5	87.6	99.4	96.8	85.8	92.0
2007																
1st quarter	90.9	95.8	105.5	89.8	100.9	98.8	84.3	92.5	90.7	95.7	105.5	89.7	100.9	98.9	84.7	92.8
2nd quarter	91.2	96.5	105.8	89.9	99.9	98.5	86.1	93.1	91.0	96.5	106.0	89.6	99.7	98.5	86.6	93.3
3rd quarter	92.1	97.1	105.4	90.3	99.7	98.0	87.7	93.5	91.9	97.1	105.7	90.0	99.4	97.9	88.2	93.7
4th quarter	92.8	97.6	105.2	91.1	99.5	98.2	88.0	93.8	92.7	97.6	105.3	91.0	99.3	98.2	88.2	93.9
2008																
1st quarter	92.1	96.6	104.9	92.0	99.4	99.9	86.3	94.0	91.9	96.6	105.0	91.9	99.2	100.0	86.4	94.1
2nd quarter	93.0	97.1	104.3	92.2	98.2	99.1	88.5	94.4	92.9	97.0	104.4	92.1	98.1	99.1	88.7	94.6
3rd quarter	93.2	96.2	103.2	93.0	97.6	99.8	89.1	95.1	93.1	96.2	103.3	92.9	97.5	99.8	89.5	95.3
4th quarter	92.7	93.4	100.7	93.9	100.8	101.3	87.2	95.1	92.6	93.2	100.7	93.8	100.8	101.4	87.8	95.5
2009																
1st quarter	93.6	91.9	98.1	91.5	99.0	97.7	91.8	95.1	93.4	91.7	98.2	91.4	98.9	97.9	92.8	95.7
2nd quarter	95.5	91.7	96.0	93.7	100.8	98.1	90.3	94.7	95.4	91.5	95.9	93.7	100.8	98.3	91.2	95.2
3rd quarter	96.9	92.1	95.1	94.3	100.6	97.3	91.4	94.7	96.6	91.8	95.0	94.2	100.5	97.5	92.3	95.2
4th quarter	98.5	93.3	94.8	94.9	100.5	96.4	93.3	95.0	98.2	93.1	94.8	94.8	100.4	96.6	93.9	95.4
2010																
1st quarter	98.9	93.7	94.8	94.3	99.6	95.4	95.5	95.4	98.7	93.6	94.8	94.3	99.6	95.5	96.2	95.8
2nd quarter	99.0	94.8	95.8	95.1	100.6	96.1	95.5	95.8	98.8	94.6	95.7	95.2	100.6	96.3	96.1	96.2
3rd quarter	99.6	95.8	96.3	95.6	100.8	96.0	96.0	96.0	99.4	95.6	96.3	95.6	100.8	96.2	96.6	96.4
4th quarter	99.9	96.5	96.6	96.1	100.4	96.1	97.3	96.6	99.8	96.4	96.6	96.1	100.5	96.3	97.5	96.8
2011																
1st quarter	99.2	96.0	96.8	97.8	101.1	98.5	95.7	97.3	99.1	95.9	96.7	97.9	101.3	98.8	95.4	97.3
2nd quarter	99.3	96.9	97.6	97.1	99.3	97.8	98.0	97.9	99.2	96.9	97.6	97.2	99.4	98.0	97.9	97.9
3rd quarter	98.9	96.9	98.0	97.8	99.4	98.9	98.2	98.6	98.8	96.9	98.0	97.9	99.5	99.1	97.9	98.6
4th quarter	99.6	98.4	98.7	96.6	97.7	96.9	101.3	98.8	99.5	98.2	98.7	96.6	97.7	97.1	101.3	98.9
2012																
1st quarter	99.9	99.5	99.6	98.9	99.4	98.9	99.7	99.3	99.9	99.4	99.5	98.9	99.5	99.0	99.7	99.3
2nd quarter	100.2	100.0	99.8	99.3	99.7	99.1	100.5	99.7	100.3	100.0	99.7	99.4	99.8	99.1	100.6	99.8
3rd quarter	100.1	100.2	100.1	99.5	99.4	99.5	101.3	100.3	100.1	100.2	100.1	99.5	99.4	99.4	101.3	100.3
4th quarter	99.8	100.3	100.5	102.3	101.5	102.5	98.4	100.7	99.8	100.4	100.6	102.1	101.4	102.4	98.3	100.6
2013																
1st quarter	100.7	101.5	100.8	100.9	99.7	100.2	102.0	101.0	100.4	101.4	101.0	100.7	99.5	100.3	101.5	100.8
2nd quarter	100.5	101.7	101.2	101.6	100.5	101.2	101.2	101.2	100.0	101.4	101.4	101.4	100.3	101.4	100.7	101.1
3rd quarter	100.8	102.7	101.9	101.3	99.6	100.5	103.1	101.6	100.4	102.4	102.0	101.2	99.5	100.7	102.8	101.6
4th quarter	101.6	103.8	102.2	102.0	99.9	100.4	104.3	102.1	101.2	103.6	102.3	101.9	99.8	100.6	104.4	102.3
2014																
1st quarter	100.7	103.3	102.6	104.0	101.3	103.3	101.5	102.5	100.3	103.1	102.8	103.9	101.1	103.6	101.5	102.7
2nd quarter	101.6	105.1	103.4	103.5	100.2	101.9	104.7	103.1	101.3	104.9	103.5	103.4	100.1	102.1	104.6	103.2
3rd quarter	102.4	106.7	104.3	104.0	100.4	101.6	105.9	103.5	102.2	106.5	104.3	104.1	100.5	101.8	106.0	103.6
4th quarter	101.8	107.5	105.5	105.0	101.7	103.1	103.9	103.4	101.7	107.3	105.4	105.2	101.8	103.4	104.0	103.7
2015																
1st quarter	102.9	108.7	105.7	106.3	103.6	103.4	102.8	103.1	102.7	108.5	105.6	106.6	103.8	103.7	103.2	103.5
2nd quarter	103.3	109.6	106.1	107.3	103.8	103.8	103.4	103.6	103.1	109.4	106.0	107.4	104.0	104.2	103.8	104.0
3rd quarter	103.3	110.0	106.5	107.6	103.7	104.1	103.6	103.9	103.1	109.8	106.4	107.8	103.9	104.5	104.0	104.3
4th quarter	102.9	110.1	107.0	107.5	103.6	104.5	102.8	103.8	102.7	109.9	106.9	107.8	103.9	104.9	103.3	104.2
2016																
1st quarter	103.2	110.8	107.4	107.6	103.7	104.2	102.7	103.6	103.0	110.5	107.3	107.8	104.0	104.6	103.5	104.1
2nd quarter	103.1	111.2	107.9	107.8	103.1	104.6	104.1	104.4	102.9	110.8	107.7	108.1	103.4	105.0	104.8	104.9
3rd quarter	103.4	111.9	108.2	108.3	103.1	104.7	104.6	104.7	103.3	111.5	108.0	108.6	103.4	105.1	105.5	105.3
4th quarter	104.4	112.8	108.0	109.8	103.9	105.1	105.1	105.1	104.0	112.5	108.1	109.7	103.9	105.5	106.1	105.8
2017																
1st quarter	104.5	113.4	108.6	110.7	104.1	105.9	105.2	105.6	104.2	113.1	108.5	110.8	104.2	106.3	105.9	106.2
2nd quarter	104.2	114.0	109.4	111.2	104.4	106.8	104.7	105.9	104.0	113.7	109.3	111.4	104.6	107.2	105.4	106.4
3rd quarter	105.1	115.0	109.4	112.7	105.3	107.3	105.3	106.4	104.8	114.8	109.5	112.8	105.4	107.6	106.1	107.0
4th quarter	105.5	116.3	110.3	114.2	105.9	108.3	105.5	107.1	105.3	116.1	110.3	114.4	106.1	108.7	106.2	107.6
2018																
1st quarter	106.1	117.6	110.9	115.0	105.7	108.4	106.6	107.6	105.8	117.3	110.9	115.1	105.8	108.8	107.4	108.2
2nd quarter	106.4	118.5	111.4	115.3	105.4	108.4	108.7	108.5	106.0	118.2	111.5	115.4	105.5	108.9	109.5	109.1
3rd quarter	106.6	119.1	111.8	116.6	106.2	109.4	108.1	108.9	106.3	118.9	111.8	116.8	106.4	109.9	109.0	109.5
4th quarter	106.7	119.6	112.0	117.1	106.2	109.7	108.7	109.3	106.4	119.3	112.1	117.3	106.3	110.2	109.5	109.9

Table 9-4. Corporate Profits with Inventory Valuation Adjustment by Industry Group, NAICS Basis

(Billions of dollars, quarterly data are at seasonally adjusted annual rates.)   **NIPA Table 6.16D**

Year and quarter	Total	Domestic industries											
		Financial			Nonfinancial								
								Manufacturing					
									Durable goods					
		Total	Federal Reserve banks	Other financial	Total	Utilities	Total	Fabricated metal products	Machinery	Computer and electronic products	Electrical equipment, appliances, and components	Motor vehicles, bodies and trailers, and parts	Other durable goods
2001	697.1	528.3	28.9	166.1	333.3	22.5	75.1	9.2	2.2	-29.1	1.1	-6.8	14.0
2002	797.4	640.6	23.5	241.9	375.3	10.5	78.3	9.9	2.9	-25.0	-0.8	-3.1	19.5
2003	955.7	796.7	20.0	282.7	494.0	13.2	123.9	8.9	2.8	-6.1	2.7	7.9	15.5
2004	1 217.5	1 022.4	20.0	326.0	676.3	21.1	186.2	12.6	8.3	1.2	0.4	-4.6	35.2
2005	1 629.2	1 403.4	26.5	383.0	993.9	32.4	279.7	19.0	16.4	15.5	-0.6	1.6	61.4
2006	1 812.2	1 572.5	33.8	379.3	1 159.4	55.2	352.9	19.3	20.8	28.5	11.7	-6.9	67.6
2007	1 708.3	1 370.5	36.0	264.2	1 070.3	49.6	321.1	21.4	23.4	24.3	-0.7	-16.3	67.1
2008	1 344.5	954.3	35.1	59.5	859.7	30.4	240.0	15.7	18.0	27.7	5.0	-39.2	39.5
2009	1 470.1	1 121.3	47.3	315.3	758.7	23.4	164.7	11.8	9.6	27.1	9.2	-54.8	33.0
2010	1 786.4	1 400.6	71.6	334.3	994.8	30.6	281.8	15.4	17.3	48.4	10.1	-10.9	43.4
2011	1 750.2	1 337.7	76.0	302.4	959.3	10.2	296.0	16.5	25.8	37.8	4.9	-0.3	49.7
2012	2 144.7	1 739.3	71.7	410.6	1 256.9	13.8	403.0	24.0	33.5	52.9	12.0	23.0	60.1
2013	2 165.9	1 767.1	79.7	351.1	1 336.3	28.3	446.9	25.3	36.5	58.7	20.4	21.5	66.6
2014	2 266.6	1 861.7	103.5	379.6	1 378.6	32.8	458.7	24.1	35.5	60.3	14.2	32.0	68.1
2015	2 184.6	1 789.4	100.7	346.5	1 342.1	20.2	427.2	25.0	24.3	68.4	24.1	26.8	66.1
2016	2 138.8	1 718.9	92.0	365.4	1 261.5	9.4	336.8	23.9	19.1	50.8	5.7	29.6	65.7
2017	2 147.9	1 649.0	78.2	357.4	1 213.3	14.0	316.8	22.6	23.0	50.5	6.3	13.3	63.9
2018	2 211.3	1 689.6	68.0	382.3	1 239.3	22.0	346.7	19.5	15.7	65.1	11.3	-2.3	69.1
2019	2 254.6	1 741.2	64.1	469.0	1 208.0	7.7	355.7	21.9	25.8	61.9	4.3	4.5	65.0
2020	2 165.9	1 711.2	92.9	409.6	1 208.7	10.4	328.8	22.7	27.9	67.0	6.6	5.6	58.9
2019													
1st quarter	2 214.9	1 716.8	61.1	461.1	1 194.6	16.4	339.5	22.8	19.8	67.6	5.0	3.3	71.2
2nd quarter	2 279.6	1 750.6	68.0	472.0	1 210.5	13.5	350.6	22.2	26.6	61.5	4.1	5.8	68.4
3rd quarter	2 255.3	1 732.8	64.0	468.1	1 200.6	4.3	365.6	20.9	28.0	56.1	4.2	5.6	61.7
4th quarter	2 268.6	1 764.5	63.3	475.0	1 226.2	-3.3	367.1	21.9	29.0	62.3	3.9	3.2	58.6
2020													
1st quarter	2 081.9	1 602.8	81.6	404.5	1 116.8	0.6	340.9	24.1	24.4	64.4	2.3	7.9	57.6
2nd quarter	1 864.0	1 455.7	89.7	410.9	955.1	11.1	246.9	11.5	18.4	63.4	6.3	6.6	26.8
3rd quarter	2 360.5	1 906.0	106.1	396.4	1 403.6	10.4	362.3	27.2	36.4	63.0	10.4	8.9	76.4
4th quarter	2 357.2	1 880.1	94.4	426.6	1 359.1	19.6	365.3	27.7	32.3	77.0	7.2	-1.1	74.8

Year and quarter	Domestic industries—*Continued*										Rest of the world, net
	Nonfinancial—*Continued*										
	Manufacturing—*Continued*										
	Nondurable goods					Wholesale trade	Retail trade	Transportation and warehousing	Information	Other nonfinancial	
	Total	Food and beverage and tobacco products	Petroleum and coal products	Chemical products	Other nondurable goods						
2001	84.5	28.5	27.5	22.0	6.6	51.1	71.3	-0.7	-26.4	140.2	168.8
2002	74.9	26.7	4.8	30.7	12.8	53.5	83.3	-6.5	5.0	151.2	156.8
2003	92.3	25.6	26.7	31.8	8.1	56.6	87.9	4.4	28.1	179.9	158.9
2004	133.0	26.2	50.8	39.4	16.6	72.7	94.0	12.0	61.6	228.8	195.1
2005	166.3	29.2	80.0	36.2	20.9	96.0	123.3	28.4	100.7	333.5	225.7
2006	211.8	34.6	82.0	68.8	26.4	105.0	133.6	40.8	115.2	356.8	239.7
2007	201.9	31.3	76.1	70.8	23.7	102.8	119.4	23.3	120.5	333.6	337.8
2008	173.3	31.5	85.0	51.5	5.3	92.7	82.2	29.3	98.8	286.3	390.2
2009	128.9	45.0	10.4	55.2	18.2	88.9	107.9	21.7	87.0	265.1	348.8
2010	158.1	45.1	26.2	63.4	23.5	99.3	115.9	44.6	102.3	320.4	385.8
2011	161.6	40.0	47.5	53.2	20.9	97.2	115.1	30.6	95.7	314.5	412.6
2012	197.5	44.7	57.7	63.5	31.5	137.9	155.7	54.4	112.0	380.1	405.4
2013	217.8	55.6	53.9	75.0	33.3	146.4	153.3	45.2	137.6	378.6	398.8
2014	224.5	58.3	65.5	72.2	28.4	150.6	157.3	55.7	126.6	397.0	404.9
2015	192.6	69.0	19.6	65.5	38.4	152.4	169.3	61.0	135.5	376.4	395.2
2016	141.9	69.2	-30.4	64.7	38.4	127.9	175.2	64.6	157.8	389.8	419.9
2017	137.3	60.4	-5.1	55.7	26.3	123.3	149.6	59.4	139.1	411.2	498.9
2018	168.3	50.6	31.5	55.0	31.2	114.5	148.1	48.6	140.3	419.1	521.7
2019	172.3	55.2	16.7	68.0	32.4	117.8	159.1	37.6	127.8	402.3	513.4
2020	140.4	74.8	-37.9	74.6	29.0	123.7	218.5	19.2	134.9	373.1	454.7
2019											
1st quarter	149.9	50.9	11.1	58.8	29.1	117.6	144.5	38.3	133.7	404.7	498.0
2nd quarter	162.1	52.3	14.0	64.7	31.1	110.7	153.6	35.2	139.0	408.0	528.9
3rd quarter	189.1	58.1	24.9	72.4	33.8	123.4	158.2	39.2	104.9	404.9	522.5
4th quarter	188.2	59.7	16.9	75.9	35.7	119.6	180.3	37.6	133.4	391.5	504.2
2020											
1st quarter	160.3	65.4	1.2	69.8	23.9	131.9	171.2	22.8	126.5	322.9	479.1
2nd quarter	113.8	76.2	-45.6	70.3	13.0	101.4	209.7	6.5	112.0	267.6	408.3
3rd quarter	140.0	78.7	-55.6	78.6	38.3	125.4	250.2	22.7	143.4	489.2	454.5
4th quarter	147.3	78.7	-51.7	79.6	40.7	136.2	242.9	24.8	157.7	412.5	477.0

NOTES AND DEFINITIONS, CHAPTER 9

General note on data on compensation per hour

This chapter includes two data series with similar names—the Employment Cost Index for total compensation and the *Index of Compensation* per hour—that often display different behavior. Both are compiled and published by the Bureau of Labor Statistics (BLS), but the definitions, sources, and methods of compilation are different. Users should be aware of these differences and of the consequent differences in the appropriate uses and interpretations for each of the two series.

The *Employment Cost Index (ECI)* (Tables 9-1 and 9-2) measures changes in hourly compensation for "all civilian workers", which is not quite as broad as it sounds, as it excludes federal government workers, farm workers, and private household workers. Indexes are also published for subgroups including state and local workers, "all private industry" (again excluding farm and private household workers), and a number of industry and occupational subgroups.

The Employment Cost Index (ECI) data from the National Compensation Survey (NCS) are used for a variety of reasons, by both the private and public sectors. Some examples include: military pay adjustments, federal pay adjustments, Medicare reimbursement adjustments, contract escalator clauses, labor cost adjustments, and collective bargaining negotiations.

The ECI is calculated and published separately for *total compensation* and for the two components of hourly compensation, *wages and salaries* and the employer cost of employee *benefits*. It is constructed by analogy with the Consumer Price Index (CPI); that is, it holds the composition of employment constant in order to isolate hourly compensation trends that take place for individual occupations, which are then aggregated, using fixed relative importance weights. The ECI is based on a sample survey and may be revised from time to time, due to updated classification, weighting, and seasonal adjustments. However, it is not subject to major benchmark revision of the underlying wage, salary, and benefit rate observations. By design, it excludes any representation of employee stock options. As it is based on a sample survey, the ECI is measured "from the bottom up," aggregating from individual employers' reports to higher levels. The ECI is frequently and appropriately used as the best available measure of the general trend of wages and of the extent of inflationary pressure exerted on prices by labor costs.

The *compensation per hour* component of the report on "Productivity and Costs" (Table 9-3) is calculated and published for total compensation in total business, nonfarm business, nonfinancial corporations, and manufacturing. The nonfarm business category is similar in scope to the "all private industry" category in the ECI. The measures in Table 9-3, however, are compiled "from the top down," starting with aggregate estimates of compensation and hours, then dividing the former by the latter. Compensation per hour is affected by changes in the composition of employment. If the composition of employment shifts toward a larger proportion of higher-paid employees and/or industries, compensation per hour will rise even if there is no increase in hourly compensation for any individual worker.

In addition, *compensation per hour* includes the value of exercised stock options as expensed by companies. Also included are other transitory payments, many of which may be of little relevance to the typical worker or to ongoing production costs. These values are not reported immediately. Instead, they are incorporated when later, more comprehensive reports are received. This process can lead to dramatic revisions in compensation per hour and in the unit labor costs index, which is based on compensation. For example, the fourth-quarter 2004 increase in compensation per hour in nonfarm business was initially reported at an annual rate of 3.1 percent. Four months later, the reported rate for the same time period was 10.2 percent. The rate of increase from a year earlier was revised from 3.6 to 5.9 percent. According to then-Federal Reserve Chairman Alan Greenspan, in testimony before the Joint Economic Committee on June 9, 2005, this reflected "a large but apparently transitory surge in bonuses and the proceeds of stock option exercises," not a potentially inflationary acceleration in the rate of labor compensation increase. More recently, it was reported in August 2009 that "first-quarter unit labor costs were revised to negative 2.7% from positive 3%." (*Wall Street Journal,* August 12, 2009, p. A2.)

These characteristics suggest that *compensation per hour* should not be considered a reliable or appropriate indicator of wage or compensation trends for typical workers. It is useful in conjunction with the productivity series, because aggregate productivity is subject to the same composition shifts—higher-productivity industries also tend to have higher-paid employees. Hence, the measure of *unit labor costs* (derived by dividing compensation per hour by output per hour in this system) is not distorted when the composition of output shifts toward higher-productivity industries. The shift affects the numerator and denominator of the ratio similarly. However, both compensation and unit labor costs can still be distorted by transitory payments, such as those discussed above.

There are other, probably less important differences between the two measures. Compensation per hour refers to the entire quarter, while the ECI is observed in the terminal month of each quarter. Tips and other forms of compensation not provided by employers are included in hourly compensation but not in the ECI. The ECI excludes persons working for token wages, business owners and others who set their own wage, and family workers who do not earn a market wage; all of these workers are included in the productivity and cost accounts. Hourly compensation excludes employees of nonprofit institutions serving individuals—about 10 percent of private workers (mostly in education and medical care) who are within the scope of the ECI. Hourly compensation measures include an estimate for the unincorporated self-employed, who are assumed to earn the same hourly compensation as other employees in the sector. Implicitly, unpaid family workers also are included in the hourly compensation measures with the assumption that their hourly compensation is zero. Both of these groups are also excluded from the ECI.

TABLES 9-1 AND 9-2

Employment Cost Indexes

SOURCE: U.S. DEPARTMENT OF LABOR, BUREAU OF LABOR STATISTICS (BLS)

The Employment Cost Index (ECI) is a quarterly measure of the change in the cost of labor, independent of the influence of employment shifts among occupations and industries. It uses a fixed market basket of labor—similar in concept to the Consumer Price Index's fixed market basket of goods and services—to measure changes over time in employer costs of employing labor. Data are quarterly in all cases and are reported for the final month of each quarter. These measures are expressed as indexes, with the not-seasonally-adjusted value for December 2005 set at 100.

Care should be used in comparing the ECI with other data sets. The "all private industry" category in the ECI excludes farm and household workers (it is sometimes, and more precisely, called "private nonfarm industry"), and the "all civilian workers" category excludes federal government, farm, and household workers.

The data for 1979 through 2019, which are presented in Table 9-2 and are the official ECI measures for that time period, were based on the 1987 Standard Industrial Classification (SIC) and 2010 Occupational Classification System (OCS).

For over 60 years, the Standard Industrial Classification (SIC) system served as the structure for the collection, presentation, and analysis of the U.S. economy. The SIC system was developed in the 1930s at a time when manufacturing dominated the U.S. economy. Developments in information services, new forms of health care provision, expansion of services, and high-tech manufacturing are examples of industrial changes that could not be incorporated under the SIC system.

Currently the ECI is compiled based on the 2012 North American Industry Classification System (NAICS) and the 2010 Standard Occupational Classification Manual (SOC). These data, along with comparable data for 2004 through 2019, are shown in Table 9-1.

Developed in cooperation with Canada and Mexico, the North American Industry Classification System (NAICS) represents one of the most profound changes for statistical programs focusing on emerging economic activities. NAICS uses a production-oriented conceptual framework to group establishments into industries based on the activity in which they are primarily engaged. Establishments using similar raw material inputs, similar capital equipment, and similar labor are classified in the same industry. In other words, establishments that do similar things in similar ways are classified together. NAICS was introduced in 1997 and is periodically revised to reflect changes in the industrial structure of the U.S. and North American economy.

For certain broad categories shown in this volume—indicated by footnote 2 in Table 9-2—the old SIC categories are roughly comparable and continuous with the data for 2006 and subsequent years. (However, they differ slightly on overlap dates, and should be "linked" if a continuous time series is desired; see the article at the beginning of this volume.) Many of the new industry and occupational categories are not continuous with the old series shown here, and some of the old categories are not being continued because BLS finds them obsolete and no longer meaningful.

Definitions

Total compensation comprises wages, salaries, and the employer's costs for employee benefits. Excluded from wages and salaries and employee benefits are the value of stock option exercises and items such as payment-in-kind, free room and board, and tips.

Wages and salaries consists of straight-time earnings per hour before payroll deductions, including production bonuses, incentive earnings, commissions, and cost-of-living adjustments. These wage rates exclude premium pay for overtime and for work on weekends and holidays, shift differentials, and nonproduction bonuses such as lump-sum payments provided in lieu of wage increases. According to BLS, wages and salaries are about 70 percent of total compensation.

Benefits includes the cost to employers for paid leave—vacations, holidays, sick leave, and other leave; for supplemental pay—premium pay for work in addition to the regular work schedule (such as overtime, weekends, and holidays), shift differentials, and nonproduction bonuses (such as referral bonuses and lump-sum payments provided in lieu of wage increases); for insurance benefits—life, health, short-term disability, and long-term disability; for retirement and savings benefits—defined benefit and defined contribution plans; and for legally required benefits—Social Security, Medicare, federal and state unemployment insurance, and workers' compensation. Severance pay and supplemental unemployment benefit (SUB) plans are included in the data through December 2005 but were dropped beginning with the March 2006 data. The combined cost of these two benefits accounted for less than one-tenth of one percent of compensation, and according to BLS, dropping these benefits has had virtually no impact on the index. According to BLS, benefit costs are about 30 percent of total compensation.

Civilian workers are private industry workers, as defined below, and workers in state and local government. Federal workers are not included.

Private industry workers are paid workers in private industry excluding farms and private households. To be included in the ECI, employees in occupations must receive cash payments from the establishment for services performed and the establishment must pay the employer's portion of Medicare taxes on that individual's wages. Major exclusions from the survey are the self-employed, individuals who set their own pay (for example, proprietors, owners, major stockholders, and partners in unincorporated firms), volunteers, unpaid workers, family members being paid token wages, individuals receiving long-term disability compensation, and U.S. citizens working overseas.

Private industry workers excluding incentive paid occupations is a new category introduced in the 2006 revision to eliminate the quarter-to-quarter variability related to the way workers (for example, salespersons working on commission) are paid. (The category *private industry workers excluding sales occupations* was intended to serve a similar purpose in the previous SIC-based classification system, but was much less accurate in separately identifying workers with highly variable compensation.)

Goods-producing industries include mining, construction, and manufacturing.

Service-providing industries include the following NAICS industries: wholesale trade; retail trade; transportation and warehousing; utilities; information; finance and insurance; real estate and rental and leasing; professional, scientific, and technical services; management of companies and enterprises; administrative and support and waste management and remediation services; education services; health care and social assistance; arts, entertainment, and recreation; accommodation and food services; and other services, except public administration.

Notes on the data

Employee benefit costs are calculated as cents per hour worked.

The July 2019 data were collected from probability samples of approximately 25,600 occupational observations in about 6,300 sample establishments in private industry, and approximately 7800 occupations within about 1,400 establishments in state and local governments. The private industry sample is rotated over approximately five years. The state and local government sample is replaced less frequently; the latest sample was introduced in September 2007.

Currently, the sample establishments are classified in industry categories based on the NAICS. Within an establishment, specific job categories are selected and classified into approximately 800 occupational classifications according to the SOC. Similar procedures were followed under the previous classification systems. Data are collected each quarter for the pay periods including the 12th day of March, June, September, and December.

Aggregate indexes are calculated using fixed employment weights. Beginning with December 2013, estimates are based on 2012 employment weight, using Occupational Employment counts. From March 2006 through June 2018, ECI weights were based on fixed employment counts for 2012 from the BLS Occupational Employment Statistics survey. Employment data from the 2012 Survey were introduced in December 2013. ECI measures were based on 1990 employment counts from March 1995 through December 2005 and 1980 census employment counts from June 1986 through December 1994. Prior to June 1986, they were based on 1970 census employment counts.

Use of fixed weights ensures that changes in the indexes reflect only changes in hourly compensation, not employment shifts among industries or occupations with different levels of wages and compensation. This feature distinguishes the ECI from other compensation series such as average hourly earnings (see Chapter 10 and its notes and definitions) and the compensation per hour component of the productivity series (see Table 9-3 and its notes and definitions, and the general note above), each of which is affected by such employment shifts.

Data availability

Data for wages and salaries for the private nonfarm economy are available beginning with the data for 1975; data for compensation begin with the 1980 data. The series for state and local government and for the civilian nonfarm economy begin with the 1981 data. All series are available on the BLS Web site at <https://www.bls.gov>.

Wage and salary change and compensation cost change data also are available by major occupational and industry groups, as well as by region and collective bargaining status. Information on wage and salary change is available from 1975 to the present for most of these series. Compensation cost change data are available from 1980 to the present for most series. For 10 occupational and industry series, benefit cost change data are available from the early 1980s to the present. For state and local governments and the civilian economy (state and local governments plus private industry), wage and salary change and compensation cost change data are available for major occupational and industry series. BLS provides data for all these series from June 1981 to the present.

Updates are available about four weeks after the end of the reference quarter. Reference quarters end in March, June, September, and December. Seasonal adjustment factors and seasonally adjusted indexes are released in late April.

References

Explanatory notes, including references, are included in a Technical Note in each quarter's ECI news release, and can be found on the BLS Web site, in the PDF version of the release.

More detailed information on the ECI is available from Chapter 8, "National compensation measures," (www.bls.gov/opub/hom/pdf/homch8.pdf) from the BLS Handbook of Methods, and several articles published in the *Monthly Labor Review* and *Compensation and Working Conditions*. The articles and other descriptive pieces are available at www.bls.gov/ect/#publications, by calling (202) 691-6199, or sending e-mail to NCSinfo@bls.gov.

TABLE 9-3A AND 9-3B

Productivity and Related Data

The indexes of productivity and costs for the entire postwar period, 1947 through 2019, have been revised to reflect the 2013 and 2014 comprehensive revisions of the National Income and Product Accounts (NIPAs).

Productivity is a measure of economic efficiency that shows how effectively economic inputs are converted into goods and services. Therefore, productivity measures relate real physical output to real input. They encompass a family of measures that includes single-factor input measures, such as output per unit of labor input or output per unit of capital input, as well as measures of multifactor productivity—that is, output per unit of combined labor and capital inputs. The indexes published in this book are indexes of labor productivity expressed in terms of output per hour of labor input. (A larger group of BLS productivity measures can be found in Bernan Press's *Handbook of U.S. Labor Statistics*.) All data are presented as indexes with a base of 2012 = 100.

Labor productivity is then the efficiency at which labor hours are utilized in producing output of goods and services, measured as output per hour of labor. (Also known as output per hour, or output per hour of all persons.)

Definitions

Current dollar output is the current-dollar value of the goods and services produced in the specified sector. *Output* is the constant-dollar value of the same goods and services, derived as current-dollar output divided by the sector *implicit price deflator* (the ratio of the current-dollar value of a series to its corresponding chained-dollar value, multiplied by 100.)

All these data are derived from components of the NIPAs; see Notes on the data below, and for general information on the NIPAs, see the Notes and Definitions to Chapter 1.

Output per hour of all persons (labor productivity) is the value of goods and services in constant dollars produced per hour of labor input. By definition, nonfinancial corporations include no

self-employed persons. Productivity in this sector is expressed as *output per hour of all employees. Output per person* is output divided by the index for employment instead of by the index for hours of all persons.

Compensation is the total value of the wages and salaries of employees, plus employers' contributions for social insurance and private benefit plans, plus wages, salaries, and supplementary payments for the self-employed. *Compensation per hour* is compensation divided by *hours of all persons*. Included in compensation is the value of exercised stock options that companies report as a charge against earnings. Stock option values are reported with a delay; consequently, recent values are estimated based on extrapolation. They are revised to actual values when the data become available; sometimes the revisions are very large. The labor compensation of proprietors cannot be explicitly identified and must be estimated. This is done by assuming that proprietors have the same hourly compensation as employees in the same sector. The quarterly labor productivity and cost measures do not contain estimates of compensation for unpaid family workers.

Real compensation per hour is compensation per hour deflated by the Consumer Price Index Research Series (CPI-U-RS) for the period 1978 through 2019 (For current quarters, before the CPI-U-RS becomes available, changes in the CPI-U are used.) Changes in the Consumer Price Index for Urban Wage Earners and Clerical Workers (CPI-W) are used for data before 1978, as there was no CPI-U (or CPIU-RS) for that period. See the Notes and Definitions to Chapter 8 for explanation of the CPI-U, the CPI-W, and the CPI-U-RS.

Unit labor costs represent the cost of labor required to produce one unit of output. Unit labor costs also describe the relationship between compensation per hour worked (hourly compensation) and real output per hour worked (labor productivity). When hourly compensation growth outpaces productivity, units labor costs increase. Alternatively, when productivity growth exceeds hourly compensation, unit labor costs decrease.

Unit nonlabor payments include profits, depreciation, interest, rental income of persons, and indirect taxes per unit of output. They are computed by subtracting current-dollar compensation of all persons from current-dollar value of output, providing the data for the index of total *nonlabor payments,* which is then divided by output.

Unit nonlabor costs are available for nonfinancial corporations only. They contain all the components of unit nonlabor payments except unit profits (and rental income of persons, which is zero by definition for nonfinancial corporations).

Unit profits, the other component of unit nonlabor payments, are also only available for nonfinancial corporations.

Labor hours are measured as annual hours worked by all employed in an industry. Data on industry and hours come primarily from the BLS Current Employment Statistics (CES) survey and Current Population Survey (CPS). Definitions and data for these data sources are fund in Chapter 10.

Hours of all persons (labor input) consists of the total hours at work (*employment* multiplied by *average weekly hours*) of payroll workers, self-employed persons, and unpaid family workers. For the nonfinancial corporations data, there are no self-employed persons; the data represent *employee hours*.

Labor share is the total dollar amount of labor compensation divided by the total current-dollar value of output.

Notes on the data

Output for the business sector is equal to constant-dollar gross domestic product minus: the rental value of owner-occupied dwellings, the output of nonprofit institutions, the output of paid employees of private households, and general government output. The measures are derived from national income and product account (NIPA) data supplied by the U.S. Department of Commerce's Bureau of Economic Analysis (BEA). For manufacturing, BLS produces annual estimates of sectoral output. Quarterly manufacturing output indexes derived from the Federal Reserve Board of Governors' monthly indexes of industrial production (see Chapter 2) are adjusted to these annual measures by the BLS, and are also used to project the quarterly values in the current period.

Nonfinancial corporate output consists of business output minus unincorporated businesses and those corporations classified as offices of bank holding companies, offices of other holding companies, or offices in the finance and insurance sector. Unit profits and unit nonlabor costs can be calculated separately for this sector and are shown in this table.

Compensation and hours data are developed from BLS and BEA data. The primary source for hours and employment is BLS's Current Employment Statistics (CES) program (see the notes and definitions for Chapter 10). Other data sources are the Current Population Survey (CPS) and the National Compensation Survey (NCS). Weekly paid hours are adjusted to hours at work using the NCS. For paid employees, hours at work differ from hours paid, in that they exclude paid vacation and holidays, paid sick leave, and other paid personal or administrative leave.

Although the labor productivity measures relate output to labor input, they do not measure the contribution of labor or any other specific factor of production. Instead, they reflect the joint effect of many influences, including changes in technology; capital investment; level of output; utilization of capacity, energy, and materials; the organization of production; managerial skill; and the characteristics and efforts of the work force.

Revisions

Data for recent years are revised frequently to take account of revisions in the output and labor input measures that underlie the estimates. Customarily, all revisions to source data are reflected in the release following the source data revision.

Data availability

Series are available quarterly and annually. Quarterly measures are based entirely on seasonally adjusted data. For some detailed manufacturing series (not shown here), only annual averages are available. Productivity indexes are published early in the second and third months of each quarter, reflecting new data for preceding quarters. Complete historical data are available on the BLS Web site at <https://www.bls.gov>.

BLS also publishes productivity estimates for a number of individual industries. A release entitled "Productivity and Costs by Industry" is available on the BLS Web site at <https://www.bls.gov>.

References

Further information is available in the Technical Notes and footnotes on the most current monthly release, available on the Web site, and from the following sources: Chapter 10, "Productivity Measures: Business Sector and Major Subsectors," *BLS Handbook of Methods*—Bulletin 2490 (April 1997) and the following *Monthly Labor Review* articles: "Alternative Measures of Supervisory Employee Hours and Productivity Growth" (April 2004); "Possible Measurement Bias in Aggregate Productivity Growth" (February 1999); "Improvements to the Quarterly Productivity Measures" (October 1995); "Hours of Work: A New Base for BLS Productivity Statistics" (February 1990); and "New Sector Definitions for Productivity Series" (October 1976).

TABLE 9-4

Corporate Profits with Inventory Valuation Adjustment by Industry Group

SOURCE: U.S. DEPARTMENT OF COMMERCE, BUREAU OF ECONOMIC ANALYSIS

Corporate profits is one of the most closely watched U.S. economic indicator. Profitability provides a summary measure of corporate financial health and thus serves as an essential indicator of economic performance. Profits are a source of retained earnings, providing much of the funding for capital investments that raise productive capacity. The estimates of profits and of related measures may also be used to evaluate the effects on corporations of changes in policy or in economic conditions.

Corporate profits represents the portion of the total income earned from current production that is accounted for by U.S. corporations. The estimates of corporate profits are an integral part of the national income and product accounts (NIPAs), a set of accounts prepared by the Bureau of Economic Analysis (BEA) that provides a logical and consistent framework for presenting statistics on U.S. economic activity.

These profits measures are derived from the NIPAs and classified according to the NAICS. See the notes and definitions to Chapter 1 for definitions, data availability, and references. Note that this industry breakdown of profits incorporates the inventory valuation adjustment (IVA), which eliminates any capital gain element in profits arising from changes in the prices at which inventories are valued, but does not incorporate the capital consumption adjustment (CCAdj), which adjusts historical costs of fixed capital to replacement costs and uses actual rather than tax-based service lives. This is because the CCAdj is calculated by BEA at an aggregate level, whereas the IVA is calculated at an industry level.

CHAPTER 10: EMPLOYMENT, HOURS, AND EARNINGS

SECTION 10A: LABOR FORCE, EMPLOYMENT, AND UNEMPLOYMENT

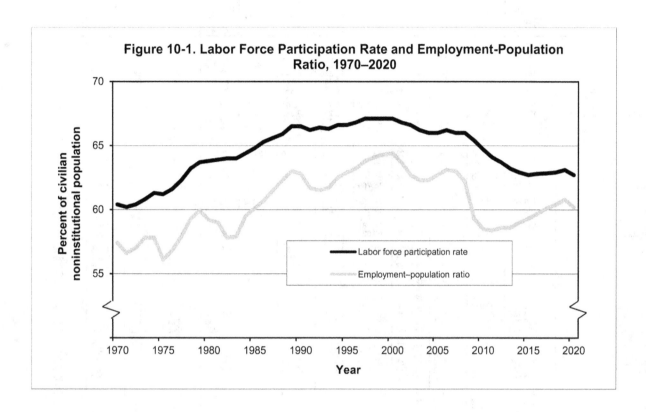

Figure 10-1. Labor Force Participation Rate and Employment-Population Ratio, 1970–2020

- The National Bureau of Economic Research (NBER) determined that the Great Recession lasted from the fourth quarter of 2007 to the second quarter of 2009, lasting seven quarters. NPER announced on July 19, 2021 that the 2020 economy fell into a recession in February 2020 due to the coronavirus pandemic and state stay-at-home orders. By April 2020, the shortest recession in the history of the United States ended. (Table 10-1A)

- Two labor force measurements that are not as commonly reported as employment are labor force participation rate and employment/population ratio. The labor force participation rate (LFPR) is the civilian labor force (employed and actively looking for a job) divided by the civilian labor force. The employment-population ratio measures the civilian labor force currently employed against the total working-working age population. (Figure 10-1.)

- Over the past 20+ years, participation and population rates has fallen in the United States faster than the other 37 countries in the Organization for Economic Co-operation and Development (OECD). The main factor for the declining rates is the aging U.S. population. Older Americans are less likely than younger ones to be in the labor force; this demographic shift reduced the overall labor participation.

- The employment-population ratio measures the civilian labor force currently employed against the total working age population. Seasonally the short-term labor force fluctuations do affect the employment-to-population ratios, thus includes those unemployed people not looking for jobs. In April 2020, the ratio was 51.3, the lowest it has been in several decades. (Table 10-1A)

Table 10-1A. Summary Labor Force, Employment, and Unemployment: Recent Data

(Thousands of persons, percent, seasonally adjusted, except as noted.)

Year and month	Civilian noninstitutional population [1]	Civilian labor force — Thousands of persons	Civilian labor force — Participation rate (percent)	Employment — Total	By age and sex — Men, 20 years and over	By age and sex — Women, 20 years and over	By age and sex — Both sexes, 16 to 19 years	By industry — Agricultural	By industry — Nonagricultural	Employment-population ratio, percent	Unemployment — Total	Unemployment — Unemployed 15 weeks and over	Rate (percent)
1970	137 085	82 771	60.4	78 678	45 581	26 952	6 144	3 463	75 215	57.4	4 093	663	4.9
1971	140 216	84 382	60.2	79 367	45 912	27 246	6 208	3 394	75 972	56.6	5 016	1 187	5.9
1972	144 126	87 034	60.4	82 153	47 130	28 276	6 746	3 484	78 669	57.0	4 882	1 167	5.6
1973	147 096	89 429	60.8	85 064	48 310	29 484	7 271	3 470	81 594	57.8	4 365	826	4.9
1974	150 120	91 949	61.3	86 794	48 922	30 424	7 448	3 515	83 279	57.8	5 156	955	5.6
1975	153 153	93 775	61.2	85 846	48 018	30 726	7 104	3 408	82 438	56.1	7 929	2 505	8.5
1976	156 150	96 158	61.6	88 752	49 190	32 226	7 336	3 331	85 421	56.8	7 406	2 366	7.7
1977	159 033	99 009	62.3	92 017	50 555	33 775	7 688	3 283	88 734	57.9	6 991	1 942	7.1
1978	161 910	102 251	63.2	96 048	52 143	35 836	8 070	3 387	92 661	59.3	6 202	1 414	6.1
1979	164 863	104 962	63.7	98 824	53 308	37 434	8 083	3 347	95 477	59.9	6 137	1 241	5.8
1980	167 745	106 940	63.8	99 303	53 101	38 492	7 710	3 364	95 938	59.2	7 637	1 871	7.1
1981	170 130	108 670	63.9	100 397	53 582	39 590	7 225	3 368	97 030	59.0	8 273	2 285	7.6
1982	172 271	110 204	64.0	99 526	52 891	40 086	6 549	3 401	96 125	57.8	10 678	3 485	9.7
1983	174 215	111 550	64.0	100 834	53 487	41 004	6 342	3 383	97 450	57.9	10 717	4 210	9.6
1984	176 383	113 544	64.4	105 005	55 769	42 793	6 444	3 321	101 685	59.5	8 539	2 737	7.5
1985	178 206	115 461	64.8	107 150	56 562	44 154	6 434	3 179	103 971	60.1	8 312	2 305	7.2
1986	180 587	117 834	65.3	109 597	57 569	45 556	6 472	3 163	106 434	60.7	8 237	2 232	7.0
1987	182 753	119 865	65.6	112 440	58 726	47 074	6 640	3 208	109 232	61.5	7 425	1 983	6.2
1988	184 613	121 669	65.9	114 968	59 781	48 383	6 805	3 169	111 800	62.3	6 701	1 610	5.5
1989	186 393	123 869	66.5	117 342	60 837	49 745	6 759	3 199	114 142	63.0	6 528	1 375	5.3
1990	189 164	125 840	66.5	118 793	61 678	50 535	6 581	3 223	115 570	62.8	7 047	1 525	5.6
1991	190 925	126 346	66.2	117 718	61 178	50 634	5 906	3 269	114 449	61.7	8 628	2 357	6.8
1992	192 805	128 105	66.4	118 492	61 496	51 328	5 669	3 247	115 245	61.5	9 613	3 408	7.5
1993	194 838	129 200	66.3	120 259	62 355	52 099	5 805	3 115	117 144	61.7	8 940	3 094	6.9
1994	196 814	131 056	66.6	123 060	63 294	53 606	6 161	3 409	119 651	62.5	7 996	2 860	6.1
1995	198 584	132 304	66.6	124 900	64 085	54 396	6 419	3 440	121 460	62.9	7 404	2 363	5.6
1996	200 591	133 943	66.8	126 708	64 897	55 311	6 500	3 443	123 264	63.2	7 236	2 316	5.4
1997	203 133	136 297	67.1	129 558	66 284	56 613	6 661	3 399	126 159	63.8	6 739	2 062	4.9
1998	205 220	137 673	67.1	131 463	67 135	57 278	7 051	3 378	128 085	64.1	6 210	1 637	4.5
1999	207 753	139 368	67.1	133 488	67 761	58 555	7 172	3 281	130 207	64.3	5 880	1 480	4.2
2000	212 577	142 583	67.1	136 891	69 634	60 067	7 189	2 464	134 427	64.4	5 692	1 318	4.0
2001	215 092	143 734	66.8	136 933	69 776	60 417	6 740	2 299	134 635	63.7	6 801	1 752	4.7
2002	217 570	144 863	66.6	136 485	69 734	60 420	6 332	2 311	134 174	62.7	8 378	2 904	5.8
2003	221 168	146 510	66.2	137 736	70 415	61 402	5 919	2 275	135 461	62.3	8 774	3 378	6.0
2004	223 357	147 401	66.0	139 252	71 572	61 773	5 907	2 232	137 020	62.3	8 149	3 072	5.5
2005	226 082	149 320	66.0	141 730	73 050	62 702	5 978	2 197	139 532	62.7	7 591	2 619	5.1
2006	228 815	151 428	66.2	144 427	74 431	63 834	6 162	2 206	142 221	63.1	7 001	2 266	4.6
2007	231 867	153 124	66.0	146 047	75 337	64 799	5 911	2 095	143 952	63.0	7 078	2 303	4.6
2008	233 788	154 287	66.0	145 362	74 750	65 039	5 573	2 168	143 194	62.2	8 924	3 188	5.8
2009	235 801	154 142	65.4	139 877	71 341	63 699	4 837	2 103	137 775	59.3	14 265	7 272	9.3
2010	237 830	153 889	64.7	139 064	71 230	63 456	4 378	2 206	136 858	58.5	14 825	8 786	9.6
2011	239 618	153 617	64.1	139 869	72 182	63 360	4 327	2 254	137 615	58.4	13 747	8 077	8.9
2012	243 284	154 975	63.7	142 469	73 403	64 640	4 426	2 186	140 283	58.6	12 506	6 996	8.1
2013	245 679	155 389	63.2	143 929	74 176	65 295	4 458	2 130	141 799	58.6	11 460	6 117	7.4
2014	247 947	155 922	62.9	146 305	75 471	66 287	4 548	2 237	144 068	59.0	9 617	4 714	6.2
2015	250 801	157 130	62.7	148 834	76 776	67 323	4 734	2 422	146 411	59.3	8 296	3 595	5.3
2016	253 538	159 187	62.8	151 436	78 084	68 387	4 965	2 460	148 976	59.7	7 751	3 163	4.9
2017	255 079	160 320	62.9	153 337	78 919	69 344	5 074	2 454	150 883	60.1	6 982	2 704	4.4
2018	257 791	162 075	62.9	155 761	80 211	70 424	5 126	2 425	153 336	60.4	6 314	2 268	3.9
2019	259 175	163 539	63.1	157 538	80 917	71 470	5 150	2 425	155 113	60.8	6 001	2 126	3.7
2020	260 329	160 742	61.7	147 795	76 227	66 873	4 695	2 349	145 446	56.8	12 947	4 511	8.1
2019													
January	258 239	163 067	63.1	156 625	80 473	71 035	5 117	2 553	154 029	60.7	7 140	2 152	4.4
February	258 392	163 032	63.1	156 904	80 775	71 155	4 974	2 470	154 385	60.7	6 625	2 206	4.1
March	258 537	163 010	63.1	156 809	80 637	71 036	5 136	2 327	154 363	60.7	6 382	2 226	3.9
April	258 693	162 737	62.9	156 741	80 648	71 134	4 960	2 356	154 360	60.6	5 387	2 099	3.3
May	258 861	162 848	62.9	156 883	80 789	71 047	5 046	2 412	154 460	60.6	5 503	2 082	3.4
June	259 037	163 046	62.9	157 131	80 760	71 140	5 231	2 320	154 802	60.7	6 292	2 163	3.8
July	259 225	163 586	63.1	157 617	80 977	71 251	5 389	2 455	155 029	60.8	6 556	2 084	4.0
August	259 432	163 861	63.2	157 861	80 992	71 657	5 213	2 430	155 546	60.8	6 203	2 091	3.8
September	259 638	163 958	63.1	158 230	81 134	71 992	5 104	2 433	155 989	60.9	5 465	2 158	3.3
October	259 845	164 278	63.2	158 356	81 120	72 052	5 184	2 450	155 991	60.9	5 510	2 162	3.3
November	260 020	164 447	63.2	158 540	81 341	71 943	5 256	2 358	156 159	61.0	5 441	2 085	3.3
December	260 181	164 579	63.3	158 735	81 373	72 172	5 190	2 531	156 189	61.0	5 503	1 997	3.4
2020													
January	259 502	164 455	63.4	158 659	81 329	72 099	5 231	2 405	156 217	61.1	6 504	2 045	4.0
February	259 628	164 448	63.3	158 732	81 235	72 171	5 326	2 455	156 240	61.1	6 218	1 928	3.8
March	259 758	162 721	62.6	155 536	79 785	70 691	5 060	2 352	153 093	59.9	7 370	1 972	4.5
April	259 896	156 478	60.2	133 937	69 975	59 938	3 457	2 379	130 982	51.3	22 504	1 767	14.4
May	260 047	158 200	60.8	137 224	71 668	61 630	3 926	2 303	134 904	52.8	20 514	2 200	13.0
June	260 204	159 797	61.4	142 100	73 605	64 321	4 174	2 257	139 840	54.6	18 072	3 265	11.2
July	260 373	160 085	61.5	143 777	74 173	65 270	4 333	2 158	141 455	55.2	16 882	7 971	10.5
August	260 558	160 818	61.7	147 276	75 903	66 667	4 706	2 194	145 216	56.5	13 742	8 129	8.5
September	260 742	160 078	61.4	147 543	76 258	66 328	4 957	2 270	145 454	56.6	12 277	7 339	7.7
October	260 925	160 718	61.6	149 669	77 013	67 534	5 122	2 515	147 255	57.4	10 620	6 185	6.6
November	261 085	160 536	61.5	149 809	76 777	67 941	5 091	2 432	147 314	57.4	10 264	5 804	6.4
December	261 230	160 567	61.5	149 830	77 004	67 872	4 955	2 461	147 351	57.4	10 404	5 529	6.5

[1] Not seasonally adjusted.

Table 10-1B. Summary Labor Force, Employment, and Unemployment: Historical Data

(Thousands of persons, percent, seasonally adjusted, except as noted.)

Year and month	Civilian noninstitutional population [1]	Civilian labor force		Employment, thousands of persons						Employment-population ratio, percent	Unemployment		
					By age and sex			By industry			Thousands of persons		
		Thousands of persons	Participation rate (percent)	Total	Men, 20 years and over	Women, 20 years and over	Both sexes, 16 to 19 years	Agricultural	Nonagricultural		Total	Unemployed 15 weeks and over	Rate (percent) [2]
14 Years and Over													
1929	...	49 180	...	47 630	...	...	...	10 450	37 180	...	1 550	...	3.2
1930	...	49 820	...	45 480	...	...	...	10 340	35 140	...	4 340	...	8.7
1931	...	50 420	...	42 400	...	...	...	10 290	32 110	...	8 020	...	15.9 (15.3)
1932	...	51 000	...	38 940	...	...	...	10 170	28 770	...	12 060	...	23.6 (22.5)
1933	...	51 590	...	38 760	...	...	...	10 090	28 670	...	12 830	...	24.9 (20.6)
1934	...	52 230	...	40 890	...	...	...	9 900	30 990	...	11 340	...	21.7 (16.0)
1935	...	52 870	...	42 260	...	...	...	10 110	32 150	...	10 610	...	20.1 (14.2)
1936	...	53 440	...	44 410	...	...	...	10 000	34 410	...	9 030	...	16.9 (9.9)
1937	...	54 000	...	46 300	...	...	...	9 820	36 480	...	7 700	...	14.3 (9.1)
1938	...	54 610	...	44 220	...	...	...	9 690	34 530	...	10 390	...	19.0 (12.5)
1939	...	55 230	...	45 750	...	...	...	9 610	36 140	...	9 480	...	17.2 (11.3)
1940	99 840	55 640	55.7	47 520	...	...	...	9 540	37 980	47.6	8 120	...	14.6 (9.5)
1941	99 900	55 910	56.0	50 350	...	...	...	9 100	41 250	50.4	5 560	...	9.9 (6.0)
1942	98 640	56 410	57.2	53 750	...	...	...	9 250	44 500	54.5	2 660	...	4.7 (3.1)
1943	94 640	55 540	58.7	54 470	...	...	...	9 080	45 390	57.6	1 070	...	1.9 (1.8)
1944	93 220	54 630	58.6	53 960	...	...	...	8 950	45 010	57.9	670	...	1.2
1945	94 090	53 860	57.2	52 820	...	...	...	8 580	44 240	56.1	1 040	...	1.9
1946	103 070	57 520	55.8	55 250	...	...	...	8 320	46 930	53.6	2 270	...	3.9
1947	106 018	60 168	56.8	57 812	...	...	...	8 256	49 557	54.5	2 356	...	3.9
16 Years and Over													
1947	101 827	59 350	58.3	57 038	...	...	...	7 890	49 148	56.0	2 311	...	3.9
1948	103 068	60 621	58.8	58 343	39 382	14 936	4 026	7 629	50 714	56.6	2 276	309	3.8
1949	103 994	61 286	58.9	57 651	38 803	15 137	3 712	7 658	49 993	55.4	3 637	684	5.9
1950	104 995	62 208	59.2	58 918	39 394	15 824	3 703	7 160	51 758	56.1	3 288	782	5.3
1951	104 621	62 017	59.2	59 961	39 626	16 570	3 767	6 726	53 235	57.3	2 055	303	3.3
1952	105 231	62 138	59.0	60 250	39 578	16 958	3 719	6 500	53 749	57.3	1 883	232	3.0
1953	107 056	63 015	58.9	61 179	40 296	17 164	3 720	6 260	54 919	57.1	1 834	210	2.9
1954	108 321	63 643	58.8	60 109	39 634	17 000	3 475	6 205	53 904	55.5	3 532	812	5.5
1955	109 683	65 023	59.3	62 170	40 526	18 002	3 642	6 450	55 722	56.7	2 852	702	4.4
1956	110 954	66 552	60.0	63 799	41 216	18 767	3 818	6 283	57 514	57.5	2 750	533	4.1
1957	112 265	66 929	59.6	64 071	41 239	19 052	3 778	5 947	58 123	57.1	2 859	560	4.3
1958	113 727	67 639	59.5	63 036	40 411	19 043	3 582	5 586	57 450	55.4	4 602	1 452	6.8
1959	115 329	68 369	59.3	64 630	41 267	19 524	3 838	5 565	59 065	56.0	3 740	1 040	5.5
1960	117 245	69 628	59.4	65 778	41 543	20 105	4 129	5 458	60 318	56.1	3 852	957	5.5
1961	118 771	70 459	59.3	65 746	41 342	20 296	4 108	5 200	60 546	55.4	4 714	1 532	6.7
1962	120 153	70 614	58.8	66 702	41 815	20 693	4 195	4 944	61 759	55.5	3 911	1 119	5.5
1963	122 416	71 833	58.7	67 762	42 251	21 257	4 255	4 687	63 076	55.4	4 070	1 088	5.7
1964	124 485	73 091	58.7	69 305	42 886	21 903	4 516	4 523	64 782	55.7	3 786	973	5.2
1950													
January	104 619	61 661	58.9	57 635	38 780	15 255	3 600	7 065	50 570	55.1	4 026	947	6.5
February	104 737	61 687	58.9	57 751	38 818	15 339	3 594	7 057	50 694	55.1	3 936	947	6.4
March	104 844	61 604	58.8	57 728	38 851	15 366	3 511	7 116	50 612	55.1	3 876	912	6.3
April	104 943	62 158	59.2	58 583	39 100	15 831	3 652	7 264	51 319	55.8	3 575	920	5.8
May	105 014	62 083	59.1	58 649	39 416	15 628	3 605	7 277	51 372	55.8	3 434	890	5.5
June	105 104	62 419	59.4	59 052	39 476	15 953	3 623	7 285	51 767	56.2	3 367	868	5.4
July	105 194	62 121	59.1	59 001	39 517	15 793	3 691	7 126	51 875	56.1	3 120	769	5.0
August	105 282	62 596	59.5	59 797	39 879	16 124	3 794	7 248	52 549	56.8	2 799	633	4.5
September	105 269	62 349	59.2	59 575	39 865	15 902	3 808	6 992	52 583	56.6	2 774	648	4.4
October	105 096	62 428	59.4	59 803	39 737	16 175	3 891	7 371	52 432	56.9	2 625	545	4.2
November	104 979	62 286	59.3	59 697	39 668	16 195	3 834	7 163	52 534	56.9	2 589	507	4.2
December	104 872	62 068	59.2	59 429	39 536	16 149	3 744	6 760	52 669	56.7	2 639	482	4.3
1951													
January	104 844	61 941	59.1	59 636	39 595	16 279	3 762	6 828	52 808	56.9	2 305	438	3.7
February	104 604	61 778	59.1	59 661	39 695	16 257	3 709	6 738	52 923	57.0	2 117	386	3.4
March	104 629	62 526	59.8	60 401	40 013	16 557	3 831	6 858	53 543	57.7	2 125	355	3.4
April	104 521	61 808	59.1	59 889	39 804	16 426	3 659	6 752	53 167	57.3	1 919	294	3.1
May	104 491	62 044	59.4	60 188	39 752	16 581	3 855	6 752	53 436	57.6	1 856	269	3.0
June	104 488	61 615	59.0	59 620	39 538	16 368	3 714	6 529	53 091	57.1	1 995	258	3.2
July	104 504	62 106	59.4	60 156	39 483	16 898	3 775	6 601	53 555	57.6	1 950	260	3.1
August	104 536	61 927	59.2	59 994	39 508	16 665	3 821	6 790	53 204	57.4	1 933	249	3.1
September	104 588	61 780	59.1	59 713	39 416	16 504	3 793	6 558	53 155	57.1	2 067	223	3.3
October	104 690	62 204	59.4	60 010	39 555	16 674	3 781	6 636	53 374	57.3	2 194	269	3.5
November	104 740	62 014	59.2	59 836	39 504	16 669	3 663	6 699	53 137	57.1	2 178	316	3.5
December	104 810	62 457	59.6	60 497	39 691	16 946	3 860	7 065	53 432	57.7	1 960	269	3.1
1952													
January	104 862	62 432	59.5	60 460	39 714	17 001	3 745	7 148	53 312	57.7	1 972	282	3.2
February	104 868	62 419	59.5	60 462	39 772	16 935	3 755	7 020	53 442	57.7	1 957	248	3.1
March	104 860	61 721	58.9	59 908	39 580	16 627	3 701	6 468	53 440	57.1	1 813	234	2.9
April	104 906	61 720	58.8	59 909	39 542	16 659	3 708	6 525	53 384	57.1	1 811	242	2.9
May	104 996	62 058	59.1	60 195	39 588	16 844	3 763	6 334	53 861	57.3	1 863	219	3.0
June	105 118	62 103	59.1	60 219	39 558	16 837	3 824	6 529	53 690	57.3	1 884	210	3.0
July	105 246	61 962	58.9	59 971	39 496	16 778	3 697	6 334	53 637	57.0	1 991	194	3.2
August	105 346	61 877	58.7	59 790	39 289	16 867	3 634	6 174	53 616	56.8	2 087	211	3.4
September	105 436	62 457	59.2	60 521	39 386	17 477	3 658	6 537	53 984	57.4	1 936	249	3.1
October	105 591	61 971	58.7	60 132	39 451	17 032	3 649	6 363	53 769	56.9	1 839	230	3.0
November	105 706	62 491	59.1	60 748	39 549	17 450	3 749	6 509	54 239	57.5	1 743	216	2.8
December	105 812	62 621	59.2	60 954	40 011	17 181	3 762	6 361	54 593	57.6	1 667	238	2.7

[1] Not seasonally adjusted.
[2] In 1930 through 1943, the official BLS data count persons on work relief as unemployed. The unemployment rates for those years shown in parentheses count persons on work relief as employed, which is more consistent with the postwar practice. See notes and definitions.
. . . = Not available.

Table 10-1B. Summary Labor Force, Employment, and Unemployment: Historical Data—*Continued*

(Thousands of persons, percent, seasonally adjusted, except as noted.)

Year and month	Civilian noninsti-tutional popu-lation [1]	Civilian labor force Thousands of persons	Civilian labor force Participa-tion rate (percent)	Total	Men, 20 years and over	Women, 20 years and over	Both sexes, 16 to 19 years	Agri-cultural	Nonagri-cultural	Employ-ment-population ratio, percent	Total	Unem-ployed 15 weeks and over	Rate (percent) [2]
1953													
January	106 594	63 439	59.5	61 600	40 256	17 482	3 862	6 642	54 958	57.8	1 839	268	2.9
February	106 678	63 520	59.5	61 884	40 546	17 321	4 017	6 463	55 421	58.0	1 636	208	2.6
March	106 744	63 657	59.6	62 010	40 648	17 397	3 965	6 420	55 590	58.1	1 647	213	2.6
April	106 826	63 167	59.1	61 444	40 346	17 242	3 856	6 362	55 082	57.5	1 723	180	2.7
May	106 910	62 615	58.6	61 019	40 323	16 983	3 713	5 937	55 082	57.1	1 596	176	2.5
June	106 978	63 063	58.9	61 456	40 358	17 301	3 797	6 361	55 095	57.4	1 607	213	2.5
July	107 034	63 057	58.9	61 397	40 378	17 341	3 678	6 267	55 130	57.4	1 660	168	2.6
August	107 132	62 816	58.6	61 151	40 352	17 108	3 691	6 319	54 832	57.1	1 665	177	2.7
September	107 253	62 727	58.5	60 906	40 192	17 063	3 651	6 198	54 708	56.8	1 821	178	2.9
October	107 383	62 867	58.5	60 893	40 155	17 236	3 502	6 096	54 797	56.7	1 974	190	3.1
November	107 504	62 949	58.6	60 738	40 163	16 974	3 601	6 345	54 393	56.5	2 211	259	3.5
December	107 623	62 795	58.3	59 977	39 885	16 599	3 493	5 929	54 048	55.7	2 818	309	4.5
1954													
January	107 763	63 101	58.6	60 024	39 834	16 574	3 616	6 073	53 951	55.7	3 077	372	4.9
February	107 880	63 994	59.3	60 663	39 899	17 162	3 602	6 590	54 073	56.2	3 331	532	5.2
March	107 987	63 793	59.1	60 186	39 497	17 022	3 667	6 395	53 791	55.7	3 607	765	5.7
April	108 080	63 934	59.2	60 185	39 613	17 015	3 557	6 142	54 043	55.7	3 749	774	5.9
May	108 184	63 675	58.9	59 908	39 467	16 975	3 466	6 210	53 698	55.4	3 767	879	5.9
June	108 267	63 343	58.5	59 792	39 476	16 894	3 422	6 162	53 630	55.2	3 551	880	5.6
July	108 344	63 302	58.4	59 643	39 467	16 777	3 399	6 222	53 421	55.0	3 659	932	5.8
August	108 440	63 707	58.7	59 853	39 582	16 868	3 403	6 087	53 766	55.2	3 854	1 002	6.0
September	108 546	64 209	59.2	60 282	39 702	17 133	3 447	6 453	53 829	55.5	3 927	1 017	6.1
October	108 668	63 936	58.8	60 270	39 618	17 209	3 443	6 242	54 028	55.5	3 666	1 009	5.7
November	108 798	63 759	58.6	60 357	39 745	17 213	3 399	5 934	54 423	55.5	3 402	975	5.3
December	108 892	63 312	58.1	60 116	39 763	17 121	3 232	5 848	54 268	55.2	3 196	827	5.0
1955													
January	109 059	63 910	58.6	60 753	39 937	17 375	3 441	6 113	54 640	55.7	3 157	882	4.9
February	109 078	63 696	58.4	60 727	39 964	17 413	3 350	5 854	54 873	55.7	2 969	826	4.7
March	109 254	63 882	58.5	60 964	40 111	17 415	3 438	6 242	54 722	55.8	2 918	816	4.6
April	109 377	64 564	59.0	61 515	40 120	17 867	3 528	6 363	55 152	56.2	3 049	811	4.7
May	109 544	64 381	58.8	61 634	40 410	17 665	3 559	6 327	55 307	56.3	2 747	734	4.3
June	109 680	64 482	58.8	61 781	40 444	17 837	3 500	6 243	55 538	56.3	2 701	668	4.2
July	109 792	65 145	59.3	62 513	40 751	18 123	3 639	6 438	56 075	56.9	2 632	640	4.0
August	109 882	65 581	59.7	62 797	40 747	18 377	3 673	6 575	56 222	57.1	2 784	535	4.2
September	109 977	65 628	59.7	62 950	40 920	18 285	3 745	6 819	56 131	57.2	2 678	558	4.1
October	110 085	65 821	59.8	62 991	40 858	18 327	3 806	6 728	56 263	57.2	2 830	572	4.3
November	110 177	66 037	59.9	63 257	40 936	18 422	3 899	6 655	56 602	57.4	2 780	564	4.2
December	110 296	66 445	60.2	63 684	41 063	18 630	3 991	6 653	57 031	57.7	2 761	581	4.2
1956													
January	110 390	66 419	60.2	63 753	41 203	18 691	3 859	6 590	57 163	57.8	2 666	561	4.0
February	110 478	66 124	59.9	63 518	41 175	18 582	3 761	6 457	57 061	57.5	2 606	545	3.9
March	110 582	66 175	59.8	63 411	41 199	18 496	3 716	6 221	57 190	57.3	2 764	521	4.2
April	110 650	66 264	59.9	63 614	41 289	18 629	3 696	6 460	57 154	57.5	2 650	476	4.0
May	110 810	66 722	60.2	63 861	41 166	18 844	3 851	6 375	57 486	57.6	2 861	506	4.3
June	110 903	66 702	60.1	63 820	41 196	18 748	3 876	6 335	57 485	57.5	2 882	516	4.3
July	111 019	66 752	60.1	63 800	41 216	18 718	3 866	6 320	57 480	57.5	2 952	523	4.4
August	111 099	66 673	60.0	63 972	41 265	18 864	3 843	6 280	57 692	57.6	2 701	543	4.1
September	111 222	66 714	60.0	64 079	41 221	19 019	3 839	6 375	57 704	57.6	2 635	577	3.9
October	111 335	66 546	59.8	63 975	41 261	18 928	3 786	6 137	57 838	57.5	2 571	530	3.9
November	111 432	66 657	59.8	63 796	41 208	18 846	3 742	5 997	57 799	57.3	2 861	575	4.3
December	111 526	66 700	59.8	63 910	41 192	18 859	3 859	5 806	58 104	57.3	2 790	567	4.2
1957													
January	111 626	66 428	59.5	63 632	41 168	18 740	3 724	5 790	57 842	57.0	2 796	509	4.2
February	111 711	66 879	59.9	64 257	41 341	19 115	3 801	6 125	58 132	57.5	2 622	530	3.9
March	111 824	66 913	59.8	64 404	41 500	19 066	3 838	5 963	58 441	57.6	2 509	514	3.7
April	111 933	66 647	59.5	64 047	41 345	18 937	3 765	5 836	58 211	57.2	2 600	516	3.9
May	112 031	66 695	59.5	63 985	41 334	18 897	3 754	5 999	57 986	57.1	2 710	538	4.1
June	112 172	67 052	59.8	64 196	41 411	18 973	3 812	6 002	58 194	57.2	2 856	526	4.3
July	112 317	67 336	60.0	64 540	41 472	19 262	3 806	6 401	58 139	57.5	2 796	535	4.2
August	112 421	66 706	59.3	63 959	41 243	19 020	3 696	5 898	58 061	56.9	2 747	542	4.1
September	112 554	67 064	59.6	64 121	41 213	19 116	3 792	5 728	58 393	57.0	2 943	559	4.4
October	112 710	67 066	59.5	64 046	41 069	19 160	3 817	5 875	58 171	56.8	3 020	650	4.5
November	112 874	67 123	59.5	63 669	40 853	19 082	3 734	5 686	57 983	56.4	3 454	674	5.1
December	113 013	67 398	59.6	63 922	40 884	19 285	3 753	6 037	57 885	56.6	3 476	731	5.2
1958													
January	113 138	67 095	59.3	63 220	40 617	19 035	3 568	5 831	57 389	55.9	3 875	879	5.8
February	113 234	67 201	59.3	62 898	40 336	18 951	3 611	5 654	57 244	55.5	4 303	1 005	6.4
March	113 337	67 223	59.3	62 731	40 180	18 968	3 583	5 561	57 170	55.3	4 492	1 128	6.7
April	113 415	67 647	59.6	62 631	40 129	18 969	3 533	5 602	57 029	55.2	5 016	1 387	7.4
May	113 534	67 895	59.8	62 874	40 253	18 978	3 643	5 647	57 227	55.4	5 021	1 493	7.4
June	113 647	67 674	59.5	62 730	40 208	19 008	3 514	5 510	57 220	55.2	4 944	1 677	7.3
July	113 727	67 824	59.6	62 745	40 270	19 039	3 436	5 525	57 220	55.2	5 079	1 796	7.5
August	113 835	68 037	59.8	63 012	40 343	19 103	3 566	5 673	57 339	55.4	5 025	1 888	7.4
September	113 977	68 002	59.7	63 181	40 564	19 033	3 584	5 453	57 728	55.4	4 821	1 795	7.1
October	114 138	68 045	59.6	63 475	40 699	19 091	3 685	5 563	57 912	55.6	4 570	1 708	6.7
November	114 283	67 658	59.2	63 470	40 684	19 157	3 629	5 571	57 899	55.5	4 188	1 570	6.2
December	114 429	67 740	59.2	63 549	40 666	19 170	3 713	5 521	58 028	55.5	4 191	1 490	6.2

[1]Not seasonally adjusted.
[2]In 1930 through 1943, the official BLS data count persons on work relief as unemployed. The unemployment rates for those years shown in parentheses count persons on work relief as employed, which is more consistent with the postwar practice. See notes and definitions.

Table 10-1B. Summary Labor Force, Employment, and Unemployment: Historical Data—*Continued*

(Thousands of persons, percent, seasonally adjusted, except as noted.)

Year and month	Civilian noninstitutional population [1]	Civilian labor force — Thousands of persons	Civilian labor force — Participation rate (percent)	Employment — Total	By age and sex — Men, 20 years and over	By age and sex — Women, 20 years and over	By age and sex — Both sexes, 16 to 19 years	By industry — Agricultural	By industry — Nonagricultural	Employment-population ratio, percent	Unemployment — Total	Unemployment — Unemployed 15 weeks and over	Rate (percent) [2]
1959													
January	114 582	67 936	59.3	63 868	40 769	19 292	3 807	5 481	58 387	55.7	4 068	1 396	6.0
February	114 712	67 649	59.0	63 684	40 699	19 167	3 818	5 429	58 255	55.5	3 965	1 277	5.9
March	114 849	68 068	59.3	64 267	41 079	19 379	3 809	5 677	58 590	56.0	3 801	1 210	5.6
April	114 986	68 339	59.4	64 768	41 419	19 498	3 851	5 893	58 875	56.3	3 571	1 039	5.2
May	115 144	68 178	59.2	64 699	41 355	19 565	3 779	5 792	58 907	56.2	3 479	965	5.1
June	115 287	68 278	59.2	64 849	41 387	19 658	3 804	5 712	59 137	56.3	3 429	963	5.0
July	115 429	68 539	59.4	65 011	41 596	19 595	3 820	5 564	59 447	56.3	3 528	889	5.1
August	115 555	68 432	59.2	64 844	41 485	19 568	3 791	5 442	59 402	56.1	3 588	889	5.2
September	115 668	68 545	59.3	64 770	41 351	19 531	3 888	5 447	59 323	56.0	3 775	895	5.5
October	115 798	68 821	59.4	64 911	41 362	19 702	3 847	5 355	59 556	56.1	3 910	883	5.7
November	115 916	68 533	59.1	64 530	41 062	19 594	3 874	5 480	59 050	55.7	4 003	982	5.8
December	116 040	68 994	59.5	65 341	41 651	19 717	3 973	5 458	59 883	56.3	3 653	920	5.3
1960													
January	116 594	68 962	59.1	65 347	41 637	19 686	4 024	5 458	59 889	56.0	3 615	915	5.2
February	116 702	68 949	59.1	65 620	41 729	19 765	4 126	5 443	60 177	56.2	3 329	841	4.8
March	116 827	68 399	58.5	64 673	41 320	19 388	3 965	4 959	59 714	55.4	3 726	959	5.4
April	116 910	69 579	59.5	65 959	41 641	20 110	4 208	5 471	60 488	56.4	3 620	896	5.2
May	117 033	69 626	59.5	66 057	41 668	20 186	4 203	5 359	60 698	56.4	3 569	797	5.1
June	117 167	69 934	59.7	66 168	41 553	20 290	4 325	5 416	60 752	56.5	3 766	854	5.4
July	117 281	69 745	59.5	65 909	41 490	20 257	4 162	5 542	60 367	56.2	3 836	921	5.5
August	117 431	69 841	59.5	65 895	41 503	20 316	4 076	5 520	60 375	56.1	3 946	927	5.6
September	117 521	70 151	59.7	66 267	41 604	20 493	4 170	5 755	60 512	56.4	3 884	982	5.5
October	117 643	69 884	59.4	65 632	41 464	20 076	4 092	5 436	60 196	55.8	4 252	1 189	6.1
November	117 829	70 439	59.8	66 109	41 543	20 384	4 182	5 513	60 596	56.1	4 330	1 223	6.1
December	118 001	70 395	59.7	65 778	41 416	20 332	4 030	5 622	60 156	55.7	4 617	1 142	6.6
1961													
January	118 155	70 447	59.6	65 776	41 363	20 325	4 088	5 422	60 354	55.7	4 671	1 328	6.6
February	118 250	70 420	59.6	65 588	41 177	20 392	4 019	5 472	60 116	55.5	4 832	1 416	6.9
March	118 358	70 703	59.7	65 850	41 273	20 459	4 118	5 406	60 444	55.6	4 853	1 463	6.9
April	118 503	70 267	59.3	65 374	41 206	20 145	4 023	5 037	60 337	55.2	4 893	1 598	7.0
May	118 638	70 452	59.4	65 449	41 139	20 261	4 049	5 099	60 350	55.2	5 003	1 686	7.1
June	118 767	70 878	59.7	65 993	41 349	20 446	4 198	5 220	60 773	55.6	4 885	1 651	6.9
July	118 889	70 536	59.3	65 608	41 245	20 252	4 111	5 153	60 455	55.2	4 928	1 830	7.0
August	119 006	70 534	59.3	65 852	41 362	20 279	4 211	5 366	60 486	55.3	4 682	1 649	6.6
September	119 107	70 217	59.0	65 541	41 400	20 112	4 029	5 021	60 520	55.0	4 676	1 531	6.7
October	119 202	70 492	59.1	65 919	41 509	20 338	4 072	5 203	60 716	55.3	4 573	1 481	6.5
November	119 153	70 376	59.1	66 081	41 556	20 330	4 195	5 090	60 991	55.5	4 295	1 388	6.1
December	119 214	70 077	58.8	65 900	41 534	20 287	4 079	4 992	60 908	55.3	4 177	1 361	6.0
1962													
January	119 300	70 189	58.8	66 108	41 547	20 501	4 060	5 094	61 014	55.4	4 081	1 235	5.8
February	119 360	70 409	59.0	66 538	41 745	20 693	4 100	5 289	61 249	55.7	3 871	1 244	5.5
March	119 476	70 414	58.9	66 493	41 696	20 567	4 230	5 157	61 336	55.7	3 921	1 162	5.6
April	119 702	70 278	58.7	66 372	41 647	20 567	4 158	5 009	61 363	55.4	3 906	1 122	5.6
May	119 813	70 551	58.9	66 688	41 847	20 558	4 283	4 964	61 724	55.7	3 863	1 134	5.5
June	119 943	70 514	58.8	66 670	41 761	20 547	4 362	4 943	61 727	55.6	3 844	1 079	5.5
July	120 128	70 302	58.5	66 483	41 671	20 592	4 220	4 840	61 643	55.3	3 819	1 049	5.4
August	120 323	70 981	59.0	66 968	41 900	20 841	4 227	4 866	62 102	55.7	4 013	1 081	5.7
September	120 653	71 153	59.0	67 192	42 200	20 982	4 190	4 867	62 325	55.7	3 961	1 096	5.6
October	120 856	70 917	58.7	67 114	42 086	20 856	4 172	4 816	62 298	55.5	3 803	1 022	5.4
November	121 045	70 871	58.5	66 847	41 985	20 794	4 068	4 831	62 016	55.2	4 024	1 051	5.7
December	121 236	70 854	58.4	66 947	41 934	20 831	4 182	4 647	62 300	55.2	3 907	1 068	5.5
1963													
January	121 463	71 146	58.6	67 072	41 938	20 933	4 201	4 882	62 190	55.2	4 074	1 122	5.7
February	121 613	71 262	58.6	67 024	41 876	21 046	4 102	4 652	62 372	55.1	4 238	1 137	5.9
March	121 824	71 423	58.6	67 351	42 047	21 162	4 142	4 696	62 655	55.3	4 072	1 087	5.7
April	121 986	71 697	58.8	67 642	42 131	21 281	4 230	4 670	62 972	55.5	4 055	1 071	5.7
May	122 162	71 832	58.8	67 615	42 145	21 225	4 245	4 729	62 886	55.3	4 217	1 157	5.9
June	122 352	71 626	58.5	67 649	42 268	21 185	4 196	4 642	63 007	55.3	3 977	1 067	5.6
July	122 521	71 956	58.7	67 905	42 427	21 268	4 210	4 694	63 211	55.4	4 051	1 070	5.6
August	122 667	71 786	58.5	67 908	42 400	21 185	4 323	4 604	63 304	55.4	3 878	1 114	5.4
September	122 821	72 131	58.7	68 174	42 500	21 317	4 357	4 650	63 524	55.5	3 957	1 069	5.5
October	123 014	72 281	58.8	68 294	42 437	21 456	4 401	4 702	63 592	55.5	3 987	1 071	5.5
November	123 192	72 418	58.8	68 267	42 415	21 553	4 299	4 694	63 573	55.4	4 151	1 054	5.7
December	123 360	72 188	58.5	68 213	42 427	21 481	4 305	4 629	63 584	55.3	3 975	1 007	5.5
1964													
January	123 560	72 356	58.6	68 327	42 510	21 462	4 355	4 603	63 724	55.3	4 029	1 057	5.6
February	123 707	72 683	58.8	68 751	42 579	21 652	4 520	4 563	64 188	55.6	3 932	1 015	5.4
March	123 857	72 713	58.7	68 763	42 600	21 685	4 478	4 366	64 397	55.5	3 950	1 039	5.4
April	124 019	73 274	59.1	69 356	42 885	22 110	4 361	4 414	64 942	55.9	3 918	934	5.3
May	124 204	73 395	59.1	69 631	43 025	22 103	4 503	4 603	65 028	56.1	3 764	975	5.1
June	124 386	73 032	58.7	69 218	42 760	21 995	4 463	4 556	64 662	55.6	3 814	1 047	5.2
July	124 567	73 007	58.6	69 399	42 998	21 846	4 555	4 591	64 808	55.7	3 608	1 002	4.9
August	124 731	73 118	58.6	69 463	42 963	22 002	4 498	4 573	64 890	55.7	3 655	934	5.0
September	124 920	73 290	58.7	69 578	43 009	21 863	4 706	4 619	64 959	55.7	3 712	917	5.1
October	125 108	73 308	58.6	69 582	43 023	21 984	4 575	4 550	65 032	55.6	3 726	903	5.1
November	125 291	73 286	58.5	69 735	43 171	21 954	4 610	4 496	65 239	55.7	3 551	922	4.8
December	125 468	73 465	58.6	69 814	43 109	22 136	4 569	4 322	65 492	55.6	3 651	873	5.0

[1] Not seasonally adjusted.
[2] In 1930 through 1943, the official BLS data count persons on work relief as unemployed. The unemployment rates for those years shown in parentheses count persons on work relief as employed, which is more consistent with the postwar practice. See notes and definitions.

Table 10-1B. Summary Labor Force, Employment, and Unemployment: Historical Data—*Continued*

(Thousands of persons, percent, seasonally adjusted, except as noted.)

Year and month	Civilian noninstitutional population [1]	Civilian labor force		Employment, thousands of persons						Employment-population ratio, percent	Unemployment		
		Thousands of persons	Participation rate (percent)	Total	By age and sex			By industry			Thousands of persons		Rate (percent) [2]
					Men, 20 years and over	Women, 20 years and over	Both sexes, 16 to 19 years	Agricultural	Nonagricultural		Total	Unemployed 15 weeks and over	
1965													
January	125 647	73 569	58.6	69 997	43 237	22 282	4 478	4 271	65 726	55.7	3 572	793	4.9
February	125 810	73 857	58.7	70 127	43 279	22 276	4 572	4 322	65 805	55.7	3 730	919	5.1
March	125 985	73 949	58.7	70 439	43 370	22 373	4 696	4 318	66 121	55.9	3 510	796	4.7
April	126 155	74 228	58.8	70 633	43 397	22 416	4 820	4 424	66 209	56.0	3 595	796	4.8
May	126 320	74 466	59.0	71 034	43 579	22 494	4 961	4 724	66 310	56.2	3 432	736	4.6
June	126 499	74 412	58.8	71 025	43 487	22 759	4 779	4 444	66 581	56.1	3 387	786	4.6
July	126 573	74 761	59.1	71 460	43 489	22 841	5 130	4 390	67 070	56.5	3 301	683	4.4
August	126 756	74 616	58.9	71 362	43 447	22 783	5 132	4 355	67 007	56.3	3 254	733	4.4
September	126 906	74 502	58.7	71 286	43 371	22 684	5 231	4 271	67 015	56.2	3 216	732	4.3
October	127 043	74 838	58.9	71 695	43 461	22 819	5 415	4 418	67 277	56.4	3 143	672	4.2
November	127 171	74 797	58.8	71 724	43 447	22 829	5 448	4 093	67 631	56.4	3 073	645	4.1
December	127 294	75 093	59.0	72 062	43 513	22 983	5 566	4 159	67 903	56.6	3 031	659	4.0
1966													
January	127 394	75 186	59.0	72 198	43 495	23 098	5 605	4 077	68 121	56.7	2 988	623	4.0
February	127 514	74 954	58.8	72 134	43 528	23 089	5 517	4 078	68 056	56.6	2 820	594	3.8
March	127 626	75 075	58.8	72 188	43 576	23 109	5 503	4 069	68 119	56.6	2 887	583	3.8
April	127 744	75 338	59.0	72 510	43 679	23 227	5 604	4 108	68 402	56.8	2 828	575	3.8
May	127 879	75 447	59.0	72 497	43 710	23 282	5 505	3 930	68 567	56.7	2 950	534	3.9
June	127 983	75 647	59.1	72 775	43 662	23 359	5 754	3 967	68 808	56.9	2 872	475	3.8
July	128 102	75 736	59.1	72 860	43 574	23 422	5 864	3 920	68 940	56.9	2 876	427	3.8
August	128 240	76 046	59.3	73 146	43 636	23 605	5 905	3 921	69 225	57.0	2 900	464	3.8
September	128 359	76 056	59.3	73 258	43 718	23 881	5 659	3 952	69 306	57.1	2 798	488	3.7
October	128 494	76 199	59.3	73 401	43 776	23 881	5 744	3 912	69 489	57.1	2 798	494	3.7
November	128 627	76 610	59.6	73 840	43 804	24 130	5 906	3 945	69 895	57.4	2 770	464	3.6
December	128 730	76 641	59.5	73 729	43 820	24 025	5 884	3 906	69 823	57.3	2 912	488	3.8
1967													
January	128 909	76 639	59.5	73 671	44 029	23 872	5 770	3 890	69 781	57.1	2 968	489	3.9
February	129 032	76 521	59.3	73 606	43 997	23 919	5 690	3 723	69 883	57.0	2 915	459	3.8
March	129 190	76 328	59.1	73 439	43 922	23 832	5 685	3 757	69 682	56.8	2 889	436	3.8
April	129 344	76 777	59.4	73 882	44 061	24 161	5 660	3 748	70 134	57.1	2 895	428	3.8
May	129 515	76 773	59.3	73 844	44 100	24 172	5 572	3 658	70 186	57.0	2 929	417	3.8
June	129 722	77 270	59.6	74 278	44 230	24 303	5 745	3 689	70 589	57.3	2 992	422	3.9
July	129 918	77 464	59.6	74 520	44 364	24 416	5 740	3 833	70 687	57.4	2 944	412	3.8
August	130 187	77 712	59.7	74 767	44 410	24 600	5 757	3 963	70 804	57.4	2 945	441	3.8
September	130 392	77 812	59.7	74 854	44 535	24 683	5 636	3 851	71 003	57.4	2 958	448	3.8
October	130 582	78 194	59.9	75 051	44 610	24 802	5 639	4 008	71 043	57.5	3 143	472	4.0
November	130 754	78 191	59.8	75 125	44 625	24 914	5 586	3 933	71 192	57.5	3 066	490	3.9
December	130 936	78 491	59.9	75 473	44 719	25 104	5 650	4 076	71 397	57.6	3 018	485	3.8
1968													
January	131 112	77 578	59.2	74 700	44 606	24 581	5 513	3 908	70 792	57.0	2 878	503	3.7
February	131 277	78 230	59.6	75 229	44 659	24 881	5 689	3 959	71 270	57.3	3 001	468	3.8
March	131 412	78 256	59.6	75 379	44 663	25 019	5 697	3 904	71 475	57.4	2 877	447	3.7
April	131 553	78 270	59.5	75 561	44 753	25 072	5 736	3 875	71 686	57.4	2 709	393	3.5
May	131 712	78 847	59.9	76 107	44 841	25 513	5 753	3 814	72 293	57.8	2 740	395	3.5
June	131 872	79 120	60.0	76 182	44 914	25 466	5 802	3 806	72 376	57.8	2 938	405	3.7
July	132 053	78 970	59.8	76 087	44 935	25 347	5 805	3 820	72 267	57.6	2 883	426	3.7
August	132 251	78 811	59.6	76 043	44 897	25 201	5 945	3 736	72 307	57.5	2 768	393	3.5
September	132 446	78 858	59.5	76 172	44 893	25 445	5 834	3 758	72 414	57.5	2 686	375	3.4
October	132 617	78 913	59.5	76 224	44 884	25 475	5 865	3 741	72 483	57.5	2 689	386	3.4
November	132 903	79 209	59.6	76 494	44 996	25 674	5 824	3 758	72 736	57.6	2 715	357	3.4
December	133 120	79 463	59.7	76 778	45 262	25 712	5 804	3 746	73 032	57.7	2 685	351	3.4
1969													
January	133 324	79 523	59.6	76 805	45 154	25 777	5 874	3 704	73 101	57.6	2 718	339	3.4
February	133 465	80 019	60.0	77 327	45 339	26 092	5 896	3 770	73 557	57.9	2 692	358	3.4
March	133 639	80 079	59.9	77 367	45 305	26 115	5 947	3 668	73 699	57.9	2 712	353	3.4
April	133 821	80 281	60.0	77 523	45 262	26 233	6 028	3 629	73 894	57.9	2 758	386	3.4
May	134 027	80 125	59.8	77 412	45 278	26 283	5 851	3 706	73 706	57.8	2 713	387	3.4
June	134 213	80 696	60.1	77 880	45 313	26 429	6 138	3 663	74 217	58.0	2 816	368	3.5
July	134 414	80 827	60.1	77 959	45 305	26 516	6 138	3 548	74 411	58.0	2 868	377	3.5
August	134 597	81 106	60.3	78 250	45 513	26 556	6 181	3 613	74 637	58.1	2 856	373	3.5
September	134 774	81 290	60.3	78 250	45 447	26 572	6 231	3 551	74 699	58.1	3 040	391	3.7
October	135 012	81 494	60.4	78 445	45 488	26 658	6 299	3 517	74 928	58.1	3 049	374	3.7
November	135 239	81 397	60.2	78 541	45 505	26 652	6 384	3 477	75 064	58.1	2 856	392	3.5
December	135 489	81 624	60.2	78 740	45 577	26 832	6 331	3 409	75 331	58.1	2 884	413	3.5
1970													
January	135 713	81 981	60.4	78 780	45 654	26 908	6 218	3 422	75 358	58.0	3 201	431	3.9
February	135 957	82 151	60.4	78 698	45 627	26 828	6 243	3 439	75 259	57.9	3 453	470	4.2
March	136 179	82 498	60.6	78 863	45 668	26 933	6 262	3 499	75 364	57.9	3 635	534	4.4
April	136 416	82 727	60.6	78 930	45 679	27 114	6 137	3 568	75 362	57.9	3 797	602	4.6
May	136 686	82 483	60.3	78 564	45 666	26 739	6 159	3 547	75 017	57.5	3 919	591	4.8
June	136 928	82 484	60.2	78 413	45 554	26 904	5 955	3 555	74 858	57.3	4 071	657	4.9
July	137 196	82 901	60.4	78 726	45 516	27 083	6 127	3 517	75 209	57.4	4 175	662	5.0
August	137 455	82 880	60.3	78 624	45 495	27 011	6 118	3 418	75 206	57.2	4 256	705	5.1
September	137 717	82 954	60.2	78 498	45 535	26 784	6 179	3 451	75 047	57.0	4 456	788	5.4
October	137 988	83 276	60.4	78 685	45 508	27 058	6 119	3 337	75 348	57.0	4 591	771	5.5
November	138 264	83 548	60.4	78 650	45 540	27 020	6 090	3 372	75 278	56.9	4 898	871	5.9
December	138 529	83 670	60.4	78 594	45 466	27 038	6 090	3 380	75 214	56.7	5 076	1 102	6.1

[1] Not seasonally adjusted.
[2] In 1930 through 1943, the official BLS data count persons on work relief as unemployed. The unemployment rates for those years shown in parentheses count persons on work relief as employed, which is more consistent with the postwar practice. See notes and definitions.

Table 10-1B. Summary Labor Force, Employment, and Unemployment: Historical Data—*Continued*

(Thousands of persons, percent, seasonally adjusted, except as noted.)

Year and month	Civilian noninsti-tutional popu-lation [1]	Civilian labor force		Employment, thousands of persons						Employ-ment-population ratio, percent	Unemployment		
					By age and sex			By industry			Thousands of persons		
		Thousands of persons	Participa-tion rate (percent)	Total	Men, 20 years and over	Women, 20 years and over	Both sexes, 16 to 19 years	Agri-cultural	Nonagri-cultural		Total	Unem-ployed 15 weeks and over	Rate (percent) [2]
1971													
January	138 795	83 850	60.4	78 864	45 527	27 173	6 164	3 393	75 471	56.8	4 986	1 113	5.9
February	139 021	83 603	60.1	78 700	45 455	27 040	6 205	3 288	75 412	56.6	4 903	1 068	5.9
March	139 285	83 575	60.0	78 588	45 520	26 967	6 101	3 356	75 232	56.4	4 987	1 098	6.0
April	139 566	83 946	60.1	78 987	45 789	26 984	6 214	3 574	75 413	56.6	4 959	1 149	5.9
May	139 826	84 135	60.2	79 139	45 917	27 056	6 166	3 449	75 690	56.6	4 996	1 173	5.9
June	140 090	83 706	59.8	78 757	45 879	27 013	5 865	3 334	75 423	56.2	4 949	1 167	5.9
July	140 343	84 340	60.1	79 305	46 000	27 054	6 251	3 386	75 919	56.5	5 035	1 251	6.0
August	140 596	84 673	60.2	79 539	46 041	27 171	6 327	3 395	76 144	56.6	5 134	1 261	6.1
September	140 869	84 731	60.1	79 689	46 090	27 390	6 209	3 367	76 322	56.6	5 042	1 239	6.0
October	141 146	84 872	60.1	79 918	46 132	27 538	6 248	3 405	76 513	56.6	4 954	1 268	5.8
November	141 393	85 458	60.4	80 297	46 209	27 721	6 367	3 410	76 887	56.8	5 161	1 277	6.0
December	141 666	85 625	60.4	80 471	46 280	27 791	6 400	3 371	77 100	56.8	5 154	1 283	6.0
1972													
January	142 736	85 978	60.2	80 959	46 471	27 956	6 532	3 366	77 593	56.7	5 019	1 257	5.8
February	143 017	86 036	60.2	81 108	46 600	28 016	6 492	3 358	77 750	56.7	4 928	1 292	5.7
March	143 263	86 611	60.5	81 573	46 821	28 126	6 626	3 438	78 135	56.9	5 038	1 232	5.8
April	143 483	86 614	60.4	81 655	46 863	28 114	6 678	3 382	78 273	56.9	4 959	1 203	5.7
May	143 760	86 809	60.4	81 887	46 950	28 184	6 753	3 412	78 475	57.0	4 922	1 168	5.7
June	144 033	87 006	60.4	82 083	47 147	28 175	6 761	3 402	78 681	57.0	4 923	1 141	5.7
July	144 285	87 143	60.4	82 230	47 244	28 225	6 761	3 461	78 769	57.0	4 913	1 154	5.6
August	144 522	87 517	60.6	82 578	47 321	28 382	6 875	3 603	78 975	57.1	4 939	1 156	5.6
September	144 761	87 392	60.4	82 543	47 394	28 417	6 732	3 568	78 975	57.0	4 849	1 131	5.5
October	144 988	87 491	60.3	82 616	47 354	28 438	6 824	3 634	78 982	57.0	4 875	1 123	5.6
November	145 211	87 592	60.3	82 990	47 529	28 567	6 894	3 517	79 473	57.2	4 602	1 040	5.3
December	145 446	87 943	60.5	83 400	47 747	28 698	6 955	3 596	79 804	57.3	4 543	1 006	5.2
1973													
January	145 720	87 487	60.0	83 161	47 701	28 596	6 864	3 456	79 705	57.1	4 326	947	4.9
February	145 943	88 364	60.5	83 912	47 884	28 995	7 033	3 415	80 497	57.5	4 452	894	5.0
March	146 230	88 846	60.8	84 452	48 117	29 110	7 225	3 469	80 983	57.8	4 394	889	4.9
April	146 459	89 018	60.8	84 559	48 098	29 304	7 157	3 407	81 152	57.7	4 459	809	5.0
May	146 719	88 977	60.6	84 648	48 068	29 432	7 148	3 376	81 272	57.7	4 329	816	4.9
June	146 981	89 548	60.9	85 185	48 244	29 505	7 436	3 509	81 676	58.0	4 363	779	4.9
July	147 233	89 604	60.9	85 299	48 452	29 592	7 255	3 540	81 759	57.9	4 305	756	4.8
August	147 471	89 509	60.7	85 204	48 353	29 578	7 273	3 425	81 779	57.8	4 305	788	4.8
September	147 731	89 838	60.8	85 488	48 408	29 710	7 370	3 342	82 146	57.9	4 350	785	4.8
October	147 980	90 131	60.9	85 987	48 631	29 885	7 471	3 424	82 563	58.1	4 144	793	4.6
November	148 219	90 716	61.2	86 320	48 764	30 071	7 485	3 593	82 727	58.2	4 396	832	4.8
December	148 479	90 890	61.2	86 401	48 902	29 991	7 508	3 658	82 743	58.2	4 489	767	4.9
1974													
January	148 753	91 199	61.3	86 555	49 107	29 893	7 555	3 756	82 799	58.2	4 644	799	5.1
February	148 982	91 485	61.4	86 754	49 057	30 146	7 551	3 824	82 930	58.2	4 731	829	5.2
March	149 225	91 453	61.3	86 819	48 986	30 293	7 540	3 726	83 093	58.2	4 634	849	5.1
April	149 478	91 287	61.1	86 669	48 853	30 376	7 440	3 582	83 087	58.0	4 618	889	5.1
May	149 750	91 596	61.2	86 891	49 039	30 424	7 428	3 529	83 362	58.0	4 705	880	5.1
June	150 012	91 868	61.2	86 941	48 946	30 512	7 483	3 386	83 555	58.0	4 927	926	5.4
July	150 248	92 212	61.4	87 149	48 883	30 869	7 397	3 436	83 713	58.0	5 063	924	5.5
August	150 493	92 059	61.2	87 037	48 950	30 662	7 425	3 429	83 608	57.8	5 022	960	5.5
September	150 753	92 488	61.4	87 051	48 978	30 569	7 504	3 460	83 591	57.7	5 437	1 021	5.9
October	151 009	92 518	61.3	86 995	48 959	30 570	7 466	3 431	83 564	57.6	5 523	1 072	6.0
November	151 256	92 766	61.3	86 626	48 833	30 424	7 369	3 405	83 221	57.3	6 140	1 128	6.6
December	151 494	92 780	61.2	86 144	48 458	30 431	7 255	3 361	82 783	56.9	6 636	1 326	7.2
1975													
January	151 755	93 128	61.4	85 627	48 086	30 343	7 198	3 401	82 226	56.4	7 501	1 555	8.1
February	151 990	92 776	61.0	85 256	47 927	30 215	7 114	3 361	81 895	56.1	7 520	1 841	8.1
March	152 217	93 165	61.2	85 187	47 776	30 334	7 077	3 358	81 829	56.0	7 978	2 074	8.6
April	152 443	93 399	61.3	85 189	47 759	30 410	7 020	3 315	81 874	55.9	8 210	2 442	8.8
May	152 704	93 884	61.5	85 451	47 835	30 483	7 133	3 560	81 891	56.0	8 433	2 643	9.0
June	152 976	93 575	61.2	85 355	47 754	30 618	6 983	3 368	81 987	55.8	8 220	2 843	8.8
July	153 309	94 021	61.3	85 894	48 050	30 794	7 050	3 457	82 437	56.0	8 127	2 943	8.6
August	153 580	94 162	61.3	86 234	48 239	30 966	7 029	3 429	82 805	56.1	7 928	2 862	8.4
September	153 848	94 202	61.2	86 279	48 126	30 979	7 174	3 508	82 771	56.1	7 923	2 906	8.4
October	154 082	94 267	61.2	86 370	48 165	31 121	7 084	3 397	82 973	56.1	7 897	2 689	8.4
November	154 338	94 250	61.1	86 456	48 203	31 135	7 118	3 331	83 125	56.0	7 794	2 789	8.3
December	154 589	94 409	61.1	86 665	48 266	31 268	7 131	3 259	83 406	56.1	7 744	2 868	8.2
1976													
January	154 853	94 934	61.3	87 400	48 592	31 595	8 967	3 387	84 013	56.4	7 534	2 713	7.9
February	155 066	94 998	61.3	87 672	48 721	31 680	8 981	3 304	84 368	56.5	7 326	2 519	7.7
March	155 306	95 215	61.3	87 985	48 836	31 842	9 007	3 296	84 689	56.7	7 230	2 441	7.6
April	155 529	95 416	61.6	88 416	49 097	31 951	9 151	3 438	84 978	56.8	7 330	2 210	7.7
May	155 765	95 847	61.5	88 794	49 193	32 147	9 155	3 367	85 427	57.0	7 053	2 115	7.4
June	156 026	95 885	61.5	88 563	49 010	32 267	8 943	3 310	85 253	56.8	7 322	2 332	7.6
July	156 276	96 583	61.8	89 093	49 236	32 334	9 204	3 358	85 735	57.0	7 490	2 316	7.8
August	156 525	96 741	61.8	89 223	49 417	32 437	9 168	3 380	85 843	57.0	7 518	2 378	7.8
September	156 779	96 553	61.6	89 173	49 485	32 390	8 968	3 278	85 895	56.9	7 380	2 296	7.6
October	156 993	96 704	61.6	89 274	49 524	32 412	9 054	3 316	85 958	56.9	7 430	2 292	7.7
November	157 235	97 254	61.9	89 634	49 561	32 753	9 055	3 263	86 371	57.0	7 620	2 354	7.8
December	157 438	97 348	61.8	89 803	49 599	32 914	9 011	3 251	86 552	57.0	7 545	2 375	7.8

[1]Not seasonally adjusted.
[2]In 1930 through 1943, the official BLS data count persons on work relief as unemployed. The unemployment rates for those years shown in parentheses count persons on work relief as employed, which is more consistent with the postwar practice. See notes and definitions.

Table 10-1B. Summary Labor Force, Employment, and Unemployment: Historical Data—*Continued*

(Thousands of persons, percent, seasonally adjusted, except as noted.)

Year and month	Civilian noninstitutional population [1]	Civilian labor force Thousands of persons	Participation rate (percent)	Employment Total	Men, 20 years and over	Women, 20 years and over	Both sexes, 16 to 19 years	Agricultural	Nonagricultural	Employment-population ratio, percent	Unemployment Total	Unemployed 15 weeks and over	Rate (percent) [2]
1977													
January	157 688	97 208	61.6	89 928	49 738	32 872	9 025	3 185	86 743	57.0	7 280	2 200	7.5
February	157 913	97 785	61.9	90 342	49 838	32 997	9 198	3 222	87 120	57.2	7 443	2 174	7.6
March	158 131	98 115	62.0	90 808	50 031	33 246	9 257	3 212	87 596	57.4	7 307	2 057	7.4
April	158 371	98 330	62.1	91 271	50 185	33 470	9 289	3 313	87 958	57.6	7 059	1 936	7.2
May	158 657	98 665	62.2	91 754	50 280	33 851	9 279	3 432	88 322	57.8	6 911	1 928	7.0
June	158 928	99 093	62.4	91 959	50 544	33 678	9 525	3 340	88 619	57.9	7 134	1 918	7.2
July	159 185	98 913	62.1	92 084	50 597	33 749	9 377	3 247	88 837	57.8	6 829	1 907	6.9
August	159 430	99 366	62.3	92 441	50 745	33 809	9 550	3 260	89 181	58.0	6 925	1 836	7.0
September	159 674	99 453	62.3	92 702	50 825	34 218	9 340	3 201	89 501	58.1	6 751	1 853	6.8
October	159 915	99 815	62.4	93 052	51 046	34 187	9 441	3 272	89 780	58.2	6 763	1 789	6.8
November	160 129	100 576	62.8	93 761	51 316	34 536	9 551	3 375	90 386	58.6	6 815	1 804	6.8
December	160 376	100 491	62.7	94 105	51 492	34 668	9 406	3 320	90 785	58.7	6 386	1 717	6.4
1978													
January	160 617	100 873	62.8	94 384	51 542	34 948	9 473	3 434	90 950	58.8	6 489	1 643	6.4
February	160 831	100 837	62.7	94 519	51 578	35 118	9 448	3 320	91 199	58.8	6 318	1 584	6.3
March	161 038	101 092	62.8	94 755	51 635	35 310	9 441	3 351	91 404	58.8	6 337	1 531	6.3
April	161 263	101 574	63.0	95 394	51 912	35 546	9 518	3 349	92 045	59.2	6 180	1 502	6.1
May	161 518	101 896	63.1	95 769	52 050	35 597	9 668	3 325	92 444	59.3	6 127	1 420	6.0
June	161 794	102 371	63.3	96 343	52 240	35 828	9 781	3 483	92 860	59.5	6 028	1 352	5.9
July	162 034	102 399	63.2	96 090	52 190	35 764	9 749	3 441	92 649	59.3	6 309	1 373	6.2
August	162 259	102 511	63.2	96 431	52 228	35 856	9 903	3 401	93 030	59.4	6 080	1 242	5.9
September	162 502	102 795	63.3	96 670	52 284	36 274	9 700	3 400	93 270	59.5	6 125	1 308	6.0
October	162 783	103 080	63.3	97 133	52 448	36 525	9 727	3 409	93 724	59.7	5 947	1 319	5.8
November	163 017	103 562	63.5	97 485	52 802	36 559	9 704	3 284	94 201	59.8	6 077	1 242	5.9
December	163 272	103 809	63.6	97 581	52 807	36 686	9 708	3 396	94 185	59.8	6 228	1 269	6.0
1979													
January	163 516	104 057	63.6	97 948	53 072	36 697	9 749	3 305	94 643	59.9	6 109	1 250	5.9
February	163 726	104 502	63.8	98 329	53 233	36 904	9 762	3 373	94 956	60.1	6 173	1 297	5.9
March	164 027	104 589	63.8	98 480	53 120	37 159	9 751	3 368	95 112	60.0	6 109	1 365	5.8
April	164 162	104 172	63.5	98 103	53 085	36 944	9 652	3 291	94 812	59.8	6 069	1 272	5.8
May	164 459	104 171	63.3	98 331	53 178	37 134	9 553	3 272	95 059	59.8	5 840	1 239	5.6
June	164 720	104 638	63.5	98 679	53 309	37 221	9 664	3 331	95 348	59.9	5 959	1 171	5.7
July	164 970	105 002	63.6	99 006	53 384	37 514	9 606	3 335	95 671	60.0	5 996	1 123	5.7
August	165 198	105 096	63.6	98 776	53 336	37 548	9 456	3 374	95 402	59.8	6 320	1 203	6.0
September	165 431	105 530	63.8	99 340	53 510	37 798	9 623	3 371	95 969	60.0	6 190	1 172	5.9
October	165 813	105 700	63.7	99 404	53 478	37 931	9 574	3 325	96 079	59.9	6 296	1 219	6.0
November	166 051	105 812	63.7	99 574	53 435	38 065	9 599	3 436	96 138	60.0	6 238	1 239	5.9
December	166 300	106 258	63.9	99 933	53 555	38 259	9 690	3 400	96 533	60.1	6 325	1 277	6.0
1980													
January	166 544	106 562	64.0	99 879	53 501	38 367	9 590	3 316	96 563	60.0	6 683	1 353	6.3
February	166 759	106 697	64.0	99 995	53 686	38 389	9 501	3 397	96 598	60.0	6 702	1 358	6.3
March	166 984	106 442	63.7	99 713	53 353	38 406	9 500	3 418	96 295	59.7	6 729	1 457	6.3
April	167 197	106 591	63.8	99 233	53 035	38 427	9 272	3 326	95 907	59.4	7 358	1 694	6.9
May	167 407	106 929	63.9	98 945	52 915	38 335	9 457	3 382	95 563	59.1	7 984	1 740	7.5
June	167 643	106 780	63.7	98 682	52 712	38 312	9 438	3 296	95 386	58.9	8 098	1 760	7.6
July	167 932	107 159	63.8	98 796	52 733	38 374	9 499	3 319	95 477	58.8	8 363	1 995	7.8
August	168 103	107 105	63.7	98 824	52 815	38 511	9 247	3 234	95 590	58.8	8 281	2 162	7.7
September	168 297	107 098	63.6	99 077	52 866	38 595	9 289	3 443	95 634	58.9	8 021	2 309	7.5
October	168 503	107 405	63.7	99 317	53 094	38 620	9 319	3 372	95 945	58.9	8 088	2 306	7.5
November	168 695	107 568	63.8	99 545	53 210	38 795	9 246	3 396	96 149	59.0	8 023	2 329	7.5
December	168 883	107 352	63.6	99 634	53 333	38 737	9 175	3 492	96 142	59.0	7 718	2 406	7.2
1981													
January	169 104	108 026	63.9	99 955	53 392	39 042	9 300	3 429	96 526	59.1	8 071	2 389	7.5
February	169 280	108 242	63.9	100 191	53 445	39 280	9 257	3 345	96 846	59.2	8 051	2 344	7.4
March	169 453	108 553	64.1	100 571	53 662	39 464	9 212	3 365	97 206	59.4	7 982	2 276	7.4
April	169 641	108 925	64.2	101 056	53 886	39 628	9 289	3 529	97 527	59.6	7 869	2 231	7.2
May	169 829	109 222	64.3	101 048	53 879	39 759	9 160	3 369	97 679	59.5	8 174	2 221	7.5
June	170 042	108 396	63.7	100 298	53 576	39 682	8 780	3 334	96 964	59.0	8 098	2 250	7.5
July	170 246	108 556	63.8	100 693	53 814	39 683	8 839	3 296	97 397	59.1	7 863	2 166	7.2
August	170 399	108 725	63.8	100 689	53 718	39 723	8 931	3 379	97 310	59.1	8 036	2 241	7.4
September	170 593	108 294	63.5	100 064	53 625	39 342	8 835	3 361	96 703	58.7	8 230	2 261	7.6
October	170 809	109 024	63.8	100 378	53 482	39 843	8 851	3 412	96 966	58.8	8 646	2 303	7.9
November	170 996	109 236	63.9	100 207	53 335	39 908	8 852	3 415	96 792	58.6	9 029	2 345	8.3
December	171 166	108 912	63.6	99 645	53 149	39 708	8 602	3 227	96 418	58.2	9 267	2 374	8.5
1982													
January	171 335	109 089	63.7	99 692	53 103	39 821	8 676	3 393	96 299	58.2	9 397	2 409	8.6
February	171 489	109 467	63.8	99 762	53 172	39 859	8 697	3 375	96 387	58.2	9 705	2 758	8.9
March	171 667	109 567	63.8	99 672	53 054	39 936	8 550	3 372	96 300	58.1	9 895	2 965	9.0
April	171 844	109 820	63.9	99 576	53 081	39 848	8 605	3 351	96 225	57.9	10 244	3 086	9.3
May	172 026	110 451	64.2	100 116	53 234	40 121	8 753	3 434	96 682	58.2	10 335	3 276	9.4
June	172 190	110 081	63.9	99 543	52 933	40 219	8 293	3 331	96 212	57.8	10 538	3 451	9.6
July	172 364	110 342	64.0	99 493	52 896	40 228	8 380	3 402	96 091	57.7	10 849	3 555	9.8
August	172 511	110 514	64.1	99 633	52 797	40 336	8 514	3 408	96 225	57.8	10 881	3 696	9.8
September	172 690	110 721	64.1	99 504	52 760	40 275	8 469	3 385	96 119	57.6	11 217	3 889	10.1
October	172 881	110 744	64.1	99 215	52 624	40 105	8 499	3 489	95 726	57.4	11 529	4 185	10.4
November	173 058	111 050	64.2	99 112	52 537	40 111	8 520	3 510	95 602	57.3	11 938	4 485	10.8
December	173 199	111 083	64.1	99 032	52 497	40 164	8 397	3 414	95 618	57.2	12 051	4 662	10.8

[1] Not seasonally adjusted.
[2] In 1930 through 1943, the official BLS data count persons on work relief as unemployed. The unemployment rates for those years shown in parentheses count persons on work relief as employed, which is more consistent with the postwar practice. See notes and definitions.

Table 10-1B. Summary Labor Force, Employment, and Unemployment: Historical Data—*Continued*

(Thousands of persons, percent, seasonally adjusted, except as noted.)

Year and month	Civilian noninstitutional population [1]	Civilian labor force		Employment, thousands of persons						Employment-population ratio, percent	Unemployment		
		Thousands of persons	Participation rate (percent)	Total	By age and sex			By industry			Thousands of persons		Rate (percent) [2]
					Men, 20 years and over	Women, 20 years and over	Both sexes, 16 to 19 years	Agricultural	Nonagricultural		Total	Unemployed 15 weeks and over	
1983													
January	173 354	110 695	63.9	99 161	52 487	40 268	8 335	3 439	95 722	57.2	11 534	4 668	10.4
February	173 505	110 634	63.8	99 089	52 453	40 336	8 159	3 382	95 707	57.1	11 545	4 641	10.4
March	173 656	110 587	63.7	99 179	52 615	40 368	8 098	3 360	95 819	57.1	11 408	4 612	10.3
April	173 794	110 828	63.8	99 560	52 814	40 542	8 094	3 341	96 219	57.3	11 268	4 370	10.2
May	173 953	110 796	63.7	99 642	52 922	40 538	8 006	3 328	96 314	57.3	11 154	4 538	10.1
June	174 125	111 879	64.3	100 633	53 515	40 695	8 448	3 462	97 171	57.8	11 246	4 470	10.1
July	174 306	111 756	64.1	101 208	53 835	41 041	8 207	3 481	97 727	58.1	10 548	4 329	9.4
August	174 440	112 231	64.3	101 608	53 837	41 314	8 379	3 502	98 106	58.2	10 623	4 070	9.5
September	174 602	112 298	64.3	102 016	53 983	41 650	8 147	3 347	98 669	58.4	10 282	3 854	9.2
October	174 779	111 926	64.0	102 039	54 146	41 597	8 010	3 303	98 736	58.4	9 887	3 648	8.8
November	174 951	112 228	64.1	102 729	54 499	41 788	8 075	3 291	99 438	58.7	9 499	3 535	8.5
December	175 121	112 327	64.1	102 996	54 662	41 852	8 089	3 332	99 664	58.8	9 331	3 379	8.3
1984													
January	175 533	112 209	63.9	103 201	54 975	41 812	7 965	3 293	99 908	58.8	9 008	3 254	8.0
February	175 679	112 615	64.1	103 824	55 213	42 196	7 958	3 353	100 471	59.1	8 791	2 991	7.8
March	175 824	112 713	64.1	103 967	55 281	42 328	7 926	3 233	100 734	59.1	8 746	2 881	7.8
April	175 969	113 098	64.3	104 336	55 373	42 512	7 988	3 291	101 045	59.3	8 762	2 858	7.7
May	176 123	113 649	64.5	105 193	55 661	43 071	7 944	3 343	101 850	59.7	8 456	2 884	7.4
June	176 284	113 817	64.6	105 591	55 996	42 944	8 131	3 383	102 208	59.9	8 226	2 612	7.2
July	176 440	113 972	64.6	105 435	55 921	42 979	8 045	3 344	102 091	59.8	8 537	2 638	7.5
August	176 583	113 682	64.4	105 163	55 930	42 885	7 809	3 286	101 877	59.6	8 519	2 604	7.5
September	176 763	113 857	64.4	105 490	56 095	42 967	7 951	3 393	102 097	59.7	8 367	2 538	7.3
October	176 956	114 019	64.4	105 638	56 183	43 052	7 862	3 194	102 444	59.7	8 381	2 526	7.4
November	177 135	114 170	64.5	105 972	56 274	43 244	7 844	3 394	102 578	59.8	8 198	2 438	7.2
December	177 306	114 581	64.6	106 223	56 313	43 472	7 933	3 385	102 838	59.9	8 358	2 401	7.3
1985													
January	177 384	114 725	64.7	106 302	56 184	43 589	8 036	3 317	102 985	59.9	8 423	2 284	7.3
February	177 516	114 876	64.7	106 555	56 216	43 787	8 020	3 317	103 238	60.0	8 321	2 389	7.2
March	177 667	115 328	64.9	106 989	56 356	44 035	8 062	3 250	103 739	60.2	8 339	2 394	7.2
April	177 799	115 331	64.9	106 936	56 374	44 000	7 958	3 306	103 630	60.1	8 395	2 393	7.3
May	177 944	115 234	64.8	106 932	56 531	43 905	7 966	3 280	103 652	60.1	8 302	2 292	7.2
June	178 096	114 965	64.6	106 505	56 288	43 958	7 680	3 161	103 344	59.8	8 460	2 310	7.4
July	178 263	115 320	64.7	106 807	56 435	43 975	8 013	3 143	103 664	59.9	8 513	2 329	7.4
August	178 405	115 291	64.6	107 095	56 655	44 104	7 714	3 121	103 974	60.0	8 196	2 258	7.1
September	178 572	115 905	64.9	107 657	56 845	44 395	7 818	3 064	104 593	60.3	8 248	2 242	7.1
October	178 770	116 145	65.0	107 847	56 969	44 565	7 889	3 051	104 796	60.3	8 298	2 295	7.1
November	178 940	116 135	64.9	108 007	56 972	44 617	7 852	3 062	104 945	60.4	8 128	2 207	7.0
December	179 112	116 354	65.0	108 216	56 995	44 889	7 826	3 141	105 075	60.4	8 138	2 208	7.0
1986													
January	179 670	116 682	64.9	108 887	57 637	44 944	7 704	3 287	105 600	60.6	7 795	2 089	6.7
February	179 821	116 882	65.0	108 480	57 269	44 804	7 895	3 083	105 397	60.3	8 402	2 308	7.2
March	179 985	117 220	65.1	108 837	57 353	44 960	7 977	3 200	105 637	60.5	8 383	2 261	7.2
April	180 148	117 316	65.1	108 952	57 358	45 081	8 058	3 153	105 799	60.5	8 364	2 162	7.1
May	180 311	117 528	65.2	109 089	57 287	45 289	7 997	3 150	105 939	60.5	8 439	2 232	7.2
June	180 503	118 084	65.4	109 576	57 471	45 621	8 024	3 193	106 383	60.7	8 508	2 320	7.2
July	180 682	118 129	65.4	109 810	57 514	45 837	7 914	3 141	106 669	60.8	8 319	2 269	7.0
August	180 828	118 150	65.3	110 015	57 597	45 926	7 920	3 082	106 933	60.8	8 135	2 276	6.9
September	180 997	118 395	65.4	110 085	57 630	45 972	7 945	3 171	106 914	60.8	8 310	2 318	7.0
October	181 186	118 516	65.4	110 273	57 660	46 046	6 977	3 128	107 145	60.9	8 243	2 188	7.0
November	181 363	118 634	65.4	110 475	57 941	46 070	7 891	3 220	107 255	60.9	8 159	2 202	6.9
December	181 547	118 611	65.3	110 728	58 185	46 132	7 769	3 148	107 580	61.0	7 883	2 161	6.6
1987													
January	181 827	118 845	65.4	110 953	58 264	46 219	7 861	3 143	107 810	61.0	7 892	2 168	6.6
February	181 998	119 122	65.5	111 257	58 279	46 444	7 969	3 208	108 049	61.1	7 865	2 117	6.6
March	182 179	119 270	65.5	111 408	58 362	46 549	7 913	3 214	108 194	61.2	7 862	2 070	6.6
April	182 344	119 336	65.4	111 794	58 503	46 746	7 916	3 246	108 548	61.3	7 542	2 091	6.3
May	182 533	120 008	65.7	112 434	58 713	47 052	8 075	3 345	109 089	61.6	7 574	2 104	6.3
June	182 703	119 644	65.5	112 246	58 581	47 102	7 857	3 216	109 030	61.4	7 398	2 087	6.2
July	182 885	119 902	65.6	112 634	58 740	47 229	7 911	3 235	109 399	61.6	7 268	1 921	6.1
August	183 002	120 318	65.7	113 057	58 810	47 322	8 232	3 112	109 945	61.8	7 261	1 878	6.0
September	183 161	120 011	65.5	112 909	58 964	47 285	7 945	3 189	109 720	61.6	7 102	1 866	5.9
October	183 311	120 509	65.7	113 282	59 073	47 533	8 074	3 219	110 063	61.8	7 227	1 794	6.0
November	183 470	120 540	65.7	113 505	59 210	47 622	8 002	3 145	110 360	61.9	7 035	1 797	5.8
December	183 620	120 729	65.7	113 793	59 217	47 781	8 092	3 213	110 580	62.0	6 936	1 767	5.7
1988													
January	183 822	120 969	65.8	114 016	59 346	47 862	8 110	3 247	110 769	62.0	6 953	1 714	5.7
February	183 969	121 156	65.9	114 227	59 535	47 919	8 025	3 201	111 026	62.1	6 929	1 738	5.7
March	184 111	120 913	65.7	114 037	59 393	48 090	7 854	3 169	110 868	61.9	6 876	1 744	5.7
April	184 232	121 251	65.8	114 650	59 832	48 147	7 937	3 224	111 426	62.2	6 601	1 563	5.4
May	184 374	121 071	65.7	114 292	59 644	47 946	7 912	3 121	111 171	62.0	6 779	1 647	5.6
June	184 562	121 473	65.8	114 927	59 751	48 146	8 193	3 111	111 816	62.3	6 546	1 531	5.4
July	184 729	121 665	65.9	115 060	59 888	48 186	8 198	3 060	112 000	62.3	6 605	1 601	5.4
August	184 830	122 125	66.1	115 282	59 877	48 467	8 201	3 119	112 163	62.4	6 843	1 639	5.6
September	184 962	121 960	65.9	115 356	59 980	48 511	8 124	3 165	112 191	62.4	6 604	1 569	5.4
October	185 114	122 206	66.0	115 638	60 023	48 859	7 961	3 231	112 407	62.5	6 568	1 562	5.4
November	185 244	122 637	66.2	116 100	60 042	49 254	7 904	3 241	112 859	62.7	6 537	1 468	5.3
December	185 402	122 622	66.1	116 104	60 059	49 257	7 966	3 194	112 910	62.6	6 518	1 490	5.3

[1]Not seasonally adjusted.
[2]In 1930 through 1943, the official BLS data count persons on work relief as unemployed. The unemployment rates for those years shown in parentheses count persons on work relief as employed, which is more consistent with the postwar practice. See notes and definitions.

Table 10-1B. Summary Labor Force, Employment, and Unemployment: Historical Data—Continued

(Thousands of persons, percent, seasonally adjusted, except as noted.)

Year and month	Civilian noninstitutional population [1]	Civilian labor force		Employment, thousands of persons						Employment-population ratio, percent	Unemployment		
		Thousands of persons	Participation rate (percent)	Total	By age and sex			By industry			Thousands of persons		Rate (percent) [2]
					Men, 20 years and over	Women, 20 years and over	Both sexes, 16 to 19 years	Agricultural	Nonagricultural		Total	Unemployed 15 weeks and over	
1989													
January	185 644	123 390	66.5	116 708	60 477	49 529	8 019	3 287	113 421	62.9	6 682	1 480	5.4
February	185 777	123 135	66.3	116 776	60 588	49 497	7 871	3 234	113 542	62.9	6 359	1 304	5.2
March	185 897	123 227	66.3	117 022	60 795	49 503	7 809	3 198	113 824	62.9	6 205	1 353	5.0
April	186 024	123 565	66.4	117 097	60 764	49 565	7 929	3 162	113 935	62.9	6 468	1 397	5.2
May	186 181	123 474	66.3	117 099	60 795	49 583	7 890	3 125	113 974	62.9	6 375	1 348	5.2
June	186 329	123 995	66.5	117 418	61 054	49 542	8 094	3 068	114 350	63.0	6 577	1 300	5.3
July	186 483	123 967	66.5	117 472	60 947	49 693	7 961	3 227	114 245	63.0	6 495	1 435	5.2
August	186 598	124 166	66.5	117 655	60 915	49 804	8 126	3 284	114 371	63.1	6 511	1 302	5.2
September	186 726	123 944	66.4	117 354	60 668	50 015	7 870	3 219	114 135	62.8	6 590	1 360	5.3
October	186 871	124 211	66.5	117 581	60 958	49 871	7 940	3 215	114 366	62.9	6 630	1 392	5.3
November	187 017	124 637	66.6	117 912	60 958	50 221	7 964	3 132	114 780	63.0	6 725	1 418	5.4
December	187 165	124 497	66.5	117 830	61 068	50 116	7 851	3 188	114 642	63.0	6 667	1 375	5.4
1990													
January	188 413	125 833	66.8	119 081	61 742	50 436	8 103	3 210	115 871	63.2	6 752	1 412	5.4
February	188 516	125 710	66.7	119 059	61 805	50 438	8 015	3 188	115 871	63.2	6 651	1 350	5.3
March	188 630	125 801	66.7	119 203	61 832	50 463	8 061	3 260	115 943	63.2	6 598	1 331	5.2
April	188 778	125 649	66.6	118 852	61 579	50 457	7 987	3 231	115 621	63.0	6 797	1 376	5.4
May	188 913	125 893	66.6	119 151	61 778	50 646	7 911	3 266	115 885	63.1	6 742	1 415	5.4
June	189 058	125 573	66.4	118 983	61 762	50 550	7 783	3 245	115 738	62.9	6 590	1 436	5.2
July	189 188	125 732	66.5	118 810	61 683	50 514	7 777	3 192	115 618	62.8	6 922	1 534	5.5
August	189 342	125 990	66.5	118 802	61 715	50 635	7 708	3 197	115 605	62.7	7 188	1 607	5.7
September	189 528	125 892	66.4	118 524	61 608	50 587	7 575	3 206	115 318	62.5	7 368	1 695	5.9
October	189 710	125 995	66.4	118 536	61 606	50 616	7 565	3 270	115 266	62.5	7 459	1 689	5.9
November	189 872	126 070	66.4	118 306	61 545	50 541	7 506	3 189	115 117	62.3	7 764	1 831	6.2
December	190 017	126 142	66.4	118 241	61 506	50 530	7 516	3 245	114 996	62.2	7 901	1 804	6.3
1991													
January	190 163	125 955	66.2	117 940	61 383	50 472	7 478	3 208	114 732	62.0	8 015	1 866	6.4
February	190 271	126 020	66.2	117 755	61 117	50 523	7 405	3 270	114 485	61.9	8 265	1 955	6.6
March	190 381	126 238	66.3	117 652	61 144	50 422	7 447	3 177	114 475	61.8	8 586	2 137	6.8
April	190 517	126 548	66.4	118 109	61 280	50 760	7 381	3 241	114 868	62.0	8 439	2 206	6.7
May	190 650	126 176	66.2	117 440	61 052	50 457	7 303	3 275	114 165	61.6	8 736	2 252	6.9
June	190 800	126 331	66.2	117 639	61 147	50 585	7 248	3 300	114 339	61.7	8 692	2 533	6.9
July	190 946	126 154	66.1	117 568	61 179	50 636	7 138	3 319	114 249	61.6	8 586	2 388	6.8
August	191 116	126 150	66.0	117 484	61 122	50 601	7 105	3 313	114 171	61.5	8 666	2 460	6.9
September	191 302	126 650	66.2	117 928	61 279	50 864	7 123	3 319	114 609	61.6	8 722	2 497	6.9
October	191 497	126 642	66.1	117 800	61 174	50 811	7 185	3 289	114 511	61.5	8 842	2 638	7.0
November	191 657	126 701	66.1	117 770	61 201	50 759	7 169	3 296	114 474	61.4	8 931	2 718	7.0
December	191 798	126 664	66.0	117 466	61 074	50 728	7 104	3 146	114 320	61.2	9 198	2 892	7.3
1992													
January	191 953	127 261	66.3	117 978	61 116	51 095	7 138	3 155	114 823	61.5	9 283	3 060	7.3
February	192 067	127 207	66.2	117 753	61 062	51 033	7 083	3 239	114 514	61.3	9 454	3 182	7.4
March	192 204	127 604	66.4	118 144	61 363	51 204	6 998	3 236	114 908	61.5	9 460	3 196	7.4
April	192 354	127 841	66.5	118 426	61 468	51 323	6 910	3 245	115 181	61.6	9 415	3 130	7.4
May	192 503	128 119	66.6	118 375	61 513	51 245	7 028	3 213	115 162	61.5	9 744	3 444	7.6
June	192 663	128 459	66.7	118 419	61 537	51 383	7 137	3 297	115 122	61.5	10 040	3 758	7.8
July	192 826	128 563	66.7	118 713	61 641	51 458	7 087	3 285	115 428	61.6	9 850	3 614	7.7
August	193 018	128 613	66.6	118 826	61 681	51 386	7 194	3 279	115 547	61.6	9 787	3 579	7.6
September	193 229	128 501	66.5	118 720	61 663	51 359	7 216	3 274	115 446	61.4	9 781	3 504	7.6
October	193 442	128 026	66.2	118 628	61 550	51 373	6 985	3 254	115 374	61.3	9 398	3 505	7.3
November	193 621	128 441	66.3	118 876	61 644	51 535	7 164	3 207	115 669	61.4	9 565	3 397	7.4
December	193 784	128 554	66.3	118 997	61 721	51 524	7 174	3 259	115 738	61.4	9 557	3 651	7.4
1993													
January	193 962	128 400	66.2	119 075	61 895	51 505	7 089	3 222	115 853	61.4	9 325	3 346	7.3
February	194 108	128 458	66.2	119 275	61 963	51 573	7 144	3 125	116 150	61.4	9 183	3 190	7.1
March	194 248	128 598	66.2	119 542	62 007	51 808	7 132	3 119	116 423	61.5	9 056	3 115	7.0
April	194 398	128 584	66.1	119 474	62 032	51 732	7 091	3 074	116 400	61.5	9 110	3 014	7.1
May	194 549	129 264	66.4	120 115	62 309	51 996	7 244	3 100	117 015	61.7	9 149	3 101	7.1
June	194 719	129 411	66.5	120 290	62 409	52 183	7 114	3 108	117 182	61.8	9 121	3 141	7.0
July	194 882	129 397	66.4	120 467	62 497	52 088	7 205	3 126	117 341	61.8	8 930	3 046	6.9
August	195 063	129 619	66.4	120 856	62 634	52 294	7 264	3 026	117 830	62.0	8 763	3 026	6.8
September	195 259	129 268	66.2	120 554	62 437	52 241	7 180	3 174	117 380	61.7	8 714	3 042	6.7
October	195 444	129 573	66.3	120 823	62 614	52 379	7 171	3 084	117 739	61.8	8 750	3 029	6.8
November	195 625	129 711	66.3	121 169	62 732	52 531	7 248	3 157	118 012	61.9	8 542	2 986	6.6
December	195 794	129 941	66.4	121 464	62 760	52 813	7 178	3 116	118 348	62.0	8 477	2 968	6.5
1994													
January	195 953	130 596	66.6	121 966	62 798	53 052	7 486	3 302	118 664	62.2	8 630	3 060	6.6
February	196 090	130 669	66.6	122 086	62 708	53 266	7 457	3 339	118 747	62.3	8 583	3 118	6.6
March	196 213	130 400	66.5	121 930	62 780	53 099	7 381	3 354	118 576	62.1	8 470	3 055	6.5
April	196 363	130 621	66.5	122 290	62 906	53 274	7 551	3 428	118 862	62.3	8 331	2 921	6.4
May	196 510	130 779	66.6	122 864	63 116	53 624	7 466	3 409	119 455	62.5	7 915	2 836	6.1
June	196 693	130 561	66.4	122 634	63 041	53 393	7 527	3 299	119 335	62.3	7 927	2 735	6.1
July	196 859	130 652	66.4	122 706	63 034	53 531	7 453	3 333	119 373	62.3	7 946	2 822	6.1
August	197 043	131 275	66.6	123 342	63 294	53 744	7 619	3 451	119 891	62.6	7 933	2 750	6.0
September	197 248	131 421	66.6	123 687	63 631	53 991	7 352	3 430	120 257	62.7	7 734	2 746	5.9
October	197 430	131 744	66.7	124 112	63 818	54 071	7 543	3 490	120 622	62.9	7 632	2 955	5.8
November	197 607	131 891	66.7	124 516	64 080	54 168	7 423	3 574	120 942	63.0	7 375	2 666	5.6
December	197 765	131 951	66.7	124 721	64 359	54 054	7 599	3 577	121 144	63.1	7 230	2 488	5.5

[1] Not seasonally adjusted.
[2] In 1930 through 1943, the official BLS data count persons on work relief as unemployed. The unemployment rates for those years shown in parentheses count persons on work relief as employed, which is more consistent with the postwar practice. See notes and definitions.

Table 10-1B. Summary Labor Force, Employment, and Unemployment: Historical Data—*Continued*

(Thousands of persons, percent, seasonally adjusted, except as noted.)

Year and month	Civilian noninstitutional population [1]	Civilian labor force		Employment, thousands of persons						Employment-population ratio, percent	Unemployment		
					By age and sex			By industry			Thousands of persons		
		Thousands of persons	Participation rate (percent)	Total	Men, 20 years and over	Women, 20 years and over	Both sexes, 16 to 19 years	Agricultural	Nonagricultural		Total	Unemployed 15 weeks and over	Rate (percent) [2]
1995													
January	197 753	132 038	66.8	124 663	64 185	54 087	7 650	3 519	121 144	63.0	7 375	2 396	5.6
February	197 886	132 115	66.8	124 928	64 378	54 226	7 659	3 620	121 308	63.1	7 187	2 345	5.4
March	198 007	132 108	66.7	124 955	64 321	54 141	7 742	3 634	121 321	63.1	7 153	2 287	5.4
April	198 148	132 590	66.9	124 945	64 165	54 366	7 774	3 566	121 379	63.1	7 645	2 473	5.8
May	198 286	131 851	66.5	124 421	63 829	54 272	7 664	3 349	121 072	62.7	7 430	2 577	5.6
June	198 452	131 949	66.5	124 522	63 992	54 020	7 850	3 461	121 061	62.7	7 427	2 266	5.6
July	198 615	132 343	66.6	124 816	63 962	54 476	7 798	3 379	121 437	62.8	7 527	2 311	5.7
August	198 801	132 336	66.6	124 852	63 875	54 434	7 910	3 374	121 478	62.8	7 484	2 391	5.7
September	199 005	132 611	66.6	125 133	64 179	54 507	7 825	3 285	121 848	62.9	7 478	2 306	5.6
October	199 192	132 716	66.6	125 388	64 272	54 692	7 774	3 438	121 950	62.9	7 328	2 272	5.5
November	199 355	132 614	66.5	125 188	63 931	54 850	7 765	3 338	121 850	62.8	7 426	2 339	5.6
December	199 508	132 511	66.4	125 088	64 041	54 674	7 768	3 352	121 736	62.7	7 423	2 331	5.6
1996													
January	199 634	132 616	66.4	125 125	64 180	54 580	7 733	3 483	121 642	62.7	7 491	2 371	5.6
February	199 772	132 952	66.6	125 639	64 398	54 844	7 688	3 547	122 092	62.9	7 313	2 307	5.5
March	199 921	133 180	66.6	125 862	64 506	54 994	7 673	3 489	122 373	63.0	7 318	2 454	5.5
April	200 101	133 409	66.7	125 994	64 481	55 067	7 774	3 406	122 588	63.0	7 415	2 455	5.6
May	200 278	133 667	66.7	126 244	64 683	55 034	7 841	3 473	122 771	63.0	7 423	2 403	5.6
June	200 459	133 697	66.7	126 602	64 940	55 177	7 739	3 424	123 178	63.2	7 095	2 355	5.3
July	200 641	134 284	66.9	126 947	65 068	55 362	7 859	3 433	123 514	63.3	7 337	2 297	5.5
August	200 847	134 054	66.7	127 172	65 216	55 525	7 731	3 395	123 777	63.3	6 882	2 267	5.1
September	201 060	134 515	66.9	127 536	65 169	55 669	7 935	3 448	124 088	63.4	6 979	2 220	5.2
October	201 273	134 921	67.0	127 890	65 460	55 750	7 980	3 463	124 427	63.5	7 031	2 268	5.2
November	201 463	135 007	67.0	127 771	65 320	55 896	7 875	3 356	124 415	63.4	7 236	2 159	5.4
December	201 636	135 113	67.0	127 860	65 435	55 849	7 883	3 445	124 415	63.4	7 253	2 124	5.4
1997													
January	202 285	135 456	67.0	128 298	65 679	56 024	7 930	3 449	124 849	63.4	7 158	2 162	5.3
February	202 388	135 400	66.9	128 298	65 758	55 955	7 948	3 353	124 945	63.4	7 102	2 140	5.2
March	202 513	135 891	67.1	128 891	65 974	56 270	7 951	3 419	125 472	63.6	7 000	2 110	5.2
April	202 674	136 016	67.1	129 143	66 092	56 347	7 974	3 462	125 681	63.7	6 873	2 176	5.1
May	202 832	136 119	67.1	129 464	66 328	56 446	7 964	3 437	126 027	63.8	6 655	2 121	4.9
June	203 000	136 211	67.1	129 412	66 308	56 573	7 849	3 409	126 003	63.7	6 799	2 085	5.0
July	203 166	136 477	67.2	129 822	66 422	56 785	7 975	3 422	126 400	63.9	6 655	2 119	4.9
August	203 364	136 618	67.2	130 010	66 508	56 852	7 922	3 359	126 651	63.9	6 608	2 004	4.8
September	203 570	136 675	67.1	130 019	66 483	56 931	7 873	3 392	126 627	63.9	6 656	2 074	4.9
October	203 767	136 633	67.1	130 179	66 511	56 982	7 876	3 312	126 867	63.9	6 454	1 950	4.7
November	203 941	136 961	67.2	130 653	66 765	57 039	8 042	3 386	127 267	64.1	6 308	1 817	4.6
December	204 098	137 155	67.2	130 679	66 643	57 219	7 923	3 405	127 274	64.0	6 476	1 901	4.7
1998													
January	204 238	137 095	67.1	130 726	66 750	56 941	8 171	3 299	127 389	64.0	6 368	1 833	4.6
February	204 400	137 112	67.1	130 807	66 856	56 992	8 137	3 284	127 522	64.0	6 306	1 809	4.6
March	204 546	137 236	67.1	130 814	66 721	57 080	8 235	3 146	127 650	64.0	6 422	1 772	4.7
April	204 731	137 150	67.0	131 209	67 151	57 074	8 071	3 334	127 852	64.1	5 941	1 476	4.3
May	204 899	137 372	67.0	131 325	67 164	57 155	8 228	3 360	127 959	64.1	6 047	1 490	4.4
June	205 085	137 455	67.0	131 244	67 054	57 156	8 268	3 380	127 874	64.0	6 212	1 613	4.5
July	205 270	137 588	67.0	131 329	67 119	57 192	8 221	3 455	127 913	64.0	6 259	1 577	4.5
August	205 479	137 570	67.0	131 390	66 985	57 332	8 289	3 509	127 970	63.9	6 179	1 626	4.5
September	205 699	138 286	67.2	131 986	67 254	57 520	8 489	3 500	128 399	64.2	6 300	1 688	4.6
October	205 919	138 279	67.2	131 999	67 433	57 529	8 347	3 593	128 389	64.1	6 280	1 582	4.5
November	206 104	138 381	67.1	132 280	67 591	57 638	8 269	3 375	128 897	64.2	6 100	1 590	4.4
December	206 270	138 634	67.2	132 602	67 548	57 840	8 340	3 246	129 320	64.3	6 032	1 559	4.4
1999													
January	206 719	139 003	67.2	133 027	67 679	58 256	8 367	3 233	129 802	64.4	5 976	1 490	4.3
February	206 873	138 967	67.2	132 856	67 498	58 129	8 399	3 246	129 647	64.2	6 111	1 551	4.4
March	207 036	138 730	67.0	132 947	67 660	58 132	8 343	3 238	129 656	64.2	5 783	1 472	4.2
April	207 236	138 959	67.1	132 955	67 542	58 260	8 334	3 336	129 615	64.2	6 004	1 480	4.3
May	207 427	139 107	67.1	133 311	67 539	58 440	8 454	3 335	129 937	64.3	5 796	1 505	4.2
June	207 632	139 329	67.1	133 378	67 700	58 641	8 175	3 386	129 982	64.2	5 951	1 624	4.3
July	207 828	139 439	67.1	133 414	67 731	58 490	8 306	3 346	130 146	64.2	6 025	1 513	4.3
August	208 038	139 430	67.0	133 591	67 768	58 707	8 208	3 234	130 366	64.2	5 838	1 455	4.2
September	208 265	139 622	67.0	133 707	67 882	58 735	8 323	3 173	130 434	64.2	5 915	1 449	4.2
October	208 483	139 771	67.0	133 993	67 840	58 921	8 394	3 229	130 758	64.3	5 778	1 438	4.1
November	208 666	140 025	67.1	134 309	68 094	59 018	8 358	3 343	130 989	64.4	5 716	1 378	4.1
December	208 832	140 177	67.1	134 523	68 217	59 056	8 370	3 260	131 257	64.4	5 653	1 375	4.0
2000													
January	211 410	142 267	67.3	136 559	69 419	59 842	8 360	2 613	133 863	64.6	5 708	1 380	4.0
February	211 576	142 456	67.3	136 598	69 505	59 887	8 359	2 731	133 912	64.6	5 858	1 300	4.1
March	211 772	142 434	67.3	136 701	69 482	59 977	8 355	2 579	134 022	64.6	5 733	1 312	4.0
April	212 018	142 751	67.3	137 270	69 519	60 358	8 458	2 505	134 806	64.7	5 481	1 261	3.8
May	212 242	142 388	67.1	136 630	69 399	59 951	8 344	2 480	134 144	64.4	5 758	1 325	4.0
June	212 466	142 591	67.1	136 940	69 629	60 027	8 308	2 445	134 528	64.5	5 651	1 242	4.0
July	212 677	142 278	66.9	136 531	69 525	60 011	8 078	2 408	134 196	64.2	5 747	1 343	4.0
August	212 916	142 514	66.9	136 662	69 823	59 719	8 280	2 433	134 311	64.2	5 853	1 394	4.1
September	213 163	142 518	66.9	136 893	69 700	60 083	8 176	2 384	134 489	64.2	5 625	1 290	3.9
October	213 405	142 622	66.8	137 088	69 762	60 238	8 124	2 319	134 808	64.2	5 534	1 337	3.9
November	213 540	142 962	66.9	137 322	69 910	60 269	8 211	2 330	134 921	64.3	5 639	1 315	3.9
December	213 736	143 248	67.0	137 614	69 939	60 503	8 258	2 389	135 194	64.4	5 634	1 329	3.9

[1] Not seasonally adjusted.
[2] In 1930 through 1943, the official BLS data count persons on work relief as unemployed. The unemployment rates for those years shown in parentheses count persons on work relief as employed, which is more consistent with the postwar practice. See notes and definitions.

Table 10-1B. Summary Labor Force, Employment, and Unemployment: Historical Data—*Continued*

(Thousands of persons, percent, seasonally adjusted, except as noted.)

Year and month	Civilian noninstitutional population [1]	Civilian labor force		Employment, thousands of persons						Employment-population ratio, percent	Unemployment		
					By age and sex			By industry			Thousands of persons		
		Thousands of persons	Participation rate (percent)	Total	Men, 20 years and over	Women, 20 years and over	Both sexes, 16 to 19 years	Agricultural	Nonagricultural		Total	Unemployed 15 weeks and over	Rate (percent) [2]
2001													
January	213 888	143 800	67.2	137 778	70 064	60 609	8 243	2 360	135 304	64.4	6 023	1 372	4.2
February	214 110	143 701	67.1	137 612	69 959	60 615	8 154	2 370	135 291	64.3	6 089	1 491	4.2
March	214 305	143 924	67.2	137 783	69 881	60 902	8 120	2 350	135 372	64.3	6 141	1 521	4.3
April	214 525	143 569	66.9	137 299	69 916	60 523	7 970	2 336	135 036	64.0	6 271	1 499	4.4
May	214 732	143 318	66.7	137 092	69 865	60 509	7 760	2 353	134 735	63.8	6 226	1 502	4.3
June	214 950	143 357	66.7	136 873	69 690	60 371	7 942	2 082	134 755	63.7	6 484	1 532	4.5
July	215 180	143 654	66.8	137 071	69 808	60 480	7 929	2 295	134 858	63.7	6 583	1 653	4.6
August	215 420	143 284	66.5	136 241	69 585	60 301	7 531	2 305	133 944	63.2	7 042	1 861	4.9
September	215 665	143 989	66.8	136 846	69 933	60 265	7 836	2 322	134 558	63.5	7 142	1 950	5.0
October	215 903	144 086	66.7	136 392	69 621	60 168	7 858	2 327	134 098	63.2	7 694	2 082	5.3
November	216 117	144 240	66.7	136 238	69 444	60 174	7 873	2 203	133 955	63.0	8 003	2 318	5.5
December	216 315	144 305	66.7	136 047	69 551	60 095	7 712	2 293	133 751	62.9	8 258	2 444	5.7
2002													
January	216 506	143 883	66.5	135 701	69 308	60 032	7 619	2 385	133 233	62.7	8 182	2 578	5.7
February	216 663	144 653	66.8	136 438	69 534	60 479	7 650	2 397	134 127	63.0	8 215	2 608	5.7
March	216 823	144 481	66.6	136 177	69 480	60 190	7 802	2 368	133 816	62.8	8 304	2 719	5.7
April	217 006	144 725	66.7	136 126	69 574	60 204	7 621	2 371	133 833	62.7	8 599	2 852	5.9
May	217 198	144 938	66.7	136 539	69 981	60 226	7 588	2 260	134 278	62.9	8 399	2 967	5.8
June	217 407	144 808	66.6	136 415	69 769	60 297	7 617	2 161	134 135	62.7	8 393	3 023	5.8
July	217 630	144 803	66.5	136 413	69 806	60 290	7 591	2 324	134 107	62.7	8 390	2 966	5.8
August	217 866	145 009	66.6	136 705	69 937	60 560	7 477	2 127	134 593	62.7	8 304	2 887	5.7
September	218 107	145 552	66.7	137 302	70 207	60 679	7 667	2 285	135 102	63.0	8 251	2 971	5.7
October	218 340	145 314	66.6	137 008	69 948	60 663	7 537	2 471	134 580	62.7	8 307	3 042	5.7
November	218 548	145 041	66.4	136 521	69 615	60 697	7 487	2 261	134 171	62.5	8 520	3 062	5.9
December	218 741	145 066	66.3	136 426	69 620	60 667	7 385	2 352	134 071	62.4	8 640	3 271	6.0
2003													
January	219 897	145 937	66.4	137 417	69 919	61 406	7 358	2 337	135 045	62.5	8 520	3 166	5.8
February	220 114	146 100	66.4	137 482	70 262	61 159	7 322	2 234	135 306	62.5	8 618	3 161	5.9
March	220 317	146 022	66.3	137 434	70 243	61 317	7 143	2 263	135 232	62.4	8 588	3 161	5.9
April	220 540	146 474	66.4	137 633	70 311	61 374	7 223	2 150	135 561	62.4	8 842	3 348	6.0
May	220 768	146 500	66.4	137 544	70 215	61 393	7 228	2 183	135 370	62.3	8 957	3 318	6.1
June	221 014	147 056	66.5	137 790	70 159	61 747	7 268	2 185	135 419	62.3	9 266	3 552	6.3
July	221 252	146 485	66.2	137 474	70 190	61 437	7 150	2 187	135 242	62.1	9 011	3 633	6.2
August	221 507	146 445	66.1	137 549	70 237	61 442	7 035	2 313	135 200	62.1	8 896	3 557	6.1
September	221 779	146 530	66.1	137 609	70 631	61 119	7 112	2 349	135 355	62.0	8 921	3 486	6.1
October	222 039	146 716	66.1	137 984	70 685	61 451	7 060	2 479	135 571	62.1	8 732	3 451	6.0
November	222 279	147 000	66.1	138 424	70 935	61 494	7 112	2 373	136 003	62.3	8 576	3 420	5.8
December	222 509	146 729	65.9	138 411	71 170	61 396	6 978	2 243	136 145	62.2	8 317	3 366	5.7
2004													
January	222 161	146 842	66.1	138 472	71 318	61 183	7 194	2 196	136 228	62.3	8 370	3 364	5.7
February	222 357	146 709	66.0	138 542	71 122	61 514	7 077	2 210	136 362	62.3	8 167	3 248	5.6
March	222 550	146 944	66.0	138 453	71 155	61 534	6 930	2 180	136 302	62.2	8 491	3 314	5.8
April	222 757	146 850	65.9	138 680	71 121	61 647	7 093	2 241	136 474	62.3	8 170	2 971	5.6
May	222 967	147 065	66.0	138 852	71 180	61 762	7 126	2 300	136 556	62.3	8 212	3 103	5.6
June	223 196	147 460	66.1	139 174	71 562	61 793	7 007	2 237	136 748	62.4	8 286	3 130	5.6
July	223 422	147 692	66.1	139 556	71 780	61 884	7 166	2 222	137 354	62.5	8 136	2 918	5.5
August	223 677	147 564	66.0	139 573	71 808	61 836	7 123	2 333	137 230	62.4	7 990	2 846	5.4
September	223 941	147 415	65.8	139 487	71 744	61 859	7 056	2 251	137 323	62.3	7 927	2 910	5.4
October	224 192	147 793	65.9	139 732	71 860	61 942	7 180	2 216	137 598	62.3	8 061	3 041	5.5
November	224 422	148 162	66.0	140 231	72 110	62 088	7 216	2 206	137 978	62.5	7 932	2 960	5.4
December	224 640	148 059	65.9	140 125	72 058	62 136	7 202	2 171	137 947	62.4	7 934	2 927	5.4
2005													
January	224 837	148 029	65.8	140 245	72 063	62 260	7 071	2 112	138 111	62.4	7 784	2 851	5.3
February	225 041	148 364	65.9	140 385	72 299	62 253	7 073	2 129	138 267	62.4	7 980	2 896	5.4
March	225 236	148 391	65.9	140 654	72 478	62 222	7 185	2 180	138 462	62.4	7 737	2 817	5.2
April	225 441	148 926	66.1	141 254	72 860	62 483	7 190	2 248	138 992	62.7	7 672	2 678	5.2
May	225 670	149 261	66.1	141 609	73 133	62 557	7 201	2 225	139 379	62.8	7 651	2 683	5.1
June	225 911	149 238	66.1	141 714	73 223	62 516	7 140	2 302	139 276	62.7	7 524	2 405	5.0
July	226 153	149 432	66.1	142 026	73 337	62 691	7 150	2 308	139 789	62.8	7 406	2 449	5.0
August	226 421	149 779	66.2	142 434	73 513	62 844	7 240	2 183	140 277	62.9	7 345	2 569	4.9
September	226 693	149 954	66.1	142 401	73 333	63 035	7 141	2 181	140 276	62.8	7 553	2 537	5.0
October	226 959	150 001	66.1	142 548	73 445	63 127	7 124	2 191	140 435	62.8	7 453	2 492	5.0
November	227 204	150 065	66.0	142 499	73 341	63 127	7 265	2 174	140 299	62.7	7 566	2 486	5.0
December	227 425	150 030	66.0	142 752	73 467	63 209	7 139	2 094	140 635	62.8	7 279	2 429	4.9
2006													
January	227 553	150 214	66.0	143 150	73 892	63 151	7 197	2 164	140 933	62.9	7 064	2 270	4.7
February	227 763	150 641	66.1	143 457	73 972	63 304	7 298	2 178	141 254	63.0	7 184	2 546	4.8
March	227 975	150 813	66.2	143 741	74 228	63 353	7 342	2 153	141 604	63.1	7 072	2 373	4.7
April	228 199	150 881	66.1	143 761	74 204	63 413	7 198	2 249	141 388	63.0	7 120	2 353	4.7
May	228 428	151 069	66.1	144 089	74 229	63 656	7 215	2 194	141 859	63.1	6 980	2 303	4.6
June	228 671	151 354	66.2	144 353	74 261	63 866	7 393	2 256	142 019	63.1	7 001	2 127	4.6
July	228 912	151 377	66.1	144 202	74 011	64 030	7 324	2 278	142 066	63.0	7 175	2 289	4.7
August	229 161	151 716	66.2	144 625	74 384	64 139	7 266	2 240	142 440	63.1	7 091	2 293	4.7
September	229 420	151 662	66.1	144 815	74 866	63 922	7 196	2 182	142 661	63.1	6 847	2 231	4.5
October	229 675	152 041	66.2	145 314	74 833	64 298	7 289	2 183	143 222	63.3	6 727	2 062	4.4
November	229 905	152 406	66.3	145 534	74 962	64 328	7 331	2 164	143 350	63.3	6 872	2 159	4.5
December	230 108	152 732	66.4	145 970	75 232	64 518	7 287	2 233	143 716	63.4	6 762	2 083	4.4

[1]Not seasonally adjusted.
[2]In 1930 through 1943, the official BLS data count persons on work relief as unemployed. The unemployment rates for those years shown in parentheses count persons on work relief as employed, which is more consistent with the postwar practice. See notes and definitions.

Table 10-1B. Summary Labor Force, Employment, and Unemployment: Historical Data—*Continued*

(Thousands of persons, percent, seasonally adjusted, except as noted.)

Year and month	Civilian noninstitutional population [1]	Civilian labor force		Employment, thousands of persons						Employment-population ratio, percent	Unemployment		
		Thousands of persons	Participation rate (percent)	Total	By age and sex			By industry			Thousands of persons		Rate (percent) [2]
					Men, 20 years and over	Women, 20 years and over	Both sexes, 16 to 19 years	Agricultural	Nonagricultural		Total	Unemployed 15 weeks and over	
2007													
January	230 650	153 144	66.4	146 028	75 238	64 621	7 240	2 214	143 785	63.3	7 116	2 156	4.6
February	230 834	152 983	66.3	146 057	75 239	64 750	7 133	2 295	143 741	63.3	6 927	2 211	4.5
March	231 034	153 051	66.2	146 320	75 386	64 928	7 061	2 178	144 153	63.3	6 731	2 255	4.4
April	231 253	152 435	65.9	145 586	75 342	64 366	6 985	2 069	143 385	63.0	6 850	2 281	4.5
May	231 480	152 670	66.0	145 903	75 386	64 724	6 888	2 081	143 773	63.0	6 766	2 231	4.4
June	231 713	153 041	66.0	146 063	75 327	64 788	7 109	1 946	144 112	63.0	6 979	2 281	4.6
July	231 958	153 054	66.0	145 905	75 247	64 766	6 953	2 016	144 041	62.9	7 149	2 364	4.7
August	232 211	152 749	65.8	145 682	75 195	64 838	6 714	1 863	143 865	62.7	7 067	2 333	4.6
September	232 461	153 414	66.0	146 244	75 273	65 086	7 001	2 095	144 148	62.9	7 170	2 355	4.7
October	232 715	153 183	65.8	145 946	75 146	64 842	7 039	2 121	143 926	62.7	7 237	2 300	4.7
November	232 939	153 835	66.0	146 595	75 683	64 985	7 071	2 148	144 413	62.9	7 240	2 366	4.7
December	233 156	153 918	66.0	146 273	75 510	64 910	7 032	2 219	144 018	62.7	7 645	2 501	5.0
2008													
January	232 616	154 063	66.2	146 378	75 551	65 058	7 015	2 205	144 168	62.9	7 685	2 540	5.0
February	232 809	153 653	66.0	146 156	75 450	65 021	6 820	2 190	143 943	62.8	7 497	2 446	4.9
March	232 995	153 908	66.1	146 086	75 294	65 074	6 813	2 172	143 871	62.7	7 822	2 491	5.1
April	233 198	153 769	65.9	146 132	75 182	65 107	6 947	2 115	143 874	62.7	7 637	2 687	5.0
May	233 405	154 303	66.1	145 908	74 953	65 137	7 182	2 113	143 737	62.5	8 395	2 780	5.4
June	233 627	154 313	66.1	145 737	74 975	65 169	6 925	2 127	143 629	62.4	8 575	2 913	5.6
July	233 864	154 469	66.1	145 532	74 950	65 103	6 909	2 134	143 519	62.2	8 937	3 114	5.8
August	234 107	154 641	66.1	145 203	74 658	65 008	6 801	2 148	143 086	62.0	9 438	3 420	6.1
September	234 360	154 570	66.0	145 076	74 456	65 078	6 850	2 231	142 796	61.9	9 494	3 626	6.1
October	234 612	154 876	66.0	144 802	74 263	65 103	6 793	2 199	142 689	61.7	10 074	3 990	6.5
November	234 828	154 639	65.9	144 100	73 943	64 885	6 612	2 207	141 962	61.4	10 538	3 923	6.8
December	235 035	154 655	65.8	143 369	73 311	64 813	6 601	2 209	141 139	61.0	11 286	4 547	7.3
2009													
January	234 739	154 210	65.7	142 152	72 724	64 209	5 218	2 147	140 029	60.6	12 058	4 764	7.8
February	234 913	154 538	65.8	141 640	72 260	64 195	5 185	2 130	139 493	60.3	12 898	5 455	8.3
March	235 086	154 133	65.6	140 707	71 629	64 027	5 051	2 031	138 664	59.9	13 426	5 886	8.7
April	235 271	154 509	65.7	140 656	71 599	64 021	5 036	2 146	138 437	59.8	13 853	6 385	9.0
May	235 452	154 747	65.7	140 248	71 410	63 807	5 031	2 145	138 036	59.6	14 499	7 022	9.4
June	235 655	154 716	65.7	140 009	71 326	63 747	4 937	2 165	137 841	59.4	14 707	7 837	9.5
July	235 870	154 502	65.5	139 901	71 273	63 761	4 867	2 126	137 819	59.3	14 601	7 839	9.5
August	236 087	154 307	65.4	139 492	71 111	63 633	4 749	2 088	137 371	59.1	14 814	7 828	9.6
September	236 322	153 827	65.1	138 818	70 844	63 324	4 649	2 033	136 734	58.7	15 009	8 402	9.8
October	236 550	153 784	65.0	138 432	70 713	63 275	4 445	2 039	136 483	58.5	15 352	8 648	10.0
November	236 743	153 878	65.0	138 659	70 774	63 422	4 463	2 098	136 640	58.6	15 219	8 755	9.9
December	236 924	153 111	64.6	138 013	70 479	63 086	4 449	2 087	135 904	58.3	15 098	8 835	9.9
2010													
January	236 832	153 404	64.8	138 451	70 506	63 515	4 430	2 131	136 390	58.5	14 953	8 903	9.7
February	236 998	153 720	64.9	138 599	70 601	63 505	4 493	2 307	136 333	58.5	15 121	8 933	9.8
March	237 159	153 964	64.9	138 752	70 876	63 378	4 498	2 211	136 588	58.5	15 212	9 096	9.9
April	237 329	154 642	65.2	139 309	71 356	63 416	4 537	2 288	136 966	58.7	15 333	9 133	9.9
May	237 499	154 106	64.9	139 247	71 378	63 436	4 433	2 197	136 998	58.6	14 858	8 892	9.6
June	237 690	153 631	64.6	139 148	71 353	63 555	4 240	2 140	136 975	58.5	14 483	8 898	9.4
July	237 890	153 706	64.6	139 179	71 457	63 415	4 307	2 172	136 934	58.5	14 527	8 704	9.5
August	238 099	154 087	64.7	139 427	71 607	63 420	4 400	2 163	137 187	58.6	14 660	8 405	9.5
September	238 322	153 971	64.6	139 393	71 592	63 533	4 268	2 161	137 209	58.5	14 578	8 444	9.5
October	238 530	153 631	64.4	139 111	71 432	63 382	4 297	2 338	136 891	58.3	14 520	8 617	9.5
November	238 715	154 127	64.6	139 030	71 140	63 494	4 396	2 191	136 872	58.2	15 097	8 697	9.8
December	238 889	153 639	64.3	139 266	71 470	63 493	4 302	2 186	137 072	58.3	14 373	8 549	9.4
2011													
January	238 704	153 198	64.2	139 287	71 544	63 413	4 330	2 270	137 036	58.4	13 910	8 430	9.1
February	238 851	153 280	64.2	139 422	71 819	63 281	4 322	2 266	137 182	58.4	13 858	8 213	9.0
March	239 000	153 403	64.2	139 655	71 834	63 461	4 360	2 260	137 471	58.4	13 748	8 184	9.0
April	239 146	153 566	64.2	139 622	71 946	63 373	4 302	2 143	137 438	58.4	13 944	8 007	9.1
May	239 313	153 526	64.2	139 653	72 120	63 267	4 266	2 230	137 395	58.4	13 873	8 189	9.0
June	239 489	153 379	64.0	139 409	71 999	63 134	4 276	2 253	137 136	58.2	13 971	8 107	9.1
July	239 671	153 309	64.0	139 524	72 008	63 293	4 223	2 225	137 215	58.2	13 785	8 151	9.0
August	239 871	153 724	64.1	139 904	72 217	63 339	4 348	2 344	137 470	58.3	13 820	8 214	9.0
September	240 071	154 059	64.2	140 154	72 409	63 372	4 372	2 232	137 904	58.4	13 905	8 282	9.0
October	240 269	153 940	64.1	140 335	72 415	63 540	4 381	2 211	138 283	58.4	13 604	7 808	8.8
November	240 441	154 072	64.1	140 747	72 861	63 489	4 396	2 251	138 500	58.5	13 326	7 713	8.6
December	240 584	153 927	64.0	140 836	73 039	63 406	4 390	2 362	138 454	58.5	13 090	7 555	8.5
2012													
January	242 269	154 328	63.7	141 677	73 083	64 219	4 375	2 211	139 437	58.5	12 650	7 467	8.2
February	242 435	154 826	63.9	141 943	73 103	64 436	4 403	2 193	139 782	58.5	12 883	7 373	8.3
March	242 604	154 811	63.8	142 079	73 181	64 521	4 377	2 246	139 888	58.6	12 732	7 216	8.2
April	242 784	154 565	63.7	141 963	73 131	64 456	4 376	2 203	139 712	58.5	12 603	7 056	8.2
May	242 966	154 946	63.8	142 257	73 245	64 600	4 412	2 278	139 980	58.6	12 689	7 069	8.2
June	243 155	155 134	63.8	142 432	73 294	64 629	4 509	2 221	140 246	58.6	12 702	7 170	8.2
July	243 354	154 970	63.7	142 272	73 301	64 456	4 515	2 212	140 020	58.5	12 698	6 946	8.2
August	243 566	154 669	63.5	142 204	73 197	64 644	4 364	2 106	140 017	58.4	12 464	6 848	8.1
September	243 772	155 018	63.6	142 947	73 677	64 857	4 414	2 178	140 773	58.6	12 070	6 728	7.8
October	243 983	155 507	63.7	143 369	73 923	64 980	4 466	2 176	141 379	58.8	12 138	6 795	7.8
November	244 174	155 279	63.6	143 233	73 807	64 962	4 465	2 126	141 110	58.7	12 045	6 563	7.8
December	244 350	155 485	63.6	143 212	73 924	64 901	4 387	2 066	141 121	58.6	12 273	6 634	7.9

[1] Not seasonally adjusted.
[2] In 1930 through 1943, the official BLS data count persons on work relief as unemployed. The unemployment rates for those years shown in parentheses count persons on work relief as employed, which is more consistent with the postwar practice. See notes and definitions.

Table 10-1B. Summary Labor Force, Employment, and Unemployment: Historical Data—Continued

(Thousands of persons, percent, seasonally adjusted, except as noted.)

Year and month	Civilian noninsti-tutional popu-lation [1]	Civilian labor force		Employment, thousands of persons						Employ-ment-population ratio, percent	Unemployment		
		Thousands of persons	Participa-tion rate (percent)	Total	By age and sex			By industry			Thousands of persons		Rate (percent) [2]
					Men, 20 years and over	Women, 20 years and over	Both sexes, 16 to 19 years	Agri-cultural	Nonagri-cultural		Total	Unem-ployed 15 weeks and over	
2013													
January	244 663	155 699	63.6	143 384	74 084	64 790	4 510	2 057	141 234	58.6	12 315	6 573	7.9
February	244 828	155 511	63.5	143 464	74 183	64 911	4 370	2 070	141 393	58.6	12 047	6 485	7.7
March	244 995	155 099	63.3	143 393	74 190	64 838	4 365	2 020	141 350	58.5	11 706	6 355	7.5
April	245 175	155 359	63.4	143 676	74 161	65 148	4 368	2 048	141 604	58.6	11 683	6 329	7.5
May	245 363	155 609	63.4	143 919	74 137	65 323	4 459	2 081	141 860	58.7	11 690	6 287	7.5
June	245 552	155 822	63.5	144 075	74 265	65 340	4 470	2 091	142 021	58.7	11 747	6 218	7.5
July	245 756	155 693	63.4	144 285	74 301	65 514	4 470	2 171	142 081	58.7	11 408	6 031	7.3
August	245 959	155 435	63.2	144 179	74 015	65 743	4 421	2 205	141 918	58.6	11 256	5 973	7.2
September	246 168	155 473	63.2	144 270	74 151	65 539	4 580	2 208	142 058	58.6	11 203	5 927	7.2
October	246 381	154 625	62.8	143 485	73 808	65 229	4 448	2 208	141 449	58.2	11 140	5 824	7.2
November	246 567	155 284	63.0	144 443	74 373	65 547	4 523	2 139	142 317	58.6	10 841	5 786	7.0
December	246 745	154 937	62.8	144 586	74 467	65 617	4 502	2 229	142 337	58.6	10 351	5 530	6.7
2014													
January	230 244	149 943	65.1	140 818	74 905	65 913	4 388	1 999	141 527	58.1	10 280	5 392	6.6
February	230 421	150 207	65.2	140 989	74 820	66 168	4 312	1 973	142 160	58.3	10 387	5 657	6.7
March	230 600	150 488	65.3	141 293	75 284	66 009	4 504	2 008	143 082	58.7	10 384	5 708	6.6
April	230 787	149 878	64.9	141 239	75 163	66 076	4 485	2 048	143 718	58.9	9 696	5 139	6.2
May	230 978	150 006	64.9	141 323	75 159	66 164	4 545	2 101	144 297	59.1	9 761	4 898	6.3
June	231 178	150 059	64.9	141 771	75 504	66 267	4 476	2 288	144 815	59.4	9 453	4 448	6.1
July	231 394	150 396	65.0	141 881	75 631	66 250	4 520	2 403	144 862	59.4	9 648	4 452	6.2
August	231 607	150 441	65.0	141 956	75 668	66 289	4 495	2 472	144 175	59.1	9 568	4 321	6.1
September	231 831	150 200	64.8	142 081	75 889	66 192	4 527	2 482	144 459	59.1	9 237	4 242	5.9
October	232 049	150 377	64.8	142 488	75 928	66 560	4 772	2 517	145 419	59.5	8 983	4 251	5.7
November	232 243	150 627	64.9	142 569	75 675	66 894	4 762	2 332	145 335	59.3	9 071	4 144	5.8
December	232 432	150 383	64.7	142 658	76 026	66 632	4 784	2 220	144 970	59.1	8 688	3 922	5.6
2015													
January	249 723	157 022	62.9	148 061	75 364	66 894	4 294	2 234	144 317	59.3	8 962	4 250	5.7
February	249 899	156 771	62.7	148 108	75 671	67 058	4 389	2 234	144 884	59.3	8 663	4 248	5.5
March	250 080	156 781	62.7	148 244	76 122	67 022	4 491	2 405	145 230	59.3	8 538	4 064	5.4
April	250 266	157 043	62.8	148 522	76 749	67 303	4 536	2 294	146 293	59.3	8 521	3 802	5.4
May	250 455	157 447	62.9	148 792	77 137	67 493	4 718	2 431	146 918	59.4	8 655	3 851	5.5
June	250 663	156 993	62.6	148 742	77 315	67 003	5 327	2 703	146 942	59.3	8 251	3 369	5.3
July	250 876	157 125	62.6	148 890	77 541	66 485	5 696	2 601	147 121	59.3	8 235	3 245	5.2
August	251 096	157 109	62.6	149 092	77 311	66 874	5 042	2 539	146 689	59.4	8 017	3 318	5.1
September	251 325	156 809	62.4	148 932	77 110	67 394	4 476	2 471	146 509	59.3	7 877	3 207	5.0
October	251 541	157 123	62.5	149 255	77 258	67 885	4 574	2 518	147 198	59.3	7 869	3 301	5.0
November	251 747	157 358	62.5	149 419	76 911	68 335	4 520	2 363	147 404	59.4	7 939	3 256	5.0
December	251 936	157 957	62.7	150 030	76 827	68 131	4 745	2 273	147 430	59.6	7 927	3 231	5.0
2016													
January	252 397	158 362	62.7	150 533	76 644	67 904	4 490	2 200	146 838	59.6	7 829	3 297	4.9
February	252 577	158 888	62.9	151 043	77 148	68 305	4 608	2 274	147 787	59.8	7 845	3 525	4.9
March	252 768	159 278	63.0	151 301	77 639	68 451	4 648	2 491	148 247	59.9	7 977	3 651	5.0
April	252 969	158 938	62.8	151 028	78 028	68 346	4 701	2 478	148 597	59.7	7 910	3 499	5.0
May	253 174	158 510	62.6	151 058	78 241	68 496	4 857	2 620	148 974	59.7	7 451	3 113	4.7
June	253 397	158 889	62.7	151 090	78 673	67 769	5 548	2 661	149 329	59.6	7 799	2 970	4.9
July	253 620	159 295	62.8	151 546	78 695	67 702	6 040	2 597	149 840	59.8	7 749	3 060	4.9
August	253 854	159 508	62.8	151 655	78 562	67 776	5 466	2 718	149 086	59.7	7 853	2 942	4.9
September	254 091	159 830	62.9	151 926	78 459	68 709	4 810	2 526	149 451	59.8	7 904	3 004	4.9
October	254 321	159 643	62.8	151 902	78 538	68 997	4 800	2 408	149 927	59.7	7 740	3 087	4.8
November	254 540	159 456	62.6	152 048	78 405	69 203	4 778	2 366	150 020	59.7	7 409	2 859	4.6
December	254 742	159 640	62.7	152 111	77 984	68 984	4 831	2 180	149 617	59.7	7 529	2 945	4.7
2017													
January	254 082	159 718	62.9	152 076	78 448	68 572	5 056	2 225	149 851	59.9	7 642	3 055	4.8
February	254 246	159 997	62.9	152 511	78 515	68 978	5 018	2 262	150 249	60.0	7 486	2 813	4.7
March	254 414	160 235	63.0	153 064	78 548	69 337	5 179	2 441	150 623	60.2	7 171	2 725	4.5
April	254 588	160 181	62.9	153 161	78 839	69 218	5 104	2 587	150 574	60.2	7 021	2 719	4.4
May	254 767	159 729	62.7	152 892	78 794	69 087	5 010	2 564	150 328	60.0	6 837	2 788	4.3
June	254 957	160 214	62.8	153 250	78 753	69 289	5 209	2 612	150 638	60.1	6 964	2 652	4.3
July	255 151	160 467	62.9	153 511	78 863	69 586	5 062	2 506	151 005	60.2	6 956	2 779	4.3
August	255 357	160 598	62.9	153 471	78 887	69 502	5 082	2 508	150 963	60.1	7 127	2 802	4.4
September	255 562	161 082	63.0	154 324	79 393	69 692	5 238	2 367	151 957	60.4	6 759	2 695	4.2
October	255 766	160 371	62.7	153 846	79 248	69 576	5 022	2 559	151 287	60.2	6 524	2 500	4.1
November	255 949	160 533	62.7	153 917	79 324	69 665	4 928	2 451	151 466	60.1	6 616	2 514	4.1
December	256 109	160 597	62.7	154 021	79 431	69 614	4 977	2 368	151 653	60.1	6 576	2 397	4.1
2018													
January	256 780	161 123	62.7	154 495	82 915	72 238	5 143	2 480	2 480	60.2	6 641	2 387	4.1
February	256 934	161 900	63.0	155 174	83 258	72 595	5 178	2 450	2 450	60.4	6 687	2 336	4.1
March	257 097	161 646	62.9	155 266	83 149	72 580	5 123	2 331	2 331	60.4	6 486	2 237	4.0
April	257 272	161 551	62.8	155 363	83 163	72 558	5 074	2 312	2 312	60.3	6 335	2 330	3.9
May	257 454	161 667	62.8	155 688	83 257	72 590	5 079	2 353	2 353	60.4	6 128	2 164	3.8
June	257 642	162 129	62.9	155 768	83 103	73 155	5 131	2 363	2 363	60.4	6 537	2 329	4.0
July	257 843	162 209	62.9	156 186	83 019	73 295	5 125	2 493	2 493	60.5	6 245	2 377	3.9
August	258 066	161 802	62.7	155 567	83 044	73 153	4 892	2 346	2 346	60.3	6 197	2 247	3.8
September	258 290	162 055	62.7	155 948	83 104	73 107	5 108	2 478	2 478	60.4	5 986	2 240	3.7
October	258 514	162 694	62.9	156 306	83 277	73 442	5 258	2 418	2 418	60.6	6 112	2 229	3.8
November	258 708	162 821	62.9	156 598	83 408	73 478	5 221	2 556	2 556	60.6	6 018	2 124	3.7
December	258 888	163 240	63.1	156 745	83 500	73 769	5 226	2 522	2 522	60.6	6 294	2 203	3.9

[1] Not seasonally adjusted.
[2] In 1930 through 1943, the official BLS data count persons on work relief as unemployed. The unemployment rates for those years shown in parentheses count persons on work relief as employed, which is more consistent with the postwar practice. See notes and definitions.

Table 10-2. Labor Force and Employment by Major Age and Sex Groups

(Thousands of persons, percent, seasonally adjusted.)

Year and month	Civilian labor force (thousands)			Participation rate (percent)			Employment (thousands)			Employment-population ratio, percent		
	Men, 20 years and over	Women, 20 years and over	Both sexes, 16 to 19 years	Men, 20 years and over	Women, 20 years and over	Both sexes, 16 to 19 years	Men, 20 years and over	Women, 20 years and over	Both sexes, 16 to 19 years	Men, 20 years and over	Women, 20 years and over	Both sexes, 16 to 19 years
1970	47 220	28 301	7 249	82.6	43.3	49.9	45 581	26 952	6 144	79.7	41.2	42.3
1971	48 009	28 904	7 470	82.1	43.3	49.7	45 912	27 246	6 208	78.5	40.9	41.3
1972	49 079	29 901	8 054	81.6	43.7	51.9	47 130	28 276	6 746	78.4	41.3	43.5
1973	49 932	30 991	8 507	81.3	44.4	53.7	48 310	29 484	7 271	78.6	42.2	45.9
1974	50 879	32 201	8 871	81.0	45.3	54.8	48 922	30 424	7 448	77.9	42.8	46.0
1975	51 494	33 410	8 870	80.3	46.0	54.0	48 018	30 726	7 104	74.8	42.3	43.3
1976	52 288	34 814	9 056	79.8	47.0	54.5	49 190	32 226	7 336	75.1	43.5	44.2
1977	53 348	36 310	9 351	79.7	48.1	56.0	50 555	33 775	7 688	75.6	44.8	46.1
1978	54 471	38 128	9 652	79.8	49.6	57.8	52 143	35 836	8 070	76.4	46.6	48.3
1979	55 615	39 708	9 638	79.8	50.6	57.9	53 308	37 434	8 083	76.5	47.7	48.5
1980	56 455	41 106	9 378	79.4	51.3	56.7	53 101	38 492	7 710	74.6	48.1	46.6
1981	57 197	42 485	8 988	79.0	52.1	55.4	53 582	39 590	7 225	74.0	48.6	44.6
1982	57 980	43 699	8 526	78.7	52.7	54.1	52 891	40 086	6 549	71.8	48.4	41.5
1983	58 744	44 636	8 171	78.5	53.1	53.5	53 487	41 004	6 342	71.4	48.8	41.5
1984	59 701	45 900	7 943	78.3	53.7	53.9	55 769	42 793	6 444	73.2	50.1	43.7
1985	60 277	47 283	7 901	78.1	54.7	54.5	56 562	44 154	6 434	73.3	51.0	44.4
1986	61 320	48 589	7 926	78.1	55.5	54.7	57 569	45 556	6 472	73.3	52.0	44.6
1987	62 095	49 783	7 988	78.0	56.2	54.7	58 726	47 074	6 640	73.8	53.1	45.5
1988	62 768	50 870	8 031	77.9	56.8	55.3	59 781	48 383	6 805	74.2	54.0	46.8
1989	63 704	52 212	7 954	78.1	57.7	55.9	60 837	49 745	6 759	74.5	54.9	47.5
1990	64 916	53 131	7 792	78.2	58.0	53.7	61 678	50 535	6 581	74.3	55.2	45.3
1991	65 374	53 708	7 265	77.7	57.9	51.6	61 178	50 634	5 906	72.7	54.6	42.0
1992	66 213	54 796	7 096	77.7	58.5	51.3	61 496	51 328	5 669	72.1	54.8	41.0
1993	66 642	55 388	7 170	77.3	58.5	51.5	62 355	52 099	5 805	72.3	55.0	41.7
1994	66 921	56 655	7 481	76.8	59.3	52.7	63 294	53 606	6 161	72.6	56.2	43.4
1995	67 324	57 215	7 765	76.7	59.4	53.5	64 085	54 396	6 419	73.0	56.5	44.2
1996	68 044	58 094	7 806	76.8	59.9	52.3	64 897	55 311	6 500	73.2	57.0	43.5
1997	69 166	59 198	7 932	77.0	60.5	51.6	66 284	56 613	6 661	73.7	57.8	43.4
1998	69 715	59 702	8 256	76.8	60.4	52.8	67 135	57 278	7 051	73.9	58.0	45.1
1999	70 194	60 840	8 333	76.7	60.7	52.0	67 761	58 555	7 172	74.0	58.5	44.7
2000	72 010	62 301	8 271	76.7	60.6	52.0	69 634	60 067	7 189	74.2	58.4	45.2
2001	72 816	63 016	7 902	76.5	60.6	49.6	69 776	60 417	6 740	73.3	58.1	42.3
2002	73 630	63 648	7 585	76.3	60.5	47.4	69 734	60 420	6 332	72.3	57.5	39.6
2003	74 623	64 716	7 170	75.9	60.6	44.5	70 415	61 402	5 919	71.7	57.5	36.8
2004	75 364	64 923	7 114	75.8	60.3	43.9	71 572	61 773	5 907	71.9	57.4	36.4
2005	76 443	65 714	7 164	75.8	60.4	43.7	73 050	62 702	5 978	72.4	57.6	36.5
2006	77 562	66 585	7 281	75.9	60.5	43.7	74 431	63 834	6 162	72.9	58.0	36.9
2007	78 596	67 516	7 012	75.9	60.6	41.3	75 337	64 799	5 911	72.8	58.2	34.8
2008	79 047	68 382	6 858	75.7	60.9	40.2	74 750	65 039	5 573	71.6	57.9	32.6
2009	78 897	68 856	6 390	74.8	60.8	37.5	71 341	63 699	4 837	67.6	56.2	28.4
2010	78 994	68 990	5 906	74.1	60.3	34.9	71 230	63 456	4 378	66.8	55.5	25.9
2011	79 080	68 810	5 727	73.4	59.8	34.1	72 182	63 360	4 327	67.0	55.0	25.8
2012	79 387	69 765	5 823	73.0	59.3	34.3	73 403	64 640	4 426	67.5	55.0	26.1
2013	79 744	69 860	5 785	72.5	58.8	34.5	74 176	65 295	4 458	67.4	54.9	26.6
2014	80 056	70 212	5 654	71.9	58.5	34.0	75 471	66 287	4 548	67.8	55.2	27.3
2015	80 735	70 695	5 700	71.7	58.2	34.3	76 776	67 323	4 734	68.1	55.4	28.5
2016	81 759	71 538	5 889	71.7	58.3	35.2	78 084	68 387	4 965	68.5	55.7	29.7
2017	82 206	72 213	5 901	71.6	58.5	35.2	78 919	69 344	5 074	68.8	56.1	30.3
2018	83 188	73 002	5 885	71.6	58.5	35.1	80 211	70 424	5 126	69.0	56.4	30.6
2019	83 737	73 906	5 896	71.6	58.9	35.3	80 917	71 470	5 150	69.2	56.9	30.9
2020	82 345	72 677	5 720	70.1	57.6	34.5	76 227	66 873	4 695	64.8	53.0	28.3
2019												
January	83 511	73 661	5 895	71.7	58.9	32.8	80 473	71 035	5 117	69.1	56.8	28.3
February	83 575	73 678	5 779	71.7	58.9	32.4	80 775	71 155	4 974	69.3	56.8	27.9
March	83 606	73 520	5 884	71.7	58.7	33.3	80 637	71 036	5 136	69.2	56.7	29.3
April	83 530	73 480	5 727	71.6	58.6	31.7	80 648	71 134	4 960	69.1	56.8	28.0
May	83 620	73 472	5 756	71.6	58.6	33.6	80 789	71 047	5 046	69.2	56.6	29.3
June	83 544	73 594	5 908	71.5	58.6	41.9	80 760	71 140	5 231	69.1	56.7	35.6
July	83 789	73 674	6 124	71.7	58.7	44.3	80 977	71 251	5 389	69.2	56.7	38.4
August	83 842	74 072	5 948	71.6	58.9	37.9	80 992	71 657	5 213	69.2	57.0	33.3
September	83 878	74 245	5 834	71.6	59.0	33.6	81 134	71 992	5 104	69.3	57.2	29.5
October	83 894	74 454	5 930	71.6	59.1	34.2	81 120	72 052	5 184	69.2	57.2	30.2
November	84 065	74 375	6 007	71.6	59.0	34.3	81 341	71 943	5 256	69.3	57.1	30.3
December	83 996	74 616	5 967	71.5	59.2	33.9	81 373	72 172	5 190	69.3	57.2	30.1
2020												
January	83 970	74 502	5 982	71.7	59.2	33.6	81 329	72 099	5 231	69.4	57.3	29.2
February	83 930	74 501	6 017	71.6	59.2	34.1	81 235	72 171	5 326	69.3	57.4	30.2
March	83 171	73 657	5 894	70.9	58.5	33.6	79 785	70 691	5 060	68.0	56.1	29.0
April	80 490	70 896	5 093	68.6	56.3	28.1	69 975	59 938	3 457	59.6	47.6	19.1
May	81 073	71 548	5 579	69.1	56.8	32.7	71 668	61 630	3 926	61.0	48.9	22.7
June	81 922	72 479	5 396	69.7	57.5	39.1	73 605	64 321	4 174	62.6	51.0	29.5
July	81 861	72 866	5 358	69.6	57.7	40.0	74 173	65 270	4 333	63.1	51.7	32.3
August	82 461	72 728	5 630	70.1	57.6	36.2	75 903	66 667	4 706	64.5	52.8	30.5
September	82 293	71 865	5 920	69.9	56.8	34.4	76 258	66 328	4 957	64.8	52.5	28.9
October	82 505	72 255	5 958	70.0	57.1	34.7	77 013	67 534	5 122	65.3	53.4	30.2
November	82 226	72 395	5 915	69.7	57.2	34.1	76 777	67 941	5 091	65.1	53.7	29.6
December	82 244	72 422	5 900	69.7	57.2	33.8	77 004	67 872	4 955	65.3	53.6	29.0

Table 10-3. Employment by Type of Job

(Thousands of persons, seasonally adjusted, except as noted.)

Year and month	By class of worker								Multiple jobholders		Employed and at work part-time	
	Agricultural	Nonagricultural industries							Total (thousands)	Percent of total employed	Economic reasons	Non-economic reasons
		Total	Wage and salary				Self-employed (unincorporated)	Unpaid family workers [1]				
			Total	Government	Private industries							
					Private house-holds [1]	Other private industries						
1970	3 463	75 215	69 491	12 431	...	...	5 221	502	...	...	2 446	9 999
1971	3 394	75 972	70 120	12 799	...	...	5 327	522	...	...	2 688	10 152
1972	3 484	78 669	72 785	13 393	...	...	5 365	519	...	...	2 648	10 612
1973	3 470	81 594	75 580	13 655	...	...	5 474	540	...	...	2 554	10 972
1974	3 515	83 279	77 094	14 124	...	...	5 697	489	...	...	2 988	11 153
1975	3 408	82 438	76 249	14 675	...	...	5 705	483	...	...	3 804	11 228
1976	3 331	85 421	79 175	15 132	...	...	5 783	464	...	...	3 607	11 607
1977	3 283	88 734	82 121	15 361	...	...	6 114	498	...	...	3 608	12 120
1978	3 387	92 661	85 753	15 525	...	...	6 429	479	...	...	3 516	12 650
1979	3 347	95 477	88 222	15 635	...	...	6 791	463	...	...	3 577	12 893
1980	3 364	95 938	88 525	15 912	...	...	7 000	413	...	...	4 321	13 067
1981	3 368	97 030	89 543	15 689	...	...	7 097	390	...	...	4 768	13 025
1982	3 401	96 125	88 462	15 516	...	...	7 262	401	...	...	6 170	12 953
1983	3 383	97 450	89 500	15 537	...	...	7 575	376	...	...	6 266	12 911
1984	3 321	101 685	93 565	15 770	...	...	7 785	335	...	...	5 744	13 169
1985	3 179	103 971	95 871	16 031	...	...	7 811	289	...	...	5 590	13 489
1986	3 163	106 434	98 299	16 342	...	...	7 881	255	...	...	5 588	13 935
1987	3 208	109 232	100 771	16 800	...	...	8 201	260	...	...	5 401	14 395
1988	3 169	111 800	103 021	17 114	...	...	8 519	260	...	...	5 206	14 963
1989	3 199	114 142	105 259	17 469	...	...	8 605	279	...	...	4 894	15 393
1990	3 223	115 570	106 598	17 769	...	...	8 719	253	...	...	5 204	15 341
1991	3 269	114 449	105 373	17 934	...	...	8 851	226	...	...	6 161	15 172
1992	3 247	115 245	106 437	18 136	...	...	8 575	233	...	...	6 520	14 918
1993	3 115	117 144	107 966	18 579	...	...	8 959	218	...	...	6 481	15 240
1994	3 409	119 651	110 517	18 293	...	...	9 003	131	7 260	5.9	4 625	17 638
1995	3 440	121 460	112 448	18 362	...	...	8 902	110	7 693	6.2	4 473	17 734
1996	3 443	123 264	114 171	18 217	...	...	8 971	122	7 832	6.2	4 315	17 770
1997	3 399	126 159	116 983	18 131	...	...	9 056	120	7 955	6.1	4 068	18 149
1998	3 378	128 085	119 019	18 383	...	...	8 962	103	7 926	6.0	3 665	18 530
1999	3 281	130 207	121 323	18 903	...	101 487	8 790	95	7 802	5.8	3 357	18 758
2000	2 464	134 427	125 114	19 248	718	105 148	9 205	108	7 604	5.6	3 227	18 814
2001	2 299	134 635	125 407	19 335	694	105 378	9 121	107	7 357	5.4	3 715	18 790
2002	2 311	134 174	125 156	19 636	757	104 764	8 923	95	7 291	5.3	4 213	18 843
2003	2 275	135 461	126 015	19 634	764	105 616	9 344	101	7 315	5.3	4 701	19 014
2004	2 232	137 020	127 463	19 983	779	106 701	9 467	90	7 473	5.4	4 567	19 380
2005	2 197	139 532	129 931	20 357	812	108 761	9 509	93	7 546	5.3	4 350	19 491
2006	2 206	142 221	132 449	20 337	803	111 309	9 685	87	7 576	5.2	4 162	19 591
2007	2 095	143 952	134 283	21 003	813	112 467	9 557	112	7 655	5.2	4 401	19 756
2008	2 168	143 194	133 882	21 258	805	111 819	9 219	93	7 620	5.2	5 875	19 343
2009	2 103	137 775	128 713	21 178	783	106 752	8 995	66	7 271	5.2	8 913	18 710
2010	2 206	136 858	127 914	21 003	667	106 244	8 860	84	6 878	4.9	8 874	18 251
2011	2 254	137 615	128 934	20 536	722	107 676	8 603	78	6 880	4.9	8 560	18 334
2012	2 186	140 283	131 452	20 360	738	110 355	8 749	81	6 943	4.9	8 122	18 806
2013	2 130	141 799	133 111	20 247	723	112 141	8 619	70	7 002	4.9	7 935	18 903
2014	2 237	144 068	135 402	20 135	820	114 446	8 602	64	7 146	4.9	7 213	19 489
2015	2 422	146 411	137 678	20 601	798	116 279	8 665	68	7 262	4.9	6 371	20 018
2016	2 460	148 976	140 161	20 630	724	118 807	8 751	65	7 531	5.0	5 943	20 680
2017	2 454	150 883	142 096	20 835	657	120 603	8 736	52	7 545	4.9	5 250	20 906
2018	2 425	153 336	144 326	20 942	777	122 607	8 941	69	7 769	5.0	4 778	21 297
2019	2 425	155 113	146 262	20 976	821	124 465	8 799	53	8 050	5.1	4 407	21 430
2020	2 349	145 446	136 881	20 599	654	115 627	8 511	55	6 687	4.5	7 227	18 348
2019												
January	2 553	154 029	145 180	20 555	799	123 809	8 883	44	7 828	5.0	5 080	20 416
February	2 470	154 385	145 720	20 638	796	124 014	8 755	38	7 706	4.9	4 291	20 743
March	2 327	154 363	145 667	20 732	808	123 994	8 747	45	7 878	5.0	4 487	21 036
April	2 356	154 360	145 741	20 919	825	124 000	8 541	37	7 814	5.0	4 640	21 031
May	2 412	154 460	145 639	20 780	807	124 031	8 711	31	7 898	5.0	4 275	21 100
June	2 320	154 802	145 908	20 897	849	124 260	8 723	19	8 150	5.2	4 245	21 090
July	2 455	155 029	145 984	20 871	808	124 410	8 897	46	8 357	5.3	3 826	21 052
August	2 430	155 546	146 471	20 918	869	124 702	8 844	76	8 312	5.3	4 281	21 258
September	2 433	155 989	146 835	21 195	842	125 011	8 844	80	8 340	5.3	4 232	21 259
October	2 450	155 991	147 126	21 490	784	124 937	8 821	66	8 151	5.1	4 277	21 231
November	2 358	156 159	147 351	21 400	824	125 165	8 893	83	8 132	5.1	4 216	21 226
December	2 531	156 189	147 501	21 307	841	125 239	8 916	70	8 024	5.1	4 119	21 248
2020												
January	2 405	156 217	147 434	21 460	801	125 147	8 846	50	8 170	5.1	4 130	21 669
February	2 455	156 240	147 439	21 054	781	125 323	8 893	45	8 064	5.1	4 304	21 801
March	2 352	153 093	144 327	21 147	712	122 327	8 799	37	7 191	4.6	5 728	19 987
April	2 379	130 982	123 374	19 268	492	103 600	7 523	23	5 411	4.1	10 739	11 986
May	2 303	134 904	126 840	19 749	498	106 551	7 928	41	5 564	4.1	10 486	14 073
June	2 257	139 840	131 306	20 765	564	110 114	8 316	64	6 266	4.4	8 939	16 718
July	2 158	141 455	132 763	20 479	708	111 741	8 462	82	6 597	4.6	8 336	17 383
August	2 194	145 216	136 168	20 988	715	114 440	8 788	77	6 802	4.6	7 439	18 257
September	2 270	145 454	136 493	20 466	683	115 601	8 675	54	6 491	4.4	6 197	18 589
October	2 515	147 255	138 539	20 678	636	117 304	8 690	70	6 669	4.5	6 552	19 029
November	2 432	147 314	138 891	20 418	626	117 902	8 570	45	6 559	4.4	6 582	18 182
December	2 461	147 351	138 971	20 709	636	117 472	8 638	66	6 460	4.3	6 082	17 846

[1] Not seasonally adjusted.

. . . = Not available.

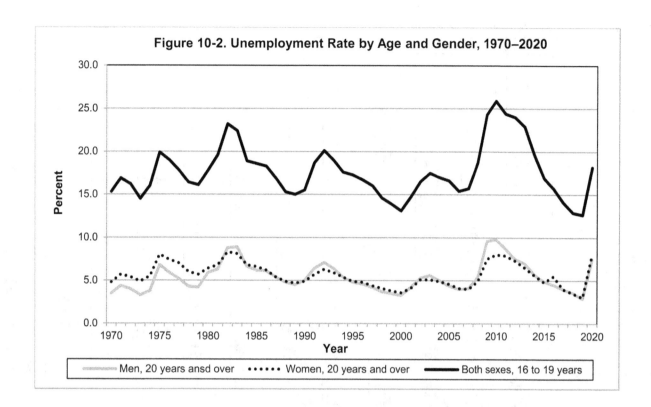

Figure 10-2. Unemployment Rate by Age and Gender, 1970–2020

- After the Great Recession, the unemployment rate peaked at 10.0 percent in October 2009, lagging, as it usually does, the business cycle trough, which was in June 2009. In 2020, once stay-at-home, lockdown and 'slow the spread' orders began in mid-March, many businesses abruptly closed. The U.S. economy teetered on the edge. The unemployment rose to 14.4 percent, more than two-fold between March and April 2020. It decline significantly, by December but at 6.5 percent, the unemployment rate was still much higher than it was in December 2019 when it was 3.4 percent. (Tables 10-1A)

- One of the most iconic graphs early in the pandemic was from the Department of Labor, Employment and Training Administration. The severity of the pandemic was illustrated in a stark chart. Unemployment compensation claims skyrocketed from 212,200 in February 2020 to 2.3 million in March, 4.7 million in April then slowly declining to 2.1 million in May, 1.5 in June and 1.4 million in July. See Table 10-6. Unemployment compensation, established with the Social Security Act of 1935, is a federal-state program that provides financial assistance to recently unemployed workers.

- Figure 10-2 depicts the unemployment rates for men over 20, women over 20 and 16-19 for both men and women. Women usually experienced higher unemployment rates and lower earnings since the surge of women entering into the workforce in the 1970s. During the Great Recession, more women retained their jobs. However, during the pandemic, millions of women left the labor force in part to take care of family members as schools and day cares closed. In April 2020, the unemployment rate was 15.5 percent for women 20 years and over compared with 13.1 percent with men. (Table 10-4).

Table 10-4. Unemployment by Demographic Group

(Unemployment in thousands of persons and as a percent of the civilian labor force in group, seasonally adjusted, except as noted.)

Year and month	Unemployment (thousands of persons)				Unemployment rate (percent)							
						By age and sex			By race			
	Total	Men, 20 years and over	Women, 20 years and over	Both sexes, 16 to 19 years	All civilian workers	Men, 20 years and over	Women, 20 years and over	Both sexes, 16 to 19 years	White	Black or African American	Asian [1]	Hispanic or Latino ethnicity
1970	4 093	1 638	1 349	1 106	4.9	3.5	4.8	15.3	4.5	. . .	. . .	. . .
1971	5 016	2 097	1 658	1 262	5.9	4.4	5.7	16.9	5.4	. . .	. . .	. . .
1972	4 882	1 948	1 625	1 308	5.6	4.0	5.4	16.2	5.1	10.4	. . .	. . .
1973	4 365	1 624	1 507	1 235	4.9	3.3	4.9	14.5	4.3	9.4	. . .	7.5
1974	5 156	1 957	1 777	1 422	5.6	3.8	5.5	16.0	5.0	10.5	. . .	8.1
1975	7 929	3 476	2 684	1 767	8.5	6.8	8.0	19.9	7.8	14.8	. . .	12.2
1976	7 406	3 098	2 588	1 719	7.7	5.9	7.4	19.0	7.0	14.0	. . .	11.5
1977	6 991	2 794	2 535	1 663	7.1	5.2	7.0	17.8	6.2	14.0	. . .	10.1
1978	6 202	2 328	2 292	1 583	6.1	4.3	6.0	16.4	5.2	12.8	. . .	9.1
1979	6 137	2 308	2 276	1 555	5.8	4.2	5.7	16.1	5.1	12.3	. . .	8.3
1980	7 637	3 353	2 615	1 669	7.1	5.9	6.4	17.8	6.3	14.3	. . .	10.1
1981	8 273	3 615	2 895	1 763	7.6	6.3	6.8	19.6	6.7	15.6	. . .	10.4
1982	10 678	5 089	3 613	1 977	9.7	8.8	8.3	23.2	8.6	18.9	. . .	13.8
1983	10 717	5 257	3 632	1 829	9.6	8.9	8.1	22.4	8.4	19.5	. . .	13.7
1984	8 539	3 932	3 107	1 499	7.5	6.6	6.8	18.9	6.5	15.9	. . .	10.7
1985	8 312	3 715	3 129	1 468	7.2	6.2	6.6	18.6	6.2	15.1	. . .	10.5
1986	8 237	3 751	3 032	1 454	7.0	6.1	6.2	18.3	6.0	14.5	. . .	10.6
1987	7 425	3 369	2 709	1 347	6.2	5.4	5.4	16.9	5.3	13.0	. . .	8.8
1988	6 701	2 987	2 487	1 226	5.5	4.8	4.9	15.3	4.7	11.7	. . .	8.2
1989	6 528	2 867	2 467	1 194	5.3	4.5	4.7	15.0	4.5	11.4	. . .	8.0
1990	7 047	3 239	2 596	1 212	5.6	5.0	4.9	15.5	4.8	11.4	. . .	8.2
1991	8 628	4 195	3 074	1 359	6.8	6.4	5.7	18.7	6.1	12.5	. . .	10.0
1992	9 613	4 717	3 469	1 427	7.5	7.1	6.3	20.1	6.6	14.2	. . .	11.6
1993	8 940	4 287	3 288	1 365	6.9	6.4	5.9	19.0	6.1	13.0	. . .	10.8
1994	7 996	3 627	3 049	1 320	6.1	5.4	5.4	17.6	5.3	11.5	. . .	9.9
1995	7 404	3 239	2 819	1 346	5.6	4.8	4.9	17.3	4.9	10.4	. . .	9.3
1996	7 236	3 146	2 783	1 306	5.4	4.6	4.8	16.7	4.7	10.5	. . .	8.9
1997	6 739	2 882	2 585	1 271	4.9	4.2	4.4	16.0	4.2	10.0	. . .	7.7
1998	6 210	2 580	2 424	1 205	4.5	3.7	4.1	14.6	3.9	8.9	. . .	7.2
1999	5 880	2 433	2 285	1 162	4.2	3.5	3.8	13.9	3.7	8.0	. . .	6.4
2000	5 692	2 376	2 235	1 081	4.0	3.3	3.6	13.1	3.5	7.6	3.6	5.7
2001	6 801	3 040	2 599	1 162	4.7	4.2	4.1	14.7	4.2	8.6	4.5	6.6
2002	8 378	3 896	3 228	1 253	5.8	5.3	5.1	16.5	5.1	10.2	5.9	7.5
2003	8 774	4 209	3 314	1 251	6.0	5.6	5.1	17.5	5.2	10.8	6.0	7.7
2004	8 149	3 791	3 150	1 208	5.5	5.0	4.9	17.0	4.8	10.4	4.4	7.0
2005	7 591	3 392	3 013	1 186	5.1	4.4	4.6	16.6	4.4	10.0	4.0	6.0
2006	7 001	3 131	2 751	1 119	4.6	4.0	4.1	15.4	4.0	8.9	3.0	5.2
2007	7 078	3 259	2 718	1 101	4.6	4.1	4.0	15.7	4.1	8.3	3.2	5.6
2008	8 924	4 297	3 342	1 285	5.8	5.4	4.9	18.7	5.2	10.1	4.0	7.6
2009	14 265	7 555	5 157	1 552	9.3	9.6	7.5	24.3	8.5	14.8	7.3	12.1
2010	14 825	7 763	5 534	1 528	9.6	9.8	8.0	25.9	8.7	16.0	7.5	12.5
2011	13 747	6 898	5 450	1 400	8.9	8.7	7.9	24.4	7.9	15.8	7.0	11.5
2012	12 506	5 984	5 125	1 397	8.1	7.5	7.3	24.0	7.2	13.8	5.9	10.3
2013	11 460	5 568	4 565	1 327	7.4	7.0	6.5	22.9	6.5	13.1	5.2	9.1
2014	9 617	4 585	3 926	1 106	6.2	5.7	5.6	19.6	5.3	11.3	5.0	7.4
2015	8 296	3 959	3 371	966	5.3	4.9	4.8	16.9	4.6	9.6	3.8	6.6
2016	7 751	3 675	3 151	925	4.9	4.5	5.5	15.7	4.3	8.4	3.6	5.8
2017	6 973	3 220	2 865	831	4.4	4.0	4.0	14.1	3.8	7.5	3.4	5.1
2018	6 306	2 971	2 575	760	3.9	3.6	3.5	12.9	3.5	6.5	3.0	4.7
2019	5 989	2 209	2 012	746	3.7	2.9	3.0	12.6	3.3	6.1	2.7	4.3
2020	12 948	6 118	5 804	1 025	8.1	7.5	8.0	18.2	7.3	11.5	8.7	10.5
2019												
January	6 516	2 484	2 130	765	4.0	3.3	3.2	12.9	3.5	6.8	3.1	4.8
February	6 181	2 324	2 028	773	3.8	3.1	3.1	13.3	3.3	6.9	3.1	4.3
March	6 194	2 310	2 038	747	3.8	3.0	3.1	12.7	3.4	6.6	3.1	4.7
April	5 850	2 234	1 907	734	3.6	3.0	2.9	12.9	3.1	6.6	2.2	4.2
May	5 938	2 128	1 976	730	3.6	2.8	3.0	12.6	3.3	6.2	2.5	4.2
June	5 985	2 191	2 072	751	3.7	2.9	3.1	12.7	3.3	6.0	2.1	4.3
July	6 027	2 208	2 036	767	3.7	2.9	3.1	12.7	3.3	5.9	2.8	4.5
August	5 999	2 183	2 001	742	3.7	2.9	3.0	12.5	3.2	5.4	2.8	4.2
September	5 753	2 132	1 941	735	3.5	2.8	2.9	12.5	3.2	5.5	2.5	3.9
October	5 857	2 118	2 038	730	3.6	2.8	3.0	12.3	3.2	5.5	2.8	4.1
November	5 811	2 134	1 992	721	3.5	2.8	3.0	12.0	3.2	5.6	2.6	4.2
December	5 753	2 064	1 981	752	3.5	2.7	2.9	12.6	3.2	5.9	2.5	4.2
2020												
January	5 796	2 641	2 404	751	3.5	3.1	3.2	12.6	3.0	6.1	3.1	4.3
February	5 717	2 695	2 330	691	3.5	3.2	3.1	11.5	3.0	6.0	2.4	4.4
March	7 185	3 385	2 966	834	4.4	4.1	4.0	14.1	3.9	6.8	4.1	6.0
April	23 109	10 515	10 958	1 636	14.8	13.1	15.5	32.1	14.1	16.7	14.5	18.9
May	20 975	9 405	9 918	1 653	13.3	11.6	13.9	29.6	12.3	16.7	14.9	17.6
June	17 697	8 317	8 158	1 222	11.1	10.2	11.3	22.6	10.1	15.3	13.9	14.5
July	16 308	7 688	7 596	1 024	10.2	9.4	10.4	19.1	9.2	14.4	11.9	12.7
August	13 542	6 558	6 061	924	8.4	8.0	8.3	16.4	7.4	12.8	10.6	10.5
September	12 535	6 036	5 537	963	7.8	7.3	7.7	16.3	7.0	12.0	8.8	10.3
October	11 049	5 492	4 721	836	6.9	6.7	6.5	14.0	6.0	10.8	7.6	8.8
November	10 728	5 449	4 453	825	6.7	6.6	6.2	13.9	5.9	10.3	6.7	8.4
December	10 736	5 240	4 551	946	6.7	6.4	6.3	16.0	6.0	9.9	5.9	9.3

[1] Not seasonally adjusted.
. . . = Not available.

Table 10-5. Unemployment Rates and Related Data

(Seasonally adjusted, except as noted.)

Year and month	Married men, spouse present	Married women, spouse present	Women who maintain families[1]	Total	Job losers and persons who completed temporary jobs	Job leavers	Reentrants	New entrants	Average (mean) weeks unemployed	Median weeks unemployed	Including discouraged workers (U-4)	Including all marginally attached workers (U-5)	Including marginally attached and under-employed (U-6)
1970	2.6	4.9	5.4	4.9	2.2	0.7	1.5	0.6	8.6	4.9	...	...	...
1971	3.2	5.7	7.3	5.9	2.8	0.7	1.7	0.7	11.3	6.3	...	...	...
1972	2.8	5.4	7.2	5.6	2.4	0.7	1.7	0.8	12.0	6.2	...	...	...
1973	2.3	4.7	7.1	4.9	1.9	0.8	1.5	0.7	10.0	5.2	...	...	...
1974	2.7	5.3	7.0	5.6	2.4	0.8	1.6	0.7	9.8	5.2	...	...	...
1975	5.1	7.9	10.0	8.5	4.7	0.9	2.0	0.9	14.2	8.4	...	...	...
1976	4.2	7.1	10.1	7.7	3.8	0.9	2.0	0.9	15.8	8.2	...	...	...
1977	3.6	6.5	9.4	7.1	3.2	0.9	2.0	1.0	14.3	7.0	...	...	...
1978	2.8	5.5	8.5	6.1	2.5	0.9	1.8	0.9	11.9	5.9	...	...	...
1979	2.8	5.1	8.3	5.8	2.5	0.8	1.7	0.8	10.8	5.4	...	...	...
1980	4.2	5.8	9.2	7.1	3.7	0.8	1.8	0.8	11.9	6.5	...	...	...
1981	4.3	6.0	10.4	7.6	3.9	0.8	1.9	0.9	13.7	6.9	...	...	...
1982	6.5	7.4	11.7	9.7	5.7	0.8	2.2	1.1	15.6	8.7	...	...	...
1983	6.5	7.0	12.2	9.6	5.6	0.7	2.2	1.1	20.0	10.1	...	...	...
1984	4.6	5.7	10.3	7.5	3.9	0.7	1.9	1.0	18.2	7.9	...	...	...
1985	4.3	5.6	10.4	7.2	3.6	0.8	2.0	0.9	15.6	6.8	...	...	...
1986	4.4	5.2	9.8	7.0	3.4	0.9	1.8	0.9	15.0	6.9	...	...	...
1987	3.9	4.3	9.2	6.2	3.0	0.8	1.6	0.8	14.5	6.5	...	...	...
1988	3.3	3.9	8.1	5.5	2.5	0.8	1.5	0.7	13.5	5.9	...	...	...
1989	3.0	3.7	8.1	5.3	2.4	0.8	1.5	0.5	11.9	4.8	...	...	...
1990	3.4	3.8	8.3	5.6	2.7	0.8	1.5	0.5	12.0	5.3	...	...	...
1991	4.4	4.5	9.3	6.8	3.7	0.8	1.7	0.6	13.7	6.8	...	...	...
1992	5.1	5.0	10.0	7.5	4.2	0.8	1.8	0.7	17.7	8.7	...	...	...
1993	4.4	4.6	9.7	6.9	3.8	0.8	1.7	0.7	18.0	8.3	...	...	...
1994	3.7	4.1	8.9	6.1	2.9	0.6	2.1	0.5	18.8	9.2	6.5	7.4	10.9
1995	3.3	3.9	8.0	5.6	2.6	0.6	1.9	0.4	16.6	8.3	5.9	6.7	10.1
1996	3.0	3.6	8.2	5.4	2.5	0.6	1.9	0.4	16.7	8.3	5.7	6.5	9.7
1997	2.7	3.1	8.1	4.9	2.2	0.6	1.7	0.4	15.8	8.0	5.2	5.9	8.9
1998	2.4	2.9	7.2	4.5	2.1	0.5	1.5	0.4	14.5	6.7	4.7	5.4	8.0
1999	2.2	2.7	6.4	4.2	1.9	0.6	1.4	0.3	13.4	6.4	4.4	5.0	7.4
2000	2.0	2.7	5.9	4.0	1.8	0.5	1.4	0.3	12.6	5.9	4.2	4.8	7.0
2001	2.7	3.1	6.6	4.7	2.4	0.6	1.4	0.3	13.1	6.8	4.9	5.6	8.1
2002	3.6	3.7	8.0	5.8	3.2	0.6	1.6	0.4	16.6	9.1	6.0	6.7	9.6
2003	3.8	3.7	8.5	6.0	3.3	0.6	1.7	0.4	19.2	10.1	6.3	7.0	10.1
2004	3.1	3.5	8.0	5.5	2.8	0.6	1.6	0.5	19.6	9.8	5.8	6.5	9.6
2005	2.8	3.3	7.8	5.1	2.5	0.6	1.6	0.4	18.4	8.9	5.4	6.1	8.9
2006	2.4	2.9	7.1	4.6	2.2	0.5	1.5	0.4	16.8	8.3	4.9	5.5	8.2
2007	2.5	2.8	6.5	4.6	2.3	0.5	1.4	0.4	16.8	8.5	4.9	5.5	8.3
2008	3.4	3.6	8.0	5.8	3.1	0.6	1.6	0.5	17.9	9.4	6.1	6.8	10.5
2009	6.6	5.5	11.5	9.3	5.9	0.6	2.1	0.7	24.4	15.1	9.7	10.5	16.2
2010	6.8	5.9	12.3	9.6	6.0	0.6	2.3	0.8	33.0	21.4	10.3	11.1	16.7
2011	5.8	5.6	12.4	8.9	5.3	0.6	2.2	0.8	39.3	21.4	9.5	10.4	15.9
2012	4.9	5.3	11.4	8.1	4.4	0.6	2.2	0.8	39.4	19.3	8.6	9.5	14.7
2013	4.3	4.6	10.2	7.4	3.9	0.6	2.1	0.8	36.5	17.0	7.9	8.8	13.8
2014	3.3	3.8	8.6	6.2	3.1	0.5	1.8	0.7	33.7	14.2	6.6	7.5	12.0
2015	2.8	3.2	7.4	5.3	2.6	0.5	1.6	0.6	29.1	11.7	5.7	6.4	10.5
2016	2.7	3.0	6.8	4.9	2.4	0.5	1.5	0.5	27.5	10.8	5.2	5.9	9.6
2017	2.4	2.7	6.2	4.4	2.1	0.5	1.3	0.4	25.0	4.6	4.6	5.3	8.5
2018	2.0	2.4	5.4	3.9	1.9	0.5	1.2	0.4	22.7	9.3	4.2	4.8	7.7
2019	1.6	2.1	4.2	3.5	1.6	0.5	1.0	0.3	20.8	9.0	3.7	4.2	6.7
2020	4.9	6.3	9.7	8.1	6.1	0.4	1.2	0.3	18.2	12.6	8.4	9.2	13.7
2019													
January	2.1	2.4	5.4	4.0	1.9	0.5	1.2	0.4	20.6	9.0	4.2	4.9	8.0
February	1.9	2.3	4.9	3.8	1.8	0.5	1.2	0.4	22.0	9.4	4.0	4.6	7.2
March	1.9	2.4	4.7	3.8	1.7	0.5	1.2	0.4	22.2	9.5	4.0	4.6	7.4
April	1.8	1.8	4.9	3.6	1.6	0.4	1.2	0.3	22.8	9.3	3.9	4.5	7.3
May	1.7	2.4	4.7	3.6	1.6	0.5	1.1	0.4	24.1	9.1	3.9	4.5	7.2
June	1.8	2.3	5.1	3.7	1.7	0.5	1.1	0.3	22.1	9.4	3.9	4.6	7.2
July	1.8	2.2	6.0	3.7	1.7	0.5	1.1	0.4	19.7	9.0	3.9	4.5	6.9
August	1.8	2.2	5.1	3.7	1.7	0.5	1.1	0.4	22.1	9.0	3.9	4.6	7.2
September	1.7	2.2	4.7	3.5	1.6	0.5	1.0	0.4	21.7	9.4	3.7	4.3	6.9
October	1.7	2.3	5.4	3.6	1.6	0.5	1.0	0.4	21.6	9.2	3.8	4.3	6.9
November	1.9	2.2	4.8	3.5	1.7	0.5	1.0	0.4	20.2	9.2	3.7	4.3	6.8
December	1.6	2.1	4.2	3.5	1.6	0.5	1.0	0.3	20.8	9.0	3.7	4.2	6.7
2020													
January	1.7	2.1	5.4	3.5	1.6	0.5	1.1	0.3	22.2	9.3	3.7	4.3	6.9
February	1.9	2.2	4.1	3.5	1.6	0.5	1.1	0.3	20.8	9.0	3.7	4.3	7.0
March	2.3	3.0	5.3	4.4	2.6	0.4	1.1	0.3	16.7	5.8	4.7	5.3	8.8
April	9.6	13.1	15.9	14.8	13.2	0.4	1.0	0.3	6.1	1.9	15.1	16.0	22.9
May	8.2	11.5	15.8	13.3	11.5	0.4	1.0	0.3	10.4	7.5	13.6	14.6	21.2
June	6.9	8.9	13.1	11.1	8.9	0.4	1.5	0.3	15.5	13.4	11.5	12.4	18.0
July	6.1	8.6	12.4	10.2	8.1	0.4	1.4	0.3	17.3	15.1	10.6	11.3	16.5
August	5.0	6.4	10.4	8.4	6.4	0.4	1.3	0.3	20.0	16.7	8.7	9.6	14.2
September	4.8	5.9	10.0	7.8	5.6	0.5	1.3	0.3	21.0	17.8	8.2	8.9	12.8
October	4.1	4.8	8.6	6.9	4.8	0.5	1.3	0.3	21.4	19.0	7.2	8.0	12.1
November	4.1	4.5	7.7	6.7	4.7	0.4	1.2	0.3	23.0	18.9	7.1	7.9	12.0
December	4.0	4.7	7.2	6.7	4.5	0.5	1.4	0.3	23.4	16.8	7.1	7.9	11.7

[1]Not seasonally adjusted.
. . . = Not available.

Table 10-6. Insured Unemployment

(Averages of weekly data; thousands of persons, except as noted.)

Year and month	State programs, seasonally adjusted			Federal programs, not seasonally adjusted			
	Initial claims	Insured unemployment	Insured unemployment rate (percent) [1]	Initial claims		Persons claiming benefits	
				Federal employees	Newly discharged veterans	Federal employees	Newly discharged veterans
1980	488	3 365	3.9	...	...	...	...
1981	451	3 032	3.5	...	...	...	...
1982	586	4 094	4.7	...	...	...	...
1983	441	3 337	3.9	...	...	...	...
1984	374	2 452	2.8	...	...	...	...
1985	392	2 584	2.9	...	2.5	21	17.5
1986	378	2 632	2.8	2	2.6	21	17.7
1987	325	2 273	2.4	2	2.7	23	18.1
1988	309	2 075	2.1	2	2.7	23	18.1
1989	330	2 174	2.1	2	2.3	22	15.1
1990	385	2 539	2.4	2	2.5	24	18.4
1991	447	3 338	3.2	3	2.9	31	22.7
1992	409	3 208	3.1	3	5.0	32	60.6
1993	344	2 768	2.6	3	3.9	32	54.4
1994	340	2 667	2.5	3	3.0	32	37.5
1995	359	2 590	2.4	5	2.5	32	29.6
1996	352	2 552	2.3	7	2.1	29	24.2
1997	322	2 300	2.0	2	1.8	24	19.6
1998	317	2 213	1.9	2	1.4	19	15.6
1999	298	2 186	1.8	1	1.2	17	14.2
2000	299	2 112	1.7	2	1.0	19	12.5
2001	406	3 016	2.4	1	1.2	18	14.0
2002	404	3 570	2.8	1	1.2	18	16.2
2003	402	3 532	2.8	2	1.5	18	19.8
2004	342	2 930	2.3	2	1.9	18	26.9
2005	331	2 660	2.1	1	2.0	17	27.6
2006	312	2 456	1.9	1	2.0	15	26.3
2007	321	2 548	1.9	1	1.7	15	22.8
2008	418	3 337	2.5	1	1.6	15	22.2
2009	574	5 808	4.4	2	2.0	20	30.4
2010	459	4 544	3.6	3	2.6	28	39.2
2011	409	3 744	3.0	2	2.6	31	39.1
2012	374	3 319	2.6	1	2.6	20	39.7
2013	343	2 978	2.3	4	2.3	22	34.8
2014	308	2 590	2.2	1	1.8	16	26.0
2015	278	2 267	1.7	1	1.4	13	19.4
2016	263	2 136	1.6	1	1.4	11	13.8
2017	245	1 961	1.4	1	0.8	11	10.2
2018	220	1 756	1.2	1	0.6	9	7.4
2019	218	1 701	1.2	2	0.5	11	6.0
2020	1 380	10 329	7.1	1	1.0	1	1.0
2018							
January	236	1 911	1.4	1	0.7	14	8.6
February	219	1 874	1.3	1	0.6	10	6.5
March	223	1 841	1.3	1	0.6	11	8.1
April	219	1 808	1.3	1	0.6	9	7.7
May	220	1 743	1.2	1	0.8	8	7.7
June	222	1 734	1.2	1	0.7	7	7.6
July	215	1 746	1.2	1	0.6	7	7.5
August	215	1 723	1.2	1	0.6	8	7.6
September	212	1 678	1.2	1	0.6	7	7.3
October	216	1 654	1.2	1	0.6	7	7.1
November	225	1 675	1.2	1	0.5	8	6.8
December	223	1 700	1.2	2	0.5	11	6.9
2019							
January	220	1 717	1.2	14	0.6	37	7.0
February	225	1 723	1.2	1	0.5	13	6.3
March	218	1 734	1.2	1	0.5	11	6.0
April	216	1 678	1.2	1	0.5	9	5.8
May	218	1 690	1.2	1	0.5	7	5.6
June	221	1 691	1.2	1	0.5	7	5.5
July	214	1 698	1.2	1	0.5	7	5.6
August	216	1 699	1.2	1	0.5	7	5.6
September	213	1 678	1.2	1	0.5	7	5.8
October	215	1 694	1.2	1	0.5	7	5.8
November	215	1 690	1.2	1	0.4	9	6.3
December	226	1 736	1.2	1	0.5	11	6.6
2020							
January	211	1 742	1.2	1	0.6	1	0.6
February	212	1 715	1.2	1	0.6	1	0.6
March	2 344	3 612	2.5	1	0.6	1	0.6
April	4 668	16 913	11.6	1	0.9	1	0.9
May	2 148	20 363	13.9	2	1.2	2	1.2
June	1 476	17 853	12.3	1	1.3	1	1.3
July	1 384	16 669	11.4	2	1.4	2	1.5
August	919	14 048	9.6	1	1.4	1	1.4
September	851	11 830	8.1	1	1.4	1	1.4
October	789	7 828	5.3	1	1.3	1	1.3
November	735	5 991	4.1	1	1.0	1	1.0
December	823	5 385	3.7	2	1.0	2	1.0

[1]Insured unemployed as a percent of employment covered by state programs.
. . . = Not available.

SECTION 10B: PAYROLL EMPLOYMENT, HOURS, AND EARNINGS

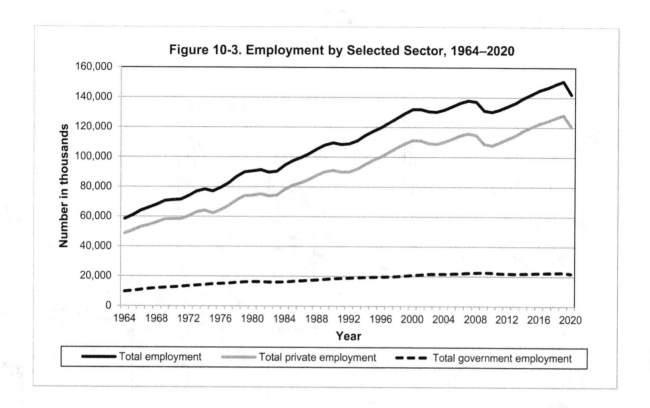

Figure 10-3. Employment by Selected Sector, 1964–2020

- Nonfarm employment includes wage and salary workers but not self-employed persons and unpaid family members working in a family business. The largest recent declines in employment occurred in 2009 due to the Great Recession and in 2020 due to the COVID-19 pandemic. Once the pandemic took hold of the country, all industries lost employment between March and April 2020. The leisure and hospitality sector was particularly impacted as employment declined 19.3 percent. (See Table 10-7)

- The U.S. economy continues to be service-oriented rather than producing goods. Manufacturing, once the economic engine of the economy, lost 23.3 percent of its workforce in the last 56 years. (Table 10-7)

- Nonfarm payroll employment peaked in January 2008 then plunged 5.7 percent, a postwar record, between then and its lowest point in December 2009. During this period, 8.4 million jobs were lost. (Table 10-9). The economy rebounded to its pre-Great Recession employment level in 2015. Of note, between February 2017 to December 2019, employment increased over 6.2 million. As more people stayed home and businesses closed temporarily or went bankrupt due to COVID-19, the number of unemployed increased from 7.3 million in March 2020 to 22.5 million in April 2020. (Table 10-1B)

- The diffusion index indicates the percentage of private industries in which employment is higher than six months earlier. Diffusion indexes measure the extent to which expansion or contraction have spread throughout the economy; indexes below 50 percent indicate recession. This index reached a low of 5.8 percent in May 2020—lower than the lowest points reached in any of the previous four recessions (1980, 1981-1982, 1990-1991, and 2001), and thus indicating the most widespread and pervasive decline in several decades. (Tables 10-7).

Table 10-7. Nonfarm Payroll Employment by NAICS Supersector

(Thousands; seasonally adjusted, except as noted.)

Year and month	Total	Private							Service-providing				
		Total	Goods-producing						Total	Private			
			Total	Mining and logging	Construc-tion	Manufacturing				Total	Trade, transportation, and utilities		
						Total	Durable	Nondurable			Total	Wholesale trade	Retail trade
1964	58 391	48 680	19 733	697	3 148	15 888	9 414	6 474	38 658	28 947	11 660	2 835	5 978
1965	60 874	50 683	20 595	694	3 284	16 617	9 973	6 644	40 279	30 089	12 121	2 945	6 264
1966	64 020	53 110	21 740	690	3 371	17 680	10 803	6 878	42 280	31 370	12 593	3 057	6 532
1967	65 931	54 406	21 882	679	3 305	17 897	10 952	6 945	44 049	32 524	12 932	3 134	6 713
1968	68 023	56 050	22 292	671	3 410	18 211	11 137	7 074	45 731	33 759	13 315	3 212	6 979
1969	70 512	58 181	22 893	683	3 637	18 573	11 396	7 177	47 619	35 288	13 833	3 320	7 297
1970	71 006	58 318	22 179	677	3 654	17 848	10 762	7 086	48 827	36 139	14 124	3 392	7 465
1971	71 335	58 323	21 602	658	3 770	17 174	10 229	6 944	49 734	36 721	14 298	3 398	7 659
1972	73 798	60 333	22 299	672	3 957	17 669	10 630	7 039	51 499	38 034	14 767	3 521	8 041
1973	76 912	63 050	23 450	693	4 167	18 589	11 414	7 176	53 462	39 600	15 327	3 661	8 374
1974	78 389	64 086	23 364	755	4 095	18 514	11 432	7 082	55 025	40 721	15 670	3 795	8 539
1975	77 069	62 250	21 318	802	3 608	16 909	10 266	6 643	55 751	40 932	15 583	3 782	8 604
1976	79 502	64 501	22 025	832	3 662	17 531	10 640	6 891	57 477	42 476	16 105	3 891	8 970
1977	82 593	67 334	22 972	865	3 940	18 167	11 132	7 035	59 620	44 362	16 741	4 025	9 363
1978	86 826	71 014	24 156	902	4 322	18 932	11 770	7 162	62 670	46 858	17 633	4 248	9 882
1979	89 933	73 865	24 997	1 008	4 562	19 426	12 220	7 206	64 936	48 869	18 276	4 452	10 185
1980	90 533	74 158	24 263	1 077	4 454	18 733	11 679	7 054	66 270	49 895	18 387	4 524	10 249
1981	91 297	75 117	24 118	1 180	4 304	18 634	11 611	7 023	67 179	50 999	18 577	4 600	10 369
1982	89 689	73 706	22 550	1 163	4 024	17 363	10 610	6 753	67 138	51 156	18 430	4 541	10 377
1983	90 295	74 284	22 110	997	4 065	17 048	10 326	6 722	68 186	52 174	18 642	4 525	10 640
1984	94 548	78 389	23 435	1 014	4 501	17 920	11 050	6 870	71 113	54 954	19 624	4 753	11 227
1985	97 532	81 000	23 585	974	4 793	17 819	11 034	6 784	73 947	57 415	20 350	4 878	11 738
1986	99 500	82 661	23 318	829	4 937	17 552	10 795	6 757	76 182	59 343	20 765	4 899	12 082
1987	102 116	84 960	23 470	771	5 090	17 609	10 767	6 842	78 647	61 490	21 271	4 966	12 422
1988	105 378	87 838	23 909	770	5 233	17 906	10 969	6 938	81 469	63 929	21 942	5 115	12 812
1989	108 051	90 124	24 045	750	5 309	17 985	11 004	6 981	84 006	66 079	22 477	5 245	13 112
1990	109 526	91 112	23 723	765	5 263	17 695	10 737	6 958	85 803	67 389	22 633	5 230	13 186
1991	108 425	89 879	22 588	739	4 780	17 068	10 220	6 848	85 837	67 291	22 247	5 147	12 900
1992	108 799	90 012	22 095	689	4 608	16 799	9 946	6 853	86 704	67 918	22 091	5 072	12 831
1993	110 931	91 942	22 219	666	4 779	16 774	9 901	6 872	88 712	69 723	22 343	5 056	13 024
1994	114 393	95 118	22 774	659	5 095	17 020	10 132	6 889	91 619	72 344	23 090	5 208	13 494
1995	117 400	97 968	23 156	641	5 274	17 241	10 373	6 868	94 245	74 812	23 793	5 393	13 900
1996	119 828	100 289	23 409	637	5 536	17 237	10 486	6 751	96 419	76 880	24 197	5 481	14 146
1997	122 941	103 278	23 886	654	5 813	17 419	10 705	6 714	99 055	79 392	24 656	5 622	14 393
1998	126 146	106 237	24 354	645	6 149	17 560	10 911	6 649	101 792	81 883	25 139	5 752	14 613
1999	129 228	108 921	24 465	598	6 545	17 322	10 831	6 491	104 763	84 456	25 722	5 848	14 974
2000	132 011	111 221	24 649	599	6 787	17 263	10 877	6 386	107 362	86 572	26 174	5 888	15 284
2001	132 073	110 955	23 873	606	6 826	16 441	10 336	6 105	108 200	87 082	25 931	5 728	15 242
2002	130 634	109 121	22 557	583	6 716	15 259	9 485	5 774	108 077	86 564	25 442	5 606	15 029
2003	130 331	108 748	21 816	572	6 735	14 509	8 964	5 546	108 515	86 931	25 228	5 556	14 922
2004	131 769	110 148	21 882	591	6 976	14 315	8 925	5 390	109 887	88 266	25 470	5 608	15 063
2005	134 005	112 201	22 190	628	7 336	14 227	8 956	5 271	111 814	90 010	25 959	5 764	15 280
2006	136 398	114 424	22 530	684	7 691	14 155	8 981	5 174	113 867	91 894	26 276	5 905	15 353
2007	137 936	115 718	22 233	724	7 630	13 879	8 808	5 071	115 703	93 485	26 630	6 015	15 520
2008	137 170	114 661	21 335	767	7 162	13 406	8 463	4 943	115 835	93 326	26 293	5 943	15 283
2009	131 233	108 678	18 558	694	6 016	11 847	7 284	4 564	112 675	90 121	24 906	5 587	14 522
2010	130 275	107 785	17 751	705	5 518	11 528	7 064	4 464	112 524	90 034	24 636	5 452	14 440
2011	131 842	109 756	18 047	788	5 533	11 726	7 273	4 453	113 795	91 708	25 065	5 543	14 668
2012	134 104	112 184	18 420	848	5 646	11 927	7 470	4 457	115 683	93 763	25 476	5 667	14 841
2013	136 368	114 504	18 700	868	5 827	12 006	7 543	4 463	117 668	95 804	25 870	5 747	15 077
2014	139 578	117 670	19 360	904	6 231	12 225	7 708	4 517	120 218	98 310	26 490	5 824	15 414
2015	142 253	120 196	19 614	778	6 490	12 346	7 769	4 577	122 639	100 582	26 938	5 843	15 631
2016	144 882	122 566	19 718	661	6 727	12 330	7 693	4 637	125 164	102 848	27 322	5 878	15 887
2017	146 608	124 258	20 048	676	6 969	12 440	7 741	4 699	126 768	104 174	27 393	5 814	15 846
2018	148 908	126 454	20 704	727	7 288	12 688	7 946	4 742	128 205	105 750	27 607	5 841	15 786
2019	150 939	128 346	21 067	735	7 492	12 840	8 059	4 781	129 873	107 279	27 715	5 903	15 644
2020	142 252	120 344	20 076	620	7 274	12 182	7 581	4 601	122 117	100 268	26 589	5 641	14 856

Table 10-7. Nonfarm Payroll Employment by NAICS Supersector—*Continued*

(Thousands; seasonally adjusted, except as noted.)

Year and month	Service-providing—*Continued*													Diffusion index, 6-month span, private nonfarm [2]
	Private—*Continued*						Government							
							Total	Federal		State		Local		
	Information	Financial activities	Professional and business services	Education and health services	Leisure and hospitality	Other services		Total	Department of Defense [1]	Total	Education	Total	Education	
1964	1 766	2 811	4 154	3 438	3 772	1 346	9 711	2 463	676	1 856	609	5 392	2 839	...
1965	1 824	2 878	4 323	3 587	3 951	1 404	10 191	2 495	679	1 996	679	5 700	3 031	...
1966	1 908	2 961	4 536	3 770	4 127	1 475	10 910	2 690	741	2 141	775	6 080	3 297	...
1967	1 955	3 087	4 739	3 986	4 269	1 558	11 525	2 852	802	2 302	873	6 371	3 490	...
1968	1 991	3 234	4 937	4 191	4 453	1 638	11 972	2 871	801	2 442	958	6 660	3 649	...
1969	2 048	3 404	5 175	4 428	4 670	1 731	12 330	2 893	815	2 533	1 042	6 904	3 785	...
1970	2 041	3 532	5 287	4 577	4 789	1 789	12 687	2 865	756	2 664	1 104	7 158	3 912	...
1971	2 009	3 651	5 348	4 675	4 914	1 827	13 012	2 828	731	2 747	1 149	7 437	4 091	...
1972	2 056	3 784	5 544	4 863	5 121	1 900	13 465	2 815	720	2 859	1 188	7 790	4 262	...
1973	2 135	3 920	5 796	5 092	5 341	1 990	13 862	2 794	696	2 923	1 205	8 146	4 433	...
1974	2 160	4 023	5 997	5 322	5 471	2 078	14 303	2 858	698	3 039	1 267	8 407	4 584	...
1975	2 061	4 047	6 056	5 497	5 544	2 144	14 820	2 882	704	3 179	1 323	8 758	4 722	...
1976	2 111	4 155	6 310	5 756	5 794	2 244	15 001	2 863	693	3 273	1 371	8 865	4 786	...
1977	2 185	4 348	6 611	6 052	6 065	2 359	15 258	2 859	676	3 377	1 385	9 023	4 859	...
1978	2 287	4 599	6 997	6 427	6 411	2 505	15 812	2 893	661	3 474	1 367	9 446	4 958	...
1979	2 375	4 843	7 339	6 768	6 631	2 637	16 068	2 894	649	3 541	1 378	9 633	4 989	...
1980	2 361	5 025	7 571	7 077	6 721	2 755	16 375	3 000	645	3 610	1 398	9 765	5 090	...
1981	2 382	5 163	7 809	7 364	6 840	2 865	16 180	2 922	655	3 640	1 420	9 619	5 095	...
1982	2 317	5 209	7 875	7 526	6 874	2 924	15 982	2 884	690	3 640	1 433	9 458	5 049	...
1983	2 253	5 334	8 065	7 781	7 078	3 021	16 011	2 915	699	3 662	1 450	9 434	5 020	...
1984	2 398	5 553	8 493	8 211	7 489	3 186	16 159	2 943	716	3 734	1 488	9 482	5 076	...
1985	2 437	5 815	8 900	8 679	7 869	3 366	16 533	3 014	738	3 832	1 540	9 687	5 221	...
1986	2 445	6 128	9 241	9 086	8 156	3 523	16 838	3 044	736	3 893	1 561	9 901	5 358	...
1987	2 507	6 385	9 639	9 543	8 446	3 699	17 156	3 089	736	3 967	1 586	10 100	5 469	...
1988	2 585	6 500	10 121	10 096	8 778	3 907	17 540	3 124	719	4 076	1 621	10 339	5 590	...
1989	2 622	6 562	10 588	10 652	9 062	4 116	17 927	3 136	735	4 182	1 668	10 609	5 740	...
1990	2 688	6 614	10 881	11 024	9 288	4 261	18 415	3 196	722	4 305	1 730	10 914	5 902	...
1991	2 677	6 561	10 746	11 556	9 256	4 249	18 545	3 110	702	4 355	1 768	11 081	5 994	43.6
1992	2 641	6 559	11 001	11 948	9 437	4 240	18 787	3 111	702	4 408	1 799	11 267	6 076	61.6
1993	2 668	6 742	11 527	12 362	9 732	4 350	18 989	3 063	670	4 488	1 834	11 438	6 206	72.5
1994	2 738	6 910	12 207	12 872	10 100	4 428	19 275	3 018	657	4 576	1 882	11 682	6 329	81.4
1995	2 843	6 866	12 878	13 360	10 501	4 572	19 432	2 949	627	4 635	1 919	11 849	6 453	70.5
1996	2 940	7 018	13 497	13 761	10 777	4 690	19 539	2 877	597	4 606	1 911	12 056	6 592	78.5
1997	3 084	7 255	14 371	14 185	11 018	4 825	19 664	2 806	588	4 582	1 904	12 276	6 759	81.0
1998	3 218	7 565	15 183	14 570	11 232	4 976	19 909	2 772	550	4 612	1 922	12 525	6 921	70.2
1999	3 419	7 753	15 994	14 939	11 543	5 087	20 307	2 769	525	4 709	1 983	12 829	7 120	70.5
2000	3 630	7 783	16 704	15 252	11 862	5 168	20 790	2 865	510	4 786	2 031	13 139	7 294	58.9
2001	3 629	7 900	16 514	15 814	12 036	5 258	21 118	2 764	504	4 905	2 113	13 449	7 479	32.4
2002	3 395	7 956	16 016	16 398	11 986	5 372	21 513	2 766	499	5 029	2 243	13 718	7 654	38.0
2003	3 188	8 078	16 029	16 835	12 173	5 401	21 583	2 761	486	5 002	2 255	13 820	7 709	40.5
2004	3 118	8 105	16 440	17 230	12 493	5 409	21 621	2 730	473	4 982	2 238	13 909	7 765	61.0
2005	3 038	8 197	16 954	18 154	12 816	5 395	21 804	2 732	493	5 032	2 260	14 041	7 856	64.5
2006	3 032	8 367	17 566	18 099	13 110	5 438	21 974	2 732	491	5 075	2 293	14 167	7 913	60.1
2007	2 984	8 348	17 942	18 613	13 427	5 494	22 218	2 734	496	5 122	2 318	14 362	7 987	57.2
2008	2 804	8 206	17 735	19 156	13 436	5 515	22 509	2 762	519	5 177	2 354	14 571	8 084	27.3
2009	2 707	7 838	16 579	19 550	13 077	5 367	22 555	2 832	545	5 169	2 360	14 554	8 079	19.2
2010	2 674	7 695	16 728	19 889	13 049	5 331	22 490	2 977	559	5 137	2 373	14 376	8 013	62.8
2011	2 676	7 697	17 332	20 228	13 353	5 360	22 086	2 859	552	5 078	2 374	14 150	7 873	73.8
2012	2 706	7 784	17 932	20 698	13 768	5 430	21 920	2 820	537	5 055	2 389	14 045	7 778	62.2
2013	2 726	7 880	18 560	21 102	14 242	5 464	21 864	2 766	524	5 048	2 393	14 050	7 783	63.0
2014	2 750	8 006	19 189	21 541	14 775	5 575	21 908	2 736	526	5 043	2 379	14 129	7 847	78.5
2015	2 794	8 149	19 705	22 140	15 266	5 620	22 057	2 761	529	5 086	2 407	14 210	7 865	64.5
2016	2 814	8 324	20 279	22 745	15 684	5 708	22 316	2 811	527	5 101	2 423	14 404	7 968	63.2
2017	2 839	8 451	20 508	23 188	16 051	5 770	22 350	2 805	531	5 165	2 479	14 379	7 922	70.2
2018	2 860	8 590	20 950	23 638	16 295	5 831	22 455	2 800	543	5 173	2 487	14 481	7 963	69.8
2019	2 860	8 746	21 313	24 177	16 576	5 893	22 594	2 834	543	5 177	2 484	14 583	8 010	63.2
2020	2 698	8 727	20 253	23 234	13 369	5 396	21 908	2 929	560	5 074	2 380	13 905	7 572	37.6

[1] Not seasonally adjusted.
[2] See notes and definitions for explanation. September value used to represent year.
. . . = Not available.

Table 10-7. Nonfarm Payroll Employment by NAICS Supersector—*Continued*

(Thousands; seasonally adjusted, except as noted.)

Year and month	Total	Private								Service-providing				
		Total	Goods-producing							Total	Private			
			Total	Mining and logging	Construc-tion	Manufacturing					Total	Trade, transportation, and utilities		
						Total	Durable	Nondurable				Total	Wholesale trade	Retail trade
2016														
January	143 211	121 097	19 754	728	6 639	12 387	7 766	4 621		123 457	101 343	27 072	5 856	15 718
February	143 448	121 318	19 747	710	6 662	12 375	7 753	4 622		123 701	101 571	27 123	5 854	15 767
March	143 673	121 507	19 752	692	6 705	12 355	7 736	4 619		123 921	101 755	27 167	5 856	15 797
April	143 826	121 665	19 743	683	6 704	12 356	7 735	4 621		124 083	101 922	27 177	5 861	15 792
May	143 869	121 682	19 699	674	6 690	12 335	7 712	4 623		124 170	101 983	27 187	5 857	15 800
June	144 166	121 951	19 705	668	6 690	12 347	7 714	4 633		124 461	102 246	27 209	5 858	15 825
July	144 457	122 200	19 731	664	6 708	12 359	7 723	4 636		124 726	102 469	27 245	5 861	15 843
August	144 633	122 343	19 707	661	6 704	12 342	7 703	4 639		124 926	102 636	27 282	5 864	15 860
September	144 882	122 566	19 718	661	6 727	12 330	7 693	4 637		125 164	102 848	27 322	5 878	15 887
October	145 006	122 698	19 727	659	6 743	12 325	7 692	4 633		125 279	102 971	27 331	5 881	15 881
November	145 170	122 876	19 762	666	6 771	12 325	7 695	4 630		125 408	103 114	27 346	5 887	15 868
December	145 325	123 026	19 794	668	6 783	12 343	7 708	4 635		125 531	103 232	27 374	5 888	15 881
2017														
January	145 627	123 325	19 865	649	6 847	12 369	7 701	4 668		125 762	103 460	27 357	5 802	15 920
February	145 815	123 496	19 928	655	6 889	12 384	7 698	4 686		125 887	103 568	27 342	5 804	15 880
March	145 944	123 619	19 964	660	6 909	12 395	7 704	4 691		125 980	103 655	27 339	5 807	15 862
April	146 141	123 811	19 985	669	6 916	12 400	7 706	4 694		126 156	103 826	27 352	5 811	15 854
May	146 296	123 964	20 007	673	6 928	12 406	7 715	4 691		126 289	103 957	27 339	5 806	15 824
June	146 512	124 166	20 050	677	6 955	12 418	7 726	4 692		126 462	104 116	27 366	5 814	15 831
July	146 727	124 368	20 056	679	6 960	12 417	7 718	4 699		126 671	104 312	27 368	5 814	15 823
August	146 911	124 554	20 135	684	6 990	12 461	7 750	4 711		126 776	104 419	27 385	5 814	15 822
September	146 929	124 563	20 161	687	7 004	12 470	7 761	4 709		126 768	104 402	27 410	5 816	15 815
October	147 196	124 827	20 206	687	7 027	12 492	7 777	4 715		126 990	104 621	27 435	5 821	15 810
November	147 421	125 028	20 273	693	7 066	12 514	7 799	4 715		127 148	104 755	27 449	5 821	15 816
December	147 551	125 170	20 326	692	7 093	12 541	7 822	4 719		127 225	104 844	27 465	5 827	15 802
2018														
January	147 672	125 317	20 371	699	7 114	12 558	7 835	4 723		127 301	104 946	27 448	5 822	15 785
February	148 078	125 672	20 494	706	7 200	12 588	7 861	4 727		127 584	105 178	27 525	5 823	15 821
March	148 254	125 850	20 530	714	7 205	12 611	7 886	4 725		127 724	105 320	27 578	5 836	15 833
April	148 391	125 977	20 577	722	7 223	12 632	7 904	4 728		127 814	105 400	27 574	5 817	15 832
May	148 669	126 238	20 648	724	7 266	12 658	7 920	4 738		128 021	105 590	27 602	5 819	15 836
June	148 888	126 429	20 698	729	7 282	12 687	7 944	4 743		128 190	105 731	27 589	5 826	15 797
July	149 024	126 562	20 739	729	7 304	12 706	7 961	4 745		128 285	105 823	27 598	5 838	15 785
August	149 268	126 778	20 791	737	7 335	12 719	7 972	4 747		128 477	105 987	27 657	5 857	15 788
September	149 348	126 859	20 834	739	7 355	12 740	7 991	4 749		128 514	106 025	27 636	5 854	15 741
October	149 549	127 064	20 884	742	7 378	12 764	8 011	4 753		128 665	106 180	27 633	5 857	15 702
November	149 683	127 197	20 897	737	7 376	12 784	8 022	4 762		128 786	106 300	27 691	5 864	15 729
December	149 865	127 370	20 948	741	7 402	12 805	8 038	4 767		128 917	106 422	27 666	5 873	15 704
2019														
January	150 134	127 628	21 023	746	7 452	12 825	8 059	4 766		129 111	106 605	27 711	5 879	15 696
February	150 135	127 622	20 994	741	7 423	12 830	8 062	4 768		129 141	106 628	27 688	5 885	15 667
March	150 282	127 754	21 011	741	7 443	12 827	8 056	4 771		129 271	106 743	27 665	5 880	15 642
April	150 492	127 939	21 039	741	7 469	12 829	8 056	4 773		129 453	106 900	27 671	5 894	15 631
May	150 577	128 026	21 050	743	7 478	12 829	8 056	4 773		129 527	106 976	27 667	5 898	15 618
June	150 759	128 206	21 076	741	7 497	12 838	8 064	4 774		129 683	107 130	27 686	5 899	15 613
July	150 953	128 366	21 085	736	7 504	12 845	8 067	4 778		129 868	107 281	27 692	5 906	15 614
August	151 160	128 523	21 087	731	7 508	12 848	8 066	4 782		130 073	107 436	27 688	5 907	15 613
September	151 368	128 718	21 106	731	7 524	12 851	8 066	4 785		130 262	107 612	27 712	5 913	15 622
October	151 553	128 908	21 086	735	7 541	12 810	8 019	4 791		130 467	107 822	27 750	5 923	15 644
November	151 814	129 155	21 131	724	7 539	12 868	8 064	4 804		130 683	108 024	27 762	5 926	15 630
December	151 998	129 319	21 136	715	7 555	12 866	8 064	4 802		130 862	108 183	27 809	5 933	15 672
2020														
January	152 234	129 445	21 096	689	7 615	12 792	8 002	4 790		131 138	108 349	27 852	5 901	15 605
February	152 523	129 688	21 137	690	7 648	12 799	8 007	4 792		131 386	108 551	27 876	5 895	15 609
March	150 840	128 066	20 949	674	7 557	12 718	7 961	4 757		129 891	107 117	27 729	5 877	15 483
April	130 161	108 335	18 571	622	6 535	11 414	7 062	4 352		111 590	89 764	24 513	5 486	13 235
May	132 994	111 680	19 262	601	7 004	11 657	7 201	4 456		113 732	92 418	24 934	5 509	13 644
June	137 840	116 487	19 767	597	7 171	11 999	7 472	4 527		118 073	96 720	25 934	5 557	14 502
July	139 566	118 010	19 827	593	7 197	12 037	7 502	4 535		119 739	98 183	26 205	5 537	14 742
August	141 149	119 076	19 880	589	7 223	12 068	7 500	4 568		121 269	99 196	26 553	5 544	14 995
September	141 865	120 008	19 971	592	7 256	12 123	7 538	4 585		121 894	100 037	26 662	5 578	15 025
October	142 545	120 962	20 078	594	7 329	12 155	7 550	4 605		122 467	100 884	26 847	5 588	15 131
November	142 809	121 321	20 146	597	7 353	12 196	7 580	4 616		122 663	101 175	26 983	5 602	15 129
December	142 503	121 047	20 228	597	7 400	12 231	7 598	4 633		122 275	100 819	26 984	5 617	15 159

Table 10-7. Nonfarm Payroll Employment by NAICS Supersector—*Continued*

(Thousands; seasonally adjusted, except as noted.)

	Service-providing—*Continued*													Diffusion index, 6-month span, private nonfarm [2]
	Private—*Continued*						Government							
								Federal		State		Local		
Year and month	Information	Financial activities	Profes-sional and business services	Education and health services	Leisure and hospitality	Other services	Total	Total	Depart-ment of Defense [1]	Total	Education	Total	Education	
2016														
January	2 763	8 207	19 877	22 334	15 443	5 647	22 114	2 771	528	5 088	2 412	14 255	7 883	63.6
February	2 773	8 213	19 902	22 408	15 488	5 664	22 130	2 777	528	5 084	2 408	14 269	7 887	65.7
March	2 779	8 231	19 928	22 443	15 537	5 670	22 166	2 781	529	5 091	2 411	14 294	7 901	68.4
April	2 781	8 249	19 994	22 495	15 552	5 674	22 161	2 769	529	5 089	2 410	14 303	7 904	66.3
May	2 739	8 263	20 022	22 544	15 561	5 667	22 187	2 791	529	5 079	2 404	14 317	7 914	61.4
June	2 780	8 280	20 081	22 603	15 610	5 683	22 215	2 798	530	5 089	2 412	14 328	7 917	57.6
July	2 778	8 300	20 165	22 644	15 652	5 685	22 257	2 802	530	5 093	2 417	14 362	7 942	64.1
August	2 778	8 315	20 196	22 697	15 673	5 695	22 290	2 805	530	5 094	2 413	14 391	7 961	62.0
September	2 786	8 324	20 279	22 745	15 684	5 708	22 316	2 811	530	5 101	2 423	14 404	7 968	63.2
October	2 780	8 330	20 334	22 790	15 695	5 711	22 308	2 817	531	5 092	2 414	14 399	7 953	67.2
November	2 768	8 342	20 380	22 821	15 739	5 718	22 294	2 811	527	5 088	2 410	14 395	7 934	65.9
December	2 762	8 364	20 416	22 871	15 744	5 701	22 299	2 819	532	5 085	2 414	14 395	7 945	66.1
2017														
January	2 819	8 399	20 338	22 938	15 878	5 731	22 302	2 815	531	5 151	2 465	14 336	7 905	64.1
February	2 814	8 401	20 347	23 012	15 910	5 742	22 319	2 813	530	5 160	2 469	14 346	7 911	67.6
March	2 813	8 409	20 376	23 051	15 922	5 745	22 325	2 811	529	5 163	2 473	14 351	7 917	66.9
April	2 809	8 424	20 406	23 101	15 986	5 748	22 330	2 800	528	5 166	2 480	14 364	7 918	65.7
May	2 804	8 432	20 463	23 139	16 021	5 759	22 332	2 808	526	5 174	2 492	14 350	7 919	64.7
June	2 807	8 448	20 498	23 167	16 063	5 767	22 346	2 806	527	5 170	2 486	14 370	7 913	68.0
July	2 809	8 460	20 540	23 227	16 134	5 774	22 359	2 805	526	5 173	2 488	14 381	7 912	67.1
August	2 815	8 469	20 568	23 264	16 138	5 780	22 357	2 802	527	5 167	2 479	14 388	7 923	67.4
September	2 811	8 477	20 571	23 295	16 065	5 773	22 366	2 802	526	5 160	2 473	14 404	7 931	70.2
October	2 812	8 482	20 619	23 322	16 156	5 795	22 369	2 803	524	5 155	2 468	14 411	7 939	70.2
November	2 813	8 494	20 649	23 374	16 170	5 806	22 393	2 792	525	5 171	2 484	14 430	7 947	69.0
December	2 819	8 498	20 683	23 383	16 190	5 806	22 381	2 794	526	5 159	2 471	14 428	7 940	68.4
2018														
January	2 815	8 504	20 738	23 437	16 193	5 811	22 355	2 801	525	5 147	2 475	14 407	7 910	68.2
February	2 815	8 533	20 781	23 491	16 218	5 815	22 406	2 793	525	5 151	2 474	14 462	7 957	69.8
March	2 826	8 538	20 823	23 523	16 220	5 812	22 404	2 793	525	5 154	2 476	14 457	7 949	73.4
April	2 839	8 545	20 868	23 538	16 217	5 819	22 414	2 795	527	5 167	2 476	14 452	7 947	73.1
May	2 837	8 567	20 914	23 576	16 263	5 831	22 431	2 792	528	5 174	2 481	14 465	7 956	73.4
June	2 837	8 586	20 948	23 617	16 310	5 844	22 459	2 796	529	5 180	2 485	14 483	7 971	74.2
July	2 841	8 594	20 968	23 644	16 349	5 829	22 462	2 798	529	5 178	2 486	14 486	7 970	70.7
August	2 841	8 607	21 009	23 691	16 350	5 832	22 490	2 801	530	5 183	2 493	14 506	7 984	71.1
September	2 839	8 629	21 042	23 716	16 326	5 837	22 489	2 804	530	5 193	2 504	14 492	7 967	69.8
October	2 851	8 647	21 079	23 767	16 358	5 845	22 485	2 805	530	5 184	2 497	14 496	7 966	70.5
November	2 850	8 657	21 102	23 790	16 368	5 842	22 486	2 811	532	5 173	2 487	14 502	7 965	68.8
December	2 854	8 665	21 128	23 844	16 415	5 850	22 495	2 809	532	5 173	2 489	14 513	7 972	71.9
2019														
January	2 843	8 676	21 126	23 900	16 496	5 853	22 506	2 811	537	5 170	2 485	14 525	7 978	69.2
February	2 841	8 690	21 144	23 918	16 473	5 854	22 513	2 814	537	5 175	2 485	14 524	7 976	71.9
March	2 851	8 707	21 176	23 981	16 494	5 869	22 528	2 815	538	5 175	2 488	14 538	7 982	69.4
April	2 845	8 721	21 226	24 046	16 507	5 884	22 553	2 823	538	5 169	2 487	14 561	7 995	68.4
May	2 853	8 727	21 253	24 076	16 519	5 881	22 551	2 826	540	5 158	2 474	14 567	7 993	68.4
June	2 865	8 732	21 294	24 131	16 526	5 896	22 553	2 829	543	5 157	2 470	14 567	7 987	62.4
July	2 862	8 753	21 337	24 204	16 528	5 905	22 587	2 831	544	5 168	2 478	14 588	8 006	60.1
August	2 861	8 768	21 377	24 262	16 570	5 910	22 637	2 857	543	5 184	2 489	14 596	8 021	63.0
September	2 866	8 771	21 402	24 323	16 631	5 907	22 650	2 857	545	5 181	2 483	14 612	8 027	63.2
October	2 865	8 792	21 444	24 363	16 701	5 907	22 645	2 844	545	5 184	2 481	14 617	8 028	61.8
November	2 874	8 804	21 481	24 436	16 744	5 923	22 659	2 850	554	5 181	2 479	14 628	8 032	67.1
December	2 883	8 814	21 503	24 465	16 784	5 925	22 679	2 847	553	5 184	2 481	14 648	8 039	65.7
2020														
January	2 910	8 849	21 437	24 513	16 858	5 930	22 789	2 852	554	5 284	2 579	14 653	8 025	61.7
February	2 914	8 875	21 469	24 565	16 915	5 937	22 835	2 863	558	5 303	2 596	14 669	8 030	62.1
March	2 898	8 850	21 318	24 347	16 133	5 842	22 774	2 879	558	5 242	2 536	14 653	8 009	37.5
April	2 633	8 596	19 082	21 722	8 691	4 527	21 826	2 883	558	5 074	2 374	13 869	7 572	7.6
May	2 594	8 613	19 247	22 107	10 146	4 777	21 314	2 877	559	5 031	2 341	13 406	7 280	5.8
June	2 602	8 634	19 568	22 671	12 158	5 153	21 353	2 876	559	5 043	2 356	13 434	7 336	7.8
July	2 592	8 646	19 715	22 885	12 824	5 316	21 556	2 897	561	5 039	2 350	13 620	7 492	6.8
August	2 617	8 674	19 915	23 084	12 963	5 390	22 073	3 153	563	5 060	2 369	13 860	7 672	8.9
September	2 659	8 712	20 055	23 152	13 357	5 440	21 857	3 117	563	5 010	2 315	13 730	7 444	11.5
October	2 650	8 746	20 296	23 235	13 622	5 488	21 583	2 975	564	4 945	2 254	13 663	7 341	81.3
November	2 650	8 756	20 391	23 278	13 632	5 485	21 488	2 888	562	4 931	2 245	13 669	7 335	81.5
December	2 659	8 774	20 550	23 249	13 134	5 469	21 456	2 892	561	4 930	2 244	13 634	7 326	79.0

[1]Not seasonally adjusted.
[2]See notes and definitions for explanation. September value used to represent year.

Table 10-8. Employment, Hours, and Earnings, Total Nonfarm and Manufacturing, Historical Annual and Monthly

(Wage and salary workers on nonfarm payrolls, seasonally adjusted.)

Year and month	All wage and salary workers (thousands)					Production and nonsupervisory workers on private payrolls							
	Total	Private			Service-providing	Number (thousands)		Average hours per week		Average hourly earnings, dollars		Average weekly earnings, dollars	
		Total	Goods-producing			Total private	Manufac-turing	Total private	Manufac-turing	Total private	Manufac-turing	Total private	Manufac-turing
			Total	Manufac-turing									
1939	30 645	26 606	11 511	9 450	19 134	...	8 163	...	37.7	...	0.49	...	18.47
1940	32 407	28 156	12 378	10 099	20 029	...	8 737	...	38.2	...	0.53	...	20.25
1941	36 600	31 874	14 940	12 121	21 660	...	10 641	...	40.7	...	0.61	...	24.83
1942	40 213	34 621	17 275	14 030	22 938	...	12 447	...	43.2	...	0.74	...	31.97
1943	42 574	36 353	18 738	16 153	23 837	...	14 407	...	45.1	...	0.86	...	38.79
1944	42 006	35 819	17 981	15 903	24 026	...	14 031	...	45.4	...	0.91	...	41.31
1945	40 510	34 428	16 308	14 255	24 203	...	12 445	...	43.6	...	0.90	...	39.24
1946	41 759	36 054	16 122	13 513	25 637	...	11 781	...	40.4	...	0.95	...	38.38
1947	43 945	38 379	17 314	14 287	26 631	...	12 453	...	40.5	...	1.10	...	44.55
1948	44 954	39 213	17 579	14 324	27 376	...	12 383	...	40.1	...	1.20	...	48.12
1949	43 843	37 893	16 464	13 281	27 379	...	11 355	...	39.2	...	1.25	...	49.00
1950	45 287	39 167	17 343	14 013	27 945	...	12 032	...	40.6	...	1.32	...	53.59
1951	47 930	41 427	18 703	15 070	29 227	...	12 808	...	40.7	...	1.45	...	59.02
1952	48 909	42 182	18 928	15 291	29 981	...	12 797	...	40.8	...	1.53	...	62.42
1953	50 310	43 552	19 733	16 131	30 577	...	13 437	...	40.6	...	1.63	...	66.18
1954	49 093	42 235	18 515	15 002	30 578	...	12 300	...	39.7	...	1.66	...	65.90
1955	50 744	43 722	19 234	15 524	31 510	...	12 735	...	40.8	...	1.74	...	70.99
1956	52 473	45 087	19 799	15 858	32 674	...	12 869	...	40.5	...	1.84	...	74.52
1957	52 959	45 235	19 669	15 798	33 290	...	12 640	...	39.9	...	1.93	...	77.01
1958	51 426	43 480	18 319	14 656	33 107	...	11 532	...	39.2	...	1.99	...	78.01
1959	53 374	45 182	19 163	15 325	34 211	...	12 089	...	40.3	...	2.08	...	83.82
1960	54 296	45 832	19 182	15 438	35 114	...	12 074	...	39.8	...	2.15	...	85.57
1961	54 105	45 399	18 647	15 011	35 458	...	11 612	...	39.9	...	2.20	...	87.78
1962	55 659	46 655	19 203	15 498	36 455	...	11 986	...	40.5	...	2.27	...	91.94
1963	56 764	47 423	19 385	15 631	37 379	...	12 051	...	40.6	...	2.34	...	95.00
1964	58 391	48 680	19 733	15 888	38 658	40 575	12 298	38.5	40.8	2.53	2.41	97.41	98.33
1950													
January	43 528	37 594	16 255	13 161	27 273	...	11 258	...	39.6	...	1.27	...	50.29
February	43 298	37 372	16 035	13 169	27 263	...	11 262	...	39.7	...	1.26	...	50.02
March	43 952	37 874	16 482	13 290	27 470	...	11 362	...	39.7	...	1.28	...	50.82
April	44 376	38 282	16 718	13 471	27 658	...	11 528	...	40.3	...	1.29	...	51.99
May	44 718	38 675	17 080	13 780	27 638	...	11 855	...	40.3	...	1.30	...	52.39
June	45 084	39 062	17 288	13 923	27 796	...	11 979	...	40.6	...	1.30	...	52.78
July	45 454	39 364	17 464	14 072	27 990	...	12 107	...	40.9	...	1.31	...	53.58
August	46 188	40 001	17 917	14 461	28 271	...	12 476	...	41.3	...	1.33	...	54.93
September	46 442	40 214	18 040	14 561	28 402	...	12 519	...	40.8	...	1.33	...	54.26
October	46 712	40 463	18 249	14 737	28 463	...	12 659	...	41.1	...	1.36	...	55.90
November	46 778	40 516	18 288	14 762	28 490	...	12 682	...	41.0	...	1.37	...	56.17
December	46 855	40 541	18 283	14 782	28 572	...	12 710	...	40.9	...	1.39	...	56.85
1951													
January	47 288	40 936	18 518	14 950	28 770	...	12 816	...	41.0	...	1.40	...	57.40
February	47 577	41 195	18 666	15 076	28 911	...	12 929	...	40.9	...	1.41	...	57.67
March	47 871	41 461	18 754	15 125	29 117	...	12 936	...	41.0	...	1.42	...	58.22
April	47 856	41 405	18 810	15 166	29 046	...	12 960	...	41.0	...	1.43	...	58.63
May	47 953	41 536	18 829	15 164	29 124	...	12 941	...	41.0	...	1.44	...	59.04
June	48 068	41 569	18 826	15 176	29 242	...	12 934	...	40.9	...	1.45	...	59.31
July	48 062	41 524	18 747	15 110	29 315	...	12 848	...	40.6	...	1.45	...	58.87
August	48 009	41 490	18 709	15 061	29 300	...	12 772	...	40.4	...	1.46	...	58.98
September	47 955	41 403	18 622	14 996	29 333	...	12 659	...	40.4	...	1.46	...	58.98
October	48 009	41 432	18 630	14 973	29 379	...	12 615	...	40.3	...	1.47	...	59.24
November	48 148	41 522	18 617	14 999	29 531	...	12 628	...	40.4	...	1.48	...	59.79
December	48 309	41 621	18 698	15 045	29 611	...	12 667	...	40.7	...	1.49	...	60.64
1952													
January	48 298	41 709	18 719	15 067	29 579	...	12 675	...	40.8	...	1.49	...	60.79
February	48 522	41 872	18 813	15 105	29 709	...	12 689	...	40.8	...	1.49	...	60.79
March	48 504	41 842	18 775	15 127	29 729	...	12 695	...	40.6	...	1.51	...	61.31
April	48 616	41 954	18 806	15 162	29 810	...	12 713	...	40.3	...	1.51	...	60.85
May	48 645	41 951	18 784	15 143	29 861	...	12 676	...	40.5	...	1.51	...	61.16
June	48 286	41 574	18 419	14 828	29 867	...	12 353	...	40.6	...	1.51	...	61.31
July	48 144	41 407	18 268	14 707	29 876	...	12 233	...	40.2	...	1.50	...	60.30
August	48 923	42 205	18 928	15 279	29 995	...	12 764	...	40.7	...	1.53	...	62.27
September	49 319	42 585	19 206	15 553	30 113	...	13 007	...	41.1	...	1.55	...	63.71
October	49 598	42 782	19 312	15 690	30 286	...	13 122	...	41.2	...	1.56	...	64.27
November	49 816	43 015	19 473	15 843	30 343	...	13 262	...	41.2	...	1.58	...	65.10
December	50 164	43 229	19 610	15 973	30 554	...	13 375	...	41.2	...	1.58	...	65.10
1953													
January	50 145	43 351	19 721	16 067	30 424	...	13 447	...	41.1	...	1.59	...	65.35
February	50 339	43 542	19 841	16 158	30 498	...	13 529	...	41.0	...	1.61	...	66.01
March	50 475	43 691	19 909	16 270	30 566	...	13 620	...	41.2	...	1.61	...	66.33
April	50 432	43 662	19 908	16 293	30 524	...	13 629	...	40.9	...	1.62	...	66.26
May	50 491	43 774	19 930	16 341	30 561	...	13 645	...	41.0	...	1.62	...	66.42
June	50 522	43 788	19 909	16 343	30 613	...	13 636	...	40.9	...	1.63	...	66.67
July	50 536	43 813	19 910	16 353	30 626	...	13 653	...	40.7	...	1.64	...	66.75
August	50 487	43 733	19 834	16 278	30 653	...	13 564	...	40.7	...	1.64	...	66.75
September	50 365	43 616	19 726	16 151	30 639	...	13 419	...	40.1	...	1.65	...	66.17
October	50 242	43 478	19 578	15 981	30 664	...	13 244	...	40.1	...	1.65	...	66.17
November	49 907	43 158	19 315	15 728	30 592	...	12 990	...	40.0	...	1.65	...	66.00
December	49 702	42 959	19 173	15 581	30 529	...	12 847	...	39.7	...	1.65	...	65.51

. . . = Not available.

Table 10-8. Employment, Hours, and Earnings, Total Nonfarm and Manufacturing, Historical Annual and Monthly—*Continued*

(Wage and salary workers on nonfarm payrolls, seasonally adjusted.)

Year and month	All wage and salary workers (thousands)					Production and nonsupervisory workers on private payrolls							
	Total	Private			Service-providing	Number (thousands)		Average hours per week		Average hourly earnings, dollars		Average weekly earnings, dollars	
		Total	Goods-producing			Total private	Manufacturing	Total private	Manufacturing	Total private	Manufacturing	Total private	Manufacturing
			Total	Manufacturing									
1954													
January	49 468	42 708	18 963	15 440	30 505	. . .	12 706	. . .	39.5	. . .	1.65	. . .	65.18
February	49 382	42 599	18 880	15 307	30 502	. . .	12 593	. . .	39.7	. . .	1.65	. . .	65.51
March	49 158	42 362	18 748	15 197	30 410	. . .	12 493	. . .	39.6	. . .	1.65	. . .	65.34
April	49 178	42 372	18 602	15 065	30 576	. . .	12 361	. . .	39.7	. . .	1.65	. . .	65.51
May	48 965	42 136	18 476	14 974	30 489	. . .	12 282	. . .	39.7	. . .	1.67	. . .	66.30
June	48 896	42 050	18 400	14 910	30 496	. . .	12 220	. . .	39.7	. . .	1.67	. . .	66.30
July	48 835	41 967	18 280	14 799	30 555	. . .	12 121	. . .	39.7	. . .	1.66	. . .	65.90
August	48 825	41 933	18 251	14 772	30 574	. . .	12 089	. . .	39.8	. . .	1.66	. . .	66.07
September	48 882	41 988	18 261	14 805	30 621	. . .	12 104	. . .	39.9	. . .	1.66	. . .	66.23
October	48 944	42 044	18 321	14 841	30 623	. . .	12 142	. . .	39.7	. . .	1.67	. . .	66.30
November	49 178	42 214	18 438	14 913	30 740	. . .	12 206	. . .	40.1	. . .	1.68	. . .	67.37
December	49 331	42 374	18 508	14 967	30 823	. . .	12 254	. . .	40.1	. . .	1.68	. . .	67.37
1955													
January	49 497	42 544	18 609	15 034	30 888	. . .	12 309	. . .	40.4	. . .	1.69	. . .	68.28
February	49 644	42 721	18 726	15 138	30 918	. . .	12 408	. . .	40.6	. . .	1.70	. . .	69.02
March	49 963	43 025	18 910	15 258	31 053	. . .	12 524	. . .	40.7	. . .	1.71	. . .	69.60
April	50 247	43 288	19 067	15 375	31 180	. . .	12 626	. . .	40.8	. . .	1.71	. . .	69.77
May	50 512	43 521	19 223	15 493	31 289	. . .	12 731	. . .	41.1	. . .	1.73	. . .	71.10
June	50 790	43 770	19 331	15 585	31 459	. . .	12 810	. . .	40.8	. . .	1.73	. . .	70.58
July	50 985	43 936	19 376	15 614	31 609	. . .	12 818	. . .	40.7	. . .	1.75	. . .	71.23
August	51 111	44 088	19 432	15 679	31 679	. . .	12 866	. . .	40.7	. . .	1.76	. . .	71.63
September	51 262	44 195	19 427	15 668	31 835	. . .	12 830	. . .	40.7	. . .	1.77	. . .	72.04
October	51 431	44 313	19 482	15 740	31 949	. . .	12 896	. . .	41.0	. . .	1.77	. . .	72.57
November	51 592	44 509	19 554	15 813	32 038	. . .	12 967	. . .	41.1	. . .	1.78	. . .	73.16
December	51 805	44 673	19 608	15 859	32 197	. . .	13 009	. . .	40.9	. . .	1.78	. . .	72.80
1956													
January	51 975	44 808	19 665	15 882	32 310	. . .	13 011	. . .	40.8	. . .	1.78	. . .	72.62
February	52 167	44 955	19 731	15 889	32 436	. . .	12 986	. . .	40.7	. . .	1.79	. . .	72.85
March	52 295	45 043	19 691	15 829	32 604	. . .	12 905	. . .	40.6	. . .	1.80	. . .	73.08
April	52 375	45 099	19 811	15 909	32 564	. . .	12 970	. . .	40.5	. . .	1.82	. . .	73.71
May	52 506	45 139	19 825	15 893	32 681	. . .	12 925	. . .	40.4	. . .	1.83	. . .	73.93
June	52 584	45 217	19 905	15 835	32 679	. . .	12 836	. . .	40.3	. . .	1.83	. . .	73.75
July	51 954	44 549	19 390	15 468	32 564	. . .	12 435	. . .	40.3	. . .	1.82	. . .	73.35
August	52 630	45 179	19 922	15 893	32 708	. . .	12 860	. . .	40.3	. . .	1.85	. . .	74.56
September	52 601	45 120	19 860	15 863	32 741	. . .	12 822	. . .	40.5	. . .	1.87	. . .	75.74
October	52 781	45 262	19 918	15 937	32 863	. . .	12 908	. . .	40.6	. . .	1.88	. . .	76.33
November	52 822	45 269	19 886	15 916	32 936	. . .	12 864	. . .	40.4	. . .	1.88	. . .	75.95
December	52 930	45 346	19 926	15 957	33 004	. . .	12 882	. . .	40.6	. . .	1.91	. . .	77.55
1957													
January	52 888	45 268	19 833	15 970	33 055	. . .	12 881	. . .	40.4	. . .	1.90	. . .	76.76
February	53 097	45 451	19 933	15 998	33 164	. . .	12 885	. . .	40.5	. . .	1.91	. . .	77.36
March	53 157	45 485	19 936	15 994	33 221	. . .	12 855	. . .	40.4	. . .	1.92	. . .	77.57
April	53 238	45 537	19 887	15 970	33 351	. . .	12 811	. . .	40.0	. . .	1.91	. . .	76.40
May	53 149	45 436	19 834	15 931	33 315	. . .	12 762	. . .	40.0	. . .	1.92	. . .	76.80
June	53 066	45 364	19 777	15 873	33 289	. . .	12 697	. . .	40.0	. . .	1.92	. . .	76.80
July	53 123	45 369	19 735	15 854	33 388	. . .	12 669	. . .	40.0	. . .	1.93	. . .	77.20
August	53 126	45 369	19 728	15 867	33 398	. . .	12 673	. . .	40.0	. . .	1.94	. . .	77.60
September	52 932	45 183	19 545	15 710	33 387	. . .	12 528	. . .	39.7	. . .	1.95	. . .	77.42
October	52 765	44 997	19 421	15 599	33 344	. . .	12 437	. . .	39.4	. . .	1.96	. . .	77.22
November	52 559	44 790	19 260	15 466	33 299	. . .	12 301	. . .	39.2	. . .	1.96	. . .	76.83
December	52 385	44 539	19 111	15 332	33 274	. . .	12 170	. . .	39.1	. . .	1.95	. . .	76.25
1958													
January	52 077	44 256	18 902	15 130	33 175	. . .	11 969	. . .	38.9	. . .	1.95	. . .	75.86
February	51 576	43 744	18 529	14 908	33 047	. . .	11 757	. . .	38.7	. . .	1.95	. . .	75.47
March	51 300	43 452	18 335	14 670	32 965	. . .	11 532	. . .	38.8	. . .	1.96	. . .	76.05
April	51 027	43 159	18 120	14 506	32 907	. . .	11 373	. . .	38.9	. . .	1.96	. . .	76.24
May	50 913	43 019	18 008	14 414	32 905	. . .	11 294	. . .	38.9	. . .	1.97	. . .	76.63
June	50 912	42 986	17 984	14 408	32 928	. . .	11 300	. . .	39.1	. . .	1.98	. . .	77.42
July	51 037	43 065	18 038	14 450	32 999	. . .	11 349	. . .	39.3	. . .	1.98	. . .	77.81
August	51 231	43 219	18 147	14 524	33 084	. . .	11 412	. . .	39.5	. . .	2.01	. . .	79.40
September	51 506	43 490	18 331	14 658	33 175	. . .	11 556	. . .	39.5	. . .	2.00	. . .	79.00
October	51 486	43 455	18 218	14 503	33 268	. . .	11 394	. . .	39.6	. . .	2.00	. . .	79.20
November	51 944	43 916	18 610	14 827	33 334	. . .	11 702	. . .	39.9	. . .	2.03	. . .	81.00
December	52 088	43 988	18 592	14 877	33 496	. . .	11 743	. . .	39.9	. . .	2.04	. . .	81.40
1959													
January	52 480	44 375	18 796	14 998	33 684	. . .	11 849	. . .	40.2	. . .	2.04	. . .	82.01
February	52 687	44 571	18 890	15 115	33 797	. . .	11 950	. . .	40.3	. . .	2.05	. . .	82.62
March	53 016	44 884	19 069	15 259	33 947	. . .	12 078	. . .	40.4	. . .	2.07	. . .	83.63
April	53 320	45 178	19 269	15 385	34 051	. . .	12 185	. . .	40.5	. . .	2.08	. . .	84.24
May	53 549	45 396	19 378	15 487	34 171	. . .	12 277	. . .	40.7	. . .	2.08	. . .	84.66
June	53 679	45 536	19 462	15 554	34 217	. . .	12 330	. . .	40.6	. . .	2.09	. . .	84.85
July	53 803	45 630	19 529	15 623	34 274	. . .	12 366	. . .	40.3	. . .	2.09	. . .	84.23
August	53 334	45 153	19 049	15 202	34 285	. . .	11 936	. . .	40.4	. . .	2.07	. . .	83.63
September	53 429	45 190	19 052	15 254	34 377	. . .	11 984	. . .	40.4	. . .	2.08	. . .	84.03
October	53 359	45 094	18 925	15 158	34 434	. . .	11 864	. . .	40.1	. . .	2.07	. . .	83.01
November	53 635	45 351	19 108	15 300	34 527	. . .	11 991	. . .	39.9	. . .	2.07	. . .	82.59
December	54 175	45 807	19 425	15 573	34 750	. . .	12 254	. . .	40.3	. . .	2.11	. . .	85.03

. . . = Not available.

Table 10-8. Employment, Hours, and Earnings, Total Nonfarm and Manufacturing, Historical Annual and Monthly—Continued

(Wage and salary workers on nonfarm payrolls, seasonally adjusted.)

Year and month	All wage and salary workers (thousands)					Production and nonsupervisory workers on private payrolls							
	Total	Private			Service-providing	Number (thousands)		Average hours per week		Average hourly earnings, dollars		Average weekly earnings, dollars	
		Total	Goods-producing			Total private	Manufac-turing	Total private	Manufac-turing	Total private	Manufac-turing	Total private	Manufac-turing
			Total	Manufac-turing									
1960													
January	54 274	45 967	19 491	15 687	34 783	...	12 362	...	40.6	...	2.13	...	86.48
February	54 513	46 187	19 605	15 765	34 908	...	12 434	...	40.3	...	2.14	...	86.24
March	54 458	45 933	19 373	15 707	35 085	...	12 362	...	40.0	...	2.14	...	85.60
April	54 812	46 278	19 446	15 654	35 366	...	12 299	...	40.0	...	2.14	...	85.60
May	54 473	46 041	19 374	15 575	35 099	...	12 218	...	40.1	...	2.14	...	85.81
June	54 347	45 915	19 240	15 466	35 107	...	12 102	...	39.9	...	2.14	...	85.39
July	54 304	45 862	19 170	15 413	35 134	...	12 047	...	39.9	...	2.14	...	85.39
August	54 271	45 799	19 105	15 360	35 166	...	11 986	...	39.7	...	2.15	...	85.36
September	54 228	45 734	19 057	15 330	35 171	...	11 956	...	39.4	...	2.16	...	85.10
October	54 144	45 642	18 952	15 231	35 192	...	11 846	...	39.7	...	2.16	...	85.75
November	53 962	45 446	18 799	15 112	35 163	...	11 726	...	39.3	...	2.15	...	84.50
December	53 744	45 147	18 548	14 947	35 196	...	11 556	...	38.4	...	2.16	...	82.94
1961													
January	53 683	45 119	18 508	14 863	35 175	...	11 473	...	39.3	...	2.16	...	84.89
February	53 556	44 969	18 418	14 801	35 138	...	11 414	...	39.4	...	2.16	...	85.10
March	53 662	45 051	18 438	14 802	35 224	...	11 410	...	39.5	...	2.16	...	85.32
April	53 626	44 997	18 432	14 825	35 194	...	11 444	...	39.5	...	2.18	...	86.11
May	53 785	45 121	18 523	14 932	35 262	...	11 544	...	39.7	...	2.19	...	86.94
June	53 977	45 289	18 618	14 981	35 359	...	11 593	...	40.0	...	2.20	...	88.00
July	54 123	45 399	18 640	15 029	35 483	...	11 639	...	40.0	...	2.21	...	88.40
August	54 298	45 534	18 725	15 093	35 573	...	11 701	...	40.1	...	2.22	...	89.02
September	54 388	45 592	18 730	15 080	35 658	...	11 679	...	39.5	...	2.20	...	86.90
October	54 522	45 717	18 805	15 143	35 717	...	11 731	...	40.3	...	2.23	...	89.87
November	54 743	45 931	18 927	15 259	35 816	...	11 842	...	40.7	...	2.23	...	90.76
December	54 871	46 035	18 981	15 309	35 890	...	11 872	...	40.4	...	2.24	...	90.50
1962													
January	54 891	46 040	18 936	15 322	35 955	...	11 865	...	40.0	...	2.25	...	90.00
February	55 187	46 309	19 109	15 411	36 078	...	11 950	...	40.4	...	2.26	...	91.30
March	55 276	46 375	19 109	15 451	36 167	...	11 970	...	40.6	...	2.26	...	91.76
April	55 602	46 680	19 258	15 524	36 344	...	12 034	...	40.6	...	2.26	...	91.76
May	55 627	46 669	19 253	15 513	36 374	...	12 011	...	40.6	...	2.27	...	92.16
June	55 644	46 644	19 186	15 518	36 458	...	12 006	...	40.5	...	2.26	...	91.53
July	55 746	46 720	19 248	15 522	36 498	...	12 004	...	40.5	...	2.27	...	91.94
August	55 838	46 775	19 251	15 517	36 587	...	11 990	...	40.5	...	2.28	...	92.34
September	55 977	46 888	19 305	15 568	36 672	...	12 033	...	40.5	...	2.28	...	92.34
October	56 041	46 927	19 301	15 569	36 740	...	12 034	...	40.3	...	2.29	...	92.29
November	56 056	46 911	19 260	15 530	36 796	...	11 977	...	40.5	...	2.29	...	92.75
December	56 028	46 902	19 219	15 520	36 809	...	11 961	...	40.3	...	2.29	...	92.29
1963													
January	56 116	46 912	19 257	15 545	36 859	...	11 974	...	40.5	...	2.30	...	93.15
February	56 230	46 999	19 228	15 542	37 002	...	11 965	...	40.5	...	2.31	...	93.56
March	56 322	47 077	19 233	15 564	37 089	...	11 990	...	40.5	...	2.32	...	93.96
April	56 580	47 316	19 343	15 602	37 237	...	12 029	...	40.5	...	2.32	...	93.96
May	56 616	47 328	19 399	15 641	37 217	...	12 066	...	40.5	...	2.33	...	94.37
June	56 658	47 356	19 371	15 624	37 287	...	12 050	...	40.7	...	2.34	...	95.24
July	56 794	47 460	19 423	15 646	37 371	...	12 080	...	40.6	...	2.35	...	95.41
August	56 910	47 542	19 437	15 644	37 473	...	12 060	...	40.6	...	2.34	...	95.00
September	57 077	47 660	19 483	15 674	37 594	...	12 088	...	40.6	...	2.36	...	95.82
October	57 284	47 805	19 517	15 714	37 767	...	12 131	...	40.7	...	2.36	...	96.05
November	57 255	47 771	19 456	15 675	37 799	...	12 072	...	40.7	...	2.37	...	96.46
December	57 360	47 863	19 493	15 712	37 867	...	12 108	...	40.6	...	2.38	...	96.63
1964													
January	57 487	47 925	19 406	15 715	38 081	39 913	12 132	38.2	40.1	2.50	2.38	95.50	95.44
February	57 751	48 170	19 570	15 742	38 181	40 123	12 165	38.5	40.7	2.50	2.38	96.25	96.87
March	57 898	48 287	19 587	15 770	38 311	40 171	12 190	38.5	40.6	2.50	2.38	96.25	96.63
April	57 922	48 278	19 593	15 785	38 329	40 209	12 211	38.6	40.7	2.52	2.40	97.27	97.68
May	58 089	48 419	19 630	15 812	38 459	40 332	12 231	38.6	40.8	2.52	2.40	97.27	97.92
June	58 221	48 552	19 682	15 839	38 539	40 448	12 255	38.6	40.8	2.53	2.41	97.66	98.33
July	58 413	48 736	19 740	15 887	38 673	40 624	12 309	38.5	40.8	2.53	2.41	97.41	98.33
August	58 619	48 887	19 810	15 948	38 809	40 771	12 354	38.5	40.9	2.55	2.42	98.18	98.98
September	58 903	49 117	19 943	16 073	38 860	41 026	12 409	38.5	40.9	2.55	2.44	98.18	99.80
October	58 794	48 949	19 723	15 821	39 071	40 828	12 224	38.5	40.7	2.55	2.40	98.18	97.68
November	59 217	49 338	20 026	16 096	39 191	41 157	12 477	38.6	41.0	2.56	2.42	98.82	99.22
December	59 421	49 524	20 111	16 176	39 310	41 307	12 551	38.7	41.2	2.58	2.44	99.85	100.53
1965													
January	59 583	49 646	20 173	16 245	39 410	41 453	12 603	38.7	41.3	2.58	2.45	99.85	101.19
February	59 800	49 826	20 216	16 291	39 584	41 583	12 644	38.7	41.3	2.59	2.46	100.23	101.60
March	60 003	49 993	20 292	16 353	39 711	41 674	12 701	38.7	41.3	2.60	2.47	100.62	102.01
April	60 259	50 208	20 317	16 418	39 942	41 885	12 752	38.7	41.2	2.60	2.47	100.62	101.76
May	60 492	50 398	20 444	16 477	40 048	42 044	12 792	38.8	41.3	2.62	2.49	101.66	102.84
June	60 690	50 562	20 522	16 554	40 168	42 183	12 854	38.6	41.2	2.62	2.49	101.13	102.59
July	60 963	50 762	20 611	16 669	40 352	42 364	12 962	38.6	41.2	2.63	2.49	101.52	102.59
August	61 228	50 957	20 726	16 732	40 502	42 537	12 994	38.5	41.1	2.64	2.50	101.64	102.75
September	61 490	51 152	20 808	16 802	40 682	42 726	13 046	38.6	41.1	2.65	2.51	102.29	103.16
October	61 718	51 340	20 895	16 864	40 823	42 871	13 100	38.5	41.2	2.66	2.52	102.41	103.82
November	61 997	51 561	21 021	16 962	40 976	43 045	13 175	38.6	41.3	2.67	2.52	103.06	104.08
December	62 321	51 822	21 151	17 051	41 170	43 270	13 243	38.6	41.3	2.68	2.53	103.45	104.49

. . . = Not available.

Table 10-8. Employment, Hours, and Earnings, Total Nonfarm and Manufacturing, Historical Annual and Monthly—*Continued*

(Wage and salary workers on nonfarm payrolls, seasonally adjusted.)

Year and month	All wage and salary workers (thousands)					Production and nonsupervisory workers on private payrolls							
	Total	Private			Service-providing	Number (thousands)		Average hours per week		Average hourly earnings, dollars		Average weekly earnings, dollars	
		Total	Goods-producing			Total private	Manufac-turing	Total private	Manufac-turing	Total private	Manufac-turing	Total private	Manufac-turing
			Total	Manufac-turing									
1966													
January	62 528	51 987	21 214	17 143	41 314	43 401	13 301	38.6	41.5	2.68	2.54	103.45	105.41
February	62 796	52 185	21 315	17 288	41 481	43 552	13 426	38.7	41.7	2.69	2.56	104.10	106.75
March	63 192	52 500	21 515	17 400	41 677	43 801	13 508	38.7	41.6	2.70	2.56	104.49	106.50
April	63 436	52 677	21 568	17 517	41 868	43 959	13 598	38.7	41.8	2.71	2.58	104.88	107.84
May	63 711	52 890	21 675	17 625	42 036	44 138	13 678	38.5	41.5	2.72	2.58	104.72	107.07
June	64 110	53 208	21 846	17 733	42 264	44 390	13 753	38.5	41.4	2.72	2.58	104.72	106.81
July	64 301	53 327	21 872	17 760	42 429	44 484	13 758	38.4	41.2	2.74	2.60	105.22	107.12
August	64 507	53 501	21 972	17 882	42 535	44 596	13 843	38.4	41.4	2.75	2.61	105.60	108.05
September	64 644	53 581	21 948	17 886	42 696	44 659	13 841	38.3	41.2	2.76	2.63	105.71	108.36
October	64 854	53 727	21 991	17 956	42 863	44 789	13 906	38.4	41.3	2.77	2.64	106.37	109.03
November	65 019	53 816	21 988	17 981	43 031	44 834	13 918	38.3	41.2	2.78	2.65	106.47	109.18
December	65 200	53 944	22 008	17 998	43 192	44 916	13 906	38.2	40.9	2.78	2.64	106.20	107.98
1967													
January	65 407	54 092	22 057	18 033	43 350	45 051	13 925	38.3	41.1	2.79	2.65	106.86	108.92
February	65 428	54 075	21 987	17 978	43 441	44 967	13 853	37.9	40.4	2.81	2.67	106.50	107.87
March	65 530	54 133	21 919	17 940	43 611	44 991	13 797	37.9	40.5	2.81	2.67	106.50	108.14
April	65 467	54 032	21 842	17 878	43 625	44 871	13 712	37.8	40.4	2.82	2.68	106.60	108.27
May	65 619	54 145	21 779	17 832	43 840	44 961	13 664	37.8	40.4	2.83	2.69	106.97	108.68
June	65 750	54 216	21 761	17 812	43 989	45 004	13 632	37.8	40.4	2.84	2.69	107.35	108.68
July	65 887	54 343	21 772	17 784	44 115	45 105	13 602	37.8	40.5	2.86	2.71	108.11	109.76
August	66 142	54 552	21 887	17 905	44 255	45 267	13 681	37.8	40.6	2.87	2.73	108.49	110.84
September	66 164	54 541	21 775	17 794	44 389	45 236	13 559	37.8	40.6	2.88	2.73	108.86	110.84
October	66 225	54 583	21 779	17 800	44 446	45 278	13 587	37.8	40.6	2.89	2.74	109.24	111.24
November	66 703	55 008	21 996	17 985	44 707	45 701	13 777	37.9	40.6	2.91	2.75	110.29	111.65
December	66 900	55 165	22 037	18 025	44 863	45 800	13 782	37.7	40.7	2.92	2.77	110.08	112.74
1968													
January	66 805	55 011	21 917	18 040	44 888	45 655	13 798	37.6	40.4	2.94	2.81	110.54	113.52
February	67 215	55 396	22 117	18 054	45 098	45 980	13 793	37.8	40.8	2.95	2.82	111.51	115.06
March	67 295	55 453	22 119	18 067	45 176	46 041	13 803	37.7	40.8	2.97	2.84	111.97	115.87
April	67 555	55 677	22 207	18 131	45 348	46 239	13 858	37.6	40.3	2.98	2.85	112.05	114.86
May	67 653	55 748	22 255	18 190	45 398	46 267	13 900	37.7	40.9	3.00	2.87	113.10	117.38
June	67 904	55 917	22 264	18 228	45 640	46 402	13 921	37.8	40.9	3.01	2.88	113.78	117.79
July	68 125	56 107	22 329	18 265	45 796	46 563	13 953	37.7	40.8	3.03	2.89	114.23	117.91
August	68 328	56 286	22 350	18 254	45 978	46 670	13 903	37.7	40.7	3.03	2.89	114.23	117.62
September	68 487	56 420	22 390	18 252	46 097	46 792	13 914	37.7	40.9	3.06	2.92	115.36	119.43
October	68 720	56 619	22 419	18 293	46 301	46 990	13 974	37.7	41.0	3.07	2.94	115.74	120.54
November	68 985	56 878	22 512	18 346	46 473	47 244	14 028	37.5	40.9	3.09	2.96	115.88	121.06
December	69 246	57 101	22 617	18 410	46 629	47 385	14 044	37.5	40.7	3.11	2.97	116.63	120.88
1969													
January	69 438	57 229	22 644	18 432	46 794	47 529	14 086	37.7	40.8	3.12	2.99	117.62	121.99
February	69 700	57 476	22 755	18 502	46 945	47 696	14 134	37.5	40.4	3.14	3.00	117.75	121.20
March	69 905	57 676	22 813	18 558	47 092	47 852	14 169	37.6	40.8	3.15	3.01	118.44	122.81
April	70 072	57 827	22 815	18 554	47 257	47 959	14 144	37.7	41.0	3.17	3.03	119.51	124.23
May	70 328	58 044	22 899	18 588	47 429	48 122	14 161	37.6	40.7	3.19	3.04	119.94	123.73
June	70 636	58 277	22 981	18 640	47 655	48 329	14 206	37.5	40.7	3.20	3.05	120.00	124.14
July	70 729	58 389	22 990	18 642	47 739	48 435	14 194	37.5	40.6	3.22	3.08	120.75	125.05
August	71 006	58 633	23 111	18 767	47 895	48 616	14 287	37.5	40.6	3.24	3.10	121.50	125.86
September	70 917	58 538	22 988	18 620	47 929	48 524	14 159	37.5	40.6	3.26	3.12	122.25	126.67
October	71 120	58 690	22 976	18 613	48 144	48 669	14 174	37.4	40.5	3.28	3.13	122.67	126.77
November	71 087	58 639	22 840	18 467	48 247	48 589	14 035	37.5	40.5	3.29	3.14	123.38	127.17
December	71 240	58 763	22 884	18 485	48 356	48 638	14 013	37.5	40.6	3.30	3.15	123.75	127.89
1970													
January	71 176	58 680	22 726	18 424	48 450	48 564	13 964	37.3	40.4	3.31	3.16	123.46	127.66
February	71 304	58 786	22 747	18 361	48 557	48 600	13 897	37.3	40.2	3.33	3.17	124.21	127.43
March	71 452	58 849	22 738	18 360	48 714	48 690	13 917	37.2	40.1	3.35	3.19	124.62	127.92
April	71 348	58 643	22 552	18 207	48 796	48 480	13 785	37.0	39.8	3.36	3.19	124.32	126.96
May	71 123	58 455	22 336	18 029	48 787	48 287	13 616	37.0	39.8	3.38	3.22	125.06	128.16
June	71 029	58 362	22 241	17 930	48 788	48 225	13 554	36.9	39.8	3.39	3.24	125.09	128.95
July	71 053	58 356	22 195	17 877	48 858	48 243	13 527	37.0	40.0	3.41	3.25	126.17	130.00
August	70 933	58 222	22 105	17 779	48 828	48 088	13 449	37.0	39.8	3.43	3.26	126.91	129.75
September	70 948	58 207	21 988	17 692	48 960	48 101	13 401	36.8	39.6	3.45	3.29	126.96	130.28
October	70 519	57 726	21 477	17 173	49 042	47 619	12 905	36.8	39.5	3.46	3.26	127.33	128.77
November	70 409	57 579	21 345	17 024	49 064	47 466	12 781	36.7	39.5	3.47	3.26	127.35	128.77
December	70 790	57 945	21 673	17 309	49 117	47 778	13 062	36.8	39.5	3.50	3.32	128.80	131.14
1971													
January	70 866	57 988	21 594	17 280	49 272	47 859	13 069	36.8	39.9	3.52	3.36	129.54	134.06
February	70 806	57 929	21 514	17 216	49 292	47 779	13 033	36.7	39.7	3.54	3.39	129.92	134.58
March	70 859	57 951	21 491	17 154	49 368	47 819	12 984	36.7	39.8	3.56	3.39	130.65	134.92
April	71 037	58 092	21 552	17 149	49 485	47 966	12 993	36.8	39.9	3.57	3.41	131.38	136.06
May	71 247	58 277	21 645	17 225	49 602	48 153	13 081	36.7	40.0	3.60	3.43	132.12	137.20
June	71 253	58 245	21 568	17 139	49 685	48 108	13 012	36.8	39.9	3.62	3.45	133.22	137.66
July	71 315	58 304	21 564	17 126	49 751	48 169	13 001	36.7	40.0	3.63	3.46	133.22	138.40
August	71 370	58 329	21 570	17 115	49 800	48 164	12 993	36.7	39.8	3.66	3.48	134.32	138.50
September	71 617	58 549	21 650	17 154	49 967	48 363	13 038	36.7	39.7	3.67	3.48	134.69	138.16
October	71 642	58 527	21 604	17 126	50 038	48 305	13 027	36.8	39.9	3.68	3.50	135.42	139.65
November	71 846	58 698	21 684	17 166	50 162	48 441	13 064	36.9	40.0	3.69	3.49	136.16	139.60
December	72 108	58 918	21 741	17 202	50 367	48 613	13 078	36.9	40.2	3.73	3.55	137.64	142.71

Table 10-8. Employment, Hours, and Earnings, Total Nonfarm and Manufacturing, Historical Annual and Monthly—*Continued*

(Wage and salary workers on nonfarm payrolls, seasonally adjusted.)

Year and month	All wage and salary workers (thousands)					Production and nonsupervisory workers on private payrolls							
	Total	Private			Service-providing	Number (thousands)		Average hours per week		Average hourly earnings, dollars		Average weekly earnings, dollars	
		Total	Goods-producing			Total private	Manufac-turing	Total private	Manufac-turing	Total private	Manufac-turing	Total private	Manufac-turing
			Total	Manufac-turing									
1972													
January	72 445	59 179	21 865	17 283	50 580	49 035	13 173	36.9	40.2	3.80	3.57	140.22	143.51
February	72 652	59 354	21 915	17 361	50 737	49 143	13 235	36.9	40.4	3.82	3.61	140.96	145.84
March	72 945	59 616	22 036	17 447	50 909	49 437	13 316	36.9	40.4	3.84	3.63	141.70	146.65
April	73 163	59 805	22 099	17 508	51 064	49 562	13 373	36.9	40.5	3.86	3.65	142.43	147.83
May	73 467	60 051	22 222	17 602	51 245	49 745	13 451	36.8	40.5	3.87	3.67	142.42	148.64
June	73 760	60 355	22 282	17 641	51 478	49 995	13 475	36.9	40.6	3.88	3.68	143.17	149.41
July	73 708	60 226	22 162	17 556	51 546	49 844	13 387	36.8	40.5	3.90	3.69	143.52	149.45
August	74 138	60 608	22 400	17 741	51 738	50 155	13 562	36.8	40.6	3.92	3.73	144.26	151.44
September	74 263	60 688	22 456	17 774	51 807	50 226	13 572	36.9	40.6	3.94	3.75	145.39	152.25
October	74 673	61 067	22 613	17 893	52 060	50 552	13 681	37.0	40.7	3.97	3.78	146.89	153.85
November	74 967	61 324	22 688	18 005	52 279	50 789	13 783	36.9	40.7	3.98	3.79	146.86	154.25
December	75 270	61 586	22 772	18 158	52 498	51 054	13 902	36.8	40.6	4.01	3.83	147.57	155.50
1973													
January	75 621	61 931	22 955	18 276	52 666	51 349	14 006	36.8	40.4	4.03	3.86	148.30	155.94
February	76 017	62 306	23 160	18 410	52 857	51 685	14 127	36.9	40.9	4.04	3.87	149.08	158.28
March	76 285	62 540	23 262	18 493	53 023	51 901	14 181	37.0	40.9	4.06	3.88	150.22	158.69
April	76 455	62 678	23 316	18 530	53 139	51 983	14 192	36.9	40.8	4.08	3.91	150.55	159.53
May	76 646	62 829	23 382	18 564	53 264	52 082	14 217	36.9	40.7	4.10	3.93	151.29	159.95
June	76 887	63 015	23 485	18 606	53 402	52 233	14 253	36.9	40.7	4.12	3.95	152.03	160.77
July	76 911	63 046	23 522	18 598	53 389	52 240	14 232	36.9	40.7	4.15	3.98	153.14	161.99
August	77 166	63 262	23 559	18 629	53 607	52 394	14 251	36.9	40.6	4.16	4.00	153.50	162.40
September	77 276	63 384	23 548	18 609	53 728	52 410	14 213	36.8	40.7	4.19	4.03	154.19	164.02
October	77 606	63 629	23 641	18 702	53 965	52 655	14 289	36.7	40.6	4.21	4.05	154.51	164.43
November	77 912	63 877	23 719	18 773	54 193	52 845	14 342	36.9	40.6	4.23	4.07	156.09	165.24
December	78 035	63 965	23 779	18 820	54 256	52 954	14 386	36.7	40.6	4.25	4.09	155.98	166.05
1974													
January	78 104	64 014	23 709	18 788	54 395	52 896	14 340	36.6	40.5	4.26	4.10	155.92	166.05
February	78 254	64 119	23 718	18 727	54 536	52 970	14 269	36.6	40.4	4.29	4.13	157.01	166.85
March	78 296	64 144	23 687	18 700	54 609	52 951	14 223	36.6	40.4	4.31	4.15	157.75	167.66
April	78 382	64 191	23 670	18 702	54 712	53 006	14 225	36.4	39.5	4.34	4.16	157.98	164.32
May	78 547	64 326	23 635	18 688	54 912	53 094	14 199	36.5	40.3	4.39	4.25	160.24	171.28
June	78 602	64 363	23 591	18 690	55 011	53 106	14 197	36.5	40.2	4.43	4.30	161.70	172.86
July	78 635	64 347	23 462	18 656	55 173	53 046	14 152	36.5	40.1	4.45	4.33	162.43	173.63
August	78 619	64 291	23 396	18 570	55 223	53 026	14 089	36.5	40.2	4.49	4.38	163.89	176.08
September	78 611	64 189	23 274	18 492	55 337	52 915	14 025	36.4	40.0	4.53	4.42	164.89	176.80
October	78 629	64 145	23 118	18 364	55 511	52 835	13 884	36.3	40.0	4.56	4.48	165.53	179.20
November	78 261	63 729	22 773	18 077	55 488	52 411	13 607	36.1	39.5	4.57	4.49	164.98	177.36
December	77 657	63 098	22 303	17 693	55 354	51 856	13 259	36.1	39.3	4.61	4.52	166.42	177.64
1975													
January	77 297	62 673	21 974	17 344	55 323	51 438	12 933	36.1	39.2	4.61	4.54	166.42	177.97
February	76 919	62 172	21 512	17 004	55 407	50 934	12 622	35.9	38.9	4.63	4.58	166.22	178.16
March	76 649	61 895	21 274	16 853	55 375	50 665	12 483	35.7	38.8	4.66	4.63	166.36	179.64
April	76 461	61 666	21 109	16 759	55 352	50 442	12 407	35.8	39.0	4.66	4.63	166.83	180.57
May	76 623	61 796	21 097	16 746	55 526	50 557	12 406	35.9	39.0	4.68	4.65	168.01	181.35
June	76 520	61 736	21 018	16 690	55 502	50 537	12 371	35.9	39.2	4.72	4.68	169.45	183.46
July	76 769	61 908	20 981	16 678	55 788	50 729	12 374	35.9	39.4	4.73	4.71	169.81	185.57
August	77 155	62 285	21 176	16 824	55 979	51 070	12 538	36.1	39.7	4.77	4.75	172.20	188.58
September	77 230	62 406	21 284	16 904	55 946	51 182	12 617	36.1	39.8	4.79	4.78	172.92	190.24
October	77 535	62 635	21 384	16 984	56 151	51 375	12 687	36.1	39.9	4.81	4.80	173.64	191.52
November	77 680	62 777	21 442	17 025	56 238	51 456	12 700	36.1	39.9	4.85	4.83	175.09	192.72
December	78 018	63 072	21 602	17 140	56 416	51 759	12 811	36.2	40.2	4.87	4.86	176.29	195.37
1976													
January	78 506	63 537	21 799	17 287	56 707	52 182	12 945	36.3	40.3	4.90	4.90	177.87	197.47
February	78 817	63 836	21 893	17 384	56 924	52 430	13 030	36.3	40.4	4.94	4.94	179.32	199.58
March	79 049	64 062	21 980	17 470	57 069	52 615	13 092	36.0	40.2	4.96	4.98	178.56	200.20
April	79 292	64 307	22 050	17 541	57 242	52 812	13 160	36.0	39.6	4.98	4.98	179.28	197.21
May	79 311	64 340	21 988	17 513	57 323	52 802	13 130	36.1	40.3	5.02	5.04	181.22	203.11
June	79 376	64 413	21 982	17 521	57 394	52 830	13 121	36.1	40.2	5.04	5.07	181.94	203.81
July	79 547	64 554	21 988	17 524	57 559	52 975	13 124	36.1	40.3	5.07	5.11	183.03	205.93
August	79 704	64 697	22 038	17 596	57 666	53 072	13 195	36.0	40.2	5.12	5.16	184.32	207.43
September	79 892	64 921	22 142	17 665	57 750	53 268	13 253	36.0	40.0	5.15	5.20	185.40	209.04
October	79 905	64 877	22 037	17 548	57 868	53 164	13 109	35.9	40.0	5.17	5.19	185.60	207.60
November	80 237	65 164	22 207	17 682	58 030	53 362	13 199	35.9	40.1	5.21	5.25	187.04	210.53
December	80 448	65 373	22 261	17 719	58 187	53 542	13 230	35.9	39.9	5.23	5.29	187.76	211.07
1977													
January	80 692	65 636	22 320	17 803	58 372	53 755	13 305	35.6	39.4	5.26	5.35	187.26	210.79
February	80 988	65 932	22 478	17 843	58 510	54 016	13 331	36.0	40.2	5.30	5.36	190.80	215.47
March	81 391	66 341	22 672	17 941	58 719	54 389	13 424	35.9	40.3	5.33	5.40	191.35	217.62
April	81 729	66 654	22 807	18 024	58 922	54 672	13 490	36.0	40.4	5.37	5.45	193.32	220.18
May	82 089	66 957	22 919	18 107	59 170	54 940	13 567	36.0	40.5	5.40	5.49	194.40	222.35
June	82 488	67 281	23 046	18 192	59 442	55 194	13 622	36.0	40.5	5.43	5.54	195.48	224.37
July	82 836	67 537	23 106	18 259	59 730	55 396	13 670	35.9	40.4	5.46	5.58	196.01	225.43
August	83 074	67 746	23 124	18 276	59 950	55 543	13 679	35.9	40.4	5.48	5.61	196.73	226.64
September	83 532	68 129	23 244	18 334	60 288	55 858	13 714	35.9	40.4	5.51	5.65	197.81	228.26
October	83 794	68 331	23 279	18 356	60 515	56 003	13 722	36.0	40.6	5.56	5.69	200.16	231.01
November	84 173	68 658	23 371	18 419	60 802	56 281	13 771	35.9	40.5	5.59	5.72	200.68	231.66
December	84 408	68 870	23 371	18 531	61 037	56 465	13 861	35.8	40.4	5.61	5.75	200.84	232.30

Table 10-8. Employment, Hours, and Earnings, Total Nonfarm and Manufacturing, Historical Annual and Monthly—*Continued*

(Wage and salary workers on nonfarm payrolls, seasonally adjusted.)

Year and month	All wage and salary workers (thousands)					Production and nonsupervisory workers on private payrolls							
	Total	Private			Service-providing	Number (thousands)		Average hours per week		Average hourly earnings, dollars		Average weekly earnings, dollars	
		Total	Goods-producing			Total private	Manufac-turing	Total private	Manufac-turing	Total private	Manufac-turing	Total private	Manufac-turing
			Total	Manufac-turing									
1978													
January	84 595	68 984	23 374	18 593	61 221	56 547	13 917	35.3	39.5	5.66	5.83	199.80	230.29
February	84 948	69 277	23 453	18 639	61 495	56 768	13 950	35.6	39.9	5.69	5.86	202.56	233.81
March	85 461	69 730	23 649	18 699	61 812	57 176	13 992	35.8	40.5	5.73	5.88	205.13	238.14
April	86 163	70 366	24 008	18 772	62 155	57 711	14 037	35.8	40.4	5.79	5.93	207.28	239.57
May	86 509	70 675	24 082	18 848	62 427	57 941	14 096	35.8	40.4	5.82	5.96	208.36	240.78
June	86 951	71 099	24 238	18 919	62 713	58 262	14 129	35.9	40.6	5.87	6.01	210.73	244.01
July	87 205	71 304	24 300	18 951	62 905	58 422	14 152	35.9	40.6	5.90	6.06	211.81	246.04
August	87 481	71 590	24 374	19 006	63 107	58 626	14 187	35.8	40.5	5.93	6.09	212.29	246.65
September	87 618	71 799	24 444	19 068	63 174	58 819	14 241	35.8	40.5	5.97	6.15	213.73	249.08
October	87 954	72 096	24 548	19 142	63 406	59 017	14 291	35.8	40.5	6.03	6.20	215.87	251.10
November	88 391	72 497	24 678	19 257	63 713	59 377	14 388	35.7	40.6	6.06	6.26	216.34	254.16
December	88 673	72 762	24 758	19 334	63 915	59 599	14 459	35.7	40.5	6.10	6.31	217.77	255.56
1979													
January	88 810	72 873	24 740	19 388	64 070	59 659	14 497	35.6	40.4	6.14	6.36	218.58	256.94
February	89 054	73 107	24 784	19 409	64 270	59 840	14 501	35.7	40.5	6.18	6.40	220.63	259.20
March	89 480	73 524	24 998	19 453	64 482	60 216	14 526	35.8	40.6	6.22	6.45	222.68	261.87
April	89 418	73 441	24 958	19 450	64 460	60 069	14 515	35.3	39.3	6.22	6.43	219.57	252.70
May	89 791	73 801	25 071	19 509	64 720	60 369	14 551	35.6	40.2	6.28	6.52	223.57	262.10
June	90 109	74 064	25 161	19 553	64 948	60 583	14 566	35.6	40.2	6.32	6.56	224.99	263.71
July	90 215	74 065	25 163	19 531	65 052	60 559	14 536	35.6	40.2	6.36	6.59	226.42	264.92
August	90 297	74 068	25 059	19 406	65 238	60 517	14 397	35.6	40.1	6.40	6.63	227.84	265.86
September	90 325	74 197	25 088	19 442	65 237	60 631	14 440	35.6	40.1	6.45	6.67	229.62	267.47
October	90 482	74 346	25 038	19 390	65 444	60 748	14 384	35.6	40.2	6.47	6.71	230.33	269.74
November	90 576	74 403	24 947	19 299	65 629	60 781	14 295	35.6	40.1	6.51	6.74	231.76	270.27
December	90 673	74 493	24 970	19 301	65 703	60 863	14 300	35.5	40.1	6.57	6.80	233.24	272.68
1980													
January	90 802	74 601	24 949	19 282	65 853	60 899	14 241	35.4	40.0	6.57	6.82	232.58	272.80
February	90 882	74 656	24 874	19 219	66 008	60 966	14 170	35.4	40.1	6.63	6.88	234.70	275.89
March	90 994	74 698	24 818	19 217	66 176	60 990	14 165	35.3	39.9	6.70	6.95	236.51	277.31
April	90 850	74 267	24 507	18 973	66 343	60 544	13 914	35.2	39.8	6.72	6.97	236.54	277.41
May	90 419	73 965	24 234	18 726	66 185	60 198	13 632	35.1	39.3	6.76	7.02	237.28	275.89
June	90 099	73 658	23 968	18 490	66 131	59 895	13 405	35.0	39.2	6.82	7.10	238.70	278.32
July	89 837	73 419	23 698	18 276	66 139	59 698	13 227	34.9	39.1	6.86	7.16	239.41	279.96
August	90 097	73 687	23 860	18 414	66 237	59 913	13 349	35.1	39.5	6.91	7.24	242.54	285.98
September	90 210	73 880	23 931	18 445	66 279	60 079	13 396	35.1	39.6	6.95	7.30	243.95	289.08
October	90 491	74 105	24 012	18 506	66 479	60 244	13 437	35.2	39.8	7.02	7.38	247.10	293.72
November	90 748	74 357	24 123	18 601	66 625	60 455	13 528	35.3	39.9	7.09	7.47	250.28	298.05
December	90 943	74 570	24 182	18 640	66 761	60 611	13 550	35.3	40.1	7.13	7.52	251.69	301.55
1981													
January	91 037	74 677	24 152	18 639	66 885	60 715	13 545	35.4	40.1	7.19	7.58	254.53	303.96
February	91 105	74 759	24 118	18 613	66 987	60 742	13 518	35.2	39.8	7.23	7.62	254.50	303.28
March	91 210	74 918	24 203	18 647	67 007	60 881	13 550	35.3	40.0	7.29	7.68	257.34	307.20
April	91 283	75 023	24 151	18 711	67 132	60 979	13 594	35.3	40.1	7.33	7.76	258.75	311.18
May	91 293	75 095	24 148	18 766	67 145	60 981	13 633	35.3	40.2	7.37	7.81	260.16	313.96
June	91 490	75 331	24 290	18 789	67 200	61 141	13 632	35.2	40.0	7.42	7.85	261.18	314.00
July	91 602	75 427	24 302	18 785	67 300	61 228	13 629	35.2	39.9	7.46	7.89	262.59	314.81
August	91 566	75 456	24 258	18 748	67 308	61 223	13 573	35.2	40.0	7.53	7.97	265.06	318.80
September	91 479	75 448	24 210	18 712	67 269	61 241	13 565	35.0	39.6	7.57	8.03	264.95	317.99
October	91 380	75 311	24 051	18 566	67 329	61 074	13 399	35.1	39.6	7.59	8.06	266.41	319.18
November	91 171	75 093	23 875	18 409	67 296	60 825	13 235	35.1	39.4	7.64	8.08	268.16	318.35
December	90 893	74 820	23 656	18 223	67 237	60 520	13 033	34.9	39.2	7.64	8.09	266.64	317.13
1982													
January	90 567	74 526	23 362	18 047	67 205	60 218	12 874	34.1	37.3	7.72	8.26	263.25	308.10
February	90 562	74 551	23 361	17 981	67 201	60 285	12 831	35.1	39.6	7.73	8.21	271.32	325.12
March	90 432	74 408	23 214	17 857	67 218	60 150	12 727	34.9	39.1	7.76	8.24	270.82	322.18
April	90 152	74 142	22 996	17 683	67 156	59 877	12 566	34.8	39.1	7.77	8.28	270.40	323.75
May	90 107	74 104	22 884	17 588	67 223	59 851	12 506	34.8	39.1	7.83	8.33	272.48	325.70
June	89 864	73 848	22 643	17 430	67 221	59 599	12 365	34.8	39.2	7.85	8.37	273.18	328.10
July	89 522	73 632	22 434	17 278	67 088	59 422	12 261	34.8	39.2	7.89	8.40	274.57	329.28
August	89 364	73 434	22 268	17 160	67 096	59 213	12 153	34.7	39.0	7.94	8.43	275.52	328.77
September	89 183	73 260	22 146	17 074	67 037	59 078	12 104	34.8	39.0	7.94	8.45	276.31	329.55
October	88 906	72 950	21 879	16 853	67 027	58 761	11 880	34.6	38.9	7.96	8.44	275.42	328.32
November	88 783	72 806	21 736	16 722	67 047	58 625	11 766	34.6	39.0	7.98	8.46	276.11	329.94
December	88 769	72 788	21 688	16 690	67 081	58 599	11 746	34.7	39.0	8.02	8.49	278.29	331.11
1983													
January	88 993	72 970	21 757	16 705	67 236	58 828	11 783	34.8	39.3	8.06	8.52	280.49	334.84
February	88 918	72 914	21 676	16 706	67 242	58 803	11 794	34.5	39.3	8.10	8.59	279.45	337.59
March	89 090	73 085	21 649	16 711	67 441	58 971	11 817	34.7	39.6	8.10	8.59	281.07	340.16
April	89 366	73 376	21 729	16 794	67 637	59 214	11 894	34.8	39.7	8.13	8.61	282.92	341.82
May	89 643	73 638	21 829	16 885	67 814	59 458	11 987	34.9	40.0	8.17	8.64	285.13	345.60
June	90 022	74 002	21 949	16 960	68 073	59 819	12 054	34.9	40.1	8.19	8.66	285.83	347.27
July	90 440	74 429	22 103	17 059	68 337	60 203	12 155	34.9	40.3	8.23	8.71	287.23	351.01
August	90 132	74 116	22 207	17 118	67 925	59 834	12 200	34.9	40.3	8.20	8.71	286.18	351.01
September	91 247	75 205	22 381	17 255	68 866	60 859	12 318	35.0	40.6	8.26	8.76	289.10	355.66
October	91 518	75 532	22 546	17 367	68 972	61 108	12 408	35.2	40.6	8.31	8.80	292.51	357.28
November	91 871	75 874	22 698	17 479	69 173	61 392	12 503	35.1	40.6	8.32	8.84	292.03	358.90
December	92 227	76 219	22 803	17 551	69 424	61 680	12 553	35.1	40.5	8.33	8.87	292.38	359.24

Table 10-8. Employment, Hours, and Earnings, Total Nonfarm and Manufacturing, Historical Annual and Monthly—*Continued*

(Wage and salary workers on nonfarm payrolls, seasonally adjusted.)

	All wage and salary workers (thousands)					Production and nonsupervisory workers on private payrolls							
		Private				Number (thousands)		Average hours per week		Average hourly earnings, dollars		Average weekly earnings, dollars	
Year and month	Total	Total	Goods-producing		Service-providing	Total private	Manufac-turing	Total private	Manufac-turing	Total private	Manufac-turing	Total private	Manufac-turing
			Total	Manufac-turing									
1984													
January	92 673	76 663	22 942	17 630	69 731	61 925	12 617	35.1	40.6	8.06	8.91	294.14	361.75
February	93 154	77 129	23 146	17 728	70 008	62 342	12 703	35.3	41.1	8.10	8.92	295.46	366.61
March	93 429	77 399	23 209	17 806	70 220	62 531	12 768	35.1	40.7	8.10	8.96	295.19	364.67
April	93 792	77 717	23 305	17 872	70 487	62 817	12 814	35.2	40.8	8.13	8.98	297.44	366.38
May	94 100	77 997	23 389	17 916	70 711	63 029	12 840	35.1	40.7	8.17	8.99	296.24	365.89
June	94 479	78 352	23 497	17 967	70 982	63 313	12 871	35.1	40.6	8.19	9.03	297.65	366.62
July	94 792	78 620	23 571	18 013	71 221	63 532	12 901	35.1	40.6	8.23	9.05	299.05	367.43
August	95 034	78 810	23 608	18 034	71 426	63 670	12 906	35.0	40.5	8.20	9.09	298.20	368.15
September	95 344	79 089	23 617	18 019	71 727	63 889	12 880	35.1	40.5	8.26	9.12	300.46	369.36
October	95 630	79 356	23 626	18 024	72 004	64 100	12 868	34.9	40.5	8.31	9.15	298.40	370.58
November	95 979	79 668	23 639	18 016	72 340	64 343	12 846	35.0	40.4	8.32	9.19	299.95	371.28
December	96 107	79 825	23 673	18 023	72 434	64 460	12 848	35.1	40.5	8.33	9.22	302.21	373.41
1985													
January	96 373	80 037	23 672	18 009	72 701	64 678	12 833	34.9	40.3	8.61	9.27	300.49	373.58
February	96 497	80 148	23 621	17 966	72 876	64 775	12 784	34.8	40.1	8.64	9.29	300.67	372.53
March	96 843	80 448	23 661	17 939	73 182	65 026	12 758	34.9	40.4	8.67	9.32	302.58	376.53
April	97 039	80 609	23 644	17 886	73 395	65 133	12 701	34.9	40.5	8.69	9.35	303.28	378.68
May	97 313	80 839	23 632	17 855	73 681	65 328	12 673	34.9	40.4	8.70	9.37	303.63	378.55
June	97 459	80 961	23 592	17 819	73 867	65 403	12 635	34.9	40.5	8.74	9.39	305.03	380.30
July	97 649	81 029	23 549	17 776	74 100	65 450	12 596	34.8	40.4	8.74	9.42	304.15	380.57
August	97 842	81 223	23 546	17 756	74 296	65 633	12 593	34.8	40.6	8.77	9.43	305.20	382.86
September	98 045	81 407	23 528	17 718	74 517	65 769	12 556	34.8	40.6	8.80	9.44	306.24	383.26
October	98 233	81 579	23 529	17 708	74 704	65 939	12 556	34.8	40.7	8.79	9.46	305.89	385.02
November	98 442	81 768	23 520	17 697	74 922	66 089	12 545	34.8	40.7	8.82	9.49	306.94	386.24
December	98 609	81 915	23 518	17 693	75 091	66 219	12 550	34.9	40.9	8.87	9.55	309.56	390.60
1986													
January	98 734	82 019	23 530	17 686	75 204	66 316	12 546	35.0	40.7	8.85	9.53	309.75	387.87
February	98 841	82 082	23 485	17 663	75 356	66 387	12 530	34.8	40.7	8.88	9.56	309.02	389.09
March	98 935	82 180	23 428	17 624	75 507	66 425	12 498	34.8	40.7	8.89	9.58	309.37	389.91
April	99 122	82 357	23 427	17 616	75 695	66 554	12 495	34.7	40.5	8.89	9.56	308.48	387.18
May	99 249	82 459	23 349	17 593	75 900	66 635	12 474	34.8	40.7	8.90	9.59	309.72	390.31
June	99 155	82 376	23 263	17 530	75 892	66 558	12 424	34.7	40.7	8.91	9.58	309.18	389.91
July	99 473	82 694	23 235	17 497	76 238	66 829	12 389	34.6	40.6	8.92	9.60	308.63	389.76
August	99 587	82 787	23 225	17 489	76 362	66 927	12 399	34.7	40.7	8.94	9.61	310.22	391.13
September	99 934	83 024	23 216	17 498	76 718	67 133	12 411	34.6	40.7	8.94	9.60	309.32	390.72
October	100 120	83 151	23 208	17 477	76 912	67 230	12 396	34.6	40.6	8.96	9.62	310.02	390.57
November	100 306	83 301	23 204	17 472	77 102	67 368	12 407	34.7	40.7	9.00	9.64	312.30	392.35
December	100 511	83 490	23 237	17 478	77 274	67 517	12 425	34.6	40.8	9.01	9.66	311.75	394.13
1987													
January	100 683	83 638	23 232	17 465	77 451	67 638	12 405	34.7	40.8	9.02	9.67	312.99	394.54
February	100 915	83 879	23 296	17 499	77 619	67 869	12 438	34.9	41.2	9.05	9.69	315.85	399.23
March	101 164	84 100	23 307	17 507	77 857	68 015	12 446	34.7	41.0	9.07	9.71	314.73	398.11
April	101 502	84 393	23 342	17 525	78 160	68 261	12 465	34.7	40.8	9.08	9.71	315.08	396.17
May	101 728	84 616	23 390	17 542	78 338	68 467	12 481	34.8	41.0	9.11	9.73	317.03	398.93
June	101 900	84 776	23 390	17 537	78 510	68 579	12 482	34.7	40.9	9.11	9.74	316.12	398.37
July	102 247	85 087	23 455	17 593	78 792	68 819	12 521	34.7	41.0	9.12	9.74	316.46	399.34
August	102 418	85 246	23 506	17 630	78 912	68 941	12 560	34.9	40.9	9.18	9.80	320.38	400.82
September	102 646	85 511	23 566	17 691	79 080	69 164	12 614	34.7	40.8	9.19	9.85	318.89	401.88
October	103 138	85 869	23 655	17 729	79 483	69 442	12 637	34.8	41.1	9.22	9.84	320.86	404.42
November	103 370	86 071	23 711	17 775	79 659	69 621	12 678	34.8	41.0	9.27	9.87	322.60	404.67
December	103 664	86 317	23 772	17 809	79 892	69 852	12 707	34.6	41.0	9.28	9.89	321.09	405.49
1988													
January	103 758	86 393	23 668	17 790	80 090	69 859	12 684	34.6	41.1	9.29	9.91	321.43	407.30
February	104 211	86 822	23 769	17 823	80 442	70 255	12 706	34.7	41.1	9.29	9.92	322.36	407.71
March	104 487	87 040	23 824	17 844	80 663	70 397	12 712	34.5	40.9	9.31	9.94	321.20	406.55
April	104 732	87 280	23 880	17 874	80 852	70 604	12 733	34.6	41.0	9.36	9.99	323.86	409.59
May	104 961	87 480	23 896	17 892	81 065	70 749	12 747	34.6	41.0	9.41	10.02	325.59	410.82
June	105 324	87 809	23 951	17 916	81 373	71 031	12 767	34.6	41.1	9.42	10.04	325.93	412.64
July	105 546	88 052	23 966	17 926	81 580	71 235	12 774	34.7	41.1	9.45	10.05	327.92	413.06
August	105 670	88 126	23 926	17 891	81 744	71 287	12 752	34.5	40.9	9.46	10.07	326.37	411.86
September	106 009	88 375	23 942	17 914	82 067	71 487	12 764	34.5	41.0	9.51	10.12	328.10	414.92
October	106 277	88 607	23 987	17 966	82 290	71 680	12 812	34.7	41.1	9.56	10.16	331.73	417.58
November	106 616	88 870	24 030	18 003	82 586	71 902	12 851	34.5	41.1	9.58	10.19	330.51	418.81
December	106 906	89 170	24 054	18 025	82 852	72 175	12 864	34.6	40.9	9.60	10.20	332.16	417.18
1989													
January	107 168	89 394	24 097	18 057	83 071	72 393	12 882	34.7	41.1	9.65	10.23	334.86	420.45
February	107 426	89 614	24 080	18 055	83 346	72 577	12 880	34.5	41.2	9.68	10.26	333.96	422.71
March	107 619	89 797	24 069	18 060	83 550	72 695	12 878	34.5	41.1	9.70	10.29	334.65	422.92
April	107 792	89 952	24 100	18 055	83 692	72 819	12 867	34.6	41.1	9.75	10.28	337.35	422.51
May	107 910	90 034	24 089	18 040	83 821	72 889	12 852	34.4	41.0	9.73	10.30	334.71	422.30
June	108 026	90 114	24 052	18 013	83 974	72 941	12 822	34.4	40.9	9.77	10.33	336.09	422.50
July	108 066	90 161	24 027	17 980	84 039	72 972	12 790	34.5	40.9	9.82	10.36	338.79	423.72
August	108 115	90 126	24 048	17 964	84 067	72 940	12 790	34.5	40.9	9.83	10.39	339.14	424.95
September	108 365	90 338	24 000	17 922	84 365	73 114	12 745	34.4	40.8	9.87	10.41	339.53	424.73
October	108 476	90 443	23 997	17 895	84 479	73 211	12 723	34.6	40.8	9.93	10.43	343.58	425.54
November	108 753	90 696	24 009	17 886	84 744	73 427	12 713	34.4	40.7	9.93	10.44	341.59	424.91
December	108 849	90 774	23 949	17 881	84 900	73 504	12 705	34.3	40.5	9.98	10.49	342.31	424.85

Table 10-8. Employment, Hours, and Earnings, Total Nonfarm and Manufacturing, Historical Annual and Monthly—Continued

(Wage and salary workers on nonfarm payrolls, seasonally adjusted.)

Year and month	All wage and salary workers (thousands)					Production and nonsupervisory workers on private payrolls							
	Total	Private			Service-providing	Number (thousands)		Average hours per week		Average hourly earnings, dollars		Average weekly earnings, dollars	
		Total	Goods-producing			Total private	Manufacturing	Total private	Manufacturing	Total private	Manufacturing	Total private	Manufacturing
			Total	Manufacturing									
1990													
January	109 183	91 032	23 981	17 796	85 202	73 738	12 738	34.5	40.5	10.02	10.52	345.69	426.06
February	109 432	91 255	24 071	17 893	85 361	73 935	12 848	34.4	40.6	10.07	10.64	346.41	431.98
March	109 647	91 353	24 023	17 868	85 624	73 995	12 821	34.4	40.7	10.11	10.70	347.78	435.49
April	109 688	91 311	23 967	17 846	85 721	73 961	12 804	34.3	40.5	10.12	10.68	347.46	432.54
May	109 838	91 239	23 887	17 796	85 951	73 873	12 755	34.3	40.6	10.16	10.74	348.49	436.04
June	109 863	91 307	23 850	17 777	86 013	73 867	12 739	34.4	40.7	10.20	10.78	351.22	438.75
July	109 833	91 273	23 745	17 703	86 088	73 807	12 673	34.2	40.6	10.22	10.80	349.52	438.48
August	109 613	91 156	23 648	17 649	85 965	73 744	12 624	34.2	40.5	10.24	10.81	350.21	437.81
September	109 525	91 088	23 571	17 609	85 954	73 636	12 596	34.2	40.5	10.28	10.86	351.58	439.83
October	109 366	90 923	23 473	17 577	85 893	73 504	12 577	34.1	40.4	10.30	10.92	351.23	441.17
November	109 216	90 766	23 283	17 428	85 933	73 351	12 439	34.2	40.2	10.32	10.89	352.94	437.78
December	109 160	90 692	23 203	17 395	85 957	73 285	12 415	34.2	40.3	10.35	10.93	353.97	440.48
1991													
January	109 039	90 565	23 060	17 329	85 979	73 143	12 351	34.1	40.2	10.38	10.98	353.96	441.40
February	108 735	90 253	22 900	17 211	85 835	72 855	12 242	34.1	40.1	10.39	10.97	354.30	439.90
March	108 577	90 089	22 779	17 140	85 798	72 704	12 191	34.0	40.0	10.41	11.00	353.94	440.00
April	108 367	89 882	22 688	17 094	85 679	72 535	12 157	34.0	40.1	10.46	11.05	355.64	443.11
May	108 240	89 742	22 617	17 069	85 623	72 438	12 148	34.0	40.1	10.49	11.09	356.66	444.71
June	108 338	89 777	22 571	17 044	85 767	72 459	12 135	34.1	40.5	10.51	11.13	358.73	450.77
July	108 302	89 704	22 507	17 015	85 795	72 427	12 130	34.1	40.5	10.54	11.17	359.41	452.39
August	108 308	89 741	22 493	17 025	85 815	72 484	12 153	34.1	40.6	10.56	11.18	360.10	453.91
September	108 340	89 797	22 466	17 010	85 874	72 501	12 140	34.1	40.6	10.58	11.22	360.78	455.53
October	108 356	89 763	22 418	16 999	85 938	72 476	12 138	34.2	40.6	10.59	11.25	362.18	456.75
November	108 299	89 672	22 316	16 961	85 983	72 405	12 102	34.1	40.7	10.61	11.26	361.80	458.28
December	108 324	89 683	22 274	16 916	86 050	72 448	12 075	34.1	40.7	10.64	11.27	362.82	458.69
1992													
January	108 378	89 690	22 214	16 840	86 164	72 490	12 013	34.1	40.6	10.65	11.24	363.17	456.34
February	108 313	89 624	22 172	16 828	86 172	72 467	12 015	34.1	40.7	10.67	11.30	363.85	459.91
March	108 368	89 653	22 127	16 805	86 241	72 484	12 006	34.1	40.7	10.70	11.32	364.87	460.72
April	108 527	89 788	22 132	16 831	86 395	72 637	12 029	34.3	41.0	10.72	11.36	367.70	464.62
May	108 654	89 901	22 135	16 835	86 519	72 752	12 046	34.3	40.9	10.74	11.39	368.38	465.85
June	108 721	89 959	22 097	16 826	86 624	72 788	12 042	34.2	40.8	10.77	11.41	368.33	465.53
July	108 790	89 973	22 075	16 820	86 715	72 809	12 049	34.2	40.8	10.79	11.43	369.02	466.34
August	108 930	90 047	22 045	16 783	86 885	72 886	12 020	34.2	40.8	10.82	11.46	370.04	467.57
September	108 966	90 137	22 020	16 761	86 946	72 988	12 002	34.3	40.7	10.82	11.45	371.13	466.02
October	109 145	90 317	22 028	16 750	87 117	73 143	11 999	34.2	40.8	10.85	11.47	371.41	467.98
November	109 284	90 443	22 042	16 758	87 242	73 294	12 012	34.2	40.9	10.87	11.49	371.75	469.94
December	109 494	90 616	22 075	16 768	87 419	73 478	12 031	34.2	40.9	10.89	11.51	372.78	470.76
1993													
January	109 805	90 904	22 133	16 791	87 672	73 754	12 060	34.3	41.1	10.93	11.55	375.24	474.71
February	110 047	91 145	22 188	16 805	87 859	74 011	12 072	34.3	41.1	10.94	11.57	375.59	475.53
March	109 998	91 091	22 142	16 795	87 856	73 928	12 074	34.1	40.8	10.99	11.59	374.76	472.87
April	110 306	91 368	22 131	16 772	88 175	74 153	12 056	34.4	41.5	10.99	11.64	378.40	483.06
May	110 573	91 622	22 189	16 766	88 384	74 410	12 056	34.3	41.1	11.02	11.66	377.99	479.23
June	110 754	91 785	22 165	16 742	88 589	74 511	12 039	34.3	40.9	11.03	11.67	378.67	477.30
July	111 053	91 993	22 184	16 740	88 869	74 706	12 043	34.4	41.1	11.05	11.69	380.46	480.46
August	111 212	92 184	22 203	16 741	89 009	74 881	12 050	34.3	41.1	11.08	11.72	380.04	481.69
September	111 451	92 410	22 252	16 769	89 199	75 072	12 080	34.4	41.3	11.10	11.76	381.84	485.69
October	111 737	92 695	22 306	16 778	89 431	75 318	12 092	34.4	41.3	11.13	11.79	382.87	486.93
November	111 999	92 931	22 347	16 800	89 652	75 537	12 119	34.4	41.3	11.15	11.83	383.56	488.58
December	112 311	93 202	22 413	16 815	89 898	75 762	12 140	34.4	41.4	11.18	11.88	384.59	491.83
1994													
January	112 583	93 436	22 465	16 855	90 118	75 967	12 181	34.4	41.4	11.21	11.89	385.62	492.25
February	112 783	93 633	22 451	16 862	90 332	76 174	12 198	34.2	40.9	11.25	11.97	384.75	489.57
March	113 248	94 058	22 550	16 897	90 698	76 536	12 234	34.5	41.7	11.25	11.95	388.13	498.32
April	113 597	94 374	22 641	16 933	90 956	76 833	12 276	34.5	41.8	11.27	11.96	388.82	498.73
May	113 931	94 667	22 704	16 962	91 227	77 112	12 304	34.5	41.8	11.29	11.98	389.85	500.76
June	114 247	94 973	22 764	17 010	91 483	77 363	12 351	34.5	41.8	11.31	12.01	390.54	502.02
July	114 624	95 323	22 806	17 025	91 818	77 658	12 367	34.6	41.8	11.34	12.02	392.36	502.44
August	114 902	95 596	22 876	17 081	92 026	77 901	12 428	34.5	41.7	11.36	12.05	391.92	502.49
September	115 253	95 916	22 947	17 114	92 306	78 166	12 459	34.5	41.6	11.39	12.09	392.96	502.94
October	115 468	96 124	22 975	17 145	92 493	78 349	12 489	34.5	41.8	11.42	12.11	394.34	506.20
November	115 887	96 520	23 050	17 186	92 837	78 697	12 529	34.5	41.7	11.45	12.15	395.03	507.87
December	116 162	96 774	23 095	17 217	93 067	78 942	12 558	34.5	41.8	11.47	12.17	396.06	508.71
1995													
January	116 487	97 090	23 146	17 261	93 341	79 181	12 593	34.5	41.8	11.49	12.19	396.41	509.54
February	116 691	97 284	23 103	17 265	93 588	79 338	12 602	34.4	41.7	11.52	12.24	396.63	510.41
March	116 913	97 486	23 151	17 263	93 762	79 518	12 600	34.3	41.5	11.55	12.25	396.17	508.38
April	117 075	97 641	23 174	17 278	93 901	79 651	12 608	34.3	41.1	11.56	12.25	396.85	503.48
May	117 059	97 641	23 120	17 259	93 939	79 673	12 590	34.2	41.2	11.60	12.28	396.72	505.94
June	117 294	97 849	23 137	17 247	94 157	79 842	12 574	34.3	41.2	11.63	12.31	398.91	507.17
July	117 395	97 958	23 118	17 217	94 277	79 909	12 538	34.1	41.1	11.67	12.38	400.28	508.82
August	117 644	98 215	23 164	17 240	94 480	80 159	12 566	34.3	41.2	11.69	12.39	401.92	510.47
September	117 885	98 455	23 207	17 246	94 678	80 356	12 567	34.3	41.2	11.73	12.41	402.34	511.29
October	118 041	98 577	23 207	17 217	94 834	80 477	12 535	34.3	41.2	11.75	12.43	403.37	512.12
November	118 189	98 726	23 200	17 209	94 989	80 551	12 515	34.3	41.3	11.78	12.45	404.05	514.19
December	118 321	98 855	23 208	17 230	95 113	80 702	12 551	34.2	40.9	11.81	12.49	403.90	510.84

Table 10-8. Employment, Hours, and Earnings, Total Nonfarm and Manufacturing, Historical Annual and Monthly—Continued

(Wage and salary workers on nonfarm payrolls, seasonally adjusted.)

Year and month	All wage and salary workers (thousands)					Production and nonsupervisory workers on private payrolls							
	Total	Private			Service-providing	Number (thousands)		Average hours per week		Average hourly earnings, dollars		Average weekly earnings, dollars	
		Total	Goods-producing			Total private	Manufac-turing	Total private	Manufac-turing	Total private	Manufac-turing	Total private	Manufac-turing
			Total	Manufac-turing									
1996													
January	118 303	98 853	23 196	17 208	95 107	80 627	12 517	33.8	39.7	11.87	12.60	401.21	500.22
February	118 735	99 250	23 281	17 230	95 454	81 019	12 533	34.3	41.3	11.87	12.55	407.14	518.32
March	119 001	99 469	23 276	17 193	95 725	81 197	12 488	34.3	41.1	11.89	12.50	407.83	513.75
April	119 165	99 650	23 316	17 204	95 849	81 364	12 505	34.2	41.1	11.96	12.69	409.03	521.56
May	119 485	99 956	23 357	17 221	96 128	81 625	12 518	34.3	41.4	11.97	12.71	410.91	526.19
June	119 774	100 246	23 399	17 226	96 375	81 838	12 522	34.4	41.5	12.03	12.76	414.18	529.54
July	120 029	100 482	23 417	17 222	96 612	82 037	12 517	34.3	41.4	12.06	12.79	413.66	529.51
August	120 202	100 698	23 479	17 255	96 723	82 234	12 546	34.4	41.5	12.09	12.83	416.24	532.45
September	120 427	100 860	23 497	17 252	96 930	82 358	12 544	34.4	41.6	12.14	12.85	417.62	534.56
October	120 677	101 123	23 546	17 268	97 131	82 606	12 559	34.4	41.4	12.16	12.83	418.30	531.16
November	120 976	101 411	23 585	17 278	97 391	82 791	12 560	34.4	41.5	12.21	12.88	420.02	534.52
December	121 146	101 575	23 598	17 284	97 548	82 960	12 571	34.4	41.7	12.25	12.95	421.40	540.02
1997													
January	121 382	101 789	23 619	17 298	97 763	83 106	12 579	34.3	41.4	12.29	12.99	421.89	537.79
February	121 684	102 086	23 686	17 316	97 998	83 387	12 592	34.4	41.6	12.32	13.00	423.81	540.80
March	122 000	102 392	23 739	17 340	98 261	83 617	12 613	34.5	41.8	12.37	13.04	426.77	545.07
April	122 293	102 690	23 766	17 350	98 527	83 868	12 618	34.6	41.8	12.39	13.03	428.69	544.65
May	122 551	102 950	23 809	17 362	98 742	84 093	12 647	34.6	41.7	12.43	13.07	430.08	545.02
June	122 818	103 158	23 834	17 387	98 984	84 232	12 647	34.3	41.5	12.46	13.09	427.72	543.24
July	123 131	103 445	23 862	17 389	99 269	84 480	12 645	34.5	41.6	12.50	13.09	431.25	544.54
August	123 092	103 475	23 952	17 452	99 140	84 427	12 699	34.6	41.7	12.57	13.17	434.92	549.19
September	123 604	103 925	23 996	17 465	99 608	84 822	12 711	34.6	41.7	12.60	13.17	436.31	549.19
October	123 945	104 207	24 053	17 513	99 892	85 032	12 746	34.6	41.8	12.67	13.29	438.38	555.52
November	124 251	104 490	24 112	17 556	100 139	85 226	12 777	34.5	41.8	12.72	13.32	440.11	556.78
December	124 554	104 788	24 184	17 588	100 370	85 459	12 800	34.6	41.9	12.75	13.35	441.50	559.37
1998													
January	124 830	105 060	24 262	17 619	100 568	85 621	12 818	34.6	41.9	12.79	13.35	442.88	559.37
February	125 026	105 240	24 283	17 627	100 743	85 790	12 828	34.5	41.7	12.84	13.39	444.61	558.36
March	125 177	105 385	24 264	17 637	100 913	85 820	12 822	34.5	41.6	12.88	13.43	444.71	558.69
April	125 456	105 640	24 340	17 637	101 116	86 040	12 814	34.4	41.3	12.92	13.40	444.79	553.42
May	125 862	105 987	24 361	17 624	101 501	86 320	12 790	34.5	41.5	12.97	13.45	448.76	558.18
June	126 080	106 201	24 387	17 608	101 693	86 470	12 769	34.4	41.4	12.99	13.43	447.20	556.00
July	126 204	106 274	24 238	17 422	101 966	86 488	12 558	34.5	41.4	13.01	13.34	448.85	552.28
August	126 551	106 592	24 420	17 563	102 131	86 774	12 702	34.5	41.4	13.08	13.46	451.61	557.24
September	126 775	106 790	24 420	17 558	102 355	86 935	12 715	34.4	41.3	13.11	13.52	451.33	558.38
October	126 971	106 970	24 405	17 511	102 566	87 085	12 673	34.5	41.4	13.15	13.53	453.68	560.14
November	127 254	107 210	24 394	17 465	102 860	87 251	12 634	34.4	41.4	13.17	13.54	453.39	560.56
December	127 601	107 522	24 454	17 449	103 147	87 517	12 625	34.5	41.5	13.22	13.56	456.09	562.74
1999													
January	127 726	107 642	24 401	17 427	103 325	87 577	12 605	34.4	41.3	13.27	13.59	456.83	561.27
February	128 137	107 993	24 434	17 395	103 703	87 891	12 575	34.4	41.3	13.30	13.63	457.52	564.28
March	128 244	108 076	24 378	17 368	103 866	87 954	12 562	34.3	41.3	13.33	13.69	457.56	565.40
April	128 619	108 382	24 424	17 343	104 195	88 183	12 540	34.4	41.4	13.38	13.73	460.62	567.05
May	128 831	108 602	24 445	17 333	104 386	88 368	12 534	34.3	41.4	13.43	13.80	460.65	571.32
June	129 092	108 820	24 434	17 295	104 658	88 543	12 503	34.4	41.3	13.47	13.86	463.71	572.42
July	129 411	109 072	24 474	17 308	104 937	88 751	12 525	34.4	41.4	13.52	13.92	465.09	576.29
August	129 578	109 203	24 468	17 288	105 110	88 862	12 502	34.4	41.5	13.54	13.93	466.12	578.10
September	129 791	109 387	24 485	17 281	105 306	89 003	12 495	34.3	41.5	13.61	13.99	467.17	580.59
October	130 192	109 735	24 506	17 273	105 686	89 307	12 484	34.4	41.4	13.64	13.99	469.22	579.19
November	130 483	109 987	24 561	17 282	105 922	89 526	12 488	34.4	41.4	13.66	14.01	469.90	580.01
December	130 778	110 238	24 582	17 280	106 196	89 745	12 490	34.4	41.4	13.70	14.06	471.62	582.08
2000													
January	131 008	110 437	24 627	17 283	106 381	89 897	12 491	34.4	41.5	13.75	14.13	473.34	586.40
February	131 138	110 539	24 608	17 284	106 530	89 977	12 481	34.4	41.5	13.80	14.15	474.72	587.23
March	131 606	110 873	24 705	17 302	106 901	90 244	12 490	34.4	41.4	13.84	14.18	476.44	587.05
April	131 893	111 091	24 688	17 298	107 205	90 468	12 477	34.4	41.6	13.90	14.23	478.50	591.97
May	132 119	110 972	24 647	17 279	107 472	90 375	12 464	34.3	41.3	13.94	14.23	478.14	587.70
June	132 074	111 187	24 674	17 298	107 400	90 544	12 468	34.3	41.3	13.98	14.30	479.86	590.59
July	132 251	111 384	24 717	17 322	107 534	90 674	12 474	34.3	41.5	14.03	14.32	481.23	594.28
August	132 237	111 400	24 684	17 288	107 553	90 698	12 431	34.2	41.0	14.07	14.36	481.19	588.76
September	132 371	111 636	24 642	17 230	107 729	90 847	12 382	34.3	41.1	14.13	14.40	484.66	591.84
October	132 357	111 614	24 639	17 218	107 718	90 835	12 357	34.3	41.1	14.18	14.49	486.37	595.54
November	132 582	111 822	24 624	17 203	107 958	90 966	12 336	34.2	41.1	14.24	14.52	487.01	596.77
December	132 724	111 920	24 576	17 182	108 148	91 015	12 307	34.0	40.4	14.29	14.50	485.86	585.80
2001													
January	132 694	111 859	24 531	17 102	108 163	90 965	12 229	34.2	40.6	14.29	14.48	489.06	587.89
February	132 766	111 860	24 473	17 027	108 293	90 923	12 155	34.0	40.5	14.37	14.55	490.02	589.28
March	132 741	111 796	24 408	16 937	108 333	90 876	12 085	34.1	40.5	14.42	14.58	492.06	590.49
April	132 460	111 468	24 254	16 802	108 206	90 640	11 982	34.0	40.5	14.45	14.64	491.64	592.92
May	132 422	111 393	24 119	16 661	108 303	90 565	11 859	34.0	40.4	14.50	14.69	493.00	593.48
June	132 293	111 156	23 967	16 517	108 326	90 369	11 739	34.0	40.3	14.55	14.74	494.70	594.02
July	132 178	110 993	23 836	16 381	108 342	90 253	11 632	34.0	40.6	14.55	14.82	495.04	601.69
August	132 020	110 802	23 668	16 233	108 352	90 100	11 495	33.9	40.3	14.60	14.85	494.94	598.46
September	131 778	110 536	23 537	16 117	108 241	89 837	11 400	33.8	40.2	14.64	14.89	495.17	598.58
October	131 454	110 179	23 379	15 973	108 075	89 552	11 286	33.7	40.1	14.66	14.90	494.38	597.49
November	131 160	109 834	23 210	15 826	107 950	89 232	11 175	33.8	40.1	14.72	14.96	497.87	599.90
December	130 989	109 634	23 095	15 712	107 894	89 142	11 081	33.9	40.2	14.75	15.01	500.36	603.40

Table 10-8. Employment, Hours, and Earnings, Total Nonfarm and Manufacturing, Historical Annual and Monthly—*Continued*

(Wage and salary workers on nonfarm payrolls, seasonally adjusted.)

Year and month	All wage and salary workers (thousands)					Production and nonsupervisory workers on private payrolls							
	Total	Private			Service-providing	Number (thousands)		Average hours per week		Average hourly earnings, dollars		Average weekly earnings, dollars	
		Total	Goods-producing			Total private	Manufac-turing	Total private	Manufac-turing	Total private	Manufac-turing	Total private	Manufac-turing
			Total	Manufac-turing									
2002													
January	130 847	109 470	22 959	15 585	107 888	89 083	10 993	33.8	40.1	14.76	15.05	499.23	603.51
February	130 714	109 324	22 875	15 514	107 839	89 048	10 951	33.8	40.3	14.78	15.11	499.90	608.93
March	130 695	109 264	22 786	15 443	107 909	89 006	10 901	33.9	40.6	14.82	15.15	502.74	615.09
April	130 615	109 172	22 689	15 392	107 926	88 851	10 859	33.9	40.6	14.84	15.17	503.08	615.90
May	130 607	109 093	22 604	15 337	108 003	88 711	10 824	33.9	40.6	14.88	15.24	504.77	618.74
June	130 664	109 115	22 579	15 299	108 085	88 636	10 797	34.0	40.7	14.94	15.27	506.81	621.49
July	130 579	109 035	22 521	15 256	108 058	88 487	10 764	33.8	40.4	14.98	15.29	506.66	617.72
August	130 564	108 975	22 450	15 172	108 114	88 414	10 697	33.9	40.5	15.02	15.34	509.52	621.27
September	130 504	108 958	22 398	15 120	108 106	88 395	10 668	33.9	40.5	15.07	15.38	511.21	622.89
October	130 629	109 070	22 326	15 061	108 303	88 469	10 631	33.8	40.3	15.12	15.46	511.39	623.04
November	130 639	109 058	22 283	14 993	108 356	88 432	10 583	33.8	40.4	15.15	15.48	512.41	625.39
December	130 481	108 893	22 189	14 912	108 292	88 246	10 523	33.8	40.5	15.21	15.53	514.44	628.97
2003													
January	130 575	108 949	22 149	14 869	108 426	88 294	10 484	33.8	40.3	15.22	15.59	514.77	628.28
February	130 422	108 798	22 024	14 782	108 398	88 148	10 416	33.7	40.3	15.29	15.63	515.61	629.89
March	130 212	108 602	21 946	14 722	108 266	87 860	10 357	33.8	40.4	15.29	15.64	517.14	631.86
April	130 167	108 572	21 864	14 609	108 303	87 815	10 256	33.6	40.1	15.27	15.62	513.74	626.36
May	130 156	108 589	21 831	14 556	108 325	87 775	10 218	33.7	40.2	15.33	15.69	516.96	630.74
June	130 166	108 560	21 788	14 493	108 378	87 764	10 165	33.7	40.3	15.36	15.72	517.97	633.52
July	130 189	108 556	21 707	14 401	108 482	87 740	10 093	33.6	40.1	15.40	15.76	517.78	631.98
August	130 148	108 592	21 707	14 377	108 441	87 806	10 084	33.7	40.2	15.42	15.79	519.99	634.76
September	130 250	108 746	21 700	14 347	108 550	87 924	10 059	33.6	40.5	15.42	15.84	518.45	641.52
October	130 446	108 888	21 691	14 334	108 755	88 022	10 054	33.7	40.6	15.43	15.82	520.33	642.29
November	130 462	108 927	21 687	14 315	108 775	88 061	10 039	33.8	40.9	15.47	15.89	523.22	649.90
December	130 586	109 040	21 703	14 300	108 883	88 130	10 031	33.6	40.7	15.47	15.91	520.13	647.54
2004													
January	130 747	109 209	21 716	14 291	109 031	88 236	10 027	33.7	40.9	15.50	15.94	522.69	651.95
February	130 791	109 241	21 692	14 278	109 099	88 250	10 012	33.8	41.0	15.54	15.98	525.59	655.18
March	131 123	109 535	21 758	14 287	109 365	88 506	10 025	33.7	40.9	15.56	16.01	524.71	654.81
April	131 372	109 758	21 803	14 316	109 569	88 752	10 060	33.7	40.7	15.59	16.06	525.72	653.64
May	131 679	110 065	21 881	14 342	109 798	89 062	10 091	33.8	41.0	15.64	16.07	528.97	660.48
June	131 753	110 152	21 885	14 332	109 868	89 200	10 087	33.6	40.7	15.67	16.11	526.85	655.68
July	131 785	110 179	21 899	14 329	109 886	89 304	10 095	33.7	40.8	15.70	16.14	529.43	658.51
August	131 917	110 291	21 943	14 344	109 974	89 440	10 115	33.8	40.8	15.74	16.20	532.35	660.96
September	132 079	110 444	21 956	14 330	110 123	89 625	10 104	33.8	40.8	15.78	16.30	533.70	665.04
October	132 425	110 769	22 004	14 332	110 421	89 840	10 103	33.8	40.6	15.81	16.27	535.05	660.56
November	132 490	110 798	21 998	14 308	110 492	89 973	10 078	33.7	40.5	15.84	16.30	534.15	660.15
December	132 619	110 926	22 006	14 288	110 613	90 116	10 063	33.7	40.6	15.87	16.34	536.74	663.40
2005													
January	132 753	111 018	21 959	14 258	110 794	90 228	10 045	33.7	40.6	15.91	16.38	536.50	665.03
February	132 992	111 248	22 037	14 274	110 955	90 456	10 052	33.8	40.6	15.93	16.43	538.77	667.06
March	133 126	111 386	22 066	14 269	111 060	90 633	10 056	33.7	40.4	15.97	16.44	538.53	664.18
April	133 489	111 735	22 136	14 250	111 353	90 972	10 048	33.8	40.4	16.01	16.46	541.48	664.98
May	133 664	111 883	22 171	14 255	111 493	91 098	10 061	33.7	40.4	16.04	16.53	540.89	667.81
June	133 909	112 146	22 186	14 228	111 723	91 350	10 047	33.7	40.4	16.08	16.54	542.23	668.22
July	134 282	112 425	22 204	14 225	112 078	91 587	10 039	33.7	40.5	16.15	16.58	544.93	671.49
August	134 478	112 615	22 227	14 202	112 251	91 773	10 043	33.7	40.5	16.17	16.63	545.27	673.52
September	134 545	112 700	22 226	14 175	112 319	91 866	10 046	33.8	40.7	16.19	16.59	547.90	675.21
October	134 629	112 800	22 292	14 192	112 337	91 967	10 073	33.8	41.0	16.29	16.69	550.94	685.96
November	134 966	113 107	22 357	14 187	112 609	92 318	10 093	33.8	40.9	16.31	16.67	551.62	681.80
December	135 125	113 246	22 377	14 194	112 748	92 471	10 112	33.7	40.8	16.36	16.67	551.67	680.14
2006													
January	135 402	113 555	22 468	14 211	112 934	92 825	10 153	33.9	41.0	16.42	16.69	557.32	684.29
February	135 717	113 839	22 536	14 210	113 181	93 092	10 164	33.8	41.0	16.48	16.69	557.36	684.29
March	135 997	114 094	22 572	14 214	113 425	93 389	10 174	33.8	41.1	16.54	16.71	559.39	686.78
April	136 179	114 260	22 631	14 226	113 548	93 568	10 190	33.9	41.3	16.64	16.75	564.44	691.78
May	136 202	114 276	22 596	14 202	113 606	93 631	10 179	33.8	41.1	16.65	16.77	563.11	689.25
June	136 279	114 357	22 597	14 212	113 682	93 695	10 190	33.9	41.2	16.72	16.79	567.49	691.75
July	136 486	114 513	22 590	14 188	113 896	93 836	10 177	33.9	41.4	16.78	16.80	569.52	695.52
August	136 670	114 659	22 571	14 158	114 099	93 978	10 158	33.9	41.2	16.83	16.83	570.88	693.40
September	136 827	114 745	22 537	14 109	114 290	94 019	10 120	33.8	41.0	16.87	16.83	570.54	691.71
October	136 829	114 761	22 455	14 074	114 374	94 039	10 071	33.9	41.1	16.94	16.90	574.61	696.28
November	137 039	114 956	22 408	14 041	114 631	94 269	10 047	33.8	41.0	16.98	16.91	574.26	693.31
December	137 210	115 122	22 404	14 014	114 806	94 447	10 041	33.9	41.1	17.05	16.97	578.33	695.77
2007													
January	137 448	115 353	22 439	14 008	115 009	94 676	10 036	33.8	41.0	17.09	17.02	577.98	697.82
February	137 536	115 405	22 334	13 997	115 202	94 706	10 035	33.7	40.9	17.16	17.06	578.63	699.46
March	137 724	115 575	22 391	13 970	115 333	94 917	10 011	33.9	41.3	17.22	17.10	584.44	706.23
April	137 802	115 627	22 350	13 945	115 452	95 003	10 006	33.9	41.3	17.28	17.21	586.47	710.77
May	137 946	115 753	22 322	13 928	115 624	95 152	10 007	33.8	41.1	17.34	17.23	586.43	709.88
June	138 017	115 810	22 322	13 910	115 695	95 265	9 996	33.9	41.3	17.41	17.28	590.88	715.39
July	137 984	115 813	22 277	13 889	115 707	95 350	9 990	33.8	41.3	17.46	17.29	590.82	714.08
August	137 968	115 742	22 166	13 829	115 802	95 304	9 944	33.8	41.3	17.51	17.35	592.18	716.56
September	138 053	115 774	22 093	13 790	115 960	95 381	9 933	33.8	41.3	17.57	17.37	594.20	717.38
October	138 135	115 838	22 055	13 763	116 080	95 486	9 911	33.8	41.2	17.58	17.37	594.54	714.82
November	138 253	115 919	22 015	13 757	116 238	95 589	9 920	33.8	41.3	17.64	17.43	596.91	719.86
December	138 350	115 974	21 976	13 746	116 374	95 679	9 924	33.8	41.1	17.70	17.44	598.60	716.78

Table 10-8. Employment, Hours, and Earnings, Total Nonfarm and Manufacturing, Historical Annual and Monthly—*Continued*

(Wage and salary workers on nonfarm payrolls, seasonally adjusted.)

Year and month	All wage and salary workers (thousands)					Production and nonsupervisory workers on private payrolls							
	Total	Private			Service-providing	Number (thousands)		Average hours per week		Average hourly earnings, dollars		Average weekly earnings, dollars	
		Total	Goods-producing			Total private	Manufac-turing	Total private	Manufac-turing	Total private	Manufac-turing	Total private	Manufac-turing
			Total	Manufac-turing									
2008													
January	138 365	115 977	21 947	13 725	116 418	95 688	9 914	33.7	41.1	17.75	17.50	598.51	719.25
February	138 279	115 862	21 898	13 697	116 381	95 592	9 888	33.7	41.2	17.80	17.57	602.32	723.88
March	138 199	115 756	21 820	13 659	116 379	95 539	9 866	33.8	41.3	17.87	17.63	604.68	728.12
April	137 985	115 535	21 680	13 598	116 305	95 359	9 810	33.7	41.1	17.92	17.62	606.37	724.18
May	137 803	115 320	21 599	13 564	116 204	95 192	9 779	33.7	41.1	17.98	17.69	606.60	727.06
June	137 631	115 114	21 483	13 504	116 148	95 008	9 721	33.7	41.0	18.04	17.75	608.62	729.53
July	137 421	114 853	21 360	13 430	116 061	94 805	9 655	33.6	41.0	18.11	17.80	609.17	729.80
August	137 162	114 595	21 250	13 358	115 912	94 590	9 586	33.7	40.9	18.18	17.80	613.34	728.02
September	136 710	114 173	21 101	13 275	115 609	94 222	9 504	33.6	40.5	18.21	17.83	612.53	722.12
October	136 236	113 687	20 897	13 149	115 339	93 822	9 384	33.5	40.5	18.27	17.91	614.21	725.36
November	135 471	112 911	20 625	13 036	114 846	93 119	9 290	33.4	40.2	18.32	17.95	612.56	719.80
December	134 774	112 218	20 323	12 851	114 451	92 532	9 137	33.3	39.8	18.38	18.00	612.72	716.40
2009													
January	133 976	111 397	19 888	12 560	114 088	91 792	8 889	33.3	39.7	18.41	18.01	613.72	715.00
February	133 275	110 699	19 576	12 381	113 699	91 235	8 741	33.2	39.6	18.45	18.08	613.20	715.97
March	132 449	109 889	19 226	12 207	113 223	90 546	8 592	33.1	39.3	18.50	18.13	613.01	712.51
April	131 765	109 088	18 893	12 029	112 872	89 846	8 453	33.1	39.6	18.51	18.17	613.67	717.32
May	131 411	108 794	18 655	11 862	112 756	89 653	8 311	33.1	39.3	18.53	18.13	614.01	712.51
June	130 944	108 368	18 422	11 726	112 522	89 262	8 203	33.0	39.6	18.57	18.18	613.14	719.93
July	130 617	108 096	18 276	11 666	112 341	89 055	8 172	33.1	39.9	18.60	18.28	616.65	730.17
August	130 401	107 864	18 150	11 625	112 251	88 869	8 148	33.1	40.0	18.66	18.33	618.31	733.60
September	130 174	107 723	18 042	11 590	112 132	88 757	8 133	33.1	40.0	18.71	18.43	619.96	736.80
October	129 976	107 452	17 917	11 540	112 059	88 525	8 100	33.0	40.2	18.75	18.39	619.41	738.88
November	129 970	107 437	17 871	11 511	112 099	88 538	8 079	33.2	40.5	18.81	18.42	624.82	745.61
December	129 687	107 205	17 794	11 477	111 893	88 401	8 050	33.2	40.6	18.84	18.41	626.15	747.85
2010													
January	129 705	107 225	17 716	11 462	111 989	88 410	8 040	33.3	40.8	18.89	18.43	629.04	751.94
February	129 655	107 187	17 635	11 453	112 020	88 365	8 032	33.1	40.4	18.91	18.46	625.92	745.78
March	129 811	107 300	17 676	11 458	112 135	88 501	8 030	33.3	41.0	18.92	18.47	630.04	757.27
April	130 062	107 492	17 735	11 493	112 327	88 646	8 053	33.4	41.2	18.96	18.51	633.26	762.61
May	130 578	107 586	17 747	11 527	112 831	88 704	8 080	33.4	41.4	19.01	18.59	634.93	769.63
June	130 456	107 696	17 756	11 543	112 700	88 816	8 101	33.4	41.0	19.03	18.58	635.60	761.78
July	130 395	107 816	17 781	11 571	112 614	88 895	8 115	33.4	41.2	19.06	18.62	636.60	767.14
August	130 353	107 933	17 792	11 550	112 561	88 971	8 093	33.5	41.2	19.11	18.65	640.19	768.38
September	130 296	108 040	17 783	11 557	112 513	89 060	8 092	33.5	41.3	19.13	18.72	640.86	773.14
October	130 537	108 239	17 795	11 557	112 742	89 240	8 090	33.5	41.3	19.22	18.72	643.87	773.14
November	130 674	108 388	17 822	11 581	112 852	89 356	8 101	33.5	41.3	19.22	18.76	643.87	774.79
December	130 745	108 482	17 788	11 592	112 957	89 464	8 110	33.5	41.3	19.22	18.78	643.87	775.61
2011													
January	130 815	108 554	17 788	11 620	113 027	89 487	8 133	33.4	41.0	19.31	18.89	644.95	774.49
February	130 983	108 777	17 855	11 653	113 128	89 657	8 160	33.5	41.3	19.31	18.90	646.89	780.57
March	131 195	109 008	17 904	11 675	113 291	89 901	8 186	33.6	41.4	19.32	18.90	649.15	782.46
April	131 517	109 328	17 967	11 704	113 550	90 166	8 213	33.6	41.4	19.36	18.91	650.50	782.87
May	131 619	109 494	18 008	11 711	113 611	90 295	8 218	33.6	41.5	19.41	18.93	652.18	785.60
June	131 836	109 680	18 036	11 723	113 800	90 461	8 224	33.6	41.3	19.42	18.91	652.51	780.98
July	131 942	109 899	18 106	11 755	113 836	90 652	8 251	33.7	41.4	19.49	18.94	656.81	784.12
August	132 064	110 024	18 122	11 763	113 942	90 751	8 256	33.6	41.4	19.49	18.90	654.86	782.46
September	132 285	110 292	18 171	11 766	114 114	90 997	8 261	33.6	41.4	19.51	18.91	655.54	782.87
October	132 468	110 469	18 177	11 773	114 291	91 151	8 269	33.7	41.6	19.55	18.99	658.84	789.98
November	132 632	110 660	18 181	11 771	114 451	91 341	8 267	33.7	41.5	19.57	18.96	659.51	786.84
December	132 828	110 882	18 236	11 798	114 592	91 564	8 293	33.7	41.6	19.57	18.99	659.51	789.98
2012													
January	133 188	111 246	18 304	11 837	114 884	91 909	8 323	33.8	41.8	19.58	19.02	661.80	795.04
February	133 414	111 474	18 327	11 859	115 087	92 152	8 352	33.7	41.8	19.60	19.01	660.52	794.62
March	133 657	111 720	18 377	11 901	115 280	92 344	8 392	33.7	41.6	19.65	19.02	662.21	791.23
April	133 753	111 822	18 396	11 916	115 357	92 444	8 400	33.7	41.6	19.70	19.09	663.89	794.14
May	133 863	111 953	18 394	11 928	115 469	92 531	8 412	33.6	41.5	19.69	19.02	661.58	789.33
June	133 951	112 028	18 411	11 939	115 540	92 579	8 414	33.7	41.6	19.72	19.08	664.56	793.73
July	134 111	112 200	18 465	11 979	115 646	92 721	8 453	33.7	41.7	19.76	19.11	665.91	796.89
August	134 261	112 336	18 452	11 956	115 809	92 847	8 426	33.6	41.5	19.75	19.06	663.60	790.99
September	134 422	112 495	18 436	11 942	115 986	92 995	8 406	33.6	41.5	19.78	19.07	664.61	791.41
October	134 647	112 750	18 452	11 947	116 195	93 220	8 411	33.6	41.5	19.80	19.10	665.28	792.65
November	134 850	112 961	18 484	11 951	116 366	93 371	8 414	33.7	41.6	19.85	19.15	668.95	796.64
December	135 064	113 176	18 536	11 965	116 528	93 543	8 416	33.7	41.7	19.89	19.14	670.29	798.14
2013													
January	135 261	113 395	18 579	11 982	116 682	93 686	8 423	33.6	41.6	19.95	19.15	670.32	796.64
February	135 541	113 658	18 651	12 004	116 890	93 903	8 429	33.8	41.9	20.00	19.22	676.00	805.32
March	135 682	113 822	18 680	12 007	117 002	94 016	8 420	33.8	41.9	20.02	19.22	676.68	805.32
April	135 885	114 010	18 669	12 001	117 216	94 175	8 414	33.7	41.8	20.04	19.21	675.35	802.98
May	136 084	114 232	18 671	11 994	117 413	94 352	8 397	33.7	41.8	20.06	19.25	676.02	804.65
June	136 285	114 433	18 684	11 991	117 601	94 505	8 391	33.7	41.9	20.12	19.28	678.04	807.83
July	136 434	114 603	18 679	11 982	117 755	94 660	8 383	33.5	41.7	20.15	19.27	675.03	803.56
August	136 636	114 783	18 696	11 990	117 940	94 815	8 390	33.7	41.9	20.17	19.33	679.73	809.93
September	136 800	114 936	18 718	11 993	118 082	94 932	8 394	33.6	41.9	20.21	19.35	680.40	811.60
October	137 037	115 183	18 756	12 011	118 281	95 172	8 410	33.7	42.0	20.25	19.37	682.43	813.54
November	137 311	115 455	18 824	12 046	118 487	95 397	8 442	33.7	42.0	20.30	19.42	684.11	815.64
December	137 395	115 541	18 811	12 053	118 584	95 471	8 444	33.5	41.9	20.35	19.45	681.73	814.96

Table 10-8. Employment, Hours, and Earnings, Total Nonfarm and Manufacturing, Historical Annual and Monthly—*Continued*

(Wage and salary workers on nonfarm payrolls, seasonally adjusted.)

Year and month	All wage and salary workers (thousands)					Production and nonsupervisory workers on private payrolls							
	Total	Private			Service-providing	Number (thousands)		Average hours per week		Average hourly earnings, dollars		Average weekly earnings, dollars	
		Total	Goods-producing			Total private	Manufac-turing	Total private	Manufac-turing	Total private	Manufac-turing	Total private	Manufac-turing
			Total	Manufac-turing									
2014													
January	137 642	115 831	18 984	12 102	117 060	95 644	8 486	33.5	41.6	20.40	19.47	683.40	809.95
February	137 830	116 006	19 031	12 122	117 766	95 860	8 512	33.5	41.6	20.48	19.49	684.37	810.78
March	138 055	116 229	19 073	12 131	118 539	96 056	8 524	33.7	42.0	20.50	19.53	690.18	820.26
April	138 385	116 542	19 131	12 142	119 454	96 322	8 534	33.7	41.9	20.52	19.48	691.19	818.16
May	138 621	116 780	19 156	12 154	120 122	96 516	8 539	33.7	42.2	20.55	19.53	692.54	824.17
June	138 866	117 052	19 190	12 177	120 426	96 772	8 561	33.7	42.1	20.59	19.54	693.88	822.63
July	139 156	117 295	19 243	12 191	119 238	96 953	8 573	33.7	42.0	20.63	19.58	694.89	822.36
August	139 369	117 504	19 277	12 205	119 551	97 118	8 588	33.7	42.0	20.68	19.59	698.65	822.78
September	139 619	117 739	19 315	12 214	120 289	97 266	8 588	33.7	42.1	20.68	19.59	696.92	826.70
October	139 840	117 957	19 349	12 237	121 362	97 388	8 601	33.7	42.1	20.72	19.64	697.93	826.84
November	140 263	118 371	19 425	12 282	121 933	97 671	8 640	33.8	42.2	20.77	19.67	702.03	830.07
December	140 592	118 690	19 489	12 301	122 095	97 923	8 663	33.8	42.1	20.72	19.64	700.67	826.84
2015													
January	140 606	118 653	19 521	12 299	121 085	97 893	8 656	33.7	42.0	20.81	19.65	701.30	825.30
February	140 844	118 875	19 542	12 306	121 302	98 087	8 661	33.7	41.9	20.82	19.73	701.63	826.69
March	140 930	118 972	19 530	12 319	121 400	98 147	8 668	33.7	41.8	20.89	19.77	703.99	826.39
April	141 192	119 207	19 560	12 321	121 632	98 292	8 665	33.6	41.8	20.92	19.80	702.91	827.64
May	141 536	119 531	19 591	12 337	121 945	98 566	8 688	33.6	41.8	20.99	19.86	705.26	830.15
June	141 742	119 726	19 603	12 338	122 139	98 720	8 691	33.7	41.8	21.00	19.88	707.70	830.98
July	141 996	119 965	19 627	12 352	122 369	98 842	8 695	33.7	41.8	21.04	19.95	709.05	833.91
August	142 153	120 080	19 624	12 347	122 529	98 957	8 688	33.7	41.8	21.10	20.01	711.07	836.42
September	142 253	120 196	19 614	12 346	122 639	99 055	8 685	33.7	41.7	21.12	20.06	711.74	836.50
October	142 574	120 510	19 656	12 353	122 918	99 308	8 698	33.7	41.7	21.19	20.05	714.10	836.09
November	142 846	120 770	19 688	12 346	123 158	99 484	8 690	33.7	41.8	21.21	20.08	714.78	839.34
December	143 085	120 987	19 730	12 359	123 355	99 715	8 698	33.8	41.7	21.26	20.13	718.59	839.42
2016													
January	143 211	121 097	19 754	12 387	123 457	99 833	8 716	33.7	41.9	21.32	20.16	718.48	844.70
February	143 448	121 318	19 747	12 375	123 701	99 989	8 703	33.6	41.8	21.33	20.20	716.69	844.36
March	143 673	121 507	19 752	12 355	123 921	100 111	8 689	33.6	41.7	21.40	20.27	719.04	845.26
April	143 826	121 665	19 743	12 356	124 083	100 179	8 679	33.6	41.8	21.46	20.39	721.06	852.30
May	143 869	121 682	19 699	12 335	124 170	100 140	8 655	33.6	41.9	21.48	20.41	721.73	855.18
June	144 166	121 951	19 705	12 347	124 461	100 376	8 668	33.6	41.8	21.53	20.42	723.41	853.56
July	144 457	122 200	19 731	12 359	124 726	100 603	8 673	33.7	42.0	21.59	20.47	727.58	859.74
August	144 633	122 343	19 707	12 342	124 926	100 690	8 653	33.6	41.8	21.62	20.56	726.43	859.41
September	144 882	122 566	19 718	12 330	125 164	100 854	8 640	33.6	41.8	21.68	20.55	728.45	858.99
October	145 006	122 698	19 727	12 325	125 279	100 987	8 634	33.6	42.0	21.72	20.61	729.79	865.62
November	145 170	122 876	19 762	12 335	125 408	101 164	8 639	33.6	41.8	21.74	20.60	730.46	861.08
December	145 325	123 026	19 794	12 343	125 531	101 372	8 656	33.6	41.9	21.80	20.63	732.48	864.40
2017													
January	145 696	123 383	19 888	12 369	125 808	101 690	8 676	33.6	41.9	21.81	20.63	732.82	864.40
February	145 896	123 587	19 964	12 390	125 932	101 872	8 699	33.6	42.0	21.85	20.65	734.16	867.30
March	145 969	123 655	19 982	12 400	125 987	101 941	8 705	33.6	41.8	21.89	20.70	735.50	865.26
April	146 144	123 829	19 998	12 410	126 146	102 074	8 718	33.7	41.9	21.94	20.79	739.38	871.10
May	146 299	123 994	20 013	12 414	126 286	102 186	8 712	33.6	41.9	21.98	20.80	738.53	871.52
June	146 538	124 214	20 048	12 428	126 490	102 395	8 716	33.7	42.0	22.02	20.85	742.07	875.70
July	146 728	124 402	20 040	12 424	126 688	102 546	8 716	33.7	42.0	22.06	20.88	743.42	876.96
August	146 949	124 610	20 115	12 463	126 834	102 713	8 745	33.6	42.0	22.11	20.93	742.90	879.06
September	146 963	124 626	20 130	12 469	126 833	102 719	8 755	33.6	41.8	22.20	20.99	745.92	877.38
October	147 234	124 903	20 168	12 489	127 066	102 980	8 772	33.7	41.9	22.18	21.05	747.47	884.10
November	147 450	125 120	20 246	12 519	127 204	103 119	8 793	33.7	41.9	22.23	21.12	749.15	884.93
December	147 625	125 294	20 328	12 558	127 297	103 244	8 822	33.8	41.8	22.31	21.21	754.08	886.58
2018													
January	147 767	125 393	20 386	12 561	127 381	103 304	8 822	33.6	41.9	22.36	21.29	751.30	892.05
February	148 097	125 697	20 497	12 592	127 600	103 549	8 837	33.8	42.2	22.40	21.34	757.12	900.55
March	148 279	125 870	20 527	12 612	127 752	103 703	8 847	33.7	42.2	22.49	21.39	757.91	902.66
April	148 475	126 054	20 587	12 634	127 888	103 853	8 864	33.8	42.4	22.55	21.46	762.19	909.90
May	148 745	126 318	20 650	12 655	128 095	104 103	8 870	33.8	42.0	22.62	21.43	764.56	900.06
June	149 007	126 554	20 706	12 687	128 301	104 294	8 900	33.8	42.1	22.67	21.48	766.25	904.31
July	149 185	126 727	20 744	12 707	128 441	104 418	8 909	33.8	42.2	22.71	21.46	767.60	905.61
August	149 467	126 973	20 794	12 715	128 673	104 624	8 914	33.8	42.2	22.80	21.55	770.64	909.41
September	149 575	127 081	20 832	12 733	128 743	104 660	8 923	33.7	42.1	22.86	21.62	770.38	910.20
October	149 852	127 366	20 892	12 762	128 960	104 921	8 944	33.7	42.1	22.90	21.69	771.73	913.15
November	150 048	127 566	20 921	12 789	129 127	105 051	8 966	33.7	42.0	22.99	21.78	774.76	914.76
December	150 275	127 790	20 961	12 809	129 314	105 244	8 987	33.7	42.0	23.09	21.85	778.13	917.70
2019													
January	150 134	127 628	21 023	12 825	129 111	105 168	8 998	33.8	42.0	23.10	21.80	781.10	917.30
February	150 135	137 622	20 994	12 830	129 141	105 109	9 000	33.6	41.7	23.20	21.90	779.20	913.60
March	150 282	127 754	21 011	12 827	129 271	105 217	8 992	33.7	41.7	23.30	22.00	284.50	915.70
April	150 492	127 939	21 039	12 829	129 453	105 335	8 979	33.7	41.6	23.30	22.00	786.20	913.50
May	150 577	128 026	21 050	12 829	129 527	105 399	8 970	33.6	41.5	23.40	22.00	786.90	914.70
June	150 759	128 206	21 076	12 838	129 683	105 503	8 968	33.6	41.6	23.50	22.10	788.60	921.00
July	150 953	128 366	21 085	12 845	129 868	105 604	8 967	33.5	41.5	23.50	22.20	788.60	920.90
August	151 160	128 523	21 087	12 848	130 073	105 731	8 968	33.6	41.5	23.60	22.20	794.30	922.10
September	151 368	128 718	21 106	12 851	130 262	105 885	8 968	33.6	41.5	23.70	22.30	796.30	923.80
October	151 553	128 908	21 086	12 810	130 467	105 992	8 931	33.6	41.4	23.80	22.30	798.30	923.20
November	151 814	129 155	21 131	12 868	130 683	106 156	8 978	33.5	41.4	23.80	22.40	797.60	926.90
December	151 998	129 319	21 136	12 866	130 862	106 300	8 980	33.6	41.4	23.80	22.40	801.00	929.00

Figure 10-4. Weekly Hours and Hourly Earnings for All Employees and Production and Nonsupervisory Workers, 2010–2020

- In March 2006, the payroll survey (Current Employment Statistics) began collecting more comprehensive hours and earnings data for all nonfarm jobs. For production and nonsupervisory workers, hours and weekly data has been collected for decades. Tables 13, 14 and 15 provide this data. Figure 10-4 displays hourly earnings and hours per week for both nonfarm workers and production and nonsupervisory employees.

- Miners and loggers continued to work the most hours during the pandemic at 44.4 hours in 2020. At the other end, service-providing sectors such as leisure and hospitality worked the least at 25.9 hours in 2019 and at 25.5 hours in 2020. In 2020, many industries did lose employees due to shutdowns but these industries did surpass their low in 2009. (Table 10-9)

- In 2020, average weekly earnings of production and nonsupervisory workers were the highest in information at $1,604.89 followed by those in mining and logging at $1,542. (Table 10-12)

- The index of aggregate hours can point to an upcoming recession. As the index falls, fewer hours are being used for the production of goods and services. Even though employment is up, but hours are not up proportionally. This reflects the trend to part-time workers and the reduction of hours in part-time workers. (Table 10-15).

Table 10-9. Average Weekly Hours of All Employees on Private Nonfarm Payrolls by NAICS Supersector

(Hours per week, seasonally adjusted.)

Year and month	Total private	Mining and logging	Construction	Manufacturing		Trade, transportation, and utilities			Information	Financial activities	Professional and business services	Education and health services	Leisure and hospitality	Other services
				Average weekly hours	Overtime hours	Total	Wholesale trade	Retail trade						
2010	34.1	43.4	37.8	40.2	3.0	34.2	38.1	31.3	36.5	36.9	35.4	32.7	25.7	31.6
2011	34.4	44.5	38.3	40.5	3.2	34.6	38.6	31.6	36.6	37.3	35.7	32.7	25.9	31.7
2012	34.5	44.0	38.7	40.7	3.3	34.6	38.7	31.7	36.6	37.4	36.0	32.8	26.1	31.6
2013	34.4	43.9	39.0	40.8	3.4	34.5	38.7	31.4	36.7	37.1	36.1	32.7	26.0	31.7
2014	34.5	34.5	39.0	41.0	3.5	34.5	38.9	31.3	36.8	37.3	36.3	32.7	26.2	31.8
2015	34.5	44.0	39.2	40.8	3.3	34.6	38.9	31.4	36.2	37.6	36.2	32.8	26.3	31.9
2016	34.4	43.4	39.0	40.7	3.3	34.3	38.9	31.0	36.0	37.5	36.1	32.9	26.1	31.9
2017	34.4	45.1	39.1	40.8	3.4	34.4	39.0	31.0	36.2	37.5	36.1	32.9	26.1	31.8
2018	34.5	46.0	39.2	40.9	3.5	34.5	39.0	31.0	36.1	37.6	36.1	32.9	26.1	31.8
2019	34.4	46.2	39.3	40.5	3.3	34.2	38.9	30.6	36.3	37.6	36.2	33.0	25.9	31.9
2020	34.6	44.4	38.9	39.9	2.9	34.2	38.5	30.8	36.6	37.6	36.4	33.2	25.5	32.2
2016														
January	34.6	43.5	39.3	40.7	3.3	34.6	38.9	31.3	36.2	37.7	36.3	32.9	26.2	31.9
February	34.5	43.1	39.2	40.7	3.3	34.5	38.9	31.2	36.0	37.7	36.1	32.8	26.2	31.9
March	34.4	42.8	38.7	40.7	3.3	34.3	38.8	31.0	36.0	37.6	36.1	32.8	26.1	31.9
April	34.4	43.0	39.1	40.7	3.3	34.4	38.9	31.1	36.0	37.6	36.1	32.8	26.1	31.9
May	34.4	43.1	39.1	40.7	3.3	34.3	38.8	31.0	36.0	37.4	36.1	32.8	26.1	31.9
June	34.4	43.0	39.1	40.7	3.2	34.3	38.8	31.0	36.0	37.5	36.0	32.9	26.1	32.0
July	34.4	43.3	39.2	40.8	3.3	34.4	38.9	31.1	36.1	37.6	36.1	32.9	26.1	32.0
August	34.3	43.6	38.8	40.6	3.3	34.2	38.9	30.8	35.9	37.5	36.0	32.9	26.0	31.9
September	34.4	43.7	38.8	40.7	3.3	34.2	38.9	30.8	35.8	37.5	36.1	32.9	26.1	31.9
October	34.4	43.9	39.2	40.8	3.3	34.2	38.9	30.8	35.9	37.3	36.1	32.9	26.0	32.0
November	34.3	43.6	39.1	40.6	3.2	34.2	38.9	30.8	36.0	37.5	36.0	32.9	26.1	31.9
December	34.4	43.7	38.9	40.7	3.3	34.4	38.9	31.1	36.1	37.4	36.0	32.9	26.0	31.9
2017														
January	34.4	44.0	39.0	40.8	3.3	34.3	38.9	30.9	36.6	37.2	36.1	32.9	26.0	31.8
February	34.3	44.5	39.0	40.6	3.3	34.2	38.9	30.8	36.3	37.4	36.1	32.9	25.9	31.8
March	34.3	45.0	38.9	40.6	3.3	34.2	38.9	30.9	36.3	37.4	36.0	32.9	26.0	31.8
April	34.4	45.2	39.1	40.7	3.3	34.5	39.0	31.2	36.3	37.4	36.1	32.9	26.2	31.8
May	34.4	45.4	39.2	40.8	3.3	34.4	39.0	31.0	36.3	37.4	36.0	32.8	26.0	31.8
June	34.4	45.0	39.1	40.8	3.3	34.4	39.0	31.0	36.2	37.6	36.1	32.9	26.1	31.8
July	34.4	45.5	39.1	40.9	3.4	34.4	39.1	31.0	36.3	37.5	36.1	32.9	26.1	31.7
August	34.4	45.0	39.0	40.8	3.4	34.4	39.1	30.9	36.1	37.5	36.0	32.9	26.0	31.7
September	34.4	45.3	39.0	40.8	3.4	34.4	39.1	30.9	36.0	37.5	36.1	32.8	26.0	31.7
October	34.4	45.4	39.2	40.9	3.5	34.4	39.0	31.0	36.1	37.5	36.0	32.9	26.1	31.7
November	34.5	45.6	39.3	41.0	3.5	34.6	39.2	31.3	36.0	37.6	36.2	32.9	26.1	31.7
December	34.5	45.6	39.2	40.8	3.4	34.5	39.3	31.1	36.1	37.6	36.0	33.0	26.2	31.8
2018														
January	34.4	45.4	38.9	40.7	3.5	34.5	39.0	31.1	35.9	37.5	35.9	32.9	26.0	31.6
February	34.5	46.0	39.3	41.0	3.7	34.5	39.0	31.1	36.0	37.6	36.2	33.0	26.1	31.7
March	34.5	45.8	39.3	40.9	3.6	34.5	39.0	31.2	36.1	37.5	36.2	32.9	26.1	31.7
April	34.5	46.0	39.5	41.1	3.6	34.5	39.0	31.0	36.1	37.6	36.2	33.0	26.1	31.8
May	34.5	46.2	39.5	40.9	3.4	34.5	39.1	31.1	35.9	37.6	36.1	32.9	26.2	31.7
June	34.6	46.4	39.2	40.9	3.5	34.6	39.1	31.1	35.7	37.7	36.2	33.0	26.2	31.8
July	34.5	46.0	39.5	41.0	3.5	34.6	39.0	31.1	36.1	37.5	36.2	32.9	26.1	31.8
August	34.5	46.1	39.2	40.9	3.5	34.5	39.1	30.9	36.1	37.6	36.1	33.0	26.1	31.8
September	34.5	45.9	39.0	40.9	3.5	34.5	39.0	30.9	36.2	37.6	36.1	32.9	26.0	31.9
October	34.5	46.0	38.9	40.8	3.5	34.4	39.0	30.8	36.2	37.8	36.2	32.9	26.0	31.9
November	34.4	45.9	38.7	40.8	3.5	34.5	39.0	30.9	36.2	37.6	36.1	32.9	25.9	31.9
December	34.5	46.2	39.3	40.9	3.5	34.3	39.0	30.6	36.3	37.6	36.1	33.0	26.0	31.9
2019														
January	34.5	46.4	39.9	40.8	3.5	34.3	39.0	30.7	36.2	37.7	36.3	33.0	26.1	31.9
February	34.4	46.3	38.8	40.7	3.5	34.2	39.0	30.6	36.2	37.7	36.2	33.0	26.0	31.8
March	34.5	46.6	39.4	40.7	3.4	34.3	39.0	30.7	36.3	37.7	36.3	33.0	26.1	32.0
April	34.4	46.8	39.2	40.6	3.3	34.3	39.0	30.7	36.2	37.7	36.2	33.0	25.9	31.9
May	34.4	46.3	39.1	40.6	3.3	34.3	38.9	30.7	36.4	37.6	36.2	33.0	25.9	31.9
June	34.4	46.3	39.3	40.6	3.4	34.2	38.9	30.7	36.4	37.5	36.2	33.0	25.9	31.9
July	34.3	46.2	39.1	40.4	3.3	34.1	38.8	30.6	36.2	37.5	36.1	33.0	25.8	31.9
August	34.4	46.2	39.4	40.5	3.2	34.2	38.9	30.6	36.5	37.7	36.2	33.0	25.8	31.8
September	34.4	46.2	39.7	40.5	3.2	34.2	38.9	30.7	36.5	37.6	36.1	33.0	25.9	31.8
October	34.4	46.1	39.3	40.3	3.2	34.2	39.0	30.6	36.4	37.7	36.1	33.0	25.8	31.9
November	34.3	45.7	39.1	40.4	3.2	34.0	39.0	30.3	36.3	37.7	36.1	33.1	25.8	31.9
December	34.3	45.8	39.0	40.4	3.2	34.1	38.8	30.6	36.3	37.5	36.1	33.0	25.8	31.8
2020														
January	34.3	45.6	39.2	40.4	3.1	34.0	38.8	30.3	36.2	37.7	36.1	33.0	25.9	31.9
February	34.4	45.6	39.2	40.7	3.2	34.2	38.8	30.7	36.2	37.6	36.2	33.1	25.8	31.9
March	34.1	45.0	39.1	40.3	3.0	34.1	38.7	30.6	36.3	37.6	36.1	33.0	24.1	31.4
April	34.2	43.0	37.9	38.0	2.1	33.8	37.7	30.5	36.5	37.6	36.0	32.7	24.2	32.2
May	34.7	43.0	38.8	38.8	2.4	34.4	38.0	31.3	36.6	37.7	36.5	32.9	25.9	32.7
June	34.6	43.6	38.8	39.1	2.5	34.4	38.2	31.3	36.6	37.5	36.4	33.1	25.7	32.3
July	34.6	44.1	38.9	39.8	2.9	34.2	38.4	30.7	36.3	37.6	36.4	33.4	25.5	32.1
August	34.7	44.3	38.9	40.1	3.0	34.2	38.5	30.8	36.7	37.6	36.4	33.4	25.8	32.2
September	34.8	44.4	39.0	40.3	3.1	34.3	38.6	30.8	36.6	37.6	36.6	33.5	26.1	32.4
October	34.8	44.7	38.9	40.4	3.2	34.5	38.7	31.0	36.7	37.7	36.6	33.5	26.0	32.4
November	34.8	45.0	39.0	40.3	3.2	34.5	38.6	30.9	36.9	37.8	36.7	33.4	25.7	32.4
December	34.7	45.0	39.2	40.0	3.2	34.1	38.6	30.4	37.1	37.7	36.7	33.5	25.2	32.4

Table 10-10. Indexes of Aggregate Weekly Hours of All Employees on Private Nonfarm Payrolls by NAICS Supersector

(2007 =100, seasonally adjusted.)

Year and month	Total private	Mining and logging	Construc-tion	Manu-facturing	Trade, transportation, and utilities			Information	Financial activities	Profes-sional and business services	Education and health services	Leisure and hospitality	Other services
					Total	Wholesale trade	Retail trade						
2010	92.4	96.1	71.9	83.4	91.7	90.5	92.0	90.3	93.0	93.1	106.5	95.9	97.2
2011	94.7	110.2	73.1	85.4	94.2	93.3	94.1	89.4	94.0	97.4	108.6	98.7	98.0
2012	97.1	117.1	75.4	87.4	95.8	95.6	95.4	89.6	95.3	101.7	111.2	102.6	99.0
2013	99.0	119.2	78.7	88.3	97.0	96.7	96.2	90.6	96.0	105.1	112.6	105.7	100.3
2014	101.5	125.5	82.7	89.8	99.1	98.5	97.7	91.5	97.4	108.8	114.6	109.8	102.0
2015	103.9	112.4	87.1	90.5	101.3	99.2	99.6	91.1	100.1	111.8	118.0	113.7	103.3
2016	105.4	91.0	90.8	90.5	101.8	99.1	99.7	91.6	101.6	113.6	121.3	116.5	104.6
2017	107.4	96.0	94.1	91.3	102.9	100.2	99.8	93.1	103.8	116.0	124.5	119.5	105.7
2018	109.6	105.1	98.7	93.4	103.9	100.6	99.3	93.6	106.0	118.8	127.1	121.3	107.0
2019	110.8	105.5	101.6	93.6	103.5	101.1	97.0	95.0	107.9	120.6	130.1	122.6	108.2
2020	104.3	86.4	97.3	87.3	99.4	95.7	92.9	90.1	107.7	115.5	126.0	115.5	100.1
2016													
January	105.2	101.0	89.8	90.9	101.8	99.4	99.9	91.8	101.4	113.6	120.0	115.5	104.2
February	104.7	96.5	89.3	90.5	101.8	99.1	100.2	91.3	101.2	113.1	120.0	115.8	104.2
March	104.9	93.1	89.5	90.4	101.7	98.9	99.8	91.6	101.4	112.9	120.2	115.7	104.3
April	105.1	91.3	90.3	90.7	101.8	99.5	99.9	91.7	101.9	113.7	120.5	115.9	104.5
May	105.1	90.0	89.9	90.5	101.6	99.0	99.6	90.5	101.5	113.1	120.9	116.0	104.3
June	105.3	88.4	90.3	90.4	101.7	98.9	99.8	92.0	101.5	113.3	121.5	116.5	104.5
July	105.6	88.4	90.8	90.6	101.8	99.2	99.9	92.3	102.6	114.2	121.8	116.8	105.0
August	105.4	88.6	90.6	90.4	101.7	99.0	99.6	92.0	102.2	113.6	122.0	116.7	105.2
September	105.9	88.6	91.5	90.6	102.0	99.5	99.7	91.9	102.3	114.3	122.3	118.0	105.1
October	106.0	88.6	91.9	90.6	102.1	99.7	99.7	92.3	102.4	114.4	122.7	117.1	105.2
November	106.2	89.0	92.2	90.1	101.8	99.5	99.2	92.4	102.2	114.6	122.9	117.9	105.4
December	106.3	89.1	91.9	90.5	102.6	99.5	100.3	92.7	102.5	114.5	123.2	117.1	105.1
2017													
January	106.5	89.3	92.2	90.6	102.4	99.5	99.9	94.2	102.4	115.1	123.2	117.7	104.7
February	106.3	91.7	92.8	90.7	102.0	99.6	99.3	93.3	102.9	115.1	123.6	117.5	105.3
March	106.4	93.6	92.6	90.5	102.0	99.6	99.5	93.2	103.0	114.7	123.8	118.1	105.3
April	106.9	94.9	93.0	90.8	103.0	100.0	100.4	93.1	103.2	115.5	124.1	119.1	105.4
May	106.7	96.0	93.4	91.1	102.3	99.9	99.3	92.7	103.3	115.5	123.9	118.9	105.6
June	107.2	95.7	93.7	91.4	102.7	100.0	99.7	93.1	104.1	116.0	124.4	119.6	105.7
July	107.4	96.9	93.8	91.4	102.8	100.3	99.3	92.9	103.9	116.3	124.8	120.1	105.6
August	107.6	96.7	94.0	91.5	102.8	100.3	99.3	92.8	104.1	116.1	125.0	119.7	105.7
September	107.6	97.5	94.1	91.5	102.6	100.1	99.2	92.7	104.1	116.1	124.8	119.4	105.5
October	107.8	97.8	95.0	91.9	103.0	100.1	99.6	92.7	104.2	116.4	125.3	120.3	105.6
November	108.3	99.2	96.0	92.3	103.6	100.7	100.5	92.6	104.6	117.2	125.5	120.5	106.1
December	108.4	99.5	96.2	92.0	103.4	101.0	99.8	93.3	104.7	116.8	126.0	120.6	106.4
2018													
January	108.2	99.5	95.5	92.0	103.3	100.1	99.7	92.3	104.5	116.8	125.9	120.1	105.9
February	108.8	102.0	97.7	92.9	103.6	100.2	99.9	92.5	105.1	117.9	126.6	120.7	106.3
March	109.0	103.0	97.6	92.8	103.8	100.4	100.3	93.1	104.9	117.9	126.4	120.8	106.2
April	109.1	104.4	98.4	93.4	103.8	100.1	99.7	93.6	105.3	118.1	126.8	120.8	106.7
May	109.3	105.1	98.9	93.1	103.9	100.4	99.7	93.0	105.6	118.4	126.6	121.1	106.6
June	109.5	106.4	98.4	93.6	104.2	100.5	99.8	92.5	106.1	118.9	127.2	121.4	107.2
July	109.6	105.3	99.4	93.7	103.9	100.4	99.4	93.7	105.9	119.0	127.0	121.7	106.9
August	109.8	106.8	98.8	93.6	104.1	101.0	99.0	93.7	106.0	118.9	127.7	121.7	107.0
September	109.6	106.6	98.1	93.5	104.0	100.7	98.8	93.9	106.3	119.1	127.4	121.1	107.4
October	110.1	107.3	98.9	93.7	103.8	100.5	98.3	94.0	107.1	119.6	127.7	121.9	107.5
November	109.8	106.4	98.8	93.8	104.2	100.9	98.7	94.3	106.7	119.4	127.8	121.0	107.5
December	110.3	107.7	101.0	94.2	103.5	101.0	97.6	95.0	106.8	119.9	128.5	121.8	107.6
2019													
January	110.5	108.5	102.7	94.2	103.7	101.1	97.8	93.9	107.2	120.3	128.8	122.8	107.6
February	110.2	107.8	99.4	93.9	103.3	101.2	97.3	93.8	107.3	119.8	128.9	122.2	107.3
March	110.6	108.4	101.0	93.9	103.6	101.2	97.2	94.2	107.6	120.5	129.2	122.8	108.3
April	110.5	108.2	101.0	93.7	103.6	101.3	97.4	94.1	107.7	120.4	129.5	122.0	108.2
May	110.5	107.6	100.8	93.6	103.6	101.1	97.3	94.9	107.6	120.5	129.7	121.6	107.8
June	110.7	107.2	101.6	93.7	103.7	101.0	97.2	95.3	107.4	120.7	130.0	122.1	108.4
July	110.5	105.8	101.1	93.2	103.4	100.8	96.9	94.8	107.9	120.5	129.9	121.7	108.6
August	110.9	104.4	101.7	93.4	103.4	101.0	96.8	95.4	108.4	121.0	130.6	122.1	108.7
September	111.1	104.2	102.4	93.4	103.8	101.1	97.2	96.1	108.2	120.8	131.0	123.0	108.3
October	111.3	104.4	101.9	92.6	103.6	101.2	97.0	95.6	108.8	121.0	131.2	123.6	108.6
November	111.1	101.8	101.2	93.4	103.0	101.4	95.8	95.7	109.0	121.2	131.5	123.9	108.8
December	111.2	100.1	101.9	93.1	103.8	101.0	97.1	95.8	108.5	121.2	131.7	123.8	108.5
2020													
January	111.5	98.7	102.9	93.0	103.3	101.0	96.0	96.2	109.3	121.3	132.1	124.6	109.1
February	112.0	98.9	103.3	93.7	104.0	100.9	97.3	96.3	109.3	121.9	132.8	124.5	109.2
March	109.6	95.3	101.9	92.2	103.2	100.3	96.2	96.1	109.0	120.7	131.2	110.9	105.8
April	93.0	84.0	85.4	78.0	90.4	91.2	82.0	87.8	105.9	107.7	116.0	60.0	84.0
May	97.3	81.2	93.7	81.4	93.6	92.3	86.7	86.7	106.4	110.1	118.8	75.0	90.1
June	101.2	81.8	95.9	84.4	97.3	93.6	92.2	87.0	106.1	111.7	122.5	89.2	96.0
July	102.5	82.2	96.5	86.2	97.8	93.8	91.9	85.9	106.5	112.5	124.8	93.3	98.4
August	103.7	82.0	96.9	87.1	99.1	94.2	93.8	87.7	106.9	113.7	125.9	95.4	100.1
September	104.8	82.6	97.5	87.9	99.8	95.0	94.0	88.9	107.3	115.1	126.6	99.5	101.6
October	105.7	83.4	98.3	88.3	101.1	95.4	95.3	88.8	108.0	116.5	127.1	101.1	102.5
November	106.0	84.4	98.9	88.4	101.6	95.4	94.9	89.3	108.4	117.3	127.0	100.0	102.5
December	105.4	84.4	100.0	88.0	100.4	95.6	93.6	90.1	108.4	118.3	127.2	94.4	102.2

Table 10-11. Average Hourly Earnings of All Employees on Private Nonfarm Payrolls by NAICS Supersector

(Dollars, seasonally adjusted.)

Year and month	Total private	Mining and logging	Construc-tion	Manu-facturing	Trade, transportation, and utilities			Information	Financial activities	Profes-sional and business services	Education and health services	Leisure and hospitality	Other services
					Total	Wholesale trade	Retail trade						
2010	22.56	27.39	25.19	23.31	19.60	26.04	15.57	30.53	27.21	27.26	22.76	13.08	20.16
2011	23.03	28.10	25.41	23.69	19.99	26.28	15.87	31.59	27.91	27.79	23.42	13.23	20.50
2012	23.49	28.76	25.73	23.92	20.45	26.79	16.31	31.83	29.26	28.16	24.01	13.37	20.85
2013	23.95	29.72	26.12	24.35	20.91	27.54	16.64	32.91	30.15	28.58	24.42	13.50	21.40
2014	24.46	30.79	26.69	24.81	21.32	27.97	17.01	34.07	30.76	29.32	24.72	13.91	21.97
2015	25.01	31.15	27.37	25.25	21.77	28.53	17.52	35.14	31.52	30.11	25.24	14.32	22.48
2016	25.64	31.91	28.12	25.99	22.26	29.36	17.88	36.67	32.29	30.82	25.74	14.87	23.05
2017	26.32	32.05	28.90	26.59	22.72	29.92	18.18	38.30	33.24	31.67	26.32	15.47	23.85
2018	27.11	32.49	29.90	27.05	23.33	30.45	18.79	40.08	34.79	32.59	27.00	15.98	24.56
2019	27.99	33.68	30.76	27.70	24.21	31.36	19.70	42.19	35.94	33.68	27.62	16.56	25.21
2020	29.35	34.73	31.66	28.77	25.23	32.36	20.87	43.81	37.83	35.18	28.52	17.08	26.57
2016													
January	25.36	31.79	27.66	25.61	22.01	28.90	17.71	35.99	32.03	30.54	25.55	14.59	22.78
February	25.39	31.82	27.75	25.66	22.03	28.92	17.78	36.24	32.02	30.57	25.58	14.63	22.81
March	25.45	31.97	27.87	25.76	22.14	29.20	17.85	36.15	32.19	30.56	25.60	14.67	22.86
April	25.53	31.98	27.97	25.86	22.18	29.29	17.83	36.25	32.15	30.69	25.68	14.74	22.91
May	25.57	32.10	28.08	25.97	22.22	29.35	17.86	36.47	32.20	30.80	25.64	14.79	22.97
June	25.63	32.08	28.12	25.99	22.29	29.34	17.95	36.52	32.21	30.88	25.69	14.86	23.04
July	25.69	31.98	28.20	26.00	22.31	29.54	17.89	36.64	32.42	30.93	25.72	14.92	23.10
August	25.72	31.63	28.20	26.13	22.34	29.53	17.91	36.85	32.48	30.92	25.71	14.98	23.16
September	25.77	31.83	28.21	26.12	22.37	29.53	17.93	37.07	32.57	30.99	25.82	15.02	23.16
October	25.88	31.98	28.42	26.28	22.49	29.70	18.00	37.38	32.44	31.09	25.89	15.08	23.32
November	25.91	31.90	28.35	26.25	22.52	29.60	18.11	37.45	32.62	31.14	25.93	15.12	23.33
December	25.94	32.04	28.43	26.32	22.44	29.70	17.96	37.51	32.69	31.21	25.98	15.16	23.38
2017													
January	26.02	32.87	28.53	26.36	22.55	29.79	18.04	37.56	32.65	31.32	25.99	15.22	23.46
February	26.08	32.19	28.52	26.40	22.55	29.82	18.02	37.58	32.83	31.37	26.09	15.29	23.65
March	26.10	32.05	28.61	26.41	22.56	29.77	18.06	37.63	32.78	31.51	26.09	15.35	23.61
April	26.18	31.83	28.61	26.55	22.59	29.87	18.07	38.01	32.89	31.60	26.20	15.39	23.66
May	26.22	31.83	28.73	26.54	22.66	29.84	18.14	38.21	32.86	31.52	26.27	15.49	23.69
June	26.27	31.88	28.89	26.57	22.70	29.87	18.17	38.50	33.07	31.54	26.27	15.46	23.77
July	26.36	32.18	28.95	26.68	22.77	29.95	18.22	38.67	33.24	31.62	26.38	15.48	23.87
August	26.38	32.02	29.00	26.61	22.77	29.89	18.26	38.71	33.36	31.66	26.42	15.54	23.93
September	26.50	31.94	29.16	26.70	22.84	30.00	18.27	38.63	33.49	31.88	26.51	15.62	24.05
October	26.48	32.02	29.12	26.74	22.82	29.88	18.28	38.50	33.71	31.80	26.43	15.59	24.10
November	26.54	32.11	29.22	26.73	22.87	30.04	18.30	38.68	33.68	31.91	26.54	15.64	24.17
December	26.64	32.16	29.30	26.77	22.95	30.12	18.35	38.80	34.03	32.02	26.62	15.70	24.21
2018													
January	26.72	32.32	29.39	26.88	22.97	30.10	18.39	38.93	34.25	32.15	26.67	15.75	24.26
February	26.75	32.26	29.54	26.84	23.01	30.13	18.45	39.13	34.22	32.11	26.69	15.74	24.27
March	26.83	32.47	29.49	26.90	23.05	30.14	18.49	39.27	34.41	32.24	26.82	15.82	24.40
April	26.91	32.38	29.66	26.95	23.12	30.13	18.60	39.48	34.44	32.31	26.85	15.87	24.46
May	26.99	32.27	29.71	26.99	23.22	30.28	18.72	39.60	34.63	32.40	26.96	15.88	24.50
June	27.04	32.47	29.78	27.03	23.23	30.44	18.67	39.81	34.67	32.49	27.02	15.94	24.54
July	27.12	32.41	29.95	27.02	23.30	30.40	18.78	39.80	34.81	32.60	27.05	16.00	24.58
August	27.22	32.57	30.02	27.09	23.41	30.51	18.87	40.18	34.91	32.78	27.13	16.06	24.60
September	27.31	32.83	30.19	27.13	23.50	30.68	18.94	40.74	35.11	32.84	27.13	16.10	24.70
October	27.36	32.59	30.25	27.16	23.56	30.67	19.04	40.98	35.06	32.88	27.18	16.16	24.76
November	27.43	32.73	30.28	27.25	23.61	30.73	19.08	41.10	35.27	32.94	27.22	16.21	24.79
December	27.55	32.67	30.46	27.30	23.80	30.97	19.23	41.50	35.34	33.04	27.28	16.28	24.87
2019													
January	27.59	32.76	30.33	27.27	23.80	30.85	19.33	41.72	35.42	33.09	27.43	16.30	25.00
February	27.68	32.99	30.43	27.41	23.93	31.00	19.41	41.78	35.48	33.23	27.46	16.38	25.02
March	27.76	32.99	30.50	27.46	24.03	31.26	19.44	41.95	35.53	33.32	27.53	16.39	25.04
April	27.80	33.30	30.63	27.48	24.01	31.09	19.49	41.96	35.72	33.42	27.49	16.44	25.08
May	27.88	33.40	30.70	27.58	24.12	31.28	19.55	42.02	35.80	33.52	27.43	16.51	25.15
June	27.96	33.57	30.74	27.67	24.20	31.39	19.66	41.90	35.91	33.64	27.54	16.55	25.16
July	28.04	33.97	30.76	27.75	24.26	31.35	19.73	42.31	35.95	33.76	27.64	16.59	25.19
August	28.16	34.00	30.88	27.82	24.37	31.60	19.80	42.98	36.19	33.86	27.71	16.62	25.28
September	28.15	34.25	30.89	27.89	24.37	31.54	19.86	42.31	36.05	33.96	27.70	16.68	25.30
October	28.24	34.53	31.00	27.93	24.41	31.64	19.90	42.38	36.21	34.07	27.83	16.71	25.37
November	28.33	34.36	31.12	28.03	24.50	31.73	19.99	42.59	36.41	34.18	27.87	16.77	25.46
December	28.36	34.38	31.16	28.14	24.47	31.62	20.03	42.63	36.51	34.24	27.84	16.79	25.53
2020													
January	28.43	34.24	31.23	28.18	24.60	31.73	20.12	42.85	36.64	34.31	27.86	16.85	25.54
February	28.51	34.41	31.36	28.23	24.65	31.81	20.18	42.95	36.85	34.43	27.90	16.90	25.59
March	28.74	34.43	31.37	28.37	24.76	31.88	20.33	43.25	36.90	34.52	28.05	16.89	25.78
April	30.07	34.74	31.38	29.31	25.62	32.45	21.10	43.66	37.37	35.83	28.41	18.00	27.79
May	29.74	34.87	31.50	29.06	25.34	32.44	20.77	43.62	37.65	35.51	28.52	17.44	27.50
June	29.35	34.94	31.63	28.64	25.02	32.25	20.64	43.51	37.88	35.22	28.51	17.02	26.91
July	29.37	34.84	31.74	28.81	25.30	32.42	20.99	44.09	37.77	35.13	28.55	16.92	26.72
August	29.47	34.80	31.82	28.95	25.41	32.49	21.19	44.00	38.10	35.29	28.64	17.06	26.59
September	29.50	34.89	31.82	28.90	25.55	32.52	21.44	43.93	38.21	35.35	28.70	17.10	26.58
October	29.52	34.89	31.87	28.86	25.41	32.66	21.11	44.77	38.66	35.38	28.72	17.12	26.51
November	29.61	34.47	31.97	28.99	25.47	32.76	21.15	44.40	38.79	35.44	28.86	17.09	26.69
December	29.91	34.67	32.09	29.00	25.67	32.87	21.33	44.28	39.06	35.59	29.45	17.15	26.85

Table 10-12. Average Weekly Earnings of All Employees on Private Nonfarm Payrolls by NAICS Supersector

(Dollars, seasonally adjusted.)

Year and month	Total private	Mining and logging	Construc- tion	Manu- facturing	Trade, transportation, and utilities			Information	Financial activities	Profes- sional and business services	Education and health services	Leisure and hospitality	Other services
					Total	Wholesale trade	Retail trade						
2010	769.57	1 189.32	952.78	937.34	670.87	991.59	488.08	1 114.65	1 003.94	964.60	743.41	336.83	637.65
2011	790.74	1 250.91	973.85	958.84	690.43	1 015.85	501.04	1 156.56	1 039.70	992.94	766.88	342.67	649.87
2012	809.46	1 263.98	997.01	973.96	707.20	1 038.30	516.10	1 166.45	1 093.00	1 014.67	787.43	349.12	659.49
2013	824.91	1 306.16	1 018.01	994.30	721.19	1 066.81	522.57	1 206.05	1 119.71	1 031.57	798.73	350.95	679.43
2014	844.80	1 380.77	1 040.85	1 016.42	735.94	1 088.33	532.88	1 252.44	1 146.22	1 063.71	809.11	364.07	698.41
2015	864.07	1 371.13	1 070.93	1 029.71	753.57	1 109.79	550.74	1 274.99	1 185.77	1 089.87	828.36	376.20	716.17
2016	881.09	1 383.16	1 100.94	1 057.77	764.27	1 140.05	554.27	1 315.74	1 208.20	1 110.34	844.80	387.80	734.90
2017	906.19	1 448.75	1 131.76	1 084.86	781.98	1 169.15	563.80	1 388.30	1 246.39	1 142.52	865.65	403.77	757.95
2018	936.37	1 494.46	1 174.87	1 107.27	804.94	1 189.45	582.14	1 447.26	1 309.49	1 178.94	889.44	416.89	781.48
2019	963.06	1 555.88	1 209.74	1 124.06	827.92	1 220.61	602.58	1 531.68	1 351.30	1 218.15	911.10	429.00	803.21
2020	1 013.94	1 542.03	1 228.75	1 146.23	864.49	1 245.35	642.96	1 604.89	1 425.75	1 280.52	947.44	435.50	855.22
2016													
January	877.46	1 395.58	1 087.04	1 044.89	761.55	1 127.10	554.32	1 310.04	1 207.53	1 108.60	840.60	382.26	728.96
February	873.42	1 374.62	1 082.25	1 044.36	760.04	1 124.99	556.51	1 304.64	1 203.95	1 103.58	839.02	383.31	727.64
March	875.48	1 371.94	1 084.14	1 048.43	761.62	1 132.96	555.14	1 301.40	1 210.34	1 100.16	839.68	382.89	729.23
April	878.23	1 371.94	1 093.63	1 055.09	762.99	1 142.31	554.51	1 305.00	1 212.06	1 110.98	842.30	384.71	730.83
May	879.61	1 380.30	1 095.12	1 059.58	762.15	1 138.78	553.66	1 312.92	1 207.50	1 108.80	840.99	386.02	732.74
June	881.67	1 376.23	1 099.49	1 057.79	764.55	1 138.39	556.45	1 314.72	1 204.65	1 111.68	845.20	387.85	734.98
July	883.74	1 381.54	1 102.62	1 058.20	765.23	1 149.11	554.59	1 322.70	1 222.23	1 119.67	846.19	389.41	739.20
August	882.20	1 379.07	1 099.80	1 063.49	764.03	1 145.76	553.42	1 322.92	1 218.00	1 113.12	845.86	389.48	741.12
September	886.49	1 390.97	1 105.83	1 065.70	767.29	1 148.72	554.04	1 327.11	1 221.38	1 118.74	849.48	393.52	738.80
October	890.27	1 400.72	1 114.06	1 072.22	771.41	1 158.30	556.20	1 341.94	1 216.50	1 122.35	851.78	392.08	743.91
November	891.30	1 397.22	1 111.32	1 065.75	770.18	1 151.44	557.79	1 348.20	1 219.99	1 124.15	853.10	394.63	744.23
December	892.34	1 400.15	1 111.61	1 071.22	771.94	1 155.33	558.56	1 354.11	1 222.61	1 123.56	854.74	392.64	745.82
2017													
January	895.09	1 439.71	1 115.52	1 072.85	773.47	1 158.83	557.44	1 374.70	1 214.58	1 130.65	855.07	395.72	743.68
February	894.54	1 432.46	1 115.13	1 074.48	771.21	1 160.00	555.02	1 364.15	1 227.84	1 132.46	858.36	396.01	752.07
March	895.23	1 448.66	1 112.93	1 072.25	771.55	1 158.05	558.05	1 365.97	1 225.97	1 131.21	858.36	399.10	750.80
April	900.59	1 438.72	1 115.79	1 080.59	779.36	1 164.93	563.78	1 379.76	1 230.09	1 140.76	861.98	401.68	752.39
May	899.35	1 445.08	1 123.34	1 082.83	777.24	1 163.76	560.53	1 383.20	1 228.96	1 134.72	861.66	402.74	753.34
June	903.69	1 434.60	1 129.60	1 086.71	780.88	1 164.93	563.27	1 397.55	1 243.43	1 138.59	864.28	403.51	755.89
July	906.78	1 460.97	1 131.95	1 091.21	783.29	1 171.05	563.00	1 399.85	1 246.50	1 141.48	867.90	404.03	756.68
August	907.47	1 440.90	1 131.00	1 085.69	783.29	1 168.70	564.23	1 397.43	1 251.00	1 139.76	869.22	404.04	758.58
September	911.60	1 446.88	1 137.24	1 089.36	783.41	1 170.00	564.54	1 394.54	1 255.88	1 147.68	869.53	406.12	762.39
October	910.91	1 450.51	1 141.50	1 093.67	785.01	1 165.32	566.68	1 389.85	1 264.13	1 144.80	869.55	406.90	761.56
November	915.63	1 464.22	1 151.27	1 095.93	791.30	1 177.57	572.79	1 392.48	1 266.37	1 155.14	873.17	408.20	766.19
December	919.08	1 469.71	1 151.49	1 092.22	791.78	1 183.72	570.69	1 404.56	1 279.53	1 152.72	878.46	409.77	769.88
2018													
January	919.17	1 464.10	1 146.21	1 094.02	792.47	1 173.90	571.93	1 397.59	1 284.38	1 154.19	877.44	409.50	766.62
February	922.88	1 483.96	1 163.88	1 100.44	793.85	1 175.07	573.80	1 408.68	1 286.67	1 162.38	880.77	410.81	769.36
March	925.64	1 490.37	1 158.96	1 100.21	795.23	1 175.46	576.89	1 417.65	1 290.38	1 163.86	882.38	412.90	773.48
April	928.40	1 492.72	1 171.57	1 107.65	797.64	1 175.07	576.60	1 425.23	1 294.94	1 166.39	886.05	414.21	777.83
May	931.16	1 490.87	1 173.55	1 103.89	801.09	1 183.95	580.32	1 421.64	1 302.09	1 169.64	886.98	414.47	776.65
June	932.88	1 506.61	1 167.38	1 108.23	803.76	1 190.20	580.64	1 421.22	1 307.06	1 176.14	891.66	416.03	780.37
July	935.64	1 487.62	1 183.03	1 107.82	803.85	1 185.60	582.18	1 436.78	1 308.86	1 180.12	889.85	417.60	781.64
August	939.09	1 501.48	1 173.78	1 107.98	807.65	1 192.94	583.08	1 450.50	1 312.62	1 183.36	895.29	419.17	782.28
September	939.46	1 506.90	1 168.35	1 106.90	810.75	1 196.52	585.25	1 474.79	1 320.14	1 185.52	892.58	418.60	787.93
October	943.92	1 499.14	1 176.73	1 108.13	810.46	1 193.06	586.43	1 479.38	1 325.27	1 190.26	894.22	421.78	789.84
November	943.59	1 505.58	1 174.86	1 111.80	814.55	1 198.47	589.57	1 487.82	1 326.15	1 189.13	895.54	419.84	790.80
December	950.48	1 509.35	1 203.17	1 116.57	816.34	1 207.83	588.44	1 510.60	1 328.78	1 196.05	900.24	423.28	793.35
2019													
January	951.86	1 516.79	1 213.20	1 112.62	816.34	1 203.15	593.43	1 510.26	1 335.33	1 201.17	905.19	425.43	797.50
February	952.19	1 527.44	1 183.73	1 115.59	818.41	1 209.00	593.95	1 512.44	1 337.60	1 199.60	906.18	425.88	795.64
March	957.72	1 537.33	1 201.70	1 117.62	824.23	1 219.14	594.86	1 518.59	1 339.48	1 209.52	908.49	427.78	801.28
April	956.32	1 555.11	1 200.70	1 115.69	823.54	1 212.51	598.34	1 518.95	1 346.64	1 209.80	907.17	425.80	800.05
May	959.07	1 549.76	1 200.37	1 119.75	827.32	1 216.79	600.19	1 529.53	1 346.08	1 213.42	905.19	425.96	799.77
June	961.82	1 561.01	1 208.08	1 123.40	830.06	1 221.07	603.56	1 525.16	1 346.63	1 217.77	908.82	428.65	802.60
July	961.77	1 572.81	1 202.72	1 121.10	829.69	1 216.38	603.74	1 531.62	1 351.72	1 218.74	909.36	428.02	803.56
August	968.70	1 570.80	1 213.58	1 126.71	833.45	1 229.24	605.88	1 564.47	1 364.36	1 225.73	914.43	428.80	806.43
September	968.36	1 582.35	1 220.16	1 129.55	835.89	1 226.91	609.70	1 548.55	1 355.48	1 225.96	914.10	432.01	804.54
October	971.46	1 595.29	1 215.20	1 125.58	834.82	1 230.80	608.94	1 542.63	1 365.12	1 229.93	918.39	432.79	809.30
November	971.72	1 573.69	1 210.57	1 135.22	833.00	1 237.47	605.70	1 546.02	1 372.66	1 233.90	919.71	434.34	812.17
December	972.75	1 578.04	1 218.36	1 136.86	836.87	1 226.86	612.92	1 543.21	1 369.13	1 236.06	918.72	433.18	811.85
2020													
January	975.15	1 561.34	1 224.22	1 138.47	836.40	1 231.12	609.64	1 551.17	1 381.33	1 238.59	919.38	436.42	814.73
February	980.74	1 569.10	1 229.31	1 148.96	843.03	1 234.23	619.53	1 554.79	1 385.56	1 246.37	923.49	436.02	816.32
March	980.03	1 549.35	1 226.57	1 143.31	844.32	1 233.76	622.10	1 569.98	1 387.44	1 246.17	925.65	407.05	809.49
April	1 028.39	1 493.82	1 189.30	1 113.78	865.96	1 223.37	643.55	1 593.59	1 405.11	1 289.88	929.01	435.60	894.84
May	1 031.98	1 499.41	1 222.20	1 127.53	871.70	1 232.72	650.10	1 596.49	1 419.41	1 296.12	938.31	451.70	899.25
June	1 015.51	1 523.38	1 227.24	1 119.82	860.69	1 231.95	646.03	1 592.47	1 420.50	1 282.01	943.68	437.41	869.19
July	1 016.20	1 536.44	1 234.69	1 146.64	865.26	1 244.93	644.39	1 600.47	1 420.15	1 278.73	953.57	431.46	857.71
August	1 022.61	1 541.64	1 237.80	1 160.90	869.02	1 250.87	652.65	1 614.80	1 432.56	1 284.56	956.58	440.15	856.20
September	1 026.60	1 549.12	1 240.98	1 164.67	876.37	1 255.27	660.35	1 607.84	1 436.70	1 293.81	961.45	446.31	861.19
October	1 027.30	1 559.58	1 239.74	1 165.94	876.65	1 263.94	654.41	1 643.06	1 457.48	1 294.91	962.12	445.12	858.92
November	1 030.43	1 551.15	1 246.83	1 168.30	878.72	1 264.54	653.54	1 638.36	1 466.26	1 300.65	963.92	439.21	864.76
December	1 037.88	1 560.15	1 257.93	1 160.00	875.35	1 268.78	648.43	1 642.79	1 472.56	1 306.15	986.58	432.18	869.94

Table 10-13. Production and Nonsupervisory Workers on Private Nonfarm Payrolls by NAICS Supersector

(Thousands, seasonally adjusted.)

Year and month	Total private	Mining and logging	Construction	Manufacturing	Trade, transportation, and utilities			Information	Financial activities	Professional and business services	Education and health services	Leisure and hospitality	Other services
					Total	Wholesale trade	Retail trade						
1965	42 302	523	2 906	12 905	10 702	. . .	. . .	1 268	2 434	3 515	3 443	3 443	1 161
1966	44 292	517	2 977	13 703	11 095	. . .	. . .	1 334	2 492	3 715	3 623	3 607	1 230
1967	45 185	501	2 903	13 714	11 369	. . .	. . .	1 365	2 585	3 890	3 818	3 734	1 306
1968	46 519	491	2 986	13 908	11 688	. . .	. . .	1 394	2 700	4 067	4 008	3 898	1 379
1969	48 246	501	3 177	14 147	12 152	. . .	. . .	1 438	2 841	4 252	4 196	4 089	1 452
1970	48 180	496	3 158	13 490	12 388	. . .	. . .	1 422	2 922	4 321	4 305	4 185	1 494
1971	48 151	474	3 238	13 034	12 502	. . .	. . .	1 392	2 978	4 354	4 372	4 286	1 521
1972	49 971	494	3 425	13 497	12 954	2 920	7 257	1 437	3 066	4 518	4 531	4 467	1 583
1973	52 235	502	3 576	14 227	13 437	3 041	7 551	1 504	3 164	4 748	4 747	4 664	1 666
1974	52 846	550	3 469	14 040	13 700	3 148	7 673	1 516	3 217	4 907	4 941	4 766	1 740
1975	51 010	581	2 990	12 576	13 578	3 121	7 714	1 416	3 227	4 939	5 088	4 821	1 795
1976	52 916	606	2 999	13 127	14 038	3 212	8 048	1 459	3 300	5 153	5 309	5 046	1 880
1977	55 207	636	3 209	13 591	14 579	3 323	8 396	1 514	3 452	5 404	5 561	5 284	1 978
1978	58 188	658	3 544	14 150	15 329	3 509	8 861	1 586	3 645	5 717	5 874	5 588	2 099
1979	60 404	737	3 760	14 458	15 843	3 667	9 113	1 650	3 825	5 993	6 158	5 772	2 209
1980	60 377	785	3 623	13 667	15 907	3 708	9 158	1 626	3 957	6 197	6 447	5 850	2 318
1981	60 967	861	3 469	13 492	16 004	3 753	9 238	1 633	4 052	6 396	6 700	5 944	2 414
1982	59 475	834	3 208	12 315	15 821	3 662	9 254	1 564	4 055	6 421	6 822	5 976	2 458
1983	60 018	698	3 240	12 121	15 999	3 639	9 494	1 502	4 128	6 581	7 045	6 161	2 542
1984	63 333	714	3 614	12 821	16 797	3 821	9 964	1 631	4 289	6 918	7 385	6 491	2 672
1985	65 456	686	3 868	12 648	17 427	3 935	10 399	1 660	4 476	7 258	7 789	6 817	2 827
1986	66 825	577	3 984	12 449	17 769	3 941	10 704	1 663	4 698	7 532	8 130	7 066	2 957
1987	68 725	541	4 088	12 537	18 196	3 989	10 986	1 717	4 861	7 859	8 513	7 310	3 104
1988	71 059	545	4 199	12 765	18 771	4 132	11 306	1 775	4 894	8 256	8 985	7 587	3 280
1989	72 960	526	4 257	12 805	19 230	4 235	11 565	1 807	4 931	8 648	9 465	7 833	3 459
1990	73 721	538	4 115	12 669	19 032	4 198	11 308	1 866	4 973	8 889	9 784	8 299	3 555
1991	72 567	515	3 674	12 164	18 640	4 122	11 008	1 871	4 914	8 748	10 257	8 247	3 539
1992	72 854	478	3 546	12 020	18 506	4 071	10 931	1 871	4 924	8 971	10 607	8 406	3 526
1993	74 671	462	3 704	12 070	18 752	4 072	11 104	1 896	5 084	9 451	10 961	8 667	3 623
1994	77 478	461	3 973	12 361	19 392	4 196	11 502	1 928	5 220	10 078	11 397	8 979	3 689
1995	79 943	458	4 113	12 567	19 984	4 361	11 841	2 007	5 199	10 645	11 829	9 330	3 812
1996	81 888	461	4 325	12 532	20 325	4 423	12 057	2 096	5 322	11 161	12 195	9 565	3 907
1997	84 313	479	4 546	12 673	20 698	4 523	12 274	2 181	5 482	11 896	12 566	9 780	4 013
1998	86 516	473	4 807	12 729	21 059	4 605	12 440	2 217	5 692	12 566	12 903	9 947	4 124
1999	88 647	438	5 105	12 524	21 576	4 673	12 772	2 351	5 818	13 184	13 217	10 216	4 219
2000	90 543	446	5 295	12 428	21 965	4 686	13 040	2 502	5 819	13 790	13 487	10 516	4 296
2001	90 202	457	5 332	11 677	21 709	4 555	12 952	2 531	5 888	13 588	13 986	10 662	4 373
2002	88 645	436	5 196	10 768	21 337	4 474	12 774	2 398	5 964	13 049	14 471	10 576	4 449
2003	87 938	420	5 123	10 189	21 078	4 396	12 655	2 347	6 052	12 911	14 726	10 666	4 426
2004	89 212	440	5 309	10 072	21 319	4 444	12 788	2 371	6 052	13 287	14 984	10 955	4 425
2005	91 401	473	5 611	10 060	21 830	4 584	13 030	2 386	6 127	13 854	15 359	11 263	4 438
2006	93 727	519	5 903	10 137	22 166	4 724	13 110	2 399	6 312	14 446	15 783	11 568	4 494
2007	95 203	547	5 883	9 975	22 546	4 851	13 317	2 403	6 365	14 784	16 261	11 861	4 578
2008	94 610	574	5 521	9 629	22 337	4 822	13 134	2 388	6 320	14 585	16 777	11 873	4 606
2009	89 556	510	4 567	8 322	21 116	4 506	12 472	2 240	6 066	13 520	17 166	11 560	4 488
2010	88 875	525	4 172	8 077	20 874	4 378	12 425	2 170	5 942	13 699	17 452	11 507	4 458
2011	90 537	594	4 184	8 228	21 234	4 443	12 647	2 148	5 900	14 251	17 736	11 772	4 491
2012	92 715	641	4 246	8 400	21 617	4 562	12 793	2 164	5 986	14 802	18 165	12 154	4 541
2013	94 580	639	4 401	8 412	21 882	4 632	12 921	2 178	6 064	15 351	18 519	12 559	4 558
2014	96 794	658	4 631	8 568	22 281	4 707	13 113	2 221	6 157	15 795	18 859	12 981	4 642
2015	98 783	592	4 866	8 683	22 629	4 702	13 264	2 226	6 278	16 133	19 337	13 360	4 678
2016	100 531	476	5 062	8 666	22 882	4 696	13 424	2 235	429	16 479	19 839	13 749	4 715
2017	102 331	504	5 186	8 728	23 121	4 742	13 491	2 205	6 569	16 875	20 320	14 047	4 771
2018	104 310	544	5 437	8 899	23 386	4 698	13 521	2 275	6 638	17 121	20 788	14 384	4 839
2019	105 617	540	5 583	8 975	23 438	4 739	13 349	2 301	6 768	17 335	21 233	14 568	4 876
2020	98 013	440	5 385	8 433	22 426	4 487	12 663	2 140	6 678	16 265	20 348	11 503	4 395
2019													
January	105 168	555	5 579	8 998	23 469	4 730	13 410	2 293	6 721	17 215	20 991	14 497	4 850
February	105 109	552	5 530	9 000	23 432	4 735	13 385	2 291	6 731	17 251	21 001	14 474	4 847
March	105 217	553	5 538	8 992	23 417	4 731	13 366	2 292	6 744	17 264	21 063	14 495	4 859
April	105 335	549	5 558	8 979	23 405	4 738	13 341	2 288	6 754	17 294	21 117	14 516	4 875
May	105 399	548	5 566	8 970	23 416	4 740	13 344	2 296	6 757	17 302	21 148	14 526	4 870
June	105 503	545	5 580	8 968	23 420	4 737	13 334	2 307	6 753	17 317	21 202	14 527	4 884
July	105 604	540	5 586	8 967	23 432	4 738	13 332	2 306	6 768	17 343	21 261	14 515	4 886
August	105 731	535	5 595	8 968	23 420	4 739	13 321	2 306	6 781	17 365	21 314	14 558	4 889
September	105 885	532	5 607	8 968	23 448	4 742	13 341	2 306	6 782	17 387	21 359	14 611	4 885
October	105 992	535	5 620	8 931	23 459	4 743	13 351	2 301	6 803	17 408	21 396	14 654	4 885
November	106 156	524	5 612	8 978	23 444	4 743	13 315	2 310	6 806	17 429	21 456	14 703	4 894
December	106 300	516	5 623	8 980	23 494	4 750	13 347	2 314	6 812	17 444	21 491	14 736	4 890
2020													
January	106 444	496	5 672	8 916	23 555	4 724	13 313	2 334	6 848	17 390	21 528	14 804	4 901
February	106 651	496	5 709	8 932	23 575	4 721	13 323	2 338	6 870	17 414	21 572	14 846	4 899
March	105 083	478	5 598	8 860	23 441	4 702	13 215	2 327	6 843	17 260	21 350	14 125	4 801
April	87 038	433	4 726	7 776	20 550	4 346	11 232	2 091	6 589	15 158	18 970	7 121	3 624
May	90 011	420	5 155	7 962	20 901	4 368	11 579	2 047	6 585	15 307	19 314	8 478	3 842
June	94 400	422	5 321	8 326	21 796	4 404	12 344	2 051	6 594	15 596	19 806	10 316	4 172
July	95 920	421	5 374	8 354	22 032	4 394	12 548	2 058	6 586	15 764	20 049	10 963	4 319
August	96 836	421	5 378	8 364	22 371	4 409	12 791	2 065	6 602	15 940	20 226	11 097	4 372
September	97 686	422	5 380	8 390	22 491	4 436	12 832	2 103	6 628	16 079	20 279	11 489	4 425
October	98 541	421	5 415	8 406	22 684	4 444	12 923	2 088	6 648	16 322	20 333	11 755	4 469
November	98 926	428	5 432	8 441	22 859	4 447	12 921	2 084	6 671	16 414	20 381	11 753	4 463
December	98 617	426	5 463	8 471	22 855	4 453	12 936	2 092	6 667	16 534	20 370	11 287	4 452

. . . = Not available.

Table 10-14. Average Weekly Hours of Production and Nonsupervisory Workers on Private Nonfarm Payrolls by NAICS Supersector

(Hours per week, seasonally adjusted.)

Year and month	Total private	Mining and logging	Construc-tion	Manufacturing		Trade, transportation, and utilities			Informa-tion	Financial activities	Profes-sional and business services	Education and health services	Leisure and hospitality	Other services
				Average weekly hours	Overtime hours	Total	Wholesale trade	Retail trade						
1965	38.6	43.7	37.9	41.2	3.6	39.6	. . .	. . .	38.3	37.1	37.3	35.2	32.5	36.1
1966	38.5	44.1	38.1	41.4	3.9	39.1	. . .	. . .	38.3	37.2	37.0	34.9	31.9	35.8
1967	37.9	43.9	38.1	40.6	3.3	38.5	. . .	. . .	37.6	36.9	36.6	34.5	31.3	35.4
1968	37.7	44.0	37.8	40.7	3.6	38.2	. . .	. . .	37.6	36.8	36.3	34.1	30.8	35.0
1969	37.5	44.3	38.4	40.6	3.6	37.9	. . .	. . .	37.6	36.9	36.3	34.1	30.4	35.0
1970	37.0	43.9	37.8	39.8	2.9	37.6	. . .	. . .	37.2	36.6	35.9	33.8	30.0	34.7
1971	36.7	43.7	37.6	39.9	2.9	37.4	. . .	. . .	37.0	36.4	35.5	33.3	29.9	34.2
1972	36.9	44.1	37.0	40.6	3.4	37.4	39.8	35.1	37.3	36.4	35.5	33.3	29.7	34.2
1973	36.9	43.8	37.2	40.7	3.8	37.2	39.6	34.8	37.3	36.4	35.5	33.3	29.4	34.1
1974	36.4	43.7	37.1	40.0	3.2	36.8	39.2	34.3	37.0	36.3	35.3	33.1	29.1	33.9
1975	36.0	43.7	36.9	39.5	2.6	36.4	39.1	34.0	36.6	36.2	35.1	33.0	28.8	33.8
1976	36.1	44.2	37.3	40.1	3.1	36.3	39.1	33.8	36.7	36.2	34.9	32.7	28.5	33.6
1977	35.9	44.7	37.0	40.3	3.4	36.0	39.2	33.3	36.8	36.2	34.7	32.5	28.1	33.4
1978	35.8	44.9	37.3	40.4	3.6	35.6	39.2	32.7	36.8	36.1	34.6	32.3	27.7	33.2
1979	35.6	44.7	37.5	40.2	3.3	35.4	39.2	32.4	36.6	35.9	34.4	32.2	27.4	33.0
1980	35.2	44.9	37.5	39.6	2.8	35.0	38.8	31.9	36.4	36.0	34.3	32.1	27.0	33.0
1981	35.2	45.1	37.4	39.8	2.8	35.0	38.9	31.9	36.3	36.0	34.3	32.1	26.9	33.0
1982	34.7	44.1	37.2	38.9	2.3	34.6	38.7	31.7	35.8	36.0	34.2	32.1	26.8	33.0
1983	34.9	43.9	37.6	40.1	2.9	34.6	38.8	31.6	36.2	35.9	34.4	32.1	26.8	33.0
1984	35.1	44.6	38.2	40.6	3.4	34.7	38.9	31.6	36.6	36.2	34.3	32.0	26.7	32.9
1985	34.9	44.6	38.2	40.5	3.3	34.4	38.8	31.2	36.5	36.1	34.2	31.9	26.4	32.8
1986	34.7	43.6	37.9	40.7	3.4	34.1	38.7	31.0	36.4	36.1	34.3	32.0	26.2	32.9
1987	34.7	43.5	38.2	40.9	3.7	34.1	38.5	31.0	36.5	36.0	34.3	32.0	26.3	32.8
1988	34.6	43.3	38.2	41.0	3.8	33.8	38.5	30.9	36.1	35.6	34.2	32.0	26.3	32.9
1989	34.5	44.1	38.3	40.9	3.8	33.8	38.4	30.7	36.1	35.6	34.2	32.0	26.1	32.9
1990	34.3	45.0	38.3	40.5	3.9	33.7	38.4	30.6	35.8	35.5	34.2	31.9	26.0	32.8
1991	34.1	45.3	38.1	40.4	3.8	33.6	38.4	30.4	35.6	35.4	34.0	31.9	25.6	32.7
1992	34.2	44.6	38.0	40.7	4.0	33.8	38.5	30.7	35.8	35.6	34.0	32.0	25.7	32.6
1993	34.3	44.9	38.4	41.1	4.4	34.1	38.5	30.7	36.0	35.5	34.0	32.0	25.9	32.6
1994	34.5	45.3	38.8	41.7	5.0	34.3	38.8	30.9	36.0	35.5	34.1	32.0	26.0	32.7
1995	34.3	45.3	38.8	41.3	4.7	34.1	38.6	30.8	36.0	35.5	34.0	32.0	25.9	32.6
1996	34.3	46.0	38.9	41.3	4.8	34.1	38.6	30.7	36.3	35.5	34.1	31.9	25.9	32.5
1997	34.5	46.2	38.9	41.7	5.1	34.3	38.8	30.9	36.3	35.8	34.3	32.2	26.1	32.7
1998	34.5	44.9	38.8	41.4	4.9	34.2	38.6	30.9	36.6	36.0	34.3	32.2	26.2	32.6
1999	34.3	44.2	39.0	41.4	4.9	33.9	38.6	30.8	36.7	35.8	34.4	32.1	26.1	32.5
2000	34.3	44.4	39.2	41.3	4.7	33.8	38.8	30.7	36.8	35.9	34.5	32.2	26.1	32.5
2001	34.0	44.6	38.7	40.3	4.0	33.5	38.4	30.7	36.9	35.8	34.2	32.3	25.8	32.3
2002	33.9	43.2	38.4	40.5	4.2	33.6	38.0	30.9	36.5	35.6	34.2	32.4	25.8	32.1
2003	33.7	43.6	38.4	40.4	4.2	33.6	37.9	30.9	36.2	35.6	34.1	32.3	25.6	31.4
2004	33.7	44.5	38.3	40.8	4.6	33.5	37.8	30.7	36.3	35.6	34.2	32.4	25.7	31.0
2005	33.8	45.6	38.6	40.7	4.6	33.4	37.7	30.6	36.5	36.0	34.2	32.6	25.7	30.9
2006	33.9	45.6	39.0	41.1	4.4	33.4	38.0	30.5	36.6	35.8	34.6	32.5	25.7	30.9
2007	33.8	45.9	39.0	41.2	4.2	33.3	38.2	30.2	36.5	35.9	34.8	32.6	25.5	30.9
2008	33.6	45.1	38.5	40.8	3.7	33.2	38.2	30.0	36.7	35.9	34.8	32.4	25.2	30.8
2009	33.1	43.2	37.6	39.8	2.9	32.9	37.6	29.9	36.6	36.1	34.7	32.2	24.8	30.5
2010	33.4	44.6	38.4	41.1	3.8	33.3	37.9	30.2	36.3	36.2	35.1	32.1	24.8	30.7
2011	33.6	46.7	39.0	41.4	4.1	33.7	38.5	30.5	36.2	36.4	35.2	32.2	24.8	30.8
2012	33.7	46.6	39.3	41.7	4.2	33.8	38.7	30.6	36.0	36.8	35.3	32.3	25.0	30.7
2013	33.7	45.9	39.6	41.8	4.3	33.7	38.7	30.2	35.9	36.7	35.3	32.1	25.0	30.7
2014	33.7	47.4	39.6	42.0	4.5	33.6	38.6	30.0	35.9	36.8	35.6	32.0	25.1	30.7
2015	33.7	45.8	39.6	41.8	4.3	33.7	38.6	30.1	35.7	37.1	35.5	32.1	25.1	30.8
2016	33.6	45.3	39.7	41.9	4.3	33.5	38.6	29.7	35.6	36.9	35.4	32.2	24.9	30.8
2017	31.2	43.4	39.8	41.9	4.4	33.8	38.9	30.2	33.4	36.9	35.4	32.2	24.9	30.8
2018	33.7	46.8	39.8	42.1	4.5	33.9	38.9	30.4	35.6	37.0	35.3	32.2	24.9	30.8
2019	33.6	47.0	39.7	41.6	4.2	33.8	38.7	30.3	35.3	36.9	35.4	32.2	24.7	30.8
2020	33.9	45.0	39.3	40.8	3.7	34.1	38.2	30.8	36.0	37.1	35.8	32.5	24.1	31.2
2019														
January	33.8	46.6	40.5	42.0	4.5	34.0	38.8	30.5	35.4	37.0	35.5	32.2	24.9	30.9
February	33.6	46.9	39.0	41.7	4.4	33.8	38.7	30.3	35.5	37.0	35.4	32.2	24.8	30.8
March	33.7	47.2	39.9	41.7	4.4	33.9	38.8	30.4	35.5	37.0	35.4	32.2	24.9	30.9
April	33.7	47.3	39.8	41.6	4.3	33.9	38.7	30.5	35.3	36.9	35.4	32.2	24.7	30.8
May	33.6	46.9	39.7	41.5	4.2	33.8	38.7	30.2	35.4	36.9	35.4	32.2	24.6	30.8
June	33.6	47.2	39.8	41.6	4.2	33.8	38.7	30.3	35.5	36.7	35.5	32.2	24.7	30.8
July	33.5	47.2	39.6	41.5	4.2	33.7	38.6	30.2	35.1	36.8	35.4	32.1	24.6	30.8
August	33.6	47.2	39.9	41.5	4.2	33.8	38.7	30.3	35.2	36.8	35.6	32.2	24.6	30.8
September	33.6	47.1	40.1	41.5	4.2	33.8	38.7	30.3	35.5	36.9	35.4	32.1	24.6	30.8
October	33.6	47.2	39.7	41.4	4.1	33.8	38.6	30.3	35.2	36.9	35.3	32.2	24.7	30.8
November	33.5	46.5	39.4	41.4	4.1	33.6	38.6	29.9	35.1	37.0	35.4	32.2	24.7	30.8
December	33.6	46.2	39.4	41.4	4.1	33.8	38.5	30.3	35.1	36.8	35.3	32.3	24.7	30.8
2020														
January	33.6	46.0	39.9	41.4	4.0	33.9	38.6	30.4	35.1	37.0	35.5	32.2	24.7	31.0
February	33.7	45.8	39.5	41.7	4.0	33.9	38.6	30.4	35.2	36.8	35.6	32.3	24.7	31.0
March	33.4	45.4	39.5	41.3	3.9	34.0	38.4	30.6	35.3	36.7	35.5	32.2	22.8	30.4
April	33.5	43.1	38.3	38.5	2.8	33.6	37.0	30.5	35.6	36.9	35.2	31.8	22.3	31.2
May	34.1	43.9	39.4	39.4	3.1	34.3	37.6	31.3	35.9	37.0	35.8	32.1	24.3	31.8
June	33.9	44.3	39.3	39.9	3.3	34.1	37.9	30.9	36.1	36.9	35.8	32.4	24.2	31.5
July	34.0	44.3	39.3	40.7	3.7	34.2	38.1	30.9	35.9	37.1	35.9	32.6	24.0	31.2
August	34.0	44.9	39.2	41.1	3.8	34.1	38.2	30.9	36.8	37.0	35.9	32.6	24.5	31.2
September	34.1	45.0	39.3	41.2	3.8	34.2	38.5	30.9	36.2	37.3	36.0	32.8	24.7	31.3
October	34.2	45.2	39.1	41.3	3.9	34.5	38.5	31.0	36.5	37.3	36.1	32.8	24.6	31.4
November	34.2	46.0	39.3	41.3	4.0	34.4	38.5	31.0	37.3	37.3	36.2	32.8	24.3	31.4
December	34.2	45.9	39.8	41.3	4.1	34.1	38.5	30.6	36.5	37.4	36.3	32.9	23.8	31.4

. . . = Not available.

Table 10-15. Indexes of Aggregate Weekly Hours of Production and Nonsupervisory Workers on Private Nonfarm Payrolls by NAICS Supersector

(2002 = 100, seasonally adjusted.)

Year and month	Total private	Mining and logging	Construc-tion	Manu-facturing	Trade, transportation, and utilities			Information	Financial activities	Profes-sional and business services	Education and health services	Leisure and hospitality	Other services
					Total	Wholesale trade	Retail trade						
1965	54.4	121.6	55.2	122.1	59.0	. . .	. . .	55.5	42.6	29.4	25.9	41.0	29.4
1966	56.8	121.1	56.8	130.2	60.5	. . .	. . .	58.3	43.6	30.8	27.0	42.2	30.9
1967	57.0	117.0	55.4	127.8	61.1	. . .	. . .	58.6	44.9	31.9	28.1	42.9	32.4
1968	58.4	114.9	56.5	130.1	62.2	. . .	. . .	59.9	46.8	33.1	29.2	44.0	33.9
1969	60.4	118.1	61.0	131.9	64.3	. . .	. . .	61.8	49.4	34.6	30.5	45.6	35.6
1970	59.4	115.7	59.8	123.3	64.9	. . .	. . .	60.4	50.3	34.7	31.0	46.1	36.3
1971	59.0	109.9	61.0	119.3	65.1	. . .	. . .	58.7	51.1	34.7	31.1	46.9	36.5
1972	61.4	115.6	63.4	125.7	67.5	68.4	64.4	61.1	52.5	36.0	32.2	48.5	37.9
1973	64.2	117.0	66.7	132.9	69.6	71.0	66.4	64.1	54.2	37.8	33.7	50.3	39.9
1974	64.2	127.7	64.5	129.0	70.2	72.7	66.7	64.0	54.9	38.8	34.9	50.8	41.4
1975	61.1	134.9	55.2	113.9	68.9	71.8	66.4	59.1	55.0	38.9	35.8	50.9	42.6
1976	63.6	142.4	56.0	120.8	70.9	73.9	68.8	61.2	56.2	40.3	37.1	52.8	44.3
1977	66.1	151.1	59.4	125.8	73.1	76.7	70.7	63.5	58.8	42.1	38.6	54.4	46.3
1978	69.3	156.9	66.2	131.3	76.1	81.0	73.4	66.6	62.0	44.3	40.5	56.6	48.8
1979	71.6	175.2	70.6	133.3	78.3	84.6	74.7	69.0	64.7	46.3	42.3	57.9	51.2
1980	70.8	187.2	68.0	124.4	77.6	84.8	74.0	67.5	67.0	47.7	44.1	57.8	53.6
1981	71.4	206.2	64.9	123.1	78.0	86.0	74.5	67.7	68.6	49.2	45.9	58.7	55.8
1982	68.8	195.5	59.7	109.9	76.4	83.4	74.2	64.0	68.6	49.2	46.7	58.7	56.8
1983	69.8	162.8	61.0	111.6	77.2	83.3	76.0	62.1	69.8	50.7	48.3	60.4	58.9
1984	74.1	169.3	69.1	119.6	81.2	87.5	79.8	68.0	73.0	53.2	50.5	63.6	61.7
1985	76.0	162.7	73.9	117.5	83.5	89.9	82.2	69.1	76.1	55.6	53.1	66.0	65.0
1986	77.3	133.5	75.5	116.3	84.5	89.8	83.9	69.1	79.9	57.8	55.4	67.9	68.1
1987	79.5	125.2	78.1	117.8	86.5	90.5	86.3	71.5	82.3	60.3	58.1	70.5	71.5
1988	81.9	125.6	80.4	120.3	88.6	93.6	88.5	73.1	82.0	63.3	61.4	73.0	75.6
1989	83.9	123.2	81.7	120.3	90.5	95.9	90.0	74.4	82.6	66.3	64.7	74.9	79.7
1990	84.2	128.6	78.8	117.7	89.5	94.9	87.5	76.2	83.1	68.1	66.7	78.9	81.8
1991	82.4	123.8	70.1	112.8	87.4	93.3	84.8	76.1	82.0	66.7	69.8	77.3	81.1
1992	83.0	113.3	67.5	112.4	87.3	92.4	85.1	76.5	82.4	68.4	72.5	79.2	80.6
1993	85.3	110.3	71.3	113.9	89.1	92.4	86.3	78.0	84.9	71.9	74.9	82.1	82.8
1994	89.1	111.0	77.3	118.3	92.7	95.8	89.8	79.2	87.2	77.0	77.9	85.5	84.5
1995	91.5	110.3	79.9	119.0	95.1	99.2	92.3	82.5	86.9	81.2	80.8	88.5	87.0
1996	93.6	112.7	84.3	118.8	96.6	100.7	93.7	86.9	89.1	85.2	83.0	90.7	89.1
1997	97.0	117.6	88.6	121.4	98.9	103.4	95.9	90.4	92.3	91.5	86.4	93.4	91.9
1998	99.4	112.8	93.4	121.0	100.3	104.8	97.2	92.6	96.4	96.7	88.7	95.5	94.3
1999	101.5	102.9	99.7	119.0	101.9	106.2	99.5	98.5	98.1	101.7	90.6	97.8	96.2
2000	103.5	105.1	104.0	117.8	103.5	107.0	101.3	105.0	98.4	106.6	92.7	100.5	97.8
2001	102.1	108.3	103.2	108.1	101.5	102.9	100.5	106.7	99.3	104.0	96.5	100.6	99.0
2002	100.0	100.0	100.0	100.0	100.0	100.0	100.0	100.0	100.0	100.0	100.0	100.0	100.0
2003	98.7	97.4	98.4	94.5	98.6	98.0	98.9	97.0	101.3	98.7	101.6	100.0	97.4
2004	100.2	104.0	101.7	94.3	99.6	98.8	99.4	98.2	101.4	101.8	103.7	103.0	96.1
2005	102.8	114.7	108.3	93.9	101.6	101.8	100.8	99.4	103.7	106.3	106.8	106.2	96.2
2006	105.8	125.8	115.4	95.6	103.3	105.7	101.1	100.2	106.3	112.1	109.4	108.8	97.4
2007	107.3	133.5	114.7	94.4	104.8	109.2	101.8	100.1	107.6	115.3	113.0	110.8	99.3
2008	106.0	137.6	106.5	90.2	103.3	108.6	99.8	100.0	106.8	113.9	116.2	109.7	99.5
2009	98.8	117.2	85.9	76.1	96.8	99.9	94.3	93.5	103.1	105.2	117.9	105.1	96.0
2010	98.9	124.5	80.2	76.2	96.8	97.7	95.0	90.0	101.3	107.6	119.4	104.6	96.0
2011	101.4	147.4	81.7	78.3	99.7	100.7	97.7	88.9	101.2	112.4	122.0	106.9	96.8
2012	104.2	158.7	83.6	80.3	101.8	104.0	98.9	88.9	103.7	117.2	125.1	111.3	97.7
2013	106.1	155.7	87.2	80.8	102.7	105.6	98.7	89.3	104.6	121.6	126.8	115.1	98.2
2014	108.8	165.5	91.8	82.7	104.4	107.1	99.6	99.0	106.5	126.0	128.7	119.4	100.0
2015	110.9	144.1	96.5	83.3	106.3	106.8	100.9	90.8	109.6	128.2	132.3	122.7	100.7
2016	112.5	114.4	100.6	83.3	107.0	106.7	101.1	90.7	111.6	130.6	136.0	125.2	101.7
2017	114.7	214.8	103.1	83.9	101.4	108.8	179.7	90.4	114.2	133.9	139.6	127.7	102.9
2018	117.3	135.2	108.4	86.0	110.8	108.5	103.9	92.5	115.7	135.3	142.9	131.0	104.5
2019	118.3	134.9	111.1	85.6	110.8	108.7	102.3	92.7	117.5	137.3	145.7	131.8	105.4
2020	110.7	105.3	106.1	79.0	107.0	101.8	98.6	88.0	116.5	130.2	140.8	101.7	96.2
2019													
January	118.5	137.4	113.1	86.8	111.6	108.9	103.5	92.6	117.0	136.6	144.1	132.2	105.1
February	117.7	137.6	108.0	86.2	110.8	108.7	102.6	92.8	117.2	136.5	144.2	131.5	104.7
March	118.2	138.7	110.6	86.1	111.0	108.9	102.8	92.9	117.4	136.6	144.6	132.2	105.3
April	118.3	138.0	110.8	85.7	111.0	108.8	103.0	92.2	117.3	136.9	145.0	131.3	105.3
May	118.0	136.6	110.6	85.5	110.7	108.9	102.0	92.8	117.3	136.9	145.2	130.9	105.2
June	118.1	136.7	111.2	85.6	110.7	108.8	102.2	93.5	116.6	137.5	145.6	131.4	105.5
July	117.9	135.4	110.8	85.4	110.4	108.5	101.9	92.4	117.2	137.3	145.5	130.8	105.5
August	118.4	134.2	111.8	85.4	110.7	108.8	102.1	92.6	117.4	138.2	146.3	131.2	105.6
September	118.6	133.2	112.6	85.4	110.8	108.9	102.3	93.4	117.8	137.6	146.2	131.7	105.5
October	118.7	134.2	111.7	84.9	110.9	108.6	102.4	92.4	118.1	137.4	146.9	132.0	105.5
November	118.5	129.5	110.7	85.3	110.2	108.6	100.7	92.5	118.5	138.0	147.3	133.0	105.7
December	119.0	126.7	110.9	85.3	111.1	108.5	102.3	92.7	118.0	137.7	148.0	133.3	105.6
2020													
January	119.2	121.2	113.3	84.7	111.7	108.2	102.4	93.5	119.3	138.0	147.8	133.9	106.6
February	119.8	120.7	112.9	85.5	111.8	108.2	102.5	93.9	119.0	138.6	148.6	134.3	106.5
March	117.0	115.3	110.7	84.0	111.5	107.2	102.3	93.8	118.2	137.0	146.6	118.0	102.4
April	97.2	99.2	90.6	68.7	96.6	95.4	86.7	85.0	114.4	119.3	128.6	58.2	79.3
May	102.3	98.0	101.7	72.0	100.3	97.5	91.7	83.9	114.7	122.5	132.2	75.5	85.7
June	106.6	99.3	104.7	76.3	103.9	99.1	96.5	84.5	114.5	124.8	136.8	91.4	92.2
July	108.7	99.1	105.7	78.1	105.4	99.3	98.1	84.3	115.0	126.5	139.4	96.4	94.5
August	109.7	100.5	105.6	78.9	106.7	100.0	100.0	86.7	115.0	127.9	140.6	99.6	95.7
September	111.0	100.9	105.9	79.4	107.6	101.4	100.3	86.9	116.4	129.4	141.8	103.9	97.1
October	112.3	101.1	106.0	79.7	109.4	101.5	101.4	87.0	116.7	131.7	142.2	105.9	98.4
November	112.7	104.6	106.9	80.0	110.0	101.6	101.4	88.7	117.1	132.9	142.5	104.6	98.3
December	112.4	103.9	108.9	80.3	109.0	101.8	100.2	87.2	117.4	134.2	142.9	98.4	98.0

. . . = Not available.

Table 10-16. Average Hourly Earnings of Production and Nonsupervisory Workers on Private Nonfarm Payrolls by NAICS Supersector

(Dollars, seasonally adjusted.)

Year and month	Total private	Mining and logging	Construc- tion	Manu- facturing	Trade, transportation, and utilities — Total	Wholesale trade	Retail trade	Information	Financial activities	Profes- sional and business services	Education and health services	Leisure and hospitality	Other services
1965	2.63	2.87	3.23	2.49	2.94	...	...	4.47	2.38	3.28	2.12	1.17	1.25
1966	2.73	3.00	3.41	2.60	3.04	...	...	4.56	2.47	3.39	2.23	1.26	1.37
1967	2.85	3.14	3.63	2.71	3.15	...	...	4.68	2.58	3.51	2.36	1.37	1.49
1968	3.02	3.30	3.92	2.89	3.32	...	...	4.85	2.75	3.65	2.49	1.53	1.62
1969	3.22	3.54	4.30	3.07	3.48	...	...	5.05	2.92	3.84	2.68	1.69	1.81
1970	3.40	3.77	4.74	3.24	3.65	...	...	5.25	3.07	4.04	2.88	1.82	2.01
1971	3.63	3.99	5.17	3.45	3.86	...	...	5.53	3.23	4.26	3.11	1.95	2.24
1972	3.90	4.28	5.55	3.70	4.23	4.58	3.52	5.87	3.37	4.50	3.33	2.08	2.46
1973	4.14	4.59	5.89	3.97	4.46	4.80	3.69	6.17	3.55	4.72	3.54	2.20	2.67
1974	4.43	5.09	6.29	4.31	4.74	5.11	3.92	6.52	3.80	5.01	3.82	2.40	2.95
1975	4.73	5.68	6.78	4.71	5.01	5.45	4.14	6.92	4.08	5.29	4.09	2.58	3.21
1976	5.06	6.19	7.17	5.10	5.31	5.75	4.36	7.37	4.30	5.60	4.39	2.78	3.51
1977	5.44	6.70	7.56	5.55	5.67	6.12	4.65	7.84	4.58	5.95	4.72	3.03	3.84
1978	5.88	7.44	8.11	6.05	6.11	6.61	5.00	8.34	4.93	6.32	5.07	3.33	4.19
1979	6.34	8.20	8.71	6.57	6.56	7.12	5.34	8.86	5.31	6.71	5.44	3.63	4.56
1980	6.85	8.97	9.37	7.15	7.04	7.68	5.71	9.47	5.82	7.22	5.93	3.98	5.05
1981	7.44	9.89	10.24	7.87	7.55	8.28	6.09	10.21	6.34	7.80	6.49	4.36	5.61
1982	7.87	10.64	11.04	8.36	7.91	8.81	6.34	10.76	6.82	8.30	7.00	4.63	6.11
1983	8.20	11.14	11.36	8.70	8.23	9.27	6.60	11.18	7.32	8.70	7.39	4.89	6.51
1984	8.49	11.54	11.56	9.05	8.45	9.61	6.73	11.50	7.65	8.98	7.66	4.99	6.79
1985	8.74	11.87	11.75	9.40	8.60	9.88	6.83	11.81	7.97	9.28	7.97	5.10	7.10
1986	8.93	12.14	11.92	9.60	8.74	10.07	6.93	12.08	8.37	9.55	8.24	5.20	7.38
1987	9.14	12.17	12.15	9.77	8.92	10.32	7.02	12.36	8.73	9.85	8.56	5.30	7.69
1988	9.44	12.45	12.52	10.05	9.15	10.71	7.23	12.63	9.07	10.22	8.95	5.50	8.08
1989	9.80	12.90	12.98	10.35	9.46	11.12	7.46	12.99	9.54	10.69	9.45	5.76	8.58
1990	10.20	13.40	13.42	10.78	9.83	11.58	7.71	13.40	9.98	11.14	9.98	6.02	9.08
1991	10.51	13.82	13.65	11.13	10.08	11.95	7.89	13.90	10.43	11.50	10.48	6.22	9.39
1992	10.77	14.09	13.81	11.40	10.30	12.21	8.12	14.29	10.86	11.78	10.85	6.36	9.66
1993	11.05	14.12	14.04	11.70	10.55	12.57	8.36	14.86	11.38	11.96	11.19	6.48	9.90
1994	11.34	14.41	14.38	12.04	10.80	12.93	8.61	15.32	11.84	12.15	11.48	6.62	10.18
1995	11.65	14.78	14.73	12.34	11.10	13.34	8.85	15.68	12.31	12.53	11.78	6.79	10.51
1996	12.04	15.09	15.11	12.75	11.46	13.80	9.21	16.30	12.75	13.00	12.15	6.99	10.85
1997	12.51	15.57	15.67	13.14	11.90	14.41	9.59	17.14	13.28	13.57	12.53	7.32	11.29
1998	13.01	16.20	16.23	13.45	12.40	15.07	10.05	17.67	14.00	14.27	12.96	7.67	11.79
1999	13.49	16.33	16.80	13.85	12.82	15.62	10.45	18.40	14.55	14.85	13.40	7.96	12.26
2000	14.02	16.55	17.48	14.32	13.31	16.28	10.87	19.07	15.04	15.52	13.91	8.32	12.73
2001	14.54	17.00	18.00	14.76	13.70	16.77	11.29	19.80	15.65	16.33	14.59	8.57	13.27
2002	14.97	17.19	18.52	15.29	14.02	16.98	11.67	20.20	16.25	16.80	15.16	8.81	13.72
2003	15.37	17.56	18.95	15.74	14.34	17.36	11.90	21.01	17.21	17.21	15.57	9.00	13.84
2004	15.69	18.07	19.23	16.14	14.58	17.65	12.08	21.40	17.58	17.48	16.08	9.15	13.98
2005	16.12	18.72	19.46	16.56	14.92	18.16	12.36	22.06	17.98	18.08	16.63	9.38	14.34
2006	16.75	19.90	20.02	16.81	15.39	18.91	12.57	23.23	18.83	19.13	17.30	9.75	14.77
2007	17.42	20.97	20.95	17.26	15.78	19.59	12.75	23.96	19.67	20.15	18.01	10.41	15.42
2008	18.07	22.50	21.87	17.75	16.16	20.13	12.87	24.78	20.32	21.18	18.75	10.84	16.09
2009	18.61	23.29	22.66	18.24	16.48	20.84	13.01	25.45	20.90	22.35	19.35	11.12	16.59
2010	19.05	23.82	23.22	18.61	16.82	21.54	13.25	25.87	21.55	22.78	19.98	11.31	17.06
2011	19.44	24.50	23.65	18.93	17.15	21.97	13.51	26.62	21.93	23.12	20.63	11.45	17.32
2012	19.74	25.79	23.97	19.08	17.43	22.24	13.82	27.04	22.82	23.29	20.94	11.62	17.59
2013	20.13	26.81	24.22	19.30	17.75	22.63	14.02	27.99	23.87	23.69	21.30	11.78	18.00
2014	20.61	26.85	24.67	19.56	18.27	23.24	14.39	28.66	24.71	24.28	21.65	12.09	18.52
2015	21.03	26.48	25.50	19.91	18.67	23.63	14.82	29.05	25.34	24.79	22.09	12.41	19.01
2016	21.54	27.05	25.97	20.43	18.99	24.18	15.05	30.04	26.11	25.42	22.53	12.85	19.36
2017	22.13	27.66	26.44	20.95	19.35	24.75	15.11	30.69	26.52	26.09	22.96	13.45	19.98
2018	22.70	28.28	27.71	21.53	19.89	25.16	15.90	31.92	26.93	26.79	23.65	13.87	20.77
2019	23.51	29.97	28.51	22.14	20.64	26.06	16.61	33.85	27.68	27.79	24.34	14.50	21.41
2020	24.68	30.45	29.19	22.79	21.41	26.79	17.61	35.71	29.07	29.26	25.40	14.71	22.60
2019													
January	23.11	29.00	28.19	21.84	20.21	25.52	16.23	33.10	27.28	27.23	24.03	14.23	21.22
February	23.19	29.05	28.17	21.91	20.34	25.75	16.30	33.24	27.46	27.32	24.06	14.29	21.24
March	23.28	29.36	28.33	21.96	20.49	26.04	16.41	33.36	27.37	27.44	24.16	14.34	21.24
April	23.33	29.88	28.45	21.96	20.53	25.98	16.49	33.41	27.50	27.52	24.14	14.38	21.27
May	23.42	29.95	28.49	22.04	20.68	26.06	16.63	33.62	27.56	27.63	24.13	14.43	21.35
June	23.47	29.86	28.50	22.14	20.65	26.10	16.60	33.67	27.65	27.75	24.21	14.44	21.39
July	23.54	29.80	28.45	22.19	20.68	26.05	16.64	33.84	27.71	27.84	24.39	14.49	21.37
August	23.64	30.17	28.58	22.22	20.78	26.28	16.72	34.16	27.82	27.96	24.45	14.55	21.47
September	23.70	30.52	28.63	22.26	20.76	26.20	16.74	34.42	27.81	28.06	24.54	14.63	21.50
October	23.76	30.85	28.68	22.30	20.80	26.28	16.77	34.53	27.89	28.16	24.67	14.67	21.55
November	23.81	30.55	28.72	22.39	20.88	26.33	16.86	34.43	28.02	28.23	24.63	14.73	21.62
December	23.84	30.68	28.88	22.44	20.83	26.15	16.88	34.44	28.06	28.28	24.72	14.77	21.71
2020													
January	23.88	30.29	28.92	22.41	20.89	26.23	16.92	34.51	28.17	28.35	24.70	14.84	21.74
February	23.96	30.79	28.96	22.50	20.96	26.25	16.98	34.65	28.25	28.45	24.77	14.91	21.79
March	24.15	30.70	29.06	22.58	20.99	26.44	17.07	34.95	28.35	28.58	24.97	14.63	22.12
April	25.16	30.98	28.69	22.72	21.59	26.87	17.63	35.76	28.82	29.86	25.35	14.68	23.50
May	25.01	30.59	28.98	22.76	21.63	26.94	17.85	35.55	29.12	29.68	25.41	14.58	23.21
June	24.77	30.49	29.31	22.62	21.65	26.84	18.12	35.76	29.03	29.36	25.36	14.58	22.71
July	24.67	30.54	29.30	22.84	21.29	26.86	17.50	36.03	29.17	29.30	25.37	14.58	22.61
August	24.81	30.35	29.39	22.87	21.57	26.92	17.75	36.16	29.43	29.51	25.47	14.72	22.57
September	24.79	30.36	29.09	23.01	21.47	26.93	17.78	36.16	29.48	29.50	25.60	14.80	22.61
October	24.83	30.27	29.40	22.99	21.57	26.98	17.87	36.50	29.62	29.39	25.67	14.84	22.65
November	24.93	29.87	29.55	23.10	21.62	27.08	17.92	36.24	29.68	29.48	25.83	14.70	22.80
December	25.15	30.16	29.64	23.12	21.74	27.12	17.96	36.19	29.68	29.66	26.28	14.66	22.93

. . . = Not available.

Table 10-17. Average Weekly Earnings of Production and Nonsupervisory Workers on Private Nonfarm Payrolls by NAICS Supersector

(Dollars, seasonally adjusted.)

Year and month	Total private	Mining and logging	Construc-tion	Manu-facturing	Trade, transportation, and utilities			Information	Financial activities	Profes-sional and business services	Education and health services	Leisure and hospitality	Other services
					Total	Wholesale trade	Retail trade						
1965	101.51	125.48	122.35	102.69	116.36	...	...	171.24	88.50	122.30	74.84	38.06	45.30
1966	105.23	132.50	130.11	107.47	118.78	...	...	174.52	91.83	125.53	78.04	40.34	48.94
1967	108.07	137.76	138.55	109.85	121.57	...	...	176.09	95.35	128.34	81.34	43.06	52.69
1968	113.82	145.26	148.22	117.73	126.69	...	...	182.65	101.18	132.47	85.02	47.07	56.81
1969	120.70	157.11	164.88	124.74	132.13	...	...	190.18	107.91	139.37	91.46	51.29	63.44
1970	125.79	165.82	179.11	128.84	137.15	...	...	195.24	112.32	144.76	97.23	54.57	69.67
1971	133.22	174.18	194.70	137.59	144.11	...	...	204.50	117.60	151.51	103.57	58.39	76.58
1972	143.87	188.76	205.04	150.23	158.09	181.98	123.57	218.72	122.86	159.88	111.12	61.78	84.14
1973	152.59	201.43	219.32	161.59	165.61	190.33	128.16	230.48	129.32	167.40	117.85	64.92	91.06
1974	161.61	222.24	233.24	172.37	174.18	200.53	134.39	241.07	137.71	176.47	126.50	69.90	99.98
1975	170.29	248.38	249.70	185.69	182.61	212.85	140.99	253.21	147.75	185.81	134.83	74.49	108.67
1976	182.65	273.69	267.00	204.41	192.62	224.66	147.21	270.80	155.54	195.61	143.47	79.47	117.85
1977	195.58	299.46	279.61	224.01	203.87	239.57	154.51	288.29	165.47	206.78	153.38	85.20	128.12
1978	210.29	334.27	302.27	244.49	217.53	258.75	163.74	306.71	177.96	218.42	163.48	92.16	138.74
1979	225.69	366.58	326.55	263.99	232.36	278.74	173.18	324.51	190.72	231.16	174.80	99.47	150.47
1980	241.07	402.51	351.49	283.35	246.60	298.24	182.25	344.38	209.21	247.64	190.16	107.52	166.32
1981	261.53	446.10	382.75	312.74	263.93	322.08	193.97	370.36	228.21	267.46	208.06	117.49	184.77
1982	273.10	469.10	410.39	325.07	274.09	340.84	200.74	385.82	245.16	284.11	224.53	124.14	201.49
1983	286.43	488.89	427.00	348.89	284.76	359.98	208.81	404.89	262.83	298.74	237.40	130.82	214.87
1984	298.26	514.77	441.28	367.77	292.99	373.78	212.82	420.45	276.50	308.24	245.16	133.49	223.33
1985	304.62	529.62	448.35	380.60	295.81	383.22	213.38	430.86	287.66	317.41	254.19	134.71	232.81
1986	309.78	529.20	451.22	390.46	298.07	389.73	214.52	439.84	302.32	327.30	263.41	136.34	242.33
1987	317.39	529.72	463.78	400.00	304.10	397.39	218.05	450.77	314.01	337.57	273.49	139.45	252.58
1988	326.48	539.63	478.74	412.62	309.58	411.71	223.67	455.59	322.87	349.89	286.57	144.51	265.83
1989	338.34	568.55	497.43	423.58	319.40	427.40	229.14	468.77	339.46	365.93	302.70	150.29	282.09
1990	349.63	602.43	513.43	436.13	331.55	444.46	235.56	479.50	354.60	380.61	318.87	156.32	297.88
1991	358.46	625.46	520.41	449.83	339.10	459.17	240.13	495.14	369.57	391.06	334.07	159.20	306.75
1992	368.20	628.94	525.13	464.43	348.60	470.41	249.66	511.95	386.31	400.64	347.70	163.70	315.08
1993	378.89	634.77	539.81	480.89	359.51	484.46	256.89	535.19	403.68	406.20	358.44	167.54	322.69
1994	391.17	653.13	558.53	501.95	370.38	501.14	265.74	551.21	420.18	414.16	367.50	172.27	332.44
1995	400.04	670.40	571.57	509.26	378.79	515.14	272.63	564.92	437.26	426.54	376.94	175.74	342.36
1996	413.25	695.04	588.48	526.55	390.67	533.36	282.74	592.45	453.05	442.81	387.50	181.02	352.68
1997	431.86	720.07	609.48	548.26	407.63	559.39	295.94	622.37	475.03	465.51	403.63	190.66	368.63
1998	448.59	727.19	629.75	557.12	423.33	582.21	310.33	646.52	503.94	490.13	417.58	200.82	384.25
1999	463.15	721.77	655.11	573.29	434.31	602.77	321.71	675.47	520.74	510.99	429.98	208.05	398.77
2000	480.99	734.88	685.78	591.01	449.96	631.24	333.41	700.92	540.39	535.07	447.82	217.20	413.30
2001	493.74	757.96	695.86	595.19	459.53	643.45	346.16	731.18	560.46	557.84	471.36	220.73	428.64
2002	506.60	741.97	711.82	618.62	471.27	644.38	360.84	737.94	578.94	574.60	490.73	227.31	439.87
2003	517.82	765.94	727.00	636.03	481.14	657.29	367.18	760.84	611.82	587.02	503.27	230.49	434.41
2004	528.89	804.01	735.55	658.52	488.51	666.79	371.13	776.72	625.53	597.54	521.24	234.86	433.04
2005	544.05	853.87	750.37	673.30	498.46	685.00	377.58	805.11	646.48	618.71	541.78	241.36	443.40
2006	567.39	907.95	781.59	690.88	514.37	718.50	383.12	850.64	673.63	662.27	561.59	250.34	456.50
2007	589.27	962.63	816.23	711.53	525.91	748.94	385.00	874.45	706.52	700.82	586.41	265.54	477.06
2008	607.53	1 014.69	842.61	724.46	536.11	769.62	386.21	908.78	729.64	737.90	608.58	273.39	495.57
2009	616.01	1 006.67	851.76	726.12	541.88	784.49	388.57	931.08	754.90	775.81	622.73	275.95	506.26
2010	636.25	1 063.11	891.83	765.15	559.63	816.50	400.07	939.85	780.19	798.54	640.60	280.87	523.70
2011	653.19	1 144.64	921.84	784.29	577.71	845.44	412.09	964.85	798.68	813.37	665.05	283.82	532.63
2012	665.82	1 201.69	942.14	794.63	588.86	860.70	422.10	973.52	840.04	822.58	675.85	290.54	539.46
2013	677.67	1 230.00	958.67	807.51	597.51	875.82	423.00	1 005.49	875.22	837.27	683.48	294.34	553.12
2014	694.89	1 271.15	977.05	822.24	613.95	897.74	431.64	1 029.73	908.43	864.12	692.41	303.83	568.90
2015	708.90	1 211.91	998.02	832.05	628.76	911.41	445.52	1 038.10	939.46	878.71	709.25	311.32	583.54
2016	723.69	1 224.33	1 031.16	855.69	636.64	933.16	447.62	1 068.25	962.73	898.76	724.40	319.52	595.73
2017	742.48	1 267.91	969.01	872.52	654.05	962.29	462.06	1 097.75	981.24	923.51	741.48	331.08	614.38
2018	766.05	1 322.86	1 103.35	906.70	674.73	979.13	482.82	1 136.98	996.57	946.74	762.23	344.94	639.69
2019	790.23	1 407.43	1 132.62	920.16	697.65	1 007.93	503.00	1 195.48	1 021.06	984.04	783.68	358.04	659.81
2020	836.79	1 369.55	1 147.96	929.04	730.43	1 023.28	542.25	1 286.92	1 077.26	1 048.05	824.48	354.18	706.08
2019													
January	781.12	1 351.40	1 141.70	917.28	687.14	990.18	495.02	1 171.74	1 009.36	966.67	773.77	354.33	655.70
February	779.18	1 362.45	1 098.63	913.65	687.49	996.53	493.89	1 180.02	1 016.02	967.13	774.73	354.39	654.19
March	784.54	1 385.79	1 130.37	915.73	694.61	1 010.35	498.86	1 184.28	1 012.69	971.38	777.95	357.07	656.32
April	786.22	1 413.32	1 132.31	913.54	695.97	1 005.43	502.95	1 179.37	1 014.75	974.21	777.37	355.19	655.12
May	786.91	1 404.66	1 131.05	914.66	698.98	1 008.52	502.23	1 190.15	1 016.96	978.10	776.99	354.98	657.58
June	788.59	1 409.39	1 134.30	921.02	697.97	1 010.07	502.98	1 195.29	1 014.76	985.13	779.56	356.67	658.81
July	788.59	1 406.50	1 126.62	920.89	696.92	1 005.53	502.53	1 187.78	1 019.72	985.96	782.92	356.45	658.20
August	794.30	1 424.02	1 140.34	922.13	702.36	1 017.04	506.62	1 202.43	1 023.78	995.38	787.29	357.93	661.28
September	796.32	1 437.49	1 148.06	923.79	701.69	1 013.94	507.22	1 221.91	1 026.19	993.32	787.73	359.90	662.20
October	798.34	1 456.12	1 138.60	923.22	703.04	1 014.41	508.13	1 215.46	1 029.14	994.05	794.37	360.88	663.74
November	797.64	1 420.58	1 131.57	926.95	701.57	1 016.34	504.11	1 208.49	1 036.74	999.34	793.09	363.83	665.90
December	801.02	1 417.42	1 137.87	929.02	704.05	1 006.78	511.46	1 208.84	1 032.61	998.28	798.46	364.82	668.67
2020													
January	802.37	1 393.34	1 153.91	927.77	708.17	1 012.48	514.37	1 211.30	1 042.29	1 006.43	795.34	366.55	673.94
February	807.45	1 410.18	1 143.92	938.25	710.54	1 013.25	516.19	1 219.68	1 039.60	1 012.82	800.07	368.28	675.49
March	806.61	1 393.78	1 147.87	932.55	713.66	1 015.30	522.34	1 233.74	1 040.45	1 014.59	804.03	333.56	672.45
April	842.86	1 335.24	1 098.83	874.72	725.42	994.19	537.72	1 273.06	1 063.46	1 051.07	806.13	327.36	733.20
May	852.84	1 342.90	1 141.81	896.74	741.91	1 012.94	558.71	1 276.25	1 077.44	1 062.54	815.66	354.29	738.08
June	839.70	1 350.71	1 151.88	902.54	738.27	1 017.24	559.91	1 290.94	1 071.21	1 051.09	821.66	352.84	715.37
July	838.78	1 352.92	1 151.49	929.59	728.12	1 023.37	540.75	1 293.48	1 082.21	1 051.87	827.06	349.92	705.43
August	843.54	1 362.72	1 152.09	939.96	735.54	1 028.34	548.48	1 330.69	1 088.91	1 059.41	830.32	360.64	704.18
September	845.34	1 366.20	1 143.24	948.01	734.27	1 036.81	549.40	1 308.99	1 099.60	1 062.00	839.68	365.56	707.69
October	849.19	1 368.20	1 149.54	949.49	744.17	1 038.73	553.97	1 332.25	1 104.83	1 060.98	841.98	365.06	711.21
November	852.61	1 374.02	1 161.32	954.03	743.73	1 041.65	555.52	1 351.75	1 107.06	1 067.18	847.22	357.21	715.92
December	860.13	1 384.34	1 179.67	954.86	741.33	1 044.12	549.58	1 320.94	1 110.03	1 076.66	864.61	348.91	720.00

... = Not available.

SECTION 10C: OTHER SIGNIFICANT LABOR MARKET DATA

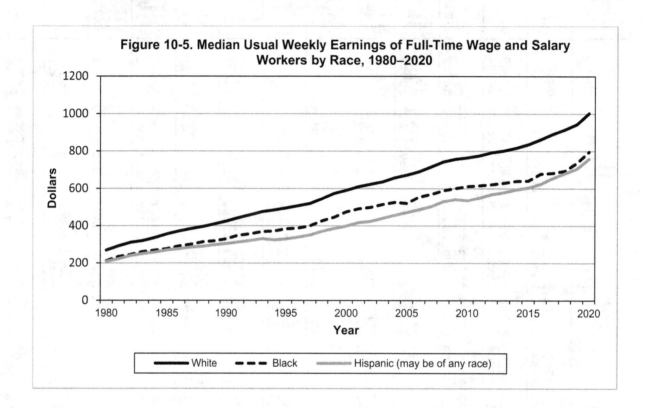

Figure 10-5. Median Usual Weekly Earnings of Full-Time Wage and Salary Workers by Race, 1980–2020

- This section of *Business Statistics* includes indicators of hours and earnings from the Current Population Statistics (household) survey that are more appropriate than similarly-named indicators produced by the payroll survey and shown in the previous section. It also incorporates annual employment data from the Bureau of Economic Analysis, produced as part of the National Income and Product Accounts (NIPA), that provide a consistent historical record of U.S. employment from 1929 through 2020.

- The gender pay gap is illustrated in Table 10-19. Using median earnings of full-time wage and salary workers; comparisons can be made by age and gender. In 2020, although the gender wage gap has narrowed, women only earned approximately 84 percent of what men earned including full and part-time workers. Women have to work approximately 42 extra days a year to earn what men earn. (Table 10-19)

- In 2000, the Census Bureau began reporting the Asian race separately. Since then, Asian workers have the highest median usual weekly earnings among all the races. In 2020, Asians had median usual weekly earnings of $1,310 compared with $1,003 for Whites, $794 for Blacks, and $758 for Hispanics. (Table 10-19).

Table 10-18. Hours at Work, Current Population Survey

(Hours per week.)

Year and month	Hours per person, all industries				Hours per person, nonagricultural industries	
	Total	Men	Women	Persons who usually work full-time	All workers	
					Total	Usually work full-time
1948	42.8	. . .	. . .	. . .	41.6	. . .
1949	42.1	. . .	. . .	. . .	40.9	. . .
1950	41.7	. . .	. . .	. . .	40.7	. . .
1951	42.2	. . .	. . .	. . .	41.3	. . .
1952	42.4	. . .	. . .	. . .	41.6	. . .
1953	41.9	. . .	. . .	. . .	41.1	. . .
1954	40.9	. . .	. . .	. . .	40.0	. . .
1955	41.6	. . .	. . .	. . .	40.9	. . .
1956	41.5	43.8	36.5	. . .	40.9	. . .
1957	41.0	43.4	36.1	. . .	40.5	. . .
1958	40.6	42.9	35.8	. . .	40.1	. . .
1959	40.5	42.8	35.6	. . .	40.0	. . .
1960	40.5	43.0	35.4	. . .	40.0	. . .
1961	40.5	43.0	35.3	. . .	40.1	. . .
1962	40.5	43.2	35.2	. . .	40.1	. . .
1963	40.4	43.2	35.1	. . .	40.1	. . .
1964	40.0	43.2	34.7	. . .	39.7	. . .
1965	40.5	42.8	35.1	. . .	40.2	. . .
1966	40.4	43.3	35.2	. . .	40.1	. . .
1967	40.4	43.2	35.2	. . .	40.0	. . .
1968	40.1	43.3	34.9	. . .	39.7	. . .
1969	39.9	43.0	34.9	. . .	39.5	. . .
1970	39.1	42.9	34.2	. . .	38.7	. . .
1971	39.3	42.0	34.3	. . .	38.9	. . .
1972	39.4	42.2	34.5	. . .	39.0	. . .
1973	39.3	42.3	34.4	. . .	39.0	. . .
1974	39.0	42.4	34.3	. . .	38.7	. . .
1975	38.7	42.0	34.1	. . .	38.4	. . .
1976	38.7	41.6	34.1	. . .	38.4	. . .
1977	38.8	41.7	34.2	. . .	38.5	. . .
1978	39.0	41.9	34.5	. . .	38.7	. . .
1979	38.9	42.1	34.5	. . .	38.6	. . .
1980	38.5	42.0	34.5	. . .	38.3	. . .
1981	38.1	41.5	34.1	. . .	37.9	. . .
1982	38.0	41.1	34.1	. . .	37.7	. . .
1983	38.3	40.9	34.5	. . .	38.1	. . .
1984	38.8	41.2	34.9	. . .	38.6	. . .
1985	39.0	41.8	35.2	. . .	38.9	. . .
1986	39.1	42.0	35.4	. . .	38.9	. . .
1987	39.0	42.1	35.3	. . .	38.8	. . .
1988	39.4	42.0	35.7	. . .	39.3	. . .
1989	39.6	42.4	35.8	. . .	39.4	. . .
1990	39.4	42.6	35.8	. . .	39.3	. . .
1991	39.2	42.3	35.8	. . .	39.1	. . .
1992	38.9	42.0	35.6	. . .	38.8	. . .
1993	39.4	41.7	36.0	. . .	39.3	. . .
1994	39.2	42.2	35.5	43.4	39.1	43.3
1995	39.3	42.2	35.6	43.4	39.2	43.2
1996	39.3	42.3	35.7	43.3	39.2	43.2
1997	39.5	42.3	36.0	43.4	39.4	43.3
1998	39.3	42.4	35.8	43.2	39.2	43.1
1999	39.6	42.2	36.2	43.4	39.5	43.3
2000	39.7	42.4	36.4	43.4	39.6	43.3
2001	39.2	42.5	36.1	42.9	39.2	42.8
2002	39.2	41.9	36.0	42.9	39.1	42.8
2003	39.0	41.8	35.9	42.9	39.0	42.7
2004	39.0	41.7	35.9	42.9	39.0	42.8
2005	39.2	41.7	36.1	42.9	39.1	42.8
2006	39.2	41.8	36.2	42.9	39.2	42.8
2007	39.2	41.8	36.1	42.8	39.1	42.7
2008	38.9	41.7	36.1	42.6	38.8	42.5
2009	37.9	41.3	35.3	41.9	37.8	41.8
2010	38.2	40.2	35.5	42.2	38.1	42.2
2011	38.3	40.5	35.6	42.4	38.2	42.3
2012	38.5	40.6	35.8	42.5	38.4	42.4
2013	38.6	40.8	36.0	42.6	38.5	42.5
2014	38.6	40.9	35.9	42.5	38.6	42.5
2015	38.6	41.0	35.9	42.4	38.5	42.3
2016	38.7	40.9	36.2	42.5	38.7	42.4
2017	38.7	41.0	36.2	42.4	38.6	42.3
2018	38.9	40.9	36.4	42.5	38.9	42.1
2019	39.0	41.0	36.6	42.6	38.9	42.5
2020	38.2	40.1	36.1	41.5	38.0	42.0

. . . = Not available.

Table 10-19 Median Usual Weekly Earnings of Full-Time Wage and Salary Workers

(Current dollars, [second quartile] except as noted; not seasonally adjusted.)

Year and quarter	Sex and age						Race and ethnicity			
	Men, 16 years and over			Women, 16 years and over			White	Black or African American	Asian	Hispanic or Latino ethnicity
	16 to 24 years	25 to 54 years	55 years and over	16 to 24 years	25 to 54 years	55 years and over				
1980	208	...	...	167	...	...	269	212	...	209
1981	218	...	...	180	...	...	291	235	...	223
1982	225	...	...	192	...	...	310	245	...	240
1983	223	...	...	198	...	...	320	261	...	250
1984	231	...	...	203	...	...	336	269	...	259
1985	241	...	...	211	...	...	356	277	...	270
1986	246	...	...	219	...	...	371	291	...	277
1987	257	...	...	227	...	...	384	301	...	285
1988	262	...	...	235	...	...	395	314	...	290
1989	271	...	...	246	...	...	409	319	...	298
1990	282	...	...	254	...	...	424	329	...	304
1991	285	...	...	266	...	...	442	348	...	312
1992	284	...	...	267	...	...	458	357	...	321
1993	288	...	...	273	...	...	475	369	...	331
1994	294	...	...	276	...	...	484	371	...	324
1995	303	...	...	275	...	...	494	383	...	329
1996	307	...	...	284	...	...	506	387	...	339
1997	317	...	...	292	...	...	519	400	...	351
1998	334	...	...	305	...	...	545	426	...	370
1999	356	...	...	324	...	...	573	445	...	385
2000	375	690	714	344	519	497	590	474	615	399
2001	391	717	742	353	547	519	610	491	639	417
2002	391	727	773	367	571	556	623	498	658	424
2003	398	736	797	371	584	584	636	514	693	440
2004	400	755	819	375	599	601	657	525	708	456
2005	409	763	829	381	610	619	672	520	753	471
2006	418	784	870	395	624	641	690	554	784	486
2007	443	809	902	409	644	657	716	569	830	503
2008	461	843	920	420	666	687	742	589	861	529
2009	458	857	944	424	683	706	757	601	880	541
2010	443	854	961	422	700	716	765	611	855	535
2011	455	864	976	421	713	738	775	615	866	549
2012	468	890	987	416	719	752	792	621	920	568
2013	479	891	999	423	733	766	802	629	942	578
2014	493	899	1 007	451	746	773	816	639	953	594
2015	510	921	1 054	450	757	774	835	641	993	604
2016	512	943	1 082	486	778	801	862	678	1 021	624
2017	547	977	1 084	499	801	843	890	682	1 043	655
2018	575	1 004	1 127	522	825	845	916	694	1 095	680
2019	607	1 045	1 150	540	864	868	945	735	1 174	706
2020	622	1 129	1 204	589	925	944	1 003	794	1 310	758
2013										
1st quarter	487	902	969	419	729	754	802	622	951	575
2nd quarter	479	890	1 018	422	735	769	799	634	973	572
3rd quarter	452	885	984	414	729	765	794	630	922	587
4th quarter	492	888	1 036	449	739	776	813	632	916	576
2014										
1st quarter	480	905	979	434	750	767	819	646	955	593
2nd quarter	481	892	993	449	744	768	802	649	954	583
3rd quarter	498	894	1 034	448	743	778	816	638	945	598
4th quarter	508	905	1 019	469	749	784	823	621	959	600
2015										
1st quarter	491	922	1 029	461	757	768	835	650	966	590
2nd quarter	497	918	1 032	444	753	782	829	647	965	601
3rd quarter	517	916	1 069	442	757	781	829	624	974	602
4th quarter	543	926	1 092	453	764	768	847	643	1 091	624
2016										
1st quarter	511	935	1 102	488	771	821	857	673	1 032	612
2nd quarter	505	944	1 049	470	774	785	854	677	1 021	618
3rd quarter	510	943	1 095	480	782	793	854	685	1 010	632
4th quarter	522	953	1 084	506	788	810	881	675	1 022	646
2017										
1st quarter	558	982	1 045	489	795	828	894	679	1 019	649
2nd quarter	524	984	1 046	496	811	859	886	689	1 103	657
3rd quarter	527	969	1 125	500	797	859	887	696	1 010	655
4th quarter	581	974	1 116	512	799	818	891	666	1 061	657
2018										
1st quarter	563	1 001	1 097	545	819	819	911	696	1 066	675
2nd quarter	528	991	1 117	511	811	868	907	683	1 083	674
3rd quarter	575	1 012	1 111	515	845	826	915	686	1 128	689
4th quarter	609	1 014	1 166	539	825	873	931	712	1 095	684
2019										
1st quarter	605	1 034	1 149	539	841	859	935	737	1 157	696
2nd quarter	601	1 035	1 141	522	852	871	933	724	1 152	696
3rd quarter	601	1 047	1 143	538	883	854	943	727	1 247	718
4th quarter	621	1 066	1 168	566	881	892	967	756	1 166	712
2020										
1st quarter	593	1 109	1 197	582	894	895	980	775	1 221	721
2nd quarter	640	1 136	1 191	594	948	977	1 017	805	1 336	786
3rd quarter	631	1 149	1 231	583	942	942	1 008	813	1 392	785
4th quarter	625	1 115	1 202	596	929	965	1 007	792	1 261	742

. . . = Not available.

NOTES AND DEFINITIONS, CHAPTER 10

General note on monthly employment data

This chapter presents data from two different data sets that measure employment monthly. Both are compiled and published by the Bureau of Labor Statistics (BLS), but each set has different characteristics. Users should be aware of these dissimilarities and the consequent differences in the appropriate uses and interpretations of data from the two systems.

One set of monthly employment estimates comes from the Current Population Survey (CPS), a large sample survey of approximately 60,000 U.S. households. The numbers in the sample are expanded to match the latest estimates of the total U.S. population. These are the most comprehensive estimates in their scope—that is, in the universe that they are designed to measure. These estimates represent all civilian workers, including the following groups that are excluded by definition from the other set of estimates: all farm workers; domestic household workers (house cleaners, gardeners, nannies, etc.); nonagricultural, nonincorporated self-employed workers; and nonagricultural unpaid family workers. See Notes and Definitions from Chapter 3 for the impact of gathering data for the CPS system.

This household survey (CPS) is designed to measure the labor force status of the civilian noninstitutional population with demographic detail. The national unemployment rate is the best-known statistic produced from the household survey. The survey also provides a measure of employed people, one that includes agricultural workers and the self-employed. A representative sample of U.S. households provides the information for the household survey.

However, official CPS data are characterized by periodic discontinuities, which occur when new benchmarks for Census measures of the total population are introduced. These updates take place in a single month—usually January—and the official data for previous months are typically not modified to provide a smooth transition. Therefore, shorter-term comparisons (for a year or two or for a business cycle phase) will be misleading if such a discontinuity is included in the period. A recent example will illustrate. Beginning with January 2019, the updated controls decreased the estimated size of the civilian noninstitutional population 16 years and over by 811,000, the civilian labor force by 524,000, employment by 507,000, unemployment by 17,000, and the number of persons not in the labor force by 287,000. The total unemployment rate, the labor force participation rate, and the employment-population ratio were not affected. Such discontinuities occur throughout the history of the series.

The CPS is a count of persons employed, rather than a count of jobs. A person is counted as employed in this data set only once, no matter how many jobs he or she may hold. The CPS count is limited to persons 16 years of age and over.

The second set of employment estimates—the payroll survey—comes from a very large sample survey of about 149,000 business and government employers at approximately 651,000 worksites, the Current Employment Statistics (CES) survey. It is benchmarked annually to a survey of all employers. Benchmark data are introduced with a smooth adjustment back to the previous benchmark, thus preserving the continuity of the series and making it more appropriate for measurement of employment change over a year or two, a business cycle, or other short- to medium-length periods. This sample is much larger than the CPS sample, including about one-third of all nonfarm payroll employees, and consequently the threshold of statistical significance for changes is lower. The minimum size of the over-the-month change required to be statistically significant is about 115,000 jobs in the payroll survey, versus about 500,000 persons in the household survey.

The payroll survey (CES) is designed to measure employment, hours, and earnings in the nonfarm sector, with industry and geographic detail. The survey is best known for providing a highly reliable gauge of monthly change in nonfarm payroll employment. A representative sample of businesses in the U.S. provides the data for the payroll survey.

Over recent years, benchmark revisions to payroll survey employment have ranged in magnitude from an upward revision of 0.6 percent, in 2006, to the March 2009 benchmark, which reduced the seasonally adjusted level of payroll employment in that month by 902,000 persons, or 0.7 percent. The most recent revision increased the level of employment in March 2019 deceased employment by 489,000, or 0.3. percent. In absolute terms (that is, disregarding the sign), revisions have ranged from 0.1 to 0.7 percentage points over the latest 13 years and averaged 0.195 percentage points. Within that range, relatively large upward revisions have been seen for strong economies, and relatively large downward revisions for weak ones.

The scope of the CES survey is smaller than that of the CPS survey, as it is limited to wage and salary workers on nonfarm payrolls. There is also a significant definitional difference, because the CES survey is a count of jobs. Thus, a person with more than one nonfarm wage or salary job is counted as employed in each job. In addition, workers are not classified by age; as a result, there may be some workers younger than 16 years old in the job count.

Persons with a job but not at work (absent due to bad weather, work stoppages, personal reasons, and the like) are included in the household survey. However, they are excluded from the payroll survey if on leave without pay for the entire payroll period.

In addition to the differences in definitions and scope between the two series, there are also differences in sample design, collection methodology, and the sampling variability inherent in the surveys.

The payroll survey provides the most reliable and detailed information on employment by industry (for example, the data shown in Table 15-1). In addition, it provides data on weekly hours per job and hourly and weekly earnings per job.

The CPS employment estimates provide information not collected in the CES on employment by demographic characteristics, such as age, race, and Hispanic ethnicity; by education levels; and by occupation. A few of these tabulations are shown in *Business Statistics*. Many more breakdowns, in richer detail, can be found in the *Handbook of U.S. Labor Statistics*, also published by Bernan Press.

The differences between the two employment measurement systems are discussed in an article on the BLS Web site, "Employment from the BLS household and payroll surveys: summary of recent trends," which is updated monthly along with the release of the monthly data, and can be found under "Publications" on the CPS homepage at https://www.bls.gov. This article also includes references to further relevant studies.

Additional annual employment data

In addition to the CPS and CES monthly and annual data series, a third set of historical, annual-only estimates of employment is presented at the end of this chapter. These estimates of "full-time and part-time employees" by industry are compiled by the U.S. Department of Commerce, Bureau of Economic Analysis, as part of the National Income and Product Accounts (NIPAs). These estimates provide the most comprehensive and consistent employment estimates for the years before 1948.

Further detail on the historical and other characteristics of all of these employment series is presented below in the notes associated with specific data tables.

TABLES 10-1 THROUGH 10-5

Labor Force, Employment, and Unemployment

SOURCE: U.S. DEPARTMENT OF LABOR, BUREAU OF LABOR STATISTICS (BLS)

Labor force, employment, and unemployment data are derived from the Current Population Survey (CPS), a sample survey of households conducted each month by the Census Bureau for the Bureau of Labor Statistics (BLS). The data pertain to the U.S. civilian noninstitutional population age 16 years and over.

Due to changes in questionnaire design and survey methodology, data for 1994 and subsequent years are not fully comparable with

data for 1993 and earlier years. Additionally, discontinuities in the reported number of persons in the population, and consequently in the estimated numbers of employed and unemployed persons and the number of persons in the labor force, are introduced whenever periodic updates are made to U.S. population estimates.

For example, population controls based on Census 2000 were introduced beginning with the data for January 2000. These data are therefore not comparable with data for December 1999 and earlier. Data for 1990 through 1999 incorporate 1990 census–based population controls and are not comparable with the preceding years. An additional large population adjustment was introduced in January 2004, making the data from that time forward not comparable with data for December 2003 and earlier; further adjustments have been made in each subsequent January and other discontinuities have been introduced in various earlier years, usually with January data. See "Notes on the Data," below, for information on adjustments in other years, including the incorporation of the 2010 Census count beginning in January 2012.

For the most part, these population adjustments distort comparisons involving the <u>numbers of persons</u> in the population, labor force, and employment. They generally have negligible effects on the <u>percentages</u> that comprise the most important features of the CPS: the unemployment rates, the labor force participation rates, and the employment-population ratios.

Beginning with the data for January 2000, data classified by industry and occupation use the North American Industry Classification System (NAICS) and the 2000 Standard Occupational Classification System. This creates breaks in the time series between December 1999 and January 2000 for occupational and industry data at all levels of aggregation. Since the recent history is so short, most CPS industry and occupation data have been dropped from *Business Statistics* in favor of other important and economically meaningful data for which a longer consistent history can be supplied. However, detailed employment data by occupation and industry can be found in Bernan Press's *Handbook of U.S. Labor Statistics*.

Pre-1948 data

The Census Bureau began the survey of households that provides labor force data in 1942, and the Census of Population supplied data for 1940. For the years before that, annual data for labor force, employment, and unemployment are retrospective estimates. The 1929-1947 estimates were made by BLS. The 1890-1929 estimates shown in Table 10-1B were made by Stanley Lebergott. Both of those used trend interpolation of labor force participation between Census years, and the Census and Lebergott estimates are identical in 1929.

From 1929 to 1947, the data collected pertained to persons 14 years of age and over. From 1947 to the present the survey pertains to persons 16 years of age and over. Table 10-1C shows summary data for both age definitions in the overlap year, 1947. In that year, the unemployment rates are the same (3.9 percent) for both age definitions. However, the labor force participation rate and the employment/population ratio are higher when the 14- and 15-year-olds are excluded. Naturally, the raw numbers for population, labor force, and employment are smaller when the 14- and 15-year-olds are excluded.

The 1940 Census and the BLS data for 1931 through 1942 did not treat government work relief employment as employment; persons engaged in such work were counted as unemployed. In the labor force survey used today, anyone who worked for pay or profit is counted as employed (see the definitions below). Therefore, today's survey would count work relief as employment and not unemployment, and the BLS figures for the period before 1942 are not consistent with today's unemployment rates. Michael Darby, a former member of NBER, calculated an alternative unemployment rate in which such workers are counted as employed, and this rate is shown in parentheses in Table 10-1B. BLS counts employment in nonprofit and private groups that provide relief under the "emergency and other relief services" industry (also referred to in some BLS data as the "community food and housing, and emergency and other relief services" industry). This employment is usually found in the "Other Services' of the NAICS supersector.

Race and ethnic origin

Data for two broad racial categories were made available beginning in 1954: *White* and *Black and other.* The latter included Asians and all other "nonwhite" races, and was discontinued after 2002. Data for *Blacks* only are available beginning with 1972; this category is now called *Black or African American.* Data for *Asians* are shown beginning with 2000. Persons in the remaining race categories—American Indian or Alaska Native, Native Hawaiian or Other Pacific Islanders, and persons who selected more than one race category when that became possible, beginning in 2003 (see below)—are included in the estimates of total employment and unemployment, but are not shown separately because their numbers are too small to yield quality estimates.

Hispanic or Latino ethnicity, previously labeled *Hispanic origin*, is not a racial category and is established in a survey question separate from the question about race. Persons of Hispanic or Latino ethnicity may be of any race.

In January 2003, changes that affected classification by race and Hispanic ethnicity were introduced. These changes caused discontinuities in race and ethnic group data between December 2002 and January 2003.

- Individuals in the sample are now asked whether they are of Hispanic ethnicity <u>before</u> being asked about their race. Prior to 2003, individuals were asked their ethnic origin <u>after</u> they

were asked about their race. Furthermore, respondents are now asked directly if they are Spanish, Hispanic, or Latino. Previously, they were identified based on their or their ancestors' country of origin.

- Individuals in the sample are now allowed to choose more than one race category. Before 2003, they were required to select a single primary race. This change had no impact on the size of the overall civilian noninstitutional population and labor force. It did reduce the population and labor force levels of Whites and Blacks beginning in January 2003, as individuals who reported more than one race are now excluded from those groups.

BLS has estimated, based on a special survey, that these changes reduced the population and labor force levels for Whites by about 950,000 and 730,000 persons, respectively, and for Blacks by about 320,000 and 240,000 persons, respectively, while having little or no impact on either of their unemployment rates. The changes did not affect the size of the Hispanic population or labor force, but they did cause an increase of about half a percentage point in the Hispanic unemployment rate.

Definitions

The employment status of the civilian population is surveyed each month with respect to a specific week in mid-month—not for the entire month. This is known as the "reference week." For a precise definition and explanation of the reference week, see Notes on the Data, which follows these definitions.

The *civilian noninstitutional population* comprises all civilians 16 years of age and over who are not inmates of penal or mental institutions, sanitariums, or homes for the aged, infirm, or needy. A recent example will illustrate. Benchmark population updates does occur annually. For example, in January 2019, the updated controls decreased the estimated size of the civilian noninstitutional population 16 years and over by 811,000, the civilian labor force by 524,000, employment by 507,000, unemployment by 17,000, and the number of persons not in the labor force by 287,000. The total unemployment rate, the labor force participation rate, and the employment-population ratio were not affected. Such discontinuities occur throughout the history of the series.

Civilian employment includes those civilians who (1) worked for pay or profit at any time during the Sunday-through-Saturday week that includes the 12th day of the month (the reference week), or who worked for 15 hours or more as an unpaid worker in a family-operated enterprise; or (2) were temporarily absent from regular jobs because of vacation, illness, industrial dispute, bad weather, or similar reasons. Each employed person is counted only once; those who hold more than one job are counted as being in the job at which they worked the greatest number of hours during the reference week.

Unemployed persons are all civilians who were not employed (according to the above definition) during the reference week, but who were available for work—except for temporary illness—and who had made specific efforts to find employment sometime during the previous four weeks. Persons who did not look for work because they were on layoff are also counted as unemployed.

The *civilian labor force* comprises all civilians classified as employed or unemployed.

Civilians 16 years of age and over in the noninstitutional population who are not classified as employed or unemployed are defined as *not in the labor force*. This group includes those engaged in own-home housework; in school; unable to work because of longterm illness, retirement, or age; seasonal workers for whom the reference week fell in an "off" season (if not qualifying as unemployed by looking for a job); persons who became discouraged and gave up the search for work; and the voluntarily idle. Also included are those doing only incidental work (less than 15 hours) in a family-operated business during the reference week.

The civilian *labor force participation rate* represents the percentage of the civilian noninstitutional population (age 16 years and over) that is in the civilian labor force. This rate includes people who have stopped looking for a job while the unemployment figure does not. Thus a low unemployment rate while the labor force participation rate is also low points to a structural problem in the labor market. When former workers become discouraged and stop looking for work, this shrinks the labor force.

The *employment-population ratio* represents the percentage of the civilian noninstitutional population (age 16 years and over) that is employed. This is traditionally called a "ratio," although it is also traditionally expressed as a percent and therefore would be more appropriately called a "rate," as is the case with the labor force participation rate. Factors that change the rate are population demographics such as baby boomers are retiring and younger individuals chose to stay in college longer.

Employment is shown by *class of worker*, including a breakdown of total employment into *agricultural* and *nonagricultural* industries. Employment in *nonagricultural industries* includes *wage and salary workers*, the *self-employed*, and *unpaid family workers*.

Wage and salary workers receive wages, salaries, commissions, tips, and/or pay-in-kind. This category includes owners of self-owned incorporated businesses.

Self-employed workers are those who work for profit or for fees in their own business, profession, trade, or farm. This category includes only the unincorporated; a person whose business is incorporated is considered to be a wage and salary worker since he or she is a paid employee of a corporation, even if he or she is the corporation's president and sole employee. These categories are now labeled "Self-employed workers, unincorporated" to clarify this definition.

Wage and salary employment comprises *government* and *private industry* wage and salary workers. Domestic workers and other employees of *private households*, who are not included in the payroll employment series, are shown separately from *all other private industries*. The series for *government* and *other private industries* wage and salary workers are the closest in scope to similar categories in the payroll employment series.

Multiple jobholders are employed persons who, during the reference week, either had two or more jobs as a wage and salary worker, were self-employed and also held a wage and salary job, or worked as an unpaid family worker and also held a wage and salary job. This category does not include self-employed persons with multiple businesses or persons with multiple jobs as unpaid family workers. For purposes of industry and occupational classification, multiple jobholders are counted as being in the job at which they worked the greatest number of hours during the reference week.

Employed and at work part time does not include employed persons who were absent from their jobs during the entire reference week for reasons such as vacation, illness, or industrial dispute.

At work part time for economic reasons ("involuntary" part time) refers to individuals who worked 1 to 34 hours during the reference week because of slack work, unfavorable business conditions, an inability to find full-time work, or seasonal declines in demand. To be included in this category, workers must also indicate that they want and are available for full-time work.

At work part time for noneconomic reasons ("voluntary" part time) refers to persons who usually work part time and were at work for 1 to 34 hours during the reference week for reasons such as illness, other medical limitations, family obligations, education, retirement, Social Security limits on earnings, or working in an industry where the workweek is less than 35 hours. It also includes respondents who gave an economic reason but were not available for, or did not want, full-time work. At work part time for noneconomic reasons excludes persons who usually work full time, but who worked only 1 to 34 hours during the reference week for reasons such as holidays, illnesses, and bad weather.

The *long-term unemployed* are persons currently unemployed (searching or on layoff) who have been unemployed for 15 consecutive weeks or longer. If a person ceases to look for work for two weeks or more, or becomes temporarily employed, the continuity of longterm unemployment is broken. If he or she starts searching for work or is laid off again, the monthly CPS will record the length of his or her unemployment from the time the search recommenced or since the latest layoff.

The civilian *unemployment rate* is the number of unemployed as a percentage of the civilian labor force. The unemployment rates for groups within the civilian population (such as males age 20 years and over) are the number of unemployed in a group as a percent of that group's labor force.

Unemployment rates by reason provides a breakdown of the total unemployment rate. Each unemployed person is classified into one of four groups.

Job losers and persons who completed temporary jobs includes persons on temporary layoff, permanent job losers, and persons who completed temporary jobs and began looking for work after those jobs ended. These three categories are shown separately without seasonal adjustment in the BLS's "Employment Situation" news release and on its Web site. They are combined, under the title shown here, for the purpose of seasonal adjustment. This is the category of unemployment that responds most strongly to the business cycle.

Job leavers terminated their employment voluntarily and immediately began looking for work.

Reentrants are persons who previously worked, but were out of the labor force prior to beginning their current job search.

New entrants are persons searching for a first job who have never worked.

Each of these categories is expressed as a proportion of the entire civilian labor force, so that the sum of the four rates equals the unemployment rate for all civilian workers, except for possible discrepancies due to rounding or separate seasonal adjustment.

Median and average weeks unemployed are summary measures of the length of time that persons classified as unemployed have been looking for work. For persons on layoff, the duration represents the number of full weeks of the layoff. The *average (mean)* number of weeks is computed by aggregating all the weeks of unemployment experienced by all unemployed persons during their current spell of unemployment and dividing by the number of unemployed. The average can be distorted by what is called "top coding" because the length of unemployment is reported in ranges, including a top range of "over __ weeks", rather than exact numbers. See the paragraph below for further explanation. The *median* number of weeks unemployed is the number of weeks of unemployment experienced by the person at the midpoint of the distribution of all unemployed persons, as ranked by duration of unemployment, and is not distorted by top coding. Like medians in other economic time series, it is likely to be a better measure of typical experience.

Beginning with the data for January 2011 and phasing in through April 2011, respondents could report unemployment durations of up to 5 years; before that time, the "top code" was up to 2 years. This change caused a sharp increase in January 2011 and continued rises through April for *average weeks unemployed.* It did not affect total unemployment, total long-term unemployment, or the *median*

weeks unemployed. Comparisons of the average weeks statistics on the old and new basis are available on the BLS Web site.

Alternative measures of labor underutilization are calculated by BLS and published in the monthly Employment Situation release. They measure alternative concepts of unused working capacity, and are numbered "U-1" through "U-6" in order of increasing breadth of the definition of underutilization.

"U-1" is persons unemployed 15 weeks or longer, as a percent of the civilian labor force. It is not shown in *Business Statistics.*

"U-2" is job losers and persons who completed temporary jobs, as a percent of the civilian labor force; it is shown in *Business Statistics* in the fifth column of Table 10-5.

"U-3" is the official rate, described above and shown in the final columns of Tables 10-1, the fifth column of Table 10-4, and the fourth column of Table 10-5.

"U-4" through "U-6" are shown in the last three columns of Table 10-5. They are based on additional labor force status questions, now included in the CPS survey, that were introduced beginning in 1994. U-4 and U-5 are increasingly broader rates of unemployment, while U-6 can be described as an "unemployment and underemployment rate."

"U-4" adds discouraged workers to unemployment and the labor force. Discouraged workers are persons not in the officially defined labor force who have given a job-market-related reason for not looking currently for a job—for example, they have not looked for a job because they believed that no jobs were available.

"U-5" adds both discouraged workers and all other "marginally attached" workers to unemployment and the labor force. "Marginally attached" workers are all persons who currently are neither working nor looking for work but indicate that they want and are available for a job and have looked for work sometime in the recent past.

"U-6" adds persons employed part time for economic reasons, as shown in Table 10-3, to the number of persons counted as unemployed in "U-5", with the same labor force definition as in "U-5." This statistic, which measures a combination of unemployment and underemployment, is often cited in media reports on the employment situation.

For more information, see "BLS introduced new range of alternative unemployment measures" in the October 1995 issue of the *Monthly Labor Review.*

Notes on the data

The CPS data are collected by trained interviewers from about 60,000 sample households selected to represent the U.S.

civilian noninstitutional population. The sample size has fluctuated between 50,000 and 60,000 households In January 1996, the size was reduced to 50,00 due to budgetary reasons. The sample size was increased back to 60,000 households, beginning with the data for July 2001, as part of a plan to meet the requirements of the State Children's Health Insurance Program legislation. The CPS provides data for other data series in addition to the BLS employment status data, such as household income and poverty) and health insurance (see Chapter 3.

The employment status data are based on the activity or status reported for the calendar week, Sunday through Saturday, that includes the 12th day of the month (the reference week). This specification is chosen so as to avoid weeks that contain major holidays. Households are interviewed in the week following the reference week. Sample households are phased in and out of the sample on a rotating basis. Consequently, three-fourths of the sample is the same for any two consecutive months. One-half of the sample is the same as the sample in the same month a year earlier.

Data relating to 1994 and subsequent years are not strictly comparable with data for 1993 and earlier years because of the major 1994 redesign of the survey questionnaire and collection methodology. The redesign included new and revised questions for the classification of individuals as employed or unemployed, the collection of new data on multiple jobholding, a change in the definition of discouraged workers, and the implementation of a more completely automated data collection.

The 1994 redesign of the CPS was the most extensive since 1967. However, there are many other significant periods of year-to-year noncomparability in the labor force data. These typically result from the introduction of new decennial census data into the CPS estimation procedures, expansions of the sample, or other improvements made to increase the reliability of the estimates. Each change introduces a new discontinuity, usually between December of the previous year and January of the newly altered year. The discontinuities are usually minor or negligible with respect to figures expressed as nationwide percentages (such as the unemployment rate or the labor force participation rate), but can be significant with respect to levels (such as labor force and employment in thousands of persons). A list of the dates of the major discontinuities follows, with BLS estimates of their quantitative impact on the national totals. (There are likely to be larger impacts on population subgroups.) The discontinuities occur in January unless otherwise indicated. Note that some of the changes caused adjustments that were carried back to an earlier year.

- 2012: Reflecting the 2010 Census, the civilian noninstitutional population was increased by 1,510,000; the civilian labor force by 258,000; employment by 216,000; and unemployment by 42,000. BLS states, "Although the total unemployment rate was unaffected, the labor force participation rate and the employment-population ratio were each reduced by 0.3 percentage point. This was because the population increase was primarily among persons 55 and older and, to a lesser degree, persons 16 to 24 years of age. Both these age groups have lower levels of labor force participation than the general population."

- 2013: Updated population estimates increased the population by 138,000, the labor force by 136,000, and employment by 127,000. The rates and ratios were not affected.

- 2014: the smallest population control adjustment on record increased labor force by 24,000 and employment by 22,000, with no effect on rates or ratios.

- 2015: civilian population aged 16 or older increased by over one-half million, the labor force by 348,000, employment by 324,000 and unemployment by 24,000. The rates and ratios were not affected.

- 2016: the population adjustments rose once again by population 265,000, labor force 218,000, employment 206,000, unemployment 12,000 and not in labor force 47,000. The rates and ratios were not affected.

- 2017: the first year since 2012, the controls decreased. Population down by 831,000, labor force, 508,000, employment 483,000, unemployment 21,000 and those not in labor force 323,000. The rates and ratios were not affected.

- 2019: Population was down 811,000 persons, labor force down 524,000, employment down 507,000, unemployment down 17,000 those in not in the labor force down 287,000.

For further information on these changes, see "Publications and Other Documentation" at https://www.bls.gov/cps.

The monthly labor force, employment, and unemployment data are seasonally adjusted by the X-12-ARIMA method. All seasonally adjusted civilian labor force and unemployment rate statistics, as well as major employment and unemployment estimates, are computed by aggregating independently adjusted series. For example, the seasonally adjusted level of total unemployment is the sum of the seasonally adjusted levels of unemployment for the four age/sex groups (men and women age 16 to 19 years, and men and women age 20 years and over). Seasonally adjusted employment is the sum of the seasonally adjusted levels of employment for the same four groups. The seasonally adjusted civilian labor force is the sum of all eight components. Finally, the seasonally adjusted civilian worker unemployment rate is calculated by taking total seasonally adjusted unemployment as a percent of the total seasonally adjusted civilian labor force.

To minimize subsequent revisions, BLS uses a concurrent technique that estimates factors for the latest month using the most recent data. Then, seasonal adjustment factors are fully revised at the end of each year to reflect recent experience. The revisions also affect the preceding four years. An article describing the seasonal adjustment methodology for the household survey data is available at https://www.bls.gov/cps/cpsrs2010.pdf.

Breakdowns other than the basic age/sex classification described above—such as the employment data by class of worker in Table 10-3—will not necessarily add to totals because of independent seasonal adjustment.

Data availability

Data for each month are usually released on the first Friday of the following month in the "Employment Situation" press release, which also includes data from the establishment survey (Tables 10-7 through 10-17 and Chapter 15). (The release date actually is determined by the timing of the survey week.) The press release and data are available on the BLS Web site at <https://www.bls.gov>. The *Monthly Labor Review*, also available online at the BLS Web site, features frequent articles analyzing developments in the labor force, employment, and unemployment.

Monthly and annual data on the current basis are available beginning with 1948. Historical unadjusted data are published in *Labor Force Statistics Derived from the Current Population Survey* (BLS Bulletin 2307). Historical seasonally adjusted data are available from BLS upon request. Complete historical data are available on the BLS Web site at <https://www.bls.gov/cps>.

Seasonal adjustment factors are revised each year for the five previous years, with the release of December data in early January. New population controls are introduced with the release of January data in early February.

BLS annual data for 1940 through 1947 are published on their Web site at <https://www.bls.gov>. The data for 1929 through 1939 were published in *Employment and Earnings,* May 1972, and in U.S. Commerce Department, Bureau of Economic Analysis, *Long-Term Economic Growth, 1860–1970,* June 1973, p. 163. The Lebergott estimates are also found in the latter volume.

The Darby alternative unemployment rate is found in Michael Darby, "Three-and-a-Half Million U.S. Employees Have Been Mislaid," *Journal of Political Economy,* February 1976, v. 84, no. 1. It is also displayed and discussed in Robert A. Margo, "Employment and Unemployment in the 1930s," *Journal of Economic Perspectives,* v. 7, no. 2, Spring 1993.

References

Comprehensive descriptive material can be found at <https://www.bls.gov/cps> under the "Publications and Other Documentation" section. Historical background on the CPS, as well as a description of the 1994 redesign, can be found in three articles from the September 1993 edition of *Monthly Labor Review*: "Why Is It Necessary to Change?"; "Redesigning the Questionnaire"; and "Evaluating Changes in the Estimates." The redesign is also described in the February 1994 issue

of *Employment and Earnings.* See also Chapter 1, "Labor Force Data Derived from the Current Population Survey," *BLS Handbook of Methods*, Bulletin 2490 (April 1997).

TABLE 10-6

Insured Unemployment

SOURCE: U.S. DEPARTMENT OF LABOR, EMPLOYMENT AND TRAINING ADMINISTRATION

Definitions

State programs of unemployment insurance cover operations of regular programs under state unemployment insurance laws. In 1976, the law was amended to extend coverage to include virtually all state and local government employees, as well as many agricultural and domestic workers. (This took effect on January 1, 1978.) Benefits under state programs are financed by taxes levied by the states on employers.

An *initial claim* is the first claim in a benefit year filed by a worker after losing his or her job, or the first claim filed at the beginning of a subsequent period of unemployment in the same benefit year. The initial claim establishes the starting date for any insured unemployment that may result if the claimant is unemployed for one week or longer. Transitional claims (filed by claimants as they start a new benefit year in a continuing spell of unemployment) are excluded; therefore, these data more closely represent instances of new unemployment and are widely followed as a leading indicator of job market conditions.

Insured unemployment and *persons claiming benefits* both describe the average number of persons receiving benefits in the indicated month or year.

The *insured unemployment rate* for state programs is the level of insured unemployment as a percentage of employment covered by state programs.

Monthly averages in this book are averages, calculated by the editor, of the weekly data published by the Employment and Training Administration. Annual data are averages of the monthly data.

Data availability

Data are published in weekly press releases from the Employment and Training Administration. These releases are available on their Web site at <https://www.doleta.gov> under "Labor Market Data," as are historical data, under the category "UI/Program Statistics."

TABLES 10-7, 10-8, 10-13, 15-1, AND 15-2

Nonfarm Payroll Employment

SOURCE: U.S. DEPARTMENT OF LABOR, BUREAU OF LABOR STATISTICS (BLS)

These nonfarm employment data, as well as the hours and earnings data in Tables 10-8 through 10-12, 10-14 through 10-17, and 15-3 through 15-6, are compiled from payroll records. Information is reported monthly on a voluntary basis to BLS and its cooperating state agencies by a large sample of establishments, representing all industries except farming. These data, formally known as the Current Employment Statistics (CES) survey, are often referred to as the "establishment data" or the "payroll data." They are also known as the BLS-790 survey.

The survey, originally based on a stratified quota sample, has been replaced on a phased-in basis by a stratified probability sample. The new sampling procedure went into effect for wholesale trade in June 2000; for mining, construction, and manufacturing in June 2001; and for retail trade, transportation and public utilities, and finance, insurance, and real estate in June 2002. The phase-in was completed in June 2003, upon its extension to the service industries. The phase-in schedule was slightly different for the state and area series.

The sample has always been very large. Currently, it includes approximately 145,000 businesses and government agencies covering about 697,000 individual worksites, which account for about one-third of total benchmark employment of payroll workers. The sample is drawn from a sampling frame of over 10.2 million unemployment insurance tax accounts.

Data are classified according to the North American Industry Classification System. BLS has reconstructed historical time series to conform with NAICS, to ensure that all published series have a NAICS-based history extending back to at least January 1990. NAICS-based history extends back to January 1939 for total nonfarm and other high-level aggregates. For more detailed series, the starting date for NAICS data varies depending on the extent of the definitional changes between the old Standard Industrial Classification (SIC) and NAICS.

Definitions

An *establishment* is an economic unit, such as a factory, store, or professional office, that produces goods or services at a single location and is engaged in one type of economic activity.

Employment comprises all persons who received pay (including holiday and sick pay) for any part of the payroll period that includes the 12th day of the month. The definition of the payroll period for each reporting respondent is that used by the employer; it could be weekly, biweekly, monthly, or other. Included are all fulltime and parttime workers in nonfarm establishments, including salaried officers of corporations. Persons holding more than one job are counted in each establishment that reports them. Not covered are proprietors, the selfemployed, unpaid volunteer and family workers, farm workers, domestic workers in households, and military personnel. Employees of the Central Intelligence Agency, the Defense Intelligence Agency, the National Geospatial-Intelligence Agency, and the National Security Agency are not included.

Persons on an establishment payroll who are on paid sick leave (when pay is received directly from the employer), on paid holiday or vacation, or who work during a portion of the pay period despite being unemployed or on strike during the rest of the period, are counted as employed. Not counted as employed are persons who are laid off, on leave without pay, on strike for the entire period, or hired but not paid during the period.

Intermittent workers are counted if they performed any service during the month. BLS considers regular fulltime teachers (private and government) to be employed during the summer vacation period, regardless of whether they are specifically paid during those months.

The *government* division includes federal, state, and local activities such as legislative, executive, and judicial functions, as well as the U.S. Postal Service and all governmentowned and governmentoperated business enterprises, establishments, and institutions (arsenals, navy yards, hospitals, state-owned utilities, etc.), and government force account construction. However, as indicated earlier, members of the armed forces and employees of certain national-security-related agencies are not included.

The monthly *diffusion index of employment change*, currently based on 271 private nonfarm NAICS industries, represents the percentage of those industries in which the seasonally adjusted level of employment in that month was higher than six months earlier, plus one-half of the percentage of industries with unchanged employment. Therefore, the diffusion index reported for September represents the change from March to September. *Business Statistics* uses the September value to represent the year as a whole, since it spans the year's midpoint. Diffusion indexes measure the dispersion of economic gains and losses, with values below 50 percent associated with recessions. The current NAICS-based series begins with January 1991. For October 1976 through December 1990, an earlier series is available based on 347 SIC industries (there are more industries using the older classification system because in SIC manufacturing industries were represented in greater detail). September values from this series are used here to represent the years 1977 through 1990.

Production and nonsupervisory workers include all *production and related workers* in mining and manufacturing; *construction workers* in construction; and *nonsupervisory workers* in transportation, communication, electric, gas, and sanitary services; wholesale and retail trade; finance, insurance, and real estate; and services. These groups account for about four-fifths of the total employment on private nonagricultural payrolls. Previously, this category was called "production or nonsupervisory workers." The definitions have not changed.

Production and related workers include working supervisors and all nonsupervisory workers (including group leaders and trainees) engaged in fabricating, processing, assembling, inspecting, receiving, storing, handling, packing, warehousing, shipping, trucking, hauling, maintenance, repair, janitorial, guard services, product development, auxiliary production for plant's own use (such as a power plant), record keeping, and other services closely associated with these production operations.

Construction workers include the following employees in the construction division of the NAICS: working supervisors, qualified craft workers, mechanics, apprentices, laborers, and the like, who are engaged in new work, alterations, demolition, repair, maintenance, and other tasks, whether working at the site of construction or working in shops or yards at jobs (such as precutting and preassembling) ordinarily performed by members of the construction trades.

Nonsupervisory employees include employees (not above the working supervisory level) such as office and clerical workers, repairers, salespersons, operators, drivers, physicians, lawyers, accountants, nurses, social workers, research aides, teachers, drafters, photographers, beauticians, musicians, restaurant workers, custodial workers, attendants, line installers and repairers, laborers, janitors, guards, and other employees at similar occupational levels whose services are closely associated with those of the employees listed.

Notes on the data

Benchmark adjustments. The establishment survey data are adjusted annually to comprehensive counts of employment, called "benchmarks." Benchmark information on employment by industry is compiled by state agencies from reports of establishments covered under state unemployment insurance laws; these form an annual compilation of administrative data known as the ES-202. These tabulations cover about 97 percent of all employees on nonfarm payrolls. Benchmark data for the residual are obtained from alternate sources, primarily from Railroad Retirement Board records and the Census Bureau's *County Business Patterns*. The latest benchmark adjustment, which is incorporated into the data in this volume, increased the employment level in the benchmark month March 2018 by 135,000 jobs, which was 0.1 percent.

The estimates for the benchmark month are compared with new benchmark levels for each industry. If revisions are necessary, the monthly series of estimates between benchmark periods are adjusted by graduated amounts between the new benchmark and the preceding one ("wedged back"), and the new benchmark

level for each industry is then carried forward month by month based on the sample.

More specifically, the month-to-month changes for each estimation cell are based on changes in a matched sample for that cell, plus an estimate of net business births and deaths. The matched sample for each pair of months consists of establishments that have reported data for both months (which automatically excludes establishments that have gone out of business by the second month). Since new businesses are not immediately incorporated into the sample, a model-based estimate of net business births and deaths in that estimating cell is added. The birth/death adjustment factors are re-estimated quarterly based on the Quarterly Census of Employment and Wages.

Not-seasonally-adjusted data for all months since the last benchmark date are subject to revision.

Beginning in 1959, the data include Alaska and Hawaii. This inclusion resulted in an increase of 212,000 (0.4 percent) in total nonfarm employment for the March 1959 benchmark month.

Seasonal adjustment. The seasonal movements that recur periodically—such as warm and cold weather, holidays, and vacations—are generally the largest single component of monthtomonth changes in employment. After adjusting the data to remove such seasonal variation, basic trends become more evident. BLS uses X-12-ARIMA software to produce seasonal factors and perform concurrent seasonal adjustment, using the most recent 10 years of data. New factors are developed each month adding the most current data.

For most series, a special procedure called REGARIMA (regression with autocorrelated errors) is used before calculating the seasonal factors; this adjusts for the length of the interval (which can be either four or five weeks) between the survey weeks. REGARIMA has also been used to isolate extreme weather effects that distort the measurement of seasonal patterns in the construction industry, and to identify variations in local government employment due to the presence or absence of election poll workers.

Seasonal adjustment factors are directly applied to the component levels. Seasonally adjusted totals for employment series are then obtained by aggregating the seasonally adjusted components directly, while hours and earnings series represent weighted averages of the seasonally adjusted component series. Seasonally adjusted data are not published for a small number of series characterized by small seasonal components relative to their trend and/or irregular components. However, these series are used in aggregating to broader seasonally adjusted levels.

Revisions of the seasonally adjusted data, usually for the most recent five-year period, are made once a year coincident with the benchmark revisions. This means that these revisions typically extend back farther than the benchmark revisions.

Data availability

Employment data by industry division are available beginning with 1919. Data for each month usually are released on the first Friday of the following month in a press release that also contains data from the household survey (Tables 10-1 through 10-5). (The release date actually is determined by the timing of the survey week.) The *Monthly Labor Review* frequently contains articles analyzing developments in the labor force, employment, and unemployment. The *Monthly Labor Review*, press releases, and complete historical data are available on the BLS Web site at <https://www.bls.gov>.

Benchmark revisions and revised seasonally adjusted data for recent years are made each year with the release of January data in early February. Before 2004, the benchmark revisions were not made until June; the acceleration is due to earlier availability of the benchmark UI (ES-202) data.

References

References can be found at <https://www.bls.gov/ces> under the headings "Special Notices," "Benchmark Information," and "Technical Notes." Extensive changes incorporated in June 2003 are described in "Recent Changes in the National Current Employment Statistics Survey," *Monthly Labor Review*, June 2003. The latest benchmark revision is discussed in an article available on the Website. See also Chapter 2, "Employment, Hours, and Earnings from the Establishment Survey," *BLS Handbook of Methods*, Bulletin 2490 (April 1997).

TABLES 10-8 THROUGH 10-10, 10-14, 10-15, 15-3 AND 15-6

Average Hours Per Week; Aggregate Employee Hours

SOURCE: U.S. DEPARTMENT OF LABOR, BUREAU OF LABOR STATISTICS (BLS)

See the notes and definitions to Tables 10-7 and related tables for an overall description of the "establishment" or "payroll" survey that is the source of these earnings data.

Hours and earnings have been reported for production and non-supervisory workers, as defined above, since the inception of the CES. Beginning with data for March 2006, such data have also been collected for all payroll employees. With sufficient history for calculation of seasonal adjustment factors, BLS began publishing all-employee hours and earnings in February 2010, and these new data are presented in *Business Statistics* Tables 10-9 through 10-12.

Definitions

Average weekly hours represents the average hours paid per worker during the pay period that includes the 12th of the month.

Included are hours paid for holidays and vacations, as well as those paid for sick leave when pay is received directly from the firm.

Average weekly hours are different from standard or scheduled hours. Factors such as unpaid absenteeism, labor turnover, part-time work, and work stoppages can cause average weekly hours to be lower than scheduled hours of work for an establishment.

An important characteristic of these data is that average weekly hours pertain to jobs, not to persons; thus, a person with half-time jobs in two different establishments is represented in this series as two jobs that have 20-hour workweeks, not as one person with a 40-hour workweek.

Overtime hours represent the portion of average weekly hours worked in excess of regular hours, for which overtime premiums were paid. Weekend and holiday hours are included only if overtime premiums were paid. Hours for which only shift differential, hazard, incentive, or other similar types of premiums were paid are excluded.

Aggregate hours provide measures of changes over time in labor input to the industry, in index-number form.

Indexes of aggregate weekly hours are calculated by dividing the current month's aggregate hours by the average of the 12 monthly figures, for the base year. The index of aggregate hours paints a good picture of the stall in the recovery. Employment is up, but hours are not up proportionally. This reflects the trend to part-time workers and the reduction of hours in part-time workers. For the series covering production and nonsupervisory workers, the base period is 2002; for the all-employee series, the base period is 2007.

Notes on the data

Benchmark adjustments. Independent benchmarks are not available for the hours and earnings series. However, at the time of the annual adjustment of the employment series to new benchmarks, the levels of hours and earnings may be affected by the revised employment weights (which are used in computing the industry averages for hours and earnings), as well as by the changes in seasonal adjustment factors introduced with the benchmark revision.

Method of computing industry series. "Average weekly hours" for individual industries are computed by dividing worker hours (reported by establishments classified in each industry) by the number of workers reported for the same establishments. Estimates for divisions and major industry groups are averages (weighted by employment) of the figures for component industries.

Seasonal adjustment. Hours and earnings series are seasonally adjusted by applying factors directly to the corresponding unadjusted series. Data for some industries are not seasonally adjusted because the seasonal component is small relative to the trendcycle and/or irregular components. Consequently, they cannot be separated with sufficient precision.

Special adjustments are made to average weekly hours to account for the presence or absence of religious holidays in the April survey reference period and the occasional occurrence of Labor Day in the September reference period. In addition, REGARIMA modeling is used prior to seasonal adjustment to correct for reporting and processing errors associated with the number of weekdays in a month (rather than to correct for the 4- and 5-week effect, which is less significant for hours than it is for employment). This is of particular importance for average weekly hours in the service-providing industries other than retail trade. For this reason, BLS advises that calculations of over-the-year changes (for example, the change for the current month from a year earlier) should use seasonally adjusted data, since the actual not-seasonally-adjusted monthly data may be distorted.

Data availability

See data availability for Tables 10-7 and related, above.

References

See references for Tables 10-7 and related, above.

TABLES 10-8, 10-11, 10-12, 10-16, 10-17, 15-4, AND 15-5

Hourly and Weekly Earnings

SOURCE: U.S. DEPARTMENT OF LABOR, BUREAU OF LABOR STATISTICS (BLS)

See the notes and definitions to Tables 10-8 and related for an overall description of the "establishment" or "payroll" survey that is the source of these earnings data.

Hours and earnings have been reported for production and non-supervisory workers, as defined above, since the inception of the CES. Beginning with data for March 2006, such data have also been collected for all payroll employees. With sufficient history for calculation of seasonal adjustment factors, BLS began publishing all-employee hours and earnings in February 2010, and these data are presented in new *Business Statistics* Tables 10-9 through 10-12.

Definitions

Earnings are the payments that workers receive during the survey period (before deductions for taxes and other items), including premium pay for overtime or late-shift work but excluding irregular bonuses and other special payments. After being previously excluded, tips were asked to be reported beginning in September 2005. This made little difference in most industries, and BLS asserts that many respondents had already been including tips. In two industries, full-service restaurants and cafeterias, there was a substantial difference, and the historical earnings data for those industries have been reconstructed to reflect the new higher level of earnings.

Notes on the data

The hours and earnings series are based on reports of gross payroll and corresponding paid hours for full and parttime workers who received pay for any part of the pay period that included the 12th of the month.

Total payrolls are before deductions, such as for the employee share of oldage and unemployment insurance, group insurance, withholding taxes, bonds, and union dues. The payroll figures also include pay for overtime, holidays, vacations, and sick leave (paid directly by the employer for the period reported). Excluded from the payroll figures are fringe benefits (health and other types of insurance and contributions to retirement, paid by the employer, and the employer share of payroll taxes), bonuses (unless earned and paid regularly each pay period), other pay not earned in the pay period reported (retroactive pay), and the value of free rent, fuel, meals, or other payment-in-kind.

Average hourly earnings data reflect not only changes in basic hourly and incentive wage rates, but also such variable factors as premium pay for overtime and lateshift work and changes in output of workers paid on an incentive basis. Shifts in the volume of employment between relatively highpaid and lowpaid work also affect the general average of hourly earnings.

Averages of hourly earnings should not be confused with wage rates, which represent the rates stipulated for a given unit of work or time, while earnings refer to the actual return to the worker for a stated period of time. The earnings series do not represent total labor cost to the employer because of the inclusion of tips and the exclusion of irregular bonuses, retroactive items, the cost of employer-provided benefits, and payroll taxes paid by employers.

Average weekly earnings are not the amounts available to workers for spending, since they do not reflect deductions such as income taxes and Social Security taxes. It is also important to understand that average weekly earnings represent earnings per job, not per worker (since a worker may have more than one job) and not per family (since a family may have more than one worker). A person with two half-time jobs will be reflected as two earners with low weekly earnings rather than as one person with the total earnings from his or her two jobs.

Method of computing industry series. Average hourly earnings are obtained by dividing the reported total worker payroll by total worker hours. Estimates for both hours and hourly earnings for nonfarm divisions and major industry groups are employment-weighted averages of the figures for component industries.

Average weekly earnings are computed by multiplying average hourly earnings by average weekly hours. In addition to the factors mentioned above, which exert varying influences upon average hourly earnings, average weekly earnings are affected by changes in the length of the workweek, parttime work, work stoppages, labor turnover, and absenteeism. Persistent longterm uptrends in the proportion of parttime workers in retail trade and many of the service industries have reduced average workweeks (as measured here), and have similarly affected the average weekly earnings series.

Benchmark adjustments. Independent benchmarks are not available for the hours and earnings series. At the time of the annual adjustment of the employment series to new benchmarks, the levels of hours and earnings may be affected by the revised employment weights (which are used in computing the industry averages for hours and earnings), as well as by the changes in seasonal adjustment factors that were also introduced with the benchmark revision.

Seasonal adjustment. Hours and earnings series are seasonally adjusted by applying factors directly to the corresponding unadjusted series; seasonally adjusted average weekly earnings are the product of seasonally adjusted hourly earnings and weekly hours.

REGARIMA modeling is used to correct for reporting and processing errors associated with variations in the number of weekdays in a month (rather than for the 4- and 5-week effect, which is less significant for earnings than for employment). This is of particular importance for average hourly earnings in wholesale trade, financial activities, professional and business services, and other services. For this reason, BLS advises that calculations of over-the-year changes, for example the change for the current month from a year earlier, should use seasonally adjusted data, since the actual not seasonally adjusted monthly data may be distorted.

Data availability

See data availability for Tables 10-7 and related, above.

References

See references for Tables 10-7 and related, above.

TABLE 10-18

Hours at Work, Current Population Survey

This table presents annual average measures of hours worked per week reported by workers in the Current Population Survey, in response to questions asking for the hours worked in the survey week by each worker in the household on all his or her jobs combined. These measures are not published in regular BLS reports but are available on request. *Business Statistics* obtained these numbers from BLS staff and presents them here in annual average form.

Do CPS respondents overestimate the number of hours they work? One study made that claim, but a careful re-examination of the data by Harley Frazis and Jay Stewart in the June 2014 *Monthly Labor Review* indicates that respondents slightly underreport the hours that they actually worked during the reference week. (On the other hand, the authors also note that the reference week overestimates the average for the entire month because of the absence of holidays.) (*Monthly Labor Review* is available online at www.bls.gov.) In any event, the CPS data give a more accurate picture of trends in the workweeks of typical American workers than does the establishment (CES) survey.

Table 10-19

Median Usual Weekly Earnings of Full-Time Wage and Salary Workers

SOURCE: U.S. DEPARTMENT OF LABOR, BUREAU OF LABOR STATISTICS

These data are from the Current Population Survey, which was described in the notes to Tables 10-1 through 10-6. Because they are earnings per worker, not per job, and are limited to full-time workers, the data are not distorted by the increasing proportion of part-time workers, as the CES earnings data are.

Definitions

Full-time wage and salary workers are those workers reported as "employed" in the CPS who receive wages, salaries, commissions, tips, pay in kind, or piece rates, and usually work 35 hours or more per week at their sole or principal job. Both private-sector and public-sector employees are included. All self-employed persons are excluded (even those whose businesses are incorporated).

Usual weekly earnings are earnings before taxes and other deductions and include any overtime pay, commissions, or tips usually received. In the case of multiple jobholders they refer to the main job. The wording of the question was changed in January 1994 to better deal with persons who found it easier to report earnings on other than a weekly basis. Such reports are then converted to the weekly equivalent. According to BLS, "the term 'usual' is as perceived by the respondent. If the respondent asks for a definition of usual, interviewers are instructed to define the term as more than half the weeks worked during the past 4 or 5 months."

The *median* is the amount that divides a given earnings distribution into two equal groups, one having earnings above the median and the other having earnings below the median.

Race and ethnicity. See the notes to Tables 10-1 through 10-6 for the definitions of these categories.

Data availability

These data become available about 3 weeks after the end of each quarter in the "Usual Weekly Earnings of Wage and Salary Workers" press release, available on the BLS Web site at <https://www.bls.gov/cps>. Recent data are available at that location. Also available are greater detail by demographic and age groups, by occupation, by union status, and by education; distributional data, by deciles and quartiles; and earnings for part-time workers. Also available are earnings in 1982 dollars using the CPI-U. (In the opinion of the editor, these give a less accurate depiction of longer-term trends, which is why *Business Statistics* provides the CPI-U-RS data explained above.) Historical data are available upon request from BLS by telephone at (202) 691-6555).

CHAPTER 11: ENERGY

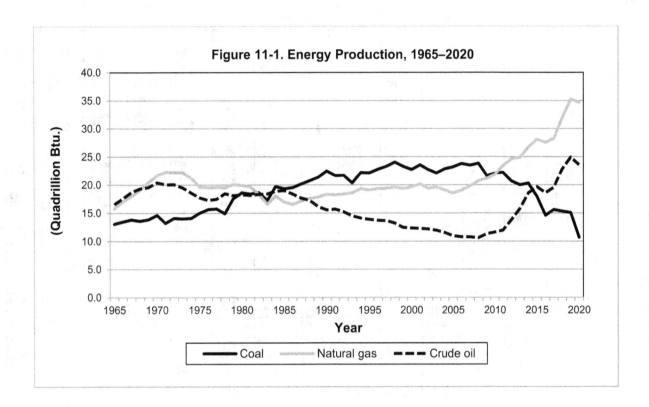

Figure 11-1. Energy Production, 1965–2020

- As seen throughout this publication, COVID-19 had a major impact on every aspect of the economy and the energy sector was no different. It experienced historic demand shocks and returning to 2019 levels could take years.

- U.S. consumption of petroleum fell to its lowest level in decades during the COVID-19 pandemic. Total petroleum demand for the week of April 10, 2020 was 13.8 million barrels per day, the lowest level published by the US. Energy Information agency, dating back to the early 1990s.

- Responses to COVID-19 caused global demand for petroleum products to fall significantly in 2020. For example, motor gasoline consumption fell to 5.3 million barrels per day during the week of April 17, 2020—a decline of 40 percent. Other petroleum products include jet fuel and diesel fuel. Diesel fuel is primarily consumed by trucking, locomotive and agriculture sectors.

- After reaching a high of $98.15 in 2008, the price of crude oil per barrel plummeted 60 percent by 2016. Between 2019 and 2020, prices rose 5.4 percent. During the pandemic, gas prices plummeted to a low of $1.77 per gallon in April 2020. By March 2021, U.S regular retail gas prices averaged at $2.85 per gallon. (Table 11-3)

Table 11-1. Energy Supply and Consumption

(Quadrillion Btu.)

Year and month	Imports	Exports	Production, by source								Consumption, by end-use sector			
			Total	Fossil fuels					Nuclear electric power	Renewable energy, total	Total	Residential and commercial	Industrial	Transportation
				Total	Coal	Natural gas	Crude oil	Natural gas plant liquids						
1965	5.892	1.829	50.644	47.205	13.055	15.775	16.521	1.853	0.043	3.396	53.953	16.485	25.035	12.432
1966	6.146	1.829	53.507	50.011	13.468	17.011	17.561	1.971	0.064	3.432	56.949	17.493	26.356	13.100
1967	6.159	2.115	56.347	52.568	13.825	17.943	18.651	2.148	0.088	3.690	58.895	18.539	26.604	13.752
1968	6.905	1.998	58.188	54.274	13.609	19.068	19.308	2.289	0.142	3.773	62.401	19.666	27.869	14.866
1969	7.676	2.126	60.501	56.252	13.863	20.446	19.556	2.386	0.154	4.095	65.596	21.003	29.087	15.507
1970	8.342	2.632	63.462	59.152	14.607	21.666	20.401	2.478	0.239	4.070	67.817	22.113	29.605	16.098
1971	9.535	2.151	62.686	58.011	13.186	22.280	20.033	2.513	0.413	4.262	69.260	22.968	29.562	16.730
1972	11.387	2.118	63.870	58.904	14.092	22.208	20.041	2.564	0.584	4.382	72.660	24.041	30.901	17.717
1973	14.613	2.033	63.528	58.207	13.992	22.187	19.493	2.535	0.910	4.411	75.652	24.441	32.591	18.613
1974	14.304	2.203	62.308	56.294	14.074	21.210	18.575	2.435	1.272	4.742	73.929	24.049	31.753	18.120
1975	14.032	2.323	61.284	54.697	14.989	19.640	17.729	2.338	1.900	4.687	71.931	24.307	29.379	18.245
1976	16.760	2.172	61.522	54.684	15.654	19.480	17.262	2.288	2.111	4.727	75.939	25.474	31.356	19.101
1977	19.948	2.052	61.970	55.059	15.755	19.565	17.454	2.286	2.702	4.209	77.920	25.870	32.221	19.822
1978	19.106	1.920	63.060	55.031	14.910	19.485	18.434	2.202	3.024	5.005	79.907	26.645	32.643	20.617
1979	19.460	2.855	65.851	57.952	17.540	20.076	18.104	2.232	2.776	5.123	80.812	26.461	33.877	20.472
1980	15.796	3.695	67.147	58.979	18.598	19.908	18.249	2.225	2.739	5.428	78.021	26.332	31.993	19.697
1981	13.719	4.307	66.910	58.488	18.377	19.699	18.146	2.266	3.008	5.414	76.057	25.878	30.662	19.514
1982	11.861	4.608	66.527	57.416	18.639	18.319	18.309	2.149	3.131	5.980	73.046	26.392	27.561	19.089
1983	11.752	3.693	64.066	54.368	17.247	16.593	18.392	2.136	3.203	6.496	72.915	26.364	27.372	19.177
1984	12.471	3.786	68.800	58.809	19.719	18.008	18.848	2.234	3.553	6.438	76.571	27.404	29.508	19.656
1985	11.781	4.196	67.661	57.502	19.325	16.980	18.992	2.204	4.076	6.084	76.334	27.493	28.757	20.088
1986	14.151	4.021	67.030	56.539	19.509	16.541	18.376	2.113	4.380	6.111	76.599	27.582	28.225	20.789
1987	15.398	3.812	67.506	57.131	20.141	17.136	17.675	2.179	4.754	5.622	79.008	28.210	29.332	21.469
1988	17.296	4.366	68.890	57.846	20.738	17.599	17.279	2.231	5.587	5.457	82.659	29.711	30.627	22.318
1989	18.766	4.661	69.285	57.448	21.360	17.847	16.117	2.123	5.602	6.235	84.740	30.987	31.282	22.479
1990	18.817	4.752	70.668	58.523	22.488	18.326	15.571	2.138	6.104	6.040	84.433	30.258	31.749	22.419
1991	18.335	5.141	70.321	57.831	21.636	18.229	15.701	2.265	6.422	6.068	84.380	30.920	31.342	22.118
1992	19.372	4.937	69.914	57.615	21.694	18.375	15.223	2.323	6.479	5.821	85.725	30.796	32.513	22.415
1993	21.218	4.227	68.273	55.780	20.336	18.584	14.494	2.366	6.410	6.082	87.266	32.029	32.559	22.671
1994	22.307	4.035	70.683	58.002	22.202	19.348	14.103	2.349	6.694	5.987	88.983	32.208	33.462	23.319
1995	22.180	4.496	71.129	57.496	22.130	19.082	13.887	2.398	7.075	6.557	90.931	33.207	33.908	23.812
1996	23.633	4.613	72.435	58.338	22.790	19.344	13.723	2.480	7.087	7.011	93.935	34.674	34.836	24.419
1997	25.119	4.493	72.420	58.806	23.310	19.394	13.658	2.445	6.597	7.017	94.507	34.644	35.134	24.723
1998	26.473	4.237	72.826	59.266	24.045	19.613	13.235	2.372	7.068	6.493	94.920	34.920	34.779	25.225
1999	27.152	3.669	71.686	57.560	23.295	19.341	12.451	2.473	7.610	6.516	96.545	35.931	34.692	25.916
2000	28.865	3.962	71.271	57.307	22.735	19.662	12.358	2.551	7.862	6.102	98.702	37.597	34.587	26.515
2001	30.052	3.731	71.675	58.485	23.547	20.166	12.282	2.491	8.029	5.162	96.064	37.175	32.653	26.242
2002	29.331	3.608	70.653	56.777	22.732	19.382	12.160	2.502	8.145	5.731	97.535	38.132	32.590	26.808
2003	31.007	4.013	69.885	55.983	22.094	19.633	11.960	2.296	7.960	5.942	97.835	38.466	32.489	26.881
2004	33.492	4.351	70.169	55.884	22.852	19.074	11.550	2.408	8.223	6.063	100.000	38.738	33.444	27.826
2005	34.659	4.462	69.377	54.995	23.185	18.556	10.974	2.280	8.161	6.221	100.100	39.467	32.374	28.261
2006	34.649	4.727	70.678	55.877	23.790	19.022	10.767	2.299	8.215	6.586	99.392	38.378	32.317	28.697
2007	34.679	5.338	71.338	56.369	23.493	19.786	10.741	2.349	8.459	6.510	100.890	39.773	32.306	28.815
2008	32.970	6.949	73.145	57.527	23.851	20.703	10.613	2.359	8.426	7.192	98.754	40.071	31.261	27.421
2009	29.690	6.920	72.592	56.612	21.624	21.139	11.340	2.508	8.355	7.625	93.942	38.970	28.380	26.592
2010	29.866	8.176	74.907	58.159	22.038	21.806	11.610	2.705	8.434	8.314	97.513	39.954	30.574	26.978
2011	28.748	10.373	78.098	60.529	22.221	23.406	12.012	2.890	8.269	9.300	96.863	39.363	30.893	26.599
2012	27.068	11.267	79.244	62.296	20.677	24.610	13.847	3.162	8.062	8.886	94.374	37.292	30.954	26.126
2013	24.623	11.788	81.846	64.184	20.001	24.859	15.872	3.451	8.244	9.418	97.117	38.981	31.525	26.612
2014	23.241	12.270	87.726	69.622	20.286	26.718	18.613	4.005	8.338	9.766	98.276	39.710	31.691	26.869
2015	23.794	12.902	88.255	70.190	17.946	28.067	19.701	4.476	8.337	9.729	97.375	38.774	31.361	27.239
2016	25.378	14.119	84.282	65.430	14.667	27.576	18.522	4.665	8.427	10.425	97.337	38.209	31.347	27.786
2017	25.458	17.946	88.066	68.447	15.625	28.289	19.546	4.987	8.419	11.200	97.599	37.786	31.798	28.014
2018	24.833	21.224	95.705	75.758	15.363	31.882	22.786	5.727	8.438	11.509	101.160	39.994	32.757	28.464
2019	22.865	23.474	101.400	81.425	14.256	35.258	25.559	6.352	8.452	11.527	100.290	39.080	32.701	28.506
2020	19.988	23.464	95.721	75.692	10.713	34.674	23.501	6.805	8.248	11.780	93.048	37.642	31.130	24.268
2019														
January	2.122	1.910	8.526	6.811	1.331	2.878	2.093	0.509	0.770	0.945	9.532	4.346	2.878	2.306
February	1.700	1.725	7.680	6.129	1.179	2.616	1.859	0.476	0.676	0.875	8.377	3.737	2.512	2.128
March	1.925	1.912	8.344	6.672	1.126	2.915	2.102	0.529	0.680	0.992	8.692	3.600	2.716	2.378
April	1.925	1.893	8.322	6.658	1.234	2.833	2.073	0.518	0.633	1.032	7.662	2.701	2.623	2.343
May	2.046	1.954	8.650	6.884	1.248	2.950	2.145	0.541	0.701	1.065	7.937	2.747	2.750	2.442
June	1.889	1.940	8.332	6.612	1.145	2.866	2.082	0.519	0.718	1.002	7.906	2.806	2.671	2.429
July	2.021	1.889	8.539	6.796	1.191	2.978	2.101	0.526	0.754	0.989	8.548	3.241	2.796	2.505
August	1.975	1.969	8.770	7.073	1.286	3.051	2.204	0.533	0.751	0.946	8.552	3.173	2.825	2.548
September	1.789	1.977	8.411	6.817	1.180	2.949	2.149	0.540	0.690	0.904	7.854	2.842	2.684	2.324
October	1.816	2.088	8.649	7.070	1.162	3.090	2.256	0.562	0.648	0.932	7.929	2.750	2.739	2.442
November	1.688	2.028	8.440	6.867	1.098	3.012	2.216	0.540	0.670	0.903	8.378	3.335	2.737	2.307
December	1.969	2.190	8.739	7.035	1.075	3.121	2.280	0.558	0.763	0.942	8.926	3.803	2.771	2.354
2020														
January	1.871	2.175	8.774	7.006	1.112	3.058	2.256	0.580	0.774	0.994	8.959	3.936	2.767	2.259
February	1.727	2.089	8.124	6.440	0.949	2.848	2.117	0.526	0.689	0.995	8.346	3.578	2.622	2.150
March	1.782	2.236	8.470	6.807	0.921	3.040	2.261	0.585	0.668	0.995	7.868	3.139	2.688	2.045
April	1.507	1.880	7.779	6.244	0.787	2.891	2.034	0.532	0.618	0.917	6.495	2.657	2.290	1.552
May	1.651	1.694	7.516	5.809	0.745	2.822	1.713	0.529	0.672	1.034	6.841	2.647	2.415	1.780
June	1.705	1.659	7.625	5.880	0.793	2.749	1.779	0.560	0.702	1.044	7.286	2.869	2.446	1.969
July	1.692	1.874	8.006	6.282	0.865	2.886	1.933	0.598	0.725	0.999	8.101	3.330	2.615	2.146
August	1.613	1.877	7.991	6.311	0.952	2.901	1.863	0.596	0.720	0.960	8.025	3.188	2.668	2.159
September	1.545	1.853	7.692	6.115	0.904	2.783	1.856	0.572	0.686	0.891	7.331	2.737	2.527	2.062
October	1.578	1.975	7.749	6.187	0.900	2.859	1.837	0.590	0.620	0.942	7.488	2.722	2.653	2.114
November	1.596	1.957	7.866	6.221	0.887	2.862	1.899	0.574	0.645	1.000	7.600	2.946	2.667	1.988
December	1.720	2.195	8.130	6.392	0.898	2.975	1.955	0.563	0.730	1.009	8.710	3.897	2.769	2.043

Table 11-2. Energy Consumption Per Dollar of Real Gross Domestic Product

Year	Primary energy consumption (quadrillion Btu)			Gross domestic product (billions of chained [2012] dollars)	Energy intensity per real dollar of GDP (thousand Btu per chained [2012] dollar)		
	Total	Petroleum and natural gas	Other energy		Total	Petroleum and natural gas	Other energy
1950	34.599	19.267	15.332	2 291.1	15.85	8.83	7.02
1951	36.954	21.456	15.497	2 475.4	15.67	9.10	6.57
1952	36.726	22.484	14.243	2 576.7	14.96	9.16	5.80
1953	37.641	23.439	14.202	2 697.5	14.65	9.12	5.52
1954	36.614	24.144	12.470	2 681.9	14.33	9.45	4.88
1955	40.178	26.223	13.955	2 873.2	14.68	9.58	5.09
1956	41.722	27.519	14.203	2 934.4	14.93	9.85	5.08
1957	41.754	28.089	13.665	2 996.2	14.63	9.85	4.78
1958	41.609	29.154	12.455	2 974.0	14.69	10.30	4.39
1959	43.423	30.997	12.426	3 180.2	14.34	10.24	4.10
1960	45.041	32.259	12.782	3 262.1	14.50	10.39	4.11
1961	45.691	33.096	12.595	3 345.7	14.35	10.40	3.95
1962	47.775	34.728	13.047	3 550.7	14.14	10.28	3.86
1963	49.589	36.049	13.540	3 705.3	14.06	10.23	3.84
1964	51.755	37.530	14.226	3 918.8	13.88	10.07	3.81
1965	53.953	38.953	15.001	4 173.4	13.58	9.81	3.77
1966	56.949	41.331	15.618	4 448.7	13.45	9.77	3.68
1967	58.895	43.219	15.676	4 570.7	13.53	9.93	3.60
1968	62.401	46.176	16.225	4 795.4	13.66	10.11	3.55
1969	65.596	48.999	16.598	4 945.2	13.92	10.40	3.52
1970	67.817	51.294	16.523	4 954.4	14.37	10.87	3.50
1971	69.260	53.008	16.253	5 117.6	14.20	10.87	3.33
1972	72.660	55.617	17.043	5 386.7	14.16	10.84	3.32
1973	75.652	57.318	18.334	5 690.9	13.95	10.57	3.38
1974	73.929	55.153	18.776	5 660.1	13.71	10.23	3.48
1975	71.931	52.647	19.284	5 648.5	13.36	9.78	3.58
1976	75.939	55.487	20.452	5 952.8	13.39	9.78	3.60
1977	77.920	57.013	20.907	6 228.1	13.13	9.61	3.52
1978	79.907	57.920	21.987	6 572.8	12.76	9.25	3.51
1979	80.812	57.741	23.070	6 780.9	12.50	8.94	3.57
1980	78.021	54.394	23.627	6 763.5	12.10	8.44	3.66
1981	76.057	51.631	24.426	6 935.2	11.50	7.81	3.69
1982	73.046	48.535	24.511	6 810.1	11.26	7.49	3.78
1983	72.915	47.218	25.698	7 122.3	10.74	6.96	3.78
1984	76.571	49.386	27.185	7 637.7	10.52	6.79	3.73
1985	76.334	48.570	27.764	7 956.2	10.06	6.40	3.66
1986	76.599	48.742	27.857	8 231.7	9.75	6.21	3.54
1987	79.008	50.457	28.551	8 516.4	9.72	6.21	3.51
1988	82.659	52.621	30.038	8 872.2	9.76	6.22	3.54
1989	84.740	53.766	30.974	9 198.0	9.65	6.12	3.53
1990	84.433	53.103	31.330	9 371.5	9.43	5.94	3.50
1991	84.380	52.822	31.558	9 361.3	9.44	5.91	3.53
1992	85.725	54.181	31.544	9 691.1	9.26	5.85	3.40
1993	87.266	54.817	32.449	9 957.7	9.18	5.77	3.41
1994	88.983	56.181	32.802	10 358.9	8.99	5.68	3.31
1995	90.931	57.012	33.918	10 637.0	8.95	5.61	3.33
1996	93.935	58.674	35.261	11 038.3	8.90	5.56	3.34
1997	94.507	59.288	35.219	11 529.2	8.21	5.15	3.06
1998	94.920	59.550	35.370	12 045.8	7.89	4.95	2.94
1999	96.545	60.641	35.903	12 623.4	7.66	4.82	2.85
2000	98.702	61.976	36.727	13 138.0	7.53	4.73	2.80
2001	96.064	60.856	35.208	13 263.4	7.25	4.60	2.65
2002	97.535	61.628	35.908	13 488.4	7.24	4.58	2.66
2003	97.835	61.538	36.297	13 865.5	7.06	4.44	2.62
2004	100.002	63.062	36.940	14 399.7	6.95	4.38	2.56
2005	100.102	62.782	37.320	14 901.3	6.72	4.22	2.50
2006	99.392	61.969	37.422	15 315.9	6.49	4.05	2.44
2007	100.893	63.030	37.863	15 623.9	6.47	4.04	2.42
2008	98.754	60.612	38.141	15 643.0	6.34	4.06	2.45
2009	93.942	58.195	35.747	15 236.3	6.19	3.97	2.35
2010	97.513	59.895	37.618	15 649.0	6.25	3.85	2.40
2011	96.863	59.594	37.269	15 891.5	6.12	3.79	2.34
2012	94.374	59.922	34.452	16 254.0	5.83	3.60	2.12
2013	97.117	61.203	35.914	16 553.3	5.89	3.11	2.17
2014	98.276	62.041	36.235	16 932.1	5.82	3.69	2.13
2015	97.375	63.559	33.816	17 390.3	5.60	3.30	2.31
2016	97.337	64.112	33.225	17 680.3	5.50	3.62	1.88
2017	97.599	64.098	33.500	18 079.1	5.39	3.54	1.85
2018	101.162	68.045	33.117	18 606.8	5.42	3.65	1.78
2019	100.293	69.063	31.230	19 032.7	5.25	3.61	1.64
2020	93.048	63.875	29.173	18 384.7	5.04	3.46	1.58

Table 11-3. Petroleum and Petroleum Products—Prices, Imports, Domestic Production, and Stocks

(Not seasonally adjusted.)

Year and month	Crude oil futures price (dollars per barrel)		Imports				Supply (thousands of barrels per day)					Stocks (end of period, millions of barrels)		
			Total energy-related petroleum products (thousands of barrels)	Crude petroleum			Petroleum and products			Domestic production		Crude oil and petroleum products	Crude petroleum	
				Thousands of barrels		Unit price (dollars per barrel)								
	Current dollars	2009 dollars		Total	Average per day		Exports	Imports	Net imports	Crude oil	Natural gas plant liquids		Non-SPR	Strategic petroleum reserve
1983	30.66	69.52	. . .	1 293 819	3 545	29.51	739	5 051	4 312	8 688	1 559	1 454	344	379
1984	29.44	63.41	. . .	1 319 683	3 616	27.68	722	5 437	4 715	8 879	1 630	1 556	345	451
1985	27.89	57.07	. . .	1 260 856	3 454	26.20	781	5 067	4 286	8 971	1 609	1 519	321	493
1986	15.05	29.56	. . .	1 634 567	4 478	13.90	785	6 224	5 439	8 680	1 551	1 593	331	512
1987	19.15	36.38	. . .	1 744 977	4 781	16.80	764	6 678	5 914	8 349	1 595	1 607	349	541
1988	15.96	29.10	. . .	1 887 860	5 172	13.69	815	7 402	6 587	8 140	1 625	1 597	330	560
1989	19.58	34.69	. . .	2 146 552	5 881	16.49	859	8 061	7 202	7 613	1 546	1 581	341	580
1990	24.50	42.53	. . .	2 216 604	6 073	19.75	857	8 018	7 161	7 355	1 559	1 621	323	586
1991	21.50	37.24	2 828 953	2 146 064	5 880	17.46	1 001	7 627	6 626	7 417	1 659	1 617	325	569
1992	20.58	34.37	2 947 582	2 294 570	6 269	16.80	950	7 888	6 938	7 171	1 697	1 592	318	575
1993	18.48	29.82	3 257 008	2 543 374	6 968	15.13	1 003	8 620	7 618	6 847	1 736	1 647	335	587
1994	17.19	26.71	3 416 045	2 704 196	7 409	14.23	942	8 996	8 054	6 662	1 727	1 653	337	592
1995	18.40	27.76	3 361 882	2 767 312	7 582	15.81	949	8 835	7 886	6 560	1 762	1 563	303	592
1996	22.03	32.11	3 622 385	2 893 647	7 906	18.98	981	9 478	8 498	6 465	1 830	1 507	284	566
1997	20.61	28.95	3 802 574	3 069 430	8 409	17.67	1 003	10 162	9 158	6 452	1 817	1 560	305	563
1998	14.40	19.20	4 088 027	3 242 711	8 884	11.49	945	10 708	9 764	6 252	1 759	1 647	324	571
1999	19.30	24.44	4 081 181	3 228 092	8 844	15.76	940	10 852	9 912	5 881	1 850	1 493	284	567
2000	30.26	36.47	4 314 825	3 399 239	9 288	26.44	1 040	11 459	10 419	5 822	1 911	1 468	286	541
2001	25.95	30.48	4 475 026	3 471 067	9 510	21.40	971	11 871	10 900	5 801	1 868	1 586	312	550
2002	26.15	29.95	4 337 075	3 418 022	9 364	22.61	984	11 530	10 546	5 744	1 880	1 548	278	599
2003	30.99	34.41	4 654 638	3 676 005	10 071	26.98	1 027	12 264	11 238	5 649	1 719	1 568	269	638
2004	41.47	44.35	4 917 591	3 820 979	10 440	34.48	1 048	13 145	12 097	5 441	1 809	1 645	286	676
2005	56.70	58.57	5 004 339	3 754 671	10 287	46.81	1 165	13 714	12 549	5 184	1 717	1 682	308	685
2006	66.25	66.42	4 880 734	3 734 226	10 231	58.01	1 317	13 707	12 390	5 086	1 739	1 703	296	689
2007	72.41	71.01	4 807 811	3 690 568	10 111	64.28	1 433	13 468	12 036	5 074	1 783	1 648	268	697
2008	99.75	98.15	4 613 444	3 590 628	9 810	95.22	1 802	12 915	11 114	5 000	1 784	1 719	308	702
2009	62.09	62.09	4 266 007	3 314 787	9 082	56.93	2 024	11 691	9 667	5 357	1 910	1 758	307	727
2010	79.61	78.11	4 279 611	3 377 077	9 252	74.67	2 353	11 793	9 441	5 484	2 074	1 772	312	727
2011	95.11	91.25	4 164 117	3 321 918	9 101	99.82	2 986	11 436	8 450	5 667	2 216	1 725	308	696
2012	94.15	89.03	3 847 545	3 097 407	8 463	101.11	3 205	10 598	7 393	6 518	2 408	1 779	338	695
2013	98.05	91.17	3 549 945	2 813 770	7 709	96.95	3 621	9 859	6 237	7 493	2 606	1 728	327	696
2014	92.91	84.12	3 381 460	2 700 939	7 400	91.23	4 176	9 240	5 064	8 787	3 015	1 825	361	691
2015	48.79	44.54	3 384 807	2 661 968	7 293	47.26	4 738	9 449	4 650	9 439	3 342	1 982	449	695
2016	43.32	39.20	3 576 378	2 806 413	7 689	36.00	5 261	10 055	2 480	8 839	3 509	2 030	485	695
2017	50.80	45.09	3 639 778	2 883 753	7 901	45.97	6 376	10 075	3 723	9 352	3 736	1 895	421	662
2018	64.81	60.27	3 464 237	2 694 326	7 382	58.22	7 601	9 943	2 342	10 990	4 369	1 912	442	649
2019	56.99	51.97	3 116 908	2 374 322	6 505	53.30	8 499	9 093	594	12 232	4 813	1 916	433	635
2020	61.65	54.77	2 719 832	2 087 168	5 718	36.66	8 508	7 857	-651	11 313	5 161	1 982	485	638
2019														
January	51.38	43.22	282 790	223 855	7 221	42.63	8 044	9 690	1 646	11 360	4 545	1 098	449	649
February	54.95	46.30	226 060	173 678	6 203	46.91	8 404	8 626	222	11 181	4 706	1 101	452	649
March	58.15	48.63	251 749	195 255	6 299	53.06	7 929	8 837	908	11 411	4 728	1 108	459	649
April	63.86	53.21	270 681	205 633	6 854	57.17	8 440	9 504	1 063	11 667	4 787	1 117	469	649
May	60.83	50.51	289 879	219 518	7 081	60.56	8 149	9 796	1 647	11 639	4 838	1 125	480	645
June	54.66	45.29	259 032	204 160	6 805	59.18	8 654	9 234	581	11 605	4 793	1 109	464	645
July	57.35	47.37	285 560	213 008	6 871	56.44	8 011	9 547	1 535	11 375	4 679	1 087	442	645
August	54.81	45.17	265 629	199 720	6 443	54.15	8 424	9 356	931	12 003	4 727	1 076	431	645
September	56.95	46.85	242 939	185 307	6 177	53.10	8 678	8 666	-12	12 029	4 989	1 071	426	645
October	53.96	44.36	251 415	188 653	6 086	52.02	8 915	8 574	-340	12 199	5 022	1 085	444	641
November	57.03	46.78	228 703	166 418	5 547	51.91	8 757	8 056	-700	12 382	4 972	1 082	447	635
December	59.88	49.06	262 471	199 116	6 423	51.48	9 594	9 159	-435	12 332	4 971	1 068	433	635
2020														
January	57.52	47.19	256 779	198 338	6 400	52.24	9 177	8 572	-605	12 755	5 145	1 078	443	635
February	50.54	41.51	236 244	183 257	6 319	48.54	9 983	8 457	-1 526	12 746	4 965	1 089	454	635
March	29.21	25.65	244 125	187 756	6 057	40.53	9 621	8 345	-1 276	12 737	5 253	1 117	482	635
April	16.55	16.56	205 548	159 479	5 316	25.65	8 452	7 236	-1 216	12 010	4 934	1 167	529	638
May	28.56	26.33	217 732	172 384	5 561	22.78	6 818	7 757	939	10 019	4 745	1 169	521	648
June	38.31	33.35	229 229	180 788	6 026	27.69	7 692	8 367	675	10 442	5 197	1 188	532	656
July	40.71	35.01	226 286	172 283	5 558	33.14	8 412	7 846	-566	10 973	5 369	1 175	519	656
August	42.34	36.08	224 011	169 412	5 465	37.56	8 498	7 465	-1 033	10 584	5 325	1 152	504	648
September	39.63	33.40	216 120	158 489	5 283	37.60	8 376	7 543	-833	10 870	5 309	1 140	497	642
October	39.40	33.12	221 117	164 429	5 304	36.37	8 356	7 372	-984	10 439	5 299	1 132	494	639
November	40.94	34.63	217 308	166 803	5 560	35.70	7 823	7 616	-207	11 168	5 323	1 139	500	638
December	47.02	40.15	225 982	173 698	5 603	38.30	8 933	7 728	-1 205	11 088	5 060	1 123	485	638

. . . = Not available.

NOTES AND DEFINITIONS, CHAPTER 11

TABLES 11-1 AND 11-2

Energy Supply and Consumption

SOURCES: U.S. DEPARTMENT OF ENERGY, ENERGY INFORMATION ADMINISTRATION; U.S. DEPARTMENT OF COMMERCE, BUREAU OF ECONOMIC ANALYSIS

Definitions

The *British thermal unit (Btu)* is a measure used to combine data for different energy sources into a consistent aggregate. It is the amount of energy required to raise the temperature of 1 pound of water 1 degree Fahrenheit when the water is near a temperature of 39.2 degrees Fahrenheit. To illustrate one of the factors used to convert volumes to Btu, conventional motor gasoline has a heat content of 5.253 million Btu per barrel. For further information, see the Energy Information Administration's *Monthly Energy Review*, Appendix A.

Production: Crude oil includes lease condensates.

Renewable energy, total includes conventional hydroelectric power, geothermal, solar thermal and photovoltaic, wind, and biomass. Hydroelectric power includes conventional electrical utility and industrial generation. Biomass includes wood, waste, and alcohol fuels (ethanol blended into motor gasoline).

The sum of domestic energy *production* and net imports of energy (*imports* minus *exports*) does not exactly equal domestic energy *consumption*. The difference is attributed to inventory changes; losses and gains in conversion, transportation, and distribution; the addition of blending compounds; shipments of anthracite to U.S. armed forces in Europe; and adjustments to account for discrepancies between reporting systems.

Consumption by end-use sector is based on total, not net, consumption—that is, each sector's consumption includes its electricity purchases as well as its own energy production. Electric utilities are not treated as a separate end-use sector. However, they are counted as primary producers in the production accounts, which measure only primary production. As a result, total national supply and consumption are in rough balance, though components may not add to exact totals, not only because of the miscellaneous adjustments described above, but also because of different sector-specific conversion factors.

References and notes on the data

All of these data are published each month in Tables 1.1, 1.2, 1.7, and 2.1 in the *Monthly Energy Review*. Annual data before 1973

are published in the *Annual Energy Review*. These two publications are no longer published in printed form but are available, along with all current and historical data, on the EIA Web site at <https://www.eia.doe.gov>.

The real gross domestic product (GDP) data used to calculate energy consumption per dollar of real GDP are from the Bureau of Economic Analysis; see Table 1-2 and the applicable notes and definitions in this volume of *Business Statistics*. The GDP numbers shown in this table reflect the comprehensive revision of July 2013, which increased the overall level of GDP by including as investment research, development, and creation of intellectual property. This changed the average level of the energy-to-GDP ratio but had little effect on its downward trend. The GDP estimate shown here also reflects subsequent revisions and updates made through June 2016.

TABLE 11-3

Petroleum and Petroleum Products—Prices, Imports, Domestic Production, and Stocks

SOURCES: FUTURES PRICES—U.S. DEPARTMENT OF ENERGY, ENERGY INFORMATION ADMINISTRATION (EIA), AND U.S. DEPARTMENT OF COMMERCE, BUREAU OF ECONOMIC ANALYSIS; IMPORTS—U.S. DEPARTMENT OF COMMERCE, CENSUS BUREAU (SEE NOTES AND DEFINITIONS FOR TABLES 7-9 THROUGH 7-14); SUPPLY (NET IMPORTS AND DOMESTIC PRODUCTION) AND STOCKS—EIA.

Definitions and notes on the data

The *crude oil futures price* in *current dollars per barrel* is the price for next-month delivery in Cushing, Oklahoma (a pipeline hub), of light, sweet crude oil, as determined by trading on the New York Mercantile Exchange (NYMEX). Official daily closing prices are reported each day at 2:30 p.m. and are tabulated weekly in Table 13 of *EIA's Weekly Petroleum Status Report*. The monthly averages shown in this volume are the average prices for the nearest future from each trading day of the month. For example, for most days in January, the futures contract priced will be for February; for the last few days in January, the February contract will have expired and the March contract will be quoted. The annual averages are averages of the monthly averages.

The *crude oil futures price* in *2009 dollars* is calculated by the editors, by dividing each month's current-dollar price by that month's chain price index for total personal consumption expenditures (PCE), with the price index average for the year 2009 set at 1.0000. The PCE chain price index is compiled by the Bureau of Economic Analysis (BEA). It is described in the notes and definitions for Chapter 1 and is also presented in Chapter 8, Table 8-2, and discussed in its notes and definitions.

The import data in Columns 3 through 6 of this table are those published as Exhibit 17, "Imports of Energy-related Petroleum Products, including Crude Petroleum," in the monthly Census-BEA foreign trade press release, FT900. *Total energy-related petroleum products* includes the following Standard International Trade Classification (SITC) commodity groupings: crude oil, petroleum preparations, and liquefied propane and butane gas.

The data in Columns 7 through 11, on exports, imports, and net imports (imports minus exports) of petroleum and products and domestic production of crude oil and natural gas plant liquids (all expressed as thousands of barrels per day), and in Columns 12 through 14, depicting stocks of crude oil in millions of barrels, are derived from the Department of Energy's weekly petroleum supply reporting system. They are published in EIA's *Monthly Energy Review*, Tables 3.1 and 3.4, which can be reached by

searching the Web site. Stock totals are as of the end of the period. Geographic coverage includes the 50 states and the District of Columbia.

Data availability

Data on futures prices, petroleum supply and stocks are available from the EIA Web site at <https://www.eia.doe.gov>, under the categories "Publications and Reports/Monthly Energy Review" and "Petroleum/Weekly Petroleum Status Report." The *Monthly Energy Review* is no longer published in printed form.

The import data are available in the FT900 report from the Census Bureau at www.census.gov. See the notes and definitions for Tables 7-9 through 7-14 for further information.

CHAPTER 12: MONEY, INTEREST, ASSETS, LIABILITIES, AND ASSET PRICES

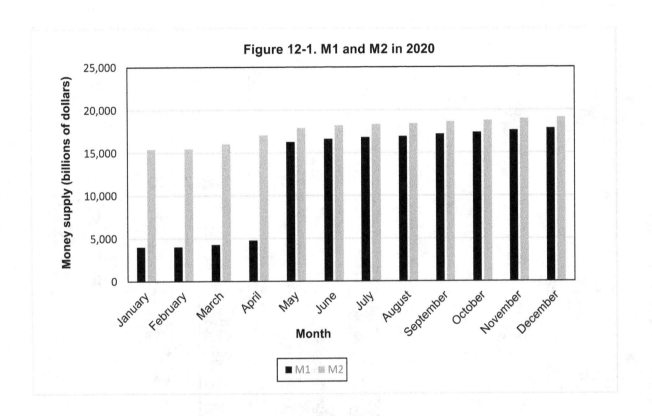

Figure 12-1. M1 and M2 in 2020

- Bank notes initially started with currency such as gold and silver coins. Demand deposits, or checking accounts, began after a 10 percent tax was instituted on the issuance of state bank notes in 1865. As new instruments were introduced, such as Negotiable Order of Withdrawal (NOW), defining the U.S. money supply took on more complexity.

- The Federal Reserve Board of Governors announced on March 15, 2020 that required reserve ratios were reduced to zero with no plans to re-institute them. In addition, Regulation D imposes reserve requirements, with zero ratio, and the Federal Reserve now classifies savings as transactions, thus these actions are added together into the new category now called "other liquid deposits." Another change was that separate deposits in thrift institutions and commercial banks do not have to be reported individually. Instead they are combined into "other checkable deposits total."

- The money supply is now composed of three components, (1) currency in circulation, (2) total other checkable deposits, and (3) other liquid deposits. See Figure 12-1. With the all these changes, M1 is significantly higher since savings deposits are now combined with the other deposits. (Table 12-1).

- The Federal Reserve revived some of the same tools used during the Great Recession such as keeping interest rates low and the Qualitative Easing (QE) program which bought bank securities. This action increased the bank's lending ability. The reduction of the reserve requirement to zero occurred during the pandemic.

Table 12-1A. Money Stock Measures and Components of M1: Recent Data

(Billions of dollars, monthly data are averages of daily figures, annual data are for December.)

Year and month	Not seasonally adjusted		Seasonally adjusted					Other checkable deposits			
	M1	M2	M1	M2	Currency	Traveler's checks	Demand deposits	At commercial banks	At thrift institutions	Total	Other liquid deposits
1965	172.6	463.1	167.8	459.2	36.0	0.5	135.3	0.0	0.1	0.1	. . .
1966	176.9	483.7	172.0	480.2	38.0	0.5	137.5	0.0	0.1	0.1	. . .
1967	188.4	528.0	183.3	524.8	40.0	0.6	146.9	0.0	0.1	0.1	. . .
1968	202.8	569.7	197.4	566.8	43.0	0.6	158.2	0.0	0.1	0.1	. . .
1969	209.3	590.1	203.9	587.9	45.7	0.7	162.0	0.0	0.1	0.1	. . .
1970	220.1	627.8	214.4	626.5	48.6	0.8	169.6	0.0	0.1	0.1	. . .
1971	234.5	711.2	228.3	710.3	52.0	1.0	180.4	0.0	0.2	0.2	. . .
1972	256.1	803.1	249.2	802.3	56.2	1.2	197.5	0.0	0.2	0.2	. . .
1973	270.2	856.5	262.9	855.5	60.8	1.3	206.7	0.0	0.3	0.3	. . .
1974	281.8	903.5	274.2	902.1	67.0	1.6	211.6	0.2	0.4	0.4	. . .
1975	295.3	1 017.8	287.1	1 016.2	72.8	2.0	218.3	0.4	0.5	0.9	. . .
1976	314.5	1 153.5	306.2	1 152.0	79.5	2.4	228.4	1.3	1.4	2.7	. . .
1977	340.0	1 273.0	330.9	1 270.3	87.4	2.7	244.0	1.8	2.3	4.2	. . .
1978	367.9	1 370.8	357.3	1 366.0	96.0	3.1	258.4	5.3	3.1	8.5	. . .
1979	393.2	1 479.0	381.8	1 473.7	104.8	3.3	266.0	12.7	4.2	16.9	. . .
1980	419.5	1 604.8	408.5	1 599.8	115.3	3.7	270.1	20.8	7.3	28.2	. . .
1981	447.0	1 760.3	436.7	1 755.5	122.5	3.9	239.4	63.0	15.6	79.0	. . .
1982	485.8	1 913.8	474.8	1 905.9	132.5	3.9	242.5	80.5	23.6	104.6	. . .
1983	533.3	2 134.0	521.4	2 123.5	146.2	4.3	247.4	97.3	34.8	132.9	. . .
1984	564.6	2 318.5	551.6	2 306.4	156.1	4.6	253.1	104.7	42.4	148.4	. . .
1985	633.3	2 504.1	619.8	2 492.1	167.7	5.2	276.9	124.7	54.9	181.2	. . .
1986	739.8	2 740.7	724.7	2 728.0	180.4	5.7	313.9	161.0	74.2	237.4	. . .
1987	765.4	2 838.3	750.2	2 826.4	196.7	6.2	298.2	178.2	81.0	261.8	. . .
1988	803.1	3 000.6	786.7	2 988.2	212.0	6.6	298.4	192.5	88.1	283.5	. . .
1989	810.6	3 165.6	792.9	3 152.5	222.3	6.5	290.9	197.4	87.7	288.2	. . .
1990	842.7	3 285.1	824.7	3 271.8	246.5	7.4	289.4	208.7	85.0	297.0	. . .
1991	915.6	3 386.4	897.0	3 372.2	267.1	7.4	302.4	241.6	90.9	336.3	. . .
1992	1 045.6	3 441.3	1 024.9	3 424.7	292.1	7.9	354.4	280.8	103.8	388.9	. . .
1993	1 153.3	3 495.1	1 129.6	3 474.5	321.6	7.7	401.8	302.6	112.0	419.4	. . .
1994	1 174.5	3 507.8	1 150.7	3 486.4	354.5	8.3	400.2	297.4	106.6	408.4	. . .
1995	1 152.7	3 653.3	1 127.5	3 629.5	372.8	8.8	407.2	249.0	107.6	360.5	. . .
1996	1 105.8	3 839.8	1 081.3	3 818.6	394.6	8.6	420.1	172.1	103.6	279.1	. . .
1997	1 097.5	4 055.1	1 072.3	4 032.9	425.3	8.3	412.4	148.4	96.7	247.9	. . .
1998	1 121.2	4 399.6	1 095.0	4 375.2	460.4	8.4	395.9	143.9	105.9	252.7	. . .
1999	1 148.2	4 664.5	1 122.2	4 638.0	517.9	8.4	371.7	139.7	103.6	246.0	. . .
2000	1 111.7	4 952.6	1 088.6	4 924.7	531.3	8.1	326.8	133.2	105.4	241.2	. . .
2001	1 208.5	5 463.8	1 183.2	5 432.7	581.2	7.9	354.3	142.2	115.6	261.1	. . .
2002	1 245.5	5 803.0	1 220.2	5 770.9	626.2	7.7	323.8	154.4	125.0	283.8	. . .
2003	1 332.5	6 097.3	1 306.2	6 065.9	662.4	7.6	343.0	175.3	134.8	315.2	. . .
2004	1 401.5	6 446.3	1 376.0	6 417.2	697.9	7.5	359.1	187.1	140.7	332.5	. . .
2005	1 397.2	6 707.2	1 374.3	6 680.1	724.7	7.2	338.3	180.6	137.7	322.5	. . .
2006	1 387.7	7 098.0	1 366.6	7 069.5	750.3	6.7	317.6	176.3	128.5	308.6	. . .
2007	1 394.9	7 502.0	1 373.4	7 469.4	760.6	6.3	315.4	171.9	132.9	309.2	. . .
2008	1 632.3	8 229.0	1 601.7	8 189.7	816.2	5.5	493.0	177.1	133.0	314.9	. . .
2009	1 724.4	8 540.8	1 692.8	8 493.1	863.7	5.1	469.4	229.1	149.0	384.1	. . .
2010	1 871.4	8 855.2	1 836.7	8 799.4	918.8	4.7	543.7	233.3	163.4	402.3	. . .
2011	2 208.1	9 726.7	2 165.7	9 657.7	1 001.9	4.3	789.0	231.1	176.0	411.5	. . .
2012	2 509.7	10 528.6	2 459.4	10 451.5	1 090.6	3.8	969.8	243.2	196.7	443.8	. . .
2013	2 715.7	11 101.6	2 662.9	11 020.3	1 160.3	3.5	1 079.0	255.6	210.7	471.2	. . .
2014	2 992.0	11 757.1	2 939.4	11 674.0	1 252.4	2.9	1 245.2	265.2	219.7	489.5	. . .
2015	3 141.1	12 424.3	3 096.3	12 340.1	1 339.2	2.5	1 278.9	276.6	238.2	519.2	. . .
2016	3 384.0	13 300.9	3 345.4	13 214.2	1 421.3	2.2	1 408.9	288.8	258.4	550.7	. . .
2017	3 652.7	13 945.8	3 618.9	13 854.8	1 525.1	1.9	1 526.7	306.4	287.0	596.7	. . .
2018	3 801.0	14 466.8	3 771.2	14 373.9	1 624.2	1.7	1 538.4	333.4	293.7	634.2	. . .
2019	4 042.4	15 431.8	4 011.2	15 325.8	1 709.7	. . .	1 648.2	367.2	306.8	681.1	. . .
2020	17 949.8	19 278.7	17 812.4	19 129.5	1 969.3	. . .	3 356.3	. . .	. . .	. . .	12 619.7
2019											
January	3 748.5	14 442.5	3 772.9	14 443.3	1 629.1	. . .	1 484.5	. . .	. . .	640.4	. . .
February	3 705.1	14 420.3	3 783.4	14 486.2	1 634.1	. . .	1 456.3	. . .	. . .	620.3	. . .
March	3 757.3	14 592.3	3 746.4	14 533.5	1 639.0	. . .	1 466.0	. . .	. . .	649.8	. . .
April	3 823.0	14 643.1	3 770.6	14 568.9	1 645.7	. . .	1 501.3	. . .	. . .	672.3	. . .
May	3 790.5	14 593.8	3 775.4	14 668.4	1 651.9	. . .	1 481.1	. . .	. . .	653.8	. . .
June	3 830.5	14 753.8	3 813.4	14 787.0	1 658.5	. . .	1 522.4	. . .	. . .	648.1	. . .
July	3 862.7	14 833.1	3 844.8	14 857.9	1 666.6	. . .	1 542.8	. . .	. . .	653.6	. . .
August	3 849.8	14 914.7	3 844.0	14 935.2	1 674.1	. . .	1 522.6	. . .	. . .	655.7	. . .
September	3 877.1	15 005.6	3 887.7	15 026.6	1 684.2	. . .	1 534.5	. . .	. . .	658.8	. . .
October	3 924.0	15 131.7	3 926.1	15 153.1	1 692.6	. . .	1 569.7	. . .	. . .	662.0	. . .
November	3 925.2	15 278.6	3 955.6	15 251.3	1 702.5	. . .	1 566.1	. . .	. . .	654.8	. . .
December	4 042.4	15 431.8	4 011.2	15 325.8	1 709.7	. . .	1 648.2	. . .	. . .	681.1	. . .
2020											
January	3 982.6	15 416.3	4 019.2	15 406.8	1 718.9	. . .	1 586.1	. . .	. . .	682.5	. . .
February	3 941.1	15 402.6	4 028.4	15 470.4	1 724.2	. . .	1 557.6	. . .	. . .	665.3	. . .
March	4 289.1	16 076.1	4 281.3	16 011.4	1 746.1	. . .	1 826.7	. . .	. . .	714.9	. . .
April	4 850.5	17 122.9	4 774.4	17 039.1	1 781.6	. . .	2 047.4	. . .	. . .	1 018.8	. . .
May	16 170.6	17 788.2	16 262.0	17 889.2	1 820.0	. . .	2 125.7	. . .	. . .	. . .	12 220.6
June	16 544.4	18 127.4	16 583.8	18 175.7	1 856.6	. . .	2 216.5	. . .	. . .	. . .	12 470.8
July	16 746.5	18 277.5	16 773.8	18 316.6	1 885.8	. . .	2 261.0	. . .	. . .	. . .	12 601.3
August	16 869.1	18 346.5	16 887.0	18 378.5	1 911.1	. . .	2 274.1	. . .	. . .	. . .	12 686.2
September	17 136.8	18 569.7	17 156.8	18 601.6	1 927.9	. . .	2 387.4	. . .	. . .	. . .	12 820.1
October	17 321.1	18 717.1	17 346.8	18 747.9	1 944.1	. . .	2 427.4	. . .	. . .	. . .	12 949.7
November	17 642.1	19 009.4	17 589.1	18 958.7	1 956.8	. . .	2 753.0	. . .	. . .	. . .	12 931.2
December	17 949.8	19 278.7	17 812.4	19 129.5	1 969.3	. . .	3 356.3	. . .	. . .	. . .	12 619.7

. . . = Not available.

Table 12-1B. Money Stock, Historical: 1892–1924

(Not seasonally adjusted, millions of dollars.)

Classification	1892	1893	1894	1895	1896	1897	1898	1899	1900	1901	1902
June 30											
Currency outside banks	1 015	1 081	972	971	974	1 013	1 150	1 181	1 331	1 395	1 431
Demand deposits adjusted	2 880	2 766	2 807	2 960	2 839	2 871	3 432	4 162	4 420	5 204	5 719
M1	3 895	3 847	3 779	3 931	3 813	3 884	4 582	5 343	5 751	6 599	7 150
Time deposits	1 929	2 007	1 994	2 088	2 220	2 305	2 397	2 617	3 015	3 315	3 565
M2	5 824	5 854	5 773	6 019	6 033	6 189	6 979	7 960	8 766	9 914	10 715
December 31											
Currency outside banks	...	...	...	...	...	...	...	...	...	...	...
Demand deposits adjusted	...	...	...	...	...	...	...	...	...	...	...
M1	...	...	...	...	...	...	...	...	...	...	...
Time deposits	...	...	...	...	...	...	...	...	...	...	...
M2	...	...	...	...	...	...	...	...	...	...	...

Classification	1903	1904	1905	1906	1907	1908	1909	1910	1911	1912	1913
June 30											
Currency outside banks	1 543	1 562	1 629	1 759	1 700	1 711	1 691	1 725	1 709	1 762	1 858
Demand deposits adjusted	5 962	6 256	7 069	7 504	7 872	7 384	7 768	8 254	8 668	9 156	9 140
M1	7 505	7 818	8 698	9 263	9 572	9 095	9 459	9 979	10 377	10 918	10 998
Time deposits	3 800	4 045	4 464	4 769	5 350	5 493	6 265	6 944	7 337	7 889	8 356
M2	11 305	11 863	13 162	14 032	14 922	14 588	15 724	16 923	17 714	18 807	19 354
December 31											
Currency outside banks	...	...	...	...	...	...	...	...	...	...	...
Demand deposits adjusted	...	...	...	...	...	...	...	...	...	...	...
M1	...	...	...	...	...	...	...	...	...	...	...
Time deposits	...	...	...	...	...	...	...	...	...	...	...
M2	...	...	...	...	...	...	...	...	...	...	...

Classification	1914	1915	1916	1917	1918	1919	1920	1921	1922	1923	1924
June 30											
Currency outside banks	1 533	1 575	1 876	2 276	3 298	3 593	4 105	3 677	3 346	3 739	3 650
Demand deposits adjusted	10 082	9 828	11 973	13 501	14 843	17 624	19 616	17 113	18 045	18 958	19 412
M1	11 615	11 403	13 849	15 777	18 141	21 217	23 721	20 790	21 391	22 697	23 062
Time deposits	8 350	9 231	10 313	11 543	11 717	13 423	15 834	16 583	17 437	19 722	21 259
M2	19 965	20 634	24 162	27 320	29 858	34 640	39 555	37 373	48 828	42 419	44 321
December 31											
Currency outside banks	...	...	...	...	...	...	...	...	...	3 726	3 696
Demand deposits adjusted	...	...	...	...	...	...	...	...	...	19 144	20 898
M1	...	...	...	...	...	...	...	...	...	22 870	24 594
Time deposits	...	...	...	...	...	...	...	...	...	20 379	22 232
M2	...	...	...	...	...	...	...	...	...	43 249	46 826

. . . = Not available.

Table 12-1C. Money Stock, Historical: January 1947–January 1959

(Averages of daily figures; seasonally adjusted, billions of dollars.)

Year and month	Money stock (M1)			Time deposits adjusted	M2 (M1 plus time deposits)
	Total	Currency component	Demand deposit component		
1947					
January	109.5	26.7	82.8	33.3	142.8
February	109.7	26.7	83.0	33.5	143.2
March	110.3	26.7	83.7	33.6	143.9
April	111.1	26.6	84.5	33.7	144.8
May	111.7	26.6	85.1	33.8	145.5
June	112.1	26.6	85.5	33.9	146.0
July	112.2	26.5	85.7	34.0	146.2
August	112.6	26.5	86.1	34.4	147.0
September	113.0	26.7	86.3	34.7	147.7
October	112.9	26.5	86.4	35.0	147.9
November	113.3	26.5	86.8	35.2	148.5
December	113.1	26.4	86.7	35.4	148.5
1948					
January	113.4	26.4	87.0	35.5	148.9
February	113.2	26.3	86.8	35.7	148.9
March	112.6	26.2	86.4	35.7	148.3
April	112.3	26.1	86.3	35.7	148.0
May	112.1	26.0	86.0	35.7	147.8
June	112.0	26.0	86.0	35.8	147.8
July	112.2	26.0	86.2	35.8	148.0
August	112.3	26.0	86.2	35.9	148.2
September	112.2	26.0	86.2	35.9	148.1
October	112.1	26.0	86.1	35.9	148.0
November	111.8	26.0	85.9	36.0	147.8
December	111.5	25.8	85.8	36.0	147.5
1949					
January	111.2	25.7	85.5	36.1	147.3
February	111.2	25.7	85.5	36.1	147.3
March	111.2	25.7	85.6	36.1	147.3
April	113.3	25.7	85.6	36.2	149.5
May	111.5	25.7	85.8	36.3	147.8
June	111.3	25.6	85.7	36.4	147.7
July	111.2	25.5	85.7	36.4	147.6
August	111.0	25.5	85.6	36.4	147.4
September	110.9	25.3	85.6	36.4	147.3
October	110.9	25.3	85.6	36.4	147.3
November	111.0	25.2	85.8	36.4	147.4
December	111.2	25.1	86.0	36.4	147.6
1950					
January	111.5	25.1	86.4	36.4	147.9
February	112.1	25.1	86.9	36.6	148.7
March	112.5	25.2	87.3	36.6	149.1
April	113.2	25.3	88.0	36.7	149.9
May	113.7	25.2	88.5	36.9	150.6
June	114.1	25.1	89.0	36.9	151.0
July	114.6	25.0	89.6	36.8	151.4
August	115.0	24.9	90.1	36.7	151.7
September	115.2	24.9	90.3	36.6	151.8
October	115.7	24.9	90.8	36.5	152.2
November	115.9	24.9	90.9	36.6	152.5
December	116.2	25.0	91.2	36.7	152.9
1951					
January	116.7	25.0	91.7	36.7	153.4
February	117.1	25.1	92.0	36.6	153.7
March	117.6	25.2	92.4	36.6	154.2
April	117.8	25.2	92.6	36.7	154.5
May	118.2	25.3	92.8	36.8	155.0
June	118.6	25.4	93.2	36.9	155.5
July	119.1	25.6	93.4	37.2	156.3
August	119.6	25.7	93.8	37.4	157.0
September	120.4	25.8	94.5	37.7	158.1
October	121.0	26.0	95.1	37.8	158.8
November	122.0	26.0	96.0	38.0	160.0
December	122.7	26.1	96.5	38.2	160.9
1952					
January	123.1	26.2	96.9	38.4	161.5
February	123.6	26.3	97.3	38.7	162.3
March	123.8	26.4	97.5	38.9	162.7
April	124.1	26.4	97.6	39.1	163.2
May	124.5	26.5	98.0	39.3	163.8
June	125.0	26.7	98.4	39.5	164.5
July	125.3	26.7	98.6	39.7	165.0
August	125.7	26.8	98.9	40.0	165.7
September	126.4	26.9	99.4	40.3	166.7
October	126.7	27.0	99.7	40.5	167.2
November	127.1	27.2	99.9	40.9	168.0
December	127.4	27.3	100.1	41.1	168.5

Table 12-1C. Money Stock, Historical: January 1947–January 1959—*Continued*

(Averages of daily figures; seasonally adjusted, billions of dollars.)

Year and month	Money stock (M1)			Time deposits adjusted	M2 (M1 plus time deposits)
	Total	Currency component	Demand deposit component		
1953					
January	127.3	27.4	99.9	41.4	168.7
February	127.4	27.5	99.9	41.6	169.0
March	128.0	27.6	100.4	41.9	169.9
April	128.3	27.7	100.7	42.1	170.4
May	128.5	27.7	100.7	42.4	170.9
June	128.5	27.7	100.7	42.6	171.1
July	128.6	27.8	100.8	42.9	171.5
August	128.7	27.8	100.9	43.2	171.9
September	128.6	27.8	100.8	43.5	172.1
October	128.7	27.8	100.9	43.9	172.6
November	128.7	27.8	100.9	44.2	172.9
December	128.8	27.7	101.1	44.5	173.3
1954					
January	129.0	27.7	101.3	44.8	173.8
February	129.1	27.7	101.5	45.2	174.3
March	129.2	27.6	101.6	45.6	174.8
April	128.6	27.6	101.0	46.1	174.7
May	129.7	27.6	102.1	46.5	176.2
June	129.9	27.5	102.3	46.8	176.7
July	130.3	27.5	102.8	47.3	177.6
August	130.7	27.5	103.2	47.8	178.5
September	130.9	27.4	103.5	47.9	178.8
October	131.5	27.4	104.1	48.1	179.6
November	132.1	27.4	104.7	48.2	180.3
December	132.3	27.4	104.9	48.3	180.6
1955					
January	133.0	27.4	105.6	48.5	181.5
February	133.9	27.5	106.4	48.7	182.6
March	133.6	27.5	106.0	48.8	182.4
April	133.9	27.5	106.3	49.0	182.9
May	134.6	27.6	107.0	49.0	183.6
June	134.4	27.6	106.8	49.2	183.6
July	134.8	27.7	107.2	49.3	184.1
August	134.8	27.7	107.0	49.3	184.1
September	135.0	27.7	107.3	49.6	184.6
October	135.2	27.8	107.4	49.7	184.9
November	134.9	27.8	107.1	49.9	184.8
December	135.2	27.8	107.4	50.0	185.2
1956					
January	135.5	27.9	107.7	49.9	185.4
February	135.5	27.9	107.7	49.9	185.4
March	135.7	27.9	107.8	50.1	185.8
April	136.0	27.9	108.1	50.3	186.3
May	135.8	27.9	107.9	50.4	186.2
June	136.0	27.9	108.1	50.7	186.7
July	136.0	28.0	108.0	50.9	186.9
August	135.7	28.0	107.8	51.2	186.9
September	136.2	28.0	108.2	51.5	187.7
October	136.3	28.0	108.2	51.6	187.9
November	136.6	28.1	108.4	51.8	188.4
December	136.9	28.2	108.7	51.9	188.8
1957					
January	136.9	28.2	108.6	52.6	189.5
February	136.8	28.2	108.6	53.1	189.9
March	136.9	28.2	108.7	53.7	190.6
April	136.9	28.2	108.7	54.0	190.9
May	137.0	28.2	108.8	54.5	191.5
June	136.9	28.3	108.6	54.8	191.7
July	137.0	28.3	108.7	55.3	192.3
August	137.1	28.3	108.8	55.7	192.8
September	136.8	28.3	108.4	56.1	192.9
October	136.5	28.3	108.2	56.6	193.1
November	136.3	28.3	108.0	57.0	193.3
December	135.9	28.3	107.6	57.4	193.3
1958					
January	135.5	28.3	107.2	57.6	193.1
February	136.2	28.2	107.9	59.2	195.4
March	136.5	28.2	108.3	60.5	197.0
April	137.0	28.2	108.7	61.5	198.5
May	137.5	28.3	109.2	62.3	199.8
June	138.4	28.3	110.1	63.2	201.6
July	138.4	28.4	110.0	64.0	202.4
August	139.1	28.4	110.7	64.6	203.7
September	139.5	28.5	111.1	64.8	204.3
October	140.1	28.5	111.6	64.9	205.0
November	140.9	28.5	112.4	65.2	206.1
December	141.1	28.6	112.6	65.4	206.5
1959					
January	142.2	28.7	113.5	66.3	208.5

Table 12-2. Components of Non-M1 M2

(Billions of dollars, seasonally adjusted; monthly data are averages of daily figures, annual data are for December.)

Year and month	Savings deposits				Small-denomination time deposits			Retail money funds	Total non-M1 M2
	At commercial banks	At thrift institutions	Total	Other liquid deposits	At commercial banks	At thrift institutions	Total		
1965	92.4	164.5	256.9	...	26.7	7.8	33.6	...	290.5
1966	89.9	163.3	253.4	...	38.7	16.3	53.4	...	306.8
1967	94.1	169.6	264.0	...	50.7	27.1	75.6	...	339.6
1968	96.1	172.8	269.0	...	63.5	37.1	97.8	...	366.8
1969	93.8	169.8	263.4	...	71.6	48.8	117.4	...	380.8
1970	98.6	162.3	259.0	...	79.3	71.9	148.8	...	407.8
1971	112.8	179.4	289.9	...	94.7	95.1	186.8	...	476.7
1972	124.8	196.6	318.7	...	108.2	123.5	228.3	...	547.0
1973	128.0	198.7	323.9	...	116.8	149.0	262.3	0.1	586.3
1974	136.8	201.8	335.4	...	123.1	164.8	284.8	1.4	621.6
1975	161.2	227.6	385.3	...	142.3	195.5	334.9	2.3	722.5
1976	201.8	251.4	449.2	...	155.5	235.2	388.1	1.7	839.0
1977	218.8	273.4	488.1	...	167.5	278.0	443.3	1.6	933.0
1978	216.5	265.4	478.1	...	185.1	335.8	519.4	5.4	1 002.9
1979	195.0	228.8	420.6	...	235.5	398.7	633.1	32.2	1 085.9
1980	185.7	214.5	397.1	...	286.2	442.3	727.9	60.3	1 185.3
1981	159.0	184.9	341.2	...	347.7	475.4	823.0	149.1	1 313.3
1982	190.1	210.0	397.2	...	379.9	471.0	851.4	179.4	1 428.0
1983	363.2	321.7	682.4	...	350.9	433.1	784.8	133.5	1 600.7
1984	389.3	315.4	702.2	...	387.9	500.9	889.7	161.9	1 753.8
1985	456.6	358.6	813.0	...	386.4	499.3	886.4	171.4	1 870.8
1986	533.5	407.4	939.0	...	369.4	489.0	858.4	203.6	2 001.0
1987	534.8	402.6	936.0	...	391.7	529.3	920.1	216.9	2 073.0
1988	542.4	383.9	925.6	...	451.2	585.9	1 035.0	236.9	2 197.5
1989	541.1	352.6	893.7	...	533.8	617.6	1 148.1	313.2	2 355.0
1990	581.3	341.6	922.0	...	610.7	562.6	1 170.9	349.5	2 442.4
1991	664.8	379.6	1 043.2	...	602.2	463.1	1 063.0	364.6	2 470.8
1992	754.2	433.1	1 185.3	...	508.1	359.7	865.8	344.6	2 395.7
1993	785.3	434.0	1 217.7	...	467.9	313.5	779.7	344.5	2 341.9
1994	752.8	398.5	1 149.7	...	503.6	313.9	815.8	367.8	2 333.3
1995	774.8	361.0	1 134.9	...	575.8	356.5	930.8	434.9	2 500.6
1996	906.0	368.7	1 271.7	...	594.2	353.7	947.0	515.1	2 733.8
1997	1 022.5	378.7	1 398.3	...	625.5	342.2	967.5	591.8	2 957.6
1998	1 187.4	416.1	1 601.8	...	626.4	324.9	951.8	724.9	3 278.5
1999	1 288.9	451.2	1 739.9	...	636.9	318.3	956.0	820.4	3 516.3
2000	1 425.3	454.3	1 882.5	...	700.8	345.3	1 047.0	911.4	3 840.9
2001	1 740.3	571.2	2 314.8	...	636.0	338.5	975.0	965.5	4 255.3
2002	2 057.9	713.1	2 775.1	...	591.3	303.5	894.6	887.9	4 557.6
2003	2 335.2	823.6	3 161.5	...	541.9	276.2	817.9	785.4	4 764.8
2004	2 633.9	872.7	3 508.2	...	552.3	276.1	828.4	708.3	5 044.9
2005	2 777.2	825.0	3 603.9	...	647.2	346.5	994.2	711.9	5 310.0
2006	2 913.1	779.9	3 696.3	...	781.4	424.6	1 207.9	806.1	5 710.3
2007	3 042.7	823.5	3 871.2	...	859.4	416.5	1 279.1	956.8	6 107.1
2008	3 323.1	765.3	4 089.4	...	1 079.6	378.0	1 461.3	1 046.1	6 596.8
2009	3 978.9	833.0	4 820.6	...	868.6	319.0	1 190.3	805.6	6 816.5
2010	4 412.3	919.2	5 347.7	...	663.9	270.5	933.7	702.4	6 983.8
2011	5 037.6	996.0	6 052.3	...	548.3	228.6	774.6	691.7	7 518.6
2012	5 727.5	955.8	6 705.6	...	469.0	176.8	642.5	670.9	8 019.0
2013	6 108.1	1 020.1	7 151.2	...	425.9	144.5	566.0	668.7	8 385.9
2014	6 495.8	1 077.2	7 599.2	...	391.4	132.0	518.3	647.6	8 765.1
2015	7 026.4	1 143.3	8 193.6	...	302.6	110.6	420.8	668.9	9 283.3
2016	7 556.1	1 258.4	8 848.1	...	251.6	101.8	363.5	705.2	9 916.8
2017	7 813.1	1 297.2	9 146.1	...	302.5	111.7	426.7	720.3	10 293.1
2018	7 926.4	1 334.6	9 289.8	...	425.4	107.6	546.1	829.9	10 665.8
2019	8 418.1	1 347.7	9 790.9	...	458.7	121.2	596.8	1 001.7	11 389.4
2020	...	...	...	12 619.7	...	...	248.3	1 080.6	13 948.6
2019									
January	...	...	9 247.7	...	...	...	567.8	878.5	10 694.0
February	...	...	9 244.5	...	...	...	591.8	879.4	10 715.2
March	...	...	9 330.8	...	...	...	611.5	892.6	10 834.9
April	...	...	9 301.1	...	...	...	624.8	894.2	10 820.1
May	...	...	9 283.4	...	...	...	628.7	891.1	10 803.2
June	...	...	9 385.3	...	...	...	638.5	899.5	10 923.3
July	...	...	9 414.1	...	...	...	638.3	918.0	10 970.4
August	...	...	9 496.9	...	...	...	635.6	932.3	11 064.8
September	...	...	9 546.8	...	...	...	629.6	952.0	11 128.4
October	...	...	9 609.3	...	...	...	619.5	978.9	11 207.7
November	...	...	9 751.1	...	...	...	608.1	994.2	11 353.4
December	...	...	9 790.9	...	...	...	596.8	1 001.7	11 389.4
2020									
January	...	...	9 842.1	...	...	...	579.7	1 011.9	11 433.7
February	...	...	9 908.0	...	...	...	549.4	1 004.0	11 461.4
March	...	...	10 223.1	...	...	...	516.4	1 047.6	11 787.1
April	...	...	10 662.3	...	...	...	498.2	1 111.9	12 272.4
May	...	...	...	12 220.6	...	...	481.1	1 136.5	13 838.2
June	...	...	...	12 470.8	...	...	452.3	1 130.6	14 053.7
July	...	...	...	12 601.3	...	...	418.8	1 112.2	14 132.3
August	...	...	...	12 686.2	...	...	381.7	1 095.6	14 163.5
September	...	...	...	12 820.1	...	...	350.4	1 082.6	14 253.1
October	...	...	...	12 949.7	...	...	315.2	1 080.7	14 345.6
November	...	...	...	12 931.2	...	...	277.0	1 090.2	14 298.4
December	...	...	...	12 619.7	...	...	248.3	1 080.6	13 948.6

... = Not available.

Table 12-3. Aggregate Reserves of Depository Institutions and the Monetary Base

(Not seasonally adjusted. Millions of dollars unless otherwise noted.)

Year and month	Reserves balances required			Reserves balances maintained			Reserves		Vault cash		
	Reserve balance	Top of penalty-free brand	Bottom of penalty-free band	Total	Balances maintaned to satisfy reserve balance requirements	Balances maintained that exceed the top of the penalty-free brand	Total	Required	Total	Used to satisfy required reserves	Surplus
1965	. . .	. . .	. . .	18 757	. . .	. . .	22 694	22 270	3 936	3 936	0
1966	. . .	. . .	. . .	19 550	. . .	. . .	23 785	23 446	4 235	4 235	0
1967	. . .	. . .	. . .	20 770	. . .	. . .	25 291	24 916	4 521	4 521	0
1968	. . .	. . .	. . .	22 455	. . .	. . .	27 192	26 766	4 737	4 737	0
1969	. . .	. . .	. . .	23 094	. . .	. . .	28 053	27 767	4 959	4 959	0
1970	. . .	. . .	. . .	23 907	. . .	. . .	29 246	28 998	5 340	5 340	0
1971	. . .	. . .	. . .	25 670	. . .	. . .	31 345	31 163	5 675	5 675	0
1972	. . .	. . .	. . .	25 317	. . .	. . .	31 415	31 131	6 098	6 098	0
1973	. . .	. . .	. . .	28 473	. . .	. . .	35 108	34 804	6 635	6 635	0
1974	. . .	. . .	. . .	29 682	. . .	. . .	36 861	36 603	7 179	7 179	0
1975	. . .	. . .	. . .	27 219	. . .	. . .	34 990	34 724	7 772	7 772	0
1976	. . .	. . .	. . .	26 689	. . .	. . .	35 237	34 964	8 548	8 548	0
1977	. . .	. . .	. . .	27 134	. . .	. . .	36 486	36 296	9 352	9 352	0
1978	. . .	. . .	. . .	31 347	. . .	. . .	41 678	41 446	10 331	10 331	0
1979	. . .	. . .	. . .	32 676	. . .	. . .	44 020	43 578	11 344	11 344	0
1980	. . .	. . .	. . .	27 354	. . .	. . .	40 660	40 146	18 149	13 306	4 843
1981	. . .	. . .	. . .	26 167	. . .	. . .	41 925	41 606	19 538	15 758	3 780
1982	. . .	. . .	. . .	24 806	. . .	. . .	41 855	41 354	20 392	17 049	3 343
1983	. . .	. . .	. . .	20 986	. . .	. . .	38 894	38 333	20 755	17 908	2 847
1984	20 898	. . .	. . .	21 734	. . .	. . .	40 693	39 858	22 193	18 960	3 233
1985	26 518	. . .	. . .	27 582	. . .	. . .	48 122	47 058	23 336	20 540	2 796
1986	35 991	. . .	. . .	37 165	. . .	. . .	59 369	58 196	24 538	22 204	2 334
1987	36 672	. . .	. . .	37 692	. . .	. . .	62 129	61 109	26 676	24 436	2 239
1988	36 703	. . .	. . .	37 765	. . .	. . .	63 678	62 616	28 204	25 913	2 291
1989	34 425	. . .	. . .	35 367	. . .	. . .	62 732	61 790	29 827	27 365	2 462
1990	28 562	. . .	. . .	30 227	. . .	. . .	59 122	57 457	31 789	28 895	2 894
1991	25 680	. . .	. . .	26 670	. . .	. . .	55 545	54 555	32 509	28 875	3 634
1992	24 246	. . .	. . .	25 401	. . .	. . .	56 578	55 423	34 541	31 177	3 364
1993	28 290	. . .	. . .	29 360	. . .	. . .	62 847	61 777	36 818	33 487	3 331
1994	23 500	. . .	. . .	24 671	. . .	. . .	61 359	60 188	40 382	36 688	3 694
1995	19 164	. . .	. . .	20 455	. . .	. . .	57 896	56 605	42 284	37 441	4 843
1996	11 913	. . .	. . .	13 332	. . .	. . .	51 176	49 757	44 527	37 844	6 683
1997	8 979	. . .	. . .	10 666	. . .	. . .	47 921	46 234	44 742	37 255	7 486
1998	7 512	. . .	. . .	9 025	. . .	. . .	45 208	43 695	44 295	36 183	8 112
1999	3 965	. . .	. . .	5 260	. . .	. . .	41 651	40 357	60 625	36 392	24 233
2000	5 594	. . .	. . .	6 920	. . .	. . .	38 371	37 045	45 246	31 451	13 795
2001	7 402	. . .	. . .	9 046	. . .	. . .	41 051	39 407	43 895	32 005	11 890
2002	7 916	. . .	. . .	9 925	. . .	. . .	40 271	38 263	43 363	30 347	13 016
2003	9 820	. . .	. . .	10 867	. . .	. . .	42 953	41 906	44 884	32 087	12 797
2004	10 136	. . .	. . .	12 045	. . .	. . .	46 847	44 938	48 555	34 802	13 754
2005	8 146	. . .	. . .	10 046	. . .	. . .	45 383	43 483	52 586	35 337	17 249
2006	6 616	. . .	. . .	8 479	. . .	. . .	43 282	41 419	53 054	34 803	18 251
2007	6 313	. . .	. . .	8 098	. . .	. . .	43 463	41 678	54 458	35 365	19 093
2008	16 312	. . .	. . .	783 631	. . .	. . .	820 876	53 558	56 029	37 245	18 784
2009	24 632	. . .	. . .	1 099 831	. . .	. . .	114 045	65 250	54 752	40 619	14 134
2010	28 438	. . .	. . .	1 035 074	. . .	. . .	107 800	71 365	55 708	42 927	12 781
2011	47 838	. . .	. . .	1 550 043	. . .	. . .	159 871	96 510	59 908	48 672	11 236
2012	58 675	. . .	. . .	1 517 425	. . .	. . .	157 038	111 634	63 846	52 959	10 887
2013	69 030	75 947	62 114	2 485 248	75 713	240 953	254 101	124 801	66 275	55 771	10 504
2014	82 770	91 061	74 481	2 606 700	90 852	251 584	266 593	142 007	69 116	59 236	9 880
2015	89 313	98 253	80 370	2 419 774	97 981	232 179	248 118	150 727	71 616	61 413	10 203
2016	105 944	116 551	95 338	2 031 007	116 285	191 472	209 528	170 224	74 751	64 280	10 471
2017	123 720	136 103	111 337	2 244 274	135 719	210 855	230 982	189 269	76 631	65 549	11 082
2018	123 703	136 085	111 322	1 691 394	135 698	155 569	175 985	192 165	80 812	68 462	12 350
2019	138 984	152 893	125 076	1 630 090	152 562	147 752	169 834	207 239	80 168	68 255	11 914
2019											
January	131 130	144 255	118 006	1 639 030	143 615	149 541	170 725	199 356	80 389	68 226	12 163
February	125 129	137 655	112 606	1 645 233	137 128	150 810	171 368	193 579	81 298	68 450	12 848
March	128 423	141 279	115 569	1 661 297	140 926	152 037	172 593	193 064	76 814	64 640	12 174
April	130 120	143 144	117 098	1 559 450	142 641	141 680	162 390	194 575	76 135	64 455	11 681
May	134 717	148 200	121 237	1 511 285	147 792	136 349	157 630	199 742	75 826	65 024	10 802
June	134 908	148 409	121 408	1 535 857	148 025	138 783	160 130	200 360	76 106	65 452	10 654
July	135 103	148 624	121 584	1 513 550	148 191	136 535	157 861	200 169	76 485	65 065	11 420
August	134 639	148 114	121 167	1 520 876	147 555	137 332	158 684	200 608	78 451	65 969	12 483
September	134 707	148 188	121 227	1 439 771	147 498	129 227	150 480	199 741	76 550	65 035	11 516
October	134 998	148 509	121 489	1 481 513	148 050	133 346	154 713	200 621	76 660	65 623	11 037
November	140 705	154 787	126 625	1 529 341	154 256	137 508	159 522	206 586	76 921	65 881	11 040
December	138 984	152 893	125 076	1 630 090	152 562	147 752	169 834	207 239	80 168	68 255	11 914
2020											
January	144 816	159 309	130 326	1 645 384	158 765	148 661	171 521	214 652	81 216	69 835	11 381
February	138 370	152 218	124 524	1 656 989	151 612	150 537	172 694	208 324	80 735	69 954	10 781
March	113 139	124 461	101 817	2 045 148	124 147	192 100	209 936	167 360	77 114	54 222	22 892
April	0	0	0	2 953 586	0	295 358	295 358	0	88 104	0	88 104
May	0	0	0	3 217 635	0	321 763	321 763	0	101 345	0	101 345
June	0	0	0	3 043 556	0	304 355	304 355	0	104 201	0	104 201
July	0	0	0	2 718 529	0	271 852	271 852	0	98 392	0	98 392
August	0	0	0	2 799 719	0	279 971	279 971	0	95 327	0	95 327

See footnotes at end of table.

Table 12-3. Aggregate Reserves of Depository Institutions and the Monetary Base—*Continued*

(Not seasonally adjusted. Millions of dollars unless otherwise noted.)

Year and month	Monetary base			Borrowings from the federal reserve					Nonborrowed reserves
	Total	Total balances maintained	Currency in circulation	Total	Primary	Secondary	Seasonal	Other credit extensions	
1965	61 022	18 758	42 264	444	...	...	0	...	22 250
1966	64 185	19 551	44 634	532	...	...	0	...	23 252
1967	67 818	20 771	47 047	228	...	...	0	...	25 064
1968	73 139	22 456	50 683	746	...	...	0	...	26 446
1969	76 752	23 095	53 658	1 119	...	...	0	...	26 934
1970	80 987	23 907	57 079	332	...	...	0	...	28 914
1971	86 798	25 671	61 127	126	...	...	0	...	31 219
1972	91 381	25 318	66 063	1 050	...	...	0	...	30 365
1973	100 143	28 474	71 669	1 298	...	...	41	...	33 810
1974	108 640	29 682	78 957	727	...	...	32	...	36 134
1975	113 125	27 220	85 905	130	...	...	14	...	34 860
1976	120 337	26 690	93 647	53	...	...	13	...	35 184
1977	129 915	27 135	102 780	569	...	...	55	...	35 917
1978	144 721	31 348	113 373	868	...	...	135	...	40 810
1979	156 653	32 677	123 977	1 473	...	...	82	...	42 547
1980	163 376	27 355	136 021	1 690	...	...	116	...	38 970
1981	170 681	26 282	144 399	636	...	...	54	...	41 289
1982	180 717	25 241	155 476	634	...	...	33	...	41 221
1983	192 191	22 002	170 189	774	...	...	96	...	38 120
1984	204 812	23 060	181 752	3 186	...	...	113	...	37 507
1985	224 722	29 494	195 229	1 318	...	...	56	...	46 804
1986	248 625	39 492	209 133	827	...	...	38	...	58 543
1987	266 878	39 632	227 246	777	...	...	93	...	61 351
1988	283 789	39 344	244 445	1 716	...	...	130	...	61 962
1989	294 323	37 558	256 765	265	...	...	84	...	62 466
1990	315 270	32 343	282 927	326	...	...	76	...	58 796
1991	335 415	30 947	304 467	192	...	...	38	...	55 353
1992	361 903	31 418	330 486	124	...	...	18	...	56 454
1993	398 638	36 191	362 447	82	...	...	31	...	62 765
1994	428 489	29 483	399 006	209	...	...	100	...	61 150
1995	445 840	26 125	419 715	257	...	...	40	...	57 638
1996	464 955	20 615	444 340	155	...	...	68	...	51 021
1997	493 078	17 728	475 350	324	...	...	79	...	47 597
1998	526 435	15 969	510 467	117	...	...	15	...	45 091
1999	612 499	12 614	599 885	320	...	...	67	...	41 331
2000	598 305	14 053	584 252	210	...	...	111	...	38 161
2001	650 775	18 499	632 276	67	...	...	33	...	40 984
2002	699 216	20 906	678 310	80	...	...	45	...	40 191
2003	739 408	23 032	716 376	46	17	0	29	...	42 907
2004	776 279	22 785	753 494	63	11	0	52	...	46 784
2005	803 124	18 406	784 718	169	97	0	72	...	45 214
2006	826 731	15 586	811 145	191	111	0	80	...	43 091
2007	837 192	14 905	822 287	15 430	3 787	1	30	...	28 033
2008	166 636	788 042	878 323	653 565	88 245	52	3	0	167 311
2009	202 622	110 179	924 426	169 927	19 025	518	37	0	970 523
2010	201 700	103 733	979 663	45 488	41	3	26	0	103 251
2011	261 958	155 257	106 701	9 526	103	0	23	0	158 918
2012	267 594	151 742	115 852	795	12	0	23	0	156 958
2013	371 745	248 524	123 220	170	13	0	59	0	254 084
2014	393 445	260 670	132 775	102	22	0	80	0	266 583
2015	383 581	241 977	141 603	106	38	0	67	0	248 108
2016	353 156	203 100	150 055	39	13	0	25	0	209 524
2017	385 096	224 427	160 669	75	43	0	33	0	230 974
2018	340 074	169 139	170 935	76	18	0	58	0	175 978
2019	342 646	163 009	179 637	21	10	0	11	0	169 832
2019									
January	334 687	163 903	170 784	26	20	0	6	0	170 723
February	335 346	164 523	170 823	19	7	0	12	0	171 366
March	338 145	166 129	172 015	15	7	0	8	0	172 592
April	328 665	155 945	172 720	30	14	0	15	0	162 387
May	324 446	151 128	173 317	56	18	0	38	0	157 625
June	327 482	153 585	173 896	80	20	0	60	0	160 122
July	326 031	151 355	174 676	120	9	0	111	0	157 849
August	327 137	152 087	175 050	117	16	0	101	0	158 672
September	320 266	143 977	176 289	101	15	0	86	0	150 470
October	325 280	148 151	177 129	63	4	0	59	0	154 707
November	331 555	152 934	178 620	26	4	0	22	0	159 519
December	342 646	163 009	179 637	21	10	0	11	0	169 832
2020									
January	344 256	164 538	179 718	6	5	0	1	0	171 521
February	345 447	165 698	179 748	3	3	0	0	0	172 693
March	388 315	204 514	183 800	40 554	19 538	0	0	21 015	205 881
April	484 494	295 358	189 135	124 461	38 299	0	0	86 162	282 912
May	514 952	321 763	193 189	111 845	22 180	0	2	89 663	310 579
June	500 197	304 355	195 842	97 671	8 456	0	11	89 204	294 588
July	470 036	271 852	198 183	92 943	4 670	0	26	88 248	262 558
August	480 739	279 971	200 767	83 126	2 851	0	38	80 237	271 659

. . . = Not available.

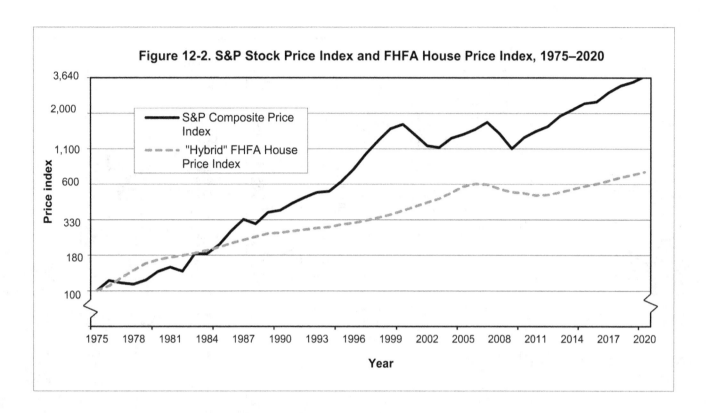

Figure 12-2. S&P Stock Price Index and FHFA House Price Index, 1975–2020

- U.S. net worth is a concept that measures the total nonfinancial wealth, including land, machines and patent rights, of the U.S. as a whole. Household net worth more than doubled between 2003 to 2017. It reached a high of $195,350 in 2018 but declined to $131,920 in 2020. (Table 12-7)

- Before the Great Recession began, consumer revolving credit reached $2,643 billion in 2008 then ballooned to $3,831 billion by 2017, a rise of 44.9 percent. As stay-at-home orders and work-at-home actions increased due to COVID, credit outstanding fell slightly between 2019 and 2020, dropping 0.2 percent. (Table 12-4)

- After the Great Recession slowly faded away, the Fed increased the fed funds rate at least six times. The lowest rate was 0.09 percent in 2014. With the pandemic, the Federal Reserve again reduced the fed funds rate to 0.38 percent in 2020. (Table 12-6)

Table 12-4. Consumer Credit

(Outstanding at end of period, billions of dollars.)

Year and month	Seasonally adjusted			Not seasonally adjusted						
	Total	By major credit type		Total [1]	By major holder					
		Revolving	Non-revolving		Depository institutions	Finance companies [2]	Credit unions	Federal government [2]	Nonfinancial businesses	Securitized pools [3]
1970	131.6	5.0	126.6	133.7	70.1	27.6	13.0	0.0	23.0	0.0
1971	146.9	8.2	138.7	149.2	79.0	29.2	14.8	0.0	26.2	0.0
1972	166.2	9.4	156.8	168.8	92.1	31.9	17.0	0.0	27.8	0.0
1973	190.1	11.3	178.7	193.0	108.1	35.4	19.6	0.0	29.8	0.0
1974	198.9	13.2	185.7	201.9	112.1	36.1	21.9	0.0	31.8	0.0
1975	204.0	14.5	189.5	207.0	116.2	32.6	25.7	0.0	32.6	0.0
1976	225.7	16.5	209.2	229.0	128.9	33.7	31.2	0.0	35.2	0.0
1977	260.6	37.4	223.1	264.9	152.1	37.3	37.6	0.5	37.4	0.0
1978	306.1	45.7	260.4	311.3	179.6	44.4	45.2	0.9	41.2	0.0
1979	348.6	53.6	295.0	354.6	205.7	55.4	47.4	1.5	44.6	0.0
1980	351.9	55.0	297.0	358.0	202.9	62.2	44.1	2.6	46.2	0.0
1981	371.3	60.9	310.4	377.9	208.2	70.1	46.7	4.8	48.1	0.0
1982	389.8	66.3	323.5	396.7	217.5	75.3	48.8	6.4	48.7	0.0
1983	437.1	79.0	358.0	444.9	245.2	83.3	56.1	4.6	55.7	0.0
1984	517.3	100.4	416.9	526.6	303.1	89.9	67.9	5.6	60.2	0.0
1985	599.7	124.5	475.2	610.6	354.8	111.7	74.0	6.8	63.3	0.0
1986	654.8	141.1	513.7	666.4	383.1	134.0	77.1	8.2	64.0	0.0
1987	686.3	160.9	525.5	698.6	399.4	140.0	81.0	10.0	68.1	0.0
1988	731.9	184.6	547.3	745.2	427.6	144.7	88.3	13.2	71.4	0.0
1989	794.6	211.2	583.4	809.3	445.8	158.5	91.7	16.0	72.2	47.3
1990	808.2	238.6	569.6	824.4	431.6	160.2	91.6	19.2	77.0	76.7
1991	798.0	263.8	534.3	815.6	412.3	153.5	90.3	21.1	74.6	103.0
1992	806.1	278.4	527.7	824.8	400.3	158.0	91.7	24.2	78.8	120.3
1993	865.7	309.9	555.7	886.2	433.6	162.0	101.6	27.2	86.3	130.5
1994	997.3	365.6	631.7	1 021.2	497.2	178.3	119.6	37.2	97.6	146.1
1995	1 140.7	443.9	696.8	1 168.2	542.4	201.5	131.9	43.5	102.0	213.1
1996	1 253.4	507.5	745.9	1 273.9	572.2	214.0	144.1	51.4	100.5	273.5
1997	1 324.8	540.0	784.8	1 344.2	562.2	240.7	152.4	57.2	109.6	320.5
1998	1 421.0	581.4	839.6	1 441.3	564.4	267.8	155.4	64.9	100.6	393.9
1999	1 531.1	610.7	920.4	1 553.6	569.5	305.7	167.9	81.8	96.1	456.7
2000	1 717.0	682.6	1 034.3	1 741.3	615.8	379.9	184.4	96.7	103.6	528.4
2001	1 867.9	714.8	1 153.0	1 891.8	639.5	453.1	189.6	111.9	98.0	597.8
2002	1 972.1	750.9	1 221.2	1 997.0	671.3	502.8	195.7	117.3	101.0	630.4
2003	2 077.4	768.3	1 309.1	2 102.9	747.3	601.5	205.9	102.9	70.6	594.8
2004	2 192.2	799.6	1 392.7	2 220.1	795.6	665.0	215.4	86.1	67.0	571.5
2005	2 290.9	829.5	1 461.4	2 320.6	816.1	691.9	228.6	89.8	68.0	609.9
2006	2 456.7	923.9	1 532.8	2 456.7	836.7	728.0	236.1	108.7	56.3	617.2
2007	2 609.5	1 001.6	1 607.9	2 609.5	894.9	776.5	236.6	115.7	58.0	652.5
2008	2 643.8	1 004.0	1 639.8	2 643.8	965.0	734.8	236.2	135.2	51.6	610.2
2009	2 555.0	916.1	1 638.9	2 555.0	906.3	627.4	237.1	232.6	47.0	572.5
2010	2 646.8	839.1	1 807.7	2 646.8	1 185.5	715.8	226.5	363.8	44.4	50.3
2011	2 756.2	840.2	1 916.1	2 756.2	1 192.6	697.0	223.0	494.8	45.0	46.2
2012	2 912.9	840.0	2 072.9	2 912.9	1 215.0	688.6	243.6	622.2	44.2	50.0
2013	3 090.5	854.1	2 236.3	3 090.5	1 271.2	688.2	265.6	735.5	38.1	49.1
2014	3 309.5	887.4	2 422.2	3 309.5	1 343.1	693.6	301.0	846.2	37.7	49.8
2015	3 400.2	898.1	2 502.1	3 400.2	1 428.3	561.3	352.6	949.7	37.1	26.4
2016	3 636.4	960.1	2 676.3	3 636.4	1 532.1	548.4	396.7	1 049.3	38.2	30.5
2017	3 830.8	1 016.8	2 813.9	3 830.8	1 611.8	541.3	439.3	1 145.6	36.2	21.4
2018	4 007.0	1 053.8	2 953.2	4 007.0	1 681.9	534.4	481.2	1 236.3	36.5	5.5
2019	4 192.2	1 092.0	3 100.2	4 192.2	1 771.0	537.7	498.0	1 319.2	35.8	3.1
2020	4 184.9	974.6	3 210.3	4 184.9	1 685.6	551.4	505.1	1 381.0	35.8	1.9
2019										
January	4 022.4	1 057.8	2 964.6	401.6	1 666.5	533.3	481.5	1 263.0	36.1	5.2
February	4 037.6	1 061.6	2 976.0	400.0	1 650.2	530.0	480.2	1 268.7	35.5	5.0
March	4 050.1	1 060.5	2 989.6	399.4	1 644.5	529.4	480.8	1 269.6	35.2	4.7
April	4 067.1	1 066.9	3 000.2	401.4	1 659.7	530.6	483.6	1 270.4	35.1	4.5
May	4 083.1	1 071.0	3 012.1	403.9	1 677.2	533.6	483.7	1 275.4	35.2	4.3
June	4 099.6	1 071.7	3 027.9	405.2	1 684.4	533.3	487.4	1 278.3	35.1	4.1
July	4 121.0	1 083.3	3 037.7	407.3	1 700.3	535.1	488.6	1 281.4	35.1	3.9
August	4 131.0	1 083.4	3 047.6	411.0	1 714.0	536.2	491.7	1 300.1	35.3	3.7
September	4 144.9	1 083.9	3 061.0	412.4	1 715.9	536.1	493.9	1 311.0	35.2	3.5
October	4 158.2	1 086.6	3 071.6	413.9	1 727.3	536.4	494.5	1 314.3	35.2	3.4
November	4 165.5	1 081.0	3 084.4	415.1	1 739.1	536.1	493.4	1 316.2	35.5	3.3
December	4 192.2	1 092.0	3 100.2	419.2	1 771.0	537.7	498.0	1 319.2	35.8	3.1
2020										
January	4 200.9	1 091.1	3 109.9	419.5	1 751.4	535.2	497.2	1 345.6	35.5	3.0
February	4 217.0	1 097.5	3 119.5	418.0	1 736.7	531.1	496.4	1 351.0	35.0	2.9
March	4 203.5	1 077.3	3 126.2	414.8	1 709.9	528.5	495.2	1 350.6	34.7	2.8
April	4 139.8	1 019.9	3 119.8	408.7	1 653.4	526.6	491.5	1 352.2	34.7	2.7
May	4 125.0	996.5	3 128.5	408.1	1 640.9	530.3	492.1	1 354.8	34.8	2.6
June	4 144.8	993.8	3 151.1	409.7	1 644.4	536.4	498.3	1 355.8	34.8	2.5
July	4 157.8	992.2	3 165.6	411.0	1 647.7	541.6	501.8	1 357.1	34.8	2.4
August	4 146.7	981.2	3 165.4	412.5	1 645.9	544.6	501.5	1 371.5	35.1	2.3
September	4 163.4	983.6	3 179.8	414.3	1 649.2	548.6	503.9	1 379.4	35.1	2.2
October	4 163.3	978.6	3 184.7	414.4	1 649.2	549.2	503.9	1 380.5	35.1	2.1
November	4 174.0	977.4	3 196.6	416.0	1 661.9	551.8	504.0	1 380.4	35.4	2.0
December	4 184.9	974.6	3 210.3	418.5	1 685.6	551.4	505.1	1 381.0	35.8	1.9

[1] Includes nonprofit and educational institutions, not shown.
[2] Student Loan Marketing Association (Sallie Mae) included in federal government sector until end of 2004, and in finance companies since then.
[3] Outstanding balances of pools upon which securities have been issued; these balances are no longer carried on the balance sheets of the loan originators.
. . . = Not available.

Table 12-5. Selected Stock and Housing Market Data

Year and month	Stock price indexes			FHFA House Price Indexes			
				House Price Index (purchases and refinance)		Purchase-Only Index	
	Dow Jones industrials (30 stocks)	Standard and Poor's composite (500 stocks) (1941–1943 = 10)	Nasdaq composite (Feb. 5, 1971 = 100)	Level at end of period (1980:I = 100)	Appreciation from same quarter one year earlier (percent)	Level at end of period (1991:I = 100)	Appreciation from same quarter one year earlier (percent)
1965	910.88	88.17	. . .	. . .	. . .	. . .	. . .
1966	873.60	85.26	. . .	. . .	. . .	. . .	. . .
1967	879.12	91.93	. . .	. . .	. . .	. . .	. . .
1968	906.00	98.70	. . .	. . .	. . .	. . .	. . .
1969	876.72	97.84	. . .	. . .	. . .	. . .	. . .
1970	753.19	83.22	. . .	. . .	. . .	. . .	. . .
1971	884.76	98.29	107.44	. . .	. . .	. . .	. . .
1972	950.71	109.20	128.52	. . .	. . .	. . .	. . .
1973	923.88	107.43	109.90	. . .	. . .	. . .	. . .
1974	759.37	82.85	76.29	. . .	. . .	. . .	. . .
1975	802.49	86.16	77.20	62.23	. . .	. . .	. . .
1976	974.92	102.01	89.90	67.26	8.08	. . .	. . .
1977	894.63	98.20	98.71	77.24	14.84	. . .	. . .
1978	820.23	96.02	117.53	87.52	13.31	. . .	. . .
1979	844.40	103.01	136.57	98.29	12.31	. . .	. . .
1980	891.41	118.78	168.61	104.59	6.41	. . .	. . .
1981	932.92	128.05	203.18	107.56	2.84	. . .	. . .
1982	884.36	119.71	188.97	111.78	3.92	. . .	. . .
1983	1 190.34	160.41	285.43	117.67	5.27	. . .	. . .
1984	1 178.48	160.46	248.88	123.17	4.67	. . .	. . .
1985	1 328.23	186.84	290.19	130.22	5.72	. . .	. . .
1986	1 792.76	236.34	366.96	139.71	7.29	. . .	. . .
1987	2 275.99	286.83	402.57	147.31	5.44	. . .	. . .
1988	2 060.82	265.79	374.43	155.61	5.63	. . .	. . .
1989	2 508.91	322.84	437.81	164.33	5.60	. . .	. . .
1990	2 678.94	334.59	409.17	166.31	1.20	. . .	. . .
1991	2 929.33	376.18	491.69	171.51	3.13	101.45	. . .
1992	3 284.29	415.74	599.26	175.63	2.40	104.17	2.70
1993	3 522.06	451.41	715.16	180.30	2.66	107.01	2.77
1994	3 793.77	460.42	751.65	183.12	1.56	110.03	2.88
1995	4 493.76	541.72	925.19	191.46	4.55	112.96	2.72
1996	5 742.89	670.50	1 164.96	196.30	2.53	116.06	2.79
1997	7 441.15	873.43	1 469.49	204.92	4.39	119.85	3.30
1998	8 625.52	1 085.50	1 794.91	215.30	5.07	126.65	5.69
1999	10 464.88	1 327.33	2 728.15	225.91	4.93	134.43	6.14
2000	10 786.85	1 320.28	2 470.52	241.90	7.08	143.78	6.95
2001	10 021.50	1 148.08	1 950.40	259.12	7.12	153.47	6.73
2002	8 341.63	879.82	1 335.51	276.49	6.70	165.20	7.63
2003	10 453.92	1 111.92	2 003.37	295.80	6.98	178.14	7.84
2004	10 783.01	1 211.92	2 175.44	326.38	10.34	196.22	10.18
2005	10 717.50	1 248.29	2 205.32	363.04	11.23	216.19	10.23
2006	12 463.15	1 418.30	2 415.29	379.47	4.53	222.32	2.87
2007	13 264.82	1 468.36	2 652.28	375.19	-1.13	216.30	-2.71
2008	8 776.39	903.25	1 577.03	348.41	-7.14	194.47	-10.12
2009	10 428.05	1 115.10	2 269.15	330.30	-5.20	189.60	-2.52
2010	11 577.51	1 257.64	2 652.87	324.20	-1.85	182.07	-3.96
2011	12 217.56	1 257.60	2 605.15	313.46	-3.31	177.38	-2.52
2012	13 104.14	1 426.19	3 019.51	315.31	0.59	185.86	4.86
2013	16 576.66	1 848.36	4 176.59	329.20	4.41	198.45	6.84
2014	17 823.07	2 058.90	4 736.05	346.12	5.14	207.57	4.63
2015	17 425.03	2 043.94	5 007.41	363.73	5.09	218.90	5.46
2016	19 762.60	2 238.83	5 383.12	383.66	5.48	231.93	5.94
2017	24 719.22	2 673.61	6 903.39	404.95	5.55	246.59	6.28
2018	23 327.46	2 506.85	6 635.28	424.89	4.92	260.68	5.65
2019	28 538.44	3 230.78	8 972.60	446.22	5.02	274.97	5.41
2020	. . .	. . .	. . .	473.81	6.18	305.45	11.01
2019							
January	24 999.67	2 704.10	7 281.74	. . .	. . .	. . .	. . .
February	25 916.00	2 784.49	7 532.53	. . .	. . .	. . .	. . .
March	25 928.68	2 834.40	7 729.32	429.57	4.59	263.56	5.05
April	26 592.91	2 945.83	8 095.39	. . .	. . .	. . .	. . .
May	24 815.04	2 752.06	7 453.15	. . .	. . .	. . .	. . .
June	26 599.96	2 941.76	8 006.24	436.69	4.39	271.03	5.07
July	26 864.27	2 980.38	8 175.42	. . .	. . .	. . .	. . .
August	26 403.28	2 926.46	7 962.88	. . .	. . .	. . .	. . .
September	26 916.83	2 976.74	7 999.34	442.23	4.46	273.85	5.01
October	27 046.23	3 037.56	8 292.36	. . .	. . .	. . .	. . .
November	28 051.41	3 140.98	8 665.47	. . .	. . .	. . .	. . .
December	28 538.44	3 230.78	8 972.60	446.22	5.02	274.97	5.41
2020							
January	28 256.03	3 225.52	9 150.94	. . .	. . .	. . .	. . .
February	25 409.36	2 954.22	8 567.37	. . .	. . .	. . .	. . .
March	21 917.16	2 584.59	7 700.10	451.30	5.06	280.04	6.23
April	24 345.72	2 912.43	8 889.55	. . .	. . .	. . .	. . .
May	25 383.11	3 044.31	9 489.87	. . .	. . .	. . .	. . .
June	25 812.88	3 100.29	10 058.77	455.78	4.37	286.73	5.83
July	26 428.32	3 271.12	10 745.27	. . .	. . .	. . .	. . .
August	28 430.05	3 500.31	11 775.46	. . .	. . .	. . .	. . .
September	27 781.70	3 363.00	11 167.51	463.92	4.90	296.20	8.20
October	26 501.60	3 269.96	10 911.59	. . .	. . .	. . .	. . .
November	29 638.64	3 621.63	12 198.74	. . .	. . .	. . .	. . .
December	. . .	. . .	. . .	473.81	6.18	305.45	11.01

. . . = Not available.

Table 12-6. Summary Interest Rates and Bond Yields

(Rates.)

Year and quarter	Federal funds interest rate	Federal Reserve discount rate	U.S. treasury bills, secondary market, 3-month	Inflation: percent change in PCE chain-type price index excluding food and energy	Bank prime rank	Treasury 10-year nominal yields	Domestic corporate bond yields Moody's Aaa	Domestic corporate bond yields Moody's Baa
1970	7.18	5.950	6.39	22.13	7.90	7.35	8.04	9.11
1971	4.66	4.880	4.33	23.17	5.72	6.16	7.39	8.56
1972	4.43	4.500	4.07	23.91	5.25	6.21	7.21	8.16
1973	8.73	6.440	7.03	24.82	8.03	6.85	7.44	8.24
1974	10.50	7.830	7.83	26.79	10.80	7.56	8.57	9.50
1975	5.82	6.250	5.78	29.03	7.85	7.99	8.83	10.61
1976	5.05	5.500	4.97	30.79	6.84	7.61	8.43	9.75
1977	5.54	5.460	5.27	32.77	6.83	7.42	8.02	8.97
1978	7.93	7.460	7.19	34.94	9.05	8.41	8.73	9.49
1979	11.19	10.280	10.07	37.49	12.66	9.43	9.63	10.69
1980	13.36	11.770	11.43	40.94	15.28	11.43	11.94	13.67
1981	16.38	13.420	14.03	44.52	18.86	13.92	14.17	16.04
1982	12.26	11.020	10.61	47.42	14.85	13.01	13.79	16.11
1983	9.09	8.500	8.61	49.84	10.79	11.10	12.04	13.55
1984	10.23	8.800	9.52	51.91	12.06	12.46	12.71	14.19
1985	8.10	7.690	7.48	54.02	9.93	10.62	11.37	12.72
1986	6.81	6.330	5.98	55.88	8.32	7.67	9.02	10.39
1987	6.66	5.660	5.78	57.68	8.20	8.39	9.38	10.58
1988	7.57	6.200	6.67	60.13	9.32	8.85	9.71	10.83
1989	9.22	6.920	8.11	62.63	10.87	8.49	9.26	10.18
1990	8.10	6.980	7.49	65.17	10.01	8.55	9.32	10.36
1991	5.69	5.450	5.38	67.50	8.46	7.86	8.77	9.80
1992	3.52	3.250	3.43	69.55	6.25	7.01	8.14	8.97
1993	3.02	3.000	3.00	71.44	6.00	5.87	7.22	7.92
1994	4.20	3.600	4.25	73.03	7.14	7.09	7.96	8.63
1995	5.84	5.210	5.49	74.63	8.83	6.57	7.59	8.20
1996	5.30	5.020	5.01	76.04	8.27	6.44	7.37	8.06
1997	5.46	5.000	5.06	77.38	8.44	6.35	7.26	7.87
1998	5.35	4.920	4.78	78.37	8.36	5.26	6.53	7.22
1999	4.97	4.620	4.64	79.43	8.00	5.65	7.04	7.88
2000	6.24	5.730	5.82	80.80	9.24	6.03	7.62	8.37
2001	3.89	3.410	3.39	82.26	6.94	5.02	7.08	7.95
2002	1.67	1.170	1.60	83.64	4.68	4.61	6.49	7.80
2003	1.13	2.100	1.01	84.84	4.12	4.01	5.67	6.76
2004	1.35	2.400	1.37	86.52	4.34	4.27	5.63	6.39
2005	3.21	4.250	3.15	88.37	6.19	4.29	5.24	6.06
2006	4.96	6.020	4.73	90.39	7.96	4.80	5.59	6.48
2007	5.02	5.790	4.35	92.38	8.05	4.63	5.56	6.48
2008	1.93	2.170	1.37	94.22	5.07	3.66	5.63	7.44
2009	0.16	0.500	0.15	95.32	3.25	3.26	5.31	7.29
2010	0.18	0.730	0.14	96.61	3.25	3.22	4.94	6.04
2011	0.10	0.750	0.05	98.14	3.25	2.78	4.64	5.66
2012	0.14	0.750	0.09	100.00	3.25	1.80	3.67	4.94
2013	0.11	0.750	0.06	101.53	3.25	2.35	4.24	5.10
2014	0.09	0.750	0.03	103.12	3.25	2.54	4.16	4.85
2015	0.13	0.770	0.05	104.41	3.26	2.14	3.89	5.00
2016	0.40	1.020	0.32	106.07	3.51	1.84	3.67	4.71
2017	1.00	1.630	0.93	107.79	4.10	2.33	3.74	4.44
2018	1.83	2.460	1.94	109.90	4.90	2.91	3.93	4.80
2019	2.16	2.750	2.06	111.67	5.29	2.14	3.39	4.37
2020	0.38	0.580	0.37	115.62	3.54	0.89	2.48	3.60

[1]Outstanding principal balances of mortgage-backed securities issued or guaranteed by the holder indicated.

Table 12-7. Derivation of U.S. Net Wealth

(Billions of dollars, amounts outstanding at the end of period.)

Year and month	Household net worth	Growth of domestic nonfinancial debt				
		Total	households	Business	State and local governments	Federal
2003	49 426	8.0	11.8	2.2	8.3	10.9
2004	55 951	9.0	11.1	5.6	11.4	9.0
2005	61 789	8.6	10.6	8.1	5.8	6.6
2006	66 073	8.4	10.5	9.8	3.9	3.9
2007	66 499	8.1	7.2	12.4	6.0	4.7
2008	56 292	5.8	0.0	5.7	1.4	21.4
2009	60 347	3.7	0.5	-3.9	4.7	20.4
2010	67 129	4.4	-0.6	-0.8	2.7	18.5
2011	67 900	3.7	0.1	2.5	-1.0	10.8
2012	72 925	4.7	0.5	5.7	-0.3	10.1
2013	81 605	4.2	2.3	4.9	-0.2	6.7
2014	87 699	3.8	1.2	6.8	-2.5	5.4
2015	90 667	4.4	2.2	7.0	0.4	5.0
2016	95 799	4.4	3.1	5.1	1.0	5.6
2017	104 553	4.2	3.9	6.1	0.0	3.7
2018	195 350	4.7	3.3	4.3	-1.6	7.6
2019	117 878	4.7	3.4	4.8	0.3	6.6
2020	131 920	12.5	3.9	9.2	2.9	24.1
2014						
1st quarter	80 940	4.1	1.9	6.1	-1.7	5.7
2nd quarter	82 627	4.2	5.2	5.1	0.1	3.5
3rd quarter	82 520	4.5	3.0	5.9	-1.7	6.0
4th quarter	84 189	4.7	2.2	7.0	1.5	5.9
2015						
1st quarter	85 798	2.7	2.0	7.4	1.6	-0.3
2nd quarter	86 434	4.4	3.8	8.0	0.5	2.7
3rd quarter	85 249	2.7	1.3	5.5	0.2	2.1
4th quarter	87 287	7.8	3.8	5.6	-1.2	15.4
2016						
1st quarter	86 811	5.5	2.5	9.2	0.7	6.2
2nd quarter	87 532	4.6	4.4	4.2	2.2	5.7
3rd quarter	89 750	5.0	3.5	6.1	0.8	6.3
4th quarter	91 583	3.1	3.7	2.4	0.4	3.6
2017						
1st quarter	95 101	3.2	3.7	5.9	-2.2	1.7
2nd quarter	97 272	4.7	3.9	6.6	-0.9	4.9
3rd quarter	98 866	4.9	2.7	6.2	-0.6	6.9
4th quarter	100 926	3.3	5.1	3.6	3.5	1.3
2018						
1st quarter	106 792	6.7	3.0	3.9	-3.2	14.3
2nd quarter	108 507	4.0	3.6	3.3	-0.4	5.7
3rd quarter	110 594	4.3	3.4	4.3	-1.4	5.9
4th quarter	107 219	3.4	2.8	4.8	-1.5	3.7
2019						
1st quarter	111 132	5.9	2.2	6.7	-0.7	9.6
2nd quarter	113 446	3.5	4.3	4.2	-1.8	3.1
3rd quarter	114 304	5.9	3.3	5.9	0.9	8.9
4th quarter	117 878	3.3	3.6	2.2	2.9	4.2
2020						
1st quarter	111 355	10.8	3.7	19.1	0.9	11.4
2nd quarter	119 626	25.6	0.1	15.2	3.5	59.2
3rd quarter	123 857	5.4	5.6	0.7	5.5	9.1
4th quarter	131 920	6.3	6.2	1.1	1.6	10.9

NOTES AND DEFINITIONS, CHAPTER 12

The Federal Reserve's mission is to promote the goals of maximum employment and stable prices by using monetary policy tools. Monetary policy in the United States comprises the Federal Reserve's actions and communications to promote maximum employment, stable prices, and moderate long-term interest rates—the economic goals the Congress has instructed the Federal Reserve to pursue.

The Fed has traditionally used three tools to conduct monetary policy: reserve requirements, the discount rate, and open market operations. Reserve requirements – see discussion for Chapter 12-3 – for further information. Discount rate is defined in the notes for Table 12-6. Open market operations (OMOs)—the purchase and sale of securities in the open market by a central bank—are a key tool used by the Federal Reserve in the implementation of monetary policy.

The Federal Reserve System is the central bank of the United States performs five general functions to promote the effective operation of the U.S. economy and, more generally, the public interest. The Federal Reserve

- **conducts the nation's monetary policy** to promote maximum employment, stable prices, and moderate long-term interest rates in the U.S. economy;

- **promotes the stability of the financial system** and seeks to minimize and contain systemic risks through active monitoring and engagement in the U.S. and abroad;

- **promotes the safety and soundness of individual financial institutions** and monitors their impact on the financial system as a whole;

- **fosters payment and settlement system safety and efficiency** through services to the banking industry and the U.S. government that facilitate U.S.-dollar transactions and payments; and

- **promotes consumer protection and community development** through consumer-focused supervision and examination, research and analysis of emerging consumer issues and trends, community economic development activities, and the administration of consumer laws and regulations.

During the Great Recession of 2007-2009, the Federal Reserve used monetary policy to achieve their goals of reducing interest rates to near-zero and increasing the money supply with its Qualitative Easing policy. In early 2020, the Federal Reserve began lowering interest rates and increasing money supply through purchasing banks' bonds in response to the spreading coronavirus pandemic.

The COVID-19 virus crisis in the United States and associated business closures, event cancellations, and work-from-home triggered a deep economic downturn of uncertain duration. The Federal Reserve stepped in with policies used during the Great Recession, such as keeping interest rates low and increasing the money supply (M1).

One action the Federal Reserve used during the pandemic and not the Great Recession was reducing reserve requirements rate 0 percent. This action allowed banks to increase their lending thereby supporting the flow of credit to households and businesses. The Fed states that the Board has no plans to reimpose reserve requirements. However the Bords may adjust reserve requirement ratios in the future.

Another action the Board of Governors of the Federal Reserve was to revise the Regulation D which had separated bank deposits and savings accounts. Savings amount are now consolidated with demand deposits with a new column called "other liquid deposits." With some accounting changes, data were zeroed out, combined with other amounts and no longer published.

Most of the data in this chapter are found on the Federal Reserve Board Web site, <https://www.federalreserve.gov>. Current releases and most historical data are found at that site by selecting Economic Research & Data/Statistical Releases and Historical Data and then selecting the appropriate report. This is the location for all data not otherwise specified.

Historical data not found online are taken from two printed volumes of statistical data that were published by the Board of Governors of the Federal Reserve System: *Banking and Monetary Statistics,* 1943, and *Banking and Monetary Statistics, 1941-1970,* 1976. These will be referred to as *B&MS* 1943 and *B&MS* 1976.

TABLES 12-1 AND 12-2

Money Stock Measures and Components

SOURCE: BOARD OF GOVERNORS OF THE FEDERAL RESERVE SYSTEM

As described above, many changes were instituted in 2020 by the Fed during the pandemic. The Federal Reserve provides financial data from banks, industrial productivity and foreign exchange rates. Two main statistical reports are "H.3 Aggregate Reserves of Depository Institutions and the Monetary Base" and "H.6 Money Stock Measures." H-3's last release was September 17, 2020. See Table 12-3 for the historical data. The only new data are for 2020 months.

Tables 12-1 and 2 reflect the major changes via the H.6 release. Table 12-1 contains the estimates of two monetary aggregates (M1 and M2) and the components of these measures are published weekly. The monthly data are averages of daily figures. In addition, these measures are revised in subsequent releases. Table 12-2 shows the savings data consolidated into the "Other liquid deposits." An accounting change allows the Federal Reserve to report monetary aggregates and not data for commercial and thrift institutions.

The Federal Reserve Board ceased publication of the M3 aggregate on March 23, 2006. Weekly publication was also discontinued for the following components of M3: large-denomination time deposits, repurchase agreements (RPs), and Eurodollars. The Board continues to publish institutional money market mutual funds as a memorandum item in this release. Measures of large-denomination time deposits continue to be published in the Financial Accounts (Z.1 release) and in the H.8 release weekly for commercial banks.

The Board ceased publication of outstanding amounts of U.S. dollar-denominated traveler's checks of nonbank issuers in early 2019.

Definitions

In response to the COVID-19 pandemic, the Federal Reserve instituted many changes, similar to changes made in response during the Great Recession

Starting in **May 2020**, the following definitions are now current.

M1 now includes (1) currency, (2) demand deposits and (3) other liquid deposits which includes savings and other checkable deposits.

M2 consists of M1 plus (1) small-denomination time deposits and (2) balances in retail money market funds.

Currency consists of currency outside the U.S. Treasury, the Federal Reserve Banks, and the vaults of depository institutions.

Traveler's checks is the outstanding amount of U.S. dollar-denominated traveler's checks of nonbank issuers. The Federal Reserve stopped reporting these amounts in early 2019.

Demand deposits consists of demand deposits at domestically chartered commercial banks, U.S. branches and agencies of foreign banks, and Edge Act corporations (excluding those amounts held by depository institutions, the U.S. government, and foreign banks and official institutions) less cash items in the process of collection and Federal Reserve float.

Other checkable deposits at commercial banks and thrift institutions are no longer reported separately. Instead only the money aggregate at a total industry level. These amounts are then reported as "checkable deposits, total."

Saving deposits are now recognized as a transaction account like the demand deposits and are combined to create "Other liquid deposits."

Small denomination time deposit are amounts less than $100,000.

Retail money funds are investment funds with capital invested by individual. Excluded are IRA and Keogh account balances at money market mutual funds.

Institutional money funds are included in the money stock report for informational purposes. They are not part of M1 or M2.

Seasonal adjustment. Seasonally adjusted M1 is calculated by summing currency, traveler's checks, demand deposits, and other checkable deposits (each seasonally adjusted separately). Seasonally adjusted M2 is computed by adjusting each of its nonM1 components and then adding this result to seasonally adjusted M1.

Revisions. Money stock measures are revised frequently and have a benchmark and seasonal factor review in the middle of the year; this review typically extends back a number of years. The monetary aggregates were redefined in major revisions introduced in 1980.

Historical: January 1947-January 1959. These data are not currently maintained online and are found in *B&MS* 1976. They are not continuous with the current data series; for that reason the values for January 1959 are shown so that users can link to the current data. The *demand deposit component* includes demand deposits held in commercial banks by individuals, partnerships, and corporations both domestic and foreign, and demand deposits held by nonbank financial institutions and foreign banks. Note that this includes demand deposit liabilities to foreign governments, central banks, and international institutions—said to be "relatively small" in the source document. *Time deposits adjusted* is time and savings deposits at commercial banks, other than large negotiable certificates of deposit (CDs), and excluding all deposits due to the U.S. government and domestic commercial banks. The editor has added this to the *Money stock (M1)* to approximate *M2*, which is not shown as such in the source document, over this period.

Historical: 1892–1946. These data are from *B&MS* 1943 and *B&MS* 1976. They pertain only to the last day of June and, after 1922, the last day of December, the "call dates" on which banks reported to the federal government. For more data and analysis concerning monetary developments in this period, including monthly money supply estimates, see Milton Friedman and Anna Jacobson Schwartz, *A Monetary History of the United States, 1867–1960,* Princeton, Princeton University Press, 1963. In Table 12-1B, *Demand deposits adjusted* refers to the elimination of interbank and U.S. government deposits and cash items in process of collection, not to seasonal adjustment, which is not applicable to call report data because they are only reported once or twice a year. The editor has retitled as *M1* the "Total" money stock shown in the source document, and has added time deposits to it in order to approximate *M2*, which is not shown in the source document.

Data availability

Estimates are released monthly in Federal Reserve Statistical Release H.6, "Money Stock Measures." Current and historical data are available on the Federal Reserve Web site.

References

Board of Governors of the Federal Reserve System, *The Federal Reserve System: Purposes and Functions*, available online at <http://www.federalreserve.gov> in the category "About the Fed/Features," includes a chapter discussing monetary policy and the monetary aggregates and a glossary of terms as an appendix.

An explanation of the 1980 redefinition of the monetary aggregates is found in the *Federal Reserve Bulletin* for February 1980.

TABLES 12-3

Aggregate Reserves of Depository Institutions and the Monetary Base

SOURCE: BOARD OF GOVERNORS OF THE FEDERAL RESERVE SYSTEM
The Board of Governors announced a reduced reserve requirement ratios on net transaction accounts to 0 percent, effective March 26, 2020. This action eliminated reserve requirement for all depository institutions. As a result, many of the items reported on Board's Statistical Release H.3 "Aggregate Reserves of Depository Institutions and the Monetary Base" are zero.
The only data reported are monthly amounts up to the end of August 2020.

Definitions before March 2020

Total reserves consists of reserve balances with the Federal Reserve Banks plus vault cash used to satisfy reserve requirements. Seasonally adjusted, break-adjusted total reserves equal seasonally adjusted, break-adjusted required reserves plus unadjusted excess reserves.

Seasonally adjusted, break-adjusted *nonborrowed reserves* equal seasonally adjusted, break-adjusted total reserves less unadjusted total borrowings of depository institutions from the Federal Reserve.

Extended credit consisted of borrowing at the discount window under the terms and conditions established for the extended credit program to help depository institutions deal with sustained liquidity pressures. Since there was not the same need to repay such borrowing promptly as there was with traditional short-term adjustment credit, the money market impact of extended credit was similar to that of nonborrowed reserves. The extended credit program was significant in the 1980s but used infrequently in subsequent years. It ended with the 2002 revision of the discount window program, effective January 9, 2003. See the explanation of the discount rate in the notes and definitions for Table 12-9A.

To adjust *required reserves* for discontinuities due to regulatory changes in reserve requirements, a multiplicative procedure is used to estimate what required reserves would have been in past periods, had current reserve requirements been in effect. Break-adjusted required reserves include required reserves against transactions deposits and personal time and savings deposits (but not reservable nondeposit liabilities).

Excess reserves, not seasonally adjusted equals unadjusted total reserves less unadjusted required reserves.

The seasonally adjusted, break-adjusted *monetary base* consists of (1) seasonally adjusted, break-adjusted total reserves; plus (2) the seasonally adjusted currency component of the money stock; plus (3) the seasonally adjusted, break-adjusted difference between current vault cash and the amount applied to satisfy current reserve requirements for all quarterly reporters on the "Report of Transaction Accounts, Other Deposits and Vault Cash" and for all weekly reporters whose vault cash exceeds their required reserves.

Federal Reserve balance sheet: total assets is as defined above--it has not been changed by the new reserve calculating and reporting system.

Data availability

Values are shown in millions of dollars. Monthly data are prorated averages of biweekly averages.

Monetary base is defined as total balances maintained plus currency in circulation.

The series *Federal Reserve balance sheet: total assets* was introduced in the 14th edition of *Business Statistics*. It demonstrates the extent to which the Federal Reserve has, beginning in 2007, undertaken "quantitative easing"—direct purchases of financial assets—in addition to conventional easing, which has consisted of reducing short-term interest rates to near zero and supporting that rate level with purchases and sales of short-term securities on the open market. The balance sheet data are accessed on a different part of the Federal Reserve Web site—"Monetary Policy" instead of "Economic Research and Data"—which features an extensive explanation and discussion of the meaning and importance of this indicator. The balance sheet is reported in millions of dollars for each Wednesday, and is shown here with the last Wednesday of the month representing the month and the last Wednesday of December representing the year. These values are not adjusted for seasonal variation.

Federal Reserve balance sheet: total assets is total assets from the Consolidated Statement of Condition of All Federal Reserve Banks, which is reported each Wednesday. The last Wednesday of the month is used to represent the month, and the last Wednesday in December is used to represent the year. Currently, the principal components of total assets are Treasury, federal agency, and mortgage-backed securities. Other types of assets representing Federal Reserve credit extension, some of which have varied during the course of the crisis, have been repurchase agreements; term auction credit; portfolio holdings of various limited liability companies

(LLCs) set up to manage assets taken over from other institutions; liquidity swaps with foreign central banks; and other loans, including traditional loans to member commercial banks made at the discount rate (see the definitions for Table 12-9). Total assets are equal to the sum of Federal Reserve liabilities and capital. The principal components of liabilities are Federal Reserve notes and the deposits of member banks representing their reserves.

For further information, see "Aggregate Reserves of Depository Institutions and the Monetary Base - H.3" at <www.federalreserve.gov> under Economic Research & Data/Statistical Releases and Historical Data.

Reserve and monetary base data are released weekly in Federal Reserve Release H.3, "Aggregate Reserves of Depository Institutions and the Monetary Base." Historical data are available on the Federal Reserve Web site.

The Federal Reserve balance sheet appears each week in the H.4.1 release, Factors Affecting Reserve Balances, released each Thursday at 4:30 p.m., and available on the Federal Reserve Web site under Economic Research and Data/Statistical Releases and Historical Data. However, to obtain the full historical data for total assets, the user must go to Monetary policy/Credit and liquidity programs and the balance sheet/Recent balance sheet trends/Total assets/View as table/All/Copy data. Other explanatory material, including a monthly report on changes in these programs, is available at the Monetary policy location.

TABLE 12-4

Consumer Credit

SOURCE: BOARD OF GOVERNORS OF THE FEDERAL RESERVE SYSTEM.

The consumer credit series cover most short and intermediate-term extended to individuals through regular business channels, excluding loans secured by real estate (such as first and second mortgages and home equity credit). In October 2003, the scope of this survey was expanded to incorporate student loans extended by the federal government and the AM Holding Corporation, the parent company of Sallie Mae (Student Loan Marketing Association. The historical data has been revised to 1977 to reflect this inclusion.

Consumer credit is categorized by major types of credit and by major holders.

Definitions and notes on the data

The major types of consumer credit are *revolving* and *nonrevolving*.

Revolving credit includes credit arising from purchases on credit cards plans of retail stores and banks, cash advances and check credit plans of banks, and some overdraft credit arrangements.

Nonrevolving credit includes automobile loans, mobile home loans, and all other loans, such as student loans, boats, trailers, or vacations. These loans may be secured or unsecured.

Debt secured by real estate (including first liens, junior liens, and home equity loans) is excluded. Credit is extended to governmental agencies and nonprofit or charitable organizations, as well as credit extended to business or to individuals exclusively for business purposes, is excluded.

Categories of *holders* include *U.S.- charted depository institutions* (comprising commercial banks and savings institutions), *finance companies, credit unions, federal government,* and *nonfinancial businesses*. In April 2020, the Federal Reserve will no longer report *pools of securitized assets*. The Student Loan Marketing Association (Sallie Mae) is included in "Federal government" until the end of 2004 at which time it became fully privatized. Beginning with the end of 2004, Sallie Mae is included in "*Finance companies.*" Retailers and gasoline companies are included in the nonfinancial businesses category.

Federal government includes student loans originated by the Department of Education under the Federal Direct Loan Program, and the Perkins Loan Program as well as Federal Family Education Loan Program loans that the government purchased under the Ensuring Continued Access to Student Loans Act.

Data availability

Current data are available monthly in the Federal Reserve Statistical Release G.19, "Consumer Credit," available along with all current and historical data on the Federal Reserve website. In the autumn of each year there is revision of several years of past data reflecting benchmarking and seasonal factor review.

Table 12-5

Stock Prices and Housing Market Data

SOURCES: BOARD OF GOVERNORS OF THE FEDERAL RESERVE SYSTEM; BUREAU OF ECONOMIC ANALYSIS; MOODY'S INVESTORS SERVICE; THE BOND BUYER; DOW JONES, INC.; STANDARD AND POOR'S CORPORATION; NEW YORK STOCK EXCHANGE; FEDERAL HOUSING FINANCE AGENCY (FHFA), PREVIOUSLY OFHEO (OFFICE OF FEDERAL HOUSING ENTERPRISE OVERSIGHT)

Definitions and notes on the data

Stock price indexes and yield

The *Dow Jones industrial* average is an average price of 30 stocks compiled by Dow Jones, Inc.

The *Standard and Poor's composite* is an index of the prices of 500 stocks that are weighted by the volume of shares outstanding, accounting for about 90 percent of New York Stock Exchange value, with a base of 1941–1943 = 10, compiled by Standard and Poor's Corporation. (Before February 1957, these data are based on a conversion of an earlier 90-stock index, and are obtained from *B&MS* 1943 and 1976.)

The *Nasdaq composite index* is an average price of over 5,000 stocks traded on the Nasdaq exchange.

The *fixed-rate first mortgage* rates are primary market contract interest rates on commitments for fixedrate conventional 30-year first mortgages. The rates are obtained by the Federal Reserve from the Federal Home Loan Mortgage Corporation (FHLMC, or Freddie Mac).

The Federal Housing Agency (FHFA) (formerly Federal Housing Enterprise Oversight (OFHEO). House Price Index (HPI) is a broad economic measure of the movement of single-family and repeat-sales in the United States. The FHFA HPI index measures changes in single-family house prices based on data covering all 50 states and over 400 cities. Extending back to the mid-70s, the HPIs are built on tens of millions of home sales and offers insight about house price fluctuations at national, census division, state metro area, county, ZIP code and census track levels.

FHFA publishes Purchases-Only Index for the house purchase subgroup of new mortgage transactions, excluding refinancing transactions. Nation-wide, this index is based on millions of transactions over the past 28 years. While this is still a large statistical base, it is subject to somewhat greater revision and is less reliable for smaller geographical.

The FHFA HI is a weighted, repeat-sales index, meaning that it measures average price changes or refinancing's on the same properties. This information is obtained by reviewing repeat mortgage transactions on single-family properties, whose mortgages have been purchased or securitized by the Fannie Mae or Freddie Mac since January 1975. In addition the repeat-sales technique helps to control for differences, in the quality of the houses comprising the sample and is the reason the FHFA HPI is referred to as a "constant quality" index or as "all transactions" hose price index.

The FHFA price indexes are subject to revision for preceding quarters and years, because each new transaction, when reported, affects the rate of price change for all periods since the last time that the property involved in the new transaction changed hands or was refinanced. Indeed, these indexes originally indicated that prices peaked in 2007. By 2020 the HPI reached 461.57, an increase of nearly 24 percent.

The national conforming loan limit that finance single-family one-unit properties increased from $33,000 in the early 1970s, to $548,250 for 2021.

The FHFA indexed do not come from a random sample of house prices, and users need to consider possible sources of bias.

Expensive houses are under-represented in general because the transactions are limited to conforming mortgages.

Seasonally adjusted data are also available for the purchase-only indexes. Seasonal price patterns appear to have some significance, especially for regional indexes. The seasonally adjusted indexes are not shown here because the year-over-change, calculated from not-seasonally-adjusted data, is the main focus of attention.

In addition to these government-supplied measures, new privately-developed house price indexes--not available for publication in *Business Statistics*--are now receiving regular media attention, and even provide the basis for a futures contract trading on the Chicago Mercantile Exchange. Standard & Poor's now issues S&P/Case-Shiller® Home Price Indexes each month. They cover resales only for houses at all price ranges, based on information obtained from county assessor and recorder offices. They are value-weighted, meaning that price trends for more expensive homes have greater influence on changes in the index. (The FHFA index weights price trends equally for all properties.) S&P/Case-Shiller data are only collected for 20 major metropolitan statistical areas.

Data availability and references

Stock market data are published monthly in *Economic Indicators,* and until 2020 annually in *Economic Report of the President,* both available online at <https://www.gpo.gov>. Some historical interest rate data that are not available on the Federal Reserve Web site were also taken from past *Economic Reports of the President.*

The FHFA house price indexes for the United States as a whole, regions, states, and metropolitan and sub-metropolitan groups are published every 3 months, approximately 2 months after the end of the previous quarter. The release and supporting data and explanatory material are available at <https://www.fhfa.gov>.

The OFHEO (now FHFA) and other price indexes for houses are discussed and compared in Jordan Rappaport, "Comparing Aggregate Housing Price Measures," *Business Economics,* October 2007, pp. 55-65.

Table 12-6

The daily effective *federal funds rate*—a principal marker for Federal Reserve monetary policy—is a weighted average of rates on trades through New York brokers. Monthly figures include each calendar day in the month. Annualized figures use a 360-day year.

The *Federal Reserve discount rate* is the rate for discount window borrowing at the Federal Reserve Bank of New York. Monthly figures include each calendar day in the month. Annualized figures use a 360-day year. Before 1945, annual averages calculated by editor.

Beginning in January 2003, the rules governing the discount window programs were revised. "Adjustment credit," which had been extended at a below-market rate (as can be seen in the average discount rates from 1978 through 2002 shown in Table 12-9, which are below the federal funds rate), was replaced by a new type of credit called "primary credit." Primary credit is available for very short terms as a backup source of liquidity to depository institutions in generally sound financial condition, as judged by the lending Federal Reserve Bank. Primary credit is extended at a rate <u>above</u> the federal funds rate, eliminating the incentive for institutions to exploit the spread of money market rates over the discount rate.

The *U.S. Treasury bills, 3-month rate* and the *U.S. Treasury bills, 6-month rate* are the yields on these securities based on their prices as traded in the secondary market. The rates are quoted on a discount basis. Annualized figures use a 360-day year. Early data are taken from *B&MS* 1943 and 1976. From 1934 to 1944, the 3-month rate is based on dealers' quotations. From 1931 through 1933, it is the average rate on new issues. For 1920 through 1930, it is the rate on 3- to 6-month Treasury notes and certificates.

The *inflation* column shown here, is the rate of change in the Personal Consumption Expenditures (PCE) chain-type price index, excluding food and energy, beginning in 1970. For monthly entries, it is the change from the same month a year earlier. This price index is calculated by the Bureau of Economic Analysis (BEA) and shown in Table 8-3. This inflation rate is shown along with other rates in Table 8-4; see the notes and definitions for that table. Before 1960, the inflation rates shown are the similarly-defined rates of change in the CPI-U.

The *real 3-month Treasury bill rate* is calculated by the editor by subtracting the inflation estimate from the nominal interest rate. Note that subtraction means changing the sign and adding; hence negative inflation (that is, price decline or deflation), as experienced in the 1930s, contributes to large positive real interest rates.

The *bank prime rate* is one of several base rates used by banks to price shortterm business loans. It is the rate posted by a majority of the top 25 (by amount of assets in domestic offices) insured U.S.-chartered commercial banks. Monthly figures include each calendar day in the month. Annualized figures use a 360-day year. Before 1949, the data are not on the Federal Reserve Web site but have been reproduced from *B&MS* 1976. In that volume, the prime rate is described as "the rate that banks charge their most creditworthy business customers on short-term loans", as posted by the largest banks. The same source goes on to write, "A nationally publicized and uniform prime rate did not emerge until the depression of the 1930s. The rate in that period—1 ½ percent—represented a floor below which banks were said to

regard lending as unprofitable. The date shown [for the beginning of a changed rate] is that on which the new rate was put into effect by the first bank to make the change. The table shows a range of rates for 1929-1933 because no information is available to indicate when the rate changed in that period." For further information, the source document cites "The Prime Rate," *Monthly Review,* Federal Reserve Bank of New York, April and May 1962, pp. 54-59 and 70-73, respectively.

U.S. Treasury securities, constant maturities. The rates shown for 1-year, 5-year, 10-year, 20-year, and 30-year securities are yields on actively traded issues adjusted to constant maturities. Yields on Treasury securities at "constant maturity" are interpolated by the Treasury Department from the daily yield curve. This curve, which relates the yield on a security to its time to maturity, is based on the closing market bid yields on actively traded Treasury securities in the overthecounter market. These market yields are calculated from composites of quotations reported by U.S. Government securities dealers to the Federal Reserve Bank of New York. The constant maturity yield values are read from the yield curve at fixed maturities. For example, this method provides a yield for a 10year maturity, even if no outstanding security has exactly 10 years remaining to maturity. The 30-year series was discontinued as of February 2002, because the Treasury Department was no longer issuing such bonds at that time. However, issuance of 30-year bonds was resumed in 2005 as an additional means of financing rising deficits, and the 30-year interest rate series resumes in 2006. The current 20-year series begins with 1993 and is not comparable with an earlier 20-year series. For further information, see the historical data series on the Federal Reserve Web site.

Before 1962, the *Treasury 10-year* is not available on the constant-maturity basis. The entries in that column are from *B&MS* 1943 and 1976 where they are labeled "United States government bonds (long-term)." Before 1941, they represent yields on bonds that were partly tax-exempt. In 1941, the yield for the partly tax-exempt series was 1.95 percent—comparable with the entries for previous years—while the entry comparable with subsequent years was 2.12 percent.

Domestic corporate bond yields, Aaa and Baa. The rates shown are for general obligation bonds based on Thursday figures, and are provided by Moody's Investors Service and republished by the Federal Reserve. The Aaa rates through December 6, 2001 are averages of Aaa utility and Aaa industrial bond rates. As of December 7, 2001, these rates are averages of Aaa industrial bonds only.

Data Availability and references

Federal funds rate, interest rates, bond yields are published in the Federal Reserve's H.15 release, "Selected Interest Rates"; the release and current and current historical data are available on the Federal Reserve website.

Table 12-7. Derivation of U.S. Net Wealth

Background

The Z-1 *Financial Accounts* provide information on macro-financial flows and aggregate balance sheets for major sectors of the economy, including households, financial institutions, nonfinancial businesses, governments and the international sector. The *Financial Accounts* also make up the financial component of *the Integrated Macroeconomic Accounts*, which are published jointly with the Bureau of Economic Analysis and which related production, income, and saving from the *National Income and Product Account*s (NIPA) to changes in net worth and financial transactions across the major economic sectors of the U.S. economy. The basic framework of the FA allows understanding of the economic relationships underlying the major sections as well for monitoring the effects of macro-financial developments in the United States and globally.

Researches and analysts have used the Financial Accounts to investigates the causes and consequences of the financial crisis and to create and analyze indicators of financial stability. However, they were not originally designed to be a comprehensive source of data for the complex financial relationships and transactions whose importance to the macro-economy were made clear during the financial crisis 2007-2009.

A new table on the derivation on U.S. net worth has been added to the summary section of the "Financial Accounts." The calculation of U.S. of U.S. net worth (Table 12-7) Household Net Worth and Growth of Domestic Nonfinancial Debt includes the value of nonfinancial assets (real estate, equipment, intellectual property products, consumer durables and inventories) held by households and nonprofit organizations and noncorporate businesses. The measure of U.S. net worth includes the market value of domestic nonfinancial and financial corporations and is adjusted to reflect U.S. financial claims on the rest of the world.

Taking all this together, net U.S. worth is defined as value of tangible assets controlled by households and nonprofits, noncorporate businesses, and government sectors of the U.S. economy, plus the market value of domestic nonfinancial and financial corporations, net of U.S. financial to the rest of the world.

Changes in net worth consists of transaction, revaluations, and other volume changes. Corporate equity and debt securities include directly and indirectly held securities. Real estate is the value of owner-occupied real estate. Other includes equity in noncorporate businesses, consumer durable goods, fixed assets of nonprofit organizations, and other financial assets apart from corporate equities and debt securities, net of liabilities, as shown on Table B.101 Balance Sheet of Households and Nonprofit Organizations.

Definition and notes on the data

The concept of U.S. *net worth* ignores all domestic financial intermediation and just counts the value of the land, machines, houses, cars, etc., plus tangible worth but does not include financial worth.

Household net worth is the value of net worth for the household and nonprofit organization sector, as reported on table B101 in the Financial Accounts. Net worth is calculated as the difference between a sector's total assets, including both financial and non-financial assets and liabilities (debts owed to other sectors) and does include financial worth.

Noncorporate businesses includes both sole proprietorships and partnerships, including noncorporate farms.

Debt equates to the sum of debt securities and loans.

Domestic Nonfinancial entities include household, corporations, nonfarm noncorporate businesses, farm businesses, federal, state and local governments.

Domestic Nonfinancial assets include housing, property, automobiles, equipment, business equity, intellectual properties such as patents, copyrights, and trademarks.

For corporate *businesses*, worth is the market value of their outstanding equity shares and is used to better capture the value of intangible assets, such as intellectual property.

A *corporation* is formed under state law by the filing of articles of incorporation with the state.

Federal Government consists of all federal government agencies and funds included in the unified budget. However, the District of Columbia government in the state and local sector.

Nonprofits include private foundations and organizations that are tax-exempt under Sections 501c(3) through 501(c)(9) of the Internal Revenue Code. Does not include religious organizations or organizations with less than $25,000 in gross annual receipts.

Revision

Data shown for the most quarters are based on preliminary and potentially incomplete information. Nonetheless, when source data are subject are revised or estimation methods are improved methods are improved, all data are subject to revision. There is no specific revision schedule; rather, data are revised on an ongoing basis.

Data availability

The "Financial Accounts" are published online and in print four times per year, about 10 weeks following the end of each calendar quarter. The publication with series mnemonics and the guide are available online: https://www.federalreserve.gov/releases/Z1.

CHAPTER 13: INTERNATIONAL COMPARISONS

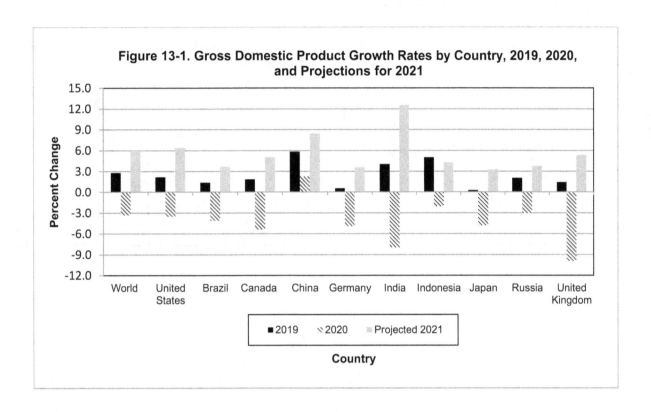

Figure 13-1. Gross Domestic Product Growth Rates by Country, 2019, 2020, and Projections for 2021

- The World Economic Outlook (WEO) is projecting a stronger recovery from COVID-19 than it did initially. Worldwide, they are projecting growth of 6 percent in 2021 and 4 percent growth in 2022. Gross domestic product in the United States is projecting to grow 6.4 percent in 2021. (Table 13-1)

- COVID-19 caused the worst economic upheaval in recent history. In 2020, the unemployment rate increased in each country listed in Table 13-1. However, the United States experienced the highest increase as it more than doubled. (Table 13-1)

- Five of the six major currencies listed in Table 13-2 including the Canadian dollar, the Euro, the Japanese yen, the British pound, and the Swiss franc are all major industrial countries whose currencies are freely traded on world markets. The other currency listed is the Chinese yuan, which is not freely traded. China can control the international values of their currencies (through, for example, direct capital controls) and keep their currencies from appreciating relative to the dollar to maintain their competitiveness in the U.S. market.

Table 13-1 International Comparisons: Percent Change in Real GDP, Consumer Prices, Current Account Balances, and Unemployment Rate, 2019, 2020, and Projected 2021

(Annual percent change.)

Country	Gross domestic product			Inflation, average consumer prices			Current account balance (percent of GDP)			Unemployment rate		
	2019	2020	2021	2019	2020	2021	2019	2020	2021	2019	2020	2021
WORLD	2.8	-3.3	6.0	3.5	3.2	3.5	0.5	0.4	0.4	. . .	. . .	. . .
Euro Area	1.3	-6.6	4.4	1.2	0.3	1.4	2.3	2.3	2.8	7.6	7.9	8.7
Germany	0.6	-4.9	3.6	1.4	0.4	2.2	7.1	7.1	7.6	3.2	4.2	4.4
United Kingdom	1.4	-9.9	5.3	1.8	0.9	1.5	-3.1	-3.9	-3.9	3.8	4.5	6.1
Brazil	1.4	-4.1	3.7	3.7	3.2	4.6	-2.7	-0.9	-0.6	11.9	13.2	14.5
Canada	1.9	-5.4	5.0	1.9	0.7	1.7	-2.1	-1.9	-0.8	5.7	9.6	8.0
China	5.8	2.3	8.4	2.9	2.4	1.2	1.0	2.0	1.6	3.6	3.8	3.6
India	4.0	-8.0	12.5	4.8	6.2	4.9	-0.9	1.0	-1.2	. . .	. . .	. . .
Indonesia	5.0	-2.1	4.3	2.8	2.0	2.0	-2.7	-0.4	-1.3	5.3	7.1	6.5
Japan	0.3	-4.8	3.3	0.5	0.0	0.1	3.7	3.3	3.6	2.4	2.8	2.8
Russia	2.0	-3.1	3.8	4.5	3.4	4.5	3.8	2.2	3.9	4.6	5.8	5.4
UNITED STATES	2.2	-3.5	6.4	1.8	1.2	2.3	-2.2	-3.1	-3.9	3.7	8.1	5.8

. . . = Not available.

Table 13-2 Foreign Exchange Rates

(Not seasonally adjusted.)

Year and month	Foreign currency per U.S. dollar					
	Canadian dollar	Chinese yuan	European currency unit	Japananese yen	Switzerland franc	British pound
1971	1.0099	. . .	. . .	347.79	4.1171	2.4442
1972	0.9907	. . .	. . .	303.12	3.8186	2.5034
1973	1.0002	. . .	. . .	271.31	3.1688	2.4525
1974	0.9780	. . .	. . .	291.84	2.9805	2.3403
1975	1.0175	. . .	. . .	296.78	2.5839	2.2217
1976	0.9863	. . .	. . .	296.45	2.5002	1.8048
1977	1.0633	. . .	. . .	268.62	2.4065	1.7449
1978	1.1405	. . .	. . .	210.39	1.7907	1.9184
1979	1.1713	. . .	. . .	219.02	1.6644	2.1224
1980	1.1693	. . .	. . .	226.63	1.6772	2.3246
1981	1.1990	1.7100	. . .	220.63	1.9675	2.0243
1982	1.2344	1.8979	. . .	249.06	2.0319	1.7480
1983	1.2325	1.9810	. . .	237.55	2.1007	1.5159
1984	1.2952	2.3303	. . .	237.46	2.3500	1.3368
1985	1.3659	2.9434	. . .	238.47	2.4552	1.2974
1986	1.3896	3.4616	. . .	168.35	1.7979	1.4677
1987	1.3259	3.7314	. . .	144.60	1.4918	1.6398
1988	1.2306	3.7314	. . .	128.17	1.4643	1.7813
1989	1.1842	3.7673	. . .	138.07	1.6369	1.6382
1990	1.1668	4.7921	. . .	145.00	1.3901	1.7841
1991	1.1460	5.3337	. . .	134.59	1.4356	1.7674
1992	1.2085	5.5206	. . .	126.78	1.4064	1.7663
1993	1.2902	5.7795	. . .	111.08	1.4781	1.5016
1994	1.3664	8.6397	. . .	102.18	1.3667	1.5319
1995	1.3725	8.3700	. . .	93.96	1.1812	1.5785
1996	1.3638	8.3389	. . .	108.78	1.2361	1.5607
1997	1.3849	8.3193	. . .	121.06	1.4514	1.6376
1998	1.4836	8.3008	. . .	130.99	1.4506	1.6573
1999	1.4858	8.2783	1.0653	113.73	1.5045	1.6172
2000	1.4855	8.2784	0.9232	107.80	1.6904	1.5156
2001	1.5487	8.2770	0.8952	121.57	1.6891	1.4396
2002	1.5704	8.2771	0.9454	125.22	1.5567	1.5025
2003	1.4008	8.2772	1.1321	115.94	1.3450	1.6347
2004	1.3017	8.2768	1.2438	108.15	1.2428	1.8330
2005	1.2115	8.1936	1.2449	110.11	1.2459	1.8204
2006	1.1340	7.9723	1.2563	116.31	1.2532	1.8434
2007	1.0734	7.6058	1.3711	117.76	1.1999	2.0020
2008	1.0660	6.9477	1.4726	103.39	1.0816	1.8545
2009	1.1412	6.8307	1.3935	93.68	1.0860	1.5661
2010	1.0298	6.7696	1.3261	87.78	1.0432	1.5452
2011	0.9887	6.4630	1.3931	79.70	0.8862	1.6043
2012	0.9995	6.3093	1.2859	79.82	0.9377	1.5853
2013	1.0300	6.1478	1.3281	97.60	0.9269	1.5642
2014	1.1043	6.1620	1.3297	105.74	0.9147	1.6484
2015	1.2791	6.2827	1.1096	121.05	0.9628	1.5284
2016	1.3243	6.6400	1.1072	108.66	0.9848	1.3555
2017	1.2984	6.7569	1.1301	112.10	0.9842	1.2890
2018	1.2957	6.6090	1.1817	110.40	0.9784	1.3363
2019	1.3269	6.9081	1.1194	109.02	0.9937	1.2768
2020	1.3422	6.9042	1.1410	106.78	0.9389	1.2829
2019						
January	1.3300	6.7863	1.1418	108.96	0.9897	1.2901
February	1.3209	6.7367	1.1349	110.44	1.0014	1.3016
March	1.3371	6.7119	1.1296	111.14	1.0005	1.3167
April	1.3378	6.7161	1.1234	111.64	1.0084	1.3029
May	1.3460	6.8519	1.1187	109.97	1.0107	1.2855
June	1.3289	6.8977	1.1295	108.07	0.9880	1.2675
July	1.3105	6.8775	1.1211	108.29	0.9880	1.2461
August	1.3273	7.0629	1.1129	106.19	0.9787	1.2160
September	1.3241	7.1137	1.1011	107.54	0.9906	1.2369
October	1.3189	7.0961	1.1058	108.14	0.9930	1.2657
November	1.3237	7.0199	1.1051	108.86	0.9929	1.2884
December	1.3169	7.0137	1.1114	109.10	0.9826	1.3109
2020						
January	1.3089	6.9184	1.1098	109.27	0.9698	1.3076
February	1.3286	6.9967	1.0911	110.03	0.9762	1.2953
March	1.3960	7.0205	1.1046	107.67	0.9593	1.2369
April	1.4048	7.0708	1.0871	107.74	0.9701	1.2420
May	1.3972	7.1016	1.0907	107.20	0.9692	1.2302
June	1.3552	7.0816	1.1259	107.58	0.9513	1.2523
July	1.3497	7.0041	1.1488	106.68	0.9327	1.2701
August	1.3229	6.9270	1.1831	106.01	0.9099	1.3143
September	1.3230	6.8106	1.1785	105.59	0.9149	1.2947
October	1.3218	6.7254	1.1768	105.21	0.9124	1.2980
November	1.3073	6.6029	1.1826	104.41	0.9110	1.3198
December	1.2809	6.5393	1.2168	103.80	0.8884	1.3434

. . . = Not available.

NOTES AND DEFINITIONS, CHAPTER 13

TABLE 13-1

International Comparisons: Gross Domestic Product Growth, Unemployment Rates, Inflation and Current Account Balances

SOURCE: APRIL AND JULY 2021 WORLD ECONOMIC OUTLOOK, PUBLISHED BY THE INTERNATIONAL MONETARY FUND

The United States trades with many countries for both goods and services. Specific countries include neighbors Canada and Mexico, European countries Germany and the United Kingdom; plus, Asian nations such as China, Japan, and India and finally Russia. Table 13-1 provides international comparisons of these nations in terms of major economic indicators. These are Real Gross Domestic Product (GDP), unemployment rates, inflation and current account balances as percent of the GDP by country for years, 2019, and 2020 and forecast for 2021.

The IMF was established in 1944 in the aftermath of the Great Depression of the 1930s. 44 founding member countries sought to build a framework for international economic cooperation. Today, its membership embraces 190 countries, with staff drawn from 150 nations.

Definitions and notes on the data

The basic measure of the overall health of an economy is the *gross domestic product* (GDP). It is the market value of all goods and services produced by labor and property located in the United States. *Real GDP* is an inflation-adjusted measure that reflects the value of all goods and services produced by an economy each year, expressed in base-year prices. See chapter 1 for in depth and historical data of GDP and its components plus notes and definitions at the end of the chapter.

The *unemployment rate* represents the number unemployed as a percent of the labor force. See Chapter 10.

The *Consumer Price Index* (CPI) measures the change in prices paid by consumers for goods and services. *Inflation/deflation* is the change over time of the CPI. See Chapter 8 for more information on the CPI and inflation.

Current *account is all transactions other than those in the financial and capital items. The major* classification are goods and services, income and current transfers. The focus of the Balance of Payment (BOP) is on transactions (between an economy and the rest of the world) in goods, services, and income. Chapter 7 provides much more historical and current data.

Table 13-1 presents the current account balance as a percent of GDP. This measure provides an indication on the level of international competitiveness of a country. Usually, countries recording a strong current account surplus have an economy heavily dependent on exports revenues, with high savings ratings but weak domestic demand. On the other hand, countries recording a current account deficit have strong imports, a low saving rates and high personal consumption rates as a percentage of disposable incomes. See Chapter 7 for International Trade information, Chapter 1 for GDP and its components and Chapter 4 for savings data and personal consumption expenditures. (PCE)

References and notes on the data

The International Monetary Fund (IMF) publishes the World Economic Outlook (WEO) on mostly annual basis with updates if there are major changes in the world economy. Tables appear in the first chapter's Annex.

TABLE 13-2

Foreign Exchange Rates

SOURCE: BOARD OF GOVERNORS OF THE FEDERAL RESERVE SYSTEM

Definitions and notes on the data

The price of a nation's currency in terms of another currency. An *exchange rate* thus has two components, the domestic currency and a foreign currency, and can be quoted either directly or indirectly. In a direct quotation, the price of a unit of foreign currency is expressed in terms of the domestic currency. In an indirect quotation, the price of a unit of domestic currency is expressed in terms of the foreign currency.

This table measures the U.S. dollar relative to the currencies of some important individual countries and relative to average values for major groups of countries. In *Business Statistics,* all these measures are defined as the foreign currency price of the U.S. dollar. When the measure is relatively high, the dollar is relatively strong—but less competitive (in the sense of price competition)—and the other currency or group of currencies named in the measure is relatively weak and more competitive.

For consistency, this definition is used in Business Statistics even in the case of currencies that are commonly quoted in the financial press and elsewhere as dollars per foreign currency unit instead of foreign currency units per dollar. Notably, this is the case for the euro and for the British pound.

The definition of the dollar's value used in *Business Statistics* is the most useful for economic analysis from the U.S. point of view and for foreign tourists in the United States. For American tourists overseas, it is easier to use the inverse of this measure, the value of the other currency; for example, the traveler in Paris can more easily translate prices into dollars by multiplying by the dollar value of the euro than by dividing by the euro value of the dollar.

The foreign exchange rates shown are averages of the daily noon buying rates for cable transfers in New York City certified for customs purposes by the Federal Reserve Bank of New York.

The introduction of the euro was in January 1999 as the common currency for 11 European countries and marked a major change in the international currency system. Over time, the Eurozone has increased to 19 countries - Austria, Belgium, Cyprus, Estonia, Finland, France, Germany, Greece, Ireland, Italy, Latvia, Lithuania, Luxembourg, Malta, Netherlands, Portugal, Slovakia, Slovenia and Spain. In addition, the euro is also the national currency in Monaco, the Vatican City and San Marino, and is the de facto currency in Andorra, Kosovo, and Montenegro. The values of the currencies of these countries no longer fluctuate relative to each other, but the value of the euro still fluctuates relative to the dollar and to currencies for countries outside the EMU. The currency and coins of the individual countries continued to circulate from 1999 through the end of 2001, but in January 2002, new euro currency and coins were introduced, replacing the currency and coins of the individual countries. Once a country has entered the monetary union, its values relative to the <u>dollar</u> will continue to fluctuate—but only due to fluctuations in the value of the euro relative to the dollar.

There is no fully satisfactory historical equivalent to the euro. For comparisons over time, the Federal Reserve Board uses a "restated German mark," derived simply by dividing each historical value of the mark by the euro conversion factor, 1.95583. The G-10 dollar index described below includes five of the currencies that later merged into the euro, but also includes the currencies of Canada, Japan, the United Kingdom, Switzerland, and Sweden.

Data availability and references

Current press releases, historical data, and information on weights and methods for exchange rates and exchange rate indexes are available on the Federal Reserve Web site at <https://www.federalreserve.gov/>; go to Data, then "Foreign Exchange Rates H10/G5," and select DDP, the new Data Download Program. The dollar value indexes are described in the article "Indexes of the Foreign Exchange Value of the Dollar," *Federal Reserve Bulletin* (Winter 2005), also available on the Federal Reserve Web site.

Additional information on exchange rates can be found on the Federal Reserve Bank of St. Louis Web site at <https://www.stls.frb.org/fred/data/exchange.html>.

PART B: INDUSTRY PROFILES

CHAPTER 14: PRODUCT AND INCOME BY INDUSTRY

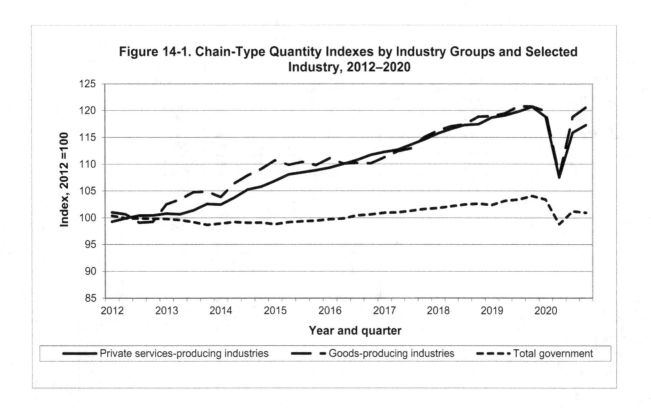

Figure 14-1. Chain-Type Quantity Indexes by Industry Groups and Selected Industry, 2012–2020

- Private services-producing industries, which accounted for 70.5 percent of total GDP in 2020, typically display less cyclical swing and more real growth than the goods sector, which was 16.9 percent of the total. Government production—the other 12.6 percent of total GDP—was comparatively stable, but this is an incomplete measurement of the counter-cyclical impact of government, as it does not include the effects of changes in tax receipts and payments. (Tables 14-1 and 14-2)

- Table 14-3 can be used to assess the share of each industry group in total gross domestic factor income and the shares paid to employees and accruing to land and capital in each industry. For these purposes factor income is a better measure than the BEA definition of value added because value added includes, but factor income excludes, taxes on production and imports.

- In private goods-producing industries in 2019, employee compensation was 52.0 percent of gross factor income, while in the less capital-intensive private services-producing industries (excluding real estate and rental and leasing), compensation was 54.4 percent of total value. (Table 14-3)

- BEA publishes quarterly measures of GDP by industrial origin, in both current-dollar and real (quantity) terms. Industry output, sometimes referred to as "gross product originating in the industry," is here termed "value added".

Table 14-1. Gross Domestic Product (Value Added) by Industry

(Billions of dollars.)

Year	Total gross domestic product	Private industries Total	Agriculture, forestry, fishing, and hunting	Mining	Utilities	Construction	Manufacturing Durable goods	Manufacturing Nondurable goods	Wholesale trade	Retail trade	Transportation and warehousing	Information	Finance and insurance	Real estate and rental and leasing
2000	10 252.3	8 929.3	98.3	110.6	180.1	461.3	924.8	625.4	622.6	685.5	307.8	471.3	743.1	1 231.7
2001	10 581.8	9 188.9	99.8	123.9	181.3	486.5	833.4	640.5	613.8	709.5	308.1	502.4	803.1	1 325.0
2002	10 936.4	9 462.0	95.6	112.4	177.6	493.6	832.8	635.7	613.1	732.6	305.7	550.6	816.4	1 400.5
2003	11 458.2	9 905.9	114.0	139.0	184.0	525.2	863.2	661.0	641.5	769.6	321.4	564.9	846.3	1 449.6
2004	12 213.7	10 582.5	142.9	166.5	199.2	584.6	905.1	703.0	697.1	795.6	352.1	620.4	872.4	1 516.7
2005	13 036.6	11 326.4	128.3	225.7	198.1	651.8	956.8	736.6	754.9	840.8	375.8	642.3	973.7	1 632.5
2006	13 814.6	12 022.6	125.1	273.3	226.8	697.1	1 004.4	789.4	811.5	869.9	410.4	652.0	1 034.2	1 709.7
2007	14 451.9	12 564.8	144.1	314.0	231.9	715.3	1 030.6	814.1	857.8	869.2	413.9	706.9	1 030.5	1 817.7
2008	14 712.8	12 731.2	147.2	392.2	241.7	648.9	999.7	801.1	884.3	848.7	426.8	743.0	873.2	1 889.5
2009	14 448.9	12 403.9	130.0	275.8	258.2	565.6	881.0	821.2	834.2	827.6	404.6	721.9	966.6	1 901.1
2010	14 992.1	12 884.1	146.3	305.8	278.8	525.1	964.3	832.7	888.9	851.5	433.0	753.3	1 003.6	1 939.4
2011	15 542.6	13 405.5	180.9	356.3	287.5	524.4	1 015.2	852.4	934.9	871.9	451.4	759.8	1 026.0	2 019.3
2012	16 197.0	14 037.5	179.6	358.8	279.7	553.4	1 061.7	865.3	997.4	908.4	472.0	759.0	1 162.8	2 098.2
2013	16 784.9	14 572.3	215.6	386.5	286.3	587.6	1 102.0	889.9	1 040.1	949.5	491.1	828.9	1 144.9	2 177.9
2014	17 527.3	15 255.9	201.0	416.4	298.1	636.9	1 134.1	916.1	1 088.2	974.5	521.8	842.4	1 282.6	2 265.4
2015	18 238.3	15 898.9	182.3	261.8	299.2	694.9	1 183.8	945.8	1 142.9	1 020.1	565.8	906.9	1 363.1	2 385.9
2016	18 745.1	16 360.2	166.6	218.0	301.7	746.9	1 186.4	913.4	1 133.6	1 052.8	582.0	968.4	1 458.0	2 488.0
2017	19 543.0	17 094.2	176.6	274.0	310.1	797.8	1 227.2	955.1	1 163.5	1 083.5	607.0	1 005.4	1 513.3	2 603.6
2018	20 611.9	18 062.2	178.6	330.8	321.8	848.2	1 287.6	1 026.8	1 210.9	1 115.8	650.7	1 059.8	1 633.6	2 738.3
2019	21 433.2	18 793.8	175.4	309.5	335.3	892.7	1 320.8	1 025.1	1 262.3	1 162.2	696.7	1 127.5	1 665.8	2 876.0
2020	20 936.6	18 290.9	175.8	192.5	336.9	897.6	1 278.2	991.0	1 217.7	1 200.9	595.9	1 161.4	1 727.1	2 933.2
2012														
1st quarter	16 019.8	13 871.1	182.6	369.7	272.4	548.3	1 050.8	864.4	979.9	901.5	465.5	755.4	1 126.1	2 069.4
2nd quarter	16 152.3	14 001.2	178.6	353.8	281.7	551.7	1 065.6	864.4	991.9	904.0	474.5	768.2	1 153.8	2 092.5
3rd quarter	16 257.2	14 096.1	175.8	349.6	283.2	552.0	1 063.7	874.1	1 003.1	910.6	474.2	760.1	1 184.5	2 115.5
4th quarter	16 358.9	14 181.7	181.3	362.1	281.3	561.6	1 066.8	858.5	1 014.5	917.6	473.6	752.1	1 186.8	2 115.2
2013														
1st quarter	16 569.6	14 375.2	218.3	369.9	287.4	571.5	1 090.0	887.9	1 027.9	943.1	483.4	812.1	1 109.3	2 146.7
2nd quarter	16 637.9	14 430.5	224.7	383.0	286.4	579.0	1 091.0	873.3	1 025.9	942.7	484.3	820.8	1 126.7	2 150.8
3rd quarter	16 848.7	14 633.7	222.2	401.3	283.2	594.3	1 107.2	882.3	1 045.0	953.8	491.6	830.2	1 143.9	2 196.1
4th quarter	17 083.1	14 850.1	197.2	391.8	288.3	605.4	1 119.6	916.3	1 061.5	958.2	505.1	852.6	1 199.8	2 217.8
2014														
1st quarter	17 104.6	14 857.1	197.3	412.2	301.1	615.5	1 101.5	892.7	1 049.0	951.3	498.5	833.6	1 228.6	2 211.8
2nd quarter	17 432.9	15 172.2	213.0	435.3	295.5	630.0	1 121.6	915.2	1 074.6	969.0	515.7	840.7	1 284.2	2 248.0
3rd quarter	17 721.7	15 443.0	196.7	431.3	297.8	644.0	1 154.5	931.0	1 108.7	982.8	531.7	845.4	1 298.2	2 289.3
4th quarter	17 849.9	15 551.2	197.0	386.7	297.9	658.1	1 158.8	925.7	1 120.4	995.0	541.5	850.0	1 319.4	2 312.6
2015														
1st quarter	18 003.4	15 685.4	181.9	289.9	299.8	673.1	1 176.7	939.7	1 134.3	1 001.3	553.2	877.7	1 352.2	2 342.2
2nd quarter	18 223.6	15 889.2	181.8	279.2	297.1	689.7	1 181.7	951.3	1 151.1	1 012.4	561.5	897.2	1 394.8	2 370.6
3rd quarter	18 347.4	15 999.3	185.4	251.7	303.0	703.0	1 191.0	962.0	1 144.8	1 030.9	573.0	917.5	1 351.8	2 405.0
4th quarter	18 378.8	16 021.6	180.0	226.2	297.0	713.9	1 185.7	930.3	1 141.3	1 035.7	575.6	935.4	1 353.7	2 426.1
2016														
1st quarter	18 470.2	16 104.6	168.7	197.4	295.4	730.8	1 185.0	912.4	1 135.2	1 044.8	575.2	957.3	1 371.0	2 452.7
2nd quarter	18 656.2	16 279.1	170.6	212.3	298.2	738.6	1 182.8	918.9	1 130.4	1 047.9	581.8	961.2	1 435.0	2 481.8
3rd quarter	18 821.4	16 428.9	167.0	222.6	306.9	748.9	1 186.0	913.1	1 132.2	1 054.8	580.4	974.4	1 494.3	2 495.1
4th quarter	19 032.6	16 628.2	160.0	239.9	306.5	769.2	1 191.8	909.0	1 136.7	1 063.9	590.5	980.7	1 531.6	2 522.4
2017														
1st quarter	19 237.4	16 816.8	183.3	259.5	304.5	785.3	1 204.5	931.6	1 145.7	1 073.6	596.2	988.7	1 500.9	2 559.9
2nd quarter	19 379.2	16 943.8	180.2	265.8	311.9	788.1	1 214.6	939.6	1 156.3	1 077.4	604.0	996.6	1 478.7	2 591.2
3rd quarter	19 617.3	17 160.2	170.5	271.1	309.0	801.0	1 232.6	958.2	1 166.8	1 087.1	609.5	1 010.8	1 520.7	2 614.4
4th quarter	19 938.0	17 456.3	172.5	299.7	315.0	816.9	1 257.3	991.0	1 185.3	1 095.9	618.3	1 025.6	1 552.8	2 648.7
2018														
1st quarter	20 242.2	17 733.1	181.0	313.2	319.9	835.4	1 270.6	1 007.7	1 190.3	1 106.8	634.4	1 029.2	1 597.0	2 690.3
2nd quarter	20 552.7	18 016.2	184.3	331.4	322.7	845.1	1 281.6	1 025.2	1 203.5	1 116.4	644.2	1 062.1	1 638.6	2 722.9
3rd quarter	20 742.7	18 176.4	172.6	342.2	317.6	851.7	1 292.8	1 027.6	1 212.6	1 118.4	653.1	1 072.1	1 672.9	2 754.6
4th quarter	20 909.9	18 323.0	176.4	336.5	327.1	860.5	1 305.5	1 046.5	1 237.0	1 121.4	671.3	1 075.8	1 626.1	2 785.4
2019														
1st quarter	21 115.3	18 508.9	170.3	316.9	329.2	880.1	1 318.2	1 005.7	1 257.0	1 139.5	682.3	1 094.7	1 649.8	2 820.6
2nd quarter	21 329.9	18 703.8	172.8	319.2	332.7	887.4	1 319.2	1 021.5	1 253.8	1 156.0	690.7	1 122.3	1 663.7	2 859.6
3rd quarter	21 540.3	18 887.2	178.0	301.2	338.6	897.7	1 317.7	1 031.0	1 268.0	1 173.2	703.6	1 137.0	1 656.5	2 901.4
4th quarter	21 747.4	19 075.1	180.4	300.6	340.6	905.5	1 328.0	1 042.1	1 270.4	1 180.3	710.0	1 156.1	1 693.2	2 922.3
2020														
1st quarter	21 561.1	18 879.0	190.2	248.3	333.8	914.6	1 309.7	1 036.6	1 258.6	1 180.7	686.0	1 156.8	1 663.9	2 943.6
2nd quarter	19 520.1	16 925.5	142.4	136.3	333.2	853.7	1 145.5	908.2	1 111.9	1 102.1	520.2	1 115.7	1 699.8	2 864.8
3rd quarter	21 170.3	18 516.6	172.5	179.6	342.9	899.5	1 324.1	1 004.9	1 244.5	1 259.2	578.5	1 175.2	1 748.3	2 953.8
4th quarter	21 494.7	18 842.4	198.2	205.7	337.6	922.5	1 333.4	1 014.3	1 256.0	1 261.5	598.8	1 198.1	1 796.3	2 970.4

Table 14-1. Gross Domestic Product (Value Added) by Industry—*Continued*

(Billions of dollars.)

Year	Professional, scientific, and technical services	Management of companies and enterprises	Administrative and waste management services	Educational services	Health care and social assistance	Arts, entertainment, and recreation	Accommodation and food services	Other services except government	Government Total government	Federal	State and local	Private goods-producing industries	Private services-producing industries	Information-communications-technology-producing industries[1]
2000	651.8	171.1	282.1	95.2	600.2	99.0	287.5	279.7	1 323.0	423.5	899.5	2 220.4	6 708.9	632.9
2001	686.8	173.6	295.1	101.7	648.2	96.7	294.0	265.6	1 392.9	430.4	962.5	2 184.1	7 004.8	610.3
2002	714.7	175.0	300.2	106.5	700.5	103.8	309.7	284.9	1 474.4	462.5	1 011.9	2 170.1	7 291.9	620.9
2003	741.3	185.6	320.5	116.8	746.0	111.0	321.1	283.8	1 552.3	498.9	1 053.5	2 302.4	7 603.5	653.1
2004	792.4	203.1	345.5	129.1	798.3	117.9	343.3	297.3	1 631.3	525.5	1 105.8	2 502.2	8 080.3	706.2
2005	852.4	214.1	379.9	133.2	837.3	122.2	359.0	310.7	1 710.3	551.3	1 159.0	2 699.3	8 627.1	755.8
2006	917.1	230.5	399.1	142.9	892.5	130.5	381.1	325.0	1 792.0	575.5	1 216.4	2 889.4	9 133.2	795.2
2007	984.9	251.2	430.6	151.5	936.4	137.4	396.1	330.5	1 887.1	601.9	1 285.2	3 018.1	9 546.7	852.5
2008	1 082.1	256.4	438.6	167.8	1 017.0	143.2	399.5	330.3	1 981.6	632.2	1 349.4	2 989.1	9 742.1	904.2
2009	1 031.3	245.0	412.4	188.3	1 079.2	144.6	388.6	326.5	2 045.1	663.3	1 381.7	2 673.6	9 730.3	888.8
2010	1 063.9	265.4	437.6	198.9	1 111.8	152.2	403.5	328.0	2 108.0	697.4	1 410.5	2 774.3	10 109.8	937.4
2011	1 124.6	278.0	454.1	206.0	1 148.7	158.3	422.6	333.1	2 137.1	712.3	1 424.8	2 929.3	10 476.3	974.4
2012	1 188.5	302.2	473.9	213.9	1 193.5	171.2	450.1	348.0	2 159.5	713.9	1 445.6	3 018.8	11 018.7	985.4
2013	1 208.5	319.7	489.1	217.5	1 229.7	177.4	473.9	356.3	2 212.5	703.8	1 508.7	3 181.6	11 390.8	1 062.6
2014	1 267.6	332.9	517.9	226.1	1 265.8	189.1	502.2	376.6	2 271.4	715.8	1 555.5	3 304.5	11 951.4	1 095.6
2015	1 348.6	348.0	540.4	233.4	1 337.6	193.5	553.3	391.6	2 339.4	731.3	1 608.2	3 268.6	12 630.3	1 182.7
2016	1 394.1	350.9	559.2	246.1	1 405.8	207.0	581.3	399.9	2 384.9	743.5	1 641.4	3 231.2	13 129.0	1 256.3
2017	1 456.7	372.6	601.7	248.5	1 458.8	216.3	608.1	414.3	2 448.7	762.5	1 686.3	3 430.9	13 663.4	1 322.8
2018	1 548.9	392.3	631.6	258.4	1 523.5	228.7	638.0	437.9	2 549.7	789.9	1 759.8	3 671.9	14 390.3	1 413.9
2019	1 638.4	411.4	660.9	269.9	1 595.6	238.6	668.6	461.3	2 639.5	813.5	1 826.0	3 723.4	15 070.4	1 511.5
2020	1 626.4	405.1	642.0	256.1	1 551.4	153.2	526.5	421.9	2 645.7	842.3	1 803.4	3 535.0	14 755.8	. . .
2012														
1st quarter	1 169.8	291.9	471.4	212.5	1 184.2	167.6	444.4	343.3	2 148.7	715.1	1 433.6	3 015.8	10 855.3	. . .
2nd quarter	1 189.1	293.5	471.7	214.3	1 186.8	170.1	447.8	346.9	2 151.0	714.8	1 436.3	3 014.2	10 987.0	. . .
3rd quarter	1 191.4	302.8	474.9	214.5	1 194.1	172.0	450.4	349.6	2 161.0	714.2	1 446.8	3 015.1	11 081.0	. . .
4th quarter	1 203.8	320.5	477.7	214.2	1 208.8	175.3	458.0	352.0	2 177.2	711.5	1 465.7	3 030.3	11 151.4	. . .
2013														
1st quarter	1 201.8	313.9	479.9	214.7	1 222.3	174.5	467.5	353.1	2 194.4	706.5	1 487.9	3 137.6	11 237.6	. . .
2nd quarter	1 197.5	319.6	484.6	215.9	1 224.9	175.2	470.3	353.9	2 207.5	704.1	1 503.4	3 151.0	11 279.4	. . .
3rd quarter	1 208.6	321.1	492.9	217.8	1 231.7	177.7	476.4	356.4	2 215.1	698.4	1 516.7	3 207.3	11 426.4	. . .
4th quarter	1 226.3	324.2	498.9	221.4	1 240.0	182.2	481.5	361.8	2 233.1	706.3	1 526.8	3 230.4	11 619.6	. . .
2014														
1st quarter	1 230.1	333.3	503.0	222.0	1 241.5	185.9	483.4	365.0	2 247.4	710.9	1 536.5	3 219.2	11 637.9	. . .
2nd quarter	1 247.6	327.7	515.2	225.4	1 254.1	188.8	496.9	373.8	2 260.7	713.7	1 547.0	3 315.0	11 857.2	. . .
3rd quarter	1 289.3	331.0	523.3	228.1	1 276.7	191.3	509.6	382.2	2 278.6	717.5	1 561.1	3 357.5	12 085.5	. . .
4th quarter	1 303.5	339.5	530.2	228.9	1 291.1	190.5	519.1	385.4	2 298.7	721.2	1 577.5	3 326.3	12 224.9	. . .
2015														
1st quarter	1 324.7	346.8	533.5	230.3	1 311.7	190.7	537.3	388.3	2 318.0	726.7	1 591.3	3 261.4	12 424.0	. . .
2nd quarter	1 342.2	348.3	536.9	231.5	1 328.4	192.4	549.1	392.0	2 334.4	729.4	1 605.0	3 283.8	12 605.4	. . .
3rd quarter	1 360.5	347.8	543.5	233.9	1 349.0	194.0	559.4	392.2	2 348.2	733.2	1 614.9	3 293.1	12 706.2	. . .
4th quarter	1 366.9	349.0	547.6	238.2	1 361.2	196.8	567.3	393.8	2 357.2	735.8	1 621.4	3 236.1	12 785.5	. . .
2016														
1st quarter	1 383.3	347.8	550.5	242.7	1 383.0	201.3	573.1	396.9	2 365.6	738.0	1 627.6	3 194.2	12 910.3	. . .
2nd quarter	1 388.6	349.4	554.0	246.0	1 401.4	204.0	577.8	398.3	2 377.2	740.8	1 636.4	3 223.1	13 055.9	. . .
3rd quarter	1 392.5	351.2	559.4	246.3	1 408.5	210.1	584.2	401.0	2 392.4	745.4	1 647.0	3 237.6	13 191.3	. . .
4th quarter	1 412.1	355.2	573.0	249.4	1 430.5	212.5	589.9	403.3	2 404.4	749.9	1 654.5	3 269.9	13 358.3	. . .
2017														
1st quarter	1 427.8	361.5	586.3	248.3	1 441.7	211.8	598.7	406.9	2 420.7	755.1	1 665.5	3 364.3	13 452.5	. . .
2nd quarter	1 446.3	367.3	597.2	247.1	1 452.0	213.6	605.5	410.5	2 435.5	758.7	1 676.8	3 388.3	13 555.4	. . .
3rd quarter	1 466.1	373.8	607.3	248.5	1 463.3	220.9	611.1	417.3	2 457.1	764.6	1 692.6	3 433.4	13 726.8	. . .
4th quarter	1 486.8	387.6	616.2	250.0	1 477.9	219.1	617.2	422.4	2 481.7	771.5	1 710.2	3 537.5	13 918.8	. . .
2018														
1st quarter	1 517.2	385.9	620.5	254.5	1 501.7	221.1	628.0	428.5	2 509.1	779.8	1 729.2	3 607.9	14 125.2	. . .
2nd quarter	1 547.2	387.2	627.8	257.1	1 516.7	230.7	635.9	435.7	2 536.4	787.0	1 749.4	3 667.6	14 348.6	. . .
3rd quarter	1 559.0	397.9	633.5	259.3	1 527.3	231.2	639.8	440.3	2 566.3	793.9	1 772.4	3 686.9	14 489.5	. . .
4th quarter	1 572.1	398.2	644.5	262.9	1 548.4	231.9	648.5	447.2	2 586.9	798.7	1 788.2	3 725.3	14 597.7	. . .
2019														
1st quarter	1 608.9	408.9	650.5	264.6	1 569.7	234.3	654.8	452.9	2 606.4	805.6	1 800.9	3 691.3	14 817.6	. . .
2nd quarter	1 624.9	412.2	656.1	267.9	1 585.6	236.3	664.0	458.1	2 626.0	809.8	1 816.3	3 720.1	14 983.7	. . .
3rd quarter	1 651.9	410.8	664.9	271.6	1 603.8	240.4	675.6	464.4	2 653.1	816.6	1 836.6	3 725.5	15 161.7	. . .
4th quarter	1 668.0	413.6	672.3	275.3	1 623.1	243.5	680.0	469.7	2 672.3	822.2	1 850.1	3 756.6	15 318.4	. . .
2020														
1st quarter	1 670.5	412.2	668.9	275.2	1 605.8	227.3	636.0	460.2	2 682.2	828.2	1 854.0	3 699.3	15 179.6	. . .
2nd quarter	1 547.4	397.6	579.9	244.6	1 374.9	98.2	378.1	371.0	2 594.6	837.7	1 756.9	3 186.0	13 739.4	. . .
3rd quarter	1 625.9	402.9	645.3	256.2	1 594.7	137.1	545.9	425.4	2 653.6	850.5	1 803.2	3 580.6	14 936.0	. . .
4th quarter	1 661.8	407.8	674.1	248.5	1 630.3	150.2	546.0	431.0	2 652.3	853.0	1 799.4	3 674.0	15 168.3	. . .

[1]Consists of computer and electronic products manufacturing; publishing, including software; information and data processing services; and computer systems design and related services.
. . . = Not available.

Table 14-2. Chain-Type Quantity Indexes for Value Added by Industry

(New Series, 2012 = 100.)

Year	Total gross domestic product	Private industries												
		Total	Agriculture, forestry, fishing, and hunting	Mining	Utilities	Construc-tion	Manufacturing		Wholesale trade	Retail trade	Transpor-tation and ware-housing	Information	Finance and insurance	Real estate and rental and leasing
							Durable goods	Nondurable goods						
2000	81.1	81.1	90.1	65.8	93.2	141.5	70.9	111.7	81.1	90.3	90.0	55.6	77.8	73.7
2001	81.9	81.7	87.0	76.2	77.0	138.6	66.4	110.5	82.7	93.6	84.0	58.9	83.8	76.9
2002	83.3	83.1	90.0	78.2	79.7	134.1	67.8	109.7	83.5	97.7	80.9	64.6	83.2	78.2
2003	85.7	85.5	97.0	69.2	77.9	136.3	72.8	113.1	88.2	102.7	83.8	66.6	83.7	79.4
2004	88.9	89.0	104.7	69.6	82.7	141.2	78.0	120.9	91.9	104.5	90.8	74.3	83.6	81.4
2005	92.1	92.5	109.2	70.8	78.4	141.8	83.4	118.8	96.1	107.9	95.1	79.3	91.4	85.8
2006	94.7	95.5	111.0	81.7	83.3	138.8	89.8	122.5	98.7	108.7	100.7	82.1	95.2	87.4
2007	96.5	97.1	98.3	88.0	84.9	134.6	94.0	124.5	102.1	105.1	99.9	90.1	92.8	91.1
2008	96.3	96.5	100.4	85.2	89.5	121.4	94.5	118.1	102.0	101.3	99.0	95.9	79.1	93.2
2009	93.9	93.5	111.4	97.7	84.8	104.3	80.9	114.7	89.7	97.0	93.1	93.6	93.9	92.0
2010	96.3	95.9	108.0	86.2	95.0	98.9	91.1	112.4	95.0	99.1	97.6	98.9	92.7	94.7
2011	97.8	97.6	103.8	89.4	98.7	97.3	97.3	104.9	96.8	99.3	99.4	100.3	92.5	97.8
2012	100.0	100.0	100.0	100.0	100.0	100.0	100.0	100.0	100.0	100.0	100.0	100.0	100.0	100.0
2013	101.8	101.9	116.6	103.9	98.9	102.5	102.5	103.8	102.3	103.1	101.5	109.1	94.1	101.9
2014	104.4	104.8	117.9	115.3	95.1	104.4	104.0	105.9	106.2	105.0	104.6	111.8	99.0	103.7
2015	107.6	108.5	126.5	125.9	95.2	109.2	106.0	106.7	110.8	108.9	107.5	123.5	102.3	106.0
2016	109.5	110.5	133.0	119.0	100.0	113.3	105.8	105.0	109.4	113.0	109.2	134.3	103.7	107.9
2017	112.0	113.3	130.1	120.1	100.3	116.9	109.4	106.6	111.2	117.0	113.4	143.0	103.6	110.1
2018	115.4	116.9	135.5	126.0	100.9	120.1	114.6	110.4	111.9	120.1	118.3	153.0	103.8	113.5
2019	117.9	119.7	135.7	140.6	102.2	120.1	116.4	113.1	109.5	123.1	122.0	163.9	104.2	115.8
2020	113.8	115.3	143.2	124.6	105.8	117.8	112.2	111.1	105.2	119.7	106.4	169.1	105.9	115.2
2012														
1st quarter	99.6	99.6	105.4	96.9	98.7	100.1	99.8	103.8	98.1	100.5	100.5	100.0	97.6	99.3
2nd quarter	100.0	100.1	101.9	101.1	101.4	99.6	100.2	101.4	100.7	98.4	100.0	101.2	99.9	99.9
3rd quarter	100.1	100.1	97.1	100.1	100.8	99.1	99.6	98.3	101.0	100.7	99.8	99.7	101.7	100.7
4th quarter	100.3	100.2	95.6	101.9	99.1	101.2	100.3	96.5	100.2	100.4	99.7	99.1	100.8	100.1
2013														
1st quarter	101.1	101.1	109.1	101.4	101.7	102.0	102.3	102.1	101.5	103.6	101.2	106.8	93.5	101.0
2nd quarter	101.3	101.2	118.3	102.6	99.3	102.0	101.8	103.5	101.0	102.9	100.3	107.6	93.7	101.1
3rd quarter	102.1	102.1	121.3	104.0	98.5	103.3	102.7	105.1	102.6	102.7	101.1	109.4	93.2	102.6
4th quarter	102.9	103.1	117.7	107.8	96.2	102.6	103.0	104.6	104.1	103.3	103.2	112.6	95.9	103.0
2014														
1st quarter	102.6	102.7	116.1	105.2	92.7	102.8	101.6	103.9	102.6	103.8	103.0	109.8	96.5	102.8
2nd quarter	104.0	104.3	117.6	111.2	94.3	104.4	103.3	106.9	104.8	105.2	103.6	111.5	99.3	103.3
3rd quarter	105.2	105.8	118.2	118.1	96.7	104.4	105.7	106.3	108.4	106.0	105.9	112.4	99.3	104.3
4th quarter	105.8	106.5	119.8	126.8	96.8	106.0	105.3	106.5	109.0	105.1	105.8	113.7	100.8	104.6
2015														
1st quarter	106.8	107.7	125.6	133.5	90.2	107.0	106.0	108.0	110.3	106.9	104.7	118.5	102.9	105.3
2nd quarter	107.6	108.5	124.6	120.0	95.6	109.2	106.0	107.3	111.4	108.8	107.0	121.6	104.9	105.6
3rd quarter	108.0	108.9	127.5	124.5	97.6	109.9	106.3	106.8	111.4	109.9	108.9	125.0	100.8	106.4
4th quarter	108.1	109.1	128.5	125.7	97.5	110.6	105.6	104.7	110.0	110.2	109.2	129.0	100.8	106.8
2016														
1st quarter	108.7	109.7	132.9	134.0	99.0	113.0	105.9	104.7	108.3	112.0	107.1	132.2	100.5	107.2
2nd quarter	109.1	110.1	132.4	116.6	99.0	112.5	105.3	105.8	108.9	112.0	109.1	133.2	102.7	108.0
3rd quarter	109.7	110.7	133.8	113.2	101.2	113.2	105.9	105.5	110.2	113.4	109.0	135.4	105.0	108.0
4th quarter	110.4	111.5	133.0	112.4	100.7	114.7	106.1	104.2	110.2	114.5	111.6	136.4	106.6	108.3
2017														
1st quarter	111.0	112.2	135.3	113.5	99.1	116.6	107.2	104.8	110.9	115.2	112.4	139.5	105.1	109.3
2nd quarter	111.5	112.7	131.7	119.5	100.0	115.8	108.1	107.2	110.8	116.2	113.2	141.3	102.0	110.1
3rd quarter	112.3	113.6	126.9	123.8	99.9	116.2	109.8	106.3	111.3	118.2	113.5	144.3	103.6	110.2
4th quarter	113.4	114.7	126.6	123.7	102.4	118.8	112.3	108.2	111.9	118.4	114.7	146.8	103.7	110.9
2018														
1st quarter	114.4	115.9	133.4	121.6	100.5	120.8	113.9	108.5	112.7	120.4	117.5	148.5	103.7	112.4
2nd quarter	115.2	116.7	136.5	126.0	102.8	120.1	114.3	109.5	111.5	119.3	117.5	153.0	104.3	113.3
3rd quarter	115.8	117.4	135.2	126.1	99.6	120.1	114.3	110.8	111.9	120.9	118.4	154.6	105.4	113.6
4th quarter	116.2	117.8	137.1	130.5	100.5	119.5	115.8	112.8	111.4	119.7	119.8	155.9	101.9	114.5
2019														
1st quarter	117.0	118.8	132.1	138.7	99.2	120.6	116.3	110.2	111.9	122.2	119.9	159.0	104.7	115.0
2nd quarter	117.4	119.2	135.4	140.4	102.7	119.8	116.1	111.9	108.9	121.2	121.2	162.7	104.2	115.5
3rd quarter	118.2	120.1	136.9	143.1	100.7	119.9	116.2	115.5	108.7	123.6	123.2	165.5	103.0	116.2
4th quarter	118.9	120.8	138.2	140.1	106.0	120.0	116.9	114.9	108.6	124.4	123.8	168.4	104.9	116.5
2020														
1st quarter	117.4	119.1	147.1	139.3	108.1	120.2	115.2	112.8	108.5	122.1	120.7	167.2	101.4	116.3
2nd quarter	106.8	107.6	131.4	122.2	105.7	111.3	99.9	104.3	97.5	111.3	93.0	164.3	104.2	113.3
3rd quarter	114.8	116.5	146.2	117.6	106.0	118.2	115.8	113.5	107.0	122.5	105.5	171.9	107.4	115.4
4th quarter	116.0	118.0	148.2	119.4	103.4	121.6	117.7	113.6	107.8	122.9	106.3	173.1	110.7	115.7

Table 14-2. Chain-Type Quantity Indexes for Value Added by Industry—*Continued*

(New Series, 2012 = 100.)

Year	Professional, scientific, and technical services	Management of companies and enterprises	Administrative and waste management services	Educational services	Health care and social assistance	Arts, entertainment, and recreation	Accommodation and food services	Other services except government	Total government	Federal	State and local	Private goods-producing industries	Private services-producing industries	Information-communications-technology-producing industries[1]
2000	71.1	91.8	71.3	71.4	70.0	80.5	94.5	124.0	91.6	87.4	93.7	94.0	77.6	38.9
2001	73.3	95.5	72.3	73.2	71.7	75.9	91.9	111.7	92.5	86.2	95.7	91.4	79.0	40.5
2002	75.1	94.6	72.0	73.6	74.9	79.3	93.8	114.8	94.2	87.9	97.3	91.6	80.8	42.8
2003	76.1	97.8	77.1	77.1	77.8	82.1	95.9	111.6	95.3	89.6	98.1	95.0	83.0	47.6
2004	78.7	92.2	81.1	81.8	81.3	84.9	100.6	113.0	96.2	91.2	98.6	100.5	85.9	54.5
2005	81.7	92.1	88.2	80.4	83.3	84.8	101.1	113.8	97.0	91.9	99.6	102.9	89.7	61.6
2006	84.9	91.8	90.2	82.4	86.9	87.5	103.7	114.4	97.6	92.3	100.2	107.4	92.3	68.1
2007	88.1	89.6	95.3	83.7	87.4	88.5	102.6	111.7	98.5	93.0	101.3	109.0	93.8	76.4
2008	94.9	90.2	95.4	89.1	93.0	89.6	99.1	107.6	100.4	95.5	102.9	104.9	94.2	84.8
2009	89.8	83.4	87.8	96.3	95.6	88.4	91.8	101.3	100.6	98.1	101.8	97.9	92.4	85.0
2010	92.0	89.2	93.8	99.1	96.3	92.9	94.9	99.4	101.1	100.3	101.4	98.7	95.2	92.7
2011	95.9	92.9	96.9	99.8	98.1	95.5	98.5	98.5	100.7	100.5	100.9	98.8	97.2	97.7
2012	100.0	100.0	100.0	100.0	100.0	100.0	100.0	100.0	100.0	100.0	100.0	100.0	100.0	100.0
2013	100.3	104.9	101.5	98.4	101.8	102.0	102.2	99.3	99.3	97.7	100.1	103.9	101.3	108.3
2014	104.6	111.9	105.4	99.5	103.8	106.6	105.6	102.1	99.1	97.1	100.0	106.8	104.3	113.3
2015	109.2	114.8	106.9	100.3	108.2	104.7	110.8	102.7	99.2	97.2	100.2	110.2	108.0	125.7
2016	112.5	116.2	107.3	103.2	111.3	108.3	111.6	101.9	100.2	98.0	101.2	110.4	110.5	137.1
2017	116.1	124.3	113.7	101.3	113.6	111.7	113.7	102.7	101.2	98.6	102.5	112.9	113.3	148.1
2018	122.2	132.8	117.9	102.9	116.9	115.7	115.5	106.0	102.3	99.2	103.7	117.4	116.8	...
2019	127.8	142.4	120.8	105.1	120.3	118.1	117.0	107.5	103.2	100.0	104.8	120.0	119.6	173.6
2020	125.8	142.6	114.6	97.4	113.7	73.4	88.8	93.9	101.1	103.0	100.3	116.8	114.9	...
2012														
1st quarter	99.0	97.3	100.0	100.3	99.9	99.9	99.2	99.6	100.4	100.4	101.0	99.3	99.3	...
2nd quarter	100.1	97.7	99.7	100.7	99.5	99.5	99.6	99.9	100.1	99.8	100.7	99.9	99.9	...
3rd quarter	100.0	99.8	100.0	100.0	99.7	99.7	99.7	100.2	99.9	99.8	99.1	100.4	100.4	...
4th quarter	100.8	105.2	100.4	99.0	100.8	100.8	101.5	100.3	99.5	100.0	99.3	100.4	100.4	...
2013														
1st quarter	100.0	101.2	100.2	98.1	101.6	101.6	101.3	99.4	99.0	100.2	102.5	100.8	100.8	...
2nd quarter	99.3	103.6	101.0	98.1	101.7	101.7	101.4	98.9	98.3	100.2	103.4	100.6	100.6	...
3rd quarter	100.3	106.5	102.1	98.3	101.8	101.8	101.4	99.0	97.3	100.1	104.8	101.4	101.4	...
4th quarter	101.5	108.4	102.8	99.3	102.2	102.2	103.9	99.7	96.1	99.9	104.9	102.6	102.6	...
2014														
1st quarter	101.8	112.4	103.5	98.4	102.3	102.3	105.5	99.9	97.5	99.6	103.8	102.4	102.4	...
2nd quarter	103.3	110.7	105.3	99.3	103.0	103.0	106.5	101.7	97.2	100.2	106.4	103.7	103.7	...
3rd quarter	106.4	111.9	106.0	100.2	104.4	104.4	107.4	103.4	96.9	100.1	107.9	105.2	105.2	...
4th quarter	106.9	112.7	106.6	100.1	105.4	105.4	107.0	103.5	96.7	100.2	109.1	105.8	105.8	...
2015														
1st quarter	107.9	114.6	106.9	100.1	107.1	107.1	104.9	103.3	97.1	99.6	110.7	106.9	106.9	...
2nd quarter	108.7	114.7	106.7	99.7	107.8	107.8	104.2	103.3	97.2	100.1	109.9	108.1	108.1	...
3rd quarter	109.9	114.9	107.2	100.0	108.7	108.7	104.5	102.4	97.2	100.4	110.4	108.4	108.4	...
4th quarter	110.4	115.2	106.9	101.5	109.3	109.3	105.4	102.0	97.3	100.5	109.8	108.8	108.8	...
2016														
1st quarter	112.1	114.8	106.5	102.9	110.6	110.6	106.5	102.1	97.6	100.7	111.1	109.3	109.3	...
2nd quarter	112.3	115.7	106.3	103.6	111.3	111.3	107.1	101.7	97.9	100.8	110.1	110.0	110.0	...
3rd quarter	112.1	116.4	107.1	103.0	111.1	111.1	108.4	101.9	98.2	101.5	110.2	110.8	110.8	...
4th quarter	113.5	118.1	109.2	103.4	112.2	112.2	111.4	101.8	98.3	101.8	110.1	111.8	111.8	...
2017														
1st quarter	114.0	119.6	111.6	102.0	112.8	112.8	109.1	101.8	98.5	102.1	111.3	112.3	112.3	...
2nd quarter	115.4	122.2	113.1	101.0	113.4	113.4	110.5	102.0	98.4	102.3	112.4	112.7	112.7	...
3rd quarter	116.6	124.5	114.4	101.2	113.7	113.7	113.9	103.1	98.6	102.6	113.0	113.7	113.7	...
4th quarter	118.2	130.7	115.8	101.0	114.4	114.4	113.2	103.9	98.8	103.0	115.1	114.6	114.6	...
2018														
1st quarter	120.2	129.0	116.4	102.3	116.1	116.1	113.1	104.9	98.9	103.2	116.3	115.8	115.8	...
2nd quarter	121.9	130.7	117.0	102.5	116.5	116.5	116.9	105.9	99.2	103.6	117.1	116.6	116.6	...
3rd quarter	122.7	135.2	118.2	103.0	117.1	117.1	116.3	106.2	99.4	103.9	117.4	117.3	117.3	...
4th quarter	123.9	136.4	120.1	103.7	118.0	118.0	116.4	107.2	99.1	104.3	118.9	117.5	117.5	...
2019														
1st quarter	125.9	140.4	120.0	103.9	119.5	119.5	117.1	107.4	98.1	104.4	118.9	118.7	118.7	...
2nd quarter	126.8	142.3	120.2	104.7	120.0	120.0	117.0	107.2	100.0	104.7	119.5	119.1	119.1	...
3rd quarter	128.9	142.8	121.1	105.5	120.6	120.6	119.3	107.9	100.7	104.7	120.8	119.8	119.8	...
4th quarter	129.9	144.3	121.8	106.3	121.3	121.3	118.8	107.4	101.1	105.5	120.8	120.7	120.7	...
2020														
1st quarter	129.5	142.9	121.0	105.4	119.0	119.0	110.1	103.7	101.6	104.3	119.9	118.9	118.9	...
2nd quarter	119.8	139.7	103.2	93.0	101.0	101.0	46.3	83.1	102.5	97.2	107.9	107.5	107.5	...
3rd quarter	125.8	142.3	114.3	97.1	116.2	116.2	65.3	94.2	104.1	100.0	118.8	115.9	115.9	...
4th quarter	128.0	145.3	119.9	94.2	118.5	118.5	71.9	94.7	103.7	99.7	120.6	117.3	117.3	...

[1]Consists of computer and electronic products manufacturing; publishing, including software; information and data processing services; and computer systems design and related services.
. . . = Not available.

Table 14-3. Gross Domestic Factor Income by Industry

(Billions of current dollars.)

NAICS industry	2007	2008	2009	2010	2011	2012	2013	2014	2015	2016	2017	2018	2019
Gross domestic factor income, total	13 469.6	13 715.7	13 480.5	13 984.8	14 498.8	15 119.0	15 655.9	16 344.6	17 020.3	17 495.0	18 238.9	19 230.4	20 015.7
Compensation of employees	7 889.4	8 068.7	7 767.2	7 933.0	8 234.0	8 575.4	8 843.6	9 259.7	9 709.5	9 974.8	10 433.1	10 960.6	11 444.5
Gross operating surplus	5 580.2	5 647.0	5 713.3	6 051.8	6 264.8	6 543.6	6 812.3	7 084.9	7 310.8	7 520.2	7 805.8	8 269.8	8 571.2
Private industries	11 563.9	11 713.7	11 412.9	11 856.1	12 339.1	12 937.0	13 418.8	14 048.0	14 656.4	15 084.3	15 764.9	16 653.8	17 348.8
Compensation of employees	6 369.8	6 475.5	6 126.3	6 241.3	6 532.0	6 871.6	7 095.3	7 468.7	7 863.2	8 088.0	8 497.0	8 944.2	9 358.3
Gross operating surplus	5 194.1	5 238.2	5 286.6	5 614.8	5 807.1	6 065.4	6 323.5	6 579.3	6 793.2	6 996.3	7 267.9	7 709.6	7 990.5
Agriculture, forestry, fishing, and hunting	146.6	148.8	131.8	147.9	180.2	178.5	214.3	196.9	180.0	167.1	175.0	179.1	185.0
Compensation of employees	41.8	42.1	42.3	41.4	41.2	48.1	48.9	51.0	50.6	53.7	56.2	55.1	57.7
Gross operating surplus	104.8	106.7	89.5	106.5	139.0	130.4	165.4	145.9	129.4	113.4	118.8	124.0	127.3
Mining	280.2	349.7	246.0	272.6	318.4	318.5	344.6	369.9	221.7	180.3	234.7	287.0	264.4
Compensation of employees	62.7	72.8	64.7	69.2	80.3	90.5	93.5	101.1	91.9	74.5	76.8	84.5	86.6
Gross operating surplus	217.5	276.9	181.3	203.4	238.1	228.0	251.1	268.8	129.8	105.8	157.9	202.5	177.8
Utilities	180.3	188.2	203.1	222.0	229.4	220.8	227.0	238.8	240.2	241.5	248.3	258.3	270.7
Compensation of employees	63.1	66.3	66.8	67.7	71.2	69.8	72.8	75.2	77.6	81.4	81.7	84.3	88.2
Gross operating surplus	117.2	121.9	136.3	154.3	158.2	151.0	154.2	163.6	162.6	160.1	166.6	174.0	182.5
Construction	707.0	641.0	558.3	517.9	517.2	545.9	579.6	628.5	686.0	737.3	787.7	837.6	881.6
Compensation of employees	440.0	433.9	368.4	343.8	347.3	365.9	388.0	422.4	458.5	485.9	520.1	557.6	592.4
Gross operating surplus	267.0	207.1	189.9	174.1	169.9	180.0	191.6	206.1	227.5	251.4	267.6	280.0	289.2
Durable goods manufacturing	1 005.4	974.0	854.9	939.1	989.9	1 036.3	1 073.2	1 104.7	1 153.5	1 157.2	1 196.9	1 256.3	1 288.4
Compensation of employees	627.4	615.5	539.2	546.2	578.7	604.4	612.0	638.6	662.7	666.0	695.1	732.1	749.7
Gross operating surplus	378.0	358.5	315.7	392.9	411.2	431.9	461.2	466.1	490.8	491.2	501.8	524.2	538.7
Nondurable goods manufacturing	775.0	761.4	772.0	781.8	798.9	811.6	834.3	861.2	890.5	857.5	896.6	968.7	968.4
Compensation of employees	316.2	316.4	296.0	301.0	303.7	312.6	319.8	334.5	343.7	347.2	359.1	369.1	381.7
Gross operating surplus	458.8	445.0	476.0	480.8	495.2	499.0	514.5	526.7	546.8	510.3	537.5	599.6	586.7
Wholesale trade	685.4	712.5	676.0	718.7	749.9	804.9	837.8	880.4	932.5	921.6	941.3	963.9	985.5
Compensation of employees	429.3	435.7	405.1	412.3	436.2	457.7	467.6	489.9	509.8	511.1	533.1	545.4	558.6
Gross operating surplus	256.1	276.8	270.9	306.4	313.7	347.2	370.2	390.5	422.7	410.5	408.2	418.5	426.9
Retail trade	688.2	670.1	661.7	673.1	684.8	713.8	744.1	760.5	803.2	829.7	851.5	875.3	912.3
Compensation of employees	506.4	500.9	474.3	478.9	495.7	510.1	526.7	545.5	573.6	587.8	606.9	628.3	650.5
Gross operating surplus	181.8	169.2	187.4	194.2	189.1	203.7	217.4	215.0	229.6	241.9	244.6	247.0	261.8
Transportation and warehousing	388.2	400.7	378.1	407.6	424.0	443.7	459.7	488.6	530.8	545.4	568.2	609.8	653.6
Compensation of employees	255.9	255.6	241.1	245.5	259.9	274.8	283.4	296.8	320.0	332.8	352.5	379.0	408.6
Gross operating surplus	132.3	145.1	137.0	162.1	164.1	168.9	176.3	191.8	210.8	212.6	215.7	230.8	245.0
Information	658.9	698.2	677.9	708.9	714.6	713.6	781.5	793.6	851.7	912.1	946.1	997.3	1 066.3
Compensation of employees	260.5	257.8	251.5	248.6	260.1	271.6	286.5	304.4	318.7	329.0	348.4	376.2	399.6
Gross operating surplus	398.4	440.4	426.4	460.3	454.5	442.0	495.0	489.2	533.0	583.1	597.7	621.1	666.7
Finance and insurance	988.2	829.5	922.9	959.5	980.9	1 117.5	1 097.8	1 225.2	1 299.6	1 391.3	1 454.2	1 558.9	1 604.5
Compensation of employees	617.4	612.1	548.0	573.3	606.5	630.1	641.3	681.1	715.7	734.2	787.5	818.4	850.5
Gross operating surplus	370.8	217.4	374.9	386.2	374.4	487.4	456.5	544.1	583.9	657.1	666.7	740.5	754.0
Real estate and rental and leasing	1 612.6	1 675.7	1 677.1	1 714.9	1 792.1	1 868.1	1 941.1	2 017.5	2 129.9	2 220.8	2 322.6	2 448.3	2 577.9
Compensation of employees	112.2	110.3	103.7	103.8	106.4	114.3	118.9	126.4	136.7	140.7	148.7	158.9	168.9
Gross operating surplus	1 500.4	1 565.4	1 573.4	1 611.1	1 685.7	1 753.8	1 822.2	1 891.1	1 993.2	2 080.1	2 173.9	2 289.4	2 409.0
Professional, scientific, and technical services	949.8	1 051.9	1 008.6	1 040.2	1 099.4	1 161.3	1 177.7	1 234.6	1 313.4	1 357.1	1 418.4	1 508.7	1 597.0
Compensation of employees	655.0	693.5	669.4	682.7	727.1	776.7	801.5	848.9	909.4	939.1	990.3	1 059.0	1 126.1
Gross operating surplus	294.8	358.4	339.2	357.5	372.3	384.6	376.2	385.7	404.0	418.0	428.1	449.7	470.9
Management of companies and enterprises	243.4	247.2	236.6	257.1	269.7	293.8	311.2	324.5	339.4	342.1	363.4	383.0	401.7
Compensation of employees	219.9	221.1	207.9	227.2	237.9	259.4	275.0	287.4	302.3	304.6	324.7	342.8	360.0
Gross operating surplus	23.5	26.1	28.7	29.9	31.8	34.4	36.2	37.1	37.1	37.5	38.7	40.2	41.7
Administrative and waste management services	421.3	429.1	403.1	427.7	443.7	463.1	477.6	505.8	528.0	546.3	587.9	617.2	646.1
Compensation of employees	310.1	314.1	289.2	306.5	321.9	341.3	353.7	376.7	398.1	409.8	439.3	463.8	482.9
Gross operating surplus	111.2	115.0	113.9	121.2	121.8	121.8	123.9	129.1	129.9	136.5	148.6	153.4	163.2
Educational services	145.2	160.9	180.7	191.0	198.1	205.9	209.2	218.0	225.0	237.2	239.1	248.8	259.9
Compensation of employees	120.9	129.4	139.9	145.5	152.8	161.4	165.2	174.9	180.4	190.5	192.0	200.1	209.4
Gross operating surplus	24.3	31.5	40.8	45.5	45.3	44.5	44.0	43.1	44.6	46.7	47.1	48.7	50.5
Health care and social assistance	913.5	993.6	1 054.6	1 087.0	1 127.8	1 169.6	1 205.4	1 241.1	1 310.4	1 376.3	1 426.9	1 490.1	1 561.0
Compensation of employees	775.1	824.6	862.4	888.5	922.0	963.6	997.3	1 028.3	1 085.1	1 136.6	1 187.2	1 247.7	1 305.7
Gross operating surplus	138.4	169.0	192.2	198.5	205.8	206.0	208.1	212.8	225.3	239.7	239.7	242.4	255.3
Arts, entertainment, and recreation	122.3	127.7	129.5	136.7	142.3	153.8	159.4	170.4	174.0	186.7	194.7	205.8	215.1
Compensation of employees	77.0	80.6	78.6	79.4	81.5	86.1	89.7	96.7	100.9	108.1	113.3	120.1	125.1
Gross operating surplus	45.3	47.1	50.9	57.3	60.8	67.7	69.7	73.7	73.1	78.6	81.4	85.7	90.0
Accommodation and food services	339.3	340.7	331.1	342.5	363.1	387.6	407.2	432.1	476.1	499.3	521.1	546.4	573.3
Compensation of employees	247.8	252.5	242.8	248.3	262.4	282.5	295.8	316.2	340.9	360.2	379.0	399.5	419.5
Gross operating surplus	91.5	88.2	88.3	94.2	100.7	105.1	111.4	115.9	135.2	139.1	142.1	146.9	153.8
Other services, except government	313.1	312.6	308.9	310.1	314.7	329.0	336.3	356.0	370.2	377.5	390.6	413.4	436.0
Compensation of employees	231.1	240.1	235.1	231.7	239.3	250.9	257.9	272.8	286.4	294.9	305.3	322.4	336.5
Gross operating surplus	82.0	72.5	73.8	78.4	75.4	78.1	78.4	83.2	83.8	82.6	85.3	91.0	99.5
Government	1 905.8	2 002.0	2 067.6	2 128.8	2 159.8	2 182.0	2 237.1	2 296.6	2 364.0	2 410.8	2 474.0	2 576.5	2 666.9
Compensation of employees	1 519.6	1 593.2	1 640.9	1 691.7	1 702.0	1 703.8	1 748.4	1 791.0	1 846.3	1 886.9	1 936.1	2 016.3	2 086.2
Gross operating surplus	386.2	408.8	426.7	437.1	457.8	478.2	488.7	505.6	517.7	523.9	537.9	560.2	580.7
Addenda:													
Private goods-producing industries	2 914.4	2 875.0	2 562.9	2 659.2	2 804.6	2 890.8	3 046.0	3 161.1	3 131.7	3 099.4	3 290.8	3 528.8	3 587.7
Compensation of employees	1 488.2	1 480.8	1 310.5	1 301.5	1 351.1	1 421.4	1 462.2	1 547.5	1 607.4	1 627.3	1 707.2	1 798.5	1 868.0
Gross operating surplus	1 426.2	1 394.2	1 252.4	1 357.7	1 453.5	1 469.4	1 583.8	1 613.6	1 524.3	1 472.1	1 583.6	1 730.3	1 719.7
Private services-producing industries	8 649.5	8 838.7	8 849.9	9 196.9	9 534.5	10 046.1	10 372.8	10 886.9	11 524.6	11 984.8	12 474.1	13 125.1	13 761.1
Compensation of employees	4 881.6	4 994.7	4 815.8	4 939.8	5 180.9	5 450.1	5 633.1	5 921.2	6 255.8	6 460.7	6 789.8	7 145.7	7 490.3
Gross operating surplus	3 767.9	3 844.0	4 034.1	4 257.1	4 353.6	4 596.0	4 739.7	4 965.7	5 268.8	5 524.1	5 684.3	5 979.4	6 270.8
Information-communications-technology-producing industries [1]	804.9	859.3	844.9	892.9	928.6	939.2	1 014.1	1 045.0	1 125.4	1 198.0	1 261.2	1 348.9	1 447.9
Compensation of employees	420.3	422.2	410.6	423.0	453.6	483.8	501.4	536.2	571.7	597.2	641.2	692.1	738.9
Gross operating surplus	384.6	437.1	434.3	469.9	475.0	455.4	512.7	508.8	553.7	600.8	620.0	656.8	709.0

[1]Consists of computer and electronic products manufacturing; publishing, including software; information and data processing services; and computer systems design and related services.

NOTES AND DEFINITIONS, CHAPTER 14

TABLES 14-1 THROUGH 14-3

Gross Domestic Product (VALUE ADDED) and Gross Factor Income by Industry

SOURCE: U.S. DEPARTMENT OF COMMERCE, BUREAU OF ECONOMIC ANALYSIS (BEA)

In the introduction to the notes and definitions for Chapter 1, it was observed that gross domestic product (GDP), while primarily measured as the sum of final demands for goods and services, is also the sum of the values created by each industry in the economy. In this chapter, selected data are presented from the industry accounts in the national income and product accounts (NIPAs). The industry accounts measure the contribution of each major industry to GDP.

New in the 25th edition of *Business Statistics* are updated quarterly estimates of current- and constant-dollar GDP by industry. They provide a complete accounting of the industrial origin of GDP, and measure the output of major industries on a more up-to-date basis than the annual measures previously available—within 120 days after the end of the reference quarter.

In recent years, estimates of GDP by industry have been prepared using a methodology integrated with annual input-output accounts in order to produce estimates of gross industry output, industry input, and the difference between the two—industry value added—with greater consistency and timeliness than was previously possible. The current integrated industry accounts also include a wealth of related information too extensive for inclusion here, such as quantity and price indexes for gross output and intermediate inputs, cost per unit of real value added allocated to the three components of value added, and components of domestic supply (domestic output, imports, exports, and inventory change).

The most precise estimates of GDP by NAICS industry begin with 1997, but the annual series were extended back to 1947, using approximations of current methods in earlier years when the source data were less comprehensive and were initially compiled on the older SIC classifications. Table 14-1B presents this "old series" current-dollar GDP for NAICS industry groups from 1947 through 2009; Table 14-2B presents "old series" indexes of real value added for each industry group.

The 2019 comprehensive benchmark revision incorporated three major types of revisions: 1) statistical changes to introduce new and improved technologies and newly available source data; 2) changes in definitions to more accurately portray the evolving U.S. economy to more accurately portray the evolving U.S.

economy and to provide consistent comparisons with data for other national economies; and 3) changes in presentations to reflect the definitional and statistical changes, where necessary, or to provide additional data or perspective for users. Also output and price measures will be expressed with 2012 equal to 100. The estimates for most tables showing real, or chained-dollar, estimates will begin with 2002.

In Table 14-3, the editor presents a measure derived from the components of current-dollar value added as published by BEA. This measure, "gross domestic factor income," enables users to obtain a clearer picture of the quantitative impact of each industry on the economy's factors of production and of the shares of capital and labor in each industry.

The 2004 revision incorporated a change in terminology. An industry's contribution to total GDP, formerly referred to as "gross product originating" (GPO) or "gross product by industry," is now called "value added." This is consistent with the use of the term "value added" in most economic writing. However, it should not be confused with a concept known as "Census value added," which is used in U.S. censuses and surveys of manufactures. Census value added is calculated at the individual establishment level and, for that reason, does not exclude purchased business services. This means that census value added, while still an important gauge of relative importance, is not a true measure of economic value added.

Definitions and notes on the data

An industry's *gross domestic product (value added)*, formerly *GPO*, is equal to the market value of its gross output (which consists of the value, including taxes, of sales or receipts and other operating income plus the value of inventory change) minus the value of its intermediate inputs (energy, raw materials, semi finished goods, and services that are purchased from domestic industries or from foreign sources).

In concept, this is also equal to the sum of *compensation of employees, taxes on production and imports less subsidies,* and *gross operating surplus.* (See Chapter 1 and its notes and definitions for more information.)

The GDP data from 1997 forward are not comparable with the "old series" data for earlier years presented in Tables 14-1B and 14-2B, the major reason being that they do not reflect the conceptual revisions introduced in the comprehensive 2018 revision of the NIPAs (see the Notes and Definitions to Chapter 1). In particular, the new data include, while the old data exclude, the capitalized values of research and development, intellectual property, and all real estate transfer costs. This does not change labor compensation values—the associated workers were always included; it was just that their costs were taken to be written off in the first year. But it does increase across the board the non-labor share of the total value of output, by the amount of capital consumption and net investment. This is seen in labor compensation shares derived from Table 14-3, compared with those that would have been calculated on the old basis last year.

Compensation of employees consists of wage and salary accruals and supplements to wages and salaries. This approximates the labor share of production, subject to the note below about proprietors' income.

Taxes on production and imports less subsidies. Although this is shown in BEA source data as a single net line item, it represents two separate components.

Taxes on production and imports are included in the market value of the goods and services sold to final consumers and therefore in the consumer valuation of those goods. Since they are not part of the payments to the labor and capital inputs in the producing industries, they must be added to the sum of the returns to those inputs in order to account for the total value to consumers. Taxes that fall into this classification include property taxes, sales and excise taxes, and Customs duties.

BEA allocates these taxes to the industry level at which they are assessed by law. Most sales taxes are considered by BEA to be part of the value added by retail trade. Some sales taxes, most fuel taxes, and all customs duties are allocated by BEA to wholesale trade. Residential real property taxes, including those on owner-occupied dwellings, are allocated by BEA to the real estate industry.

Subsidies to business by government are included in the labor and/or capital payments made by that industry. Since they are payments to the industry in addition to the market values paid by consumers, they are *subtracted* from the values of the labor and capital inputs to make them consistent with the market values as defined in value added. The role of subsidies is obvious in the source data for the agricultural sector, where the net "taxes on production and imports less subsidies" has a negative sign: farm subsidies more than offset this industry's taxes on production and imports, which mainly consist of property taxes, since sales, excise, and import taxes are not levied on farms.

For private sector businesses, *gross operating surplus* consists of business income (corporate profits before tax, proprietors' income, and rental income of persons), net interest and miscellaneous payments, business current transfer payments (net), and capital consumption allowances. For government, households, and institutions, it consists of consumption of fixed capital and (for government) government enterprises' current surplus. This

approximates the share of the value of production ascribable to capital and land as measured in the NIPAs accounts; however, as BEA notes, "an unknown portion [of proprietors' income] reflects the labor contribution of proprietors." (*Survey of Current Business*, June 2004, p. 27, footnote 7.) Another aspect to be noted is that gross operating surplus includes the return to owner-occupied housing in the real estate sector. Because there is in the NIPAs no employee compensation attributed to owner-occupied housing, the capital share in that industry as measured by gross operating surplus is very large.

Quantity indexes for value added. Measures of the constant-dollar change in each industry's gross output minus its intermediate input use are calculated by BEA, using a Fisher index-number formula which incorporates weights from two adjacent years. The changes for successive years are chained together in indexes, with the value for the year 2012 set at 100. The indexes are multiplied by 2012 current-dollar value added to provide estimates of value added in "chained 2012 dollars," but because the actual weights used change from year to year, components in chained 2012 dollars typically do not add up to total GDP in 2009 dollars—and do not contain any information not already summarized in the indexes. For that reason, only the indexes are published here.

Gross domestic factor income (not a category published as such in the NIPAs) is calculated by the editor as the sum of "compensation of employees" and "gross operating surplus," which the same as value added minus "taxes on production and imports less subsidies." The effect of this procedure is to take out the specified taxes, and to leave in the subsidies embedded in the employee compensation and gross operating surplus components. The editor believes that this provides a valuable alternative basis for assessing the importance of different industries in the economy, by measuring the value paid for by its labor and capital inputs, and for calculating the shares of labor and capital in each industry's output. The components shown in this table are found on the BEA website in a table entitled "Components of Value Added by Industry."

The editor's reasoning is based on the facts that more than half of these taxes are sales, excise, and import taxes, and the assignment of these taxes to industries is economically arbitrary. BEA assigns them to the industry with the legal liability to pay, not to the entity bearing the major incidence of the tax. Yet economists have demonstrated that most of the burdens of sales and excise taxes and import duties are not borne by the factors in the legally liable industry; instead, they are passed on to consumers. In addition, because the wholesale and retail trade industries are classified as "services-producing," BEA's allocation of those taxes has a very peculiar result: taxes on goods are represented as paid by "service" industries. The process adopted instead by the editor in Table 14-3, which excludes these taxes and focuses on "gross domestic factor income," has the effect (for example) of keeping the wholesale trade industry from appearing to be both larger and more heavily taxed than it really is.

Private goods-producing industries consists of agriculture, forestry, fishing, and hunting; mining; construction; and manufacturing.

Private services-producing industries consists of utilities; wholesale trade; retail trade; transportation and warehousing; information; finance, insurance, real estate, rental, and leasing; professional and business services; educational services, health care, and social assistance; arts, entertainment, recreation, accommodation, and food services; and other services, except government.

Information-communications-technology-producing industries is a category that cuts across the goods and services framework, consisting of computer and electronic products manufacturing; publishing industries (which includes software) from the information sector; information and data processing services; and computer systems design and related services.

Data availability and references

The comprehensive revision of the industry accounts from 1997 forward and the new quarterly statistics are described in "Industry Economic Accounts: Results of the Comprehensive Revision, Revised Statistics for 1997-2012" (*Survey of Current Business,* February 2014); "New Quarterly Statistics Detail Industries' Economic Performance," BEA news release, April 25, 2014; and "Prototype Quarterly Statistics on U.S. GDP by Industry, 2007-2011," June 2012, a "BEA Briefing." All are available on the BEA website, https://www.bea.gov. To access the historical data at <https://www.bea.gov>, click on "Annual Industry Accounts" and click on "Interactive Tables" under "Gross Domestic Product (GDP) by Industry."

"Old basis" annual GDP by industry data shown here were recalculated back to 1947 consistent with the 2009 comprehensive revision of the NIPAs. They were most recently presented and described in "Annual Industry Statistics: Revised Statistics for 2009-2011," *Survey of Current Business*, December 2012.

CHAPTER 15: EMPLOYMENT, HOURS, AND EARNINGS BY NAICS INDUSTRY

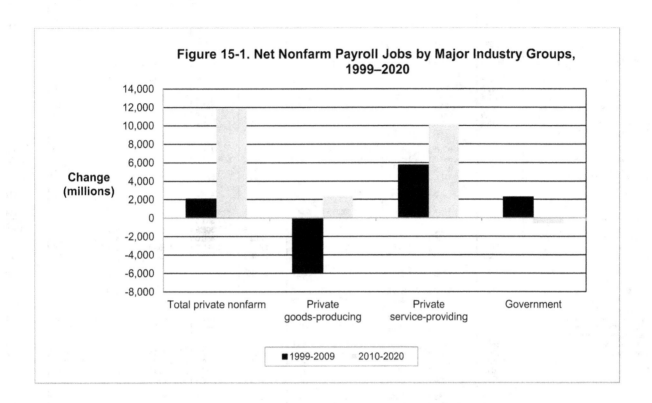

Figure 15-1. Net Nonfarm Payroll Jobs by Major Industry Groups, 1999–2020

- In 2020, total nonfarm employment decreased 5.8 percent after increasing for nine consecutive years. It decreased in all major sectors falling 4.6 percent in goods-producing industries, 6.0 percent in service-providing industries, and -3.1 percent in government. In 2020, employment began to decline due to the global pandemic. (Table 15-1)

- During the Great Recession, employment declined dramatically. In 2014, employment finally exceeded 2007 employment. In 2007, there were 137.9 million nonfarm employees versus 138.9 million in 2014, an increase of 0.7 percent. Employment declined significantly again in 2020 but employment levels remained above 2007 levels. (Table 15-1)

- Although the number of service-providing jobs declined in 2020, service-providing employment was still 13.7 percent higher than it was twenty years earlier in 2000. In contrast, goods-producing employment has declined 18.6 percent since 2000. (Table 15-1)

- The average workweek for production and nonsupervisory workers increased in 2020 after decreasing in 2019. In 2020, goods-producing workers averaged 40.3 hours per week while private service-providing workers averaged far less at 32.8 hours. (Table 15-3)

- Average hourly earnings for production and nonsupervisory workers in 2020 ranged from a low of $14.72 in the leisure and hospitality sector to $39.21 in petroleum and coal products manufacturing. (Table 15-4)

Table 15-1. Nonfarm Employment by Sector and Industry

(Wage and salary workers on nonfarm payrolls, thousands.)

Industry	1999	2000	2001	2002	2003	2004	2005	2006	2007	2008	2009
TOTAL NONFARM	129 228	132 011	132 073	130 634	130 331	131 769	134 034	136 435	137 981	137 224	131 296
Total Private	108 921	111 221	110 955	109 121	108 748	110 148	112 230	114 462	115 763	114 714	108 741
Goods-Producing	24 465	24 649	23 873	22 557	21 816	21 882	22 190	22 530	22 233	21 335	18 558
Mining and logging	598	599	606	583	572	591	628	684	724	767	694
Logging	80.8	79.0	73.5	70.4	69.4	67.6	65.2	64.4	60.1	56.6	50.4
Mining	517.4	520.2	532.5	512.2	502.7	523.0	562.2	619.7	663.8	709.8	643.3
Oil and gas extraction	131.2	124.9	123.7	121.9	120.2	123.4	125.7	134.5	146.2	160.5	159.8
Mining, except oil and gas [1]	234.5	224.8	218.7	210.6	202.7	205.1	212.8	220.3	223.4	226.0	208.3
Coal mining	78.6	72.2	74.3	74.4	70.0	70.6	73.9	78.0	77.2	81.2	81.5
Support activities for mining	151.7	170.6	190.1	179.8	179.8	194.6	223.7	264.9	294.3	323.4	275.2
Construction	6 545	6 787	6 826	6 716	6 735	6 976	7 336	7 691	7 630	7 162	6 016
Construction of buildings	1 586.3	1 632.5	1 588.9	1 574.8	1 575.8	1 630.0	1 711.9	1 804.9	1 774.2	1 641.7	1 357.2
Heavy and civil engineering	908.7	937.0	953.0	930.6	903.1	907.4	951.2	985.1	1 005.4	964.5	851.3
Specialty trade contractors	4 049.6	4 217.0	4 283.9	4 210.4	4 255.7	4 438.6	4 673.1	4 901.1	4 850.2	4 555.8	3 807.9
Manufacturing	17 322	17 263	16 441	15 259	14 509	14 315	14 227	14 155	13 879	13 406	11 847
Durable goods	10 831	10 877	10 336	9 485	8 964	8 925	8 956	8 981	8 808	8 463	7 284
Wood products	622.7	615.4	576.3	557.0	539.5	551.6	561.0	560.6	517.1	457.7	360.2
Nonmetallic mineral products	540.8	554.2	544.5	516.0	494.2	505.5	505.3	509.6	500.5	465.0	394.3
Primary metals	625.0	621.8	570.9	509.4	477.4	466.8	466.0	464.0	455.8	442.0	362.1
Fabricated metal products	1 728.4	1 752.6	1 676.4	1 548.5	1 478.9	1 497.1	1 522.0	1 553.1	1 562.8	1 527.5	1 311.6
Machinery	1 468.3	1 457.0	1 370.6	1 231.8	1 151.6	1 145.2	1 165.5	1 183.2	1 187.1	1 187.6	1 028.6
Computer and electronic products [1]	1 780.5	1 820.0	1 748.8	1 507.2	1 355.2	1 322.8	1 316.4	1 307.5	1 272.5	1 244.2	1 136.9
Computer and peripheral equipment	310.1	301.9	286.2	250.0	224.0	210.0	205.1	196.2	186.2	183.2	166.4
Communications equipment	228.7	238.6	225.4	179.0	149.2	143.0	141.4	136.2	128.1	127.3	120.5
Semiconductors and electronic components	630.5	676.3	645.4	524.5	461.1	454.1	452.0	457.9	447.5	431.8	378.1
Electronic instruments	498.3	487.7	483.6	456.8	435.4	436.9	441.0	444.5	443.2	441.0	421.6
Electrical equipment and appliances	588.0	590.9	556.9	496.5	459.6	445.1	433.5	432.7	429.4	424.3	373.6
Transportation equipment [1]	2 088.6	2 057.1	1 939.1	1 830.0	1 775.1	1 766.7	1 772.3	1 768.9	1 711.9	1 608.0	1 347.9
Motor vehicles and parts	1 312.5	1 313.6	1 212.9	1 151.2	1 125.3	1 112.8	1 096.7	1 070.0	994.2	875.5	664.1
Furniture and related products	665.2	680.1	642.9	604.7	573.7	574.1	566.3	558.3	529.4	478.0	384.3
Miscellaneous manufacturing	724.0	728.0	709.5	683.3	658.3	650.6	647.2	643.7	641.7	628.9	584.4
Nondurable goods [1]	6 491	6 386	6 105	5 774	5 546	5 390	5 271	5 174	5 071	4 943	4 564
Food manufacturing	1 549.8	1 553.1	1 551.2	1 525.7	1 517.5	1 493.7	1 477.6	1 479.4	1 484.1	1 480.9	1 456.4
Textile mills	397.1	378.2	332.9	290.9	261.3	236.9	217.6	195.0	169.7	151.2	124.4
Textile product mills	232.4	229.6	217.0	204.2	187.7	183.2	176.4	166.7	157.7	147.2	125.7
Apparel	540.5	483.5	415.2	350.0	303.9	278.0	250.5	232.4	214.6	199.0	167.5
Paper and paper products	615.6	604.7	577.6	546.6	516.2	495.5	484.2	470.5	458.2	444.9	407.0
Printing and related support activities	814.6	806.8	768.3	706.6	680.4	662.6	646.3	634.4	622.0	594.1	521.9
Petroleum and coal products	127.8	123.2	121.1	118.1	114.3	111.7	112.1	113.2	114.5	117.4	115.3
Chemicals	982.5	980.4	959.0	927.5	906.1	887.0	872.1	865.9	860.9	847.1	804.1
Plastics and rubber products	947.0	950.9	896.2	846.8	814.3	804.7	802.3	785.5	757.2	729.4	624.9
Service-Providing	104 763	107 362	108 200	108 077	108 515	109 887	111 843	113 905	115 748	115 889	112 739
Private Service-Providing	84 456	86 572	87 082	86 564	86 931	88 266	90 039	91 931	93 530	93 380	90 184
Trade, transportation, and utilities	25 722	26 174	25 931	25 442	25 228	25 470	25 892	26 206	26 556	26 219	24 834
Wholesale trade	5 848.0	5 888.4	5 728.0	5 605.5	5 556.4	5 607.8	5 705.7	5 841.9	5 948.4	5 874.9	5 520.9
Durable goods	3 310.2	3 342.4	3 221.4	3 103.7	3 044.5	3 062.5	3 118.8	3 202.7	3 257.3	3 190.6	2 944.0
Nondurable goods	2 126.8	2 131.1	2 097.3	2 084.6	2 079.9	2 091.1	2 109.2	2 133.9	2 160.7	2 148.2	2 063.3
Electronic markets, agents, and brokers	411.1	414.9	409.3	417.3	432.1	454.2	477.8	505.3	530.4	536.1	513.7
Retail trade	14 973.9	15 283.6	15 242.4	15 029.0	14 921.7	15 062.7	15 284.5	15 358.5	15 525.5	15 288.8	14 527.9
Motor vehicle and parts dealers [1]	1 796.6	1 846.9	1 854.6	1 879.4	1 882.9	1 902.3	1 918.6	1 909.7	1 908.3	1 831.2	1 637.5
Automobile dealers	1 179.7	1 216.5	1 225.1	1 252.8	1 254.4	1 257.3	1 261.4	1 246.7	1 242.2	1 176.7	1 018.2
Furniture and home furnishings stores	524.4	543.5	541.2	538.7	547.3	563.4	576.1	586.9	574.6	531.1	449.2
Electronics and appliance stores	624.2	647.7	633.0	595.2	574.4	572.0	585.5	581.1	583.1	570.2	516.3
Building material and garden supply stores	1 101.6	1 142.7	1 152.3	1 177.1	1 185.7	1 227.8	1 276.8	1 324.8	1 310.1	1 248.8	1 156.4
Food and beverage stores	2 984.5	2 993.0	2 950.5	2 881.6	2 838.4	2 821.6	2 817.8	2 821.1	2 843.6	2 862.0	2 830.0
Health and personal care stores	898.2	927.6	951.5	938.8	938.1	941.1	953.7	961.1	993.1	1 002.8	986.0
Gasoline stations	943.5	935.7	925.3	895.9	882.0	875.6	871.1	864.1	861.5	842.4	825.5
Clothing and clothing accessories stores	1 306.6	1 321.6	1 321.1	1 312.5	1 304.5	1 364.3	1 414.6	1 450.9	1 500.0	1 468.0	1 363.9
Sporting goods, hobby, book, and music stores	582.7	602.7	601.1	591.8	584.7	585.9	597.9	606.0	623.3	621.9	589.2
General merchandise stores [1]	2 751.8	2 819.8	2 842.2	2 812.0	2 822.4	2 863.0	2 934.3	2 935.0	3 020.6	3 025.6	2 966.2
Department stores	1 694.2	1 739.5	1 752.5	1 668.5	1 605.2	1 589.8	1 579.5	1 541.5	1 575.0	1 524.1	1 456.9
Miscellaneous store retailers	985.5	1 007.1	993.3	959.5	930.7	913.5	899.9	881.0	865.4	842.5	782.4
Nonstore retailers	474.5	495.3	476.3	446.7	430.5	432.3	438.2	436.7	442.1	442.3	425.4

[1]Includes other industries, not shown separately.

Table 15-1. Nonfarm Employment by Sector and Industry—*Continued*

(Wage and salary workers on nonfarm payrolls, thousands.)

Industry	2010	2011	2012	2013	2014	2015	2016	2017	2018	2019	2020
TOTAL NONFARM	130 345	131 914	134 157	136 364	138 940	141 825	144 336	146 608	148 908	150 905	142 185
Total Private	107 855	109 828	112 237	114 511	117 058	119 796	122 112	124 258	126 454	128 292	120 276
Goods-Producing	17 751	18 047	18 420	18 738	19 226	19 610	19 750	20 084	20 704	21 037	20 068
Mining and logging	705	788	848	863	891	813	668	676	727	727	619
Logging	49.7	48.7	50.8	51.8	52.0	52.4	51.0	49.6	49.5	49.0	45.8
Mining	654.8	739.2	797.2	811.0	838.5	760.4	616.8	626.1	677.8	678.0	573.1
Oil and gas extraction	158.7	172.0	187.4	193.5	197.7	193.4	169.8	143.9	142.3	143.6	136.2
Mining, except oil and gas [1]	204.5	218.4	218.7	209.6	207.2	197.8	180.9	185.8	191.3	190.4	178.5
Coal mining	80.8	87.3	84.7	78.1	73.2	64.2	50.8	51.5	51.6	50.5	41.6
Support activities for mining	291.6	348.8	391.1	407.9	433.6	369.2	266.2	296.4	344.2	344.0	258.4
Construction	5 518	5 533	5 646	5 856	6 151	6 461	6 728	6 969	7 288	7 493	7 269
Construction of buildings	1 229.7	1 222.1	1 240.2	1 285.9	1 358.0	1 423.7	1 493.2	1 545.2	1 625.3	1 661.0	1 620.3
Heavy and civil engineering	825.1	836.8	868.3	885.0	912.3	937.6	951.6	996.4	1 050.7	1 082.2	1 047.8
Specialty trade contractors	3 463.4	3 474.4	3 537.1	3 684.4	3 880.6	4 099.7	4 283.0	4 427.2	4 612.5	4 750.0	4 601.2
Manufacturing	11 528	11 726	11 927	12 020	12 185	12 336	12 354	12 439	12 688	12 817	12 179
Durable goods	7 064	7 273	7 470	7 548	7 674	7 765	7 714	7 741	7 946	8 039	7 580
Wood products	342.1	337.1	339.1	353.2	371.6	382.5	392.7	397.0	406.0	408.7	395.3
Nonmetallic mineral products	370.9	366.6	365.3	373.4	384.1	398.0	406.1	409.8	416.5	419.0	397.4
Primary metals	362.3	388.3	402.0	395.3	398.7	394.0	374.5	371.3	380.2	387.3	354.5
Fabricated metal products	1 281.7	1 347.3	1 409.8	1 432.3	1 454.2	1 457.8	1 421.5	1 425.2	1 469.6	1 485.6	1 394.6
Machinery	996.1	1 055.8	1 098.5	1 104.5	1 127.3	1 120.8	1 076.5	1 079.1	1 116.9	1 126.6	1 060.7
Computer and electronic products [1]	1 094.6	1 103.5	1 089.0	1 065.6	1 048.7	1 052.8	1 048.4	1 039.2	1 054.1	1 075.1	1 072.0
Computer and peripheral equipment	157.6	157.4	157.4	157.5	159.8	160.3	162.7	155.6	156.6	160.7	162.2
Communications equipment	117.4	115.3	108.2	101.1	93.2	88.4	86.2	86.7	84.9	84.3	85.6
Semiconductors and electronic components	369.4	383.4	383.1	374.9	367.4	369.5	367.3	362.1	368.9	375.7	370.1
Electronic instruments	406.4	404.2	399.7	393.7	390.8	398.9	396.8	400.5	410.1	422.0	421.4
Electrical equipment and appliances	359.5	366.1	373.2	374.1	377.8	383.7	382.8	386.3	399.6	402.8	379.6
Transportation equipment [1]	1 333.1	1 381.5	1 461.1	1 508.8	1 559.0	1 604.9	1 630.3	1 643.2	1 702.3	1 729.3	1 580.5
Motor vehicles and parts	678.5	717.7	777.3	824.8	872.1	913.7	944.3	963.4	998.4	993.5	871.8
Furniture and related products	357.2	353.1	351.4	359.9	370.3	381.0	389.8	394.9	392.7	387.5	354.1
Miscellaneous manufacturing	566.8	573.7	580.1	580.5	581.9	589.9	590.9	594.5	608.2	617.7	590.9
Nondurable goods [1]	4 464	4 453	4 457	4 472	4 512	4 571	4 640	4 699	4 742	4 778	4 600
Food manufacturing	1 450.6	1 458.8	1 468.8	1 473.7	1 484.4	1 511.8	1 556.5	1 598.0	1 620.8	1 645.0	1 616.7
Textile mills	119.0	120.1	118.7	117.2	117.0	116.6	114.5	112.6	111.8	108.4	95.6
Textile product mills	119.0	117.6	116.3	114.4	115.0	116.1	116.2	116.2	116.0	113.4	103.8
Apparel	156.6	151.7	148.0	144.7	140.1	136.5	130.9	119.3	113.8	110.1	90.4
Paper and paper products	394.7	387.4	379.8	378.0	373.3	372.7	370.8	366.2	365.5	365.3	356.6
Printing and related support activities	487.6	471.8	461.8	452.0	453.7	450.3	447.6	440.2	432.3	425.1	377.8
Petroleum and coal products	113.9	111.8	112.1	110.4	111.6	112.9	112.5	114.6	115.2	114.3	106.3
Chemicals	786.5	783.6	783.3	792.7	803.0	807.3	811.9	823.8	835.3	851.0	841.6
Plastics and rubber products	624.8	635.2	645.1	659.2	674.3	689.4	702.4	716.9	730.3	731.6	709.9
Service-Providing	112 594	113 867	115 737	117 626	119 713	122 215	124 586	126 524	128 205	129 867	122 117
Private Service-Providing	90 104	91 781	93 817	95 773	97 832	100 186	102 362	104 174	105 750	107 254	100 209
Trade, transportation, and utilities	24 565	24 990	25 399	25 783	26 303	26 806	27 179	27 393	27 607	27 723	26 590
Wholesale trade	5 386.5	5 474.7	5 595.2	5 660.3	5 739.5	5 780.4	5 786.9	5 813.5	5 840.9	5 888.6	5 639.9
Durable goods	2 848.3	2 905.2	2 977.9	3 012.7	3 056.0	3 079.6	3 082.5	3 108.3	3 148.7	3 201.9	3 084.0
Nondurable goods	2 025.7	2 040.5	2 070.8	2 091.8	2 121.0	2 137.2	2 145.2	2 152.8	2 151.4	2 162.3	2 070.0
Electronic markets, agents, and brokers	512.5	528.9	546.6	555.9	562.5	563.6	559.2	552.5	540.7	524.4	485.9
Retail trade	14 446.0	14 673.7	14 846.8	15 084.7	15 363.4	15 610.9	15 831.6	15 845.7	15 786.3	15 619.9	14 853.1
Motor vehicle and parts dealers [1]	1 629.2	1 691.2	1 737.0	1 793.1	1 862.2	1 929.0	1 979.6	2 004.6	2 015.2	2 026.3	1 907.6
Automobile dealers	1 011.5	1 056.9	1 095.5	1 138.4	1 187.9	1 238.7	1 279.0	1 293.3	1 296.6	1 300.3	1 210.7
Furniture and home furnishings stores	437.9	438.9	439.4	445.8	455.9	466.8	470.9	476.2	477.2	473.5	405.2
Electronics and appliance stores	523.0	528.1	508.1	497.3	497.8	523.0	522.4	503.3	490.6	474.6	425.0
Building material and garden supply stores	1 132.6	1 146.6	1 175.1	1 208.5	1 229.0	1 235.3	1 267.8	1 276.7	1 302.7	1 292.4	1 351.1
Food and beverage stores	2 808.2	2 822.8	2 861.3	2 929.7	3 004.0	3 062.3	3 090.3	3 086.2	3 072.9	3 071.9	3 101.5
Health and personal care stores	980.5	980.9	997.9	1 015.8	1 022.5	1 033.7	1 053.3	1 066.7	1 063.0	1 043.4	958.6
Gasoline stations	819.3	831.0	843.5	866.3	881.3	905.3	923.1	929.8	931.6	946.8	930.7
Clothing and clothing accessories stores	1 352.5	1 360.9	1 391.4	1 390.9	1 370.4	1 353.7	1 359.3	1 374.4	1 358.5	1 292.1	949.1
Sporting goods, hobby, book, and music stores	579.1	577.9	582.2	602.5	618.8	623.2	620.4	606.4	573.3	552.0	460.0
General merchandise stores [1]	2 997.7	3 085.2	3 065.4	3 060.4	3 102.0	3 131.4	3 169.4	3 125.9	3 097.7	3 028.8	3 029.8
Department stores	1 485.2	1 521.7	1 439.0	1 334.0	1 335.3	1 312.5	1 267.2	1 173.6	1 137.7	1 063.3	948.6
Miscellaneous store retailers	761.5	772.4	794.0	802.5	818.3	828.0	831.8	828.4	834.5	842.9	749.5
Nonstore retailers	424.8	437.9	451.6	471.9	501.3	519.3	543.2	567.2	569.2	575.2	584.8

[1]Includes other industries, not shown separately.

Table 15-1. Nonfarm Employment by Sector and Industry—*Continued*

(Wage and salary workers on nonfarm payrolls, thousands.)

Industry	1999	2000	2001	2002	2003	2004	2005	2006	2007	2008	2009
Transportation and warehousing	4 291.9	4 400.7	4 361.2	4 211.7	4 172.7	4 235.6	4 348.0	4 457.0	4 528.0	4 495.9	4 224.8
Air transportation	586.3	614.4	615.3	563.5	528.3	514.5	500.8	487.0	491.8	490.7	462.8
Rail transportation	205.1	205.6	198.1	186.7	184.2	190.9	192.6	192.4	197.6	195.4	184.6
Water transportation	51.7	56.0	54.0	52.6	54.5	56.4	60.6	62.7	65.5	67.1	63.4
Truck transportation	1 391.8	1 406.1	1 387.1	1 339.6	1 325.9	1 352.1	1 397.9	1 436.2	1 439.6	1 389.4	1 268.6
Transit and ground passenger transportation	374.5	376.3	379.8	386.4	388.8	391.9	396.4	406.5	419.4	430.4	428.3
Pipeline transportation	46.9	46.0	45.4	41.7	40.2	38.4	37.8	38.7	39.9	41.7	42.6
Scenic and sightseeing transportation	26.1	27.5	29.1	25.6	26.6	27.2	28.8	27.5	28.6	28.0	27.6
Support activities for transportation	526.5	546.4	548.7	534.7	530.6	545.6	562.8	581.2	595.0	602.9	558.9
Couriers and messengers	585.9	605.0	587.0	560.9	561.7	556.6	571.4	582.4	580.7	573.4	546.3
Warehousing and storage	497.2	517.5	516.9	519.9	531.9	562.0	598.9	642.5	669.8	676.9	641.7
Utilities	608	601	599	596	577	564	554	548	553	559	560
Information	3 419	3 630	3 629	3 395	3 188	3 118	3 061	3 038	3 032	2 984	2 804
Publishing industries, except Internet	1 004.8	1 035.0	1 020.7	964.1	924.8	909.1	904.1	902.4	901.2	880.4	796.4
Motion picture and sound recording industries	384.4	382.6	376.8	387.9	376.2	385.0	377.5	375.7	380.6	371.3	357.6
Broadcasting, except Internet	329.4	343.5	344.6	334.1	324.3	325.0	327.7	328.3	325.2	318.7	300.5
Telecommunications	1 270.8	1 396.6	1 423.9	1 280.9	1 166.8	1 115.1	1 071.5	1 047.6	1 030.6	1 019.4	965.7
Data processing, hosting, and related services	307.1	315.7	316.8	303.9	280.0	267.1	262.5	263.2	267.8	260.3	248.5
Other information services [1]	121.9	157.1	146.5	123.6	115.9	116.9	117.7	120.8	126.3	133.5	135.0
Internet publishing and broadcasting	78.1	110.8	100.4	76.3	67.2	66.1	67.2	69.1	72.9	80.6	83.3
Financial activities	7 753	7 783	7 900	7 956	8 078	8 105	8 197	8 367	8 348	8 206	7 838
Finance and insurance	5 770.2	5 772.8	5 862.0	5 922.2	6 020.5	6 019.4	6 062.9	6 194.0	6 179.1	6 076.3	5 843.9
Monetary authorities–central bank	22.6	22.8	23.0	23.4	22.6	21.8	20.8	21.2	21.6	22.4	21.0
Credit intermediation and related activities [1]	2 591.0	2 547.8	2 597.7	2 686.0	2 792.4	2 817.0	2 869.0	2 924.9	2 866.3	2 732.7	2 590.2
Depository credit intermediation [1]	1 752.1	1 722.8	1 743.6	1 776.1	1 794.4	1 796.7	1 814.3	1 846.9	1 864.4	1 852.0	1 787.9
Commercial banking	1 357.1	1 325.2	1 334.4	1 355.8	1 361.5	1 361.1	1 375.5	1 401.9	1 425.0	1 424.3	1 378.6
Securities, commodity contracts, investments, and funds and trusts	782.2	851.1	879.0	836.4	803.9	813.1	834.2	868.9	899.6	916.2	862.1
Insurance carriers and related activities	2 374.5	2 351.1	2 362.3	2 376.4	2 401.5	2 367.5	2 338.9	2 379.1	2 391.6	2 405.1	2 370.6
Real estate and rental and leasing	1 982.5	2 010.6	2 038.4	2 033.3	2 057.5	2 085.5	2 133.5	2 172.5	2 169.1	2 129.6	1 994.0
Real estate	1 302.6	1 316.0	1 343.4	1 356.6	1 387.1	1 418.7	1 460.8	1 499.0	1 500.4	1 485.0	1 420.2
Rental and leasing services	653.1	666.8	666.3	649.1	643.1	641.1	645.8	645.5	640.3	616.9	547.3
Lessors of nonfinancial intangible assets	26.8	27.8	28.7	27.6	27.3	25.7	26.9	28.1	28.4	27.7	26.5
Professional and business services	15 994	16 704	16 514	16 016	16 029	16 440	17 003	17 619	17 998	17 792	16 634
Professional and technical services [1]	6 375.5	6 732.1	6 901.3	6 680.6	6 637.0	6 784.2	7 064.5	7 399.3	7 704.5	7 845.3	7 552.9
Legal services	1 051.4	1 065.7	1 091.3	1 115.3	1 142.1	1 163.1	1 168.0	1 173.2	1 175.4	1 161.5	1 124.9
Accounting and bookkeeping services	838.1	866.9	872.7	837.8	815.9	806.5	849.9	889.7	936.6	951.8	914.9
Architectural and engineering services	1 168.7	1 238.5	1 275.3	1 246.7	1 227.6	1 258.9	1 311.7	1 386.6	1 433.1	1 440.2	1 325.5
Computer systems design and related services	1 137.2	1 258.7	1 302.2	1 157.4	1 121.6	1 153.9	1 201.0	1 290.8	1 378.7	1 446.3	1 429.0
Management and technical consulting services	640.4	694.3	736.5	730.3	742.5	789.4	852.6	916.6	984.8	1 034.8	1 026.5
Management of companies and enterprises	1 777.5	1 799.7	1 782.7	1 709.3	1 691.5	1 729.0	1 763.8	1 816.1	1 872.0	1 910.1	1 872.4
Administrative and waste services	7 841.0	8 171.9	7 829.6	7 625.6	7 700.9	7 927.3	8 174.7	8 403.2	8 421.6	8 036.8	7 208.5
Administrative and support services [1]	7 530.5	7 859.0	7 512.3	7 307.3	7 378.8	7 598.7	7 837.0	8 055.1	8 066.6	7 680.0	6 856.8
Employment services [1]	3 582.3	3 850.0	3 468.9	3 274.0	3 327.3	3 456.4	3 607.8	3 681.9	3 547.1	3 134.1	2 481.8
Temporary help services	2 470.1	2 636.1	2 338.1	2 194.1	2 224.7	2 387.7	2 549.9	2 638.0	2 598.1	2 349.0	1 823.8
Business support services	781.8	788.1	781.2	758.0	751.3	759.5	768.2	794.8	819.5	834.4	822.1
Services to buildings and dwellings	1 534.7	1 570.5	1 606.2	1 606.1	1 636.1	1 693.7	1 737.5	1 801.4	1 849.5	1 839.8	1 753.3
Waste management and remediation services	310.5	312.9	317.3	318.3	322.1	328.6	337.6	348.1	355.0	356.8	351.7
Education and health services	14 939	15 252	15 814	16 398	16 835	17 230	17 676	18 154	18 676	19 228	19 630
Educational services	2 320.4	2 390.4	2 510.6	2 642.8	2 695.1	2 762.5	2 835.8	2 900.9	2 941.4	3 039.7	3 090.4
Health care and social assistance	12 618.3	12 861.1	13 302.9	13 755.2	14 139.6	14 467.8	14 840.4	15 253.2	15 734.5	16 188.2	16 539.9
Health care	10 690.9	10 857.8	11 188.1	11 536.0	11 817.1	12 055.3	12 313.9	12 601.8	12 946.8	13 289.9	13 543.0
Ambulatory health care services [1]	4 226.6	4 320.3	4 461.5	4 633.2	4 786.4	4 952.3	5 113.5	5 285.8	5 473.5	5 646.6	5 793.4
Offices of physicians	1 748.9	1 801.1	1 870.9	1 926.3	1 960.3	2 004.6	2 049.4	2 102.5	2 155.1	2 205.0	2 231.0
Outpatient care centers	413.1	425.2	440.0	454.5	469.0	493.7	517.3	537.9	558.4	580.8	605.6
Home health care services	629.6	633.3	638.6	679.8	732.6	776.6	821.0	865.6	913.8	961.4	1 027.1
Hospitals	3 935.5	3 954.3	4 050.9	4 159.6	4 244.6	4 284.7	4 345.4	4 423.4	4 515.0	4 627.3	4 667.4
Nursing and residential care facilities [1]	2 528.8	2 583.2	2 675.8	2 743.3	2 786.2	2 818.4	2 855.0	2 892.5	2 958.3	3 016.1	3 082.2
Nursing care facilities	1 501.0	1 513.6	1 546.8	1 573.2	1 579.8	1 576.9	1 577.4	1 581.4	1 602.6	1 618.7	1 644.9
Social assistance [1]	1 927.5	2 003.3	2 114.7	2 219.2	2 322.5	2 412.5	2 526.5	2 651.4	2 787.7	2 898.3	2 996.9
Child day care services	674.0	695.8	714.6	744.1	755.3	764.7	789.7	818.3	850.4	859.4	852.8

[1]Includes other industries, not shown separately.

Table 15-1. Nonfarm Employment by Sector and Industry—*Continued*

(Wage and salary workers on nonfarm payrolls, thousands.)

Industry	2010	2011	2012	2013	2014	2015	2016	2017	2018	2019	2020
Transportation and warehousing	4 179.2	4 289.3	4 403.7	4 486.0	4 648.6	4 858.6	5 003.5	5 178.2	5 426.4	5 664.9	5 555.0
Air transportation	458.3	456.9	459.2	444.3	444.2	458.6	477.5	491.5	496.9	504.9	430.3
Rail transportation	183.0	192.9	195.1	195.6	199.7	203.7	183.6	181.9	181.7	174.3	149.2
Water transportation	62.3	61.3	63.9	65.3	67.3	65.8	65.6	65.0	65.1	66.6	61.0
Truck transportation	1 250.8	1 301.0	1 349.8	1 382.6	1 417.7	1 452.7	1 448.1	1 457.0	1 496.2	1 528.8	1 465.6
Transit and ground passenger transportation	436.2	446.9	447.5	455.6	473.7	485.0	490.2	494.9	494.7	493.9	374.8
Pipeline transportation	42.3	42.9	43.6	44.5	47.0	49.7	49.8	48.8	49.7	51.5	50.9
Scenic and sightseeing transportation	27.3	27.5	28.0	29.1	30.6	32.9	34.5	35.2	34.6	35.5	23.3
Support activities for transportation	552.9	572.9	590.7	609.2	636.9	663.1	677.9	700.6	729.3	753.8	700.0
Couriers and messengers	528.1	529.2	534.1	543.9	576.5	612.8	644.8	676.1	739.5	826.9	957.1
Warehousing and storage	638.1	657.9	691.9	716.0	754.8	834.3	931.6	1 027.3	1 138.8	1 228.7	1 342.7
Utilities	553	553	553	552	552	556	556	555	553	549	542
Information	2 707	2 674	2 676	2 706	2 726	2 750	2 794	2 814	2 839	2 864	2 694
Publishing industries, except Internet	759.0	748.6	739.5	732.7	726.9	726.5	730.3	728.6	738.5	764.8	762.0
Motion picture and sound recording industries	370.2	362.1	362.3	370.5	379.3	397.9	426.1	432.6	441.3	437.8	282.9
Broadcasting, except Internet	290.3	283.2	285.1	283.7	282.8	276.7	270.5	268.0	269.8	266.9	248.3
Telecommunications	902.9	873.6	856.8	853.2	838.5	810.9	801.1	780.8	749.7	714.6	691.3
Data processing, hosting, and related services	243.0	245.8	254.9	269.6	279.5	296.2	303.9	318.0	331.0	343.2	356.1
Other information services [1]	141.7	160.0	177.2	196.2	219.0	241.4	262.3	285.8	308.8	336.8	353.9
Internet publishing and broadcasting	92.0	109.6	125.2	142.3	163.3	184.3	203.5	223.8	245.1	271.4	290.2
Financial activities	7 695	7 697	7 784	7 886	7 977	8 123	8 287	8 451	8 590	8 754	8 724
Finance and insurance	5 761.0	5 769.0	5 828.4	5 886.1	5 930.9	6 034.9	6 148.1	6 261.9	6 337.0	6 433.3	6 499.6
Monetary authorities–central bank	20.0	18.3	17.5	18.0	18.2	18.0	18.6	19.2	19.6	19.8	20.2
Credit intermediation and related activities [1]	2 550.0	2 554.1	2 583.3	2 614.1	2 564.0	2 570.7	2 609.7	2 644.9	2 651.2	2 648.9	2 655.1
Depository credit intermediation [1]	1 762.9	1 770.0	1 774.1	1 768.6	1 735.7	1 717.2	1 732.3	1 748.0	1 759.1	1 776.4	1 768.2
Commercial banking	1 366.3	1 375.4	1 381.3	1 373.7	1 348.3	1 338.3	1 361.5	1 375.0	1 381.4	1 392.8	1 382.9
Securities, commodity contracts, investments, and funds and trusts	850.4	860.1	859.3	865.0	882.9	907.8	927.1	938.3	953.6	962.3	966.3
Insurance carriers and related activities	2 340.6	2 336.4	2 368.3	2 388.9	2 465.8	2 538.3	2 592.7	2 659.6	2 712.7	2 802.3	2 858.1
Real estate and rental and leasing	1 933.8	1 927.4	1 955.2	2 000.2	2 045.7	2 088.4	2 138.8	2 189.2	2 253.3	2 320.7	2 224.0
Real estate	1 395.7	1 400.8	1 420.0	1 458.7	1 487.1	1 517.1	1 556.8	1 605.5	1 662.9	1 717.7	1 698.3
Rental and leasing services	513.5	502.2	511.0	517.7	535.0	547.5	558.3	560.1	567.2	579.9	503.1
Lessors of nonfinancial intangible assets	24.6	24.4	24.2	23.7	23.7	23.8	23.8	23.7	23.3	23.0	22.6
Professional and business services	16 783	17 389	17 992	18 575	19 124	19 695	20 114	20 508	20 950	21 274	20 246
Professional and technical services [1]	7 485.8	7 712.5	7 940.5	8 169.9	8 385.5	8 658.4	8 880.8	9 057.8	9 281.7	9 535.7	9 426.3
Legal services	1 114.2	1 115.7	1 124.0	1 128.5	1 119.0	1 118.6	1 123.7	1 136.8	1 142.0	1 150.7	1 123.4
Accounting and bookkeeping services	887.2	899.6	909.7	932.3	949.3	969.3	981.4	996.6	1 003.8	1 020.8	995.8
Architectural and engineering services	1 276.2	1 294.3	1 323.4	1 346.5	1 376.2	1 401.6	1 404.6	1 435.3	1 474.4	1 514.5	1 510.9
Computer systems design and related services	1 455.5	1 542.5	1 628.4	1 709.5	1 797.8	1 915.8	1 993.2	2 051.2	2 118.0	2 194.6	2 188.0
Management and technical consulting services	1 031.1	1 098.2	1 152.4	1 215.2	1 267.7	1 318.1	1 394.2	1 433.1	1 481.5	1 534.6	1 527.0
Management of companies and enterprises	1 877.8	1 939.3	2 029.3	2 109.0	2 174.6	2 213.6	2 251.6	2 308.1	2 373.9	2 419.8	2 351.2
Administrative and waste services	7 419.1	7 737.3	8 021.8	8 296.5	8 564.1	8 823.3	8 981.2	9 141.5	9 294.3	9 318.9	8 468.1
Administrative and support services [1]	7 061.8	7 372.0	7 649.9	7 919.1	8 178.0	8 426.8	8 577.1	8 726.3	8 858.0	8 867.6	8 022.4
Employment services [1]	2 723.5	2 943.2	3 135.2	3 269.7	3 408.1	3 528.3	3 537.9	3 595.1	3 656.6	3 617.6	3 062.6
Temporary help services	2 094.2	2 313.6	2 496.0	2 617.6	2 760.8	2 877.6	2 889.1	2 939.7	2 988.5	2 950.2	2 471.3
Business support services	810.7	816.7	830.7	858.3	879.7	895.9	912.0	904.4	895.3	875.7	807.4
Services to buildings and dwellings	1 745.0	1 788.6	1 830.0	1 884.7	1 943.9	2 006.6	2 062.8	2 111.2	2 144.8	2 173.7	2 096.5
Waste management and remediation services	357.3	365.3	371.9	377.5	386.1	396.5	404.1	415.2	436.3	451.3	445.7
Education and health services	19 975	20 318	20 769	21 086	21 439	22 029	22 639	23 188	23 638	24 163	23 235
Educational services	3 155.1	3 249.6	3 341.1	3 354.4	3 416.6	3 471.9	3 569.5	3 668.4	3 714.9	3 741.4	3 459.6
Health care and social assistance	16 820.0	17 068.6	17 428.1	17 731.1	18 022.2	18 557.4	19 068.8	19 519.6	19 922.6	20 421.1	19 775.8
Health care	13 776.9	14 025.9	14 281.6	14 491.5	14 676.5	15 042.3	15 413.5	15 716.6	15 964.3	16 269.1	15 836.5
Ambulatory health care services [1]	5 974.7	6 136.2	6 306.5	6 476.5	6 631.5	6 855.5	7 080.0	7 297.3	7 477.4	7 704.4	7 483.9
Offices of physicians	2 263.9	2 294.6	2 339.8	2 378.0	2 411.2	2 471.0	2 526.5	2 581.4	2 615.8	2 673.2	2 620.2
Outpatient care centers	648.7	670.2	699.0	731.1	763.7	805.7	853.0	897.2	931.4	969.1	973.3
Home health care services	1 084.6	1 140.3	1 185.0	1 230.3	1 262.4	1 314.7	1 365.3	1 419.6	1 467.0	1 518.5	1 492.4
Hospitals	4 678.5	4 721.7	4 779.0	4 785.8	4 786.8	4 895.8	5 015.2	5 071.8	5 129.8	5 189.7	5 143.1
Nursing and residential care facilities [1]	3 123.7	3 168.1	3 196.2	3 229.2	3 258.2	3 290.9	3 318.3	3 347.5	3 357.2	3 375.0	3 209.5
Nursing care facilities	1 657.1	1 669.6	1 662.8	1 653.8	1 650.3	1 648.3	1 641.5	1 627.1	1 606.8	1 596.3	1 498.5
Social assistance [1]	3 043.1	3 042.6	3 146.5	3 239.6	3 345.6	3 515.1	3 655.3	3 803.0	3 958.3	4 152.0	3 939.3
Child day care services	848.0	849.4	851.3	843.3	854.0	878.0	911.2	943.1	972.7	1 021.2	869.1

[1]Includes other industries, not shown separately.

Table 15-1. Nonfarm Employment by Sector and Industry—*Continued*

(Wage and salary workers on nonfarm payrolls, thousands.)

Industry	1999	2000	2001	2002	2003	2004	2005	2006	2007	2008	2009
Leisure and hospitality	11 543	11 862	12 036	11 986	12 173	12 493	12 816	13 110	13 427	13 436	13 077
Arts, entertainment, and recreation	1 709.1	1 787.9	1 824.4	1 782.6	1 812.9	1 849.6	1 892.3	1 928.5	1 969.2	1 970.1	1 915.5
Performing arts and spectator sports	361.1	381.8	382.3	363.7	371.7	367.5	376.3	398.5	405.0	405.7	396.8
Museums, historical sites, zoos, and parks	103.1	110.4	115.0	114.0	114.7	118.3	120.7	123.8	130.3	131.6	129.4
Amusements, gambling, and recreation	1 244.9	1 295.7	1 327.1	1 305.0	1 326.5	1 363.8	1 395.3	1 406.3	1 433.9	1 432.8	1 389.2
Accommodation and food services	9 833.7	10 073.5	10 211.3	10 203.2	10 359.8	10 643.2	10 923.0	11 181.1	11 457.4	11 466.3	11 161.9
Accommodation	1 831.7	1 884.4	1 852.2	1 778.6	1 775.4	1 789.5	1 818.6	1 832.1	1 866.9	1 868.7	1 763.0
Food services and drinking places	8 002.0	8 189.1	8 359.1	8 424.6	8 584.4	8 853.7	9 104.4	9 349.0	9 590.4	9 597.5	9 398.9
Other services	5 087	5 168	5 258	5 372	5 401	5 409	5 395	5 438	5 494	5 515	5 367
Repair and maintenance	1 222.0	1 241.5	1 256.5	1 246.9	1 233.6	1 228.8	1 236.0	1 248.5	1 253.4	1 227.0	1 150.4
Personal and laundry services	1 220.3	1 242.9	1 255.0	1 257.2	1 263.5	1 272.9	1 276.6	1 288.4	1 309.7	1 322.6	1 280.6
Membership associations and organizations	2 644.4	2 683.3	2 746.4	2 867.8	2 903.6	2 907.5	2 882.2	2 901.2	2 931.1	2 965.7	2 936.0
Government	20 307	20 790	21 118	21 513	21 583	21 621	21 804	21 974	22 218	22 509	22 555
Federal	2 769.0	2 865.0	2 764.0	2 766.0	2 761.0	2 730.0	2 732.0	2 732.0	2 734.0	2 762.0	2 832.0
Federal, except U.S. Postal Service	1 879.5	1 984.8	1 891.0	1 923.8	1 952.4	1 947.5	1 957.3	1 962.6	1 964.7	2 014.4	2 128.5
U.S. Postal Service	889.7	879.7	873.0	842.4	808.6	782.1	774.2	769.7	769.1	747.4	703.4
State government	4 709.0	4 786.0	4 905.0	5 029.0	5 002.0	4 982.0	5 032.0	5 075.0	5 122.0	5 177.0	5 169.0
State government education	1 983.2	2 030.6	2 112.9	2 242.8	2 254.7	2 238.1	2 259.9	2 292.5	2 317.5	2 354.4	2 360.2
State government, excluding education	2 725.6	2 755.9	2 791.8	2 786.3	2 747.6	2 743.9	2 771.6	2 782.0	2 804.3	2 822.5	2 808.8
Local government	12 829.0	13 139.0	13 449.0	13 718.0	13 820.0	13 909.0	14 041.0	14 167.0	14 362.0	14 571.0	14 554.0
Local government education	7 120.4	7 293.9	7 479.3	7 654.4	7 709.4	7 765.2	7 856.1	7 913.0	7 986.8	8 083.9	8 078.8
Local government, excluding education	5 708.6	5 844.6	5 970.0	6 063.2	6 110.2	6 144.1	6 184.6	6 253.8	6 375.5	6 486.5	6 474.9

¹Includes other industries, not shown separately.

Table 15-1. Nonfarm Employment by Sector and Industry—*Continued*

(Wage and salary workers on nonfarm payrolls, thousands.)

Industry	2010	2011	2012	2013	2014	2015	2016	2017	2018	2019	2020
Leisure and hospitality	13 049	13 353	13 768	14 254	14 696	15 160	15 660	16 051	16 295	16 586	13 327
Arts, entertainment, and recreation	1 913.3	1 919.1	1 968.6	2 029.7	2 103.1	2 166.4	2 251.5	2 333.2	2 382.5	2 436.9	1 782.4
Performing arts and spectator sports	406.2	394.2	402.4	419.2	443.3	450.4	464.4	493.8	506.4	518.9	344.0
Museums, historical sites, zoos, and parks	127.7	132.7	136.1	140.3	146.9	153.0	159.6	165.6	169.5	172.6	138.4
Amusements, gambling, and recreation	1 379.4	1 392.2	1 430.1	1 470.2	1 512.9	1 563.1	1 627.5	1 673.8	1 706.6	1 745.4	1 300.1
Accommodation and food services	11 135.4	11 433.6	11 799.7	12 224.2	12 592.9	12 993.8	13 408.4	13 717.9	13 912.9	14 148.8	11 544.1
Accommodation	1 759.6	1 800.5	1 825.1	1 864.9	1 894.5	1 923.0	1 960.3	2 002.9	2 034.7	2 082.4	1 522.1
Food services and drinking places	9 375.8	9 633.1	9 974.6	10 359.2	10 698.3	11 070.8	11 448.1	11 715.0	11 878.2	12 066.4	10 022.1
Other services	5 331	5 360	5 430	5 483	5 567	5 622	5 691	5 770	5 831	5 891	5 394
Repair and maintenance	1 138.8	1 168.7	1 194.0	1 216.6	1 242.1	1 277.2	1 293.1	1 310.6	1 326.7	1 346.9	1 283.7
Personal and laundry services	1 265.3	1 288.6	1 313.6	1 341.7	1 371.2	1 405.0	1 444.3	1 478.4	1 506.6	1 535.0	1 251.1
Membership associations and organizations	2 926.4	2 903.0	2 922.4	2 924.6	2 953.6	2 939.5	2 953.3	2 981.0	2 997.9	3 008.7	2 859.0
Government	22 490	22 086	21 920	21 853	21 882	22 029	22 224	22 350	22 455	22 613	21 909
Federal	2 977.0	2 859.0	2 820.0	2 769.0	2 733.0	2 757.0	2 795.0	2 805.0	2 800.0	2 831.0	2 929.0
Federal, except U.S. Postal Service	2 318.1	2 227.6	2 209.2	2 174.5	2 140.4	2 160.0	2 185.8	2 189.4	2 191.8	2 224.0	2 326.2
U.S. Postal Service	658.5	630.9	611.2	594.9	593.0	596.9	608.8	615.4	608.5	607.2	602.1
State government	5 137.0	5 078.0	5 055.0	5 046.0	5 050.0	5 077.0	5 110.0	5 165.0	5 173.0	5 206.0	5 074.0
State government education	2 373.1	2 374.0	2 388.5	2 393.3	2 389.3	2 401.4	2 429.2	2 478.7	2 486.9	2 515.2	2 380.0
State government, excluding education	2 764.1	2 703.7	2 666.4	2 652.8	2 660.5	2 675.6	2 680.9	2 686.4	2 686.4	2 690.9	2 693.8
Local government	14 376.0	14 150.0	14 045.0	14 037.0	14 098.0	14 195.0	14 319.0	14 379.0	14 481.0	14 576.0	13 906.0
Local government education	8 013.4	7 872.5	7 777.9	7 776.7	7 814.9	7 870.9	7 905.1	7 921.5	7 963.0	8 000.9	7 574.1
Local government, excluding education	6 362.9	6 277.7	6 266.8	6 260.1	6 283.4	6 324.0	6 414.1	6 457.5	6 518.0	6 574.9	6 331.9

¹Includes other industries, not shown separately.

Table 15-2. Production and Nonsupervisory Workers on Private Nonfarm Payrolls by Industry

(Wage and salary workers on nonfarm payrolls, thousands.)

Industry	1999	2000	2001	2002	2003	2004	2005	2006	2007	2008	2009
Total Private	88 636	90 534	90 200	88 649	87 948	89 230	91 426	93 759	95 243	94 660	89 616
Goods-Producing	18 067	18 169	17 466	16 400	15 732	15 821	16 145	16 559	16 405	15 724	13 399
Mining and logging	438	446	457	436	420	440	473	519	547	574	510
Construction	5 105	5 295	5 332	5 196	5 123	5 309	5 611	5 903	5 883	5 521	4 567
Manufacturing	12 524	12 428	11 677	10 768	10 189	10 072	10 060	10 137	9 975	9 629	8 322
Durable goods	7 651	7 659	7 164	6 530	6 152	6 140	6 220	6 355	6 250	5 975	4 990
Wood products	516	507	470	450	434	445	454	451	407	358	278
Nonmetallic mineral products	426	440	427	399	375	388	387	391	384	363	303
Primary metals	492	490	447	396	370	364	363	363	358	348	272
Fabricated metal products	1 305	1 326	1 254	1 147	1 092	1 109	1 129	1 162	1 171	1 143	960
Machinery	978	961	891	787	732	730	749	770	774	772	641
Computer and electronic products	933	949	876	744	673	656	700	756	744	730	654
Electrical equipment and appliances	433	433	402	352	320	307	300	303	305	305	266
Transportation equipment [1]	1 526	1 498	1 399	1 310	1 269	1 265	1 277	1 304	1 274	1 177	948
Motor vehicles and parts	1 076	1 073	987	931	906	903	894	873	804	696	510
Furniture and related products	532	544	509	475	444	444	436	433	409	364	284
Miscellaneous manufacturing	509	510	490	469	442	432	424	423	425	416	382
Nondurable goods [1]	4 872	4 769	4 513	4 238	4 037	3 932	3 841	3 782	3 725	3 653	3 332
Food manufacturing	1 229	1 228	1 221	1 202	1 192	1 178	1 170	1 172	1 184	1 184	1 161
Textile mills	334	315	276	242	217	194	174	158	137	122	99
Textile product mills	187	183	174	162	148	147	143	135	123	115	98
Apparel	458	404	341	286	242	219	193	182	173	163	132
Paper and paper products	474	468	446	421	393	374	365	357	350	344	313
Printing and related support activities	585	576	544	493	471	460	447	447	443	424	369
Petroleum and coal products	85	83	81	78	74	77	75	72	73	77	70
Chemicals	595	588	562	532	525	520	510	508	504	512	479
Plastics and rubber products	746	753	704	662	633	626	620	608	592	572	476
Private Service-Providing	70 569	72 365	72 734	72 249	72 216	73 409	75 282	77 200	78 838	78 936	76 217
Trade, transportation, and utilities	21 535	21 923	21 665	21 292	21 029	21 268	21 776	22 109	22 486	22 277	21 059
Wholesale trade	4 638	4 651	4 520	4 437	4 358	4 402	4 538	4 676	4 798	4 768	4 453
Retail trade	12 775	13 043	12 955	12 777	12 658	12 792	13 033	13 114	13 322	13 139	12 476
Transportation and warehousing	3 633	3 743	3 707	3 599	3 550	3 624	3 761	3 876	3 922	3 920	3 678
Utilities	489	485	483	478	464	450	443	443	444	450	451
Information	2 351	2 502	2 531	2 398	2 347	2 371	2 386	2 399	2 403	2 388	2 240
Financial activities	5 818	5 819	5 888	5 964	6 052	6 052	6 127	6 312	6 365	6 320	6 066
Professional and business services	13 214	13 819	13 617	13 080	12 942	13 321	13 892	14 487	14 828	14 631	13 565
Education and health services	13 217	13 491	13 998	14 491	14 753	15 018	15 401	15 832	16 318	16 842	17 240
Leisure and hospitality	10 216	10 516	10 662	10 576	10 666	10 955	11 263	11 568	11 861	11 873	11 560
Other services	4 219	4 296	4 373	4 449	4 426	4 425	4 438	4 494	4 578	4 606	4 488

[1]Includes other industries, not shown separately.

Table 15-2.   Production and Nonsupervisory Workers on Private Nonfarm Payrolls by Industry
—Continued

(Wage and salary workers on nonfarm payrolls, thousands.)

Industry	2010	2011	2012	2013	2014	2015	2016	2017	2018	2019	2020
Total Private	88 940	90 605	92 766	94 573	96 688	98 769	100 555	102 411	104 169	105 570	97 951
Goods-Producing	12 774	13 005	13 287	13 481	13 858	14 141	14 215	14 450	14 876	15 073	14 245
Mining and logging	525	594	641	636	653	592	471	490	541	535	439
Construction	4 172	4 184	4 246	4 423	4 640	4 866	5 074	5 230	5 437	5 579	5 377
Manufacturing	8 077	8 228	8 400	8 422	8 565	8 683	8 670	8 730	8 898	8 959	8 429
Durable goods	4 829	4 986	5 152	5 185	5 282	5 350	5 303	5 315	5 464	5 532	5 132
Wood products	269	269	272	283	298	306	309	311	319	321	309
Nonmetallic mineral products	284	278	273	275	280	297	306	305	311	312	294
Primary metals	275	301	317	306	310	307	293	292	295	302	273
Fabricated metal products	935	994	1 050	1 063	1 071	1 069	1 036	1 045	1 087	1 106	1 022
Machinery	616	662	700	699	716	711	686	691	716	709	645
Computer and electronic products	629	630	628	610	589	594	596	598	612	638	646
Electrical equipment and appliances	251	248	249	245	248	258	259	253	261	262	245
Transportation equipment [1]	937	972	1 024	1 053	1 103	1 139	1 150	1 149	1 188	1 199	1 070
Motor vehicles and parts	525	556	598	642	690	718	739	753	780	768	650
Furniture and related products	263	260	259	266	276	284	286	290	290	288	257
Miscellaneous manufacturing	370	373	380	386	390	384	382	381	384	394	371
Nondurable goods [1]	3 248	3 241	3 248	3 237	3 283	3 333	3 367	3 415	3 434	3 427	3 297
Food manufacturing	1 152	1 158	1 169	1 169	1 176	1 189	1 212	1 251	1 272	1 290	1 275
Textile mills	96	98	96	92	91	90	90	88	87	85	73
Textile product mills	92	89	85	83	86	88	89	89	85	78	71
Apparel	120	112	109	106	103	104	99	88	82	74	65
Paper and paper products	302	295	288	279	277	277	275	278	275	271	263
Printing and related support activities	342	327	316	310	312	310	312	305	296	285	256
Petroleum and coal products	70	70	72	70	72	74	76	80	77	77	72
Chemicals	474	480	491	490	497	507	516	525	546	559	535
Plastics and rubber products	472	482	487	497	518	532	536	543	548	548	521
Private Service-Providing	76 166	77 600	79 479	81 093	82 830	84 628	86 340	87 961	89 293	90 497	83 706
Trade, transportation, and utilities	20 816	21 174	21 554	21 811	22 217	22 566	22 842	23 094	23 348	23 451	22 419
Wholesale trade	4 324	4 388	4 505	4 563	4 638	4 644	4 634	4 660	4 688	4 728	4 487
Retail trade	12 430	12 652	12 798	12 928	13 112	13 269	13 433	13 486	13 488	13 332	12 657
Transportation and warehousing	3 618	3 693	3 810	3 875	4 022	4 206	4 328	4 500	4 728	4 952	4 844
Utilities	444	441	441	445	446	447	447	447	444	440	431
Information	2 170	2 148	2 164	2 194	2 209	2 226	2 252	2 268	2 286	2 305	2 139
Financial activities	5 942	5 900	5 986	6 068	6 155	6 278	6 430	6 571	6 654	6 774	6 677
Professional and business services	13 744	14 298	14 851	15 352	15 818	16 183	16 455	16 751	17 079	17 301	16 261
Education and health services	17 531	17 818	18 230	18 505	18 827	19 337	19 859	20 365	20 763	21 221	20 352
Leisure and hospitality	11 507	11 772	12 154	12 590	12 968	13 360	13 782	14 139	14 334	14 571	11 465
Other services	4 458	4 491	4 541	4 573	4 637	4 678	4 720	4 775	4 828	4 874	4 394

[1] Includes other industries, not shown separately.

Table 15-3. Average Weekly Hours of Production and Nonsupervisory Workers on Private Nonfarm Payrolls by Industry

(Hours.)

Industry	1999	2000	2001	2002	2003	2004	2005	2006	2007	2008	2009
Total Private	34.3	34.3	33.9	33.9	33.7	33.7	33.8	33.9	33.8	33.6	33.1
Goods-Producing	40.8	40.7	39.9	39.9	39.8	40.0	40.1	40.5	40.6	40.2	39.2
Mining and logging	44.2	44.4	44.6	43.2	43.6	44.5	45.6	45.6	45.9	45.1	43.2
Construction	39.0	39.2	38.7	38.4	38.4	38.3	38.6	39.0	39.0	38.5	37.6
Manufacturing	41.4	41.3	40.3	40.5	40.4	40.8	40.7	41.1	41.2	40.8	39.8
Overtime hours	4.9	4.7	4.0	4.2	4.2	4.6	4.6	4.4	4.2	3.7	2.9
Durable goods	41.9	41.8	40.6	40.8	40.8	41.3	41.1	41.4	41.5	41.1	39.8
Overtime hours	5.0	4.8	3.9	4.2	4.3	4.7	4.6	4.4	4.2	3.7	2.7
Wood products	41.3	41.0	40.2	39.9	40.4	40.7	40.0	39.8	39.4	38.6	37.4
Nonmetallic mineral products	42.1	41.6	41.6	42.0	42.2	42.4	42.2	43.0	42.3	42.1	40.8
Primary metals	43.8	44.2	42.4	42.4	42.3	43.1	43.1	43.6	42.9	42.2	40.7
Fabricated metal products	41.7	41.9	40.6	40.6	40.7	41.1	41.0	41.4	41.6	41.3	39.4
Machinery	42.3	42.3	40.9	40.5	40.8	42.0	42.1	42.4	42.6	42.3	40.1
Computer and electronic products	41.5	41.4	39.8	39.7	40.4	40.4	40.0	40.5	40.6	41.0	40.4
Electrical equipment and appliances	41.8	41.6	39.8	40.1	40.6	40.7	40.6	41.0	41.2	40.9	39.3
Transportation equipment [1]	43.6	43.3	41.9	42.5	41.9	42.5	42.4	42.7	42.8	42.0	41.2
Motor vehicles and parts	43.8	43.3	41.7	42.6	42.0	42.6	42.3	42.2	42.3	41.4	40.1
Furniture and related products	39.3	39.2	38.3	39.1	38.9	39.5	39.2	38.8	39.2	38.1	37.7
Miscellaneous manufacturing	39.3	39.0	38.8	38.7	38.4	38.5	38.7	38.7	38.9	38.9	38.5
Nondurable goods [1]	40.5	40.3	39.9	40.0	39.8	40.0	39.9	40.6	40.8	40.4	39.8
Overtime hours	4.6	4.5	4.1	4.2	4.1	4.4	4.4	4.4	4.2	3.7	3.2
Food manufacturing	40.2	40.1	39.6	39.6	39.3	39.3	39.0	40.1	40.7	40.5	40.0
Textile mills	41.0	41.4	40.0	40.6	39.1	40.1	40.3	40.6	40.3	38.7	37.7
Textile product mills	39.1	38.7	38.4	39.0	39.4	38.7	38.9	39.8	39.7	38.6	37.9
Apparel	35.4	35.7	36.0	36.7	35.6	36.1	35.8	36.5	37.2	36.4	36.0
Paper and paper products	43.6	42.8	42.1	41.8	41.5	42.1	42.5	42.9	43.1	42.9	41.8
Printing and related support activities	39.1	39.2	38.7	38.4	38.2	38.4	38.4	39.2	39.1	38.3	38.0
Petroleum and coal products	42.6	42.7	43.8	43.0	44.5	44.9	45.5	45.0	44.1	44.6	43.4
Chemicals	42.8	42.2	41.9	42.3	42.4	42.8	42.3	42.5	41.9	41.5	41.4
Plastics and rubber products	41.3	40.8	40.0	40.6	40.4	40.4	40.0	40.7	41.3	41.0	40.2
Private Service-Providing	32.7	32.7	32.5	32.5	32.3	32.3	32.4	32.4	32.4	32.3	32.1
Trade, transportation, and utilities	33.9	33.8	33.5	33.6	33.5	33.5	33.4	33.4	33.3	33.1	32.8
Wholesale trade	38.6	38.8	38.4	38.0	37.9	37.8	37.7	38.0	38.2	38.3	37.7
Retail trade	30.8	30.7	30.7	30.9	30.9	30.7	30.6	30.5	30.2	30.0	29.9
Transportation and warehousing	37.6	37.3	36.6	36.7	36.7	37.2	37.0	36.8	36.9	36.4	36.0
Utilities	42.0	42.0	41.4	40.9	41.1	40.9	41.1	41.4	42.4	42.7	42.0
Information	36.7	36.8	36.9	36.5	36.2	36.3	36.5	36.6	36.5	36.7	36.6
Financial activities	35.8	35.9	35.8	35.6	35.6	35.6	36.0	35.8	35.9	35.9	36.1
Professional and business services	34.4	34.5	34.2	34.2	34.1	34.2	34.3	34.6	34.8	34.8	34.7
Education and health services	32.1	32.2	32.3	32.4	32.3	32.4	32.6	32.5	32.5	32.4	32.2
Leisure and hospitality	26.1	26.1	25.8	25.8	25.6	25.7	25.7	25.7	25.5	25.2	24.8
Other services	32.5	32.5	32.3	32.1	31.4	31.0	30.9	30.9	30.9	30.8	30.5

[1] Includes other industries, not shown separately.

Table 15-3. Average Weekly Hours of Production and Nonsupervisory Workers on Private Nonfarm Payrolls by Industry—*Continued*

(Hours.)

Industry	2010	2011	2012	2013	2014	2015	2016	2017	2018	2019	2020
Total Private	33.4	33.6	33.7	33.7	33.7	33.7	33.6	33.7	33.8	33.6	33.9
Goods-Producing	40.4	40.9	41.1	41.3	41.5	41.2	41.2	41.3	41.5	41.1	40.3
Mining and logging	44.6	46.7	46.6	45.9	47.3	45.8	45.3	46.1	46.8	46.9	44.9
Construction	38.4	39.0	39.3	39.6	39.6	39.6	39.7	39.7	40.0	39.8	39.2
Manufacturing	41.1	41.4	41.7	41.8	42.0	41.8	41.9	41.9	42.2	41.6	40.7
Overtime hours	3.8	4.1	4.2	4.3	4.5	4.3	4.3	4.3	4.6	4.3	3.7
Durable goods	41.4	41.9	42.0	42.2	42.5	42.1	42.3	42.3	42.5	42.0	40.9
Overtime hours	3.8	4.2	4.3	4.4	4.7	4.3	4.5	4.4	4.7	4.3	3.7
Wood products	39.1	39.7	41.1	42.7	42.0	41.3	41.8	42.1	41.9	41.5	41.7
Nonmetallic mineral products	41.7	42.3	42.2	42.5	43.3	42.4	42.0	42.9	44.2	43.8	43.4
Primary metals	43.7	44.6	43.8	43.8	44.2	43.8	43.4	43.1	44.6	43.8	42.1
Fabricated metal products	41.4	42.0	42.0	42.2	42.6	42.3	42.1	42.2	42.2	41.7	40.7
Machinery	42.1	43.2	42.8	42.9	43.0	41.9	42.1	42.7	42.7	42.4	41.0
Computer and electronic products	40.9	40.5	40.4	40.5	40.8	40.9	41.2	41.2	40.9	40.5	40.0
Electrical equipment and appliances	41.1	40.8	41.6	41.8	41.7	42.2	42.9	43.1	42.6	41.4	40.7
Transportation equipment [1]	42.9	43.2	43.8	43.6	43.6	43.7	44.1	43.9	44.4	43.4	41.5
Motor vehicles and parts	43.4	43.4	44.2	43.7	43.8	44.1	44.7	44.0	44.7	43.4	42.3
Furniture and related products	38.5	39.9	40.0	40.3	40.9	39.8	40.0	39.3	39.3	39.4	39.6
Miscellaneous manufacturing	38.7	38.9	39.2	40.1	40.2	40.1	40.8	39.9	39.5	39.7	38.4
Nondurable goods [1]	40.8	40.8	41.1	41.2	41.3	41.4	41.2	41.3	41.6	41.1	40.5
Overtime hours	3.8	4.0	4.1	4.3	4.3	4.3	4.1	4.2	4.4	4.2	3.8
Food manufacturing	40.7	40.2	40.6	40.8	40.8	41.0	41.4	41.7	42.0	41.5	41.3
Textile mills	41.2	41.7	42.6	41.5	41.5	42.5	41.2	40.6	42.3	43.5	43.7
Textile product mills	39.0	39.1	39.7	38.4	38.0	37.0	37.7	38.4	39.3	37.8	38.5
Apparel	36.6	38.2	37.1	38.1	38.5	38.2	36.4	36.5	37.7	37.0	36.6
Paper and paper products	42.9	42.9	42.9	43.1	43.7	43.0	42.7	42.5	43.1	42.1	42.4
Printing and related support activities	38.2	38.0	38.5	38.6	39.0	39.8	39.2	39.5	39.3	38.8	38.1
Petroleum and coal products	43.0	43.8	47.1	46.4	46.1	45.2	44.2	45.0	45.6	48.3	43.8
Chemicals	42.2	42.5	42.4	42.9	42.7	42.6	41.8	41.7	42.1	41.8	40.8
Plastics and rubber products	41.9	42.0	41.8	41.9	42.3	42.5	42.4	42.5	42.1	41.0	39.5
Private Service-Providing	32.2	32.4	32.5	32.4	32.4	32.4	32.3	32.4	32.5	32.4	32.8
Trade, transportation, and utilities	33.3	33.7	33.8	33.7	33.6	33.7	33.5	33.8	33.9	33.8	34.1
Wholesale trade	37.9	38.5	38.7	38.7	38.6	38.6	38.6	39.0	38.9	38.7	38.2
Retail trade	30.2	30.5	30.6	30.2	30.0	30.1	29.7	30.2	30.4	30.3	30.8
Transportation and warehousing	37.1	37.8	38.0	38.5	38.4	38.7	38.8	38.4	38.4	37.9	38.3
Utilities	42.0	42.1	41.1	41.7	42.3	42.4	42.5	42.5	42.7	42.4	42.6
Information	36.3	36.2	36.0	35.9	35.9	35.7	35.5	35.8	35.6	35.3	36.1
Financial activities	36.2	36.4	36.8	36.7	36.7	37.1	36.9	37.0	37.0	36.9	37.1
Professional and business services	35.1	35.2	35.3	35.4	35.6	35.5	35.4	35.4	35.4	35.4	35.8
Education and health services	32.0	32.2	32.3	32.1	32.0	32.1	32.2	32.2	32.2	32.2	32.5
Leisure and hospitality	24.8	24.8	25.0	25.0	25.1	25.1	24.9	24.9	24.9	24.7	24.1
Other services	30.7	30.8	30.7	30.8	30.7	30.7	30.8	30.7	30.8	30.8	31.2

[1]Includes other industries, not shown separately.

Table 15-4. Average Hourly Earnings of Production and Nonsupervisory Workers on Private Nonfarm Payrolls by Industry

(Dollars.)

Industry	1999	2000	2001	2002	2003	2004	2005	2006	2007	2008	2009
Total Private	13.48	14.01	14.54	14.96	15.36	15.68	16.12	16.74	17.41	18.06	18.60
Goods-Producing	14.71	15.27	15.78	16.33	16.80	17.19	17.60	18.02	18.67	19.33	19.90
Mining and logging	16.33	16.55	17.00	17.19	17.56	18.07	18.72	19.90	20.97	22.50	23.29
Construction	16.80	17.48	18.00	18.52	18.95	19.23	19.46	20.02	20.95	21.87	22.66
Manufacturing	13.85	14.32	14.76	15.29	15.74	16.14	16.56	16.81	17.26	17.75	18.24
Excluding overtime [1]	13.08	13.55	14.06	14.54	14.96	15.29	15.68	15.96	16.43	16.97	17.59
Durable goods	14.46	14.93	15.38	16.02	16.45	16.82	17.33	17.68	18.20	18.70	19.36
Wood products	11.18	11.63	11.99	12.33	12.71	13.03	13.16	13.39	13.68	14.19	14.92
Nonmetallic mineral products	13.97	14.53	14.86	15.39	15.76	16.25	16.61	16.59	16.93	16.90	17.28
Primary metals	16.00	16.64	17.06	17.68	18.13	18.57	18.94	19.36	19.66	20.19	20.10
Fabricated metal products	13.34	13.77	14.19	14.68	15.01	15.31	15.80	16.17	16.53	16.99	17.48
Machinery	14.77	15.21	15.48	15.92	16.29	16.67	17.02	17.20	17.72	17.97	18.38
Computer and electronic products	14.37	14.73	15.42	16.20	16.68	17.27	18.39	18.94	19.94	21.04	21.87
Electrical equipment and appliances	12.90	13.23	13.78	13.98	14.36	14.90	15.24	15.53	15.93	15.78	16.27
Transportation equipment [2]	18.24	18.89	19.47	20.63	21.22	21.48	22.09	22.41	23.03	23.85	24.98
Motor vehicles and parts	18.49	19.11	19.66	21.09	21.68	21.71	22.26	22.13	22.00	22.21	21.86
Furniture and related products	11.28	11.73	12.14	12.62	12.99	13.16	13.45	13.80	14.32	14.54	15.04
Miscellaneous manufacturing	11.55	11.93	12.45	12.91	13.30	13.84	14.07	14.36	14.66	15.20	16.13
Nondurable goods [2]	12.85	13.31	13.75	14.15	14.63	15.05	15.27	15.33	15.67	16.15	16.56
Food manufacturing	11.40	11.77	12.18	12.55	12.80	12.98	13.04	13.13	13.55	14.00	14.39
Textile mills	10.90	11.23	11.40	11.73	11.99	12.13	12.38	12.55	13.00	13.58	13.71
Textile product mills	10.04	10.31	10.49	10.85	11.15	11.31	11.61	11.86	11.78	11.73	11.44
Apparel	8.35	8.61	8.83	9.11	9.58	9.77	10.26	10.65	11.05	11.40	11.37
Paper and paper products	15.58	15.91	16.38	16.85	17.33	17.91	17.99	18.01	18.44	18.89	19.29
Printing and related support activities	13.67	14.09	14.48	14.93	15.37	15.71	15.74	15.80	16.15	16.75	16.75
Petroleum and coal products	22.22	22.80	22.90	23.04	23.63	24.39	24.47	24.11	25.21	27.41	29.61
Chemicals	16.40	17.09	17.57	17.97	18.50	19.17	19.67	19.60	19.55	19.50	20.30
Plastics and rubber products	12.25	12.70	13.21	13.55	14.18	14.59	14.80	14.97	15.39	15.85	16.01
Private Service-Providing	13.09	13.62	14.18	14.58	14.98	15.28	15.72	16.40	17.09	17.75	18.33
Trade, transportation, and utilities	12.80	13.28	13.68	13.99	14.31	14.55	14.90	15.36	15.74	16.13	16.44
Wholesale trade	15.59	16.24	16.74	16.94	17.33	17.62	18.13	18.87	19.54	20.08	20.78
Retail trade	10.45	10.87	11.30	11.67	11.90	12.09	12.36	12.58	12.76	12.87	13.02
Transportation and warehousing	14.50	15.00	15.27	15.71	16.20	16.46	16.65	17.21	17.67	18.36	18.74
Utilities	22.03	22.75	23.58	23.96	24.77	25.61	26.68	27.40	27.88	28.83	29.48
Information	18.40	19.07	19.80	20.20	21.01	21.40	22.06	23.23	23.96	24.78	25.45
Financial activities	14.55	15.04	15.65	16.25	17.21	17.58	17.98	18.83	19.67	20.32	20.90
Professional and business services	14.86	15.53	16.34	16.82	17.22	17.49	18.09	19.14	20.16	21.19	22.36
Education and health services	13.40	13.91	14.58	15.15	15.56	16.07	16.62	17.28	17.99	18.73	19.34
Leisure and hospitality	7.96	8.32	8.57	8.81	9.00	9.15	9.38	9.75	10.41	10.84	11.12
Other services	12.26	12.73	13.27	13.72	13.84	13.98	14.34	14.77	15.42	16.09	16.59

[1]Derived by assuming that overtime hours are paid at the rate of time and one-half.
[2]Includes other industries, not shown separately.

Table 15-4. Average Hourly Earnings of Production and Nonsupervisory Workers on Private Nonfarm Payrolls by Industry—*Continued*

(Dollars.)

Industry	2010	2011	2012	2013	2014	2015	2016	2017	2018	2019	2020
Total Private	19.04	19.43	19.73	20.13	20.60	21.03	21.53	22.05	22.71	23.51	24.67
Goods-Producing	20.28	20.67	20.94	21.24	21.59	21.96	22.58	23.18	24.00	24.75	25.41
Mining and logging	23.82	24.50	25.79	26.80	26.84	26.48	26.97	27.44	28.27	29.92	30.48
Construction	23.22	23.65	23.97	24.22	24.67	25.20	25.97	26.74	27.75	28.52	29.22
Manufacturing	18.61	18.93	19.08	19.30	19.56	19.91	20.44	20.90	21.54	22.15	22.79
Excluding overtime [1]	17.78	18.03	18.16	18.34	18.57	18.93	19.43	19.87	20.42	21.07	21.79
Durable goods	19.81	20.11	20.18	20.35	20.66	20.97	21.48	21.89	22.51	23.08	23.76
Wood products	14.85	14.81	14.99	15.47	15.57	16.16	16.81	17.47	17.88	18.50	19.18
Nonmetallic mineral products	17.48	18.16	18.15	18.40	19.16	19.92	20.30	20.34	21.41	22.10	22.66
Primary metals	20.13	19.94	20.70	21.94	22.41	22.47	23.10	23.10	23.31	23.44	23.96
Fabricated metal products	17.94	18.13	18.26	18.35	18.68	19.02	19.66	20.15	20.55	21.29	22.16
Machinery	18.96	19.54	20.17	20.58	21.00	21.34	21.80	22.41	23.06	23.82	24.62
Computer and electronic products	22.78	23.32	23.34	23.41	23.36	23.30	24.27	24.58	25.09	25.20	25.59
Electrical equipment and appliances	16.87	17.96	18.03	18.04	18.28	18.85	19.29	19.72	20.59	20.42	20.59
Transportation equipment [2]	25.23	25.34	24.57	24.57	24.96	25.05	25.06	25.36	26.31	27.16	28.01
Motor vehicles and parts	22.02	21.93	21.27	21.08	21.38	21.49	21.59	21.72	22.76	23.51	23.63
Furniture and related products	15.06	15.24	15.46	15.59	15.67	16.09	16.82	17.52	17.87	18.33	19.02
Miscellaneous manufacturing	16.56	16.82	17.05	17.03	17.31	17.72	18.44	19.04	19.15	19.62	20.77
Nondurable goods [2]	16.80	17.06	17.29	17.56	17.75	18.16	18.74	19.32	19.95	20.60	21.27
Food manufacturing	14.41	14.63	15.02	15.44	15.55	15.90	16.52	16.92	17.49	18.19	18.89
Textile mills	13.56	13.79	13.51	13.90	14.15	14.72	15.71	15.97	16.46	16.59	17.46
Textile product mills	11.79	12.21	12.77	12.88	13.35	13.31	13.64	14.80	15.31	15.52	16.03
Apparel	11.43	11.96	12.89	13.21	13.51	13.65	13.73	14.35	15.33	15.92	16.90
Paper and paper products	20.04	20.28	20.42	20.32	20.35	21.46	21.71	21.75	21.89	22.47	23.32
Printing and related support activities	16.91	17.28	17.28	17.77	18.01	18.31	18.59	18.61	18.74	18.98	20.06
Petroleum and coal products	31.31	31.75	32.15	34.58	35.39	37.32	38.88	39.95	40.24	41.36	39.21
Chemicals	21.07	21.45	21.45	21.40	21.49	21.76	22.71	24.29	25.46	25.46	26.03
Plastics and rubber products	15.71	15.95	16.05	16.20	16.51	16.82	17.17	17.63	18.49	19.38	20.20
Private Service-Providing	18.78	19.17	19.48	19.90	20.39	20.83	21.31	21.82	22.44	23.25	24.52
Trade, transportation, and utilities	16.78	17.10	17.38	17.69	18.21	18.61	18.93	19.29	19.88	20.63	21.41
Wholesale trade	21.46	21.88	22.13	22.52	23.14	23.52	24.07	24.58	25.17	26.06	26.81
Retail trade	13.25	13.52	13.82	14.03	14.40	14.83	15.05	15.33	15.91	16.62	17.60
Transportation and warehousing	19.10	19.42	19.47	19.73	20.43	20.66	20.83	21.22	21.75	22.36	22.75
Utilities	30.04	30.82	31.61	32.27	32.86	34.02	35.33	36.22	36.76	36.91	38.47
Information	25.87	26.62	27.04	27.98	28.70	29.05	30.05	30.74	31.97	33.93	35.72
Financial activities	21.55	21.93	22.82	23.87	24.71	25.34	26.12	26.57	26.93	27.68	29.09
Professional and business services	22.80	23.14	23.31	23.74	24.31	24.81	25.43	26.05	26.82	27.79	29.27
Education and health services	19.95	20.60	20.91	21.29	21.64	22.09	22.52	23.03	23.64	24.34	25.40
Leisure and hospitality	11.31	11.45	11.62	11.78	12.09	12.41	12.85	13.38	13.87	14.50	14.72
Other services	17.06	17.32	17.59	18.00	18.51	19.01	19.36	20.10	20.78	21.40	22.58

[1]Derived by assuming that overtime hours are paid at the rate of time and one-half.
[2]Includes other industries, not shown separately.

Table 15-5. Average Weekly Earnings of Production and Nonsupervisory Workers on Private Nonfarm Payrolls by Industry

(Dollars.)

Industry	1999	2000	2001	2002	2003	2004	2005	2006	2007	2008	2009
Total Private	463.09	480.90	493.53	506.48	517.68	528.65	543.94	566.94	589.09	607.10	615.82
Goods-Producing	599.99	621.86	630.01	651.65	669.13	688.32	705.28	730.16	757.50	776.63	779.68
Mining and logging	721.77	734.88	757.96	741.97	765.94	804.01	853.87	907.95	962.63	1 014.60	1 006.60
Construction	655.11	685.78	695.86	711.82	727.00	735.55	750.37	781.59	816.23	842.61	851.76
Manufacturing	573.29	590.92	595.19	618.62	636.03	658.49	673.34	690.88	711.53	724.46	726.12
Durable goods	606.55	624.38	624.38	652.97	671.35	694.06	712.67	731.93	754.73	767.92	771.24
Wood products	461.46	476.97	481.33	492.07	514.06	530.15	526.65	533.12	539.41	547.53	557.65
Nonmetallic mineral products	587.42	604.76	618.91	647.00	664.96	688.33	700.63	712.67	716.78	711.11	705.54
Primary metals	700.80	734.83	723.86	749.17	767.15	799.69	815.90	843.79	843.42	851.12	817.70
Fabricated metal products	555.86	576.68	576.60	596.30	610.44	628.83	647.24	668.91	687.16	701.57	689.22
Machinery	625.04	643.94	632.72	645.38	664.44	699.45	716.13	728.81	754.34	760.27	738.06
Computer and electronic products	596.37	609.97	613.18	642.77	674.69	697.97	735.59	766.75	809.10	861.58	883.02
Electrical equipment and appliances	538.98	550.48	548.03	560.33	583.27	607.00	618.88	637.04	656.46	645.60	639.34
Transportation equipment [1]	795.57	817.56	816.74	877.50	889.42	912.56	937.72	957.47	986.75	1 000.80	1 028.50
Motor vehicles and parts	809.47	828.41	818.84	898.57	910.20	925.07	940.54	934.38	930.47	920.36	876.34
Furniture and related products	443.68	459.95	464.87	493.95	505.26	519.61	527.49	535.90	561.08	553.90	566.75
Miscellaneous manufacturing	454.14	464.80	483.07	499.01	510.54	533.27	545.01	555.87	570.12	591.95	620.74
Nondurable goods [1]	520.06	536.89	548.30	566.75	582.48	602.53	608.95	622.00	639.96	652.22	658.57
Food manufacturing	458.73	472.09	481.81	497.25	502.92	509.55	508.55	526.02	551.21	566.88	575.40
Textile mills	447.38	464.51	456.64	476.52	469.33	486.68	498.47	509.39	524.40	525.00	516.86
Textile product mills	392.46	398.93	402.53	423.05	438.67	437.89	451.36	472.10	467.80	453.06	433.09
Apparel	295.62	307.51	317.63	334.24	340.73	352.04	366.93	389.05	411.57	415.10	408.86
Paper and paper products	679.05	681.38	689.76	705.20	719.55	754.17	764.15	772.57	795.58	809.57	806.19
Printing and related support activities	534.15	552.15	560.89	573.05	587.58	603.97	604.73	618.92	632.02	642.50	635.68
Petroleum and coal products	947.60	973.53	1 003.30	990.88	1 052.30	1 095.00	1 114.50	1 085.50	1 112.70	1 222.00	1 284.40
Chemicals	701.06	721.41	735.57	759.56	784.26	819.93	831.79	833.84	819.51	809.29	841.18
Plastics and rubber products	505.52	517.60	528.95	550.06	572.60	590.08	591.68	608.69	635.57	649.41	643.81
Private Service-Providing	427.95	445.66	460.97	473.61	484.32	493.95	509.00	532.11	554.05	573.23	587.37
Trade, transportation, and utilities	433.44	448.78	458.58	469.97	480.00	487.37	497.07	512.82	524.57	534.44	540.19
Wholesale trade	601.78	630.09	642.08	643.40	656.36	665.96	683.99	717.42	747.08	768.14	782.62
Retail trade	321.74	333.48	346.31	360.92	367.28	371.23	377.58	383.25	385.18	386.44	388.74
Transportation and warehousing	544.81	559.63	559.22	576.77	594.70	611.99	615.26	633.23	651.78	667.57	674.19
Utilities	924.40	955.09	977.25	979.26	1 017.40	1 048.00	1 095.90	1 135.50	1 182.60	1 230.60	1 239.30
Information	675.47	700.92	731.18	737.94	760.84	776.72	805.11	850.64	874.45	908.78	931.08
Financial activities	520.73	540.42	560.46	579.08	611.99	625.50	646.51	673.66	706.52	729.64	754.90
Professional and business services	511.39	535.56	558.32	575.00	587.68	597.88	619.65	662.80	701.42	738.31	776.30
Education and health services	429.76	447.80	471.33	490.38	503.05	521.06	541.40	561.02	585.44	607.82	622.30
Leisure and hospitality	208.05	217.20	220.73	227.31	230.49	234.86	241.36	250.34	265.54	273.39	275.95
Other services	398.77	413.30	428.64	439.87	434.41	433.04	443.40	456.50	477.06	495.57	506.26

[1]Includes other industries, not shown separately.

Table 15-5. Average Weekly Earnings of Production and Nonsupervisory Workers on Private Nonfarm Payrolls by Industry—*Continued*

(Dollars.)

Industry	2010	2011	2012	2013	2014	2015	2016	2017	2018	2019	2020
Total Private	636.02	652.72	665.56	677.62	694.74	708.70	723.20	742.48	766.99	790.44	836.58
Goods-Producing	818.96	844.85	861.39	877.09	895.09	905.43	930.34	956.83	996.67	1 017.90	1 023.80
Mining and logging	1 063.10	1 144.60	1 201.60	1 229.70	1 270.90	1 211.90	1 221.60	1 265.90	1 322.40	1 402.30	1 368.90
Construction	891.83	921.84	942.14	958.72	977.11	998.02	1 031.80	1 061.90	1 108.50	1 135.70	1 145.90
Manufacturing	764.99	784.29	794.67	807.37	822.03	832.08	855.77	876.10	908.01	921.68	928.28
Durable goods	819.06	841.85	848.35	859.69	877.31	882.91	909.23	926.85	956.74	968.43	970.99
Wood products	580.74	587.77	615.76	661.10	653.87	666.82	703.47	735.06	749.63	767.64	798.92
Nonmetallic mineral products	728.22	768.35	766.16	782.69	829.79	844.77	852.66	873.01	947.10	968.08	982.57
Primary metals	880.46	889.34	907.23	960.61	991.13	984.77	1 003.40	995.41	1 038.40	1 026.90	1 007.40
Fabricated metal products	742.61	762.14	767.52	775.35	795.62	804.67	827.74	849.82	866.83	886.87	902.26
Machinery	797.62	843.10	863.99	883.03	903.42	894.61	918.23	957.16	985.50	1 010.00	1 009.70
Computer and electronic products	932.26	943.88	944.02	948.79	952.82	953.04	999.76	1 012.10	1 026.60	1 021.50	1 022.90
Electrical equipment and appliances	693.49	732.16	749.91	753.07	763.08	794.79	827.24	850.47	877.69	846.07	837.25
Transportation equipment [1]	1 081.60	1 094.40	1 075.00	1 070.80	1 088.20	1 094.00	1 105.90	1 113.90	1 167.90	1 178.80	1.00
Motor vehicles and parts	956.39	952.34	940.00	920.56	936.90	948.30	964.46	956.61	1 017.10	1 019.30	999.78
Furniture and related products	579.66	608.00	617.74	628.36	641.27	640.01	672.60	689.02	702.49	722.52	752.99
Miscellaneous manufacturing	640.85	654.90	668.95	682.97	695.67	709.56	751.91	759.06	756.91	778.42	797.89
Nondurable goods [1]	685.07	696.03	710.13	723.53	733.64	751.05	771.47	798.20	829.93	846.35	861.84
Food manufacturing	586.52	588.19	609.69	629.70	634.95	652.26	683.74	705.82	734.72	754.14	780.23
Textile mills	559.13	574.61	575.75	577.18	586.40	625.84	647.60	648.43	696.84	722.32	762.80
Textile product mills	459.46	477.49	507.00	494.76	507.19	493.03	513.89	568.47	602.46	587.20	617.68
Apparel	418.28	456.97	478.33	503.01	520.57	520.73	499.82	524.59	578.04	589.21	618.13
Paper and paper products	858.65	870.53	877.14	874.85	888.07	923.13	926.10	924.75	942.38	945.46	989.21
Printing and related support activities	646.11	655.81	665.45	685.33	701.55	729.57	728.41	734.43	736.06	736.74	764.85
Petroleum and coal products	1 345.70	1 390.80	1 513.30	1 605.00	1 630.80	1 685.20	1 719.80	1 796.50	1 832.90	1 998.30	1 716.20
Chemicals	888.25	910.88	910.02	918.69	917.96	927.83	950.00	1 012.30	1 071.90	1 064.40	1 063.30
Plastics and rubber products	658.39	669.70	670.94	678.38	697.81	713.84	728.44	750.04	778.83	794.71	797.35
Private Service-Providing	604.91	620.78	632.87	644.65	661.42	675.83	689.13	707.04	728.42	752.56	804.25
Trade, transportation, and utilities	558.05	575.88	587.09	595.36	611.77	626.54	633.77	652.11	674.74	697.95	730.72
Wholesale trade	814.04	842.06	857.06	871.89	894.06	907.72	929.09	957.95	979.82	1 007.40	1 023.80
Retail trade	400.38	412.29	422.35	423.44	431.97	446.01	447.69	463.10	483.03	503.06	542.15
Transportation and warehousing	707.93	734.06	739.12	758.79	785.50	800.14	807.25	813.69	835.39	847.97	870.56
Utilities	1 262.80	1 296.90	1 298.20	1 344.70	1 388.90	1 444.00	1 502.00	1 540.20	1 569.30	1 566.90	1 639.20
Information	939.85	964.85	973.52	1 003.60	1 030.10	1 038.10	1 068.20	1 100.00	1 139.50	1 198.90	1 288.20
Financial activities	780.25	798.68	839.84	875.04	908.15	939.46	962.95	982.09	997.26	1 020.40	1 078.60
Professional and business services	799.43	814.74	823.37	839.86	865.25	879.63	899.79	922.51	949.18	984.35	1 048.30
Education and health services	639.37	663.04	674.48	683.24	692.56	709.25	723.91	741.55	761.86	783.66	824.80
Leisure and hospitality	280.87	283.82	290.54	294.31	303.81	311.32	319.67	332.54	345.21	358.27	355.00
Other services	523.70	532.63	539.46	553.77	568.92	583.54	595.68	617.91	640.70	659.07	705.41

[1]Includes other industries, not shown separately.

Table 15-6.   Indexes of Aggregate Weekly Hours of Production and Nonsupervisory Workers on Private Nonfarm Payrolls by Industry

(2002 = 100.)

Industry	1999	2000	2001	2002	2003	2004	2005	2006	2007	2008	2009
Total Private	101.4	103.5	102.0	100.0	98.7	100.2	102.8	105.8	107.4	106.0	98.8
Goods-Producing	112.6	113.1	106.6	100.0	95.7	96.8	98.9	102.5	101.7	96.5	80.2
Mining and logging	102.9	105.1	108.3	100.0	97.4	104.0	114.7	125.8	133.5	137.6	117.2
Construction	99.7	104.0	103.2	100.0	98.4	101.7	108.3	115.4	114.7	106.5	85.9
Manufacturing	119.0	117.7	108.1	100.0	94.5	94.3	93.9	95.6	94.4	90.2	76.1
Durable goods	120.5	120.4	109.3	100.0	94.3	95.2	96.1	98.9	97.4	92.2	74.7
Wood products	118.5	115.8	105.0	100.0	97.8	100.8	101.2	99.9	89.3	76.7	57.8
Nonmetallic mineral products	106.9	109.1	106.1	100.0	94.3	98.0	97.4	100.3	96.9	91.2	73.8
Primary metals	128.4	128.9	113.0	100.0	93.4	93.3	93.1	94.2	91.4	87.4	66.1
Fabricated metal products	116.7	119.2	109.3	100.0	95.3	97.7	99.3	103.1	104.5	101.3	81.3
Machinery	129.8	127.6	114.1	100.0	93.6	96.0	98.8	102.2	103.3	102.3	80.7
Computer and electronic products	131.1	133.1	117.9	100.0	92.1	89.8	94.8	103.6	102.2	101.2	89.4
Electrical equipment and appliances	128.3	127.7	113.4	100.0	92.0	88.7	86.4	88.0	89.1	88.5	74.1
Transportation equipment [1]	119.5	116.3	105.3	100.0	95.5	96.5	97.3	99.9	98.0	88.6	70.1
Motor vehicles and parts	118.8	117.3	103.6	100.0	95.9	97.0	95.2	92.9	85.8	72.7	51.6
Furniture and related products	112.6	114.7	104.8	100.0	93.0	94.3	91.9	90.4	86.1	74.6	57.6
Miscellaneous manufacturing	110.3	109.5	104.7	100.0	93.6	91.8	90.6	90.4	91.0	89.2	81.1
Nondurable goods [1]	116.1	113.3	106.0	100.0	94.7	92.7	90.3	90.4	89.6	86.9	78.1
Food manufacturing	103.7	103.4	101.4	100.0	98.4	97.1	95.8	98.6	101.1	100.6	97.5
Textile mills	139.1	132.4	112.2	100.0	86.3	79.0	71.3	65.1	56.3	47.9	37.8
Textile product mills	115.6	112.3	105.5	100.0	92.4	90.2	88.0	85.0	77.5	70.5	58.5
Apparel	154.6	137.5	117.1	100.0	81.9	75.1	65.7	63.4	61.5	56.7	45.4
Paper and paper products	117.2	113.5	106.6	100.0	92.5	89.2	88.0	86.9	85.8	83.5	74.2
Printing and related support activities	120.9	119.4	111.5	100.0	95.3	93.4	90.9	92.5	91.6	86.1	74.1
Petroleum and coal products	107.6	105.8	105.6	100.0	98.7	102.6	102.4	96.9	95.6	102.4	90.2
Chemicals	113.2	110.4	104.7	100.0	99.0	99.0	95.9	96.1	94.1	94.6	88.3
Plastics and rubber products	114.6	114.2	105.0	100.0	95.2	94.2	92.4	92.0	91.1	87.2	71.3
Private Service-Providing	98.3	100.9	100.8	100.0	99.5	101.1	103.8	106.7	108.9	108.6	104.1
Trade, transportation, and utilities	102.0	103.6	101.6	100.0	98.6	99.6	101.6	103.2	104.8	103.2	96.7
Wholesale trade	106.3	107.1	102.9	100.0	98.0	98.7	101.6	105.5	108.9	108.3	99.5
Retail trade	99.5	101.3	100.5	100.0	98.9	99.4	100.8	101.1	101.8	99.8	94.3
Transportation and warehousing	103.3	105.7	102.8	100.0	98.7	101.9	105.2	107.9	109.5	107.9	100.2
Utilities	105.0	104.1	102.3	100.0	97.4	94.2	93.1	93.8	96.2	98.3	97.0
Information	98.5	105.0	106.7	100.0	97.0	98.2	99.4	100.2	100.1	100.0	93.5
Financial activities	98.0	98.4	99.2	100.0	101.3	101.3	103.7	106.3	107.6	106.8	103.1
Professional and business services	101.6	106.5	104.0	100.0	98.7	101.8	106.4	112.2	115.4	114.0	105.3
Education and health services	90.4	92.6	96.5	100.0	101.7	103.8	107.0	109.6	113.2	116.5	118.3
Leisure and hospitality	97.8	100.5	100.6	100.0	100.0	103.0	106.2	108.8	110.8	109.7	105.1
Other services	96.2	97.8	99.0	100.0	97.4	96.1	96.2	97.4	99.3	99.5	96.0

[1]Includes other industries, not shown separately.

Table 15-6. Indexes of Aggregate Weekly Hours of Production and Nonsupervisory Workers on Private Nonfarm Payrolls by Industry—*Continued*

(2002 = 100.)

Industry	2010	2011	2012	2013	2014	2015	2016	2017	2018	2019	2020
Total Private	99.0	101.4	104.3	106.1	108.6	110.9	112.5	114.9	117.2	118.3	110.7
Goods-Producing	78.8	81.2	83.5	85.1	87.8	89.1	89.5	91.1	94.4	94.8	87.7
Mining and logging	124.5	147.4	158.7	155.0	164.3	144.1	113.4	120.2	134.5	133.3	104.7
Construction	80.2	81.7	83.6	87.7	92.0	96.5	100.9	104.0	108.8	111.2	105.6
Manufacturing	76.2	78.3	80.3	80.9	82.6	83.3	83.3	84.0	86.1	85.6	78.8
Durable goods	75.0	78.4	81.4	82.3	84.3	84.6	84.3	84.5	87.2	87.2	78.8
Wood products	58.5	59.3	62.1	67.3	69.6	70.2	72.0	72.9	74.3	74.2	71.6
Nonmetallic mineral products	70.5	70.1	68.9	69.7	72.4	75.0	76.7	78.1	82.1	81.6	76.2
Primary metals	71.7	80.1	82.7	79.8	81.7	80.1	75.8	74.9	78.4	78.8	68.3
Fabricated metal products	83.1	89.6	94.7	96.4	97.9	97.0	93.6	94.6	98.4	98.9	89.3
Machinery	81.2	89.6	94.0	94.0	96.6	93.4	90.6	92.5	95.9	94.3	82.9
Computer and electronic products	87.2	86.4	86.0	83.7	81.4	82.3	83.1	83.4	84.9	87.6	87.4
Electrical equipment and appliances	73.2	71.6	73.4	72.4	73.5	77.2	78.6	77.3	78.8	77.0	70.7
Transportation equipment [1]	72.1	75.3	80.4	82.4	86.3	89.3	91.1	90.6	94.7	93.4	79.8
Motor vehicles and parts	57.5	60.9	66.6	70.7	76.2	79.8	83.2	83.6	87.9	84.0	69.3
Furniture and related products	54.4	55.8	55.6	57.6	60.7	60.8	61.6	61.3	61.3	61.0	54.7
Miscellaneous manufacturing	79.0	80.0	82.2	85.3	86.3	84.9	85.8	83.8	83.7	86.3	78.6
Nondurable goods [1]	78.0	77.9	78.6	78.6	80.0	81.2	81.6	83.1	84.2	82.9	78.7
Food manufacturing	98.5	97.7	99.6	100.1	100.8	102.4	105.3	109.5	112.2	112.3	110.6
Textile mills	40.2	41.6	41.7	39.0	38.4	39.1	37.8	36.3	37.4	37.6	32.4
Textile product mills	56.5	55.2	53.3	50.5	51.5	51.5	53.3	54.1	53.2	46.8	43.3
Apparel	42.0	40.7	38.4	38.5	38.0	37.8	34.3	30.5	29.4	26.2	22.7
Paper and paper products	73.5	71.9	70.0	68.2	68.5	67.5	66.6	67.0	67.1	64.8	63.3
Printing and related support activities	69.0	65.6	64.3	63.2	64.2	65.2	64.6	63.7	61.4	58.5	51.6
Petroleum and coal products	89.1	91.2	101.6	96.8	98.5	100.1	100.7	107.0	104.7	111.0	93.8
Chemicals	88.9	90.6	92.6	93.6	94.4	96.1	96.1	97.4	102.3	103.9	97.2
Plastics and rubber products	73.6	75.3	75.8	77.4	81.4	84.0	84.7	86.0	85.9	83.7	76.6
Private Service-Providing	104.5	107.0	110.0	112.0	114.5	117.0	118.9	121.5	123.5	124.8	117.0
Trade, transportation, and utilities	96.8	99.7	101.8	102.6	104.4	106.3	106.9	109.2	110.8	110.9	107.0
Wholesale trade	97.4	100.2	103.5	104.8	106.4	106.4	106.2	107.8	108.3	108.5	101.7
Retail trade	95.0	97.7	98.9	98.8	99.5	101.0	101.1	103.1	103.6	102.1	98.6
Transportation and warehousing	101.5	105.7	109.5	112.8	117.0	123.3	126.9	130.6	137.4	142.1	140.3
Utilities	95.4	94.9	92.6	94.9	96.3	97.0	97.1	97.2	96.9	95.6	93.9
Information	90.0	88.9	88.9	89.8	90.5	90.8	91.4	92.6	93.0	93.0	88.0
Financial activities	101.3	101.1	103.7	104.7	106.5	109.6	111.6	114.3	116.0	117.5	116.5
Professional and business services	107.7	112.6	117.3	121.4	125.9	128.3	130.2	132.6	135.2	137.0	130.2
Education and health services	119.8	122.3	125.4	126.6	128.5	132.3	136.1	139.8	142.7	145.7	140.9
Leisure and hospitality	104.6	106.9	111.3	115.2	119.3	122.7	125.6	128.7	130.6	131.9	101.3
Other services	96.0	96.8	97.7	98.7	99.9	100.7	101.8	102.9	104.4	105.3	96.2

[1] Includes other industries, not shown separately.

NOTES AND DEFINITIONS, CHAPTER 15

TABLES 15-1 THROUGH 15-6

Employment, Hours, and Earnings by NAICS Industry

SOURCE: U.S. DEPARTMENT OF LABOR, BUREAU OF LABOR STATISTICS

See the notes and definitions for Tables 10-8 through 10-18 regarding definitions of *employment, production and nonsupervisory workers, average weekly hours, overtime hours, average hourly earnings, average weekly earnings*, and the *indexes of aggregate weekly hours*. Availability and reference information is also provided in those notes and definitions.

Definitions

The North American Industry Classification System (NAICS) is the standard used by Federal statistical agencies in classifying business establishments for the purpose of collecting, analyzing, and publishing statistical data related to the U.S. business economy. NAICS defines industries according to a consistent principle: businesses that use similar production processes are grouped together.

NAICS is the product of a cooperative effort on the part of the statistical agencies of the United States, Canada, and Mexico. This system is the hierarchical, numerical system used by the Federal government to classify businesses by industry, in order to collect, analyze, and publish statistical data related to the U.S. business economy.

There are 20 high-level industrial sections and are listed below.

Sector	Description
11	Agriculture, Forestry, Fishing and Hunting
21	Mining, Quarrying, and Oil and Gas Extraction
22	Utilities
23	Construction
31-33	Manufacturing
42	Wholesale Trade
44-45	Retail Trade
48-49	Transportation and Warehousing
51	Information
52	Finance and Insurance
53	Real Estate and Rental and Leasing
54	Professional, Scientific, and Technical Services
55	Management of Companies and Enterprises
56	Administrative and Support and Waste Management and Remediation Services
61	Educational Services
62	Health Care and Social Assistance
71	Arts, Entertainment, and Recreation
72	Accommodation and Food Services
81	Other Services (except Public Administration)
92	Public Administration *(not covered in economic census)*

CHAPTER 16: KEY SECTOR STATISTICS

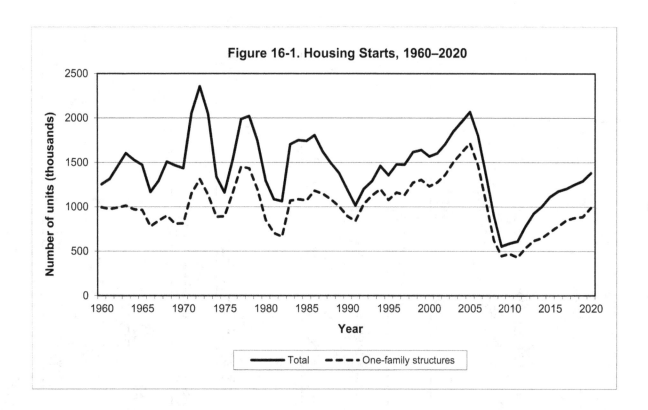

Figure 16-1. Housing Starts, 1960–2020

- The housing sector and associated financial excesses had the leading role in the boom and bust cycle of 2001–2009. In 2005, as shown in Figure 16-1, nearly 2.1 million housing units were started, the highest since 1972. Of those, 1.7 million were one-family homes, an all-time record. By 2009, both total and single-family starts had plunged to the lowest levels of their 50-year history. With very modest recovery in the years following 2009, starts remained at levels once viewed as recessionary. In 2020, the housing starts more than doubled the 2009 low—to 1.38 million. (Table 16-2)

- New orders for nondefense capital goods excluding aircraft and parts at U.S. manufacturing firms is a widely followed advance indicator for production of investment goods. The value of such orders fell nearly 39 percent from 2007 to 2009 which was greater than their decline between 2000 and 2002. Their recovery in the four years following 2009 was faster than it was in the 4 years following 2002, and the value of new orders in 2013 surpassed the peak in 2007 but declined 5.5 percent between 2013 and 2019. In 2020, new orders for nondefense capital goods declined significantly again, dropping nearly 27 percent in just one year, (Table 16-5)

- E-commerce grew from 2.7 percent of total retail sales at the beginning of 2006 to 13.6 percent (seasonally adjusted) at the end of 2020. (Table 16-9)

- Sales of new passenger cars dropped to its lowest rate in decades in 2020, marking six consecutive years in which sales have declined. (Table 16-7)

Table 16-1. New Construction Put in Place

(Billions of dollars, monthly data are at seasonally adjusted annual rates.)

Year and month	Total	Private Total¹	Residential	Office	Commercial Total¹	Multi-retail	Health care	Educational	Amusement and recreation	Transportation	Communication	Power	Manufacturing
1980	273.9	210.3	100.4	...	...	...	...	...	...	...	...	...	...
1981	289.1	224.4	99.2	...	...	...	...	...	...	...	...	...	...
1982	279.3	216.3	84.7	...	...	...	...	...	...	...	...	...	...
1983	311.9	248.4	125.8	...	...	...	...	...	...	...	...	...	...
1984	370.2	300.0	155.0	...	...	...	...	...	...	...	...	...	...
1985	403.4	325.6	160.5	...	...	...	...	...	...	...	...	...	...
1986	433.5	348.9	190.7	...	...	...	...	...	...	...	...	...	...
1987	446.6	356.0	199.7	...	...	...	...	...	...	...	...	...	...
1988	462.0	367.3	204.5	...	...	...	...	...	...	...	...	...	...
1989	477.5	379.3	204.3	...	...	...	...	...	...	...	...	...	...
1990	476.8	369.3	191.1	...	...	...	...	...	...	...	...	...	...
1991	432.6	322.5	166.3	...	...	...	...	...	...	...	...	...	...
1992	463.7	347.8	199.4	...	...	...	...	...	...	...	...	...	...
1993	485.5	358.2	208.2	20.0	34.4	11.5	14.9	4.8	4.6	4.7	9.8	23.6	23.4
1994	531.9	401.5	241.0	20.4	39.6	12.2	15.4	5.0	5.1	4.7	10.1	21.0	28.8
1995	548.7	408.7	228.1	23.0	44.1	12.0	15.3	5.7	5.9	4.8	11.1	22.0	35.4
1996	599.7	453.0	257.5	26.5	49.4	13.3	15.4	7.0	7.0	5.8	11.8	17.4	38.1
1997	631.9	478.4	264.7	32.8	53.1	12.2	17.4	8.8	8.5	6.2	12.5	16.4	37.6
1998	688.5	533.7	296.3	40.4	55.7	13.3	17.7	9.8	8.6	7.3	12.5	21.7	40.5
1999	744.6	575.5	326.3	45.1	59.4	15.2	18.4	9.8	9.6	6.5	18.4	22.0	35.1
2000	802.8	621.4	346.1	52.4	64.1	14.9	19.5	11.7	8.8	6.9	18.8	29.3	37.6
2001	840.2	638.3	364.4	49.7	63.6	16.4	19.5	12.8	7.8	7.1	19.6	31.5	37.8
2002	847.9	634.4	402.0	44.3	62.5	15.6	27.1	73.9	17.3	25.8	18.5	36.8	22.9
2003	891.5	675.4	451.3	39.4	61.5	15.4	29.3	74.3	16.8	24.7	14.6	41.5	21.5
2004	991.4	771.2	538.4	42.4	67.1	18.8	32.2	74.3	16.7	25.1	15.5	35.6	23.4
2005	1 116.8	882.7	624.6	37.3	66.6	22.8	28.5	12.8	7.5	7.1	18.8	29.2	28.4
2006	1 161.3	905.9	607.8	45.7	73.4	29.2	32.0	13.8	9.3	8.7	22.2	33.7	32.3
2007	1 148.0	858.9	488.8	53.8	85.9	34.8	35.6	16.7	10.2	9.0	27.5	54.1	40.2
2008	1 077.3	768.6	359.2	55.5	82.7	32.0	38.4	18.6	10.5	9.9	26.3	69.2	53.6
2009	911.8	596.9	252.8	37.3	51.1	18.4	35.3	16.9	8.4	9.1	19.7	76.1	57.4
2010	813.0	509.0	245.7	24.4	37.2	12.5	29.6	13.4	6.5	9.9	17.7	66.1	40.6
2011	791.2	504.8	247.0	23.7	39.2	13.4	28.9	14.1	6.7	9.5	17.5	64.3	39.8
2012	854.4	575.1	273.7	27.4	44.3	14.9	31.4	16.6	6.2	10.9	16.0	86.4	46.8
2013	914.6	643.9	329.6	30.1	50.9	16.7	29.7	16.9	6.9	11.0	17.6	81.3	51.8
2014	1 015.3	739.2	377.5	38.9	60.9	19.5	28.9	16.6	7.7	12.2	17.1	98.2	60.1
2015	1 140.2	846.4	431.8	47.9	64.5	20.0	30.9	17.7	10.0	13.6	21.5	99.5	82.4
2016	1 223.7	926.7	479.4	59.8	75.5	22.4	31.8	20.0	12.6	13.1	22.0	102.3	78.9
2017	1 279.8	983.3	539.0	59.9	84.5	24.0	33.5	21.2	14.5	14.8	23.6	89.8	70.0
2018	1 333.2	1 023.0	557.6	66.8	82.8	20.8	34.0	22.3	15.7	17.9	24.3	94.4	72.0
2019	1 391.0	1 046.7	546.6	77.5	80.3	14.6	36.8	21.6	15.8	17.2	22.1	110.4	80.5
2020	1 469.2	1 107.9	628.9	75.3	82.7	10.7	38.3	18.3	13.4	15.9	22.4	107.9	71.8
2018													
January	1 341.6	1 041.4	571.8	62.2	86.9	23.1	34.3	22.2	14.5	17.3	24.9	105.2	68.9
February	1 361.8	1 059.6	578.9	64.6	90.9	23.4	34.6	23.0	14.9	17.6	25.1	104.0	71.7
March	1 353.9	1 047.8	575.1	64.6	86.8	23.2	33.8	22.4	15.3	17.9	26.4	102.1	69.8
April	1 360.8	1 049.8	576.6	64.9	87.0	23.1	34.3	22.6	15.8	18.2	24.6	100.5	70.0
May	1 366.6	1 053.9	579.5	66.9	87.3	22.1	34.5	23.1	16.1	18.0	24.4	97.0	71.9
June	1 345.3	1 032.6	570.1	65.5	82.9	21.7	33.3	22.3	16.5	17.8	24.1	94.9	70.9
July	1 336.2	1 021.9	559.4	67.2	82.3	21.2	33.2	22.0	16.4	18.0	24.0	93.5	70.1
August	1 334.7	1 014.1	548.7	68.6	81.6	20.6	34.1	21.8	16.3	18.0	23.4	91.7	73.6
September	1 320.6	1 011.2	548.7	68.6	81.9	19.1	34.0	22.1	15.8	17.7	23.3	88.7	74.8
October	1 303.7	992.5	533.3	70.2	79.6	18.5	34.2	23.0	15.4	17.3	23.7	86.0	73.7
November	1 291.5	983.9	535.1	67.6	74.8	17.5	32.7	22.2	15.6	18.1	23.8	85.2	73.1
December	1 285.0	974.8	516.3	70.5	73.9	16.1	34.8	22.0	15.6	18.9	24.4	86.7	75.4
2019													
January	1 304.4	983.1	519.6	72.6	77.5	16.3	35.5	22.3	15.7	19.6	22.3	83.7	77.7
February	1 321.9	989.4	520.0	72.2	75.8	15.6	35.4	22.0	16.1	18.7	21.8	88.2	81.5
March	1 335.7	1 001.6	521.7	74.2	76.3	15.4	36.1	22.4	16.1	18.0	22.4	94.2	82.3
April	1 363.6	1 010.0	527.3	75.3	75.1	14.0	35.2	21.7	16.0	15.9	22.4	100.1	82.3
May	1 368.7	1 024.1	532.9	76.4	77.4	15.0	35.7	21.3	15.6	16.8	21.9	107.6	80.7
June	1 385.3	1 041.9	541.7	75.3	80.4	15.1	36.2	21.1	15.6	16.6	21.8	113.2	81.3
July	1 409.1	1 061.5	552.0	80.7	80.8	14.6	37.1	21.7	15.2	16.9	21.8	115.8	81.1
August	1 419.3	1 073.5	556.7	82.7	82.0	13.9	36.3	22.0	16.0	17.6	22.2	119.3	80.4
September	1 427.9	1 076.4	559.6	79.5	82.3	14.0	37.4	21.9	15.9	17.8	22.2	122.6	80.3
October	1 429.8	1 080.8	561.3	80.2	84.0	14.0	37.6	21.3	15.9	17.0	22.0	124.2	79.3
November	1 450.2	1 099.1	572.4	80.6	86.9	14.5	39.2	21.1	16.3	16.4	21.9	124.5	81.5
December	1 458.5	1 101.5	581.5	79.5	83.9	13.0	39.3	20.8	15.5	16.0	22.8	125.6	78.8
2020													
January	1 486.4	1 118.5	591.5	82.1	88.3	12.8	39.1	20.5	15.1	16.1	22.6	127.4	77.5
February	1 501.6	1 130.2	609.7	81.9	88.3	12.9	39.1	20.1	15.1	16.5	22.4	122.6	76.2
March	1 507.1	1 132.4	617.6	83.0	87.9	12.4	39.9	19.8	15.1	16.4	22.7	117.4	76.3
April	1 452.4	1 086.2	597.7	76.5	85.8	11.6	38.7	18.4	13.9	16.3	22.9	109.7	71.8
May	1 437.7	1 063.3	584.2	75.9	84.1	10.7	37.8	18.6	13.5	16.1	22.6	105.6	71.5
June	1 435.0	1 070.9	590.4	76.3	84.9	10.2	39.3	18.5	12.7	16.2	22.5	106.2	70.9
July	1 439.6	1 083.6	608.6	74.3	81.2	10.0	38.9	18.4	13.0	16.1	22.7	105.3	72.8
August	1 455.0	1 098.9	632.7	73.0	79.2	10.1	38.2	17.6	12.7	15.4	22.4	104.2	72.1
September	1 459.3	1 107.1	648.3	72.5	78.2	9.9	36.9	17.3	12.6	15.5	22.6	102.6	69.1
October	1 471.7	1 120.1	664.1	71.3	79.9	9.7	37.7	17.1	12.7	15.4	21.9	99.9	69.7
November	1 487.2	1 131.8	684.5	69.5	78.7	9.4	37.1	17.1	12.4	15.3	21.6	98.1	68.0
December	1 504.2	1 147.0	704.8	69.0	77.2	9.3	36.5	16.6	11.8	15.5	21.8	100.0	65.9

¹Includes categories not shown separately.
. . . = Not available.

Table 16-1. New Construction Put in Place—*Continued*

(Billions of dollars, monthly data are at seasonally adjusted annual rates.)

Year and month	Total	Public													Federal
		State and local													
		Total [1]	Residential	Office	Health care	Educational	Public safety	Amusement and recreation	Transportation	Power	Highway and street	Sewage and waste disposal	Water supply	
1980	63.6	54.0	...	...	...	...	...	...	...	...	...	...	...	9.6
1981	64.7	54.3	...	...	...	...	...	...	...	...	...	...	...	10.4
1982	63.1	53.1	...	...	...	...	...	...	...	...	...	...	...	10.0
1983	63.5	52.9	...	...	...	...	...	...	...	...	...	...	...	10.6
1984	70.2	59.0	...	...	...	...	...	...	...	...	...	...	...	11.2
1985	77.8	65.8	...	...	...	...	...	...	...	...	...	...	...	12.0
1986	84.6	72.2	...	...	...	...	...	...	...	...	...	...	...	12.4
1987	90.6	76.6	...	...	...	...	...	...	...	...	...	...	...	14.1
1988	94.7	82.5	...	...	...	...	...	...	...	...	...	...	...	12.3
1989	98.2	86.0	...	...	...	...	...	...	...	...	...	...	...	12.2
1990	107.5	95.4	...	...	...	...	...	...	...	...	...	...	...	12.1
1991	110.1	97.3	...	...	...	...	...	...	...	...	...	...	...	12.8
1992	115.8	101.5	...	...	...	...	...	...	...	...	...	...	...	14.4
1993	127.4	112.9	3.4	2.8	2.3	24.2	4.6	4.3	9.8	7.4	34.5	11.2	6.4	14.4
1994	130.4	116.0	4.2	3.0	2.4	25.3	4.5	4.7	9.2	5.1	37.3	12.0	6.4	14.4
1995	140.0	124.3	4.5	3.3	2.6	27.5	5.0	5.1	9.6	5.7	38.6	13.0	7.3	15.8
1996	146.7	131.4	3.7	3.6	2.8	31.0	5.5	5.0	10.4	4.8	40.6	13.6	7.7	15.3
1997	153.4	139.4	3.3	3.8	2.9	34.3	5.6	5.7	10.3	4.4	44.4	13.1	8.1	14.1
1998	154.8	140.5	3.2	3.7	2.3	35.1	6.1	6.2	10.5	2.8	45.4	13.2	8.9	14.3
1999	169.1	155.1	3.2	3.6	2.5	39.8	6.2	7.2	11.4	2.9	51.0	14.5	9.6	14.0
2000	181.3	167.2	3.0	4.5	2.8	46.8	5.9	7.6	13.0	5.5	51.6	14.0	9.5	14.2
2001	201.9	186.8	3.5	5.6	2.9	52.8	6.1	9.1	15.9	5.3	56.4	14.2	11.4	15.1
2002	213.4	196.9	3.8	6.3	3.5	59.5	6.0	9.2	17.3	3.8	56.7	15.3	11.7	16.6
2003	216.1	198.2	3.7	6.1	4.0	59.3	5.8	8.4	16.5	6.8	56.3	15.6	11.7	17.9
2004	220.2	201.8	4.1	6.0	5.0	59.7	5.5	7.8	16.4	7.0	57.4	17.1	12.0	18.3
2005	234.2	216.9	4.0	5.2	5.1	65.8	6.0	7.3	16.3	8.3	63.2	18.3	13.5	17.3
2006	255.4	237.8	4.3	5.6	5.6	69.8	6.6	9.4	17.7	7.8	71.0	21.5	14.3	17.6
2007	289.1	268.5	5.1	7.2	7.0	78.4	8.4	10.7	21.1	11.4	75.5	23.3	15.0	20.6
2008	308.7	285.0	4.9	8.5	7.0	84.5	9.7	10.9	23.2	11.0	80.4	24.1	16.0	23.7
2009	314.9	286.5	5.8	9.2	6.8	83.7	9.4	10.6	25.5	11.8	81.3	23.5	14.8	28.4
2010	304.0	272.8	7.6	8.3	6.2	71.9	7.6	9.7	26.5	10.8	81.3	24.6	14.4	31.1
2011	286.4	254.8	6.0	7.4	7.0	68.0	7.2	8.5	23.3	9.5	78.4	21.2	13.4	31.7
2012	279.3	252.4	4.7	6.1	7.0	65.6	7.6	8.9	24.8	9.8	79.7	20.9	12.7	26.9
2013	270.7	247.0	4.5	5.2	6.9	60.0	6.6	8.1	25.9	11.0	80.6	21.0	12.9	23.7
2014	276.1	253.7	4.1	5.4	6.2	61.2	6.4	8.7	27.8	10.7	84.0	21.9	12.7	22.4
2015	293.8	271.2	6.0	5.9	5.5	65.8	5.9	10.0	29.4	10.3	90.8	23.4	12.8	22.5
2016	297.0	274.7	5.9	5.7	5.7	69.9	5.8	10.7	27.9	8.5	92.1	23.2	13.6	22.2
2017	296.5	275.3	6.2	6.0	6.4	74.0	6.2	11.6	29.3	5.4	88.3	22.4	13.7	21.3
2018	310.2	288.2	5.8	6.9	6.5	77.2	7.1	11.9	32.8	4.6	90.4	23.2	14.9	22.0
2019	344.3	318.1	6.1	8.1	6.5	85.2	8.1	14.2	37.6	7.1	97.5	25.0	15.6	26.3
2020	361.2	331.0	8.2	9.4	7.0	87.5	9.0	13.6	40.6	6.7	98.2	25.6	17.8	30.3
2018														
January	300.1	278.9	6.2	6.5	6.7	75.1	7.2	11.1	31.7	3.9	85.2	24.0	14.9	21.2
February	302.2	281.8	6.4	6.7	6.7	75.7	6.6	11.2	32.3	4.1	86.2	23.9	16.0	20.4
March	306.2	285.8	6.3	7.0	6.6	78.8	7.0	11.5	32.0	4.9	87.0	24.0	14.5	20.4
April	311.0	290.0	6.3	7.1	6.6	78.4	7.2	11.5	32.2	4.5	90.0	25.3	14.8	20.6
May	312.7	291.4	6.3	7.3	6.8	78.5	7.4	11.9	32.5	5.0	90.2	23.5	15.5	21.2
June	312.7	291.9	5.7	7.4	6.3	75.3	7.2	12.3	33.1	4.8	91.6	24.2	16.7	20.8
July	314.3	293.0	6.1	7.1	6.8	74.9	7.1	12.8	35.0	5.0	92.6	22.7	15.9	21.2
August	320.6	297.7	5.7	7.3	6.7	79.3	7.1	12.1	33.6	4.4	95.0	23.3	15.7	22.9
September	309.4	287.4	5.4	6.5	6.3	77.9	7.1	12.2	32.5	4.1	92.3	21.7	13.9	22.0
October	311.2	286.8	5.3	6.7	6.4	76.7	7.1	12.4	33.0	4.9	90.5	22.5	13.9	24.4
November	307.7	283.3	5.1	6.6	6.3	77.0	7.0	11.9	32.8	5.0	90.1	21.7	12.9	24.4
December	310.2	286.1	5.0	6.7	6.1	80.7	7.2	11.8	32.3	4.6	88.5	23.1	13.2	24.0
2019														
January	321.4	296.6	5.3	7.1	6.2	82.2	7.2	12.3	35.0	6.2	91.4	23.2	13.3	24.8
February	332.5	306.6	5.6	7.1	6.1	82.4	7.6	13.8	35.1	6.2	99.2	22.8	14.2	26.0
March	334.1	309.5	5.5	7.3	6.4	82.4	7.1	14.0	35.4	5.3	99.9	24.1	15.1	24.6
April	353.5	327.6	5.8	7.3	6.4	84.6	7.4	14.1	36.6	7.0	112.0	24.3	15.5	25.9
May	344.6	319.9	5.6	7.5	6.4	83.4	7.8	14.1	37.9	6.9	102.9	25.6	15.0	24.7
June	343.4	317.1	6.0	7.6	6.3	83.3	7.6	14.9	37.8	6.4	99.3	25.3	15.3	26.3
July	347.6	321.3	5.8	8.4	6.6	85.2	8.3	14.4	38.9	7.3	97.9	25.4	15.7	26.3
August	345.8	320.0	6.4	8.6	6.7	85.1	8.5	14.7	38.9	7.9	95.3	25.6	15.2	25.9
September	351.5	324.8	6.7	8.8	6.5	87.0	8.2	14.1	37.8	8.0	97.0	27.2	16.3	26.7
October	349.0	321.4	6.9	8.6	6.7	90.2	8.9	14.2	37.5	7.7	91.4	24.8	16.9	27.5
November	351.2	322.6	6.7	8.7	6.7	89.4	9.0	14.7	39.1	7.8	89.9	25.4	17.7	28.6
December	356.9	328.2	7.2	9.2	6.9	87.3	8.9	14.9	40.0	8.4	95.6	25.7	16.9	28.7
2020														
January	367.9	338.1	8.2	9.4	6.5	89.3	9.3	14.9	41.5	7.4	100.7	25.9	17.8	29.8
February	371.4	341.7	8.2	9.6	6.8	90.7	9.5	14.8	41.0	7.9	102.6	25.5	17.5	29.7
March	374.7	344.7	8.0	9.6	6.8	91.6	9.8	13.8	40.7	8.1	106.4	25.0	17.5	30.0
April	366.2	333.3	7.5	9.2	6.8	90.7	9.7	13.0	39.3	7.0	100.0	25.3	17.8	32.9
May	374.4	342.2	8.0	9.4	7.0	93.9	9.7	13.2	42.0	6.8	101.8	25.1	18.0	32.2
June	364.2	331.1	8.1	9.7	6.8	87.5	9.2	13.3	40.5	5.9	98.5	26.1	18.3	33.0
July	356.0	322.6	8.4	9.7	6.8	83.5	9.2	13.4	39.9	6.0	93.3	26.5	18.3	33.4
August	356.2	324.3	8.3	9.5	7.2	83.2	8.5	13.8	42.5	6.2	94.3	25.3	18.2	31.8
September	352.2	322.4	8.4	9.5	7.4	84.6	8.4	13.8	41.1	6.2	92.1	26.0	17.8	29.8
October	351.7	324.9	8.3	9.0	7.4	83.5	8.4	13.5	39.2	6.3	98.5	25.4	17.7	26.8
November	355.4	328.9	8.5	9.1	7.1	86.6	8.4	13.0	39.1	6.5	100.4	25.8	17.1	26.5
December	357.2	331.1	8.3	8.8	7.3	87.3	8.2	13.3	40.5	6.6	100.9	25.8	16.8	26.0

[1] Includes categories not shown separately.
. . . = Not available.

Table 16-2. Housing Starts and Building Permits; New House Sales and Prices

	Housing starts and building permits										New house sales and prices			
	New private housing units (thousands)									Shipments of manufactured homes (thousands, seasonally adjusted annual rate)	Seasonally adjusted		Median sales price (dollars)	Price index (2005 = 100)
	Started (not seasonally adjusted)			Seasonally adjusted annual rate							Sold (thousands, annual rate)	For sale, end-of-period (thousands)		
				Started			Authorized by building permits							
Year and month	Total [1]	One-family structures	Five units or more	Total [1]	One-family structures	Five units or more	Total [1]	One-family structures	Five units or more					
1980	1 292	852	331	1 292	852	331	1 191	710	366	222	545	342	64 600	38.9
1981	1 084	705	288	1 084	705	288	986	564	319	241	436	278	68 900	42.0
1982	1 062	663	320	1 062	663	320	1 000	546	366	240	412	255	69 300	43.0
1983	1 703	1 068	522	1 703	1 068	522	1 605	901	570	296	623	304	75 300	43.9
1984	1 750	1 084	544	1 750	1 084	544	1 682	922	617	295	639	358	79 900	45.7
1985	1 742	1 072	576	1 742	1 072	576	1 733	957	657	284	688	350	84 300	46.2
1986	1 805	1 179	542	1 805	1 179	542	1 769	1 078	583	244	750	361	92 000	48.0
1987	1 621	1 146	409	1 621	1 146	409	1 535	1 024	421	233	671	370	104 500	50.6
1988	1 488	1 081	348	1 488	1 081	348	1 456	994	386	218	676	371	112 500	52.5
1989	1 376	1 003	318	1 376	1 003	318	1 338	932	340	198	650	366	120 000	54.6
1990	1 193	895	260	1 193	895	260	1 111	794	263	188	534	321	122 900	55.7
1991	1 014	840	138	1 014	840	138	949	754	152	171	509	284	120 000	56.4
1992	1 200	1 030	139	1 200	1 030	139	1 095	911	138	211	610	267	121 500	57.2
1993	1 288	1 126	133	1 288	1 126	133	1 199	987	160	254	666	295	126 500	59.4
1994	1 457	1 198	224	1 457	1 198	224	1 372	1 068	241	304	670	340	130 000	62.9
1995	1 354	1 076	244	1 354	1 076	244	1 333	997	272	340	667	374	133 900	64.3
1996	1 477	1 161	271	1 477	1 161	271	1 426	1 069	290	363	757	326	140 000	66.0
1997	1 474	1 134	296	1 474	1 134	296	1 441	1 062	310	354	804	287	146 000	67.5
1998	1 617	1 271	303	1 617	1 271	303	1 612	1 188	355	373	886	300	152 500	69.2
1999	1 641	1 302	307	1 641	1 302	307	1 664	1 247	351	348	880	315	161 000	72.8
2000	1 569	1 231	299	1 569	1 231	299	1 592	1 198	329	250	877	301	169 000	75.6
2001	1 603	1 273	293	1 603	1 273	293	1 637	1 236	335	193	908	310	175 200	77.9
2002	1 705	1 359	308	1 705	1 359	308	1 748	1 333	341	169	973	344	187 600	81.4
2003	1 848	1 499	315	1 848	1 499	315	1 889	1 461	346	131	1 086	377	195 000	86.0
2004	1 956	1 611	303	1 956	1 611	303	2 070	1 613	366	131	1 203	431	221 000	92.8
2005	2 068	1 716	311	2 068	1 716	311	2 155	1 682	389	147	1 283	515	240 900	100.0
2006	1 801	1 465	293	1 801	1 465	293	1 839	1 378	384	117	1 051	537	246 500	104.7
2007	1 355	1 046	277	1 355	1 046	277	1 398	980	359	96	776	496	247 900	104.9
2008	906	622	266	906	622	266	905	576	295	82	485	352	232 100	99.5
2009	554	445	97	554	445	97	583	441	121	50	375	232	216 700	95.1
2010	587	471	104	587	471	104	605	447	135	50	323	188	221 800	95.0
2011	609	431	167	609	431	167	624	418	184	52	306	150	227 200	94.3
2012	781	535	234	781	535	234	830	519	285	55	368	148	245 200	97.6
2013	925	618	294	925	618	294	991	621	341	60	429	186	268 900	104.7
2014	1 003	648	342	1 003	648	342	1 052	640	382	64	437	212	288 500	110.2
2015	1 112	715	386	1 112	715	386	1 183	696	455	71	501	235	294 200	112.9
2016	1 174	782	381	1 174	782	381	1 207	751	421	81	561	257	307 800	120.4
2017	1 203	849	343	1 203	849	343	1 282	820	425	93	613	294	323 100	126.8
2018	1 250	876	360	1 250	876	360	1 329	855	434	97	617	348	326 400	132.4
2019	1 290	888	389	1 290	888	389	1 386	862	481	95	683	327	321 500	135.5
2020	1 380	991	377	1 380	991	377	1 471	979	445	94	822	302	336 900	140.0
2018														
January	92	60	31	1 309	883	414	1 352	861	445	103	610	292	329 600	. . .
February	90	62	26	1 289	902	369	1 332	877	407	101	644	294	327 200	. . .
March	107	73	34	1 327	886	427	1 407	858	508	100	680	296	335 400	129.8
April	118	85	31	1 285	916	348	1 391	871	478	99	658	299	314 400	. . .
May	124	89	34	1 354	957	385	1 331	860	435	98	680	301	316 700	. . .
June	112	84	28	1 199	865	324	1 320	859	422	97	598	310	310 500	131.0
July	112	82	30	1 193	860	327	1 328	878	421	95	600	315	327 500	. . .
August	114	81	32	1 288	896	375	1 264	829	397	97	582	320	321 400	. . .
September	110	75	34	1 238	867	362	1 289	850	396	96	584	327	328 300	132.5
October	106	75	29	1 208	862	327	1 275	840	398	93	546	333	328 300	. . .
November	91	59	32	1 183	786	386	1 318	841	436	89	618	335	308 500	. . .
December	76	53	22	1 095	777	298	1 338	821	476	87	566	345	329 700	135.1
2019														
January	87	64	22	1 244	940	288	1 295	805	445	87	628	344	305 400	. . .
February	80	55	25	1 142	788	349	1 304	812	454	90	675	339	320 800	. . .
March	98	70	28	1 203	843	355	1 316	825	454	91	721	335	310 600	129.9
April	117	82	33	1 282	880	380	1 337	802	488	94	689	332	339 000	. . .
May	118	78	39	1 303	843	448	1 337	833	467	94	619	334	312 700	. . .
June	115	83	31	1 237	864	361	1 276	842	387	96	711	331	311 800	133.9
July	114	84	29	1 224	887	326	1 369	852	471	95	636	331	308 300	. . .
August	121	81	39	1 371	899	457	1 479	895	542	96	677	326	327 000	. . .
September	113	79	34	1 285	910	364	1 439	894	509	98	706	324	315 700	137.7
October	115	77	37	1 318	889	417	1 509	924	539	99	703	323	322 400	. . .
November	103	68	34	1 350	917	414	1 509	940	530	99	700	323	328 000	. . .
December	108	69	38	1 547	1 012	515	1 453	938	472	97	733	322	329 500	137.1
2020														
January	113	67	45	1 589	992	588	1 550	980	527	98	756	322	328 900	. . .
February	112	73	37	1 589	1 055	515	1 478	1 009	421	104	730	325	331 800	. . .
March	105	74	30	1 277	895	369	1 382	895	440	96	623	328	328 200	135.7
April	85	63	21	938	685	238	1 094	673	387	75	582	321	310 100	. . .
May	95	68	27	1 046	733	305	1 246	753	449	82	704	312	317 100	. . .
June	119	87	31	1 273	903	363	1 296	850	405	87	839	301	341 100	137.5
July	139	94	44	1 497	995	492	1 542	993	500	94	972	291	329 800	. . .
August	123	92	28	1 376	1 023	331	1 522	1 055	414	95	977	286	325 500	. . .
September	126	95	31	1 448	1 105	338	1 589	1 121	422	96	971	286	344 400	142.4
October	131	100	30	1 514	1 162	337	1 595	1 141	394	98	969	284	346 900	. . .
November	118	88	29	1 551	1 182	353	1 696	1 155	487	101	865	290	350 800	. . .
December	115	90	25	1 661	1 315	336	1 758	1 233	476	103	943	299	365 300	144.6

[1]Includes structures with 2 to 4 units, not shown separately.
. . . = Not available.

Table 16-3. Manufacturers' Shipments

(Millions of dollars, seasonally adjusted.)

Year and month	Total	Total durable goods[1]	Total nondurable goods[1]	By topical categories									
				Construction materials and supplies	Information technology industries	Capital goods					Consumer goods		
							Nondefense					
						Total	Total	Excluding aircraft and parts	Defense	Total	Durable	Nondurable
1994	3 238 112	1 764 061	1 474 051	332 734	264 092	616 435	538 203	512 327	78 232	1 192 098	314 931	877 167
1995	3 479 677	1 902 815	1 576 862	353 198	291 885	666 167	590 578	565 729	75 589	1 256 611	324 036	932 575
1996	3 597 188	1 978 597	1 618 591	371 401	311 028	704 635	630 932	605 295	73 703	1 292 955	328 402	964 553
1997	3 834 699	2 147 384	1 687 315	399 880	349 846	779 232	702 971	665 074	76 261	1 358 516	360 193	998 323
1998	3 899 813	2 231 588	1 668 225	418 756	362 564	821 736	747 046	695 717	74 690	1 351 812	373 404	978 408
1999	4 031 887	2 326 736	1 705 151	434 138	374 384	839 754	768 799	713 042	70 955	1 424 828	412 646	1 012 182
2000	4 208 584	2 373 688	1 834 896	444 812	399 751	875 396	808 345	757 617	67 051	1 500 532	391 463	1 109 069
2001	3 970 499	2 174 406	1 796 093	424 517	353 237	801 999	728 495	678 288	73 504	1 480 495	367 522	1 112 973
2002	3 914 723	2 123 621	1 791 102	424 008	284 799	728 585	652 342	609 595	76 243	1 494 575	395 953	1 098 622
2003	4 015 388	2 142 589	1 872 799	429 183	274 829	719 602	634 273	600 616	85 329	1 584 329	418 821	1 165 508
2004	4 308 970	2 264 667	2 044 303	463 148	287 837	752 905	661 740	629 146	91 165	1 700 835	419 182	1 281 653
2005	4 742 077	2 424 844	2 317 233	509 865	295 447	821 906	730 368	686 939	91 538	1 895 119	422 555	1 472 564
2006	5 015 552	2 562 194	2 453 358	546 866	319 890	884 199	794 638	744 282	89 561	1 980 031	421 860	1 558 171
2007	5 319 457	2 687 028	2 632 429	560 208	322 846	936 404	836 426	768 662	99 978	2 106 081	421 822	1 684 259
2008	5 468 994	2 616 667	2 852 327	543 819	319 032	955 412	840 250	774 775	115 162	2 254 007	357 546	1 896 461
2009	4 423 779	2 056 829	2 366 950	426 663	271 678	820 521	697 469	642 555	123 052	1 849 113	268 036	1 581 077
2010	4 911 277	2 280 712	2 630 565	443 880	270 118	858 123	727 818	674 747	130 305	2 058 913	323 432	1 735 481
2011	5 491 894	2 479 086	3 012 808	471 598	274 110	923 876	803 248	740 848	120 628	2 373 512	344 299	2 029 213
2012	5 696 728	2 627 582	3 069 146	500 848	272 578	1 000 585	884 994	799 591	115 591	2 437 147	373 352	2 063 795
2013	5 814 127	2 698 831	3 115 296	523 741	271 471	1 010 075	893 660	800 926	116 415	2 496 007	401 442	2 094 565
2014	5 889 007	2 797 291	3 091 716	548 111	265 000	1 022 566	909 950	807 734	112 616	2 499 624	427 266	2 072 358
2015	5 533 033	2 781 867	2 751 166	554 163	258 289	995 652	883 796	779 425	111 856	2 257 336	457 847	1 799 489
2016	5 363 596	2 716 122	2 647 474	554 018	256 501	951 323	834 891	727 502	116 432	2 187 429	471 353	1 716 076
2017	5 548 795	2 767 416	2 781 379	574 239	256 478	978 816	854 811	736 908	124 005	2 273 113	453 465	1 819 648
2018	5 890 664	2 928 056	2 962 608	607 949	263 462	1 029 474	903 094	784 070	126 380	2 433 606	475 039	1 958 567
2019	5 731 193	2 883 305	2 847 888	602 578	266 344	1 016 160	883 213	789 022	132 947	2 361 128	469 811	1 891 317
2020	5 356 798	2 708 974	2 647 824	595 369	276 510	965 746	832 650	787 577	133 096	2 144 407	412 826	1 731 581
2017												
January	457 211	227 906	229 305	46 832	21 201	79 244	69 463	59 778	9 781	189 472	39 208	150 264
February	457 371	227 225	230 146	47 408	21 349	80 151	69 546	59 987	10 605	188 304	37 887	150 417
March	457 258	228 825	228 433	47 561	21 223	80 797	70 530	60 681	10 267	186 734	37 851	148 883
April	454 701	225 880	228 821	47 212	21 298	79 763	69 618	60 445	10 145	186 056	36 759	149 297
May	458 333	231 080	227 253	47 625	21 278	81 293	71 014	61 109	10 279	186 221	38 487	147 734
June	457 509	229 506	228 003	47 506	21 283	80 787	70 691	60 720	10 096	186 051	37 891	148 160
July	456 756	227 835	228 921	47 227	21 426	81 658	71 499	60 854	10 159	185 372	36 272	149 100
August	462 402	231 191	231 211	47 734	21 499	82 106	71 818	61 707	10 288	188 972	37 452	151 520
September	465 409	232 277	233 132	48 325	21 332	82 905	72 479	62 405	10 426	189 942	37 247	152 695
October	470 226	233 905	236 321	48 738	21 533	82 490	71 977	62 741	10 513	193 090	38 042	155 048
November	479 071	237 514	241 557	49 263	21 761	84 558	73 912	63 498	10 646	198 047	38 547	159 500
December	479 474	236 874	242 600	49 806	21 490	83 681	73 144	63 977	10 537	197 855	37 908	159 947
2018												
January	482 452	238 168	244 284	49 691	21 734	83 834	73 052	63 556	10 782	199 922	38 579	161 343
February	484 165	239 603	244 562	49 854	21 369	83 751	73 518	64 012	10 233	200 659	39 130	161 529
March	485 100	240 699	244 401	50 121	21 375	84 673	74 725	63 867	9 948	200 213	39 106	161 107
April	486 234	241 571	244 663	50 623	21 883	82 843	71 796	65 011	11 047	201 544	40 379	161 165
May	490 275	241 504	248 771	50 952	21 773	85 258	74 939	65 092	10 319	201 765	37 026	164 739
June	494 812	244 776	250 036	51 064	21 981	86 501	76 089	65 980	10 412	204 191	39 060	165 131
July	492 982	243 079	249 903	51 214	22 390	83 091	72 717	66 517	10 374	205 266	39 865	165 401
August	497 255	246 322	250 933	51 236	22 143	86 970	76 473	66 126	10 497	205 691	39 619	166 072
September	498 389	246 777	251 612	50 823	21 809	87 336	76 923	65 978	10 413	207 338	39 961	167 377
October	499 513	248 208	251 305	50 919	22 362	87 556	76 694	66 450	10 862	208 158	40 916	167 242
November	491 389	247 710	243 679	50 471	22 278	87 749	77 051	65 739	10 698	201 248	40 492	160 756
December	487 054	248 181	238 873	50 581	22 321	88 289	77 218	66 066	11 071	197 892	40 993	156 899
2019												
January	484 548	246 094	238 454	50 480	22 156	88 049	76 675	65 825	11 374	197 290	40 351	156 939
February	486 932	246 587	240 345	50 527	22 177	88 179	77 208	65 952	10 971	199 573	40 104	159 469
March	483 965	245 026	238 939	50 316	22 074	86 652	75 582	65 892	11 070	199 030	40 335	158 695
April	480 104	240 555	239 549	49 865	22 763	84 838	73 553	66 315	11 285	198 417	38 680	159 737
May	479 366	241 185	238 181	50 292	22 414	85 028	73 658	66 597	11 370	197 129	39 025	158 104
June	478 958	243 543	235 415	50 581	22 155	85 743	74 429	66 297	11 314	195 692	40 353	155 339
July	476 073	239 122	236 951	50 187	22 267	82 975	71 967	65 881	11 008	196 997	39 891	157 106
August	475 168	239 085	236 083	50 289	22 096	83 617	72 462	65 847	11 155	195 746	39 226	156 520
September	473 597	237 657	235 940	50 412	22 010	82 963	72 015	65 250	10 948	195 451	38 731	156 720
October	472 370	236 757	235 613	50 030	21 829	84 047	72 980	65 403	11 067	195 231	38 029	157 202
November	472 012	235 839	236 173	50 085	22 255	82 839	71 789	65 034	11 050	195 512	37 932	157 580
December	472 893	235 184	237 709	49 855	22 497	83 297	72 726	65 223	10 571	196 323	37 424	158 899
2020												
January	468 624	233 064	235 560	50 360	22 353	81 490	70 011	65 297	11 479	193 233	36 637	156 596
February	468 676	236 700	231 976	50 012	22 530	83 202	72 063	64 967	11 139	192 094	38 187	153 907
March	443 429	223 698	219 731	49 383	22 462	82 894	72 329	64 064	10 565	172 769	30 165	142 604
April	380 636	180 607	200 029	43 953	22 099	72 508	61 490	59 402	11 018	143 123	13 834	129 289
May	389 858	188 696	201 162	45 624	22 144	73 196	62 225	60 874	10 971	146 604	17 244	129 360
June	432 181	217 741	214 440	48 124	22 325	76 685	65 822	63 672	10 863	174 428	33 949	140 479
July	452 585	233 068	219 517	49 926	23 013	78 421	67 433	65 681	10 988	185 910	42 276	143 634
August	455 568	234 208	221 360	50 423	23 325	81 491	70 436	67 055	11 055	184 791	39 761	145 030
September	457 690	235 293	222 397	50 937	23 530	81 153	70 375	67 319	10 778	185 769	40 119	145 650
October	463 216	238 958	224 258	51 386	24 067	84 385	73 155	68 790	11 230	185 777	39 283	146 494
November	466 345	239 759	226 586	51 789	23 986	83 722	71 862	69 601	11 860	188 467	40 123	148 344
December	475 283	244 387	230 896	52 807	24 053	85 691	74 546	70 042	11 145	193 052	41 112	151 940

[1]Includes categories not shown separately.

Table 16-4. Manufacturers' Inventories

(Current cost basis, end of period; seasonally adjusted, millions of dollars.)

Year and month	Total	Total durable goods	Durables total by stage of fabrication			Total nondurable goods	Nondurables total by stage of fabrication		
			Materials and supplies	Work in process	Finished goods		Materials and supplies	Work in process	Finished goods
1994	399 934	253 095	78 482	106 521	68 092	146 839	57 113	24 444	65 282
1995	424 802	267 437	85 545	106 634	75 258	157 365	60 778	25 776	70 811
1996	430 366	272 428	86 265	110 527	75 636	157 938	59 157	26 485	72 296
1997	443 227	280 730	92 253	109 714	78 763	162 497	60 175	28 523	73 799
1998	448 373	290 071	93 406	114 928	81 737	158 302	58 156	27 049	73 097
1999	463 004	296 009	97 722	113 805	84 482	166 995	60 975	28 791	77 229
2000	480 748	306 002	105 848	110 909	89 245	174 746	61 465	30 090	83 191
2001	427 353	267 409	91 168	93 768	82 473	159 944	55 671	27 157	77 116
2002	423 028	260 476	88 445	92 343	79 688	162 552	56 571	28 133	77 848
2003	408 302	246 922	82 330	88 608	75 984	161 380	56 866	27 251	77 263
2004	441 222	264 895	92 122	90 934	81 839	176 327	61 917	30 341	84 069
2005	474 639	283 712	98 652	98 400	86 660	190 927	67 224	33 226	90 477
2006	523 476	317 406	111 687	106 352	99 367	206 070	70 601	37 548	97 921
2007	563 043	334 628	116 506	117 496	100 626	228 415	75 570	45 290	107 555
2008	543 273	329 781	117 709	110 840	101 232	213 492	72 866	41 193	99 433
2009	505 025	294 755	100 633	106 167	87 955	210 270	71 913	42 137	96 220
2010	553 726	321 441	106 899	122 157	92 385	232 285	76 592	45 922	109 771
2011	607 035	352 897	119 445	133 306	100 146	254 138	82 059	50 675	121 404
2012	625 216	367 335	125 059	138 670	103 606	257 881	83 389	51 167	123 325
2013	631 755	372 017	126 265	141 504	104 248	259 738	84 678	52 417	122 643
2014	642 723	389 654	133 735	146 860	109 059	253 069	84 024	49 279	119 766
2015	638 073	393 090	130 633	152 032	110 425	244 983	84 255	45 742	114 986
2016	635 921	380 629	126 560	143 614	110 455	255 292	85 151	47 231	122 910
2017	658 885	390 073	132 845	141 810	115 418	268 812	89 874	50 341	128 597
2018	677 647	407 177	144 209	141 354	121 614	270 470	91 180	49 784	129 506
2019	713 305	431 260	147 831	158 927	124 502	282 045	93 423	53 972	134 650
2020	709 607	433 212	150 011	165 017	118 184	276 395	93 140	49 706	133 549
2017									
January	637 187	380 369	127 039	142 962	110 368	256 818	85 267	47 507	124 044
February	638 057	380 789	126 909	143 299	110 581	257 268	85 743	47 796	123 729
March	637 605	380 806	127 390	142 795	110 621	256 799	85 645	46 954	124 200
April	638 884	381 440	128 850	141 460	111 130	257 444	86 684	46 823	123 937
May	638 713	381 717	129 215	140 884	111 618	256 996	86 687	46 958	123 351
June	638 970	382 264	129 853	140 029	112 382	256 706	86 159	47 499	123 048
July	642 059	383 883	130 340	139 874	113 669	258 176	86 056	48 355	123 765
August	644 842	385 022	130 805	139 881	114 336	259 820	86 782	48 907	124 131
September	649 579	387 567	132 038	140 363	115 166	262 012	88 575	48 933	124 504
October	651 969	388 407	131 916	141 123	115 368	263 562	88 014	49 447	126 101
November	655 218	388 878	132 215	141 631	115 032	266 340	88 798	49 910	127 632
December	658 885	390 073	132 845	141 810	115 418	268 812	89 874	50 341	128 597
2018									
January	660 606	391 210	133 079	142 710	115 421	269 396	89 478	50 529	129 389
February	663 493	393 570	134 291	143 586	115 693	269 923	89 735	50 292	129 896
March	662 481	392 858	134 796	142 411	115 651	269 623	89 740	51 299	128 584
April	664 755	394 453	135 844	142 453	116 156	270 302	89 839	51 198	129 265
May	666 095	395 918	136 858	142 432	116 628	270 177	89 816	51 038	129 323
June	667 089	395 035	138 415	139 081	117 539	272 054	90 152	51 317	130 585
July	673 326	400 715	139 743	143 322	117 650	272 611	91 185	51 086	130 340
August	673 619	399 755	140 661	140 922	118 172	273 864	92 014	51 340	130 510
September	677 727	402 821	141 971	141 465	119 385	274 906	92 691	52 019	130 196
October	679 399	403 688	142 797	141 296	119 595	275 711	92 640	51 394	131 677
November	677 796	405 335	143 799	141 277	120 259	272 461	91 617	50 167	130 677
December	677 647	407 177	144 209	141 354	121 614	270 470	91 180	49 784	129 506
2019									
January	682 289	409 902	145 156	142 442	122 304	272 387	91 820	50 656	129 911
February	685 262	411 595	144 960	144 261	122 374	273 667	91 972	50 937	130 758
March	688 720	412 437	144 680	145 048	122 709	276 283	91 875	52 381	132 027
April	691 675	414 411	144 587	147 059	122 765	277 264	92 161	52 607	132 496
May	694 633	416 540	144 309	148 942	123 289	278 093	92 430	52 815	132 848
June	697 873	418 745	145 017	149 577	124 151	279 128	92 997	52 370	133 761
July	701 126	421 336	145 745	150 713	124 878	279 790	92 550	52 771	134 469
August	702 772	423 785	146 191	152 344	125 250	278 987	92 807	52 429	133 751
September	705 549	426 064	146 982	153 858	125 224	279 485	92 544	52 784	134 157
October	707 846	427 964	147 678	155 260	125 026	279 882	92 319	53 276	134 287
November	710 068	429 158	147 862	156 786	124 510	280 910	92 913	54 184	133 813
December	713 305	431 260	147 831	158 927	124 502	282 045	93 423	53 972	134 650
2020									
January	711 101	430 674	147 186	159 632	123 856	280 427	93 201	53 176	134 050
February	707 384	429 514	147 163	159 552	122 799	277 870	92 684	51 922	133 264
March	700 122	430 921	147 998	161 507	121 416	269 201	91 128	48 576	129 497
April	698 387	431 811	151 638	160 433	119 740	266 576	90 186	47 726	128 664
May	698 049	430 889	151 247	160 291	119 351	267 160	90 112	49 015	128 033
June	702 389	431 221	149 461	162 134	119 626	271 168	91 598	50 117	129 453
July	698 776	427 849	148 050	161 463	118 336	270 927	91 821	50 010	129 096
August	699 708	427 552	147 669	161 813	118 070	272 156	92 156	50 088	129 912
September	699 720	428 719	146 966	164 176	117 577	271 001	91 330	49 570	130 101
October	701 183	429 890	147 755	164 216	117 919	271 293	91 177	48 613	131 503
November	706 402	433 286	148 540	165 370	119 376	273 116	91 659	49 299	132 158
December	709 607	433 212	150 011	165 017	118 184	276 395	93 140	49 706	133 549

Table 16-4. Manufacturers' Inventories—*Continued*

(Current cost basis, end of period; seasonally adjusted, millions of dollars.)

Year and month	Construction materials and supplies	Information technology industries	Capital goods				Consumer goods		
			Total	Nondefense		Defense	Total	Durable	Nondurable
				Total	Excluding aircraft and parts				
1994	40 879	41 538	123 368	103 320	85 717	20 048	109 536	23 948	85 588
1995	43 420	46 936	129 709	111 563	94 673	18 146	116 404	25 316	91 088
1996	44 124	43 556	132 746	115 211	93 441	17 535	116 351	24 752	91 599
1997	45 725	48 094	137 556	122 598	98 870	14 958	119 660	24 905	94 755
1998	46 500	45 333	145 048	127 108	97 362	17 940	117 343	24 895	92 448
1999	48 541	46 174	146 244	126 278	99 610	19 966	124 220	26 097	98 123
2000	50 518	52 719	148 992	131 655	110 122	17 337	130 823	27 295	103 528
2001	46 341	42 967	128 670	114 908	93 305	13 762	121 377	25 410	95 967
2002	46 698	39 083	122 538	108 147	88 529	14 391	124 904	25 687	99 217
2003	45 448	35 222	114 917	99 119	81 660	15 798	125 052	25 017	100 035
2004	51 244	33 132	117 611	98 900	83 687	18 711	134 390	26 240	108 150
2005	55 094	39 215	127 158	110 573	92 903	16 585	145 446	28 104	117 342
2006	60 864	39 914	139 499	122 442	101 760	17 057	154 185	27 686	126 499
2007	62 522	38 748	150 191	131 347	104 706	18 844	172 565	27 729	144 836
2008	61 386	38 048	150 665	134 264	107 682	16 401	155 212	24 151	131 061
2009	50 915	36 649	145 498	125 685	97 529	19 813	159 016	21 207	137 809
2010	53 287	37 550	160 079	139 469	103 618	20 610	174 664	21 989	152 675
2011	57 661	39 635	174 551	154 445	113 807	20 106	188 238	22 900	165 338
2012	60 166	39 375	184 247	163 894	118 325	20 353	191 814	25 053	166 761
2013	61 262	38 321	186 652	166 409	117 579	20 243	193 690	26 169	167 521
2014	65 407	37 126	193 925	173 756	121 689	20 169	186 589	27 549	159 040
2015	64 346	37 683	201 306	179 703	119 806	21 603	183 790	28 568	155 222
2016	64 830	36 786	191 913	171 797	115 534	20 116	192 346	28 178	164 168
2017	68 456	36 740	188 730	167 722	119 090	21 008	202 126	29 322	172 804
2018	74 293	37 886	191 099	172 712	127 127	18 387	202 162	30 715	171 447
2019	74 848	39 547	212 734	192 554	129 512	20 180	218 875	33 538	185 337
2020	73 639	40 120	218 756	198 405	129 331	20 351	213 164	32 458	180 706
2017									
January	65 138	36 757	191 274	170 736	115 794	20 538	193 377	27 949	165 428
February	65 274	36 726	191 204	170 525	115 888	20 679	193 387	27 786	165 601
March	64 996	36 889	191 221	170 906	116 131	20 315	192 470	27 918	164 552
April	65 953	36 683	189 872	168 901	116 004	20 971	192 894	28 088	164 806
May	66 097	36 653	189 360	168 499	116 456	20 861	191 924	27 964	163 960
June	66 441	36 711	189 046	168 038	116 816	21 008	191 744	28 365	163 379
July	66 875	36 755	188 969	167 410	117 435	21 559	193 044	28 610	164 434
August	67 320	36 761	188 979	167 348	117 772	21 631	194 483	28 699	165 784
September	67 612	36 489	189 031	167 691	118 136	21 340	196 696	28 965	167 731
October	67 778	36 631	189 030	167 596	118 444	21 434	197 572	28 967	168 605
November	68 205	36 611	188 775	167 707	118 551	21 068	199 905	28 812	171 093
December	68 456	36 740	188 730	167 722	119 090	21 008	202 126	29 322	172 804
2018									
January	68 751	36 653	189 129	168 462	119 459	20 667	203 107	29 388	173 719
February	69 254	36 897	190 399	169 748	120 152	20 651	203 607	29 498	174 109
March	69 684	36 763	189 268	168 971	120 338	20 297	203 499	29 617	173 882
April	70 392	36 850	189 459	169 627	121 137	19 832	203 937	29 645	174 292
May	70 973	37 105	189 276	169 583	121 496	19 693	204 171	30 029	174 142
June	71 719	37 232	187 399	167 404	122 434	19 995	204 839	29 929	174 910
July	72 404	37 031	190 700	170 967	122 776	19 733	205 081	30 169	174 912
August	72 894	37 228	188 542	169 332	123 545	19 210	206 055	30 424	175 631
September	73 796	37 606	190 161	171 138	124 955	19 023	206 720	30 316	176 404
October	73 827	37 716	190 619	171 740	125 636	18 879	207 260	30 270	176 990
November	74 058	37 609	190 798	172 081	126 222	18 717	204 411	30 664	173 747
December	74 293	37 886	191 099	172 712	127 127	18 387	202 162	30 715	171 447
2019									
January	74 444	38 096	193 027	174 339	127 985	18 688	204 338	31 189	173 149
February	74 408	38 308	194 093	175 344	127 956	18 749	206 893	31 744	175 149
March	74 320	38 484	195 969	176 621	128 496	19 348	209 497	31 690	177 807
April	74 119	38 430	197 386	177 887	128 288	19 499	211 190	32 096	179 094
May	74 235	38 500	199 544	179 885	128 479	19 659	212 280	32 559	179 721
June	74 480	38 644	200 971	181 209	128 712	19 762	213 498	32 904	180 594
July	74 769	38 792	203 586	183 506	129 632	20 080	214 335	33 092	181 243
August	74 866	38 917	205 742	185 800	129 639	19 942	214 215	33 436	180 779
September	74 961	39 140	207 449	187 254	129 938	20 195	215 326	33 656	181 670
October	75 098	39 210	209 615	189 096	129 905	20 519	216 065	33 665	182 400
November	74 908	39 296	210 668	190 064	129 350	20 604	217 330	33 738	183 592
December	74 848	39 547	212 734	192 554	129 512	20 180	218 875	33 538	185 337
2020									
January	74 988	39 395	212 747	192 352	128 971	20 395	217 255	33 296	183 959
February	74 644	39 373	212 505	192 201	128 559	20 304	214 693	33 048	181 645
March	74 574	39 486	213 585	193 445	128 982	20 140	206 516	32 785	173 731
April	74 886	39 838	214 269	193 890	129 533	20 379	203 516	32 075	171 441
May	74 034	39 889	214 875	194 542	129 479	20 333	204 335	32 224	172 111
June	73 223	39 952	216 933	196 429	129 100	20 504	208 932	32 633	176 299
July	71 860	39 837	217 023	196 733	128 432	20 290	208 822	32 400	176 422
August	71 650	39 812	217 066	196 552	128 538	20 514	209 676	32 092	177 584
September	71 762	39 896	218 030	197 356	128 099	20 674	208 156	32 003	176 153
October	72 167	39 889	218 166	197 459	127 962	20 707	208 516	32 348	176 168
November	72 769	39 972	219 731	199 397	128 651	20 334	211 089	33 131	177 958
December	73 639	40 120	218 756	198 405	129 331	20 351	213 164	32 458	180 706

Table 16-5. Manufacturers' New Orders

(Net, millions of dollars, seasonally adjusted.)

Year and month	Total [1]	Total durable goods [1]	By topical categories								
			Construction materials and supplies	Information technology industries	Capital goods					Consumer goods		
					Total	Nondefense		Defense	Total	Durable	Nondurable
						Total	Excluding aircraft and parts				
1995	3 426 503	1 849 641	355 161	297 605	680 857	612 132	576 769	68 725	1 256 721	324 146	932 575
1996	3 567 384	1 948 793	373 536	310 074	737 268	648 797	607 174	88 471	1 293 537	328 984	964 553
1997	3 779 835	2 092 520	403 860	352 700	792 859	728 362	676 119	64 497	1 360 010	361 687	998 323
1998	3 808 143	2 139 918	419 330	365 723	809 727	745 600	698 279	64 127	1 352 708	374 300	978 408
1999	3 957 242	2 252 091	435 034	389 160	840 603	772 703	728 089	67 900	1 425 617	413 435	1 012 182
2000	4 161 472	2 326 576	446 792	409 500	910 933	831 335	767 754	79 598	1 501 810	392 741	1 109 069
2001	3 868 855	2 072 762	420 817	336 935	775 315	691 552	656 944	83 763	1 477 201	364 228	1 112 973
2002	3 823 145	2 032 043	423 561	273 788	698 865	622 403	589 148	76 462	1 494 106	395 484	1 098 622
2003	3 975 812	2 103 013	431 569	282 289	737 032	636 821	608 175	100 211	1 585 029	419 521	1 165 508
2004	4 289 001	2 244 698	468 746	293 836	787 748	688 813	643 997	98 935	1 701 565	419 912	1 281 653
2005	4 764 032	2 446 799	516 797	300 367	896 672	814 286	703 796	82 386	1 894 021	421 457	1 472 564
2006	5 089 646	2 636 288	549 467	332 649	992 499	889 370	775 156	103 129	1 979 165	420 994	1 558 171
2007	5 397 027	2 764 598	564 717	324 248	1 061 415	957 485	786 665	103 930	2 105 784	421 525	1 684 259
2008	5 452 124	2 599 797	543 218	318 571	1 006 627	879 429	781 810	127 198	2 252 724	356 263	1 896 461
2009	4 205 737	1 838 787	413 497	265 602	690 674	587 116	608 664	103 558	1 848 693	267 616	1 581 077
2010	4 895 899	2 265 334	450 921	272 817	885 135	747 708	685 492	137 427	2 058 565	323 084	1 735 481
2011	5 511 660	2 498 852	471 284	286 080	994 126	861 040	765 584	133 086	2 373 717	344 504	2 029 213
2012	5 709 710	2 640 564	500 617	274 254	1 051 261	932 086	803 417	119 175	2 437 479	373 684	2 063 795
2013	5 898 932	2 783 636	524 553	256 251	1 134 933	1 035 998	807 568	98 935	2 496 304	401 739	2 094 565
2014	5 952 546	2 860 830	547 944	260 335	1 114 942	1 005 179	806 881	109 763	2 499 685	427 327	2 072 358
2015	5 433 340	2 682 174	554 821	250 876	950 523	844 588	761 235	105 935	2 257 164	457 675	1 799 489
2016	5 295 968	2 648 494	552 175	260 653	959 105	829 099	723 458	130 006	2 187 809	471 733	1 716 076
2017	5 492 320	2 710 941	575 439	261 257	999 429	873 987	742 671	125 442	2 273 215	453 567	1 819 648
2018	5 815 784	2 853 176	613 610	265 421	980 538	844 518	787 193	136 020	2 434 388	475 821	1 958 567
2019	5 801 304	2 953 416	607 003	267 500	1 125 054	978 713	786 765	146 341	2 360 786	469 469	1 891 317
2020	5 198 635	2 550 811	595 737	278 847	854 949	717 976	795 405	136 973	2 145 442	413 861	1 731 581
2017											
January	447 001	217 696	46 974	21 855	77 464	67 500	60 419	9 964	189 507	39 243	150 264
February	445 123	214 977	46 666	22 155	74 411	70 817	60 740	3 594	188 498	38 081	150 417
March	450 248	221 815	48 422	21 445	80 233	70 515	61 013	9 718	186 663	37 780	148 883
April	451 986	223 165	47 242	21 425	82 646	72 450	61 308	10 196	186 083	36 786	149 297
May	448 086	220 833	47 672	21 486	77 913	68 206	61 404	9 707	186 174	38 440	147 734
June	466 961	238 958	47 252	21 240	97 972	85 939	60 378	12 033	186 034	37 874	148 160
July	450 373	221 452	47 266	21 827	82 264	70 660	61 535	11 604	185 391	36 291	149 100
August	453 992	222 781	47 755	21 285	80 198	69 936	61 552	10 262	189 094	37 574	151 520
September	466 658	233 526	48 652	22 279	90 333	72 265	64 088	18 068	189 879	37 184	152 695
October	466 004	229 683	48 718	21 948	84 347	74 029	63 703	10 318	193 048	38 000	155 048
November	478 454	236 897	49 644	22 673	90 308	78 091	63 645	12 217	198 115	38 615	159 500
December	477 642	235 042	50 213	21 736	84 678	77 235	63 795	7 443	197 788	37 841	159 947
2018											
January	469 659	225 375	49 841	21 478	74 961	66 762	63 324	8 199	200 119	38 776	161 343
February	474 929	230 367	50 545	21 117	77 240	65 432	64 087	11 808	200 718	39 189	161 529
March	483 526	239 125	51 137	21 376	84 105	74 918	63 553	9 187	200 463	39 356	161 107
April	484 494	239 831	51 566	21 890	82 717	73 318	64 909	9 399	201 643	40 478	161 165
May	489 859	241 088	51 685	22 125	85 528	73 228	66 231	12 300	201 808	37 069	164 739
June	491 414	241 378	51 448	22 321	83 660	71 540	67 247	12 120	204 329	39 198	165 131
July	483 690	233 787	51 669	22 759	76 552	67 546	68 749	9 006	205 416	40 015	165 401
August	499 107	248 174	51 537	22 466	91 684	76 158	66 798	15 526	205 556	39 484	166 072
September	496 571	244 959	50 975	21 758	84 384	70 677	66 399	13 707	207 391	40 014	167 377
October	490 790	239 485	51 270	22 906	81 423	68 792	67 104	12 631	208 194	40 952	167 242
November	473 094	229 415	50 787	22 614	73 701	61 183	64 292	12 518	201 173	40 417	160 756
December	481 244	242 371	50 871	22 469	86 340	77 051	64 894	9 289	197 863	40 964	156 899
2019											
January	490 759	252 305	51 032	22 116	98 752	87 707	65 841	11 045	197 196	40 257	156 939
February	483 586	243 241	50 761	21 838	88 679	78 666	65 221	10 013	199 434	39 965	159 469
March	494 863	255 924	50 447	22 436	101 593	87 567	66 457	14 026	198 872	40 177	158 695
April	492 222	252 673	50 362	23 035	100 264	87 403	65 737	12 861	198 365	38 628	159 737
May	478 025	239 844	50 702	22 514	88 713	75 899	65 271	12 814	197 200	39 096	158 104
June	480 142	244 727	51 218	22 566	89 857	83 610	66 139	6 247	195 786	40 447	155 339
July	486 699	249 748	50 729	22 435	97 168	85 570	65 823	11 598	196 931	39 825	157 106
August	481 697	245 614	50 935	22 211	93 226	80 583	65 593	12 643	195 749	39 229	156 520
September	481 257	245 317	50 486	22 314	92 871	79 282	65 187	13 589	195 378	38 658	156 720
October	486 286	250 673	49 971	22 168	101 805	85 421	65 642	16 384	195 246	38 044	157 202
November	470 340	234 167	50 692	21 983	82 609	73 379	65 189	9 230	195 531	37 951	157 580
December	478 052	240 343	50 078	22 196	89 468	73 181	65 045	16 287	196 350	37 451	158 899
2020											
January	464 438	228 878	50 239	22 643	79 758	69 305	65 765	10 453	193 199	36 603	156 596
February	462 877	230 901	49 579	22 603	81 797	67 026	64 885	14 771	192 112	38 205	153 907
March	402 748	183 017	48 187	22 457	47 735	33 454	64 103	14 281	172 905	30 301	142 604
April	361 862	161 833	42 672	22 486	60 070	49 074	59 872	10 996	142 998	13 709	129 289
May	380 125	178 963	45 081	22 389	67 680	56 607	61 297	11 073	146 838	17 478	129 360
June	413 666	199 226	48 247	22 434	62 136	51 686	64 300	10 450	174 571	34 092	140 479
July	438 265	218 748	49 997	23 264	68 213	56 504	66 189	11 709	186 135	42 501	143 634
August	444 422	223 062	50 873	23 542	74 308	63 005	67 791	11 303	184 966	39 936	145 030
September	449 061	226 664	51 670	23 596	76 979	67 182	68 646	9 797	185 878	40 228	145 650
October	453 094	228 836	52 035	24 165	77 818	66 282	69 626	11 536	185 814	39 320	146 494
November	460 424	233 838	52 484	24 189	80 724	68 915	70 563	11 809	188 571	40 227	148 344
December	468 324	237 428	53 981	24 545	80 178	71 026	71 619	9 152	193 085	41 145	151 940

[1]Includes categories not shown separately.

Table 16-6. Manufacturers' Unfilled Orders, Durable Goods Industries

(End of period, millions of dollars, seasonally adjusted.)

Year and month	Total [1]	Transportation equipment		Construction materials and supplies	Information technology industries	By topical categories				Consumer durable goods
		Nondefense aircraft and parts	Defense aircraft and parts			Capital goods				
						Total	Nondefense		Defense	
							Total	Excluding aircraft and parts		
1995	447 510	109 506	42 360	27 155	84 919	313 963	199 613	118 006	114 350	5 282
1996	489 147	130 580	45 203	29 436	84 227	346 596	217 605	120 276	128 991	5 821
1997	513 317	143 183	40 842	33 584	87 704	360 636	243 413	132 076	117 223	7 330
1998	496 363	137 228	37 711	34 268	90 930	348 398	241 565	134 417	106 833	8 262
1999	505 667	126 256	35 616	35 246	105 883	349 497	245 603	149 679	103 894	9 035
2000	549 507	138 159	42 421	37 405	115 679	384 834	268 323	159 844	116 511	10 349
2001	509 910	124 656	52 002	33 580	98 908	357 539	230 560	137 637	126 979	6 988
2002	479 610	114 352	57 383	33 233	88 083	327 423	200 536	117 571	126 887	6 593
2003	506 423	109 736	63 441	35 701	95 736	344 824	203 047	125 283	141 777	7 296
2004	558 457	122 946	56 998	41 467	101 278	378 930	229 584	140 211	149 346	8 205
2005	653 074	187 614	54 421	48 493	106 404	451 740	311 502	157 208	140 238	7 245
2006	795 263	264 577	58 648	50 972	119 047	557 632	404 587	188 224	153 045	6 443
2007	944 036	375 979	61 975	55 394	120 159	681 761	524 218	206 323	157 543	6 169
2008	994 104	416 404	71 589	54 682	119 729	735 435	563 945	213 446	171 490	4 639
2009	825 089	342 911	61 144	41 183	113 546	606 897	456 046	178 858	150 851	4 205
2010	871 076	349 923	61 939	48 404	116 251	635 475	476 681	190 027	158 794	3 726
2011	952 436	388 754	65 509	48 161	128 181	704 201	533 254	215 229	170 947	3 884
2012	1 015 260	444 476	75 809	47 999	129 972	756 491	582 093	219 247	174 398	4 173
2013	1 142 130	586 750	75 572	48 905	114 993	877 635	720 793	226 115	156 842	4 460
2014	1 255 669	694 551	74 816	48 798	110 643	972 683	817 239	225 391	155 444	4 473
2015	1 205 811	675 556	70 265	49 550	103 235	927 567	779 473	206 696	148 094	4 371
2016	1 186 562	661 557	75 427	47 668	107 377	933 564	771 886	202 682	161 678	4 746
2017	1 184 960	651 133	67 940	48 907	112 058	956 898	793 838	208 360	163 060	4 904
2018	1 166 319	594 452	69 329	54 689	113 919	911 342	739 248	211 553	172 094	5 690
2019	1 285 367	699 020	88 308	59 183	115 038	1 018 120	832 472	209 182	185 648	5 337
2020	1 180 385	579 219	84 445	59 504	117 464	910 678	720 791	217 074	189 887	6 392
2017										
January	1 181 428	655 637	74 506	47 810	108 031	931 784	769 923	203 323	161 861	4 781
February	1 173 110	653 556	73 905	47 068	108 837	926 044	771 194	204 076	154 850	4 975
March	1 170 446	650 321	73 507	47 929	109 059	925 480	771 179	204 408	154 301	4 904
April	1 171 819	649 892	74 095	47 959	109 186	928 363	774 011	205 271	154 352	4 931
May	1 165 772	644 601	73 396	48 006	109 394	924 983	771 203	205 566	153 780	4 884
June	1 179 581	657 863	71 928	47 752	109 351	942 168	786 451	205 224	155 717	4 867
July	1 177 370	653 688	72 190	47 791	109 752	942 774	785 612	205 905	157 162	4 886
August	1 173 163	649 807	71 362	47 812	109 538	940 866	783 730	205 750	157 136	5 008
September	1 178 746	645 708	69 621	48 139	110 485	948 294	783 516	207 433	164 778	4 945
October	1 178 723	645 042	68 253	48 119	110 900	950 151	785 568	208 395	164 583	4 903
November	1 182 494	647 134	67 075	48 500	111 812	955 901	789 747	208 542	166 154	4 971
December	1 184 960	651 133	67 940	48 907	112 058	956 898	793 838	208 360	163 060	4 904
2018										
January	1 176 704	644 719	66 516	49 057	111 802	948 025	787 548	208 128	160 477	5 101
February	1 171 780	636 174	65 336	49 748	111 550	941 514	779 462	208 203	162 052	5 160
March	1 174 543	637 321	63 855	50 764	111 551	940 946	779 655	207 889	161 291	5 410
April	1 177 167	639 449	61 944	51 707	111 558	940 820	781 177	207 787	159 643	5 509
May	1 181 237	637 386	62 687	52 440	111 910	941 090	779 466	208 926	161 624	5 552
June	1 182 294	632 020	64 581	52 824	112 250	938 249	774 917	210 193	163 332	5 690
July	1 177 292	624 643	63 544	53 279	112 619	931 710	769 746	212 425	161 964	5 840
August	1 183 495	624 311	63 570	53 580	112 942	936 424	769 431	213 097	166 993	5 705
September	1 186 034	617 640	67 756	53 732	112 891	933 472	763 185	213 518	170 287	5 758
October	1 181 669	609 235	67 931	54 083	113 435	927 339	755 283	214 172	172 056	5 794
November	1 167 806	594 492	70 430	54 399	113 771	913 291	739 415	212 725	173 876	5 719
December	1 166 319	594 452	69 329	54 689	113 919	911 342	739 248	211 553	172 094	5 690
2019										
January	1 176 844	605 835	70 508	55 241	113 879	922 045	750 280	211 569	171 765	5 596
February	1 178 041	608 681	71 013	55 475	113 540	922 545	751 738	210 838	170 807	5 457
March	1 193 183	620 343	72 585	55 606	113 902	937 486	763 723	211 403	173 763	5 299
April	1 209 663	634 902	74 302	56 103	114 174	952 912	777 573	210 825	175 339	5 247
May	1 212 737	638 448	75 169	56 513	114 274	956 597	779 814	209 499	176 783	5 318
June	1 218 203	648 566	75 182	57 150	114 685	960 711	788 995	209 341	171 716	5 412
July	1 233 115	662 820	75 239	57 692	114 853	974 904	802 598	209 283	172 306	5 346
August	1 243 849	671 857	76 909	58 338	114 968	984 513	810 719	209 029	173 794	5 349
September	1 255 650	680 768	79 294	58 412	115 272	994 421	817 986	208 966	176 435	5 276
October	1 273 734	693 442	85 574	58 353	115 611	1 012 179	830 427	209 205	181 752	5 291
November	1 276 134	697 039	85 117	58 960	115 339	1 011 949	832 017	209 360	179 932	5 310
December	1 285 367	699 020	88 308	59 183	115 038	1 018 120	832 472	209 182	185 648	5 337
2020										
January	1 285 182	699 083	87 340	59 062	115 328	1 016 388	831 766	209 650	184 622	5 303
February	1 283 515	694 349	86 069	58 629	115 401	1 014 983	826 729	209 568	188 254	5 321
March	1 246 883	655 376	88 957	57 433	115 396	979 824	787 854	209 607	191 970	5 457
April	1 232 127	643 066	89 218	56 152	115 783	967 386	775 438	210 077	191 948	5 332
May	1 226 441	637 378	88 781	55 609	116 028	961 870	769 820	210 500	192 050	5 566
June	1 212 060	622 195	87 695	55 732	116 137	947 321	755 684	211 128	191 637	5 709
July	1 201 879	610 548	88 074	55 803	116 388	937 113	744 755	211 636	192 358	5 934
August	1 194 899	602 032	87 648	56 253	116 605	929 930	737 324	212 372	192 606	6 109
September	1 190 796	596 462	85 885	56 986	116 671	925 756	734 131	213 699	191 625	6 218
October	1 184 751	588 392	85 474	57 635	116 769	919 189	727 258	214 535	191 931	6 255
November	1 183 067	584 177	84 556	58 330	116 972	916 191	724 311	215 497	191 880	6 359
December	1 180 385	579 219	84 445	59 504	117 464	910 678	720 791	217 074	189 887	6 392

[1] Includes categories not shown separately.

Table 16-7. Motor Vehicle Sales and Inventories

(Units.)

Year and month	Retail sales of new passenger cars						Retail inventories of new domestic passenger cars (thousands of units, end of period)		
	Thousands of units, not seasonally adjusted			Millions of units, seasonally adjusted annual rate			Not seasonally adjusted	Seasonally adjusted	Inventory to sales ratio
	Total	Domestic	Foreign	Total	Domestic	Foreign			
1977	11 046.0	8 971.2	2 074.8	11.046	8.971	2.075	1 731.0	1 743.0	2.300
1978	11 164.0	9 163.9	2 000.1	11.164	9.164	2.000	1 729.0	1 731.0	2.300
1979	10 558.8	8 230.1	2 328.7	10.559	8.230	2.329	1 691.0	1 667.0	2.400
1980	8 981.8	6 581.4	2 400.4	8.982	6.581	2.401	1 448.0	1 440.0	2.600
1981	8 534.3	6 208.8	2 325.5	8.535	6.209	2.326	1 471.0	1 495.0	3.600
1982	7 979.4	5 758.2	2 221.2	7.979	5.758	2.221	1 126.0	1 127.0	2.200
1983	9 178.6	6 793.0	2 385.6	9.179	6.793	2.386	1 352.0	1 350.0	2.000
1984	10 390.2	7 951.7	2 438.5	10.391	7.952	2.439	1 415.0	1 411.0	2.100
1985	10 978.4	8 204.7	2 773.7	10.979	8.205	2.774	1 630.0	1 619.0	2.500
1986	11 405.7	8 215.0	3 190.7	11.406	8.215	3.191	1 499.0	1 515.0	2.000
1987	10 170.9	7 080.9	3 090.0	10.171	7.081	3.090	1 680.0	1 716.0	2.800
1988	10 545.6	7 539.4	3 006.2	10.545	7.539	3.006	1 601.0	1 601.0	2.300
1989	9 776.8	7 078.1	2 698.7	9.777	7.078	2.699	1 669.0	1 687.0	3.100
1990	9 300.2	6 896.9	2 403.3	9.300	6.897	2.403	1 408.0	1 418.0	2.600
1991	8 175.0	6 136.9	2 038.1	8.175	6.137	2.038	1 283.0	1 296.0	2.600
1992	8 214.4	6 276.6	1 937.8	8.215	6.277	1.938	1 276.0	1 288.0	2.300
1993	8 517.7	6 734.0	1 783.7	8.518	6.734	1.784	1 364.9	1 377.3	2.359
1994	8 990.4	7 255.2	1 735.2	8.990	7.255	1.735	1 436.6	1 445.3	2.319
1995	8 620.4	7 114.1	1 506.3	8.620	7.114	1.506	1 618.5	1 629.8	2.565
1996	8 478.6	7 206.3	1 272.3	8.478	7.206	1.272	1 363.4	1 422.5	2.478
1997	8 217.7	6 862.3	1 355.4	8.218	6.862	1.356	1 329.9	1 399.7	2.368
1998	8 084.9	6 705.1	1 379.8	8.085	6.705	1.380	1 324.4	1 369.7	2.222
1999	8 637.7	6 918.8	1 718.9	8.638	6.919	1.719	1 367.6	1 406.6	2.369
2000	8 777.7	6 761.6	2 016.1	8.778	6.762	2.016	1 377.0	1 397.2	2.810
2001	8 352.1	6 254.4	2 097.7	8.352	6.254	2.098	955.7	976.9	2.267
2002	8 042.1	5 816.5	2 225.6	8.043	5.817	2.226	1 132.0	1 229.8	2.533
2003	7 555.6	5 472.6	2 083.0	7.556	5.473	2.083	1 115.8	1 227.1	2.713
2004	7 482.5	5 333.6	2 148.9	7.482	5.333	2.149	1 034.2	1 144.8	2.405
2005	7 660.4	5 473.6	2 186.8	7.661	5.474	2.187	930.6	1 012.2	2.289
2006	7 761.3	5 416.7	2 344.6	7.762	5.417	2.345	1 031.7	1 105.5	2.498
2007	7 562.1	5 197.1	2 365.0	7.562	5.197	2.365	906.8	985.3	2.272
2008	6 769.2	4 491.0	2 278.2	6.769	4.491	2.278	1 144.2	1 215.5	4.115
2009	5 401.5	3 558.4	1 843.1	5.401	3.558	1.843	686.4	733.2	2.162
2010	5 635.7	3 791.5	1 844.2	5.636	3.792	1.844	759.1	796.7	2.402
2011	6 092.9	4 146.0	1 946.9	6.093	4.146	1.947	813.0	806.7	2.255
2012	7 245.1	5 119.8	2 125.3	7.245	5.120	2.125	1 069.5	1 067.8	2.374
2013	7 586.4	5 433.2	2 153.2	7.586	5.433	2.153	1 259.3	1 231.0	2.812
2014	7 708.0	5 609.9	2 098.1	7.708	5.610	2.098	1 249.4	1 218.0	2.522
2015	7 528.5	5 595.1	1 933.4	7.529	5.595	1.933	1 178.6	1 156.0	2.600
2016	6 883.3	5 145.6	1 737.8	6.883	5.146	1.738	1 209.8	1 143.9	2.700
2017	6 089.2	4 593.0	1 496.2	6.089	4.593	1.496	967.6	862.8	2.444
2018	5 310.3	4 086.9	1 223.4	5.310	4.087	1.223	802.6	722.5	2.172
2019	4 719.7	3 543.9	1 175.8	4.720	3.544	1.176	579.0	496.2	1.743
2020	3 401.8	2 559.8	842.1	3.402	2.560	0.842	518.3	426.5	1.884
2018									
January	366.4	280.5	85.9	5.467	4.139	1.328	988.2	868.4	2.518
February	422.3	329.0	93.3	5.509	4.193	1.316	995.9	867.2	2.482
March	537.6	416.1	121.5	5.374	4.114	1.260	971.1	870.3	2.539
April	429.1	326.9	102.1	5.330	4.094	1.237	973.1	884.6	2.593
May	513.7	394.9	118.8	5.381	4.097	1.285	917.9	867.2	2.540
June	483.5	372.4	111.1	5.231	4.031	1.201	891.1	839.8	2.500
July	417.2	321.3	96.0	5.179	4.048	1.131	815.6	810.9	2.404
August	441.3	338.1	103.2	5.065	3.915	1.150	775.7	780.4	2.392
September	430.3	329.6	100.8	5.226	3.987	1.240	752.1	734.7	2.211
October	420.4	329.2	91.3	5.573	4.385	1.188	790.5	709.2	1.941
November	401.3	306.4	94.9	5.227	4.049	1.178	821.5	702.3	2.081
December	447.1	342.6	104.6	5.161	3.992	1.169	802.6	722.5	2.172
2019									
January	353.6	277.2	76.4	5.251	4.062	1.190	838.3	724.7	2.141
February	365.5	284.5	81.1	4.795	3.641	1.154	839.7	715.4	2.358
March	483.0	371.9	111.1	4.978	3.799	1.179	786.6	678.0	2.142
April	395.6	295.2	100.4	4.807	3.606	1.201	748.3	655.0	2.180
May	455.0	339.5	115.5	4.789	3.548	1.241	695.6	641.1	2.168
June	440.0	322.1	117.9	4.878	3.569	1.309	698.0	637.5	2.143
July	382.9	277.5	105.4	4.651	3.421	1.230	643.3	626.6	2.198
August	434.2	322.2	112.0	4.586	3.402	1.183	612.7	625.9	2.208
September	339.5	255.0	84.4	4.588	3.466	1.122	637.4	619.4	2.144
October	343.8	254.7	89.1	4.427	3.284	1.143	640.4	567.9	2.075
November	352.6	261.4	91.3	4.409	3.313	1.097	627.9	524.1	1.898
December	374.1	282.9	91.3	4.477	3.416	1.061	579.0	496.2	1.743
2020									
January	293.2	223.6	69.6	4.364	3.294	1.071	607.4	490.8	1.788
February	346.5	267.0	79.5	4.269	3.193	1.075	630.9	504.6	1.896
March	264.7	208.1	56.6	2.902	2.266	0.637	665.9	544.7	2.885
April	166.4	124.9	41.5	1.974	1.485	0.489	576.6	462.0	3.733
May	258.5	181.5	77.0	2.675	1.867	0.807	451.9	362.9	2.332
June	251.2	178.3	72.9	2.892	2.059	0.833	459.9	366.5	2.136
July	292.6	217.4	75.2	3.469	2.616	0.853	474.0	423.9	1.944
August	299.8	226.7	73.1	3.477	2.657	0.820	473.7	441.6	1.994
September	304.8	233.9	71.0	3.744	2.856	0.888	508.2	449.4	1.888
October	313.6	240.1	73.5	3.859	2.963	0.896	542.1	439.3	1.779
November	277.6	211.0	66.7	3.778	2.917	0.861	545.8	435.6	1.792
December	332.9	247.4	85.6	3.600	2.700	0.900	518.3	426.5	1.884

Table 16-7. Motor Vehicle Sales and Inventories—*Continued*

(Units.)

Year and month	Retail sales of new trucks and buses								Unit sales of cars and light trucks (millions of units, seasonally adjusted annual rate)		
	Thousands of units, not seasonally adjusted				Millions of units, seasonally adjusted annual rate						
	Total	0–14,000 pounds		14,001 pounds and over	Total	0–14,000 pounds		14,001 pounds and over	Total	Domestic	Foreign
		Domestic	Foreign			Domestic	Foreign				
1977	3 813.0	3 112.8	323.1	377.1	3.818	3.116	0.324	0.378	14.486	12.087	2.399
1978	4 256.8	3 481.1	335.9	439.8	4.249	3.469	0.340	0.440	14.973	12.633	2.340
1979	3 589.7	2 730.2	469.4	390.1	3.599	2.740	0.469	0.390	13.768	10.970	2.798
1980	2 487.4	1 731.1	484.6	271.7	2.482	1.731	0.480	0.271	11.193	8.312	2.881
1981	2 255.6	1 581.7	447.6	226.3	2.255	1.585	0.444	0.226	10.564	7.794	2.770
1982	2 562.8	1 967.5	410.4	184.9	2.569	1.971	0.413	0.185	10.363	7.729	2.634
1983	3 117.3	2 465.2	463.3	188.8	3.130	2.480	0.461	0.189	12.120	9.273	2.847
1984	4 093.1	3 207.2	607.7	278.2	4.086	3.199	0.609	0.278	14.199	11.151	3.048
1985	4 741.7	3 618.4	828.3	295.0	4.760	3.634	0.831	0.295	15.444	11.839	3.605
1986	4 912.1	3 671.4	967.2	273.5	4.918	3.676	0.969	0.273	16.051	11.891	4.160
1987	4 991.5	3 792.0	912.2	287.3	4.978	3.783	0.907	0.288	14.861	10.864	3.997
1988	5 231.9	4 199.7	697.9	334.3	5.225	4.194	0.697	0.334	15.436	11.733	3.703
1989	5 055.9	4 113.6	630.3	312.0	5.065	4.123	0.629	0.313	14.529	11.201	3.328
1990	4 837.0	3 956.8	602.7	277.5	4.840	3.960	0.602	0.278	13.862	10.857	3.005
1991	4 355.4	3 605.6	528.8	221.0	4.361	3.612	0.528	0.221	12.315	9.749	2.566
1992	4 892.2	4 247.0	395.9	249.3	4.893	4.247	0.398	0.248	12.860	10.524	2.336
1993	5 667.8	5 000.5	364.5	302.8	5.658	4.991	0.365	0.302	13.874	11.725	2.149
1994	6 407.3	5 658.0	396.3	352.8	6.408	5.659	0.395	0.354	15.044	12.914	2.130
1995	6 496.4	5 705.9	402.1	388.4	6.498	5.706	0.402	0.390	14.728	12.820	1.908
1996	6 977.6	6 179.8	438.7	359.1	6.976	6.180	0.439	0.357	15.097	13.386	1.711
1997	7 280.4	6 324.7	579.5	376.2	7.280	6.325	0.579	0.376	15.122	13.187	1.935
1998	7 882.4	6 802.0	656.1	424.3	7.883	6.802	0.656	0.425	15.543	13.507	2.036
1999	8 777.3	7 480.7	775.3	521.3	8.777	7.481	0.775	0.521	16.894	14.400	2.494
2000	9 033.9	7 719.7	852.3	461.9	9.033	7.720	0.852	0.461	17.350	14.482	2.868
2001	9 120.4	7 789.0	981.3	350.1	9.120	7.789	0.981	0.350	17.122	14.043	3.079
2002	9 096.5	7 707.8	1 066.3	322.4	9.096	7.708	1.066	0.322	16.817	13.525	3.292
2003	9 411.9	7 856.3	1 227.2	328.4	9.411	7.856	1.227	0.328	16.639	13.329	3.310
2004	9 815.8	8 138.0	1 246.2	431.6	9.813	8.138	1.246	0.429	16.866	13.471	3.395
2005	9 784.4	8 072.4	1 215.5	496.5	9.784	8.072	1.215	0.497	16.948	13.546	3.402
2006	9 287.0	7 396.0	1 346.6	544.4	9.288	7.396	1.347	0.545	16.505	12.813	3.692
2007	8 897.9	7 138.7	1 388.1	371.1	8.900	7.139	1.388	0.373	16.089	12.336	3.753
2008	15 408.6	5 329.2	9 780.9	298.5	6.724	5.329	1.097	0.298	13.195	9.820	3.375
2009	5 200.5	4 116.5	884.2	199.8	5.200	4.117	0.884	0.199	10.402	7.675	2.727
2010	6 136.6	5 020.3	898.7	217.6	6.137	5.020	0.899	0.218	11.556	8.812	2.743
2011	6 955.5	5 666.5	982.4	306.6	6.954	5.666	0.982	0.306	12.743	9.812	2.929
2012	7 534.3	6 127.3	1 060.7	346.3	7.534	6.127	1.061	0.346	14.435	11.247	3.186
2013	8 296.4	6 704.5	1 239.3	352.6	8.296	6.705	1.239	0.352	15.530	12.138	3.392
2014	9 151.9	7 384.3	1 359.9	407.7	9.150	7.384	1.360	0.406	16.452	12.994	3.458
2015	10 328.8	8 097.4	1 782.1	449.3	10.329	8.097	1.782	0.449	17.131	13.692	3.715
2016	10 995.0	8 436.2	2 157.7	401.0	10.995	8.436	2.158	0.401	17.465	13.582	3.895
2017	11 475.9	8 651.8	2 409.1	415.0	11.476	8.652	2.409	0.415	17.137	13.245	3.905
2018	12 402.5	9 153.4	2 761.3	487.9	12.403	9.153	2.761	0.488	17.214	13.240	3.985
2019	12 768.4	9 621.7	2 619.7	527.1	12.768	9.622	2.620	0.527	16.938	13.166	3.795
2020	11 479.5	8 614.8	2 455.2	409.5	11.480	8.615	2.455	0.410	14.472	11.175	3.297
2018											
January	816.3	600.8	184.8	30.7	12.083	8.982	2.674	0.427	17.123	13.120	4.003
February	906.8	665.0	207.4	34.4	12.061	8.847	2.742	0.472	17.099	13.040	4.058
March	1 150.9	844.5	265.9	40.5	12.342	9.093	2.767	0.481	17.234	13.207	4.027
April	963.1	714.6	210.9	37.7	12.476	9.172	2.844	0.460	17.346	13.265	4.080
May	1 113.8	824.5	249.3	40.0	12.340	9.039	2.830	0.471	17.250	13.136	4.114
June	1 104.1	811.3	249.8	42.9	12.430	9.079	2.860	0.490	17.171	13.110	4.061
July	986.8	728.7	217.9	40.2	12.230	9.039	2.703	0.488	16.921	13.087	3.835
August	1 087.0	803.6	238.2	45.2	12.259	9.160	2.598	0.501	16.823	13.075	3.748
September	1 045.5	774.8	227.8	42.9	12.586	9.289	2.778	0.519	17.293	13.276	4.018
October	986.5	727.4	213.5	45.6	12.582	9.327	2.739	0.516	17.639	13.712	3.927
November	1 021.8	754.2	227.9	39.7	12.627	9.334	2.789	0.503	17.351	13.383	3.968
December	1 219.9	903.9	267.9	48.1	12.801	9.480	2.810	0.511	17.451	13.472	3.978
2019											
January	818.4	598.1	181.9	38.3	12.061	8.886	2.639	0.536	16.776	12.947	3.829
February	923.4	680.7	205.9	36.8	12.312	9.090	2.719	0.503	16.604	12.731	3.873
March	1 160.5	870.1	246.4	43.9	12.860	9.703	2.630	0.527	17.311	13.502	3.809
April	977.8	745.2	186.4	46.1	12.358	9.329	2.466	0.562	16.602	12.935	3.667
May	1 173.8	897.4	229.8	46.6	13.080	9.937	2.592	0.552	17.318	13.485	3.833
June	1 115.5	856.6	213.9	45.1	12.870	9.825	2.512	0.533	17.215	13.394	3.821
July	1 061.6	803.9	210.2	47.4	12.883	9.774	2.552	0.557	16.977	13.194	3.782
August	1 251.7	946.2	258.9	46.6	13.021	9.847	2.640	0.534	17.073	13.249	3.824
September	976.7	729.7	198.5	48.5	13.062	9.842	2.657	0.563	17.087	13.308	3.779
October	1 037.3	776.1	215.0	46.2	12.857	9.642	2.697	0.518	16.766	12.926	3.840
November	1 086.7	820.4	231.0	35.3	13.038	9.884	2.689	0.465	16.982	13.197	3.785
December	1 185.1	897.3	241.6	46.2	12.821	9.697	2.649	0.475	16.823	13.113	3.710
2020											
January	875.2	659.4	183.9	31.9	12.956	9.856	2.653	0.446	16.874	13.150	3.724
February	1 037.2	786.7	217.4	33.1	12.955	9.845	2.663	0.448	16.776	13.038	3.738
March	758.6	582.5	142.7	33.4	8.848	6.819	1.639	0.390	11.361	9.085	2.276
April	576.9	436.0	112.9	28.0	7.088	5.291	1.456	0.341	8.721	6.776	1.945
May	884.2	645.6	215.0	23.6	9.737	7.081	2.358	0.299	12.113	8.948	3.165
June	880.2	631.5	218.3	30.4	10.468	7.445	2.686	0.337	13.023	9.504	3.519
July	975.9	725.7	218.4	31.8	11.533	8.575	2.586	0.372	14.630	11.191	3.439
August	1 054.6	794.3	223.9	36.3	12.063	9.178	2.456	0.429	15.111	11.835	3.276
September	1 074.8	822.6	213.6	38.6	12.989	9.904	2.653	0.432	16.302	12.760	3.541
October	1 085.8	823.1	222.3	40.4	12.979	9.866	2.647	0.466	16.372	12.830	3.543
November	957.6	709.1	212.4	36.1	12.414	9.224	2.713	0.477	15.714	12.141	3.574
December	1 318.5	998.3	274.3	45.9	13.054	9.876	2.720	0.458	16.229	12.592	3.637

Table 16-8. Retail and Food Services Sales

(All retail establishments and food services; millions of dollars; not seasonally adjusted.)

Year and month	Retail and food services, total [1]	Retail (NAICS industry categories)											Food services and drinking places
		GAFO (department store type goods), total [2]	Motor vehicles and parts	Furniture and home furnishings	Electronics and appliances	Building materials and garden	Food and beverages	Health and personal care	Gasoline	Clothing and accessories	General merchandise	Nonstore retailers	
1995	2 450 628	650 040	579 715	63 470	64 770	164 561	390 386	101 632	181 113	131 333	300 498	103 516	233 012
1996	2 603 794	682 613	627 507	67 707	68 363	176 683	401 073	109 554	194 425	136 581	315 305	117 761	242 245
1997	2 726 131	713 387	653 817	72 715	70 061	191 063	409 373	118 670	199 700	140 293	331 363	126 190	257 364
1998	2 852 956	757 936	688 415	77 412	74 527	202 423	416 525	129 582	191 727	149 151	351 081	133 904	271 194
1999	3 086 990	815 665	764 204	84 294	78 977	218 290	433 699	142 697	212 524	159 751	380 179	151 797	283 900
2000	3 287 537	862 739	796 210	91 170	82 206	228 994	444 764	155 233	249 816	167 674	404 228	180 453	304 261
2001	3 378 906	882 700	815 579	91 484	80 240	239 379	462 429	166 532	251 383	167 287	427 468	180 563	316 638
2002	3 459 077	912 707	818 811	94 438	83 740	248 539	464 856	179 983	250 619	172 304	446 520	189 279	330 525
2003	3 612 457	946 114	841 588	96 736	86 442	263 463	474 385	275 187	178 694	178 694	468 771	206 359	349 726
2004	3 846 605	1 003 891	866 372	103 757	93 896	295 274	490 380	324 006	324 006	190 253	497 382	228 977	373 557
2005	4 085 746	1 059 599	888 307	109 120	100 461	320 802	508 484	378 923	378 923	200 969	528 385	255 579	396 463
2006	4 294 359	1 110 155	899 997	112 795	105 477	334 130	525 232	421 976	421 976	213 189	554 256	284 343	422 786
2007	4 439 733	1 143 426	910 139	111 144	106 599	320 854	547 837	451 822	451 822	221 205	578 582	308 767	444 551
2008	4 391 580	1 136 376	785 865	98 720	105 317	301 833	569 276	246 573	503 639	215 583	595 041	319 152	456 265
2009	4 064 476	1 088 197	671 772	84 749	95 364	261 637	568 418	252 794	391 234	204 475	588 918	311 152	452 005
2010	4 284 968	1 114 374	742 913	85 205	97 396	260 566	580 530	260 435	448 349	213 286	603 757	340 957	466 920
2011	4 598 302	1 155 666	812 938	87 586	99 928	269 480	609 137	271 612	533 457	228 606	624 766	376 344	495 350
2012	4 826 390	1 191 843	886 494	91 542	102 060	281 533	628 205	274 000	555 419	239 493	642 313	408 171	524 161
2013	5 003 332	1 213 772	962 173	95 734	103 536	299 561	641 546	280 043	553 763	245 045	653 575	429 984	543 484
2014	5 218 529	1 241 461	1 026 997	100 510	102 897	313 497	670 536	295 584	547 064	251 102	670 614	464 182	576 602
2015	5 352 218	1 262 662	1 103 938	107 816	100 257	323 930	687 473	309 489	455 747	256 926	680 138	498 361	624 099
2016	5 506 136	1 267 631	1 151 917	112 260	93 973	337 787	702 162	319 171	436 143	261 207	682 713	543 845	657 923
2017	5 732 863	1 274 977	1 185 696	115 309	92 424	349 365	728 843	323 866	476 152	261 396	691 891	608 194	692 649
2018	5 985 075	1 298 524	1 204 803	119 094	94 002	366 225	750 000	337 765	521 453	266 881	707 094	676 183	732 038
2019	6 184 582	1 305 943	1 239 767	120 517	90 536	372 432	773 647	342 569	512 377	268 735	716 476	761 664	773 545
2020	6 215 073	1 245 270	1 244 316	115 563	76 680	425 577	865 095	348 713	430 116	204 196	739 679	924 559	621 483
2018													
January	444 286	90 650	88 243	8 878	7 290	23 535	60 393	27 699	38 954	15 780	50 594	53 006	54 478
February	435 373	92 611	89 728	8 701	6 972	23 507	56 483	25 667	36 879	18 424	50 770	48 632	54 702
March	508 383	108 401	109 760	10 185	7 581	29 753	63 791	28 477	42 186	22 207	59 068	54 589	63 389
April	480 373	98 990	99 466	9 365	6 835	32 034	59 571	27 155	42 573	20 463	53 805	52 528	60 128
May	527 991	110 609	109 239	10 114	7 397	37 940	64 527	28 960	47 442	23 560	60 281	55 618	63 941
June	507 106	106 035	104 879	9 921	7 504	34 966	62 765	27 655	46 750	21 294	58 091	51 733	63 529
July	505 209	105 372	103 830	9 916	7 378	33 133	63 399	27 467	47 089	21 733	57 383	53 542	63 442
August	520 544	111 811	108 381	10 399	7 861	32 075	63 628	28 904	47 873	23 121	60 099	55 160	64 514
September	477 137	100 372	95 966	9 759	7 280	29 354	61 186	26 846	44 442	19 782	54 945	51 314	59 965
October	503 602	105 419	99 033	9 966	7 335	32 490	62 554	29 355	47 071	21 203	57 771	57 620	61 724
November	518 457	121 812	95 230	10 770	9 565	29 908	63 656	28 786	42 017	25 364	66 319	69 356	59 138
December	556 614	146 442	101 048	11 120	11 004	27 530	68 047	30 794	38 177	33 950	77 968	73 085	63 088
2019													
January	456 538	91 540	87 889	8 818	7 290	26 620	62 829	28 639	36 439	16 155	51 708	58 403	57 077
February	442 274	90 967	89 623	8 629	6 972	24 039	56 898	26 772	35 514	17 961	50 626	54 156	57 307
March	513 845	106 564	110 355	10 018	7 581	29 916	63 504	28 786	42 065	22 059	58 788	58 091	66 690
April	506 920	102 978	103 370	9 579	6 835	34 033	62 402	28 402	44 270	21 500	56 991	59 140	63 999
May	544 203	110 415	111 785	10 296	7 397	37 235	66 510	29 487	47 387	23 079	60 909	63 232	68 306
June	515 269	105 867	104 650	9 759	7 504	33 517	64 479	27 642	44 876	21 116	58 979	58 740	66 674
July	528 710	107 090	109 183	10 188	7 378	33 691	66 428	28 142	46 392	21 742	58 759	62 532	66 613
August	541 951	114 131	114 591	10 616	7 861	32 375	66 937	28 528	45 949	23 829	61 777	62 064	68 469
September	493 076	100 240	99 612	10 116	7 280	29 963	62 420	27 297	42 751	19 567	54 785	58 886	63 520
October	522 195	106 921	103 856	10 272	7 335	32 629	64 849	29 551	44 348	21 400	58 872	65 195	65 759
November	532 130	121 457	101 242	11 037	9 565	29 793	66 363	27 844	41 424	25 170	66 356	71 509	63 127
December	587 471	147 773	103 611	11 189	11 004	28 621	70 028	31 479	40 962	35 157	77 926	89 716	66 004
2020													
January	480 301	94 549	93 367	93 367	7 079	26 966	64 567	28 987	39 696	16 873	53 203	62 245	61 567
February	478 467	97 552	97 828	97 828	6 687	26 237	61 962	27 756	36 963	19 232	54 596	58 864	62 956
March	478 267	95 501	82 387	82 387	5 816	32 152	80 990	30 888	34 261	10 969	63 624	66 414	47 740
April	407 227	68 637	69 534	69 534	3 040	35 916	71 064	25 724	26 810	2 744	54 576	73 022	30 017
May	504 607	91 042	107 362	107 362	3 952	42 422	76 438	26 251	32 045	8 787	63 381	78 134	42 321
June	532 678	102 574	114 228	114 228	5 608	42 092	71 799	28 279	36 314	16 442	60 501	76 015	51 473
July	549 416	106 664	116 233	116 233	6 555	39 430	75 085	29 573	38 876	17 779	61 674	79 072	54 511
August	545 307	109 556	115 928	115 928	6 839	36 664	72 353	28 918	38 730	18 968	62 304	77 168	56 358
September	530 987	104 834	113 058	113 058	6 459	36 930	69 741	29 462	37 231	18 790	58 567	75 540	54 740
October	553 114	111 528	114 679	114 679	6 865	37 582	71 957	30 630	38 161	20 088	63 203	81 386	57 392
November	543 273	117 962	103 220	103 220	8 296	34 662	71 879	28 575	34 394	21 287	66 964	91 542	50 911
December	611 429	144 871	116 492	116 492	9 484	34 524	77 260	33 670	36 635	32 237	77 086	105 157	51 497

[1] Includes store categories not shown separately.
[2] Includes furniture, home furnishings, electronics, appliances, clothing, sporting goods, hobby, book, music, general merchandise, office supplies, stationery, and gifts.

Table 16-8. Retail and Food Services Sales—*Continued*

(All retail establishments and food services; millions of dollars; seasonally adjusted.)

Year and month	Total	Retail and food services — Retail (NAICS industry categories)										
		Total	GAFO (department store type goods) ²	Motor vehicles and parts	Furniture and home furnishings	Electronics and appliances	Building materials and garden	Food and beverages — Total ¹	Groceries	Beer, wine, and liquor	Health and personal care	Gasoline
1995	2 450 628	2 217 613	650 040	579 715	63 470	64 770	164 561	390 386	356 409	22 007	101 632	181 113
1996	2 603 794	2 361 546	682 613	627 507	67 707	68 363	176 683	401 073	365 547	23 157	109 554	194 425
1997	2 726 131	2 468 765	713 387	653 817	72 715	70 061	191 063	409 373	372 570	24 081	118 670	199 700
1998	2 852 956	2 581 761	757 936	688 415	77 412	74 527	202 423	416 525	378 188	25 382	129 582	191 727
1999	3 086 990	2 803 088	815 665	764 204	84 294	78 977	218 290	433 699	394 250	26 476	142 697	212 524
2000	3 287 537	2 983 275	862 739	796 210	91 170	82 206	228 994	444 764	402 515	28 507	155 233	249 816
2001	3 378 906	3 062 267	882 700	815 579	91 484	80 240	239 379	462 429	418 127	29 621	166 532	251 383
2002	3 459 077	3 128 552	912 707	818 811	94 438	83 740	248 539	464 856	419 813	29 894	179 983	250 619
2003	3 612 457	3 262 731	946 114	841 588	96 736	86 442	263 463	474 385	427 987	30 469	275 187	178 694
2004	3 846 605	3 473 048	1 003 891	866 372	103 757	93 896	295 274	490 380	441 136	32 189	324 006	324 006
2005	4 085 746	3 689 283	1 059 599	888 307	109 120	100 461	320 802	508 484	457 667	33 567	378 923	378 923
2006	4 294 359	3 871 573	1 110 155	899 997	112 795	105 477	334 130	525 232	471 699	36 016	421 976	421 976
2007	4 439 733	3 995 182	1 143 426	910 139	111 144	106 599	320 854	547 837	491 360	38 128	451 822	451 822
2008	4 391 580	3 935 315	1 136 376	785 865	98 720	105 317	301 833	569 276	511 222	39 504	246 573	503 639
2009	4 064 476	3 612 471	1 088 197	671 772	84 749	95 364	261 637	568 418	510 033	40 245	252 794	391 234
2010	4 284 968	3 818 048	1 114 374	742 913	85 205	97 396	260 566	580 530	520 750	41 401	260 435	448 349
2011	4 598 302	4 102 952	1 155 666	812 938	87 586	99 928	269 480	609 137	547 476	42 392	271 612	533 457
2012	4 826 390	4 302 229	1 191 843	886 494	91 542	102 060	281 533	628 205	563 645	44 365	274 000	555 419
2013	5 003 332	4 459 848	1 213 772	962 173	95 734	103 536	299 561	641 546	575 476	45 647	280 043	553 763
2014	5 218 529	4 641 927	1 241 461	1 026 997	100 510	102 897	313 497	670 536	601 498	47 395	295 584	547 064
2015	5 352 218	4 728 119	1 262 662	1 103 938	107 816	100 257	323 930	687 473	616 086	49 156	309 489	455 747
2016	5 506 136	4 848 213	1 267 631	1 151 917	112 260	93 973	337 787	702 162	627 871	51 252	319 171	436 143
2017	5 732 863	5 040 214	1 274 977	1 185 696	115 309	92 424	349 365	728 843	653 178	52 622	323 866	476 152
2018	5 985 075	5 253 037	1 298 524	1 204 803	119 094	94 002	366 225	750 000	671 330	55 088	337 765	521 453
2019	6 184 582	5 411 037	1 305 943	1 239 767	120 517	90 536	372 432	773 647	693 015	56 805	342 569	512 377
2020	6 215 073	5 593 590	1 245 270	1 244 316	115 563	76 680	425 577	865 095	773 741	66 852	348 713	430 116
2018												
January	491 492	432 148	107 591	100 279	9 875	7 847	29 261	61 935	55 465	4 520	27 671	42 760
February	493 759	434 106	108 619	99 817	9 910	7 941	30 076	62 026	55 520	4 520	27 510	43 184
March	493 373	433 232	107 377	100 129	9 937	7 880	29 792	62 166	55 631	4 564	27 674	42 612
April	495 025	435 610	108 236	100 463	10 113	7 994	29 807	62 516	55 999	4 573	27 937	42 403
May	500 719	439 996	110 084	100 878	9 974	7 945	30 546	62 516	55 953	4 601	28 309	43 525
June	499 631	438 191	108 423	100 593	9 971	7 991	30 974	62 350	55 828	4 575	28 076	43 773
July	502 962	440 703	108 795	101 183	10 006	7 916	30 991	62 713	56 158	4 600	28 258	44 174
August	501 913	439 278	108 286	99 709	9 885	7 940	30 601	62 510	56 007	4 556	28 533	44 616
September	500 362	438 985	107 777	99 414	9 818	7 778	30 735	62 813	56 203	4 629	28 319	44 089
October	506 010	444 038	108 637	99 879	9 907	7 770	31 505	63 056	56 414	4 638	28 555	45 878
November	506 973	445 242	109 261	100 696	9 917	7 714	30 855	63 138	56 478	4 669	29 077	43 722
December	496 593	434 803	107 535	101 771	9 884	7 579	30 971	62 979	56 359	4 664	27 944	40 962
2019												
January	502 724	440 751	107 814	99 605	9 787	7 619	32 451	63 940	57 299	4 660	28 639	39 781
February	502 627	439 996	107 153	100 353	9 862	7 508	30 745	62 493	55 865	4 667	28 756	41 440
March	510 320	447 167	108 744	103 240	10 008	7 571	31 106	63 724	57 045	4 704	28 700	42 662
April	512 326	448 709	109 319	102 189	10 073	7 519	30 959	63 950	57 255	4 686	28 545	43 487
May	513 870	449 552	108 851	102 619	10 074	7 590	30 338	64 071	57 417	4 683	28 684	43 276
June	515 911	450 927	109 081	102 956	10 071	7 549	30 385	64 557	57 849	4 736	28 615	42 617
July	519 447	454 012	109 662	103 680	10 067	7 652	30 679	65 344	58 581	4 760	28 398	43 398
August	521 833	456 500	109 339	105 600	10 082	7 572	31 270	65 328	58 549	4 783	28 414	42 783
September	518 605	452 849	108 996	103 712	10 177	7 618	30 806	64 871	58 117	4 764	28 434	42 538
October	521 114	455 486	109 047	104 097	10 120	7 446	31 118	64 915	58 172	4 742	28 718	43 266
November	522 805	457 658	108 946	106 580	10 219	7 514	31 312	65 212	58 406	4 798	28 499	43 240
December	523 862	458 055	109 703	104 823	9 990	7 497	31 952	65 676	58 877	4 829	28 359	44 093
2020												
January	526 930	460 586	110 605	105 162	10 475	7 467	32 920	65 321	58 546	4 875	28 872	43 195
February	525 810	459 610	110 253	105 520	10 456	7 381	32 904	65 326	58 441	4 901	29 064	41 625
March	480 593	434 467	99 049	78 046	8 225	6 135	32 894	82 758	75 026	5 730	30 462	34 607
April	410 120	380 193	72 279	68 198	4 156	3 527	32 306	72 069	65 033	5 281	25 958	26 156
May	484 339	444 897	89 127	100 942	7 349	4 272	36 338	73 724	65 931	5 749	26 251	29 399
June	526 860	476 347	106 140	110 574	10 104	6 004	36 538	72 538	64 685	5 757	28 336	34 258
July	534 295	481 627	107 240	109 646	10 346	6 981	35 662	72 734	64 944	5 701	29 811	36 164
August	538 646	483 716	107 116	110 195	10 812	6 986	36 543	71 780	63 861	5 825	29 599	36 503
September	549 528	493 327	112 966	114 374	10 843	6 886	36 676	71 774	63 823	5 790	29 972	37 009
October	550 038	493 991	111 682	114 247	10 864	7 114	36 685	71 191	63 383	5 675	29 941	37 194
November	542 583	488 652	108 932	112 202	10 705	6 851	37 002	72 198	64 371	5 727	29 550	36 473
December	535 972	484 782	107 735	114 447	10 621	6 456	37 099	71 382	63 775	5 543	29 929	39 098

¹Includes store categories not shown separately.
²Includes furniture, home furnishings, electronics, appliances, clothing, sporting goods, hobby, book, music, general merchandise, office supplies, stationery, and gifts.

Table 16-9. Quarterly U.S. Retail Sales: Total and E-Commerce

Year and quarter	Retail sales (millions of dollars)		E-commerce as a percent of total sales	Percent change from prior quarter		Percent change from same quarter a year ago	
	Total	E-commerce		Total sales	E-commerce sales	Total sales	E-commerce sales
NOT SEASONALLY ADJUSTED							
2019							
1st quarter	1 231 583	124 384	10.1	-11.7	-19.8	1.3	11.4
2nd quarter	1 367 413	134 714	9.9	11.0	8.3	3.0	13.2
3rd quarter	1 365 135	140 538	10.3	-0.2	4.3	3.8	16.8
4rd quarter	1 446 906	178 865	12.4	6.0	27.3	3.7	15.3
2020							
1st quarter	1 264 772	141 521	11.2	-12.6	-20.9	2.7	13.8
2nd quarter	1 320 701	193 624	14.7	4.4	36.8	-3.4	43.7
3rd quarter	1 460 101	191 573	13.1	10.6	-1.1	7.0	36.3
4rd quarter	1 548 016	235 957	15.2	6.0	23.2	7.0	31.9
SEASONALLY ADJUSTED							
2007							
1st quarter	985 713	31 728	3.2	1.3	5.3	2.3	20.1
2nd quarter	994 838	33 524	3.4	0.9	5.7	2.8	22.5
3rd quarter	1 001 953	34 841	3.5	0.7	3.9	3.0	20.8
4th quarter	1 014 852	35 784	3.5	1.3	2.7	4.3	18.7
2008							
1st quarter	1 007 189	36 017	3.6	-0.8	0.7	2.2	13.5
2nd quarter	1 011 101	36 514	3.6	0.4	1.4	1.6	8.9
3rd quarter	999 159	36 292	3.6	-1.2	-0.6	-0.3	4.2
4th quarter	910 187	33 040	3.6	-8.9	-9.0	-10.3	-7.7
2009							
1st quarter	888 604	34 132	3.8	-2.4	3.3	-11.8	-5.2
2nd quarter	892 284	35 282	4.0	0.4	3.4	-11.8	-3.4
3rd quarter	912 858	37 404	4.1	2.3	6.0	-8.6	3.1
4th quarter	919 242	38 108	4.1	0.7	1.9	1.0	15.3
2010							
1st quarter	932 930	39 289	4.2	1.5	3.1	5.0	15.1
2nd quarter	949 236	41 303	4.4	1.7	5.1	6.4	17.1
3rd quarter	953 120	43 474	4.6	0.4	5.3	4.4	16.2
4th quarter	981 272	45 073	4.6	3.0	3.7	6.7	18.3
2011							
1st quarter	1 005 074	47 038	4.7	2.4	4.4	7.7	19.7
2nd quarter	1 020 787	48 851	4.8	1.6	3.9	7.5	18.3
3rd quarter	1 029 157	50 187	4.9	0.8	2.7	8.0	15.4
4th quarter	1 046 972	53 191	5.1	1.7	6.0	6.7	18.0
2012							
1st quarter	1 068 960	55 290	5.2	2.1	3.9	6.4	17.5
2nd quarter	1 064 910	56 563	5.3	-0.4	2.3	4.3	15.8
3rd quarter	1 073 811	58 551	5.5	0.8	3.5	4.3	16.7
4rd quarter	1 089 355	60 837	5.6	1.4	3.9	4.0	14.4
2013							
1st quarter	1 108 381	62 316	5.6	1.7	2.4	3.7	12.7
2nd quarter	1 108 048	64 027	5.8	0.0	2.7	4.1	13.2
3rd quarter	1 118 548	65 932	5.9	0.9	3.0	4.2	12.6
4rd quarter	1 124 609	68 343	6.1	0.5	3.7	3.2	12.3
2014							
1st quarter	1 134 215	70 305	6.2	0.9	2.9	2.3	12.8
2nd quarter	1 161 895	73 329	6.3	2.4	4.3	4.9	14.5
3rd quarter	1 169 524	75 729	6.5	0.7	3.3	4.6	14.9
4th quarter	1 170 880	77 649	6.6	0.1	2.5	4.1	13.6
2015							
1st quarter	1 162 225	80 228	6.9	-0.7	3.3	2.5	14.1
2nd quarter	1 181 538	82 914	7.0	1.7	3.3	1.7	13.1
3rd quarter	1 192 546	85 656	7.2	0.9	3.3	2.0	13.1
4th quarter	1 187 795	88 350	7.4	-0.4	3.1	1.4	13.8
2016							
1st quarter	1 189 765	91 163	7.7	0.2	3.2	2.4	13.6
2nd quarter	1 203 089	94 194	7.8	1.1	3.3	1.8	13.6
3rd quarter	1 213 656	96 929	8.0	0.9	2.9	1.8	13.2
4th quarter	1 226 066	100 137	8.2	1.0	3.3	3.2	13.3
2017							
1st quarter	1 246 204	104 149	8.4	1.6	4.0	4.7	14.2
2nd quarter	1 247 934	108 598	8.7	0.1	4.3	3.7	15.3
3rd quarter	1 260 424	111 556	8.9	1.0	2.7	3.9	15.1
4th quarter	1 291 373	117 203	9.1	2.5	5.1	5.3	17.0
2018							
1st quarter	1 299 486	121 570	9.4	0.6	3.7	4.3	16.7
2nd quarter	1 313 797	125 386	9.5	1.1	3.1	5.3	15.5
3rd quarter	1 318 966	127 471	9.7	0.4	1.7	4.6	14.3
4th quarter	1 324 083	130 743	9.9	0.4	2.6	2.5	11.6
2019							
1st quarter	1 327 914	135 629	10.2	0.3	3.7	2.2	11.6
2nd quarter	1 349 188	141 716	10.5	1.6	4.5	2.7	13.0
3rd quarter	1 363 361	147 965	10.9	1.1	4.4	3.4	16.1
4rd quarter	1 371 199	151 218	11.0	0.6	2.2	3.6	15.7
2020							
1st quarter	1 354 477	154 575	11.4	-1.2	2.2	2.0	14.0
2nd quarter	1 301 259	203 796	15.7	-3.9	31.8	-3.6	43.8
3rd quarter	1 458 670	201 382	13.8	12.1	-1.2	7.0	36.1
4rd quarter	1 467 425	199 665	13.6	0.6	-0.9	7.0	32.0

Table 16-10. Retail Inventories

(All retail stores; end of period, millions of dollars.)

Year and month	Not seasonally adjusted			Seasonally adjusted							General merchandise	
	Total	Excluding motor vehicles and parts	Motor vehicles and parts	Total	Excluding motor vehicles and parts	Motor vehicles and parts	Furniture, home furnishings, electronics, and appliances	Building materials and garden	Food and beverages	Clothing and accessories	Total	Department stores [1]
1995	317 304	220 921	96 383	322 216	228 842	93 374	21 817	26 337	28 718	29 298	59 530	43 455
1996	328 160	227 888	100 272	333 255	236 015	97 240	22 253	27 447	29 658	29 778	60 591	44 124
1997	338 790	234 270	104 520	343 825	242 518	101 307	22 109	28 897	29 891	31 079	60 715	44 309
1998	351 255	245 400	105 855	356 518	253 888	102 630	22 665	30 921	30 837	32 308	61 542	43 438
1999	378 813	259 879	118 934	384 078	268 567	115 511	24 096	33 005	32 635	33 735	64 297	43 835
2000	400 394	268 982	131 412	405 931	277 829	128 102	25 622	34 269	32 108	36 753	64 929	42 667
2001	387 859	266 370	121 489	393 638	274 796	118 842	24 497	34 235	33 165	35 627	64 790	40 464
2002	409 314	271 757	137 557	415 174	280 277	134 897	25 853	36 123	32 907	37 401	66 006	38 750
2003	425 748	277 471	148 277	431 199	285 668	145 531	27 152	37 398	32 504	38 503	66 655	36 823
2004	454 848	297 561	157 287	460 335	305 941	154 394	30 043	41 593	33 433	41 417	70 969	37 230
2005	465 791	310 227	155 564	471 616	318 849	152 767	30 550	45 072	33 784	43 003	74 179	38 030
2006	480 338	324 005	156 333	486 403	332 972	153 431	30 807	47 010	34 700	47 272	75 592	37 133
2007	494 372	334 566	159 806	500 489	343 476	157 013	31 356	49 074	36 484	47 381	75 820	36 428
2008	471 330	323 360	147 970	477 148	331 531	145 617	27 772	46 496	37 273	45 958	72 777	33 090
2009	423 380	114 772	114 772	429 159	315 870	113 289	25 710	42 707	37 254	40 811	69 575	30 817
2010	449 059	320 671	128 388	454 548	327 909	126 639	28 006	40 737	38 613	41 931	73 290	30 933
2011	465 191	331 392	133 799	471 361	339 195	132 166	26 680	43 354	40 194	44 273	76 774	31 374
2012	500 096	341 424	158 672	507 157	349 988	157 169	27 501	44 644	41 092	46 716	78 497	30 406
2013	537 918	357 477	180 441	544 700	366 354	178 346	27 566	47 255	42 647	49 764	81 434	30 394
2014	554 891	366 511	188 380	561 120	375 140	185 980	27 468	48 092	44 079	51 033	82 032	28 965
2015	581 724	380 339	201 385	587 580	388 822	198 758	27 336	49 574	45 443	52 476	83 972	29 235
2016	603 998	387 143	216 855	611 019	395 696	215 323	27 235	50 969	46 933	52 757	83 225	27 908
2017	617 178	394 470	222 708	626 342	403 411	222 931	27 781	52 361	48 795	53 016	81 023	26 024
2018	645 007	408 258	236 749	653 741	416 992	236 749	27 853	55 310	50 479	54 251	82 544	24 494
2019	649 680	415 682	233 998	657 537	423 985	233 552	27 001	57 497	51 471	53 720	80 747	22 075
2020	614 176	419 978	194 198	620 612	427 488	193 124	25 511	61 515	53 000	48 171	83 416	20 087
2017												
January	606 590	385 455	221 135	613 976	395 056	218 920	27 247	51 087	46 845	52 660	82 671	27 859
February	610 623	386 507	224 116	615 321	394 071	221 250	27 415	51 005	46 845	52 834	81 979	27 412
March	619 625	391 738	227 887	617 948	394 986	222 962	27 348	51 183	46 977	53 032	82 121	27 467
April	616 234	388 644	227 590	617 333	393 883	223 450	27 236	51 046	47 351	52 591	82 126	27 444
May	612 278	387 071	225 207	618 727	394 582	224 145	27 516	51 115	47 717	52 731	81 226	26 869
June	616 261	389 325	226 936	621 665	396 559	225 106	27 555	51 105	47 447	52 743	81 646	26 712
July	606 571	387 864	218 707	622 262	397 063	225 199	27 574	51 452	47 595	52 641	81 441	26 584
August	614 305	394 772	219 533	625 467	398 602	226 865	27 596	51 440	47 895	52 631	81 140	26 316
September	623 520	406 671	216 849	620 755	398 415	222 340	27 693	51 629	47 847	52 639	81 037	26 099
October	647 009	425 701	221 308	621 348	399 878	221 470	27 558	51 877	48 038	52 719	80 948	26 002
November	653 904	429 229	224 675	623 348	401 461	221 887	27 499	52 113	48 419	52 752	80 963	25 997
December	617 178	394 470	222 708	626 342	403 411	222 931	27 781	52 361	48 795	53 016	81 023	26 024
2018												
January	621 033	394 523	394 523	627 539	403 538	224 001	27 499	52 608	49 073	53 031	81 026	26 146
February	627 553	398 091	398 091	630 704	404 803	225 901	27 637	53 156	49 404	53 641	81 287	26 134
March	629 345	400 602	400 602	629 260	404 065	225 195	27 647	53 242	49 059	53 292	80 708	25 470
April	631 839	401 292	401 292	632 025	406 068	225 957	27 555	53 442	48 594	53 690	81 417	25 904
May	628 352	399 932	399 932	633 740	407 013	226 727	27 388	53 878	48 973	53 274	82 219	26 027
June	628 254	400 717	400 717	635 890	408 933	226 957	27 205	54 630	49 181	53 410	81 917	25 840
July	621 900	400 018	400 018	637 091	409 279	227 812	27 513	54 843	49 345	53 229	82 205	25 721
August	630 283	406 431	406 431	640 946	410 483	230 463	27 761	55 103	49 706	53 284	82 645	25 611
September	643 484	417 539	417 539	642 870	410 311	232 559	27 751	55 011	49 632	53 087	82 554	25 555
October	673 410	439 540	439 540	646 556	413 112	233 444	28 581	54 966	49 794	53 766	83 168	25 654
November	675 473	437 365	437 365	644 954	410 018	234 936	27 364	54 880	49 924	53 373	81 597	24 520
December	645 007	408 258	408 258	653 741	416 992	236 749	27 853	55 310	50 479	54 251	82 544	24 494
2019												
January	652 247	410 190	410 190	657 715	418 818	238 897	28 155	56 121	50 439	54 601	82 955	24 330
February	659 262	415 127	415 127	660 773	420 904	239 869	28 487	55 841	50 599	54 491	83 648	24 253
March	658 829	417 424	417 424	660 222	421 083	239 139	28 146	56 016	50 711	54 448	83 097	24 007
April	662 496	417 911	417 911	661 146	421 885	239 261	28 199	56 492	51 076	54 311	82 777	23 686
May	658 495	416 196	416 196	663 154	423 067	240 087	28 025	56 767	51 201	54 372	82 200	23 538
June	653 380	414 090	414 090	663 177	423 146	240 031	27 716	56 805	51 215	53 994	82 289	23 431
July	649 771	414 109	414 109	664 835	423 542	241 293	27 616	57 212	51 267	54 193	82 326	23 300
August	650 831	417 507	417 507	664 058	422 933	241 125	27 340	57 007	51 328	54 089	81 994	23 217
September	665 716	430 625	430 625	664 378	423 269	241 109	27 345	57 382	51 199	54 028	82 471	23 235
October	692 590	452 547	452 547	665 027	426 028	238 999	27 654	57 725	51 465	53 953	82 254	23 192
November	688 890	451 554	451 554	660 583	425 130	235 453	27 190	57 566	51 514	53 851	81 821	22 790
December	649 680	415 682	415 682	657 537	423 985	233 552	27 001	57 497	51 471	53 720	80 747	22 075
2020												
January	652 807	417 371	417 371	657 485	425 337	232 148	27 228	57 091	52 048	53 676	81 133	22 210
February	652 801	418 612	418 612	655 065	424 167	230 898	26 862	57 023	51 668	53 681	80 822	22 048
March	662 952	417 907	417 907	662 232	420 379	241 853	26 881	56 779	48 742	54 941	79 198	22 006
April	638 563	412 303	412 303	636 067	415 471	220 596	25 817	55 112	50 200	53 955	76 721	20 869
May	589 281	400 143	400 143	597 501	408 047	189 454	24 405	53 607	50 297	52 253	75 318	20 278
June	571 861	395 990	395 990	579 905	404 105	175 800	23 617	54 101	51 012	49 754	73 870	19 149
July	572 642	396 962	396 962	584 548	405 582	178 966	23 531	54 999	51 467	48 730	74 671	18 951
August	578 323	402 979	402 979	590 490	409 100	181 390	24 059	55 742	51 858	47 975	76 666	19 445
September	603 914	421 863	421 863	600 447	414 661	185 786	24 590	56 901	52 433	47 447	78 685	19 682
October	633 606	444 720	444 720	608 412	419 987	188 425	25 501	59 357	52 577	47 817	81 100	19 955
November	639 528	445 806	445 806	614 004	421 271	192 733	25 364	60 206	52 660	47 844	81 855	20 193
December	614 176	419 978	419 978	620 612	427 488	193 124	25 511	61 515	53 000	48 171	83 416	20 087

[1]Excluding leased departments.

Table 16-11. Merchant Wholesalers—Sales and Inventories

(Millions of dollars.)

Year and month	Not seasonally adjusted						Seasonally adjusted					
	Sales			Inventories (current cost, end of period)			Sales			Inventories (current cost, end of period)		
	Total	Durable goods establishments	Nondurable goods establishments	Total	Durable goods establishments	Nondurable goods establishments	Total	Durable goods establishments	Nondurable goods establishments	Total	Durable goods establishments	Nondurable goods establishments
1995	2 158 980	1 141 701	1 017 279	239 275	151 709	87 566	2 158 980	1 141 701	1 017 279	238 392	154 089	84 303
1996	2 284 343	1 190 342	1 094 001	241 396	154 207	87 189	2 284 343	1 190 342	1 094 001	241 058	156 683	84 375
1997	2 377 845	1 256 384	1 121 461	258 900	165 371	93 529	2 377 845	1 256 384	1 121 461	258 454	168 089	90 365
1998	2 427 120	1 306 545	1 120 575	272 575	175 994	96 581	2 427 120	1 306 545	1 120 575	272 297	178 918	93 379
1999	2 599 159	1 406 371	1 192 788	290 382	187 738	102 644	2 599 159	1 406 371	1 192 788	290 182	190 899	99 283
2000	2 814 554	1 486 673	1 327 881	309 710	198 525	111 185	2 814 554	1 486 673	1 327 881	309 191	201 797	107 394
2001	2 785 152	1 422 195	1 362 957	298 577	182 521	116 056	2 785 152	1 422 195	1 362 957	297 536	185 517	112 019
2002	2 835 528	1 421 503	1 414 025	302 715	182 150	120 565	2 835 528	1 421 503	1 414 025	301 310	185 048	116 262
2003	2 978 282	1 466 158	1 512 124	310 115	186 435	123 680	2 978 282	1 466 158	1 512 124	308 274	189 325	118 949
2004	3 330 011	1 689 588	1 640 423	341 642	213 590	128 052	3 330 011	1 689 588	1 640 423	340 128	216 704	123 424
2005	3 638 496	1 830 347	1 808 149	369 380	233 199	136 181	3 638 496	1 830 347	1 808 149	367 978	236 438	131 540
2006	3 941 257	2 005 139	1 936 118	400 297	256 731	143 566	3 941 257	2 005 139	1 936 118	398 924	260 115	138 809
2007	4 223 473	2 101 969	2 121 504	426 254	263 195	163 059	4 223 473	2 101 969	2 121 504	424 344	266 628	157 716
2008	4 525 024	2 127 382	2 397 642	446 222	280 065	166 157	4 525 024	2 127 382	2 397 642	445 681	283 785	161 896
2009	3 830 607	1 746 786	2 083 821	399 543	232 966	166 577	3 830 607	1 746 786	2 083 821	397 806	236 547	161 259
2010	4 339 199	2 001 087	2 338 112	445 003	255 818	189 185	4 339 199	2 001 087	2 338 112	442 743	260 109	182 634
2011	4 887 628	2 232 235	2 655 393	490 374	284 563	205 811	4 887 628	2 232 235	2 655 393	488 255	289 164	199 091
2012	5 211 528	2 393 081	2 818 447	526 560	309 102	217 458	5 211 528	2 393 081	2 818 447	524 721	314 336	210 385
2013	5 403 968	2 474 180	2 929 788	550 294	325 287	225 007	5 403 968	2 474 180	2 929 788	549 169	330 959	218 210
2014	5 629 073	2 579 807	3 049 266	586 237	348 791	237 446	5 629 073	2 579 807	3 049 266	584 584	354 998	229 586
2015	5 386 511	2 553 141	2 833 370	597 465	350 965	246 500	5 386 511	2 553 141	2 833 370	595 716	357 457	238 259
2016	5 338 174	2 548 980	2 789 194	613 246	353 243	260 003	5 338 174	2 548 980	2 789 194	610 731	359 397	251 334
2017	5 700 968	2 732 543	2 968 425	635 233	369 524	265 709	5 700 968	2 732 543	2 968 425	632 013	375 611	256 402
2018	6 099 945	2 920 076	3 179 869	673 933	402 503	271 430	6 099 945	2 920 076	3 179 869	671 212	408 791	262 421
2019	6 087 908	2 911 955	3 175 953	683 596	406 200	277 396	6 087 908	2 911 955	3 175 953	680 387	412 283	268 104
2020	5 823 889	2 849 860	2 974 029	675 240	390 452	284 788	5 823 889	2 849 860	2 974 029	668 675	396 699	271 976
2017												
January	432 365	202 907	229 458	616 719	356 924	259 795	466 813	221 826	244 987	610 134	358 629	251 505
February	416 930	194 605	222 325	616 310	359 024	257 286	468 154	221 595	246 559	611 236	359 412	251 824
March	493 190	236 267	256 923	618 939	360 949	257 990	465 345	220 226	245 119	612 878	361 831	251 047
April	449 454	213 212	236 242	613 285	362 933	250 352	468 352	226 185	242 167	610 671	362 508	248 163
May	487 152	229 913	257 239	609 042	365 239	243 803	463 342	224 976	238 366	613 898	364 816	249 082
June	491 921	238 993	252 928	611 767	366 156	245 611	467 646	224 748	242 898	618 993	366 822	252 171
July	448 806	213 488	235 318	614 955	372 391	242 564	468 495	225 288	243 207	621 635	368 775	252 860
August	499 192	242 299	256 893	616 191	374 028	242 163	475 717	229 121	246 596	625 989	372 304	253 685
September	479 819	234 990	244 829	626 162	375 651	250 511	481 735	231 069	250 666	629 698	373 514	256 184
October	509 535	247 264	262 271	629 458	374 786	254 672	488 355	234 761	253 594	627 331	373 186	254 145
November	498 065	239 868	258 197	635 618	375 138	260 480	495 961	237 519	258 442	631 071	375 250	255 821
December	494 539	238 737	255 802	635 233	369 524	265 709	503 199	239 916	263 283	632 013	375 611	256 402
2018												
January	470 555	221 482	249 073	622 618	373 545	249 073	493 904	235 261	258 643	637 743	375 324	262 419
February	444 370	210 451	233 919	612 744	378 825	233 919	498 409	238 624	259 785	642 454	379 376	263 078
March	516 020	248 983	267 037	648 307	381 270	267 037	498 533	238 414	260 119	644 228	381 602	262 626
April	494 967	233 129	261 838	643 731	381 893	261 838	502 783	240 370	262 413	644 680	381 461	263 219
May	545 534	251 253	294 281	677 068	382 787	294 281	516 153	245 052	271 101	645 149	382 680	262 469
June	524 635	251 113	273 522	658 746	385 224	273 522	513 319	244 326	268 993	645 491	385 626	259 865
July	505 677	238 846	266 831	658 110	391 279	266 831	513 661	244 696	268 965	648 028	387 363	260 665
August	540 526	261 667	278 859	671 489	392 630	278 859	516 331	247 572	268 759	654 406	390 957	263 449
September	500 547	244 374	256 173	651 919	395 746	256 173	516 408	247 574	268 834	657 251	393 648	263 603
October	550 872	266 166	284 706	685 956	401 250	284 706	515 469	246 043	269 426	662 217	399 721	262 496
November	509 795	246 999	262 796	664 659	401 863	262 796	508 353	244 545	263 808	664 299	402 500	261 799
December	496 447	245 613	250 834	653 337	402 503	250 834	504 821	247 041	257 780	671 212	408 791	262 421
2019												
January	478 211	229 074	249 137	658 902	409 765	249 137	499 854	241 757	258 097	676 724	411 809	264 915
February	448 446	215 478	232 968	645 455	412 487	232 968	502 505	243 412	259 093	679 978	413 260	266 718
March	513 145	247 283	265 862	678 862	413 000	265 862	509 937	244 106	265 831	679 830	413 225	266 605
April	515 523	241 445	274 078	691 856	417 778	274 078	508 078	241 576	266 502	686 011	417 021	268 990
May	537 600	250 536	287 064	704 536	417 472	287 064	510 593	244 789	265 804	687 928	417 773	270 155
June	506 586	244 627	261 959	680 244	418 285	261 959	509 484	245 254	264 230	687 924	418 633	269 291
July	516 225	243 648	272 577	694 428	421 851	272 577	510 674	242 829	267 845	687 388	417 863	269 525
August	520 225	250 304	269 921	690 271	420 350	269 921	509 426	243 514	265 912	687 661	418 727	268 934
September	505 734	247 688	258 046	678 230	420 184	258 046	509 505	244 180	265 325	683 131	418 267	264 864
October	539 209	260 731	278 478	696 060	417 582	278 478	503 587	240 146	263 441	681 141	416 325	264 816
November	495 606	236 017	259 589	673 457	413 868	259 589	508 279	241 993	266 286	681 042	414 059	266 983
December	511 398	245 124	266 274	672 474	406 200	266 274	506 534	238 942	267 592	680 387	412 283	268 104
2020												
January	489 192	227 968	261 224	668 764	407 540	261 224	511 747	240 365	271 382	674 481	409 607	264 874
February	458 477	216 460	242 017	646 943	404 926	242 017	505 830	241 897	263 933	668 928	405 272	263 656
March	498 129	239 778	258 351	665 119	406 768	258 351	477 347	228 874	248 473	663 606	406 167	257 439
April	406 588	191 420	215 168	620 491	405 323	215 168	397 426	190 656	206 770	663 770	404 387	259 383
May	419 831	202 268	217 563	614 785	397 222	217 563	421 472	209 033	212 439	656 147	396 390	259 757
June	487 333	243 030	244 303	634 313	390 010	244 303	463 822	229 691	234 131	650 768	389 991	260 777
July	493 859	242 989	250 870	641 493	390 623	250 870	488 848	241 770	247 078	649 348	387 519	261 829
August	489 422	242 922	246 500	637 637	391 137	246 500	495 626	244 245	251 381	652 766	389 737	263 029
September	508 430	256 801	251 629	644 277	392 648	251 629	496 735	246 045	250 690	657 361	390 943	266 418
October	531 237	268 240	262 997	656 993	393 996	262 997	509 720	254 187	255 533	665 365	392 570	272 795
November	500 026	249 766	250 260	645 111	394 851	250 260	512 500	255 304	257 196	666 483	395 009	271 474
December	541 365	268 218	273 147	663 599	390 452	273 147	519 893	254 613	265 280	668 675	396 699	271 976

. . . = Not available.

Table 16-12. Manufacturing and Trade Sales and Inventories

Year and month	Sales, billions of dollars					Inventories, billions of dollars, end of period, seasonally adjusted				Ratios, inventories to sales, seasonally adjusted [1]			
	Not seasonally adjusted, total	Seasonally adjusted				Total	Manufac-turing	Retail trade	Merchant wholesalers	Total	Manufac-turing	Retail trade	Merchant wholesalers
		Total	Manufac-turing	Retail trade	Merchant wholesalers								
1999	9 434.1	9 431.7	4 033.3	2 801.4	2 597.0	1 137.3	463.0	384.1	290.2	1.40	1.35	1.59	1.30
2000	10 006.4	9 998.9	4 202.4	2 979.4	2 817.1	1 195.9	480.7	406.0	309.2	1.41	1.35	1.59	1.29
2001	9 817.9	9 819.3	3 971.2	3 062.2	2 785.9	1 118.6	427.4	393.7	297.5	1.42	1.38	1.58	1.32
2002	9 878.8	9 881.5	3 917.4	3 129.6	2 834.5	1 139.5	423.0	415.2	301.3	1.36	1.29	1.55	1.26
2003	10 256.4	10 255.7	4 016.6	3 261.6	2 977.4	1 147.8	408.3	431.2	308.3	1.34	1.25	1.56	1.22
2004	11 112.0	11 071.7	4 295.3	3 460.9	3 315.6	1 241.7	441.2	460.4	340.1	1.30	1.19	1.56	1.17
2005	12 069.9	12 073.8	4 743.7	3 686.6	3 643.6	1 314.3	474.6	471.7	368.0	1.27	1.17	1.51	1.17
2006	12 828.4	12 839.3	5 016.8	3 876.6	3 946.0	1 408.8	523.5	486.4	398.9	1.28	1.20	1.49	1.17
2007	13 538.1	13 538.6	5 320.1	3 997.4	4 221.1	1 487.6	562.7	500.6	424.3	1.28	1.22	1.49	1.17
2008	13 929.3	13 882.9	5 448.0	4 226.3	4 507.3	1 465.7	543.3	476.7	445.7	1.47	1.42	1.62	1.38
2009	11 866.9	11 870.5	4 427.7	3 613.0	3 829.8	1 331.4	505.0	428.5	397.8	1.28	1.29	1.39	1.17
2010	13 068.5	13 065.6	4 914.3	3 816.6	4 334.7	1 450.0	553.7	453.5	442.7	1.27	1.28	1.38	1.17
2011	14 482.5	14 492.3	5 053.3	4 102.0	4 893.9	1 566.7	607.0	471.4	488.3	1.26	1.30	1.35	1.16
2012	15 210.5	15 192.1	5 692.5	4 297.0	5 202.6	1 657.1	625.2	507.2	524.7	1.29	1.30	1.39	1.19
2013	15 677.9	15 675.9	5 816.7	4 459.6	5 399.7	1 725.6	631.8	544.7	549.2	1.30	1.29	1.44	1.19
2014	16 160.0	16 148.2	5 889.8	4 636.5	5 621.8	1 788.4	642.7	561.1	584.6	1.35	1.35	1.44	1.26
2015	15 647.7	15 638.3	5 533.7	4 724.1	5 380.5	1 821.4	638.1	587.6	595.7	1.42	1.44	1.48	1.36
2016	15 550.0	15 513.5	5 353.5	4 832.6	5 327.5	1 857.7	635.9	611.0	610.7	1.39	1.39	1.48	1.32
2017	16 290.0	16 314.8	5 555.7	5 045.9	5 713.1	1 917.2	658.9	626.3	632.0	1.35	1.37	1.45	1.26
2018	17 243.6	17 244.1	5 889.6	5 256.3	6 098.1	2 002.6	677.6	653.7	671.2	1.40	1.39	1.50	1.33
2019	17 230.1	17 236.1	5 736.0	5 411.7	6 088.5	2 051.2	713.3	657.5	680.4	1.43	1.51	1.44	1.34
2020	16 774.3	16 736.5	5 354.1	5 581.4	5 801.0	1 998.9	709.6	620.6	668.7	1.35	1.49	1.28	1.29
2016													
January	1 140.8	1 269.3	442.1	394.7	432.4	1 821.6	634.8	591.0	595.8	1.44	1.44	1.50	1.38
February	1 187.3	1 268.7	441.6	398.1	429.0	1 816.6	631.6	593.1	592.0	1.43	1.43	1.49	1.38
March	1 338.2	1 272.9	442.6	396.9	433.5	1 822.7	631.6	597.8	593.2	1.43	1.43	1.51	1.37
April	1 269.3	1 279.9	444.3	398.2	437.4	1 829.1	631.5	598.7	598.9	1.43	1.42	1.50	1.37
May	1 314.2	1 282.5	443.9	400.1	438.5	1 834.1	631.7	601.6	600.7	1.43	1.42	1.50	1.37
June	1 356.0	1 300.1	448.4	404.8	446.9	1 835.2	631.6	602.4	601.1	1.41	1.41	1.49	1.35
July	1 254.1	1 292.6	444.1	403.7	444.8	1 836.4	632.2	603.9	600.4	1.42	1.42	1.50	1.35
August	1 349.9	1 297.4	445.8	404.0	447.6	1 836.7	633.2	604.2	599.4	1.42	1.42	1.50	1.34
September	1 320.2	1 301.1	447.7	406.0	447.4	1 839.8	631.8	606.8	601.2	1.41	1.41	1.49	1.34
October	1 310.3	1 308.6	448.3	407.4	452.9	1 841.2	632.1	606.8	602.2	1.41	1.41	1.49	1.33
November	1 307.7	1 307.4	447.5	406.1	453.8	1 853.2	634.8	611.4	607.0	1.42	1.42	1.51	1.34
December	1 401.9	1 333.1	457.1	412.6	463.3	1 857.7	635.9	611.0	610.7	1.39	1.39	1.48	1.32
2017													
January	1 220.1	1 340.1	457.2	416.1	466.8	1 861.3	637.2	614.0	610.1	1.39	1.39	1.48	1.31
February	1 207.0	1 341.0	457.4	415.5	468.2	1 864.6	638.1	615.3	611.2	1.39	1.40	1.48	1.31
March	1 404.1	1 337.2	457.3	414.6	465.3	1 868.4	637.6	617.9	612.9	1.40	1.39	1.49	1.32
April	1 302.2	1 339.9	454.7	416.9	468.4	1 866.9	638.9	617.3	610.7	1.39	1.41	1.48	1.30
May	1 395.5	1 336.2	458.3	414.5	463.3	1 871.3	638.7	618.7	613.9	1.40	1.39	1.49	1.32
June	1 401.4	1 341.7	457.5	416.5	467.6	1 879.6	639.0	621.7	619.0	1.40	1.40	1.49	1.32
July	1 300.8	1 342.0	456.8	416.7	468.5	1 886.0	642.1	622.3	621.6	1.41	1.41	1.49	1.33
August	1 414.1	1 355.3	462.4	417.2	475.7	1 896.3	644.8	625.5	626.0	1.40	1.39	1.50	1.32
September	1 372.2	1 373.6	465.4	426.5	481.7	1 900.0	649.6	620.8	629.7	1.38	1.40	1.46	1.31
October	1 406.9	1 385.5	470.2	426.9	488.4	1 900.6	652.0	621.3	627.3	1.37	1.39	1.46	1.28
November	1 408.6	1 406.2	479.1	431.2	496.0	1 909.6	655.2	623.3	631.1	1.36	1.37	1.45	1.27
December	1 457.0	1 416.0	479.5	433.3	503.2	1 917.2	658.9	626.3	632.0	1.35	1.37	1.45	1.26
2018													
January	1 308.8	1 408.5	482.5	432.1	493.9	1 925.9	660.6	627.5	637.7	1.37	1.37	1.45	1.29
February	1 274.2	1 416.7	484.2	434.1	498.4	1 936.7	663.5	630.7	642.5	1.37	1.37	1.45	1.29
March	1 472.7	1 416.9	485.1	433.2	498.5	1 936.0	662.5	629.3	644.2	1.37	1.37	1.45	1.29
April	1 397.7	1 424.6	486.2	435.6	502.8	1 941.5	664.8	632.0	644.7	1.36	1.37	1.45	1.28
May	1 518.7	1 446.4	490.3	440.0	516.2	1 945.0	666.1	633.7	645.1	1.34	1.36	1.44	1.25
June	1 487.7	1 446.3	494.8	438.2	513.3	1 948.5	667.1	635.9	645.5	1.35	1.35	1.45	1.26
July	1 423.4	1 447.3	493.0	440.7	513.7	1 958.4	673.3	637.1	648.0	1.35	1.37	1.45	1.26
August	1 515.8	1 452.9	497.3	439.3	516.3	1 969.0	673.6	640.9	654.4	1.36	1.35	1.46	1.27
September	1 423.4	1 453.8	498.4	439.0	516.4	1 977.8	677.7	642.9	657.3	1.36	1.36	1.46	1.27
October	1 507.5	1 459.0	499.5	444.0	515.5	1 988.2	679.4	646.6	662.2	1.36	1.36	1.46	1.28
November	1 450.2	1 445.0	491.4	445.2	508.4	1 987.0	677.8	645.0	664.3	1.38	1.38	1.45	1.31
December	1 463.5	1 426.7	487.1	434.8	504.8	2 002.6	677.6	653.7	671.2	1.40	1.39	1.50	1.33
2019													
January	1 329.0	1 425.2	484.5	440.8	499.9	2 016.7	682.3	657.7	676.7	1.42	1.41	1.49	1.35
February	1 285.6	1 429.4	486.9	440.0	502.5	2 026.0	685.3	660.8	680.0	1.42	1.41	1.50	1.35
March	1 464.2	1 441.1	484.0	447.2	509.9	2 028.8	688.7	660.2	679.8	1.41	1.42	1.48	1.33
April	1 440.7	1 436.9	480.1	448.7	508.1	2 038.8	691.7	661.1	686.0	1.42	1.44	1.47	1.35
May	1 510.9	1 439.5	479.4	449.6	510.6	2 045.7	694.6	663.2	687.9	1.42	1.45	1.48	1.35
June	1 451.1	1 439.4	479.0	450.9	509.5	2 049.0	697.9	663.2	687.9	1.42	1.46	1.47	1.35
July	1 442.5	1 440.8	476.1	454.0	510.7	2 053.3	701.1	664.8	687.4	1.43	1.47	1.46	1.35
August	1 484.7	1 441.1	475.2	456.5	509.4	2 054.5	702.8	664.1	687.7	1.43	1.48	1.45	1.35
September	1 419.6	1 436.0	473.6	452.8	509.5	2 053.1	705.5	664.4	683.1	1.43	1.49	1.47	1.34
October	1 483.6	1 431.4	472.4	455.5	503.6	2 054.0	707.8	665.0	681.1	1.43	1.50	1.46	1.35
November	1 421.1	1 437.9	472.0	457.7	508.3	2 051.7	710.1	660.6	681.0	1.43	1.50	1.44	1.34
December	1 497.2	1 437.5	472.9	458.1	506.5	2 051.2	713.3	657.5	680.4	1.43	1.51	1.44	1.34
2020													
January	1 347.3	1 441.0	468.6	460.6	511.7	2 043.1	711.1	657.5	674.5	1.42	1.52	1.43	1.32
February	1 320.2	1 434.1	468.7	459.6	505.8	2 031.4	707.4	655.1	668.9	1.42	1.51	1.43	1.32
March	1 395.5	1 355.1	443.4	434.3	477.3	2 025.8	701.0	662.1	663.6	1.50	1.58	1.52	1.39
April	1 165.2	1 158.0	380.6	379.9	397.4	1 997.6	698.4	635.5	663.8	1.73	1.83	1.67	1.67
May	1 274.4	1 256.0	389.9	444.6	421.5	1 950.8	698.0	596.6	656.1	1.55	1.79	1.34	1.56
June	1 424.9	1 372.3	432.2	476.3	463.8	1 933.1	702.4	579.9	650.8	1.41	1.63	1.22	1.40
July	1 429.6	1 423.1	452.6	481.6	488.8	1 932.7	698.8	584.5	649.3	1.36	1.54	1.21	1.33
August	1 441.8	1 434.9	455.6	483.7	495.6	1 943.0	699.7	590.5	652.8	1.35	1.54	1.22	1.32
September	1 458.5	1 447.8	457.7	493.3	496.7	1 957.5	699.7	600.4	657.4	1.35	1.53	1.22	1.32
October	1 501.4	1 466.9	463.2	494.0	509.7	1 975.0	701.2	608.4	665.4	1.35	1.51	1.23	1.31
November	1 442.1	1 467.5	466.3	488.7	512.5	1 986.9	706.4	614.0	666.5	1.35	1.51	1.26	1.30
December	1 573.4	1 480.0	475.3	484.8	519.9	1 998.9	709.6	620.6	668.7	1.35	1.49	1.28	1.29

[1] Annual data are averages of monthly ratios.

Table 16-13. Real Manufacturing and Trade Sales and Inventories

(Billions of chained [2012] dollars, ratios; seasonally adjusted; annual sales figures are averages of seasonally adjusted monthly data.)

NIPA Tables 1BU, 2BU, 3BU

Year and month	Sales, monthly average				Inventories, end of period				Ratios, end-of-period inventories to monthly average sales			
	Total	Manufac-turing	Retail trade	Merchant wholesalers	Total	Manufac-turing	Retail trade	Merchant wholesalers	Total	Manufac-turing	Retail trade	Merchant wholesalers
2001	1 111.0	473.4	311.7	328.0	1 525.2	644.5	466.5	418.6	1.37	1.36	1.50	1.28
2002	1 128.4	470.9	320.6	338.1	1 558.3	642.3	496.8	419.7	1.38	1.36	1.55	1.24
2003	1 150.6	471.9	332.8	345.9	1 570.5	631.6	515.8	421.3	1.37	1.34	1.55	1.22
2004	1 195.0	481.7	346.0	367.0	1 631.0	638.3	543.3	446.3	1.37	1.33	1.57	1.22
2005	1 248.2	503.5	358.9	385.9	1 689.2	665.4	549.3	472.6	1.35	1.32	1.53	1.23
2006	1 283.1	509.8	370.2	402.9	1 742.7	687.6	560.5	493.2	1.36	1.35	1.51	1.22
2007	1 311.3	522.0	375.4	414.0	1 781.6	709.1	568.2	502.9	1.36	1.36	1.51	1.22
2008	1 261.8	494.7	358.7	408.8	1 741.2	692.1	535.3	513.1	1.38	1.40	1.49	1.26
2009	1 144.5	428.0	338.5	377.6	1 604.0	662.5	478.7	462.6	1.40	1.55	1.41	1.23
2010	1 198.7	449.8	349.0	399.9	1 663.9	687.1	493.1	483.7	1.39	1.53	1.41	1.21
2011	1 238.6	465.5	359.8	413.3	1 709.4	711.7	494.6	503.1	1.38	1.53	1.38	1.22
2012	1 279.7	473.9	371.7	434.1	1 784.0	730.8	522.1	531.0	1.39	1.54	1.41	1.22
2013	1 319.9	483.2	387.1	449.6	1 878.7	758.4	558.9	561.2	1.42	1.57	1.44	1.25
2014	1 358.6	486.2	404.7	467.8	1 947.2	776.9	574.5	595.7	1.43	1.60	1.42	1.27
2015	1 389.5	482.4	428.6	478.8	2 042.7	815.3	604.2	623.0	1.47	1.69	1.41	1.30
2016	1 411.7	476.6	448.6	486.8	2 077.4	817.2	628.8	629.7	1.47	1.72	1.40	1.29
2017	1 443.4	477.3	465.4	501.3	2 116.4	822.3	645.6	646.3	1.47	1.72	1.39	1.29
2018	1 474.2	483.7	480.1	511.1	2 187.8	840.8	670.8	673.6	1.48	1.74	1.40	1.32
2019	1 483.7	472.2	498.4	514.8	2 256.5	887.8	681.5	685.4	1.52	1.88	1.37	1.33
2020	1 473.2	450.4	521.4	504.5	2 214.6	878.1	663.0	672.1	1.50	1.95	1.27	1.33
2016												
January	1 395.8	477.5	439.4	479.2	2 047.6	814.0	607.8	625.2	1.47	1.71	1.38	1.31
February	1 407.1	479.9	447.4	479.8	2 046.8	813.6	609.5	623.0	1.46	1.70	1.36	1.30
March	1 407.6	479.5	443.8	484.5	2 053.8	816.0	612.4	624.6	1.46	1.70	1.38	1.29
April	1 406.0	478.5	442.6	485.1	2 059.2	815.7	613.5	629.1	1.47	1.71	1.39	1.30
May	1 398.6	474.6	444.8	479.3	2 060.4	814.5	616.3	628.5	1.47	1.72	1.39	1.31
June	1 406.8	475.2	448.8	483.0	2 057.8	813.2	617.2	626.3	1.46	1.71	1.38	1.30
July	1 405.2	471.1	450.6	483.8	2 055.0	811.2	618.4	624.0	1.46	1.72	1.37	1.29
August	1 416.3	474.9	451.4	490.4	2 056.5	812.5	619.6	623.0	1.45	1.71	1.37	1.27
September	1 418.0	475.8	452.1	490.5	2 060.9	811.0	623.8	624.4	1.45	1.71	1.38	1.27
October	1 420.1	474.3	452.0	494.2	2 061.7	812.1	623.8	624.2	1.45	1.71	1.38	1.26
November	1 420.6	474.9	452.0	494.2	2 072.5	816.0	627.1	627.7	1.46	1.72	1.39	1.27
December	1 437.8	482.8	457.9	497.5	2 077.4	817.2	628.8	629.7	1.45	1.69	1.37	1.27
2017												
January	1 431.6	478.9	458.0	495.2	2 079.8	816.5	633.7	627.7	1.45	1.71	1.38	1.27
February	1 428.3	476.9	458.5	493.3	2 078.4	814.5	634.2	627.7	1.46	1.71	1.38	1.27
March	1 425.5	475.2	458.3	492.4	2 076.9	810.3	635.4	629.0	1.46	1.71	1.39	1.28
April	1 422.9	470.4	460.4	492.6	2 074.7	810.4	635.6	626.5	1.46	1.72	1.38	1.27
May	1 427.9	474.8	461.0	492.6	2 078.1	808.5	637.2	630.0	1.46	1.70	1.38	1.28
June	1 432.7	473.2	464.1	495.9	2 084.8	807.3	639.7	635.3	1.46	1.71	1.38	1.28
July	1 438.2	473.1	465.7	500.1	2 090.5	810.2	640.3	637.6	1.45	1.71	1.38	1.28
August	1 445.6	476.5	464.3	505.4	2 099.6	813.1	643.0	641.0	1.45	1.71	1.39	1.27
September	1 452.4	476.5	469.6	507.0	2 104.1	817.9	639.8	644.2	1.45	1.72	1.36	1.27
October	1 460.5	480.0	471.4	509.7	2 103.7	818.6	641.4	641.5	1.44	1.71	1.36	1.26
November	1 473.1	486.1	474.9	512.7	2 111.8	820.4	644.0	645.2	1.43	1.69	1.36	1.26
December	1 482.7	486.1	478.1	519.1	2 116.4	822.3	645.6	646.3	1.43	1.69	1.35	1.25
2018												
January	1 465.4	486.4	473.9	505.6	2 124.7	824.1	646.9	651.4	1.45	1.69	1.37	1.29
February	1 469.8	486.0	475.9	508.5	2 135.9	826.9	651.1	655.5	1.45	1.70	1.37	1.29
March	1 467.3	485.4	475.4	507.1	2 134.1	825.1	650.2	656.5	1.45	1.70	1.37	1.29
April	1 467.0	483.4	476.3	508.0	2 138.2	827.8	652.6	655.5	1.46	1.71	1.37	1.29
May	1 475.6	481.3	480.8	514.3	2 137.9	827.3	654.1	654.1	1.45	1.72	1.36	1.27
June	1 473.8	483.9	479.0	511.5	2 139.8	828.1	656.5	652.7	1.45	1.71	1.37	1.28
July	1 475.2	481.3	482.6	512.2	2 148.1	833.5	657.9	654.1	1.46	1.73	1.36	1.28
August	1 482.3	485.4	481.8	515.9	2 157.0	834.9	660.0	659.6	1.46	1.72	1.37	1.28
September	1 481.9	485.9	480.9	515.8	2 163.8	839.4	660.5	661.5	1.46	1.73	1.37	1.28
October	1 478.8	483.4	485.0	511.2	2 172.9	841.5	663.7	665.3	1.47	1.74	1.37	1.30
November	1 477.1	479.7	488.9	509.6	2 171.1	838.8	663.1	666.7	1.47	1.75	1.36	1.31
December	1 476.5	482.4	481.4	513.6	2 187.8	840.8	670.8	673.6	1.48	1.74	1.39	1.31
2019												
January	1 484.5	482.7	489.5	513.4	2 203.3	847.2	673.6	679.9	1.48	1.76	1.38	1.32
February	1 483.8	483.4	488.2	513.1	2 214.7	851.9	677.1	683.1	1.49	1.76	1.39	1.33
March	1 483.4	476.2	493.7	515.0	2 218.6	857.4	675.6	683.2	1.50	1.80	1.37	1.33
April	1 469.2	469.0	492.6	509.2	2 224.7	860.4	674.3	687.7	1.51	1.84	1.37	1.35
May	1 473.4	468.7	494.5	511.9	2 229.5	862.5	675.5	689.2	1.51	1.84	1.37	1.35
June	1 485.6	473.0	497.6	516.6	2 234.8	866.2	676.7	689.6	1.50	1.83	1.36	1.34
July	1 485.1	469.2	501.6	516.2	2 242.7	871.7	678.2	690.5	1.51	1.86	1.35	1.34
August	1 493.2	470.7	505.7	518.8	2 246.2	874.6	677.8	691.6	1.50	1.86	1.34	1.33
September	1 491.3	470.3	501.8	521.1	2 249.4	878.7	680.4	688.2	1.51	1.87	1.36	1.32
October	1 482.1	467.4	503.5	513.3	2 250.7	881.6	681.0	686.1	1.52	1.89	1.35	1.34
November	1 488.1	467.2	505.8	517.2	2 252.5	884.3	680.4	685.9	1.51	1.89	1.35	1.33
December	1 485.1	468.4	506.8	512.0	2 256.5	887.8	681.5	685.4	1.52	1.90	1.35	1.34
2020												
January	1 486.5	463.8	508.9	516.1	2 255.7	885.6	686.2	681.9	1.52	1.91	1.35	1.32
February	1 491.7	467.6	509.4	517.0	2 256.3	883.7	691.2	679.1	1.51	1.89	1.36	1.31
March	1 432.3	448.3	486.4	499.8	2 255.0	876.1	698.7	677.1	1.57	1.95	1.44	1.36
April	1 267.3	397.0	434.9	437.5	2 241.5	877.9	680.6	680.9	1.77	2.21	1.57	1.56
May	1 368.6	401.5	509.9	461.0	2 208.6	881.6	650.1	676.3	1.61	2.20	1.28	1.47
June	1 473.4	442.8	538.6	495.5	2 193.6	888.4	638.3	667.2	1.49	2.01	1.19	1.35
July	1 512.2	459.5	541.2	514.8	2 189.0	881.8	643.5	663.5	1.45	1.92	1.19	1.29
August	1 515.4	460.5	540.4	517.9	2 193.1	880.4	646.9	665.3	1.45	1.91	1.20	1.29
September	1 524.6	462.0	549.8	516.3	2 199.2	876.3	653.8	668.2	1.44	1.90	1.19	1.29
October	1 539.6	465.4	551.6	526.2	2 208.5	875.3	658.1	673.8	1.44	1.88	1.19	1.28
November	1 536.7	466.7	546.6	526.9	2 210.3	878.6	658.3	672.1	1.44	1.88	1.20	1.28
December	1 530.6	469.8	539.0	524.9	2 214.6	878.1	663.0	672.1	1.45	1.87	1.23	1.28

Table 16-14. Selected Services—Quarterly Estimated Revenue for Employer Firms

(Millions of dollars.)

2012 NAICS code	Kind of business	4th quarter 2019	1st quarter 2020	2nd quarter 2020	3rd quarter 2020	4th quarter 2020	1st quarter 2021
SEASONALLY ADJUSTED							
51	**Information**	449 927	450 195	433 762	459 578	482 547	504 760
5112	Software publishers	85 605	88 194	92 343	96 535	99 398	106 318
512	Motion picture and sound recording industries	27 986	24 582	18 576	19 468	22 677	22 606
54	**Professional, Scientific, and Technical Services**	525 831	526 524	470 796	493 189	513 905	535 156
5411	Legal services	79 785	79 195	72 343	73 889	79 290	84 790
5412	Accounting, tax preparation, bookkeeping, and payroll services	42 623	42 249	37 530	43 863	44 148	43 244
56 pt	**Administrative and Support and Waste Management and Remediation Services**	280 647	273 704	241 778	261 160	273 952	290 141
5613	Employment services	109 754	107 528	98 210	102 626	111 090	122 307
5615	Travel arrangement and reservation services	16 818	13 312	2 736	5 559	5 637	6 826
562	Waste management and remediation services	28 445	28 488	25 420	27 741	28 375	29 049
622	**Hospitals**	301 450	285 232	279 389	304 973	317 524	315 335
NOT SEASONALLY ADJUSTED							
51	**Information**	471 074	440 291	429 424	452 225	505 709	493 655
511	Publishing industries (except Internet)	112 155	106 486	108 931	112 205	125 216	124 278
51111	Newspaper publishers	6 113	5 408	4 680	4 892	5 465	5 041
51112	Periodical publishers	6 662	5 916	5 040	5 602	6 122	5 283
5111 pt	Book, directory and mailing list, and other publishers	8 981	7 321	7 514	9 424	8 963	7 742
5112	Software publishers	90 399	87 841	91 697	92 287	104 666	106 212
512	Motion picture and sound recording industries	29 245	24 262	18 632	18 787	23 697	22 290
515	Broadcasting (except Internet)	48 683	44 776	39 723	43 563	51 007	45 952
5151	Radio and television broadcasting	24 418	22 620	18 418	20 737	26 310	22 369
5152	Cable and other subscription programming	24 265	22 156	21 305	22 826	24 697	23 583
517	Telecommunications [1]	165 664	158 055	155 502	158 967	167 481	163 698
5171	Wired telecommunications carriers	81 614	79 000	78 107	78 465	80 815	79 997
5172	Wireless telecommunications carriers (except satellite)	72 458	67 416	65 534	68 684	74 591	71 492
54	**Professional, Scientific, and Technical Services** [1]	536 348	513 361	475 504	490 723	524 183	521 777
5411	Legal services	89 120	70 800	71 620	74 037	88 250	75 972
5412	Accounting, tax preparation, bookkeeping, and payroll services	37 295	49 220	39 782	39 521	38 762	50 163
5413	Architectural, engineering, and related services	89 709	86 177	79 639	79 768	79 680	82 865
5415	Computer systems design and related services	126 602	125 510	120 476	118 838	122 350	120 950
5416	Management, scientific, and technical consulting services	73 450	69 984	63 283	66 507	71 307	70 667
5417	Scientific research and development services	49 405	47 893	45 927	50 837	53 769	53 053
5418	Advertising and related services	37 840	33 554	27 235	30 544	35 533	33 292
56	**Administrative and Support and Waste Management and Remediation Services** [1]	285 641	266 205	242 065	262 141	280 057	282 521
561	Administrative and support services	257 395	238 771	216 060	233 873	251 909	254 460
5613	Employment services	115 571	106 453	94 576	101 908	117 200	120 962
5615	Travel arrangement and reservation services	15 943	12 793	2 840	5 854	5 344	6 553
562	Waste management and remediation services	28 246	27 434	26 005	28 268	28 148	28 061
61	**Educational Services**	18 832	17 256	13 192	15 618	16 646	17 003
62	**Health Care and Social Asistance**	717 432	683 295	638 186	700 164	747 410	721 534
71	**Arts, Entertainment, and Recreation**	76 144	57 871	32 071	47 922	51 397	50 292
81	**Other services (Except Public Administration)**	167 775	126 648	126 284	144 045	170 185	153 850

[1] Includes components not shown separately.

NOTES AND DEFINITIONS, CHAPTER 16

TABLE 16-1

Construction Put in Place

SOURCE: U.S. DEPARTMENT OF COMMERCE, CENSUS BUREAU

The Census Bureau's estimates of the value of new construction put in place are intended to provide monthly estimates of the total dollar value of construction work done in the United States.

The United States Code, Title 13, authorizes the Survey of Construction and provides for voluntary responses. Construction statistics are collected from building permits, housing starts and housing completions.

Definitions and notes on the data

The estimates cover all construction work done each month on new private residential and nonresidential buildings and structures, public construction, and improvements to existing buildings and structures. Included are the cost of labor, materials, and equipment rental; cost of architectural and engineering work; overhead costs assigned to the project; interest and taxes paid during construction; and contractor's profits.

The total value put in place for a given period is the sum of the value of work done on all projects underway during this period, regardless of when work on each individual project was started or when payment was made to the contractors. For some categories, estimates are derived by distributing the total construction cost of the project by means of historic construction progress patterns. Published estimates represent payments made during a period for some categories.

The statistics on the value of construction put in place result from direct measurement and indirect estimation. A series results from direct measurement when it is based on reports of the actual value of construction progress or construction expenditures obtained in a complete census or a sample survey. All other series are developed by indirect estimation using related construction statistics. On an annual basis, estimates for series directly measured monthly, quarterly, or annually accounted for about 71 percent of total construction in 1998 (private multifamily residential, private residential improvements, private nonresidential buildings, farm nonresidential construction, public utility construction, all other private construction, and virtually all of public construction). On a monthly basis, directly measured data are available for about 55 percent of the value in place estimates.

Beginning in 1993, the Construction Expenditures Branch of the Census Bureau's Manufacturing and Construction Division began collecting these data using a new classification system, which bases project types on their end usage instead of on building/nonbuilding types. Data collection on this system for federal construction began in January 2002.

With the changes in project classifications, data presented in these tables for 1993 to date are not directly comparable with data for previous years, except at aggregate levels. For that reason, *Business Statistics* shows earlier historical data only at these aggregate levels. Although some categories, such as lodging, office, education, and religion, have the same names as categories in previously published data, there have been changes within the classifications that make these values non-comparable. For example, private medical office buildings were classified as "office" buildings previously, but are categorized as "health care" under the new classification.

The seasonally adjusted data are obtained by removing normal seasonal movement from the unadjusted data to bring out underlying trends and business cycles, which is accomplished by using the Census X-12-ARIMA method. Seasonal adjustment accounts for month-to-month variations resulting from normal or average changes in any phenomena affecting the data, such as weather conditions, the differing lengths of months, and the varying number of holidays, weekdays, and weekends within each month. It does not adjust for abnormal conditions within each month or for year-to-year variations in weather. The seasonally adjusted annual rate is the seasonally adjusted monthly rate multiplied by 12.

Residential consists of new houses, town houses, apartments, and condominiums for sale or rent; these dwellings are built by the owner or for the owner on contract. It includes improvements inside and outside residential structures, such as remodeling, additions, major replacements, and additions of swimming pools and garages. Manufactured housing, houseboats, and maintenance and repair work are not included.

Office includes general office buildings, administration buildings, professional buildings, and financial institution buildings. Office buildings at manufacturing sites are classified as *manufacturing,* but office buildings owned by manufacturing companies but not at such a site are included in the *office* category. In the state and local government category, *office* includes capitols, city halls, courthouses, and similar buildings.

Commercial includes buildings and structures used by the retail, wholesale, farm, and selected service industries. One of the subgroups of this category is *multi-retail,* which consists of department and variety stores, shopping centers and malls, and warehouse-type retail stores.

Health care includes hospitals, medical buildings, nursing homes, adult day-care centers, and similar institutions.

Educational includes schools at all levels, higher education facilities, trade schools, libraries, museums, and similar institutions.

Amusement and recreation includes theme and amusement parks, sports structures not located at educational institutions, fitness centers and health clubs, neighborhood centers, camps, movie theaters, and similar establishments.

Transportation includes airport facilities; rail facilities, track, and bridges; bus, rail, maritime, and air terminals; and docks, marinas, and similar structures.

Communication includes telephone, television, and radio distribution and maintenance structures.

Power includes electricity production and distribution and gas and crude oil transmission, storage, and distribution.

Manufacturing includes all buildings and structures at manufacturing sites but not the installation of production machinery or special-purpose equipment.

Included in *total private construction*, but not shown separately in these pages, are lodging facilities (hotels and motels), religious structures, and private public safety, sewage and waste disposal, water supply, highway and street, and conservation and development spending.

Included in *total state and local construction*, but not shown separately in these pages, are state and local construction of commercial buildings, conservation and development (dams, levees, jetties, and dredging), lodging, religious facilities, and communication structures.

Public safety includes correctional facilities, police and sheriffs' stations, fire stations, and similar establishments.

Highway and street includes pavement, lighting, retaining walls, bridges, tunnels, toll facilities, and maintenance and rest facilities.

Sewage and waste disposal includes sewage systems, solid waste disposal, and recycling.

Water supply includes water supply, transmission, and storage facilities.

Among the data sources for construction expenditures are the Census Bureau's Survey of Construction, Building Permits Survey, Consumer Expenditure Survey (conducted for the Bureau of Labor Statistics), Annual Capital Expenditures Survey, and Construction Progress Reporting Survey; also included are data from the F.W. Dodge Division of the McGraw-Hill Information Systems Company, the U.S. Department of Agriculture, and utility regulatory agencies.

Data availability

Each month's "Construction Spending" press release is released on the last workday of the following month. The release, more detailed data, and a discussion of methodologies can be found on the Census Bureau's Web site at <https://www.census.gov/constructionspending>. Current data at this site may reflect benchmarking since Table 16-1 was compiled.

TABLE 16-2

Housing Starts and Building Permits; New House Sales and Prices

SOURCES: U.S. DEPARTMENT OF COMMERCE, CENSUS BUREAU

These data are mainly found in two major Census Bureau reports, "New Residential Construction" and "New Residential Sales." They cover new housing units intended for occupancy and maintained by the occupants, excluding hotels, motels, and group residential structures. Manufactured home units are reported in a separate survey.

Definitions

A *housing unit* is a house, an apartment, or a group of rooms or single room intended for occupancy as separate living quarters. Occupants must live separately from other individuals in the building and have direct access to the housing unit from the outside of the building or through a common hall. Each apartment unit in an apartment building is counted as one housing unit. As of January 2000, a previous requirement for residents to have the capability to eat separately has been eliminated. (Based on the old definition, some senior housing projects were excluded from the multifamily housing statistics because individual units did not have their own eating facilities.) Housing starts exclude group quarters such as dormitories or rooming houses, transient accommodations such as motels, and manufactured homes. Publicly owned housing units are excluded, but units in structures built by private developers with subsidies or for sale to local public housing authorities are both classified as private housing.

The *start* of construction of a privately owned housing unit is when excavation begins for the footings or foundation of a building primarily intended as a housekeeping residential structure and designed for nontransient occupancy. All housing units in a multifamily building are defined as being started when excavation for the building begins.

One-family structures includes fully detached, semi-detached, row houses, and townhouses. In the case of attached units, each must be separated from the adjacent unit by a ground-to-roof wall to be classified as a one-unit structure and must not share facilities such as heating or water supply. Units built one on top of another and those built side-by-side without a ground-to-roof wall and/or with common facilities are classified by the number of units in the structure.

Apartment buildings are defined as buildings containing *five units or more.* The type of ownership is not the criterion—a condominium apartment building is not classified as one-family structures but as a multifamily structure.

A *manufactured* home is a moveable dwelling, 8 feet or more wide and 40 feet or more long, designed to be towed on its own chassis with transportation gear integral to the unit when it leaves the factory, and without need of a permanent foundation. Multiwides and expandable manufactured homes are included. Excluded are travel trailers, motor homes, and modular housing. The shipments figures are based on reports submitted by manufacturers on the number of homes actually shipped during the survey month. Shipments to dealers may not necessarily be placed for residential use in the same month as they are shipped. The number of manufactured "homes" used for nonresidential purposes (for example, those used for offices) is not known.

Units authorized by building permits represents the approximately 97 percent of housing in permit-requiring areas.

The *start* occurs when excavation begins for the footing or foundation. Starts are estimated for all areas, regardless of whether permits are required.

New house *sales* are reported only for new single-family residential structures. The sales transaction must intend to include both house and land. Excluded are houses built for rent, houses built by the owner, and houses built by a contractor on the owner's land. A sale is reported when a deposit is taken or a sales agreement is signed; this can occur prior to a permit being issued.

> Once the sale is reported, the sold housing unit drops out of the survey. Consequently, the Census Bureau does not find out if the sales contract is cancelled or if the house is ever resold. As a result, if conditions are worsening and cancellations are high, sales are temporarily overestimated. When conditions improve and the cancelled sales materialize as actual sales, the Census sales estimates are then underestimated because the case did not re-enter the survey. In the long run, cancellations do not cause the survey to overestimate or underestimate sales; but in the short run, cancellations and ultimate resales are not reflected in this survey, and fluctuations can appear less severe than in reality.

A house is *for sale* when a permit to build has been issued (or work begun in non-permit areas) and a sales contract has not been signed nor a deposit accepted.

The *sales price* used in this survey is the price agreed upon between the purchaser and the seller at the time the first sales contract is signed or deposit made. It includes the price of the improved lot. The *median sales price* is the sales price of the house that falls on the middle point of a distribution by price of the total number of houses sold. Half of the houses sold have a price lower than the median; half have a price higher than the median. Changes in the *sales price* data reflect changes in the distribution of houses by region, size, and the like, as well as changes in the prices of houses with identical characteristics.

The *price index* measures the change in price of a new single-family house of constant physical characteristics, using the characteristics of houses built in 2005. Characteristics held constant include floor area, whether inside or outside a metropolitan area, number of bedrooms, number of bathrooms, number of fireplaces, type of parking facility, type of foundation, presence of a deck, construction method, exterior wall material, type of heating, and presence of air-conditioning. The indexes are calculated separately for attached and detached houses and combined with base period weights. The price measured includes the value of the lot.

Notes on the data

Monthly permit authorizations are based on data collected by a mail survey from a sample of about 9,000 permit-issuing places, selected from and representing a universe of 20,000 such places in the United States. The remaining places are surveyed annually. Data for 2014 to the present includes approximately 20,100 places while data for 2004 to 2013 included 19,300 places.

Data for 1994 through 2003 represented 19,000 places; data for 1984 through 1993 represented 17,000 places; data for 1978 through 1983 represented 16,000 places; data for 1972 through 1977 represented 14,000 places; data for 1967 through 1971 represented 13,000 places; data for 1963 through 1966 represented 12,000 places; and data for 1959 through 1962 represented 10,000 places.

Housing starts and sales data are obtained from the Survey of Construction, for which Census Bureau field representatives sample both permit-issuing and non-permit-issuing places.

Effective with the January 2005 data release, the Survey of Construction implemented a new sample of building permit offices, replacing a previous sample selected in 1985. As a result, writes the Census Bureau, "Data users should use caution when analyzing year over year changes in housing prices and characteristics between 2004 and 2005." In the newer sample, land may be more abundant, lot sizes larger, and sales prices lower.

For 2004, the permit data were compiled for both the new 20,000 place universe and the old 19,000 place universe. Ratios of the new estimates to the old were calculated by state for total housing units, structures by number of units, and valuation. For the United States as a whole, the new estimate was 100.9 percent of the old estimate.

Effective with the data for April 2001, the Census Bureau made changes to the methodology used for new house sales, including discontinuing an adjustment for construction in areas in which building permits are required without a permit being issued. It was believed that such unauthorized construction has virtually ceased. The upward adjustment was not phased out but dropped completely in revised estimates as of January 1999. The total effect of these changes was to lower the number of sales by about 2.9 percent relative to those published for earlier years.

The data used in the price index are collected in the Survey of Construction, through monthly interviews with the builders or owners. The size of the sample is currently about 20,000 observations per year.

Data availability and references

Housing starts and building permit data have been collected monthly by the Bureau of the Census since 1959.

The monthly report for "New Residential Construction" (permits, starts, and completions) is issued in the middle of the following month. The monthly report and associated descriptions and historical data can be found at <https://www.census.gov/construction/nrc>.

The monthly report for "New Residential Sales" (sales, houses for sale, and prices) is issued toward the end of the following month. The monthly report and associated descriptions and historical data can be found at <https://www.census.gov/construction/nrs>.

The manufactured housing data (not seasonally adjusted) and background information can be found at <https://www.manufacturedhousing.org/statistics>. Data with and without seasonal adjustment can be found at <https://www.census.gov/construction/mhs>.

Data and background on the price index for new one-family houses can be found at <https://www.census/gov>, in the alphabetical index under the category "Construction price indexes."

TABLES 16-3 THROUGH 16-6

Manufacturers' Shipments, Inventories, and Orders

SOURCE: U.S. DEPARTMENT OF COMMERCE, CENSUS BUREAU

These data are from the Census Bureau's monthly M3 survey, a sample-based survey that provides measures of changes in the value of domestic manufacturing activity and indications of future production commitments. The sample is not a probability sample. It includes approximately 4,300 reporting units, including companies with $500 million or more in annual shipments and a selection of smaller companies. Currently, reported monthly data represent approximately 60 percent of shipments at the total manufacturing level.

One important technology industry, semiconductors, is represented in the shipments and inventories data in this report but not in new or unfilled orders. This affects the new and unfilled orders totals for computers and electronic products, durable goods industries, and total manufacturing. Based on shipments data, semiconductors accounted for about 15 percent of computers and electronic products, 3 percent of durable goods industries, and 1.5 percent of total manufacturing. Since semiconductors are intermediate materials and components rather than finished final products, the absence of these data does not distort new and unfilled orders data for important final demand categories, such as capital goods and information technology.

Definitions and notes on the data

Shipments. The value of shipments data represent net selling values, f.o.b. (free on board) plant, after discounts and allowances and excluding freight charges and excise taxes. For multi-establishment companies, the M3 reports are typically company- or division-level reports that encompass groups of plants or products. The data reported are usually net sales and receipts from customers and do not include the value of interplant transfers. The reported sales are used to calculate month-to-month changes that bring forward the estimates for the entire industry (that is, estimates of the statistical "universe") that have been developed from the Annual Survey of Manufactures (ASM). The value of products made elsewhere under contract from materials owned by the plant is also included in shipments, along with receipts for contract work performed for others, resales, miscellaneous activities such as the sale of scrap and refuse, and installation and repair work performed by employees of the plant.

Inventories. Inventories in the M3 survey are collected on a current cost or pre-LIFO (last in, first out) basis. As different inventory valuation methods are reflected in the reported data, the estimates differ slightly from replacement cost estimates. Companies using the LIFO method for valuing inventories report their pre-LIFO value; the adjustment to their base-period prices is excluded. In the ASM, inventories are collected according to this same definition.

Inventory data are requested from respondents by three stages of fabrication: finished goods, work in process, and raw materials and supplies. Response to the stage of fabrication inquiries is lower than for total inventories; not all companies keep their monthly data at this level of detail. It should be noted that a product considered to be a finished good in one industry, such as steel mill shapes, may be reported as a raw material in another industry, such as stamping plants. For some purposes, this difference in definitions is an advantage. When a factory accumulates inventory that it considers to be raw materials, it can be expected that that accumulation is intentional. But when a factory—whether a materials-making or a final-product producer—has a buildup of finished goods inventories, it may indicate involuntary accumulation as a result of sales falling short of expectations. Hence, the two types of accumulation can have different economic interpretations, even if they represent identical types of goods.

Like total inventories, stage of fabrication inventories are benchmarked to the ASM data. Stage of fabrication data are benchmarked at the major group level, as opposed to the level of total inventories, which is benchmarked at the individual industry level.

New orders (durable goods), as reported in the monthly survey, are net of order cancellations and include orders received and filled during the month as well as orders received for future delivery. They also include the value of contract changes that increase or decrease the value of the unfilled orders to which they relate. Orders are defined to include those supported by binding legal documents such as signed contracts, letters of award, or letters of intent, although this definition may not be strictly applicable in some industries.

New orders (nondurable goods) are equal to shipments, as order backlogs are not reported for these industries.

Unfilled orders (durable goods) includes new orders (as defined above) that have not been reflected as shipments. Generally, unfilled orders at the end of the reporting period are equal to unfilled orders at the beginning of the period plus net new orders received less net shipments.

Series are adjusted for seasonal variation and variation in the number of trading days in the month using the X-12-ARIMA version of the Census Bureau's seasonal adjustment program.

Benchmarking and revisions

The data shown in the volume have been benchmarked to the 2007 Economic Census and to ASMs through 2011. In each benchmark revision, new and unfilled orders are adjusted to be consistent with the benchmarked shipments and inventory data, seasonal adjustment factors are revised and updated, and other corrections are made.

Data availability and references

Data have been collected monthly since 1958.

The "Advance Report on Durable Goods Manufacturers' Shipments, Inventories and Orders" is available as a press release

about 18 working days after the end of each month. It includes seasonally adjusted and not seasonally adjusted estimates of shipments, new orders, unfilled orders, and inventories for durable goods industries.

The monthly "Manufacturers' Shipments, Inventories, and Orders" report is released on the 23rd working day after the end of the month. Content includes revisions to the advance durable goods data, estimates for nondurable goods industries, tabulations by market category, and ratios of shipments to inventories and to unfilled orders. Revisions may affect selected data for the two previous months.

Press releases, historical data, descriptions of the survey, and documentation are available on the Census Bureau Web site at <https://www.census.gov>, under the category "Manufacturing" in the alphabetic listing there.

TABLE 16-7

Motor Vehicle Sales and Inventories

SOURCE: U.S. DEPARTMENT OF COMMERCE, BUREAU OF ECONOMIC ANALYSIS

The Bureau of Economic Analysis (BEA) collects data on retail sales and inventories of cars, trucks, and buses from data from the American Automobile Manufacturers Association, Ward's Automotive Reports, and other sources. Seasonal adjustments are recalculated annually. Data are available on the BEA Web site at <https://www.bea.gov> as a part of the national income and product accounts data set; they are found under the "Supplemental Estimates" heading.

Definitions

Product	Description
Autos	All passenger cars, including station wagons.
Light trucks	Sport utility vehicles. Prior to the 2003 Benchmark Revision light trucks were up to 10,000 pounds.
Heavy trucks	Trucks more than 14,000 pounds gross vehicle weight. Prior to the 2003 Benchmark Revision heavy trucks were more than 10,000 pounds
Domestic sales	United States (U.S.) sales of vehicles assembled in the U.S., Canada, and Mexico
Foreign sales	U.S. sales of vehicles produced elsewhere
Domestic auto production	Autos assembled in the U.S
Domestic auto inventories	U.S. inventories of vehicles assembled in the U.S., Canada, and Mexico.

Data Availability

Auto and truck sales are updated by the end of the third business day after the end of the month. Auto production and inventories are available by the end of the second week after the end of month.

TABLES 16-8 AND 16-10

RETAIL AND FOOD SERVICES SALES; RETAIL INVENTORIES

SOURCE: U.S. DEPARTMENT OF COMMERCE, CENSUS BUREAU

Every month, the Census Bureau prepares estimates of retail sales and inventories by kind of business, based on a mail-out/mail-back survey of about 5,500 retail businesses with paid employees.

In June 2019, the monthly retail sales estimate is based on the results of the 2017 Annual Trade Survey and the service annual service. The annual retail trade survey (ARTS) produces national estimates of total annual sales, e-commerce sales, sales taxes, end-of-year inventories, purchases, total operating expenses, gross margins, and end-of-year accounts receivable for retail businesses located in the united states.

Retail sales and inventories are now compiled using the new NAICS classification system, which replaced the old SIC system. Historical data have been restated on the NAICS basis back to January 1992. In NAICS, Eating and drinking places and Mobile food services have been reclassified out of retail trade and into sector 72, Accommodation and food services, which also includes Hotels. The retail sales survey still collects and publishes sales data for Food services and drinking places. It no longer includes them in the Retail total, but they are included in a new Retail and food services total.

Subtotals of durable and nondurable goods are no longer published. They were always imprecise for retail sales, since general merchandise stores (including department stores) were included in nondurable goods, yet obviously sold substantial quantities of durable goods.

Definitions

Sales is the value of merchandise sold for cash or credit at retail or wholesale. Services that are incidental to the sale of merchandise, and excise taxes that are paid by the manufacturer or wholesaler and passed along to the retailer, are also included. Sales are net, after deductions for refunds and merchandise returns. They exclude sales taxes collected directly from customers and paid directly to a local, state, or federal tax agency. The sales estimates include only sales by establishments primarily engaged in retail trade, and are not intended to measure the total sales for a given commodity or merchandise line.

Inventories is the value of stocks of goods held for sale through retail stores, valued at cost, as of the last day of the report period. Stocks may be held either at the store or at warehouses that maintain supplies primarily intended for distribution to retail stores within the organization.

Leased departments consists of the operations of one company conducted within the establishment of another company, such as jewelry counters or optical centers within department stores. The values for sales and inventories at department stores in Tables 16-9 and 16-10 exclude sales of leased departments.

GAFO (department store type goods) is a special aggregate grouping of sales at general merchandise stores and at other stores that sell merchandise normally sold in department stores—clothing and accessories, furniture and home furnishings, electronics, appliances, sporting goods, hobby, book, music, office supplies, stationery, and gifts.

Notes on the data

The data published here have been benchmarked to the 2012, 2007, 2002, 1997, and 1992 Economic Censuses and the Annual Retail Trade Surveys for 2012 and previous years. Each year, the monthly series are benchmarked to the latest annual survey and new factors are incorporated to adjust for seasonal, trading-day, and holiday variations, using the Census Bureau's X-12-ARIMA program.

The survey sample is stratified by kind of business and estimated sales. All firms with sales above applicable size cutoffs are included. Firms are selected randomly from the remaining strata. The sample used for the end-of-month inventory estimates is a sub-sample of the monthly sales sample, about one-third of the size of the whole sample.

New samples, designed to produce NAICS estimates, were introduced with the 1999 Annual Retail Trade Survey and the March 2001 Monthly Retail Trade Survey. On November 30, 2006, another new sample was introduced, affecting the data for September 2006 and the following months. The sample is updated quarterly to take account of business births and deaths.

Data availability and references

An "Advance Monthly Retail Sales" report is released about nine working days after the close of the reference month, based on responses from a sub-sample of the complete retail sample.

The revised and more complete monthly "Retail Trade, Sales, and Inventories" reports are released six weeks after the close of the reference month. They contain preliminary figures for the current month and final figures for the prior 12 months. Statistics include retail sales, inventories, and ratios of inventories to sales. Data are both seasonally adjusted and unadjusted.

The "Annual Benchmark Report for Retail Trade" is released each spring. It includes updated seasonal adjustment factors; revised and benchmarked monthly estimates of sales and inventories; monthly data for the most recent 10 or more years; detailed annual estimates and ratios for the United States by kind of business; and comparable prior-year statistics and year-to-year changes.

All data are available on the Census Bureau Web site at <https://www.census.gov/retail>.

TABLE 16-9

Quarterly Retail Sales: Total and E-Commerce

SOURCE: U.S. DEPARTMENT OF COMMERCE, CENSUS BUREAU

Beginning with the fourth quarter of 1999, the Census Bureau has conducted a quarterly survey of retail e-commerce sales from the Monthly Retail Trade Survey sample. (The monthly survey does not report electronic shopping separately; it is combined with mail order.)

E-commerce sales are the sales of goods and services in which an order is placed by the buyer or the price and terms of sale are negotiated over the Internet or an extranet, Electronic Data Interchange (EDI) network, electronic mail, or other online system. Payment may or may not be made online. The quarterly release is issued around the 20th of February, May, August, and November, and is available along with full historical data on the Census Bureau Web site at <https://www.census.gov>. It can be located under the heading "Retail" in the alphabetical Web site index, under "E" for "Economic data and information."

These estimates reflect the NAICS definition of retail sales, which excludes food service. Online travel services, financial brokers and dealers, and ticket sales agencies are not classified as retail and are not included in these estimates; they are, however, included in the annual survey of selected services.

TABLE 16-11

Merchant Wholesalers—Sales and Inventories

SOURCE: U.S. DEPARTMENT OF COMMERCE, CENSUS BUREAU

The Annual Wholesale Trade Survey (AWTS) produces national estimates of total annual sales, e-commerce sales, end-of-year inventories, inventories held outside of the United States, purchases, total operating expenses, gross margins, and commissions (for electronic markets, agents, and brokers) for wholesale businesses located in the United States. The sample consists of about 8400 establishments, with a response rate of about 62

percent; missing reports are imputed based on reports of similar reporters.

These data are now based on the new NAICS classification system, which replaced the old SIC system. Historical data have been restated on the NAICS basis back to January 1992.

Classification changes in NAICS

NAICS shifts a significant number of businesses from the Wholesale to the Retail sector. An important new criterion for classification concerns whether or not the establishment is intended to solicit walk-in traffic. If it is, and if it uses mass-media advertising, it is now classified as Retail, even if it also serves business and institutional clients.

Definitions

Merchant wholesalers includes merchant wholesalers that take title of the goods they sell, as well as jobbers, industrial distributors, exporters, and importers. The survey does not cover marketing sales offices and branches of manufacturing, refining, and mining firms, nor does it include NAICS 4251: Wholesale Electronic Markets and Agents and Brokers.

Notes on the data

Inventories are valued using methods other than LIFO (last in, first out) in order to better reflect the current costs of goods held as inventory.

A survey has been conducted monthly since 1946. New samples are drawn every 5 years, most recently in 2009. The samples are updated every quarter to add new businesses and to drop companies that are no longer active.

Data availability and references

"Monthly Wholesale Trade, Sales and Inventories" reports are released six weeks after the close of the reference month. They contain preliminary current-month figures and final figures for the previous month. Statistics include sales, inventories, and stock/sale ratios, along with standard errors. Data are both seasonally adjusted and unadjusted.

The "Annual Benchmark Report for Wholesale Trade" is released each spring. It contains estimated annual sales, monthly and yearend inventories, inventory/sales ratios, purchases, gross margins, and gross margin/sales ratios by kind of business. Annual estimates are benchmarked to annual surveys and the most recent census of wholesale trade. Monthly sales and inventories estimates are revised consistent with the annual data, seasonal adjustment factors are updated, and revised data for both seasonally adjusted and unadjusted values are published.

Data and documentation are available on the Census Bureau Web site at <https://www.census.gov>, under "Economic Indicators" and in the alphabetic index under "E" for economic data.

TABLES 16-12 AND 16-13

Manufacturing and Trade Sales and Inventories

SOURCES: U.S. DEPARTMENT OF COMMERCE, CENSUS BUREAU (CURRENT-DOLLAR SERIES) AND U.S. DEPARTMENT OF COMMERCE, BUREAU OF ECONOMIC ANALYSIS (BEA; CONSTANT-DOLLAR SERIES)

The current-dollar data on which these tables are based bring together summary data from the separate series on manufacturers' shipments, inventories, and orders; merchant wholesalers' sales and inventories; and retail sales and inventories, all of which are included in this chapter. Generally, current-dollar inventories are collected on a current cost (or pre-LIFO [last in, first out]) basis. See the notes and definitions for Tables 16-3, 16-4, 16-8 16-10, and 16-11 for further information about these data.

Based on these current-dollar values and relevant price data, BEA makes estimates of real sales, inventories, and inventory-sales ratios. Note, however, that annual figures for sales are shown as annual totals in Table 16-12 but as averages of the monthly data in Table 16-13, reflecting the practices of the respective source agencies. Also note that constant-dollar detail may not add to constant-dollar totals because of the chain-weighting formula; see the discussion of chain-weighted measures in the notes and definitions for Chapter 1. The constant-dollar estimates shown in this volume of *Business Statistics* are stated in 2009 dollars.

Inventory values are as of the end of the month or year. In Table 16-13, annual values for monthly current-dollar inventory-sales ratios are averages of seasonally adjusted monthly ratios. However, for the real ratios in Table 16-14, annual figures for inventory-sales ratios are calculated by BEA as year-end (December) inventories divided by the monthly average of sales for the entire year; this means that the annual ratios will not be equivalent to averages of month ratios. In all cases, the ratios in these two tables (like those in Table 1-8) represent the number of months' sales on hand as inventory at the end of the reporting period.

Data availability

Sales, inventories, and inventory-sales ratios for manufacturers, merchant wholesalers, and retailers are published monthly by the Census Bureau in a press release entitled "Manufacturing and Trade Inventories and Sales." Recent and historical data are available on the Census Bureau Web site at <https://www.census.gov/mtis/www/mtis.html>. They can also be found by going to the general Census website, <https://www.census.gov>, going to the alphabetical index, finding "Economic Data and Information" under "E" and then finding "Manufacturing and trade" under "Manufacturing" or "Sales."

Sales and inventories in constant dollars are available on the BEA Web site at <https://www.bea.gov>. To locate these data on that site, click on "National Economic Accounts." Scroll down to "Supplemental Estimates," click "Underlying Detail Tables," and then click on "List of Underlying Detail Tables." For the most recent data, if there is more than one table with the same title, select the last table listed.

TABLE 16-14

Selected Services, Quarterly: Estimated Revenue for Employer Firms

SOURCE: U.S. DEPARTMENT OF COMMERCE, CENSUS BUREAU

Census data on quarterly revenue for selected service industries are based on information collected from a probability sample that has been expanded over recent years to approximately 19,000 employer firms (firms with employees), chosen from the sample for the larger Service Annual Survey and expanded to represent totals—for employer firms only—for the selected industries. The sample is updated quarterly to account for business births, deaths, and other changes. Industries are defined according to the 2012 NAICS.

The scope of the survey and the size of the sample have increased several times since the inception of this survey in 2004. More industries are now available than are shown here in Table 16-15, which focuses on industries with a longer statistical history.

Definitions and notes on the data

These data are collected in current dollars only. See the Producer Price Indexes in Chapter 8 for indicators of price trends in various sectors.

Both taxable and tax-exempt firms are covered unless otherwise specified.

Generally, government enterprises are not within the scope (that is, the industries it is designed to cover) of the survey. *Utilities* excludes government-owned utilities and *Transportation and warehousing* excludes the U.S. Postal Service.

Private industries that are not within the scope of the survey are NAICS 482, rail transportation; 525, funds, trusts, and other financial vehicles; 51112, offices of notaries; 6111, 6112, and 6113, elementary, secondary, and post-secondary schools; 8131, religious organizations; 81393 (labor unions and similar), 81394 (political organizations, and 814 (private households).

Totals shown for sectors and subsectors may include data for kinds of business that are in the scope of the survey but are not shown separately in the detail beneath.

Data for selected industry groups are adjusted for seasonal varia-tion using the Census Bureau's X-13 ARIMA-SEATS program.

Data availability and references

The quarterly release "U.S. Government Estimates of Quarterly Revenue for Selected Services" is available on the Census Web site at <https://www.census.gov/>, as "Quarterly Services Survey" listed under Q in the alphabetic index; historical, technical, and background information, including sampling errors, is also available there.

INDEX

CPSIA information can be obtained
at www.ICGtesting.com
Printed in the USA
BVHW091250090122
624249BV00004B/12

9 781636 71003